TRIALS OF THE DIASPORA

TRIALS OF THE DIASPORA

A HISTORY OF ANTI-SEMITISM IN ENGLAND

ANTHONY JULIUS

OXFORD

UNIVERSITY PRESS

OXFORD
UNIVERSITY PRESS

Great Clarendon Street, Oxford OX2 6DP

Oxford University Press is a department of the University of Oxford.
It furthers the University's objective of excellence in research, scholarship,
and education by publishing worldwide in

Oxford New York

Auckland Cape Town Dar es Salaam Hong Kong Karachi
Kuala Lumpur Madrid Melbourne Mexico City Nairobi
New Delhi Shanghai Taipei Toronto

With offices in

Argentina Austria Brazil Chile Czech Republic France Greece
Guatemala Hungary Italy Japan Poland Portugal Singapore
South Korea Switzerland Thailand Turkey Ukraine Vietnam

Oxford is a registered trade mark of Oxford University Press
in the UK and in certain other countries

Published in the United States
by Oxford University Press Inc., New York

© Anthony Julius 2010

British Library Cataloguing in Publication Data

Data available

Library of Congress Cataloging in Publication Data

Data available

Typeset by SPI Publisher Services, Pondicherry, India
Printed in Great Britain
on acid-free paper by
Clays Ltd, St Ives plc

ISBN 978-0-19-929705-4

Katarina, this book is for you.

Contents

Acknowledgements

Earlier versions of chapters, or parts of chapters, have appeared in Paul Iganski and Barry Kosmin (eds.), *A New Antisemitism?* (London, 2003), in the online journal *Engage*, on the website <http://www.z-word.com>, and in David Kertzer (ed.), *Old Demons, New Debates* (New York, 2005), as well as in *Critical Quarterly*, the *Jewish Chronicle*, the *Times Literary Supplement*, the *London Review of Books*, and the *Guardian*.

I owe specific debts of gratitude to Jane Ashworth, Hadassa Ben-Itto, Lily Bloch, Shimon Cohen, Simon Cohen, Stan Cohen, Jonathan Cummings, Jeffrey Davis, Michael Ezra, Ofir Frankel, R. M. Ginsbury, Daniel Hochhauser, Jonathan Hoffman, Jenifer Howie, Oliver Kamm, Irene Lancaster, Richard Landes, Noam Leshem, James Libson, Robert Jan Van Pelt, Antony Polonsky, Daniel Reisner, Andrew Roberts, Ann Robinson, Bill Rubinstein, Paul Usiskin, and Michael Yudkin. I am particularly grateful to Todd Endelmann, Deborah Lipstadt, and Ken Stern for convening a one-day conference in NYC on my manuscript.

Elena Schiff has been indefatigable on the book's behalf. I thank her for all her work on it; I cannot imagine completing it without her help. It was at Andrew Wylie's suggestion that I started to think about writing this book— I thank him, and Tracey Bohan too.

The following read all, or some part, of the book: John H. Arnold, Jane Ashworth, Anthony Bale, Steve Bayme, Paul Bew, Marcel Borden, Ben Cohen, Nick Cohen, Deborah Dwork, Richard Evans, David Feldman, Geoffrey Field, Jonathan Freedland, Norman Geras, Sander L. Gilman, Dean Godson, Bernard Harrison, David Hirsh, Dan Jacobson, Howard Jacobson, Menachem Kellner, Michael Kotzin, Shalom Lappin, Deborah Lipstadt, Colin McCabe, Derek Penslar, David Plante, Felix Posen, Aviva Raz-Shechter, W. D. Rubinstein, Ken Stern, Michael Yudkin, and Steve Zipperstein. These are all very busy people; I am grateful to them for taking the time and for offering their comments. Each one of them has improved the book.

Trials of the Diaspora began as a project under the vigilant, engaged care of the late Nikos Stangos, my very dear and still-mourned friend, and the editor of two of my earlier books. I hope he would have been pleased with the final product, even though it appears under the imprint of a publishing house other than his own. In the event, I could not have wished for a better publisher than OUP. I was lucky enough to have Luciana O'Flaherty as my editor (and thank you Claire Pinder for the introduction). She has been exemplary, both patient and enthusiastic.

Writing this book has been somewhat like swimming long-distance through a sewer. Family, friends, and colleagues, have provided welcome distractions, and I thank them all—the children, especially. Max helped with some research early on, Laura kept me politically in line, Chloe contributed some scholarship on John Singer Sargent, Theo read the whole manuscript shortly before it was finalized, all the while negotiating GCSE and physical training commitments, and Elon took a special interest in the book's length (word count, number of pages), sitting on his perch at my desk. The book's dedication is a token of my dedication.

'I do not wish to take up the cudgels for the Jews in this pamphlet. It would be useless. Everything rational and everything sentimental that can possibly be said in their defence has been said already.'

Theodore Herzl, *The Jewish State*

'...it is easy to be a Jew in England...'

Chaim Weitzmann, *Statement to the Palestine Royal Commission* (1936)

'If you want to know the character of any nation, ask the Jews.'

Chaim A. Kaplan, *Warsaw Diary*

'The Jews have contrived, in these few years of unconditional freedom, to place themselves again on trial before public opinion.'

Anonymous contributor, *London Quarterly Review*, October 1882

'In the modern world, the Jew has perpetually been on trial; still *today* the Jew is on trial, in the person of the Israeli—and this modern trial of the Jew, this trial which never ends, begins with the trial of Shylock.'

Philip Roth, *Operation Shylock*

Introduction

Experiences of many kinds go into the writing of a book—more of them, indeed, than the writer himself can ever know. Only some of them survive as memories.

Many years ago, I took a train journey to Birmingham with my father and a non-Jewish business associate whom I will call 'Arthur'. I was ten or eleven years old at the time, and I would often tag along on these business trips, when school allowed. My father owned a number of menswear shops, mainly in the West Country. He had enjoyed considerable success in business, and it was a familiar experience for me to see him in the company of other businessmen seeking his advice or asking for favours. Arthur was one such man, and his conversations with my father always had a slightly cloying, ingratiating quality. I remember that on this occasion he was talking about his daughter, who was about my age but whom I had not met. Arthur rambled on, my father patiently listening, while I read a book.

And then Arthur said something like the following: 'Do you know, Morris, she has got a special little friend, a Jewish girl, and we had the girl over for tea last weekend. I must say, the child has got the most beautiful manners.' He beamed. I had a sense of the temperature in the compartment rising, but nothing else was said on the subject, and after a short period, Arthur wandered off to the dining car to buy a drink. My father turned to me, fuming. 'Did you hear what he said? I am supposed to be impressed that he actually had a Jewish girl over to his house for tea? And that she had beautiful manners?' 'So what are you going to say, Daddy?' I asked. 'Nothing, of course. What is there to say?' Shortly afterwards, Arthur returned, and the two men resumed their conversation, chatting together until we arrived at our destination.

That evening, we took quite a late train home, and found ourselves sharing an open carriage with the players of a First Division football team. They had just played an 'away' match and were going back to London. At that time, stories about the violent activities of 'football hooligans' filled many columns of the Sunday papers. The train stood in the station, and the football fans packed the platform. Autograph books were being pushed through the small aperture at the top of the carriage's sealed windows, and the players were laughing and calling across to each other and to their fans. They were also swearing volubly, and this began to irritate my father. After a few minutes, he got up and went over to the table where some of them were sitting. 'My young son is with me. Would you please moderate your language?' I was horrified. There was a moment out of time, when the players stared at my father, he stared back at them, and the fans outside continued to stare in to the compartment. And then, miraculously, the players quietened down. The fistfight I had anticipated between my father and assorted players and fans did not take place.

It was an astonishingly brave thing for him to have done, and I told my school friends about it the next day. I was both embarrassed and proud. (We knew all the words. We were unshockable; why didn't our parents recognize that we were practically adults now, etc.—still, what a father, to stand up to the players and their fans.) But I did not tell them about the conversation earlier that day, nor about my father's failure to confront Arthur, though I have reflected on it many times since then. It was not a failure in courage on his part, for certain. I do not think that he ever in his life retreated from a fight.

It had instead something to do with an unwillingness to condescend to being offended, a refusal to acknowledge the hurt caused by the insult implicit in Arthur's remark—that it is always noteworthy when Jews behave well. It is as if my father thought: 'I'm not going to let him see that he's got to me.' But it also had something to do with not wanting to appear to be 'touchy'. 'Over-sensitivity' to slights—worse, *imagined* slights—is commonly supposed to be a characteristic of Jews.[1] Arthur intended to please my father, not to offend him, so why take offence? Indeed, perhaps he meant no more than that the little girl had the kind of manners that Jewish children everywhere are celebrated as possessing.[2] Let Arthur see that he is dealing with another Englishman, and not with an excitable Jew. Last, it had something to do with the conviction that there are certain things that will always remain unsaid between Jews and non-Jews, among which is the acknowledgement that offence has indeed been taken. Such an acknowledgement will not be understood; it cannot be communicated; it is best left alone. The Jew who does not 'speak out' is thus to be regarded as a realist, not a coward. There is no shame in silence in these circumstances. My father could perhaps have said, quite gently, 'It's not so remarkable, Arthur, that a Jewish girl has manners.' But I am sure that he knew what kind of reaction he would have prompted—confusion, embarrassment, resentment. It would have been an excruciating moment for both men.

Or so I suppose my father might have reasoned, if he had been driven to justify his decision to let Arthur's remark pass. I am sure that it was not the first time that he had thus been tried. There was in his tone, more than in the content of what he actually said to me, the implication that remarks of this kind were familiar to him—even, that he had learned to expect them. And yet there was nothing in either the tone or the content of his vexed, impatient words to suggest that he had quite settled the question of what he should do in just such circumstances. It was as if he did not have in his repertoire of responses to life's challenges a response that quite met Arthur's challenge—however inconsequential it was.

I was interested in what my father might do, mainly because I assumed it would teach me what to do if I found myself in similar circumstances. I took for granted that I would grow up to be just like him, and in time would therefore have to deal with Arthurs of my own. And yet, on those few occasions when I have been spoken to with that kind of condescension, it is not so much offence I have felt as a kind of impersonal bemusement, as if present at some odd display, one that has no real connection to me, even though directed at me. It has come at me as if from the margins, the manifestation of some absurd confusion of mind, a mental spasm. It is always unpleasant, but at the same time preposterous—the noises or gestures of a person who has embraced that tangled bundle of sentiments and beliefs known in shorthand as 'anti-Semitism'.

I do not think that this reaction of mine has much to do with any greater social confidence on my part. I think it is almost entirely generational, reflecting the diminished part played by that kind of anti-Semitism in England today. It no longer represents a threat because it no longer speaks for anything that is substantial, anything that could injure or even impede. There remain in circulation other, more potent, kinds of anti-Semitism, of course.

My father's exchange with Arthur was, among other things, a tiny episode in the history of Anglo-Jewry. Among the various promptings towards this book, the memory of that day, and the unresolved questions it provoked, are the furthest back in time.

★★★

A reader beginning a long book on anti-Semitism is entitled to wonder about the author's own experience of his subject. I am Jewish. I have met anti-Semitism both as a lawyer and as a literary critic. I have acted for clients in a number of cases where anti-Semitism was an issue and I have written about T. S. Eliot's anti-Semitism. But though I have thus seen anti-Semitism in action, I have rarely been the object of its attention. It has been to me both a subject and a spectacle; it has rarely confronted me directly, as an antagonist. I have read about the abuse and the violence; I have been present when Jews in general have been under verbal attack (at rallies, in courtrooms, and so on), and I have experienced, on those occasions, some sense of a common plight. Further, when reading anti-Semitic works of literature, I have had an uneasy sense that I am not wanted among the author's audience—though that is perhaps a little precious of me. But I have endured nothing of the unpleasant, and often worse than unpleasant, personal attacks that are still made on Jews because they are Jews—the lethal and non-lethal violence, the bullying and the intimidation. I have not been bombed or shot, stabbed or punched. I have not been chased down roads with shouted slanders and insults (it still happens, even in London).[3] I have not suffered expulsion or exclusion. There have been no traumas, no scenes of humiliation. I have no collection of outrages to be exhibited on special occasions.[4] It would be indecent—a mere affectation or pose[5]—for me to put myself in the company of Jews who have been persecuted thus.

Of course, one could not grow up as a Jew, living in part among Jews, without some sense of anti-Semitism. For Anglo-Jewry in general, it is the background noise against which we make our lives. Almost always barely audible, one then must strain to detect it—though very occasionally it irrupts into a dissonant, heart-stopping din. The question of the extent of my experience of anti-Semitism, then, is perhaps best answered thus: *just enough.* That is, just enough for it to inform my understanding of the subject, but not so much as to overwhelm me. I can see it. It has shape and depth to me, and I can therefore describe it. But it is not advancing upon me; certainly, I am not in flight before it.

My great-grandparents were late nineteenth-century immigrants from Russia. I did not know them, nor did I ever hear very much about them. Of my grandparents, I knew my paternal grandfather not at all and remember Lily, my paternal grandmother, best. She outlived both her husband and her only child, and died in the late 1980s when she herself was in her late eighties. She was an impassive, taciturn person, remote from the received notion of the Jewish grandmother. Self-contained, rarely given to any show of emotion, she lived her life as if at some distance from her family. Very little surprised her; practically nothing impressed her. Six of her eight siblings had emigrated in the aftermath of World War I, all except one of them to South Africa. She kept up correspondence with each of them for decades, but wrote most frequently to her youngest brother, Jack, who had settled in Port Elizabeth. She would sometimes show me her letters to him, and would often press on me his letters to her. They were full of references to local and world events. Jack would attach clippings from local newspapers, mostly about civil unrest in South Africa. My grandmother would respond with clippings from the *Jewish Chronicle* detailing anti-Semitic incidents—graffiti, arson, desecrations, assaults. They wrote to each other a great deal about Israel too. Their correspondence comprised a limited set of variations on a single theme: they had been lucky so far, but disaster, to be inflicted on Jews by the Gentile world, was imminent.

Though my grandmother never spoke in a hostile way about non-Jews, it was always clear when it was a non-Jew about whom she was speaking. The tone would invariably have a quality of wariness, as if she was concerned that she might be overheard. She took it for granted that Jews and Christians were divided by unbridgeable differences. If she wanted to indicate that a person was Jewish, she would say that he was '*unserer*' ('one of us'); if Gentile, he would be '*zeyricher*' ('one of them') or just 'English'. Still, I heard very little from her about anti-Semitism, and nothing at all about her own exposure to it. This was, perhaps, because she had not seen very much of it—though she had lived in the East End through the Mosley period.[6] Or it might have been because she did not consider it sufficiently exceptional to be worthy of comment. Though my mother's mother, Mary, died when I was much younger, I likewise do not remember hearing from her any stories of persecution or oppression.

I did hear a few such stories from my parents, though in the main they were concerned to protect me from the news that Jews had enemies. (On the twentieth anniversary of the end of World War II, when the newspapers were full of references to Hitler, I asked my father who he was. 'A bad man, and someone you don't need to know about', was his reply.) Their worst stories of anti-Semitism were from their childhood—mainly wartime stories of evacuation, though my father had tales of impassable streets in the East End, where Gentile kids prowled, ready to attack the Jewish kids on their way to school. But this was street-gang stuff, spiced by available abuse—name-calling, half-understood, in the main used to provoke a response. 'Stick a lump of pork / Upon a fork / And give it to the Jew boy / J-e-w b-o-y-s.'[7] Or the staple accusation, 'You killed Christ', or even, simply, 'You're a Jew!'[8] Wartime evacuation was for both of my parents their real point of entry into a hostile non-Jewish world.

In 1940, my father was evacuated to Isleham, a village near Cambridge. He was twelve years old. He was packed up by my grandmother, and seen off by her at a London train station in the company of many other children. The families that took the children in were mostly paid to do so. Some would have taken children anyway, without compensation; others doubtless just did it for the money. My father and his friend Izzy Cohen were delivered to a farm, where they stayed for some months. On that first night away from home, Izzy wet his bed. The next afternoon, returning from their temporary school, the two boys saw sheets hung out on the line, still stained, for the whole street to witness. The farmer's wife was standing outside the house, near the washing line. When she saw the boys, she began to chant in the direction of passers-by and neighbours, 'Look what the dirty Jews did.'[9]

I heard this story from my father on more than one occasion. He usually told it along with another one, about how a bag of sweets that he had with him when he arrived at the farm was taken by the farmer and his wife, never to be seen again. The tone in which he told these stories communicated the message, 'this is how unkind some people can be to small children'. It was never, 'this is anti-Semitism'. He never connected Izzy's undoubted humiliation, and his own, to the wartime horrors perpetrated by the Nazis and their allies. If someone had suggested to him that there was a connection—any connection, of any kind, however remote—I think he would have dismissed it as far-fetched. I think he would have felt that it was making too much of a momentary discomfort.

My mother was seven years old at the start of the war. Like my father, she too left London but, in her case, in the company of her parents and her brother. They settled in Maidenhead, and my mother was sent to the local primary school. She was the only Jewish child there. It was not long before the other children found out that she was Jewish, and they would taunt her during playtime, shouting 'she's a Jew, she's got horns in her head', and then running away.[10] She did not understand, she tells me, what they meant. After a while, she did not want to go to school, and she spent most of each day crying. Her parents went to see the headmaster. He was sympathetic and soon put a stop to the bullying. Once things had settled down, she had many friends back to her house to play. Yet the invitations were never reciprocated, and though there was never any unpleasantness, she knew to stay at the door when she called round to collect her friends at their homes. In her last year at the school, she was appointed head girl.

When war broke out, my mother's father became an air-raid warden. Cyril, my mother's brother, joined the Royal Engineers, clearing landmines and laying pontoon bridges, up to his shoulders in water. He was just seventeen years old when he enlisted, and when he announced it to the family, my grandfather, in a state of momentary shock, slapped him across the face. Cyril took part in the D-Day landings and for a time was reported missing. He served in France and then in Germany and, at the end of the war, he was posted to Palestine. I once asked him whether in the army he had ever been given a hard time for being Jewish. He said that he had not, except once from a soldier in his platoon, but that he had been able to warn him off. He had done this, he said, by staring intently at the man, all the while meditatively tapping a knife against the palm of his hand. I remember being thrilled by this story.[11]

In due course, my parents met and married and settled down in Southgate, a North London suburb. They had four sons, of whom I am the eldest. We were sent to non-denominational schools, where we had mostly non-Jewish friends (home invitations, always reciprocated), while our parents confined their own social contacts to members of my mother's extended family and the mainly Jewish business associates of my father. Much of their time was devoted to working for charities—mostly, but certainly not exclusively, Jewish ones. My father raised money for Israel, and donated his own money too, made with enterprise and hard work as a retailer. In the last ten years of his life—he died in 1978 aged 50—Israel's cause mattered more to him than practically anything else in his life. Arab enmity was taken for granted, but I do not recall there being much talk at home about Arab anti-Semitism.

At my primary school, when the pupils stood in the main classroom to recite the Lord's Prayer, the Jewish boys also stood, but squashed together in the unlit, slightly dank cloakroom next door. It was always hot, there was no space to move, and there was a certain amount of near-silent jostling. Every day, we overheard the Lord's Prayer, standing in darkness. At my secondary school, morning prayers were conducted with slightly more respect for the Jewish pupils. The sixth form sat on a platform in the school hall behind the headmaster. After announcements, he would nod to the 'Head Jewish

Boy', who would then stand up, and lead the Jewish pupils out of the hall. We would assemble in a number of classrooms for 'Jewish prayers', which consisted of the older boys shouting at the younger boys to shut up and listen, though to what we never heard. In due course, I became Head Jewish Boy, chosen by the headmaster from a group of Jewish sixth-form volunteers. I did not think the position an odd one, and I was pleased to have been chosen to fill it.

As with many Anglo-Jews of my generation, I have had some experience of formal and informal 'quotas', the ceiling figures placed on Jews' admission to (most often) schools and social clubs—the English equivalent of the 'numerus clausu', so much a feature of the post-emancipation anti-Semitism of Continental Europe and the United States. When I sat the examination for secondary school, I was given a 'reserve place'. It was explained to my parents that if a Jewish boy dropped out, I would be admitted. My parents accepted this, as did I. To the extent that it troubled me, the cause was embarrassment that I had not won outright one of the restricted places. When, ten or eleven years later, in 1977, I applied to law firms for a training contract, I was told by the elder brother of a friend of mine that there were certain law firms—in the main, the largest ones—to which I should not bother to apply. They were known not to take Jews—or if they did, prospects of promotion were dim. I checked their partner lists for Jewish names, and didn't write to those without any. I ended up at a predominantly Jewish firm, where I have been ever since.

Most Anglo-Jews nowadays infer the existence of English anti-Semitism from a bias that they perceive in media reporting of events in the Middle East. The bias dismays them; it is an intrusive presence in their lives; they take it to derive from a hostility to the Jewish State of Israel; they relate this hostility to a broader animus towards Jews. Yet they would not maintain that the hostility they sense, however demoralizing it is *to* them, is directed *at* them. They would probably regard as exceptional, for example, a newspaper columnist's statement, made a few years ago, that he ignores letters about Israel written by correspondents with Jewish names.[12] The animus is instead an ambience. And this is consistent with a more general sense of how English anti-Semitism operates—by stealth, by indirection, by tacit understandings and limited exclusions. So, for it to make itself directly known to one, for it to address itself to one as unmistakably and unarguably what it is—Jew-hatred without any disguise or pretence—one has either to be unlucky or else zealous in seeking it out.

I am among those Jews who have sought out anti-Semitism, or more precisely, placed myself across its path. I have done this as an English literature student at Cambridge University, and then as a lawyer in a firm that represents many Jewish institutions and bodies. Though it has not in itself defined either my academic or my professional work, this engagement with anti-Semitism has been sufficiently substantial to satisfy my curiosity about it, and given me opportunities to demonstrate the solidarity I feel with other Jews, especially when they are under attack. I should add that it has not exposed me to any harm—indeed, it has been almost wholly free of risk of any kind.

★★★

I came across instances of anti-Semitism early on in my reading in the English literary canon. They gave me a nasty surprise,[13] often because they seemed out of place in the texts in which they figured, and always because they jarred with my sense of literature's purpose. One reason, though not the only one, for my decision to study English at university was that I wanted to make sense of these instances. To that extent at least, however, my time at university was a failure. I did not get the measure of English literary anti-Semitism at Cambridge, even though I spent three years there in an on-and-off study of it.

I was at Cambridge between 1974 and 1977. The English Faculty was an unhappy, divided place during that period. There was a distinctive radical faction and a less distinctive, somewhat more ragged and embattled, but institutionally more powerful, conservative faction. Students were expected to declare their allegiance to the one or the other, and it came to be believed by us that the grading of our exam scripts would depend upon the match of ideological position between examiner and examinee.

The radical faction was where the most interesting arguments and books were to be found, and it was the side I found myself drawn towards, almost from my first term. Its values derived from a combination of the then current French literary theory, nineteenth-century German philosophy, Freud and the version of psychoanalysis associated with the maverick analyst Jacques Lacan, and the line of Western Marxist thinking that can be traced from the Austro-Marxists through to Antonio Gramsci and the Frankfurt School and closing with Louis Althusser. The conservative faction had nothing to say about most of this, and seemed to me to be demoralized, even impotent, before its cumulative force. The radicals staged confrontations between the English empiricist tradition and the tradition of Continental European philosophy in which the former, associated with the conservative faction, always lost. The received practices of English literary criticism were deprecated for their systematic exclusion of 'theory' or 'philosophy'.[14] The radicals tended to be indifferent to claims made by the conservatives on behalf of the literary canon, to disregard mere literary history, and to repudiate the supposed 'Englishness' of English literature. Their idiom was one of critique rather than celebration; they promoted a notion of intellectual rigour that was oppositionist in all its implications. There was a politics attached to this set of positions, and much time was spent considering the precise nature of art and literature's 'relative autonomy' from the economic 'base', as first and inadequately described by Marx in the Preface to his *Contribution to the Critique of Political Economy* (1859).[15]

It was not so easy to discern the principles that governed the positions taken by the conservative faction. This faction was much less programmatic, and was less inclined to wear its arguments, so to speak, on the very surface of its prose. It esteemed intelligence, understood as the free play of the mind, free of the dogmatisms of system. It valued disinterestedness, taken to be the mark of the genuine critic, and what distinguished him from 'the man with a system, an advocate'.[16] It held to the implicit conviction that literature was superior to philosophy and science, and in some sense the successor or at least an alternative to religion. The values of the conservative faction had a more local origin to those of the radical faction. They derived most proximately from positions taken by F. R. Leavis (1895–1978). He may be regarded as the principal ideologist of 'Cambridge English', the analytical study of the English secular scriptures.[17] His approach to literature was self-consciously in the line of the great English poet-critics, Johnson, Coleridge, and Arnold.[18] English literature was to him matchless in its diversity and range, full and profound in its registration of changing life. It gave us a precious continuity with the past,[19] and was thus much more than merely one university 'subject' among others. To Leavis, the study of English literature promoted 'the non-specialist intelligence' and the foundation at Cambridge towards the close of World War I of the English degree (or 'Tripos') was an important event in history.[20] Leavis's positions resonated with positions taken in the cultural politics of the 1920s and 30s. The government-appointed Newbolt Committee (1921), in its report *Teaching English in England*, extolled literature and warned that the nation that 'reject[ed] this means of grace, and which despises this great spiritual influence, must assuredly be heading for disaster'.[21] Literature, in a word, was redemptive. It seemed odd to me that this claim, so much greater than anything the radicals claimed for literature, was so utterly 'untheorized' (as we used to say) by the conservatives. They simply made the claim, and took assent for granted.

Nevertheless, the division between the factions did not, so to speak, go all the way down. There was a tacit consensus on certain, mostly pedagogic, values. It was agreed, for example, that 'practical criticism', the distinctive characteristic of Cambridge English, was valuable and to be promoted. Practical criticism requires intelligence; it is not supine; it does not adopt a worshipful posture towards the literary work.[22] It is ready to judge a work—*any* work—to be a failure.[23] It is more than just 'close reading', though it always entails the most scrupulous consideration of the literary work under examination. Literary criticism, which begins in practical criticism, is an immensely serious business. It is not a matter of scholarship, or the patient editing of texts; it is not a matter of giving an account of the pleasure one has taken in this or that literary work. It is not literary history; it is not philosophy. (At this point disagreements began to emerge. The conservatives tended to hold that the study of literature was associated with, but not dependent upon, extra-literary studies;[24] the radicals were much readier to dissolve literary studies in the study of broader discursive formations.) It was further agreed by the factions that there were both limiting and enabling intellectual or critical perspectives on literature. The ideal critic confines himself to what is discussable about a work of art. He engages in detailed analysis, holding that literary criticism can be demonstrated and therefore argued about. He is serious-minded; he is the ideal reader, rigorous and disinterested; he does not bring his own prejudices to the work under examination; he understands that writing about literature is not a mystic rapture but a process of the intelligence; he deprecates 'personal responses' to literature as self-indulgent, and often mawkish. While he acknowledges that a literary work has its own internal logic, he does not consider that this exempts it from intellectual scrutiny. He does not believe that every literary work is as valuable as every other work. (Once again, disagreements thereafter emerged. The radicals related this critical tough-mindedness to more general political and philosophical positions, while the conservatives did not.)

Though the radical and conservative factions were themselves fractured, common to practically all was a deprecating of what was termed 'reductionism'—in all its available versions.[25] This meant, among other things, writing about a poem as if it could be reduced to mere prose summary, writing about a novel or a play as if it could be reduced to a 'reflection' of the time and place of its composition, or writing about literary works in general as if they were manifestos of their authors, mere vehicles of opinion or doctrine. The absence of interest among English Faculty members in English literary anti-Semitism, which was so entrenched as to exclude consideration of the question almost entirely, can be attributed in part at least to this distaste for anything that smacked of reductionism. The radicals were embarrassed by the willingness of earlier generations of radicals to 'reduce' literature to a mere effect or reflection of society; the independence or autonomy of literature was for the conservatives one of the very premises of their critical faith.

English literary anti-Semitism was not on any syllabus; it was not taught; it was not 'examined'; fundamentally, it was not *noticed*. It was not addressed in any of the classics of Cambridge literary criticism—I. A. Richards's *Principles of Literary Criticism* (1924) and *Practical Criticism* (1929), William Empson's *Seven Types of Ambiguity* (1930), F. R. Leavis's *New Bearings on English Poetry* (1932), *Revaluation* (1936), *The Great Tradition* (1948), and *The Common Pursuit* (1952). It was not mentioned in the immensely influential literary criticism of T. S. Eliot, one of the architects of Cambridge English.[26] The New Critics in the United States disregarded it. In a critical moment in the history of modern literary criticism, the award of the 1949 Bollingen Prize for poetry to Ezra Pound, 'literary criticism', most generally considered, made it plain that a poet's anti-Semitism, even when it was to be found in his poetry, had no bearing on his work's merit.[27] Notwithstanding an emergent Feminist literary criticism, in which literature's systemic misrepresentation of women was scrutinized, there was no parallel interest in Jewish stereotypes. Literary anti-Semitism was inassimilable, a kind of blind spot in Cambridge English. This was an *institutional* and *ideological* blind spot of course, not the product of anti-Semitism among Faculty teachers.[28]

I should add that I did not find George Steiner's work especially useful in this respect. In the months between school and university, I had gone to Israel, where I had read his book of essays, *Language and Silence* (1969). It was the breadth of his cultural reference that most struck me, and his willingness to address questions that mainstream English literary criticism, such as I understood it to be at the time, failed to confront. He wrote about the connections between literature and philosophy, and about English culture as part of European culture. He wrote about the Holocaust, and about what it meant to be a Jew in a post-Holocaust world. He did not shy away from references to his own life; the 'personal' did not embarrass him. There was a rawness and an urgency of appeal about his writing that compared well, in my judgement, with the detached civilities of more conventional literary criticism. Steiner's work seemed to me to be one great dissent from 'Cambridge English'. But in the end he did not help me sort out my problems with English literature, partly because he was no longer teaching at Cambridge when I arrived there, but more importantly because—though he rejected literature's ability to redeem the unregenerate, the wicked—he too took for granted literature's own essential goodness. His critique of literature as humanism, or what he termed, in a much later book, 'the correlations between the humanities and the inhumane',[29] failed to address the inhumane *inside* the humanities. This is the moral problem of literary anti-Semitism, and Steiner's investigations stopped short in front of it. Later on, I also had misgivings about his anti-Zionism, which seemed to me to be no more than a trivial romanticizing of the exilic condition. 'Six thousand years of self-awareness are a homeland',[30] he wrote—to which the only proper response can be, 'No, they are *not*.' Homelessness is not the Jewish vocation.[31]

So, while I investigated English literary anti-Semitism at Cambridge, I did so in spite of Cambridge. I found that I was studying anti-Semitic literature in my own time and that there was, in this regard, little connection between what I was being taught and my own experience of part, at least, of what I was reading. The few critical works on the subject gave me little direction—Montague F. Modder's *The Jew in the Literature of England to the End of the 19th Century* (1939), Edgar Rosenberg's *From Shylock to Svengali* (1960), and Harold Fisch's *The Dual Image* (1959; 1971). In 1976 I made my own, very small contribution to this body of writing, contributing a piece, 'Jewish faces', for the Cambridge University Jewish Society magazine. I protested about English literary anti-Semitism in language that I would not now use: 'Jewish students of literature, ever compelled to qualify their admiration, ever shrinking from the vulnerability of a complete response, read Marlowe or Boswell, or Cobbett, or Carlyle, or Ezra Pound, and find themselves eloquently condemned, vilified . . . ' etc. This slightly frantic tone is to be explained, I think, by my inability to find a critical language appropriate to my subject. I did not want my writing to be 'personal' (with all that that entailed in loss of critical poise), but adopting an 'impersonal' idiom seemed to shut out the very possibility of addressing literary anti-Semitism altogether. I was not a dissenter from Cambridge English; I had made its principles my own. But I was also aware that they made impossible the kind of inquiry I wanted to undertake. It was only ten years after I graduated, when I started a PhD on T. S. Eliot, that I was able to reject them—and even then, it took me some time to do so.[32]

I did, however, have one Cambridge experience that had a bearing on my study of English literary anti-Semitism. In my third year, just before Passover, a pamphlet was pushed through the front door of the house where I rented some rooms. My landlady brought it up to me, though my name was not written anywhere on it. The pamphlet comprised just four sheets of photocopied, typed pages. It warned its readers against any contact with Jews during the coming month, and urged parents to keep their children indoors or under close supervision. Gentiles everywhere, but especially Gentile boys, it said, were at risk of abduction and murder. It was the time of year when Jews preyed upon Gentiles for the blood they needed to make matzos, the unleavened bread eaten at Passover. Ritual murder, the pamphlet announced, is a reality that we overlook at our peril. The tone was self-consciously restrained. Multiply footnoted, with bogus references to well-known scholarly works, the pamphlet purported to give considered, thoroughly factual, advice. The publisher was the 'Little St Hugh of Lincoln Society'. I came to realize, long after I had graduated, that many of the literary works I was then reading play variations on aspects of just this calumny of the Jews. This is a major theme in the present book.

★★★

Upon graduation, I took up law studies, and sat the examinations necessary to qualify as a solicitor. Within two years of qualifying, I was defending a libel case for the Board of Deputies of British Jews, the representative body of Anglo-Jewry. During the 1983 General Election, the Board had distributed flyers in a marginal constituency drawing the local electorate's attention to the fact that the Conservative Party's candidate was formerly a member of the National Front, a political party of the Far Right. He was duly defeated in the poll, notwithstanding a national swing in favour of the Conservatives. Blaming the Board for his defeat, he sued, arguing that the implication of the flyer was that he was, among other disreputable things, anti-Semitic. But he abandoned the case before it came to court, so the proposition of the defence, that one was entitled to infer anti-Semitism from membership of the National Front, was not tested. More than a decade later, in a case that did come to court, I found myself engaged once again in litigation with someone complaining that he had been defamed as an anti-Semite.

The complaint was about a book, *Denying the Holocaust*, written by Deborah Lipstadt, an American university professor. The book described the well-known writer David Irving as a Holocaust denier. He did not care for the description, and sued both Lipstadt and her publishers, Penguin Books, for defamation. They were separately represented in the proceedings, with my firm acting for Lipstadt herself. Irving could have sued in the USA, but he chose to sue in England because English law gives certain advantages to libel claimants. He complained that the book represented him to be a Nazi apologist, a manipulator of the historical record, a Holocaust denier, a racist, and a consorter with racists. The defendants broadly agreed that that was indeed how the book characterized him, and they insisted that it was the truth about him. They added that he was an anti-Semite too. The bad history he wrote was a consequence of the bad politics he espoused. Irving also claimed that he was the victim of an international Jewish conspiracy to silence and discredit him. Here the defendants did not agree, and nor in due course did the judge.[33]

The only witnesses to the Holocaust Irving accepted were those who saw nothing. Euphemistic or otherwise evasive documents were taken at face value; documents that were candid about the extermination process were dismissed as forgeries or otherwise explained away or ignored. An unattainable standard of proof was demanded to 'prove' the Holocaust; anything, however flimsy and unreliable, was accepted to 'disprove' it. Consistency could not be found at the level of methodology, only at the level of politics. It was by the systematic application of 'double standards'[34] that Irving honoured Hitler's memory. By the time it came to trial, Irving had utterly lost control of his case. He was embattled, defensive—unable to cope. Required to disclose his library of speeches, diaries, and other written materials, he thereby secured the defendants' case against his politics. Confronted by expert reports that he was unable to counter, he thereby conceded their case against his historiography. The disclosure hanged him; the expert evidence hanged him a second time over. Irving was not especially dextrous as a litigant. His advocacy at trial comprised a combination of quibbles, abuse, and self-pity. There was a quality of play-acting about his performance. 'Irving', noted one trial observer, 'switched with bewildering rapidity from one persona after another.'[35] When he gave evidence, he displayed a misplaced, incoherent ingenuity. Challenged, for example, with the obvious falsification of a document, he first offered the defence, 'a silly misreading', and when that turned out to be unsustainable, explained it away as a slip of the memory. When that too failed, he claimed that dictionary definitions of the falsified word would bear him out—but was then unable to produce the dictionaries.[36]

The case began on 11 January 2000 and lasted ten weeks. The evidence of expert witnesses dominated the proceedings; no Holocaust survivors were called; Lipstadt herself did not give evidence. Mr Justice Gray heard the case without a jury. He delivered his 335-page judgment on 11 April 2000. The judge decided the case in favour of the defendants, Lipstadt and Penguin. There was never any real doubt that they would win. Irving's falsifications and distortions were so egregious, and his animus towards Jews so plain, that he won the case for them. They had proved the truth of their allegations against Irving not by proving the truth of the Holocaust (which was never in issue) but by proving the truth of Irving's manipulation of the historical record (which became *the* issue in the case). The multiple concessions made by Irving during the course of the trial[37] did not save him from the judgment that he was indeed a Holocaust denier. The judge also decided that he was an anti-Semite, a racist, a falsifier of the historical record, and 'a right-wing, pro-Nazi polemicist'.[38] An interim costs order was made against Irving in the sum of £150,000. Irving, who had represented himself at trial, instructed lawyers to represent him on his appeal. The appeal was heard in June 2001 and dismissed. Penguin then enforced the costs order and when Irving did not pay, bankrupted him. After the trial, he was asked, 'Will you stop denying the Holocaust on the basis of this judgment?' Irving replied, 'Good Lord, no.'[39] The case attracted a great deal of attention, and large claims continue to be made for its significance. By contrast, Holocaust deniers were quick to dismiss it. 'Gray's verdict', said one denier, 'was predictable, given the display of naked Jewish power during the trial.'[40]

Anti-Semitism is always a base folly, but Holocaust denial is an egregious, especially degraded folly. In anti-Semitism's abject history, there is nothing quite so cranky, nothing quite so ignominious, as the insistence, contrary to all evidence, that Nazi Germany and its allies did not murder European Jews, systematically and in their millions, by gassing and by shooting. This insistence, invariably made in bad faith, has a certain relation to that other nonsensical proposition, that the Jews are an international conspiracy whose activities were revealed when minutes of some of their meetings were discovered and then published. The one eliminates from existence an immense crime, the other summons into existence a non-existent manuscript. But both purport to reveal a concealed truth; both blame the Jews for its concealment. They also need each other. If the Jews truly were murdered in such numbers, then the fantasy of Jewish power implicit in the *Protocols* must be wrong. Denial is an attempt at extermination on paper; it revives the dead in order to strike at the living.[41] Deniers seek to unwrite the history of the Holocaust. Their desire is not to explain, but to explain *away*. They wish to add grievous insult to even more grievous injury by denying the truth of that injury. They delight in their impiety—their dishonouring of the Jewish dead, their tormenting of Jewish survivors.[42] Holocaust denial is in this sense the discursive equivalent of cemetery desecration—another sport of anti-Semites.

Our relations with Penguin were difficult on occasion. Their stance, unflinchingly hostile to Irving, was determined by considerations of freedom of speech. When asked to explain why they were resolved upon fighting Irving, when commercial considerations pointed towards settling with him, they cited their company's tradition of 'upholding the right to publish'.[43] Lipstadt's stance was more complex. As an American, she too had an instinctive, almost unreflective, commitment to freedom of speech—she had argued against the censorship of Holocaust deniers in her book on just those grounds. But defending her own right to free speech was too abstract a proposition to support the conflict with Irving. She was motivated instead by fidelity to the memory of the Jewish dead, the victims of the Shoah. Indeed, this lent passion and vigour to the efforts of us all. We felt that we were engaged in a great undertaking, one characterized by both piety and resistance. There was a sense that battle had been joined with an anti-Semite in which, for once, the oppressor did not have the upper hand. Victory gave comfort both to survivors and to their families; it was even taken by some to vindicate the memory of the dead. Jews and non-Jews of goodwill came together in defence of the historical truth of the Holocaust.

It was perhaps inevitable that these two perspectives on the case would sometimes collide. Certainly, by the end of the case, I had formed the impression that Penguin had become rather disaffected with our approach to the case, and were casting about for some symbolic gesture of detachment from us. The opportunity arose for them sooner than anyone could have anticipated. Within weeks of it being given, Penguin published Mr Justice Gray's judgment, and donated the sale proceeds to a hospital specializing in the treatment of cancer patients. I took the donation to be a rejection of what they took as our specifically Jewish perspective. Everyone suffers from cancer; it is no respecter of ethnicity. The donation felt like a snub. Was it? Was I being too 'touchy'?

The importance attached by Jews to the Irving case surprised me. By the survivors among them, I suspect it may have something to do with an intense, unsatisfied desire to be rescued, one that survives their liberation. Perhaps also present was a desire to repeat their witness, even if vicariously, and thereby to ease the burden of what must still remain an essentially incommunicable experience.[44] I do not know. But the engagement with the case of Jews of my own, and my children's, generation is more easily explained. Many such Jews have come to define themselves most sharply, to live their lives most intensely as Jews, by reference to anti-Semitism. They realize themselves as Jews in resistance to their persecutors, or (more typically) by reliving the resistance to persecution of *other* Jews. Studying these histories—almost always, Holocaust histories—has now become a major aspect of Jewish self-understanding. Alain Finkielkraut has subjected this tendency to trenchant criticism, articulated in appropriately self-lacerating language: 'I inherited a suffering to which I had not been subjected, for without having to endure oppression, the identity of the victim was mine. I could savour an exceptional destiny while remaining completely at ease. Without exposure to real danger, I had heroic stature.'[45] And yet, among the people that constitute the present generation, it is given to no one to say: I am the child of Auschwitz. 'The Holocaust', Finkielkraut writes, 'has no heirs.'[46] I agree.

To find myself in a major set-piece fight with a Holocaust denier was the purest chance. One could be fully committed to Jewish communal defence, actively engaged daily and for years, without confronting Holocaust denial, save when researching it. Holocaust denial itself is an utterly marginal phenomenon—in England, at least.[47] It is so limited in appeal, indeed, that it functions as a kind of shibboleth among the denizens of the Far Right, the sign by which they choose to declare themselves to each other. It is against a quite different mobilization of the Holocaust that Jews now have to contend, not Holocaust denial but a kind of perverse Holocaust *affirmation*, in which it is asserted that the Jews are the beneficiaries as well as the victims of the Holocaust *and* that they are the perpetrators of a new holocaust against the Palestinians. I refer, of course, to a certain kind of contemporary, abusive, and historically illiterate version of anti-Zionism, one that has the potential of even further degradation, sliding into anti-Semitism—specifically that version of anti-Semitism represented by hatred of Israel, the Jew among the nations. Any Jew writing about anti-Semitism today is likely to have this version at the forefront of his or her mind. Certainly, it has figured prominently in the present book.

The litigating of quarrels that bear upon Israel has comprised a substantial part of my legal practice in the last few years. I acted for Ariel Sharon in connection with the PCC complaint described in Chapter 7. I have defended the Board of Deputies against the charity Interpal. I represented the Middle East Media Research Institute (MEMRI) against London's then Mayor, Ken Livingstone. I have represented Haifa University and the Hebrew University of Jerusalem against the Association of University Teachers (AUT), and the interests of Israeli universities and Jewish academics more generally against the National Association of Teachers in Further and Higher Education (NATFHE), and the University and College Union (UCU). I have, indeed, been active for some time in arguing against academic and cultural boycotts of Israel.[48] These commitments have contributed towards my understanding of the nature and limits of contemporary anti-Semitism in England.

★★★

This is all quite different from being the subject of an anti-Semitic attack. The only time in my legal career I have had *that* experience is during the period that I represented Diana, Princess of Wales.

I acted for Diana in the last four years of her life. An existing client had introduced her to my firm. My first job was to sue the person who had surreptitiously photographed her exercising at a gym. I then acted for her in her divorce from the Prince of Wales. She telephoned me one afternoon and asked me to come to see her at her home in Kensington Palace. She had received two letters, one from her husband and one from her mother-in-law. Both required of her that she agree to a divorce. The letters had arrived within an hour of each other. She asked me to review them with her. Could I help her draft replies to them? Could I act for her in the inevitable divorce? I told her that it would be my first divorce case. She replied that it didn't matter—this would be her first divorce. Until then, I had avoided doing divorce work; it had no appeal to me. In the event, the Wales' divorce was not complicated. The parties behaved well. Terms were agreed relatively quickly; there were no contested court hearings; there were no unpleasant exchanges about the children.

Diana herself lived as if in a vacuum. She was under-educated in the approved style of her class and gender. She was very receptive to new experiences, which meant that she was sometimes taken by odd fancies. She had a strong desire to please, to leave her interlocutor happy, but often without quite understanding what that person was 'about'. She was intuitive, but not always accurate in her assessments of people. Sometimes, she went wildly wrong—not just in the big things, but also in odd misreadings of moods or sentiments. I never had the feeling that she set out to impress—perhaps she had surrendered that ambition as a child. But she wanted to be valued. She would talk about her 'work', by which she meant her charities. She was interested in Jews, but had no idea about them, save that Jewish men (she had heard) were more likely than the men of her own class and background to treat women decently. She was happy to take Jews to be hostile to everything to which she herself was hostile. She once said to me that she should never have married into a German family. She was interested in everything that was outside her own world; she had a tendency to esteem a thing just because it was *not* part of her world—even more if it was excluded by her world. She herself was not quite of that world, but did not belong to any other either. She gave the impression of living in a general condition of alienation, but that did not prevent her from operating very successfully in many different milieus.

Since everything about and around her was of interest to the media, I myself became of interest to the media. Several newspapers and magazines published profiles of me, in the main composed out of clichés. As a Jew I was an 'outsider', not 'Establishment', and this confirmed Diana's own 'outsider' status. I was also an 'intellectual', a contrast to the unacademic Diana. My background was middle-middle class, a contrast with Prince Charles's lawyer, Fiona Shackleton, a partner at the Royal Family's law firm. The profiles tended to be uncertain how to assess the significance of my Jewish identity, save that they all took it to be of *immense* significance. I also started receiving odd letters during this time. Some gave me advice, some chastised me for disrespect towards the monarchy, and some were anti-Semitic. It was all rather bemusing, but nothing more than an intermittent, minor distraction from the negotiations themselves.

The item in the Saturday 13 July 1996 edition of the *Telegraph* was of an entirely different order. The newspaper had been markedly friendlier to Charles than to Diana during the course of the divorce. The item appeared the day after the settlement between them had been announced. Under the headline 'Solicitors with irreconcilable differences' it read:

> It became clear almost immediately that the incompatibility of the Prince and Princess of Wales stretched even to the solicitors they had employed.
>
> The Prince, as expected, had chosen the bridge-playing Fiona Shackleton, 39, of Farrer and Co., who had also represented the Duke of York in his separation agreement.

One of the country's most respected family law specialists, much of Shackleton's career has been geared to arranging favourable divorce settlements for her clients. She adopts a conciliatory approach.

Unfortunately, her softly-softly approach is at odds with the more bullish attitude of the Princess's solicitor.

Anthony 'Genius' Julius, 39, is not a divorce lawyer but a specialist in media law, acting for Robert Maxwell and once employed by the *Daily Mail*.

His background could not be further from the upper-class world inhabited by his opposite number. He is a Jewish intellectual and Labour supporter, and less likely to feel restrained by considerations of fair play. 'I'd be very worried if I were the Royal Family,' says a Cambridge don who taught him. 'He'll get lots of money out of them.'

The author went on to speculate about whether I had in fact secured a good settlement for the Princess.

I had touched on this kind of anti-Semitism in my book on Eliot.[49] It is rather well expressed in a Kipling poem, 'The Waster, 1930':

> Slack by training and slow by birth,
> Only quick to despise,
> Largely assessing his neighbour's worth
> By the hue of his socks or ties,
> A loafer-in-grain, his foes maintain,
> And how shall we combat their view
> When, atop of his natural sloth, he holds
> There are Things no Fellow can do?
> (Which is why he is licked from the first by the Pict
> And left at the post by, etc.)[50]

The poem relates cleverness to unscrupulousness, and contrasts it with 'character'. It presents itself as an exercise in fair-mindedness; indeed, it insists upon its fair-mindedness. The waster is feckless, superficial in judgement, 'quick to despise'. But he is a gentleman, because he has been schooled in the tacit constraints of civilized life. He has character; he plays by the rules. He is, to return to the language of the *Telegraph*, 'likely to feel restrained by considerations of fair play'. The Pict and the 'etc.' do not consider themselves to be restrained thus. And the 'etc.' is, of course, the Jew—the word that conforms to the poem's *abab* rhyming scheme, and is intimated by 'do' in the first and last stanzas. For the *Telegraph*, I was just such a Jew.

I did not see the item until I was told about it. Several people telephoned me on the following Monday. The legal director of the *Telegraph* Group also called me, late that morning. Complaints had been received. I should know that the journalist had written '*outmoded* considerations of fair play'. It was a sub-editor who had cut down the phrase to 'fair play', and she was Jewish herself. Still—what would I like the paper to do? I said that it could do what it liked. The next day, at the foot of another story about the royal divorce, the following item appeared:

> Our royal divorce coverage last Saturday included profiles of the legal principals involved, Anthony Julius, of Mishcon de Reya, for the Princess of Wales, and Fiona Shackleton, of Farrer and Co. for Prince Charles.
>
> Intended to compare and contrast their styles, but without in any way seeking to question his professional integrity, we referred to Mr. Julius's background as a Jewish intellectual in a context which we now recognise, to our profound regret, to have appeared pejorative.
>
> Many readers have taken the strongest exception to this paragraph, making clear that they regard it as a racial slur. In acknowledging the force of this criticism, we offer our sincere apologies to Mr. Julius and to all those who took offence.

This was an edgy, easily embarrassed, anti-Semitism, quick to run for cover.

Not so edgy or embarrassed was the treatment I received at about the same time in a pamphlet entitled 'Who are the Mindbenders? The people who rule Britain through control of the mass media.' It was published in 1997, and a 'revised edition' appeared two years later. It is still in circulation today, a kind of contemporary version of H. H. Beamish's *The Jews' Who's Who* (1920). It was first published anonymously, though the author was later revealed to be Nick Griffin, who is now the leader of the British National Party.[51] Griffin is a Holocaust denier and an admirer of David Irving. In 1998, he was convicted of inciting race hatred and received a two-year suspended sentence. He was, I imagine, somewhat less troubled than the *Telegraph* by the possibility that what he had to say about me might be thought anti-Semitic.

The pamphlet's general argument is that British democracy is a sham because the media, which is controlled by the Jews, determines what the electorate thinks. The Jews pursue a specific programme. They denigrate British race pride and promote race intermarriage. They are protective of their own racial group, and act in concert. Griffin explains that he is not an anti-Semite, if by that is meant a person who wants to hurt or even kill Jews. The Jews will be safe provided that they obey the law, remain loyal, and desist from poisoning the minds of the British people. It is the usual fantasy: a brainless and hypnotized mass at the mercy of the Jewish conspiracy.[52] It plays on right-wing populist anxieties about the 'takeover of our brains'[53] by the modern media, and gives them an anti-Semitic twist.

There are three passages in the pamphlet about me:

> **Anthony Julius**—the Princess of Wales's lawyer and author of a vicious attack
> on the great poet T. S. Eliot, whom he regards as anti-Semitic...

> In *T. S. Eliot, Anti-Semitism and Literary Form*, lawyer and literary critic
> **Anthony Julius** launched a virulent attack on the late Anglo-American
> literary giant as an 'anti-Semite.' Among the evidence produced for this
> heinous crime was Eliot's alleged 'hostility to a type largely of anti-Semitism's
> own invention, the anarchic intellectually subversive Jew.'

> [Inside tramlines, and next to a photograph of me:] **Anthony Julius**. Princess
> Diana's divorce lawyer and author of a ferocious attack on T. S. Eliot.
> To **Julius**, and others like him, any criticism of Jews by Gentiles—even
> when justified by facts and experience—is 'anti-Semitism.' In reality, such
> paranoid over-sensitivity often creates hostility to innocent Jews where none
> existed before.

The pamphlet, a witless piece of work, is indebted to the writings of the
neo-Nazi William L. Pierce (whom it describes as an 'American patriot'). It
conforms in every particular to a form of discourse recently examined by an
American philosopher—that is, it is bullshit.[54] Griffin does not submit to the
constraints imposed by any genuine endeavour to provide an accurate
representation of reality. He is not even trying to get it right. It is not just
that he does not tell the truth (though he does not). It is that he also does not
respect the truth. He is indifferent to how things really are.

The contrast between the *Telegraph* item and pamphlet is plain, I think, and
allows an initial understanding of the difference between mainstream and
fringe English anti-Semitism. Both complain about the Jews' unfair advantage
over Gentiles. For the *Telegraph*, the advantage arises because individual Jews
do not, on the whole, 'play the game'. For 'Mindbenders', it arises because
Jews stick together and dominate society by manipulating the minds of its
Gentile members—most of whom are too dumb to realize what is happening.

★★★

It would be trite to seek to draw lessons from these experiences. But if they do
not themselves teach very much, they do, inescapably, inform my own
perspective on the threats that now bear down on Jews. In summary, I have
a sense of the malignity of many of the current attacks on Jews and the Jewish
State, made possible by a more general ignorance about Jews, Israel, and anti-
Semitism. I have a strong sense of the persistence in this country of an obdurate,
harsh anti-Semitism resistant both to reason and considerations of decency. But
I also have a sense of the need to make distinctions between opponents of

specific Jewish projects and enemies of Jews; between old and new kinds of anti-Semitism; between ignorance of anti-Semitism and anti-Semitism itself; and within instances of anti-Semitism, between the lesser and the greater.

I have written these opening pages because one should be open with one's readers about one's motivation and background, and because one's own history can be useful in the explication of broader historical events.[55] And it seems both fair and useful to say, in explicating contemporary English anti-Semitism, 'I was there'. But there is a limit to this usefulness. This book is more than an account of present times. It may be rooted in a specific political and cultural conjuncture, but it is not a report on that conjuncture. Indeed, it attempts, in its grave ambition, to make sense of one aspect of 850 years of English history. If for this reason alone, the relevant genre within which I have written it has had to be the impersonal work of scholarship. My book could not be a memoir, and the expressly autobiographical element in it has had to be confined to these prefatory words only. And now to my subject.

English anti-Semitisms

English anti-Semitism is not quite understood. In certain respects, it is misunderstood. Its complexity and its strength tend to be underestimated; its history tends to be disregarded; its literature is misinterpreted—or worse, under-interpreted. English anti-Semitism was at one time both lethal and innovative; it continues to be innovative, precisely in the respects in which it is now *non*-lethal. It once threatened Jewish lives; it has for some centuries weakened Jewish morale. And it has been the principal contributor to the anti-Semitic literary canon.

There are many kinds of anti-Semitism, and among that number there are four that have an English provenance, either wholly or in substantial part:

- a radical anti-Semitism of defamation, expropriation, murder, and expulsion—that is, the anti-Semitism of medieval England, which completed itself in 1290, when there were no Jews left to torment (Chapter 3)

- a literary anti-Semitism—that is, an anti-Semitic account of Jews continuously present in the discourse of English literature, from the anonymous medieval ballad 'Sir Hugh, or the Jew's Daughter' through to present times (Chapter 4)

- a modern, quotidian anti-Semitism of insult and partial exclusion, pervasive but contained—that is, the everyday anti-Semitism experienced by

Jews from their 'readmission' to England in the mid-seventeenth century through to the late twentieth century (Chapters 5–6)

- a new configuration of anti-Zionisms, emerging in the late 1960s and the 1970s, which treats Zionism and the State of Israel as illegitimate Jewish enterprises. This perspective, heavily indebted to anti-Semitic tropes, now constitutes the greatest threat to Anglo-Jewish security and morale (Chapters 7–8). By 'tropes' I mean those taken-for-granted utterances,[56] those figures and metaphors through which more general positions are intimated, without ever being argued for.

The hostility directed at Jews in England today is thus a mix of several kinds of anti-Semitism.

(England also had powerful traditions adverse to these versions of Jew-hatred or Jew-contempt. I address them in some of the chapters that follow. One cannot write a book about a nation's anti-Semitism without mentioning instances of esteem for, or indifference towards, Jews or Judaism. The anti-Semitism needs to be set against counter-instances. They comprise a past glory, however. Philo-Semitism, as an aspect of English public discourse, did not survive the passing of the twentieth century.)

While further kinds of anti-Semitism may emerge—new angles of attack on Jews, new configurations of the Jewish 'enemy'—there are unlikely to be any new *English* kinds. Indeed, the fourth kind is more European than English, save in the burden of its history—that is, the intimacy of association between England and the Zionist project from the early twentieth century through to the mid-1950s, and in the plurality of its versions, namely a secular-leftist version and several confessional versions.

Medieval English anti-Semitism, which was in many respects[57] as original as it was violent, amounted to a war against the Jews. A predatory State, an antagonistic Church, and an intermittently but then homicidally violent populace, made Jewish lives always difficult, often intolerable, and finally impossible. Taxable at will, and subject to unrelenting financial depredations, the once wealthy Jewish community was finally degraded to an impoverished rump. Hostilities began in or about 1144, when the ritual murder allegation was first deployed—an allegation that became, in subsequent iterations, the 'blood libel'. The final blow was administered in 1290, when the entire Jewish community was expelled. The years 1144 and 1290 were precedents for persecutions of Jews elsewhere. What England initiated, other European nations tended to imitate; what the universal

Church initiated, the English Church tended to extend. (England, writes one literary scholar, was an enthusiastic innovator and producer of anti-Semitic material.)[58] The worsening relations between Christians and Jews in twelfth- and thirteenth-century Europe found, writes one medieval historian, 'particular expression' in England;[59] the violent anti-Semitism of so original and complicated a cleric as Robert Grosseteste (c.1170–1253), writes another medieval historian, is indicative of the 'precocity of English anti-Semitism'.[60] Church and State were as mobs that howled at the door.[61] Indeed, hatred of the Jews in England was 'vast, abysmal and intense'.[62] The year 1290 marked the first national, enduring expulsion of an entire Jewish population in history.[63] And then the Jews became a mere memory.

Over time, this memory—refracted by a murderous, legend-laden, but most of all triumphant, anti-Semitism—took material form in works of literature. Absent from England itself, the Jews soon became a constant in the English cultural imagination. They figured, and to a diminished extent still figure, in England's oral literature of ballad and song, in its quotidian drama and fiction and poetry, and, last, in some major works in its literary canon—works that adversely characterize Jews, Jewish history, and Judaism. This literature is indebted to, but also constrained by, that first, early medieval Jew-hatred. It is marked by England's decisive defeat of the Jewish enemy. It is further marked by its belligerence towards Jews, a stance realized in the representation of Jews as aggressors. And it is marked by its more than occasional literary merit.

English literary anti-Semitism does not comprise a distinct genre or sub-genre within English literature. It has instead distinct tropes and themes, deployed without respect for genre boundaries. The master trope supposes a well-intentioned Christian placed in peril by a sinister Jew or Jews. The Christian is often a boy; if one Jew acts alone, he acts in conformity with his Jewish character and/or his ritual duties, and if more than one Jew is involved, they act in concert; caught, the victim does not protest, and submits to the malevolent attentions of the Jew; if the victim escapes death, it is by a miracle; if he dies, the facts of the crime, and the location of his body, are revealed by a miracle; the Jew or Jews are often apprehended and punished. It is from within these variables that the first work of literary anti-Semitism, the ballad, 'Sir Hugh, or The Jew's Daughter' (late thirteenth century?),[64] and the three canonic works of literary anti-Semitism—Chaucer's 'Prioress's Tale', one of the *Canterbury Tales* (c.1387–400); Shakespeare's *The Merchant of Venice* (1596–7?); and Dickens's *Oliver Twist* (1837–9)—are all written. These works comprise fictional re-enactments of a unique crime, the Deicide. The pub-lication in a Sunday newspaper of Tom Paulin's poem 'Crossfire' (2001), and the staging of Caryl Churchill's *Seven Jewish Children—A play for Gaza* (2009), is evidence of the trope's continuing appeal to the English literary imagin-ation. English literary anti-Semitism has a certain ubiquity;[65] it is flourishing, its vibrant life evident in both endlessly circulating canonic works and regularly emerging new works.

The modern, everyday anti-Semitism of the last 350 years, inadequately described as 'genteel', 'social', or 'polite', has by its contained, temperate nature ensured its own longevity. It accompanied the completion of Jewish emancipation; it did not impede Jewish entrepreneurial accomplishment; its existence has not inhibited Jews from celebrating England as a place of opportunity and liberty, a 'happy land of freedom'.[66] It is an anti-Semitism that continues to mislead itself about Jews, and thus to be surprised by them. It is often mixed with a certain wary regard for Jews (usually, the product of misconceptions about their qualities). In its most representative moments, it keeps Jews at a certain distance. It is, in this respect, an anti-Semitism of rebuff and of insult, not of expulsion and murder. Its votaries confer in golf clubs; they do not conspire in cellars.[67] In its most aggravated form, this anti-Semitism questions whether Jews can ever be wholehearted members of the English nation, given their assumed adherence to their own nation. It is capable of accusing Jews of entertaining 'dual loyalties'. It is informed—as are most anti-Semitisms—by a measure of historic Christian perplexity and hurt. It has a populist or 'leftist' aspect, and a 'City' or business aspect, in each case stimulated by fear of Jewish financial power. But none of this—questions and accusations, suspicions and resentments, perplexity and hurt, and even fear—has ever put in serious jeopardy Jewish civil rights or communal security. This quotidian anti-Semitism even lacks drama. There have been few trials and riots, very little violence, and no ideo-logical clashes or cultural ferment.[68] It is not, however, wholly discon-tinuous with the radical anti-Semitism of medieval England.[69] It coexisted for some time with the immense ideological anti-Semitisms of the Euro-pean Continent, in part replicating them (but in diminished form), and in part repudiating them. It also continues to coexist with a native literary anti-Semitism, from which it is radically dislocated. This is a distinctively English yoking together of extremes. While the blood libel dominates literary anti-Semitism, it rarely figures in non-literary, public discourse about the Jews.

This fourth, most recent kind of English anti-Semitism is a composite of
anti-Zionisms, principal among which is the 'new anti-Zionism' in many of its
articulations. This composite is so polluted by anti-Semitic tropes that it has
been named the 'new anti-Semitism'. Though its English version largely
replicates a hatred of international dimensions, in several of its iterations it is
burdened by specifically British imperial guilts (the Balfour Declaration, the
Palestine Mandate, the Suez Crisis) just as it is bloated with the contributions of
certain Muslim radicals granted asylum in the 1990s.[70] It denies to Jews the
rights that it upholds for other, comparable peoples. It adheres to the principle
of national self-determination, except in the Jews' case. It affirms international
law, except in Israel's case. It does not understand that supporting the cause of
Palestinian nationhood is one thing, while denying the right of Jews to live in
their own state is quite another.[71] It is outraged by the Jewish nature of the State
of Israel, but is untroubled (say) by the Islamic nature of Iran or of Saudi Arabia.
It regards as racist the social inequalities between Jew and Arab in Israel, while
being indifferent to the legal inequalities between Muslim and non-Muslim in
Iran, Saudi Arabia, and other Muslim states. It regards Jewish nationalism (i.e.,
Zionism) as uniquely pernicious, rather than as merely another nationalism,
just as earlier generations of anti-Semites regarded Jewish capitalists as uniquely
pernicious, rather than as heterogeneous members of a much larger capitalist
class. It is indifferent to Jewish suffering, while being sensitive to the suffering of
non-Jews. It writes out of the history of the Israeli–Palestinian conflict the
massacres of Jews in, say, Hebron (August 1929), Jerusalem (February 1948),
and Kfar Etzion (May 1948),[72] while treating the massacre of Arabs at Deir
Yasin (April 1948) as proof of fundamental Zionist iniquity. It is reluctant to
take a position on (say) the Chinese occupation of Tibet,[73] while holding the
Israeli occupation of the West Bank an indefensible evil of global consequence.
It makes an *exception* of the Jewish State.[74] It is hostile to the United States,
which it believes is dominated by Jews and acts at their bidding. It plays
variations on well-established anti-Semitic tropes and deploys some new
ones of its own (principally, that Israel may suitably be compared with Nazi
Germany and/or Apartheid South Africa). It treats UN, and UN committee
and council, resolutions on Israel as if passed by impartial, apolitical bodies.[75] It
denies the existence of Islamic anti-Semitism, save perhaps as a Western import
and of no practical consequence; anti-Semitism in general is dismissed either as
a phantasm exploited by Jews to pursue their own goals or as no more than a
rational judgement on them. While it excoriates racist sentiments found among
Israelis, or in the complex history of Zionism, it refuses to acknowledge the

racist themes towards Jews to be found in many currents of Arab nationalism.[76] It overstates, on every occasion, and beyond reason, any case that could be made against Israel's actions or policies (e.g., 'No other country has such a record of lawlessness: not one of the world's tyrannies comes close'),[77] and *wildly* overstates the significance of the Israeli–Palestinian conflict in world affairs—indeed, it puts Jews at the centre of world affairs.[78] Many 'new anti-Zionists' are either anti-Semites or fellow travellers with anti-Semitism; long-standing anti-Semites now embrace 'anti-Zionism' as a cover for their Jew-hatred. This is because, in relation to Israel, the anti-Semite finds a protected voice.[79] The desire to destroy Jews is reconfigured as the desire to destroy or dismantle the Jewish State. It is no longer the 'Jewish peril' but the 'Israeli peril' that constitutes the risk to global peace and security, and which therefore must be combated. The new anti-Zionism has become a cause for some English academics and political activists; it is most commonly found in the universities and in student and university teacher associations.[80] Anti-Zionism has renewed anti-Semitism, and given it a future.

In England today, anti-Semitism subsists in a state of some complexity. Though the blood libel continues to circulate in several barely disguised versions, medieval anti-Semitism itself is barely remembered—though the British National Party held several 'Remembrance Day' rallies in York, described as the historic site of English resistance to 'alien money-lenders'.[81] English literary anti-Semitism persists, not least because of the popularity of *The Merchant of Venice* and *Oliver Twist*, but also because it still provides themes for writers hostile to Jews or to Jewish projects. Quotidian anti-Semitism has been waning, but in the last decades it has been supplemented by an anti-Semitic anti-Zionism that many English Jews find truly frightening. These two quite different kinds of anti-Semitism—essentially, one of condescension and contempt, and one of an aggressive, ostensibly fearful hostility—can coexist in the very same place, and at the very same time. In the House of Lords, for example, within a single decade:

- Upon the archbishop of Canterbury being introduced to the House as a peer by Lord Janner, two Conservative peers were overheard: 'Who's that introducing the Archbishop?' 'Oh, just some Jew.'[82]

- In a speech on the Middle East, Baroness Tonge asked, 'Why can Israel continue its actions when other countries have sanctions imposed, or are invaded, for less?' The answer, she explained, was to be found in the power of the 'Israel Lobby'.[83]

The peers in these stories would certainly deny that their remarks were anti-Semitic—the former, because they comprised nothing more than casual disparagement and certainly not ideological Jew-hatred; the latter, because they concerned Israel and its 'lobby' rather than Jews in general, and were accompanied by an express repudiation of anti-Semitic intent. Against this, however, it is the argument of the present book that both casual disparagement of Jews and 'Lobby talk' *can* be anti-Semitic.

These then are England's gifts to Jew-hatred. The anti-Semitism of no other country has this density of history. The anti-Semitism of no other country is so continuously innovative. On many occasions in the history of anti-Semitism, as will become plain in the chapters that follow, England arrives *first*. Against that tendency in contemporary historiography to relieve English history of the burden of being earliest in everything,[84] my emphasis is therefore on English priority. English anti-Semitisms are exemplary, while the anti-Semitisms of other nations are in most instances but variants of them (often, of course, immensely aggravated variants). These English anti-Semitisms—this English exceptionalism, in the matter of anti-Semitism—are among the trials of the Diaspora.

Some preliminary problems in writing about English anti-Semitism

The term 'anti-Semitism' is of course itself problematical. It implies a Jewish racial identity, and it dignifies vicious and degraded sentiments with the status of an ideology. It was invented, indeed, to serve precisely these objects. In a century of ideologies, Jew-haters were troubled by the absence of a coherent ideology of Jew-hatred; the stupidity of mere Jew-baiting embarrassed them. They did not want to be thought of as mere purveyors of prejudice; they insisted that they were not 'vulgar'—that is, popular, unreflective—Jew-haters. They wanted their hatred to be both diagnostic and programmatic, that is to say to explain precisely *how* 'Jews' constituted precisely *what* 'problem', and how that problem should be solved. The term 'anti-Semitism' addressed precisely this ambition. It was the coinage of a Jew-hater, Wilhelm Marr, who wanted to make Jew-hatred intellectually respectable, even necessary. He wanted, that is, to elevate a miscellany of hostilities into a theory, and then to put that theory onto a neutral, scientific footing. Though he failed in this ambition, the term itself went into general circulation. By 1884, it had already been adopted in England,[85] and the usage was confirmed in the entry 'anti-Semitism' in *The Jewish Encyclopedia* (1901): 'While the term "Anti-Semitism" should be restricted in its use to the modern movements against the Jews, in its wider sense it may be said to include the persecution of the Jews at all times and among all nations...'. This 'wider sense' has indeed been adopted, with the consequence that hatred of Jews tends to be viewed as a continuously present, integral aspect of a single 'mentality', summarily identified as 'Western civilization'.

This has been very unfortunate, not least because it is false. On several occasions, 'anti-Semitism' provoked the Jewish philosopher and political scientist Leo Strauss to dismissive anger. It is 'certainly a most improper term', he wrote. 'Our worst enemies are called... "anti-Semites",' he also wrote, 'a word which I shall never use, and which I regard as almost obscene.' 'Why not', he asked, 'call it as we Jews call it? It is *rish'us*, "viciousness".'[86] I am sympathetic to Strauss's position. So while I have not myself departed from common usage, and therefore write of 'anti-Semitism', I nonetheless reject most of the term's implications—and all of its claims. I regard anti-Semitism as a discontinuous, contingent aspect of a number of distinct *mentalités* and milieus, none of which has so dominated the West as to make dissenting perspectives impossible. It is a heterogeneous phenomenon, the site of collective hatreds, and of cultural anxieties and resentments. The search for a single, unified theory of anti-Semitism is an idle one. There is no essence of anti-Semitism. It is instead in the irreducible plurality of its forms of existence that 'anti-Semitism' is to be understood and studied.[87] These anti-Semitisms share certain resemblances, of course— somewhat like members of a single family. When I write of 'anti-Semitism' in the singular (as I often do), it is this family name that I have in mind. Of course, there are more anti-Semites than there are anti-Semitisms. Jew-hatred of any kind impoverishes Jew-haters, impressing their minds with concepts that leave them helpless before the world's reality; dulling their capacity to react to the diversity of humankind; driving their thinking into predetermined grooves; making them unresponsive to new experiences, to fresh ways of understanding their own and other societies, and to their own and other lives. Anti-Semitism forces Jews *and* anti-Semites into pre-sized boxes—the Jews in fantasy, the anti-Semites in reality. It is in this respect, so to speak, *doubly* Procrustean.

How best, then, to conceive of anti-Semitism? Perhaps as a repertoire of attitudes, myths, and defamations in circulation at any given time. It is a kind of discursive swamp, a resource on which religious and political movements, writers and artists, demagogues, and the variously disaffected, all draw, without ever draining. It is not a political philosophy, or anything close to one.[88] It is not a conception of the world; it is merely an *idée fixe*—a hatred, dressed up as a conviction. Even the more reflective anti-Semites mostly just misappropriate the ideas of others, polluting these ideas with their own Jew-hatred. They misappropriate a theology of Jesus' martyrdom in order to incriminate Jews, the 'Deicides'. They misappropriate a critique of capitalism in order to defame Jews, the 'plutocrats'. They misappropriate a sentiment of national pride in order to exclude Jews, the 'internal enemies'. Anti-Semitism cannot claim the equivalent of a St Paul, a Locke, or a Marx. Anti-Semitism gives lumpen-thinkers the opportunity to barge into debates of genuine intellectual consequence. It is not an ideology; it is instead a protean, unstable combination of received ideas, compounded by malice. Anti-Semitism has a place in the history of ideas only in the sense that a burglar has a place in a house.

How to identify it?

Anti-Semitism has become a contested, and on occasion a litigated, phenomenon.[89] Some do not see it; some see it in many places and contexts. Some argue that what others construe to be anti-Semitism is no more than a provocation, or an innocent remark, or a distraction from real politics, or even justified criticism of Israel or of Zionism. Those others may then respond, 'No, all this is anti-Semitic.' This in turn elicits the further response, especially from critics of Israel: 'We are *not* anti-Semitic, and to say otherwise is nothing but a smear, intended to silence us.'[90] (And this too is now being litigated.)[91] The argument, which has a pre-history,[92] thus plays out on two levels. There are confrontations over anti-Semitic statements or events, and there are confrontations over whether certain statements or events properly can be described as anti-Semitic. In this, as in many other respects, anti-Semitism differs from other forms of racism. There is no serious dispute about the nature of racism; racist events are rarely ambiguous in their form. Anti-Semitism is different; or it has become different. It now needs to be *explained*. Few anti-Semites are now as obliging as the early nineteenth-century German Karl Wilhelm Grattenauer, who published a bestselling pamphlet with the unambiguous title, *Against the*

Jews;[93] or the late nineteenth-century Pole, Stanislaw Staaszic, who left his readers in no doubt regarding his anti-Semitism by publishing a pamphlet entitled *Concerning the Reasons for the Obnoxiousness of the Jews*;[94] or as forthright as either the pseudonymous correspondent of Cecil Chesterton's *New Witness*, who signed himself as 'Anti-Semite',[95] the British diplomat who confessed in a private communication at the turn of the twentieth century, 'I hate Jews',[96] or the American Arabist and man of affairs, Charles R. Crane (1858–1939), who explained that he considered the term 'anti-Semite' to be a 'title of honour'.[97] The current confusion, as well as much deliberate obfuscation, about what counts as anti-Semitism derives from a combination of factors, chief among which is a collective amnesia in respect of anti-Semitism's history, an impoverished understanding of the Holocaust, and the desire above all else to distinguish hatred of Israel from hatred of Jews.

Disagreements about what counts as anti-Semitic are quite new to anti-Semitism's history, partly because until recently, there was no shame in being hostile to Jews, and partly because the hostile measures taken against them were incapable of being misunderstood as anything *other* than hostile. This changed, in England, around the turn of the twentieth century. The immediate occasion was the debate over Jewish immigration, and it took place in the context of widely reported persecution of Jews in both Western and Eastern Europe. Many campaigners against Jewish immigration into England were anxious to distance themselves from the unreasoned, inequitable, destructive passions associated with the Dreyfus Affair in France and the State-sponsored pogroms in Russia. They said, in effect, 'We are not anti-Semitic, we are merely concerned about the impact of uncontrolled immigration on the nation's well-being, and what is more, there are Jews who agree with us.'[98] Or they said, when pushed to acknowledge that they did indeed have Jews in their sights: 'We are not anti-Semitic, because we are not against Jews as such—not, that is, against *all* Jews. We are against one kind of Jew alone.'[99] In due course, this became a reflex.[100] They claimed the right to interpret their own words and policies. They were always acquitting themselves of anti-Semitism, though they were almost always wrong to do so. (Anti-Semites lie to or deceive themselves, just as many other people do.)[101] It is too generous to them to commend them for their restraint in not abusing *all* Jews: their anti-Semitism was *predicated* upon a false distinction between 'good' and 'bad' Jews.[102]

The anti-Semitic A. H. Lane, for example, believed that the government was 'being dictated to or inspired by foreigners bent on wrecking the British Empire and working in conjunction with aliens and traitors living in it', and attacked the influence of 'the Prussian Jew, Karl Marx', the 'internationalists among whom those of the Jewish faith predominate' and who 'control Bolshevism', and even the 'Free Trade Movement', which 'has always been well supported and financed by Jews'. Yet he also insisted, 'This criticism of Jewish influence is not anti-Semitic.' It is as if the mere making of the statement is to be taken as sufficient in itself to refute the charge. It was most unfortunate, Lane continued in his book *The Alien Menace* (1932), that the Jews' 'persistent attempt to dominate and control the financial and political policies of the nations of the world' would inevitably 'create friction and disturbances'.[103] The foolish, sinister Jews caused the very anti-Semitism that they then complained about. The Jews' true friends were those like Lane, ready to expose Jewish plots in the interests both of the plotters and those against whom they were plotting. Lane was an early elaborator of this trope of anti-Semitic discourse. Certainly, there are few anti-Semites today who are not also declared enemies of 'anti-Semitism'.

How much time to devote to it?

This is a very long book.

In 1927, Freud received a request from Arnold Zweig (1887–1968), the German-Jewish novelist and man of letters. Zweig had just completed the writing of a book on anti-Semitism, one that drew on psychoanalytical concepts. Would Freud permit Zweig to dedicate it to him? There is then a small gap in the published correspondence, and the next letter is from Freud telling Zweig how proud he was of the message in the dedication. He turns to the subject of the book:

> With regard to anti-Semitism I don't really want to search for explanations; I feel a strong inclination to surrender to my affect in this matter and find myself confirmed in my wholly non-scientific belief that mankind on the average and taken by and large are a wretched lot.[104]

Freud's texts in those years contain scattered remarks on anti-Semitism that are consistent with this surrender to affect. In the *Interpretation of Dreams* (1900),[105] Freud glanced at anti-Semitism as an aspect of his own formation. In 'Analysis of a phobia in a five-year-old boy'—the 'Little Hans' study, first published in 1905—he confined to a footnote the thought that perhaps the castration complex is the deepest unconscious root of anti-Semitism (because it gives Gentile boys a right to despise Jews).[106] In *Civilisation and its*

Discontents (1930), he offers this mordant observation: 'unfortunately, all the massacres of Jews in the Middle Ages did not suffice to make that period more peaceful and secure for their Christian fellows'.[107] But witticisms did not in the end satisfy him. In 1934, he wrote to Zweig explaining the genesis of his final completed work *Moses and Monotheism* (1939). 'Faced with the new persecutions, one asks oneself again how the Jews have come to be what they are and why they have attracted this undying hatred. *I soon discovered the formula*: Moses created the Jews.'[108] (Italics added.) In this strange book, written in response to the unignorable Nazi threat, Freud posits that Moses was an Egyptian murdered by the Hebrews to whom he introduced monotheism. Their valiant fidelity to monotheism as an ideal, however, has ensured its survival.

This journey of Freud's, from an exasperated, generalized misanthropy ('mankind are a wretched lot') to a single, encompassing theory of anti-Semitism ('I soon discovered the formula'), has an exemplary significance. When confronted by anti-Semitism, most Jews, indeed, are likely to hesitate between versions of just these responses.

The first is to arrange one's defences, and then spend no further time on the matter. Anti-Semites are wicked people, unless restrained they can do a great deal of damage, and they therefore have to be resisted, but (so to speak) *that's it*. They do not merit study; they have nothing to say of intrinsic interest. There will always be people hostile to Jews. They will be hostile for their own reasons, which we do not always care to investigate. 'The great majority who hate Jews [do so] because they are wicked from birth', wrote the Yiddish essayist, Hillel Zeitlin. 'There is enough wickedness in the hearts of men.'[109] The challenge that they pose is rather like the 'challenge' of the litterbug. If a person drops litter on your front lawn, you will want to chase him away, and you will have to clear up the litter. But you will not be interested in the character and motivation of the litterbug; you will not want to scrutinize the litter before depositing it in your dustbin. You may conclude that the litterbug has a 'nasty nature'.[110] You will want to do only what is minimally necessary to deal with the problem he presents, and you will then return to your own pursuits. You will not be interested in writing up the details of your adventure with the litterbug. It will not be a story that holds any interest for you. Certainly, it will not *fascinate* you. It will not be a story that will shape the way in which you regard yourself. You may conclude, 'The world was and always will be a sty.'[111] If the nuisance persists, of course, you may become demoralized. Paul Celan wrote to his fellow poet, Nelly Sachs, following a wave of neo-Nazi activities, 'What can I say to you? Every day, baseness comes into my house, every day, believe me. What is in store for us Jews?'[112] But dealing with anti-Semites is not a vocation for Jews, it is a chore—often a time-consuming one, and sometimes a frightening one too. Anti-Semitism is just baseness, utter baseness. When it invades one's life (one's 'house'), it can lay it to waste. And that is all that needs to be said. Anti-Semitism is rubbish.

Or you can ponder this anti-Semitism, try to understand it in all its implications, make it an object of investigation. You will do this because it figures in your world and you cannot live in a world in which any aspect of it remains unanalysed. Further, the threat it represents is potentially so overwhelming, and so profound, that unless it receives your full attention, it will immobilize you. It must be studied so that it can better be combated. It is a goad to you; in part, because studying it is a way of paying respect to its victims, and ensuring that the record of their suffering is not lost or misrepresented; and, in part, because you have such an intimacy of relation with anti-Semitism that to study it is a means of self-examination. To understand anti-Semitism is to understand yourself as a Jew, even as a human being. You become inward with it. You reject the litterbug analogy, then. Instead, you regard anti-Semitism as an important, perhaps the most important, question in your life. You *commit* yourself to studying it, and in the intervals when it does not actually pose any immediate threat to you, you address anti-Semitism in its historical and theoretical aspects. You work to refute its calumnies; your encounters with it will be high points in the psychodrama of your life. You take it seriously. In due course, anti-Semitism will contribute to defining the person that you are.

Freud made the first kind of response, and then made the second kind. For a long time, he tended to disregard anti-Semitism; but in the last years of his life, he gave up his time to an inquiry into its character and origins. It finally got his attention, that is, but I think he then paid it both too much, and the wrong kind of, attention. In his preoccupation with it,[113] he misunderstood it. While *Moses* tells us a great deal about Freud, the book tells us only very little about anti-Semitism.[114] In a move that another independent-minded Jew, Arthur Koestler, somewhat paralleled forty years later,[115] Freud attempted to break the connection between modern Jewry and its self-understood origins. Both Freud and Koestler concluded, having pursued quite different lines of inquiry, that since the Jews are not what they think they are, they are not what everyone else assumes them to be either.

I have written this book as an alternative to both these approaches of Freud's. First, while I acknowledge that anti-Semitism needs to be examined, I do not do so with any relish. It is only because so much anti-Semitic rubbish has now accumulated on England's lawns (to pursue the metaphor), that a clean-up of the kind represented by this book has become necessary. But I have derived no benefit, either in self-understanding or education, from the undertaking. Secondly, and again contrary to Freud, while my approach to anti-Semitism is systematic, I offer no *formula*. Indeed, my object has been to demonstrate that it is by reference to its heterogeneity—that is, in the diversity of its appeal and the plurality of its versions—that anti-Semitism is best conceptualized.

How to write about it?

A specific question of fairness arises when making claims about a person derived from quotations from his or her work or from the foundational texts that govern his or her perspective on the world. Such an approach on its face should be the least susceptible to misrepresentation, because it confines itself to self-descriptions. Do not these quotations comprise the material for the most authoritative, least prejudiced account? Quotations can be trusted.[116]

Consider the following passage from Noam Chomsky's book about the United States, Israel, and the Palestinians, *The Fateful Triangle* (1999):

> The settlers are quite open about the measures they take towards Arabs and the justification for them, which they find in the religious law and the writings of the sages. In the journal of the religious West Bank settlers we find, for example, an article with the heading 'Those among us who call for a humanistic attitude towards our [Arab] neighbours are reading the Halacha [religious law] select-ively and are avoiding specific commandments.' The scholarly author cites passages from the Talmud explaining that God is sorry that he created the Ishmaelites, and that Gentiles are a people 'like a donkey.' The law concerning 'conquered people' is explicit, he argues, quoting Maimonides on how they must 'serve' their Jewish conquerors and be 'degraded and low' and 'must not raise their heads in Israel but must be conquered beneath their hand . . . with complete submission.' Only then may the conquerors treat them in a 'humane manner.' 'There is no relation,' he claims, 'between the law of Israel [*Torat Yisrael*] and the atheistic modern humanism,' citing again Maimonides, who holds 'that in a divinely-commanded war [*milhemet mitzvah*] one must destroy, kill and eliminate men, women and children' (the rabbinate has defined the Lebanon war as such a war). 'The eternal principles do not change,' and 'there is no place for any "humanistic" considerations.'[117]

The author, Yedidia Segal, is a 'settler' and a 'scholar', and he is cited both as representative of all settlers and as reliable on the subject of Judaism. What, then, could be more persuasive of the settlers' general position than this author's article? The settlers stand condemned by their own words; the 'rabbinate' stands condemned by its endorsement of the Lebanon war as 'divinely-commanded';[118] Judaism itself stands condemned in the citing of its most authoritative texts. There is nothing more damning than the self-damning. Yet if one takes the trouble to track down the article, in the journal *Nekuda*, this is what one finds.

It is expressly a response to two earlier articles by *other* settlers, both of whom urge respect and consideration towards Palestinians, a stance mandated, they proceed to argue, by Jewish law. Segal replies, taking a contrary position.[119] He criticizes his fellow settlers for 'crude selectivity' in their choice of texts. They rely only on what suits them; they ignore everything else. He then himself makes a selection, identifying other texts that he considers to be truly authoritative. These texts appear to prescribe a quite different, and much harsher, stance towards the Palestinians, as well as being uncomplimentary to Arabs and to non-Jews in general. *These* are the authentic expressions of Jewish law, writes Segal, and not the texts chosen by the other writers. Jewish law (or *Halacha*), he argues, is one thing, while the moral principles accepted today in the West are a completely different thing. *Halacha* makes a fundamental distinction between Jew and non-Jew; the 'West' refuses precisely this and any comparable distinction. What then, Segal asks, should a religious Jew do, if he rejects the false solution impliedly proposed in the earlier two articles, namely of a reconciliation between these opposing perspectives? But having thus drawn the starkest possible contrast between Jewish law on the one hand, and what he unflinchingly refers to as 'humane considerations' on the other, Segal ends his article *with the question unanswered*—save that he ponders whether, even if Jewish law (as he understands it) *does* apply to the Palestinians, the government of Israel has the right to implement it, because 'the Government's position in [the Land of] Israel is unclear from a Halachic standpoint'.

Now, it can be said that, while he does not expressly answer the question, he certainly pushes his readers in the direction of an answer, and that is the one that Chomsky attributes to him. But Chomsky was *not* entitled to represent as definitive of the settlers' perspective an article that at best comprised only one side of an argument within the then settler movement. The movement has always been divided on this question of the status of non-Jews in Israel,[120] though there is certainly a substantial body of opinion dismissive of even the possibility of Jewish–Arab coexistence and harshly sceptical of Arab intentions.[121] What Chomsky does here is in fact quite common in anti-Zionist polemicizing—citing an ostensibly objectionable passage from an article or speech or diary entry of a Zionist thinker or activist and then attributing it to the entire Zionist movement. (Yet Chomsky elsewhere showed himself sensitive to the politics of the incriminatory quotation.)[122] I address this topic in greater detail in Chapter 7; I touch on it here mainly because of its cautionary value. Quotations are made to do a great deal of work in *Trials of the Diaspora*. The Chomsky example is evidence of the risk that reliance on self-incriminatory, or ostensibly self-incriminatory, quotations represents. It can make an argument appear authoritative, while in reality misleading its audience.

How to avoid this risk? By ensuring that one does not quote out of context, and that one interprets fairly; by not allowing quotation to do the work of a proper summary of the author's position; by considering what the author *did*, as well as what he or she *said*;[123] by recognizing that people change their minds, and that they also often say or write things that they do not mean even at the time of saying or writing them; and by not over-burdening individual quotations with the responsibility of speaking for the politics of entire collectives—groups, classes, nations, cultures, religions.[124] These are all matters of judgement, and in the many pages that follow there are likely—notwithstanding my best intentions—to be at least some misjudgements of my own. On many occasions when I offer a quotation as a representative specimen of a particular position I can no doubt be answered, 'no, this is aberrant, not typical at all'. Overstating what would otherwise be a somewhat commonplace observation, Martin Heidegger commented:

> an interpretation is never a presuppositionless apprehending of something presented to us. When one is engaged in...exact textual interpretation, one likes to appeal to what 'stands there,' [but] one finds that what 'stands there'...is nothing other than the obvious undiscussed assumption of the interpreter.[125]

It is the 'nothing other', of course, that is the overstatement. But Heidegger was right to warn against reading one's own assumptions into the ostensible givenness of quoted material.

What does 'English' mean in the phrase 'English anti-Semitism'?

By 'English', I mean to refer to England and *not* to the multinational United Kingdom of Great Britain and Northern Ireland. There will be times when I write 'Britain', or 'British', and here it is the British government or government policy that I have in mind. I quite understand the vice of confusing the part with the whole[126]—though 'part' and 'whole' are themselves terms not altogether free from difficulty in this context. The Welsh, the Scots, and the Irish had their own perspectives on the Jews, no doubt in many respects congruent with those of the English. But I have not studied them, and am not competent to offer opinions on them. 'England' itself began as an array of territories;[127] in many respects, it is still lacking in cultural and political homogeneity. But unless I indicate otherwise, when I write about English anti-Semitism, I do not distinguish between regional variants—save to acknowledge the special case of the East End of London, which had a certain anti-Semitic political culture of its own between the last decade of the nineteenth century and the first half of the twentieth century.[128] There is a point at which a commitment to respecting the *differentia* of a subject risks frustrating the effort to give an account of it; writing about regional English anti-Semitism represents that point for me.[129] It is the *national* disposition[130] towards certain kinds of anti-Semitism that is my concern in *Trials of the Diaspora*.

To what extent is this book a history of Anglo-Jewry?

Trials of the Diaspora is much more concerned with English anti-Semites than with English Jews. It looks away from the Anglo-Jewish community and towards the shifting, unstable and ignominious communities of English Jew-haters. It is not a history of England's Jews; it is not even a history of Anglo-Jewry's response to anti-Semitism. It may be situated, however, in relation to certain developments in Anglo-Jewish historical writing.

From the late nineteenth century, for about a hundred years, Anglo-Jewish historical writing concerned itself with Jewish personalities and institutions. Though its premise was a calamitous first settlement and a secure second settlement, it paid little attention to English anti-Semitism (typically dismissed as a matter of 'sparse manifestations' only).[131] It was in part a work of historical reconstruction, and in part a work of historical apologetics. It was alive to the differences between the Jewish experience in England and in Continental Europe. England was taken to be liberal and tolerant; abroad, considerably less so. Shaped by the experience of anti-Semitism, it yet neglected the study of it.[132] It was patriotic, celebrating England by celebrating the history of England's Jews.[133] It tended to divide Anglo-Jewry into a dominant London community and subordinate provincial communities, but otherwise to assume its indivisibility. It was undertaken mainly by non-professional enthusiasts, who deferred in turn to one or two Jewish academic histor-ians, first among whom was Cecil Roth. Its principal achievements are the volumes of *Transactions of the Jewish Historical Society*, and Roth's own *History of the Jews in England*. This way of writing Anglo-Jewish history went into decline in the 1960s and 1970s, under pressure from four distinct historiographical dissents.

First, there was a dissent from the assumption of an indivisible commu-nity, adequately represented by communal bodies. Attention was paid instead to religious, social, and political divisions—between Jewish elite and Jewish poor, between Orthodox and Reform Jews, between Sephardic and Ashkenazi Jews, between Zionists and non- (and anti-) Zionists, and so on. In addition to marking these 'centrifugal tendencies',[134] attention was also paid to the deficiencies and divisions in communal representation. Anglo-Jewry was shown to be generally 'fragmented and frightened'.[135] It was noted that in the emancipation struggles in the middle decades of the nineteenth century Anglo-Jewry did not act as a distinct Jewish body,[136] and that it was militant, non-official communal organizations within the Jewish community, exasperated by the timidity of the Board of Deputies, which led the protests against the Russian pogroms, then against the anti-alienists' agitations,[137] then defended Anglo-German Jews[138] and (slightly later) Anglo-Russian Jews[139] during World War I; and later still, which campaigned against the British Union of Fascists[140] and pre-war Nazi Germany,[141] and then spoke up for the Jews being slaughtered in their hundreds of thousands by the Nazis and their allies.[142] It is through the work of these dissenting historians that we have learned, for example, that the *Jewish Chronicle* chastised communal bodies for their timidity, often taking upon itself the task of rebutting anti-Semitic calumnies;[143] that the historian Lewis Namier mocked communal leaders as 'The Order of Trembling Israelites';[144] that Tom Driberg MP took up the cause of Polish Army anti-Semitism 'against the advice—the almost lachrymose pleading—of the official spokesmen of the Jewish commu-nity in Britain';[145] that in June 1940, anxious about anti-refugee anti-Semitism, and convinced that it was caused by the refugees themselves, the Board instructed refugees to spy on each other;[146] and that in 1944, a Foreign Office minute praised the Board as 'a very moderate body, representing the best in British Jewry',[147] a reputation that the Board enjoyed in official circles for several reasons, no doubt, but one of which being that it accepted that anti-Semitic sentiment was caused in part by Jewish misconduct, and endeavoured both to fight and to appease anti-Semitism by attacking both the 'defamers without' and the 'delinquents within'.[148]

(The work of these historians thus contains all the evidence needed to demonstrate that there has never been a 'Jewish Lobby', in the sense of a centrally directed, clandestine, and powerful body successfully promoting Jewish interests. On the contrary, the preponderant evidence points to a multiply divided and docile community, with forms of representation that were and continue to be similarly submissive, divided, and weak.[149] The Board has always acted in conformity with mainstream Anglo-Jewry's 'eternal quest for respectability in the eyes of the Gentiles', its desire to preserve a certain 'image' trumping 'religious or ethnic solidarity'.[150] It has typically sought an accommodation with the dominant community by acts of communal submission, not haranguing or complaining of broken promises, but placating and flattering, swallowing grudges and praising the fairness of the politically responsible classes and the political system. It has maintained a 'low profile'.[151] The relation between state and minority community has indeed been asymmetric, but it is the Jews who have been the weaker party—by far.)[152]

Secondly, there was a dissent from the assumption of a constitutive English liberalism, one taken to be unqualifiedly tolerant and accommodating towards Jews.[153] The dissent worked itself out in a number of directions, of course. Some historians concentrated on non-liberal sentiment, thereby pointing to the incompleteness of liberalism's reach in English political culture.[154] They excavated alternative political traditions, inhospitable towards Jews, and attributed to them a greater significance than had hitherto been considered appropriate. Others argued that liberalism itself was problematic. These historians supposed the existence of an 'emancipation contract', which demanded of Jews that they surrender or at least rein in their Jewish identity in return for equality.[155] David Feldman's *Englishmen and Jews* (1994) demonstrated that English liberalism was not secular and cosmopolitan, but Christian and national, and that its reservations about Jews and Jewish emancipation did not (as in France, say) derive from a universalist perspective, but rather from notions of England as a national religious community. In combination, these dissents encouraged some historians and literary scholars to adopt a discourse of disparagement, in which there was much talk of the 'myths' of 'Britain's essential tolerance and decency', British society's 'supposed decency', the 'necessary but painful task of quashing the myths of Britain's essential "fairness" ', and so on.[156] 'Liberalism' was given something of the character of a fairytale villain, ostensibly fair and beautiful but in reality a malignant crone.[157] Others, however, while acknowledging liberalism's imperfections, esteemed its 'emphasis on gradualism and individual transformation'.[158]

Thirdly, and relatedly, there was a dissent from the assumption that English anti-Semitism, when medieval, was typical of its time,[159] and when modern, was inconsequential.[160] Todd M. Endelman concluded his *The Jews of Britain 1656–2000* (2002) by asserting, 'the history of the Jews in Britain is not the success story that Roth claimed'.[161] (A typical Roth claim: 'There was something prodigious in the speed with which Jews acclimatised themselves in the life of England, and the manner in which they were accepted before long in all circles of society.')[162] The most thoroughgoing dissent was Colin Holmes's *Anti-Semitism in British Society 1876–1939* (1979), which demonstrated the continuity of English anti-Semitic cultures, both on the political left and the political right. Other historians offered more qualified dissents. They had as little time for received Anglo-Jewish historiography as Holmes did, but they distinguished their own position from his by holding 'anti-Semitism' to be too blunt a conceptual tool with which to analyse 'the Jews' in the English imagination.[163] There was, of course, a potential tension between these two positions, deploring the failure to acknowledge the reality of English anti-Semitism and arguing for the inutility of 'anti-Semitism' as a concept.[164] The tension tended to be resolved by expanding the meaning of 'anti-Semitism' to include more 'ambivalent' sentiments,[165] or by rejecting 'anti-Semitism' in favour of 'Jewish difference'[166] or 'semitic racial representations',[167] which could then be located at the very 'centre of literary production and more widespread social and political discourses'.[168] And work has also been done relating anti-Semitism to other 'forms of racism and intolerance',[169] on the assumption of the existence of a 'common identity of the oppressed'.[170]

Fourthly, there was a dissent from the assumption that the proper focus of Anglo-Jewish historical writing is on the internal history of the community and (but only secondarily) on its contribution to the national community.

The leading, dissenting work in this respect is David S. Katz's *The Jews in the History of England* (1996), the very title announcing the author's dissent.[171] Its focus is on the national, not the communal, and it is interested in the latter mainly to the extent that it figured in the former. It is broader and more episodic than Roth's work, and concerns itself with the Jewish 'thread' in English history. Relatedly, a perspective emerged that interpreted discourse about Jews as being in certain respects related, sometimes even central, to broader discourses—about national identity, about modernity, about race, about the nature of the liberal state, and so on.[172]

What then followed was a dissent from the dissent, in the work of William D. Rubinstein. In his *A History of the Jews in the English-Speaking World: Great Britain* (1996), he took an expressly neo-Rothian position. Anglo-Jewish history was a 'success story', one attributable to several factors: the effects of the Reformation, the pervasiveness of anti-Catholic sentiment, the commercially vanguard role of Protestant dissenters, Protestant philo-Semitism, the absence of radical Jews with reformist or revolutionary agendas, the separation of finance from industry in the evolution of Victorian capitalism, the dominant political traditions of democracy, pluralism and liberalism, and the specifically English values of toleration and fairness. Rubinstein did not attach much weight either to English literary anti-Semitism or to the specifically English aspects of contemporary anti-Zionism. Nor did he comment on the precedential significance of medieval English anti-Semitism or the exemplary quality of modern English anti-Semitism. He was not, however, blind to the existence of anti-Semitism in post-Readmission England ('there has never been a lack of anti-semites, racists and Jew-haters of all descriptions'), and noted distinct anti-Semitic periods or 'outbursts' from 1917 to 1922 and 1946 to 1948, but he emphasized Anglo-Jewry's general good fortune, a life 'astonishingly free of hostility'—'no ghettoes, no crusades, no pogroms, no Holocaust'. He quarrelled with the 'younger school' of historians, sharply criticizing them for their undue emphasis on anti-Semitism, their neglect of philo-Semitism, their attacks on Anglo-Jewish institutions for pusillanimity, and their tendency to judge pre-Holocaust anti-Semitism from a post-Holocaust perspective. Jews, he argued, 'were seldom or never central to any widely-held "construction of reality" as was so common on the European continent'. He concluded his work, however, with expressions of concern about the prevalence of anti-Israel sentiment among intellectuals, in the news media and on campus.[173]

While it is not a history of Anglo-Jewry, then, my book takes into account, and in places builds upon, these developments and counter-developments in the historiography. It perhaps goes without saying, however, that I do not myself recoil from the use of 'anti-Semitism', 'anti-Semitic', or 'anti-Semite'. Indeed, I believe that the term continues to have utility, among other reasons, because it assists in the resisting of a common tendency to collapse Jew-hatred into a more generalized racism. Anti-Semitism is not most usefully to be understood as 'but one species in the whole extent of prejudice'.[174]

What is the present conjuncture?

'All of Prague is anti-Semitic today', one commentator wrote in 1893; no, a second commentator responded somewhat later, 'that is putting it mildly, the whole Czech nation, with very few exceptions, was anti-Semitic'.[175] How to measure the quantity of anti-Semitism in any given society? And what quantity produces an anti-Semitic consensus?[176] Opinion polls and other survey-based studies are hardly conclusive; public discourse is often unreliable as a guide to private attitudes.[177] One would want to take into account parliamentary fortunes, and newspaper perspectives[178]—but with what allowances? The evidence of what is not said certainly matters—but then, how to assess *that*?[179] Since *identifying* anti-Semitism is so much easier than assessing its *prevalence*, most historians understandably concentrate on the former, addressing the latter rather more perfunctorily. The path-breaking Colin Holmes, for example, concluded that 'hostile attitudes towards Jews' in British society between 1876 and 1939 were 'not uncommon'.[180] What, a reader might reasonably wish to know, is my own view about the commonness of 'hostile attitudes towards Jews' across the very much longer period under review in the present book? In very summary form, I think the following. In the medieval period, anti-Jewish sentiment was radical and normative (that is, in general circulation and broadly subscribed to), rarely challenged, and lethally destructive in its consequences for Jews. Between the mid-seventeenth and mid-twentieth centuries, a somewhat different kind of anti-Jewish sentiment was moderate and normative, more frequently the subject of intensification *and* challenge, and injurious in mostly subtle and almost always non-lethal ways to Jews. In the contemporary period, which I take to run from the late 1960s to the present, a still further kind of anti-Jewish sentiment is somewhat intense in expression, and has acquired a distinctive political character, troubling to Jews though only intermittently afflicting them with violence or the threat of violence. An anti-Semitic literary discourse of some aesthetic distinction connects these medieval, modern, and contemporary periods. The question of the weight of anti-Semitic sentiment at any particular historical conjuncture, however, must remain a matter for judgement. It requires some capacity for nuance, given in almost every instance the diversity of both public and private attitudes, the plurality of factors motivating policy decisions, the complex burden of inherited circumstances, and so on. *Trials of the Diaspora* has been written across a period of rising violence and abuse directed at English Jews.[181] Of the present conjuncture, then, my provisional judgement is that it is quite bad, and might get worse. Certainly, it would seem that the closed season on Jews is over.[182]

PART
I
Contexts

I
Enmities

It is the most calamitous, though by no means the most salient, fact of Jewish existence that during a period in excess of two millennia, Jews have been oppressed by the attentions of many kinds of enemies.

Four kinds of enemy

Jews have enemies in much the same way that non-Jews do—that is, they experience enmities neither caused nor sustained by Jew-hatred. Not every hostile encounter is a consequence of anti-Semitism. The only Jews who believe otherwise are the ones who populate Jewish jokes. There is nothing more that needs to be said about this category of enemy.

Jews have additional enemies, however, to whom their Jewish character *is* relevant, because these enemies find themselves in conflict with a genuine Jewish project or stance. I call these *rational* enemies, within which category a further distinction should be made between the *involuntary* rational enemy (for whom the enmity is implicit in the given circumstances of his material existence) and the *voluntary* rational enemy (for whom the enmity is a free choice). I give only a minimal content to 'rational'—it is enough that the Jewish project is a real one, and that the interests of the enemy conflict, or are perceived to conflict, with that project in some genuinely arguable way. And 'enemy' may in many cases safely be exchanged for 'adversary' or 'opponent'—the opposition need not be coloured by hatred or malice. Judaism is the principal Jewish 'project', so to speak, and Christian anti-Judaism therefore need not be anti-Semitic. For example, the Christian conviction that Jews ought to convert, because adherence to Judaism bars the Jew from salvation, is not in itself anti-Semitic. Nor even is the conviction that in their refusal to acknowledge the truth of the Christian

Scriptures, the Jews make themselves the enemies of the Church[1] (though this refusal may lead to persecutions indistinguishable in their effect to the persecutions pursued by anti-Semites). Towards the end of the nineteenth century, the Bolshevik confronted the Bundist in enmity, as did the anti-Zionist Palestinian Arab, the Zionist Jew. 'Zionism is directly opposed to Arab nationalism; we must resist it', declared a 1938 text of the Arab Students' Congress.[2] A more local and specific instance of a rational enmity was the Ottoman opposition to Zionist settlement,[3] and more consequentially, the conflict between Britain and the *Yishuv* (Jewish Palestine) between 1945 and 1948.[4] Israel has become the principal political project of the Jews in the late twentieth and early twenty-first centuries; indeed, approximately 38 per cent of all Jews now live in Israel. It would be a mistake in analysis to regard confrontations with Zionism and Israel as taking place between Jews and anti-Semites alone—*not* because Jews take positions on both sides (there have always been Jews ready to side with anti-Semites), but because real interests were and in certain respects continue to be at stake.

Jews also have enemies who prey upon them in their vulnerability *as Jews*. These are *opportunistic* enemies. They do not oppose Jewish projects; they exploit Jewish weakness. They arm themselves, so to speak, with anti-Semitism, the better to pursue their Jewish victims or adversaries. But they are not infected by any special animus towards Jews (or not at first). They merely take advantage of opportunities created for them by anti-Semites. They choose the side that allows them the greatest leeway for their own depravity—often the strongest side. They may be teenage children—street gangs glad of the chance to bully and to harass.[5] They are often brigands and criminals, ready to join whatever group will give them a gun.[6] They may be Jews themselves—preying dockside on newly arrived immigrants, using their knowledge of Yiddish to win over and then defraud their victims.[7] Many are extortionists—such as the parents who hid their daughter, announced that she had been killed by her Jewish employer, and then told the man that they would continue to keep her in hiding unless he gave them a large sum of money.[8] They are also wartime profiteers preying on vulnerable Jews, making the most of the opportunities for extortion, double-dealing, price-gouging, 'shake-downs', looting, and the like. But they may also be politicians and bureaucrats. There has always been money to be made out of anti-Semitism.[9] At the extreme, anti-Semitism has an instrumental value for sadists, for example, when it reduces Jews to mere playthings.[10] Such people are not cruel because they are anti-Semites; they are anti-Semites because they are cruel. These sadists may adopt anti-Semitic positions, but cynically, because it provides a justification for their actions; it gives them alibis for aggression;[11] it panders to their urge to destroy.[12] Over time, of course, these positions may come to be sincerely held. A special category of opportunistic enemy is made up of those writers who exploit anti-Semitism for literary effect—the available villain, the ready trope. And then there is that further category of opportunistic enemy comprising of Jews themselves.[13] In addition, we should take notice of a certain *counter*-category to the opportunistic enemy, that is the enemy who is an anti-Semite out of cowardice. He does not persecute Jews because it is to his advantage; he persecutes them because to fail to do so would be to his disadvantage. He attacks Jews out of fear of anti-Semites.[14]

Lastly, Jews have enemies to whom their Jewish character is determinative, but whose enmity does *not* derive from opposition to any genuine Jewish project or stance. The hatred of these enemies mostly derives from imaginary grievances, imputed to an imaginary collective entity, 'the Jews' or 'Judaism' ('*Le Judaïsme voilà l'enemi!*' affirmed a late nineteenth-century French political poster).[15] Their enmity is determined not by Jewish *projects* but by their own *projections*. Jews become the bearers of these irrational projections.[16] These are the anti-Semites, the irrational enemies of the Jews; grievances or complaints are pretexts for defamation and persecution. They make war on Jews, though Jews are not at war with them. The malevolence of the Jew, this racially constituted, cohesive, politically active subject, this single and singular actor, is taken to be murderous.[17] At the clinical extreme, the anti-Semites' hatred thus has a paranoid quality. They suppose themselves to be innocent, victimized, and under siege, and the Jews, guilty persecutors intent upon their domination or extermination.[18] Though Jews put no interest of theirs in jeopardy, their hatred of the Jews is intense, compelling. No army engaged in a real war against a real enemy, observed Norman Cohn, has ever engaged in such self-exaltation as Jew-killers engaged in their one-sided struggle against an imaginary conspiracy of Jews.[19] The Jew is the 'aggressor', the 'real enemy'[20]—whether in the guise of banker, newspaper proprietor, revolutionary, or Zionist. Jews, declare the anti-Semites, are our 'permanent antagonist', our 'inveterate enemies'.[21] 'The Jews are guilty of everything!' explained the Reich Propaganda Directorate.[22]

It follows that while every anti-Semite is an enemy of the Jews, not every enemy of the Jews is an anti-Semite. Only the Jews' irrational enemies can be described as anti-Semitic, though the boundary that separates them from the Jews' rational and opportunistic enemies is a porous one. Many rational enemies of the State of Israel, for example, routinely traverse this boundary. Opportunistic enemies are often also, or become in consequence, anti-Semites—Poland's post-war anti-Semitism was embedded in the society's opportunistic wartime behaviour.[23] Rational enmity is often infected by irrationality. Anti-Semitism can even over time colour enmities of the first kind, where the Jewish element was at first altogether absent. Applying this typology to medieval England, for example, we may say that the Jews were exploited by opportunistic enemies and persecuted by irrational enemies.

This distinction between rational and irrational enemies, the second and the fourth kinds of enemies identified above, derives from the account given in the Hebrew Scriptures (the *Tanach*) of the distinct enmities of Balak and Amalek towards the Israelites. Balak may be understood as a rational enemy; Amalek is the type of the irrational enemy. That the Israelites met Amalek before they met Balak perhaps encouraged later generations of Jews to view Balak-type enemies through Amalek-type lenses—not always to the advantage of clarity of understanding. I will touch on this further below. But first, the distinction between rational and irrational enmity requires some elaboration.

The rational enemy

The story of Balak is told in Numbers 22–4. The Israelites must pass through the land of the Emori. They send a message to Sihon, king of the Emori. Let us pass through your land. We will not turn aside into the fields or the vineyards, and we will not drink from your wells. We will go along your highway until we pass beyond your border. But Sihon does not accept their assurances. Anxious that they will *not* just pass through, or not on the terms that they promise, he musters an army and opposes the Israelites' entry. His army is defeated, and his worst fears then materialize. The whole of his land is occupied by the Israelites. 'Thus Yisra'el dwelt in the land of the Emori' (22:31). They then move on, and are met by another king, and they defeat him too.

Balak, the Moabite king, sees all this happening, and (what is more) receives none of the assurances given to Sihon. He doubts his ability to defeat the Israelites in battle, and so he calls on the prophet Balaam to curse them (22:5–6). But Balaam finds that his curses become blessings. He is an intellectual who involuntarily speaks truth to power. He tells the assembled enemies of the Israelites what fate awaits them. He predicts the conquest of the Edomites, the Amalekites, the Kenites, the Moabites, and the Midianites. 'A star rises from Jacob, a sceptre comes forth from Israel' (24:17–23). Unquestionably, Israel confronts these nations in enmity. Indeed, later God instructs Israel 'utterly to destroy' the Canaanites and other, kindred nations (Deuteronomy 20:17). They are idolaters, they practise abominations, and they must be destroyed. And so, quite understandably, they fight back.

For an understanding of political enmity, one may go to the twentieth-century German jurist Carl Schmitt. 'An enemy', he proposes, 'exists only when, at least potentially, one fighting collectivity of people confronts a similar collectivity.'[24] When the Moabites faced the Israelites, they did so as one Schmittian 'fighting collectivity' facing another such collectivity. Balak is thus the type of the rational enemy; his enmity was reciprocated. He feared the Israelites; he feared for his kingdom. He conceived his enmity in consequence of a real conflict with his adversary. He opposed a Jewish project, because he believed that it conflicted with his own interests. He believed, indeed, that this project put the very existence of the Moabites in jeopardy.

The Jews have not for millennia comprised in their totality a political collectivity—still less, a 'fighting' one. Rarely have they been in the mundane sense even a *potential* collectivity. A fraction, from time to time, has cohered to pursue a Jewish project. There have only been a few such moments in Jewish history. The Jews' rejection of Jesus, though genuine and corporate, was less a positive project, more a matter of steadfastness in faith. Indeed, Zionism is the only truly consequential collective project undertaken by Jews since the loss of Jewish sovereignty at the beginning of the Common Era. It is thus at least possible for anti-Zionists, and in particular Palestinian anti-Zionists, to be rational enemies of those Jews who constitute themselves as Israelis.

Their enmity is in certain respects unjust. They have not pursued it with due regard to the interests of Jews; they have prosecuted it on occasion without moral restraint. They have disregarded the demerits of their own position; they have disregarded the merits of the Jewish position. Some among them have sought to buttress their position with fabrications and libels. It is even arguable that many have not understood the true character of their interests (which may lie in cooperation, rather than conflict). But the enmity is not one-sided, and it too has been pursued with its own measure of injustice, its own disregard of the interests of Palestinians, its own misunderstandings of where Israel's true interests lie. It is indeed the reciprocal nature of the enmity that allows these enemies to reason with each other, and for appeals to be made to principles that are held in common. It is possible, that is, for these enemies to compromise. 'The Jews will always have sufficient enemies,' wrote Herzl, 'much as every other nation has.'[25] Israel's Palestinian enemies comprise the very type of enemy that Herzl imagined that Jews *would* have, once enstated.

Since so much of the opposition to Zionism has come from entities and individuals not engaged in the contest over land and statehood, the distinction between rational and irrational enemies needs to be supplemented by a distinction within the category of the rational enemy between the voluntary and the involuntary enemy. By 'voluntary enemy' I mean here in particular those Western supporters of, or fellow-travellers with, the Arab, and (more narrowly) the Palestinian, cause.

The voluntary enemy opposes a Jewish project—let us say, Zionism—because he believes that it conflicts with his values, that is to say with what he understands to be universal values. It is to just such a person that Edward Said appealed when he argued, 'Palestine provides the test-case for a true universalism on such matters as terror, refugees, and human rights.' The Palestinian cause represents 'an idea of justice and equality around which many others could rally'.[26] This person, one of these 'others', the voluntary enemy, associates himself with a conflict, and makes it a cause. It is not his cause until he *makes* it his cause, by a free act of will. He decides, to borrow George Orwell's phrase (used by him in connection with the Spanish Civil War), that it is a cause 'worth fighting for'.[27] It often answers to the volunteer's sense of vocation as an intellectual—after all, as Sartre remarked, an intellectual is precisely someone who gets involved in something that doesn't concern him or her.[28] Voluntary enemies tend to be of a politically progressive disposition. In search of a cause with which to associate themselves in the aftermath of Vietnam and South Africa, they have—for the moment—alighted on the Israeli–Palestinian conflict. It need not, perhaps, have been this one, but in the event, it is. Palestine has become a 'universal cause'.[29] There is something about their distance from the conflict, and the absence of any real personal or national interest at stake in it, that makes for a certain crassness—an attitudinizing, a frivolousness—in some of the positions taken by these voluntary enemies of Israel. There is also a quality of ingratiation about some of their interventions. And at the same time they intimate what might be termed an ideology of the disinterested observer.

They are impartial, they can negotiate the claims of the two people, and so on.[30] Their anti-Zionism may also relieve a certain residual, historic guilt concerning the Holocaust. The blamers have become blameworthy, the Jews have become Nazi-like; by attacking its former victims, paradoxically, Nazism itself can belatedly be contested.[31] All this has arisen in the context of a broader Western interest in the conflict that is itself surprising in its intensity.

Voluntary enemies figure prominently in nineteenth and twentieth century international politics. The British philhellenes were first in the series, partisans of the Greek struggle against the Ottoman Empire for independence. They were romantic, enthusiastic, passionately engaged in the defence of liberty, civilization, and humanity. Most among them disregarded Greek atrocities against the Turks; despotism, barbarism, and mass murder were taken to be exclusively Ottoman (I am following Gary J. Bass's account here).[32] Voluntary enemies contribute both to the class of its most idealistic and self-sacrificing heroes and to the contrasting class of its most immoral posturers. Among the heroes one can count the foreign Loyalist dead in the Spanish Civil War.[33] Among the posturers may be counted the Western defenders of Stalin's terror, the fellow-travellers. Of course—it was an irony of those times that one could be *both* hero *and* posturer. Nowadays, and specifically in relation to the Israeli–Palestinian conflict, the posturing is somewhat more salient than the heroic. Many of these volunteers to the conflict figure prominently among the attention-seekers in political life, their positions expressed with great extravagance, while rarely more than gestural in effect. Not for them, the modest activism that might further the cause of a just peace.[34] The following are among the key words in the voluntary enemy's vocabulary: 'solidarity', 'compassion', 'humane' and 'inhumane', 'suffering', 'ethical', 'cause', 'campaign', 'values' (as in 'civilized values'), and 'rights' (as in 'universal, or human rights'). In the context of the Middle East conflict, even the suicide bomber has become the beneficiary of Israel's voluntary enemies' solidarity—and sometimes sympathetic identification.[35]

There are two aspects to the distinction between voluntary and involuntary enemies. First, while the involuntary enemy tends to promote or defend a personal or collective interest, the voluntary enemy tends to promote or defend a general value or principle (not, of course, that interests are value-free—nor values interest-free, for that matter). The voluntary enemy tends to be disinterested; he acts without regard to his own interests, rather than in their defence. Both his identification with one party to a dispute and his enmity towards the other party are matters of personal choice. They are not thrust upon him. His solidarity is voluntary. It is, namely, an act of will. He 'passeth by, and meddleth with strife belonging not to him' (Proverbs 26:17). The voluntary enemy intervenes in an existing conflict; it is one that comes to his attention. His own future is not bound up with the outcome of the conflict, unless he chooses to make it so. Less is at stake for him than for the involuntary enemy whom he supports—often, from a great distance. The voluntary enemy is an interferer, often for good reason. He makes other people's business his own. Involuntary enemies cannot choose whether they engage in the conflict; they are usually its prisoners until it is concluded (though some may have the power and the skill to free themselves and others).

Secondly, though the enmity of both kinds of rational enemy can be infected by irrationality, the risk of infection is greater for the voluntary enemy. He is detached from the conflict, his sources of information about it may be unreliable, and he may be predisposed to favour one side for reasons unrelated to the merits of the conflict. He may not understand what is truly at stake in the conflict.[36] (An example: the West's medieval Crusading zeal emerged in Europe's power centres, not in the border lands, where a spirit of live-and-let-live seems to have prevailed.)[37] Some voluntary enemies can become so infected with irrationality that they cease to be rational at all. They then become irrational enemies, in relation to which (of course) the involuntary/voluntary distinction does not apply.

Enemies of all kinds are to be distinguished from judges. The judge reaches a determination on the evidence and then acquits or condemns. He is impartial; his perspective is universal. A judge is not, and a rival or competitor need not be, hostile. But enemies, and in particular voluntary enemies, sometimes pose as judges. In the judicial discourse frequently adopted by voluntary enemies, the master formulation is something like this: 'I do not oppose you, I condemn you, and I do so not in the name of any interests of mine on which you have encroached, but rather in the name of justice itself.' Israel's voluntary enemies, for example, commonly address it in this way. They draw indictments against a whole people.[38] When the judicial discourse combines with the discourse of fantasy (that is to say, when the rational enemy's enmity becomes infected by irrationality), Israel finds itself condemned by its enemies for committing imaginary, sometimes impossible, crimes.

Both kinds of rational enemy are to be distinguished from the irrational enemy, the kind who opposes what he takes to be a Jewish project but which is nothing of the kind—say, the killing of Gentile children or the domination of the world. This 'opposition', prompted by nothing other than the irrational enemy's own ill will, is merely a pretext for defamation and persecution. It is not undertaken in defence of real interests, because no such interests are truly threatened. This opposition will therefore always be unjust—essentially and not merely contingently unjust. It is not possible to reason with such an enemy; it is not possible to compromise with him—at best, one can contain him. He is the classic type of the anti-Semite, of course; the type of enemy that Herzl believed that the Jews would *not*, once enstated, have to confront at their borders.

The irrational enemy

There is a strand in Jewish tradition that takes Amalek to be the type of the anti-Semite.[39] To understand anti-Semitism, it is thought, one need only understand his story, an affair of murderous assaults, blameless victims, and his own groundless hatred. Needless to say, there have also been challenges from within the tradition, both to this characterization and to the broader identification of anti-Semitism with 'Amalekism'.[40] Jewish critics of certain tendencies within Zionism, for example, have written of an 'Amalek complex'—separatist, antagonistic, ready to assume the worst of the Gentile world.[41] Other Jews, too many even though only few, are tempted to draw an analogy between Amalekite and Palestinian hostility towards 'Israel' and the Jewish State of Israel, respectively.[42] By radical contrast, though with comparable depth of unreason, elements among the anti-Zionist ultra-Orthodox, in their hatred of Zionist secularism and their desire both to exculpate the conduct of their own rabbinical leaders during World War II and to explain the calamity of the Holocaust, have stooped to describe the Zionist movement as 'Amalek's accomplices', holding it jointly responsible with Nazi Germany for the destruction of European Jewry.[43]

Anti-Semites *are* 'Amalekites', but not quite in the sense commonly understood.

The war waged by Amalek against Israel is inaugurated at the moment of exodus from Egypt (Exodus 17:8–16; Deuteronomy 25:17–19). It is on its face inexplicable. The Israelites do not threaten Amalek himself; they are not passing through his land;[44] they have made no claim to it; Amalek is not a Canaanite.[45] Yet his assault on them is direct, violent, and merciless. He attacks the stragglers, the 'hindmost'—those who are feeble and weary, unable to defend themselves. He does not seek an equal fight; he is contemptible, cowardly. He wishes the destruction of the Israelites as a whole. This battle is the Israelites' first military engagement.[46] They regroup, and with God's help, they defeat the Amalekites. (Somewhat later on, when they return to their attack, it does not then go so well for them.) They are instructed to blot out the memory of Amalek, and yet never to forget him (Deuteronomy 25:19).

How can they do both, remember *and* forget? It is a paradoxical instruction, impossible on its face to fulfil in its entirety, and it contains a clue about how to interpret the story of Amalek. It invites us to read the story as itself constructed out of paradoxical, or contradictory formulations. These formulations are developed in the Midrash, a body of rabbinic commentary on the *Tanach*. The injunction to forget and to remember is in this sense an invitation to us to turn from the Torah to the Midrash. It is in the Midrashic amplification of the scriptural narrative, a form of interpretation by narrative augmentation,[47] that the connection between Amalekite and anti-Semitic hatreds is disclosed.

The founding or primary contradiction in the story concerns the state of Amalek's knowledge of the Israelites. It is to be inferred from the Torah that he did not know whom he was attacking. The Torah does not ascribe any motive to Amalek's attacks; his viciousness is to be understood as motiveless—pure evil, pure pleasure in destruction. But if one consults the Midrash, Amalek knew *precisely* whom he was attacking. His first attack follows the parting of the Red Sea; his second attack follows the giving of the Torah (Numbers 15:43–5). These were constitutive events in the formation of Israel, and Amalek witnesses them.[48] He is an antagonistic witness to the constituting of the Jews as a distinct people.

This is one contradiction in a series of contradictions. Amalek is a God-defying blasphemer; he defiles Israelite corpses, throwing their severed members heavenward, shouting to God, 'Here is what you delight in!'[49] But he is *also* God's own agent; he attacks the Israelites just as they murmur 'Is the LORD among us or not?'[50] He is Esau's grandson and therefore kin to the Israelites, but he is *also* unrelated to the Israelites. God tells them: 'This nation [the Amalekites] is not forbidden to you as are the children of Esau.' Amalek is to be imagined *as if* he were a Canaanite, only so that the Israelites may not, by waging war against him, disturb the ties of kinship.[51] But while he is thus the external enemy, he is *also* each one of us— he represents an aspect of our nature. Amalekite hatred is not to be understood as anti-Semitism (not *just* as anti-Semitism), but as aggressive, hating tendencies in general.[52] The Amalek that resides in the human heart is to be eradicated; the Amalekite is the person who holds on to his anger forever.[53] The Amalekites themselves were destroyed,[54] but Amalek is *also* to be fought until the end of days. Lastly, in two paradoxical instructions, Moses is enjoined by God to write down that Amalek's name must be erased, and Israel is enjoined to remember to forget him. One imagines the name written under erasure, thus: ~~Amalek~~.[55]

This is the truth of Amalek's story, the reason why it is Amalek and not his grandfather Esau who is the type of the anti-Semite. Anti-Semitism is constructed out of, indeed *driven* by, the contradictions that comprise Amalek's hatred of the Israelites. Anti-Semites hate the Jews for what they know about them *and* for what they do not know about them (that is, in consequence of their false beliefs about them). Anti-Semites are kin to Jews, intimates in hatred, and often intimate with individual Jews too—indeed, sometimes are Jews themselves. Further, the ugly, destructive emotions on which anti-Semitism feeds—envy, resentment, fear, perplexity—are emotions that afflict each one us from time to time. And yet anti-Semites are *also* opposed to Jews, alien to them, alienated from them.

In due course, anti-Semitism takes on the character of both perverted or 'partial' truths and the sheerest of fantasy. But it started, we might say, with a polarity. Amalek knew nothing about the Jews *and* he was witness to miracles and revelation. It is in the career of Haman, Amalek's descendant, that one begins to see a blurring of these two aspects of Amalek's irrational enmity: perfect knowledge and utter ignorance. Haman's story is told in Esther, a late addition to the *Tanach*. His understanding of the Jews is a corrupt mixture of the true and the false. He is animated by resentment; if he also fears the Jews, the fear is without foundation. He poisons the king against the Jews, telling him that they are a nation within a nation and therefore a threat to his kingdom. But this familiar protest is merely the cover story. It is personal affront, humiliated pride, which motivates him. Though he complains that the Jews keep their own laws and not the king's, what actually angers him is the Jew Mordecai's refusal to bow to him. This refusal by *one* Jew to observe *Haman's* 'law' thus becomes, in a typical anti-Semitic twist, a refusal by *all* Jews to observe the *king's* law. A threat to Haman's self-esteem becomes a threat to the well-being of the kingdom. Nazi anti-Semitism, as one might expect, provides the most instances of this kind of generalizing enmity, pursued to its deadly terminus. 'The Jews', declared Himmler, 'are the sworn enemies of the German people and must be eradicated.'[56] Edmund Veesenmeyer, a Nazi bureaucrat, wrote in a report: 'The Jew is our Enemy Number One.'[57] This was written *in December 1943*. The Nazis continued to affirm, until the very last days of the war, that the Jews were the most dangerous enemies of the Third Reich.

The uses of anti-Semitism

Anti-Semitism, itself protean, has diverse uses.[58] These uses comprise much of its appeal.

It legitimates cruelty   Anti-Semitism presents itself *both* as a pseudo-ethical obligation *and* as a sanctioned exception to the rules of ethical behaviour. That is to say, it has a moral appeal and yet also seeks the suspension of the categorical imperative in respect of Jews. On each side of this antinomy, however, viciousness towards Jews stands justified. Anti-Semitism is a discourse of denunciation. Hatred represents itself as an exercise in virtue, spite masquerades as righteous indignation. The Jew is injured in the interests of justice, and in order to defend the interests of the poor, the disadvantaged, the downtrodden, etc. (G. K. Chesterton remarked: compassion for the poor and speaking openly about the Jews' harmful influence are of a piece.)[59] The anti-Semite is taken to be an 'idealist', and his viciousness, praiseworthy. 'I hold the Jewish race', declared the composer Richard Wagner, 'to be the born enemy of pure humanity and everything noble in it.'[60] Anti-Semitism is a humanism; opposing humanity's enemies, it comes to the defence of mankind.[61] Anti-Semitism is thus not inconsistent with what is commonly referred to as the moral sense, the weakness of which is such that any sincere bigot may possess it to an even exemplary extent.[62] It is an intoxication, yes, but a moral one. 'To be an anti-Semite today does not mean being dominated by the narrow and strict views of national or religious exclusivism', asserted a late nineteenth-century anti-Semite. 'It *does* mean being a dedicated fighter against a materialistic current which places money before honour, virtue and the highest sentiments of the dignity of human nature' etc., etc.[63] Anti-Semites fancy themselves to be participants in a movement of revolt, of resistance.[64] A further instance: to the French intellectual Maurice Barrès, a true, national ethics, one predicated on a certain conception of France, *obligated* an anti-Semitic posture towards the Jews. The true Frenchman acted most morally when he acknowledged the absence of any moral obligation to the Jew, 'a creature apart'.[65] In the anti-Semite, then, virtues are displayed in bad actions.[66] The emphasis, indeed, is precisely on this display—anti-Semites wish to be moral *celebrities*.[67] Persecutors act out of duty; pogromists act in an ecstasy of unselfish outrage.[68] Anti-Semites are shameless. It is impossible to behave disgracefully to a people in disgrace; all the ordinary restraints may therefore be put aside.

Anti-Semitism invites us to take a moral holiday. We may act as badly as we please, without risk of censure. It is a luxury. We may bait, we may bully—and our ignominious conduct will be overlooked. We might even overlook it in ourselves. We may act on whims. We may kill and be excused our crime, just like Trotsky's imagined pogromist, 'gorged with blood' and 'capable of everything', 'daring everything'. 'He is king: the White Tsar has permitted him everything.'[69] To Hans Frank, Nazi governor of conquered Poland, it was 'a pleasure finally physically to assault the Jewish race, the more die, the better'.[70] Jews may be tortured and killed in good conscience; their occult power demands no less a response. Anti-Semitism can create contexts in which it becomes socially acceptable to harm another person; moreover, it allows the subject to do this under the guise of advancing a socially valued cause, 'combating Jewry' (or, indeed, on occasion, 'combating Israel'). It is not just—as Stanley Milgram demonstrated in his well-known experiment—that people will obey instructions, even when obedience requires them to be cruel. It is also that people will *choose* to behave cruelly when given the excuse to do so, which is something that Milgram rejected.[71] They will take pleasure in acts of cruelty; it will be 'sport', a recreational evil. In the fourteenth century, gangs of self-styled 'Jew-bashers' (*Judenschläger*) beat and murdered Jews in Alsatia, the Rhineland, and Swabia. They operated under the protection of noblemen who claimed that they had been divinely inspired to inflict on Jews the injuries inflicted by the Jews on Jesus.[72] Six centuries later, Hitler's *SA* (the *Sturmabteilung*, or 'Storm Division') bombed synagogues and Jewish-owned shops, and beat up and killed Jews. They operated under an analogous mandate. Jew-bashers and Brown-shirts alike were no doubt fanatical in their hatred—but we must also imagine them to be happy as they went about their tasks.[73] To injure, to kill, and then to be praised for it—could such people ask more from life? One of Stalin's torturers, V. I. Komarev, a vicious anti-Semitic psychopath, was in the habit of announcing to his victims, 'Your fate's in my hands and I'm not a man, I'm a beast.' And then he would add, 'All Jews are lousy bastards!'[74] To be tortured by someone who considers himself your moral superior must be utterly intolerable. It is the peculiar misfortune of Jews that their persecutors have been drawn from the ranks of the sanctimonious, the kind of people who do not 'walk forth stark naked in all the majesty of [their] scoundrelism',[75] but who instead cloak it in a moral purpose.

It allows others to be blamed for the anti-Semite's own failures   It has allowed an evasion of personal responsibility in the harshness of a judgement upon Jews. Anti-Semitism presents itself as an alternative (though a false one) to despair. It thus permits the luxury of self-pity, and the moral status associated with being a victim, without any of the perils that define that condition. Indeed, as the persecution intensifies, the need for the anti-Semite to cast himself as the victim itself grows. Seen in this aspect, anti-Semitism has correctly been described as the religion of the inadequate.[76] We have been deprived of what is justly ours by an unconquerable, malevolent power, a Jewish world-conspiracy. We are not to blame; no one could triumph over it. Among the Vichy government's first acts was to sponsor a propaganda campaign placing the blame for the French defeat on the national decadence caused by the Jewish politicians and financiers of the Third Republic.[77] It is likewise perhaps not surprising that in the Arab world there was an exponential increase in anti-Semitism following the 1967 Six-Day War.[78] And in August 2001, amid the ruins of the Zimbabwean economy, the author of the calamity, Robert Mugabe, accused South African Jews of trying to take control of his country's industries. 'Jews in South Africa, working in cahoots with their colleagues here,' he declared, 'want our textile and clothing factories ... to close down.'[79] The readiness to blame the Jews can become a reflex in a culture already saturated with anti-Semitism. 'In Saudi Arabia', writes Ayaan Hirsi Ali, 'everything was the fault of the Jews. When the air conditioner broke or suddenly the tap stopped running, the Saudi woman next door used to say the Jews did it.'[80] Whenever one hears 'the Jews' being blamed for something, one is in the presence of an anti-Semite. The repeated Jewish failure to protect Jewish life in modern times (say, from the collapse of efforts on behalf of Romanian Jewry in the late 1870s, to the feebleness of efforts on behalf of European Jewry in World War II),[81] let alone any less fundamental interests, does not faze such a person. He is convinced that 'Jewish power' is ruthless, self-seeking, and indomitable.

It gives the anomic a spurious experience of solidarity   The joys of partisanship are not of course confined to worthy causes. One of the pleasures of persecution for the persecutor lies in the camaraderie it promotes among his fellows.

During the Dreyfus Affair, for example, anti-Semitism fostered a temporary sense of community among otherwise disparate groupings.[82] It was through hatred of the Jews, reputedly powerful but in reality defenceless, that Hitler set about erasing differences of class, party, and religious denomination in Germany.[83] Persecution is a collective act, even when it is most personal. It depends upon a collective sanction. It is aggression, qualified in three respects: against a vulnerable person, without good cause, and under cover of legitimacy. It does not have to be violent; it rarely even leads to violence. It strengthens a common bond—'this is who we are, and we are not like them'. When it is also covert—'we can speak freely among ourselves, we trust each other'—it is a guilty pleasure, offering a slightly more intense feeling of camaraderie. In weaker versions, it offers the security of acting in accordance with received wisdom, even with having fashionable opinions. It is, furthermore, one of the oddities of anti-Semitic irrationality that it tends to produce among anti-Semites the characteristics that they impute to Jews. Among these characteristics is a strong sense of mutual solidarity and of 'chosen-ness'; they own the truth about the world, and they have the leadership responsibilities that this knowledge confers.

It provides members of religions rejected by Jews a larger, more crushing rejection in response The Jews rejected Christianity's claims for itself. 'We do not accept that Jesus was the Messiah', they said. 'We do not accept that his ministry brought Judaism to an end; we reject you.' To which the early Christians tended to respond, angry and wounded, 'No, *we* reject *you*.' Or as Pope Pius X put it to Herzl, 'The Jews have not recognised our Lord, therefore we cannot recognise the Jewish people, and its aspiration to a national existence.'[84] The effect is to allow Jews no more than a relational existence; they may exist only in their imputed antagonistic relation with those whom they reject. Judaism becomes nothing more than a denial of Christianity, Jewish practice nothing more than a shunning of Christians. 'The essence of the faith of Judaism', explained a bishop during an 1848 debate in the House of Lords, is 'an intense and perfect denial of all that constitutes the faith of a Christian'.[85] Therefore, Jews should not be allowed to sit in the legislature. Their rejection breeds a reciprocating rejection. But because the Jewish rejection was first, the Christian rejection is both the hollower one and the more urgent and violent in its expression. Anti-Semitism addresses the hollowness, offering language to Christians in which to articulate their counter-rejection. Jews tend to contemplate Christianity with indifference;[86]

Christian anti-Semites are preoccupied with Jews. This preoccupation founds
a hatred. The Jews must have rejected Christ out of pure wickedness; only
malice could drive them to reject a truth that would liberate them from
disgrace and oppression.[87] Rejecting them back, *hating them*, becomes a
necessary, moral response. It merely returns what is taken to be the Jews'
malice, measure for measure. Jews recoil from Christians who come bearing
glad tidings of Jesus' divinity; they remain distinct, even aloof, from their
Gentile neighbours. They pay the price in subordination, exclusion, boycott,
expulsion. This sense that the Jews stood apart, in unwarranted conviction of
their superiority, of their 'chosen-ness', was in due course secularized—what
Daniel Deronda's mother, in George Eliot's novel of that name, describes as
'the pelting contempt that pursues Jewish separateness'.[88] The persecutors of
Jews claim that they are merely getting their retaliation in first. Imagine,
invited Dostoyevsky, what Jews would do to Gentiles if they acquired
sovereignty over them. 'Would they permit them to acquire equal rights?
Would they permit them to worship freely in their midst? Wouldn't they
convert them into slaves? Worse than that: wouldn't they skin them
altogether? Wouldn't they slaughter them to the last man, etc.'[89] I return to
Dostoyevsky in Chapter 6.

It makes available the pleasures of social condescension   Anti-Semitism encourages
feelings of superiority (or 'ego-inflation');[90] the anti-Semite is given a position
of moral ascendancy over Jews, one that he is at liberty to translate into
political terms, if only he has the will. There are two versions of this
condescension. *Either*: while I may count for little, and suffer indignities and
humiliations at work and at home, the Jew is even less worthy of respect, a
legitimate object of contempt to contemptible me. Anti-Semitism, suggested
Sartre, is the 'poor man's snobbery';[91] it can be a balm to damaged or low self-
esteem.[92] In its most aggressive form, it is the revenge of the Gentile
disempowered upon the Jewish privileged. *Or*: I consider myself at the
summit of society; the Jews are social upstarts and thus to be despised. The
parvenu Jew conceals his origins because quite correctly they embarrass him.
Jewish men are comical in their attempts, say, to pass themselves off as English
gentlemen. Of these versions, the first is politically more dangerous than
the second.

It gives a focus to otherwise diffuse social anxieties   Writes one author of a study
of an anti-Semitic 'panic', a rumour that spread in a French city of Jewish
white-slaving: 'The spectre of the Jew is liable to appear in our civilisation

whenever and wherever anxiety exists.'[93] This 'anxiety' takes several forms. Say, for example: I consider myself to have a fixed position in a social hierarchy, and yet this hierarchy is under threat. It may even be collapsing. Though the source of this threat is obscure, the damage it does is intensely painful to me. That I do not know who is responsible for this damage makes my distress even greater. Only an enemy would do this to me, yet his face is covered. If I could identify him, I could confront and defeat him. Perhaps it is the Jews? They have no fixed place in the hierarchy, they seem to be benefiting from the very dislocations that torment me—it *must* be them. At least now I know my enemy. *Or*: my world has ceased to be familiar to me. I can no longer trust people that I chance to meet. They have become threatening strangers. I am disoriented and alone. The Jews, by contrast, are cohesive and appear to be at ease. I no longer have my own 'home'; they exclude me from theirs. They are responsible for my own (sense of) dispossession. They should try harder to 'fit in'. They do not share the painful feelings of helplessness I experience.[94]

It makes envy politically defensible   A chronicler of the 1190 riots against the Jews in London and the provinces deprecated the mob's motives: '[their violence] was not indeed sincere, that is, solely for the sake of faith, but in rivalry for the luck of others or from envy of their good fortune'.[95] Anti-Semitism can satisfy the desire of the envious to pull down or to discredit the objects of their envy. It is a leveller. The Jews are perceived to have skills, assets, in which the anti-Semite is deficient. To the envious, there is only one thing greater than being able to boast of one's friendship with the envied person, and that is to scorn him. I am not intimate with Rothschild; I look down on him. He does not deserve his status or the respect that he is given. It is falsely won, and I (at least) know it. The Jews triumph not because of their merit but by their mastery of blacker skills: solidarity, cunning, ruthlessness. They know how to come off best.[96] It is only thus that they succeed. This is the perspective, say, of the 'vanquished competitor'. His anti-Semitism allows him both to act on his envy and to disown it. My objections to the Jews are principled, disinterested—but when the Jews go, my business difficulties will likewise disappear.[97] Anti-Semitism is the way that this kind of person protects himself from the knowledge of his envy.[98] The Nazi persecution was, wrote Adorno, an 'explosion' of 'dammed-up malice and envy'.[99] It was not mere jealousy—the desire to appropriate Jewish wealth, a destructive acquisitiveness.[100] It was not enough for the Jews to be dispossessed of property, rights, even life itself. They had to be denied the very possibility of condescending to an 'Aryan' German. And so, in the middle of the war, when things could not have been going worse for the Jews in lands under Nazi control, trouble was taken to enact a law that prohibited them from using their professional titles when dealing with German officials.[101]

It can be exploited to gain a competitive advantage   Anti-Semitism can be used to despatch Jewish rivals, or to discredit non-Jewish rivals by associating them with Jews; in such instances, opportunistic and irrational enmity often become one. 'Don't buy from/sell to/hire/consult Jews; it is well known that they are dishonest/disloyal/self-seeking etc. Buy from/sell to/hire/consult me instead', or 'Don't buy from/sell to/hire/consult these non-Jews; it is well known that they are associated with dishonest/disloyal/self-seeking (etc.) Jews. Buy from/sell to/hire/consult me instead.' The Jews are objectionable *both* because they were separatist, unsociable, aliens *and* because they are integrated, competitive, fellow-traders—a typical contradiction of anti-Semitism.[102] In the Middle Ages, the 'evident superiority of Jews to their Christian counterparts in literacy, numeracy and legal sophistication' prompted jealous courtiers to invent and circulate defamatory tales of Jewish wrongdoing: 'no tale of intrigue was too far-fetched to believe or too shocking to relay'.[103] In the mid-seventeenth century, when Jews applied for permission to return to England, the merchants resisted, and were prominent in circulating libels about Jewish threats to the well-being of the nation. In the electoral campaigns in 1920s Germany, many of the political parties attacked each other for being soft on the Jews, or for enjoying their support.[104]

It satisfies a certain desire to be 'in the know', to see beyond the surface of things, to understand the 'real story'[105]   Anti-Semitism is the sophistication of the ignorant. Though it is thought-impeding, not thought-enabling,[106] it allows for a certain posturing, even a claim to seer-like capacity. Arnold White (1848–1925), social reformer, advocate of empire, and prominent campaigner against the Jews (and specifically against Jewish immigration), announced in his anti-Semitic tract, *The Modern Jew* (1899): 'To make the people of England think is the object of this book. If they refuse to think betimes, they will wake up one morning only to discover that they have parted with the realities of national life, and are dominated by cosmopolitan and materialist influences fatal to the existence of the English nation.'

He would reveal the Jews' 'complex and mysterious power'.[107] Later generations of anti-Semites, themselves 'Jew-wise',[108] urged comparable insights upon often unpersuaded audiences; in the months immediately prior to the outbreak of World War II, for example, English anti-Semites were emphatic in their denunciations of the coming 'War of the Jews' Revenge', and strove to get others to notice what they themselves had divined, 'the hidden hand in European affairs', 'the secret forces working for war'.[109] When these insights were rejected, they despaired, attributing the rejection to brainwashing by a 'Jew-controlled media'. By then, the anti-Semite had acquired the character of a man with a mission. His object was to open the eyes of his fellow citizens to a peril of which they were incompletely aware. He knew the truth about Jews. He had to speak this truth, by whatever means at his disposal. The inertia of the general population was maddening. That they refused to see what he saw so clearly, could itself only be explained by Jewish power. Their refusal to accept his message about Jewish power was itself proof of Jewish power. It was this evangelical commitment to the uncovering of a concealed 'truth', the conviction that he was using his 'brains',[110] that allowed the anti-Semite to pose as an intellectual. Has any anti-Semite carried his anti-Semitic convictions tentatively? Never: sometimes ironically or pseudo-ironically, but never open-mindedly.

It satisfies the desire for simple explanations It is a 'cognitive simplification', the consequence of an inability to master reality. It is reality denying, a retreat from the possibility that the world might be 'ill-contrived';[111] it is thus always a failure of intelligence, a travesty of thought. Jew-hatred represents a kind of temptation for the intellectual, an invitation to accept its nonsenses and *then* that terrible burden of thought, thought without end, investigation without conclusion, can be lifted, and the intellectual will have certainty. Complex phenomena are reduced to a slogan, a formula— *cherchez le juif.*[112] 'I know', the anti-Semite Wilhelm Marr confided in his 'Testament', 'the *Jewish Question* is the axis around which the wheel of world history revolves.'[113] Anti-Semitism is an alternative to the 'tedious and not always successful labour of strict reasoning' (John Locke's formulation).[114] Early in his career, the anti-Semitic Charles Maurras (1868–1952) explained, 'Everything seems impossible; or frightfully difficult, without the providential arrival of anti-Semitism, through which all things fall into place and are simplified.'[115] It is a principle of deliverance.

In a comparable formulation, a century later, another anti-Semite explained, 'Most anything bad that happens, prices going up, whatever, this can usually be attributed to the IMF and the World Bank, which are synonymous with the United States. And who controls the United States? The Jews do.'[116] These anti-Semites belong among the *terrible simplificateurs*. They are sincere only to the extent of their credulity; they have minds blinded by anti-Semitism.[117] Anti-Semitism subverts that impulse to thought stimulated by life's perplexities, drawing it away from real inquiries and the possibility of true answers, and driving it instead towards absurdities. What is the cause of our suffering? The Jews. Who controls our world? The Jews. 'The International Jew' is the 'world's foremost problem'[118]—solve it, and all will be well. Conclusions of this kind, reached by uncommonly angry minds,[119] are mystifications of reality that pose as *de*mystifications. 'Don't bullshit ME', raged Ezra Pound, in a canto replete with anti-Semitic bullshit.[120] Of course, at some point, anti-Semitism ceases altogether to possess the form of thought and becomes non-thought instead—a spasm of hate or fear, the consequence of a total collapse in reasoning, a comprehensive defeat of the mind.

It offers an 'education'   That there is no connection between a person's educational standard and the depth of his anti-Semitism[121] may perhaps be conceded, notwithstanding that the principal anti-Semite of the twentieth century was an ill-educated beer-hall demagogue and racist bigot.[122] Yet anti-Semitism also provides its own tutorials: 'I began a searching inquiry into the Jewish Question . . . ', a Nazi party anti-Semite recounted.[123] This Nazi received a training in anti-Semitism.[124] Hypnotized by an idea,[125] he then committed his life to its propagation. Whereupon, he and others like him joined milieus thronging with all the varieties of lumpen-intellectual: publicists, demagogues, hacks, propagandists, and doctrine-teachers. 'The significance of the Jewish question as a social issue dawned on me', wrote another young man, after attending a few Nazi Party meetings—he was taken in, but experienced his hoodwinking as a revelation.[126] At a somewhat later date in the history of Nazism, inductees into killing units were provided with a complement of 'ideas' about German racial superiority, the German right to empire in Eastern Europe, the menace posed by Jews and Bolsheviks, etc.—vicious, stupid banalities inculcated by written materials, lectures, courses, and the like.[127] The 'education of the anti-Semite' is something of a trope in the autobiographical literature of that milieu.[128] 'The scales are falling more and more from my eyes about the Jewish Question', wrote

Marr.[129] '[The English anti-Semite] Arthur Kitson introduced me to the Jewish Menace', related the English anti-Semite Arnold Leese, 'of which hitherto I had no real knowledge . . . I have been conducting research on the Jew Menace ever since.'[130] 'Bit by bit, it started coming home to me,' wrote an English anti-Semite of a later generation, John Tyndall, 'in the form of incontrovertible evidence, that there was present in Britain and around the world a definite Jewish network wielding immense influence and power . . . The truth was inescapable.'[131] *Spearhead*, the newspaper of John Tyndall's party, the National Front, regularly invited readers to join special 'study groups' and 'book clubs', in which texts exposing the international Jewish conspiracy could be examined.[132]

It is a resource for charlatans The charlatan speaks authoritatively about matters on which he is not an authority, and does so to impress others, and to enlist them in an enterprise of benefit to himself—to his reputation, or his pocket, or both. He is a fraudster; his pretences will always be self-interested. He speaks or writes in a lofty, bogus tone; he will make large, unverifiable claims. He lives dangerously, just one-step ahead of exposure; he is reckless, a risk-taker. He is engaged in bluffs, deceptions. He is engaged in parody versions of inquiry; he is averse to undertaking anything that requires 'hard thinking & close self-energy to master' (Coleridge).[133] It is the philistine in the study; disgorging 'ideas' but without the capacity for ideation. His point of departure is also his point of return; he never reads anything that challenges the premises of his 'inquiry'. He is typically a purveyor of some species of junk science or junk thought[134]—some glib, unfalsifiable theory with large pretensions; a quack, cure-all medicine; or a quack, cure-all ideology. He is always also a confidence-trickster,[135] a hoodwinker, and sometimes also a false prophet. If he is messianic in his pretensions, he is ever crooked in his practices. Lewis Namier once remarked to Isaiah Berlin that Marx was 'a typical half-charlatan, who got hold of quite a good idea and then ran it to death just to spite the Gentiles'.[136] A complete charlatan, presumably, runs a *bad* idea to death out of spite. And so the anti-Semitic charlatan is the person who runs a bad idea to death just to spite the Jews. The Holocaust denier is a good contemporary instance of the anti-Semitic charlatan. Deniers create the impression of scholarship with false or misleading references, bogus footnotes, and recycled quotations shorn of context and taken from books unread. They pose as experts, overstating when not simply inventing credentials for themselves.[137] They crave respect; they seek respectability. But they are no more than rascals.[138]

It champions irrationality, and excuses stupidity   Anti-Semitism thrives on ignorance, of course. A 1954 study of London working-class anti-Semites, for example, found that complaints about Jews driving English shopkeepers out of business came chiefly from men in occupations having no connection with those businesses, such as lorry-drivers and carpenters. They just did not know what they were talking about.[139] But there is also a positive championing of ignorance by some anti-Semites. This is the sequence of thoughts: (1) Jews may understand things that we do not, (2) but Jews are also vicious, (3) and therefore our incomprehension is proof of our virtue. Brainless Jew-haters hug their ignorance like a prize won; their witlessness, their merit. Their enemies are the 'Jewish intellectuals', and their hatred of intelligence is also a fear of intelligence, masquerading as a contempt for arguments, a misology.[140] They embrace a 'backwoods' anti-Semitism. They are afflicted by fantasies of dark mysteries and conspiracies;[141] they view experts with suspicion.[142] They are the 'know nothings' of anti-Semitic milieus, the people for whom the disparagement of reason and the disparagement of Jews are but two versions of the same animus. And the violence that these anti-Semites seek to inflict on Jews derives precisely from their stupidity. Brutality itself is stupid—*applied* stupidity, or stupidity in action.[143] Anti-Semitism thus appeals to a certain kind of person impatient with mere ratiocination, with the burden and solitariness of thinking, who wants instead to *act*. 'I have finished with those who think', Oswald Mosley is reputed to have said, when founding his Fascist movement. 'Henceforth, I shall go with those who feel.'[144] The Weimar era 'Free Corps' included young intellectuals in uniform, recruited into the army out of university or school, but who, alienated from civilian society, refused to be demobilized and to accept defeat. They formed themselves into fighting gangs and experienced the abject joys of unthinking, unreflective action when breaking bones.[145] They gave a metaphysical justification to their thuggery, which was the product of a certain kind of will to stupidity.

It provides opportunities for demagoguery   When sincere, anti-Semites tend to be disgruntled, troubled, disaffected, resentful, incoherent; when insincere, they are unscrupulous, opportunistic, cynical, mendacious. Public, career anti-Semites are demagogues, disparagers, defamers, scandal-mongers. They live for scandal; they cannot speak without lying. They are provocateurs: the

Holocaust, claimed David Irving, is 'the blood libel on the German people'.[146] Anti-Semitism is attractive to ideological conmen, demagogues on the make, manipulators of the public mood, agitators, and cynics. It appeals to political mountebanks.[147] While they believe and yet do *not* believe the tales they tell, cynical or naïve, their Jew-hatred is always a performance. The anti-Semitic demagogue does not *reason*; his speeches are flights of ideas,[148] without internal coherence or connecting logic. Anti-Semitism can thus be mobilized as a political programme. It conforms with propaganda's essential qualities: *simplification*—everything 'boils down to' the confrontation between friend and enemy; *disfiguration*—the enemy is everything that is bad, rotten etc.; *transfusion*—manipulating the audience's views to track the propagandist's own message; *unanimity*—presenting the propagandist's opinion as if the opinion of all right-thinking people; and *orchestration*—endlessly repeating the same message, but in different variations and combinations.[149] Anti-Semitism consists of a limited number of affirmations, lacking all proof. 'The more concise an affirmation is, the more destitute of every appearance of proof and demonstration, the more weight it carries',[150] wrote the student of crowds, Gustav Le Bon. Anti-Semitism is just such an 'affirmation'. It is impatient for supporters; it feeds on discontent; it was at one time the best slogan for organizing the masses.[151] It is ever on the hunt for the 'guilty party', who always turns out to be a Jew. Demagogic anti-Semites live inside the popular mind, in order to prey upon it. These demagogues exploit anti-Semitic resentments. Edouard Drumont (1844–1917), the French journalist and author of the bestselling *La France Juive* (1886), was perhaps the most capacious conduit of anti-Semitic discourse in the nineteenth century, and was thus a master of just this kind of rhetoric. His adopted tone was one of aggressive complaint. He was always defeated *and* defiant, utterly gloomy *and* yet insouciantly triumphalist. The Jews control everything—and yet, we can remove them by a simple act of will. They are the kings of the epoch, they are our masters, France itself has become Jewish—and yet, all will be well. 'A brave captain' will vanquish the Jewish capitalists and bankers.[152] Anti-Semites make displays of courage and fortitude, while facing no real threat. 'From the outset of my political career', declared the Fascist agitator William Joyce (1906–46), 'I was always told how unwise it was to mention the Jews.' He bravely persisted, however. 'I worked to break this evil superstition, and I believe that I have succeeded.'[153]

It provides topics for literature   Anti-Semitic notions, or memes,[154] propagate themselves by replication in our minds; in the process, we modify them, even play variations on them. It is only then that we relaunch them. But though there is thus a creative aspect to anti-Semitism, it is not rich in strictly literary possibilities. Those poets, novelists, and playwrights who draw on its tropes mostly produce dross. But there are some writers, inventive and resourceful, who have mastered the heterogeneous mass of material that comprises anti-Semitic discourse. They are able to turn this material into art. They can compress anti-Semitism into single, powerfully charged images, or realize it in powerfully drawn characters. Their anti-Semitism is creative. They rise above the anti-Semitism of their times by putting it to imaginative use. They exploit anti-Semitism for its literary effects.[155]

Anti-Semitism's exceptional functionality did not escape notice. An eighteenth-century English commentator, reviewing the language of opponents of a limited measure of Jewish relief, the so-called 'Jew Bill' of 1753, remarked that 'Judaism' had become a cant word, 'a mere Babel of ideas according to the character of the man that uses it'. The word could mean almost anything; it served as a receptacle for everything that one most rejected:

> In the mouth of a Jacobite, Judaism is another name for the revolution of 1688, a limited monarchy, the Hanover legacy, and the royal family . . . In the mouth of a pretended patriot and flaming bigot, Judaism is a Whiggish administration and House of Commons, a Protestant Bench of Bishops, liberty of conscience and an equitable toleration.[156]

In the mouths of later generations of anti-Semites, Judaism became 'another name' for the French Revolution, for the Russian Revolution, and for modernity itself. In the exceptional heterogeneity of its appeal, anti-Semitism is thus among the most versatile of hatreds. Its malignant solicitations[157] address many different kinds of person: the anti-Semite is a more complex composite than, say, the Balkan war criminal now commonly deployed in the discourse of moral philosophers.[158]

Though anti-Semitism is often generated by an obsessive animosity,[159] it is more than just an individual disorder or 'prejudice'. Men and women are socialized into anti-Semitism. It is among the strong ideas that come, in Michael Walzer's phrase, unchosen into our lives.[160] There are people who thus become Jew-haters in consequence of being exposed to the anti-Semitism of others. They have found themselves in the path of its dissemination. It is sometimes said of them that anti-Semitism has infected them, as if by a kind of mental contagion or virus.[161] So it is tempting to write about anti-Semitism as if it were a disease of thought,[162] an artificial mental illness,[163] both contagious and destructive.[164] Certainly, it shares some characteristics with diseases. As an irrational discourse, it falls to be investigated by reference to causes, not reasons.

Moreover, anti-Semitic libels often spread from single points, and then become 'epidemic':

> When the ground has been prepared, a visiting company of 'specialists' appears. They spread sinister rumours among the ignorant masses: the Jews are planning an attack on the Russians, some socialists have defiled a holy icon, some students have torn up the Tsar's portrait. Where there is no university, the rumour is made to fit the liberal rural council or even the high school. The wildest news travels along the telegraph wires, sometimes bearing an official stamp.[165]

Anti-Semitic libels disseminated in this way tend to be directed at audiences predisposed to violence against Jews. They are examples of what Le Bon termed the 'contagious suggestion', namely is a claim that is especially suscep-tible to dissemination.[166] Claims about Jewish misdeeds are often 'contagious suggestions'. For example, in May 1969, a rumour swept through Orléans that white slave traders were at work in the city.[167] Women were being abducted to the East as prostitutes. The women were customers of Jewish-owned dress shops; they had been drugged and bound in the fitting-rooms. In an evocation of the blood libel, it was said that Jews were trafficking in innocent flesh. All the Jews were accessories to these crimes, which the police and the press were not investigating because the Jews had bought them off. *Yet no one had even been reported missing.* There was indeed nothing in the rumour that was true. Those in Orléans who believed the rumours to be true were inclined to do so even before they had heard them. They were not merely gullible, which is itself a vice.[168] They were also predisposed to think the worst of Jews, though they may not all have identified themselves as anti-Semites.[169] Their iniquity, as it were, was comprised of stupidity *and* malice. They were roused by a 'false alarm'. Indeed, in some sense, anti-Semitism itself is a 'false alarm'.

Anti-Semitic 'contagious suggestions' lack the power to *make* anti-Semites; they are more likely to aggravate existing levels of anti-Semitism. These rumours—even entire anti-Semitic themes—can only be sustained in soci-eties in which there already exists a predisposition to believe them to be true.

This disposition must come from a general conception about Jews. Suppose, then, a *general conception* of Jews as malign. This enables, among other themes, the *theme* that the Jews are child-killers. And this theme, in turn, will lead to the circulation from time to time of *rumours* that a Jew has killed a child. Rumours derive from themes; themes, in turn, derive from a general conception. It is this 'general conception' that allows the audiences of themes and rumours to make sense of them. It is a 'given', part of the received wisdom or 'common sense' of the society. To write about anti-Semitism as a 'contagion' thus misses, in its focus upon 'outbreaks' and 'epidemics', anti-Semitism's embeddedness in the social imagination—which may be described as a society's common understanding, the normative notions and images that underlie its social practices and shared sense of legitimacy.[170] It also risks misrepresenting anti-Semitism as in some sense 'natural', a product of non-human causes, acting upon individuals impersonally, and causing them to injure others in ways for which they are not morally responsible. It collapses, that is, the distinction between a natural evil and a moral evil.[171]

Jews as irrational enemies of Jews

History is full of examples of Jews or part-Jews[172] who have been anti-Semitic or who have made common cause with anti-Semites. Though somewhat more of an obstacle than merely having Jewish friends or (say) situating oneself on the political Left, being of Jewish origin is not an *insuperable* obstacle to the adopting of anti-Semitic positions. (There were, for example, Anglo-Jewish politicians who spoke on behalf of the anti-Jewish immigration British Brothers' League in the first years of the twentieth century.)[173] There is some confusion, however, on this subject of anti-Semitic or 'renegade' Jews. There are indeed several kinds of Jews routinely but mistakenly taken for anti-Semites.

There are, first, *independent-minded* Jews. It is never the case that all Jews will stand in a common relationship to their given society. There will always be Jews who take their own course, but in the consciousness of some inner solidarity with the Jews as a people—that is, with what they understand to be 'their' people. Freud begins his *Autobiographical Study* (1925): 'I was born on 6th May 1856, at Freiburg in Moravia, a small town in what is now Czechoslovakia. My parents were Jews, and I have remained a Jew my-self.'[174] A year later, in an address to fellow Jews, he explained that what 'bound [him] to Jewry' was 'a clear consciousness of inner identity, the safe privacy of a common mental construction'. Being a Jew freed him from 'many prejudices that restricted others in the use of their intellect'.[175] And what of Jewish projects? In the preface to the Hebrew translation of *Totem and Taboo* (1930), he described himself as one 'completely estranged from the religion of his fathers', and unable to 'share nationalist ideals', but yet one who 'has never repudiated his people, who feels that he is in his essential nature a Jew and who has no desire to alter that nature'. Freud then added, '[my book] adopts no Jewish standpoint and makes no exceptions in favour of Jewry'.[176] His firm, even obdurate, refusal to 'repudiate his people' led him on other occasions, however, to a warm appreciation of collective Jewish projects, especially when of a defensive nature. In 1935, for example, he wrote of the financial arm of World Zionist Organisation, 'I well know how great and blessed an instrument this foundation has become in its endeavour to establish a new home in the ancient land of our fathers. It is a sign of our invincible will to survive which has, until now, successfully defied two thousand years of severe oppression! Our youth will continue the struggle.'[177] A Jewish perspective colours Freud's work throughout— even if (or perhaps, because) it is one that is very much his own.[178] Writing to his devoted Arnold Zweig about *Moses and Monotheism*, he both defends its thesis and acknowledges his 'Jewish consciousness'.[179] The book prompted some Jews—some of them having failed to persuade Freud not to publish it[180]—to describe him as a 'renegade'.[181] But he was not. On the contrary. He was one of those non-religious or 'godless'[182] Jews (as Leo Strauss once pointed out) who hold everything that is best in themselves attributable to their Jewish origins. Freud knew that he was a Jew, he knew that he belonged to the Jewish people, and he knew that the root of his problem was that he could not believe what his ancestors believed. This led him to a dedicated concern with the truth of the Jewish tradition.[183] There is something estimable, even noble, about this Jewish project of Freud's, which may be regarded as a horizon of aspiration for contemporary Jews.

There are also *oppositionist* Jews. There has always been in Jewish circles the harshest self-criticism. These criticisms foster the taking of public stands by some Jews against their community or its established institutions. They often preface their criticisms with the phrase, 'As Jews, we ...',[184] by implication claiming to champion the 'true' Jewish perspective—an embattled, minority position, for sure, calling for a certain moral heroism, and articulating fidelity to an idea of Jewishness, rather than more mundane solidarity with Jews. In modern times, they often deprecated Jewry's 'narrow-minded provincialism', 'narrow bigotry', 'religious intransigence',

and so on—what Bruno Bettelheim disparaged as 'ghetto thinking'.[185]
Some oppositionists have rather complex relations with Judaism that repay
study; others are no better than posturers, without real knowledge or
understanding of the religion. There are oppositionists who are prophetic
excoriators of Israel, and they speak or write out of a love of Israel. There are
an equivalent number (perhaps a greater number) of oppositionists, who
lack that commitment, and are driven instead by embarrassment, fear, or a
desire to ingratiate themselves with non-Jews or to distance themselves from
their fellow Jews' reprehensible conduct—or some combination of these
motives. Oppositionist Jews are often mistaken for anti-Semites. For sure,
and even more than independent-minded Jews, oppositionist Jews stretch
the patience and understanding of more conventional Jews. Hannah Arendt
was one such person. She is especially esteemed by some for her criticisms of
pre-war Jewish acts of terror, her criticisms of Zionism, and her criticisms of
the Eichmann trial. Many oppositionist Jews have now taken up positions as
scourges of the Jewish State. Out of perversity, some oppositionist Jews now
place themselves in the company of anti-Semites.

There are *'converts'* or otherwise *'assimilated'* Jews. There are Jews who set
themselves apart from their former community, without passion or acri-
mony, in detachment rather than in active, continuing denial. Their path
takes them to new allegiances: Christianity or Islam in pre-Enlightenment
centuries, or more often a secular identity, frequently with a political character, in more recent times.[186] They will no longer regard themselves as
Jewish, though many will acknowledge themselves as 'Jewish-born'; they
will reject the truth of Judaism; they may avoid the society of Jews, though
without expressing hostility towards them. Some may conscientiously wish to
educate their new co-religionists in the beliefs and practices of the Jews; some
may even champion the interests of Jews. For example, the self-described
'converted Jew', Hyam Isaacs, published a book in 1836 with the express
purpose of 'exciting the Christian world to do good to my highly esteemed
brethren of the seed of Abraham'. He claimed 'the exercise of Christian
hospitality on behalf of nearly seven million's of God's ancient race'. They
are, he conceded, 'completely in the dark' regarding the Gospel, and they
subscribe to 'the most absurd [Rabbinic] traditions', yet they have endured
all kinds of persecution, they have kept the ancient Bible pure to this day,
the apostles were themselves Jews, as was Jesus. It is by the blood of this Jew
that all must be saved.[187] 'In spite of his conversion', George Eliot commented
in her notebook, '[Isaacs] seems . . . still to love the Jews better than the

Xtians.'[188] He was not alone. Daniel Chwolsohn, who converted to Christianity in 1855 to become a professor at St Petersburg University, remained
actively involved in Jewish affairs and wrote a vigorous defence of the
Talmud against its anti-Semitic defamers.[189] And Heine once remarked,
of his own newly Christian status, 'I have merely been baptized, not converted.'[190] Not every defector therefore was a danger,[191] certainly, not an
unqualified danger—even the notorious Joseph Pfefferkorn (d. c.1522). He
was among the most infamous convert-adversaries of Judaism of his time,
proposing the confiscation and destruction of all the Jews' Hebrew books,
with the exception of the Bible, 'since by these means they grow more firmly
planted in their faithlessness'. And yet, he remonstrated with his Christian
readers ('*you* Christians') about the 'illegal and unjust' actions taken against
Jewish property, and dismissed the blood libel as pernicious nonsense. 'We
are making fools of ourselves and exposing the Christian faith to ridicule and
contempt.'[192] In the following centuries, there were many other converts,
more steadfast than Pfefferkorn, who also gave truthful evidence against blood
libellers and other enemies of the Jews, writing books or protesting to the
press ('We the undersigned, by nation Jews . . . ').[193]

Lastly, there are *persecuted* Jews and *opportunist* Jews. These kinds make a
pair, neither type believing the truth of their incriminating anti-Semitic
testimony, but coerced or seduced into giving it by torture or the promise
of reward. Among the unhappy Jews tortured into slanderous invention,
was the fifteenth-century Spaniard Benito Garcia, who withstood for five
days the pain of 200 lashes, water torture, suffocation, and partial garrott-
ing, but finally confessed to conspiring with others to cast a spell lethal
over Christians, having first made them mad. The purpose of the plot was
to obtain Christian wealth, destroy Christianity, and gain supremacy for
Jews and Judaism. Garcia later said to a fellow-prisoner that he had told
more than he knew.[194] Thus was the blood libel of El Santo Niño de La
Guardia launched.

We have arrived at the Jewish anti-Semite. Jewish anti-Semitism is a
complex phenomenon, not to be captured in the summary phrase, 'Jewish
self-hatred'—which itself need be no more than cultural self-deprecation
induced by persecution, a kind of 'negative chauvinism' or 'Jewish disidenti-
fication'.[195] The Jew who hates *other* Jews is not necessarily a self-hating Jew.
He may hate Jews, or classes of Jews, for qualities he does not believe that he
himself possesses. Though the effect of his actions may be to wrong himself
too, he sets out only to wrong others. Indeed, his anti-Semitism may even be

an aspect of his vanity. 'I am a universalist Jew, while you are a mere tribal Jew', some may be taken to say. 'I am a radical Jew, while you are a typical Jewish financier', others might say. 'I am not a Jew at all, though my parents were Jewish. I dislike Jews, I don't consider myself to be one, and I resent the fact that others—especially Jews themselves—consider me to be one', others may be taken to say. There is thus more than one native variant of anti-Semitism, more than one way to be a Jewish anti-Semite.[196]

Among Jewish anti-Semites, there are, first, those who simply adopt anti-Semitic accounts of Jews. They accept as a reality the 'mirage' of themselves generated by their 'reference group' (that is, the group in society upon which they confer the right of defining them).[197] They do not always make common cause with anti-Semites against Jews. They become divided against themselves, in recoil from what they cannot detach themselves from—other than through deception and self-deception. It is intolerable for them, this internalizing of hatred.[198] They have no defence against the hatred of others. They are destructive and self-destructive. They remain what they despise; they are Jews against their will, and endure a distressing self-contempt.[199] They are the recipients of anti-Semites' false compassion: 'the poor man was inconsolable over his Jewish heritage and all my words could not appease his feelings; certainly this grief played a part in his early death'.[200] The more creative among them do not merely adopt, they *elaborate* upon, the anti-Semitism of others; the best known such Jewish anti-Semite was Otto Weininger (1880–1903), author of *Sex and Character* (1903). According to Weininger, it made complete sense that the 'bitterest anti-Semites' were to be found among the Jews themselves. Whoever detests the Jewish disposition detests it most in himself.[201] The Jew's hatred of Jews is a frustrated dream of self-liberation.

By contrast, there is a *second* class of Jewish anti-Semite whose members, Jewish by origin, assume a new identity (typically, through conversion) with which they are entirely comfortable, and who make common cause against their former co-religionists. They make little of their religion of origin; it does not figure (at least, not overtly) in their hostilities against Jews. Friedrich Julius Stahl (1802–61), born a Jew, a convert to Lutheranism, and the founder of the Prussian Conservative Party, was one such Jewish anti-Semite. He disparaged the 'Jewish tribe', and opposed Jewish emancipation. They should be kept separate from the generality of the German people. They were entitled to civil rights, but not to political rights. He conceived of Prussia as a Christian state; his slogan was 'Authority, not Majority'.[202] He was the prophet of a small but powerful party that sought the restoration of medievalism, with all its enslavement and obscurantism. He provided the party with a 'few shreds of ideas and catch-words' or slogans, wrote the Jewish historian, Heinrich Graetz. Its programme included a 'systematic Jew-baiting', and its journal disseminated calumnies against Jews and Judaism among kindred circles outside of Germany.[203] The Austrian Chancellor Bruno Kreisky (1911–90) was another such Jew—in his case, however, attacking Jews from the left. He was a radical anti-Zionist. He once remarked, 'if the Jews are a people, then they are a repulsive people'.[204] These Jewish anti-Semites have foresworn in themselves what they despise in Jews. They do not consider themselves part of Jewry; they do not mobilize their former membership in their campaigns, they do not claim any special or 'inside' knowledge of Jews. It is as if what they now are is what they always were; their new identity has eradicated their identity of origin.

Then there is a *third* class of Jewish anti-Semite, whose members are discomfited by their Jewish origins and strive to escape them by more or less public acts of repudiation, often to the injury of their former co-religionists. Anti-Semitism provides one way in which Jewish converts to Christianity (or Islam),[205] insecure in their new faith, can declare their commitment to it. Many proverbs about former Jews circulated in early modern Europe—'It is difficult to teach converts and dogs new tricks'; 'When cats are gobbled by mice, Jews will become true followers of Christ.'[206] Converts struggled to overcome Christian suspicion.[207] They were monitored with all the wariness shown to an enemy who has suddenly switched sides.[208] Anti-Semitism appealed to some apostate Jews. It was a way of announcing their membership of, and their loyalty to, the new group.[209] The role of the Jewish convert in attacking the Jews in the public forum cannot be overrated.[210] The English novelist W. M. Thackeray (1811–63) identified the type in his novel *Barry Lyndon* (1844):

> You remember Monsieur de Geldern, the police minister. He was of Dutch extraction, and, what is more, of a family of Dutch Jews. Although everybody was aware of this blot in his scutcheon, he was mortally angry if ever his origin was suspected; and made up for his father's errors by outrageous professions of religion, and the most austere practices of devotion. He visited church every morning, confessed once a week, and hated Jews and Protestants as much as an inquisitor could do. He never lost an opportunity of proving his sincerity, of persecuting one or the other whenever occasion fell his way.[211]

That 'everybody was aware' of his origins exasperated de Geldern, and drove him to his acts of persecution. The type came in for slightly gentler mockery in a *Punch* cartoon, 'The Anti-Semitic Movement'. Overhearing an exchange on the persecution of the Jews in Berlin, 'Baron von Meyer (who flatters himself, on the strength of his personal appearance, that no one can suspect his origin). "Hear! Hear! You neffer shboke a druer vort zan zat." '[212]

There is a *final* class of Jewish anti-Semite, whose members choose to make a great deal of their Jewish origins, the better to collaborate in enterprises hostile to Jews and to traduce their practices and beliefs. These renegade Jews, specifically speaking as Jews or former Jews, give false testimony about Jews or Judaism to the Jews' enemies. A renegade Jew thus remains engaged with Jewry or Judaism, but in hatred.[213] He is still tied to the community, but in enmity towards it, or some substantial part of it. 'I am a Jew who has been brought to the point where he so loathes his people that he thinks in terms of their destruction', wrote Samuel Roth. 'I don't know how I shall ever again live contentedly with them.'[214] This kind of Jewish anti-Semite trades on his Jewish affiliations to give an air of authority and impartiality to his slanders. He will offer ostensibly authoritative disclosures of 'inside' information, slanted presentations of 'facts', exaggeration, etc.; he will thereby earn the applause, even the admiration, of his non-Jewish audience. 'There have at all times been no greater enemies of Judaism', a late nineteenth-century journal observed, 'than the idealists among the Jews themselves.'[215] The converts among them made themselves interesting and valuable to their new co-religionists by exposing Judaism's secrets and 'confessing' Jewish misdeeds.[216] Jews were among the first medieval polemicists against Judaism, and they wrote as self-described former Jews: Petrus Alfonsi, for example, constructed his early twelfth-century *Dialogue Against the Jews* as a series of exchanges between his present (Petrus) and former (Moses) selves.[217]

The motive of such converts was dual, even contradictory. By their revelations, they thereby both affirmed their normative status as Christians *and* drew attention to their extraordinary status as former Jews ('I took off the cloak of falsehood . . .').[218] They represented themselves to be quintessential Christians *because* they were converts; they took Paul as their model.[219] Christian controversialists eagerly exploited their dark disclosures and indictments,[220] impressed by the authority with which they spoke.[221] In early eighteenth-century Poland, for example, at the instigation of clerical anti-Semites, a converted Jew testified for the prosecution at a blood-libel trial and then wrote a work purporting to expose secret, lethal Jewish ceremonies.[222] The late nineteenth-century Russian anti-Semitic activist, Jacob Brafman was a converted Jew, a Professor at a Russian Orthodox seminary, *and* a Russian police spy. He wrote tracts 'exposing' national and international Jewish conspiracies against Russian interests.[223] He served as 'Jewish expert' for the governor-general of the North-West Region of Russia. His *Book of the Kahal* (1869) became a text for government officials in the Pale of Settlement, and was taken up by Dostoyevsky in his own polemicizing against the Jews.[224] It proposed that the Russian-Jewish institutions of self-government operated for the benefit of international Jewry and were directed by the *Alliance Israélite Universelle* in Paris.[225] In every city, he claimed, there was a Jewish executive committee striving to exploit and enslave non-Jews, by applying *Talmudic* prescriptions.[226] Élie de Cyon (or Ilya Tsion) (1843–1912), likewise a converted Jew, Russian agent, physiologist, and journalist, was an abettor of anti-Semitic conspiracy theories and an influence on Edouard Drumont.[227] There were other such converts—not a huge number, but more than a few.[228] Jews thus regarded these 'informer-apostates'[229] as utterly malevolent, 'an offshoot of evil, of the root of the serpent'.[230] Certainly, the 'special enthusiasm' or 'zeal' of the convert posed dangers to Jewish life and security.[231]

Nicholas Donin (*fl.* early thirteenth century) remains perhaps the best instance of this last kind of Jewish anti-Semite. He had a slow exit from Judaism. His Jewish adversaries alleged that he had always had rationalist or Karaite leanings;[232] in due course, he came to reject entirely the authority and teachings of the rabbis. In 1225, his Jewish teachers anathematized him. He then subsisted for some years, an excommunicant from Judaism, but not yet a convert to Christianity. When he did finally convert, he probably joined the Franciscans. From some time in the mid-1230s, he began to take steps against the Jews, with angry attacks and denunciations.[233] His first act might have been to incite Crusaders against the Jews of Anjou and Poitou: as a result, 3,000 Jews were said to have died, and 500 were forcibly baptized.[234] Several years later, he was among the experts invited by Emperor Frederick II in 1236 to answer the question, do Jews ritually murder Christian children? He confirmed, so it seems, that indeed they did so.[235] And then, in 1238, he went to Gregory IX to ask him to condemn the Talmud. It contained, Donin said, 'a multitude of deceptions and shameful things repugnant to decent people and a cause for horror among those who hear them'.[236] He added (endeavouring, no doubt, to stoke fears of homicidal Jewish enmity), that the sages of the Talmud assert that all those who do not observe what they teach deserve to die.[237] In 1240, Donin—assisted by other converts[238]—disputed at Paris with four rabbis appointed to defend the Talmud. He claimed that it permitted the cheating and murdering of Christians;[239] that it blasphemed against Jesus and Mary, and attacked the Church; that it contained numerous stupidities and revolting tales.[240] One of his disputants, Rabbi Yehiel ben Joseph, addressed Donin: 'From the day that you left our community fifteen years ago, you have looked for a pretence to impugn us malicious slander.' Donin retorted: 'As you have conspired against us, so it is just to do so to you.'[241] Another Jewish contemporary, the Spanish scholar Jacob ben Eli, accused Donin of being the originator of the blood libel.[242] In 1242, Donin was at the side of Louis IX, the King of France, when copies of the Talmud were burned in Paris.[243] He led a disputatious life. Towards the end of his life, Pope Nicholas III reprimanded him for having attacked the Franciscans; it was later rumoured that he had been murdered for having given offence to certain powerful, influential men.[244]

It is sometimes said, a person cannot be anti-Semitic if he or she is Jewish. Among the many things that this statement overlooks is the very character of Judaism itself. To be a Jew, one must be a Jew by choice, even if one is also born into the Jewish faith.[245] In a sense, it is not enough to have a Jewish mother; one also must become a Jew oneself. In the language of the *Talmudic* tractate *Pirke Aboth*, 'the Torah is not an inheritance'.[246] That is, it is not simply *given*. It has to be taken possession of, and this requires work. According to the opening verses of the first of the Psalms:

> Blessed is the man who hath not walked astray
> In council of the wicked, and i' the way
> Of sinners hath not stood, and in the seat
> Of scorners hath not sat. But in the great
> Jehovah's law is ever his delight,
> And in his law he studies day and night.[247]

This is Milton's translation, which leaves open the question of to whom the possessive pronoun in the last line refers—whose law is studied, Jehovah's, or the blessed man's? The common view, reflected in other translations of the psalm,[248] is that it is the former. It is God's law that is studied; the second reference substitutes 'his' for 'Jehovah's' merely to avoid an infelicitous repetition within the sentence. But the Talmud offers the alternative gloss. By studying the Torah, 'God's law', the blessed man makes it his own. It becomes *his* law. And then, in a gloss on the Talmud's gloss, the great Jewish commentator, the Maharal of Prague (1525–1609), adds that the Jew is born incomplete, and may only be completed through study.[249] In becoming inward with the law one realizes oneself as a Jew. It does not simply happen to a person—George Eliot's insight in *Daniel Deronda*. 'I shall call myself a Jew', declares Deronda.[250] Jewish existence precedes Jewish essence; being Jewish is always a work in progress. The Jew who gives false testimony against fellow Jews acts in destructive and self-destructive repudiation of this project of Jewish self-actualization.

Jews ready to speak ill of fellow Jews or Judaism are high-value witnesses for non-Jewish anti-Semites, because their evidence may be taken to be both authoritative and free of malice. They are most likely to know the truth; they are least likely to wish to misrepresent it. Why, after all, would they wish to injure their own people? The anti-Semitic Nesta H. Webster (1876–1960), for example, who was mired in fantasies of Jewish conspiracies but fearful of being regarded as a conspiracy fantasist, was glad to be able to report to her readers that an unidentified 'Christian Jew, no renegade to his race but deeply concerned for their future development', told her:

> The growing materialism amongst Jews has made them the most destructive force in the world. The only hope for them is to accept Christianity. At present, they are the greatest danger that Christian civilisation has to face.

In the same book, a few pages later, she cites 'a Jew named Morel':

> What can the wisest measures of the authorities of all countries do against the vast and permanent conspiracy of a people which, like a network as vast as it is strong, stretched over the whole globe, brings its force to bear wherever an event occurs that interests the name of Israelite?[251]

Elsewhere, in a pamphlet, she quotes Hitler to the effect that the Jews are incapable of religion 'according to Aryan conceptions', and then adds:

> This statement entirely accords with those made to me by two Jews, quite independently of each other, who assured me with deep regret that the Jews of Western Europe rarely believed in God or the immortality of the soul; their outlook is entirely material.[252]

This is something of a stylistic tic in her work. She writes of 'a conversation I once had with a young Jew who asked me for an interview':

> 'I come to you,' he said, 'to thank you for what you have written. Do not suppose I come as an anti-Semite, since I am a Jew to the marrow of my bones. But in studying the question of Pan-Judaism, I came across your books, and they explained to me much that I had never understood before. You are perfectly right in saying the Jews desire world domination, all my life I have heard them speak of it.'[253]

I return to Webster in Chapter 6. I return to the topic of self-incriminating statements by unnamed or misnamed Jewish witnesses in Chapter 7.

Are philo-Semites irrational enemies of the Jews?

During the course of World War II, J. B. Priestley wrote a play for the British Armed Forces intended 'to clarify . . . minds on current issues'. The work, *Desert Highway*, addressed the question, why are we fighting? The principal character is Sergeant Ben Joseph, whom Priestley describes thus:

> A well-built, thoughtful Jew of the best type, aged about 30. His ascendancy over the other men is due to his personality rather than to his rank, he has no Jewish accent, but speaks as an ordinary London secondary school boy would speak. He is a sensitive fellow but very virile.

It is given to this exemplary Jew to explain to the men in his platoon the Nazi threat. He tells them what is happening to Jews—'packed into sealed trucks and gassed to death', 'raped and then butchered', 'buried alive', 'their brains bashed out'. 'It's mad and filthy', a soldier responds. 'We're fighting to stop it.' And then another soldier says, 'Mind you, Sergeant, with all due respect to you, I know people who don't like Jews and sometimes they seem to have good reasons.' The first soldier protests, but Joseph responds:

> No, that's all right. I can understand that. We're a people who've had our wits sharpened—and sometimes been made unscrupulous—by hundreds of years of persecution and insecurity. A lot of our people behave rather badly. They're too sharp, too smart, make too much noise, are too pleased with themselves. But that's not what Hitler and the Nazis dislike about the Jews, nor why they want to destroy us. Their anti-Jewish madness is something quite different from ordinary prejudice.

Joseph explains that the Nazis hate the Jews because of their 'idea of the great invisible Lord of Hosts, the one God of righteousness'.[254] Priestley's concessions to everyday anti-Semitic sentiment might surprise contemporary readers.

It does not require any special sympathy for Jews to see through the stupidities of anti-Semitism. Indeed, it takes nothing more than a gift for incredulity—that is, level-headedness, a certain capacity to disbelieve the hostile nonsense that is spoken and written about Jews. This is all that most Jews ask for. So these Jews tend to react somewhat immoderately to *philo*-Semitism. They can be immoderately *grateful*; but they can also be immoderately *suspicious* or immoderately *resentful*.

They are *grateful*, sometimes out of a sense of unworthiness, or as a strategy of communal accommodation,[255] but mostly for the very good reason that philo-Semitism tends to be a minority position, many times maintained in the face of intense hostility and at high personal cost. Non-Jews willing to risk social ostracism, injury, or even death, to protect Jewish reputations or lives, are admirable beyond ordinary measure; they brave not just physical perils, but the contempt of their own communities. In England in particular, they have had to resist invitations to collude in disparagements—'What, Lord Randolph,' inquires an aristocratic country-house guest of Winston Churchill's father, 'you've not brought your Jewish friends?' 'No,' Randolph Churchill celebratedly replied, 'I did not think they would be very amused by your company.'[256] Many such individuals are perhaps better described as *anti*-anti-Semites, not philo-Semites;[257] they have no special, developed view of Jews—they merely recognize oppression when they see it, and it impels them to intervene. They write out of reason, not love; they regard the Jew as 'just like anyone else'; they are 'proof against *The Protocols of the Elders of Zion*, and also against invitations to pro-Jewish excesses'; they 'champion, not the Jew, but an attitude of common sense regarding the Jew';[258] they insist that there is 'nothing to show that the Jews are remarkable for their bad morals in this country'.[259] While some among them are ready to find a kind of corporate virtue in Jews, if only in consequence of persecution, they resist any tendency to idealize.[260] They are advocates, they are friends, they are vindicators of the Jews—but they are not besotted with them. And then there are stories such as this one, told by A. N. Wilson, which are moving beyond words. One morning in 1940, in a German PoW camp, several hundred British PoWs were lined up. Their sergeant major had been requested by the camp commandant to

identify the Jews in the unit. 'All those who are Jews, three paces forward.'
Every single soldier took those three steps.[261]

Jews are *suspicious*, because philo-Semitism is often banal, a matter
of 'saccharine superlatives'[262]—and condescending too, as in, 'the Jews
of every land have always faced persecution with courage and insult
with composure. They have not yet learned the more difficult lessons of
prosperity.'[263] The impeccably liberal W. E. H. Lecky (1838–1903), a
declared enemy of anti-Semitism, was yet also eloquent on the Jews'
deficiencies. Adulation, servility, falsehood, and deception became common
among this persecuted people, he explained. Slavish conditions produced
slavish characteristics. Excluded from honours, they valued riches; hitherto
excluded from polite society, they have the defects of *parvenus*.[264] Beyond
Lecky's well-intentioned prejudices,[265] expressions of warm appreciation
coexist with less friendly sentiments towards Jews.[266] This is a philo-Semitism
of mixed signals. Ostensible compliments can be covert disparagements, and a
glorification of Jews can pass suddenly into a neurotic anti-Semitism.[267] The
pseudonymous 'Philojudaeus', for example, wrote a letter to *The Times* that
both praised the Jews ('I admire them as a race, I respect their religion . . . ')
and condemned them for engineering the Russian Revolution ('[they] play a
principal part in the Bolshevist conspiracy all over the world . . . ').[268] A few
years later, Britain's colonial secretary commended the Jews' 'brains and
character', and expressed the hope that their 'subtle influence', which allowed
them to 'dominat[e] much bigger nations [than their own]', was 'working for
the good'.[269] Some philo-Semites are enthusiastic about the prospects of
reforming Jews, making them less 'singular', more like the philo-Semites
themselves. 'Why', asked one friend of the Jews, 'should they not be
reclaimed? Even the worst Jew has, in common with the rest of the human
race, an inborn principle of rectitude.'[270] Philo-Semites often just concede too
much of the anti-Semites' case against the Jews.[271] Most personal friendships
suffer from certain ambiguities—how could a friendship towards an entire
nation ever be simple?[272] At the very least, the friendship can indicate a
preoccupation with 'Jewishness' unwelcome in its intensity, its singularity
of focus. But philo-Semitism is often merely ostensible, the product of some
ulterior motive—say, to disparage one class of Jews by appearing to praise
another class, *or* to convert Jews or otherwise detach them from their given
allegiances, *or* to restate the anti-Semite's case against the Jews as parasitic,
money-minded, lacking elevated feelings, and so on, while purporting to
excuse these vices by reference to 'two thousand years of persecution', and

the like. Further, to speak well of Jews can mean esteeming them for capabilities they neither possess nor wish to possess. 'Some people like Jews and some do not. But no thoughtful man can deny the fact that they are beyond question the most formidable and the most remarkable race which has ever appeared in the world' (Winston Churchill).[273] This is a view many anti-Semites embrace and *ex*-anti-Semites will often retain, however much else they might discard. Such a misconception can only with difficulty comprise the premise for philo-Semitism. The Jews are *not* collectively formidable. They are weak, divided, heterogeneous. They have constituted themselves as a nation only with difficulty, and never such as to secure the consent of the entirety of Jewry. Finally, there is something dubious about the making of *any* general statement about Jews—however favourable. It cannot but simplify and therefore misrepresent the diversity of actual Jews. In its denial of their diversity, it does each one of them a distinct injustice—though we may acknowledge that false esteem is not the most burdensome of injustices. There is, lastly, a certain pose—what Paul Lawrence Rose describes as 'the pose of the disappointed friend'[274]—that claims the status of the philo-Semite the better to deliver an attack upon Jews or a Jewish enterprise. 'I regret to say, and I say it as one who considers himself to be a friend of the Jews', etc.—that kind of thing.

They are *resentful* when they find themselves the object of pity. Just as tolerance is an inferior version of respect, so pity is an inferior version of compassion. It is the tug of feeling for the unfortunate, the disadvantaged. There is a moral inadequacy about pity. It is a form of charity—and charity creates a multitude of sins, as Oscar Wilde remarked.[275] It can blind its possessors, wrote J. A. Hobson, to the wholesome claims of social justice.[276] It is tainted with egotism. It is apt to become morbid. It can also be cruel— 'I pity you' can never be said with pity. Pity may register the pains of persecution, but it often stands perplexed before the true character of the persecuted. It is also limiting, confining regard for the sufferer to the fact of his suffering. Hannah Arendt, in her essay 'We refugees', written in 1943, explained, 'If we are saved, we feel humiliated, and if we are helped, we feel degraded.'[277] Jews will sometimes greet philo-Semitic gestures with a cold silence, then.[278] Pity for Jews is also consistent with a great deal of casual anti-Semitism. Consider, for example, Louis MacNeice's poem, 'Refugees', written in September 1940. The poem opens, 'With prune-dark eyes, thick lips, jostling each other / These disinterred from Europe throng the deck . . .' These 'disinterred' are about to arrive in New York.

They are '[t]hinking, each of them, the worst is over / And we do not want any more to be prominent or rich, / Only to be ourselves, to be unmolested / And make ends meet...'[279] The poet's sympathy is with the refugees, of course, and not with their persecutors. But, as if by some effect of gravitation, he is also pulled towards the banalities of anti-Semitic physiognomy and sociology—Jews have full lips and dark eyes, they are all prominent or rich, etc.[280]

Against this, there is a story in the Talmud that points to the character of the philo-Semite. It is in *Avodah Zarah*, a tractate concerned with the laws governing Jews in their relations with idolaters. Like all the Talmud's stories, it requires a certain amount of interpretation.

There once was a Caesar who hated the Jews and wished to do them harm. He summoned prominent members of his government to solicit their assent to his plans. Though the Talmud does not name him, it was probably Domitian, one of the bloodier Caesars, who reigned from 81 to 96 CE. I will assume that it was he. This is the question that he put to his council. 'If a person has a wart on his foot, what should he do with it? Should he cut it away, and thus live in comfort, or should he leave it, and suffer discomfort?' It is not a question that anticipates anything other than the response, 'cut it away', though it allowed Domitian to pose as a ruler ruling upon advice. Not a tyrant, then, but solicitous of the views of others. Everyone present knew that Domitian was not asking a medical question. It was understood that he was expressing the view, just as any one of us would cut away a sore on our foot, so we must remove the Jews.

Domitian spoke as he did in order to present his policy of extermination as the common-sense solution. The homely analogy made assent practically irresistible, while also making his ministers complicit in his plans. They become collaborators in its formulation. He did not tell them to act on his plan; he invited their observations on its wisdom. What is more, referring to Jews as 'warts' makes then somewhat less than human, and justifies their murder as a matter of hygiene. It is perhaps also wise—and it seems to be the custom—to speak in code if one is planning murder.

(Hitler himself avoided issuing explicit written directives relating to the killing of the Jews, relying instead on oral instructions to single individuals or very small groups. The mass extermination of Jews was a state secret, and it was also Hitler's secret.[281] Secrecy was essential: if breached, the annihilation process would be put in jeopardy, it would be used in anti-German propaganda, and there would be a risk of retaliation by the Allies. What is

more, extermination had to be concealed from the German public; while
the policy was well known, details of its execution were withheld.[282]
Secrecy was preserved by many means, including the pervasive employment
of euphemism. The attendees at the Wannsee conference, for example,
were invited to assist Heydrich 'make all necessary organisational and
technical preparations for a comprehensive solution of the Jewish Question'.[283] Euphemisms of this order also assisted the perpetrators in keeping at
bay the reality of the murder of millions of people. Like Domitian, Hitler
also used homely analogies.)[284]

Domitian gets the response he wants, but there is one dissenter. The
name he is given in the story is the Hebrew one, Keti'ah bar Shalom,
though he was a high-ranking Roman. This is what the Talmud reports
Keti'ah as saying to his emperor.

> In the first place, you cannot do away with all of them, for it is written, 'For I
> have spread you abroad as the four winds of the heavens.' Now what does this
> verse indicate? Were it to mean that Israel was to be scattered to the four
> corners of the world, then instead of saying 'as the four winds,' the verse
> would have said 'to the four winds.' It can only mean that just as the world
> cannot exist without winds, so the world cannot exist without Israel. And
> what is more, your kingdom will be called a crippled kingdom.

The verse quoted is from Zechariah. Though his arguments are quite
complex, Keti'ah's stance is clear enough. You intend to injure the Jews.
The policy is misconceived, because it will fail. You cannot destroy the
Jews, however hard you may try. It is also dangerous, because it will damage
the Empire.

Keti'ah is dismissive of Domitian's evasions. 'You cannot kill all of
them'—he does not bother even to say, 'the Jews'. He does not affect
uncertainty about the true object of Domitian's inquiry. It is as if he is
saying, 'Let us be frank with each other, we are talking about the Jews.' He
also does not pretend that the policy has been formulated by anyone other
than the emperor. It is not 'We cannot kill them.' He makes it plain to
Domitian that the emperor, and no one other than the emperor, will be
held responsible for the murders.

The citing of Zechariah has a larger purpose. First, it demonstrates that it
is possible to discover the truth about the Jews. No person who wishes to
know the Jews, and to understand their religion, need rely on defamatory
rumour. The Hebrew Scriptures can be read; the people themselves can be

known. If hatred of the Jews proceeds from ignorance about them, then the citing of Zechariah demonstrates that it is not a necessary, unavoidable ignorance. Secondly, Zechariah was a prophet whose message was one of comfort. God will take action on Israel's behalf. He is determined to forgive. He will defend Jerusalem. He will defeat all those who oppose His will. Never again shall destruction be decreed, and Jerusalem shall dwell secure. This is consistent with Keti'ah's own gloss on Zechariah's words. The dispersion of the Jews is not to be interpreted as a punishment of them, but as an indication of their indispensability to the world. The world needs the Jews, and cannot survive without them. Zechariah is a text often cited as a warning to those threatening harm to Jews.[285] Keti'ah's advice is thus both pragmatic and prophetic, or reliant upon the prophetic. There is an appeal to self-interest too. We need the Jews; our reputation will suffer if we persecute them. We might also thereby jeopardize a valuable resource. Keti'ah adopts, in a qualified way, the perspective of his sovereign. The arguments that are deployed are intended to be persuasive. He does not say, 'This is wrong, you should not do it.' He argues on policy grounds. But his sympathy for the Jews is plain. As Domitian hates the Jews, so Keti'ah loves them. Domitian's reply is prompt, and lethal. 'You have spoken very well. However, he who contradicts Caesar is executed.' Note the confirmation that advice was not being sought; note also the implication that Keti'ah's reasoning has been accepted. We may take it that Keti'ah was aware of the danger in speaking up for the Jews.

As he is being led away, a Roman matron is heard cryptically to remark, 'Pity the ship that sails towards the harbour without paying the harbour tax.' It is not obvious what she means. Further oblique language, then, from another Roman. Keti'ah himself appears to understand her to mean that he is on a journey to the next world, but that he will not be allowed entry unless he becomes a Jew. This is consistent with his response, which is promptly to circumcise himself, declaring, 'I have paid the tax, and I will enter the world to come.' But the matron is not to be taken as an authority on Judaism, not least because conversion demands more than circumcision alone. Keti'ah is to be regarded as such an authority (evidenced by the citing of Zechariah), and thus would know both that he did not by his self-circumcision thereby become a Jew and that to die a Gentile did not in itself exclude him from the world to come. It follows that he does not circumcise himself out of a kind of misconceived, self-interested shrewdness, as if to declare: 'Though Caesar will not recognize my merit, God now will.' So what then does she mean, and why does Keti'ah respond as he does? I take her to be mocking Keti'ah. There is no real pity in her remark. She sees him go to his death, and she mocks him. Your sacrifice will not be rewarded. You will perish, and that will be that. You think that you are dying a meritorious death, but you are not. Your own people have rejected you; the Jews will not accept you either. You think that you are as good as the Jews; you think that you are a Jew. But you are not. And so you have made yourself ridiculous. Now make yourself even more ridiculous, and circumcise yourself. It is as if she is daring him: how far will you go in this infatuation, this futile identification with a people utterly alien to you?

And Keti'ah responds with his own mockery. He confronts the matron. I hold my Roman identity to be of no value. See, I will even circumcise myself. There is no line that divides me from identification with the Jews and with Judaism. If you think that circumcision deters me, you are wrong. I am ready to take that step too. It was a radical act. The Greeks and Romans regarded circumcision as a physical deformity, akin to castration.[286] It was the butt of many jokes. 'The circumcised' was a stock epithet used to describe the Jews. Though pagan intellectuals were divided in their views on most Jewish practices and beliefs, none praised circumcision.[287] Circumcision was unlawful in Rome. The punishment for the circumciser was death, and for the circumcised, exile and confiscation of property.[288] It represented that irreversible moment for pagan 'God fearers', no longer Roman, now Jewish.[289]

Speaking up for the Jews, especially in the way that he does, takes Keti'ah to the brink of conversion—by which I mean a kind of spiritual abandonment to Judaism. He loves Jews; he gives himself up to Judaism. By quoting Zechariah, Keti'ah indicates that he is not just a scholar of Judaism, familiar with its texts and capable of interpreting them, but also a believer in its prophecies. He is already ready to affirm their truth. At that moment, sympathy for the Jews, and a conviction that their religion is the true one, meets hatred of the Jews, and a threat to their survival. It precipitates a crisis. Sympathy for the Jews becomes identification with them. To argue for them now means becoming one of them, as if as an advocate adopting the cause he represents. Keti'ah's last words, just as he is being cast into the furnace, are to leave all his possessions 'to Rabbi Akiva and his friends'. He leaves everything he owns to them; he leaves everything he once was for them.

It is possible to construct an ideal of the philo-Semite from this story. There are many people who take a scholarly interest in Judaism, but who would not be willing to come to the aid of Jews. And there are many who, though knowing nothing about Judaism, have yet performed heroic, selfless acts when Jewish lives have been threatened. The 'rescuers', the 'righteous Gentiles', of the Holocaust, whose lives have been celebrated in memoir and film, are exemplary of this latter group. Their acts of rescue often entailed the breach of many norms of conduct: murder, disloyalty, dishonesty, deceit, forgery, bribery, deliberate falsification of paternity tests,[290] desertion from one's military unit, and so on.[291] Some of these people even entertained hostile feelings towards Jews.[292] Telling the truth about Jews, but not coming to their aid, *or* coming to their aid, while still cleaving to lies about the Jews—these make for something less, or other, than a complete or ideal philo-Semite. The exemplary philo-Semite is the person who tells the truth about Jews *and* comes to their defence, or is ready to do so. Keti'ah is this ideal. He is learned in the Jews' culture, and resolute in their defence. His engagement with Judaism leads him towards becoming a Jew; he resists evil at the cost of his own life. He is the answer to those who believe that the *philo*-Semite is never anything more than a special kind of *anti*-Semite.[293]

Passages from rational or opportunistic enmity to irrational enmity

The history of anti-Semitism is thick with instances of opportunistic and irrational enemies of the Jews making common cause. The Russian 'Black Hundreds', for example, were full of thuggish anti-Semites, combative and profane,[294] for whom violence against Jews was both instrument and end. Sergey Witte, minister of finance, wrote of the organization:

> Most of its leaders are political upstarts, people with unclean ways of thinking and feeling; they have not a single viable political idea and concentrate all their efforts on unleashing the lowest possible impulses in the benighted, savage masses. Sheltered by the wings of the two-headed eagle this party can instigate the most frightful pogroms and convulsions, but it is incapable of anything positive. It embodies a wild, nihilistic patriotism that thrives on lies, slander and deceit, it is a party of wild and cowardly despair but has no room for courageous, far-sighted, creative thinking. The bulk of the membership comes from the wild, ignorant masses, its leaders are political villains, it has secret sympathisers in court circles and among nobles with all kinds of titles— people who seek their salvation in lawlessness . . .[295]

Similarly, but far more consequentially for contemporary anti-Semitism, there are many connections between the irrational and the rational, between enemies of 'the Jews' and enemies of distinct Jewish projects, between anti-Semites and *non*-anti-Semites. The two categories are not mutually exclusive; much rational enmity is coloured by irrationality. There are indeed multiple connections between them.

The anti-Semite will always insist that his enmity is rational It is by exposure to anti-Semitism, not to Jews, that one becomes an anti-Semite.[296] Yet for the anti-Semite himself, there is *only* rational enmity towards the Jews, and he is its clear-eyed advocate. He will pretend that he is rational; he will seek to establish rational grounds for his enmity towards Jews. He may insist that he merely opposes a Jewish project, even though on examination it is not a project at all—say, the killing of Gentile children or mastery of the world. With the necessary patience, the anti-Semite may be exposed by reference to the contradictory, and thus self-cancelling, character of anti-Semitism's most familiar 'propositions'.[297] Jews are obtrusively, conspicuously Jewish *and* are adept at concealing their Jewish identity by name change, conversion, etc.; Jews seek the most luxurious, sensual style of life *and* are dirty, smelly, and unattractive; Jews stick together *and* take our jobs; Jews are economic parasites *and* our financial masters; Jews are capitalists *and* revolutionaries; Jews are nationalists *and* agents of national dissolution; and so on. The propositions of anti-Semitic anti-Zionism are similarly contradictory. Israel lacks the essential characteristics of a state, but it *also* has the power to assert itself as a strong nation; Israel could not survive without the United States, but *at the same time*, it has the power to manipulate the United States for its own purposes; Israel is a cowardly, ephemeral entity but it *also* displays a 'Nazi' arrogance and cruelty.[298]

Rational enmity can become irrational by a process of accretion Christians complain of the Jews' rejection of Jesus' claim to be the Messiah (or the claim made on his behalf). Muslims complain of the Jews' rejection of Mohammed's claim to be a prophet. True enough. But some Christian and Muslim anti-Semites then go on to complain that these rebuffs are attributable to the essentially wicked nature of the Jews—a theme that they then elaborate upon, adding more and more fantastic particulars. These anti-Semites begin by using a version of the truth to justify their oppression of the Jews, but then further justify it by reference to lies. These lies are easier for the anti-Semite than the truth; they seem more 'objective'. They do not require him to expose his resentment at the religious rebuff, and they can be given an appearance of verisimilitude. They are not obvious as lies; owning up to one's resentment at a rejection would, by contrast, be a painful, self-exposing affair. It is now almost impossible to scrape the accretions of the irrational from Christianity's necessary confrontation with Judaism. (I will return to this theme below.)

Both rational and irrational enmities may be helped into existence through the ill-considered actions of a Jew or Jews   This is a difficult point, easily misstated. It is distinct from the point that anti-Semites will always seek to exploit such actions. It is perhaps best approached by means of a story. According to the Talmud (*Sanhedrin* 99b), there once was a pagan of royal descent who wished to become a Hebrew. Her name was Timna, and she lived in the time of the Patriarchs. She went to Abraham, Isaac, and Jacob, but each one of them rejected her. In despair, she became the concubine of Esau's son. She decided that she would rather be a servant in Israel than a princess of another people. Amalek was a child of that union (Genesis 36:12), and this, says the Talmud, was in punishment for the Patriarchs' unrelenting stance towards his mother. Had they accepted Timna, Amalek would not have come into existence— not, at least, as kin to Israel itself. Emmanuel Levinas finds in the story a warning against haughtiness of spirit, an idolatry of the Torah.[299] The point of the story is not, then, that the Jews brought all the evil they thereafter suffered on their own heads, but rather that rejection can be the indirect cause of pain, much later on, to the rejecter. Rejection creates its own, malign connection between rejecter and rejected.

Both rational and irrational enmity can divide Jews   Precisely because Jews do not comprise a single, homogeneous group, they will divide in their responses to both rational and irrational enemies. The diversity of response will often be radical—not just a matter of differing strategies of defence, but taking the enemy's part. This is commoner in cases of rational enmity, which often set Jews against each other. Think, say, of issues of policy in relation to the Middle East peace process, or of competing positions within Zionism. But it is also true that there will always be Jews who side with anti-Semites, sometimes because they embrace anti-Semitism itself, sometimes for more personal, though equally ignominious reasons, and sometimes because they misread an irrational enmity as a rational one. I consider these Jews further in Chapter 8.

There are positions taken that, though not anti-Semitic in themselves, are enabling of anti-Semitism The commonest of these positions, to be located in the lower realms of sociological thinking, is as follows. People divide naturally into groups. Each group has its own practices and traditions, and an understanding of itself as distinct and separate from other groups. There is a 'natural' tendency towards 'group-centredness' or 'ethnocentrism'.[300] Groups will always view other groups with some wariness; sometimes their posture will be one of active belligerence. One or more groups in any particular society may dominate that society. There will thus be 'in-groups' and 'out-groups'. Inter-group enmity is taken to be rational.[301] The differences between ethno-racial groups are similarly taken to be indelible, unbridgeable.[302] The anti-Semite appropriates this position, almost ready-made for his convenience, and asserts that the Jews constitute a group, one with which another group (Gentiles, the white race, the Aryan race, etc.) must compete. It is unnecessary to inquire what the Jews have done; it is instead sufficient to understand who they *are*. They are an alien people; to know one is to know all. Anti-Semites misrepresent the quarrel they have picked with 'the Jews' as a quarrel that Jews have picked with Gentiles, or with the white race, or with the Aryan race, etc. It is in contesting precisely these positions that the enemy of anti-Semitism is led to the truth that *no* person is reducible to an essence, either collective or individual. These 'essences' are mere imaginary retreats from acknowledging the irreducible heterogeneity of our existence.[303]

The deadlier the enmity, the more irrational it is likely to be The persecution of Jews is unjustifiable, yet it is always accompanied by justifications. The more lethal the persecution, the more compelling its justification has to be. What is it that justifies murder? Only self-defence. When the anti-Semite kills, it is in purported self-defence. He defends himself against murderous attacks, and against plots intended to enslave him. They are of course imaginary attacks and plots. His life is not in jeopardy; he does not risk enslavement. But those staples of anti-Semitism, the blood libel and the libel of a Jewish global conspiracy, allow him to claim otherwise. Fantasy is never far away. Members of the Pétainist political police, the Milice National, had to take this oath: 'I swear to fight against democracy, against Gaullist insurrection, and against Jewish leprosy.'[304] Leprosy? Anti-Semitism cleaves to 'absolute lies' when it has become delusional, that is to say utterly without any rational element.[305] 'Hatred' is thus an indispensable concept in the analysis of anti-Semitism.[306] The irrational enemy is always a *mortal* enemy—*Todfeind* was Hitler's word.[307] The enmity derives from the imagination of the anti-Semite and is absolute—it is absolute *because* it is imaginary. The anti-Semite constitutes 'the Jew' as his enemy, and he himself thereby becomes the enemy of every Jew.

The greater the irrationality, the greater the misreading of events and personalities   In 1898, Colonel Henry under interrogation confessed to having forged the incriminating document upon which Dreyfus was convicted. In despair, convinced that the army had abandoned him, he killed himself while in detention. And the reaction of the anti-Dreyfusards to these events? Committed to Dreyfus's guilt as a matter of faith, one that could not be disturbed by mere contrary evidence, they chose to celebrate Henry as a hero, and to praise his act of fabrication as patriotic. The forgery was the product of a 'daring spirit of enterprise', Maurras wrote. Henry had misled his superiors, his friends, and his colleagues, 'for the welfare of all'.[308] The anti-Dreyfusards' misjudgements flowed from their anti-Semitism. In this they were exemplary, but hardly alone. Consider the far greater evil of Nazi anti-Semitism. For as long as Nazism had the capacity to destroy, it did not need to understand. But whatever it could not destroy, it stood before in perplexity. Consider, for example, Hitler's judgements on Churchill. The British prime minister was, Hitler said, 'the puppet of Jewry, who pull his strings'. He always acted 'on the order of his Jewish paymasters'.[309] One cannot make sense of the world if one believes that Jews run it; one cannot make sense of what motivates one's enemies, if one believes that they are all either Jews or controlled by Jews. Most ludicrously of all, but indicative of the essential fatuity of the Nazis' ideological position, Himmler announced to the Swedish representative of the World Jewish Congress, in the course of his overtures in April 1945 to enlist the West in a crusade against Bolshevism, that he wanted 'to bury the hatchet between us and the Jews'. This was ludicrous, but then, writes a Holocaust historian, 'Nazi ideology itself was ludicrous, and so was practically everything that continued to be done in its name until the final moments of the war.'[310] Anti-Semitism is in its essence, then, a malign credulity, a willingness to believe *anything* about the Jews, however fantastic.

The relations between the rational and the irrational have their own distinct complexities; the distinction between rational and irrational enmity is itself not free of complexity. It follows that, in the analysis of particular instances of anti-Semitism, differences of emphasis and approach between scholars will emerge. But these differences are to be distinguished from the more culpable confusions of the rational with the irrational that disfigure some contemporary writing on anti-Semitism. I return to this topic in Chapter 3.

Passages from irrational enmity to 'ideology'

Towards the end of the nineteenth century, the two distinct follies of race theory and conspiracy theory came together, establishing a new, 'ideological' version of anti-Semitism. Indeed, it is *only* in relation to Jews that racist and conspiracist theories combined. This conjunction was made possible by the absence of any empirically grounded concepts from either racism or 'conspiracism' (as I will term it). Race theory was derived from a mistake about language; conspiracy theories were grounded in nothing more than fantasy—that is to say, not 'grounded' at all. The data of genuine political ideologies—class, religion, nation, state, subject, and citizen—all have a certain reality. But 'race' and 'conspiracy' exist only inside the minds of their advocates. There is no racial order, there are no world-controlling plots. Racist-conspiracist anti-Semitism, which was political and programmatic, was thus driven to rely upon bogus science and bogus documents. Of course, many individual anti-Semitic works rely on false conceptions about Jews, or forgeries or 'improvements' of official records.[311] There will always be this element of the dishonest, the bogus, in anti-Semitism, which will often coexist with naïve belief. But racism depends *utterly* upon pseudo-scientific rubbish; conspiracism depends *utterly* upon lies, forgeries, and fabrications. And by an odd dynamic, this anti-Semitism was *both* more thoroughly nonsensical in its beliefs *and* more pretentious in the claims it made for them than any version of anti-Semitism that preceded it. It was drivel that aspired to the status of an independent belief-system. It was a delusion masquerading as an ideology. It aped religious dogma *and* scientific method. An 'Anti-Semites' Catechism', for example, was composed (in 1887 by Thomas Frey), containing the following article of faith, 'All Jews of all nations and all languages work for the Jewish domination of the world.'[312] This sentence, with various essentially unimportant modifications (perhaps not all Jews, but instead Israel, its Jewish supporters, and their creature, the United States of America), is one to which most anti-Semites would even now subscribe. Indeed, subscribing to it marks them out as anti-Semites.

Let me examine the components of this version of anti-Semitism more closely.

Racism

Racism is infected by a mania for classification; indeed, it is a slave to false taxonomies. Yet it is itself an elusive, slippery doctrine. It is supreme in its ability to fuse the visual and ideological. Racist stereotypes make theory come to life in a simple, direct manner. 'Race' was disregarded, save at the margins of their work, by all philosophers or social theorists of consequence. It appealed instead to second-rate thinkers, publicists, and synthesizers (and cranks—ethnomaniacs of various stripes). They elevated into a racial principle certain nineteenth-century bourgeois virtues: cleanliness, honesty, moral earnestness, hard work, family life. They appropriated the ideas of more serious minds; they took something from Darwin, something from Lombroso, something from Galton. Racism is thus a scavenger ideology. It has also always been a scourge; in its working-out in the mid-twentieth century it realized itself in the Holocaust.[313] Racism continues to be effective, in part because it is so banal and so eclectic. It is ethnicism made hierarchical—an unjustifiable prioritizing, derived from a misconceived 'essentializing' of differences.[314]

In its late nineteenth- and early twentieth-century formulations, this crazy doctrine[315] borrowed from eugenics. According to received eugenic theory, the spread of estimable and inferior qualities was race-neutral. Selective breeding was necessary for all groups wishing to improve their 'stock'. Francis Galton was not an anti-Semite; he did not hold that the Jews were racially inferior or racially corrupting. The support given by some leading eugenicists to Hitler's racial policies in the 1930s was not a necessary implication of eugenics doctrine itself. There is no eugenicist mandate, for example, to treat a nation as if it were a biological organism afflicted by alien parasites. However, eugenics, or what has been (slightly generously) termed '*pseudo-eugenics*', *was* at the doctrinal root of the forced sterilizations and killings by the Nazis of homosexuals, the elderly, the disabled, and the chronically sick.[316] Natural selection could not be relied upon to eliminate the degenerate; the task thus fell to the state.[317] It was eugenicist language, and the brutality implicit in eugenicist policy, that racism adopted. The eugenics movement itself did not survive the revelations of what Nazism had done in its name.[318]

In more recent formulations, it has taken on a certain cultural complexion. It is no longer an affair of blood. Racism once concerned itself with
physical differences between notional groups of human beings; now it
concerns itself with ineradicable, insurmountable cultural differences.[319] It
now presents itself as derived from social science, not natural science. Racists
have abandoned—they say that they have abandoned—claims for superiority of one race over all others. They now content themselves with arguing
that 'races' or 'people' cannot peaceably live together. They must separate,
which always means that the *other* race or people must go. 'Separation'
mandates expulsion—which is characterized as repatriation, a return home,
voluntary emigration, and the like. Violence is very regrettable, we do not
promote it, of course, but it is unavoidable, much better for both sides
to separate, etc. This new 'cultural essentialism'[320] is merely the successor
version to the racisms of the nineteenth and early to mid-twentieth centuries.
Like the 'old' racism, it promotes authoritarian values—duty, discipline, the
family, patriotism; it seeks to protect 'our way of life'; it values 'the company
of one's own kind'; it retains a pseudo-scientific language, part biology, part
anthropology—'ethnic stock', 'the territorial imperative', etc.

Though racism cannot now be imagined without its anti-Semitic aspect,
it did not quite begin that way. One of its founders, Arthur de Gobineau
(1816–82), for example, thought well of the Jews, and was not an anti-
Semite. For a time, respectable intellectuals believed that it was possible, in
the spirit of scientific inquiry, to study the supposed racial characteristics of
Jews—including of course their fabled noses (the problem of 'nostrel-
isity').[321] Jews were a problem for racists. The black/white binarism was
easy enough. Everything that was good, and beautiful, and true, could be
assigned to the right side, and everything that was vicious, and ugly, and
false, could be assigned to the left side. But what of the Jews? Were
they black or white? Did they comprise a pure race, or were they a
'mongrelized' non-race? Were they an inferior, or a superior, people?
(Certain Darwinian positions encouraged the conclusion that the Jews
were a superior race.) Jews were taxonomically slippery. They eluded
classification, and in the very perplexity they caused—the sense that they
could not quite be categorized, that they were beyond or behind the
ordinary frames of reference by which the world was to be understood—
they began to be regarded as a threat. Who are they? What do 'they' intend
for us? In the matter of the Jews, race thinking slides into conspiracy
thinking.

Conspiracism

'Anti-Semitic conspiracists' are people who believe in the existence of a conspiracy by Jews to rule the world. These conspiracists are members of a wider circle of 'conspiracy theorists', and tend to be conspirators themselves. The truth is always hidden (and thus appearances are always deceptive); secret societies or 'syndicates'[322] direct history's course; these societies are of venerable age; by chance, their activities have been exposed, and the opportunity has thus arisen to defeat them; they are best combated by similarly clandestine entities. The conspiracists' theory of history is thus characterized by a false concreteness; they personify the historical process.[323] These conspiracists often also adopt broader, populist positions, pitting a financial elite against the generality of good, honest folk. This slides very easily into anti-Semitism, and fulminations against a specifically Jewish 'money-power'.[324] Anti-Semitic conspiracists derive their notions from a misreading of the history of Jewish collective endeavour, which provides evidence only of the lamentable inability of Jews adequately to defend themselves. A people without the enterprise to ensure its own safety cannot be relied upon to complete the immeasurably more ambitious project of world domination.[325] But Jewish history does not faze these anti-Semites. For them, the Jews are everywhere, and everywhere well-organized. They are our masters. And yet, with the appropriate resolve, they can be defeated.

Though anti-Semitic conspiracy theories comprise the great political stupidity of modern times, there have for centuries been allegations against the Jews that they are engaged in clandestine, collective action of a malign, even Satanic, character, all the time ensuring by various sinister means the secrecy of these schemes, and suppressing the truth about them (it is the perennial complaint of anti-Semites, regardless of their access to the public sphere, that they are being silenced).[326] It was central to the Christian indictment of the Jews for their collective act of Deicide. In 1009–10, the Jews of Europe were accused of conspiring with the Caliph of Jerusalem to destroy the Holy Sepulchre (the site of Jesus' crucifixion), and as a result many Jewish communities were forcibly converted, expelled, or slaughtered.[327] Conspiracy was also an aspect of the medieval libels of ritual murder, host desecration and well-poisoning. The alleged conspiracies were both international and local, the Jews acting as a single corporate body worldwide and as a series of national and regional communities. The belief in a Jewish conspiracy was also an aspect of Luther's hostility to the Jews; they perpetrated their perfidies under a mantle of secrecy, he was convinced.[328] It was a feature of certain kinds of emancipationist anti-Semitism too. The Jews, it was said, are incapable of emancipation, because that would mean their incorporation in several states and they will not submit to being split in this way; 'even now', wrote one such opponent of emancipation, 'there is a secret Jewish alliance throughout Europe'.[329] By the mid-nineteenth century, the dimensions of the Jewish conspiracy had expanded. The Jews sought no less than the control of the entire world; they comprised those 'hidden, anonymous, irresponsible dynasties' already controlling the destinies of European nations.[330] And then, conveniently enough, documents proving the existence of just this plot fell into Gentile hands. The 'Jewish peril', as it was beginning to be known, was revealed. This was a great deliverance. The modern world was a puzzling, frightening place. But armed with the *Protocols*, declared the former Member of Parliament and career anti-Semite, Captain A. H. Ramsay, what formerly appeared to be a 'somewhat confused picture' became 'a concerted and connected human drama'.[331] (As noted above, this is a typical move in the anti-Semite's autobiography: 'I once was blind, but now I can see . . .')

There is more than one such 'document', and every one of them is a fabrication. The forgeries known as 'The Rabbi's Speech' and the *Protocols of the Elders of Zion* are the two most important, and the second, by far the more consequential of the two. Conspiracy theorists in general tend to rely on forgeries.[332]

'The Rabbi's Speech' began as a chapter in a novel, *Biarritz* (1868), written by one Herman Goedsche under the pseudonym Sir John Retcliffe. The novel has a chapter entitled 'In the Jewish Cemetery in Prague'. It relates a meeting of Jews to review their progress towards world-domination. They meet thus every hundred years. The Devil addresses them, 'I greet you, heads of the twelve tribes of Israel.' The Jews respond, 'We greet you, son of the accursed.' The Jews boast about how their financial power has given them control of governments; they affirm the critical importance of the press and their intention to capture it; they describe their plans to demoralize the Gentiles by undermining Church and Army. The novel's two heroes spy upon them, and they resolve to defeat the Jewish plotters.[333] The chapter was printed as a pamphlet in St Petersburg four years later. It was acknowledged to be fictitious, but said to be derived from fact. Similar pamphlets later appeared in Moscow, Odessa, and Prague. By the time it arrived in France, in 1881, it was presented as a factual account, and vouched for by an English diplomat, 'Sir John Readclif'.

The speeches by the Prague Cemetery Jews became a single speech, by a Chief Rabbi, and the text was entitled 'The Rabbi's Speech'. It enjoyed an extended life, and was endlessly reprinted; it was distributed in advance of the 1903 Kishinev pogrom;[334] it was read with special appreciation in the Germany of the Weimar Republic and the Third Reich.[335]

The *Protocols* were compiled by the promiscuous plagiarizing of several texts—principally, a political work in defence of liberalism, in which Jews do not figure, *Dialogue aux Enfers entre Montesquieu et Machiavel*, written by Maurice Joly, and published in 1864. The 'Rabbi's Speech' is another text filched by the forgers; it appeared as an appendix to one of the earliest versions of the *Protocols*.[336] The fabrication was perpetrated in France at the instigation of the Russian secret police. There were five versions of the *Protocols* in circulation between 1903 and 1906, and two shortened versions, one of which appeared as a monograph in 1917.[337] It was only when the *Protocols* came into the possession of one Sergey Alexandrovich Nilus that it was really launched on the world. Nilus was a Russian, a former landowner who had lost everything, a theoretical anarchist who became an Orthodox Christian and mystic, and an educated man who (it appears) mostly believed the *Protocols* to be true, notwithstanding the evidence to the contrary with which he was from time to time confronted. He republished the *Protocols* as an item in the second edition of his work, *The Great in the Small: Antichrist considered as an imminent political possibility* (1905). It was then reprinted various times. The 1911 reprint appeared in a German émigré magazine in 1920. It was translated into several languages, and published in London in 1920, in Berlin in 1922, and in Paris in 1927.[338] New forgeries have been added to the *Protocols*, to keep them up to date.[339]

The *Protocols* comprise twenty-four chapters, or 'protocols', which purport to be the minutes of secret meetings of Jewish leaders. They describe how the Jews will gain supremacy, and thereby bring about the messianic age, by the manipulating of national economies, control of the media, and the promoting of intellectual doubt and religious conflict. Their ultimate success will be marked by the establishment of a world-state, despotically ruled by a Jewish sovereign from the House of David. The Freemasons are a (mostly involuntary) part of this conspiracy.[340] Disparaging references are made throughout to 'the *goyim*', 'goy stupidity', and 'these *goy* cattle', who are brutish, gullible, and content with mere 'outside appearances'; self-admiring references are similarly made throughout to 'our special agents', 'our directorate', 'our newspaper militia', 'the aristocracy of our educated class headed by the aristocracy of money', and so on; and contrasts are everywhere pointed between the two classes, as in 'the goyim have lost the habit of thinking unless prompted by the suggestions of our specialists'.[341] The Jews will only come out of the shadows when they have become unbeatable: '[Our power] will remain invisible until the moment when it has gained such strength that no cunning can any longer undermine it.'[342] The tone is one of triumphant, arrogant cynicism. 'Our goal is now only a few steps off... The Press... with a few exceptions that may be disregarded, is already in our hands.'[343] The language of the *Protocols* is, of course, the language of anti-Semitism: 'the *goyim* are a flock of sheep and we are their wolves'.[344]

The exact formulation of the Jewish character of the conspirators has varied. At first, it was a Jewish–Masonic conspiracy; then it was a Judeo–Bolshevik conspiracy; more recently, it has been a Zionist conspiracy—though it has *also* always been a Zionist conspiracy (the English anti-Semitic publicist, H. H. Beamish referred to the 'Zionist Protocols' in his 1920 work, *The Jews' Who's Who*). The *Protocols* were said to be minutes of the first Zionist Conference, convened in Basel, Switzerland, in 1897. Herzl's *Jewish State* (1896) is one of the plagiarized texts; the *Protocols* have been read, indeed, as a parody of this founding text of Zionism. The references to Zionism are followed through in the notes and commentaries incorporated in later editions of the work.[345] As early as the 1920s, they were known in White Russian circles as the *Zionist Protocols*.[346] The Jews' campaign for a state was but one further step (it was said) in their greater project of world domination.

Though Philip Graves, writing in the London *Times*, exposed the fraudulent character of the *Protocols* in August 1921,[347] and returned to the subject two years later, in order to controvert arguments advanced by the forgery's defenders,[348] there have been promoters of the *Protocols* across every decade of the twentieth century and in most nations. Within months of its exposure, English anti-Semites were still insisting, 'it is the handiwork of Jews'.[349] In Germany, the Nazi theorist Alfred Rosenberg published *The Protocols of the Elders of Zion and Jewish World Policy* (1923). The *Protocols* themselves were distributed very widely.[350] In the United States of America, Henry Ford published *The International Jew: The world's foremost problem* (1920), and he promoted the *Protocols* in his newspaper, the 'Dearborn Independent' (1919–27, circulation, c.300,000).[351] In 1918, the Palestinian leader Moussa Kassem al-Husseini questioned Chaim Weitzmann about it; at the Inquiry into the 1929 Arab riots, the Grand Mufti of Jerusalem cited the *Protocols* as an indisputable source for understanding Zionist plans in Palestine; Frances

Newton, the English missionary's daughter and committed campaigner in the Arab cause, would show the *Protocols* to guests who came to her home in Jaffa in the 1920s.[352] In the 1970s and later, Louis Farrakhan's 'Nation of Islam' argued for the fabrication's authenticity,[353] and sold the *Protocols* in the bookshop attached to its Harlem mosque.[354] In Japan, from the mid-1980s, dozens of books based on the *Protocols* were published, and millions of copies were sold. The thrust of these volumes was to the effect that the Jews control the United States government.[355] In addition to the *Protocols*, there are also very many derivative texts, repeating the conspiracy story, but with differing emphases. These derivative texts tend to be hysterically anti-Israel, replacing the mostly latent anti-Zionism of the *Protocols* by an obsession with Zionist plots masterminded by the government of Israel and its puppet, the government of the United States of America. As a Soviet pamphleteer put it, *Beware: Zionism.*[356]

The *Protocols* have been exposed as a fabrication many times (London, 1921; Grahamstown, South Africa, 1934; Berne, 1934–5; Washington, 1964; Moscow, 1993), but the text is resilient, and continues to flourish. Its defenders respond to the fabrication charge by arguing that the truth of the *Protocols'* contents has been confirmed by events. If the contents are true, then the document itself must be genuine, is the reasoning. Or alternatively, if indeed it is a fabrication, then the fabricators themselves were experts on Jewish matters and merely distilled their research in fictional form. It is 'the most sinister compilation that has ever appeared', wrote an enthusiast.[357] Some, including Hitler, insisted that only the Jews, and those in their pay, claimed that the *Protocols* were a fabrication, which itself was proof of their genuineness.[358] For anti-Semites, the *Protocols* were too valuable a resource to be surrendered, regardless of their provenance. Told that the *Protocols* were mere 'vicious nonsense', the German philosopher Martin Heidegger responded, 'But the dangerous international alliance of the Jews still exists.'[359]

Of course, conspiracy talk does not depend upon the *Protocols*. Nor is it always spoken in simple hostility. There is a pseudo-philo-Semitism that praises the Jews for their conspiratorial skills, inviting other minority communities to emulate them. In *Black England* (1977), the Guyanan-born lawyer and political activist, Rudy Narayan (1938–98) reproached his own black community for lacking the political skills, and the ruthless singularity of purpose, of the Jewish community. The Jews, he explained, are planning their own destiny hundreds of years in advance and, in doing so, also determining the lives of millions of other people. This kind of planning is denied to the 'West Indian mind'. Jewish loyalty and closeness is the high-est; the Jewish child is taught from birth that he is different from other peoples; Jews are ready to give their lives when another Jew is threatened; their decisions are the products of their own thinking. Narayan then warms to his theme. The Jews own most of Britain; their control over the media is absolute; they have quietly infiltrated the political parties and the judiciary. They are Jews first and British second. It is likely that they operate inter-nationally according to a Master Plan, the blueprint for a Jewish takeover of the world. All very unlike, Narayan bitterly remarks, the West Indian community.[360]

Anti-Semitism in the twentieth century is a tale of two 'Protocols': the Russian fabrication, and a German document known as the 'Wannsee Protocol' (which set out Nazi plans to exterminate the Jews).[361] The two documents are related: Nazi anti-Semitism has been traced back, only slightly fancifully, to the very moment when Alfred Rosenberg read the *Protocols*.[362] 'We are too strong,' exult the Jews of the *Protocols*, 'there is no evading our power' (V, para. 5). And then, forty or so years later, millions of powerless Jews found themselves unable to evade Nazi power. How could world-dominators be so stupid as to allow themselves to be exterminated in their millions? The Holocaust should have put paid to fantasies of Jewish conspiracy. And certainly, writing in 1967, the author of a study of the *Protocols* noted that 'today, the whole story is already almost forgotten—so much so that it is quite rare, at least in Europe, to meet anyone under the age of forty who has even heard of those strange ideas'.[363] But the *Protocols* have since then enjoyed a resurgence in Europe. *Protocols* 'talk' has now become very common, and 'Jewish conspiracy' talk, commoner still.[364] In the 23 March 2006 issue of the *London Review of Books* a long essay appeared about the 'Israel Lobby', in which the authors made the anxious disclaimer that their thesis—that a malign and powerful entity was directing American foreign policy in the interests of the Jewish State—should not be taken as an endorsement of the *Protocols*.[365] I return to this topic in Chapter 8.

Racism and conspiracism in combination

It is therefore in respect of the Jews—indeed, *only* in respect of the Jews—that the two most debased, and deadliest, ideological fantasies of the nineteenth century, the racist and conspiracist, meet and coalesce. This race-conspiracy anti-Semitism regards the Jews as a malignant single entity, the only thing that stands between our present misery and future happiness and prosperity. They are both an internal, and external, enemy. They are at our door, and on our hearth. The logic of this anti-Semitism goes something like as follows. The imperatives of race cannot be overcome. It follows from this that race determines both the characteristics and the objectives of all the members of the race. So all (for example) are implicated in the pursuit of those objectives. Race is thus the answer to the dissent: surely not *all* Jews? To which the racist anti-Semite responds: yes, this is what all Jews are like, and that is what all Jews want.

In this account, the Jews' defining characteristics are taken to comprise a lack of spirituality, an absence of scruple, a commercial nature, an ability to create financial structures that will cheat the conscientious, hard-working Aryan, physical ugliness, and rootlessness and cultural barrenness (attributable to their origins as a nomadic people of the desert). The Jews' objective is the enslavement of the world. Why? Some racists said: because the Jews themselves do not understand freedom. The ancient Germans and Celts were free men, coerced neither by their own rulers nor foreign powers. The Jews want to rob these peoples of what they themselves never possessed, out of malignity and a kind of self-defining envy. They will enslave Gentiles by promoting 'miscegenation' (which will weaken their race rivals), by communism and by capitalism. The Jews are the eternal enemy in a race war without end. The Aryan race represents the life force itself. Thus did the heterogeneity of political and religious conflicts—interpreted by reference to those vague but incendiary terms, the Aryan and the Semitic, the labels of life and death for millions of men, women, and children—make way for a single, awful confrontation.[366]

For various reasons, race-conspiracy anti-Semitism came relatively late to England. There were intimations of it in the speeches and journalism of some of the domestic opponents of the Boer War in 1899–1902 (taken to be one fought on behalf of Jewish financial interests), and then again in certain Foreign Office officials' assessments of the Young Turk movement in 1908–10 (taken to be a Latin-influenced international Jewish Freemason conspiracy).[367] In each case, immense, and somewhat occult, power was attributed to Jews. But this version of anti-Semitism only really emerged in the years immediately prior to the outbreak of World War I. It fastened onto two financial and political scandals, the Marconi affair and the Indian Silver affair (see Chapter 5), and was thereafter taken up by proto-fascist, fascist, and Nazi-sympathizing groups in the 1920s and 1930s. This version of anti-Semitism

was given succinct expression in 1911 by the right-wing journalist Leo
Maxse, editor of the *National Review*:

> If the hateful truth may be told, there is a large and powerful international
> syndicate, with ramifications in every capital, including London and Paris,
> working chiefly through corrupt or cosmopolitan papers, inspired or con-
> trolled by that hateful figure, the International Jew.[368]

The certainty is adamantine, quite unresponsive to mere truth—save for the
self-betraying equivocation, 'inspired or controlled', so broad as to make
nonsensical the allegation, even in its own terms. In any event, and aided by
other, comparable equivocations—for example, 'backed', 'mainly controlled', etc.),[369] such a message became a rallying call, as in this passage
from a speech given by the Conservative MP Rowland Hunt in 1913:

> We are really in danger of being ruled by alien votes and foreign gold. The
> aliens and foreign plutocrats are driving out British blood.[370]

This fantasy of malevolent power dominated the thinking of the generation
of anti-Semites who came of age during 1914–18. It found literary expression in John Buchan's *The Thirty-Nine Steps* (1915), in which the hero,
Richard Hannay, receives an early lesson from an American stranger concerning the 'subterranean movement going on, engineered by very dangerous people'—that is, 'Jew-anarchists' and 'capitalists who rake in the
shekels'. The anarchists create the chaos, and the financiers 'make fortunes
by buying up the wreckages'. The 'real boss' of this 'conspiracy' is 'a little
white-faced Jew in a bath-chair with an eye like a rattlesnake'. This is 'the
man who is ruling the world just now'. What the American says 'explained
a lot that had puzzled' Hannay. He comes to understand that though 'the
Jew is everywhere', 'you have to go far down the backstairs to find him'.[371]
A similar point is made in T. S. Eliot's poem, 'Burbank with a Baedeker:
Bleistein with a Cigar'.[372]

Nazi anti-Semitism

Among the problems with race-conspiracy anti-Semitism, three stand out.
It is not true; it is confused about whether the Jews constitute a pure race; it
is not a political doctrine. Nazism addressed these problems by glossing over
the first two and presenting itself as the solution to the third.

In Nazism, anti-Semitism completes itself. It represents anti-
Semitism's strongest attempt to realize itself as an independent ideology. If

anti-Semitism is always a contingent quality of an ideology and never the ideology itself—that is to say, always an adjective and never a noun—then Nazism represents the struggle of the adjective to become a noun. While there are both anti-Semitic and non-anti-Semitic versions of (say) Christianity and Liberalism, Nazism is always and essentially anti-Semitic. Anti-Semitism thus reaches a kind of terminus in Nazism. Jew-hatred was not here a version of an ideology; it had itself become the ideology. All roads lead to the Jew;[373] Jew-baiting, which became Jew-murder, was the most perfect expression of the Nazi spirit.[374] This was apparent to both victim and observer. 'What distinguishes National Socialism from other forms of fascism', wrote Victor Klemperer, 'is a concept of race reduced solely to anti-Semitism and also fired exclusively by it.'[375] 'Anti-Semitism was the only clear idea Hitler had when he founded the Party', wrote the political scientist Stephen H. Roberts, whose 1937 book was written 'for the man-in-the-street who wishes to have some idea of the Nazi experiment'. Hitler, he explained, 'capitalised the lowest features of a traditional racial hatred, and thus gave his movement a certain emphasis on destructiveness from the beginning'.[376]

In a speech made in April 1921, Hitler declared, 'solving the Jewish question is the central question of National Socialists'.[377] The Jewish 'problem' was Hitler's obsession. He had convinced himself that the correct understanding of Jews was the key to history.[378] Hitler gathered around him other anti-Semites of a similarly obsessive, murderous disposition. Julius Streicher's loathing for the Jews, for example, absorbed his whole being.[379] Anti-Semitism was everything; and it was always fiendish, implacable. The Nazi war criminal Richard Ley explained:

> We believed that [the Allies] were all only the tools of the Jew...The disastrous end of the last war [i.e., World War I] had already been attributed to the Jew. Then, particularly, the disintegration of Germany after the war, morally and economically, had to be ascribed to the increasing unhealthy influence of, above all, the Eastern Jews. There is a great deal of evidence to support this. During the war itself, we believed that the inhumane bombarding of our cities and even villages was due to Jewish influence on the enemy side.... We ended up seeing everything through anti-Semitic eyes.[380]

While there were thus no internal constraints on the expression of the Jew-hatred, the very absence of constraint meant that Nazism was peculiarly inadequate as an ideology. It was both a total ideology of Jew hatred, and it was just rubbish. The ideology itself was no more than 'homicidal non-sense',[381] the accumulated 'refuse of international political thought'.[382] The commentators closest to the scene saw this clearly enough. In 1935, Leonard Woolf described Hitler as a political quack, with all the catchwords, patter and magic remedies current among the impoverished and resentful Germans of his time.[383] Leon Trotsky, writing at the very end of his life, saw that the 'sole feature of fascism which is not counterfeit is its will to power, subjugation and plunder'.[384] And Louis Bondy, reflecting on Nazism in the year of its defeat, understood that professional mischief-makers, unemployed warmongers, political murderers, desperadoes and evildoers of all kinds formed the spearhead of Hitler's brown army. The Nazis labelled self-admiration, cupidity, envy, and hatred noble sentiments; they sanctioned persecution and even murder in the name of a holy crusade; these failures and outcasts of society found a savage satisfaction in outlawing others.[385] Nazism was no more than Hitlerism, and Hitlerism was no more than Hitler's own egotism, his fantasies and his enmities. It was entirely rooted in Hitler's own sense of himself. What distinguished him from any conceivable predecessor, writes Joachim Fest, was a complete lack of any sense of responsibility beyond the merely personal, of any clear-headed, selfless ethos of service and of any historical morality. It was all egocentricity. He had countless harmless people killed for his own personal gratification.[386] Hitler was a gambler turned politician. 'Nothing', observed his contemporary, Sebastian Haffner, 'is more misleading than to call Hitler a Fascist.'[387] He was uninterested in the state; the state existed for him solely as a war machine at the service of the nation/race.

The Nazis pursued a course that never went beyond killing and looting. They were not ideologues; they were criminals, political gangsters.[388] Unlike any other expansionist, imperialist programme in history, Nazism had absolutely no civilizing ideas. The Nazis came as enemies to the lands that they conquered; they made it plain that they intended to remain there as enemies. Their propaganda was not rooted in any praxis; it was not derived from any political philosophy. Kurt Schumacher correctly understood Nazi propaganda to be nothing other than a 'ceaseless appeal to the filthy beast in man';[389] Thomas Mann correctly understood Nazi anti-Semitism to be nothing other than a 'mania for torture'.[390] Nazism's political ideas are not worthy of any respect, and are only to be taken seriously because they were for a time so commanding in their appeal and so lethal in their execution.[391] Talk of a 'New Order', for example, was never anything more than a pretext, as George Orwell observed in 1942. When they could, 'the Germans [came] forward quite undisguisedly as a nation of slave-masters', with the intention of 'keep[ing] the other European races in subjection and plundering them of their food and other goods'.[392]

Nazism was endlessly resourceful in finding substitutes for *thinking*. In its place it promoted discipline, hatred, loyalty, violence, cruelty, salutes, military music and uniforms, mass rallies, a sentiment of 'belonging', and bogus pieties about the dead. It cultivated a meretricious solemnity among its adherents: 'Fascism is not a doctrine. It is a time-honoured will, obscure and very ancient—and it is written into our soul. If it is different for each nation, that is because each nation possesses its way of saving itself. Such knowledge can be found only at the heart of things . . .' etc.[393] But Nazism was in truth little more than an impure nihilism.[394] An early Nazi fighting song promised to 'Smash everything to pieces'.[395] Hitler himself said early on that his stance amounted to a 'declaration of war . . . against *any* and *all* existing world-views'.[396] Goebbels revealed something of the Nazi regime's true motivation when he remarked with regret of Austria's failure to resist the *Anschluss*, 'We could have smashed everything.'[397] The waging of racist war was the Nazi reason for existence.[398] The Nazis destroyed what they could; they left nothing behind as a memorial, save for concentration camps and death camps.[399] Yet while Nazism was in some sense the final moment in the *development* of anti-Semitism, it was not the final moment in the *history* of anti-Semitism.

The Holocaust should have altogether put paid to anti-Semitism. It should have rebutted once and for all the principal anti-Semitic fantasy of malign Jewish power; it should have satiated the appetite of the most murderous anti-Semites for Jewish death. And yet instead it precipitated new anti-Semitic versions or tropes: (a) Holocaust denial, (b) the characterizing of Zionism as an avatar of Nazism, and (c) the cluster of allegations that the Jews are exploiting the Holocaust in support of false compensation claims, the defence of Israeli policies, the defence of Zionism, etc.[400] Many Arab and Muslim anti-Semites somewhat promiscuously embrace all three tropes—denying the Holocaust, praising Hitler,[401] and representing Israel as the successor to the Nazi state.

Of these three, Holocaust denial has the most intimate relation with the Holocaust itself, and is most directly a continuation of Nazism's own project. Holocaust denial is really no more than a vampire version of Nazism—no more than the sum of its hatreds of the Jews and of Israel, combined with a desire to salvage the fantasy of Jewish power in the face of overwhelming Jewish catastrophe. It too has 'left' and 'right' versions. In the former version, the 'story' of the Holocaust is a bourgeois device to obscure the daily horrors of life under capitalism and to promote the false notion that divisions *within* the capitalist order—i.e., Nazism versus the 'democracies'— comprise the sum of all possible political divisions.[402] The latter version, simply enough, has as its objective the rehabilitation and return of Nazism. There is also an Islamic version,[403] which collides with the wish to characterize Jews/Israelis as comparable to the Nazis or even as 'new' Nazis. Islamist, neo-Nazi, and 'leftist' websites often share the same Holocaust denial material.[404]

The components of the ideological discourse of Holocaust denial are German nationalism, neo-Nazism, anti-communism, anti-Semitism, and anti-Zionism.[405] The Holocaust denier is also of course an anti-Zionist. He does not like Jewish power, and he sees Israel as an expression of that power. Anti-Zionism is an absolute necessity to Holocaust denial.[406] Some Holocaust deniers expressly identify themselves with the Palestinians. Indeed, they style themselves the Palestinians of Europe; their pamphlets, the stones of a new Intifada.[407] Some opportunistically propose that opposition to Zionism and a concern for Palestinian rights motivates their Holocaust denial.[408] 'The big lie' of the Holocaust, wrote David Irving, 'allows Israel to torture Arabs and ignore UN resolutions.'[409] Holocaust denial remains an affair of anti-Semitic coteries, though it surfaces on occasion in mainstream newspapers and journals.

What, then, is 'anti-Semitism'?

By 'anti-Semitism', I understand, first, beliefs about Jews or Jewish projects that are both false and hostile, and secondly, the injurious things said to or about Jews or their projects, or done to them, in consequence of those beliefs. Anti-Semites wrong Jews, and they are wrong *about* Jews. They direct their hatred at Jews in their collective aspect—as a people, as a religious community, as a nation state. Anti-Semites pass judgements on Jews that are unjust; and their posture towards Jews is determined by malice. The distinctions that non-Nazi anti-Semites usually make between classes of Jew—typically of the character, 'most Jews bad, some Jews good'—do not qualify the offence that these anti-Semites give to Jews in general. Many anti-Semites also want to hurt Jews or deny to them freedoms or rights enjoyed by *non*-Jews. Anti-Semitism, which always begins as a discourse, poses many distinct threats to Jews.

It can be *life-threatening*, endangering individual Jews, entire Jewish communities, even the sovereign Jewish State. In August 2006, Jasmine Kranat, a thirteen-year old London Jewish girl was riding home from school on a bus. Fellow students demanded that she tell them whether she was 'English or Jewish'. When she paused, they robbed her and then beat her unconscious, breaking her cheekbone in the process.[410] Many who kill Jews today, or endorse the killing of Jews, act with the energy of innocence; perhaps they experience a moral 'rush' when going about their murderous business; they are certainly protected from doubt and remorse by the attributed character of their 'enemy', the personification of every quality the political morality of the last half-century has taught them to hate: racism, imperialism, the supremacy of money.[411]

Anti-Semitism can also be *security-threatening*, impairing the quality of Jewish life, inducing apprehension among Jews and promoting feelings of insecurity. Chants at demonstrations, threats of violence, abusive behaviour, damage to communal property, desecration of Jewish graves, graffiti sprayed on synagogue walls ('Nuke the Jews, You're next', 'Free Palestein [*sic*], fuck Israel'),[412] deny Jews peace of mind. Jewish schoolchildren, university students, and academics; synagogue congregants and employees; Jewish politicians, business-people, and communal representatives have all been targets. There are anti-Semites whose wish it is that no Jew should feel at ease either in his home, or in any public spaces. Radical threats made against Israel fall into this category.

It can be *equality-threatening*, discriminating against Jews and thereby disadvantaging them in relation to their non-Jewish fellow citizens. Certain anti-Semites will, when they can, legislate against Jews, denying them rights that non-Jews enjoy. It can have the effect of driving Jews out of representative bodies, thereby limiting their opportunities to participate in political processes. For example, in April 2005 a Jewish member of the executive of the National Union of Students resigned, citing the complicity of some if its members with the anti-Semitic activities of pro-Palestine activists.[413] Fear of anti-Semitism can drive Jews out of public schools and off the streets, or encourage them to conceal outward signs of their Jewish identity—*kippah*, *tzitzit*, the *Magen David* (Star of David). A sense of insecurity thus fostered will limit Jews' participation in the public life of the nation, encouraging them to retreat towards private, more secure spaces.

It can be *morale-threatening*, making Jews anxious about the manner in which they are regarded in the world at large, or dividing them among themselves (setting one class of Jews against another, the one treated as acceptable, the other objectionable). Defamations of Jews, or the Jewish community, are *both* security-threatening *and* morale-threatening. Holocaust-denial material, for example, characterizes Jews as self-interested liars and thus exposes them to unwarranted censure and attack. Anti-Semites put into general circulation 'canards' against the Jews—sensational reports, misrepresentations, or fabrications, all intended to deceive the public.[414] Anti-Semitism can make Jews think the poorer of themselves. In extreme cases—say, atrocity stories, or libels on Judaism's foundational texts—it can foster feelings of worthlessness or turn Jews into that self-destructive thing, the Jewish anti-Semite. The force of common prejudice, the persuasive wisdom of what 'everyone knows', can even lead Jews themselves into believing that what is said about them is true, or at least not altogether false. Contempt *for* Jews, when sufficiently widespread, can foster self-contempt *among* Jews. Anti-Semitism is a form of evil, and like all evils, being exposed to it can shatter one's trust in the world.[415] Even when it poses no greater threat, it remains an immense distraction to Jews. It pollutes their lives with its nonsense. It can overwhelm them with its insults.[416]

What of anti-Semitism's threats to, and injuries of, non-Jews? By denying Jews the opportunity of making contributions of benefit to society as a whole, anti-Semitism injures all society's members. It also encourages misconceptions about the real causes of suffering, deprivation, and injustice, and thereby prolongs their existence. It stupefies; it makes people stupid. It corrupts political discourse by its appeal to our capacity for hatred. It impedes the settling of conflicts between Jewish and non-Jewish parties by misleading the latter about the character and objectives of the former.[417] The intolerance of Jews that anti-Semitism promotes is often allied with (and in any event itself promotes) intolerance of other groups, thereby making an open, pluralist society less possible. And while in this respect anti-Semitism thus specifically hurts non-Jewish minorities, it also hurts everyone else—though not in the same degree. It even injures anti-Semites. They become self-deceiving, if only in consequence of their need to justify to themselves and others their participation in acts of persecution. It degrades them, and the worst among them lose their humanity. 'Much casual death', writes the poet Anthony Hecht of the Nazis, 'had drained away their souls.'[418] At times, the threat posed by anti-Semitism has been so great as to convince some among its adversaries that it places civilization itself in jeopardy.[419] The Jews' evil is also the world's evil.[420]

Anti-Semitism is an affair of ignorance, stupidity, and baleful prejudice.[421] The typical anti-Semite is like no one so much as an imbecile with a gun—an angry, malicious imbecile. We take him seriously only because of the harm that he can do to us. Were it not for his destructive tendencies, he would not merit our attention. Indeed, anti-Semitism is his way—perhaps his only way—of *getting* our attention. He has not arrived at his beliefs by any accredited process of reasoning. He has no good grounds for supposing—as opposed merely to desiring or hoping—his beliefs about Jews to be true. He is indifferent to consistency, and is therefore untroubled by inconsistencies in his beliefs. He does not hold these beliefs critically, and he has no interest in justifying them. They do not meet minimal criteria of rationality.[422] Whenever an anti-Semite speaks, it is as a propagandist for a lie. While anti-Semitism refutes itself, in its incoherence and folly, anti-Semites themselves are rarely amenable to reason, evidence, or moral persuasion.

2

Defamations

All versions of anti-Semitism libel Jews. These libels may be grouped under three headings: the blood libel, the conspiracy libel, and the economic libel. The *blood libel* holds that Jews entertain homicidal intentions towards non-Jews, and that Jewish law underwrites these intentions; the *conspiracy libel* supposes that Jews act as one, in pursuit of goals inimical to the interests of non-Jews; the *economic libel* supposes that Jews, who are self-interested, acquisitive, and unproductive by nature, financially exploit non-Jews. The libels share the premise that Jews hate or despise non-Jews. Of the three libels, the blood libel is the master one.[1] The enmity towards non-Jews it supposes is of the deadliest kind; it is an aggravated version of the conspiracy libel; it is a routinely deployed metaphor of the economic libel.[2] It nests inside most versions of anti-Semitism. Needless to say, the blood libel has also played a major part, complex and contradictory (invented, adapted, repudiated, redeployed), in the history of English anti-Semitism. An account of the blood libel therefore comprises the second of my introductory chapters. I address its specifically English features in Chapters 3 and 4.

The charge

The blood libel is the generic term for a number of related charges against Jews. These charges are all false—fantastical, pernicious nonsense. They are known collectively as the *blood* libel partly because they suppose that Jews wish to kill non-Jews (at first, Christians, now more usually Muslims), partly because some of them involve the claim that Jews require non-Jewish blood for ritual purposes, and partly because so much Jewish blood has been shed in consequence of them. They are *libellous* because they are damaging to the good name of the Jewish people.

Jewish enmity

In the narrative of these libels, Jews are both fantasy perpetrators and real victims; the only 'ritual murders' that take place are the judicial executions of falsely accused Jews. To those who believe the blood libel to be true, it is a matter of indifference that Jews are enjoined by their religion not to commit murder, not to consume blood (Leviticus 3:17, 7:26, 17:10–14; Deuteronomy 12:15–16, 20–4), and to regard child sacrifice with horror (Leviticus 20:2–5; Kings 21:6; Jeremiah 7:31). Blood is not sacred to Jews. The prohibition in Jewish law against consuming blood is *not* an affirmation of its magical properties. Blood sustains life, of course. But the shedding of blood brings no benefit to the slaughterer; it does not give him access to the divine. The Jews were prohibited from consuming blood precisely to teach them these truths. This prohibition amounts not to a sacralization, but a *de*sacralization, of blood. It is a repudiation of the pagan illusion that power is to be secured in the violation of living energy. The sacrificial rituals prescribed by Jewish law are extreme only in the chastity of their symbolism, thereby reducing the frisson of violation to a minimum, taking it out of private hands, limiting its venue and occasions, and thus weaning Israel away from the notion of propitiation.[3] More broadly, Jewish law puts many obstacles in the way of Jews who might otherwise be inclined to adopt superstitions regarding the efficacy of blood—superstitions that were widespread in ancient and medieval times (blood was thought to cure leprosy and inflammations of the throat, menstrual blood was thought to alleviate gout, etc.).[4] Indeed, the prohibition against consuming blood was regarded by Maimonides as an application of the most fundamental of all probations in Jewish law—that is, the prohibition against idolatry.[5] The blood libel is thus not just an attack on Jews; it is an attack on Judaism. It does not just assert, 'This is what Jews do.' It asserts, 'This is what Judaism *demands*.' It proposes that Jews secretly embrace what they insist that their religion rejects. It thus makes of Jews liars as well as murderers. It turns Jewish self-understanding on its head. It makes the killing of children Judaism's object, rather than the object of its most defining repudiation. The blood libel is anti-Semitism's most radical break with reality.

The principal charge is that Jews kidnap and then kill non-Jewish children; the murder is usually preceded by abuse and torture. The motives attributed to Jews are diverse. The Jews murder to repeat the Crucifixion; they murder because they cannot bear the victim's innocence and purity;

they murder because they are offended by his (or much less frequently, her) joyous, laudatory singing in celebration of the Christian faith; they murder, because they erroneously believe that the blood of a Christian will redeem them, rather than Christ's own blood;[6] the Jews will never obtain their freedom or return to the land of their fathers without the shedding of blood;[7] they are obliged, by an ancient and secret ordinance, daily to shed Christian blood in honour of God;[8] they offer up the child as a sacrifice in conformity with a practice initiated by God's command to Abraham to sacrifice his son Isaac; they seek to avenge their condition of subordination by acts of violence on Christians.[9] Blood sacrifices constitute the essence of Judaism; notwithstanding the destruction of the Jewish Temple, the rites of sacrifice continue.[10] The child's blood has medicinal[11] or aphrodisiac properties; the blood is used to make unleavened bread for Passover, or in the preparation of a surrogate Eucharist,[12] or to sprinkle in a synagogue,[13] or to celebrate the Red Sea turning into blood and destroying the Egyptian army;[14] the Jews need blood transfusions to fortify themselves following the experience of the Nazi death camps (a version of the libel that circulated in post-War Poland);[15] blood guilt for Jesus' death afflicts the Jews with a disease that can only be palliated by the use of Christian blood;[16] the coming of the Messiah will be hastened by the blood of sacrificed Gentile virgins.[17] According to the Catholic theologian, Johannes Eck (1486–1543), blood was indispensable to Jewish ritual. In addition, he claimed, blood was used to anoint rabbis, to cure eye ailments, to remove body odours, to mix with the ashes made to commemorate the destruction of the Temple,[18] and to remove from Jewish babies the two tiny fingers stuck to their foreheads at birth.[19] The Jews are held to be masters of blood.[20] They are bloodthirsty; they are 'blood-eaters'.[21] 'The Jews slaughtered a Christian', went an old German song, 'for them it was a blameless deed'.[22] Jewish law is said to enjoin ritual murder or ritual cannibalism (the principal versions of the blood libel); the Jews are thus most law-fearing when they are most criminal—they 'unscrupulously combine holiness with ungodliness'.[23]

The blood libel meant that local Jews would be blamed if a corpse was found washed up on a riverbank, abandoned in a wood, hidden by the murderer on a Jew's property, or even if a child had merely disappeared and was reported missing. This defamatory assumption assisted the authorities by indicating to them the most likely class of suspects. There rarely were witnesses. No one would report actually having *seen* a murder being committed, though it is a feature of the blood libel that humble Christians in Jewish service sometimes report strange or sinister happenings.[24] The Jewish suspects arbitrarily chosen were often tortured; confessions were extracted (any failure to confess could be attributed to Satan's intervention);[25] 'experts' would confirm the truth of the slanders. Occasionally, elements among the local populace would find themselves in conflict with sceptical representatives of the authorities. Many Jews died in consequence of these blood libels, some by judicial means, others at the hands of local mobs. In several instances, whole communities were expelled. In two cases, the Church honoured the deceased child: Blessed Andreas of Rinn, St Simon of Trent. Sometimes the Jews were able to avert disaster—as in Moravia in about 1343, when a woman offered her child to some Jews for a price. She was asked to return the following morning, whereupon the authorities, notified by the Jews, were waiting to arrest her.[26]

Jews are supposed to be most active at Eastertime, while being opportunistically ready to kill throughout the rest of the year. Eastertime is chosen both because it commemorates the Passion and because it coincides with the Jewish festival of Passover. Blood binds the plagues—the first was the plague of blood, the tenth, the death of the firstborn males of Egypt. It was in the execution of this tenth plague that the Angel of Death passed over ('Passover') the Jewish firstborn children, killing only the Egyptian children. The Jews were ordered to slaughter lambs, and to make red signs on their doorposts with the lamb's blood. The Jews thus celebrate their survival by the sacrifice of lambs, or the symbolic lamb's bone on the Seder plate. Christians identified the Passover lamb with Christ. The blood libel supposes this sequence: The Jews consume the Passover lamb each year; the Jews killed Jesus, the Lamb of God; the Jews kill a Gentile child each year. Passover thus acquires the character of a national religious crime.[27]

Jews are also thought to be active during *Purim*, taken to be another favoured killing time. *Purim* is the festival that commemorates the events related in Esther; some of the early stories of Jewish murders of Christians relate them to ritual re-enactments of Haman's execution. Esther was not much admired in the Christian tradition, and the commemorative Jewish festival of *Purim*, even less so. Luther commented that the Jews 'love the book of Esther, which so well fits their bloodthirsty, vengeful, murderous greed and hope'.[28] Jewish high-spirits were always to be deprecated, while the hanging of effigies of Haman was frequently misunderstood[29] as a blasphemous parody of the Passion. The fifth-century historian, Scholasticus Socrates relates an incident concerning some drunken Syrian Jews at

Purim time. They put a Christian boy on a cross, he says, and then abused and killed him.[30]

Ritual murder was taken to be indicative of the depth of Jewish enmity towards Christians. 'Throughout the centuries the Jews' hatred of Christ and Christians was enormous', wrote the seventeenth-century Bollandists. 'They cursed Christians daily and atrociously persecuted them, stealing Christian children in secret and cruelly killing them.'[31] Their fabled cruelty was held to be both innate and general in application; indeed, Jews were said on occasion to have killed even their own children. The narratives of Masada, of the First Crusade,[32] and of the York massacre, were all taken to confirm their readiness to make this intolerable sacrifice. During the violence of the Crusades, chroniclers were appalled to find that many Jewish mothers, in particular, would rather kill their children than have them (as the Jews saw it) scalded in the 'seething waters' of baptism[33] or (as the Christians saw it) nourished by the Eucharist.[34] The killing of Jewish children by their fathers, upon discovery that the child has converted, or wishes to convert, was likewise an established story in sermon literature. The miraculous rescue of one such child is depicted in the Lady Chapel in Winchester.[35] (I return to this theme in Chapter 4; it is part of the cultural context of *The Merchant of Venice*.) In any event, why, so the reasoning went, would Jews ready to kill their own children be troubled by any call on them to kill the children of Gentiles?[36]

Christian derivations

The blood libel is substantially derived from three distinct aspects of Christian thinking and practice.

First, in accordance with typological principles, Christians interpreted various events and practices in the *Tanach* as prefigurations or anticipations of the Passion. The meaning of the binding of Isaac, for example, or the ritual sacrifice of animals, was made manifest by the Passion; Jesus was to them as the reality is to the shadow. The Passion completed them, or made them perfect. To Christian anti-Semites, however, these prefigurations were also taken to demonstrate a specifically Jewish culpability for Jesus' sacrifice and death. Indeed, they enlisted other stories in the *Tanach* in support of their charge against the Jews. The story of Cain and Abel loomed especially large. Cain is the Jew; Abel is Jesus and the Church. Cain is the rejected one, the killer of his brother, the man condemned to wander. Abel is the one embraced by God, Cain's victim. 'You reject the Jews like the hateful Cain,' wrote the cleric Peter the Venerable (*c.*1092–1156), 'and you do not light a fire on their offerings. But you do desire the hosts of the Christian people, just like the offerings of Abel.'[37] The Cain and Abel story was a favourite of the blood libellers.[38]

Secondly, the blood libel is Christianity's deicide libel against the Jews, but subject to an endless repetition. It converts the singular event of the Passion into an open series of murders. Just as Jesus' death is projected back into the *Tanach*, so it is projected forward into secular history. Just as Abel is Jesus, so too is every Christian child slaughtered by the Jews. The Jews renew in their victims the death of Christ.[39] The blood libel supposes a singular, lethal confrontation between Jew and Gentile. In the extreme poverty of its understanding, the whole of human history, both sacred and secular, is reduced to a set of variations upon one scene—the murderous Jew, knife in hand, facing the passive Gentile, blessed by God and pure in spirit. The Christian dies, while the Jew survives, to kill again—endlessly repeating his crime. In this sense, modern Jewry is a composite *anti*-Simeon. Simeon is a devout Jew who appears briefly in Luke's Gospel. He witnesses the Christ child and then dies, content. 'It was revealed unto him by the Holy Ghost that he should not see death, before he had seen the Lord's Christ' (2:25).[40] Instead of witnessing the Christ child and then dying, the infant-killing Jews insist on living, putting to death instead Christ's proxy, the innocent Christian child.

Thirdly, Jesus' blood—what John Donne refers to as 'the bottomless sea of the blood of Christ Jesus'[41]—has renewed humankind. We are now 'justified by [Christ's] blood', and so 'we shall be saved from wrath through him' (Romans 5:9). 'We have redemption through his blood' (Ephesians 1:7; Colossians 1:14). 'The blood of Christ, who through the eternal Spirit offered himself without spot to God, [shall] purge your conscience from dead works to serve the living God' (Hebrews 9:14). '[You will be redeemed] with the precious blood of Christ, as of a lamb without blemish and without spot' (1 Peter 2:19). Jesus is both High Priest and sacrificial offering, atoning for the whole world by the shedding of his own blood.[42] He addressed the Jews, saying:

> Except ye eat the flesh of the Son of man, and drink his blood, ye have no life in you. Whoso eateth my flesh, and drinketh my blood, hath eternal life; and I will raise him up at the last day. For my flesh is meat indeed, and my blood is drink indeed. He that eateth my flesh, and drinketh my blood, dwelleth in me, and I in *him*. (John 6:53–6)

Christians, according to Paul's letter to the Hebrews, are both washed in the blood of the lamb and drink it.[43] This blood language, the 'adoration of the flesh of Christ in the mysteries' (Ambrose),[44] tended at first to be interpreted somewhat allegorically; the belief in the conversion in the Eucharist of the whole substance of the bread into the body and of the wine into the blood of Christ, leaving only the appearances of bread and wine,[45] took a thousand years to establish itself.[46] It was at the Fourth Lateran Council of 1215 that this doctrine of transubstantiation (or 'Real Presence') was proclaimed as dogma. In the Middle Ages, the Eucharist, the sacrament of the Lord's Supper, was at the centre of Christian faith. It was indeed the central symbol of an entire culture,[47] the incarnation of the Incarnation.[48] Celebrants were commanded: 'Behold and believe!'[49] The Eucharist was the foremost sacrament, the holy mystery of the Lord's body. The entire salvation of the world was said to lie in this mystery.[50] Christ is immolated every time the sacrament is performed. It is thus not just a sacrament; it is also a sacrifice. The doctrine was celebrated in Christian devotional poetry. George Herbert's poem 'Conscience' (1633), for example, frankly embraces the implications of Jesus' sacrifice: 'My saviour's blood: whenever at his board / I do but taste it, straight it cleanseth me, / . . . / The bloody cross of my dear Lord / Is both my physic and my sword.'[51] And John Donne declared in a sermon, 'The blood of Christ Jesus only is my cordial.'[52] The Eucharist represented the Church as a community of believers sharing Christ's Eucharistic body; the medieval historian Jacques Le Goff has written of the 'great medieval project to form one body'.[53] It was a body, of course, from which Jews were expressly excluded.[54]

It was a common medieval miracle for the bread of the Eucharist to be transformed in the priest's hands into a small, living child, then slain and dismembered in front of the congregation.[55] Such miracles persuaded doubters,[56] rebuked heretics,[57] rewarded the faithful, raised the dead, and caused Jews to convert. They offered 'proofs by blood'[58] and were a vindication of church doctrine.[59] The truth, however, is that the Eucharist was deeply shocking to Jews,[60] and in due course, Protestants appropriated that shock to advance their own objections to the Catholic Mass. The theologian and Church of England clergyman, Thomas Becon (1512(?)–67), related the story of an 'honest, civil' Jew invited to attend a church service. 'But when he saw the people fall down and worship the bread and cup, he marvelled greatly at their madness.' And so, Becon concludes, the Jew refused to be made a Christian.[61]

The blood libel supposes two practices, then—the ritual consumption of Jesus and the ritual murder of Christian children. The one is fundamental to Christian worship, the other fundamental to Jewish criminality. This is the Jews' historic, inherited guilt. What they did openly then, they do covertly now. If they were able to, they would crucify Jesus anew every day.[62] All Jews are implicated in these crimes. They plan them collectively; their crimes are committed in the name of Judaism. The Jews may indeed be taken to declare in respect of their victims, 'may their blood be upon our heads'.

Related libels

Related libels that emerged in the thirteenth and fourteenth centuries, host-desecration and well-poisoning, were taken up with what a nineteenth-century English author termed 'an eager credulity'.[63]

It was rumoured that Jews were in the habit of stealing communion wafers, torturing them in symbolic torture of Jesus himself. The wafer would take on the appearance of a child, identifiable as Jesus. It would bleed, just as the ritually murdered child bleeds. But while the child is merely a metaphor of Christ, the wafer *is* Christ—by the miracle of transubstantiation. By libelling the Jews thus, Church dogma was affirmed (though there were some contemporaries who saw through this 'pious fraud').[64] Anti-Semitism was given a role in the teaching of Christian doctrine.[65] The tortured child and the tortured wafer are Christ's proxies. Through their suffering, Jesus suffers. This vicarious suffering, a re-cruci-fixion, re-enacts the Passion. The murdered are martyrs; they are witnesses to Christianity's truth. Christ is thus the ultimate object of this imagined Jewish violence. The Jews are 'blasphemers and desecrators of the Passion'[66] and are ever ready to crucify or otherwise profane images of the crucified Christ.[67] Bleeding host shrines were built on sites where the Jews had allegedly desecrated the Eucharist.[68] Somewhat later, in the mid-fourteenth century, and in explanation for the ravages of the Black Death, Jews were said to be poisoners of wells, mass murderers of Christians. There was no special symbolism in the method of the killing; it was a genocidal malignity. It appeared that one Christian every year no longer satisfied them; they were ready to discard ritual in the realizing of their greater plan—to destroy Christendom and rule the world.[69] In Strasbourg alone, on 14 February 1349, 900 Jews were burned at the stake because of this defamation.[70] Many hundreds more Jews died elsewhere that year.

Host-desecration libels, utterly dependent for their credibility on Catholic dogma, did not survive the decline of the Middle Ages.[71] The allegations dwindled, as did sermonizing on the topic, and by the end of the fifteenth century host-desecration ceased to serve as a theme for plays. The poisoning libel, by contrast, when interpreted as indicative of Jewish misanthropy, was much more robust. Drumont alleged that the Jews poison Christian minds with false doctrines, replacing violence with ruse;[72] during the pogrom of 1892 in the Russian mining town of Iuzovka, the mob shouted that Jewish doctors had 'poisoned our brothers';[73] at the height of the Soviet propaganda campaign against Trotsky—a campaign steeped in anti-Semitic invective—his son was indicted by the Soviet authorities for plotting a mass poisoning of workers;[74] in his final 'political testament', Hitler described 'International Jewry' as 'the universal poisoner of all peoples'.[75] In the *Protocols*, the Jews declare their aim to be 'utterly [to] exhaust humanity' by, among other devices, 'the inoculation of diseases'.[76] The libel continued to circulate in the twentieth century, and into the twenty-first. In May 1988, for example, an African-American activist alleged that Jewish doctors had been injecting black babies with AIDS as part of a plot to take over the world.[77] There is, or was at one time, a widespread belief among Palestinians that Yasir Arafat was killed, poisoned by the Israelis.[78] The poisoning libel is thus exemplary of every conspiracist fantasy about the Jews—they plot together, they are tireless in advancing their own interests, and *they wish us harm*.

In the late nineteenth and early twentieth centuries, a further, related libel emerged. It was alleged by anti-Semites that Jews played a leading, and not just a conspicuous, part in the prostitution rackets—trafficking in young women, operating brothels, and other kinds of commercial sexual vice. 'No Jew', claimed the English anti-Semite Joseph Banister (1862–1953), 'is more of a hero among his fellow tribesmen than the one who can boast of having accomplished the ruin of some friendless, unprotected Christian girl.'[79] This sexualization of the ritual murder charge imagined Gentile females, rather than Gentile males, as victims, and supposed their social death (sexual abuse, exclusion, ignominy) rather than their physical death (torture, murder, unconsecrated burial). This 'white slavery' libel was frequently paired with the blood libel, to the acute distress of Jewish communal advocates, who feared that the element of truth in the former libel would make more plausible the utterly fantastic latter libel.[80]

By these and similar means, and for more than 850 years, Jews have been 'incontinently indicted'.[81] It is a simple misconception to hold that these indictments were confined to the Middle Ages; it is a more sophisticated misconception to hold them to be medieval in character. What was regarded in the Middle Ages as a religious obligation, in more modern times has come to be regarded as a racial or national imperative. Either way, the Jews are *driven* to act criminally. The blood libel is immensely versatile, immensely fecund—and immensely resilient. It has survived all its refutations and the acquittal of every single unjustly accused Jew. It has been a millennial disaster for Jews; it was responsible—together with its derivatives, the host-desecration libel and the poisoning libel—for the deaths of thousands of Jews in the Middle Ages; it continues to overshadow many Jews' lives today. It affects the honour of all Jews.[82]

The instances

The incidence of blood-libel allegations, and the development of the blood libel as a discourse, can be divided into six periods.[83]

The first period

A proto-version of the blood libel, a rumour of Jewish cannibalism, circulated in pre-Christian times. The rumour was sustained by perplexity and by malice. Their monotheism made the Jews a puzzling phenomenon in the pagan world. Their disavowal of human sacrifice was an even greater puzzle. Perhaps the disavowal was a lie, perhaps it concealed an especially horrible ritual, one conceived in enmity toward non-Jews, murderous and secret? Or so the pagan world seems to have reasoned. Speculation of this sort attached itself to the early Christians, and they retaliated in kind against their pagan enemies. They accused the Carthaginians and Phoenicians of child sacrifice in efforts to refute pagan charges that Christians themselves killed and even ate adults or children.[84] But these fantastic rumours, derived from nothing more than an inventive ill-will and only ever half-believed, should not be confused with the blood libel, a Christian invention of several centuries later.

The first period, then, begins in the mid-twelfth century and lasts until the mid-sixteenth century. By the fifteenth century, it was already standardized, commercialized and widely disseminated.[85] The incidence of the blood libel—that is, specific deaths or disappearances of children attributed to local Jews—is confined in this period largely to Western and Central Europe. The Norwich libel is the first recorded instance; of the sources for the affair, the most detailed by far is Thomas of Monmouth's *The Life and Miracles of St William of Norwich*. According to Thomas, the child was crucified, but not bled. It was not until 1235, in the German town of Fulda, that it was alleged against Jews that their primary object was to obtain blood.[86] The blood libels of this period all had a strong theological complexion, which contributed to the emergence of the host desecration libel. Versions of the blood libel thereafter proliferated. In Blois in 1171, more than thirty Jews were executed for the ritual murder of a Christian, even though no victim was ever discovered or even reported.[87] The archbishop of Mainz demanded in 1187 of the Jews of his town that they take an oath not to kill Christians on the eve of Passover.[88] There were also related, lesser charges—in 1220, for example, it was alleged that Jews in the English town of Stamford had played a game that mocked Christianity.[89] Jews were tortured, convicted, and executed (hundreds were killed, often by burning), and there was much regulated and unregulated collective punishment—pogroms, massacres, burnings, and expulsions. Rulers exploited the libels for purposes of extortion; some used it to justify harshly anti-Semitic measures. It was deployed, for example, in the mid- to late-fifteenth century by senior clerics of the Spanish Inquisition to justify the expulsion of the Jews.[90] On occasion, however, high authorities intervened to suppress prosecutions or reverse verdicts; others legislated against it;[91] several popes[92] and an Emperor, issued powerful condemnations of it.

Events unrelated to the blood libel came to be interpreted by reference to it; it was the lens through which a wide range of Jewish activities was viewed. In the Bray incident of 1192, for example, the Christian murderer of a Jew was handed over by their overlord (Countess Mary of Champagne) to the Jewish community for execution. On the Jewish account of the affair, written by Ephraim of Bonn, the murderer was hanged on *Purim*; but on the Christian account, by the monk Rigord, the execution took place during Easter. The former interprets the affair as a version of the danger-and-salvation Esther narrative; the latter interprets the affair as a version of the blood-libel narrative, the repetition by the Jews of the great sin of their corporate existence, the crucifixion of Jesus. They bribed Countess Mary to surrender the Christian to them, and then 'inspired by ancient hatred, led

[him], with hands bound behind his back, crowned with thorns, beating him, throughout the entire town, and later hung him on a cross'. The king of France then intervened to punish the Jewish community for executing the Christian murderer. Large numbers of Jews were killed.[93]

At the end of this period, the blood libel emerged as an aspect of intra-Christian polemic. Johann Eck, for example, characterized the Reformers as defenders of Jewish criminality: 'It is the devil who speaks through you Lutherans; he would like nothing better than to acquit the Jews of their murders.'[94] (This was somewhat unfair, given Martin Luther's own commitment to the blood libel.)[95] There were no blood libels in England after 1290—but only because there were no longer any Jews. Following the mid-sixteenth century, there were very few cases reported anywhere else in Europe until the mid-nineteenth century, save for Poland-Lithuania.

The second period

In this second period, which stretched from the sixteenth to seventeenth century, the blood libel developed in two distinct directions. In very summary terms, while the blood libel as an accusation against European Jewish communities moved eastwards, it flourished as a topic for literature in the West.[96] This latter shift from the forensic to the aesthetic was of greatest consequence in England, where a highly developed literary discourse of the blood libel had already emerged by the late sixteenth century. This discourse is of sufficient importance, indeed, to merit analysis as a distinct form of English anti-Semitism. I address it in Chapter 4.

El Niño Inocente de La Guardia, by the Spanish playwright, Lope de Vega (1562–1635), is exemplary of this 'aestheticizing' of the blood libel. It was written in or about 1603, first performed in 1640, and was still being staged in 1997.[97] It gives the blood libel a material, visible reality. The play claims the sanctity of scripture, the truth of history, *and* the licence of drama. It was entirely, or almost entirely, in consequence of this work that the La Guardia blood libel achieved very wide currency in the Spanish-speaking world.[98] It draws on non-literary accounts of the blood libel of Toledo (*c.*1490), which concerned one Christopher of Toledo, also known as Christopher of La Guardia, supposedly a pious young boy said to have been murdered by Jews and Jewish *conversos*. The story was in fact concocted by the Inquisition, for the purpose of justifying the Jews' expulsion. The Inquisition 'discovered', in consequence of sixteen months' 'investigation' by many agents, two tribunals, and the Inquisitor-General himself, a Jewish plot to paralyse its operations and kill all Christians by a magic spell. Eleven men were sentenced to death and burnt in Ávila at an *auto de fé* on 16 November 1491.[99] It was Spain's only ritual murder trial.[100] One of the hapless victims described the charge as 'the greatest lie in the world'.[101] His torturers invented the tale, and then tortured him into confirming its truth.[102] 'Christopher' was never found, no one had even reported a child missing, yet a cult without relics, a 'virtual' cult, quickly developed. The case was first written up in 1544,[103] and a book followed in 1583.[104] A further book about the 'martyr' appeared in 1786, written by the then parish priest of La Guardia. The almost certainly non-existent child was canonized by Pope Pius VII in 1805. In 1955, a pocketbook devoted to the cult of the 'santo niño' was published.[105]

One should not be too categoric about the migration from West to East of blood-libel cases. In 1670, for example, Raphael Lévy was condemned to death and burned alive in the French city of Metz for stealing and murdering a Christian child. And in the early 1760s, two Jews were condemned to death in Nancy for host desecration.[106] But in the main, the blood libel was restricted to Poland-Lithuania, the main centre and reserve of world Jewry during this period,[107] where there was a continuous series of separate allegations against Jews, in many instances leading to prosecutions. Several of these trials dragged on for a number of years. According to one assessment, between 1547 and 1787, there were no less than eighty-one cases of ritual murder accusations;[108] in the mid-eighteenth century, they became practically annual events.[109] Additionally, earlier host-desecration accusations continued to resonate during this period.[110] A class of so-called 'experts' emerged, posing as 'specialists on the Jewish question',[111] ready to propagandize against Jews in general, and to testify against Jewish defendants at trials. Towards the end of this period, and in response to the frequency of the blood libel, it appears that Jews abandoned the practice of using red wine during the Passover Seder meals, for fear that it would be taken for blood.[112]

The Sandomierz blood libel of 1710–13 is a representative incident. A prostitute threw the body of her dead illegitimate son into the yard of the rabbi of the local Jewish community. On advice from senior members of the community, he fled the town. Several other Jews were then arrested, among them the rabbi's son, Abraham. He confessed under protracted torture and was baptized. At trial, he gave evidence, along with another new convert, that the Jews of his community had received orders from the

Jewish elders of Raków to deliver Christian blood. After deferrals and a transfer of the proceedings, the Jewish defendants were convicted and executed.[113] Throughout the affair, a local priest actively propagandized against the Jews, intervening in the trial, publishing his own work on ritual murder and arranging for a Jewish convert to publish a second version of the trial, which was republished several times and as late as 1934 'continued to enjoy a certain vogue'.[114] By the end of the eighteenth century, ritual murder trials disappeared in Poland, in part because of the stance taken by the Apostolic See, and in part because of the abolition of torture in court proceedings by the Sejm (the Polish parliament) in 1776.[115]

The blood libels that followed, in the mid- to late-nineteenth century, were part of a broader Eastern Europe phenomenon.[116]

The first and second period in blood libel discourse

During the first and second periods, most of the themes in the blood-libel discourse were established. While the series of blood libels was coming to an end in Poland, in Western Europe—and specifically in France—the blood-libel discourse was enlarged to take in post-Christian aspects.

Until the eighteenth century at least, the blood libel was always to be found inside a broader Christian discourse. It was affirmed, and disseminated, in poems and hagiographies; woodcuts, engravings, and paintings;[117] and in festivals, commemorative rites, and pilgrimages.[118] It became an aspect of folk belief; it was something taken for granted, circulating in the culture. It was fortified by images: monasteries acquired paintings of martyred children, represented at the moment of death, Jews at work on their helpless bodies. The paintings themselves became objects of devotion, attracting thousands of pilgrims, often centuries after the alleged events portrayed by them. The façade of the Posen church—which displayed the image of a rabbi cutting the throat of a child, assisted by other Jews, holding bowls to collect the blood—reminded worshippers that hatred of Jewish perfidy was an aspect of Christian devotion. The mural of St Simon of Trent in Frankfurt daily reminded the city's citizens that Jewish wickedness was an aspect of European history.[119] The blood libel was what everyone knew about the Jews. That the Jews were guilty was taken for granted, both because of their character as enemies of humanity and as God's persecutors.

The blood libel also prompted much bogus scholarship. The medieval stories were related with additional glosses and supporting observations. So, for example, in the *Nova legenda angliae*, the English historian and theologian John Capgrave (1393–1464) augmented the received accounts of the circumstances of the 1255 Lincoln blood libel ('little Hugh of Lincoln'— see Chapter 3) with the suggestion that the child 'was eviscerated—it is said for purposes of necromancy or augury'.[120] The seventeenth-century Jesuit Bollandists of Antwerp and Louvain confirmed the medieval blood-libel stories in their forensic restatement of the lives of the saints, the *Acta Sanctorum*.[121] One might think that at least on occasion, the extravagance of invention would have made a sceptic of even the most credulous reader,[122] yet it would not appear so. A few decades later, in 1710, Andreas Eisenmenger's immensely influential *Judaism Exposed* purported to demonstrate that 'the Jews do not scruple to kill a Christian'—not only adults but also 'young, innocent children'. They sometimes buy or steal children in order to torture them. They kill them mostly at Easter because that was when they crucified Jesus. But they will kill whenever it is convenient for them to do so; that is, when the murders can be committed secretly and without danger. The murders are often accompanied by the words, 'Let us kill him, just as we did the God of the Christians, Jesus, who is nothing. Thus must all our enemies perish.'[123] This two-volume work was in print practically continuously through the eighteenth and nineteenth centuries. Eisenmenger's work was plagiarized by Röhling in his *The Talmud-Jew* (1870). In the late nineteenth and early twentieth centuries, Italian Jesuits published essays in the Catholic journal *La civiltà cattolica* relating blood libels as established facts. Even some recent Catholic scholarship has not been clear enough about the falsity of the blood-libel allegations.[124]

The discourse served many purposes, one of which was to offer plausible explanations for the relative infrequency of ritual murder. Arguments developed during the first and second periods are still deployed today by blood libellers. The Bollandists, for example, suggested that the Jews 'vented their rage in the blood of innocent Christians more frequently than it would please historians to report in chronicles or than God would permit to become known publicly'.[125] Eisenmenger had a different idea: 'because in former days Jews were dealt with very sharply when such crimes were committed, it is not to be doubted that they now refrain from shedding blood solely because of the fear of punishment'.[126] Later writers proposed that the Jews buy up and destroy any books that describe their crimes—the very paucity of material that affirms the blood libel is itself proof of the libel's truth.[127] Alternatively, it was said that few crimes are discovered, because the nations are foolish and their police are weak.[128]

A counter-discourse emerged as well. Though the blood libel was a collective hallucination,[129] even in medieval times, it never took possession of the *whole* of Europe. There were condemnations of the libel by both secular authorities (Frederick II in 1236, Duke Boleslav of Greater Poland in 1264,[130] A. Golitsyn, minister for ecclesiastical affairs, on behalf of the Tsar in 1817)[131] and ecclesiastical ones (Popes Innocent IV in 1247, Gregory X in 1272, Paul III in 1540, and Cardinal Lorenzo Ganganelli—later, Pope Clement XIV—in 1759). There were also scholars' refutations. The tract composed by Andreas Osiander (1498–1552), *Whether It Be True and Credible That the Jews Secretly Strangulate Christian Children and Make of Their Blood* (1529), advanced what had become standard defences, effective against everyone but anti-Semites. Osiander observed that Jewish law forbids murder and the ritual use of blood. He further observed that the early Christians were likewise accused of ritual murder. He also observed that in every case of alleged ritual murder, the guilty parties turn out to be Christians. And he asked, if the Jews need Christian blood, then how do the Jews of Turkey fare?[132] But this scholarly, mocking refutation was never likely to undo the blood libel, while the papal condemnations were compromised both by the complicity of local churches and priests in allegations of ritual murder and the failure of the Church itself to repudiate the cults of two beatified children, said to have been murdered by Jews in hatred of Jesus Christ.[133]

In the eighteenth century, there were two developments. First, the blood libellers extended their attack on the Jews to an attack on their Scriptures. But second, those engaged against the blood libel were able to characterize their opponents as victims of superstition, and everything that was reactionary, benighted. More needs to be said about each one of these developments. There were augmentations both to the blood libel, and to defences against the blood libel.

First, the augmentations. Between the twelfth and seventeenth centuries, Christian anti-Semites tended to advance one or more of the following 'proofs'. They said: the Jews themselves have confessed. They also said: the Talmud mandates the sacrifice of Gentiles. (This lie continues in circulation today—see below.) And they said: human sacrifice is a secret doctrine that is passed down orally from generation to generation. But they did *not* say: the *Tanach* demands it, and ritual murder follows the practices of the Jews of the Hebrew Scriptures. They did not say this because it would have meant a repudiation of the very texts that they themselves had appropriated. They could reject the Jews; they could not reject the Jews' Scriptures. They could condemn the ancient Jews for killing their prophets; but they could not condemn them for killing the prophets in accordance with Jewish law.[134] This was the state of affairs as at the mid-eighteenth century. Enlightenment anti-Semitism changed all that. It was left to the first generations of post-Christian anti-Semites to root the blood libel in the *Tanach* itself. Anti-Semites unembarrassed by conventional Christian beliefs were ready, as Christians were not, to attack the Jews through their Scriptures. In the *Philosophical Dictionary*, for example, Voltaire writes, 'Why should the Jews not have been cannibals? It would have been the only thing the people of God lacked to be the most abominable on earth.'[135] This line of defamatory speculation was then developed in the nineteenth century into the notion that Jews were acolytes of the cult of Moloch, a Phoenician–Carthaginian cult of child sacrifice. This in turn was then given a metaphorical twist, with the Jews being represented as economic blood-shedders or parasites. Moloch gave way to Mammon.[136]

What, then, of the new defences? Here is an early instance, *Lettres chinoises* (c.1742), a work by the French Enlightenment deist, the Marquis d'Argens:

> What use would it be to the Jews to sacrifice a child on the day of the death of the Christians' lawgiver? In which of their books is there the slightest trace of a like custom? How is it that in countries where they enjoy great freedom ... nothing similar has ever been attributed to them? Moreover, what is the purpose of this ridiculous sacrifice?[137]

Ridicule, then, was the new note that was struck, and superstition, the new charge. The characterizing of certain beliefs as 'superstitions' began as a Reformation practice, as ammunition to be directed by Protestants against Catholics. In the eighteenth century, Christianity itself became vulnerable to this kind of characterization.[138] 'The superstition about the use of Christian blood was so deeply instilled in me', wrote Masaryk, 'that whenever I chanced to meet a Jew I never went close to him. I always stared at his fingers to see if there was blood on them. This stupid habit remained with me a long time.'[139]

The third period

Whereas the eighteenth century marked the emergence of a non-Christian or post-Christian version of the blood libel, the nineteenth century marked the emergence of an Islamic version. It is in this period, that is, that the blood libel first appeared in Islamic lands. There were numerous blood libels in the Ottoman Empire in the second half of the nineteenth century. Their appearance may be attributed to the growing financial and cultural penetration of the Empire by the European powers and, in particular, to the European-backed wars of the Greeks against the Turks—from the 1860s, there was hardly a year without a blood libel of Greek origin. The Turkish government rejected the libels;[140] the stance of its subjects was somewhat more complex. Though the blood libel had been known in Turkey in the fifteenth and sixteenth centuries, its appearance, or reappearance, in the nineteenth century seems to have been largely the work of foreign monks, distributing blood-libel material in Arabic translation.[141] The English writer Harriet Martineau (1802–76), for example, travelling through the Middle East, reported that 'our monk-guide at Nazareth told us, in all earnestness, that the Jews had crucified a child in the Holy Week just passed'.[142] Gradually, the blood libel came to infect Muslim public opinion. It did not have to overcome especially strong resistance, it would seem. Travellers to Syria in the first decades of the nineteenth century had noticed considerable Muslim hostility towards Jews;[143] by the early twentieth century, the blood libel figured as part of an anti-Jewish campaign in Egyptian Muslim newspapers.[144]

The principal instance in this period was the Damascus blood libel of 1840. On 5 February 1840, two residents of Damascus, Father Tommaso, an Italian Friar of the Capuchin Order, and Ibrahim Amara, his Moslem servant, disappeared. Their bodies were never recovered, and the cause of their deaths remains unknown (if indeed they did die at that time). Since Roman Catholics in the Ottoman Empire were then under the protection of France, the French consul in Damascus, Count de Ratti-Menton, undertook the investigation into the disappearance of the Friar and his servant. A Jewish barber was arrested and tortured into implicating some prominent local Jews in the commission of his own non-existent crime. The consul also retained astrologers to confirm that these Jews were responsible for the murder.[145] They were arrested and tortured. Two were tortured to death, and one converted to Islam and was then released. The others refused to confess and were held prisoner until, upon the intervention of European powers, and the urgent petition of a deputation of Jews from England and France, they were released by order of Mehemet Ali, the ruler of Egypt, who at that time also controlled Syria. During the period of their imprisonment, many more Jews—approximately seventy in total—were tortured to secure confessions or evidence, and a further sixty-four Jewish schoolboys were detained to pressure their parents to cooperate with Ratti-Menton's bogus investigation. In Damascus at that time, the total population was in the order of 75,000 Muslims, 14,000 Christians and 6,000 Jews.[146] We must suppose that these 6,000 Jews lived in a state of terror for months.

Ratti-Menton was a somewhat seedy, disreputable character. He was reactionary in his politics, and careless in his private affairs. He had been bankrupted twice; he had been recalled from two previous postings; he had, reported the London *Times*, 'everywhere rendered himself obnoxious'.[147] His fits of temper were notorious. For no reason other than his own anti-Semitism,[148] he concluded that Jews had ritually murdered the two men. His excuse for seizing on the Jews—that the two men were said to have been seen on the morning of their disappearance in the Jewish Quarter—was flimsy in the extreme, though entirely in accord with the received blood-libel narrative, in which the 'Jewish Quarter' is always a place of danger for non-Jews. He was very quick to reject evidence from both Moslem and Jewish witnesses who had seen the men elsewhere, and on the afternoon of their disappearance. He urged the governor-general on to greater and greater acts of torture in order to secure confessions.[149] Yet he pretended that he had been driven to his conclusions. 'It is with real distress that, bit by bit, I have had to discard my scepticism in the face of the evidence', he wrote in a report.[150] This was a lie. He was greedy for corroboration, however flimsy, and indifferent to exculpatory evidence, however compelling. He accused the Jews of a calculated affront to French interests. 'It is a challenge to the tutelary action of His Majesty's Government and as such as well as because of the outrage to human society of these fiendish sacrifices, it is advisable to impose a salutary terror upon the Jews...'[151] Ratti-Menton did not relent. He went so far as to have an Italian pamphlet on the blood libel translated into Arabic and then had copies given away to the Damascene population.[152] When the Affair was over, and French prestige was not so caught up in Ratti-Menton's defence, questions began to be asked in Paris about his fitness for employment in the foreign service. Baron James de Rothschild was consulted. 'My sentiments never permit me', the Baron replied, 'to hit a man when he's down.'[153]

Ratti-Menton had the active support of the governor of Damascus, Sherif Pasha.[154] He also had support in France, at the highest levels. The then prime minister of France, Thiers, rebuked a critic of Ratti-Menton's, 'You protest in the name of the Jews, and I protest in the name of a Frenchman who has hitherto fulfilled all his duties with honour and fidelity' (which of course was not true—but how easily this rebuke must have come to Thiers, and how it must have stung the critic, the distinguished French statesman, Achille Fould). Ratti-Menton was opposed by the Austrian consul, G. G. Merllato, and also in due course by the Austrian and British governments. He enjoyed, however, the support of the local English consul, N. W. Werry. In the latter's despatches, he reported the 'horrible assassination' committed by 'seven of the most influential Jew merchants' in Damascus. The murders were 'sacrifices'; Jews have throughout the country 'immolated clandestinely Christians to obtain their blood to celebrate their feasts therewith in their religious ceremonies'; the perpetrators have confessed and 'the facts minutely proved'; 'too much praise cannot be given to the French consul'; measures should be taken against 'the Jew people to prevent a repetition of such horrible crimes'. 'The Jews' were resorting to 'ingenuity of argument [and] every species of intrigue, both of influence and pecuniary' to establish their innocence. Happily, the French consul ('this virtuous man') has been able, 'by his firmness' to frustrate these 'infamous practices'. No consul here could 'remain passive and for the sake of Hebrew gold and influence, shut his eyes to the horrible murder of a Minister of Christ'. All attempts to prove the men's innocence—'to prove black white!'—will fail. 'Every impartial and conscientious person' must conclude, 'the Jews are guilty'. What is more, 'extracts from the Talmud warrant these enormities'. Werry was indignant when accused of 'entertaining illiberal and uncharitable sentiments against the Jew nation'. He wrote, 'I give you my word of honour that I . . . am entirely innocent of [these charges].'[155]

It is in this period that the blood libel first acquired some of the characteristics of a *cause célèbre*. It divided nations; it got caught up in power politics. The affair had something of the character of a war by proxy; the opposing stances on the Affair taken by the French on the one hand, and the British and Austrians on the other, mirrored the Great Power divisions in respect of Mehemet Ali and Turkey. The blood libel also acquired a different kind of international resonance; the events were followed as they unfolded. A strongly philo-Semitic sentiment developed, characterized by a campaigning advocacy undertaken by non-Jews on behalf of Jews. There was also the parallel emergence of Jewish organizations, accompanied by utterly fantastic overstatements by anti-Semites of their influence. The affair was interpreted by many Jews as evidence of their continuing, post-emancipation vulnerability: 'I realised', wrote the German socialist and proto-Zionist Moses Hess, 'that I belonged to a slandered people, forsaken by all the world, spread in all lands, but not dead.'[156] Promoters of the blood libel began to make a distinction between the generality of Jews and what comes to be described as a fanatical, backward sect within Jewry. Opponents of the libel, for their part, struggle to formulate a decisive refutation— perhaps, one suggested, all the rabbis of Europe should be assembled and invited to swear that Judaism does not prescribe human sacrifice?[157] Last, in those circles in which the blood libel was dismissed as so much pernicious nonsense, it was taken for granted that nothing quite so nonsensical could ever arise in what was customarily described as a 'civilized' nation.[158]

Following the events of 1840, blood libels recurred throughout the region. In the vicinity of Damascus alone, there were nine incidents between 1840 and 1900. In Palestine, there were four incidents during the same period. In 1844, there were two incidents in Egypt, one in Cairo, instigated by Muslims, and one in Alexandria, instigated by the Greek Orthodox. The historian Tudor Parfitt continues the account:

> In 1866, in Hamadan in western Iran, eighteen Jews were massacred following a ritual murder accusation—two more were burnt alive while the rest of the community only managed to escape the fury of the mob by converting *en masse* to Islam; there were further libels in Alexandria in 1870, in Smyrna in 1871, and Damanhur (Egypt) in 1871 and 1873, initiated by Muslims, and again in Smyrna in 1873. In 1875 there was a blood libel in Aleppo, as a result of which the Pasha of Aleppo had to send troops to guard the Jewish quarter. In 1876 there was another blood libel in Smyrna and one in Constantinople, while 1877 saw libels in Damanhur and Mansura, where the local Muslims accused the Jews of kidnapping a Muslim child and killing it in order to use its blood for *matzot*.[159]

In short, the blood libel had arrived in the East.

The fourth period

In this period, from the late nineteenth century to the early twentieth century, far more limited in duration than either the first or second periods, there were numerous libels, across much of Europe. While there were blood-libel incidents in Germany, Hungary, Russia, Bulgaria, Romania, France, and of course in Poland too, the preponderance of incidents remained east of the Rhine.[160] (Medieval instances, of course, continued to be memorialized in twentieth-century Western Europe.)[161] Accurate information on the number of instances is unavailable. On one account in the five-year period between 1887 and 1891, at least twenty-two cases were raised in Europe.[162] On another account, there were 128 public accusations between 1881 and 1900 (an assessment derived mainly from examination of German and Austrian newspapers). On a third account, there were seventy-nine public accusations between 1891 and 1900, mainly in Austria-Hungary, Germany, and Bulgaria. Between 1879 and 1913, there were six major trials, including at Tisza-Esler (Hungary, 1882–3), at Polnà (Austrian Bohemia, 1899–1900), and at Kiev (Russian Ukraine, 1911–13).[163] There were twelve trials between 1867 and 1914 in Germany and the Austrian Empire alone;[164] not every trial ended in a conviction.[165] Put it another way. There were more recorded instances of the blood libel between 1870 and 1940 than in the entire preceding period of some 700 years.[166] There has been much speculation among historians about the reasons for this revival and intensification of ritual murder charges in Central Europe.[167]

These were, in any event, part of a more general intensification of anti-Semitic activity. There were anti-Semitic pamphlets, newspapers, books, movements, and parties; riots and pogroms (Pomerania, 1881; Galicia, 1898; Kishinev, 1903; among others); ritual murder trials (Tisza Eszlar, 1882; Xanten, 1891; Polnà, 1899; among others); the first anti-Semitic international congress (Dresden, 1882); and the Dreyfus Affair.[168] The blood libel became a staple of anti-Semitic agitation and polemic. It was exploited for the purposes of incitement, if only because it was understood by professional Jew-haters to be the aspect of anti-Semitism that had the most immediate appeal to the masses. To some of these propagandists, it could be mobilized to evoke the terror and menace of Eastern Europe, a place where ritual murder and other depravities are endemic. 'The seeds of this horrific monomania', wrote Drumont, 'are present there in a state of constant incubation . . .'[169]

Thus, while these libels were *on the one hand* dismissed by enlightened opinion as 'malicious charges', 'monstrous fables', 'foul slanders', and 'base falsehoods' that should 'long since have been thrown into the lumber-room of exploded opinions'[170] deriving from 'fanatical suspicion' and 'ancient delusion',[171] and evidence of a residual, medieval barbarism (though in fact anticipating an entirely modern barbarism that came to power a half-century later), they were *on the other hand* defended as the work of unregenerate, primitive Jews who still practised the murderous rites of their forefathers.[172]

But both sets of responses, and in particular the manner of their expression, were indebted to the Damascus precedent. The international interventions, febrile press coverage, the involvement of 'experts',[173] became typical of blood-libel cases after 1840. The new instances of the libel were in any event taken up by anti-Semitic campaigners, and exploited by political parties. Sensationalist newspapers dedicated to the dissemination of anti-Semitic lore played an important role in the promoting of blood libels.[174] Crooks, charlatans, men 'on the make', defrocked priests[175] and demagogues searching for a constituency, all exploited the blood libel to advance or revive their careers. Anti-Semitic propagandists manipulated the folkloric aspects of Jewish distinctness for their own purposes.[176]

Incidents in Polnà and Kiev are exemplary of the 'modern reworkings'[177] of the blood libel in this period.

Polnà

Agnes Hruza was murdered on 29 March 1899 in a forest near Polnà, a town on the Bohemian–Moravian border. Her body was discovered on 1 April, the day before Easter Sunday. It was said that the body had been drained of blood. The rumour soon spread of ritual murder. Leopold Hilsner, the son of a poor Jewish widow, was arrested. He was a lazy, feckless person, supported by his mother and rarely in work. He was tried twice, and each time convicted of murder (on the second occasion, he was also convicted of a second murder). The evidence was entirely circumstantial; it was, indeed, preposterous.[178] An opportunistic 'Young Czech' politician volunteered to represent the dead woman's family at the first trial, and in his courtroom addresses drew on the imagery and vocabulary of the blood libel.[179] 'Just imagine', he said, 'the plight of this virtuous young girl when her clothes were torn off, when she saw herself at the mercy of three strangers, who obviously belonged to a different race, obnoxious to her, when they threw themselves on her, the sacrificial lamb.' And then he added: '[The Jews living in the vicinity of Polnà] wanted to murder a Christian person, an innocent girl, in order to get her blood.'[180] Neither Hilsner's innocence, nor the best efforts of Thomas Masaryk,[181] then a Professor at the Czech University in Prague, could protect him from the anti-Semites on the juries and the bench and in the press. The state prosecutor concluded: 'I was not present, and there were no witnesses to see what he did and who delivered the fatal blow. But I am absolutely convinced that Hilsner was present at the murder.' Hilsner was sentenced to death, though the sentence was later commuted to life imprisonment. In 1918, he was pardoned, and he died in 1928. In 1968, Agnes's brother confessed on his deathbed to the murder.[182]

Kiev

On 12 March 1911, a 13-year old boy disappeared; eight days later, his mutilated body was found in a cave. Menachem Beilis (1874–1934), a Jewish clerk who worked at a nearby brick factory, was arrested and charged with murdering the boy. He was tried in September–October 1913. Two experts testified that the murder was a ritual one; other experts testified to the falsity of the blood libel. At least one of the prosecution expert witnesses was bribed, while another was I. B. Pranaitis, a charlatan-priest. Though the author of *The Talmud Unmasked* (1892), a compilation of fabricated, and falsely translated, quotations plagiarized from earlier such compilations, he was utterly incompetent even to read the Jewish texts on which he claimed to rely.[183] 'In the beginning', Beilis later wrote, 'it all seemed so ludicrous.' He was acquitted; there was never any real doubt that the charges against him had been fabricated. In his directions to the jury, the judge had said, 'You must ... remember just one thing: a Christian child has been murdered.'[184] The jury also held, therefore, that the boy had been ritually murdered (a view shared by the Tsar, among others). The authorities had let the case go to trial knowing the identities of the true culprits—members of a criminal gang who had murdered the boy to stop him informing on them.[185] In his closing address, the prosecutor remarked:

> I don't want to speak against the Jews, but when one reads the Jewish press, Jewish publications, and Jewish defence organs, one cannot escape the conclusion that in criticising them, one invites instant rebuke and disapproval. In doing so, you are either a reactionary, an obscurant, or a member of the Black Hundred. Having monopolised the press, they've become so arrogant as to believe that no one will dare level such an accusation against them ...[186]

The prosecutor's complaint is a familiar one. Criticize the Jews (now, Israel or the 'Israel Lobby'), and they respond with smears, orchestrating the vilification of their accusers, believing themselves to be beyond criticism, deploying their control of the media, etc. In 2006, the allegations against Beilis were revived in a Ukrainian periodical,[187] and the country's largest university published material purportedly containing fresh evidence for Beilis' guilt and proposing that the Jews may have been complicit in other, more recent deaths too.[188]

Though each of these cases was described as a Dreyfus Affair for its respective nation, this was a misdescription. The Dreyfus Affair was a *cause célèbre*; the Polnà and Kiev cases were mere scandals. The scandal is a cut-price, low rent version of the *cause célèbre*. People behave badly, and even those engaged on the side of justice take no pleasure in their involvement. A scandal raises no new issues, no national interests are at stake, it does not enlarge understanding, and it is miserable, undistinguished, and sordid.

During this period, and notwithstanding its proliferation, the blood libel also seemed somewhat on the defensive, somewhat diminished in its authority. This was reflected in the uncertain handling of the trope in contemporaneous anti-Semitic discourse. First, anti-Semitic polemicists often deployed it merely as a makeweight. Following Dreyfus's conviction, for example, it was said that the Jews would revenge themselves on France by engineering 'an immense financial crash, a Franco-German bloodletting' and—oh yes, as if in afterthought—'a series of ritual murders'.[189] Even when not a makeweight, the blood libel was subordinated to ostensibly more pressing, secular themes. During the pogroms of 1903–6, for example, it was a common combination to allege both that the Jews were conspiring with the Japanese (with whom Russia was at war) *and* were engaged in acts of ritual murder.[190] Secondly, in certain contexts, killing Jews barely seemed to require any pretext. During the first wave of pogroms in Russia, the pogroms of 1881–4, the violence against Jews was not provoked by any fabricated or misrepresented acts of the Jews at all, let alone the murder of a child.[191] Lastly, there were acquittals; it could no longer be assumed that a prosecution would produce a conviction. An anti-Semitic paper plaintively asked its readers: 'Can we, after the outcomes at Skurz and Xanten and after today's expected outcome at Konitz, still have confidence that murders of Christian children will be punished and expiated?'[192] In the first decades of the twentieth century, Jews—and other, less personally threatened students of anti-Semitism—might have been forgiven for believing that the blood libel, at least, was fast becoming a thing of the past.

The fifth period

That is to say, the Nazi period, 1933–45. There were no trials, and barely even any 'incidents'—few fresh reports of missing children, few unsolved murders attributed to Jews. But there was a persistent, even unrelenting, agitation on the subject, undertaken principally by Julius Streicher in his

weekly newspaper, *Der Stürmer*.[193] He was first prosecuted for the libel in
1921, and further prosecutions followed thereafter;[194] even during the war,
the blood libel remained a regular theme for him, with a lengthy series of
articles beginning in 1943.[195] Repetitious though these allegations were,[196]
Streicher outdid himself on 17 May 1934, when the entire edition of the
Stürmer was dedicated to the subject of ritual murder.[197] The front-page
headline announced, 'The Jewish murder plot against non-Jewish humanity is uncovered'.[198] Grisly detail was invented: 'The procedure is as
follows. The family head empties a few drops of the fresh and powdered
blood into a glass, wets the fingers of the left hand with it . . .' etc.[199] This is
what Jews do; this is what Jews have done on this occasion. The only
constraint was the imagination of the fabricator; no detail would be too
salacious, too horrible to be rejected by readers. The detail could go in any
direction; it was a kind of pornography. The Nazis also promoted the
obverse theme, Jewish racial pollution, the defiling properties of *Jewish*
blood.[200] That the Jews practice ritual murder is proof that they comprise
nothing more than a well-organized gang of murderers and criminals,[201]
wrote Streicher, on behalf of his own gang of murderers and criminals.
The 17 May 1934 issue was made available in England through the British
Union of Fascists.[202]

The Nazis believed that the blood libel would assist in turning their
enemies towards anti-Semitism. Himmler, for example, encouraged his
chief of security police to arrange for extracts of a book on the blood libel
to be broadcast to England and America.[203] The book itself he ordered
distributed to the *Einsatzkommandos*, 'especially to those actively engaged in
the Jewish question'.[204] The British traitor Jack Amery told an audience in
Occupied France that 'the victory of the German armies was necessary in
order that small children shall no longer be the victims of the Jews'.[205] But
little further use was made of the blood libel for domestic consumption. The
date of the *Stürmer* issue is significant. The Jews were still—just about—
members of civil society. The blood libel is about murders perpetrated by
neighbours, that is, people living within the same social space. It assumes
a certain intimacy of relation between Jew and non-Jew, as well as access
to a common system of justice. As the persecutions escalated, and the
segregation of Jews became a reality, the Nazis went beyond the blood
libel. Of course Streicher continued to prate on about ritual murder, but
genocide called for a greater justification. The blood libel did not answer, so
to speak, to the immense, metaphysical threat posed by the Jews to the

world as a whole, one which could only be combated by the killing of all the world's Jews, without exception.

World War II was framed by two pogroms, each with a certain symbolic significance. The first one took place in Tunisia in August 1940. Local Arab mobs, made up in part of demobilized conscripts in the defeated French army, rioted in the towns of Kef, Ebba Ksour, Moktar, and Siliana, injuring Jews and looting Jewish property. The pretext for the riots was a rumour that Jews had kidnapped a young Muslim girl.[206] The second pogrom took place on 4 July 1946 in Kielce, Poland. Forty-two Jews were killed, and as many as eighty wounded, by a mob drunk on rumours of a child-kidnapping.[207] This was the worst attack of many such attacks across the period 1944 to 1947, which left between 1,500 and 2,000 Jews dead. They were pulled from trains to be beaten and murdered and Jewish institutions were bombed; there were pogroms in about a dozen cities and towns. Many of these pogroms were accompanied by blood libels.[208] The first one, in Rzeszów, took place on 12 June 1945;[209] Kielce was the last and worst of the pogroms.[210] It was in all a year-long terror, and it had the effect of driving most of Poland's remaining Jews out of the country for good. An epilogue: in the mid-1980s, a documentary filmmaker recorded interviews with inhabitants of Kielce. One interviewee said, so many people believed the charge of ritual murder to be true, 'there had to be something in it'. Another interviewee said, with a noncommittal smile, 'It is their [i.e., the Jews'] secret.'[211] The Middle East, Europe—where could the Jews live in safety?

The sixth period

This runs from the 1950s to the present, and is symptomatic of the broader shift in the centre of global anti-Semitism from Nazi Germany to the Arab world.[212] The new developments are first, an immense increase in the blood libel's dissemination in Muslim lands,[213] and second, the abandonment of prosecutions as a vehicle for renewing the libel. There is a connection between these two developments, of course. Unconstrained by forensic considerations, the blood libel becomes a free-floating trope of Jewish criminality. It was as vampiric Jews, consumers of the blood of Gentiles, that a Jerusalem Arab notable described the Zionists to the King-Crane Commission in 1919:

It is impossible for us to make an understanding with [the Jews] or even live
with them ... Their history and all their past proves that it is impossible to
live with them. In all the countries where they are present they are not
wanted ... because they always arrive to suck the blood of everybody.

The notable added that the country would become 'a river of blood' if the
League of Nations did not heed his warning.[214] Little changed in the
intervening decades; blood-libel pamphlets and reports circulated in 1920s
Palestine;[215] the blood libel continues to provide the governing trope in
characterizations of Israel and the Zionist project. Against such deployments
of the libel, Jews are mostly powerless. It is almost impossible to refute
generalized charges—though there has been some success in exposing
manipulations of filmed or photographed deaths. Individual libels often
survive after they have been discredited.

The contemporary dissemination of the blood libel explicitly rehearses
earlier themes. The leading newspaper of the Arab world, *Al-Ahram*, reports
that Jews may only live in their 'sacred cities' (Jerusalem, Hebron, Safed,
Tiberias) when they have eaten blood *matzot*.[216] In a newspaper cartoon,
Ariel Sharon stands on a pile of infants' corpses, hands dripping with their
blood, holding another infant aloft, and with a Star of David hanging from
his neck. In another cartoon, a religious Jew wearing a large skullcap is
putting a baking tray in an open oven, and on the tray is a Palestinian
child.[217] And so on. *Purim* has excited the attention of blood libellers.[218] And
as one might expect, there are also vindications of the Damascus blood
libel—principally in the best-seller *The Matzah of Zion* (1983), written by
Mustafa Tlas (b. 1932), the very long-serving Syrian minister of defence.[219]
According to its cover blurb 'this study describes in fine detail and with
scientific precision, the blood rites of the Jews, who slaughter Christians and
Muslims so they can mix their blood into the matzoth they use on Yom
Kippur'.[220] The Syrian government printing house publishes the book; the
Syrian delegate to the UN Commission on Human Rights at its annual
meeting in 1991 defended it as a true account.[221] It has been continuously in
print for over twenty years; Tlas was reported in 2001 to have sold the rights
to an Egyptian producer who intended to film it as a response to *Schindler's
List*.[222] There have been other deployments of the Damascus blood libel by
Arab politicians and diplomats.[223] There are also restatements of what can be
called basic blood-libel doctrine. For example, in *Human Sacrifices in the
Talmud* (1962), published by the Egyptian Ministry of Education, the Jews
are characterized as 'a people that does not recoil from resorting to the vilest

methods in order to achieve its aims, irrespective of whether it involves killing, money or debauchery'.[224] The book was a reprint of an 1890 work, revised for twentieth-century readers.

But more innovative versions of the blood libel have also been put into circulation—mostly in cartoon form. These cartoons have all Jews in their sights. Their most immediate precedents are the cartoons of Philip Ruprecht ('Fips') that appeared in *Der Stürmer* from December 1925 until 1945;[225] their somewhat earlier precedents are to be found among the woodcuts and engravings of medieval times.

The blood libel has acquired an anti-Zionist character

'In becoming child-murderers', declared a recent Franco-Muslim pamphlet, 'the Zionists have finally unmasked themselves.'[226] It is now commonplace for Zionists/Israelis to be characterized as child-murderers.[227] The death of Mohammed al-Dura on 30 September 2000 in circumstances that are still unclear,[228] but which were not the consequence of deliberate action by Israeli forces, was widely represented in the Palestinian media and elsewhere as disclosing the criminal essence of Zionism. And Zionism in turn was represented as 'Judaism Unmasked'. The Zionist does openly what his co-religionists hitherto did in secret.[229] The Syrian-produced TV series *Al-Shatat* ('Diaspora'), first broadcast on Hizbollah's Al-Manar television channel during Ramadan 2003, tells the story of Zionism from 1812 up to the establishment of the State of Israel in 1948. It rehearses a basic medieval version of the blood libel, showing Jews baking Passover *matza* with Gentile blood. Two Iranian channels also aired *Al-Shatat* during Ramadan 2004.[230]

The poisoning libel has been revived, but as a variation on the blood libel

One may write now of an *infanticide libel*. For example, in 1983, a rumour developed that Israel was infiltrating school classrooms with a colourless, odourless, poison gas.[231] And in 1997 it was alleged that Israeli doctors were deliberately injecting the AIDS virus into Palestinian children.[232] The libel inevitably grew into a *genocide allegation*. In November 1999, Suha Arafat accused the Israeli forces of causing 'severe damage . . . by the intensive daily use of poison gas'.[233] During the al-Aqsa Intifada, Yassir Arafat and his spokesmen broadcast similar allegations, and further alleged that depleted uranium projectiles were being used against Palestinian civilians.[234] Every new poisoning allegation against Jews or the Jewish State is historically freighted, containing within it every previous such allegation—just as every call to boycott Jews or the Jewish State contains within *it* every previous such call. Anti-Semitism's discursive history makes this unavoidable. A poisoning allegation, a boycott call, can never be innocent.

A vampire theme has emerged[235]

Cartoons represent Jews as consumers of human blood. For example—an Israeli soldier gives his mother a bottle filled with the blood of a Palestinian child; the Jews drink the American people's blood through a straw; Israeli politicians toast each other with Arab blood; Ariel Sharon celebrates the New Year by drinking from a bottle labelled 'Martyrs' blood', or drinks Palestinian blood from a straw, sitting on and squashing the globe; the Israeli electorate drinks blood from a bottle provided by Ariel Sharon.[236] In a satirical television programme, shown on an Abu Dhabi television channel in 2001, Ariel Sharon runs a bottling plant manufacturing cola made with Arab blood.[237] In March 2002, a Saudi newspaper claimed that 'Jewish vampires' torment their victims by placing them in a barrel filled with needles. The blood these Jews extract is then mixed into holiday pastries to be consumed on *Purim*.[238]

The old stories have been given topical twists

The Jews slaughtered the Arabs of Sabra and Shatila to use their blood for baking *matzos*, it is alleged, one lie wrapped inside another lie.[239] The Jews want peace because they need their victims to be well-disposed towards them; hatred contaminates blood, and so hatred of Jews is the best defence against them.[240] A film about the Damascus blood libel has been announced, in which Father Tomas is murdered to prevent him speaking about a Zionist plot to move Jews from Damascus to Palestine.[241]

Christian and post-Christian themes are exploited

Palestinians are often pictured nailed to a cross; the Jews crucify Arafat, or the Palestinians, as they once crucified Jesus. The French newspaper, *Libération* published a cartoon of Sharon, gripping nails between his teeth, and spitting out the mordancy, 'No Christmas for Arafat, but he's welcome to an Easter.'[242] But there are also representations of the 'Jewish God', hungry for human sacrifice. In one cartoon, God holds a fat bag of dollars, bearing the names of major Jewish organizations; in another cartoon, God outstretches his hand to Bush, who slaughters a child on an altar to improve his chances for a second term of office.[243]

Cartoons now comprise the principal vehicle in the dissemination of the blood libel[244]

Indignation is the presiding note, the visual equivalent of a shrill, abusive scream. A token satire is put at the service of an incontinent anti-Semitism. Most of the cartoonists are no freer than their journalist colleagues to express their own views.[245] They must work within prescribed perspectives; they may only attack prescribed targets. But if they are not free to choose their enemies, they compensate in the violence with which they attack those allowed to them. These cartoonists are thus subversive of nothing but human decency. The independent-minded few who operate outside these constraints tend to live outside the Muslim world, and/or die unnatural deaths—consider the career of the late Naji Salim al-Ali, murdered in London in 1987.[246] The safest topics tend also to be the ones most susceptible to dishonest treatment—and none is safer, or more dishonest, than the topic of the blood libel. In the blood-libel cartoons, the cartoonists' pencils lie.[247] These lies are especially dangerous because cartoons are hard to contest; it is difficult to argue with them, because they themselves are not discursive. They comprise not so much an allegation as a representation of reality. They simplify, condense, and intensify. They cross linguistic and national borders.

Versions and derivatives of the blood libel now comprise a significant resource for the rallying of Israel's adversaries, and for the teaching of Israel's history, and the history of Zionism; they also provide material for the abuse of Jews and others perceived to be supporters of Israel. On 2 June 2001, members of the Association of Ilford Muslims heckled the local MP Mike Gapes with the taunts 'Racist', 'Murderer' and 'How many children have you killed today?'[248] At a Hamas-organized children's rally in Gaza City on 12 August 2006, 'the children chanted in one voice "Death to child-killers, death to enemies of the people, and death to enemies of freedom." '[249] The rhetoric is much the same in Ilford as in Gaza. It did not matter, then, to the hecklers whether Gapes himself was a child murderer. It was not as if he himself was charged with presiding over a war against insurgents. It was enough for the hecklers that he was a Jew—in the event, mistakenly *assumed* to be a Jew.[250] The Jews are the worst people in the world; the worst, therefore, may be believed about them.[251] And so, beyond even the blood libel, lies the genocide libel. In September 2001, the *Syria Times*, an English-language official gazette, attributed the following statement to Ariel Sharon: 'If I became a prime minister [*sic*], I would wipe out all Arabs, kill every newly-born Palestinian baby and knife the abdomen of every woman pregnant from an Arab. Those dogs should not be close to the chosen people of god.'[252]

How is all this to be explained? It *cannot* be explained by reference to the given facts. Both Israelis and Palestinians have cause to grieve. The circumstances of the deaths of Palestinian children, the casualties of a political and territorial dispute (and sometimes, of infighting between Palestinian factions),[253] do not warrant the deployment against Israel of blood-libel motifs. This deployment is part of a broader discursive assault upon the Jewish State. It recasts a 120-year conflict between two peoples as a 60-year old war waged by Jewish adults upon Palestinian children, and thereby provides an opening for the blood libel. Its incontinent deployment also betrays a certain anxiety both about the killing of Israeli children and the use of Palestinian children for that purpose. It attributes to Israel what is most characteristic of a certain kind of indiscriminate terror, a sanctification of armed struggle,[254] one that replicates the blood libel's principal theme.

Of course, in addition to the Muslim appropriation and exploitation of the blood libel, and its echoes in the West,[255] the blood libel continues to be a theme in the literature and on the websites of the Far Right.[256] In 1960, a Dagestan newspaper, 'Kommunist', reported as true the libel that Jews mixed Moslem blood with water for ritual purposes; following international protest, the provincial authorities characterized the article as a 'political error'.[257] It would seem that belief in the essential truth of the blood libel remains widespread among some sections of the population in Russia,[258] Poland,[259] and perhaps elsewhere too in Europe. (In Russia, the libel has attached itself to accounts of the execution of the Tsar and his family, a 'ritual Jewish sacrifice'.)[260] The libel continues to fasten upon particular instances of unexplained murder or disappearance. In February 2005, twenty Russian MPs signed a letter, along with 500 intellectuals, accusing Jews of ritual murder and Satanism, and calling for all Jewish organizations to be banned.[261] In March 2008, hundreds of leaflets were distributed in the city of Novosibirsk advising residents to 'Keep watch over your children before the coming of April 2008, the Jewish holiday of Passover. These disgusting people still engage in ritual practice to their gods.'[262]

This sixth period is, then, an epitome of the blood-libel discourse. All the elements in earlier periods are present, often in jumbled form; all the themes of the blood libel are recapitulated. The whole world is now alive to the discourse, but without any consciousness of its history in fabrication and persecution. The blood libel began in England, it spread through Western Europe, and it then reached the Muslim lands. It is now a global phenomenon. In the Middle Ages, there were popes and emperors ready to deny its truth. Until the last decades of the twentieth century, it was taken to be symptomatic of everything that was reactionary, oppressive, and false. But now it is mostly[263] tolerated, even when it is recognized for what it is. It has thus become, once again, unabashed:

> Mohammed Salmawy, who edits the state-owned newspaper, *Al-Ahram Hebdo*, defends the use of old European myths like the blood libel—the accusation that Jews use the blood of Christians when making the matzo bread for Passover. He says journalists are merely digging around—using the equivalent of Greek myths or fairy stories—to convey their horror at the Israeli occupation. 'The real question is why the actions of some people bring to mind these myths: Sharon's policy is bloody and discriminating and anti-Semitic—and remember, the Palestinians are also Semites.'[264]

The blood libel, then, has ceased to be a 'real question'.

A conclusion

The blood libel has a greater density of reference, a greater historical and ideological resonance, than the more commonplace, everyday lies that people tend to tell. But the blood libel will always be a lie, nonetheless. It is a demonstration of that great counter-intuitive truth that sometimes there *can* be smoke without fire.

At the end of the eleventh century the armies of the First Crusade made their way through the Rhineland killing, raping, and plundering Jews. Entire communities were destroyed; hundreds of lives were lost, while the lives of those Jews who survived were ruined. Among the leaders of these massacring bands was one Count Emicho. He and his cohorts fell upon the city of Worms on 18 May 1096, and immediately encountered a problem. How to incite the local populace to assist them in their planned assault on the city's Jews?

> They took a trampled corpse of theirs, which had been buried thirty days previously, and carried it through the city, saying, 'Behold what the Jews have done to our comrade. They took a Gentile and boiled him in water. They then poured the water into our wells in order to kill us.'[265]

That is to say, they just made it up. It was a *ruse de guerre*, or more accurately, a *ruse de massacre*. The lie seems to have worked; almost the entire community was killed. The lie also seems to have been a new one. The received historical wisdom is that the allegation of well-poisoning was not made until early in the fourteenth century.[266] The lie is perhaps best regarded as a preparatory to far greater, more consequential lies. But it invites one conclusion. What began in deceit and defamation continues to this day in deceit and defamation. It has throughout been an affair of 'unlawful hatreds, false accusations, abusive contumely'.[267] When Trotsky gazed at the spectacle of the Beilis blood-libel trial, in all its vicious absurdity, its cruelty, and its charlatanism, he was consumed by a 'feeling of physical nausea'.[268] Who could not similarly be affected, surveying the history of this foul lie against the Jewish people?

PART II

Versions

3
Medieval English Anti-Semitism

The first Anglo-Jewish community

French Jews first arrived in England in the wake of the Norman Conquest;[1] more Jews came some thirty years later, in flight from massacring crusaders. The Jews brought their capital with them, and began to lend it on commercial terms to the cash-starved—the Crown, ecclesiastical institutions, and landowners. Some Jews became great financiers. The Jews' pursuits were not limited to moneylending, however. Among the earliest Jewish immigrants there were those who came at the request of Archbishop Gerard of York, to assist him in his scholarly pursuits. There were rabbis, scholars, and Talmudic students; there were physicians, traders, goldsmiths, and ballad-singers,[2] and even some soldiers, fishmongers, and cheese makers.[3] This first Anglo-Jewish community lasted for little more than 200 years. England, last among the countries of Western Europe to receive Jews, was the first to expel them. The Expulsion was welcomed as a precedent by later generations of anti-Semites in other countries.[4]

In law, the Jews were, uniquely, *both* legal persons *and* negotiable property. They could be sold or mortgaged—indeed, they were mortgaged by Henry III to his brother, Richard, against a loan of 5,000 marks, and later mortgaged to Henry's son, Edward, to secure his loyalty and in return for an annual payment of 3,000 marks.[5] As chattels of the king, their property was the king's property. But they were also considered a distinct collective entity, addressed collectively through their leaders. To this extent, then, it may be said that the Jews had an acknowledged separate legal status.[6] They constituted a *communa* with which the king could deal as a single whole.[7] However, the Jews remained a juridical anomaly; England never had a

'Jewry law' of the kind that emerged in continental Europe. This was in part because the Expulsion cut short the development of such a law, in part because the Justinian Code, which restricted Jews' freedoms, never formed part of English law, and in part because the revival of Roman law in Continental Europe therefore left England untouched.[8] The charters issued by the Angevin kings described the Jews' status in the most perfunctory terms. They were '*just like* our own chattels' (Richard I), or '*just as* our own chattels' (John)[9] (emphasis added)—that is, items of possession. The 1275 Statute of Jewry (or *Statute de Judaismo*) defined them as 'the King's serfs',[10] as if finally settling the problem of status. In relation to all men save the king the Jew was free, that is, free of any obligation of duty.[11] But that amounted to a condition of total *un*freedom. 'The Jew', explained the thirteenth-century English jurist, Henry de Bracton, 'can have nothing that is his own, for whatever he acquires, he acquires not for himself, but for the king.'[12] He was Crown property.[13] An attack on Jews was thus an attack on the monarch's prestige. In 1203, for example, the king intervened on behalf of the Jews of London, addressing himself to the Mayor: 'If I give my peace even to a dog, it must be kept inviolate.'[14]

The kings' charters were mere statements of the Crown's position in relation to the Jews at the time of issue.[15] The Jews needed protection, and though the charters' combination of privileges and restrictions purported to give them that, the Jews were not safe from their ostensible protector. Certainly, the English kings were fickle, predatory protectors. The Crown always acted within its rights towards Jews, but only because it was free to do whatever it wished with them. As against the Crown, the Jews had no rights. If the king chose to override their privileges in any particular case, he could do so; he could act against them on a whim[16] (he was not similarly free to act thus against any other class of person). So for example, in 1234 the king intervened in a case, ordering the justices not to hear it. The plaintiff was a Jewish woman suing her former husband, a convert, for a dower payment. She should have converted too, the king thought.[17] Moreover, the limited protection that the king did offer was itself conditional, and came at a considerable price: King John, for example, charged the Jews for the 1201 Charter.[18] Notwithstanding all this, it would appear that the Jews attracted jealous, resentful comment for what was per-ceived as their privileged position at law.[19] This was a *mis*perception.

At first, however, the Jews thrived. Small communities sprang up across the country; by 1189, there were no less than twenty-four of them. There were communities spread through the south and east of England, with further scattered, small communities in the north and west. The largest community was in London. Provided that they enjoyed the protection of a local patron with a castle to hand in case of emergency, the Jews were relatively secure.[20] Anglo-Jewry comprised an essentially urban population. Though the Jews tended to live in close proximity to each other, there were no ghettoes. They were not segregated from their new Christian neighbours; synagogues stood near churches. These Jews at first belonged to a single Anglo-Norman Jewish community; there was little that was specifically English about them. They maintained their strong ties with Normandy.[21]

Conditions for the Jews began to deteriorate in the mid- to late-twelfth century. The blood libel made its first recorded appearance; the Crown stopped borrowing from the Jews and instead started taxing them; there was popular violence. In the late 1170s, the Exchequer turned the extorting of money from England's wealthiest Jews into a project.[22] There were riots and massacres in 1189–90 following Richard I's coronation. In 1210 King John ordered a 'general captivity' of England's Jews, and on his return from Ireland, imposed a levy (known as a 'tallage') of £40,000. There were hangings and acts of torture. The provincial communities, diminished in number by the 1190 riots, shrank further in consequence of these financial depredations. And yet Anglo-Jewry displayed extraordinary resilience. Even at the very end, there were still some active Jewish entrepreneurs, surviving (if not prospering) under the most adverse of conditions.[23] They sustained the brief moments of revival in Anglo-Jewry's fortunes in the middle decades of the thirteenth century. But by 1258, Anglo-Jewry as a whole was pretty much ruined. Thereafter, the sequence was inexorable: a prohibition on lending, with the consequent criminalization of a substantial fraction of the adult Jewish population (1275), the judicial killing of alleged and genuine coin-clippers (1278–9), an acceleration of local expulsions from provincial centres, and then a general expulsion (1290).

The history of medieval English Jewry is thus in large measure the history of the *persecution* of medieval English Jewry. The economics of the community cannot be understood other than by reference to the state's fiscal depredations. The demography of the community cannot be understood other than by reference to the restrictions placed on the Jews' rights of abode. The general relations between the Jews and the English are more completely characterized by hostility than at any other time in England's history. England was not, of course, one vast torture-chamber. The murders and executions visited upon the Jews by mob and state were relatively infrequent. Many Jews lived and died peaceful lives; more than a few Jews prospered; friendships, and other relationships of trust, were formed between Jews and Christians.[24] The king's courts were open to Jews, and there is much evidence of them litigating their contracts, or appearing as accusers in criminal cases, and receiving justice according to the character of the times.[25] But life was always uncertain and circumscribed, and it was often worse than that. From time to time, the persecution paused, and only on occasion did it embrace all Jews—in the case of certain fines, legislative restrictions imposed by the Church and the state, and the Expulsion. There were even moments when favour was shown to Jews, and arrangements made that gave them some protection, at however high a price. But the fact remains that in twelfth- and thirteenth-century England, Jews were massacred with impunity, and robbed with the express sanction of the state, when not at its actual instigation. This was a war against the Jews that ultimately left them all dead or exiled.

Themes

In medieval England, then, Jews were defamed, their wealth was expropriated, they were killed and injured, they were subjected to discriminatory and humiliating regulation, and they were, finally, expelled.

Sociologists distinguish between different kinds of violence. There is, first, the distinction between institutional and popular violence; that is, between the legally sanctioned exercise of power by those in authority and the unregulated exercise of power by those without authority. In the case of medieval England, however, the violence came both from above *and* from below. The state was implicated in violence against Jews in support of extortion, by judicial sanctions for false charges, by its tacit support for mob violence and its refusal to prosecute the murderers of Jews. The Church both practised violence and incited others to violence by its pursuit of persecutory legislation, by its preaching, and by other coercive measures. Mob violence was radical, merciless, and (quite often) skilfully directed. There is, secondly, the distinction between instrumental and expressive violence. Instrumental violence is violence used as a means to achieve some external end. Expressive violence is violence as the affirmation of a value or stance. Once again, in medieval England there was a full measure of both kinds. The extortion of money from Jews by torture was both instrumental *and* expressive. They were tortured in order to extract money from them; their bodies were symbolically treated as treasure chests to be prised open. The Jews were assets that could be hurt into surrendering their value. Lastly, there is the distinction between physical and discursive violence. In medieval England, discursive violence colluded in, when it did not positively incite, physical violence. Local expulsions were incited by clerics who preached against the Jews, while blood libels led directly to judicial executions. This is the critical point. England was exceptional in the completeness of its violence against Jews. The violence was both institutional and popular, both instrumental and expressive, both physical and discursive.

Defamation

In the twelfth and thirteenth centuries, Anglo-Jewry was tormented with two distinct defamations. According to the first, Jews periodically trapped, tortured and then killed Christian boys 'in mockery and scorn of the Lord's passion'.[26] The earliest documented instance of this allegation was directed at the Jews of Norwich, following the death there in 1144 of a young boy named William. According to the second defamation, Jews debased the currency, principally by clipping metal from coins. In the years 1278–85, hundreds of Jews were executed for coin-clipping. While the first defamation, which came to be known as the blood libel, was without any truth, there may indeed have been some coin-clipping—particularly towards the end of the late thirteenth century, when the Jews had been driven out of legitimate moneylending into dishonesty and penury. One Jewish chronicler criticized coin-clippers and 'currency falsifiers who have led to the destruction of our brethren, the inhabitants of France and [England]'.[27] At a certain abstract level, these two defamations are connected, because each conceives of Jews as enemies of Christians, bleeders of Gentile bodies or of the Gentile body politic. To the chronicler Matthew Paris (*c.*1200–59), the murders and the frauds were but different aspects of a single Jewish criminality.[28]

Beginning in Norwich, and with what must then have appeared to the Jews a bewildering rapidity, one terrifying instance followed another— these perplexing, fantastical allegations of child murder. They could not have been anticipated; how could they have been adequately resisted? The Jews tried denials; there was also some manoeuvring on jurisdiction.

The learned defences—Jewish law prohibits murder, prudence advises against it, etc.—only came many centuries later. Two disasters loomed largest in this particular history: the Norwich blood libel, both because it was the first and because it was itself written up in a work with distinct literary properties, and the Lincoln blood libel, both because it took so many Jewish lives and because it was written up in so many subsequent works of literature (at first, by express reference, and later, by general character). But there were many others both between 1144 and 1255, and then in the short interval between Lincoln and the Expulsion. With perhaps one exception, all the early reports of the incidence of the blood libel in medieval England assume the truth of the allegations against the Jews.

Let me begin with Norwich, drawing mainly on *The Life and Miracles of St William of Norwich* (*c.*1173), a hagiographical work written by Thomas of Monmouth, a monk at the Norwich Benedictine monastery. On 24 March, the eve of Easter 1144, in the long chaos of Stephen's reign, a body was discovered in a wood just outside this provincial town. (On one account, the body was hung on a tree by a thin flaxen cord; on another account, it was buried.)[29] It was the corpse of one William, a young apprentice, about twelve years old. It may be that he lost consciousness during a fit, and was taken for dead by his relatives,[30] or it may be that he died in some other set of circumstances—it is impossible to say.[31] In the immediate aftermath of the discovery of his remains, the priest Godwin Sturt, William's uncle, accused the Jews of murder. The accusation was made at a meeting of the diocesan synod, presided over by Bishop Eborard. The evidence of cruci- fixion, Sturt told the clerics, was plain on the boy's body. As further proof, he added, there were his wife's visions and the fact that crucifying children is 'what the Jews are obligated to do'. He proposed trial by ordeal. The Jews, he said, should be required to submit to some physically dangerous test— immersion in water, say, or the holding of hot coals. This would establish their guilt or innocence of the charge, because of the principle that God protects the innocent. In response, the bishop ordered the Jews to appear to answer the charge but they refused and successfully sought the sheriff's protection. The bishop was told that he lacked jurisdiction to try the case and the trial was then adjourned, no doubt to the immense dissatisfaction of everyone but the Jews themselves.

And that was it for a few years, until ruffians in the service of a local knight, Sir Simon de Novers, killed Eleazer, a Norwich Jew to whom Sir Simon was indebted. They lured him into the forest, fell upon him, and left his body exposed to dogs and birds. (Thomas says that it was in Eleazer's house that William was killed, and that this second death was the working out of divine justice.) The Jews complained to the king, and he heard the case in Norwich. In Thomas's 'imaginary sketch of the trial', the Jews first addressed the king, and then Eborard's successor, Bishop Turbe, spoke for the defence. He denied the charge. Unknown thieves killed Eleazer, and it was just bad luck that the knight's man happened to be there at the time (evidently only one of the ruffians was in court). In any event, 'we Christians ought not to have been called upon to reply to an accusation of this kind from the Jews, before they themselves were purged of the murder of one of us, a Christian'. It was only because of the sheriff's intervention, he continued, that 'the Christians were unable to have justice executed upon them'. He called for a trial of the Jews for the murder of William. The king adjourned the matter to the next council of clergy and barons in London. Everyone travelled down there, Turbe and his retinue no doubt full of eager anticipation, the Jews, fearful for their lives. But once again, there was no resolution. The king addresses Turbe: 'My Lord, we have been fatigued by a good deal of discourse today, and have yet some business which keeps us. We are unable to give the requisite attention to so weighty a matter . . . Let us therefore defer the case to another season . . .' For Thomas, it is clear: the king and all his counsellors have been bribed by the Jews, 'that most crafty and avaricious race'.[32]

There were thus two abortive trials. But then Thomas began his investigations, eventually writing a work that in effect put the Norwich Jews on trial for a third time. And on this occasion, they did not escape condemnation. At first, Thomas encountered some opposition to his campaign. Though Bishop Turbe was an ally, Thomas's prior, Elias, was sceptical of the martyrdom story. Turbe was Elias's predecessor as prior. When he became bishop in 1146, it is likely that Elias was elected his successor as prior with the support of those monks sceptical of the William story.[33] Thomas's partisanship divided the monastery. In the end, however, Thomas, Turbe, and their supporters prevailed. The campaign took on momentum: new supporters were acquired, new miracles were reported, and Thomas had further visions. At one point, he announced that the boy's remains were to be moved to a worthier spot; Elias, ill by now and under pressure from Turbe, reluctantly agreed. The new prior, Richard de Ferrariis, elected following Elias's death, was an ardent advocate of William's martyrdom.[34] Though the blood libel did not return to Norwich, stories about religiously motivated Jewish criminality persisted there.[35] Well over a hundred years later, Jews were prosecuted as part of a gang of church robbers, and it was alleged that they had broken open a pyx (a container in which wafers for the Eucharist are kept), and deliberately crushed underfoot the Host.[36] The cult of William itself persisted, especially in East Anglia.[37]

The next instance was in Gloucester in 1168. A young boy, Harold, 'is said to have been carried away secretly by Jews, in the opinion of many', reports the chronicler, cautiously.[38] The story was that all the Jews of England assembled in Gloucester as if to celebrate a circumcision, but in fact to abduct a Christian child, and torture him to death. It was said that they kidnapped him on 21 February, and killed him on 17 March. The body was discovered floating in the Severn River. While there was no witness to the circumstances of death, and no Jew confessed to it, 'the whole convent of monks of Gloucester, and almost all the citizens of that city, and innumerable persons coming to the spectacle'[39] saw marks on the body that were taken to be indicative of ritual murder. By his careful account, the chronicler both affirmed the truth of the libel and provided the grounds for doubting it, perhaps because he himself was drawing on an earlier chronicle for the story.[40]

In 1181, there was an accusation against the Jews of Bury St Edmunds. The alleged events were related a few years later in the prosaic Jocelin of Brakelond's *Chronicle of the Abbey of Bury St Edmunds* (1202):

> While the Abbacy was vacant, Augustine, archbishop of Norway, stayed here in the abbot's lodgings, as the king had allowed him 10s a day from the abbot's income. He was very influential in obtaining our free election, testifying in our favour and speaking out publicly before the king from his own experience of us. It was at this time also that the saintly boy Robert was martyred and was buried in our church: many signs and wonders were performed among the people, as I have recorded elsewhere.[41]

While it is true that Jocelin wrote a separate account of Robert (which is now lost), and while it is also true that the *Chronicle* is concerned with the Abbey, not with St Edmunds itself, it is still noteworthy that the only reference to the boy's death takes second place within a paragraph that opens with an account of a clerical visit. There is a matter-of-factness about the conjunction 'also'. For Jocelin, the blood libel had become *established*. Some thirty-odd years after Norwich, it had already, perhaps, come to be understood as one of the everyday crimes of the Jews.

There was then something in Bristol, in or about 1183. The tale was recorded in a manuscript written some hundred years later. A Jew named Samuel, a serial murderer of Christians, it was said, crucified three boys, and then tortured and crucified a further boy, Adam. The Jew taunted him, calling him the *deus christianorum* or the *corpus dei christianorum*.[42] And then Adam called out in Hebrew, in his agony, 'I am the God of Abraham, the God of Isaac, the God of Jacob, whom thou hast for a fourth time nailed to a cross.' This miracle moved Samuel's wife to confess her complicity in these atrocities, and she and her son announced that they wished to convert. Samuel thereupon killed them too.[43] This fantastical, allegedly true story parallels more avowedly exemplary tales circulating at the time, pitting unregenerate Jewish fathers against wives and sons who would ultimately convert to Christianity. The blood libel was, among other things, a gendered discourse.[44]

It was said that in Winchester, in 1192, a young boy who had recently arrived with a friend from France was murdered at Passover by his Jewish employer. The main account of the libel is in the *Chronicle* of Richard of Devizes (*fl.* late twelfth century), a monk at St Swithens.[45] There is also a record of expenses paid for escorting the Jews of Winchester to trial at Westminster.[46] The boy disappeared, and was never traced—probably because he went back home to France, though his friend may have murdered him and hidden the body. It was this friend who accused the Jews, claiming that a French Jew had conspired with their Jewish employer in Winchester to crucify the lad. The local authorities prosecuted the employer, but he denied the charge and was acquitted at trial—as a result of a bribe, Richard claims.

In 1202, there were incidents in Lincoln and Bedford. In Lincoln, the Jews were suspected of murder, when a child's body was found just outside the walls of the city, but nothing was done.[47] In Bedford, a Jew was accused of emasculating and killing a boy. The rumour was that Jews first circumcise the children they intend to crucify, so that they more closely resemble Jesus. But this Jew was tried before a jury and acquitted.[48]

In 1225 and 1232, Winchester's Jews were accused of various murders.[49] In one, the child was found alive; in another, two of the five Jewish defendants were convicted; in the third, the mother was taken into custody pending trial (or fled the city, in another version).[50] In this last case, the finders of the body alleged that it had been dismembered, castrated, and its eyes and heart plucked out. The sheriff imprisoned the city's entire Jewish population, releasing them only upon payment of a 20 mark fine.

In 1230, three Jews in Norwich were accused of having circumcised the five-year old son of a Christian physician. It was said that they did so in contempt of Christ and the Crucifixion; in another version of the story, they were intending to crucify him at Easter.[51] The child was possibly the son of a converted Jew, and had been reclaimed by the community.[52] They were convicted and executed several years later, in 1240. Their property was forfeit to the Crown. In 1235, Norwich Jews were set upon in the street; houses were set on fire; Jewish property was plundered. The attacks, it is thought, were prompted by the continuing scandal of the affair.

Then in London, on 1 August 1244, in an account given by Matthew Paris,[53] a boy's unburied body was found in a London cemetery. An inscription, written in Hebrew characters, was found on his arms and legs and under his chest. Converted Jews, housed at the nearby *Domus Conversum*, were summoned to translate the words. After some delay, during which time they were perhaps considering their options, they claimed to be able to make out the names of the boy's parents, and the statement that he had been sold to the Jews. It was thought by the gathering crowd that the boy had been killed by the Jews 'as a taunt and insult to Jesus Christ'—either crucified, or tortured to death. They reached this view, comments Paris, 'not without reason'. Those involved in the affair said that Jews did indeed sometimes perpetrate such deeds. The London Jews who had attracted suspicion in the matter 'suddenly and clandestinely took to flight, and never returned'. The canons of St Paul's hurried the body away, burying it near the great altar in the church. The Anglo-Jewish community was fined the immense sum of 60,000 marks in respect of this alleged crime.

And then in 1255 the blood libel came to Lincoln. Of the four sources for the affair, Matthew Paris gives the fullest account, though the other sources contradict him in places. Hugh, an eight or nine-year old child, disappeared on 31 July. It was said that he had been enticed away by the Jews, and then tortured, crucified, killed, and lastly disembowelled by them ('for the purpose of their magic arts'). The crime was committed by the common consent, it was further said, of all the Jews of England;[54] a council of Jews had passed sentence on the boy, in parody of a judicial process, an innocent indicted by criminals. When the child was at last dead, the Jews threw his body into a stream. But the stream threw him back onto dry land, and so they buried him instead. By morning, however, the body had reappeared on the ground's surface. In despair, and fearing discovery, they tipped the body down a well. But the well became illuminated with a bright light, a

sweet smell pervaded the place, and the body floated upwards. After the boy
had been missing for some days, the mother began 'diligently' to search for
him. Local people reported that the boy had been seen playing with some
Jewish boys and had gone into a Jew's house. The body was discovered on
29 August in or near a property belonging to a Jew named Jopin. He
incriminated his fellow Jews (it would be wrong to write 'confessed'), on
being told that his life would thereby be spared. But Henry III, on visiting
Lincoln, ordered Jopin's execution, and had ninety-one of Lincoln's Jews
sent to London, where eighteen were executed. These were the Jews who
had refused to submit to the verdict of a Christian jury. A trial of the others
followed, and they were all condemned to death. (Richard of Cornwall later
intervened and had them released.) Henry III was the first monarch to have
had Jews executed for ritual murder.[55]

(This calumny against Lincoln's Jews persisted into the twentieth century. In 1911, a brochure written by a local author purported to identify the
house in which Hugh's murder took place and the well into which his body
was thrown after his crucifixion.[56] The author acknowledged that doubts
have been expressed about the murder, and cites 'the great architect' A. W.
Pugin to settle the matter: 'there are no reasonable grounds for disbelieving
any portion of the history. The Jews are well known to have perpetrated
similar atrocities at various periods, and as a complete refutation of modern
calumnies the body of the blessed Hugh...was found a few years since,
adjacent to the place where the shrine formerly stood.'[57] The author added,
'if we acquit the Jews, we at once charge their accusers with a most
barbarous judicial crime'. In 1928, public discussion prompted by a council
decision to demolish the house but preserve the well led a local workman to
disclose that he had built the well only a few years earlier.[58] The plaque at
Lincoln Cathedral commemorating Hugh's death was not removed until
1959.)[59]

The blood libel returned to London at some time in the late 1260s. The
libel is mentioned in some correspondence between Edward I and his
justices. The king told them that the London Jews were insisting upon
their acquittal of charges in connection with the death of a child some
years earlier, during Henry III's reign. If they are correct, the king added,
the judges should not trouble with the matter. But the judges replied that a
crime had indeed been committed. The Jews crucified him 'in offence of the
name of Jesus Christ and against the peace of the realm'. The king responded
that he wished to consult the judges about this 'detestable...deed',[60] and

that they should do nothing further against the Jews for the time being. It has been suggested that these exchanges may have been a contrivance by Edward to extort money from the Anglo-Jewish community.[61]

The last recorded blood libel in medieval England was in Northampton, some time between 1277 and 1279. It was rumoured that on Good Friday, the Jews crucified, but failed to kill, a young boy. In consequence, many Jews were dragged through the streets, and then hanged in London. For well over one hundred years, then, that Jews killed Christian children was the common belief. It was, as the legal historian Maitland put it, 'the mere "common form" charge against the Jews'.[62]

This final blood-libel allegation in medieval England coincided with the bloodiest of all state acts against the Jews, the prosecution of Jews for coin-clipping offences—what have become known as the 'coin-clipping massacres'—in the late 1270s. The main offences against coinage were clipping and counterfeiting; there were related offences, such as exchanging specie or coin at any place other than an official exchange. There was an increasing incidence of these offences in the thirteenth century, and no doubt among the offenders there were Jews[63] as well as Christians (sometimes, indeed, they worked together).[64] The 1275 statute had contributed to this criminal conduct, by making it very difficult for Jews to earn livelihoods lawfully. The Jews were far from being the major offenders, as the sustained post-Expulsion coin-clipping activities confirm.[65] Though many convictions were secured on inadequate, perjured evidence,[66] the exceptional,[67] persecutory character of the coin-clipping prosecutions of Jews is best demonstrated by comparative execution figures. In the period 1278–9, while there were more Christian convicted defendants than Jewish ones (the ratio was about 5:4), ten times the number of Jewish men and women were executed than Christians.[68] Across a longer period, the second half of the thirteenth century, Christian convicted defendants outnumbered Jewish ones by more than two to one, but the execution ratio was about three Jews for every Christian.[69] This is in part because of the inherent bias of the criminal justice system[70] and in part because coinage prosecutions were often pursued against Jews as a judicial means of confiscating their wealth—it appears that practically all heads of Jewish households were imprisoned for several months in the late 1270s on suspicion of having committed coinage offences.[71] The judges hearing coinage cases were also instructed to investigate Jews' blasphemies, thereby giving an extra, prejudicial charge to the proceedings against Jewish defendants.[72] Opportunists were able to extort money from Jews by threatening to report them to the authorities for coinage offences (even when none had been committed). The arrests and prosecutions encouraged popular, non-judicial acts of violence against Jews which sheriffs belatedly were ordered to suppress.[73] In summary, during this brief period perhaps as many as half the country's adult Jewish males were executed—the greatest massacre of Jews in English history.

As with so many aspects of English anti-Semitism, these two libels have an exemplary significance. The blood libel is the paradigmatic instance of a total fabrication;[74] the coin-clipping libel is a similarly paradigmatic instance of a prejudicially formulated partial truth. The more sophisticated anti-Semite attacks Jews by deploying partial truths rather than fabrications.[75] This makes him a more accomplished, more circumspect, liar; both fabrications and partial truths are falsehoods. The fabrication is usually some fantastic lie, deriving from received understandings of Jews, Jewish history, and/or Judaism. The partial truth is a charge against the Jews, or a representative fraction of them, that has some foundation in fact, but is characterized by overstatement, suppression, 'singling-out', and malice. These are the falsifying elements. *Overstatement*, because the charge will exaggerate the numbers of Jews committing the alleged offence, and/or the relevance of their Jewish character, and/or its gravity—the negligent is taken to be the intentional, the individual becomes the collective, and so on. *Suppression*, because any material that might explain or contextualize the offence will be withheld. *Singling-out*, because special attention will be paid to the Jews for reasons unrelated to objective need. Action will be urged against Jews that will be said to be more pressing than in relation to any other group—but for no good reason. A 'double-standard' will be applied. *Malice*, in that the person making the charge is already predisposed to be hostile to Jews, and uses the charge both to express this hostility and persuade others that it is justified. Anti-Semitic partial-truths are thus often merely qualified versions of anti-Semitic fabrications. It follows that they are not to be defended by reference to some notional 'rational kernel'.[76]

In the late medieval and early modern period, the Talmud and, in modern times, Israel and the Zionist project have been attacked with both fabrications and partial truths. It was said of the Talmud that it imposes on Jews the duty to kill Christian children. This is simply untrue; it is a fabrication. It was also said that the Talmud contains grossly anthropomorphic accounts of God.[77] This is a partial truth, in that there *are* anthropomorphic accounts, but the correct way to read them is midrashically, that is to say as passages that require a specific kind of interpretation, transformative of their meaning,[78] or as accounts intended for readers incapable of abstract thought (in accordance with the principle of accommodation, that is 'the Scriptures speak the language of man').[79] As for today's anti-Semitic anti-Zionism, it deploys both fabrications and partial truths. It is a *fabrication* that Zionism is an instrument of the Jewish conspiracy to take control of the world, while it is a *partial truth* that there is an Israel lobby in the United States that is influential in formulating aspects of US foreign policy. Partial truths do not cause anti-Semitism, they are windfalls for anti-Semites.[80] To think otherwise is fundamentally to misunderstand anti-Semitism.

State violence, mob violence

England's Jews were injured or killed in pursuit of taxes and fines *by* the state; they were also injured or killed by debtors as agents *of* the state. They were injured or killed by malcontents for the offence of murdering Christ or for no offence at all, simply for the pleasure killing gave to the perpetrators. The London community and most provincial communities were exposed to assault, murder, and massacre. Few recovered—though curiously one that did was York, the place of the most infamous massacre of all.

There were four major episodes of violence against Jews in medieval England: the massacres of 1189–90 (discussed below), the Lincoln blood-libel trial of 1255 (discussed above), the Barons' War of 1263–7 (also discussed below), and the coin-clipping massacres of 1278–9 (also discussed above). The violence was not, however, limited to these episodes. For example, in 1215, during a period of civil war, London was occupied, and the houses in the Jewry were demolished to repair the city walls. In 1275, a mixed band of men and women broke into some Bristol Jews' homes, robbing and injuring them and their families, and then setting fire to the entire Jewry. The perpetrators escaped punishment.[81] Violence also usually accompanied the Crown's exercises in extortion. In order to recover the enormous sum the Jews were ordered to pay by John in 1210 (the so-called 'Bristol tallage'), all the Jews of the kingdom were arrested, and their contracts seized and investigated. The houses of some Jewish debtors were demolished to realize value in building materials. Other Jews were prosecuted for concealing assets, and some were hanged. Against one recalcitrant Jew, John ordered the daily forced extraction of a tooth, until he paid the sum demanded of him.[82] (The story of the Bristol Jew was still being told in the nineteenth century.)[83] Even the poorest Jews had to pay a levy of 40 shillings or else leave the kingdom.[84] So many Jews left that one chronicler writes of a general expulsion.[85] A further inquiry into concealment of assets followed three years later, in 1213. Jews were imprisoned often at great distances from their communities—the Hampshire Jews were sent to Bristol, the Bristol Jews, to London. Houses were confiscated and given to royal favourites. During the 1240 census there were further arrests and the imprisonment of whole families for non- or partial payment of their share of a 20,000-mark tallage. In 1244, in addition to the blood-libel fine, there was a minor levy of 4,000 marks so that Henry III could repay a loan to Italian merchants, accompanied by the threat that the wealthiest Jews would be sent overseas to Ireland. Many Jews sent their families into hiding, and as punishment, were outlawed and their property confiscated. In 1254, the king demanded the immediate payment of 8,000 marks 'on pain of being hanged'.[86]

Throughout the history of this first Anglo-Jewish community, neither Jewish life nor Jewish property was ever wholly secure from attack. And from 1181, by virtue of the Assize of Arms, Jews were forbidden to wear weapons—which made them even more vulnerable.[87] Even their most commonplace, least consequential, of social encounters with Christians were freighted with danger for Jews.[88]

During the massacres of 1189–90, mobs slaughtered very many Jews, in London and in almost all of the provincial communities. These anti-Semitic riots were the first riots against Jews instigated by local populations.[89] The massacres on the Continent, by contrast, tended to be instigated by non-locals (that is, Crusaders), and then executed jointly with the local population.[90] Though the English mobs were unlike the 'locust bands'[91] of the Crusades, people from out of town sometimes supplemented them; in the case of York, country-dwellers joined the young men from the city itself. These English mobs were doubtless moved, in however degraded a manner, by broad enthusiasm for the Crusades. One imagines them, robbing, raping, burning, and killing—all the time, self-righteously. Measures taken to punish the persecutors of Jews were unpopular. The criminals themselves often could not be identified. Local people of means were fined, but by reference to their wealth rather than the degree of their culpability.

The London massacre was known as the 'coronation riot' because it began on 3 September 1189, the day of Richard I's coronation. He had forbidden the Jews from entering the precincts of the church where he was to be crowned, or the palace where the coronation banquet was to be held. They came anyway, and waited at the palace gates with gifts for the king. A crowd began to abuse them, encouraged by the king's prohibition and affecting indignation at the Jews' presumption. First, there were blows, and then stones and sticks. The Jews attempted to flee. Some were then clubbed to death; others were trampled to death. One chronicler reports 'much blood was shed'; another, that 'thirty men [were] slain and others... slew themselves and their children'.[92] Two of York's most prominent Jews, Josce and Benedict, were present. Josce escaped, but Benedict was not so fortunate. Repeatedly assaulted, he was dragged half-dead to a church where he was forcibly baptized. The chronicler, William of Newbury, continues: 'In the meantime a pleasing rumour spread with incredible rapidity through all London, namely that the king had ordered all the Jews to be exterminated.'[93]

A mob, made up of local people and visitors from the provinces, 'breathing slaughter and spoil against the people by God's judgment hated by all',[94] went searching for Jews to kill. The London Jews fled back to their homes, and the provincial Jews with them. The mob surrounded the houses, making repeated attempts to break in, but without success. As the sun was setting; the mob, despairing of ever getting into the houses, set fire to the roofs. The fire soon spread, killing Jews and Christian householders alike. The Jews who ran out of their homes were killed by the mob. Then the looting began, with fighting breaking out within the mob, as they squabbled over ownership of the Jews' goods. There was some reckoning with the perpetrators of these crimes. Three were hanged, two for starting a fire that burned down a Christian's house, and one for robbing a Christian. But there were too many of them, and a number were related to the nobles dining with the king at the banquet.

The first attack outside London was at Lynn in January 1190. Foreign traders joined the mob. There were many fatalities; there was also much looting. The Jewry was burned to the ground. The authorities did not intervene. News of the massacre spread through East Anglia. On 6 February, all Norwich's Jews, other than those who had fled to the castle, were slaughtered. The community never recovered. At the Lenten Fair in Stamford, 7 March, young Crusaders, 'heaven-fearing wolves',[95] murdered all the town's Jews. On Palm Sunday, fifty-seven members of the Jewish community living in Bury St Edmund's were murdered. In Lincoln the Jews were luckier. Most were able to escape to the castle. In Dunstable, the entire community submitted to baptism in order to escape massacre. As with other pogroms in Jewish history, this murderous violence was socially sanctioned. The moral economy of medieval England evidently allowed for the murder of Jews; the violence did not appear to have shocked people; it no doubt even prompted drunken celebration; Jews were killed with gusto; it would seem that on such occasions everyone was very much at their ease with what they were doing.[96]

The York massacre was a protracted affair. It was also the only provincial massacre engineered by a conspiracy.[97] Among the conspirators, there were nobles who owed money to the Jews, there were some who had lost their lands to the Jews, and there were some who were about to join the Crusade. They led a hunting crowd, thirsty for blood and loot.[98] They went at night to Benedict's house, killing his widow, his children, and the other Jews living there. (It would seem that Benedict himself had by then died of the injuries sustained in London.)[99] The lay leader of the community, Josce, who must have been terrified, begged the warden of the castle for protection. He agreed, and so all the Jewish families in the city came, many bringing everything they had in cash and portable valuables. Later that day, the warden returned to the castle, only to be denied entry by the terrified Jews. The warden, in a fury, complained to the sheriff, who happened to be in York with a large body of county soldiers. The Jews, he said, have cheated me out of my castle. Troops were despatched to lay siege to the castle; the local people were summonsed for assistance. They answered his call with such immoderate alacrity that he began to have second thoughts, but it was too late. The siege lasted several days. The Jews, without food or arms, were in a desperate position. Engines to storm the castle were brought into position. During the night before the final assault, the besiegers were unusually quiet, contemplating the morning's victory. The Jews debated what they should do. They made a fire of their possessions. And then they began to kill themselves. Josce killed his wife, Anna, and their two sons. The rabbi then killed Josce, 'so that he might be more honoured than the rest',[100] and the other Jews who were party to the plan followed suit. The rabbi himself killed 60 of the 150 Jewish men and women in the tower. At daybreak, the surviving Jews appeared at the gates and on the ramparts of the tower, and asked for clemency. They offered to submit to baptism and they defamed the dead. They were encouraged out with false promises, and then murdered. The conspirators then headed for York Minster. They seized the bonds deposited there, records of their indebtedness, and burned them in the middle of the cathedral. They then dispersed, some overseas to join the Third Crusade, others, into the countryside or Scotland.[101]

The 1189–90 riots took the government by surprise; it was inexperienced in dealing with such phenomena. Richard I sent messengers throughout England ordering that the Jews should be left in peace, but it was not enough. The murders in York enraged the king (says William of Newbury) 'both for the insult to his royal majesty and for the great loss to the treasury'.[102] York castle was badly damaged. Moreover, there was substantial loss of revenue following the destruction of the bonds evidencing the debts owed to the Jews. Popular violence could get out of hand. The riots were also an affront to the monarch's authority. Assaults on Jews were an assault on the king, partly because they were the king's property, and partly because he guaranteed their protection. It thereafter became necessary, from time to time, for the king to remind his subjects of that fact. In July 1204, for example, King John wrote to the mayor of London. You know the Jews are under our special protection, he said. How then is it that you allow harm to be done to them? It is clearly against the peace of the realm. It is only in London that Jews are not left in peace. If any attempt is made to do them harm, you must come to their aid with an armed force. The discreet ought to check the folly of the unwise. 'We say this for our Jews and for our peace, for if we have granted our peace to anyone it should be observed inviolably.'[103]

But this peace could not be guaranteed to the Jews when civil war withdrew the protection of the king's peace from all his subjects. The Jews suffered with the rest of the population during the Barons' Wars of 1263–7, and they also suffered as Jews. The principal agent of their persecution was Simon de Montfort, Earl of Leicester (1208–65). His first act as lord of Leicester was to expel its Jews (1231–2), which was approved by Robert Grosseteste (c.1170–1253), then archdeacon of Leicester.[104] De Montfort himself characterized the Expulsion as a demonstration of concern for the townspeople and of his own piety. In Easter week 1264, he occupied London, encouraging the massacre and plundering of its Jewish population. Very many Jews, perhaps in the order of 500, are said to have died. His supporters also sacked the Jewries of Canterbury, Winchester, and Northampton, confronting Jewish women (in particular) with the choice of death or conversion.[105] Cecil Roth writes of de Montfort's 'personal religious prejudice' and his 'extreme anti-Jewish bias', which was aggravated by his sense that the Jews were an instrument of royal power, and his own indebtedness to them.[106] The Jews suffered in consequence of what one of de Montfort's biographers describes as the earl's 'religious zealotry' *and* his 'acquisitive eye for his own advantage'.[107] His parents also set him early examples. His father was a persecutor of Jews and Albigensians in Provence; his mother gave the Jews of Toulouse the choice of baptism or death.[108] Evesham Abbey, where his remains were buried, became the centre of a pilgrimage. Two hundred miracles allegedly occurred within a few years of his death.

His fellow rebels shared this hostility to the Jews as the king's agents. During the period of the Revolt, Gilbert de Clare, the Earl of Gloucester, captured Canterbury and sacked the Jews' quarter, killing or expelling almost the entire Jewish population of the city. Jews in Lincoln and Cambridge were also massacred. In Bedford, Cambridge, Canterbury, Bristol, and elsewhere, the *archae* were stolen.[109] In Bristol, de Montfort's men killed two Jews when sacking the city's Jewry.[110] In Lincoln, the rebels stormed the synagogue, tearing up the Torah scrolls.[111] In their struggle for the enlargement of their own liberties, the Barons were enthusiastic circumscribers of the liberties of the Jews. Even before the Revolt, there had been serious outbreaks of violence against the Jews. In February 1262, the Earl of Derby massacred the Jews of Worcester and destroyed the financial records stored in the city registry. Though the Revolt ended with the barons' defeat at Evesham and the death of de Montfort, there was some guerrilla warfare thereafter, with Jews as the particular target of the barons' violence.[112]

State extortion

In medieval England, as elsewhere and in other times, there were institutions and individuals who wished to finance projects that required capital they themselves did not possess. These individuals and institutions often found it difficult to go to fellow-Christians (though there were money lenders among them), because the Church forbad lending money at interest. So instead they tended to go to Jews ready to finance their projects and charge them interest on the money that they advanced. This had immense, calamitous consequences for the reputation of Jews in general. It fostered the misconception that the typical Jewish milieu is a commercial one, and that Judaism itself is especially hospitable to moneymaking.[113]

Notwithstanding that theological opinion was unanimous on the iniquity of payment merely for the act of lending,[114] successive English kings happily appropriated much of the profit made by the Jews on these transactions. The king was commonly described as the Jews' 'sleeping partner' or even as the 'arch-usurer of the kingdom'.[115] The Jews, for their part, became known as the 'royal milch-cow'. The history of the Jews' relations with the Crown is thus the history of the exploitation of the Jews by the Crown.

The Crown's financial dealings with the Jews fell into three periods.

Period One: as borrower, c.1070–1180

In a regime of diverse lenders, Jews and Christians, the Jews played their part. But when the Christian lenders disappeared, and other lines of credit dried up, leaving only the Jews, the Crown's practice of borrowing from them, rather than just taking from them, lost its point. By about 1164, the king had turned from Christian to Jewish moneylenders, and by 1179 or 1180, he had ceased to borrow from them, and instead simply took money as and when he wished.[116] If the Jews were already the property of the king, to borrow from them was to borrow from oneself. So a gap opened up. The Jews *lent* as before to individuals and institutions, but *gave* to the king.[117] This defined the second and longest period, from the mid-twelfth through to the late thirteenth century.

Period Two: as revenue-raiser, c.1180–1275

In this period, Jews comprised England's main source of credit.[118] The Crown's revenue-raising measures were heterogeneous and inventive. The Jews were repeatedly and oppressively taxed, subject to special levies and fines, and their commercial transactions routinely and corruptly undone by royal commutations, or appropriated to royal advantage. At the same time, legal constraints were placed incrementally on Jewish lending. The Crown squandered the Jews as a resource by grabbing their wealth greedily, incontinently. These exactions were accompanied by the fiercest and most terrifying of coercions, including imprisonment, torture, mutilation, and expulsion.[119] In the middle decades of the thirteenth century the Crown moved from sustainable, long-term participation in the Jews' financial activities, to short-termist exploitation of the Jews, without regard to their survival as a community. The majority of Jews was impoverished; the wealthier minority lost the greater part of their working capital. Communal life became unsustainable; and because the formerly wealthy Jews could no longer support themselves, the charitable institutions through which they supported the poor of the community collapsed. The relationship of Jewish creditors with their Christian debtors and with the state foundered through a combination of competition, over-exploitation, and persecution. This spelled the end of the community.

There are several specifically anti-Semitic aspects to this second period. The Jews were kept under exceptional, close surveillance, and informing was encouraged; the incidence and intensity of taxation was consistent with broader anti-Semitic trends; the Jews were the unprotected victims of corrupt practices.

The efficient taxing of the Jews required the keeping of complete records of their transactions, and the events of York in 1190 demonstrated that this would not be possible unless the Crown ensured it. So the Ordinances of the Jews (1194) was enacted,[120] which provided for the registration of all the debts, pledges, mortgages, lands, houses, rents, and possessions of the Jews. The statute was a response to the anti-Semitic violence of 1189–90, and sought to protect the Jews' asset value to the Crown. Registries of Bonds, or *archae* ('arks'), were to be established in towns with sizeable Jewish populations. All contracts were to be made before two Jewish lawyers, two Christian lawyers, and two legal registrars. One part of the contract was to stay with the Jewish lender, and one part stored 'in the common chest'. The chest was to have three locks, one key with the Jewish lawyers, one with the Christian lawyers, and the third with the registrars. A roll containing transcripts of the contracts (or 'charters') was to be kept. Jews were to swear that all their assets (and not just their contracts) have been recorded. If any Jew knew of any other Jews who had concealed their assets, or were guilty of coin-clipping, 'he shall secretly reveal it to the Justices'. Any assets concealed, and the Jew concealing them, were to be forfeited to the king. The object of the statute was to give the Crown a complete picture of its property's property.

The burdensome taxation of the Jews was consonant with their theological status as God's rejected people. They did not deserve any better treatment; it was doing God's work to ensure that they did not prosper. Of the various means of extracting money from Jews, many were improvised, most had a surface legality, and all were confiscatory in effect. 'Tallages', the principal means of exaction, were arbitrary levies declared by the Crown and imposed on Jews. Jews were also taxed along with the Crown's other subjects, but on discriminatory terms. In 1188, for example, the Saladin Tithe (the purpose of which was to finance the proposed Crusade) fixed the Jews' contribution at one-quarter of their property, whereas for everyone else it was but one-tenth.[121] The community as a whole was repeatedly 'tallaged' in immense amounts, right up to the 1280s.[122] 'Amerciaments', were paid to secure the king's 'mercy' following conviction of some offence, or otherwise acting contrary to the king's desires (for example, lending money to men under the king's displeasure). Sums were also payable by Jews in respect of major and not-so major events in their lives. 'Reliefs' were paid by a deceased Jew's heirs to buy back from the Crown the debts owed to the deceased at his death. Estates of usurers were forfeited to the Crown, which meant that loans were bets against the life of the Jewish lender; if the loan was unpaid at the date of his death, a deal could be done with the Crown. Prison was the usual penalty for non-payment. Sometimes, the Crown would deal direct with Christian debtors of Jews, forgiving part of the debt in return for payment of the balance direct to itself.[123] The Jews were also charged with sums to maintain Jewish converts.[124] The Crown was also ready to exploit the blood libel, as we have seen. In addition to these regular methods of obtaining money, there were even more direct extortions—feudal taxes not properly payable by them,[125] and demands for money backed up by threats or sanctions. In 1168, for example, certain foreign ambassadors were loaded with presents by Henry III, who paid for them by taking the richer Jews hostage ('causing them to cross the straits'),[126] only releasing them upon payment of a ransom of 5,000 marks.

With the Jews' financial transactions under much tighter state control, the opportunities for their corrupt exploitation grew. In his *History of the Jews in England*, Cecil Roth described the operations of the senior officials in the newly established Jewish Exchequer. They imprisoned Jews in order to have them ransomed. They manipulated the Jews' taxes. They made Jews pay inflated sums for licences to reside in particular places. They interfered in transactions—by whim or for their own corrupt purpose, compelling the Jewish creditors to reduce debts or return pledges. They charged 'commissions' for the most nominal assistance, and extorted gifts in money and jewels on the slightest pretext or none at all. The Exchequer itself was alleged not to be safe from their audacity: on one occasion, when the Jews were to pay a tallage of £500, they were assessed for no less than £700, of which, however, the king only received £462.[127] On one occasion, and with reluctance, Henry III dismissed some of these officials, but restored them to their offices only two years later.

Period Three: as liquidator, c.1275–90

In 1275, the Statute of Jewry made moneylending unlawful. No future loans could be made; existing loans could no longer accumulate interest. Jews who still had some capital could trade in goods; others were expected to undertake physical labour. Though some Jews made the transition to trade, their sales and purchases were at risk under the statute as disguised financing transactions.[128] The statute made the pursuit of alternatives to moneylending difficult by prohibiting Jews from living anywhere other than in towns and cities that held chirograph chests (records of the Jews' financial transactions), prohibiting Christians from living in Jews' houses, and requiring Jews over the age of twelve to pay an annual tax of 3 pence, and Jews over the age of seven to wear a yellow felt badge—this last followed a requirement imposed on Jews in Islamic lands.[129] Jews were not allowed to contribute to any taxes payable by merchant communities in towns or cities, thereby ensuring that they could never become full members of those communities (it was a provision certain to cause resentment among the Christian merchants towards their new Jewish competitors). The Jews respectfully protested the terms of the statute to the king; there is no evidence any attention was paid to their plea.[130] Following their expulsion, Edward received at least £1,000 from the sale of Jewish-held properties. The Crown also took over the Jews' contracts, and it was only in 1326 that the last debts were written off.[131]

The Jews were denied the possibility of any viable mode of existence. The Statute of Jewry cannot be regarded as an attempt at 'integration';[132] it was not an attempt at 'radical social engineering';[133] it was not a 'well-meaning experiment'[134] or an attempt 'to re-align'[135] the Jews with Christian society. There is no evidence to support the proposition that Edward I 'made a real effort to deal with the Jewish question from the standpoint of the general needs of state and society'.[136] It is almost impossible to suppose that the framers of the legislation expected anything constructive to come of it. It required Jews to abandon their distinctive and customary livelihood, while insisting at the same time that they become more visible as Jews. Caught in the contradictory thrusts of the statute, England's Jews were not so much at risk of transformation as of extinction. This model—banning Jews from their existing occupations while blocking their access to alternative ones—re-emerged in 1930s Central and Eastern Europe.[137] In this respect, as in several others, medieval England was thus innovative and precedent-establishing in its anti-Semitism.

(This reflex of the medieval states, to extort money from the Jews whenever it found itself in straitened financial circumstances, had not altogether disappeared in the centuries between the Expulsion and the Readmission of the Jews. In 1689, Parliament sought to impose an annual tax of £100,000 on the London Jews. The war with France had to be financed, and so why not extract the money from the Jews? This reversion to the practices of the twelfth and thirteenth centuries caused great anxiety among the Jews. One wrote to an Antwerp agent that the ill will in England towards them made it impossible to continue there as a merchant. But instead of leaving, the Jews responded with a pamphlet, 'The Case of the Jews Stated'. There were too few of them, they said, to be able to afford such a levy—only twenty merchants of any substance. What is more, the effect of the tax would be to destroy the diamond trade, either by driving the Jews out of England, or by impoverishing them. They very pointedly identified their role: 'The market for diamonds in the East Indies was formerly at Goa (belonging to the Portuguese) and by the means and industry of the Jews the market has been brought to English factories, and by that means England has in a manner the sole management of that precious commodity, and all foreigners bring their monies into this kingdom to purchase the said diamonds.' Times had changed. It was a pamphlet appealing to commercial self-interest, not a petition begging for mercy. The Jews won the argument. There was no tax. The policy of attracting private capital to England and the English colonies prevailed.)[138]

The Jews thus began as lenders; they became taxpayers; and then, broken, they became candidates for expulsion. It is an open question whether the breaking of the Jewish community contributed to the financial crises of the last years of the thirteenth century.[139] The disregarding of the economic interests of the nation in the pursuit of anti-Semitic objectives had its own particular resonance in twentieth-century Europe.

Ecclesiastical oppression

In their ordinary, day-to-day lives, Jews had to contend with a certain Christian militancy, with aggressive assertions of Christian dominance.[140] There were religious processions and ceremonial entries, and there were celebrations of festivals—all opportunities for displays of political might and spiritual privilege.[141] There was occasional violence associated with these events; Christians were troubled by the possibility of Jewish mockery, and even of blasphemy. (In 1250, writes Matthew Paris, a Jew killed his wife for secretly cleaning a statue of the Virgin that he had been in the habit of defecating on.)[142] There were exemplary incidents, minatory in their general effect—in 1222, for example, a convert to Judaism, formerly a deacon, was burned at the stake.[143] There were also major outbreaks of violence, not associated with religious events, when the English bishops usually declined to intervene on the Jews' side or take steps to keep them safe. The Church did not condemn atrocities committed against Jews—the archbishop of York, for example, remained silent following the massacres in 1190.[144] To adopt language from another time, but appropriate to the twelfth and thirteenth centuries, the Church was a complicit bystander. (It did not need to be; there were bishops on the Continent who did not collude thus in violence against Jews, a kind of collusion by inaction.) There was no restraining influence exercised by the Church either on the Crown or on the mob. When Edward I asserted in the 1275 Statute that he was granting the Jews his 'peace and protection' because 'Holy Church wishes and suffers that they live and be looked after',[145] and not because he himself wished it, he was not thereby acknowledging any ecclesiastical championing of the Jews.

The very occasional rulings of the bishops against harming Jews were abstract, and unrelated to any actual threat or incident of violence against a particular community. Bishop Grosseteste, for example, merely rehearsed received Augustinian doctrine when he advised the Countess of Winchester that it was the duty of rulers to protect the Jews from being killed. They have given us their books; we may hope with St Paul that a remnant will be saved.[146] It is in Grosseteste's violent animadversions against the Jews, rather than his formulaic defence of their very limited rights, that the character of the medieval English Church is shown. The Jews, Grosseteste wrote, were guilty of murdering the Saviour of the world. God had punished them by condemning them to be wanderers, and slaves of all nations. Rulers had a duty to keep them captive, allowing them to live by the sweat of their brow. They were the descendants of Cain, cursed by God, but not to be killed. They should not be allowed lives of ease on the profits of usury. Rulers who profit from the Jews' usurious activities drink the blood of their victims; these rulers' hands and garments are steeped in blood.[147] Grosseteste made a significant contribution to that shift in Church thinking about Jews that contributed ultimately to their expulsion. Why indeed should the Jews be tolerated, asked another English cleric, Alexander of Hales (1183–1245)? Alexander was one of the giant intellects of the thirteenth-century Church, and an almost exact contemporary of Grosseteste. He regarded the Jews as blasphemers and hardly better than the pagans against whom the Church was waging war in the Holy Land.[148] It was precisely in consequence of the writings of clerics such as Grosseteste and Alexander that the Augustinian position ultimately collapsed, introducing instead perspectives on Jews in which almost everything was permitted—forcible conversion, expropriation, expulsion, slaughter.

There were exceptions, of course—Christians who 'grieved over and bewailed the sufferings of the Jews' (to quote Paris again) or were ready to assist them in times of adversity. There was, for example, a twelfth-century monk named William, who lived in the Abbey of Bury St Edmunds. He was known, writes the chronicler, as 'the father and patron of the Jews, for they enjoyed his protection'. He had also incurred on the abbey's behalf very substantial debts to them. By William's leave:

> Jews had free entrance and exit, and went everywhere throughout the monastery, wandering by the altars and round the shrine while Mass was being celebrated. Their money was deposited in our treasury, in the sacrist's custody. Even more incongruous, during the troubles [of 1173–4], their wives and children were sheltered in our pittancy.[149]

The Jews needed a place of refuge, and William gave it to them. He was among the opponents of Samson, the (in the event, successful) candidate to succeed the late Abbot Hugh. Samson was an enemy of the Jews, expelling them in 1190—a sign, remarks the chronicler, of his 'great goodness'. Samson ordered that any Christian who received Jews back or gave them lodging was to be excommunicated.[150] (The king's justices were driven to rule, in response, that Jews would be allowed back for two days to Bury St Edmund's following their expulsion, in order to recover their debts.)[151] William's actions were not, however, of the kind that cause anti-Semites to conceal, let alone cease, their attacks upon Jews. There was no *anti*-anti-Semitic opinion with which they had to contend, no pro-Jewish party,[152] no defence of the Jews that challenged the opinion that the persecutors had of themselves. Philo-Semitism was not an intellectual possibility; the exploiters of the Jews and the anti-Semites had a pretty clear run.[153]

The Church borrowed money from Jews, providing Church land and chattels as security (including vessels used in divine services, and even upon relics of the saints).[154] These transactions were regularly forbidden, and regularly undertaken. Some monasteries were also unofficial partners of Jewish financiers, and trafficked in Jewish debt until changes in the law, quite late in the thirteenth century, made this impossible.[155] In these respects, it did not materially differ from other commercial parties in medieval England; clerical and lay entrepreneurs profited alike from their dealings with Jews. But the Church also engaged in three *distinctive* ways with the Jews—as proselytizer, as legislator, and as theological adversary.

Proselytizer

Christianity is a proselytizing religion, and the Church did nothing to impede the conversion of Jews. Converts were welcomed; steps were taken to ensure that they had means of support, once they had left their communities.[156] The principle that conversion must be voluntary, however, was generally upheld in medieval England. In accordance with the received Augustinian position, the Jews were to be allowed to practise their religion. In the immediate aftermath of the London coronation riots, for example, one of the Jews forcibly converted, Benedict, recanted his conversion. Archbishop Baldwin of Canterbury, contemplating this reversion to Judaism, was contemptuous, but did not object: 'If he will not be a Christian, let him be the Devil's man.'[157] The English Church was, however, zealous in hunting out lapsed converts,[158] and was also responsible for many minor provocations towards Jewish communities—erecting crosses at their expense, threatening excommunication of friendly Christians, and so on. But as for the taking of active steps to convert Jews, a distinction must be made between the eleventh- and twelfth-century Church and the thirteenth-century Church.[159]

During the eleventh and twelfth centuries, very broadly, the established monastic orders, the Benedictines, the Cistercians, and the Augustinians undertook little proselytizing. As for the Crown, it positively opposed any conversionary activity. It had adverse economic implications, because while converts' assets were forfeit to the Crown, as Christians they were no longer able to engage in finance, and thereby generate profits to be tallaged or otherwise extracted. These perspectives changed in the thirteenth century. In this period, the Church was active against the Jews. The new orders, the

Dominicans (who arrived in England in 1221) and the Franciscans, played a leading part in this new proselytizing activity. The Dominicans tended to establish institutions in or near Jewish quarters; upon their arrival in Oxford, for example, they installed themselves in the very midst of the Jewry—a compelling assertion of Christian power.[160] Although the Dominicans and Franciscans developed a new Christian ideology that denied the Jews any space in the Christian world, and became vigorous persecutors of the Jews on the Continent,[161] their stance in thirteenth-century England towards the Jews was almost protective (one or other of the two orders interceded on the Lincoln Jews' behalf after their conviction in London)[162]—protective, that is, in the context of their conversionary activity. The Oxford Franciscan Roger Bacon (1214–92) advocated the study of Hebrew and preaching to the Jews. Many souls are lost, he wrote, because no one knows how to reason with Jews in the language in which their Scriptures were composed.[163] The friars received support at the highest level for their proselytizing. Archbishop John Peckham, 'a grim enemy of Israel',[164] was himself an active campaigner for Jewish conversion.[165] The objectives of all this conversionary activity were twofold: to secure both the salvation of individual Jewish souls *and* a uniformly Christian society.[166]

Legislator

There was a further intensification of the Church's campaign against the Jews in the latter part of the thirteenth century. In 1284, Peckham issued a decree that in London all synagogues except one should be demolished and no synagogues in private houses should be allowed.[167] Pope Honorius IV, two years later, addressed a Bull to the archbishop and his colleague at York denouncing the 'accursed and perfidious' Jews of England who have done 'unspeakable things and horrible acts to the shame of our Creator and the detriment of the catholic faith'. The study of the Talmud, a book of 'manifold abominations, falsehoods, heresies and abuses', was condemned. The English Church was instructed to take steps against the Jews. In 1287, the bishop of Exeter summoned his clergy to a synod in order to renew previous ecclesiastical enactments against the Jews, especially those of Pope Clement IV at the Synod of Vienna in 1267. Jews and Christians were not to visit each other nor join in any festivities; Christians were not to take medicine from a Jewish doctor; on Easter Day no Jew was to remain outdoors; Jews were to pay taxes to the parish clergy; the wearing of the badge of the Tables of the Law was to be strictly enforced.[168]

The principal English Church legislation against the Jews consisted of the implementation of the Third (1179) and Fourth (1215) Lateran Councils. Stephen Langton (c.1155–1228), archbishop of Canterbury, was a leading spirit at the Fourth Lateran Council[169] and was very energetic—indeed, 'over-meticulous'[170]—in implementing its provisions against the Jews.[171] England was the first European country consistently to enforce them.[172] The 1222 Council of Oxford reiterated the Lateran restrictions, with some elaborations. Similar provisions to those contained in the 1222 Oxford decrees were enacted in the canons of other synods held elsewhere in England during the thirteenth century.[173] On the Continent, Jews had to wear the badge from the age of thirteen; in England, it was seven. It was to be worn on the outermost garments, two fingers wide and four fingers long, and of a colour other than that of the garment itself.[174] Jews should not employ Christians, the Council of Oxford insisted, adding its own reason to the reasons already advanced by the Lateran Council. It is absurd, the bishops declared, for the children of the free woman (the Church) to be subservient to the children of the bondswoman (the Synagogue).[175] In this 'overheated atmosphere of widespread Jew-baiting',[176] a certain competitiveness between the bishops developed.[177] William of Blois, the bishop of Worcester, was even fiercer against the Jews than Langton, introducing many of the same anti-Jewish provisions as were contained in the Oxford decrees, but several years earlier. He also petitioned the papacy to persuade Langton to enforce against the Jews the requirement that they wear a distinguishing badge.[178] At the 1222 Canterbury Council, Langton threatened with excommunication any Christians who had any familiar dealings with Jews. They should not be spoken to; they should not be sold provisions.[179] (This was a threat that the regent, Hubert de Burgh, had to counter with one of his own, that denying Jews provisions would lead to imprisonment.)[180] In his first pastoral circular following election as bishop of Lincoln, Robert Grosseteste enjoined his archdeacons, 'as far as you are able, study to prevent the dwelling of Christians with Jews'.[181] The bishop of Worcester forbade the employing of Christian wet-nurses by Jews, or the accommodating of female Christian servants in Jewish homes.[182] The Jews were to be boycotted.[183]

In themselves, these restrictions were standard—the medieval law books were full of them.[184] What distinguished the English Church was both the vigour with which it sought to enforce them and their practice of repeatedly supplementing them with ad hoc directions to the faithful to boycott the

Jews.[185] The Jews were thus trapped in a skein of discriminatory, often humiliating, regulations. At first, these regulations were enforced somewhat patchily, and to the extent that they encroached on the Crown's jurisdiction, they were mostly repelled.[186] In the decades preceding the Expulsion, however, they were enforced with a rigour that amounted at times to something like an ecclesiastical terror. In 1275, for example, Bishop Giffard instructed the deans of Westbury and Bristol to excommunicate certain Jews of Bristol and to forbid all traffic with them.[187] (This somewhat crazy act—how could *Jews* be excommunicated?—was an indication that at that time, as against the Jews, anything was possible.) And in 1278, the bishop of Lincoln tried to arrest and excommunicate thirteen Christians for the offence of being employed by Jews. Edward added his own weight to this campaign, responding positively to requests from the bishops to take action against individual Jews. There were also blasphemy trials; in 1279, a Norwich Jew was burned at the stake.

Theological adversary

Ecclesiastical, clerical anti-Semitism was a matter of animosity, exploitation, and persecution. Though there were no public burnings of the Talmud in England (unlike in France),[188] there was probably some suppression of Jewish literature.[189] To the extent that there was a theological encounter with the Jews, it was similarly uncompromising. The position in England differed from the Continent only in the absence in England of any public disputations between Jews and Christians, save perhaps for one very unusual and very early encounter, staged by William Rufus (1087–1100), at which the king announced that if the Jews 'conquered the Christians and confuted them with open argument he would join their sect' (as was recorded by a scandalized chronicler).[190] William Rufus's remarks were exceptional in their spirit—a kind of amused and lazy tolerance of the Jews, a delight in teasing the Church's most senior clergy, a certain secularism of outlook, a conviction that piety is for clerics and not monarchs. But it would appear that the Church itself in that early period was, if not similarly indulgent, at least not as animatedly antagonistic, not so utterly disparaging and repressive, of Jews, as in the two centuries that followed.

So, for example, in Gilbert Crispin's 'Disputation of a Jew with a Christian about the Christian faith', written in the late eleventh century, and addressed to St Anselm,[191] then archbishop of Canterbury, the Jewish interlocutor is allowed to refer to Christian 'animosity' towards his co-religionists.[192] If you accept that there is a duty to follow the law, the Jew asks, then why do you persecute those who fulfil that duty? Jews are treated like dogs, beaten with sticks and pursued everywhere. Yet they do no more than observe the law given by God. What is there in reason or scripture that compels a person to believe that God can become a man? How can the figurative interpretation of the Hebrew Scriptures be defended? It is no more than an arbitrary set of readings, which could be applied with equal logic to produce many other predictions. Is not Christianity a form of idolatry? You worship images of God, 'a wretch hanging on the beam of the cross transfixed with nails—a horrible sight'. The tone is not hostile. It is, indeed, far more amicable than most medieval encounters of the sort.[193] 'The Jew', writes Crispin, 'would often come to see me as a friend, and as often as we came together we would soon get talking in a friendly spirit about the Scriptures and our faith.' His objections were 'consequent and logical'. Crispin responds at one point to his Jewish interlocutor: '[your] demands are completely reasonable and your questions are well worth posing'.[194]

The work is quite different in tone to Peter of Blois' 'Against the perfidy of the Jews',[195] written about a hundred years later (between 1194 and 1198), and addressed to the bishop of Worcester. This marked shift towards an aggressive stance appears to reflect a more general hardening of the Church's stance towards the Jews.[196] In Peter's work, the Jews are said to be inconstant and shifty, their Messiah is the Antichrist, and their father is the devil. Peter (c.1135–c.1205) was born in France, studied in Bologna and Paris, and went into Henry II's employment in about 1173. He belonged to the first generation of urban medieval intellectuals;[197] he was also one of the leading anti-Jewish controversialists of his time.[198] Among his writings is an exhortation to take part in the Third Crusade. He begins his polemic on the Jews by remarking that the bishop has 'made long and anxious complaint' that he is 'surrounded by Jews and heretics' and is 'attacked by them'. Peter has composed his treatise, he writes, to aid the bishop in his fight against them. The Jews are obdurate. There is no point in debating matters of faith with them. 'It seems to me wiser for our faith to conceal the injury done to it for the time rather than enter into discussion with a people stiff-necked and of a stubbornness truly bestial.' 'It is because of illicit and unwise discussions that the insidious growth of heresies has become so rampant.'[199] But, he adds, since you complain bitterly about not having the means to meet the arguments of these Jews and heretics, and thus are unable to 'evade their machinations, I will not keep back from you what I know'. It would seem, however, that Peter rarely exercised restraint on the subject of the Jews—I will return to him later on in this chapter. Other contributors to this genre expressed similar caution about entering into debate with Jews.[200]

There was, of course, no engagement with Judaism, either in the sense of any openness to persuasion, any assumption of risk in the encounter, or in the sense of recognizing Judaism as a living religion. It was taken at most as a challenge to Christianity comparable to radical scepticism in epistemology— that is, without integrity but potentially subversive, and thus a test for the philosophically complacent. These and other similar works written in the twelfth century purported to respond to contemporary attacks on the Christian faith. They were written in the idiom of defence; the authors represented themselves as controversialists coming to the aid of an embattled Church. But there is little reason to suppose that 'Jews and heretics' truly assailed Christians. The increasing bitterness of tone in this controversial literature is to be attributed more to a general intensification of anti-Semitism rather than to any specific resentment at Jewish critiques (of which there were precisely none, it would appear).[201] In this respect, the relevant factors comprise the growing authority and power of the Church, the Crusades, the belief that the Jews were intriguing against Christendom and that the Talmud blasphemed against Christ, and the emergence of popular religious movements.[202] There may also have been a certain proselytizing purpose in some of these works, and a consequent impatience at the rate of success.[203]

The treatment of Judaism in the work of English clerics rarely rises above the trite or formulaic. The greatest biblical scholar of the later twelfth century,[204] Stephen Langton, in a typical (if extreme) supersessionist gloss, interpreted Jacob's dispossession of Esau as Christianity's dispossession of Judaism. 'When Esau weeps, he announces the distress of the Jewish people at the end of the world; they will lament because they have lost the blessing of favour... Or even: the Jewish people lament at seeing the Christian people preferred over them.'[205] The writings of Alexander Nequam (1157–1217) may be taken as representative. Nequam taught at Oxford, was elected abbot of Cirencester in 1213, and attended the Fourth Lateran Council in 1215. He knew some Hebrew, and writes of his exchanges with *litteratores hebrei*. There are five quotations from the Talmud in his homiletic writings, all dismissive, disparaging. He records that he found the Talmudic glosses on the 'Song of Songs' undeveloped and 'infantile', because they failed to recognize the presence in the text of teachings about Christ and the

Church.[206] The Jews were often thus chastised for missing the true—that is, Christological—meaning of their sacred texts.[207] Or consider the work of Robert Grosseteste. He was a person of considerable learning, and made great contributions to medieval thought and culture. He was known both as a student of Hebrew and as an enemy of the Jews.[208] He was the author of conventionally supersessionist texts on the Ten Commandments,[209] on the subject of the expiry of the law (*De cessatione legalium*), and on St Paul's letter to the Galatians.[210] Nothing of Jewish law survives Christ, he writes, bar its moral content. His writings indicate some interest in the 'Judaizing' tendencies in the early Church, but none at all in Judaism. These are not polemicizing works; Grosseteste is not writing as a controversialist.[211]

Crown and Church

There was a complex convergence between Church and Crown with regard to Jewish affairs, one that may be said ultimately to have suffocated the Jews. The Crown's financial stance in relation to the Jews changed, and as it did so, it ceased to conflict with the Church's conversionary strategy. The Crown added its own influence to the Church's newly energetic conversionary activities. The Crown gradually came to support and even to replicate Church legislation against the Jews.

Conversionary and taxing activities converged in the mid-century on what might, in retrospect at least, be seen as a common liquidation strategy. The Church sought the religious liquidation of the Jewish community, while the Crown sought its financial liquidation. If the Jews were no longer being regarded as a 'going concern'—no longer, that is, a long-term investment—then there no longer needed to be a tension between the Crown's financial interests and the Church's conversionary interests. Since Jewish finance was doomed anyway, conversion, with its immediate financial benefit of forfeiture of assets, sacrificed nothing of value to the Crown. This is apparent in the conduct of Henry III, who was as sentimental about conversion as he was ruthless about taxation. Between 1240 and 1255 he collected more than £70,000 from the Jews, thereby destroying an entire generation of lenders. They were forced to sell their bonds at deep discounts to Christian lenders to raise the money to pay the king. The effects on the community as a whole were even more calamitous. The internal structures of support were damaged; conflict broke out between the Jews appointed to assess the taxes and the taxpayers themselves. The number of Jewish destitute mounted, just as the number of converts peaked, in the 1240s and 1250s.

Institutional pressure on Jews to convert also came from the Crown, in particular during the reign of Henry III. He was an enthusiast for Jewish conversion;[212] in 1231, he granted part of the Jewish cemetery in Oxford as a building site to the hospital of St John the Baptist, which then gave way to Magdalene College in the fifteenth century.[213] Henry even assumed responsibility for the financial support of the new Christians, a weekly payment to men (10d.) and to women (8d.).[214] In 1232, a *domus conversorum* (converts' house) was established in London on the site of a former synagogue. Some time between 1268 and 1272, the king intervened to come to the aid of a church, which shared a wall with a *yeshiva* (house of study). The friars of the church complained about the noise that the Jews made—their 'continuous caterwauling' (*continuum ululatum*)—and so the king gave an order that the *yeshiva* should be pulled down.[215] The partnership between the new orders and Crown survived Henry's death. In 1277, Edward sent a Jew to parliament to be punished for blasphemy.

For an extended period, the Crown was at first willing to turn a profit by intervening in Church regulation of Jews. Jews could buy exemption from aspects of regulation. Royal financial records of 1221 show that both individuals and whole communities were exempted from compliance with the discriminatory provisions of the 1215 Lateran Council—particularly, the badge—against substantial payments.[216] But things changed for the worse in the mid-century, as the Crown aligned itself with the Church. It inaugurated a policy of appeasing the prelates.[217] Henry III's 1253 anti-Jewish statute confirmed the provisions of the 1222 Council, and elaborated on them; the king had taken the Cross three years earlier, and this oppressive legislation was consistent with the mentality of a crusader.[218] No Jews were to live without special licence in any but the recognized towns for settlement; no synagogues could be built other than in cities with a Jewish population as at the date of the statute; no Jews could remain in England unless they had guarantors and had the means to pay taxes; Jewish prayers were to be said in a low voice; no Christian women were to be servants of Jews; no Jew was to disparage Christianity nor debate religious matters with Christians; Jews and Christians were not allowed to have sexual relations with each other; Jews were to wear the identifying badge on their chests; no Jew was allowed in a church; no Jew was to dissuade prospective converts; Jews were not allowed to eat meat during Lent.[219] The year 1253 marked an irreversible degradation in the legal status of the Jews.[220] Thereafter, matters only deteriorated further. In 1280, for example, Edward I, who was very close to both the Dominicans and the Franciscans,[221] issued instructions to Jews to attend Dominican sermons. They were required to listen 'without tumult, contention, or blasphemy'.

Expulsion

In 1233, an ordinance regulating dealings between Christians and Jews provided for the expulsion of those Jews who were not serviceable to the king.[222] It does not appear, however, that any Jews were actually expelled. Twenty years later, a similar ordinance was made.[223] By coincidence, either that year or within two years of it, the Jewish community petitioned the King for permission to emigrate. They had had enough, weakened by relentless taxing and (it may be inferred) intimidated by similarly relentless conversionary activity. The king's response was to close the ports. He was not yet ready to let them go.[224] This general prohibition on emigration was preceded by incidents involving individual Jews trying to escape abroad. In 1251, for example, two Jews were arrested while trying to flee with their families from England and from the king's most recent tallage.[225]

The national Expulsion had been preceded by restrictions on rights of settlement and local expulsions. The first recorded expulsion was from Bury St Edmunds in 1190, at the instigation of the local abbot, but with the consent of the king. Other local expulsions followed: Newcastle and Warwick in 1234, High Wycombe in 1235, Southampton in 1236, Berkhampstead in 1242, Newbury and Speenhamland in 1244, Derby in 1261, and Romsey in 1266.[226] In 1253, the Jews were restricted to towns where they were 'accustomed to live'. In the early part of the 1270s, they were ordered to concentrate in the main towns. In 1273 they were prohibited from living in Winchelsea; in 1274 they were prohibited from living in Bridgnorth. In 1275 further restrictions were placed on Jewish settlement and Jews were expelled from the Queen Mother's dower towns. There was considerable displacement during that year; settlement was restricted to *archa* towns, that is towns where documents recording the Jews' financial transactions were kept. In 1283, Jews were expelled from Windsor.

These dislocations were not preparatory, as first steps in a single plan, to the 1290 Expulsion. It is not quite correct to regard the national Expulsion as merely in general form the conclusion to a whole series of local expulsions from provincial centres. But they were consistent with the Expulsion; they derived from the same perspective on Jews—a community perceived to have no attachment to the place of their birth or residence but, more than that, with no more right to be in one place as distinct from any other. As much suppose that cash has the right to be deposited in one particular bank, as suppose that the Jews had the right to choose their place of residence. So for example, as part of the arrangements for the first Edwardian tallage, instructions were given that, in order to facilitate tallage, all the Jews should come to the main towns and remain there until April 1274. Further instructions were given that any Jews who failed to meet their tallage obligations were to be expelled. To quote from the Patent Roll: 'if any Jew fail to pay on the day appointed him, they shall cause him to leave the realm with his wife and children . . . and they shall assign such Jews the port of Dover within three days after the day of payment to depart never to return, their lands, houses, rents and all the goods of them and theirs to be saved to the king'.[227]

Seven years after the last local expulsion, the general Expulsion of Jews from England was ordered, by exercise of the royal prerogative. Its implementation bears the marks of committee; it has a bureaucratic character—staged, orderly,[228] and heartless. On 18 June 1290, secret orders were given to seal the *archae*. On 18 July, the Expulsion was announced. The Jews were to leave England by 1 November. The edict was read out in synagogues. There was no resistance from the Jews, either individually or as a national community. Some Jews continued to do business, registering debts as late as in August and September that year.[229] As against France, where the Jews were expelled and readmitted several times (1306, 1322, 1394), England's Jews did not come back. All connection with the country was severed. About 2,000 Jews were forced out[230]—that is, the entire Anglo-Jewish community, save for converts and those few who might have stayed on illegally.

Among the Jews expelled, a number set sail from Queensborough. Within minutes of their departure, they were put down on a sandbank just off the coast. Invited to stretch their legs, they disembarked, leaving their goods on board. The captain and crew promptly raised anchor, and left them to drown as the tide rose. 'Pray to Moses to save you', the captain, Henry Adrian, is reported to have jeered. He was jailed for two years for this crime. There were other victims; among the legal records of the time there are pardons given to sailors for murdering Jews on the high seas. There were killings, then, and there was also some robbery.[231] Other than some court records, there are few official documents, and no memoirs, that bear on this period. What the Jews suffered may therefore only be guessed at, perhaps by consulting accounts of other expulsions. It must have been a time of multiple dislocations, multiple losses—loss of possessions, loss of livelihood, and partial loss of identity. There must have been fear and anxiety. There were children to pack up and to distract. The Jews needed to reconcile themselves to losing England, having once thought of it as their home. There must have been homesickness and perhaps even discomfort at the loss of use of the language. And they were by no means assured of a welcome elsewhere. Philip IV of France refused admission to the exiles. The Parlement of La Chandeleur of 1291 decreed that all Jews arriving from England or Gascony were to be speedily expelled.[232]

There was not quite a single policy of expropriate and expel, though there is a sense that Jews had for some time been under a general sentence of expulsion, suspended only for as long as they remained of use. The decision was probably prompted by several considerations, including those of expediency. It appears to have been a personal one on the part of King Edward. The decision was not the product of any special lobbying. It followed an expulsion of Jews from Edward's continental territories. The decision was taken in secret,[233] and the text of the decree has not survived.

First, there were considerations of Christian piety. The Church had long harboured misgivings about the relationship between the Crown and the Jews. 'It is surprising', wrote the theologian Thomas of Chobham (*c.*1160– *c.*1233), 'that the Church abets princes who with impunity transfer to their own use the money they have received from Jews . . . and thus become the accomplices of usurious practices and of usurers themselves. But the Church does not punish them, because they are powerful, which is no excuse in God's sight.'[234] The Church, and in particular, the new mendicant orders, had been campaigning against the Jews, though not expressly advocating their expulsion. There were religious objections to the Jews remaining, unconverted. There was a fear of apostasy; there also appears to have been anxiety about Jewish proselytizing. (It is an overstatement, however, to assert that the Church had begun to fear Judaism as a rival.)[235] There was a widespread conviction that the conversionary project had failed. There was also Edward's own hostility to the Jews,[236] and one may speculate about his susceptibility to the rumours circulating about them.[237] He was closely associated with the construction of the shrine to Little St Hugh in Lincoln Cathedral in the early to mid-1290s.[238] In response to a petition from the bishops urging him address the Jews' 'malice', Edward said he 'simply ha[d] lost all hope of coping with it'.[239] Edward had taken the Cross a few years earlier, and had soon thereafter expelled the Jews from his continental lands. That the Jews of England would shortly share their co-religionists' fate could not have been hard to predict.

Secondly, Edward could anticipate that the decision would be popular, and one that would be rewarded. (He was not altogether wrong, if this indeed was his calculation—in the months between Expulsion edict and the Expulsion itself, both parliament and clergy voted him subsidies.) Royal favourites were buying up unredeemed Jewish bonds at a discount, and the lands of senior barons were in consequence being lost. Baronial hostility was intense at this capitalizing of their feudal rights.[240] Edward's decision could not have been implemented without popular support,[241] though the extent of that support cannot now be gauged with any precision.[242] Edward himself would have expected to gain in stature in consequence of his actions; getting rid of the Jews was a commendable thing for a Christian prince to do.[243] There was no protest at the policy (or none that has survived); but neither was there any significant violence that accompanied its execution. The clergy were confronted by a particular dilemma. They could anticipate that in place of Jews as both tax collectors and taxpayers, the king would rely upon Italian bankers as collectors, and the clergy as payers. How could they be enthusiastic about expulsion when the effect would be to expose themselves to royal depredations?[244]

Thirdly, there was a residual financial benefit for the Crown—a final liquidation of Jewish assets.[245] It is an open question whether these last debtors would have preferred their own Jewish creditors or the king as creditor. In any event, the number of Jews' debtors by 1290 was very small.[246] Though he was certainly in need of ready cash, Edward realized only a small profit from the confiscation of Jewish properties; his financial gain from the Expulsion was not great.[247]

Fourthly, there was perceived and actual Jewish misconduct. Entries in the public records explain the Expulsion by reference to the Jews' crimes and their perfidy.[248] The crimes were taken to be part of both divine and contemporary history. There was the Jews' crime against God, repeated in their crucifying of Christian children; there were also their financial crimes. The Jews covertly continued to lend money, in breach of the 1275 statute. John Peckham, archbishop of Canterbury, petitioned Edward in 1285, asking the King when he was going to bring the lending activities to an end. Edward replied that he was doing the best he could.[249] The best he could do proved to be enough. There is some evidence that Edward himself gave as his reason for the Expulsion the Jews' continued, though covert, moneylending.[250] Perhaps the Jews' greatest offence was their refusal to convert and assimilate.

Fifthly, and most broadly, the Expulsion was in keeping with the spirit of the times.[251] There had been local expulsions in England and on the Continent. Developments in Christian theology also had a part to play in the deteriorating condition of the Jews; in particular, the theological posture of the Dominicans and Franciscans was consistent with the policy of expulsion.[252] There was a great rebirth of preaching in the thirteenth century;[253] the new message of total intolerance of the Jews communicated by the new mendicant orders (who were specialists in preaching) spread fast and wide. The growth of the monetary economy, threatening old Christian values, and the revival of the value of poverty, which promoted those values, made usury one of the major issues of the period.[254] It was also an era of intense crusading enthusiasm;[255] Jew-hatred flowed from Muslim-hatred, a misperception of threat from the Jews flowing from encounters with, and anxieties about, Muslim expansionism. Anti-Semitism was integral to the emergence of a persecuting society, one that attacked heretics and lepers as well as Jews.[256] The Jews were expelled because economic considerations no longer trumped these Jew-hating complexities.

The royal decree was reported without praise or explanation. Though Edward's expulsion of 'the faithless multitude of Jews and unbelievers' was praised by one of his obituarists,[257] the event itself receded to close to vanishing point in public memory. There is no Anglo-Jewish record of the Expulsion extant—no reflection on it, no memorializing of the catastrophe.[258] The community mostly disappeared into Rouen.[259] Among late sixteenth- and seventeenth-century pamphleteers and antiquarians, the explanation for the Expulsion was to be found in the king's wish both to purify the land of corruption and to profit from doing so: 'To purge England from such corruptions and oppressions as it groaned under and not neglecting therein his own particular gain, the King banished the Jews...'[260] Other pamphleteers, advocates of the Jews' return, argued that the Civil War was God's punishment for the mistreatment of the Jews, and that readmission would appease God's wrath and bring peace to England.[261] In the mid- to late nineteenth century (in certain respects the high point of philo-Semitism in England), there were historians ready to make a much harsher judgement. 'If it could be said with strict precision of language that a nation can commit a crime,' wrote Luke Owen Pike, 'it would be true that one of the greatest national crimes ever committed was committed in England, when the Jews were expelled through the combined influence of the clergy, the traders, and the barons.'[262] England never suffered any culture-guilt[263] concerning its treatment of the Jews, however—and some anti-Semites praised Edward's decision.[264]

Conclusion

Three medieval English anti-Semites

Let me conclude this chapter with a glance at some representative medieval English anti-Semites. Their lives illuminate the following three aspects of medieval English anti-Semitism: first, its pervasiveness; secondly, its independence of any rational objections to Jewish social or religious practices; and thirdly, the intimacy of its connection with brutality, cruelty, and dishonesty.

Thomas of Monmouth

Such was the pervasiveness of Jew-hatred in the culture, circulating in sermons and religious images, in stories of Jewish perfidy, and in the rumours and calumnies attaching themselves to this most conspicuous of minority communities, it polluted many aspects of medieval life ostensibly unrelated to Jews—say, a heightened, even exalted, sense of Christ's suffering, the cult of the Virgin and her miracles, and the commercial benefits to local communities of having their own saints. It is in relation to these latter aspects that Thomas may perhaps best be understood. He does not appear to have felt any special animus against the Jews. From the evidence of his book, his principal concern was to praise William and to edify his readers and the general population of Norwich. The very introduction of the crucifixion element in the story served not so much to demonize the Jews as to elevate William's sanctity. 'Thomas did not lack in imagination', the historian Gavin Langmuir writes. 'He crucified William and thereby made him a notable saint.' But Thomas 'betrays no overriding obsession with Jews. He does not interrupt his narrative with irrelevant outbursts against them.'[265] A saint meant protection, as patron and mediator with the divine; a saint *also* meant the possibility of a cult; a cult meant pilgrimages, ready financing for shrines and related buildings, feast days and venerations, and so on; the promotion of a cult required a *Life*.[266] Thomas was an opportunist.[267] He took advantage of a situation presented to him, perhaps caring little about the Jews themselves. We may conclude that among the Jews' enemies were many whose motives for persecution were more complicated than mere Jew hatred alone. There was in twelfth-century Norwich, as elsewhere in England, a craving for the miraculous—a craving, that is, for confirmations of God's providence. The Jews were available to meet this need. Their religion, their very lives, could be appropriated for such a purpose; in themselves, they counted for little.

Peter of Blois

The author of 'Against the Perfidy of the Jews' was a borrower from Jews in London and Canterbury. Writing to his friend the bishop of Ely in about 1174, he begged for help in paying off his debts:

> Drawn by extreme urgency, I am going to Canterbury in order to be crucified by the perfidious Jews who torture me by their debts and afflict me with their usury. I expect to bear the same cross through the London Jews, unless you liberate me out of your piety, and I feel sure that you will show me an abundance of compassion and will redeem me. Therefore, my father and dearest friend, I pray that you will remove this cross from me, and take upon yourself the payment of £6 that I owe Samson the Jew . . . [268]

The language is faintly comic, of course—self-pitying, self-dramatizing, and utterly self-serving. But it is also, in respect of the Jews, a *common* language. This is how anti-Semites wrote when they corresponded with each other. The Jews are perfidious; they will crucify Christians when they can; it is the duty of their victims' friends to help if *they* can. It is plain that debt did not turn Peter into a Jew-hater. He was a Jew-hater already. And this gives the lie to that commonplace view of anti-Semitism as in some sense explicable by the Jews' moneylending activities.[269] For sure, while the Jews were not the only moneylenders in existence,[270] they were both the most visible among them and the ones most intimately connected with the oppressive aspects of royal finance. The purely financial aspects of the relations between Jewish lenders and Christian creditors were complicated—neither wholly antagonistic nor wholly amicable. The Jews were *not*, typically, lenders of last resort. They were more concerned with the providing of capital for projects than with lending to individuals and institutions already trapped by debt. The ideological nature of the objection to Jews in general preceded particular instances of hostility that some Jews may have prompted by their activities.[271] If certain borrowers hated Jewish lenders more than those Christian purchasers of Jewish bonds (sold by Jews at discount to pay tallages),[272] this had nothing to do with the burden of the debt. It was instead because the borrowers were vigorous, aggressive anti-Semites.

Richard Malebisse

Richard Malebisse (b. *c*.1155), was the ringleader of the York massacre.[273] He was born into a well-to-do knightly family that gloried in its destructive, violent tendencies—the family name means 'evil beast', a horizon of aspiration for those who bore it. Malebisse himself was well known for his belligerent temperament. He was a substantial landowner and one of the county's leading knights. He busied himself on the fringes of power, and mixed with powerful, influential personalities. He involved himself in political powerplays, but his part was always a subordinate one, and he often found himself on the losing side. (He was, for example, a conspirator-ally of John's against Richard I.) In relation to the Church, he was both a benefactor and a predator. He was wealthy, but not as wealthy as he would have liked, and throughout the 1180s he was heavily indebted to Aaron of Lincoln. He was a violent, violently prejudiced man, dismissive of others' interests, harsh and contemptuous towards his perceived inferiors. He was also an aggressive litigant, exceptional in the frequency of his recourse to the courts. He had a strong sense of his position and prestige; unable to assert himself as he would have wished in the circles in which he mostly moved, he must have been unbearable to those to whom he *could* be unbearable. He was an intemperate bully. And during those few days in York, he organized a band of conspirators both incontinent enough to kill with abandon and yet self-possessed enough to remember to destroy the records of their financial dealings with York's Jews. (During the Barons' Wars, the pattern was repeated: first murder the Jews, then destroy the records.) It would appear that the very heavy fine imposed on him for his part in the York massacre was waived. One of John's first acts as king was to pardon him and restore to him his possessions. Absurdly and yet entirely in accordance with his expectations, late in life Malebisse was appointed a Justice.[274] There were still Jews ready to lend to him, and he thus continued to be a heavily indebted, troublemaking baron until his death in 1210. He remained to the end a leading member of his society. Malebisse very comfortably inhabited a milieu in which corruption and cruelty were endemic, and in which the most violent and murderous of hatreds were given free rein.

The distinctiveness of medieval English anti-Semitism

The medieval English war against the Jews, in its breadth and depth, was not to be repeated by any of the English anti-Semitisms that followed—the literary, the modern, or the anti-Semitic anti-Zionist. These latter have been, and for the moment they continue to be, more limited affairs of defamation and discrimination. Physical assaults have been rare, the killings and expulsions have been confined to fiction, and there has been no extortion. The blood libel, however, has had a continuing resonance. It provides the connection, for example, between the first and second of the anti-Semitisms under review in the present book. With the Jews gone, anti-Semitism might have been expected to disappear too. That it did not is attributable to the poets and playwrights.[275] Jew-hatred was preserved in the medium of their art; it was also transformed by their art. They created English literary anti-Semitism, the subject of the following chapter. What first happened to the Jews of medieval England was thereafter visited upon the fantasy Jews of English literature: humiliation, expropriation, forced conversion, and death, in consequence of allegations of ritual murder, usury, child abuse, avarice and misanthropy, and hatred of Christians and the Church.

4

English Literary Anti-Semitism

'I am their musick'

Every year, on the fast day of *Tishah be'Av*, the Book of Lamentations is recited in synagogues. Jews listen to the recitation sitting on the floor, so that they may experience something of the abjection of exile and foreign rule, and as if in mourning. *Lamentations*, or *Eicha* as it is known in the Jewish tradition, intimates a pain so extreme as to defeat adequate expression. The author grieves over the defeat of Israel by the Babylonians. The people are without their city and Babylon exults in its new mastery. Jerusalem has been lost; the Temple has been destroyed. Israel must now live among the dispossessed. The ties that make the nation whole have been sundered. Israel's mothers are as widows, and Israel itself has been orphaned. *Eicha* is a bleak work, read on the bleakest day in the Jewish calendar.

This annual recital renews Jewish memory of the Babylonian exile and of those other moments of national calamity by convention remembered on this day—among others, the destruction of the Second Temple by the Romans in 70 CE, and the expulsion of the Jews from Spain in 1492. In its slow accumulation of disasters, *Tishah be'Av* encourages the regarding of catastrophe as the defining quality of Diaspora existence. This sits somewhat awkwardly with the present circumstances of Anglo-Jewry, and yet evokes a remote, collective memory of a time when catastrophe was indeed the defining quality of Anglo-Jewish existence. By tradition, the Jews were expelled from England on *Tishah be'Av*.[1] On this day, Jews are meant to remember that catastrophe too.

Midway, near the end of the third of *Eicha*'s five chapters, the poet addresses God: 'Thou hast seen all their vengeance and all their imaginations against me. Thou hast heard their reproach, O Lord, and all their imaginations against me. The lips of those that rose up against me, and their device against me all the day. Behold their sitting down, and their rising up. *I am their musick'* (3:60–3). This is in the translation of the Authorized Version. In Hebrew, the italicized sentence is '*Ani manginotam'*. In alternative English versions, this has been translated as 'I am their song' (*Soncino*), 'I am the burden of their songs' (*Revised Standard Version*), 'I am the butt of their gibes' (*JPS*).

These versions of this sentence, and the sentences that immediately precede it, converge on the following meanings. Israel is powerless before its conqueror's scorn; the conquest of Israel has been memorialized in the culture of its conquerors; the conquest, further, is the subject of continuous, unremitting celebration; the celebration is collective, diverse in literary and musical form, and insulting and triumphalist in character. *Eicha* remembers Israel's defeat, while also teaching that victors remember it too, with memories that themselves comprise further defeats of the Jewish people.

It is what happens to a people when they have been subjugated. They find that they have become material for song. This is among the bitterest of consequences for them. The threat that they posed (or were perceived to pose) can now be invoked by the enemy ceremonially. Their conquerors have relaxed into balladeers; their defeat is given an aesthetic aspect. These songs, or ballads, which are retold endlessly, and which deny to the defeated the pathos of their defeat, both follow acts of barbarism and are themselves barbaric. They are pitiless; they can be persecutory. Or so I suppose it must have seemed to the author of *Eicha*, contemplating just these commemorations of the catastrophe he himself memorialized so despairingly, and so it might seem to any conquered or dispossessed people, staring into the distorting mirror of their vanquisher's literature.

England's former Jews could have assembled to voice just such a lament, as they contemplated from their overseas refuges the emergent literature of their late homeland, a literature proliferating texts (plays, poetry, and, somewhat later, novels) in which the crimes of predatory Jews are uncovered, and their perpetrators punished. English literary anti-Semitism is a collective 'counter-' or 'anti'-*Eicha*, not a lament but a celebration. And the burden of this celebration? That while the Jews are wicked, they are also ignominious, and when they set out to cause harm, they can be defeated.

Literary anti-Semitism

All anti-Semitic accounts of Jews are fictional in the received sense of being false.[2] There is, however, a special class of such accounts that are fictional in a further, narrower sense. I refer here to works of literature, and by 'literature' I mean works that conform to certain metrical and/or rhetorical norms.[3] English literature, for example, is replete with adverse, untrue things said about Jews and about Judaism. It contains adverse representations of Jews as a whole, and of individual, fictional Jews taken to be representative of Jews as a whole. It is a persecutory discourse; it puts Jews on trial. These anti-Semitic poems, plays, and novels comprise accounts of Jews that may be taken to acknowledge their own fictional status. This acknowledgement both subverts and strengthens the force of their anti-Semitism. It subverts it, because it concedes that the story it relates is not a true one; it strengthens it both because the story it relates is offered as typical of all Jews, and because the anti-Semitism is given a certain aesthetic dignity. Anti-Semitic literary works, even though not received as reports of true occurrences, may foster a predisposition to think ill of Jews. The strengthening, in particular, of the Jew-hating aspect of anti-Semitic works of literature by the very fact of their 'literariness' raises the question whether this double or compound fictionality creates a distinct kind of discursive anti-Semitism, one that demands analysis in its own terms, by the application of separate and distinct criteria.

The tendency among those who study such matters has been to respond to this question, 'no, or hardly at all'. They have been inclined to treat the anti-Semitic literary work *either* as an undifferentiable instance of a broader discursive assault on Jews *or* as a reflection of a non-discursive reality (that is, of what people 'thought' about Jews). There is something to be said for both of these approaches, and indeed much good work has been produced in conformity with one or other of them. But there is also something to be said for a differentiated analysis, one that respects the specificity of anti-Semitic literary discourse. This is especially so in the case of English literary anti-Semitism. To be precise, there is the following to be said.

First, literature contains imaginary worlds that only incompletely and imperfectly correspond to our non-literary, given world. One consequence of this lack of 'fit' between the literary and the *non*-literary is that literary anti-Semitism does not reliably reflect any non-literary variant. Literature instead has its own mode of existence. It has its own internal history. It has its own inner laws, its own distinct properties. It follows its own line of development. It has integrity, and commands the loyalty of its practitioners.[4] It is an object of knowledge *sui generis*; a case can be made for it comprising a distinct linguistic domain,[5] or even having a distinct ontological status.[6] What literature tells us is not verifiable; it is useless to try to seek confirmation of its content in some other place.[7] Even when a literary work is a representation of something else it is always also an event in itself, and the totality of such events form their own system, relating to each other often across very extended time periods[8]—'rousing the sense of union, with what is remote' (George Eliot).[9] Literature, further, has a distinct relation with its audiences, who in turn bring to it a distinct set of expectations. It is the object of a distinct kind of theorizing. While literature is just one among many discourses circulating in any given society, it is thus also unique.[10] It stands slightly apart from the generality of those other discourses. Poets and novelists compose their work by using themes (or 'topics') that are ready to hand, and often invest the outworn among them with fresh vigour. These topics comprise the writer's 'stockroom' or 'treasure house' (or, indeed, 'arsenal').[11] Writers draw on topics while bearing in mind uses made of them by writers of earlier generations.

The conjunction is therefore possible in a nation's life of a rich *literary* anti-Semitism and a meagre *political* anti-Semitism—that is, anti-Semitic poems, plays, and novels, but not anti-Semitic parties, pogroms, and legislation. It is indeed precisely this conjunction that characterizes the anti-Semitism of fourteenth- to twentieth-century England.[12] It is an error to suppose that a culture that energetically persecutes fictional Jews will always be ready to persecute real Jews too. There is no necessary connection between these two kinds of persecutions. This is not to say, of course, that anti-Semitic works may not on occasion lead their audiences to their own acts of Jew-baiting, or otherwise encourage a low, hostile view of Jews.[13] (How many 'thousands of Christians', pondered an American visitor to nineteenth-century London, have been prejudiced against 'the whole tribe of Israel' by Shakespeare's Shylock, though they have never seen a Jew?)[14] But what is being said about Jews in plays, poems, and novels will not always be continuous with what is being said about them in (say) journals, public addresses, and treatises—and certainly, what is being said *about* Jews will not always reflect what is being done *to* Jews. It would be wrong, then, to maintain that English literary anti-Semitism comprises works in which England showed its hand as an anti-Semitic nation. One may not 'read off' national character from a national literature, as if the latter gave reliable access to the former.[15] This overstates and simplifies the relation. Anti-Semitic literature is not simply to be read as a mediated, and highly wrought, kind of perpetrator testimony— so to say, 'this is what we did, this is what we think'.

Secondly, it is only in literature that written anti-Semitism need not be both degrading and degraded, composed by blackguards for blackguards.[16] The generality of literary works about Jews are for sure no more than vulgar incitements. The anti-Semitic play, *The Sons of Israel*, that made the rounds of Russia's provincial theatres in 1901–2, for example, provoked many violent disturbances among its audiences. It was, it would appear, little more than an incitement to a pogrom.[17] And Lord Alfred Douglas's poem 'In Excelsis' is merely execrable:

> The leprous spawn of scattered Israel
> Spreads its contagion in your English blood;
> Teeming corruption rises like a flood
> Who fountain swelters in the womb of hell.
> Your Jew-kept politicians buy and sell
> In Markets redolent of Jewish mud,
> And while the 'Learned Elders' chew the cud
> Of liquidation's fruits, they weave their spell.[18]

The rhyming of 'mud' and 'cud' is the least of the poem's offences. But not every anti-Semitic literary work can be thus dismissed. A literary work, in its distinctive merit, can elevate as well as affirm given anti-Semitic discourse; it can also subvert the discourse, complicating it by formal or ethical counter-tendencies. Lope's *El Niño Inocente de La Guardia* (c.1607),[19] for example, has an aesthetic dignity that distinguishes it from the generality of anti-Semitic material—oral execrations and apocalyptic ravings, insults and slanders, pseudo-scholarly treatises and inciting pamphlets, exclusionary or discriminatory statutes and decrees, wall newspapers,[20] and all manner of other instruments of persecution and oppression. Anti-Semitism energizes the play, which finds its voice, in all its clarity and force, in the pure joy of justified Jew-hatred. It is a creative connivance with falsehood.[21] I address subversions of anti-Semitic discourse, which includes anti-Semitic works complicated by counter-tendencies, below.

These two reasons are capable of applying to all anti-Semitic literary works, regardless of their nationality (literary works have a nationality, though not in the same way that human beings do). But there are additional reasons why English literary anti-Semitism merits special, separate attention.

Thirdly, if it is the case that among anti-Semitism's many products there are only a few literary works that deserve general esteem and thus challenge the self-respect of Jewish readers and spectators, then English literature has most of them. Indeed, it is because of *The Prioress's Tale*, *The Merchant of Venice*, and *Oliver Twist*, and a handful of other, mainly English works of literature, that a distinctly *literary* anti-Semitism came into existence. *The Merchant of Venice*, and *Oliver Twist* are national assets, and they resonate powerfully in the cultures of other nations. Walter Benjamin once remarked of Baudelaire's *Les Fleurs du mal* that it was the last book of poems to have had 'a European-wide reverberation'.[22] Shakespeare's play and Dickens's novel have this kind of 'reverberation'. They have influenced generations of novelists and playwrights. The play itself is endlessly performed; the novel has never been out of print. Both works have been adapted in several media; they are immensely popular. They are world masterpieces; Shylock and Fagin themselves are alive in global culture. The texts enjoy a perpetual contemporaneity; their principal characters are literary entities that live among us.[23] While there are several national literatures that contain substantial anti-Semitic works, England was the principal promoter, and indeed in some sense the inventor, of literary anti-Semitism.

Fourthly, English literary anti-Semitism emerged in a period of peculiar disengagement from the persecution of Jews. For about 400 years, from expulsion to readmission, English anti-Semitism subsisted without Jews. There were no Jews to persecute; there were no Jews even to address. There was no legislation to enforce, there were no taxes to levy, and no depredations to negotiate with the Jews' representatives. In consequence, anti-Semitism took on an especially alienated character, developing in something of a social void. It was unimpeded by any contact with Jews, let alone subject to any counter-thrusts by them. The non-identity of sign and referent could not have been starker. English anti-Semitism in this period *is* literary anti-Semitism. By the time of the Jews' return, the literature about them was already formed, and substantially insulated, if not quite or forever closed off, from influence by the presence of Jews themselves.

Fifthly, English literary anti-Semitism has unusual integrity and coherence. It comprises a single, albeit complex, discourse; it extends with varying strength across several literary periods, and it exploits most literary genres. The blood libel is the largely unnoticed,[24] master theme of this discourse, its 'ur-story', its 'matter'. Jews were probably last tried on blood libel charges in Northampton in 1277 or 1279, and thereafter the blood libel circulated entirely at the level of discourse. It comprised a body of narrative material allowing for any number of written works[25] that either replicated the libel's essential structure or developed distinct aspects of it—say, Jewish criminality, or Jewish legalism. It makes the Jew the aggressor, where necessary rewriting its given material in conformity with this rule—as in Graham Greene's *Brighton Rock* (1938), for example, where a news story about a race course razor-attack *on* a Jewish bookmaker and his Jewish clerk is rewritten as a race course razor-attack *by* a Jewish gang on the Roman Catholic Pinkie.[26] English literary anti-Semitism has not been a discourse for professional anti-Semites—even though it deploys a limited class of 'stereotypes' of Jews, namely pejorative simplifications of an imputed 'Jewish character'.[27] It is hegemonic. For an English writer to write fictionally about Jews means writing within the regime of literary anti-Semitism— against which it is of course possible to struggle. There are works that diminish or subvert the blood libel, though there are far more that affirm it, and give it ethical weight.

Lastly, English literary anti-Semitism has a specific place within English literature. Indeed, its relative autonomy as an anti-Semitic discourse is in part achieved by its incorporation into a broader, and very strong, literary discourse. English literary anti-Semitism stands distinctively within the dominant tendency of English literature towards the antinomian. (By 'antinomian' I have something more general in mind than the Protestant sectarian heresy, or with the few literary works that take this heresy as their theme.) English literature is disposed towards lawbreaking—genre breaking, the promoting of love over law, the celebration of *le bonheur dans le crime*,[28] the transgressive, and a hostility to formalism of all kinds. It accommodates anti-Semitism, then, but on its own terms. It tends to conceive of Jews as legalistic lawbreakers. This makes Jews adversaries of much of what English literature itself may be taken to champion. 'Jews'—by which I mean a certain conception of Jews, ultimately theological in character—were available to stand for a set of values antithetical to those advanced by the English literary project itself. This huge topic is a project for another book; I can only gesture towards its essential dimensions here.[29]

Insisting in relation to anti-Semitic discourse upon *either* an impermeable demarcation between the literary and the non-literary *or* their common identity are errors comparable in their dogmatism. Literature is immersed in its time and place *and* yet somehow also pulls out and away from both.[30] The relations between the literary and the non-literary are therefore best understood in strategic terms. In this chapter, I tend towards maintaining a demarcation; in other chapters, I tend to elide it. In those other chapters, I tend towards a New Historicist position, that is to say I assume the 'mutual embeddedness of art and history', with 'art' defined widely to include literature. I treat all of the written and visual traces of a particular culture as a mutually intelligible network of signs,[31] and literary works as mere 'sites of representations' of Jews—sharing a single 'cultural space'[32] with newspaper and journal articles, memoirs, political tracts, works of psychology and social analysis, speeches, popular songs and entertainments, and so on.

I am, for example, open to Stephen Dedalus' judgement that 'Shylock chimes with the jewbaiting that followed the hanging and quartering of the queen's leech Lopez, his jew's heart being plucked forth while the sheeny was still alive.'[33] I am similarly ready to regard Svengali, Dracula, rumours about the Jewish identity of Jack the Ripper, reports from France of the Dreyfus trials,[34] and preoccupations with successfully insinuating Jews, Jewish control of finance and the arts, and Eastern European Jewish immigration, as all creations of the 1890s,[35] contributing to a single complex discourse about Jews in circulation during that period.[36] I am ready to read as summarizing a whole climate of anti-Semitic snobbery John Galsworthy's play *Loyalties* (1922), in which a socially ambitious Jew is ostracized for accusing a fellow house guest of theft (correctly, as it turns out).[37] I am also open to biographical readings of literature—to an interpretation, say, of Benjamin Disraeli's fiction as a series of fantasies of Jewish genius and influence, defensive substitutions for received notions of Jewish ignominy.[38] And I understand why anti-Semites have sought to use anti-Semitic literary works in their polemicizing against Jews—why, for example, the anti-Semite H. H. Beamish praised 'Gehazi', Kipling's poem about Rufus Isaacs.[39]

However, in this chapter I am concerned with contests internal to literature, and so I avoid New Historicist positions and tend instead towards Russian Formalist positions. The Russian Formalists were a group of literary theorists active in the first decades of the twentieth century. 'Formalist' was a highly pejorative term in the controversies of that time, and its practitioners defended themselves against their orthodox Marxist adversaries by insisting that they were 'specifiers' instead. That is to say, they insisted both upon the specificity of the literary work and its constituent parts and upon the autonomy of literary scholarship.[40] There is an inescapably formalist aspect to literature, if only because literary works outlive the immediate contexts of their creation and have significances that exceed any intentions of their authors, and because literary forms are themselves limited, constraining authors in the creative choices that they make. For their own purposes, the Russian Formalists made this formalist aspect a special object of inquiry. For quite different purposes, I too bracket it for particular consideration in what follows. That is to say, I write without reference to non-literary factors external to the literary works themselves.[41]

Moment 1: the context of *The Prioress's Tale*

Thomas of Monmouth's *Life and Miracles of St William of Norwich*

The blood libel's fortunes in England were bound up with literary values from the outset. Thomas of Monmouth's *Life and Miracles of St William of Norwich*, the earliest extant narrative of ritual murder, borrows from the collections of saints' lives then in circulation,[42] which derived in turn from events related in the Gospels. Thomas's book is a work of hagiography,[43] establishing parallels between William's suffering and Christ's Passion whenever it can. In these respects, it is commonplace. But it is not *wholly* commonplace. Quite independently of its distinction as an innovative defamation, it has innovative literary properties too.

The detective story

Shorn of its religious language, Thomas's work has a distinctly modern timbre. It is a narrative of a certain type of scandalous, even sensational, set of circumstances. Its establishing premise is that an extraordinary, secret, and criminal act has been perpetrated by a shadowy, sinister group of people, and that this crime has been covered-up by the bribing of influential figures. It is at this point that the narrator himself then arrives upon the scene, a stranger who thus cannot possibly be involved in the crime.[44] He unmasks the criminals, confounds their protectors, and restores (indeed, elevates) the good name of the victim. He does so by patient and tenacious forensic work, which means in part refusing to accept the first answers he is given by those he questions. He is a man of great natural resources and strength of character; he acts without reward or hope of reward.

Thomas's work thus reaches across the centuries to, say, Ibsen's *A Public Enemy* (1882), in which a principled physician, Dr Stockmann, discovers that his town's public baths are causing serious illness to their users, and then to his surprise finds himself confronting the townspeople's reluctance to do anything about the baths for fear of losing tourist revenue. Thomas of Monmouth is that physician—an intrepid investigator, a redoubtable campaigner, and stalwart in the face of opposition. The Jews are the equivalent in the economy of Thomas's work to the public baths in Ibsen's work. 'I, a second David, hasten to confound the abusive Philistines, running forth from the opposite ranks', declares Thomas;[45] 'the strongest man in the world is the man who stands alone', echoes Stockmann.[46]

But there is more than just a parallel between distinct literary works to be drawn here. A more substantial claim may be made on behalf of Thomas's work. Thomas of Monmouth may indeed have been the inventor of the blood libel; but he also has a good claim to be regarded as the inventor of the detective story. Certainly, his book is the first instance of this particularly English literary genre;[47] according to convention, it may therefore be treated as the parent of the genre. When read as a detective novel rather than a hagiography, it yields up its most essential properties. There is a body, a mystery, an investigation, and the identifying of the murderers. Thomas is an amateur detective, the murderers' method is bizarre, and clues comprise an essential element in the narrative. It is the job of the priest, no less than the detective, to identify the evil in the community, then to purge it, and in consequence to return the community to a state of purity. The detective story has thus been described as the folk-myth of the twentieth century.[48] Thomas's work is a 'whodunit'; Thomas himself is a twelfth-century Father Brown, a Chestertonian priest who relies on imagination as much as deduction.[49]

The 'anti-' Arthuriad

The mirror image of the detective story, wrote W. H. Auden, is the Quest for the Grail[50]—because while the detective is a 'Quester', he is in search of an offender against God, rather than the vessel of God's grace. Thomas is one such Quester.

Blood libel stories invert or 'mirror' Grail Quest stories. Both these narratives return to the Passion, the one in an act of retrieval, the other in an act of repetition. Both the knights' quest and the Jews' quest are collective projects, though the one comprises a fellowship and is holy, while the other is a conspiracy and perpetrates atrocities. Both concern blood-carrying or blood-soaked items: the one, a vessel that once contained Jesus' blood; the other, *matza*. Both narratives engage the deepest passions: the one, of chivalry and love; the other, of murderous hatred. Both are paradigmatic: the one, of Christian virtue, the other, of Jewish vice. Both are detached from everyday experience: the one, elevated above it, and demanding supererogatory qualities of its participants; the other, utterly debased and infamous, and demanding fanaticism and sadism of *its* participants.

Somewhat remarkably, these structural, conceptual opposites, the blood libel and the legends of the Grail, emerged into written discourse at roughly the same time in roughly the same part of England,[51] and in works of comparable mendacity. Thomas of Monmouth lied about the cause of William's death *in* his work; Geoffrey of Monmouth lied about the origins *of* his work, the *History of the Kings of Britain*.[52] The blood libel and the 'Matter of Britain' (as the legends relating to Arthur and his knights, and the quest for the Grail, were collectively known) thereafter took roughly the same course through Continental Europe. The medievalist Norman Cantor, who draws attention to this 'curious and disconcerting fact of cultural history', proposes that the blood libel and Grail literature were of comparable significance to the medieval Christian sensibility. 'The child-killing Jew and Sir Lancelot', he writes, were 'fixtures of the medieval mind and embedded inextricably in the same romantic culture.'[53] They comprised novel contributions by medieval Europe to global culture and politics.[54]

The symmetry is not complete, however. While the 'prodigious vogue'[55] of Arthurian romance in the Middle Ages remained largely in the realm of the literary, blood-libel tales enjoyed a rather different kind of appeal, and routinely traversed the judicial and literary realms. More consequentially, while the Grail literature dominates medieval English literature, the blood libel is marginal to it. Against the very many English romances concerned with aspects of the Arthurian legend (nearly one-fourth of all the surviving romances of the period),[56] one may set only a handful of works concerned with the blood libel. This is not just a matter of quantity. There is no blood-libel poem that compares in quality with the late-fourteenth century *Gawain and the Green Knight*—though perhaps the late fourteenth-century *Prioress's Tale* comes close. In early modern literature, and in the literature of successive centuries, the balance changes somewhat. The writing of new works with an Arthurian theme radically declines as it ceases to be fashionable,[57] while the blood libel reaches canonic status in Shakespeare and is mockingly subverted in Marlowe. In the nineteenth century, the blood libel takes further canonic form in Dickens's *Oliver Twist* (1838), while Tennyson revives the 'Matter of Britain' in his *Idylls of the King* (1856–85).

So far as I am aware, however, in only one instance do a blood libel tale and an Arthurian tale occupy adjacent literary spaces. This is in Chaucer's *Canterbury Tales*, where the Prioress's tale of Jewish child-murderers immediately precedes the Wife of Bath's tale of the adventures of a knight of King Arthur's court.

The Gothic

It would be unreasonable to expect from Thomas's work so complete an anticipation of any further genre, but the elements in it that correspond to the literary genre of the 'Gothic' are striking in their number.

The English Gothic novel announces itself as a genre upon its very first appearance, the publication of Horace Walpole's *The Castle of Otranto* (1764). Walpole writes proudly in the preface to the second edition of the 'novelty' of his 'attempt'. It is a composite of certain effects and themes. It is set in an indeterminate 'dark ages'. It is, he explains, a 'blend [of] two kinds of romance, the ancient and the modern'.[58] The 'ancient' has imagination but is improbable; the 'modern' is prosaic, but probable. Walpole proposes a novel that 'reconciles the two kinds'. He wishes to represent ordinary men and women in extraordinary positions. These are 'personages' who 'never lose sight of their human character', even though they are 'under the dispensation of miracles'. The novel does not depart from the 'common life', even when relating the most uncommon events. In the execution of the plan, however, he somewhat erred towards the uncommon—the novel is overprovided with horror, corpses, and supernatural events. 'Terror', writes Walpole, when pretending merely to be his novel's translator, 'is the author's principal engine'.[59] The Gothic novel shares with the detective story a fascination with extreme criminal behaviour.

There are parts of Thomas's work that read as if written to Walpole's prescription. His account of William's exhumation, for example, contains the same combination of mysterious visions and everyday experiences, the miraculous and the mundane, the terrifying and the prosaic. And in its fanciful solemnity, there is also the same tacit invitation to satire. Thomas's work is not a Gothic text, but it contains elements that will cohere several centuries later in that genre. It contains possibilities; it has a certain literary pregnancy. And among these other, further possibilities is the intimation, by the equivalent of an additional mirror-effect, of the theme of the Wandering Jew.

The 'anti-' Wandering Jew

The Wandering Jew legend, according to its leading historian G. K. Anderson, took shape in the later Middle Ages.[60] The *Flowers of History* (*c.*1235), a chronicle history of England from the Saxons to 1235, contains one of its earliest documentary appearances. An English monk, Roger of Wendover, wrote the book. Roger records that during a visit to England in 1228, an Armenian bishop told of one Joseph, formerly named Cartaphilus, condemned to live until Jesus' return. The bishop relates that he knows the man well, that many people visit him from different parts of the world, and that he 'explains all doubts on the matters on which he is questioned'.[61] The chronicler Matthew Paris reproduced Roger's story in his own work, *Chronica majora*, and the story thus took its place alongside blood-libel stories and other post-biblical material relating to the Jews.

Both the Wandering Jew and the Jewish child-murderers are witnesses to the truth of the Christ story, and thus serve Christian propaganda:[62] the one, by the circumstances of his original offence and his longevity; the others, by their compulsion to re-enact the crucifixion and the curative value they mistakenly attach to Christian blood. But in all essential respects they are opposites of each other. He is a dignified, solitary, named figure; they are sordid, nameless conspirators. He has a wife and children, whom he must abandon because of the curse; they destroy Christian families, separating mother from son. He is fastidiously contrite, with 'grieved conscience';[63] they are heart-hardened sinners. His was a non-lethal offence; theirs, a lethal one. He teaches religious truths ('if he hears anyone curse . . . he tells them that they crucify their God again'),[64] they affirm theological falsehoods. His existence is governed by the endless punishment of his single offence; theirs, by an endless multiplication of offences. He wins love; they inspire hatred. His merit will earn eventual death; their crimes demand their immediate death. He cures; they torture. He gives life; they take it. He has faith, and rarely eats ('I will not eat, the Lord Jesus is sufficient for me');[65] they are perfidious, and are greedy, cannibalistic eaters. He is often consumed by a terrible thirst; they slake their thirst on blood. He loves children ('he has a great delight in [them], because his great master loved them');[66] they hate children. And of course, there is this too—while there were many charlatans and impostors over the centuries who claimed to be the Wandering Jew,[67] Jews everywhere lived in fear of the blood-libel accusation. While Jewish writers have themselves on occasion adopted the Wandering Jew theme, the blood libel has only appealed to the worst renegades among them. We may conclude: the Wandering Jew legend is the binary opposite of the Blood Libel legend.

This intimacy between the two themes, the 'blood libel' and the 'Wandering Jew', a kind of tacit pairing, is made unusually explicit in Matthew Lewis's Gothic novel, *The Monk* (1794), though they are coupled elsewhere too.[68] In the novel's sub- or parallel plot, two young people, Raymond and Agnes, fall in love. Agnes is confined in a haunted castle; the ghost, known as 'the bleeding nun', appears on the fifth of May of every fifth year. The lovers hatch a plot. On 5 May, the young woman will disguise herself as the nun; no one will challenge her thus dressed; she will escape with her beloved, who will be waiting for her in a fast carriage. On the day, the young man is in position, opens the carriage door to the person he believes is his lover, they take off, but...it's the nun who has climbed into the carriage! A storm rages, the carriage crashes, and Raymond is knocked unconscious. He is taken to an inn, and when he revives he is told that no one answering the description of Agnes was with him at the time of the accident. The nun visits him every night in his rooms in the inn, 'pressing her lips to [his], touching [him] with her rotting fingers', and murmuring 'Raymond, Raymond, thou art mine!...' He sinks into a lethargic despair, 'so faint, spiritless and emaciated that [he] could not cross the room without assistance'. She is, it is intimated, a vampire.[69] But one day his servant Theodore tells him of a mysterious figure who might help him. This is the person who will reveal himself as the Wandering Jew. The stranger comes to his place of confinement, and they converse. 'No one', the man explains, 'is adequate to comprehending the misery of my lot! Fate obliges me to be constantly in movement...' But he can exorcise the ghost. '*My hand alone can dry up the blood*', he explains. He is a blood-stauncher, not a blood-letter.[70]

Notwithstanding this work (which contains the fullest portrait of the Wandering Jew in Gothic literature),[71] the best efforts of the Romantic poets (Coleridge, Shelley, Wordsworth, Byron), and the adventures of the mysterious and powerful Jew, Sidonia, in Disraeli's novels *Coningsby* (1844), *Sybil* (1845), and *Tancred* (1847),[72] it cannot be said that the Wandering Jew has enjoyed a salience in English literature comparable to that of the blood libel. Medieval English literary allusions subsequent to *Flowers of History* and *Chronica majora* were inconsequential, and limited to a few references; the resurgence of interest in seventh-century England produced little work of any merit, and the story is the same for later centuries too. It remains an

essentially Continental legend, where it was so overburdened with meaning, it was largely useless to anti-Semites.[73] None of the English popular
versions has the vitality, Anderson argues, of the Continental European
ones. He ascribes their 'stunted growth' (they are 'mean', 'trivial', or 'poor
specimens')[74] to English 'matter-of-factness', to a Puritan deprecating of
fantasy, to the preference of native legends to migratory imported ones, and
to the 'small proportion of Jews' in England. Even when the theme attracted
the attention of major literary figures in the English canon, they tended to
denude it of its specifically Jewish character (Marmaduke, in Wordsworth's
The Borderers (1842)),[75] or to assimilate it to the Cain story (Byron's *Cain*
(1821)) or incorporate it as an element in their own distinct, fresh conception (Coleridge's 'Rime of the Ancient Mariner' (1798)).[76] Evelyn Waugh
offered what he took to be a humorous Wandering Jew, a travelling
salesman in incense, in his novel *Helena* (1950): 'I always respect religion.
It's my bread and butter . . . You have to take a long view in my business.'[77]
This resonates with the authentic tone of quotidian, modern English anti-
Semitism—condescending, unimpressed, dismissive. Within the English
literary discourse of the Jew, then, the blood libel is dominant, while
the theme of the Wandering Jew subsists as its unequal and insubstantial
opposite, or counter.

An early parody—Richard of Devizes

The hagiographic—of course—prompts parodies. In the story of the Winchester blood libel, as related by Richard of Devizes (*fl.* late twelfth
century), a young French boy, recently arrived in Winchester, disappears
and is believed dead. It is Passover, and his friend accuses the missing boy's
Jewish employer of murder. The Jew is prosecuted but he bribes the judge
and is acquitted. Richard begins his story in France, and there is a long set-
piece speech in which a French Jew, in the course of advising the boy to go
to Winchester, describes a number of English cities, including Winchester,
'the city of cities'. The story is the occasion for digressions, for pauses for the
sake of local colour, and for jokes at the expense of the French and of
England's principal cities. The blood libel itself is a device, the vehicle for
literary self-display. Richard's chronicle is believed to have circulated
among a small group of friends; it is perhaps best described as an instance
of a professional's self-irony—a piece of fun.[78] Only two versions are known
to have survived.

Richard establishes the fictional status of the story in the opening paragraph:

> Because Winchester had not to be deprived of her due reward for preserving peace for the Jews [exceptionally among the places with Jewish settlements, it had not rioted against the Jews in 1190], the Jews of Winchester, studious for the honour of their city, in their Jewish way, earned renowned glory for themselves by martyring a boy at Winchester, as was shown by the indications of the deed *although the deed itself was absent.*

The sentence undoes itself—the Jews committed a crime that they did not commit. Condemned in general terms, the Jews are exculpated of the particular crime. But in the course of this exculpation, in a work that contains many formulaic but disobliging statements about Jews, several literary and proto-literary forms are parodied.

This passage is followed by a passage that further destabilizes meaning, making even more unreliable the account of the boy's disappearance and presumed death. Speaking of Winchester, the French Jew says:

> There is one vice there, and one alone. I would say, with all due respect to the learned men and to the Jews (*salua pace litteratorum dixerium et Iudeorum*), that the people of Winchester lie like sentries.[79]

It is the French Jew's speech, but it is Richard's voice that we hear. I am a learned man of Winchester, and the truth is that I cannot be relied upon to tell a truthful story. The truth is, I am a liar. In an alternative translation of the sentence, the French Jew says:

> With the exception I should say of the learned and the Jews, the Winchester people tell lies like watchmen.

In this reading of the Latin, the learned man who asserts the truth of the blood libel and the Jews who deny it are both telling the truth, alone among the inhabitants of Winchester.

Richard of Devizes tells a tale of an uncommitted crime, a deed that was absent, one that becomes the occasion for several other tales, in a meandering narrative that concludes with an utterly fantastic series of events. Two young men are working for a Winchester Jew. When one of them does not turn up for work, the other accuses the Jew of crucifying him. When he notices a crowd gathering around him, be becomes 'more fearless', and rants 'That Jew is a devil; he has torn my heart from my breast; he has butchered my comrade; I even fancy he has eaten him.' The Jew is then 'seized and carried before the judge'. But there are no accusers. The boy himself is under-age, and the evidence of a wet-nurse employed by the Jew, who insists that she saw the missing boy disappear into the Jew's cellar, is rejected. (Christians were prohibited from working for Jews; she was 'infamous' because she breached this law.) Even so, the chronicler concludes, the Jew 'won over the judges by gold'.

The medieval chronicle is a genre that encourages digression and idio-syncrasy. But Richard goes further. His chronicle can also be read both as parodying certain other genres, and opening a satiric space between what is generally thought to be the case and what is truly the case—in combination, the blood libel as *comedy*, made possible by the absence of a body. Richard uses the Winchester case to air his amusement with the conventions of ritual-murder literature. By his parody, he draws attention to the literary properties of texts that purport to convey reality. He is not 'philo-Semitic', of course. Richard plainly despised Jews. But his impulse is to deflate. 'It gives his observations the excitement of being faintly shocking at the expense of being shallow', writes the literary scholar Nancy Partner. She regards Richard's work as a deliberate parody of Thomas of Monmouth's. He is not concerned to vindicate the Jews but to mock a popular hagiographic work. Its style and substance made it an irresistible target for Richard's wit. Richard is consistently more concerned with literature and style than with religion and crime among vulgar people. This was a singular perspective. The child-martyr narrative is a *jeu d'esprit*, a sarcastic epilogue to a literature that must have seemed to Richard to have become stale and conventional.[80]

'Sir Hugh, or the Jew's Daughter'

In the particular story that I am telling, the story of the migration of a murderous anti-Semitism into a national literature, the ballad 'Sir Hugh, or the Jew's Daughter' may be regarded both as an initial episode and as a continuing episode, because by its longevity it continuously accompanies the development of English literary anti-Semitism. This ballad came into existence in the century following the expulsion. It relates Hugh of Lincoln's murder by a cruel Jew's crueller daughter. It thus alludes, by its name and certain details of its narrative, to the Lincoln blood libel of 1255. Immensely, tellingly durable, 'Sir Hugh' was one of only a few similarly ancient ballads still in oral circulation at the beginning of the twentieth century. Renamed 'Little Sir William', it was set to music by the English composer Benjamin Britten (1913–76).[81] It was one of the most popular of the traditional ballads.[82]

It is by song that members of non-literate cultures keep themselves informed both of their history and of current events. They tend to share a common repertoire of tunes; song-versions of events of common interest tend to emerge very quickly; these versions are modified, elaborated upon, as they circulate in the culture.[83] Ballads, wrote the eighteenth-century antiquarian Thomas Percy, comprise the means by which 'the memory of illustrious actions [are] preserved and propagated'.[84] To which can be added, wicked actions followed by miraculous reverses too. 'Sir Hugh' is a work both of mourning and of celebration, and therefore of remembrance. It is among the oldest of ballads, though not the oldest. *That* ballad, already preserved in a thirteenth-century manuscript, is 'Judas'.

This is the story of 'Sir Hugh'. A child is playing outside the house of a Jew. He accidentally kicks the ball through a window of the house. Seeing the Jew's daughter inside the house, the boy asks her to return his ball. She demurs, instead inviting him into the house to get it for himself. He is reluctant to do so. Who, indeed, would want to enter a dark house, separated from one's friends, in order to negotiate with such a fiend? Even for a plucky young boy, intent on rescuing a prized ball, it would be daunting. If I come in, says the boy, I fear that you will do to me what you did to my father—what you Jews, that is, did to Jesus.

The Jew's daughter does not give the boy a direct response. Instead, she promises an apple to him if he will master his fears and accept her invitation. He walks towards her. She takes him indoors, and leads him through shuttered, unlit rooms, until finally laying him out on a table and sticking him like a swine. We may imagine the boy to be passive, submissive—Christ-like, according to convention. The blood flows: first the thick blood, then the thin blood, and last, in his agony, the heart's blood. (The three types of blood shed by the child correspond to the three types of blood shed by Jesus on the Cross.)[85] This wicked daughter of a wicked Jew thereupon rolls the body in a cake of lead, and drops it in a well ('our Lady's draw-well'), thus confirming all the boy's most dreadful fears, and our own.

When he fails to return home, his mother sets out to find him, calling out his name at the Jew's house (or 'castle') and at the Jew's garden, and then at the well. It is only by a miracle, however, that she finds her son. Here I am, mother dear, the dead boy cries, go home and prepare my shroud, is his message. He will meet her, he says, in the city on the following day. And as if in affirmation of this miracle, further miracles then occur (in one version only): the city's bells rings, but without hands, and books are read, but without tongues. The burial that follows is finer than any that the city has seen before: 'And ne'er was such a burial / Sin Adam's days begun.'

The daughter's malevolence is as her father's, while the child's suffering is resonant of *his* father's, though here it is the divine father. The murder is one kind of violation of nature, or of the natural order; the miracles are another kind, a redeeming, healing kind, which discloses the Jews' true character. These parallels and equivalences are the consequence of a certain understanding of history, one that takes for granted its patterned, static character. Jews confront Christians with the same disbelief in each generation, menacing them with the same conspiracies and attacks. Christians meekly endure these persecutions, giving witness to the truth of their belief by the manner of their deaths and the miracles attendant upon them.

This is an outline of the ballad that exists in at least twenty-one versions. It was included in Percy's *Reliques of Ancient English Poetry* (1765),[86] and then in Francis James Child's *English and Scottish Popular Ballads* (1884–98). While the ballad contains memory-traces of the death of Hugh of Lincoln, it deviates from what was then the given historical record of the event. Among these deviations is the manner of the boy's murder, which is not by crucifixion but by expert stabbing, the manner of the body's disposal, which is not painstaking but perfunctory, and the treatment of the perpetrator, who appears to escape punishment (unlike the Lincoln Jews, eighteen of whom were executed). That the historical Hugh was killed by a conspiracy, while the ballad Hugh is killed by one woman acting alone, is not a deviation of the same order, however. Literary anti-Semitism does not need conspiracies to incriminate Jews as a whole; it merely makes its Jewish characters representative Jews.

Geoffrey Chaucer, *The Prioress's Tale*

There is a literary process known in Formalist aesthetics as the canonization of the junior branch. The term signifies literature's tendency to draw upon motifs and devices of sub-literary genres in order to renew itself. Products of popular culture, leading a precarious existence on the periphery of literature, are thus raised to the status of *bona fide* literary art. That is to say, they are 'canonized'. Dostoyevsky—to take an obvious example—raises to the dignity of a literary norm the devices of the detective story. A comparable elevation occurs in English literature in respect of the blood libel. Chaucer raises to the dignity of a literary norm its devices; Shakespeare and Dickens, among others, then submit the blood libel to distinct elaborations.[87] Their blood-libel texts sit solidly inside English literature's principal literary forms: the poem, the play, and the novel—the dominant forms, respectively, in medieval, Renaissance, and modern, literature. The literary canon is made up of those texts that have become central to the imagination of successive generations of writers, are taught in schools and universities, and contribute to a certain national self-understanding. They comprise an authoritative tradition.[88] The pre-eminent authors of the English literary canon are Chaucer, Shakespeare, and Dickens. Anti-Semites take pleasure in the fact they are also the pre-eminent authors of the English literary *anti-Semitic* canon.[89]

Chaucer was born in or about 1343, some sixty years after the expulsion. He is the first English poet—that is, the first poet to write in English, for and of England. *The Canterbury Tales*, his last, unfinished work, is an innovative, even experimental undertaking, one that concludes a poetic career devoted to the resourceful 'Englishing' of precedents drawn from continental Europe. It purports to relate tales told by English men and women engaged in an act of Christian devotion, a pilgrimage to the shrine of St Thomas à Becket at Canterbury. Pilgrimages do not expose the faithful to adherents of opposing faiths, and can therefore be leisurely, agreeable affairs. Chaucer's pilgrims meet non-Christians only in the safety of their narratives.

Jew-hatred, of a distinctly sophisticated and aesthetically accomplished kind, is a feature of *The Canterbury Tales*. In the tale told by the Prioress, a Christian child gives offence to Jews and is therefore kidnapped and killed by them. But the child, throat cut and lifeless, leads his mother by song to the place where his body has been thrown. The Jews are tortured and executed, while the child is declared a martyr and given a fine burial. In the disarraying of the world and its setting to right again, the tale affirms Christianity's sovereignty, one which gives meaning to suffering and punishes those who cause it. The tale is barely 200 lines, the shortest of all the tales told by the Canterbury pilgrims. It is a tale of moral extremes, and the characterization, such as it is, serves not to complicate but to deepen the contrast between the innocence of the child and the wickedness of his murderers. It has melodramatic aspects, with twists and turns in the narrative calculated to dismay and to gratify its audience. It is exceptional among the tales that comprise Chaucer's work in the heterogeneity of its allusiveness (invoking scriptural and historical parallels), in the exoticism of its location, and in the politics implicit in its contrasting of the interests of ruler and ruled. Its dominant quality is one of piety, and it is listened to in silence. When the Prioress concludes her tale, we are encouraged to imagine the audience of pilgrims chastened into prayerful sobriety.

Though set 'in Asia, in a great city', this is a European tale. In the enmity it assumes towards Jews, and their own murderous enmity towards Christians, in the sufferings of an innocent child, and the retribution of an outraged community, the tale rehearses a familiar narrative, drawn from a tradition invented in Norwich, sustained by misreported events in Lincoln and elsewhere, and kept in circulation by song and sermon, and by legal proceedings and the reports of those proceedings. Chaucer's contribution to the libel was to compose a tale that, by the elaboration of the theme of the child's bond with his mother, by the narrating of her initial failure to find her seven-year-old son, and by the irreversibility of his death, gave it fresh qualities of pathos and suspense. What is more, by eliminating the magical and ritual elements in the murder, and giving the Jews half a motive for their hostility (if not for their crime), Chaucer gives the tale a certain psychological plausibility.

The little boy is brought up by his mother to honour the Virgin and sings a hymn in her praise on his trips through the Jewish ghetto, to and from school. This is a mistake, because the Jews are Satan's agents in the world, and his piety thus outrages them. The Jews hire a killer (a 'cursed Jew'), who lies in wait for the boy. He seizes him, drags him into an alley, cuts his throat, and dumps his body in an open pit.

The Prioress apostrophizes the Jews, 'O cursed folk of Herod all new'. The tale becomes a re-enactment of a scriptural killing, Herod's precautionary massacre of the 'innocents'. Herod feared a challenge to his authority; he feared that the Jews would rally to a new religious leader. He questioned the priests and scribes on the whereabouts of 'he that is born king of the Jews'. Bethlehem, they answered, quoting Micah, 'out of thee [Bethlehem] shall he come forth unto me that is to be ruler in Israel' (5:2). So Herod sent some of them there, explaining that he desired to worship the infant. But he was planning murder. God warned the wise men in a dream of Herod's intentions, so they did not return to him. Joseph was also warned in a dream, and took Mary and Jesus to Egypt to await Herod's own death. Herod thereupon ordered the murder of all infants, aged two years and under, in Bethlehem 'and the coasts thereof'. If the Jesus child could not be identified, he would die in the general cull. Whenever children are massacred in pursuit of the persecution of Christians, it is as if they were Herod's own innocents. They join a holy congregation, tormented by the Jews, hereditary felons all.

The child's mother waits up all night for her son. By the following morning, she is desperate. He has not returned home. She goes to all the places where he might be, or might have been. Then she hears that he was seen in the ghetto. Her frantic, dread-filled searching is narrated across several stanzas in suspenseful verse. She finally seeks him 'among the cursed Jews'. She is the type of all mothers, her anxiety and grief, the anxiety and grief of all mothers, including the mother of Jesus (see Luke 2:41–50). We may imagine the mother's sense of foreboding when she enters the Jewry. She must fear the worst at this moment. She asks the Jews whom she comes across if they have seen her son, but they answer 'nay'. Jesus then puts into the mother's mind the thought that her son's body is in the pit. When she gets there, she hears the *Alma redemptoris* sung 'so loud that all the place began to ring'. It is a miracle. The voice of her son's blood cries out to her from the ground, as the slain Abel's does to God (Genesis 4:10). The child tells his tale, and a crowd gathers. The 'Provost', the magistrate, is sent for, and arrives without delay. Praising Christ and His Mother, he orders the Jews to be bound. They are dealt with brutally and perfunctorily. The Prioress tells us that 'with torment and with shameful death each one / This provost doeth [causes] these Jews for to sterve [die] / That of this murder wiste [knew], and that anon [without delay].' That is to say, there is a mass murder of Jews.[90]

Still singing, the boy's corpse is carried off to the abbey, in solemn procession. As for his desolate mother, she is a 'new Rachel', grieving for her dead son. She knows the limit of this miracle: she will not get her son back. 'A voice was heard in Ramah, lamentation and bitter weeping; Rachel weeping for her children refused to be comforted for her children, because they were not' (Jeremiah 31:15). The Gospel appropriates this verse when writing of the Massacre of the Innocents. 'In Rama was there a voice heard, lamentation, and weeping, and great mourning, Rachel weeping for her children, and would not be comforted, because they are not' (Matthew 2:18). The Prioress in turn appropriates the Gospel. What began as Jewish lamentation ends in anti-Semitic calumny. It is no longer Israel that suffers, but its victims. The dispossessed has become the persecutor. Jeremiah's metaphor is confirmed or 'fulfilled' (Matthew 2:17) by the brutality of Herod's murders, and then confirmed again by the murder of the little boy.

Though *The Prioress's Tale* is a double fiction, a story told by a person who is herself but a character in a story, it resonates with what might be termed a 'truth-effect'—not truth itself, but an impression of truthfulness. Her account of the death of this pious Christian child works is a kind of solvent, burning through fiction's boundaries in the urgency of its warning, addressing both pilgrims and readers, joining the fictional and the real in a community of the innocent, reminding us in this tale of what our own children once risked. The specific truths that the tale affirms are the following. First, that it is both in the Jews' nature and in accordance with their laws for them to hate Christians and seek to do them harm. Secondly, that what happened to the little boy in the tale is what has happened to other little boys too. Indeed, there will be child-murders for as long as there are Jews allowed to live among us. Thirdly, that England is to count itself fortunate that it no longer has any Jews. The tale thus thrills its English audience with the thought of dangers no longer real for them. The Jewish menace has become fictional and historical, fictional *because* now historical. This English literary anti-Semitism is not a response to the real presence of Jews; it is not a 'reflection' of given Jewish–Christian relations. Rather, it is a product of the absence of Jews, of their empirical invisibility.

Chaucer's work was an intervention in an existing, rich discourse of Jewish child-murder. This discourse took various narrative forms. Closest to Chaucer's were those texts that related a murdered child's miraculous restoration to vocal life. Chaucer established something of a precedent in narrating a miracle within a form that was, quite openly, fictional in nature. The Prioress, an invented person, of complex and not wholly attractive character, tells a tale that does not even pretend to be a report of events derived from her own knowledge. The Jews and their misdeeds have at this point become material for literature; they now submit to the law of the writer's imagination (which prescribes: everything is permitted). Nothing else has changed. The defamation of the Jews continues, but in a new, better, an *additional* register. Lying acquires a literary character.

In 1801, Wordsworth 'modernized' some selections from Chaucer—*The Cuckoo and the Nightingale*, part of *Troilus and Cressida*, and *The Prioress's Tale*. Why *this* tale? It must have seemed to Wordsworth himself that the decision needed some justifying, because he prefaced his version with a short note. 'The fierce bigotry of the Prioress', he explains, 'forms a fine background for her tender-hearted sympathies with the Mother and Child, while the mode in which the story is told amply atones for the extravagance of the miracle.' It was perhaps the ballad revival then sweeping across Europe[91] that led him to *The Prioress's Tale*, because behind this work, of course, stands 'Sir Hugh'. But it is also evidence of the continuing appeal of the blood libel to the English literary imagination, however much it may be mediated by the individual author's more humane and sceptical sentiments.

Host desecration literature

The Jew-hatred attendant upon meditations on the Passion was sealed inside late medieval literature. Similarly confined were literary works concerning host desecration. The stories themselves emerged towards the end of the thirteenth century,[92] but only took definite, brief literary form some 200 years later. *The Croxton Play of the Sacrament*, alternatively, 'the play of the Conversion of Sir Jonathan the Jew by Miracle of the Blessed Sacrament',[93] is English literature's 'host desecration' work. This late fifteenth-century play is set in Spain. A party of Jews procure a host, in part to be avenged on the sacrament and in part to disprove its allegedly magical powers ('The belief of these Christian men is false . . . / For they believe in a cake . . . / And all they say how the priest doth it bind / And by the might of his word make it flesh and blood'). They pay a wayward Christian to steal it from the local church and then they subject it to various indignities and torments. The wafer at first bleeds, and then becomes the resurrected Christ. Jesus addresses the Jews: 'Why are you to your own king unkind? Why put you me to a new torment?' At this spectacle, the Jews convert ('Now are we bound to keep Christ's law . . . '), the Christian thief repents, and the miracle of the Eucharist is triumphantly affirmed.[94] The Jews thereby fulfil the roles of both assailants of and witnesses to the faith.[95]

The action in the play is transacted on three planes. There is the drama of Jewish and Christian criminality, of miraculous happenings, and conversion and redemption. There is the symbolic presentation of the Eucharist ritual, one that concludes with prayer and song in which the audience is expected to participate. And last, there is the symbolic re-enactment of the Passion— it expressly offers a 'new Passion'.[96] The play was performed near Bury St Edmunds, where three centuries earlier Jews had been accused of ritual murder. It is a work of gruesome and sometimes comic violence (one Jew loses his hand as he tries to detach it from the nailed host), while yet intimating no threat to its audience. There is no sense of the contemporary reality of its Jews.

The context of the Passion

Behind the blood libel, of course, lies the Passion. The blood libel emerged in the context of a new sympathy with Christ's humanity and an accompanying new hostility to the Jews, understood to be the principal agents of his suffering. In place of the Christ conqueror, king, emperor (*Christus vincit, Christus regnat, Christus imperat*) of the tenth and eleventh centuries, it is the suffering man-God, who patiently endures torments for our sake,[97] and who was humiliated under the hands of his enemies, his own people. Consider the following, from *The Book of Margery Kempe*. Margery witnesses many indignities and cruelties visited upon Jesus by the Jews:

> And than she thought, in her soul, she heard our Lady say to the Jews, 'Alas, you cruel Jews, why do you treat my sweet son like this, and he never did you any harm? You fill my heart full of sorrow.' And then she thought the Jews spoke back roughly to our Lady, and moved her away from her son. Then she [i.e., Margery]... cried out to the Jews and said, 'You cursed Jews, why are you killing my Lord Jesus Christ? Kill me instead, and let him go.'[98]

Margery (*c.*1373–1438) cries out against the Jews; her implication is that the particular form of religious devotion, the meditation upon the Passion of Christ, requires casting oneself in an adversarial relation with Jews.[99] 'The Jews with me made great variance', as a late medieval song went.[100] There is a fourteenth-century text in the preaching book of the friar John Grimestone in which the Virgin addresses the Jews:

> Why have you no ruthe [pity] on my child?
> Have ruthe on me full of mourning,
> Take down on rode [cross] my dearworthy child
> Or prek [nail] me on rode with my darling.

The poem continues with imprecations uttered by the Virgin against the Jews.[101] In another text, Jesus complains from the Cross, 'I suffer Jews on me to spit.'[102] In William Langland's *Piers the Ploughman*, a masterpiece of the fourteenth century, 'Faith' curses the Jews for their wickedness towards Jesus, 'you shall become serfs, and all your children with you; never again shall you prosper, never have land or dominion or plough the soil again. But you shall lead barren lives, and make your money by usury...'[103] In the fifteenth-century Morality play, *The Castle of Perseverance*, the 'unquert [hostile] Jews' prepare a cup of vinegar and force the suffering Jesus to drink it; notwithstanding the extremities of his agony, they '[do] not cease'[104] to torment him. In the roughly contemporaneous Wakefield 'Buffeting', part of the *Play of Corpus Christi*, Jews, described as 'torturers' in the text, torment Christ. They address him as if an animal; they abuse him as a rascal; they boast that they will procure his death sentence; they taunt him with references to their instruments of torture; Caiphas, the High Priest, announces that he will bless the man that 'knocks [Jesus] the best'; they blindfold him, and then take turns to strike him, mocking him the while; beaten almost unconscious, they drag him to Caiphas; Jesus revives, and is driven out of Caiphas' hall.[105] These texts are consistent with a late medieval perspective on the Jews, one that regards them as having deliberately willed their unbelief and hence engaged in malicious acts against Jesus.[106]

The perspective was dominant, but it did not altogether silence dissenters. Julian of Norwich (*c*.1342–after 1416), a religious recluse, or 'anchoress', experienced visions of Christ when ill. She was shown a crucifix and saw blood flowing from Jesus' face. She meditated on these visions, and composed a work, *Revelations of Divine Love*, which exists in two versions. The theology was heterodox: God is both mother as well as father, He/She is not prone to anger, and all Christians will be saved. Julian was concerned to emphasize her adherence to orthodox positions, especially when making her more heterodox pronouncements.

Julian wished for a vivid perception of Jesus' Passion, and to suffer his torments with him. She witnessed him hung upon the Cross, enduring contempt and spitting, dirt and blows, and many lingering pains. She saw Christ's body, bleeding abundantly, hot and freshly and vividly. The beauty and vividness of this blood were like nothing else. The spectacle moved her with love for her fellow Christians. We should contemplate the Passion with compassion and contrition, she urged. She did not see sin in her visions; God does not blame her for sinning. There can be no anger in God. He takes away all our blame and watches over us with compassion and pity, like children, not hateful but innocent. In those who shall be saved, all is included, for in man is God, and God is in everything. God is love. He is always loving, gentle, and kind. Jesus Christ, who does good for evil, is our true mother.

In taking on our human nature, he gave us life; in his blessed death on the cross, he gave us birth into life everlasting. And throughout, she believes everything that the Holy Church believes, preaches, and teaches. The faith of the Holy Church was continually before her, and she never wished or intended to receive anything that was at variance with it.[107]

And this is what she has to report on the Jews:

> I saw the Passion of Christ in several different showings . . . and although I felt some of the sorrow of our Lady and of the true friends who saw him suffer, yet I did not see the Jews who did him to death specified individually, although I knew by my faith that they were cursed and damned forever except for those who are converted through grace.[108]

She simply does not see them. Julian makes her bow in the direction of prevailing sentiments, but her imagination is engaged in quite another direction. Remarkably enough, Julian was an older contemporary of Margery Kempe's. She demonstrated that compassion for Christ's suffering did not *entail* hostility towards Jews. But it was Margery who was representative of her times, not Julian.

The sentimental hatred of the Jews, which was an aspect of this late medieval affective piety, evident in Margery, and represented in Chaucer's Prioress, over time either ceased to figure in English devotional literature altogether,[109] or gave way to a chastisement of self for being no better than the Jews—or indeed, *worse* than the Jews. See, for example, George Herbert's (1593–1633), poem 'Self-Condemnation',[110] or John Donne's (1572–1631) eleventh 'Divine Meditation'.[111] By the early seventeenth century, it would seem, reflecting on the humanity of Christ no longer required inhumanity towards Jews. These poets, though imaginatively 'st[anding] in the selfsame room in Calvary',[112] rarely felt the need, in their meditations on the Passion, even to evoke the Jewish presence.[113] It is as if the very topic of Jewish hatred, and its theological corollary, hatred of Jews, was then understood to be a diversion from—perhaps even a *sub*version of—the true meaning of Jesus' sacrifice. To concern oneself with the Jews was self-exculpatory, it was to misunderstand their role in the divine story, and it obscured Christ's own triumph. Indeed, it amounts to a double shift away from the pieties of which Margery may be taken to have once been representative. First, that is, away from an empathetic identification with Jesus towards an acknowledgement of a common position with his persecutors. And secondly, away from a sense of Christ in opposition to the Jews towards a broader sense of Christ in opposition to the world. The effect of these departures is to make Jesus' enemies general, and somewhat abstract[114]—that is, to disengage devotional poetry from Jew-hatred.

Accounts of the Passion, hostile to Jews, of course continued to be written. Lord Alfred Douglas, for example, declared himself ready to 'Fac[e] with Christ the fury of the Jews'.[115] Consider the following two works, written at the end of the nineteenth century, and in the mid-twentieth century, respectively.

The Jesus of Marie Corelli's immensely popular novel *Barabas* (1893)[116] is 'so unlike the Jewish race in the fair openness and dignity of His countenance'. Pilate exclaims to the Jewish crowd, 'I am innocent of the blood of this just person!' And the 'multitude' 'understood and accepted this position'. Corelli then continues:

> they, the elect of God, the children of Judea, eagerly embraced, and not for the first time in their annals, the righteous opportunity of slaying the innocent. And with one mighty roar they responded, men and women alike, 'His blood be upon us and our children!' The hideous, withering, irrevocable curse rose shuddering up to Heaven, there to be inscribed by the Recording Angel in letters of flame as the self-invoked doom of a people.

To Pilate, the Jews and their 'devilish priest' are 'accursed'. The Roman executioner reflects on the Jews, 'dark and bloody are their annals . . . they have been known to murder their own children to please the savage deity they worship'. Jesus is slaughtered 'to satisfy the blood-thirstiness of the God-elected children of Israel'. Corelli's novel swims in blood. The Jews are 'athirst for blood'; the 'chiefs of the Sanhedrin' are 'blood-thirsty'; 'Israel unregenerate' has 'tainted blood'; Caiphas, the 'Christ-murderer', a man of 'bloodshot eyes', pursues 'revenge, bloodthirstiness and fear'; Pilate's wife dreams of an 'ocean of human blood' that 'covers all the earth'; the Jews' 'Jehovah-Jireh' 'craves for murder and thirsts for vengeance'. And the Crucifixion itself? It is 'this singular Jewish festival of blood'.[117]

In 1942, the BBC broadcast a twelve-play cycle, *The Man Born To Be King*, written by Dorothy L. Sayers. In the notes accompanying the text of the plays, Matthew is said to be 'as vulgar a little commercial Jew as ever walked Whitechapel. . . . He has oily black hair and rapacious little hands', and a 'common little soul'. The Jews did not know that they were engaged in crucifying God; they were just fearfully unprepared for their great opportunity. But it is the penultimate play, dealing with the Crucifixion itself, which invites special comment in the context of the present chapter. The crowd chooses Barabas over Jesus. Pilate remonstrates with the Jews: 'But Jesus is innocent. He has done no harm to anyone.' They reply: 'Who cares?' and 'We don't want Jesus' and 'Crucify him!' Pilate becomes angry: 'Be quiet there, you Jews! Why should Jesus be crucified? What crime has he committed?' The High Priest, Caiphas, replies for them all: 'We have a law, and by that law he ought to die, because he claims to be the Son of God.' Jesus is whipped. Pilate makes one last appeal: 'Jews, hear reason. I have examined this man Jesus . . .' But, 'intoxicated with excitement', the Jews only chant back at him, 'Crucify! Crucify! Crucify! A'rrh! A'rrh! A'rrh!' This 'rhythmic blood-yelling', says Sayers, is the 'frightful wild-beast noise made by Nazis and boxing-fans'. In the next play, the penultimate one, Caiphas reflects on the Jews' political condition: 'It is the curse of our people that we cannot learn to live as citizens of a larger unit. We can neither rule nor be ruled.'[118]

Moment 2: the context of *The Merchant of Venice*

We may assume by the mid-sixteenth century a certain fossilizing in the received literary account of the Jew. It becomes the object of Christopher Marlowe's ironic, iconoclastic attention in his play *The Jew of Malta*, first performed in 1592.

The Jew of Malta

The name of this Jew, Barabas, is itself a provocation. Barabas was the prisoner released by acclamation of the Jews, in preference to Jesus, Pilate's candidate (see Matthew 27:16–26). In the Wakefield 'Scourging', the Jews respond to Pilate, 'Nay, nay, but Barabas! And Jesus in this case to death ye dam [condemn] this day!'[119] Barabas lives, and Jesus dies. By choosing the murderer, the Jews choose to murder Jesus. When they free Barabas, they condemn Jesus to death. To choose Barabas over Christ, is thus to choose evil over good, vice over virtue, hell over heaven. It is the existential choice made by all wicked men. Marlowe's Barabas is thus not just *a* Jew, he is *all* Jews—fickle, wanton Deicides.

Barabas first appears in his counting house, with heaps of gold. But he is not Shylock, who knows exactly what he has down to the last ducat, or

Fagin, poring over the sum of his stolen goods, parsimoniously counting them out. Barabas is overwhelmed by the fecundity, the sheer massiveness of what he has. If he can count it, he is not interested in it. 'Fie; what a trouble 'tis to count this trash!' He wishes neither for Christian poverty nor Christian monarchy. He cares nothing for religion and is alive to the hypocrisies of faith ('I can see no fruits in their faith / But malice, falsehood, and excessive pride'). He does not care for anything or anyone other than his daughter Abigail and his wealth. He does not care whether the Turks rule or the Christians. He revels in his status as a pantomime villain, guying the audience's most potent fears. He practises medicine to kill his patients; he intervenes in wars to slaughter both friend and enemy; his usuries fill the jails with bankrupts, put orphans in almshouses, and drive men mad. And that is not all. 'As for myself, I walk abroad a-nights, / And kill sick people groaning under walls; / Sometimes I go about and poison wells . . . ' (II.iii).

Barabas prizes his Jewishness as an aspect of his superiority. He is pure ego: 'For so I live, perish may all the world.' He is 'framed of finer mould than common men'; he is not one of 'these swine-eating Christians / Unchosen nation, never circumcised.' But he is indifferent to Judaism's precepts, refuses its consolations ('What tell you me of Job?'), and when plotting his crimes only asks for God's help as an afterthought. His daughter's conversion to Christianity is a personal affront only—'she that varies from me in belief / Gives great presumption that she loves me not'. He has no sense of himself as an object of contempt; he is not a man of resentment. He will ingratiate himself with Christians not for self-protection, but the better to deceive them ('We Jews can fawn like spaniels when we please; / And when we grin we bite'). When being Jewish no longer suits, he is ready to convert. 'Is't not too late now to turn Christian?' he asks friars, on being confronted with his villainy. The friars themselves know him to be capable of anything. What now, one of them asks, 'has he crucified a child?'

Marlowe's insouciance is breathtaking. He takes all the things that his audience supposes it knows about Jews, and exaggerates that 'knowledge' or mocks it,[120] or just glories in it for the opportunities it presents for his special kind of sensationalizing theatricality. (Villains celebrating their own wickedness in soliloquy were a staple of Jacobean drama; the Jewish villain, *ludicrously* boastful, parodies the convention.)[121] Barabas himself is an antinomian presence in a play that itself defies the rules of genre and the demands of verisimilitude. Marlowe freights his farce with the resources of medieval anti-Semitism; the play may be read as a parodic dictionary of received ideas about Jews. Its anarchic indifference to convention is exceptional even in Elizabethan drama, *itself* exceptional in the history of drama for *its* antinomian subversions of genre, verisimilitude, and received opinion. If *The Merchant of Venice* is an affirmation of the capacities of literary anti-Semitism, then *The Jew of Malta* is a joke at its expense. Had Shakespeare not responded to Marlowe, English literary anti-Semitism might well have been laughed into extinction.

The Merchant of Venice

The medieval poem *The Prioress's Tale* is a representation of sentimental Jew-hating piety, one that embraces death both as martyrdom and punishment. The Elizabethan play *The Merchant of Venice* is a revenge comedy in which no single voice rules, in which it is only the threat of death, not death itself, that tests Christian fortitude, and in which the Jewish villain is humiliated, not executed. The poem is so rarely read now that no knowledge of it can be assumed; the play is so well known that its language is the stuff of cliché ('pound of flesh', 'quality of mercy', etc.). The study of the poem is limited to universities; the play is regularly performed in schools and in commercial and subsidized theatres. Interpretations of the poem are confined to scholarly publications; the play is the object of widespread exegetical activity—nearly every literate person has an opinion on *The Merchant of Venice*. The poem will make most readers simply recoil; the play is so ambiguous, so troubling, both in its anti-Semitism and in its insights into anti-Semitism, that it mostly causes a perplexed unhappiness, though it has been used often enough in the centuries since its composition to promote ignoble elation at the spectacle of a Jew's humiliation. To pass from the one literary work to the other is thus to stumble over so many discontinuities of genre, theme, tone, and reception, that it may seem odd to propose the two as members of a single class. One passes, that is, as if from one literary order to another.

Yet consider the following reading of *The Merchant of Venice*. Antonio, a well-intentioned Christian, performs an act of charity by agreeing to secure his friend Bassanio's finances. This good deed brings him into contact with Shylock, whom we are invited to regard as a representative Jew. Antonio has long been the object of Shylock's enmity, and his good deed, in its selflessness, gives special offence to the Jew. And so Shylock conceives a murderous trap, a bond, innocuous on its face, because so extravagantly menacing. The ingenuous Antonio agrees to enter into it, and thereafter submits without protest to the Jew's malevolent attentions at his subsequent trial—knife-wielding Jew hovering over sacrificial Christian victim. His stance throughout is one of Christian resignation. But he is saved by the miracle of a cross-dressed woman, masquerading as a lawyer; her ingenuity is a secular version of Marian intervention. Shylock is then punished for his malevolent plan by being deprived of his wealth, or control over his wealth, and by being forced to choose death or conversion (he makes the coward's choice). That this reading of the play—Christian artlessness and Jewish malice; a potentially lethal trap; a miraculous event; the punishment of the Jewish villain—parallels *The Prioress's Tale* is more than a striking coincidence. The works are alike because they are both blood libel narratives.

Shakespeare's play, however, is a blood-libel narrative subject to considerable elaboration. Indeed, it is as if it has been written for the express purpose of investigating precisely how far English literary anti-Semitism can be taken—written as if, that is, in response to the challenge, with how much can the blood libel be burdened without it fracturing, disintegrating? Of what is it *capable*, aesthetically speaking? But that is Shakespeare in his every creative act—pushing hard against limits, putting the received material (his 'sources') under the greatest pressure.

Shakespeare develops the blood libel into a confrontation between law and
love, giving it theological depth, while at the same time secularizing it

The play is articulated through pairs of opposites. The financial bond secured by Shylock from Antonio stands both against the bonds of friendship that bind Antonio to Bassanio, and against the bonds of love that bind Bassanio to Portia, Jessica to Lorenzo, etc. The conflict between Shylock and Antonio, in which Shylock pursues his revenge and is frustrated, stands against Bassanio's courtship of Portia, in which their love is affirmed, and tested, and then reaffirmed in marriage. Shylock seeks to trap Antonio in a trial that ends badly for him. Portia imposes a trial on Bassanio, which ends well for both of them. Bassanio's trial is near the beginning of the play; Antonio's trial is near the end. And while Antonio's trial is a kind of legal process, Bassanio's is, in Freud's phrase, a 'trial of fortune'.[122] Though each trial concerns a legal document (a bond, a will) that calls for ingenuity in its proper interpretation or application, the bond is both a consensual document, agreed between the parties, yet malign in intention on the part of one of them, while the will, though it is *not* consensual, the testator imposing upon the beneficiary without reference to her wishes, is conceived in love.

How are these pairs of opposites to be interpreted?

They can, of course, be understood as conflicts between relationships of love and relationships of hatred. It is Antonio's love for Bassanio, for example, that makes him vulnerable to Shylock's hatred for him. The content of the love, and the content of the hatred, are themselves conceived in opposition to each other. Shylock's hatred is pinched, destructive, and ultimately impotent. By contrast, there is great richness to the play's representations of love. It is love as a kind of surrender, which at times has something of the martyred about it. It is patient; it does not flinch from suffering; it resonates with the divine. It is a plenitude. In relations of hatred, the desire of each is to have the other in his power; in relations of love, the desire of each is to submit to the will of the other, or rather, to find in the other's will one's own. The play thus puts Antonio in Shylock's power, and then puts Shylock in Antonio's power ('so he will let me have / The other half in use . . .'), while celebrating the mutual dependencies of the pairs of lovers.

These oppositions can also be understood, however, as conflicts between principles of love and *law*. Shylock's hatred is articulated through fidelity to law—both to what Jewish law commands him, and to what he believes Venetian law will give to him. This adherence is a kind of criminality, as we discover at the end of the trial scene. In blood-libel narratives, there is always this felonious adherence on the part of the Jews to their ritual law, and a matching adherence to principles of Christian love on the part of their victims. It is indeed precisely this confrontation between Jewish criminality and Christian martyrdom in *The Prioress's Tale* that explains the motto on her brooch, *Omnia vincit amor*, 'love conquers all'. But it is in Shakespeare's play that love conquers most completely. Jessica says to Lorenzo, 'love is blind, and lovers cannot see / The pretty follies that themselves commit . . .' (II vi 36–7). 'Love is blind' because it refuses to make judgements on the beloved; by contrast, 'justice is blind' because it does nothing but make judgements. The one separates the beloved from the rest of the world, elevating him/her above all else; the other refuses all distinctions between people, submitting all to exactly the same rule. Lovers commit 'follies' in a more complicated sense than mere ill-advised actions. There are things that are 'follies' in ordinary human relations that are *not* follies in the context of love—complete trust, a willingness to expose one's innermost thoughts, a kind of ready nakedness. Love is an estimable, praiseworthy folly.

This opposition of love and law in the play has certain theological resonances—specifically, Pauline resonances. St Paul's own immediate context in his writings is the two proto-Christian communities, the Jews, who follow the law, and the Gentiles, 'which have not the law' (Romans 2:14), and his immediate object is to effect the erasure of all differences between them, and therefore the erasure or enlargement of law itself, in the enfolding love of God. But his work is confined neither to this context nor by this objective, and it opens out instead onto law and love in many distinct registers. There is God's love for us, our love for God, our love for each other as members of a community of believers or as husband and wife, and our love of things. Love is self-sacrifice, the willing abandonment of self in favour of another or others. There is law as the 'old dispensation', in relation to which Christ's arrival is not an incremental, additional, good, but a revolutionary one, not reforming the law but abolishing it, substituting a new dispensation, one of grace, which is both law and not-law: 'the law of the Spirit of life in Christ Jesus hath made me free from the law of sin and death' (Romans 8:2). But law is also the key to decent community life; Paul affirms the liberation of the believer from the Law, only to subject him to the authority of Christ's example and the Church. It is indeed in the plurality of these registers, the intricacy of the many distinct confrontations between law and love that he stages, that Paul's work is to be understood and Shakespeare's play is to be analysed. Every Pauline letter celebrates love,[123] which he describes as the 'law of Christ' (Galatians 6:2); every Pauline letter engages warily with law. Paul is a great poet both of the *differentia* of love and of law, and of the retreat of law before love.

It is a simplification of Paul's thought to regard him as an antinomian (*anti-nomos*, anti-law). 'What shall we say then? Is the law sin?', Paul asks. '*God forbid*' (Romans 7:7). Antinomians ignore the Paul of this 'God forbid'. In the antinomian imagination, adherence to the law is regarded as mere 'legalism', and the Jew comprises the very type of the legalist. (The conception of Jews as legalists, and of Judaism as a legalism is also consistent, however, both with normative Christian perspectives and with normative biblical scholarship.) The antinomian simplification has at times exercised considerable appeal in Christianity's history; it has also fostered many considerable works in the English literary tradition—principal among them, *The Merchant of Venice*.

The play is similarly subtle about law and love, *but* in this instance, with an antinomian purpose. Hence it criminalizes its representative Jew's adherence to law. Shylock is a legalist in his indifference to equity, to charity, and to conscience. He practises an impoverished hermeneutics; he embraces an impoverished morality. He reads literally, and thus incompletely; he holds that by following rules we discharge our obligations to our friends and to strangers. He is rigorous when he should be generous or 'charitable'. He lacks imagination and makes a virtue of his dull-wittedness. He prizes above all else fidelity to the law, and thereby misunderstands law's purpose. He will not submit law to morality's authority. The given law *is* his morality. He lacks the means to distinguish good laws from bad ones, and is as ready to rely upon the one kind as the other. For Shylock, law circumscribes justice and trumps love: 'What judgment shall I dread, doing no wrong?' (IV i, l. 88). He would make the world into a courthouse; but he perverts law to suit his revenge. His religion is mired in petty regulation, adhering to legalities in a misconceived effort to attain holiness. It gives equal weight to ethical and ritual commandments. The letter of the law is its idol.[124] It is indifferent to religious motive, concerning itself only with precision of performance. It is preoccupied with nuances of observance. It is pedantic; it is censorious. It delights in the drawing of distinctions; it is most content when proscribing or persecuting. It is joyless. It is a legislated misanthropy. It supposes God to be a tyrant, capable only of issuing capricious commands, and it supposes mankind to be no better than moral slaves, fearing God's lash. It knows nothing of love—not love of God, not love of fellow man. Not for nothing is Shylock's resourcefulness, his creativity, bent towards serving his hatreds; not for nothing is Shylock an outcast—*most* cast out when willingly embracing Christianity. The moment of his final departure from the stage is also the moment of his submission to the Christian faith.

The effect is to unbalance any feasible relation between law and love. Love conquers all; there is no saving 'God forbid' in the play. To the extent that Shylock is capable of love, it is only the love of things, that most degraded of attachments: 'the love of money is the root of all evil: which while some coveted after, they have erred from the faith, and pierced themselves through with many sorrows' (1 Timothy 6:10). In Shylock's case, however, it both pierces self and others. Shylock's love of money animates his hatred of Antonio. The love for his daughter is jumbled in his mind with this love of money; the love for his wife is made deliberately ridiculous by its material comparator, a 'wilderness of monkeys'. This unbalancing of law and love is best understood by reference to Shakespeare's later work, *Measure for Measure*. It is customary to elide the two plays (for example, '*The Merchant of Venice* and *Measure for Measure* make us think about the conflicting demands of mercy and justice').[125] But this is to collapse two quite different works. There is *no* conflict between 'mercy' and 'justice' in *The Merchant of Venice*. It confronts justice with injustice; there is, in the end, nothing to say for Shylock's position. *Measure for Measure*'s very title is an invitation to reflect upon principles of justice, just as its content— for example, how may Angelo's escape from punishment be justified?—is an affront to those principles.[126] Not so with *The Merchant of Venice*. Shylock's punishment is condign; the only puzzle is why he accepts it. While *Measure for Measure* is serious about law, *The Merchant of Venice* is not. It is instead to the exploration of love that the play devotes its attentions, and the story of the Jew is but one aspect of its undertaking. He does not stand for law as an independent principle; he is instead everything that love is not. He is love's 'other'—law in several of its aspects, and the capital vices of wrath and avarice.

In *The Merchant of Venice*, then, Shakespeare goes beyond Paul to uncover antinomianism as a major theme for English literature.

Shakespeare introduces the theme of Jew-hatred

Though Shakespeare understood something of the psychology of anti-Semitism, his best account of the anti-Semitic personality is to be found in *Othello* rather than in *The Merchant of Venice*. If not the type of all anti-Semites, Iago is the type of a certain kind of extravagantly destructive anti-Semite. He is both relentless and servile in his hatred, his motives are obscure to himself, he is envious, he has an essentially pornographic imagination, he is fascinated and repelled by sexuality, he is a nihilist, a deliberate creator of chaos for the pleasure that it brings. That the object of his malice is a black soldier and not a Jewish moneylender is mere chance.

Nevertheless, there is enough attention paid in *The Merchant of Venice* to the character and effects of Jew-hatred to allow the judgement that the play is *both* an anti-Semitic play *and* a representation of anti-Semitism.

The play's anti-Semitism follows a certain logic It shows a bad Jew; it encourages us to think badly of him; it encourages us to regard him as broadly representative of all Jews; it encourages us therefore to think badly of all Jews; further, it encourages us to think badly of Judaism ('We perceive', noted the German critic A. W. Schlegel, 'a light touch of Judaism in everything he says or does');[127] it has been staged many times for this express purpose. The reception history of the play confirms that Shylock is taken by reader and audience to be a representative Jew.[128] The pathos of his great Act III speech ('Hath not a Jew . . . ?') is limited. It does not make the claim that a Jew is specifically capable of love—it is instead about the body's capacities only ('affections' and 'passions' in the seventeenth-century sense of temperament, rather than specific attachments), save for the reference to revenge. Shylock only becomes fully human when he revenges, which is his tragedy. Antonio is a merchant, but before that, a friend. He is ready to subordinate the opportunities of commerce to the obligations of friendship. And more importantly, he is ready also to change his view of Shylock, though he is justified in his contempt for the Jew by the play's events. He trusted Shylock and as a result was tricked into an agreement, one that he was encouraged not to take seriously. His offers of payment were refused, because while the Jew may thrive on Christian money, he needs Christian blood. His magnanimity towards Shylock did him credit and was an act of Christian charity to his enemy. It gave Shylock the benefit of Christianity. Shylock is an *Englishman's* Jew—wicked, malignant, but ultimately conquerable.

Its representations of anti-Semitism are by contrast diverse   It exposes the hypocrisy of Shylock-haters; it makes Shylock-baiting ugly; it gives Shylock at least one fine speech (which later authors have supplemented with their own speeches for him);[129] it subverts some of the binarisms on which anti-Semites predicate their Jew-hatred. Shylock is tolerated as a financier but despised as a Jew. His daughter betrays him. He is frustrated in his revenge by a super-legalism, and punished by partisan laws. He is then humiliated in his defeat—Antonio's mercifulness, a refined cruelty, only makes the punishment sting the more. Antonio heaps coals of fire on Shylock, the public foreswearing of vengeance granting sophisticated pleasures:

> Dearly beloved, avenge not yourselves, but rather give place unto wrath: for it is written, Vengeance is mine; I will repay, saith the Lord. Therefore if thine enemy hunger, feed him; if he thirst, give him drink: *for in so doing thou shalt heap coals of fire on his head.* (Romans 12:19–20)

When Jessica absconds, Shylock treats her as dead, but Antonio forces a humiliating reversal, compelling the Jew to recognize her afresh, to bring her back to life. He will be forced to work for his daughter for the rest of his life, in mockery of paternal devotion, and notwithstanding her betrayal of him. Not for Shylock, then, the freedom to dictate the terms of a daughter's inheritance. And the conversion is an additional degradation, all the more humiliating by being a choice, however coerced. Antonio robs Shylock of both material and spiritual consolation. He becomes, as Milton's Samson, 'a moving grave, / Buried, yet not exempt / By privilege of death and burial / From worst of other evils, pains and wrongs.'[130] There is enough here, then, to merit the observation that in this play Shakespeare inaugurates the literary investigation of anti-Semitism. Later writers, of course, pursue this investigation in a somewhat less divided manner.

This binarism, anti-Semitic drama/dramatization of anti-Semitism, is an instance of what has been taken to be a law of the Shakespearean universe: that is, that it embraces contradictory perspectives. These are articulated in part by the play's characters, and in part by the disposition of the narrative itself. Persuasive interpretations of the plays will identify their perspectives without, however, attempting to resolve them. Indeed, they *cannot* be resolved—something that clumsier interpreters fail to understand. This argument was first made by William Hazlitt at the end of the eighteenth century; it was then restated and revised by Jonathan Bate, at the end of the twentieth.

For Hazlitt, Shakespeare seemed scarcely to have an individual existence of his own, but to borrow that of others at will, and to pass successively through 'every variety of untried being'. He immersed himself in the mingled interests and feelings belonging to this wide range of imaginary reality. He was nothing in himself; he was all that others were, or that they could become. His genius shone equally on the evil and the good. When he conceived of a character, he entered into all its thoughts and feelings. Shylock is an instance of Shakespeare's power of identifying himself with the thoughts of men, their prejudices, and almost instincts. His imagination is of the same plastic kind as his conception of character or passion. To read *Coriolanus* is to save oneself the trouble of reading both Burke and Paine on the French Revolution; the arguments for and against aristocracy or democracy, the privileges of the few and the claims of the many, and so on, are all deployed. Hazlitt praises Shakespeare's utter fidelity to the '*local* truth of imagination and character' (italics added).[131]

Bate develops Hazlitt's notion of the 'local', giving it a specifically twentieth-century character. Shakespeare gives a voice to every disposition, thereby dissolving the ready distinction between virtue and vice. He is a master in making many different voices persuasive. His key gift, which did not belong to Marlowe, was experience as an actor. He offers an education in humanity, not a sermon in morality. His genius lies in his open-mindedness, his freedom from bias, his capacity to see both sides of a question, and to empathize equally with all. He was not a moral philosopher or deliverer of homilies. His interest was in dramatizing 'matter' and if there is a principal 'moral' to be derived from his work it is that any position may be answered by a counter position. In *The Tempest*, for example, a critique of Prospero is built into the play. *Henry V* is both a celebration of patriotism and a critique of it. Shakespeare refuses the 'either/or' in favour of the 'both/and'. These contraries are equally true. Bate terms this the 'aspectuality of truth'. All good literary works are aspectual; drama is fully aspectual, because it disperses the authorial voice; Shakespeare's drama is perhaps *supremely* aspectual. Alternative universes coexist in his work.[132]

There is an implication in Bate that the contradictory positions exist in a relation of equality; Hazlitt is subtler, because more empirical. In *Coriolanus*, for example, he maintains that Shakespeare 'lean[s] to the arbitrary side of the question'. Though Shakespeare 'describe[s] both sides of the question', he gives one side 'more quarter than it deserve[s]'.[133] In *The Merchant of Venice*, I suggest, he gives the anti-Semites more quarter than *they* deserve. What Hazlitt refers to elsewhere as 'the principle of repugnance'[134] is directed against the Jew rather than against Antonio or Portia, his principal adversaries. The trial scene is reminiscent of the medieval disputations between Christians and Jews. Shylock gets in some good shots, but the outcome is never in doubt. And by agreeing to convert, his defeat becomes a capitulation. He *embraces* his humiliation, and Shakespeare thereupon shoos him off stage, his sentence of conversion hastily and dishonourably accepted. Indeed, he slopes off even before the fourth Act has come to an end; it is as if Act V exists to make the point that anything is more important than the fate of this Jew. The Act affirms nothing other than Shylock's insignificance. That the testing of the lovers' fidelity, a process without either suspense or interest, is inconsequential is precisely its point. (Several of the play's eighteenth-century critics, missing just this point, thought the last scenes at Belmont superfluous: why, one of them wondered, ask us to turn our attention from the ocean to the fishpond?)[135] The play is in this respect in striking contrast to the final part of Tolstoy's *Anna Karenina*

(1877), which yet also despatches its principal character in its penultimate 'part'. Divided into eight parts, Anna's suicide occurs at the very end of the seventh: 'And the candle by the light of which she had been reading that book...sputtered, grew dim, and went out for ever.'[136] The eighth part opens out onto both the irenic routines of daily farm life and the organized violence of war, and Anna's story, placed in this vast space, itself 'melts into the immensity of time governed by forgetting'.[137] But while Anna's catastrophe resonates in this final part, until it becomes the faintest echo, Shylock's ignominious defeat is forgotten, utterly, almost as soon as he leaves the stage for the last time. Tolstoy intimates that it is only time and space, understood in their largest dimensions, that ultimately overcome the heroine of his work; it is but the pettiest of Venetian society's triumphs, however, to subdue Shakespeare's anti-hero. Only a conviction of solidarity with Shylock, unprompted by the play itself, might lead us to exit the theatre when the beaten Jew makes his own exit.

The characters in the play are also its interpreters   They comment on the drama as it unfolds, and invite the audience to see it their way. All their voices are heard. But this 'aspectualism' itself counts against the Jew. One might be inclined to read the play by analogy with Freud's concept of the 'compromise-formation', a symptom that is the product of a conflict between expressive and repressive impulses.[138] Perhaps the play is the product of, or a 'compromise' between, hostile *and* sympathetic perspectives on the Jews? Certainly, both perspectives are present in the work. But let me return once more to Hazlitt, and in particular his essay on *Coriolanus*. He suggests a reason for Shakespeare's inclination towards the 'arbitrary'—aristocracy, privilege, and the like. Shakespeare, says Hazlitt, is not much taken with 'the cause of the people'. This is because of a property of poetry itself. 'The language of poetry naturally falls in with the language of power.' The 'principle of poetry is a very anti-levelling principle...it is everything by excess'. It 'puts the individual for the species, the one above the infinite many'.[139] The 'one' and the 'individual' are what, in another context, Hazlitt refers to as the 'local'. This is *love's* commitment too. Poetry resists the general; it does not conform to rules. It favours love above law, and so, in *The Merchant*, it must favour Shylock's persecutors above Shylock. It is precisely this refusal to submit to the law of a single perspective, this creative, carnivalesque, dialogic refusal to allow one voice to dominate, which does for the Jews. Law constrains, but love forgives, and thus allows space for everything, celebrating it in its protean diversity.

Multiplying the Jews

The character of Shylock is taken to be greater than the play; he escapes Shakespeare's intentions. He is one of those Shakespearian figures who seem to break clean away from their play's confines. He is immense. One is led to ponder whether *The Merchant of Venice* should not be renamed *Shylock*, or perhaps *The Moneylender of Venice*. This immensity is consistent with a modest qualifying of his representativeness. But there is a further reason to qualify this representativeness, and its name is Jessica. In respect of Shylock's daughter, Jessica, Shakespeare of course had the precedent of *The Jew of Malta*'s Abigail. She confines herself to a nunnery and is killed by her father. But Shakespeare was also heir to two medieval discourses about Jews and their children (several centuries later, a further discourse of the 'Jewess' emerged, in turn in part derived from Shakespeare's).[140]

First, there is the predatory Jewish daughter discourse—which participates, in part, in that long and complex discourse of female cruelty inaugurated by classical mythology and then passes into European literature.[141] In 'Sir Hugh', though the villain is the Jew's daughter it could just as well be the Jew himself. The Jewish daughter is an undifferentiated part of Jewry; perhaps her wickedness is to be contrasted with the natural feelings of a mother. Shakespeare instead divides the Jew against his daughter. He thereby opens up the possibility of diversity in the representation of Jews. In rewriting the relation between Jewish father and daughter, he thereby creates two proxies for the murdered Gentile child of medieval lore. In place of Hugh, that is, there is Jessica and Antonio. Both are objects of Shylock's murderous desires. He wishes his daughter dead; he plots Antonio's death. In the received blood-libel narrative, the child is killed and the mother grieves. In Shakespeare's rewriting, the child repudiates, and is repudiated by the father.

Secondly, there is the Jewish child-convert discourse. In these stories, a Jewish child wishes to convert, his outraged father attempts to kill him, he survives the attempt by a miracle, and his mother also then converts. Only the tyrannical male Jew is culpable.[142] These stories had reached England by the twelfth-century, and circulated in sermons, in hand-held prayer books, and in collections of Marian tales and miracle tales.[143] Shakespeare both secularizes and to a certain extent ironizes this discourse. There is no genuine conversion, no attempted murder, no saving miracle, and the mother is already dead. The remaining Jewish parent is impotent before the child's decision. But even when it is not elevated, as in Jessica's love, it is a foil to Shylock. With Jessica, remarked Schlegel, 'Shakespeare contrives to throw a veil of sweetness over the national features.'[144] The Jewish woman's love has to go outside Judaism, and be lavished on a Christian. Shylock is the law's dead-end.

Jessica makes the running with Lorenzo; she shrugs off her Judaism. She is predatory in her relations with her lover, and indifferent to her ancestral faith. She is a sexy, lissom Jewish woman, the kind 'admired' in the vulgar connoisseurship of a certain kind of worldly male discourse—where the talk is of 'full-bosomed Jewesses',[145] and so on. Jessica is the low route to love. But she does not have to carry the burden of representing love. The pathos of love across class, religion, etc.—Shakespeare is not interested in this here. She merely takes her place within love's regime. It is a subordinate place. Jessica is a comic, or 'low', Portia. While they choose related men, the one chooses a husband in accordance with her father's wishes, the other contrary to them. They each dress in men's clothing at a critical moment: Jessica, when she escapes ('transformed to a boy'), Portia when she secures Antonio's escape.

Hybridity of genre

Samuel Johnson observed that Shakespeare's plays were not, in the 'rigorous and critical sense' either tragedies or comedies, but 'compositions of a distinct kind'.[146] The Merchant of Venice is one such composition. It combines two ostensibly incompatible genres, the revenge tragedy and the comedy. It is that odd hybrid, then: a revenge comedy.

In revenge tragedy a great crime or affront to the revenger drives him to retaliate, to his own disaster and to the disaster of his enemy. The Merchant of Venice bears down especially hard on two aspects of the genre. In relation to the first aspect, the play is broadly continuous with the genre's conventions; in relation to the second aspect, the play diverges from them.

The revenger is the prisoner of his hatred Shylock hates Antonio both because the merchant insults him and because he lends money at no interest. Yet he cannot escape the contempt of Venice; he cannot compel Christians to lend on commercial terms. His wish to avenge these affronts is thus unrealizable. His hatred cannot be satiated; his revenge will never be adequate to its object. Shylock in this respect is typical of the revenger, only more so. Every revenger is trapped inside his desire for revenge. It consumes him; he can think of nothing else. It makes him reckless; it makes him stupid; it is disabling. He *becomes* his revenge: Shylock the revenger is a Jew in part because wanting revenge is commonly supposed to be the Jews' national characteristic. His sense of injury so grows that nothing short of murder can satisfy him; but even that is not enough. He wishes to kill the object of his hatred, and then kill him all over again. The original injury is thus one disaster for the revenger; the desire to avenge it can be another, still greater, disaster. It is Shylock's disaster. He cannot get over his hatred, and yet he fails to consummate it in revenge. Denied the consolation of death, he is forced to live in hatred, working for the benefit of the very objects of that hatred. That is Antonio's revenge on Shylock, which masquerades as love, just as Shylock's revenge masqueraded as law. In its subtlety and scope, Antonio's revenge is far superior to Shylock's—not least because within the play's logic it is just, and thus has the effect of ending the revenge cycle. Antonio's sentiments are akin to Caponsacchi's in Browning's *The Ring and the Book* (1868–9), contemplating the murderer Guido Franceschini's fate: 'leave Guido all alone / Back on the world again that knows him now! / I think he will be found . . . / Not to die so much as slide out of life, / Pushed by the general horror and common hate / Low, lower,—left o' the very ledge of things . . .'[147]

The revenger is also the original offender   Shakespeare gives Shylock's revenge project a theological aspect. The enmity between Shylock and Antonio is coloured by the greater enmity between Jews and Christians. Within the normative Christian perspective, it was the Jews who struck the first blow. They rejected Jesus' teachings and procured his execution; they persecuted his earliest followers; they now kill the children among those who worship Him. Every act against the Jew is no more than justified vengeance for these unforgivable outrages to God and His Church. Shylock's defence of his right of revenge is in fact an admission that he has no such right: 'If you prick us do we not bleed? . . . if you poison us do we not die? And if you wrong us shall we not revenge?' (III i, ll. 58–60). Hearing this, Elizabethan audiences would think of well-poisoning and child-murdering, and they would both be angered by and enjoy the irony of Shylock's claim to the right of vengeance. It is the *Jews* who poison and prick; it is *Christians* who have the right of justified vengeance. This speech of Shylock's is full of self-pity, and there are few spectacles more ludicrous than that of an aggrieved, ignominious villain. He is a whinger.

He has exchanged the vocation of deicide for the opportunity to lend money at interest. This diminishing of the Jews' threat prepares the way for their emergence as figures of comedy.

In Shakespearian comedy pleasure's enemies are defeated. Principal among these enemies are 'churls', who are miserly, snobbish, or priggish characters, mostly old men. They are 'blocking characters',[148] the 'agelasts', the 'non-laughers', as George Meredith defined them, joyless 'men who are in that respect as dead bodies, which, if you prick them, do not bleed'.[149] Churls are grouchy and can spoil the fun; but the fun is usually too powerful for them, and overwhelms them, so that they either join in it at the end, or else are excluded from it, which itself becomes part of the entertainment. They are the butt of cruel jokes and jeering. The inflicting of pain upon them is *sanctioned*; they may be persecuted without guilt, because the persecution is no more than a response to their own malevolence. It is at this point that a connection can be glimpsed between erotic or romantic love, anti-Semitism, and Shakespearian comedy—a connection that helps explain *The Merchant of Venice*'s aesthetic integrity. Love is a departure from the regulated, general way of relating to other people. Sometimes violent and scandalous, other times pacific and esteemed, love nonetheless always entails a rupture with the everyday world. Anti-Semitism celebrates the possibilities of persecuting Jews, exculpating the persecutors of all guilt, even of any responsibility. The beloved may be loved immoderately, freely; the Jew may be wounded with impunity. Shakespearian comedy mediates between the two, both celebrating love and targeting the refusers of festivity—killjoys who put obstacles in the way of young lovers, or who lock up the food and drink rather than dispensing it.[150] A remark of Freud's about festivals is relevant:

> A festival is a permitted, or rather an obligatory excess, a solemn breach of a prohibition. It is not that men commit the excesses because they are feeling happy as a result of some injunction they have received. It is rather that excess is of the essence of a festival; the festive feeling is produced by the liberty to do what is as a rule prohibited.[151]

This 'festive feeling'—the 'liberty to do what as a rule is prohibited'— characterizes the intimacy of lovers in their relations with each other, it further characterizes the predatory hatred of anti-Semites for Jews, and it is a defining aspect of the aesthetic of Shakespeare's comedies. Transgression in each case is of their essence.

What then of the play as a *revenge comedy*? It is a revenge comedy in part because both the revenger and his enemy survive (though Shylock does not survive as a Jew); in part because the revenge plot is enfolded inside a love plot, in which the lovers are never even in jeopardy; and in part because Shylock's use of a legal process for the purposes of revenge is itself richly comic. This last aspect needs some elaboration. Shylock is an inept revenger. His plot is both effete and unintelligent. It is *effete* in comparison with the plots of those other anti-heroes of Elizabethan and Jacobean revenge dramas, which do not have as their object the trapping of their victims in a disadvantageous contract, and then enforcing it. It is *unintelligent* because when the bargain is struck, it is overwhelmingly likely that Antonio will be able to repay the loan. Moreover, Shylock ought to have understood the difficulties in the interpretation of the bond. He also ought to have known about the Venetian law that finally does for him. What, asks Kenneth Gross, could he have been thinking? That he would be allowed to take the life of a Christian merchant?[152] He has a naïve faith in the authority of legal institutions and the neutrality of the state. Though his idol is the law, he does not actually understand it very well. He finds himself trapped inside his own legalisms. He chooses the wrong revenge, and the audience has fun with his mistake. He is a comic villain. His catastrophe is an aspect of that broader upward change in fortune enjoyed by the play's other principal characters, and his suffering the prelude to their celebration.

Public understanding of the play as anti-Semitic has somewhat waned. But in the eighteenth century, there was little doubt about its Jew-hating character. During the Jew Bill controversy in 1753, the *London Evening-Post* published a satirical piece, anticipating the kind of announcements that might appear in the *Hebrew Journal* (the renamed *London Gazette*) once the Jews had established their ascendancy in the country. Among notices of public circumcisions and celebrations marking the anniversary of the Crucifixion, there was the following:

> Last Sunday an Order came from the Lord Chamberlain's Offices to the Managers of both Theatres, forbidding them, under the severest Penalties, to exhibit a certain scandalous Piece, highly injurious to our present happy Establishment, entitl'd, The Merchant of Venice . . . [153]

As late as the 1940s, there were still to be found anti-Semites who regarded the play as a brave challenge to Jewish power, and a work that the Jews would like to suppress.[154]

Moment 3: the context of *Oliver Twist*

The literary taming of the Jew in fiction

In the course of the eighteenth century, the account of the Jew in drama slips into inconsequentiality, though Shylock's menace comes to be restated in revivals of *The Merchant of Venice*. The proliferating accounts of Jewish criminality in novels are of a comparably tame kind, something akin to a scaling-back or domestication of Jewish vice—just as, in the same period, reports and accounts of the Wandering Jew tended to give way to reports and accounts of Jewish itinerants, peddlers, dealers in old clothes, and the like.[155] A point of origin for the literary treatment of villainous Jews is Thomas Nash's *The Unfortunate Traveller* (1594), a picaresque work with an episode of utter Jewish depravity, in which one Jew, Zadok, sells to another Jew, Zachary, one Christian for the purposes of medical experiment, while keeping a second Christian for his own violent pleasure. Facing expulsion and ruin, Zadok makes wild threats: 'I'll 'tice all the young children into my house that I can get and, cutting their throats, barrel them up in powdering beef tubs...' His plotting is uncovered, and he is executed most grue-somely.[156] The closest the eighteenth-century English novel gets to the blood libel, by contrast, is a kind of adjacency. Child-murder takes place in narrative proximity to Jews but is not threatened, still less perpetrated, by them.

The best instance of this adjacency is Daniel Defoe's *Roxana* (1724). It was his last novel, though not his last published work. Roxana makes a bad marriage when fifteen years old to a brewer. He squanders the family money and then abandons her and their five children. She farms them out and begins an affair with her landlord, a jeweller. But he is killed when the two of them are in Paris, and she takes up with a French aristocrat. When he decides to bring the affair to an end, Roxana resolves to sell up and return to England. But a devilish Jew to whom she attempts to sell her jewellery makes trouble for her ('putting himself into a thousand shapes, twisting his body, and wrings up his face this way, and that way', 'stamping with his feet, and throwing abroad his hands').[157] So with the help of a Dutch merchant, she flees instead to Holland. There she becomes the mistress of, but refuses to marry, the merchant. After a time, she does go back to England, and lives the independent life of a high-class courtesan, giving extravagant parties at one of which she dances in a Turkish dress, and is named 'Roxana'. She has further affairs, but then picks up again with the Dutch merchant, whom she finally marries.

That is where her story could have ended, with Roxana living in contented security. By bad luck, however, one of her long-lost daughters finds her way into Roxana's service, and because of what she knows about her mother's past, unintentionally poses a threat. Roxana finds herself at risk of exposure. Her long-standing servant, Amy, anxious to protect her mistress, murders the girl. She does, that is, what Roxana herself tells her she would not do herself: 'I wou'd not murder my child, tho' I was otherwise to be ruined by it.'[158] But she does not quite mean it, and does nothing to impede Amy. This is the second point at which the novel could have ended, with Roxana's exposure, and her implication in the murder of her child, or a swift decline into insanity and ruin burdened by undisclosed guilt. Instead, and at least for a while, she enjoys 'some few years of flourishing, and outwardly happy circumstances'. It is only in the last few lines of the novel, and then in the most perfunctory manner, that the novel intimates a final decline in fortune. 'I fell', she writes, 'into a dreadful course of calamities... the blast of heaven seem'd to follow the injury done the poor girl... and I was brought so low again, that my repentance seem'd to be only the consequence of my misery, as my misery was of crime.'[159]

Here, then, is the grieving mother, and the murdered child, and there is a wicked Jew in the story too. But he is disconnected from the drama of the child's death. He is involved instead in the marginal affair of the jewellery. He is 'cursed' and 'Satanic', in Roxana's excited but commonplace language, but nothing more than a trivial, odious crook—squalid, unpleasant, for sure, but also unresourceful, and easily outwitted. He is incidental to the plot, a genre character, part of the furniture that makes a novel.

Mockery, raillery etc.

In the line initiated by Richard of Devizes, and elaborated by Marlowe, one also finds in this period a certain readiness to mock the conventions of the blood libel. Consider, for example, the following pamphlet, commonly attributed to Alexander Pope but published anonymously:[160]

A Strange but True Relation how Edmund Curll, of Fleet-street, Stationer, Out of an extraordinary Desire of Lucre, went into Change Alley, and was converted from the Christian religion by certain Eminent Jews: And how he was circumcis'd and initiated into their Mysteries [1720].[161]

Curll was a bookseller who had earned Pope's hostility because of his publication of pirate editions of some of Pope's poetry. This lampoon was the third of three works that Pope directed at Curll. It is raillery, rather than abuse. The contents of the lampoon bear no relation to Pope's grievance. It supposes that the avaricious Curll, learning of the money made by Jews promoting 'bubbles', abandons his stationer's business to seek his fortune on 'Change Alley'. He falls into the company of Jews, who first attempt to convert him by promises of paradise and the advantages of the hereafter. He responds that he is more interested in the present. He will become rich, he is then assured, if he converts. He gives up his Christian name, but adheres to his black puddings. A further investment induces him to give up the Four Evangelists, and he becomes a Jew in all but circumcision and black pudding. The story then elaborates upon his coerced circumcision, which goes wrong (he is 'too much circumcis'd'). The piece concludes with this 'Prayer':

> Keep us, we beseech thee, from the hands of such barbarous and cruel Jews, who, albeit, they abhor the blood of black puddings, yet thirst they vehemently after the blood of white ones. And that we may avoid such like calamities, may all good and well-disposed Christians be warn'd by this unhappy wretch's woeful example to abominate the heinous sin of avarice, which sooner or later will draw them into the cruel clutches of Satan, Papists, Jews, and Stock-jobbers. Amen.

This comical, if slightly ponderous, text, so teasing and droll, touches on an association of circumcision and ritual murder that was long standing, and conventional in the culture.[162] Pope himself was a Roman Catholic and thus included himself among the Papists, Jews, and Stock-jobbers ready to savage 'good and well-dispos'd Christians'.

Speaking up for Jews

Hostility to Jews prompts defence of Jews; literary conformism stimulates experiment. It is in the nature of literary activity, just as it is in the nature of public life, that there will be those who wish to make departures from existing practices and norms, or even to take up dissenting positions. Certainly, anti-Semitism has never enjoyed an altogether unopposed run.

There have always been challenges, reversals of given narratives, counter-measures, counter-*texts*—and, among them, works of literature.[163] These estimable literary works are made in the pursuit of truth, in the presence of accepted untruths. They are written in defence of Jews. Jews are spoken up for, within literature's precincts. This is the artist as truth-teller, declaring with Browning, 'it is the glory and good of Art, / That Art remains the one way possible / Of speaking truth, to mouths like mine, at least'.[164] At the turn of the eighteenth century and the beginning of the nineteenth century, three literary works, a play and two novels gave accounts of Jews that countered or modified the then received literary account of them: Cumberland's *The Jew*, Edgeworth's *Harrington*, and Scott's *Ivanhoe*. They sought to speak the truth about Jews—to 'strip the creeper' of 'prejudice' from 'the British oak'.[165]

In *The Jew* (1794), Sheva, a Jewish moneylender, comes to the aid of a young man disinherited by his father for marrying beneath his station. This is but the first of his acts of philanthropy. Further acts follow, and previous acts are revealed. He loves his money, he concedes, but he loves his fellow-creatures a little better. He performs his good deeds in secret. At the end of the play he is praised as 'the widow's friend, the orphan's father, the poor man's protector, the universal philanthropist'. Sheva is given several opportunities to bemoan the Jews' lot. 'We have no abiding place on earth—no country, no home. Everybody rails at us, everybody flouts us, everybody points us out for their maygame and their mockery', etc. He complains about the literary representation of Jews: 'If your playwriters want a butt, or a buffoon, or a knave to make sport of, out comes a Jew to be baited and buffeted through five long acts for the amusement of all good Christians.' Of course, the general mockery and the literary accounts derive from the same general sentiments of contempt and censure. 'I am called ... a blood-sucker, an extortioner, a Shylock.' In the course of the play he is able to expose what hitherto he 'has shown to no man, Sheva's real heart'.[166] *The Jew* was a critical and commercial triumph.[167]

In *Harrington* (1817), a young man, terrified into Jew-hatred at nursery age by a malignant maidservant (apparently, a common experience),[168] then educates himself out of it, partly by self-interrogation, partly by a gentlemanly recoil from the spectacle of the bullying of a Jewish boy, and partly through the influence of a noble Jew, Montenero, and his beautiful daughter, Berenice, with whom he falls in love. The maidservant threatens the infant Harrington with Jews who 'steal poor children for the purpose of killing, crucifying, and sacrificing them at their secret feasts and midnight abominations'; the noble Jew reveals to Harrington that he has brought up his own child as a Protestant, 'according to the promise' made to his wife, the 'daughter of an English gentleman of good family'.[169] The novel celebrates 'the filial affection [Berenice, an anti-Jessica] feels for her father—though he be a Jew';[170] it is written expressly against *The Merchant of Venice*, and as an extended refutation of the blood libel. As a child, Harrington is menaced not by the attentions of malignant Jews, but malignant anti-Semites. The novel also breaks with Edgeworth's own habitual representations of Jews as villains—for example, her novel *The Absentee* switches roles between Christian parent and child, making the dying parent the Jews' victim, and the child, his father's comfort.[171] Reviewers of *Harrington* were somewhat perplexed by the weight Edgeworth attached to anti-Semitism as a social problem; the novel itself, however, tended to represent it as a *literary* problem, the consequence of 'the indisputable authority of printed books'.[172]

In *Ivanhoe* (1819), the Jewish moneylender, Isaac of York, and his beautiful daughter, Rebecca, are marginal to the main action, which binds a love story and a political story, around the person of Ivanhoe. He loves Rowena, his father Cedric's ward, but is opposed by Cedric, who wants her to marry another man. He is loyal to King Richard, and is opposed to Prince John, the king's brother, who plots with Norman nobles to depose Richard. Following a tournament, and then the siege of a castle, Ivanhoe overcomes his father's objections to him marrying Rowena, and assists Richard in overcoming John's 'cabal'. Richard succeeds in 'blending the hostile blood of the Normans and Anglo-Saxons'[173] under his rule, though it is 'wilfully careless'.[174] Rebecca, tried on charges of witchcraft, but acquitted through trial by combat, leaves England with her father (they have no part to play in the building of the nation). She of course remains brokenheartedly in love with Ivanhoe, her champion. The novel has made friends for the Jews.[175] The chapters that concern Isaac carry epigraphs from *The Merchant of Venice*, 'Hath not a Jew eyes?' and 'My daughter! O my ducats!' The narrator explains that the 'mean and unamiable' national characteristics of the Jews are attributable 'perhaps' to the 'hatred and persecution' visited on them by the 'credulous and prejudiced' populace, and the 'greedy and rapacious nobility'. Their 'passive courage' is inspired by 'their love of gain'. Their 'obstinacy and avarice' was balanced by the 'fanaticism and tyranny' of those under whom they lived. Isaac is a 'son of a rejected people', 'an outcast . . .

like his people among the nations'. He makes many false protestations of poverty. At the tournament, an angry yeoman reminds Isaac that his wealth is derived from 'sucking the blood of his miserable victims' and that this had 'swelled him like a bloated spider'. This is contradicted by the assistance Isaac gives to Ivanhoe for the purchase of horse and weapons.[176] Scott rewrites the relation between Jewish father and daughter as a loving one, rather than a conspiratorial one ('Sir Hugh') or an antagonistic one (*Merchant of Venice, Jew of Malta*). Rebecca herself is always 'the beautiful Rebecca', 'the beautiful daughter of Zion', 'the very model of perfection', 'the Rose of Sharon', a 'pearl of Zion', and so on.[177] This Jew's daughter is a healer, not a killer, one among several beautiful Jewish Rebecca's in literary fiction.[178]

The specific contribution these works make to *anti*-anti-Semitic literary discourse is to introduce anti-Semitism as a subject for literary inquiry. Later literary works built on this innovation. Consider, for example, three plays of the 1930s. In T. S. Eliot's play, *The Rock* (1934), Blackshirts address the Chorus, 'Your vesture, your gesture, your speech and your face, / Proclaim your extraction from the Jewish race.' They will not, they declare, 'descend to palaver with anthropoid Jews'.[179] In Stephen Spender's play, *Trial of a Judge* (1938), the men of the play's 'Black Chorus' *do* 'descend', but in order to murder an anthropoid Jew—to be precise, a 'gross-lipped fawn-eyed nigger-skinned / Hook-nosed intellectual', Polish Communist Jew. 'When we struck him', they boast, 'there was enough blood.' They 'kill', they further boast, 'the pascal lamb'.[180] *Trial of a Judge* turns the blood libel back against the Jews' accusers. While they rave, '[the Jews] secretly channel our blood abroad', it is the murdered Jew whose 'corpse . . . is a witness', and whose 'wounds are mouths speaking red words'.[181] And last, consider the following speech in George Bernard Shaw's *Geneva* (1938), made by its anti-Semite: 'I hate, loathe and abhor [the Jew]. He would steal my child and cut him in pieces and sprinkle its blood on his threshold.' The Commissar replies, 'Come to Russia. Jews do not do such things there. No doubt they are capable of anything when they are corrupted by Capitalism.'[182] These plays give the Jews' persecutors a self-discrediting voice. They make anti-Semitism their subject, rather than submitting to it as the condition of their own literary existence.

There is also the kind of literary work that stands against one version of anti-Semitism while affirming another version. Exemplary of such works are T. S. Eliot's poem, 'Sweeney Among the Nightingales' (1920), Dorothy L. Sayers' murder-mystery, *Whose Body?* (1923), and Christopher Isherwood's novels, *Mr Norris Changes Trains* (1935) and *Goodbye to Berlin* (1939). The poem circumscribes anti-Semitism while adopting it, flirting with but ultimately refusing the notion of a Jewish conspiracy.[183] In the murder-mystery, the Jewish businessman Sir Reuben Levy is the murder-victim, not the murderer, and the detective, Lord Peter Wimsey, solves the mystery of his death, not his crime. Isherwood's novels combine a trenchant attack on Nazi anti-Semitism with occasional disparagements of received Jewish types—'fat Jewish slum-lawyer', 'dirty old Jew producer', etc.[184] All these works affirm an anti-Semitism of condescension and disregard. I return to Sayers' work in Chapter 6.

Let me now return to the early nineteenth century, and that general enervation of English literary anti-Semitism the consequences of which are to be seen in the works of Edgeworth and Scott. It is at precisely this moment that *Oliver Twist* is written, a startling reaffirmation of literary anti-Semitism's potential.

Charles Dickens's *Oliver Twist*

Oliver Twist was serialized in the monthly magazine, *Bentley's Miscellany*, from February 1837 to April 1839. The first edition of the novel was published in November 1838, before the serialization was complete. It was revised for publication, and then further revised by Dickens in editions published in 1846, 1850, 1858, and 1867. It was Dickens's second novel. His first, *The Pickwick Papers*, had been very well received, but *Oliver Twist* exceeded it in popularity, and has never been out of print. It is not surprising—indeed, it is perhaps even predictable—that the third canonic account of Jews in English literature (which is also the third canonic work of English literary anti-Semitism) should concern a guileless Christian boy lost to his mother, whose life is put in peril when he falls into the hands of a sinister Jew, but who by a miracle is rescued (twice over, each time by proxies for his mother), while the Jew is apprehended, and executed. The novel celebrates what Dickens describes in his Preface as 'the principle of Good surviving through every adverse circumstance, and triumphing at last'.

The plot features confinements and escapes, rescues and recaptures. There are the expected reversals in fortune: those with power at the beginning of the novel are cast down, and those without power, either triumph or die affectingly. It is highly convoluted, and best understood as two stories with a common hero and an overlapping cast of characters. There is the story of a young boy who finds himself in a workhouse, leaves it, has various adventures that expose him to danger, but is rescued from his Jewish captor, Fagin, by kindly strangers, one of whom adopts him. Then there is the story of a young boy who at the beginning of the novel does not know his parentage, but by the end, through a series of happy, chance encounters, discovers who he is. The two stories are stitched together by a series of coincidences.

The novel is a Christian fable, a version of Bunyan's *Pilgrim's Progress*. Chapter VIII in the 1867 edition of the novel is entitled 'The Young Pilgrim's Progress'. *Oliver Twist* is a tale of a parish boy's 'progress' through all the wickedness of London before his eventual rescue and redemption. It was, said Dickens's first biographer, John Forster, 'the primary purpose of the tale to show its little hero, jostled as he is in the miserable crowd, preserved everywhere from the vice of its pollution by an exquisite delicacy of natural sentiment which clings to him under every disadvantage'.[185] He is a somewhat colourless presence, little more than an innocent anonymous consciousness registering suffering and bewilderment.[186] The novel also therefore plays on a very familiar Dickensian theme, the sufferings of vulnerable, isolated children. As Catherine Gallagher and Stephen Greenblatt write of *Great Expectations*, for example, 'imperilled children are so common in this novel, and their families so routinely blood-thirsty or uncaring, that its whole social world appears to be one Moloch's feast'.[187] In *Oliver Twist* it is Fagin and Sikes who take Moloch's part.

Almost as soon as Oliver arrives in London, a young pickpocket befriends him. The child takes him to Fagin, a Jew notorious for operating a gang of child pickpockets. He rules over them as a life-giving and life-forfeiting sovereign. Oliver witnesses Fagin drooling over his treasures, and comes close to being killed by him. He sees Fagin 'laying his hand on a bread-knife.... Even in his terror, Oliver could see that the knife quivered in the air.' Dickens offers a fantasy of the child's death as Fagin's prisoner: 'he looked like death'.[188] Fagin complains of Oliver that he is not like other boys: 'I had no hold upon him to make him worse.' He tries hard, however, and begins 'slowly instilling in his soul the poison which he hoped would blacken it'.[189] Fagin corrupts the boys, draining them of life as he morally drains them. He is what was known then as a 'kidsman', a thief trainer.[190] His infant captives have no future; they live hand-to-mouth, day-by-day. In this living death, Fagin is something akin to a vampire. He is a slayer of children, the suppressor of a new generation, the destroyer of fresh life and the thwarter of its promise.[191] He has immense power over his young charges; he subdues them by the force of his will. There is a mesmeric aspect to his personality.[192]

Fagin is a poisoner. When the violent criminal Bill Sikes demands liquor from the Jew, he warns him, 'And mind you don't poison it.' It is said in jest, but if Sikes 'could have seen the evil leer with which the Jew bit his pale lip as he turned round to the cupboard, he might have thought the caution not wholly unnecessary'.[193] Sikes is right to be concerned and later on Fagin indeed does plan to have Sikes's mistress, Nancy, poison him. Fagin is also akin to a serpent or other reptile. 'He glides stealthily along, creeping beneath the shelter of walls and doorways'; at night he seeks out 'some rich offal for a meal'; 'like some loathsome reptile', it is as if he was 'engendered in the slime and darkness'.[194] And Fagin is a spectre: 'some hideous phantom, moist from the grave, and worried by an evil spirit'.[195] The threat posed by this malevolent, shape-shifting Jew registers in 'little Oliver's blood'.[196]

The blood-libel stories, of which *Oliver Twist* is one, are about the judicial confounding of the Jews. In *The Prioress's Tale*, they are dragged and then executed. It is not clear how many are so treated; it is not clear whether the punishments (torture, execution) follow any proper adjudication. The executions have a quality of judicially sanctioned mob violence. In *The Merchant of Venice*, the punishment of the Jew Shylock is similarly summary, though in this instance not lethal. The trial of Shylock—as distinct from the trial of Antonio—is perfunctory in the extreme. It is as swift as the trial of the Jews in Chaucer's text. One reason why neither Chaucer nor Shakespeare dwells on the legal proceedings against the Jews or Jew at the end of each work is because their entire poem and play comprises a trial of the Jews. What then of the Jew Fagin? Dickens does not describe his trial, nor identify either the charges against him or the evidence supporting them. Perhaps the evil Fagin represents is too vast to be circumscribed by any single charge. At the moment when Fagin is convicted and the death sentence pronounced,

> The [court] building rang with a tremendous shout, and another, and another, and then it echoed deep loud groans that gathered strength as they swelled out, like angry thunder. It was a peal of joy from the populace outside, greeting the news that he would die on Monday.[197]

Dickens describes the emotions of a mob at the prospect of a lynching—a kind of ecstasy of licensed cruelty, Dickens himself found great difficulty in keeping his 'hands off Fagin and the rest of them'. He couldn't rest until Fagin, who was 'such an out and outer' that he didn't 'know what to make of him', had been tried and hanged.[198]

Oliver Twist is a work of melodrama, as has often been noted.[199] Melodrama, the melodramatic imagination, has been authoritatively examined by Peter Brooks in his literary study, *The Melodramatic Imagination*. Melodrama, he writes, polarizes and hyperdramatizes forces in conflict. It has an ethical aspect, evoking confrontations and choices in which we put our lives on the line. It expresses a moral Manichaeism: every gesture, however apparently frivolous, is charged with the struggle between good and evil, light and darkness, salvation and damnation. It is a drama of either/or, and all or nothing; there can be no compromise. But it also values heightening and sensation for their own sake. It is a dramaturgy of hyperbole, excess, grandiose antitheses, and excitement. It constitutes a refusal of the dailiness of the everyday. It refuses, that is, to content itself with the accommodations and disappointments of the real. It is a sense-making system; it is schematizing; it makes the universe morally legible. It is about masked relationships and secret societies, dark plottings, hidden and magical powers, conspiratorial realms, a world of occult manipulators and dupes, puppet-masters and puppets. It is also about overt villainy, the accumulation of menace, the persecution of the good, and the final reward of virtue. It uses a vocabulary of clear, simple, moral and psychological absolutes; its language is inflated and sententious. It refuses all nuance. Its heroes and villains are monochromatic. They repeatedly volunteer their moral and emotional states. It stages an expulsion of evil. It urges us towards an active, lucid confrontation with evil.[200] It denies the ambiguous—anything that is difficult, resistant to a categoric reading, or difficult.[201] Is this not anti-Semitism too? If one asked the question, what literary form does the anti-Semitic imagination most efficiently take? The answer might be, 'melodrama'. Another answer might be, 'read *Oliver Twist*'. The answers would be the same. *Oliver Twist* makes an innovative contribution to the anti-Semitic literary canon precisely in its elaboration of the proposition, anti-Semitism is homologous to the melodramatic imagination.

Dickens had the gift of rendering as if fresh and new themes of the greatest literary resonance. He was not a novelist of fashion; he did not merely rehearse received views. He was able to mine deeper, longer-lasting cultural notions. G. K. Chesterton wrote particularly well about this aspect of Dickens's genius. There is, he suggested, a peculiar quality of pre-existence to Dickens's characters. Not only did they exist before we heard of them, they existed before *Dickens* heard of them. He showed himself to be an original man by always accepting old and established topics. His subjects are stock subjects; throughout his writing he is engaged in the happy pursuit of pre-existing themes.[202] In *Oliver Twist*, he plays on the association 'children/Jews/danger',[203] and reaches past the conventional early nineteenth-century representations of Jews to more archaic representations—nursery tales of children-hating Jews, Sunday School tales of Jesus-persecuting Jews, ballads and songs, popular poetry and broadsheet narratives, the Jew-specific terrors, sedimented in the oral culture of the nation.

In response to a protest from a Jewish woman of his acquaintance, Mrs Eliza Davis, Dickens dropped most of the references to 'the Jew', and substituting 'Fagin' instead. This made the character's villainy personal rather than racial and supported the case for regarding him as a bad Jew. Dickens defended him as local, specific, of a certain limited type:

> Fagin, in *Oliver Twist*, is a Jew, because it unfortunately was true of the time to which that story refers, that class of criminal almost invariably was a Jew. But . . . he is called a 'Jew' not because of his religion, but because of his race. If I were to write a story, in which I described a Frenchman or a Spaniard as 'the Roman Catholic,' I should do a very indecent and unjustifiable thing; but I make mention of Fagin as the Jew, because he is one of the Jewish people, and because it conveys that kind of idea of him which I should give my readers of a Chinaman, by calling him a Chinese.

Dickens also introduced the character Riah—'Riah the Jew'[204]—in his thirteenth and last completed novel, *Our Mutual Friend*. The novel was a negative imprint of *Oliver Twist*, the first and most radical of the 'modifications' of the novel.[205] It is also a negative imprint of the blood libel. Riah houses and educates two teenage girls, one an orphan, and the other a victim of parental abuse. He is described as the girls' 'fairy godmother'; when the abusive father dies, his daughter 'hid[es] her face in [Riah's] Jewish skirts'. The Gentile father is the persecutor; the feminized Jewish father ('godmother', 'skirts') is the fairytale rescuer.[206] In his response to a further letter from Mrs Davis, in which she thanked him for Riah, he described himself as 'the best of friends with the Jewish people'.[207]

There are two canonic works, then, *The Merchant of Venice* and *Oliver Twist*, each bearing the name of the Gentile victim of a Jew, and they thrive in a continuous present, endlessly circulating in the culture, studied, performed, adapted.[208] And if one asks the question of English culture, which Jews today are the most potently, most vividly, *present?* The answer will be Shylock and Fagin. They represent a character-prison from which actual Jews still struggle to escape.[209]

Moment 4: literary anti-Semitism in retreat

There is a general retreat from the blood libel, following Dickens. This retreat takes many forms. There is, first, a *reversion* to tamer accounts of Jewish criminality. There is a striking *subversion* of the blood libel in George Eliot, a kind of counter-instance to the whole discourse of English literary anti-Semitism. And last, there are *swerves* away from the blood libel, or variations on it that distance themselves from its deadlier implications.

Reversions

There is then a certain reversion to the eighteenth-century practice of casting Jews as criminals, with occasional allusions to the blood libel, but occupying modest, even marginal, positions in the narrative. Thackeray's fiction is exemplary in this regard. His fictional Jews are marginal in his work, and they themselves are represented as marginal to their society. They are also tamer than the principal, menacing figures in the discourse of English literary anti-Semitism.[210]

Trollope's reversions maintain the strongest connection with the blood libel among the novels of the last quarter of the nineteenth century. In *The Way We Live Now* (1875), the fraudster Melmotte is a great monster, a fraud and a cheat as well as being a bad, violent parent, and a person who preys upon the family relations of others. 'People' say of him, it is reported, 'he was fed with the blood of widows and children'.[211] In *The Prime Minister* (1875–6), a Jewish adventurer, Ferdinand Lopez, woos Emily Wharton, and marries her against her father's wishes. It is a kind of trap he sets for her, a subtle kidnapping, even (one achieved with the engineered consent of the victim). He had 'robbed [Wharton] of his daughter'. This variously described 'swarthy son of Judah', 'Jew-boy', 'greasy Jew adventurer out of the gutter', 'black Portuguese nameless Jew, [with] a bright eye, a hook nose, and a glib tongue', attempts to extort money from the father, thereby alienating his wife. Emily, witnessing Ferdinand's schemings, thinks of him as 'thirsting for blood'. She has a child that dies within days of its birth ('nothing thrives that I have to do with', Lopez remarks); she is herself repeatedly referred to as a child. Lopez threatens her father that he will take her off to Guatemala if he does not give him money. The father is resolute, and a miracle happens—Lopez kills himself, thereby freeing Emily to marry her truly beloved, Arthur Fletcher, the very model of an English gentle-man.[212] (This variation on the blood-libel theme, the Jew enticing the child in order to prey on the parent, is taken up by Hilaire Belloc in his novel *Emmanuel Burden* (1904), but without Trollope's happy ending—the Jew does not die, the parent does. The Jewish fraudster I. Z. Barnett admits an innocent young man into his dishonest business scheme so that he can raise money for it from the young man's father.)

Subversions—*Daniel Deronda*: a counter-instance

There are two strands to George Eliot's *Daniel Deronda* (1876). In one, the spirited but hard-up Gwendolen Harleth marries Grandcourt, a tyrannical bully, even though she does not love him and despite her discovery that he has abandoned his mistress and children. In the other, a young man, Daniel Deronda, the ward of an English gentleman, and brought up as a gentleman himself, finds himself drawn towards Judaism and the Jewish people, only then to discover his own Jewish origins. Both Gwendolen and Deronda come to self-awareness, Gwendolen through her disastrous marriage, Deronda through revelatory, chance encounters, the first being with a young Jewish woman, Mirah, whom he saves from suicide by drowning, and the second, with her visionary brother, Mordecai. It became the convention to admire the first strand and deprecate the second, though George Eliot herself was adamant that she meant everything to be related to everything else.[213] But while the two strands entwine, they do not become one. Deronda does not marry Gwendolen and settle in England; he marries instead the Jewish Mirah and sets out for the East, intent upon assisting in the realization of Mordecai's dream of reviving Jewry's organic centre.[214]

The break

The novel was recognized as a break with her earlier fiction. It is the only one to be set in the present, the only one set in part in London, the only one set in part on the European Continent.[215] But there was more to its distinctive novelty than these thematic innovations. A reviewer of the novel suggested that Eliot had both inaugurated a new way of writing and returned to the literary form of the romance; later critics have found in the work a protracted, creative struggle with the protocols of literary realism[216] or an attempt to create a new conception of fictionality.[217] Neither reviewers nor critics recognized, however, that the novel is also a break not only with the normative discourse of English literary anti-Semitism, but also with both the mocking subversions of it in Richard of Devizes, Marlowe, and Pope, and the amends-making or apologetic writing of Cumberland, Edgeworth, Scott, and Dickens.

The extent of its break is best grasped by setting its themes against the themes deployed in English literary anti-Semitism's three canonic works.

As against *The Prioress's Tale*, and other tales of Christian children murdered by Jews and lost to their grieving mothers and communities, *Daniel Deronda* opens with a 'melancholy little boy', neglected by his mother, 'deeply engaged at the roulette-table',[218] and then explores alternative relations between parents or parent-surrogates and forsaken children.[219] It supposes the existence of honourable Jews (Deronda, the jolly Ezra Cohen) who rescue 'spoilt' (Gwendolen) or suicidal (Mirah) or infirm (Mordecai) children. It also supposes a useless, inconsequentially bad Jewish parent (Lapidoth), who steals away with his daughter, to her mother's grief ('her cry from the depths of anguish and desolation—the cry of a mother robbed of her little one'),[220] only then himself to be rescued by his admirable children (Mirah and Mordecai). And it supposes another, more complicatedly forsaking Jewish parent (Princess Halm-Eberstein) reunited with her even more admirable child (Deronda). Her act of abandonment is understood to be an act of love, however misconceived.[221] The theme of abandoning parents and abandoned children is indeed pursued in all the novel's plot lines; at its most pessimistic, the novel insists that the connectedness of mothers and children can be ensured only at the moment of birth.[222] The Arrowpoints at first disown their daughter when she declares her intention to marry the foreign musician Klesmer, but then relent. Deronda himself is both rescuing Jew and lost child—abandoned by his mother, and rescuer of the lost Mirah. Likewise Gwendolen both abandons others and is rescued herself. She does not intervene to protect Grandcourt's illegitimate children, just as she fails to save Grandcourt himself; she is rescued by Deronda at the beginning of the novel, when he retrieves her jewels, and is then rescued again, but also then abandoned, by him at the end of the novel, when by his example he redeems her but fails to marry her.

George Eliot's novel breaks from *The Merchant of Venice* and other tales of powerful, avaricious Jews and their renegade, beautiful daughters, and of Christians and Christian anti-Semites, living in foreign lands or foreign times:

- It contains no conversion narrative, and no marriage across the religious divide. Deronda does not need to convert to Judaism, because he is already a Jew. (In her essay 'Silly Novels by Lady Novelists' (1856), Eliot had mocked the author of *Adonijah: A Tale of the Jewish Dispersion* (1856) in which the hero, a Jewish captive, and the heroine, a Roman vestal, convert to Christianity 'after the shortest and easiest method approved by the "Society for Promoting the Conversion of the Jews"'.)[223] Her own novel admits instead the radical possibility that a person might *become* a Jew by a process of moral growth and self-education. In place of conversion Deronda realizes himself in the self-discovered faith of his birth.

- It breaks with the confining characterization of Jews as always and essentially Jewish, and comprising in their impoverished variety no more than one typical father and one typical daughter—hitherto to be found everywhere, even in her admired Scott, 'the unequalled model of historical romanticists'.[224] Instead, it opens out onto a diversity of Jewish characters, among other places representatively found at the dinner table (in the Cohens' home) and at debate (in the 'Philosophers' Club', where one Jew among the number takes an anti-national, liberal line, anticipating *Ulysses*' Leopold Bloom's rejection of Zionism).

- It parallels and inverts Shakespeare's double plot, both works being concerned with the exposition of Jewish character (plot 1) and courtship and marriage (plot 2), but while the effect of this double plot in the play is to set love, in its manifold forms, against Jews and Judaism, the effect in the novel is quite the opposite, and it is only in the Jewish context, that is, in plot 1, that one finds any elaboration of love—in the harmonious family life of the Cohens, in the love between Mirah and her brother Mordecai, in the developing love between Deronda and Mirah, and so on. Grandcourt's courtship of and marriage to Gwendolen, by contrast, is vicious to its core.

- It merely glances at anti-Semitism, what George Eliot calls 'unfairness and ridiculous exaggeration',[225] preferring instead to stand inside Judaism and

Jewish life, and to explore Jewish purpose as if both external and internal constraints (Gentile ill will, Jewish powerlessness) counted for nothing. Gwendolen's early, casual disregard for Jews ('Jew pawnbrokers')[226] is exemplary of her moral undevelopment, just as Deronda's discovery that 'in his anxiety about Mirah's relatives, he had lately been thinking of vulgar Jews with a sort of personal alarm', is evidence of his growing self-understanding.[227] But the novel does not stage a hostile confrontation between a 'Christian' world and a 'Jewish' world.[228] Grandcourt, the wickedest man in the novel, is not represented as an anti-Semite.

- It punishes its Christians, not its Jews. It is Grandcourt who dies; it is Gwendolen who is left bereft at the end of the novel. England itself is experienced as a kind of desolation.

Lastly, as against *Oliver Twist*, and other tales in which the eponymous character is the Christian victim/exemplar, in which the Jewish villain dies or is otherwise punished, and which unfold through narrative contrivances of unacknowledged implausibility, *Daniel Deronda* celebrates the coincidences—the secular miracles—that drive its narrative. The epigraph to Chapter XLI cites Aristotle: 'It is a part of probability that many improbable things will happen.' Deronda only by the sheerest of chances comes across Mirah, but then finds her brother, Ezra Cohen, by a double implausibility: he chances on the name Ezra Cohen, itself remote, only to discover that Mirah's 'Ezra' is living with this Ezra and his family. Deronda returns by a self-authored miracle to his Jewish origins. To understand his development, wrote one early Jewish admirer, we must 'break for ever with commonplace hypothesis'.[229]

Within the canon of English literary anti-Semitism, then, *Daniel Deronda* is the first genuinely counter-canonic work. It sets an enervated, conventionally Christian set of religious observances against an energetic, impassioned Jewish piety, and a rootless English society against Jewish communal cohesion. It is the *Jew*'s tale, not Gwendolen's—that is, it breaks with those earlier tales of Christian suffering and Jewish wickedness, the Prioress's tale, Antonio's tale, and Oliver's tale.

'Knowledge' vs received ideas

Until *Daniel Deronda*, literary 'knowledge' of the Jews consisted of *received* knowledge. Deronda has a low view of Jews because of the 'facts he knows about them', the 'ugly stories of Jewish characteristics and occupations', and 'very disagreeable images'; 'like his neighbours, [he] had regarded Judaism as a sort of eccentric fossilized form'.[230] These facts, stories and images substantially make up what 'everyone'—every person and his or her 'neighbour'—may be taken to know about Jews. Received knowledge is what passes for knowledge; it is the knowledge that is taken for granted; it is any given society's common sense. Or, to adopt social science jargon: commonly held cognitions accumulate to make up a cognitive culture map.[231] 'Jews' have a place on this map.

In many places in her fiction, Eliot is apt to acknowledge the force of received knowledge. In *Felix Holt* (1866), for example, Mrs Transome is said to know how to adopt an air of serious dignity when reciting something from her 'store of correct opinions'. She knows that the history of the Jews ought to be preferred to any profane history; she knows of the Pagans that they were 'of course' vicious and their religions quite nonsensical, but that they were responsible for classical learning; she knows that the Middle Ages were dark and papistical; she knows that the Italians are famous for painting; and so on. She has a whole 'stock of idea', supplemented by a good deal of proverbial wisdom: 'it is a lucky eel that escapes skinning'. Eliot does not mock her for any of this, but nor are we invited to admire the lady's readiness to adopt accepted wisdom. Towards the end of the novel, however, Mrs Transome delivers herself of a judgement that is wholly original to her, and born of great suffering: 'I would not lose the misery of being a woman, now I see what can be the baseness of a man.'[232] All her many opinions are as nothing against this terrible truth, and mean nothing to her. She does not quite arrive at wisdom, but we may imagine that she does leave behind the commonplaces that had sustained her hitherto.

Not just her, of course. And not just the commonplaces identified by Eliot. Among many others circulating at that time (early to mid-nineteenth century, though they persist beyond then), there were many about Jews—additional, that is, to a belief in the superior merit of their early history. Scott's *Ivanhoe* contains something like an inventory of these commonplaces: 'the unyielding obstinacy of [Isaac's] nation', 'the exclusive spirit arising out of [the Jews'] condition', and so on. His innovation is not to break with these 'of course' assumptions about Jews[233] but to bring them into creative collision with a different set of commonplaces concerning the Middle Ages: 'the universal prejudices of his age and religion', 'he had not the usual resources of bigots in that superstitious period', and so on.[234] Out of this collision comes similarly familiar, hand-me-down tales—such as the one concerning King John and the recalcitrant Jewish debtor (told by Maria Edgeworth too, of course).[235] The novel stays within 'thinking as usual', the discourse of what is 'taken-for granted'; it does not stray, that is, beyond the precincts of what everybody already knows about the Jews. It disturbs nothing; it does not trouble the reader's preconceptions. Everything, so to speak, is left in its rightful place.

The kind of 'knowledge' purveyed by Scott to his readers was given the name 'cultural code' by the French critic Roland Barthes. The cultural code in a novel comprises a résumé of received ideas. It is what we know 'naturally'; it is stereotypical knowledge. The utterances of this code are implicit proverbs, a farrago that forms the everyday 'reality' in relation to which we all adapt ourselves. Barthes recoiled from this 'knowledge', de-scribing it as a 'nauseating mix of common opinions', 'a smothering layer of received ideas'. Literary texts are clotted with such knowledge;[236] they appeal to the 'endoxal', the unexamined assumptions of a common culture or class.[237] Eliot breaks with that aspect of the cultural code relating to Jews (that is, the common stock of knowledge about the Jews), by burdening it with a depth and range of learning that it cannot accommodate.

So, on reading Book IV of *Daniel Deronda*, John Blackwood, George Eliot's publisher, wrote to his author: 'Where did you get your knowledge of the Jews?'[238] Well—Eliot learned Hebrew, cultivated friendships with Jews,[239] visited synagogues in Amsterdam and Frankfurt but, above all, she *read*. The notebooks she filled when preparing to write the novel are evidence of much more than merely conscientious research; they amount instead to a record of an English writer's intellectual journey beyond the received boundaries of her culture. She read books on the Talmud, and on the different generations of commentators on the Talmud, books on the Kabbalah and medieval Jewish philosophy, books on Jewish liturgy, books on Hebrew grammar, and books on the early, medieval, and modern history of the Jews; she studied the controversies within Judaism, and the divisions between Jews; she made long lists of Hebrew words, of fast days and festivals in the Jewish calendar, of Hebrew names and places, and of Talmudic sayings and Yiddish proverbs; she thereby made herself intimate with the inner life of modern Judaism (the title of one of the works read by her).[240] In consequence, her understanding of Jews and Judaism, like Deronda's, came to be 'fed with wider knowledge'[241] than the generality of her readers possessed. Indeed, the novel, wrote a Jewish admirer, was a 'Jewish book'. Eliot had acquired, concluded David Kaufmann, in *George*

Eliot and Judaism: An attempt to appreciate Daniel Deronda (London, 1877), 'the most minute knowledge of her subject'. She has selected 'unfamiliar quotations'; she expresses very different opinions to those held by 'all the world'; 'she is as familiar with the views of Jehuda ha-Levi as with the dreams and longings of the Cabbalists, and as conversant with the splendid names of our Hispano-Arabian epoch as with the moral aphorisms of the Talmud and the subtle meaning contained in Jewish legend'. She has thereby revealed Jews and Judaism, 'the Great Unknown of Humanity', to her readers. They are, one might say, *actively* unknown, because they are the object of 'calumny and obtuseness', and the most 'revolting treatment' by 'public opinion'.[242]

Eliot notes, in the course of the novel, the process of the 'wakening of a new interest—this passing from the supposition that we hold the right opinions on a subject we are careless about, to a sudden care for it, and a sense that our opinions were ignorance ... '[243] This moment, when the sense of ignorance first dawns, need not always be a pleasurable one. At the end of the novel, during their final interview, when Deronda lays out his plans to Gwendolen, she asks, 'Can I understand the ideas, or am I too ignorant?'[244] There is little sense of this tentativeness among reviewers of the novel. The *Tablet* found 'Daniel's acceptance of Judaism as a religion ... revolting'.[245] Another reviewer complained of 'a somewhat lavish profusion of sententious utterances, a preference for technical terms ... and a proneness to rank certain debateable positions ... among the truths to which it is safe to demand universal assent'. She uses words 'not generally known', a still further reviewer complained. She 'departs from the usual speech of [her] day and generation'. Her 'affections ... separate [her] from a wide sympathy with the heart and life of the people'. In addition, it was complained, 'the phase of Judaism' exhibited in the novel did not have 'sufficient connection with broad human feeling to be stuff for prose fiction to handle'. The novel, indeed, was considered to evince an 'ostentatious separation from the universal instinct of Christendom', subsiding instead into 'Jewish hopes and aims'.[246]

Eliot so *over*burdened the cultural code in respect of the Jews that she thereby created confusion, even boredom, in her readers, taking them beyond what they already knew, for sure, but also beyond what they were capable of readily assimilating. *Daniel Deronda* induced a kind of momentary crisis in the 'thinking as usual' about the Jews by putting it under intolerable pressure. The novel was an ambush on received opinion—it took Victorian readers by surprise, they did not expect to have their preconceptions so comprehensively subverted, to see everything that they took for granted exposed to scrutiny, the unquestionable questioned. Eliot anticipated something of this. She confided to her journal, 'The Jewish element seems to me likely to satisfy nobody.' Several months later, in December 1876, she wrote, 'I have been made aware of much repugnance or else indifference towards the Jewish part of *Deronda*, and of some hostile as well as adverse reviewing.'[247] In May 1877, she regretted 'the prejudice and ignorant obtuseness' which met her effort to ennoble Judaism in the thinking of the Christian community.[248]

The stupidity of anti-Semitism

One wants to write of *Felix Holt*'s Mrs Transome both that her readiness to embrace received ideas indicates her stupidity, and that the ideas themselves made her stupid, or contributed to her stupidity. Stupidity reigns where all seems self-evident.[249] To be *satisfied* with received ideas, to be comfortable with them—that is the mark of a stupid person. But stupidity's reach can be general; it need not mark out a limited class of person. The 'power of ignorance', that 'blind giant',[250] casts a long shadow. 'The quickest of us', wrote Eliot in *Middlemarch* (1871), 'walk about well wadded with stupidity.'[251] In *Daniel Deronda*, Eliot examined a specifically *national* stupidity— and part of that stupidity or wilful ignorance was a stupidity about the Jews. In a letter to Harriet Beecher Stowe, she records her pleasure that the response to the book has not been quite as hostile as she had expected, given the usual attitudes of Christians towards Jews—notwithstanding that these attitudes are both 'impious' and 'stupid' in the light of Christian principles. Indeed, she adds, the 'spirit of arrogance and contemptuous dictatorialness' shown by the English to all 'oriental peoples' is a 'national disgrace'. But we have a 'peculiar debt' to, and a 'peculiar thoroughness of fellowship in religious and moral sentiment' with, the Hebrews. And she continues:

> Can anything be more disgusting than to hear people called 'educated' making small jokes about eating ham, and showing themselves empty of any real knowledge as to the relation of their own social and religious life to the history of the people they think themselves witty in insulting? They hardly know that Christ was a Jew. And I find men educated at Rugby supposing that Christ spoke Greek. To my mind, this deadness to the history which has prepared half our world for us, this inability to find interest in any form of life that is not clad in the same coat-tails and flounces as our own lies very close to the worst kind of irreligion. The best that can be said of it is, that it is a sign of

the intellectual narrowness—in plain English, the *stupidity* which is still the average mark of our culture.[252]

In an early, tone-establishing chapter, Eliot examines both the broadest cultural stupidity and the pitiful limitations of individual minds. The musician and composer Klesmer, 'a felicitous combination of the German, the Sclave, and the Semite', disparages Gwendolen's 'puerile state of culture'.[253] The narrator has already chastised Gwendolen:

> self-confidence is apt to address itself to an imaginary dullness in others; as people who are well off speak in a cajoling tone to the poor, and those who are in the prime of life raise their voice and talk artificially to seniors, hastily conceiving them to be deaf and rather imbecile. Gwendolen, with all her cleverness and purpose to be agreeable, could not escape that form of stupidity: it followed in her mind, unreflectingly, that because Mrs. Arrowpoint was ridiculous she was also likely to be wanting in penetration, and she went through her little scenes without suspicion that the various shades of her behaviour were all noted.[254]

Stupidity is both a state of mind and a state of culture. It means in this novel, in Deronda's own phrase, owning a 'merely English attitude'.[255] It consists of making unwarranted assumptions; it has an element of condescension. It has a moral dimension—'moral stupidity' is one of Eliot's harshest judgements.

At about the same time that Eliot was writing *Daniel Deronda*, Gustave Flaubert was writing *Bouvard et Pécuchet*, published in 1881, the year after his death. In this unfinished work, two retired copyists undertake an examination of various fields of knowledge, testing received opinion to the breaking point. A 'Dictionary of Received Ideas', probably intended by Flaubert to comprise part of the novel's second volume, is a *sottisier*, an anthology of foolish commonplaces. It is a manual of instruction and of etiquette; it guides to the safety of the commonplace all aspirant holders of opinions; it lists both what one needs to know about certain topics, and what one does not need to know; it provides correct characterizations and appropriate responses to the remarks or observations of others. It is miscellaneous, but seeks to be encyclopaedic. Occasionally it steps out of its frame of reference, and the author may be heard, direct. An epigraph to the 'Dictionary' asserts that all public beliefs and received ideas (*toute idée publique, tout convention reçue*) are necessarily stupid.[256] Flaubert endeavours to put on display the stupidity of a whole culture, then, a whole age. 'The whole dream of democracy', he wrote, 'is to raise the proletariat to the level of stupidity attained by the bourgeoisie.' Upon the outbreak of the Franco–Prussian War, he wrote, 'whatever happens, we shall remain stupid'.[257] Stupidity is incurable, and is present everywhere, in the thinking of geniuses and fools alike.[258]

Daniel Deronda comprises Eliot's own investigation of the stupidity of received ideas, and it too was a last novel, though in Eliot's case, it was followed by a further and very curious work, *Impressions of Theophrastus Such*, in which the forms of fiction are further fractured, and which contains Eliot's account of contemporary anti-Semitism, 'The Modern Hep! Hep! Hep!' She opens with a scornful account of contemporary discourse on the Jews:

> It would be difficult to find a form of bad reasoning about them which has not been heard in conversation or been admitted to the dignity of print; but the neglect of resemblances is a common property of dullness which unites all the various points of views—the prejudiced, the puerile, the spiteful and the abysmally ignorant.[259]

And she goes on to examine 'the usual level of thinking in polite society concerning the Jews'—what 'is said', and what 'is felt', about them.[260]

There are differences between the two great novelists, of course. In Flaubert, one finds a certain disdain for the smug, self-assured platitudes of a fraction of his own class; he was always ready to mark as 'stupid' anything and everything that he disliked; there was a self-protective, even self-isolating, quality to his scorn. The recording of stupid remarks, the narrating of stupid thoughts and actions, comprise in some sense the whole of Flaubert's literary project—writing, conceived as an immersion in stupidity.[261] 'The horror', wrote Henry James, 'that haunted all his years was the horror of the cliché, the stereotyped, the thing usually said and the way it was usually said, the current phrase that passed muster.'[262] This cannot be said of George Eliot. She, for her part, rarely evinced horror of this kind; her discomfort with the commonplace was more qualified; it was not class-conditioned; there is a stronger moral—even, moralizing—emphasis in her analyses. But in both, there is a deliberate blurring of that notional line that may be drawn between the stupidity of the few and the received ideas of the many. And the effect, in George Eliot's case, is to permit a subversion of literary anti-Semitism not by substituting a set of complimentary received ideas about the Jews for the more usually deployed denigratory received ideas (that repertoire of anti-Jewish clichés),[263] nor even by mobilizing the truth against received falsehoods, but by exposing to critical scrutiny the national culture that breeds and sustains those falsehoods.

After George Eliot

Of course, just as realist novels continued to be written after *Ulysses*, so literary works *within* the discourse of literary anti-Semitism continued to be written after *Daniel Deronda*—indeed, promptly and aggressively reasserting the hegemony of that discourse. An anonymous sequel to the novel was published in the United States, *Gwendolen: A sequel to George Eliot's Daniel Deronda* (1878), in which Deronda abandons his religion upon witnessing Jewish cruelties that cause the death of a family, including an infant child. He concludes that 'as a nation, [the Jews] had been scattered for cause'.[264]

A counter-*Deronda*, of a more interesting kind, is Dorothy Richardson's *Deadlock* (1921). The heroine, Miriam Henderson, has a strong sense of herself as alien in her culture.[265] A Russian Jew, Michael Shatov, is one of her interlocutors. He is a Deronda figure. Miriam learns from him, testing her own ideas against his—especially ideas about Englishness. It was 'one of the charms of talking to Michael Shatov, finding out thoughts, looking at them when they were expressed and deciding to change them, or think them more decidedly than ever . . . ' She is intrigued by his ability to detect fellow Jews—they look no different than anyone else.[266] And later:

> He spoke with extreme gentleness, and Miriam looked uneasily ahead, wondering whether with this strange knowledge at her side she might be passing forward to some fresh sense of things that would change the English world for her. English prejudices. He saw them as clearly as he saw that she was not beautiful. . . . The pity she found herself suddenly feeling for all English people who had not intelligent foreign friends gave her courage to go on.[267]

She gets the measure of him. She does not marry him—marriage, at one time, seemed a possibility. She moves on. She becomes aware of a certain 'talked-out indolent vacuity'. The 'mysterious fact of [his] Jewishness' was 'the hidden flaw'.[268] But he is not rejected as a Jew; he is rejected as a man. She resists the implied subordination of the female in the marital relation.[269]

Swerves

There were novels written in the aftermath of *Daniel Deronda* that were professedly, straightforwardly, sympathetic to Jews—addressing Jewish suffering in foreign lands, commending Jewish virtues, and so on. Written within a received anti-Semitic discourse, of course, these novelists tended still to rely upon anti-Semitic tropes, while endeavouring to negate their anti-Semitic implications. In Hall Caine's novel *The Scapegoat* (1890), for example, the Jew's daughter converts to Islam, doing so not in repudiation of her father's faith but in order to save his life. She uncomprehendingly rejects Judaism the better to cleave to her father—'while her father was with her, then only did Naomi seem to live', 'she knew nothing of religion, she loved her father better than God', etc. And of course, she *adores* children—'she had always loved little children... Their lisping tongues, their pretty broken speech, their simple words', etc. The 'scapegoat' of the novel is Israel ben Oliel, the tax-collector for the oppressive Moroccan ruler, Basha Ben Aboo. 'Basha,' Israel cries, 'you are a tyrant, and have made me a tyrant also; you have sucked the blood of your people, and made me to drink it.'[270] Among the less cloying, less hysterical, engagements with anti-Semitic tropes, ones conducted at a somewhat more challenging literary level, are works by Rudyard Kipling, George du Maurier, Bram Stoker, and H. G. Wells. They may be read as swerving away from certain implications or themes in the discourse of literary anti-Semitism, without directly countering it.

Kipling

In Rudyard Kipling's 'Jews of Shushan', in *Life's Handicap* (1891),[271] Efraim is a debt collector, despised by the local population, and a ritual slaughterer of animals, esteemed by his own, very small Jewish community. His deepest wish is for a community large enough to permit collective prayer and thus to require a rabbi. But plague hits Shushan and most of the Jews are killed. The remainder, this 'broken colony', leaves the city. Among the casualties of the plague are Efraim's two children. Their mother, distraught at their death, leaves the relative safety of the home as if in search of them. 'She heard them crying behind every bush, or drowning in every pool of water in the fields, and she begged the cartmen... not to steal her little ones from her.' She too dies of the plague. Now, Efraim's debt collecting and ritual slaughtering point towards an account of predatory Jews, this 'dread breed', because both activities evoke ritual murder. 'A glimpse of Efraim busied in one of his religious capacities was no thing to be desired twice.' But having set it up thus, Kipling then swerves away, and it is the Jewish children (among others, of course) who die, and the Jewish mother who sets out to find them even though they are already dead. Her fears and fantasies precisely evoke elements in the blood-libel narrative. And last, the Jewish exile is self-imposed. The Jews are not the cause of the plague; they have not been banished following a trial or pogrom.

Du Maurier

Though the title of George du Maurier's *Trilby* (1894) bears the name of the Jew's victim rather than the Jew himself, in accordance with the standard practice of English literary anti-Semitism, it would be wrong to think of Trilby as entirely and uncomplicatedly Svengali's victim. Notwithstanding that she dies in consequence of her association with him, and is described as 'a gentle martyr on earth, a blessed saint in heaven',[272] Svengali is not her murderer.

The novel opens in Paris. Trilby, an artist's model of mixed Irish-Scottish origins and heavily French in her ways, is on friendly terms with a group of young British artists, 'three nice clean Englishmen', the 'three musketeers of the brush'.[273] The artists are all quite conventional, and they encourage her to give up her bohemian lifestyle in favour of more English, womanly proprieties.[274] Into this comradely marriage *à quatre*[275] comes the odious Svengali, who is both a sponger and a talented musician. He is as dirty, sordid, fetid, as the three friends are well-scrubbed—more importantly, he is as repulsive as they are well-proportioned. He discovers that she has a great talent as a singer, but one that can only be realized through hypnosis or 'mesmerism'. When she is not under his influence, she is tone-deaf, and sings execrably. In consequence of these competing pressures and influences, she gives up her old life, becoming both more 'English' and more musical—itself a paradox within the novel's cultural logic. Svengali makes her an immense success as a singer. She lives with him as his wife and is known on the concert circuit as 'La Svengali'. Svengali's health suffers a series of violent reverses, and at a concert, when Trilby is on stage but yet to perform, he dies of a heart attack—whereupon she immediately loses her ability to sing. She too dies, somewhat later on, weakened by her repeated trances, and with Svengali's name on her lips. The story is not wholly original—precedents have been found in works of Thackeray's, for example.[276]

'There is no question', George Orwell commented, 'that the book is antisemitic.'[277] Svengali is 'shabby and dirty'; he has 'bold, brilliant black eyes, with long, heavy lids, a thin, sallow face, and a beard of burnt-up black, which grew almost from under his eyelids...' etc. He has, that is, a 'sinister' appearance.[278] He is the string-pulling, hidden manipulator drawn from anti-Semitism's most fevered imaginings. He is a spider, trapping and feeding off the people caught in his extended web. (Though unlike Isaac of York he is not a *bloated* spider—when thus described, Svengali has yet to profit from his predatory ways.) Svengali is an artist, but of the most parasitic kind. He does not create, he appropriates. The three friends influence

Trilby, and she changes—experiencing a 'dawning self-respect'.[279] She becomes 'as upright and straight and honourable as a man'; it is a 'strange metamorphosis'.[280] Svengali, by contrast, merely takes control of her, mesmerizing her and fixing her with his name. Until he has her fully in his power, Trilby's sense of him is as 'a dread, powerful demon', who 'oppressed and weighed on her like an incubus'.[281] In addition, therefore, to giving an anti-Semitic twist both to the Pygmalion myth (the 'unconscious Trilby of marble')[282] and the generic fairytale (Beauty put to sleep by the wicked wizard, not to awaken until he is destroyed),[283] the novel is also a counter to *Daniel Deronda*—against Mordecai's seer-like stare and his Mirah's effortlessly beautiful singing voice, there is Svengali's malignant stare and 'the two Trilbys', the 'one who could not sing one single note in tune', and the one who 'was just a singing-machine'.[284]

Entirely unsurprisingly, then, the novel has a family resemblance to those other works of English literary anti-Semitism that improvise on blood libel themes. Svengali's first glance at Trilby communicates an 'intent to kill', the complete control he later exercises over her is akin to an imprisonment, and when she sings it is as if she 'had ceased to exist . . . *our* Trilby was *dead*'. She is no more than a 'flexible flageolet of flesh and blood'. And yet, Svengali's command of Trilby actually brings her great celebrity. The novel is not quite a tale of abduction and death; it is also one of healing (Svengali cures her neuralgia), kindness ('He was always very kind!'), and—for a while, at least—renown and material success. Svengali unlocks Trilby's capacity for song, and when she does sing it is not to disclose her whereabouts, nor to expose the Jew, but for the pleasure of her audience. 'The like of that voice has never been heard, nor ever will be again.' The singing is a miracle engineered *by* the Jewish Svengali, not deployed *against* him. And it is not the ingenuous Gentile who dies under the Jew's knife, but rather the Jew himself who suffers a knife blow, the final assault upon him prior to his collapse and death (though du Maurier is careful to point out that the attack did not itself *cause* Svengali's death). The novel may be read, then, as a subversion of the blood libel. For sure, its anti- and *anti*-anti-Semitic aspects jostle without ready resolution.[285]

Stoker

The first English poem with a vampire theme was Robert Southey's *Thalaba the Destroyer* (1797); the first English vampire story was written by the physician who accompanied Byron on his Grand Tour; Byron himself was much taken with vampires, and all the major Romantic poets wrote works that explored vampiric themes[286]—the spectral, the involuntary transfer of energy, predatory love, and the erotics of death. Dickens's Miss Petowker gives a spirited performance of 'The Blood Drinker's Burial' in *Nicholas Nickleby* (1839), terrifying her infant audience, 'who were all but frightened into fits'.[287] The literary topic of vampires seemed exhausted when Bram Stoker came to write his work. He revived it by giving the topic an anti-Semitic complexion. *Dracula* is exceptional in the subgenre of vampire fiction in part because it draws on English literary anti-Semitism's principal trope, the blood libel.

The story begins with Jonathan Harker, a solicitor, travelling to Transylvania to meet his client, Count Dracula, for whom his firm has bought a London suburban estate. While Harker is detained in the castle he has several terrifying experiences, the cumulative effect of which is to drive him temporarily insane. In the meantime, Dracula has arranged to have himself transported to England amid wooden boxes or coffins 'filled with mould'.[288] Once there, he turns one woman vampire and exposes another one to the same fate. Dedicated vampire-slayers destroy Dracula's coffins using slivers of consecrated host. Dracula himself flees back to Transylvania, but is defeated there by his adversaries, who stab him through the heart and behead him.

Preying upon small children for their blood is early introduced as a topic in the novel. Harker witnesses the feasting on a 'half-smothered child' by female vampires, and then a few days later witnesses a distraught mother at the castle wall, crying 'Monster, give me my child!', before she herself is killed. Later, in the London section of the novel, the newly vampired Lucy preys upon small children who stray onto Hampstead Heath. Dracula himself shares with the Wandering Jew the 'curse of immortality'. The vampire 'is known everywhere that men have been. In old Greece, in old Rome . . . and in China, so far from us in all ways, there even is he, and the peoples fear him at this day.' On departing England, Dracula swears revenge: 'My revenge is just begun! I spread it over centuries, and time is on my side.' This conjunction of the two tropes—the blood libel, the Wandering Jew—establishes, by a kind of reversal, a connection between *Dracula* and Lewis's *The Monk*, in which the two are set in opposition.[289]

Dracula was published just as the modern ritual-murder accusation in Central and Eastern Europe was at its most intense,[290] and when comparing Jews to vampires was practically commonplace: '[we must] defang the

Jewish vampire that sucks [the German people's] unsuspecting heart's blood'.[291] But there is a more local conjunction. The immensely successful *Trilby* was published three years before the immensely successful *Dracula*.[292] It can be said that almost everyone who read the one would also have read the other. A suggestive comparison has thus been drawn between Svengali and Dracula: the master-mesmerist Dracula seems like a derivation from Svengali.[293] Both Svengali and Dracula are from the 'poisonous East';[294] both are tall and thin; both are sinister in appearance; both have magical powers; both prey upon women; and both have animal-like characteristics (Svengali is likened to an 'uncanny black spider-cat', a rook, and a dog,[295] while Dracula is variously related to dogs, wolves, and bats). And then there is the matter of blood. Du Maurier rhapsodizes over Jewish blood: 'that strong, sturdy, irrepressible, indomitable, indelible blood which is such priceless value in diluted homeopathic doses... Fortunately for the world, most of us have in our veins at least a minimum of that precious fluid.'[296] Jews themselves may be problematic, but a homeopathic quantity of their blood confers great benefits.[297] To read about Dracula is thus to have Svengali in mind.

Indeed, Dracula possesses many of the characteristics attributed, in medieval or contemporary times, to Jews. He recoils from the Cross; he has 'a smile that Judas in hell might be proud of'; he has a distinctive, foul odour; he is infernal (travelling in London under the name 'Mr de Ville'); he is from the East; he is parasitic; he is both hyper-mobile and acquisitive; he describes himself as a 'stranger in a strange land'. And then, of course, there is the matter of blood. Vampires and Jews are consumers of blood—revived but not redeemed by its consumption, their desire for it driving them to extremes of depravity. They are shape-shifters, capable of altering their appearance and thus concealing their identity. The vampire's skill at transmutation is akin to the Jew's skill at social climbing, name-changing, etc., as well as the more sinister arts of self-concealment and conspiracy. The insinuations of Dracula's affinity with the Semitic are many, and relentlessly pressed.[298]

And yet—nowhere is Dracula identified as a Jew. He describes himself as belonging to a 'conquering race', but also explains 'in our veins flows the blood of many brave races'.[299]*Dracula* is not about Jews—its one, very minor Jewish character, is objectionable but trivial in the economy of the novel[300]—Stoker does not write about Jews; it is a misreading of the novel to regard Dracula as a form or 'incarnation' taken by the Jew in the literary imagination.[301] Stoker scavenges from many discursive fields and makes his monster out of bits and pieces of science and literature.[302] His research does not converge on a fuller and more complete representation of a single, complex phenomenon; it has instead a miscellaneous quality, one that has the effect of exceeding the confines of wholly 'Jewish' representations. The anti-Semitism in the novel thus has a somewhat blurred, out-of-focus quality. T. S. Eliot was similarly opportunistic in his scavenging of anti-Semitic discourse, but whereas in Stoker this discourse is dissolved into a larger composition, in Eliot it is compacted, intense.

Wells

Wells's *Tono-Bungay* (1909) is a tale of dishonest entrepreneurship and murder, the making of a fortune by the peddling of a worthless, even dangerous, patent medicine ('slightly injurious rubbish'),[303] in deception of consumers and breach of the law, and the killing of a man, remorselessly, and without consequence for the murderer. It is also a tale of Jewish plutocrats, and the new dominance they have secured in English society. The two tales are not the same. The first occupies almost the whole book; the second is merely glanced at in the opening pages. It is not the Jews who menace the health of society. *Tono-Bungay* is subtitled 'A Romance of Commerce', and Wells described it as 'perhaps my most ambitious novel'.[304] The narrator, George Ponderevo, describes the rise and fall of his uncle Edward, the fraudulent businessman, for a time a magnate, and then a bankrupt. During the course of his account, George also describes how he killed a 'native' while on an expedition to Mordet Island, somewhere on the African coast. He commits the murder at a moment when he 'hates all humanity'. Having killed the man, he sets about hiding him, but by the next day the body is dragged out from its burial place, so when George returns, he reburies the corpse. Two days later, when George pays a second visit, the body has gone. In his dreams, he imagines the African 'no longer . . . dead, but acutely alive and perceiving'. Journeying home, he finds to his relief that he is 'released from the spell of that bloodstained black body'.[305]

What then of the second tale? It is barely a tale at all. In a restatement of what might be called, in the context of the present chapter, 'Defoean adjacency', the Jews' offences are contiguous with, but not causative of, the greater offences that are the subject of the first tale. Edward Ponderevo is Roxana the fraudster; George Ponderevo is Roxana the murderer. The marginal Jews of Defoe's novel become the *utterly* marginal Jews of Wells's novel. We are introduced to them at the very beginning of the novel; they are mentioned again a little later on, and then they drop out of the work altogether. The renting of a stately pile, Bladesover House, to Sir Reuben Lichtenstein is taken to be indicative of a national decline. 'The prevalence of [the Lichtensteins] and their kind is but a phase in the broad slow decay of the great social organism of England.' The Jews, of whom Sir Reuben is representative, are not so much a new gentry as 'pseudomorphous' after the old, English gentry—shape-shifters who take the form of the gentry, contrary to their own natural form. They have no 'fresh vitality', there is 'nothing creative' about them, they speak for nothing more than 'a disorderly instinct of acquisition'. They feed as if on dead matter.[306] But they do not matter in the novel, however much Edward Ponderevo insists they matter in English society. Indeed, there is a striking and revealing asymmetry in the tales told by this unreliable narrator. He insists upon the significance of Sir Reuben, while denying the significance of the murder: 'And once (though it is the most incidental thing in my life) I murdered a man . . . '[307] The Jews are responsible for everything ('the clue to all England');[308] he bears no responsibility even for his own actions. Wells offers a subtle account of an anti-Semite in *Tono-Bungay*, one that may draw on his own views.[309] Wells's stance on what he described as 'the Jewish question' is problematical, and I discuss it further in Chapter 6.

It should not be thought, however, that English literary anti-Semitism, and in particular the blood-libel trope, suffered some altogether conclusive and complete rebuff in this period. Consider E. W. Hornung's short story, 'A Costume Piece'. Hornung (1866–1921), the brother-in-law of Arthur Conan-Doyle ('to whom I owe a very great deal'),[310] wrote stories about the adventures of the gentleman-burglar A. J. Raffles. Public school-educated and a keen amateur cricketer,[311] Raffles has an 'indolent, athletic figure' and 'pale, sharp, clean-shaven features'; he 'might have been a minor poet instead of an athlete of the first water'.[312] His accomplice, Bunny, formerly his school fag, is akin to the 'little boy' of Chaucer's and Dickens's imagining—though Bunny is not Raffles's child, more a parent's fantasy of a child, subordinate and adoring, while also being a friend and fellow adventurer.[313] In 'A Costume Piece', one of the stories in *Raffles: The Amateur Cracksman* (1899), Raffles and Bunny plan to rob Reuben Rosenthal, a Jewish diamond millionaire. Rosenthal, newly arrived back in London from South Africa, has 'a great hook nose, and the reddest hair and whiskers you ever saw'.[314] He is a criminal, and a 'devil'.[315] For Raffles, stealing from him is thus an act of 'conscience', or no more than 'pure mischief'. Raffles and Bunny break into Rosenthal's very grand house, but are quickly discovered. Raffles manages to escape, while Rosenthal holds Bunny at gunpoint. In the nick of time, Raffles returns, disguised as a policeman, and gets Bunny out. An 'ignominious captive' in the Jew's house, a place of peril, shot at by the Jew and thus in imminent danger of losing his life, Bunny's parent-figure rescues him by a combination of luck and resourcefulness, that is to say by a kind of miracle. It is perhaps the calculatedly reactionary tone to these detective stories, and their archaic echoes of deeds of chivalry undertaken by knight and squire, that make them susceptible to the blood-libel theme.

Moment 5: the context of *Ulysses*

The discourse of English literary anti-Semitism, then, is interrupted periodically by counter-texts. The first such challenge is Richard Devizes's. The tone of his work is cynical and worldly. There is no compassion in it, only a lofty refusal to participate in a moral panic. He does not remove the Jews from the crime scene; he instead denies the very existence of a crime. The second challenge to the discourse is Julian of Norwich's, and stands in radical contrast to Richard's. She writes Jews out from her work; they disappear under her humane, exculpating gesture of erasure. The third challenge is Marlowe's. *The Jew of Malta* is neither elevated, like Julian's work, nor ironic, like Richard's; it is instead comic—raw, extreme, mocking. It parodies literary anti-Semitism's solemn defamations. It does not deny the Jews' crimes, or remove them from the crime scene, it instead celebrates Jewish criminality for its subversive, truth-exposing energy.

And then comes *The Merchant of Venice*, which both restates and interrupts literary anti-Semitism, arresting for 250 years the development of both discourse and counter-discourse. It is in stagings of the play, both hostile and sympathetic to Jews, that the discourse and its counter subsist, though a novelistic account of Jews also begins to emerge, one that is secular in character, and somewhat tamer than the drama and poetry that precede it. Immensely worthy works (Cumberland, Edgeworth, and Scott) appear that are the very opposite of Marlovian comedy—earnest, expressly rehabilitative. And once again, the discourse of literary anti-Semitism is in danger.

But then, as with Shakespeare hard on Marlowe's heels, comes Dickens, hard on Scott's and Edgeworth's heels. When *Oliver Twist* announces its massive presence, English literary anti-Semitism's canonic accounts of the Jew are complete. Thereafter, the discourse divides, turns in on itself, and is met by increasingly strong challenges.

As worthy as Cumberland and Edgeworth, but far more interesting and experimental, *Daniel Deronda* takes its stand against English literary anti-Semitism, with the effect that the counter-discourse begins to make the running. And what then happens? *Dracula, Trilby*—that is to say, on the one hand, a dispersal of Jewish characteristics in one powerfully resonant figure, but a restatement of the blood libel, and on the other hand, a distillation of Jewish characteristics in another such figure, but a swerve away from the blood libel. In each case, there is a descent from the canonic, into popular, mass-market literature.

And then—*Ulysses*, which is where we now are in this chapter. It is commonly held to be the most famous literary work, in any language, in the twentieth century.[316] This is the first 'moment' *defined* by a counter-text; there is nothing in the discourse that is strong enough to set against *Ulysses*, though T.S. Eliot's early poetry represents the strongest challenge. The moment of *Ulysses* is a kind of caesura in the history I have been outlining. It is a summary of the history so far; it is also a break with it. All the elements of the discourse, and of the counter-discourse too, are present and visible *as elements*.

The novel

An Irishman living in self-imposed exile on the European continent wrote *Ulysses*. It is a contribution to world literature, and the work of a *world* author.[317] Nevertheless, for the purposes of this chapter I am treating it as 'English', in part because it is written in the English language, in part because it expressly situates itself within the English literary tradition (among other things, comprising 'an encyclopaedia of English literary technique'),[318] and in part because it puts English literary anti-Semitism under review, adversarially.

Ulysses is divided into eighteen chapters or episodes, and takes place across eighteen hours on one day, 16 June 1904. It continues the story of Stephen Dedalus, whose early years were the subject of an earlier work, *A Portrait of the Artist as a Young Man* (1916). He has returned from Paris, his mother is recently dead, and he is now living in a tower, in the company of two other young men. He has a job teaching at a school. To the continuation of Stephen's story Joyce adds a new story, concerning Leopold Bloom, a 38-year-old man, a commercial traveller. Bloom is a thrice-baptized[319] son of a Gentile mother and a Jewish father, a Hungarian convert to Protestantism.[320] His wife, Molly Bloom, is conducting an affair with 'Blazes' Boylan, one of the novel's usurpers. After several sightings of Stephen by Bloom, and a few brief encounters, they find themselves in each other's company in a brothel. Stephen gets into a fight with a soldier, and is knocked down. Bloom comes to his aid, and they walk back together to Bloom's house, spending some time in discussion there before they separate. Bloom then goes up to his wife, joining her in the matrimonial bed. Joyce, the 'great master of anti-climax',[321] offers no satisfying resolution.

Following explanations given by Joyce to a friend, Stuart Gilbert, early critics gave names to the novel's episodes, which are now in general use. The names correspond to episodes in Homer's *Odyssey*; but they represent, as Joyce put it, a 'ground plan' only.[322] There are other correspondences, similarly imperfect, that together make up a complex, misleading grid. Bloom is Ulysses, the Homeric traveller; Molly is Penelope, Ulysses' faithful wife; Stephen is Telemachus, Ulysses' son. However, Stephen has repudiated his own father, and Bloom has lost his own son, Rudi, who died aged eleven days. The novel is a 'triumph in form' (Pound).[323] It is a comic novel; it is also an instance of a form for which there is as yet no agreed generic name.[324] It is both the last word in realism, and the opposite of realism—and one way in which it is the opposite is by being the last word. It is novel and meta-novel; it is also novel and novel-parody; and it is novel and *anti*-novel.[325]

The Jew, Leopold Bloom

It is possible to identify a distinct series of English fictional Jews, one that was inaugurated in the eighteenth century, when the novel form itself emerged from its pre-history in criminal narratives and Christian fables. This series contains Jewish characters that can be grouped under the headings: 'fixity', 'incoherence', 'elusiveness', 'alternation', and 'deliquescence'. They make for a rough sequence.

Fixity

When Jews first appear in the novel, they display considerable fixity of identity and character, they have no great individuality, and they are without capacity for development. This is true of hostile (Defoe), mixed (Scott), and sympathetic (Edgeworth) representations. Scott's Isaac of York, for example, is a Jew instantly recognizable from a gallery of such Jews. The very first time he appears, so to speak, he *re*-appears. His features are 'keen and regular'. He has 'an aquiline nose, and piercing eyes'. His 'high and wrinkled forehead, and long grey hair and beard, would have been considered as handsome, had they not been the marks of a [Jewish] physiognomy'.[326] This kind of thing was a constant. At the end of the century, even Joyce was ready to reproduce it:

> A rich man, with that horrible cast of countenance, so common among the sweaters of Israël. I mean, the face whose line runs out over the full forehead to the crest of the nose and then recedes in a similar curve back to the chin, which, in this instance, is covered with a waspish, tapering beard.[327]

The physical presence of this kind of Jew, necessarily unchanging, is the sign of his unchanging character. He is a given, just like his body. His identity is as fixed as the arrangement of his limbs. In the case of Scott's Isaac of York, he does not differ greatly from the other characters in the novel. There is a congruity in the representations. None of the characters has an interior life; none has the capacity for change. Fagin is the most intensely realized and also the last canonic instance of this kind of Jew.

Heterogeneity

Next in the series, and as if in repudiation of precisely that former fixity, there are novels in which Jewish characters comprise no more than an amalgam of heterogeneous, typical qualities. It is almost as if anything may be attributed to them; the identity 'Jew' becomes an empty vessel to be filled with whatever the novel's plot requires. Consider Bulwer-Lytton's novel, *Leila* (1837), for example. It is set in late fifteenth-century Granada, and concerns the intrigues of the 'Hebrew' or 'Israelite' Almamen. Almamen, his Jewish identity for much of the time hidden, is a magician, a misanthrope and a schemer, but also an idealist and man of science and reason. He has travelled and studied; he does not share 'the character of his tribe'. He is a man of great wealth. He has 'sagacity and strength', and 'keen, sharp Arab features'. He is critical of Jewry's moral condition, 'bowed, like a crawling reptile', no more now than 'usurers and slaves'. He plots to achieve the Jews' 'earthly restoration and triumph'; he will 'avenge [his] nation'; he also awaits the day when 'the reign [is] restored to the eldest faith and the eldest tribe'. Though he may have 'deserted' the Jews' 'creed', he has not deserted their 'cause'. He is a widower, and has a daughter, Leila, whom he offers as hostage to King Ferdinand, to her great distress. When she later converts to Christianity, he kills her (in a chapter entitled 'The Sacrifice'), notwithstanding his devotion to her and his commitment to reason. 'Serpent as he was, he cared not through what mire of treachery and fraud he trailed his baleful folds.' The novel details the persecutions of the Jews by both Muslim and Christian rulers, while having Leila acknowledge that the Jews were responsible for first introducing 'the awful crime of persecution for opinion's sake', and are thus 'rightly punished' themselves. The novel also details the Jews' 'dark conspiracy', while characterizing them as a 'peaceable people'. The tropes are so tired; the shuffling of attributes so arbitrary. Everything is familiar; it is merely the order in which they appear that is unusual. This is a momentary thing, and as if in reaction to the constrained character of previous representations. But it has the effect of loosening the coherence of subsequent representations.[328]

Elusiveness

As if the product of a radical collision of the fixed with the protean or heterogeneous, Trollope's fraudster Melmotte—in *The Way We Live Now*—is an elusive character, both Jewish and not-Jewish at once. Melmotte is 'a large man, with bushy whiskers and rough thick hair, with heavy eyebrows, and a wonderful look of power about his mouth and chin'. His 'countenance and appearance' are 'unpleasant' and 'untrustworthy'. He 'looked as though he were purse-proud and a bully'. Madame Melmotte is somewhat easier to categorize. She is 'fat and fair,—unlike in colour to our traditional Jewesses; but she had the Jewish nose and the Jewish contraction of the eyes'.[329] So, when John Sutherland asks whether Melmotte is a 'Jewish crook', he is driven to answer: 'Yes, he is. But he is also a Gentile, an Irish, an American, a German, and an English crook.'[330] It is as if the representation of Melmotte is magnetically drawn at one and the same time both back to the fixities of romance and forward to the indeterminacies of modernism—a consequence of what one critic terms Trollope's principle of 'genealogical uncertainty'. In Trollope's fiction generally, he writes, 'Jewish identity is represented as a suspicion or rumour that haunts certain characters.'[331]

Alternation

Deronda is fixedly a Gentile and *then* fixedly a Jew, *both* Ivanhoe *and* Isaac. (His Jewish and non-Jewish characteristics run consecutively, as opposed to Melmotte's, which are concurrent.) He is one character and two characters. Deronda is definitely a Jew and definitely not a Jew. He does not so much have the capacity for development as for transformation—but it is a paradoxical transformation, one that merely returns him to his original identity as a Jew. To contain both possibilities, Deronda must be strategically under-described in the novel. When Deronda first appears he is a physiognomic blank. Refusing to conform her Jewish character to the received stereotype, the most that George Eliot can do is to deny him a face altogether. The snobbish, anti-Semitic Pulcheria, in Henry James's 'Daniel Deronda: A Conversation' (1876) remarks: 'I am sure he had a nose, and I hold that the author has shown great pusillanimity in her treatment of it. She has quite shirked it.'[332]

Deliquescence

One Joyce critic has written of the 'deliquescence of character' in *Ulysses*, by which he means the provisional and tenuous nature of personality in the novel, amounting to an uncertainty of self, even a certain implication of human interchangeability (Molly's lovers, for example).[333] Bloom is one among these deliquescent persons, and is Joyce's contribution to this series of fictional Jews. There is a hint in *Daniel Deronda* of a dissatisfaction with all forms of characterization, an intimation that they will always fall short of the truth: 'Attempts at description are stupid: who can all at once describe a human being? Even when he is presented to us we only begin that knowledge of his appearance which must be completed by innumerable impressions under differing circumstances.'[334] *Ulysses* is a flight from precisely this form of stupidity, which is, of course, among other things, the stupidity of anti-Semitism—that is, the belief that a human being who is also a Jew can adequately be described in a short number of hostile adjectives.

Bloom is, as Ezra Pound remarked, Joyce's 'second character'.[335] He marks Joyce's entry to fiction, which is also fiction's own departure from the given conventions of the late nineteenth-century novel. Bloom is rendered by 'innumerable impressions under differing circumstances'. Specifically, he is throughout the novel a figure of Greek myth, the primary representation, the 'Ulysses' of the title. Leopold Bloom 'is' Ulysses. He possesses many of the Greek hero's characteristics; his adventures on 16

June 1904 parallel Ulysses' own, several millennia earlier. He is also a figure from the Hebrew Scriptures. And he is on one occasion, a figure of romance: 'Who comes through Michan's land, bedight in sable armour? O'Bloom, the son of Rory: it is he. Impervious to fear is Rory's son: he of the prudent soul.'[336] (Bloom is 'lost Jewish, active Irish'.)[337] But the plurality of his representations does not end here. He is also a figure from Christian fantasy: Deasy says, 'they are wanderers on the earth to this day';[338] the citizen says of Bloom, very unfriendly, 'Virag from Hungary! Ahasuerus I call him. Cursed by God.'[339] (Bloom was early on identified as Joyce's 'Wandering Jew'.)[340] And he is a 'stage Jew', a stereotype—just as Molly, in one aspect, is an amalgam of sexist clichés.[341] 'In reality, there is no Mr. Bloom at all', wrote Wyndham Lewis, '[Joyce] has merely out of books and conversations collected facts, witticisms and generalisations about Jews'.[342] But Bloom is also King Hamlet, Sinbad the Sailor, the Ancient Mariner, Robinson Crusoe—Ulysses is not an 'A=B' allegory.[343] And he is a character in a work of literary realism. Ulysses produces the illusion of unmediated mind, of unstructured consciousness,[344] albeit in a highly structured and allusive text. It stands at the juncture of two extremes: artifice and realism.[345]

And still the representations multiply. Bloom is a figure in an expressionist drama, 'Circe'. In this episode of the novel, thoughts and experiences are externalized, and find themselves in character, with names, as Stephen's and Bloom's mental projections. It is a phantasmagoria, in which representation by stream of consciousness gives way to a dramatizing of the Unconscious— that is, the opaque part of a person's mind. Bloom's Jewish aspects are on particular display, and the episode discloses the new womanly man, a feminization of Bloom attributable to Joyce's reading of Weininger.[346] Lastly, Bloom is also a figure in a modernist novel, one that 'discredits the subject', 'puts a question mark over the subject [or] the notion of a *unified* subject', 'decentres the subject', in Hélène Cixous's formulations.[347] That is to say, *Ulysses* explores human subjectivity's triple vulnerability—its *discontinuities* (Bloom reflects, 'I was happier then. Or was that I? Or am I now I?'),[348] its *opacities* (Bloom is not transparent to himself), and its *derivativeness* (Bloom's internal monologues, so far from displaying Bloom as most privately and wholly himself, most sovereignly 'Bloom', comprise a multitude of texts, over which he has only incomplete control).[349] Here is Borges, writing in 1922: 'I want to tear down the exceptional pre-eminence now generally awarded to the self. . . . There is no whole self.'[350] In *Ulysses* Joyce explores the creative possibilities of precisely this destructive endeavour.

The fact that Bloom is more than one of those things is itself a departure. Multiple forms of representation are themselves innovatory in the history of the novel, and contribute to that characteristic of Joyce's writing, in which no one style can be traced.[351] *Ulysses* is a critical reflection on the history of the novel. Indeed, as Milan Kundera writes, taken outside the novel's history, Joyce's work would be 'no more than a caprice, the incomprehensible extravagance of a madman'.[352] The relating of Bloom to the history of Jewish representations or 'stereotypes' may be considered an aspect, then, of the novel's sanity. Kafka once remarked: 'What do I have in common with the Jews? I don't even have anything in common with myself.'[353] *Ulysses* may be taken to pose a similar question. What can Bloom have in common with Jewish stereotypes when he does not even have anything in common with himself?

An exploration of received thinking

Wyndham Lewis made an early case against *Ulysses*, arguing that it was no better than the clichéd language and thought it purported to transcribe.[354] Hugh Kenner replied by acknowledging but celebrating the novel's relation with cliché: *Ulysses*, he maintained, exposed the vulgarity of contemporary life, and its essential thoughtlessness. It was to be read, then, as a revised version of Flaubert's 'Dictionary'.[355] Certainly, the novel is a compendium of received opinions held both about Jews and by the Jews.

Much of the received opinion held of the Jews derives from what might be termed saloon-bar scholarship: 'Well, they're still waiting for their redeemer, says Martin. For that matter, so are we.—Yes, says J.J., and every male that's born they think it may be their Messiah. And every jew is in a tall state of excitement, I believe, till he knows if he's a father or a mother.'[356] These and other ideas are always within the mind or mouth of a character; they never become the doctrine of the novel itself. (Contrast *Daniel Deronda*. Deronda is confronted by a 'face, unmistakeably Jewish',[357] and somewhat later, there is a reference to Mordecai's 'finely typical Jewish face'.[358] 'The Jew is proud of his loyalty', Eliot comments in parenthesis.)[359] In its energetic, comic deployment of anti-Semitic commonplaces, *Ulysses* evokes *The Jew of Malta*. Joyce knew, observed an astute critic, the standard responses in the catechism of anti-Semitism.[360]

The novel is also a compendium of Bloom's received thinking, including a perhaps typically Jewish perspective on the Eucharist ('Rum idea: eating bits of corpse . . . ').[361] Bloom holds many of the conventional enlightened opinions of the time:[362] 'So they start talking about capital punishment and of course Bloom comes out with the why and the wherefore and all the codology of the business . . . '[363] 'Codology' is hoaxing, humbugging. The *OED* attributes the first use to *Ulysses*. This kind of talking encouraged some readers to regard Bloom as a 'dull babbler', a person of no intellectual or moral consequence, and to read *Ulysses* itself as containing a satiric, disparaging account of Bloom—and *therefore*, an anti-Semitic one.[364] This is a misreading. As the critic S. L. Goldberg argued, despite his own habitual use of clichés, Bloom also initiates the reader's own critical rejection of cliché. Bloom has a kind of unthinking wisdom, distinguishable from stupidity.[365] If he speaks platitudes, they are the platitudes of truth.[366] Bloom's 'wanderings' are also verbal—his mind darts from topic to topic, his conversation often meanders. His thoughts wander, his remarks often have a rambling quality. Their content is limited by the modest education of a person of his class and occupation, though they are not altogether confined by the received knowledge of his society. Bloom dares on occasion to go beyond it. Though his conversational style is mocked—'I had to laugh at Pisser Burke taking them off chewing the fat and Bloom with his *but don't you see?* and *but on the other hand.*' And then: 'You don't grasp my point, says Bloom. What I mean is . . . '[367]—it represents an effort to be fair, and to think beyond unreflective certainties.

Unlike George Eliot, Joyce does not deploy his own scholarship against misconceptions about Jews. The scholarship in the novel is not in its correcting of received ideas but in its comprehensive listing of them. *Ulysses* is 'an encyclopaedia of citational references'.[368] The novel does not construct the binarism, bad received ideas/good knowledge. Bloom is not Deronda—restlessly, relentlessly, acquiring the truth of Judaism in the face of pervasive, half-educated misconceptions about it. Bloom makes many mistakes about Jewish practices and beliefs; he is not much more reliable about Jews, Jewish history, or Judaism than the anti-Semites who challenge him.[369] Joyce stages these received ideas, which are also misconceptions, drawing out their comic value, setting them on collision courses with each other.

Anti-Semitism

Writing to his brother, Stanislaus, Joyce mentioned a newspaper column of Oliver St John Gogarty's, attacking the Jews, and of 'England becoming Jewry'. Joyce describes it as 'stupid drivel'.[370] *Ulysses* expressly interrogates this drivel. It does so in three stages: in episodes that concern Stephen, in episodes that concern Bloom, and then in episodes that concern both men, when they are together.

Stephen

During the opening episode, 'Telemachus', Haines speaks:

> —Of course I'm a Britisher, Haines' voice said, and I feel as one. I don't want to see my country fall into the hands of German jews either. That's our national problem, I'm afraid, just now.[371]

In the next episode, 'Nestor', Stephen falls into conversation with Mr Deasy, the headmaster of the school where he teaches. Deasy is Protestant Irish, an Orangeman:

> Mark my words, Mr Dedalus, he said. England is in the hands of the jews. In all the highest places: her finances, her press. And they are the signs of a nation's decay. Wherever they gather they eat up the nation's vital strength. I have seen it coming these years. As sure as we are standing here the jew merchants are already at their work of destruction. Old England is dying.

Stephen demurs:

> —A merchant, Stephen said, is one who buys cheap and sells dear, jew or Gentile, is he not?
> —They sinned against the light, Mr Deasy said gravely. And you can see the darkness in their eyes. And that is why they are wanderers on the earth to this day.

Stephen's mind turns to the Jews of the Paris Stock Exchange, 'goldskinned men quoting prices on their gemmed fingers'. As he completes his conversation with Deasy, 'From the playfield the boys raised a shout. A whirring whistle: goal.'[372]

What is the sin against the light? 'They are of those that rebel against the light; they know not the ways thereof, nor abide in the paths thereof' (Job 24:13). 'Light' is clarity of understanding, and the true path directed by God. It is also God Himself, as in 'the light of thy countenance' (Psalms 4:6), or God's most essential quality, as in 'O send out thy light and thy truth: let them lead me' (Psalms 43:3). It is also Jesus' followers, as in 'Ye are the light of the world' (Matthew 5:14). And it is his teaching, as in 'the light of the glorious gospel of Christ' (2 Corinthians 4:4). There is also a specifically Protestant meaning of conscience—'light' as in 'the knowledge and dictates of your spirits'.[373] Against Deasy's objections, freighted with theology and history, Stephen's responses are somewhat enervated, if cogent. He dissolves the 'jew' into larger collectives. Jews are as all merchants; we have all sinned against the light. It is a conventionally benevolent stance.

Bloom

The 'Cyclops' episode takes place in and around the pub. Bloom is under attack from one-eyed men, principal among them the person identified as 'the citizen'. He is a Fenian nationalist, and a Dublin barfly too. The narrator colludes with him.[374] While Bloom is talking, the dog is sniffing at him, 'I'm told those Jewies does have a sort of queer odour coming off them'[375]—anticipating a reference to the *'fetor judaicus'* in a later episode, 'Circe'.[376] He haplessly offers some liberal pieties (the history of the world is full of persecution, hatred between nations is deplorable), only to be mocked for his definition of a nation. If a 'nation is the same people living in the same place', one of the men remarks, then he himself is a nation, because he has been living in the same place for the past five years:

> So of course everybody had a laugh at Bloom and says he, trying to muck out of it:
> —Or else living in different places.
> —That covers my case, says Joe.
> —What is your nation if I may ask, says the citizen.
> —Ireland, says Bloom. I was born here. Ireland.
> The citizen said nothing only cleared the spit out of his gullet . . .

Bloom is trying to maintain an argument within the conventions of civility, but he is out of his depth among shallower, destructive people:

> —And I belong to a race too, says Bloom, that is hated and persecuted. Also now. This very moment. This very instant.

He means: you are persecuting me. The discussion winds away for a moment. And then:

> —And after all, says John Wyse, why can't a jew love his country like the next fellow?
> —Why not? Says J.J., when he's quite sure which country it is.
> —We don't want him, says Crofter the Orangeman or Presbyterian.
> —Who is Junius? Says J.J.
> —He's a perverted jew, says Martin, from a place in Hungary . . .

It is hopeless. Bloom offers some final words:

And says he:

—Mendelssohn was a jew and Karl Marx and Mercadante and Spinoza. And the saviour was a jew and his father was a jew. Your God.

—He had no father, says Martin. That'll do now. Drive ahead.

—Whose God? says the citizen.

—Well, his uncle was a jew, says he. Your god was a jew. Christ was a jew like me. Gob, the citizen made a plunge back into the shop.

—By Jesus, says he, I'll brain that bloody jewman for suing the holy name. By Jesus, I'll crucify him so I will. Give us that biscuitbox here.[377]

Bloom makes a hasty departure, and is imagined ascending in a chariot.

Stephen and Bloom

A bit later on (in 'Eumaeus'), Bloom tells Stephen about his row with the citizen:

> He called me a jew, and in a heated fashion, offensively. So I, without deviating from plain facts in the least, told him his God, I mean Christ, was a jew too, and all his family, like me, though in reality I'm not. That was one for him. A soft answer turns away wrath. He hadn't a word to say for himself as everyone saw. Am I not right?

Bloom's appeal to Stephen is not wholly successful, though the young man responds with some Vulgate Latin, to the effect that Christ came from the Jews, according to the flesh. Bloom rambles on, trying to ingratiate himself with Stephen, who is bored, tired. 'Jews, he softly imparted in an aside in Stephen's ear, are accused of ruining. Not a vestige of truth in it, I can safely say'[378]—across the generations, the Jews' urgent, clichéd appeals to the Gentile conscience. Yet Bloom suffers a rebuff from Stephen in the following episode, 'Ithaca'. He chants lines from the *Hatikva*, the Zionist anthem, and in response, Stephen sings the ballad, or 'chanted legend' of 'Little Harry Hughes'. Stephen sings the first few lines, about a little boy who breaks a Jew's windows with his ball, and this makes Bloom smile. But then Stephen sings the rest, and Bloom is dismayed. 'With mixed feelings. Unsmiling, he heard and saw with wonder a jew's daughter, all dressed in green.' It makes him think of the blood libel:

> He weighed the possible evidences for and against ritual murder: the incitation of the hierarchy, the superstition of the populace, the propagation of rumour in continued fraction of veridicity, the envy of opulence, the influence of retaliation, the sporadic reappearance of atavistic delinquency, the mitigating circumstances of fanaticism, hypnotic suggestion and somnambulism.[379]

In its title, structure and content *Ulysses* returns the reader to Homer's work, which stands at the originary, inaugural moment of European literature. And in its deployment of the ballad of the football-kicking 'Little Harry Hughes', it returns the reader to the originary, inaugural moment of English literary anti-Semitism, first intimated by the boys' game of football overheard by Stephen in 'Nestor'.

Post-*Ulysses*?

Bloom, the 'victim predestined', is said to be 'sad' at Stephen's recitation of 'Little Harry Hughes' because 'He wished that a tale of a deed should be told of a deed not by him should by him not be told.' This could mean:[380]

- He wished that Stephen had told a tale that did not implicate him (i.e., Bloom): an anti-Semitic poem about Jewish violence implicates all Jews, and thus made a villain of Bloom.

or

- He wished that Stephen had told a tale of a deed that did not implicate him (i.e., Stephen): an anti-Semitic poem discredits the reciter, and in the given context thus alienates Bloom from Stephen.

The Jewish listener stands before the inaugural moment of English literary anti-Semitism, its 'predestined victim', cast as villain, alienated from a discourse that he wants to embrace but which is addressed to him in rejection. He wants a tale, that is, but what he gets is one that wants nothing to do with him. Having given an account of the discourse itself, Joyce then gives an account of the Jew's relation to that discourse. In the matter of English literary anti-Semitism, then, what could follow *Ulysses*?

Just as no novelist—not even a great novelist—can exit from the history of the novel,[381] so no novelist can bring the novel's history to an end. *Ulysses* did not even kill off the blood libel. Just over ten years later, in 1933, Daphne du Maurier published the bestselling novel, *The Progress of Julius*, in which an anti-Bloom, son of a Jewish father and Christian mother, kills both his mother and his daughter—the mother, at the beginning of the novel, when he himself is a child, and the daughter, at the end of the novel, when he is an old man ('She opened her mouth: "Papa—Papa . . . Papa . . ." A last cry, a last choking struggle . . . ').[382] This aspect of the blood-libel trope, the implication of a Jew or Jews in the sundering of the parent–child

bond, was then put to more creative use in a somewhat later novel, Kingsley
Amis's *Stanley and the Women* (1984). Here, a young man comes under the
control of his father when he begins to suffer paranoid delusions about the
Jews. The father cannot help him; there is no miracle. The anti-Semitism of
Stanley's son is a symptom of his insanity, but Stanley himself makes anti-
Semitic remarks. The novel sets up a contrast between the son, Steve's,
'violent babblings and scribblings (EVIL LIVE VILE LEVI)' and the father-
narrator's 'unexamined and inherited prejudice', Martin Amis has written.[383] He describes the book as 'superproblematic' and a 'hate novel'.
This does not quite do it justice. The novel is anti-Semitic, indeed—but
it also addresses anti-Semitism. It conditions its perspective, while also being
the object of its attention. *Stanley and the Women* is thus a contribution both
to the canon and to the *counter*-canon of English literary anti-Semitism,
partly in consequence of Amis's slightly Marlovian delight in offending
against rules of social decency—the Amis who signed himself, in an early
letter to Philip Larkin, as 'Kingsley Ikonoklastes',[384] Amis 'the contrarian,
the unpopularity-courter'.[385]

The contemporary moment: the context
of 'Killed in Crossfire'

In *The Prioress's Tale*, the Jews kidnap and kill a child, who is then miraculously recovered by his mother. In *The Merchant of Venice*, a Jew traps a
mature businessman, but he miraculously escapes by the intervention of a
woman young enough to be his daughter. In *Oliver Twist*, a Jew traps and
menaces a boy, who is then miraculously rescued. In *Daniel Deronda*, the
Jewish mother surrenders her child who then as an adult falls in with Jews,
only to seek out his mother. In *Svengali*, a young Gentile woman comes
under the power of an older Jewish man. In *Ulysses*, a young Gentile man
comes into the company of an older Jew. And so on. It might seem as if the
permutations have been exhausted. The original account, however, can
always be restated.

Tom Paulin's poem, 'Killed in Crossfire', was published on 18 February
2001, in the *Observer*, a liberal Sunday newspaper with a substantial circulation. Paulin describes the poem as a 'squib', 'a short composition of a
satirical and witty character' (*OED*). The squib, we might say, is the poetic

equivalent of the 'remark'. It is specific to its context; limited to the expression of a particular emotion; to be taken seriously, of course, but not to be understood as the statement of a general position. It can be a political poem, that is to say a public poem, often beginning in a direct response to a current event, just as a pamphlet or a piece of journalism springs from and addresses a particular historical moment.[386] The problem with Paulin's poem is that it did not stop with the moment. It was seduced by the resonances of the blood libel.

It appeared a few months after the breaking of the Mohammed al-Dura story. Al-Dura was a young boy then alleged to have been shot by Israeli soldiers on 30 September 2000 at the Netzarim Junction in Gaza.[387] The poem's epigraph is taken from the wartime diaries of the German-Jewish Victor Klemperer (1881–1960), in which he records his opinion that 'the Zionists, who want to go back to the Jewish State of 70 AD, are just as offensive as the Nazis. With their nosing after blood, their ancient "cultural roots," their partly canting, partly obtuse winding back of the world, they are altogether a match for the National Socialists'. And then the poem:

> We're fed this inert
> this lying phrase
> like comfort food
> as another little Palestinian boy
> in trainers jeans and a white teeshirt
> is gunned down by the Zionist SS
> whose initials we should
> —but we don't—dumb goys—
> clock in the weasel word *crossfire*.

That is to say, the gunning down of Palestinian boys by the Zionist SS is deliberate, though dishonestly attributed by them to 'crossfire'. However, they are caught out by the very word they use, because its middle letters spell out the true character of their actions, though dumb goys that we are, we do not realize it. We are treated as children, and fed the comfort food of lies.

Several questions of meaning arise in this very short poem. First, who, to begin with, is doing the feeding? Is it, say, the news media? The poem leaves the answer to this question somewhat open. In an article written within days of the al-Dura incident, the journalist Robert Fisk wrote that 'crossfire', when applied to a violent death in the Middle East, 'almost always means that the Israelis have killed an innocent person'. And yet, he complained, 'BBC World Service Television was still saying yesterday morning that

Mohammed al-Durah was caught in the crossfire of a battle.'[388] But if indeed the BBC and other news media are culpable, as Paulin's poem suggests, they are merely agents of a greater power. The implication of 'dumb goys' (not a phrase the BBC would use) is that it is a Jewish power. Secondly, to what event does the poem refer? Though by implication, it is to the al-Dura incident, the phrase '*another* little Palestinian boy' implies a practice, perhaps even a policy. This is what IDF soldiers do: they kill children. They do this, the poem further suggests, because they are the Zionist version of, or no better than, the '*SS*', Hitler's *Schutzstaffel*, which directed many of the mass killings on the Eastern Front[389] and whose officers were praised by Himmler for their role in 'the extermination of the Jewish people'.[390] Thirdly, against whom is the poem written? Though the poem's anger appears to be limited to the IDF, it implicates all Zionists (it is the '*Zionist* SS') in its indictment. Indeed, by the use of 'goys' the poem implicates all Jews. The word is not in its Hebrew plural form, '*goyim*'. It is not Israelis, not even the 'Zionist SS', who would say 'goys'. The word is used instead by Diaspora Jews, as reported by anti-Semites. The poem thus has in sights Jews in general. Lastly, what of the deployment of Klemperer? The implication is that if a Jew—and a victim of the Holocaust, no less—has made a comparison between Zionists and Nazis, and (as we know) Jews cannot be anti-Semitic, then the comparison is good for all to make.

The most vulgar anti-Semitism speaks in 'Crossfire'.

It reprises the anti-Semitic trope that Jews privately view gentiles with contempt.[391] The disparagement of '*goyim*' is a central trope in the *Protocols*: The *goyim* are a flock of sheep and we are their wolves, our purpose is to turn the *goyim* into unthinking, submissive brutes, etc.[392] Paulin has penetrated this ostensibly secret Jewish language. He is the specialist in the inner nature of the Jewish IDF.[393] The truth of their practices, their crimes, has been revealed to him, as if by miraculous intuition, a kind of 'illumination' comparable to the 'divine illumination' which guided the nun in Thomas of Monmouth's story to William's corpse.[394] The Jews thought to conceal the body, but 'our Lord showed that he was a martyr'.[395] Paulin similarly uncovers the martyrdom of 'another little Palestinian boy'. This trope is allied with a newer one. The Jews, it is now being said, are no better than the Nazis. The Jews *are* Nazis. Paulin's poem joins those many other discursive instances in which Jews are—with what wit!—identified with their arch-persecutors. The trope then articulates, in a form that does not invite argument, the proposition that the Jews have become as their oppressors.

The poem has several specifically *literary* anti-Semitic resonances. In its theme of the killing of Gentile children by perfidious Jews, and the miraculous disclosure of these crimes, the poem alludes to 'Little Sir Hugh' and *The Prioress's Tale*. Chaucer's Prioress frequently describes the Jews' victim as 'little'; in several versions of 'Sir Hugh', the boy is said to be 'little'. In its use of the phrase 'dumb goys', the poem alludes to Pound's 'Pisan Cantos', written just after World War II, where 'the goyim are cattle' that 'go to saleable slaughter' without resisting.

The slaughter to which Pound refers is the wartime killing of millions, done to death in a conflict promoted by Jews, ritual murder on an international scale.[396] (Pound probably got the image of Gentile cattle from Carlyle, writing about Disraeli: 'A superlative Hebrew Conjuror, spell-binding all the great Lords, great parties, great interests of England, . . . leading them by the nose, like helpless, mesmerised somnambulant cattle.')[397] Jews manipulate, exploit, or otherwise prey upon Gentiles, but the poor dumb beasts do not see what is happening, until the sage or the poet arrives to explain it.

Entirely voluntarily, but without any good reason whatever, Paulin has made himself a prisoner of anti-Semitic discourse. 'Crossfire' invites the judgement: an anti-Semite has written this poem, or a person who does not care whether he is taking up an anti-Semitic position. Yet Paulin has insisted that what he has written is true. 'Palestinian boys are being deliberately gunned down', he has said.[398] But he does not know that IDF soldiers are hunting down Palestinian children with the object of killing them, as SS Death Squads once hunted down Jews (Jewish children among them) with the object of killing *them*. He knows that Palestinian boys have been shot and killed, just as he knows that militants deployed Palestinian children in the Second Intifada,[399] that Jewish children have also been killed in the conflict (a number of whom indeed deliberately gunned down).[400] The totality of what Paulin knows has been subordinated, however, to an anti-Semitic trope. One can test this, conveniently, by reference to a parallel set of facts unrelated to the actions of Jewish soldiers. In the course of an essay on Conor Cruise O'Brien, Paulin recalls a 1969 incident when 'members of the RUC fired machine-guns indiscriminately at Divis Flats near the centre of Belfast, killing a nine-year-old boy and a young British soldier who was home on leave'.[401] The RUC was the Royal Ulster Constabulary, Northern Ireland's then police force. Paulin does not compare the RUC to the SS; the death of *this* child did not prompt a poem.

Writing to the *Observer* (4 March 2001) Paulin complained that the insinuation that he was an anti-Semite was wrongly, even discreditably, made. And in a later poem, 'On Being Dealt the Anti-Semite Card', he returned to the theme:

> The first answer is Beckett's
> in another context—to 'Mr Beckett
> they say that you are anti-English?'
> he answered 'au contraire'
> —he didn't say 'I am not dot dot'
> which plays their game
> —in this case the ones who play the a-s card
> of death threats hate mail talking tough
> the usual cynical Goebbels stuff
> so I say the same . . . [402]

And then Paulin rehearses events in the history of anti-Semitism— Auschwitz, expulsions, the Crusaders, the Dreyfus case, 'the list is endless / it turns one's bowels'. He is appropriately, if somewhat impersonally, self-chastising: 'historic guilt / is and must be always with us'. But what is missing from his miscellaneous list is the blood libel. The poem is expansive on every kind of anti-Semitic atrocity *except the defamation that the Jews wantonly murder Gentile children*. The reason for this omission is not hard to discern. To acknowledge the blood libel would mean confronting its presence in his own earlier poem, and Paulin is a poet incapable of turning his very considerable resources of indignation inward.

He might, however, be a writer with the capacity to inaugurate a revival of English literary anti-Semitism. A few years after the publication of 'Crossfire', Caryl Churchill's play, *Seven Jewish Children*, was performed at the Royal Court Theatre, London. It is the dramatic equivalent of a squib and, in its content, closely related to Paulin's poem. It stages several Jews discussing amongst themselves how to explain to their children moments in twentieth-century Jewish history. The horrors of the Holocaust demand one kind of comforting obfuscation, the horrors of Israel's foundation ('Don't tell her they said it was a land without a people') and subsequent history ('Tell her we're entitled / Tell her they don't understand anything except violence'), another kind. These Jews are liars. They abuse their own children by lying to them, in order to conceal their greater, more lethal abuse of Palestinian children. 'Tell her we killed the babies by mistake / Don't tell her anything about the army.' And: 'Tell her I look at one of their children covered in blood and what do I feel? Tell her all I feel is happy it's not her.' The murder of children is merely an aspect of a more genocidal ambition: 'Tell her I wouldn't care if we wiped them out.' This is an ambition founded in Judaism itself: 'Tell her I don't care if the world hates us, tell her we're better haters, tell her we're chosen people.'[403]

5

Modern English Anti-Semitism

Introduction

The study of anti-Semitism tends to gravitate towards its starkest and most lethal versions—pogrom, massacre, genocide. Other versions are typically then interpreted by reference to these limit ones, which by implication are taken to disclose anti-Semitism in its essence. This approach is wrong. Much energy has been expended arguing for the uniqueness of the Holocaust in history; often overlooked is the corollary that it was also unique in the history of anti-Semitism. The Holocaust, the project of targeting every living Jew for murder,[1] is not a model for understanding anti-Semitism in its selectivity, its diversity, its heterogeneity. It is not true that the anti-Semite is always a murderer in his heart. Sometimes, he is no more than a snob. A readiness to think ill of Jews does not always lead to the readiness to kill them for the offence of being Jewish, or even to be complicit in their murder. We still need a theory of anti-Semitism in *non*-extreme situations, one that is predicated on its distinctness, and not regarded as merely a watered-down version of genocidal Jew-hatred. The quotidian anti-Semitism of England between the 1660s and the 1960s was exemplary of just this non-lethal, or 'minor', anti-Semitism. 'Minor' is to be preferred over 'mild', though that adjective has its claim to due consideration.[2] In modern times, and until 1936, it was Italy and not England that had the mildest, in the sense of the least, anti-Semitism of the Western democracies.[3]

Among the circumstances that established the conditions for the emergence of this minor anti-Semitism, the first is the rupture in Anglo-Jewish history, that just under 400 years' break (call it 'the Expulsion period'), when England was without Jews—or almost without Jews.[4] This has a significance that can only with difficulty be overestimated. In consequence of this rupture there was no continuous national experience either of

Christian persecution or Jewish self-government. England's Jews never became a people of the ghetto.

The *second* circumstance, accompanying this near-complete absence of actual Jews, is the continuing influence of the 'spectral', 'theological', 'virtual', 'protean', 'hermeneutical', or 'paper' Jew,[5] a figure rampant in the English cultural imagination during the Expulsion period. The 'Jew' represented both abstract evil (Deicide, child-murderer, usurer) and everyday commercial vice (usurious, greedy, self-seeking). The 'Jews' carried the dignity and perfidy of their various scriptural roles. This composite character was demonic and dangerous, yet also somewhat shadowy and elevated. It was disseminated by the New Testament, by sermons, by saints' and miracle tales, by ballads, plays and poetry, and even by joke books.[6] There were also rumours and reports, including rumours and reports brought back from abroad by merchants and pilgrims. Some new vices were added: for example, the Jews took on the additional character of well-poisoners.[7] The blood libel underwent various mutations. For example, in his Christmas Day 1625 sermon, John Donne preached of the Jews' 'barbarous and inhumane custom' of keeping 'in readiness the blood of some Christian' for the purpose of anointing the Jewish dead, 'with these words, if Jesus Christ were the Messiahs, then may the blood of this Christian avail thee to salvation'.[8] By the early part of the seventeenth century, the meaning of 'Jew' had expanded. To be a 'Jew' was to have any of the wicked characteristics cumulatively attributed to Jews. 'By Jews in the Text, then, we may aptly understand, not only the people of the Jews, but *people of any Nation or Language whatsoever, that shall be so Jewish as to . . . ,*' began a Royalist pamphlet.[9] The wickedness of Jews had become the stuff of proverbial wisdom—'I hate thee as I do a Jew', 'I would not have done so to a Jew', 'None but a Jew would have done so.'[10] To behave as Jews was a reproach to Christians.[11] The figure of the 'Jew', to adapt some lines from another context, had become 'a common sink / For all the filth and rubbish of men's tongues / To fall and run into'.[12]

The *third* circumstance, somewhat in conflict with the second, is a compound of new perspectives and understandings of the Hebrew Scriptures developed by religious scholars, of the 'Judaizing' or 'Traskite'[13] tendencies among the more radical of Christian dissenters, and of the millenarian beliefs and expectations so widely diffused throughout early to mid seventeenth-century England. In combination, these aspects helped to constitute, for the first time since 1290, the continued exclusion of Jews as a problem. The merit of keeping Jews out of England, that is to say, could no longer be taken for granted; the Jews' absence became visible, one might say. A general appreciation of the Jews as a 'distinct and unconfounded nation',[14] of the Church of England as rooted in the institutions of ancient Judaism, and of Jewish and Christian practices as overlapping,[15] and quite widely held beliefs that the nation's political institutions could be renewed by reference to Israelite precedent,[16] that the conversion of the Jews would be facilitated by their exposure to English Protestantism (which in turn would thereby hasten the return of the Messiah), and that the time had come for Jewish national restoration in the Holy Land—all this made the Jews of sympathetic interest to scholars and clergymen, Judaizing heretics, and all manner of Protestant sectarians, and thus of assistance to the Jews and their supporters during the Readmission controversy. What is more, the disinterested study of post-biblical Jewish literature undertaken by John Selden and others had the effect of frustrating the emergence of works of Talmud-defamation, so significant in anti-Semitic propagandizing elsewhere in Europe.[17]

(It is in certain instances artificial to separate out these second and third circumstances. For example, the strong, Protestant restatement of Christianity did not always encourage sympathetic perspectives on the Jews. John Foxe's *Acts and Monuments of the Church* (1563), more commonly known as the *Book of Martyrs*, characterized unreformed Christianity as polluted by Judaism. Rome was anti-Christian, indeed, drawing 'the people' back to a Jewish way of thinking about religion.[18] Most generally, across these decades, the late sixteenth century and the early seventeenth century, original, innovative engagements with Judaism took place. Some were hostile, some friendly and some neutral—and some, a combination of all three. The question of the boundaries between Judaism and Christianity, and the related question of the Jews, in each case in their broadest formulations, fell open for fresh consideration. Nothing was taken for granted. In the heat of religious and political division, commonplace thinking relaxed for a while its grip on the public imagination.)

The *fourth* circumstance is the character both of the England to which the Jews returned and of the returning Jews themselves. Commerce was established, and lending at interest had become lawful. England was now Protestant, and had lost its appetite for wars of religion. The rejection of the Catholic faith, civil war, the killing of a king, revolution, republican government—the Jews returned in the immediate aftermath of this immeasurable turmoil, these immense dislocations. In particular, there was a new religion 'question', one that left Jews almost entirely untouched. It was instead defined, institutionally, as the Established Church in its relation to the Roman Catholic Church and the Nonconforming interests, and theologically, as Anglicanism in its relation to Roman Catholicism and Protestant dissent. The question only became further entrenched in the eighteenth century.[19] A plurality of sectarian, and national enmities ensured that the Jews never became the principal focus of hostility.[20] The Jews themselves were different; they were more 'European', less distinctive in language and dress.

The *fifth* and least important circumstance is the intermittent presence of Jews in English society during the Expulsion period. There were the converts who remained behind; there were the occasional Jewish merchants from abroad; there were rabbis who visited at the invitation of Tudor Hebraists; there was a Marrano community in London; and there was the physician, Roderigo Lopez, a secret Jew of Sephardic origin, executed in 1594 by Elizabeth I following conviction at trial on charges of high treason and attempted murder, probably justly. His trial and conviction did not lead to speculation about Jewish—as against Spanish-inspired and Catholic-led—conspiracies, and it thus did not found a discourse in English political culture to that effect. Indeed, the whole process cannot be characterized as in any sense *driven* by anti-Semitic sentiments—though Lopez was, of course, the 'vile Jew' to his prosecutors, and the crowd at his execution found his profession of Christian faith amusing.[21]

It was, then, to an England shaped by these five sets of circumstances that the Jews returned. How best to grasp, in very summary form, the trajectory of anti-Semitism in the centuries that *followed* the return?

In 1680, narrating the efforts of the Jewish community to retrieve one of their number who had converted, Gilbert Burnet (1643–1715) warned his readers ('the Nation') what 'sort of people these Jews are, whom we harbour so kindly among us'. They 'lie under the guilt of that Innocent Blood which their Fathers wished might rest on them and their Children'; they persist in an 'obstinate infidelity'; they 'thirst after the blood of such of their Nation as believe in Him whom their Fathers crucified'; they are the 'Enemies of Christ'; etc.[22] Of perspectives on Jews in the eighteenth century, Todd Endelmann writes:

> It was believed by many persons that the Jews continually blasphemed Jesus in their prayers and writings; that they considered it meritorious to plunder Christians; that they murdered Christian children in order to obtain their

blood; that they were children of the Devil, the incarnation of Evil, the synagogue of Satan and Antichrist; that they had one eye smaller than the other; that they were distinguished by a peculiar smell; that their skin was impregnated with an inordinate amount of filth; and that they had a mark of blood on one shoulder and a malignant blackness underneath their eyes that bespoke their guilt as murderers.[23]

Though many of these specific attributes had somewhat faded in the English imagination by the turn of the nineteenth century,[24] and blood-libel tales in particular were rejected by the more advanced thinkers of the time,[25] the general condition of Jews was lamentable. Sympathetic observers found the Jews to be 'merely tolerated inhabitants', living in a state of 'abject degradation', 'despised, [like] Indian Parias', 'absolutely proscribed from the social compact', and so on.[26] Of course, to *less* sympathetic observers writing at about the same time, the position of 'this stiff-necked generation' was undeservedly high. Robert Southey complained in his 1807 work, *Letters From England*, 'The Jews have nothing to complain of.' England, he added, 'is the heaven of the Jews'.[27]

One hundred and fifty years passed. By the middle of the twentieth century, the more absurd beliefs about Jews had disappeared, while only traces remained of many others. A study of working class anti-Semites in the London Borough of Bethnal Green (mentioned in Chapter 1), recorded the following views on Jews:

> [The extreme or 'outspoken' anti-Semites] accuse Jews of being firebugs, swindlers, warmongers, and traitors. Jews will burn down buildings to get insurance without worrying if there are people in them (fire-engine sirens are 'Jewish wedding-bells'). They also state that Jews have too much political and economic power, occupy the best houses, are lazy, cowardly, are selfish. The war with Germany was due to them and now they want one against Russia. They are the main capitalists and the main communists. [The less extreme anti-Semites] are more vague in their descriptions, ascribe fewer character-istics to Jews, avoid accusations of most crimes (though the giving and receiving of bribes is referred to rather frequently) . . . Physical characteristics begin to make an appearance—Jews are referred to as big, fat, large-nosed, and dark-haired. [All anti-Semites refer to the Jews'] group solidarity. The favourite word to describe this quality of solidarity is 'clannish'.[28]

Within a decade or so, these sentiments had themselves diminished some-what, though a certain residual wariness persisted, a discomfort barely able to articulate itself. Representative of this mute though not altogether harmless prejudice is a story told by the former MP, Matthew Parris (b. 1949). When competing for selection as a parliamentary candidate, he relates, a 'handful (no more)' of the constituency association had been heard 'muttering about [Parris's rival] being Jewish'. The rejected candidate was Michael Howard, who went on to become the leader of the Conservative Party.[29] At the end of the period under review in this chapter, we may say, anti-Semitism had largely contracted to the 'mutterings' of a minority, if not a 'handful'. In 1963, the Anglo-Jewish critic and writer John Gross answered affirmatively the question, 'Is anti-Semitism dying out?' It is 'little more than a minor nuisance', he suggested. Overt anti-Semitism is on the wane; social relations between Jews and non-Jews are growing steadily easier. And he added, 'The existence of Israel is taken for granted.' It 'has won a good deal of sympathy, and at the same time given the lie to the old accusations that Jews could never make soldiers, farmers, etc.' Burnett's pamphlet and Gross's article may be taken as opening and closing texts for the period under review in this chapter.

Moments of crisis: the ascent to equality (1650s–1850s)

Between the middle of the twelfth and the end of the thirteenth century, anti-Semitism was intense, periodically spiking at moments of crisis for the first Anglo-Jewish community. The intensity generated the crises. By contrast, from the 1660s to the 1960s, the anti-Semitism was *not* intense, and the moments of crisis for the second Anglo-Jewish community tended to have more complex causes. In consequence, though these latter moments have an anti-Semitic aspect, they rarely are to be *defined* by their anti-Semitism. The moments divide into two: (a) between the 1660s and the 1860s, the Anglo-Jewish ascent to equality, and (b) from the 1860s to the 1960s, the challenges to Anglo-Jewish security.

Through the medieval and early modern period, state and ecclesiastical authorities allowed the autonomy of European Jewish communities while resisting demands for equality of treatment, and later, emancipation. Even allowing for significant differences between national histories, England is exceptional in respect of both autonomy and emancipation. Anglo-Jewry had no autonomy of the kind enjoyed by Jews in Eastern Europe; the emancipation of Anglo-Jewry did not follow the Central and Western European model. Anglo-Jewish institutions of self-government remained underdeveloped, and were of a voluntary, and inconsequential kind; few impediments were put in the way of Anglo-Jewry's ascent to full civil and political equality. There is thus nothing that is momentous about Jewish emancipation in England—though there is much that is protracted about it. By the time that Lionel Rothschild took his seat in the House of Commons Jews had long won the right to sit in the legislative assemblies of the other states of Western and Central Europe.

The Readmission debate

In the Autumn of 1655, Oliver Cromwell was petitioned by a representative of the Jews, Menasseh ben Israel, for permission to settle in England. Permission was probably not needed (since there was no law that barred them), but it was certainly sensible to ask. Cromwell's Council of State appointed a subcommittee to consider the petition, which duly reported back, endorsing readmission subject to many conditions and restrictions. A conference was then convened in December to advise on the adequacy of the recommended terms. Many of those present at this 'Whitehall Conference' (as it became known) argued against allowing back the Jews on *any* terms. The merchants were concerned about commercial competition; some of the clerics were concerned about religious competition (one among them suggested that the Jews might offer children to Moloch);[30] and many in both groups doubted whether a Christian state could accommodate non-Christians. Both advocates and enemies of readmission published furious pamphlets. The final public session of the Conference was adjourned to avert an unfavourable vote. Cromwell, unfazed by this opposition to the Jews' petition gave tacit consent to their readmission, and over time, a small, open community established itself in London. The propaganda against the Jews, one historian of the episode has concluded, was significant for its 'artificial, *ad hoc* character'.[31] On 30 November 1660, merchants petitioned the new king to reverse Cromwell's policy and expel the Jews, but to no avail.[32] Twenty-five years later, there was some litigation concerning the Jews' status: were they native religious Dissenters or were they foreign merchants and therefore subject to additional taxes? And immediately following the Glorious Revolution of 1688, attempts were made to extract large sums of money from the resident Jewish population of London.³³ But no serious effort was made to impede Jewish resettlement in the years of the Restoration, thus confirming in this respect as in others, the irreversibility of the Revolution and its works.

The anti-Jewish pamphleteers flinched from no allegation, however base. In addition to *legal* arguments (only an Act of Parliament can authorize readmission), *anti-millenarian* arguments (England has no special role to play in leading the Jews to salvation; Protestantism would be no more attractive to them than Catholicism; the Jews would be the proselytizers, thereby encouraging Judaizers and putting vulnerable Christians at risk), *demographic* arguments (England is already overpopulated), *scriptural* arguments (the truth of Christianity was proved in the Old Testament, which the Jews obstinately refuse to acknowledge), and *economic* arguments (the Jews would bring no economic benefit; the competition would disadvantage English traders, and allow Dutch penetration of their markets),³⁴ opponents of Readmission were also ready to accuse Jews of torturing Christian children and putting them to death in re-enactment of the Crucifixion.³⁵ The medieval chroniclers' allegations were accepted as simple truth. The Jews' principal pamphleteer-adversary, William Prynne (1600–69), alleged that they avoided punishment for the murder of William of Norwich by payment of a bribe. The Jews, he further alleged, murdered other Christian children, in conformity with a doctrine that all Jews must observe, not only the Jews of England.³⁶ The anonymous 'W.H.' argued that the people of medieval England hated the Jews both because of these murders and because they counterfeited money. The pamphleteers insisted that they were reflecting popular sentiment. Prynne wrote that old soldiers and other beggars had stopped him, troubled by the government's pro-Jewish policy. 'We must now all turn Jews', they complained.³⁷ So far from the Jews' return leading to *their* conversion, the Jews' own conversionary activity would constitute a threat to the Christian character of the state.

Prynne was a Puritan polemicist of unusual passion and thoroughness. In his long public career he wrote over 200 pamphlets, some of very considerable length. He was several times jailed, and suffered humiliating, excruciating punishments (ears cut off *twice*, nose slit, cheeks branded). He was an implacable enemy of Catholics, and saw Jesuit and Romanist conspiracies everywhere. He was an early defender of Parliament in the Civil War but resolutely against Cromwell—a usurper, and too soft on Jews, Quakers, and Papists. He was indefatigable, obsessional. 'The more I am beat down,' Prynne declared, 'the more am I lift up.'³⁸ His work against the Jews, the

Demurrer (1655–6), was divided into two parts, the first part going through two editions in a matter of weeks. It displays immense if deliberately misapplied learning, and took him several months of intensive work to write and then expand upon—the second edition was longer by many pages. Following his efforts of 1655 and 1666, Prynne wrote no further against the Jews, and though he maintained his hatred of the Jews until the end of his life[39] (one cannot be a *sporadic* anti-Semite),[40] Jew-hatred was not among the themes that characterized his work as a whole. It is for precisely this reason, rather than mere priority, that the 'learned, malevolent Prynne',[41] as the Jewish historian Cecil Roth described him, may be regarded as the first English intellectual anti-Semite of modern times.

The *Demurrer* is an extended piece of anti-Semitic invective, the first of its kind in the history of European anti-Semitism. There had been Christian polemics, of course—dialogues between Christian and Jew, discourses on the falsity of Judaism, the falsity of the Talmud, and other works of execration directed against Jews and their religion. But this was the first anti-Semitic work of at least partly secular character. For sure, the *Demurrer* was saturated in Christian conviction: Prynne insisted that hating the Jews was meritorious in all good Christians, and that victory for the Jews would ensure the defeat of Christianity itself.[42] But the pamphlet was not con-versionist in its object; it had not been written for the confutation of the Jews in the name of Christian truth. It had one specific, secular policy goal, and that was to promote 'a perpetual bar to the Antichristian Jews' readmis-sion into England, both in this new-fangled age and all future generations'.[43] It drew on all the available calumnies, as well as inventing some fresh ones. It relied heavily on archival records, tendentiously selected and interpreted, and frequently quoted John Foxe, whom the intensely anti-Catholic Prynne greatly admired. It presented arguments against readmission organ-ized into three capacious categories: Laws; Scriptures; and Theological, Political, and mixed Reasons. Prynne's resourcefulness was in addition extravagantly verbal. The Jews were, he wrote, 'a most rebellious, disobedi-ent, gainsaying, stiff-necked, impenitent, incorrigible, adulterous, whorish, impudent, froward, shameless, perverse, treacherous, revolting, back-slid-ing, idolatrous, wicked, sinful, stubborn, untoward, hard-hearted, hypo-critical . . . People . . . given up to a blind, obdurate, impenitent, stupid heart and spirit, a reprobate sense, a cauterized conscience'.[44] Though the *Demurrer* was not reprinted after 1656, it was frequently plagiarized.

Prynne's labours in the chaotic and rat-infested archives of the Tower of London earned him the title of 'father' or originator of Anglo-Jewish historiography. He correctly dated the beginning of Jewish settlement in England; he correctly dated the Statute of Jewry; he published, in full or part, hundreds of documents from the public records. Prynne was thus *both* liar *and* historian, and to be assessed as both, with the second not just disappearing into the first. This liar-historian—by no means the last in English intellectual life—falsified the historical record whenever it suited his purpose. He committed every historiographical crime other than utterly outright fabrication (though he came close to it, trying to argue into existence the non-existent Act of Parliament expelling the Jews). There were numerous, tendentious errors of transcription, similarly tendentious misinterpretations of documents; he suppressed relevant parts of documents, and overstated claims for documents of only limited significance; he treated exceptional cases as if typical of the rule;[45] and when challenged to produce documents which he had cited, he would sometimes argue that though they had once existed, time had destroyed them.[46]

A pro-admission pamphleteer responded that the accusations of usury and child murder against the Jews were invented to justify the hostile stance of the state towards them, and the reluctance of the Jews' debtors to repay their debts.[47] Menasseh ben Israel, the prime mover of the campaign for Readmission, understated the appeal to his opponents of the libel: 'Our adversaries who have been a little more learned, and consequently a little more civil than the vulgar, have made a halt at this imputation.'[48] In any event, the refutation of the blood libel became the most prominent aspect of his defence of his people. Of the three works he composed in support of Readmission, the second, in 1655, makes his positive case, only noticing in passing some of the calumnies directed at the Jews. The third, *Vindiciae Judaeorum* (1656), addresses the calumnies at greater length.

The Jewish Naturalization Bill, or 'Jew Bill', 1753

Aliens could not own land, or a British ship, and if they engaged in foreign trade were required to pay alien duties. Non-Jewish aliens who were wealthy enough could pay for the promotion in parliament of a private naturalization bill; Jews could not. Native-born Jews had no need of naturalization: they comprised about one-half of the approximately 8,000 Jews resident in England at that time.[49] Foreign-born Jews in England thought the discrimination against them was unfair, and disadvantageous to English interests too, because of its deterrent-effect on wealthy Jewish traders abroad.[50] The country's Whig rulers were sympathetic to their request for full property rights and commercial equality, and in due course the 'Jew Bill' of 1753 was enacted: 'persons professing the Jewish religion' might 'upon application for that purpose, be naturalised by parliament without receiving the sacrament of the Lord's supper'. It was approved by the Lords without a debate, and in the Commons by a strong majority. The Tory minority, however, made many objections, several of a radical nature: the Jews should not have the right to practise their faith; conversion should be the precondition to naturalization; Jews threaten the livelihood of Christian merchants and shopkeepers and they will come to threaten Christian political hegemony and Edward I is thus to be commended for his policy towards the Jews; it is proper to reciprocate in some measure Jewish enmity towards Christianity; the Jewish nation is cursed. The bill's supporters responded: 'from the Jews we have nothing to fear', and they prevailed.[51] But the Commons debate was but the prelude to a most extraordinary outcry once the bill had been passed. Its opponents over-whelmed the government and the Act was repealed. It was not until 1825 that the right of naturalization was finally extended to Jews—without even mentioning the Jews by name,[52] and without any public outcry. But the repeal of the 'Jew Bill' did not cause great hardship. The Jewish community continued to expand, and to prosper.

Pamphlets and petitions, newspaper and journal articles, satirical prints and cartoons, party slogans and written instructions to MPs, pelted down on Whigs and Jews—indeed, 'Jew' and 'Whig' became synonymous, to their mutual discredit. 'Nothing could be more absurd in its nature or more contrary to the maxims of our own policy, than to allow the natural enemies of the Christian religion to be the natural subjects of the Christian state', fulminated one pamphleteer. The bill was 'palpably irreconcilable with Holy Writ'. To admit 'crucifiers' would be to become implicated in the Jews' own inherited guilt. 'Let us not so degenerate from our ancestors, as to take these serpents into our bosoms.' The Jews were 'the professed enemies of Christianity'. English landed estates would fall into Jewish hands, and Jewish political influence would in consequence rocket. 'God have mercy upon such of the natives as shall continue Christian; for I am sure our rulers the Jews would have none.' Newspaper correspondents with names like 'Old England', 'Philo-Libertas', and 'Britannicus' warned readers of the bill's dire consequences for the country. There would soon be 'a Jewish King upon the Throne, with a Jewish House of Lords and a Jewish House of Commons'. The election slogan in Somerset was, 'No Judaism; Christianity for ever.' It was alleged that the Jews had bribed the administration: 'Dis be de Puss collected by our Tribe for de great Favour', says a Jew in a cartoon, entitled, 'The Grand Conference, or the Jew Predominant'. Cartoonists revived the medieval *Judensau* theme. The oldest canards were revived. The Jews 'frequently crucify Christian children on Good Friday'; their 'thirst for the blood of Christians' is 'insatiable'. They are currency-debasers, sweating and filing coins just like their pre-expulsion forebears. The Jews have no God, no King, and no Country, and act on nothing higher than self-interest; they are thieves, receivers of stolen goods and cheats. Other pamphleteers found a 'malignant blackness underneath' Jews' eyes, 'bespeaking guilt and murder'; the Jews were 'wretched usurers', 'subjects to the devil', 'in perpetual hostility to Christ'. The Jews seek power, and once secured, they use it to murder Christians. Opponents of the bill searched out news stories discreditable to Jews, generalizing upon them. At political dinners, anti-Jew-Bill hostesses served pork and ham and other 'anti-Judaic food'; women took to wearing crosses or ribbons with inscriptions, advertising their opposition to the bill. As with the Readmission debate, the clergy joined forces with merchants to attack the perceived Jewish interest. (It was only in the third contest, over admission to Parliament, that the City took the Jews' part.) The parish clergy sermonized against the danger to the Church, and recounted biblical tales of Jewish wickedness. They 'thundered out anathemas, and preached up the pious doctrine of persecution', reported one satirical observer of the clamour. The City's anti-immigration stand derived from a conception of the national economy as static, and the belief that each branch of trade was already full (or even 'over-stocked'). It followed that any new entrants to the market would diminish the share of it available for existing traders. Admit 'foreigners', or make trading easier for them, and the 'bread would be taken out of the mouths' of 'natives' one City MP insisted. The merchants also argued that showing favour to the Jews would impair trade with Spain and Portugal, nations that 'hate the Jews out of measure'. But the violence directed at Jews was discursive only; it had as its object a general election, not a pogrom. And the discursive violence itself was as much indicative of the general tone in which political debate was conducted as of the strength of anti-Semitic feeling.[53]

The bill's supporters found themselves embarrassed. While their opponents advanced an ideological case to defeat a very minor measure, inflating 'a most inoffensive Bill into a national grievance', as one supporter complained, only rarely was any *counter*-ideological case in its favour made—certainly not for an enlarged English polity (one whose membership was not limited to native Protestants), certainly not for the Jews' entitlement to rights and freedoms, and not as frequently as they should for the principles of economic and religious liberalism. In place of such full-throated possible responses, there were instead mostly self-interested, pragmatic arguments—foreign Jews would make good patriots, Jews look after their own poor, rich foreign Jews will only settle here if they can be naturalized, land prices would go up in response to the entry of new Jewish bidders for estates, and—most ignominious of all—the bill would benefit a few Jews only. The Christian pieties and expressions of sympathy ('Have we not all one Father? Hath not one God created us?' '[The Jews are] a most unhappy people, and rather the objects of our compassion than hatred') with which these arguments were leavened were insufficient; the expressions of elite contempt for 'popular gusts' were positively counter-productive. Although the archbishop of Canterbury spoke of being 'ashamed for the spirit of our country', the ideological case against the bill was left essentially unanswered, and so, when the 'inflamed and unthinking populace' protested, the bill's supporters lost heart, the government folded, and the Act was repealed within the very year in which it had been enacted. 'If it gives disturbance to weak minds,' advised the Prime Minister, Henry Pelham, 'it is right to indulge them.' The administration won the general election in the following year.[54]

How to explain the violence of the opposition? Was it mere political opportunism ('a Tory stick with which to beat the Whigs', 'an election gimmick'),[55] or anti-Semitism, or both ('the primary motive ... was political ... but its very magnitude and success suggest that anti-Semitism was very far from being dead'),[56] or perhaps something else altogether? Horace Walpole (1717–97) thought it was both opportunism *and* anti-Semitism—'obscure men' with political ambitions, inciting 'the grossest and most vulgar prejudices' of the age.[57] Certainly, the propaganda was as much anti-ministerial as anti-Semitic. A French observer, however, saw only anti-Semitism: '*en Angleterre l'animosité contre les Juifs augmente de plus en plus* ... '[58] That it was principally anti-Semitic then became a commonplace among nineteenth-century commentators: 'the ancient rancour of the English people [had] been resuscitated',[59] 'the old jealousies only slumbered—they were not extinguished'.[60] Yet it is striking that the bill's opponents, while making a principled objection to the most minor of reforms, did not argue for anything more radical than repeal—they did not argue, that is, for, say, expulsion or the stripping of native-born Jews' civil rights. Thomas W. Perry suggests why not, and thereby offers an alternative explanation. It was at bottom an argument about immigration, not about Jews. It was principled, *not* opportunistic, but it was anti-alien, *not* anti-Jewish. The anti-Jewish language was mobilized by the Tories against the Whigs because in this instance the relevant immigrant group was Jewish. That the foreigners were Jews just made it worse. The Tories were commended for being against 'every Bill that has the least tendency to let in a swarm of foreigners, especially Jewish foreigners, to lord it over Englishmen and Christians'. On an earlier occasion, the immigrant group had been Huguenot, and there too, the Tories had taken an 'exclusionist' stance.[61] In Tory memory, however, there was no doubt that it was against a measure specifically for the benefit of Jews that protest was directed. Writing fifty years later, Robert Southey commemorated the affair thus: 'During the last reign an attempt was made to naturalise [the Jews], in a body; and the measure would have been effected had it not been for the indignant outcry of the people, who very properly regarded it as an act of defiance, or at least of opposition, to the express language of prophecy.'[62]

The admission to Parliament

This was the question: could a person elected to the House of Commons take his seat without swearing an oath on the true faith of a Christian? The question went under the name of 'removal of Jewish disabilities', though most had already been removed, or under the name 'Jewish emancipation', though the Jews were already living in a mostly emancipated condition. It was also referred to as the 'Jew Question'.[63] The question was debated in Parliament periodically over nearly three decades. It had at first been posed theoretically; then, in 1847, the City of London actually elected a Jew, Lionel Rothschild, and the question became real. What was to be done about Rothschild and his electors? It was now as much about the freedom of Christians to elect Jews as about the freedom of Jews to be elected. After several rebuffs, he was at last allowed to take his seat in the House of Commons. This was in 1858, more or less the hundreth anniversary of the Jew Bill, and the two-hundredth anniversary of the Readmission. (By this time, the Anglo-Jewish community numbered between 30–35,000, the great majority of whom lived in London.)[64] As with these earlier episodes, it was a less than perfect success—a compromise, in fact. Each House was left to devise its own oath, and in this way the deadlock between the Commons and the Lords on the more general question was broken. Rothschild was finally admitted to his seat, though he served without distinction. In 1869, Queen Victoria rejected Gladstone's recommendation of a peerage for Rothschild. She wrote to her Prime Minister, of a 'feeling of which she cannot divest herself, against making a person of the Jewish religion, a Peer', and added that Rothschild was no more than a gambler 'on a gigantic scale', and thus 'far removed from that legitimate trading which she delights to honour'.[65]

Whenever a bill was introduced to give effect to the desire of reformers for Jews to sit in the House of Commons, its opponents mostly adopted an elevated tone, and were careful to exclude overt anti-Semitic animus.[66] Lord Salisbury's opposition, for example, derived from the conviction that any sincere Jew elected to the House of Commons must be 'opposed to all in a religious sense that [the present Members] were there to uphold'. This Jew would be obliged by his own religious convictions, Salisbury suggested, to take a view 'hostile to their whole body, and to all their institutions'.[67] For Salisbury, the 'spirit which abhors a national church has been found also to abhor the institutions which give political predominance to the educated classes'.[68] Though Lord Ashley, for example, felt unable to support the bill, he would defer to no man in his admiration for the Jews, and was certain that the Jews 'merited every [other] concession that could contribute to their honour and comfort'. Extravagant praise was heaped on Jews by many of the opponents of admission. During the 1830 debate in the House of Lords, the archbishop of Canterbury declared that he regarded the Jews as the most remarkable people on earth. They are to be both pitied and admired—pitied for their sufferings and errors, admired for their constancy. They retain their original character as vouchers of divine truth; they are estranged brothers; Christians and Jews share a moral and social code.[69] During the 1847 debate in the Commons, another opponent insisted that he 'was not actuated by any of the old prejudices or unworthy feelings against the Jews, whom he admired almost as much as Disraeli did'.[70]

Still, the opposition had considered responses to the case made by the Jews' advocates. Once Nonconforming Protestants and Catholics had been admitted to Parliament, consistency did *not* require support for admitting Jews, they argued. The differences between Christians were of little consequence; the difference between Christian and non-Christians was fundamental. Precedent did not assist, because the cases were not alike: the Jews are 'haters of Christianity'. They had no right to the removal of disabilities; they were no more than voluntary strangers. They had no more entitlement to participate in the government of the country than does a lodger to participate in the management of the house in which he is temporarily domiciled; they were entitled to 'shelter and kindness', but not 'political privileges'. They comprised a nation within a nation; they were 'totally distinct in every respect'; they were 'citizens of the world, rather than citizens of England'. Parliament would be 'desecrated' were Jews to be admitted. Excluding them was a matter of 'self-defence', securing Parliament against the violation of a sacred principle.[71] Towards the end of the campaign, the language became more extreme among the parliamentary diehards. According to one Tory MP, for example, the campaign for emancipation was a Talmudic plot, itself part of a Catholic conspiracy, directed by the Jesuits to destroy Britain's religion, constitution, and prosperity.[72] The Jews, it was said, were religious fanatics: they were looking forward to the time when they would trample Gentiles underfoot. But they were also unethical opportunists: they cared little about principle, a great deal about interest.[73] The admission of Jews to Parliament would 'send a shock quivering through every institution'; it would 'shiver' the nation's institutions into 'fragments'.[74] The extra-parliamentary opposition tended to be even less irenic. Admitting the Jews to Parliament, one pamphleteer claimed, would be a repudiation of God's own punishment of the Jews for rejecting Christ. There were allegations that Lionel Rothschild had bought up votes; one prominent Tory elector declared that the candidate should be 'one of the princes of Judah, in the land of Judah', rather than seeking to enter the British legislature. Thomas Carlyle wrote to a leading Commons politician in advance of a vote on Jewish disabilities, 'how can a real Jew . . . try to be a senator, or even citizen, of any country, except his own wretched Palestine, whither all his thoughts and steps and efforts tend?' 'We won't have you, / you little Jew', ran the lines of a campaign ditty directed against Lord John Russell, a well-known supporter of the Jews.[75] But this was all quite tame—certainly, when compared to the events of 1656 and 1753.

Those who advocated Jewish admission were brisker, tending to characterize the oath, and the exclusion it implied, as anachronistic, an 'absurd restriction', derived from 'ancient prejudices', the 'last remnant of religious persecution', 'fanaticism and bigotry', 'the last relic of the old system of intolerance', a 'moral stain', a 'penalty . . . in principle exactly the same as . . . inflicting punishment of death'.[76] This, for example, was Macaulay's position. In his maiden speech on 5 April 1830, however, when he spoke in support of the second reading of one of the reforming bills, he also advanced a rather different argument. He called for the recognition of Jewish power:

> The power of which you deprive the Jew consists in maces, and gold chains, and skins of parchment with pieces of wax dangling from their edges. The power which you leave the Jew is the power of principal over clerk, or master over servant, of landlord over tenant. . . . Does not wealth confer power? How are we to permit all the consequences of that wealth but one?[77]

Of course, both supporters and opponents of the various bills declared that they were acting on Christian principle.[78] But supporters were able to insist that they were also campaigning in 'the great cause of civil and religious freedom'.[79] What, one pro-emancipationist asked, did religion have to do with 'the discharge of duties purely political and temporal'?[80] Pro-emancipationists considered themselves to be in step with the spirit of the times. When Gladstone finally came down on the pro-emancipationist side, Walter Bagehot praised his willingness to change his position. These changes, he wrote, 'do credit to [his] good sense; they show that he has a susceptible nature, that he will not live out of sympathy with his age'. Public opinion was broadly with the emancipationists; the Jews' success was but one instance, wrote the jurist A. V. Dicey, of the concessions made by the legislature to the demand of dominant liberalism for the extension of religious and civil equality.[81] 'The City of London having elected Lionel Rothschild one of her representatives,' wrote the then leader of the Tories, George Bentinck, in September 1847, 'it is such a pronouncement of public opinion, that I do not think the party, as a party, would do themselves any good by taking up the question against the Jews.' By failing to take his advice, he later wrote, the party had 'degenerated into a No Popery, No Jew Party'. 'Bigotry' was driving it, he concluded.[82]

The vote had one consequence for the later development of anti-Semitic sentiment in England. After ten years' silence on the question, Disraeli voted against his party in favour of the remission of Jewish disabilities. He made fine if eccentric interventions, speaking with a passionate conviction that some observers found to be uncharacteristic. It was usual to regard him as a man of masks, either concealing his beliefs or without any beliefs—raffish, cynical, manipulative. But then, the apparent revelation—he cared about his own people, his 'nation'. It was his moment of redemption, this open, sincere act, contrary to the sentiments of his political colleagues. But it was also the moment at which he was taken to have revealed his true loyalties, and they were alien. The liberal academic, E. A. Freeman, drew out these implications. A mocker about everything else, he has been thoroughly serious about his national sympathies. It was the most honourable action of his life, when he forsook his party for the sake of his nation. On that day this Jew was a gentleman in the highest sense. He acted as one who could brave much and risk much for real conviction. His zeal for his own people is really the best feature in his career.[83]

Conclusion

These contests, if viewed as a whole, have a number of features distinctive to England. Together they contribute to the case for a certain English 'exceptionalism' in the matter of modern anti-Semitism.

First, there was no pre-existing state of 'non-'emancipation, no Jews confined in ghettoes, the object of speculative, fearful attention, alien and yet present in an otherwise homogeneous national community. Most of their civil restrictions or 'disabilities' applying to Jews on their return applied to non-Protestants generally; on occasion, they found themselves caught in a trap set for others.[84] The passage in the Church of England prayer book of 1549, 1552, and 1662, 'Have mercy upon all Jews, Turks, infidels and heretics', reflects this generally undiscriminating perspective. Jews were thus entitled to think of themselves as a section of Nonconformist society. Furthermore, the restrictions were in the main quite modest, and in certain instances, only casually observed. While, for example, constituency returning officers could require (until 1835) an elector to swear a Christian oath as a pre-condition to the casting of his vote, many did not impose that requirement, and so there was a Jewish electorate (though not a 'Jewish vote') long before there was a Jewish Member of Parliament. Certain measures clarified the law as much as reforming it: in 1833, for example, a declaratory act confirmed the Jews' right to own freehold land.[85] By imperceptible degrees, England's Jews became English Jews. The Jews' emancipation was a modest affair, and did not involve any radical elevation of status, or any radical increase in social visibility. There was steady, unsensational progress; a measured, orderly collapsing of the barriers holding Jews back from participation in politics, in high society, in the cultural life of the nation. There was no single emancipation date, no proclamation, no abolition of Jewry laws, no tearing down of ghetto walls. It is the gradualism of change that is striking, and this includes the very late date by which English Jews' last disabilities were removed. It was not until 1871, with the Promissory Oaths Act, that Jews were altogether free of constraint—by contrast, Prussian Jewry was emancipated, finally and by courtesy of Bismarck, in 1869.

But secondly, and exceptionally in European history, there were no less than three protracted, staged public contests over the rights of Jews, separated by approximately one-hundred-year intervals. These were the key moments when the relation between the Jews and the state came up for review, when the Jews were most visible, when questions relating to them were pressed with the greatest force, and when they dominated public discourse. First, there was the Whitehall Conference (4–18 December 1655), which debated Jewish readmission; then almost exactly one hundred years later, in 1753, there were the civil disturbances over a law (the 'Jew Bill') to naturalize foreign Jews; and last, about one hundred years after that, a conclusion was reached in the parliamentary debates on Jewish admission to the House of Commons (1830–58—in all, fourteen attempts by Jews and their parliamentary advocates).[86] The Readmission controversy and the Jew Bill controversy were the first occasions in Europe when Jewish rights were publicly debated. The distinctiveness of Anglo-Jewish history is evident as much in this curious alternation between modest advance and public contest or, better, this serial punctuating of a single, incremental process, as it is in the absence of show trials, pogroms, boycotts, and other persecutions that characterized the travails of Continental Jewry.[87] The position of Jews was debated nowhere else so thoroughly, so repeatedly, or so early on as in England. The status of the Jews was not so protractedly elevated, yet nor from so advanced a starting point, as in England.

Thirdly, these contests encouraged the emergence of a strongly philo-Semitic body of opinion, which in turn fostered robust advocacy in support of Jewish interests, an appreciation for Judaism and the character of the Jewish people, and an ardent belief in the commonality of interest of the English and Jewish nations. There was a strong Christian character to these positions; at times, they acquired an almost doctrinal authority. God honours the Jews, and it is incumbent upon Christians to imitate Him; He punishes those who oppress the Jews and rewards their benefactors; Christians are brethren to the Jews; and so on.[88] There was also a strong, mostly complementary, liberal aspect, the Jews' campaigns for the removal of their disabilities being regarded as integral to broader campaigns for social and civic equality.[89] (On the question of admission to Parliament, for example, the sequence was Protestant dissenters in 1828, Catholics in 1829, and then Jews in 1858. How, it was argued, could one support the first and the second, yet not the third?) Convictions of this kind carried the Jews along, beyond the triumph of 1858, and ensured support for their tormented co-religionists in Russia and then, much more consequentially, for the Zionist project. The content of this philo-Semitism was thus substantially different to the equivalent positions taken in the emancipation debates on the Continent. There, much was made of the degeneracy of the Jews, and the potential of emancipation for their reform. Shut out from the political nation, subject to humiliations, and limited in the economic roles they were able to perform, it was not surprising—so the argument went—that they were a benighted people. Persecution had made them vicious; toler-ance would improve them. In England, by contrast, this argument was more typically found in literary works (call it the 'Walter Scott' or '*Ivanhoe*' line). Political support for the Jews only infrequently touched on the theme, tending either to avoid altogether arguments compromised by such preju-diced, adverse perspectives, or else to phrase them conditionally, as in '*if* [the Jews] are vicious it is we who have made them so'.[90] It was left to polemicists more frankly hostile to the Jews to embrace the notion of the Jews as degenerate, and unregenerate too. If circumstances had made of Jews an unlovely people, they argued, this character was now fixed.[91]

Fourthly, while the achievements of emancipation have never been in jeopardy, and Jews have for at least 150 years now enjoyed a strong sense of juridical and political equality, what remains is a residual sense of constraint, and on occasion, a sense of vulnerability. If the ultimate end of emancipa-tion is for members of the subject group to move freely in civil society, and for the group as a defensive entity itself to dissolve,[92] Anglo-Jewry has yet to complete its journey. It remains on its guard. It displays certain anxieties about status and security that are not altogether misconceived. At times, the organized part of Anglo-Jewry behaves as if it is a party to an 'emancipation contract', in which membership of an international collective has been exchanged for citizenship in a national one, and civil rights secured in return for the ready adoption of specifically British perspectives.

Fifthly, the absence of an organized anti-Semitic interest in Parliament was a significant aspect of the protracted emancipation process. This continued to be a feature of English political life. Further, it proved entirely possible to take a pro-readmission/naturalization/emancipation line and yet also entertain hostile feelings towards the Jews. One might support them in their efforts to attain the same legal status as other subjects of the Crown (that was only fair), without at the same time thinking well of them. Lord George Bentinck, who lost his position as Tory leader because of his pro-emancipation vote, and who was memorialized by Disraeli, told a parliamentary colleague, 'as for the Jews themselves, I don't care two strokes about them and heartily wish they were all back in the Holy Land'.[93] This too was significant in the unfolding of English anti-Semitism. What it meant, among other things, is that when the legal status of Jews was not in issue, the hostility to them could be somewhat greater.

Lastly, at no time during this period did the Jews act collectively. They were always divided; they never functioned as a coherent corporate body. And this is true for the entire emancipation process, from the mid-seventeenth century to the mid-nineteenth century.[94] They were, if anything, even more divided in their responses to the challenges to their security. The Jewish community as a whole usually failed correctly to identify its true interests; on some occasions, the leading communal organizations behaved foolishly, even ignominiously. Very often, Jewish self-defence was left to maverick entities, quite outside established communal structures. Communal cohesiveness deteriorated still further in the decades following the period under review in this chapter, that is to say, from the late 1960s to the present. Yet it is a curious fact that just when the Jewish community was thus perhaps at its least effective as a collective entity, that is to say, least endowed with effective, public leaders, capable of open and persuasive advocacy and defence of communal interests, the notion emerged in the public sphere of a 'Jewish lobby', possessing immense, even somewhat occult power, and operating to the disadvantage of all who opposed it or the interests it represented.

Moments of crisis: the challenges to security (1860s–1960s)

Writing in 1867, a sympathetic observer of the Jewish scene commented, 'the greater intercourse with the Jews, consequent on their naturalisation in England, has broken down most of the prejudices against them, and has enabled us to form a truer conception of their character than that which was formerly maintained'.[95] He spoke too soon. Across the decades that followed, from the 1870s to the 1940s, Jewish individuals or groups became the object of harsh discursive assault: Disraeli, Russian-Jewish immigrants, South African Randlords, Liberal politicians and plutocrats, Bolsheviks, Zionists. These were agitations principally about Britain's foreign or imperial policy, or about the influence of foreign affairs on Britain, or about 'pauper aliens' and 'plutocratic aliens'—that is, types of foreign Jew.[96] Why, it was demanded, was Disraeli siding with the Moslem Turks against Christian Russia? If England had been drawn into war over the Eastern Question, it was said, 'it would have been a Jewish war, a war waged with British blood to uphold the objects of Jewish sympathy, or to avenge Jewish wrongs'.[97] And then, twenty or so years later, a 'Jewish war' *was* waged. Why, it was asked, was the British government fighting a war of gold against the Boers on behalf of Jewish magnates? At the same time, and on the home front, what damage did Russian-Jewish refugees pose to the moral health of the nation? A decade or so later, a fresh question emerged. What was the precise nature of the threat posed by the Russian Revolution, in which Jews appeared to have played the leading part? And then—why was Britain committing resources to the establishment of a Jewish home in Palestine? And *then*—why was Britain picking a fight with Hitler on behalf of the Jews? Why were Zionists attacking and killing British soldiers in Palestine? Framed in anti-Semitic terms, these questions duly generated anti-Semitic responses.

Disraeli and the Eastern Question

The 'Great Eastern Crisis' of 1876–8 was an episode in the history of the 'Eastern Question'—the question being, how to deal with the consequences for Europe of the declining Ottoman Empire? The British answer for much of the nineteenth century had been, essentially, maintain Turkey to contain Russia. Defeating Russian designs in Asia, the 'Great Game', was pursued single-mindedly by generations of British civilian and military officials; the disappearance of the Ottoman Empire, it was thought, would be the first step towards the disappearance of Britain's.[98] This was the doctrine of the 'independence and integrity' of the Ottoman Empire. The doctrine came under intense pressure in the late 1870s from Nonconformists and Liberals. Their campaigning perplexed Disraeli, because they thereby disregarded the long-standing British objective of exercising control over the eastern Mediterranean and the routes to India. His was what might be termed a 'realist' perspective: 'human rights' concerns should not trump national self-interest. He was not much concerned with the suffering of the Ottoman Empire's minorities, but nor was he a Turcophile.[99] His entire object was to maintain national prestige and the national interest—that is, *British* prestige, and *British* interest. Indeed, he expressly contrasted his perspective with the cosmopolitan principles of his political opponents. His position had no 'Jewish' quality;[100] the Jewish community itself was divided along broader, national party lines.[101] Yet some of the criticism of him had an anti-Semitic quality.

Disraeli's Jewish origins were the subject of sniping throughout his public career. A spat with Daniel O'Connell, for example, provoked the Irish leader into uncharacteristic anti-Semitic abuse.[102] In an 1849 letter, Disraeli acknowledged the 'great anomaly' of being the Tories' 'chief', given the 'prejudices' that existed against his 'origin'.[103] But it was only during the most violent passages of the Eastern Question during Disraeli's second ministry, when he became the object of particular vituperation, that his Jewishness acquired real salience in the public imagination.[104] He was held to have taken sides against the Christian party in favour of the Muslim party, and against small nations striving for independence in favour of a decaying and alien empire.[105] Worst of all, in June 1876 he had trivialized atrocities committed by Ottoman forces on Bulgarian Christians. Never mind that he himself took his patriotism as an Englishman for granted. His detractors represented him as 'un-English' or even anti-English, 'a Jew in race, in heart, and in practice' who 'controls all England by skilfully playing upon the prejudices and weaknesses of those around him'.[106] He bamboozles the British public into viewing as a British policy a policy that is in fact Jewish ('a Hebrew policy'),[107] and has the pursuit of Jewish interests as its objective.

In the manner of anti-Semitic discourse, the abuse was both inventive and stale. Disraeli was a 'lump of dirt', a 'Fagin'. He was 'Judas', 'Jewish Dizzy', the 'Jewish chief', 'Sir Benjamin de Judah', and 'Chief Rabbi Benjamin'. He was 'a very Hebrew of Hebrews', the 'Jew Earl, Philo-Turkish Jew and Jew Premier', and the 'traitorous Jew', the 'haughty Jew', and the 'abominable Jew'. He was a leader of the 'Turkophile party', its 'most rabid element' consisting of 'the race of Shylock'. He was the premier of a 'Jew government'. He was a wizard, a conjurer, a magician, an alchemist. He was a 'man of the East', an 'Asiatic'. 'For the past six years we have had an Asiatic ruler.' He was a 'wandering Jew', 'sprung from a race of migratory Jews'. He was 'born in a foreign country [i.e., England]', and raised 'amid a people for whose ideas and habits he has no sympathy and little respect'. He was a 'sham Christian and a sham Englishman'. He was the 'charioteer' of a 'Juggernaut car', 'drag[ging] the whole of Christendom' over the rights of the Christian subjects of the Ottoman Empire. Most cartoons gave him an immense nose and curly black hair; he was represented as Shylock ('our modern Shylock'); many related him to the Devil ('the most authentic incarnation of the Evil One'); two represented him in the act of ritually murdering the infant Britannia, and in one of these Gladstone is the distressed mother, arriving perhaps too late to save her child.[108] And there was a note sounded for the first time, but to be repeated many times thereafter: the Jews want war, against the national interest. The socialist William Morris (1834–96) wrote to the *Daily News*, praising Freeman's 'manly and closely reasoned letters', and condemning Disraeli, the 'clever trickster', for being 'determined to drag us into a shameful and unjust war'.[109] It was as if all the anti-Semitic discourse in general circulation in the culture was drawn in that time towards this one man, just as iron filings, thinly spread across a surface, fly towards a newly introduced magnet, when of sufficient power.

As before, there were both parliamentary and extra-parliamentary as-saults. W. E. Gladstone and E. A. Freeman attacked Disraeli in the name of national self-determination, the 'real course of national feeling in this great cause of justice, mercy and faith', and everything that was 'purely generous, purely unselfish'.[110] But they also held that his policy was in some sense 'Judaic', and therefore alien to the character and interests of Christian Europe. Disraeli hates 'Christian liberty and reconstruction', wrote Glad-stone. It was his 'crypto-Judaism', his 'Judaic feeling' that drove him to favour the Turks: 'The Jews of the East bitterly hate the Christians who have not always used them well.'[111] (This was especially absurd—the 'Jews of the East' had equal reason to 'hate' the Ottomans—as was pointed out by a Jewish apologist at the time.)[112] 'We cannot sacrifice our people, the people of Aryan and Christian Europe, to the most genuine belief in an Asian mystery' wrote Freeman. 'We cannot have England governed by a Hebrew policy.' The Jews survived their rejection of Christ, he maintained, only as an 'instrument of Satan to buffet all other people'.[113] Gladstone and Freeman would no doubt have rejected angrily the charge of anti-Semitism, had it been made (the very decade in which the term was invented), and might even have characterized it as deliberately diversionary. Certainly, responding to expressions of concern, Gladstone held to his position that 'Judaic sympathies' were influencing 'the question of the East', which he 'deeply deplore[d]'. They denied any desire to see the Jews harmed. Gladstone, indeed, expressed concern that their support for the Turks might prejudice them in the Christian states under Turkish dominion.[114] As for Freeman, he insisted, 'No one wishes to place the Jew . . . under any disability as compared with the European Christian.' 'But,' he added, 'it will not do to have the policy of England, the welfare of Europe, sacrificed to Hebrew sentiment.'[115] Freeman felt himself personally engaged in 'the warfare with Turk and Jew'.[116] The two men might also have argued that Disraeli was at least partly responsible himself for the character of some of the attacks on him, both because of the way he spoke and wrote about Judaism's special genius, and the way he dealt with the public reaction to the Bulgarian atrocities (which reflected something of the *Jewish Chronicle*'s perspective—why this outrage at atrocities perpetrated on Bulgarian Christians, it asked, when comparable violence committed against Rumanian Jews excites barely a murmur?).[117] Both Gladstone and Freeman exploited anti-Semitism at a particular juncture, and in support of a particular cause, though it was Freeman who drove the implications of their common perspective the hardest. Comrades in the struggle against Disraeli, Gladstone later rewarded Freeman with the Regius Professorship of Medieval History at Oxford.[118]

'Mr. Disraeli', wrote the liberal Henry Dunckley, 'is a Jew by birth, and a Christian by accident.'[119] Disraeli's early biographers shared this essential perspective. J. A. Froude admired Disraeli's success, achieved 'in the teeth of prejudice, without support save in his own force of character'. Disraeli, he wrote, 'was not given to veneration, but if he venerated anything it was the genius and destiny of his own race'. 'Though calling himself a Christian,' Froude went on, 'he was a Jew in his heart.' His thoughts on religious questions 'ran on Asiatic rather than European lines'. 'He was English only by adoption.'[120] Banal and absurd from the outset, this quickly became a cliché in commentary on Disraeli's career. G. K. Chesterton, in his very widely read *A Short History of England* (1917), for example, described Disraeli as a 'brilliant Jewish adventurer', whose 'pro-Turkish settlement' reflected his 'native indifference to the Christian subjects of Turkey'.[121] Support for these Christian communities tended to be both high-minded and racist—better, high-mindedly racist. Turkish crimes were vilified, as was Jewish complicity with them; Christian suffering was sanctified. This mistrust of Disraeli thus survived his death. T. S. Eliot, writing to a private correspondent, gave an account of his own impossible Toryism that took in Disraeli's taken-for-granted phoniness: 'My own "toryism" ', he explained, 'is only intelligible on the understanding that there are no Tories in politics at all, and that I don't much like any government since Charles I, and that Disraeli was a Jew film producer only commendable because so much less intolerable than Gladstone.'[122]

Eliot's drollery contains a clue to Disraeli's place in English anti-Semitism's history. It was complex and in certain measure contradictory. His career and public opinions provided material for anti-Semites while also acting as a restraint on their wilder speculations. (In contrast, say, to the public career of the German statesman and industrialist Walter Rathenau, assassinated in 1922 by right-wing fanatics, Disraeli's career did not lead to the mobilization of any anti-Semitic movement.)[123] Something of this contradictory perspective is evident in Frank Harrison Hill's series of articles on Disraeli, published in the *Fortnightly Review* in 1878. On the one hand, he 'can scarcely be classified, no one but himself can be his parallel'; on the other hand, he is 'one of the most remarkable illustratory ornaments' of an 'historic race', and the 'most remarkable illustration of his own doctrine of the ascendancy of Hebrew genius in modern Europe'. The 'secret of Lord Beaconsfield's life lies in his Jewish blood'. On the one hand, his 'political character is, in the situation which he holds, a danger and defiance to England, and a threat to the peace of the world'. On the other hand, he is nothing more than 'a grotesque foreign accident in our English political history', and the 'situation' he has created is 'more ridiculous and annoying than dangerous'. On the one hand, he is an exhibitionist, an attention-seeker, a 'humour[er] [of] the prejudices of the people among whom he has been thrown' (and in these respects, he 'has been of some use to the British public'—a diversion, an entertainment). On the other hand, he speaks for Jewish power. We live 'under a Mosaic dispensation'. 'In administration, in finance, and in journalism, Jewish influences notoriously shape and guide English politics.' 'The rulers of the synagogue are more largely than is suspected the rulers of England.' But Disraeli goes too far! He overstates Jewish influence: 'Judaism and the Jews have been thrust by him with an almost unnecessary pertinacity into English politics and literature.' This Jewish politician, Hill implies, is a bore on the subject of the Jews. The truth is that his career has been about no more than personal opportunism—

'to climb higher and higher, to fix more and more steadily the public gaze, to wield power, to receive and distribute honours, to be the talk of his coterie, of England, of Europe'. His 'statesmanship' on the Eastern Question was the product of nothing more than 'An erratic Oriental imagination' rather than 'a European intelligence'. His career has been described as 'demoralising to the national character, and as lowering the standard and aims of English politics'. But, Hill argues, these are misjudgements: his influence has not been 'depraving', it has been 'privative'—by which Hill means a kind of moral vacuum. It has not been possible to think of political morality with him, and therefore 'it has escaped injury or deterioration'. However, Disraeli is typical yet unique, a mere diversion, yet the public face of Jewish power. Thus was English anti-Semitism typically frustrated in the very moments of its elaboration. The most powerful Jew in nineteenth-century England was in the end, though a threat, probably harmless. Hill's succinct formulation, 'more ridiculous and annoying than dangerous', may be taken as modern English anti-Semitism's final judgement on the Jews.[124]

The Boer War

The Dutch began to settle at the Cape of Good Hope in 1652; over the generations, the settlers became known as 'Boers'. About 150 years later, a British expeditionary force arrived at the Cape, and then another one, eleven years after that. In 1815, Britain annexed the Cape, and twenty years later, slavery was abolished in the Cape Colony. From 1834 to 1840, the Boers migrated inland, a process known as the 'Great Trek'. Over the next fifty years, they settled in three regions of Southern Africa: Natal, Transvaal, and what became known as the Orange Free State. The British ruled the Cape Colony. In consequence first of British colonization, and then of the discovery of diamonds near Kimberley and of gold in the Transvaal, many British and others emigrated to South Africa, comprising a substantial presence in both the British and Boer territories. The Boers referred to these speculators and entrepreneurs as *Uitlanders* or 'outsiders', that is, non-Dutch-origin whites. The most successful among them were termed 'Randlords', after Witwatersrand, the place where gold was discovered. The Boers lost their independent polities, repeatedly. They lost Natal in 1843; then they lost Transvaal in 1877, only to get it back four years later. Then they lost it again, and the Orange Free State in 1902. During this period, they fought two wars against the British Empire. The first was a short one, the second, a rather longer one, lasting from October 1899 until May 1902. The first ended in a victory for the Boers, the second, in their defeat, with a face-saving promise of limited self-government. The British suffered several reverses and disasters before finally triumphing in this second 'Boer War', the last great colonial war and the first modern war.

It was in South Africa that the doctrines of British imperialism were articulated most forcefully, and implemented with the greatest force. It was also in South Africa that the relations between imperialism and finance were both most frankly acknowledged and most intimate. The common denominator was Cecil Rhodes. He was among the most vigorous advocates of British expansion in Southern Africa, and among the most successful of British entrepreneurs there too. He was for a while prime minister of the Cape Colony; he was a major player in the diamond industry. In his first role, he kept company with Joseph Chamberlain, the Colonial Secretary, and Alfred Milner, high commissioner for Southern Africa and governor of Cape Colony. In his second role, he kept company with the Randlords, Sir Alfred Beit (1853–1906) and Barny Barnato (1852–97). They deferred to him in political matters.[125]

The Boer War precipitated new, dissenting thinking about empire. These radical critics regarded South Africa not as a *limit-case* of late nineteenth-century British imperialism, but as a *typical* case. This was what it was like, in its ambition, in its disregard for subject people, in its complicity with high finance, and in its use of newspapers to manipulate popular support for its endeavours. But then their positions diverged into the liberal and the revolutionary.

Within the range of liberal positions, there were those who developed a critique of the new imperialism, distinguishing it from earlier imperialisms. It was no longer a national expansion, but an affair of conspiracies, contrary to the national interest; a coterie profited, while the nation, not to mention the colonies, paid. There were those who were concerned with the brutalities attendant upon the suppression of the Boer revolt: the barbarism of the concentration camps and of the 'scorched earth' policy. And there were those who argued for reform: colonial estates should not be developed by entrepreneurs and speculators, but by disinterested authorities, benefiting both the colonized and the wider global community.[126] The range of revolutionary positions was much narrower. It was open to Marxists, taking their line from Marx himself, to treat imperialism as a progressive force, conferring certain benefits (though brutally, and without regard for any interests but its own), and precipitating a final, systemic crisis. The Social Democratic Federation tended not to do this, however, or not, at any rate, in relation to the Boer War, which they characterized as a 'war for the Transvaal and its gold' against the Boers, 'a peaceful people', and nothing less than 'Mammon worship'.[127] They thus came closer to the liberal position, deploying a different vocabulary to the same polemical end. If only for this reason, the liberal positions were more developed than the revolutionary ones. J. A. Hobson at one time or another advanced most of them. It was not until Lenin that a specifically Marxist theory of imperialism emerged, which nonetheless drew substantially upon Hobson's work.

What then of anti-Semitism? It derived from the false thesis that the Jewish origins of some South African Randlords or 'gold bugs', and of some English financiers and newspaper proprietors, had explanatory value. It was not enough that the war was a 'capitalist' one;[128] it had to be a 'Jew-Capitalist' one. This thesis omitted critical facts and falsified others. For example, so far from Europe's press being controlled by Jews, as anti-Semitic anti-War critics alleged, it was pro-Boer, and tended to characterize the British as dupes of Jewish financiers.[129] Again, non-Jewish Randlords, such as Herman Eckstein, of German Protestant origins, were said to be Jewish, so as to give a stronger impression of Jewish dominance.[130] This impression coloured liberal political discourse of the time. In L. T. Hobhouse's *Democracy and Reaction* (1904), for example, which refers in passing to 'the extravagant Orientalism of Disraeli, with its correlatives of hostility to Russia and support for Turkey', there is a footnote to the effect that in Australia the personification of Britain is no longer John Bull, but 'a far more sinister term'. For the Australians, 'John Bull-Cohen is now the impersonation of British Imperial policy.'[131] Hobhouse does not expressly endorse the new term; the implication, however, is that there is something in it.

In the 1890s, as in the 1870s, the liberal position was to support small nations against empires. In the 1870s, it was the Balkan nations as against the Ottomans; in the 1890s, it was the Boers, as against Britain itself. In each case, some liberals cast a Jew (Disraeli) or Jews (the Randlords) as the enemy. The case against the 'Randlords' became a case against Jews in general. If the Jews engineered the war, it must follow that it was being fought in pursuit of their interests. Hilaire Belloc, as might be expected, insisted that it had been 'openly and undeniably provoked and promoted by Jewish interests in South Africa'.[132] But J. A. Hobson, too, contributed his authority and prestige to this fantasy of a tribal conspiracy. He saw Jews acting in concert to promote Jewish interests, when he should have seen financiers of various origins, pursuing their own interests, often in competition with each other, and with no special Jewish consciousness.[133] Hobson had some history on the subject of the Jews; I return to him in the next chapter.

Hobson's positions were substantially reproduced, though without the supporting economic doctrine, in *Reynolds's Newspaper*, which had a considerable working-class readership, and was at the relevant time owned by the Liberal MP, James Henry Dalziel, and edited by W. H. Thompson. Following correspondence on the 'Jewish Question', the editor made the newspaper's position clear. The Jews would 'probably' establish 'international dominancy', in consequence of their refusal to inter-marry and their ever-growing control of the money markets and the press. That they are a 'chosen people' is an absurd assumption that the world cannot admit. Their worship of the tribal war-god Jehovah could not be more opposed to the worship of the Christ of the New Testament. The Jews are wanderers on the face of the earth largely through their own fault. The whole world cannot be wrong and they right. Passages from Deuteronomy and Isaiah ('Jehovah on the Jews', 'Isaiah on the Jews') were cited, critical of the Jews. A correspondent was then allowed to add: The 'chosen people' seem to possess the power to command John Bull. He is helpless in the merciless grip of the Jew Gold Bug. This miserable Shylock, whose precious hide has been looked after, will have the pickings when the war is over, and John Bull will resignedly assist the bloodsucker. The newspaper went on to quote Hyndman approvingly: 'In the City today the Jews were openly boasting that they had won the Dreyfus case and dragged England into the Transvaal war.'[134] In the following year, the newspaper returned to the theme of the 'Capitalist-cum-Jewish war', explaining its debt to Hobson's analysis. It is 'strictly impartial', and touches upon 'many deeply interesting questions'. Hobson shows that, though there were a few Englishmen among the early financial pioneers in the Transvaal, 'as soon as the vast possibilities of its gold production became apparent' it was 'immediately over-run by German Jews, true as the vulture to scent its prey'. According to Hobson, it continues, Johannesburg is the New Jerusalem, dominated by this 'tribe without a country'. The Jews own the dynamite monopoly, the drink trade, and nearly the whole Press. 'Verily the Jew has led the Gentile captive.' The complicated financial dealings between these Jews remind us of the extraordinary bargains made among 'the poor Jews of the East End' (which leads to 'so much sordid litigation that the English people have to support a county court' in Whitechapel just for the settlement of their disputes). The Stock Exchange pulls the strings, and the British government dances, 'but behind the Stock Exchange is the sinister figure of the financial Jew', 'enmeshing the world' in the 'money-web' spun by this 'great racial free-masonry'. Then there is the standard disclaimer: 'We make no sweeping charges against the whole Jewish race, but . . .' and so on.[135]

The Marxist case should have been more resistant to anti-Semitic pollution, because it did not elevate conspiracy to the status of an explanatory principle. Certainly, much that was anti-Semitic in the Social Democratic Federation position could be dismissed as opportunistic, deriving from the well-tested principle that a case against capitalism could best be made in the guise of a case against Jewish capitalists—the target was more manageable, less abstract, smaller. 'HRH is practically in the hand of the Jews', alleged its weekly newspaper, *Justice*. 'We have no special animosity against rich Jews', it went on. 'But there are still a few chauvinist Englishmen left who may object to seeing the crown of England in the pocket of an international Jew loan-monger.'[136] Nevertheless, the anti-Semitic character of *Justice*'s line during the Boer War was in accord with the generally anti-Semitic character of the newspaper since its inception, almost twenty years' earlier,[137] and which in turn reflected a broader leftist perspective, where the figure of the 'Jewish financier' was taken to be the very type of the international capitalist, not merely representative of the genus, but its most sinister and destructive species. 'The Jew', explained the English socialist and trades unionist Ben Tillett, is 'the most consistent and determined money-grubber we know.'[138] The libertarian Edward Carpenter complained that British politicians were 'being led by the nose by the Jews'.[139] *Justice* explained, 'We have no feeling against Jews as Jews, but as nefarious capitalists and poisoners of the well of public information, we denounce them.'[140]

Readers of *Justice* were told both that the Jews owned the press and the politicians, and that they had started the war to advance their own financial ends. 'In Paris, in Berlin, and especially in Vienna, the power of the capitalist Jews over the press is enormous, and in some cases none the less injurious for being unseen', asserted *Justice*. The Jewish proprietors are more dangerous than Christian owners, it added, 'because they act practically in accord with their fellow capitalist Jews all over the world'.[141] It published on its front page a list of the 'Jew-owned and Jew-edited papers in London, in all of which, of course, considerations of "bishness" and financial interests—Israel in Egypt—holds first place'.[142] *Justice*'s attacks on the 'Jew-Jingo press', the 'Jew-Jingo owners of the *Daily Telegraph*', 'our loathsome yellow sheets and their Jew-Jingo backers',[143] etc., were unceasing. This was a theme since 1890.[144] So when *Justice* explained in 1899 that the 'Jew financiers' and their 'Jew-Jingo backers' in the press were 'gold-greedy ghouls thirsting for blood',[145] this did not come as any great surprise to its readers. Two weeks later, in case any reader had missed the point, *Justice* explained again: 'The Jew capitalists have been specially prominent in this nefarious business, and it is the Jew-owned yellow press which has been specially virulent in exciting the jingo mob here and inciting rowdies to violence.'[146] Rhodes was described as the mere 'tout of Jewish capitalists'.[147] The war was nothing more than a buccaneering attempt to grab the rich country of the Rand for a gang of cosmopolitan plunderers, without any concern for the British Empire, or patriotism, or anything else.[148] Indeed, this was not the first war started by the Jews. The Mexican war of France's Second Empire was also undertaken at the instance of Jews and stockjobbers who had obtained control of the Emperor's entourage. 'It was a Jews' war, and dearly did France pay for the subservience of her rulers to the power of the Semitic money-bags.'[149]

There were rebukes, criticisms of what was characterized as *Justice*'s 'anti-Semitic campaign',[150] and this led to a debate in *Justice* in October and November 1899. A letter was published from a correspondent 'by birth a Jew, by conviction an atheist', protesting *Justice*'s denunciations of 'the Jew capitalist'.[151] One comrade, Th. Rothstein, complained: Hyndman gives vent to prejudices against the Jews, and his bias cannot be explained away; he has an 'anti-Semitic mind', singling out among the sinful goats the *Jew*-goats and marking them for a special offering; *Justice* preaches from its pulpit rank anti-Semitism; it confirms to the Zionists their argument that anti-Semitism will be rampant in any society, capitalist or socialist, and that the Jews therefore need a country of their own. The Wimbledon branch wrote that he continued to use the word 'Jew' in a manner calculated to inflame racial feeling.[152] In the following issue, E. Belfort Bax also wrote in. Why mention the racial origin of the financier unless you hold it to be significant? Yet in reality it has no significance. It is only of significance to anti-Semites. It is only anti-Semites who object to the financial Jew *as Jew*. There are both Jews and non-Jews among the guilty. You overcome this objection by maintaining that the non-Jews are the 'tools' of the Jews. But that is absurd.

'I confess to an intellectual capacity for conceiving either Chamberlain or Rhodes as a "tool" '. As for the press, 'is *The Times* a Jew organ, or the *Daily Mail*, or the *Pall Mall*, or the *Standard*?' This singling out of Jews for special obloquy is a disgrace to our movement.

Harry Quelch replied to Bax, denying that the newspaper was anti-Semitic. The fact that we are publishing your piece, he wrote, is proof that 'the socialist movement' is not 'drifting into anti-Semitism'. But *you* display race-antipathy—though to Britons, rather than Jews. What is more, why should the Jews be protected from our outrage? 'Is it permissible to de-nounce all capitalists and money-grabbers in unmeasured terms, except when they are Jews, and is it then alone that we must speak with bated breath and whispering humbleness?' In the next issue, other correspondents added their weight to this line, strengthening its specifically anti-Semitic component. One asked, why are the Jews unpopular? It is because they are a parasitic tribe. There may indeed be British financiers, but there are also British soldiers, miners, shipbuilders, and sailors. These are not Jewish occupations—though there are Jew camp followers ready to strip the clothes from dead combatants, and there are Jew dealers and diminutive, degenerate Jew fish jobbers. The Jews are not engaged in productive work, they are not of the soil of this or any other country; they are exclusive and apart from every other people. Of course, *nobody find fault with the Jew because he is a Jew*, but because he is a parasite. Another correspondent observed that the Jews who complained as soon as *Justice* calls a Jew a Jew are not 'internationalist' but 'thin-skinist'. Our Scotch, Irish, or English comrades do not complain when capitalists of their nation are condemned. Yet the Jew capitalist is worse than the English capitalist: 'I have worked for both, and I know which I prefer.' Quelch added, the 'Jew capitalists' have been especially prominent in this scandalous business, it is a 'Jew-capitalist war', and the 'wolfish fury of the Jewish press' has overstepped the bounds of the ordinary capitalist press. We deplore anti-Semitism, he explained, but we fear that 'unscrupulous wealthy Jews', by their ferocious pretence of jingoism and their greed for gold, are going the right way to stir it up. A correspondent added: 'the rich Jews (who really are the influence and the power) will be to blame if any sort of anti-Semitism breaks out here'.[153] Hyndman himself insisted that he numbered among his 'intimate acquaintances, Jews', for whom he had 'great esteem and admiration'.[154] And so on. The anti-Semitism was denied, then, but not repudiated. This controversy did produce one small modifi-cation in the newspaper's position, however. To the Jews were added the

Jesuits. If the Jews were the 'principal promoters of the war', it declared, then the 'leading agents' to turn the war to our disadvantage will be the Jesuits.[155]

In a speech delivered in Battersea Park on 20 May 1900, at a rally organized by the ' "Stop the War" Committee', the radical MP John Burns fulminated against 'the financial Jew', the 'directing and financial power' in South Africa:

> The South African Jew has . . . no bowels of compassion. Appetite grew by what it fed upon; the slave of the centuries, the persecuted of all time, released from the restraint of disciplined control, gained a cash ascendancy, and having gained it by speculation, sustained it by corruption and fraud till his vulgar insolence and arrogant assumptions warned the Boers that a new danger had entered amongst them. The Jew capitalist had arrived. . . .
>
> Every institution and class had been scheduled by the Jew as his heritage, medium and dependent. Where he could not intimidate, he corrupted; where he could not corrupt, he defamed. . . .
>
> [The Boers] defend their land, not from a nation armed, vindicating a righteous cause, but against a militant capitalism that is using our soldiers as the uniformed brokers' men turning out the wrong tenants in South Africa for the interests of Jews. . . .
>
> With wisdom, foresight, kindliness, we may yet retain South Africa for the Empire and humanity, even though we lose it for the Jews.[156]

We are the true patriots; we do not confuse the real interests of the nation with the phoney interests covertly promoted by the Jews. This was a theme in Burns' oratory. In a speech made in the Commons earlier that year, he described the British army as the 'janissary of the Jews', and told the House, 'wherever we examine, there is the financial Jew operating, directing, inspiring, the agencies that have led to this war'. (He later had the speech printed as a pamphlet, 'The Trail of the Financial Serpent', with subheadings, among others, 'England as the janissary of the Jews', and 'Everywhere the financial Jew'.)[157] Notwithstanding interventions of this kind, anti-Semitic agitation, both liberal and revolutionary, was mostly the work of extra-parliamentary agitators, operating on the left and left-liberal margins of political life. There, anti-Semitism was commonplace—to be found wherever there was discussion of the war. The *ILP News*, for example, was happy to assert that the 'stock-exchange Jew' was 'the incarnation of the money idea' and that the 'Jew financier controls the policy of Europe';[158] at the 1900 TUC Conference, the mover of a resolution on the War claimed that '£100m of taxpayers' money had been spent in trying to secure the goldfields of South Africa for cosmopolitan Jews, most of whom had no patriotism and no country.'[159] Inside the House of Commons, the anti-Jewish language tended to be more moderate, though there were still MPs ready to condemn the 'financial gang which has engineered this war' and call for them to meet its cost, to contrast 'the falsehoods of the [Jewish] press' with the 'testimony of manly and honest men with English names', to condemn 'Mr. Rhodes and his associates—generally of the German Jew extraction', 'Mr. Rhodes and German Jew associates', and to disparage Jewish courage, 'how many of these millionaire masters of Her Majesty's Government are now at the front with your soldiers?' 'Mr Rhodes...has had the courage to face the music in Kimberley. But then his name is Rhodes and not Rhodes-stein.'[160] But the Liberal leader, Campbell-Bannerman, refused to characterize the war as a Jewish one, and rejected the anti-Semitic language of its radical opponents. The official opposition would not endorse any account of the war as a Jewish capitalist conspiracy, yet it remains the case, as David Feldman has argued, that the view that the war was a Jewish one was commonplace among its opponents.[161]

'Anti-alienism'

In the four decades preceding the outbreak of World War I, more than 2 million Jews migrated westwards from Eastern Europe, about 80 per cent to the United States.[162] Between 120,000 and 150,000 Jews settled in Britain, many of them in East London. A parliamentary committee reported in 1888 that these were 'the poorest and worse' of the immigrants.[163] Fifteen years later, a Royal Commission recommended limited restrictions on immigration, and in 1905, the Aliens Act was passed which gave immigration officers the power to exclude 'undesirable aliens'. Even though the word 'Jew' appears nowhere in the legislation, both advocates and opponents of the measure accepted Jews would be disproportionately affected by it. One month after enactment, the Conservative administration was defeated in a general election, and many anti-alien MPs lost their seats. The new Liberal Home Secretary, Herbert Gladstone, gave the Act a generous interpretation, one so favourable to immigrants that anti-alien campaigners complained he had eviscerated it.[164]

These campaigners were stalwart in their advocacy, marshalling many arguments against the presence of these Jews from abroad. The arguments resonated with arguments made against Jews in earlier times. Though the campaigners' efforts culminated in the passing of the 1905 Act, the Act barely reflected the content of their case.

There was a *health-threat* argument. Immigrant Jews comprised a threat to the health of the nation. Only the poorest and most disadvantaged left their countries of origin, and USA medical restrictions meant that only the least healthy among this element would come to Britain. Arthur Balfour suggested that Britain had become 'a sieve...which lets through the fit to North and South America, but which retains the unfit in the process'.[165] Upon arrival, the Jews were content to live in overcrowded conditions, and tolerated lower standards of cleanliness. They had, it was said, 'no regard to any provision for sanitation, and scanty regard for cleanliness'. They 'nearly approach the condition of animal life'.[166] According to *The Lancet*, in 1884, 'the foreign Jews, who for many years have been flocking to the East End of London, are so numerous that their presence seriously affects the social and sanitary condition of this part of the metropolis'.[167] Beyond this, they depress the morale of the native poor. 'The presence of thousands of foreign-faced men and women crowding into the dense parts of the poorer quarters of [London] does not so much anger our own people as it saddens them.' It is remarkable that there has never been a 'Jew-hunt'—'may it never come!'[168]

Then there was a *social-cost* argument. The labour market would be 'flooded'—'our own, edged out'.[169] 'The Polish Jew drives the British workman out of the labour market just as a base currency drives a pure currency out of circulation.'[170] Tailors and garment manufacturers feared for their livelihoods; they faced the threat of unemployment, or at least wage-depression. Jews had a 'lower standard of living', which allowed them to compete on favourable terms with local workers. They worked on a Sunday, and then cheated by opening on Saturdays too. They worked longer hours. They discriminated against non-Jewish traders, preferring to buy from other Jews.[171] Those who were not paupers, a 'burden on the rates', pauperized others by 'sweating' them. They were bad employers and bad employees. Jewish workers, one trades union leader claimed, 'exhibited an unmistakeable ambition to become sweaters'. They were 'self-assertive and individualistic', potential blacklegs, possessing 'but the faintest idea of the principles of trades unionism', and each one an entrepreneur in the making, 'a sweating master'. They would not be organized as workers. They were 'incorrigible, either sweaters or sweated'. The 'unfair competition of the Jew' had driven English workers to the 'verge of starvation'.[172] What is more, the Jews created housing problems too, driving out local inhabitants and overcrowding urban spaces, making the East End habitable only to their own kind. Their presence over time would lead, claimed a Tory parliamentary candidate, to 'the extermination of the British working-man' in that part of London.[173] This extravagantly expressed fear opened out onto a more general concern, of the kind embraced by Beatrice Webb, that clever, purposive Jews were in some sense a danger to the less-intelligent native population.[174]

And there was a *public-order* argument, which shaded into a *political-order* argument. Anti-alien campaigners claimed concern for Jews at the anti-Semitism that inevitably followed upon unrestricted immigration. 'A *Judenhetz* [is] brewing in East London', it was said, owing to 'the foreign Jews of no nationality', who are 'becoming a pest and a nuisance to the poor native-born East Ender'.[175] But violence against Jews was merely one aspect of the disruption to the social fabric caused by Jewish immigration. There were dangerous elements among these foreign Jews—criminals, radicals. They were 'pro-Boer', political 'incendiarists', 'anarchists'. They were, at the very least, 'politically unfit to be transplanted into democratic institutions'.[176] Yiddish pamphlets circulating in the East End were said to contain 'the vilest political sentiments'.[177] They were not the victims of political persecution; they were agents of political unrest. They brought a 'social contagion' that had the effect of 'seriously deteriorating the life of those compelled to be his neighbour'. The 'destitute foreign immigrant' was 'diseased in both mind and body', 'a physical plague-spot', 'a bad citizen', 'a breaker or evader of the law', a 'sedition monger' and an 'enemy of this country'.[178]

Lastly, there was a '*threat to the character of England*' argument. The slogans 'Great Britain for the British' and 'England for the English' were widely adopted.[179] The immigration of destitute aliens, wrote the anti-alien Arnold White, ran counter to that 'crystallisation of national life from native elements only, and the rejection of alien constituents' characteristic of modern times.[180] Responding to criticism of his position by John A. Dyche, a Russian immigrant, White complained that this 'guest' wrote with 'the air of a conqueror indifferent to the feelings of the vanquished'.[181] Though London's East End had always been a dismal place, the new immigrants were held responsible for its worst features. 'There is no end to them in Whitechapel and Mile End. It is Jerusalem.' It is 'a foreign country', 'Jew-town'.[182] There was much talk of 'invasion', an aspect of a more general 'reverse colonisation'[183]—that is, a counter-exploitation of imperial Britain by subject or weaker races, and a certain perception of national decline or enervation. And contradictory objections were taken, on the one hand, to the Jews corrupting the nation's 'racial stock'[184] (expressed as 'mongrelization'), and on the other, to the refusal of Jews to assimilate. Joseph Banister's *England Under the Jews* (London, 1901) is a typical expression of the former objection:

> The absorption of this scrofula-laden blood is going on constantly. English gentlemen sell their daughters to Jew millionaires, and British noblemen refill their private exchequers by marrying the millions of Semitic heiresses. In the next generation, half-caste and full-blooded Jews will have become so numerous in the House of Lords that a visitor will imagine he has entered a Hampstead synagogue.[185]

The 'Yiddishites', 'Yiddish money-pigs', 'Yiddish rats', 'Yiddish vermin', 'cosmopolitan money-pigs', 'cosmopolitan plutocrats', 'Jewish wire-pullers', or 'Asiatics' were an 'alien invasion', let in by England's 'cowardly, Jew-dominated rulers'. Banister's work was a capacious restatement, in abusive, violent language, of anti-Semitism's then preoccupations. The Jews are 'usurers, perjurers, white-slave traffickers, obscene literature promoters, fraudulent bankrupts, receivers of stolen goods', etc. Yet 'they are forever whining about the wickedness and injustices of anti-Semitism'. Unless one praises the Jews, one risks 'the grave charge of anti-Semitism, which brings down on [one's] head the wrath of almost every daily journal in London'.[186] Concern about the broader damaging consequences of unrestricted immigration persisted well after these controversies had passed. In the 1920s, for example, eugenicists who insisted that 'indiscriminate immigration' was 'destructive of all true progress', warned that Jewish immigration should be 'checked' in the interests of 'the maintenance and improvement of [English] stock'.[187]

Beneath and below these arguments, were fantasies of Jewish destructive power and a denial of the reality of Jewish suffering in Eastern Europe. (Even after the savage pogroms that followed upon the 1905 Revolution, there were anti-alien campaigners ready to argue that Jewish immigrants from Russia were *not* refugees from persecution.)[188] Much colourful, abusive language was deployed. 'Loathsome wretches who come grunting and itching to our shores.' 'Swarms', 'alien invasion', 'an unpleasant, indecent people', 'a seething mass of refuse and filth', 'the refuse of Europe', 'filthy rickety jetsam of humanity, bearing on their evil faces the stigmata of every physical and moral degradation'.[189] Somewhat inevitably, the abuse created a context for violence, with local gangs preying on Jewish newcomers.[190]

Though the British Brothers League, an alliance of East End workers and Tory MPs, dominated the organized response to Jewish immigration, it was shopkeepers who were the anti-alien campaigners' most zealous constituents. Among no other group was anti-alienism fiercer, nor the commonly insisted distinction between anti-alienism and anti-Semitism less convincing.[191] But anti-alienism also for a time attracted support from the labour movement.[192] In 1895, for example, the TUC formulated questions to be put to parliamentary candidates, including one demanding restrictions on Jewish immigration.[193] Trades Union leaders were vigorous in their attacks. The celebrated Ben Tillett, of the ILP, wrote in the *Labour Leader* in December 1894:

> If getting on is the most desirable thing in this earth then the Jew, as the most consistent and determined money grubber we know is worthy of the greatest respect. That his money grubbing is not universally respected only proves that the bulk of civilised nations, even now, do not believe in the commercialistic idea of clean hands and blood-stained money.[194]

Harry Quelch of *Justice* concurred, complaining that Jewish workers were 'always dreaming of becoming master men'.[195] Robert Blatchford argued in an 1895 article that immigration controls against Jews were a matter of 'legitimate self-preservation'.[196] (The Bootmakers Union was especially active against Jewish immigrants, even though there were never more than 10,000 Jews employed in the bootmaking industry, less than 2.5 per cent of its total workforce.)[197] Trades unionists were mostly keen to insist that their objections were not to Jews 'as Jews', provoking one trades union leader to insist to the Royal Commission, in exasperation, 'most of [the immigrants] are Jews, and we may as well speak of them as Jews, because it is known all over the country that this is a Jewish question'.[198] While the main socialist parties, and radical newspapers, with varying degrees of enthusiasm, condemned the aliens legislation as reactionary and unnecessary,[199] in part through hatred of the Conservative administration that promoted it, they found it difficult to resist the 'rich Jews bad'/'poor Jews good' argument. The ILP, for example, published a pamphlet against control in 1904, *The Problem of Alien Immigration*, while attacking 'the rich Jew who has done his best to besmirch the fair name of England and to corrupt the sweetness of our national life and character'.[200] John Burns opposed the Aliens Bill (why legislate merely because 'a few poor Jews came to this country and worked for low wages'?), while calling for legislation to exclude another kind of Jew, 'the rich Jews of Bayswater, Fitzjohn's Avenue, Hampstead':

but the Government dare not include these people in the schedule of the Bill. The political power and financial influence of these rich Jews were so great that they could pull the Government from Dan to Beersheba . . . We [have] lost 22,000 precious lives, and we [will] lose South Africa because of the rich Jew. . . . The rich Jew suborned judges and corrupted Parliaments, made raids, organised rebellions, and did not hesitate to do things to make himself richer still.

The 'anti-Jewish feeling' growing in the country was 'mostly propagated in newspapers owned by Jewish proprietors'. That all this was just nonsense was irrelevant. Burns had got in another hit against the 'power' of 'rich Jews'. This rhetoric—of what the government could not 'dare' to do, what by implication it would take immense courage to do, and the identification of a protected class of 'poor Jews'—parallels the rhetoric of today's fulminators against the power of the 'Jewish Lobby', and their praise of those Jews willing to oppose it. The MP who followed Burns in the debate remarked that his parliamentary colleague 'appeared to be suffering from "Jew on the brain" '.[201] Burns himself told the House 'Jew salesmen from Covent Garden and Billingsgate had engaged ruffians to smash his windows and morally and physically intimidate him'.[202] It would not appear that his anti-Semitism attracted much censure from the Labour movement.[203] The view that the Tories were attacking the wrong kind of Jew appears to have been widely held in left and liberal circles of that time.[204]

As for more mainstream Liberals, though they were often the staunchest of pro-alien advocates, there were East End activists who were defiantly anti-Semitic. In 1901, for example, the Bethnal Green Liberal and Radical Club passed the resolution, 'That in future, no candidate will be accepted as a member if he be one of the Jewish race.' Two years later, another local Liberal and Radical Club rejected a candidate put up by the local Labour Party for a joint ticket because he was a Jew. The bitterness of the feeling against 'the Jewish population', it was noted, meant that he would be defeated, and why go into an election with a losing candidate?[205]

There were also 'anti-alien' Jews, who sought to deny to their co-religionists advantages that they themselves enjoyed, for fear that those advantages would be lost if too many Jewish immigrants arrived to claim them too. Indeed, in the matter of anti-alien advocacy, Jews stole a march on anti-Semites. Jewish efforts to dissuade East European immigration preceded the anti-alien agitation by at least a decade. In 1888, for example, Britain's most senior rabbi despatched a circular to his East European colleagues asking them 'to publicise the evil which is befalling our brethren who have come here, and warn [their congregants] not to come to the land of Britain'. The Jewish Board of Guardians concurred: 'bitter and evil is the lot of the foreigners who come'. And well before then, the Jews already in England were discomfited by the arrival of poor, unskilled Jews from Holland and northern Germany.[206] It was only the emergence of a non-Jewish anti-Semitic anti-alienism that drove Jewish organizations, encouraged by the *Jewish Chronicle*, into a defensive position on behalf of the aliens.[207] Anti-alien activists found Jewish support of immense value. How, one leading activist asked, could the campaign be anti-Semitic when its support drew on all classes and creeds?[208] The Conservative MP for Islington, Benjamin Cohen, supported the proposed restrictions on immigration, voted for the Aliens Act in 1905, and denied that the anti-alien measures were anti-Semitic.[209]

Most anti-alien campaigners sought to distinguish between immigrants and Jewish immigrants, and between Jewish immigrants and Jews in general. They hotly denied the charge of anti-Semitism, while worrying aloud, for example, that there might be 'an outbreak of [anti-Semitic feelings] of very grave proportions' unless something was done about 'the influx of aliens'. The 'uneducated classes', one campaigner explained, 'naturally take a hatred to the Jewish people'. You 'cannot persuade them it is not a racial question when they are being turned out of their homes'. If the Jewish community 'range themselves against the natural and rising feeling of the people' they will cause the very anti-Semitism that they falsely claim to find among advocates of restricted immigration.[210] The essential argument appeared to be: we are not anti-Semitic, but unless the Jews are checked as we propose, they might make anti-Semitic trouble for themselves. Government spokesmen, for example, dismissed the allegations that the Aliens Bill was intended to strike at Jews, and the founder of the 'British Brothers' League' explained that he had made it his first condition on starting the organization that 'the word "Jew" should never be mentioned'.[211] The more extravagant the anti-Semitic language, the more heated the denial of anti-Semitism. Thus the incorrigibly anti-Semitic anti-alien campaigner Arnold White insisted to the Royal commission, 'I absolutely refuse to regard this as a Jewish question... I have not gone into the religions of these people and do not intend to do so.'[212]

Anti-alienism did not have a free run. Yes, it was conceded, there may be dislike of foreigners in the East End, but that dislike was without any real ground. The problems of 'sweating' were best dealt with by anti-sweating legislation. The immigrants tended in fact to be healthier than the indigenous population. Their sanitary habits were better, in any event they showed a great capacity for improvement, and they were responsive to official pressure. Jewish parents took better care of their children. They did *not* bring infectious diseases. Such medical conditions as afflicted them were treatable.[213] It was the best that came over, not the weakest. (The authors of *The Jew in London* (1900), subtitled, 'A study of racial character and present-day conditions', were sure that, 'whatever may be thought of the Jewish character in itself, there is no doubt that an infusion of Jewish blood would introduce an admirable strain into the breed of Englishmen'.)[214] The rule of the survival of the fittest ensured that only the strongest could embark upon, and survive, the journey from Eastern Europe. They were independent by their nature, and in any event, could rely on the philanthropy of their already established co-religionists. They would never become a 'burden on the rates'. And even if every foreign Jew resident in England had been sent back to his birthplace, wrote Beatrice Webb, the bulk of the sweated workers would not have been affected, for better or worse.[215] What is more, the anti-alien agitation was an attack on the principle of political and religious asylum, a proud English tradition. What was objectionable about the immigrants to anti-alienists commended them to pro-alienists—liberal pro-alienists in particular: they were impoverished Jewish refugees, in flight from persecution. Anti-alien sentiment, the liberals added, was protectionist in character, got up by trades unionists and socialists, attacking principles of freedom of labour and economic self-advancement. To defend the alien was to reassert Liberal values, free trade among them. They tended to idealize the Jewish immigrant, his 'self-denial and private economy'. He was industrious, self-reliant, and thrifty. As early as 1893, the House of Lords Sweating Committee had concluded, after extensive investigation, 'undue stress has been laid on the injurious effect caused by foreign immigration', because the 'evils complained of', obtain in trades without foreign workers or employers. 'Sweating' was far from a Jewish monopoly.[216] Pro-alien advocates were also ready to acknowledge the anti-Semitic character of the anti-alien attacks. Charles Dilke told the House of Commons, 'an anti-Jewish feeling has been aroused'.[217] He identified the 'prohibition of alien immigration' as a 'sham remedy for very grave evils in the labour market'.[218] He warned Conservatives 'they had raised a devil which they will find difficult to lay'. His colleague Charles Trevelyan spoke of a 'frankly anti-Semitic movement'.[219]

Scandals and swindles

In the immediate pre-war period, 1912–13, reactionary political sentiment fastened onto the issue of political corruption, as a means both of attacking the then Liberal government, and of discrediting democracy, which they characterized as mere plutocracy, or rule by an ignoble elite. The anti-Semites among them gave this issue an anti-Semitic twist, exploiting two scandals—or more precisely, since there was little that was actually scandalous about the events, two series of events that came to be characterized as scandals. They caused great alarm to Anglo-Jewry, already on the defensive, and in addition having to contend with attacks of the following kind:

> Sir Marcus Samuel is a typical Jew. He is a pronounced Jew. You could never take him for anything else. He is stout, swarthy, black-haired, black-moustached, thick-nosed, thick-lipped, bulge-eyed—in short, he fulfils every expectation that one habitually forms of the prosperous Jew...

This was from—of all journals—the *Sporting Times*.[220] Nahum Sokolow probably had this kind of thing in mind when he reported to the Zionist Executive that anti-Semitism had 'become epidemic in England'.[221]

The Marconi Affair

Government ministers bought shares in one company, while another company was given a government contract. Though the two companies shared the same name (Marconi), and were connected in other ways too, the share price of the former company was not affected by the good fortune of the latter—the only point that actually mattered. However, there was the whiff of impropriety, made more noisome by evasiveness on the part of some of the ministers when questioned in the House of Commons. Three of the parties involved were Jewish: two ministers, Sir Rufus Isaacs and Herbert Samuel, and the managing director of one of the companies, Godfrey Isaacs (Rufus's brother). This gave Cecil Chesterton, editor of the *New Witness* and a confirmed anti-Semite, his opportunity to raise a stink. He hoped to draw the ministers into a libel action, but was sued by Godfrey instead—and lost. Cecil's brother, the celebrated G.K., thought that the scandal would be regarded as a turning point in English history, but he was wrong. The scandal-mongering anti-Semites, however, remained obsessed with it, and ten years later, were still trying to use it against their Jewish enemies.[222]

The Indian Silver Affair

In parallel with the Marconi scandal was the 'Indian silver' or 'little Marconi' scandal. The Indian government's silver requirements were obtained secretly, through a private bank, rather than openly, through the Bank of England, to avoid speculators pushing the price of silver up, thereby making the metal more expensive to buy. It was a sensible, prudent move. But because the person responsible on behalf of the Indians for the purchase was also on the board of the bank's own parent company, there was the risk of a conflict of interest. What is more, one of the partners in the bank, Sir Stuart Samuel, was also an MP; the under-secretary of state for India was a cousin. There was an impression of collusion, a family affair. All these individuals were Jewish, as was the assistant under-secretary of state (through whom the business was contracted), and so anti-Semites cried foul. The anti-Semites, perhaps distracted by the parallel Marconi Affair, and somewhat bemused by the commercial rationale of the dealings, were unable to make much of the Indian Silver Affair. Conservative attempts were made to 'demonstrate' that the Jews were in control of the Liberal Party. Samuel was required to resign his Whitechapel seat and stand for re-election. He was returned, though with a reduced majority; the Conservative candidate complained that his rival had exploited 'the bogey of anti-Semitism' when canvassing Jewish electors.[223]

If the Marconi Affair lacked the longer-term consequences for Jews that the anti-Semites desired, the Indian Silver Affair was a disappointment from the start. Neither precipitated a turn in public sentiment towards political anti-Semitism; neither attracted to anti-Semitism hitherto non-anti-Semitic intellectuals or writers; neither contributed to the political formation of a generation; neither could be characterized as a crisis. In each respect, the contrast with the Dreyfus Affaire was stark. Belloc told the Parliamentary Select Committee on Marconi that the two affairs had had the effect of shaking 'the old apathy' towards the Jewish Question.[224] He was wrong. It would take more than that—*much* more than that, in the event. It required, as it turned out, war, revolution, and a fabricated document evidencing a global conspiracy, to invigorate English anti-Semitism.

War, revolution, and conspiracy

In the period 1914–17, and in consequence of world war and revolution, English anti-Semitism intensified, expanding its vocabulary and pushing the logic of its positions to terminal points.

War

In the first years of the war, there were demonstrations of hostility towards Jews living in the East End. Jews applying for Poor Law relief were discriminated against; the rioting following the sinking by a German submarine of the *Lusitania* did not distinguish between Jewish and German targets.[225] But then the question of conscription became the focus of special conflict—at first, even when there was no conscription of British subjects. Jewish aliens inevitably benefited from business opportunities created by the absence in the trenches of British soldiers, it was said.[226] Then the Conscription Act of 1916 made military service compulsory for British males between eighteen and forty-one, and for naturalized foreigners and 'friendly' or 'neutral' aliens. Russians, however, were excepted—mostly Russian Jews. The Home Secretary, Herbert Samuel, thought it wrong to require them to fight for (in effect) the Tsar, given that they were mostly refugees from Tsarist persecution. They were free to volunteer, of course, though few did. In February 1917, with the Tsar gone, however, there was no reason not to conscript Russians—they should serve or be deported, it was said. In June 1917, there was a riot in Leeds. According to Selig Brodetsky, a mob of over a thousand broke into the Jewish quarter, smashing windows and looting shops. A bigger mob came the next day, and at night grew to thousands, hurling stones and bricks, and shouting 'Kill the Jews!'[227] In July, conscription was extended to Russian Jews; the press then complained that they were evading the draft. They were cowards; they were 'shirkers'; they were doing well at home while British boys were dying at the Front; they were 'war profiteers'. In September, there was a riot in Bethnal Green, part of London's East End. Over two days, 5,000 people were drawn into an incident that began, apparently, with an argument between a discharged soldier and a Russian-Jewish alien, about whether the soldier had been a 'fool' to join up.[228] Jews were attacked and Jewish property was damaged. The proximate cause of these riots was resentment at what was perceived to be an alien community exempt from conscription and of dubious loyalty to the state. The rioters were quite quickly dispersed, with only minor damage done, and the most minor of injuries sustained. Some Jewish families were kept under siege in their homes for several hours. Stones were thrown. Though the riot demonstrated the marginal status of East End Jewry, it was not typical of everyday relations between Jewish and non-Jewish East End communities.[229]

At the same time, naturalized Jews in elite circles came under attack for their German affiliations. They were taken to be men of dubious loyalty—or worse. The campaign against them preceded the outbreak of war itself. As early as 1911, L. J. Maxse, editor of the *National Review*, was denouncing 'Jews... who simply use the hospitality and social distinctions accorded them in this country to intrigue against British interests and to work for our German enemies'.[230] He complained of 'our excessive tolerance'.[231] When war came, there were calls for resignations, expulsions, and recipro-cating expressions of patriotism ('loyalty-letters'),[232] angry counter-protests and even libel actions. Jewish observers were concerned to note that *The Times* had begun to use 'German' and 'Jew' interchangeably, and attributed 'to Jews or Jewish influence every enemy manoeuvre'. *The Times* reported that the sinking of the *Lusitania* had caused joy among 'the Jewish financial press'.[233]

Revolution

That the Russian Revolution benefited Germany, and many of the revolu-tionaries were of Jewish origin, encouraged the belief that the events of October 1917 were engineered by 'adventurers of German-Jewish blood and in German pay' (as *The Times* put it).[234] Russia was now open to industrial exploitation by German-Jewish finance. This was merely a step in a more general programme of global domination. The Jews already controlled the capitalist West; they had now turned the autocratic East communist, and controlled that too. They had murdered the Tsar; they were murdering priests (but not rabbis, one Unionist MP suggested); they had erected a statue to Judas Iscariot in Moscow.[235] The Judaeo-Bolshevik conspiracy must be defeated, declared anti-Semitism, lost inside the stupid-ity of its analysis of the Revolution. For a while, the Allied intervention in Russia, from early 1918 to late 1919, gave this account a military dimension. A war against the Bolsheviks was a war not just against Revolution and against German militarism ('the Boche is still fighting us, through the Bolshevist');[236] it was also a war against the Jews. This war, promoted by the White Russian troops of General Denikin, led to the deaths in the Ukraine of no less than 100,000 Jews and the dispossession of no less than 500,000 Jews. British propaganda directed at the Red Army exploited what was taken to be widespread anti-Semitism among the troops: 'we the soldiers of Free Russia... call to you to throw off the Jewish yoke.... It is now two years since the Jews have been running our country and have been trying in the person of Russia to avenge themselves on the entire world . . . '[237] That in Russia 'the Jews rule supreme' approached the status of a commonplace in the British political culture of the early 1920s.[238] It even had a parliamentary champion in the short-lived, right-wing National Party.[239] None of this was quite good enough for G. K. Chesterton, however. Talk of Jewish Bolshevism risked overlooking the true extent of Jewish power, its reach, and its age. 'It is stupid of the *Morning Post* to talk as if Jews came on earth to spread Bolshevism, for all the world as if the Tory Party had not been led by Disraeli and run by Rothschild.'[240] (The newspaper liked to claim that the 'Jewish quarters of Germany and Russia' comprised the centre of the 'Bolshevist movement'.)[241] Nevertheless, anti-Semitic anti-Bolshevism remained the most durable theme in the Catholic press during the 1920s.[242]

Conspiracy

That Jews have a corporate existence, that their interests are collective, that the effect of their practices and beliefs is to separate them from other nations, that they hold those other nations in contempt, wish them ill and conspire against them—these are the commonplaces of much modern anti-Semitism. They cohere in the fantasy of a Jewish world-conspiracy, given documentary form in the *Protocols*. Their influence may also have been felt in less radical anti-Semitic positions, and in particular in the turn taken by English anti-Semitism in the first decades of the twentieth century. Though the full-blown fantasy or 'myth' attracted few subscribers, a more diffuse conviction of the operating of Jewish influence, secret and ill-intentioned, may be detected in the political programmes and politicians' speeches, the books and articles, the newspaper reports and readers' letters, the cartoons and graffiti, and the private diaries and opinion-polling of the times.

The first intimations of self-interested, secret Jewish activity were in the financial scandals in the pre-war years. And then came the war. During World War I, there was much talk of an unidentifiable, malign force operating against British interests. It was referred to as 'the hidden hand' and the 'unseen hand', the guiding intelligence commanding Britain's diverse enemies. It frustrated British efforts to bring the war to a speedy conclusion; it was behind every military reverse; it spread demoralizing rumours, and betrayed military secrets; it was the organizer of conspiracies, spy-networks, and all manner of clandestine operations. Nothing happened by chance; whatever was contrary to Britain's interests was a contrivance of her enemies. 'If Lord Kitchener is dead,' declared one journal, 'the Unseen Hand killed him.' (It was in fact a mine that did for him.) It achieved its ends by underhand, secretive methods—bribery, blackmail, the exploitation of every human weakness and vice. European chancelleries intrigued with master criminals; traitors lurked everywhere; scheming foreigners hid behind English names and identities. (Names *were* changed, not the better to conspire, but to throw off any residual foreign identity, and for self-protection.)[243] Berlin was the occult centre of operations, both plutocratic and Bolshevik Jews were on its secret payroll, and no naturalized English Jew of German origin could be trusted.[244] In this way, anti-German sentiment merged with anti-Jewish sentiment, with which it shared certain themes in any event.[245]

While it was thus not a great leap to pass from an unseen or hidden hand to the *Protocols*, the notoriety of the document itself was bound up with the reception to the Russian Revolution. The one was the blueprint for the other, a Judaeo-Bolshevik plot. It appeared in an English translation in February 1920, in time, that is, to explain the Revolution. It was ignored until the *Times* article, 'The Jewish Peril', on 8 May. It asked, was the document a forgery? If so, whence comes this uncanny note of prophecy? The British government should not, in any event, be dealing with the representatives of the 'Jewish world government' in Moscow. Later that year, H. A. Gwynne, the editor of the *Morning Post* argued that, genuine or otherwise, the Bolshevik programme matched 'almost to the letter the programme outlined in the *Protocols*'. He found the *Protocols* to be 'a most masterly exposition—very high-falutin' of course, as would be expected in an oriental race—a distinct programme intended to achieve the aim of the political Jews, which is the domination of the world'.[246] This was in the context of a great deal of panicky, angry talk about 'the wave of mad Communism—the work of Jew Bolsheviks', etc.[247] It was quite possible in those years both to affirm the existence of a Jewish conspiracy and to deny the genuineness of the *Protocols*. Some anti-Semites made a connection between Bolshevism and Zionism, as if they were merely two Jewish masks assumed by international Jewry for the purposes of most effectively dominating Russia and Palestine respectively. Philip Graves, the *Times* journalist who exposed the *Protocols*, noticed that 'the British people' were affected 'to a slight extent by the anti-Semitic attitude of certain political groups, and by a vague idea that Zionists, being Jews, may also turn out to be Bolshevists'.[248] The *Protocols* circulated among British officers in the Middle East.[249] This brings me to the Palestine Mandate.

Two months before the Bolshevik Revolution, the *Morning Post* advised its readers:

> The Jews are a great nation, emphatically a nation, and the able statecraft of their secret rulers has kept them a nation through forty centuries of the world's history. ... It may be doubted whether all that is best in Jewry the world over will not ere long find cause deeply to regret what seems, in the light of the latest revelations, something like a Jewish alliance with Old Testament Germany to regain temporal power upon the earth.[250]

Within a very short period, the notion of an 'alliance', which implied a certain equality of arms, had given way before the new notion of an exclusively Jewish endeavour, drawing support opportunistically from Germany, for sure, but from New York and elsewhere too. The 'hidden hand' became a signifier for Jews in general: 'Jews camouflaged as nationals *are* the Hidden Hand.'[251] As the new notion developed, taking into account Zionist advances in Palestine, as well as Communist advances in Central and Eastern Europe, so Germany joined the ranks of international Jewry's victims, before becoming, fifteen years later, its most resolute adversary.

The Balfour Declaration and the Zionist project, 1917–39

On 2 November 1917, Arthur Balfour, the British foreign minister, wrote to Lord Rothschild a 'declaration of sympathy with the Jewish Zionist aspirations' confirming the government's support for the establishment of a national home for the Jewish people in Palestine, then part of a province of the Ottoman Empire. British wartime success, and the subsequent military occupation of Palestine, gave it the power to implement this promise. By decision of the League of Nations at San Remo on 24 July 1922, and then confirmed by Parliament, Britain was awarded the Mandate for Palestine. It incorporated in its preamble the language of the Balfour Declaration, which provided that nothing was to be done to prejudice either the civil and religious rights of existing non-Jewish communities in Palestine, or the rights and political status of Jews in any other country. There had been strong Arab opposition to the Zionist project from its inception; when the British added their endorsement to the project, the conflict became triangular. Each side complained that Britain favoured the other, though until the end of the 1930s, the Arab side had the better case in that respect, by far. Immigration and land sales quickly became the most contentious issues. The Arabs pressed for a complete block on both; the Jews pressed for no limits on either.

I am concerned here only with the anti-Semitic aspects of British policy. I am not concerned with British policy in general, which was incoherent, reactive, and indecisive, nor am I concerned with the anti-Semitic aspects of Arab opposition to the Zionist project.

The Balfour Declaration

The Balfour Declaration was the product of several considerations, among which were conventional 'Great Power' ones—principally, the containing of French influence in the Middle East, and the soliciting of American-Jewish support for the war effort. There were also less self-interested considerations at work.[252] In consequence, Jews have long tended to regard it as an act of great generosity, and its author, Balfour, has been celebrated as a philo-Semite of heroic proportions. Indeed, the enthusiasm of the Jewish population of Palestine for him was, wrote his niece, Blanche Dugdale, 'almost embarrassing'.[253] But it has also been said, against him, that he was an anti-Semite (even, a 'notorious anti-Semite'),[254] a characterization that serves also to impugn the motives of the British government and indeed the character of Zionism itself.

Certainly, he was ready to argue for the exclusion of Jewish immigrants; to speculate about the deleterious influence on the national polity of too many Jews; and to look the other way when confronted with evidence of the Russian government's policy of pogroms. He was not, observed Christopher Sykes, a 'natural Judeophile';[255] according to Leonard Stein, there was 'a certain ambivalence in Balfour's feelings about the Jews'.[256] One may grant all this (though Dugdale would deny it, and wrote only of his 'moral indignation' regarding anti-Semitism),[257] without conceding that his support for Zionism was itself anti-Semitic. There is no reason to suppose that this charge is true.

Zionism to Balfour meant the Jews 'developing, in peace and quietness under British rule, those great gifts which hitherto they have been compelled to bring to fruition in countries that know not their language and belong not to their race'.[258] He came to Zionism in the middle years of his political career. It developed into a passion. 'The more he thought about Zionism,' wrote Dugdale, a passionate Zionist herself, 'the more his respect for it, and his belief in its importance, grew.'[259] His interest in the Jews was lifelong, she writes. It originated in the Old Testament training of his mother; as he grew up, his intellectual admiration and sympathy for Jewish philosophy and culture grew;[260] the problem of the Jews in modern age seemed to him to be of immense importance. He considered that Christian civilization owed to Judaism an immeasurable debt, shamefully ill repaid.

His interest in Zionism was whetted in 1905, when the Zionist movement rejected the British offer of land in British East Africa. He was put in contact, one year later, with Chaim Weizmann, who was at that time a lecturer in organic chemistry at Manchester University. Their meeting was intended to last fifteen minutes; they were together for over an hour. An immediate, 'unusual sympathy' emerged between them. Balfour told Dugdale, 'It was from that talk with Weizmann that I saw that the Jewish form of patriotism was unique. Their love for the country refused to be satisfied by the Uganda scheme. It was Weizmann's absolute refusal even to look at it which impressed me.' At the end of his life, Dugdale continues, Balfour told her that 'what he had been able to do for the Jews had been the thing he looked back upon as the most worth his doing'.[261]

What then of opposition to the Declaration? It was at first an almost entirely Jewish affair.[262] Leon Simon's 1917 pamphlet *The Case of the Anti-Zionists: A reply* was directed entirely against 'a small group of Jews who are opposed to Zionism';[263] even as late as 1928, Jews remained Zionism's 'most implacable enemies' according to one well-informed Anglo-Jewish observer.[264] When the idea of the Declaration came to be debated by the prime minister and his Cabinet, the two ministers who were Jewish, Herbert Samuel and Edwin Montagu, took opposing sides.[265] These cousins argued respectively for the 'party' of Jewish nationalists, and the 'party' of Jewish religionists, thereby reflecting a long-standing, if intermittent, division within Jewry.[266] To the latter party, Zionists were at best defeatists, capitulating to anti-Semitism, when indeed not actively colluding with it. Zionism also made credible the anti-Semites' assertions that Jews could not be trusted as citizens of any land other than their own, and would never assimilate. Essentially, two arguments were deployed in support of this position.

First, then, Zionism was retrograde, in that it sought to reverse the gains of emancipation. It wanted to rob the Jews of their citizenship; it wanted to send them away. Within a week of the Balfour Declaration, Anglo-Jewish notables formed the League of British Jews, with the declared object of 'resisting the allegation that Jews constitute a separate political entity'.[267] Edwin Montagu, Isaiah Berlin wrote, used to address his colleagues with anger and indignation, declaring that the Jews did not wish—and did not think they deserved—to be sent back to the ghetto. He would buttonhole his friends in various drawing rooms in London and ask them vehemently whether they regarded him as an oriental alien and wanted to see him 'repatriated' to the eastern Mediterranean.[268] The Zionists considered Montagu to be their main opponent.[269] 'I have been striving all my life', he declared, 'to escape from the Ghetto.'[270] The Balfour Declaration had 'dealt an irreparable blow at Jewish Britons'.[271] He was not a contented 'Jewish Briton', though. Judaism was for him, it has been argued, a troublesome inheritance, void of positive content, and an obstacle to his full integration into British society. Not so for Claude Montefiore (1858–1938), however, another Jewish opponent of the Balfour Declaration. Unlike Montagu, he did not reject his Jewish identity; he merely rejected the Zionist version of Jewish identity.[272] To Montefiore, Zionism turned Jews inward, and tended to emphasize the distinctness of the Jews as a people. It thereby encouraged anti-Semitism. Judaism was evolving in the 'desired direction of denationalization'; 'Jewish reform' would 'make of Judaism a religion, and nothing more than a religion'. Zionism ran counter to this welcome development. Montefiore wished Anglo-Jews to maintain the distinctness of their religious character, but to regard England rather than Palestine as their national home. Jewish nationalism was a disease. It had put the clock back; in 1874, the tendency in all countries was to regard assimilation as a fact as well as an ideal. In his last years, he would declare himself a 'die-hard'; he refused to bend the knee to the fashionable Zionist Baal. His old ideal of the Englishman of the Jewish faith, he continued to insist, would ultimately prevail. Hitlerism was at least partially, Weizmann's creation.[273]

Secondly, there was a sense that Zionism invited the accusation of 'dual loyalties'. During a Jewish disabilities debate, Lord John Russell said: 'One ground that has been stated for the exclusion of the Jews is that they are a separate nation. But the Jews themselves utterly deny this allegation. . . . It is obvious to all the world that *their attachment is to England, and to no other country*' (italics added).[274] A mere seventy years later, it is not surprising that many Jews feared that the very argument used against them in the parliamentary debates would be revived, in a context in which the possibility of a second allegiance would be much more than merely notional.[275] (Indeed, Hilaire Belloc made precisely this argument in 1922.)[276] The fear that certain classes of British subject might have religious–political allegiances that would trump their allegiance to the Crown was a constant in the national political discourse from the time of the Reformation. This preoccupation afflicted Catholics principally, but in later centuries bore down on Jews too.

It would appear that it continues to be a problem for them.[277] In the 2007 ADL Survey, 50 per cent of those surveyed in the UK believed that it was 'probably true' that Jews were more loyal to Israel than to the UK.[278]

In combination, these two arguments comprised what has been termed the 'classic Anglo-Jewish doctrine'. No cause should be embraced that might have the effect of alienating Jews from other Englishmen, or create suspicions concerning their patriotism.[279] To Blanche Dugdale, the most formidable English foes of Jewish nationalism were Jews themselves.[280] She regarded their opposition to Zionism as somewhat craven—fear of provoking anti-Semitism, lack of sympathy with co-religionists of a different class, a simplistic British patriotism, a lack of political imagination. This was a harsh judgement. The opposition was, on the whole, neither mean nor destructive. Why should the real achievements of emancipation be endangered by the quest for an unrealizable, undesirable fantasy?[281] In most cases, this opposition did not persist in the face of the reality of the growing Yishuv. For much of its duration, this 'West End' Jewish anti-Zionism was complemented by an 'East End' Jewish indifference to Zionism. It was not until 1945 that Zionism won the wholehearted support of the Jewish community.[282] In the meantime, the Zionists continued to contend with both internal and external enemies.[283]

The early years of the Mandate

Early dismay at aspects of the Mandate was expressed by opposition politicians, mainly the 'Diehards' of the Conservative Party (William Joynson-Hicks, among others),[284] and by certain newspapers, already hostile to Lloyd George's coalition government, mainly the *Morning Post* and *The Times*. Indeed, the press would appear to have been almost uniformly hostile to the Zionist project.[285] Their dismay took the form of concern about the financial burden imposed by the Mandate on British taxpayers ('Why is the British ass forced to bear the burden of Judah?'),[286] about its injustice to the Arabs and the threats to civil order in consequence of their opposition to it, and about whether the terms of the Mandate were not so hopelessly contradictory—how could a national home be established that would *not* prejudice the Arab's civil and religious rights?—as to be impossible to realize. Furthermore, Jews could not be trusted with power. The Zionists were all Bolsheviks, Bolshevik-sympathizers, or worse than Bolsheviks; they would stimulate anti-Semitism ('it will be their grave responsibility if the overwhelming anti-Zionist feeling in England develops into . . . anti-Semitism');[287] they were conspirators and blackmailers; 'Jewry and the British Government have become interchangeable';[288] and so on. The 'best Jews' know all this to be so:

> Zionism has already divided Jewry, it may yet imperil the British Empire . . . In the opinion of the best Jews, its crude materialism, its mean, sterile programme, its prostitution of all those ideals which have given to Judaism its fire and permanence, have doomed it to failure.[289]

(There is a sense in which certain contemporary Anglo-Jewish anti-Zionists are the successors to this first generation of 'best Jews'.) The newspapers' concerns were thus often expressed in language immoderately hostile to the Zionist project itself. *The Times* found the Jews of Palestine to be 'pushful, grasping and domineering'.[290] The *Morning Post* complained that British taxpayers were being 'compelled to pay for establishing a national home for Zionist Jews'. The *Daily Mail* argued that Britain should not be engaged in seeking to 'convert an old Arab state into a sham Jewish one'. The 750,000 Arabs would never accept the 80,000 Jews; the British should not be trying to force the Zionists on an unwilling, hostile native population. Britain should 'give back the Mandate'. In 1923, the *Catholic Herald* gave an anti-Zionist account of events in Palestine under the heading 'The Jewish Menace'.[291] All this greatly alarmed Chaim Weizmann, who wrote at the time to a correspondent of 'the general anti-Semitic campaign which is being so vigorously pressed in certain circles'. 'An anti-Semitic crusade has been initiated', he wrote to another correspondent.[292]

There was opposition, too, both from officials in the relevant government departments (the Foreign Office, then the Colonial Office) in London, and from the Palestinian administration (military, then civil). The military administration, known as 'OETA',[293] did not look with favour on Zionist activity.[294] In 1919, the *New Statesman* published a letter from a 'British Officer' written on behalf of 'every officer with whom I have discussed the matter'. The Jews, he wrote, are to the Mohammedan mind the very worst people to be given charge of the country. The hatred of the Jews is such that constant police protection has to be given to any Jewish visitor to Nablus. The people look upon the Jew as their natural enemy. In the Jewish colonies, the Mohammedan does the hard work. The Jew finds the money and runs the organization, but exploits Mohammedan cheap labour. He employs methods of usury and cunning; he is a modern Shylock.[295] General Money, chief administrator of Palestine between 1918

and 1919, confided to his diary his dislike of Jerusalem's Jews, 'Pharisees of
the New Testament', bringing up their children to be 'dirty idle wasters',
and among whose women there were 'more prostitutes than the rest of the
population put together'. And in an official report, Money explained that
the Jews were 'as a class inferior morally and intellectually' to the Muslim
and Christian inhabitants. Money reflected quite widespread attitudes in the
British army.[296] In July 1921, Weizmann was already worrying about 'an
anti-Zionist kink in some official minds'.[297] It was a 'kink' that derived, at
least in part, certainly, from exposure to local Zionist leaders, but mediated
by received, hostile notions about essential Jewish characteristics. According
to Isaiah Berlin, these officials 'tended to look on the Jews in Palestine
as aggressively self-assertive, shrill, touchy, neurotic, cliquish, devious, ill-
mannered, ungrateful, contemptuous of their Arab neighbours, unutterably
tiresome and exhausting to deal with'.[298] As for the Palestinian bureaucrats, a
local Jewish observer, married to Palestine's Attorney General no less, had
this to report in 1920:

> Feelings between . . . the Jews and the British are worse than ever. . . . It is said
> by otherwise intelligent British people here that the newspapers at home are
> entirely controlled by Jews, and only express the Jewish point of view, because
> they criticise the management of affairs here. They forget the *Morning Post* and
> its violently anti-Jewish attitude! Some of the British even believe that
> there 'may be something behind the *Protocols of the Elders of Zion*,' that
> violently anti-Semitic publication recently resuscitated, which is freely quoted
> in the Arab press.[299]

In letters home, Helen Bentwich wrote that most of the English people in
Palestine were 'outspokenly anti-Jewish'. 'The average Englishman here',
she wrote, 'is anti-Semitic.' 'There are such a lot of English people one can't
meet on equal terms now, because of their anti-Semitism.'[300] 'Your Brit-
isher here', wrote the Rev. H. Danby in 1920, 'is obsessed by the notion that
Zionism is incipient Bolshevism.'[301] There was also some social anti-Semitism of a very recognizable kind—remarks about 'bloody Jews', 'Moses,
Aaron & Co.', 'pound of flesh', and so on. The expatriate British community continued to entertain hostile sentiments towards the Jews, even in the
war years—there was anger at the emergent, dissident Jewish terrorism
directed at British targets, and there was a broader impatience with the
Jews' refusal as a single body to make a choice between, so to speak, national
or confessional status. They wanted both, or some wanted both, or some

wanted one, and others wanted the other—it was exasperating. 'What the Jews have got to decide is this', an oil executive remarked to a foreign newspaper correspondent. 'Are they a race or a religion? If they're a race then every Jew should be given a Palestinian passport . . .'[302]

'I dislike them equally', wrote one senior British officer of Jews and Arabs. 'The whole lot of them is not worth a single Englishman!'[303] Not every British official was so even-handed in his contempt, however. In the very first years of the British rule, the acting senior judicial officer, one Colonel Scott, was well known as a 'strong anti-Semite', ultimately forced to resign in consequence of abusing some Jews standing in a courthouse corridor: 'Don't make so much noise—this is not a synagogue!'[304] But E. T. Richmond is a more interesting example. He was an architect who had served before the war in the Egyptian Public Works Administration. In 1920, he was appointed Assistant Civil Secretary (Political), with responsibility for liaising with the Muslim community, resigning in 1924 in protest at the government's pro-Zionist policy. He returned to Palestine as director of antiquities in 1927, retiring in 1937. In his first period of office, Richmond was an appointment of High Commissioner Herbert Samuel's, and was given special responsibility for Arab affairs. He supported Haj Amin as candidate for Grand Mufti, intriguing on his behalf. When Haj Amin was defeated in the election for Mufti (he came a poor fourth), Richmond proposed that the result should be set aside. While not attacking the actual fairness of the election process, he argued that 'a very large number of people . . . believed that the elections have been arranged under Jewish influence', and that 'the vast majority of the people' wanted Haj Amin to be Mufti. Samuel submitted to Richmond's urgings. In a memorandum to the Colonial Office, prepared in 1922, he described Zionism as a movement 'with a decidedly Communistic bias'. He urged 'the establishment of an Administration' free of 'partiality'—that is, without Jews. In his letter of resignation, he described the inspiring spirit of the Mandate's administration as 'evil'.

Following his resignation in 1924, Richmond contributed an article to the political journal, the *Nineteenth Century*, entitled 'England in Palestine'. England's perspective on the Arabs is akin to twelfth-century Crusaders, namely unsympathetic and even hostile. The Arabs of Palestine, this unoffending people, do not have the machinery of a highly organized Press, with all the wealth and influence that that implies. By contrast, the Jews enjoy considerable advantages. They are regarded as pitiable, because dispersed; they have penetrated the life of all nations while remaining Jews; their financial interests are worldwide, and their political influence is in proportion to their wealth; their money and power are effective substitutes for force of arms. Long before the war, the Jews coveted Palestine; the Zionists are predators. Britain had been rendered blind to ordinary standards of conduct by financial and quasi-religious considerations; it is shackled to international Jewry. Following his retirement in 1937, Richmond contributed a further article to the *Nineteenth Century*, 'Dictatorship in Palestine'. Britain has been committing a twenty-year act of aggression against the Arab people, who are wholly unorganized for defence. This aggression has been carried out under the direction and control, not of British democracy, but of a special, ad hoc, conjunction of interests and influences. It comprises a hidden dictatorship, one that is wholly un-English, indeed, neither Christian nor English. This fantastic project has nothing that is characteristically English about it; we seek in vain for anything that is characteristically English. There is no sense of justice or fair play; the prevailing spirit is materialist; it is nothing more than atheistic barbarism. The conflict is a religious one. We need to change—away from dictatorship and back to things English. This may of course be considered a reversion to 'narrow nationalism', and thus be 'too painful for the delicate international susceptibilities of the Geneva Sanhedrin' (i.e., the Zionist movement). Weizmann found Richmond 'particularly malicious'.[305] To the historian Bernard Wasserstein, Richmond's views were 'extreme, but not altogether unrepresentative' of Mandate officials. The 'general balance of *idées reçues* about Jews was profoundly unfavourable'.[306]

The Mandate soon attracted the attention of political commentators. J. M. N. Jeffries's *The Palestine Deception* (London, 1923) and Philip Graves's *Palestine, the Land of Three Faiths* (London, 1923) are indicative of a certain conventional range of opinion regarding the Zionist project, from the unqualifiedly hostile to the qualifiedly sympathetic.

Jeffries's book was originally published as a series of articles in the *Daily Mail*. British policy is entirely wrong; we ought to evacuate Palestine. We ought to give the Arabs their independence, and not force them to submit to the rule of Zionists. It is revolting that Britain, a Christian country, should give the Holy Land to 'free-thinking young Judaeo-Slavs'. So far from Zionist money benefiting Arabs, the country is heading for bankruptcy. We pledged ourselves through McMahon to an independent Arab kingdom, with boundaries including Palestine. The illicit Balfour

Declaration was no more than a bigamist's second vow—dishonest and fraudulent. The Zionists enjoy an artificial predominance in Palestine thanks to the British, who will not benefit from this gift. Graves likewise declares himself to be against political Zionism, the 'artificial Judaization' of Palestine by 'the importation of large numbers of Jews in the hope that this will lead to Jewish political dominance'. But he is 'equally sceptical' of the ability of the Palestinian Arabs to 'make anything' of the country 'unaided by Jewish brains and capital and by British administrators'. He is opposed to newspaper demands—'tinged at times with anti-Semitism'—that Britain pull out of Palestine. We would lose our bridgehead to the Suez Canal and one of our principal stations on the air route to the East. Anti-Jewish feeling in Palestine may be explained by the grave tactical errors committed by many Zionists, by the growth of Arab nationalism, by the revival of pan-Islamism, and by the fears of a backward people when exposed to more advanced strangers. But these factors do not quite account for that dread of Zionism found among highly educated Arabs, among Europeans and Americans, 'including a few British officials': 'Over their minds', writes Graves, 'broods the spectre of Jewish revolutionary domination, anti-Christian, narrowly nationalist and communist, a doctrinaire, machine-like power, wielded in accordance with the instructions laid down in the notorious *Protocols of the Elders of Zion*.' Yet Zionism, of a practical and moderate kind, can be of great assistance to Palestine. The British Empire can honourably work for the realization of Ahad Ha'am's hope that Palestine will be a national spiritual centre of Judaism. We must plod on.[307]

The later, pre-war years of the Mandate

The period is framed by violence and terror: by the small catastrophe of the 1929 Arab riots and the immense catastrophe of the Nazi genocide, by a small assertion of Zionist strength at the beginning of the decade and a complete collapse of Jewish defences at its end. Disputes over immigration comprised its most constant theme. The 1930 White Paper proposed limits on Jewish entry to Palestine, which were then waived; the 1939 White Paper imposed limits, which were so strictly enforced that actual immigration fell short of them. Analysing the anti-Semitic aspect of British policy in this period is the least of it; it is the consequences for Jews of that policy, considered as a whole, which matters rather more.

The Arab riots prompted an inquiry, which in turn prompted a White Paper, which in turn prompted an attack on the paper by Weizmann and others, thereby prompting the MacDonald letter. The inquiry concluded that the Arabs were to blame; the White Paper concluded that their violence had to be appeased; the MacDonald letter concluded that the appeasement went too far. Official sentiment in London tended to the view that Arab violence was born of frustration and a certain inability to argue its case in more pacific contexts. When General Smuts tried to persuade Lord Passfield to withdraw the 1930 White Paper, he was abruptly told, 'It's very unfair that those Jews are so well represented. They have got Mr. Weizmann, whereas the poor Arabs haven't.'[308]

There is a specific Labour Party aspect to these developments. The riots coincided with its brief period in office. It was reassessing its position, and was less convinced than before that Zionist settlement was the route to modernization of the region. While Socialist Zionism impressed it hardly at all, it found Arab opposition to Jewish immigration very troubling indeed. It understood Britain to be an imperial power; it interpreted Britain's mandate responsibilities as imperial objectives; its anti-imperialism supported 'native' self-government; it did not regard the Jews as 'natives'. The Colonial Secretary, Lord Passfield, was the most anti-Zionist Secretary of State with whom the Zionists had to deal at any time.[309] His wife, Beatrice Webb, extended his lack of sympathy for Zionism to Jews in general. Her observation to Chaim Weizmann regarding the mass killing of Hebron's Jews in 1929 was the following: 'I can't understand why the Jews make such a fuss over a few dozen of their people killed in Palestine. As many are killed every week in London in traffic accidents, and no one pays any attention.'[310] Jewish anti-Zionists reacted somewhat differently. Harold Laski, for example, demanded the dismissal of Passfield and the revoking of the White Paper. He explained to the prime minister that while his views on Zionism 'had not changed':

> as a Jew I resent a policy which surrenders Jewish interests, in spite of a pledged word, to the authors of an unjustifiable massacre. No doubt when the Arabs kill the next lot of Jews, Webb will be allowed to expel all Jews from Palestine.[311]

(I consider this formulation, 'as a Jew', in Chapter 8. It now tends to preface statements of position that favour Palestinian Arab interests.)

Between White Papers, there were further riots, and then partition proposals were made, somewhat despairingly, that duly foundered upon Arab opposition. The Arab riots of 1936–8 took place in a very different context to the riots of 1929. They were more disciplined, and indicated an emergent Palestinian national consciousness, though they too degenerated into score-settling and intra-Arab murder. Among the victims of the rioters were nineteen Jews in Tiberias, eleven of them children (mostly burnt alive in their nursery).[312] The Partition proposals made by the Peel Commission, had the parties accepted them, might have led to the creation of a small Jewish state before the hostilities of World War II began. An Israel would then have been able to issue passports. It would have made citizens of stateless Jews or Jews persecuted by the states of which they were still members. It would have provided a refuge for many, though by no means all, Jews at risk. The Nazis recognized this danger to their interests.[313]

Something of the weight of the Zionist movement's difficulties in the 1930s can be gauged by an examination of the career of a senior civil servant, George Rendel. Rendel was the head of the Eastern Department of the Foreign Office from 1930 to 1938. To him, Jewish interests should not be served at the price of quarrelling with the Arab world. The Jews had lived in Arab lands unmolested and at peace, until the Palestine question became acute. This question, which he regarded as central in Middle East affairs, had to be solved to the satisfaction of the Arabs if British interests were to be protected. In 1936, he favoured promising the Arab Higher Committee that upon the cessation of violence, immigration would be suspended, and thereafter regulated to ensure Arab continued dominance. Rendel's response to the murder by Arabs in 1937 of the district commissioner for Galilee was that Britain had brought the violence on itself. He endorsed the views of a *New Statesman* correspondent who described the murdered official 'from the point of view of the great majority of Arabs as a spy, who represented the hated British autocracy in its most objectionable form'. (Rendell added in the margin, against 'British autocracy', the phrase 'or Zionist policy'.) He worried that a Jewish State would 'rapidly spread its influence and control over all the neighbouring countries'. It would also acquire 'a very Teutonic complexion', becoming a 'spiritual colony' of Germany once the 'active Jew-baiting' there had ceased. He persuaded the Cabinet to reject the Peel Report. Raids, attacks, and massacres would follow partition, he warned. The violence would engulf Syria, Iraq, and even Muslim India.[314] Rendel was himself indifferent to the anti-Semitic aspect of Arab opposition to the Zionist project, though he was astute enough to wish to conceal this aspect from general view.[315]

Newspapers and polemicists, often in language that drew on established anti-Semitic themes, fostered a certain mystification of Zionist power, and a false impression of its ambitions. As late as in December 1938, for example, the *Weekly Review* explained to its readers that the Zionist movement was the cause of the Nazi persecution of the Jews. The movement's object, it said, 'though not definitely avowed, is to secure world domination for the members of its race'.[316] At precisely this time, the Yishuv's impotence was in fact starkly demonstrated. The prime minister, Neville Chamberlain, was heard to remark, 'If we must offend one side, let us offend the Jews rather than the Arabs.'[317]

The 1939 White Paper limited Jewish immigration into Palestine to 75,000 for the next five years. Thereafter, no further Jewish immigration would be permitted without the consent of 'the Arabs of Palestine'.[318] Though their consent was not solicited, had it been, it would doubtless have been refused. Even today, many Palestinian activists—very ready to condemn the Western powers for denying refuge to Germany's Jews—still refuse to acknowledge the Palestinian role in barring the last escape route from Nazi Europe.[319] (One of the principal demands made by the Arab delegation at the 1939 London conference was for the immediate cessation of Jewish immigration to Palestine.)[320] In any event, not satisfied with this immense political victory, the leader of the Palestinians, Haj Amin al-Husseini, continued to intrigue against the Jews. That 75,000 more Jews would be allowed in was intolerable to him; when the Arab National Defence Party indicated that for their part they would accept that number, a member of the group was murdered by one of the Mufti's men.[321] As for Arab assistance to the Allies, as Churchill telegraphed in January 1944 to Eden and Attlee: 'the Arabs have done nothing for us during this war, except for the rebellion in Iraq'.[322] Though Churchill opposed the 1939 White Paper at the time, he did not reverse it during his premiership.

Curiously, and notwithstanding Arab success in blocking Partition, when Jeffries returned to an analysis of the Zionist project, some sixteen years following his 1923 book, he continued to complain of injustice. In *Palestine: The reality* (London, 1939), he wrote that the Arabs' case had remained unheard before the court of public opinion. They were suffering from a supreme injustice. British subterfuge, fraud, and perfidy had deprived the Arabs of their natural and inherent rights over their native land. Their remote ancestors were Canaanites. They were first in the land. Jewish tenure of the land was never complete and lasted a mere seventy years.

Palestine was but a section of the larger natural unit of Syria. 'There is no reason why it should be a country. It is too small, its boundaries are artificial in the main, there is nothing to distinguish it from the territory just to the north, its sacred character has not the slightest national character.'[323] He maintained that in the early 1920s, the government and the Zionists had plotted against the Arabs. The professions of concern addressed to the Arabs had all been fraudulent. Insofar as Britain had enemies in Germany, it had done its best to push the Arabs into their arms. The Peel Partition recommendation was intolerable. There should be a single state, with all its inhabitants enjoying equal rights, and the rights of minorities specifically guaranteed. In due course, Palestine will be naturally absorbed into Syria. The industrialization of Palestine must stop.[324]

The build-up to World War II

There is very little that may be said in praise of the 1930s. And the decade's pervasive anti-Semitism, an anti-Semitism that was said to be 'in the air',[325] was among its least attractive aspects. Doing the best that he could in his *English History 1914–1945*, A. J. P. Taylor acknowledged this endemic but 'quiet' anti-Semitism, one that excluded Jews from golf clubs and limited their access to public schools, but he insisted upon the utterly different character of the Nazi persecutions. Even England's anti-Semites, he wrote, were offended by what the Nazis were doing to German Jewry. They joined with all other Englishmen in condemning Hitler's anti-Semitism, even if they were also annoyed that he had made it impossible for them to express their own reservations about Jews. Taylor concluded, 'the persecutions did more than anything else to turn English moral feeling against Germany, and this moral feeling in turn made English people less reluctant to go to war'.[326] The argument seems to be that Nazi anti-Semitism inhibited an English anti-Semitism already mostly innocuous in its effects.

Taylor's view has not survived detailed examination by more recent historians of the decade. The current view is that the anti-Semitism of those years was deep and broad, and that it bore the weight of the preceding half-century of anti-Semitic practice, which itself contributed to an indigenous proto-fascist political tradition.[327] This strength and depth was evident in the emergence of fascist parties, in certain aspects of the policy of appeasement, in the reception of Jewish refugees, and in the apparently quite widely held view in late 1939 that 'the Jews' were to blame for the anticipated war.[328] For the first time, then, a party with an explicitly anti-Semitic programme had gained some support (though not enough to win a parliamentary seat); the violent, programmatic anti-Semitism of a Continental power was viewed sympathetically in influential political circles, when not positively excused or condoned; Jews at their least threatening and in most need of humanitarian assistance were generally addressed with something less than compassion, and were regarded by many as seeking to engineer a world war for their advantage. In parallel with these developments, but also informing them, was the English press's failure throughout much of the 1930s adequately to take the measure of Nazi anti-Semitism, a failure attributable in part to the belief that the Jews were no worse treated in Germany than elsewhere in Central and Eastern Europe, in part to the belief that Britain had no right to interfere in the domestic policies of the democratically elected and popular government of a sovereign nation, and in part to what has been described as its fundamental inability to understand the potential depths of Nazi brutality.[329]

Fascism

The scholar Norman Cohn identified 'a subterranean world where pathological fantasies disguised as ideas are churned out by crooks and half-educated fanatics for the benefit of the ignorant and superstitious'.[330] This is the anti-Semitic underworld. Gangsters, hooligans, Holocaust deniers, defamers of Judaism, charlatans and buffoons, crackpots and autodidacts, faddists of 'secret knowledge',[331] subscribers to the 'underground of rejected knowledge',[332] and misfits of one kind or another with a taste for violence, drift in and out of it; cranks intrigue against each other; disaffected, extra-parliamentary agitators attempt to establish reputations in this underworld; and uniformed or irregular para-military groupings recruit there. The mediocrity of this miscellany of misfits, their weakness, their venality, their resentments and their obsessiveness, their reluctance to allow challenges to their fantasizing—none of these characteristics makes a life beyond the environs of fellow-believers congenial to them and, in consequence, they usually remain self-segregated from society. When circumstances allow, however, they invade their society's public spaces, and even come to influence its political life. The threat that they then pose to Jews becomes more considerable. In the 1920s, it appeared that a threat of this order had arisen, but then the threat subsided. In the 1930s a further threat arose, greater in both breadth and intensity than the previous decade's, and one that took somewhat longer to subside.

In the 1920s, the Bolshevik Revolution and its aftermath in Civil War, and then the publication of the *Protocols*, encouraged anti-Semitic coteries to believe that they could mount an assault upon mainstream political opinion. These events appeared to them to be incontestable demonstrations of Jewish power, and of an order that dwarfed the petty financial scandals before the war. From Samuel, Isaacs, and Montagu to Lenin, Trotsky, and the Elders of Zion—what a transition! At last the enemy was standing plain in view, visible to all. What had been suspected beforehand was now triumphantly confirmed. (G. K. Chesterton exulted, 'The popular press is now naming the Jewish influence quite openly.')[333] In 1921, the chairman of the Conservative Party attributed Tory by-election defeats to 'the strong anti-Semitic feeling which is very prominent at the present time'.[334] It appeared to some vanguard Jew-haters that English anti-Semitism, so long an exasperatingly inert and limited affair, might well be developed into something more dynamic and substantial.[335] It could be made to catch up with Continental anti-Semitism. Groups were formed,[336] books and pamphlets were written, publishing houses, fresh newspapers and journals were founded, already-established newspapers and journals were infiltrated, and affiliations were made with overseas parties and other entities. But disappointment was in store for them, as it was for the extra-parliamentary, Radical Right in general.[337] By the mid-1920s, the purchase that the notion of an international Jewish conspiracy had on the public mind weakened, and these committed, preoccupied anti-Semites were forced to resume their practice of talking mostly to themselves and to each other.[338] More outward-facing groups, such as 'The Britons', which aimed to eradicate 'alien influence',[339] went into decline or just collapsed. (By 1925, when The Britons was finally wound up, its founder, Henry Hamilton Beamish, had for several years been travelling the world promoting anti-Semitism, looking for larger and more congenial audiences, and in flight from an English court judgment against him.)[340] Of course, anti-Semitism did not altogether retire to the private sphere. William Joynson-Hicks, Conservative Home Secretary from 1924 to 1929, made Jews anxious from time to time, for example. The cumulative force of his anti-alienism, anti-Bolshevism, and anti-Zionism, together with disobliging remarks made to and about Jews in election campaigns in 1906 and 1908, produced a general impression of anti-Semitism.[341] In addition, the open channels between the fascist and Conservative Right during the period intensified the more pervasive, received anti-Semitism in the political culture, encouraging a somewhat more acute consciousness of the Jewish peril (Maurice Cowling's delicate formulation) than hitherto.[342] This anti-Semitism, the everyday kind, which was 'rife',[343] was also somewhat sharper, and more menacing in its implications, than in previous decades.

In the matter of anti-Semitism, the difference between the 1920s and the 1930s is the difference between Joynson-Hicks and Oswald Mosley. Encouraged by Continental successes and then by the threat of war, fascist and fascist-sympathizing groupings emerged, as if from a miasma, both to participate in and to challenge mainstream politics. They became noticeable; they were monitored by the security services; for the very first time, they represented a credible threat. One among them in particular, the British Union of Fascists, was able to subsist almost entirely outside what would otherwise have been its typical milieu. It had a national organization of sorts; it had youth sections; it was a presence on the streets of some major cities; it had newspapers; and above all, it had in Oswald Mosley (1896–1980) a well-known leader, a person of real political standing who had himself at one time or another been esteemed by each one of the main political parties. He had been a Conservative MP, then an independent MP, and then (after a flirtation with the Liberals), a Labour MP and member of the party's National Executive Committee until resigning to form a new political party in February 1931, The New Party. In October 1932, he founded the BUF (from 1936, the 'British Union of Fascists and National Socialists'), and on 20 June 1940 it was banned. It would seem that Mosley did not always regard anti-Semitism as a comprehensive explanation of social ills, though he was capable of reacting to Jews anti-Semitically under certain conditions, came from a family in which the taking of adversarial positions regarding Jews was not unprecedented, and took positions himself, even in the 1920s, which were implicitly anti-Semitic.[344] He understood that he needed anti-Semitism to retain the devotional core of his BUF members and supporters; in late 1933, Jews were excluded from membership of the party;[345] the BUF 'drifted' towards open, campaigning anti-Semitism in the mid-1930s,[346] with Mosley mimicking supposed Jewish accents in public speeches, to great applause (he was always ready to attack 'Jewish rascals', 'the yelping of a Yiddish mob', 'warriors of class war—all from Jerusalem', 'the force of international Jewish finance', and so on);[347] in May 1935, Mosley addressed a public telegram to Julius Streicher declaring, 'the power of Jewish corruption must be destroyed in all countries before peace and justice can be achieved in Europe'.[348] Mosley from the outset recognized the propaganda utility of concentrating on a single enemy and 'capitalism' was too abstract and impersonal a force to be an object of hatred; he happily coexisted for some time with his lieutenants, A. K. Chesterton and William Joyce, and with leading rank-and-filers, Mick Clarke, Jock Houston, and Bill Bailey, aggressive, implacable anti-Semites all;[349] and he used anti-Semitism as a weapon in his 'peace' campaign, constituting the Jews as a lobby for war, seeking to create 'a land fit for Hebrews to live in'.[350] In a somewhat opaque passage in his pamphlet *Tomorrow We Live* (1938–9), he proposed expulsion for Jews 'who have indulged in practices alien to British character and tradition', and demotion to 'foreigner' status for the rest of the Jewish population: '[They] will be treated as the majority of their people have elected to be treated', that is, as 'a state within the nation'.[351] To Evelyn Waugh, writing in 1938, English fascism was now no more than 'a form of anti-Semitism in the slums'.[352] In the post-war years, Mosley promoted Holocaust denial, condemning the Nuremberg trials and questioning the existence of a Hitler 'order' sanctioning any genocide.[353] Still, writing in 1961, Mosley himself denied that he was *ever* an anti-Semite, according to his own definition of anti-Semitism. All he did was to defend his movement against misconceived attacks on it by Jews, and to criticize 'certain Jewish interests' for attempting 'to drag us into war with Germany'. As for Suez, 'for the second time we have been dragged towards war by international Jewish finance'. His Union Movement, he explained, is the only force that 'dares' to stand up to 'Jewish financial interests'.[354] These were long-standing themes of Mosley's.[355]

Though the BUF never won a parliamentary seat, the fascist perspective was not altogether unrepresented in the House of Commons—not, at any rate, in its anti-Semitic aspects. The Conservative MP, Capt Maule Ramsay, was active against the Jews throughout much of the 1930s. He established the 'Right Club' with the object of educating the Conservative Party about the Jewish menace. He fought and lost a libel case in July 1941; his position at trial was that the war was a 'Jewish ramp', namely run by Jews and in the interests of Jews. The judge commented: 'I don't believe that any man outside of a lunatic asylum could persuade himself of that.'[356] But Ramsay's career was representative of the dismal trajectory of Anglo-fascist anti-Semites—detained for much of the war under Regulation 18B, he became a political fugitive after the war, publishing an absurd book in 1952,

The Nameless War, in which he speculated that Calvin was a Jew, characterized the term 'director' as 'characteristically Jewish', cited Hitler with approval, fulminated against 'Zionists', defended the authenticity of the *Protocols*, and detected Jewish influence *everywhere*. The 'nameless war', of course, was the war waged by International Jewry against the Gentile world, its victories misdescribed as the 'French' and 'Russian' 'Revolutions', and 'World War II'. He was not, he declared an 'anti-Semite' or even 'anti-Jew'; he was 'Jew-wise'.[357]

The other expressly anti-Semitic groups were substantially more marginal; indeed, marginality was written into their very character and composition. There was, for example, Arnold Leese and his 'Imperial Fascist League'. Leese (1878–1956) was a retired veterinary surgeon and full-time anti-Semitic activist—a self-described 'anti-Jewish camel-doctor' and 'opponent of secret Jewish power'.[358] He believed the Aryan race to be at risk of Jewish corruption, and the Jews themselves to be a mongrel conglomeration, part Khazar. He entertained the possibility of genocide, promoted the blood libel, and disparaged the BUF ('the Imperial Fascist League has absolutely no connection with the pro-Jewish so-called "Fascism" of Sir Oswald Mosley'). Whatever he did not like, he described as 'Jewish'.[359] There was Alexander Ratcliffe and his 'British Protestant League'. Ratcliffe became an early denier of Nazi atrocities, writing in March 1943 'there is not a single authentic case on record of a single Jew having been massacred or unlawfully put to death under the Hitler regime'.[360] And then there were the 'Militant Christian Patriots', who gave away free copies of the *Protocols* to subscribers to its newspapers.[361] They were stalwart anti-Zionists. 'A decisive battle must be fought', they thundered, 'against the enslavers of our race whose power is concentrated in Zionism.'[362] There was Admiral Sir Barry Domvile and his 'Link', its object being 'to promote Anglo-German understanding'. In March 1938, it had 1,800 members, and by June 1939, over 4,300; it had branches across the country, some more strenuously anti-Semitic than others.[363] 'I object to being dubbed anti-Jewish', Domvile wrote. 'I am not, but I am fully alive to the harmful activities of the most powerful section of Jewry...'[364] And there was the 'Nordic League', which described itself as 'an association...of race-conscious Britons'. It put itself at the service of 'patriotic bodies...engaged in exposing and frustrating the Jewish stranglehold on our Nordic realm'. It was an upper-middle class group, and drew on BUF membership for stewards for its meetings. Typical of those meetings was a speech of

A. K. Chesterton's, received with great relish, in which he spoke of 'greasy little Jew-boy pornographers'. It pursued a strongly anti-Zionist line.[365]

One needs a certain scholarly resolve to write at any length about these individuals and groups. They contributed nothing to the understanding of their times; they included no thinkers or strategists of distinction or even mediocrity; there was nothing original or even engaging in their pro-grammes; they produced nothing of political or cultural value; their news-letters and pamphlets were dreary, somewhat hysterical, and most of all just *wrong* about the events they reported; British fascism itself was an abject failure.[366] In France during the 1930s, non-fascists read the *Action Française* for its book reviews;[367] in England, no one other than the already converted would bother with the *Patriot, Fascist, British Lion, Action, Blackshirt, BUF Quarterly*, or any of the other sectarian proto-fascist or fascist, anti-Semitic newspapers and journals. Subject to this, of course, each group had its own distinctive features. The *Patriot*, owned by the Duke of Northumberland, was preoccupied with the Judeo-Bolshevik threat to the British Empire, holding Jews and Bolsheviks responsible for unrest in India, Ireland, and Egypt (while denying that its position was 'fanatically anti-Semitic' because it condemned only a 'section' of Jewry).[368] Leese was keen, as we have seen, on the ritual-murder topic; the MCP talked up the threat of Zionism; Lymington tended towards a certain pessimism regarding the weakening of England's racial 'stock'; the British People's Party (another pro-Nazi group) adopted the tactic of not referring to Jews directly, and using code words or expressions instead; the Anglo-German Fellowship, a society of businessmen sharing an enthusiasm for Nazi Germany, comprised ostensibly moderate members and dedicated anti-Semitic activists, and so on. Some groups accented the pro-German, others the anti-Semitic, in their propa-gandizing. Once war had broken out, most were immobilized by the tension between their patriotic and fascist loyalties.

From the early 1920s, the Palestine question attracted the attention of the Far Right. The *Patriot* opposed the Mandate, regarding it as 'weak senti-mentalism', a subvention of 'international Jewish finance', and likely to lead to the Bolshevization of Palestine; secular Zionism itself aided 'the enemies of Christianity and civilisation'.[369] As World War II approached, the hos-tility became more acute. In Mosley's pamphlet, *Tomorrow We Live*, he proposed that the Jews should be transported to one of the 'many waste places on earth', where they will thereby escape the 'curse of no nationality'; Palestine itself is not available to them, because it is the home of Arabs, and we would not want to wrong 'the Arab ally'.[370] (This was an echo of Beamish's proposal, that the Jew should be transported to Madagascar.)[371] In 1938, Nesta Webster wrote in the *Patriot* that the 'Jewish Question' had to be faced 'fairly and squarely, here and in Palestine', and proposed the removal of 'the whole Jewish race' to the 'vast unpeopled spaces of Soviet Russia', where they would enjoy 'the government of pro-Semite rulers'.[372] Elsewhere, she commended Joynson-Hicks's observation that the Jewish immigrants to Palestine were 'the sweepings of the ghettos of Central Europe'. The 'sanguinary riots' of 1929, she wrote, were the product of 'provocations [the Arabs] had long endured'.[373] Ramsay warned at a pro-Nazi meeting shortly before the war that the Jews controlled the press, and that they were both godless communists and international financiers. They exercise immense power in Europe and the United States, he said, and now they have set their sights on Palestine. The Mayor of Bethlehem had handed revolvers to his three sons with the command that they shoot every Jew they saw, Ramsay recounted. And then, addressing his son, sitting next to him on the platform, 'I may have to do this with you before long.'[374] In February 1939, George Mansur, a senior representative of the Arab League spoke at a meeting of the Nordic League. He explained that the concessions made to Zionism by the British government proved 'the power of Jewish gold'. The government was 'under the domination of the Jews'. He was proud to associate himself with the Nordic League, which was committed to 'crush-ing that dominating power'. League members returned the compliment, praising the Arab method with the Jews: 'extermination is the only solution to the Jew problem in Palestine, [and there is] no better one for this country'.[375] William Joyce condemned the 'persecution of the Arabs' and the 'campaign of murder, torture, and arson' carried out against them; the administration of the Mandate was proof of 'the Jewish control of Brit-ain'.[376] This 'anti-Zionist' theme remained a constant on the Far Right. Writing in May 1948, Mosley attributed the creation of the State of Israel to the 'International money power', which as 'ardently desired a Jewish state in Palestine as it previously wanted the destruction of the German state'.[377] The so-called 'Cotswold Agreement', concluded in August 1961, commit-ted British and American neo-Nazi groups to 'combat and utterly destroy the international Jew-Communist and Zionist apparatus of treason and subversion'.[378] Martin Webster, a Far Right activist, warned against 'the might of international finance, which is dominated by persons of a Jewish and pro-Zionist background'.[379] By the 1970s, it had become standard practice to collapse 'the Jews' into 'the Zionists'. 'Zionism is the issue', declared the National Front newspaper, *Spearhead*, in 1975.[380]

Anti-Semitic expression in the decade took various forms. There were rallies and open-air meetings, of course. There was also a good measure of overt 'Jew-baiting' and 'Jew-bashing'—a product of what Keynes called 'the philo-fisticuffs of the Right'.[381] In London's East End, there were attacks on Jews, damage to Jewish property, as well as more creative acts of vandalism, such as nailing pigs' heads or rashers of bacon to synagogue doors or waving a severed pig's head at a march.[382] There were provocative marches in areas with a substantial Jewish population—'The Yids! The Yids!', the marchers would chant, 'We gotta get rid of the Yids!'[383] There was a great deal of graffiti—'Britain before Aliens' was often found, commonly next to a BUF symbol. 'Perish Judah' or 'P.J.' was a familiar sight on walls in some parts of London. There were BUF 'chalk squads', and activists who affixed on walls and shop windows 'sticky backs' bearing anti-Semitic messages.[384] There was some poetry, 'His hair was sleek and full of oil, / And so his manner too, / His hands were far too soft for toil, / The Son, of a Son, of a Jew', etc., and adaptations of popular songs, 'Abie, Abie, now that we've tumbled you, / You'll go crazy before we are done with you,' etc.[385] Synagogue walls were defaced with swastikas. In one public library, the *Jewish Chronicle* was defaced so frequently that it was withdrawn from open access, and was available only upon special request.[386] In October 1936, a gang of 150 BUF members and supporters smashed the windows of and looted forty-five Jewish shops in the East End; they threw a man and a girl through a plate-glass window, and set a motor car on fire, all the time chanting 'Down with the Yids.'[387] The anti-Semites were furious letter-writers too. It was the conduct of the Jews that 'nourished anti-Semitic feeling in Britain', one newspaper was informed. The Jews 'lustily sing the International during renditions of the National Anthem',[388] another correspondent reported. Several of the groups had their own newspapers and journals, and there were a few books published. A. K. Chesterton attempted, in the *BUF Quarterly*, to patronize Jews while also encouraging a 'passionate and wholesome rage' against them, but incitement and condescension do not sit well together, and it is unlikely that readers even finished his 'Apotheosis of the Jew'. In summary, none of these activities could command respect; they did not speak for a party or parties about to take charge of the country.

The strategy was to exploit given fears on local political issues, especially following the BUF's decision to concentrate its strength in London's East End. They would, say, seek to enlist the support of local clergy concerned about Sunday trading or the erosion of parish congregations because of Jewish migration.[389] They would seek to enlist labour and trades union support by exploiting resentment towards 'sweat shops', foreign cheap labour, slum dwellings, and so on. ('The big Jew puts you in the unemployment queue by the million, and the little Jew sweats you.')[390] They would seek to enlist the support of small businesses by complaining about Jewish 'cut-price' grocers, and exploiting Jewish–Gentile rivalry in the furniture trade. (There was an alliance between the BUF and the Stoke Newington Grocers' Association.)[391] In the early months of the war, popular discontents about the effects of the blackouts, wartime bureaucracy, shortage of goods, etc. would all be blamed on the Jews.[392] Questions would be posed that implied prejudicial answers—why do Jews get the best council houses? Why do ratepayers 'pay subsidies to house foreigners cheaply'?[393]

Bigger issues were also given an anti-Semitic twist. Protectionist trade positions—say, calling for the expansion of the domestic market for British manufacturers, or for the privileging of goods produced in the Empire, or for the penalizing with tariffs of foreign goods—were simplified, and supplemented with attacks on cosmopolitan financiers, wealthy rootless Jews, and the like. Jews were accused of being insufficiently patriotic, and beneficiaries of the main political parties' betrayal of British farmers and manufacturers. They were condemned as practitioners of a capitalism indifferent to national boundaries, to the distinction between 'our' goods and 'foreign' goods, and so on.[394] But the anti-Semites could never *contain* their anti-Semitism; it was constantly swamping their message. Maule Ramsay, for example, composed the following hymn of hatred, which was distributed around London, 'Land of dope and Jewry / Land that once was free'. It went on to condemn the plunder of the nation by the Jews, the sacrifice of its sons to 'feed the guns', the 'Jewish lies' told in 'press and books and movies', and so on.[395] It left far behind anti-Semitic twists to issues of broader political concern; it instead demanded assent to an entirely anti-Semitic account of contemporary events.

It might be thought, given the development of anti-Semitism from the 1910s to the 1920s, and then from the 1920s to the 1930s, that were it not for the outbreak of war, anti-Semitism would have commanded the programme of a political party with a decent chance of electoral success. But the complex truth is that the BUF had substantially failed before the war, while it was the advent of war that briefly revived it (the extent of the revival is an open question).[396] The party suffered a rapid turnover of membership, and was only effective in a limited number of local areas, chief among which was the East End of London. As its message became shriller, so its appeal declined. The revival in its fortunes following the invasion of Czechoslovakia—a revival attributable at least in part to the success of the allegation that Jews were dragging England into a war with Hitler—could not withstand the patriotic commitment to the war effort. This is not to minimize either the July 1939 rally at Earls Court Stadium, attended by over 20,000 people ('a million Britons shall not die in your Jews' quarrel')[397] nor the very well-attended meeting at the Criterion Restaurant on 1 March 1940 ('the real reason' why Britain had declared war on Germany was because it 'was controlled by Jews and they desired to see the end of the present German government so that they could resume their exploitation of the German people').[398]

The absence of ideas favourable to fascism, the consequent absence of any sustainable fascist political tradition in this country, the paucity of fascism's intellectual appeal, the limited number of fascist fellow-travellers among intellectuals, the complete electoral failure of the BUF, the strength of the Conservative Party,[399] the very positioning of Britain against fascism in World War II, the utter marginality of fascists in the political culture, has meant that it makes no sense to speak of an English anti-Semitism that is fascist in nature.[400] (Unity Mitford, complained to Julius Streicher, editor of the *Stürmer*: 'In general, the English have no notion of the Jewish menace. The English Jews are always called "decent".')[401] The political system was a barrier against fascism. It was very efficient; it enjoyed an unchallengeable legitimacy. The hegemony of party politics in British political life was preserved, not least because every important social group was adequately represented in Parliament.[402] In addition, the exceptional heterogeneity of the Far Right's interests (tariff reformers, Imperial isolationists, anti-industrial 'ruralists', anti-German conspiracy theorists, distributists, fascists, Social Credit enthusiasts, etc.) frustrated the emergence of any coherent anti-Semitic politics, certainly for the long-term. Anti-Semitism was never strong enough to constitute a positive principle around which diverse interests could group; and these interests were mostly so at odds with each other that they were unable to find common ground independently of anti-Semitism. They came together as 'single issue' coalitions, on occasion sustaining 'intense but transient bursts of anti-Semitism';[403] the coalitions then disintegrated once the perceived threat receded from view. Lastly, the political Right was too factionalized, too fissured by rivalries and disloyalties, to allow for any novel political proposition—say, that the Jews were to blame for the nation's ills, and had to be defeated if there was to be a national revival—to stand even a chance of commanding general support. The combined effect was a kind of ideological indecision, amounting to paralysis. In due course English fascism became the ideology of treason—'disloyal in heart and soul to our King, our Government, and our people', as the judge in the Beamish case put it.[404]

And then the war came and, with that, administrative detention under Defence Regulation 18B, the discrediting of pro-fascist positions as treasonable, and the retreat of organized anti-Semites back into coteries that were smaller and more embattled than at any time before. All the progress that had been made since the Marconi and Indian Silver 'scandals'—the popular indignation at German Jewish plutocrats and Russian Jewish shirkers during World War I, the conspiracy fantasies fuelled by the 1917 Revolution, the immense gift of the *Protocols*, the proliferation of public, openly anti-Semitic organizations, with real membership lists and offices and newspapers and rallies—all this, as if overnight, was reversed, and just disappeared. Or so it must have seemed. These committed, organized, one-eyed anti-Semites soldiered on, of course, leading what has been described as 'a fragile and often shadowy existence'.[405] On Mosley's arrest, the BUF newspaper, *Action*, defiantly announced, 'We carry on', and 'We can take it' (though they didn't, and they couldn't). But a journal, the *Patriot*, campaigned on behalf of 18B detainees; pacifist organizations were infiltrated; other organizations were simply taken over; new groups were formed. But what once had pretensions to the mainstream had shrivelled to its former condition, a fetid milieu.[406]

The question of appeasement

Of course, the fascists were appeasers—more than appeasers. Many of them identified themselves with the Nazi project. Appeasement itself, which was by no means limited to those sympathetic with Nazism, came to mean giving in to Hitler's demands in the hope that he would desist from making further demands, a policy of Danegeld.[407] At its inception, it was by no means ignominious; leniency towards Germany was not at first dictated by weakness or cowardice, but by some generosity of spirit and even courage.[408] At its terminal point, however, the policy appeared to most people to have led to national humiliation.[409] Each one but the last of Hitler's provocations (euphemistically, unilateral Treaty revisions) were met with the feeblest of responses: the military occupation of the Rhineland, the *Anschluss* with Austria, the grabbing of the Sudetenland from Czechoslovakia, and the Munich agreement-violating occupation of Czechoslovakia itself. The persecution of Jews, however, was not considered a provocation at all. Appeasement did not work: at the end, many appeasers reversed their positions, acknowledging the misjudgements they had made.[410] But it did not begin like that.

It was predicated on reasonable positions: the error of encirclement of Germany in 1904 and 1907, the injustice of the 1919 Versailles Treaty, the simplistic analysis underlying the Treaty's 'war guilt' clause ('Germany accepts the responsibility . . . for causing all the loss and damage . . . '), the cogency of Germany's grievances. In appeasement's early repudiation of the post-World War I slogan, 'Germany must pay', it applied the venerable principle of 'fair play'. In its later acknowledgement of Britain's unpreparedness for war, the policy of some appeasers to strive for peace while preparing for war, was not altogether ignoble. And it assumed what only the war itself refuted, that internal violence and external aggression are two quite separate vices. In its post-1933 version, it took an odd view of Hitler, one that required the putting aside of everything he actually said, regarding him as 'sincere' when expressing a desire for peace. He was no 'ogre'; he could be 'separated from his extremists'.[411] (As late as 1937, Lord Halifax met Goering, and found him 'frankly attractive, like a great schoolboy, full of life and pride in what he was doing', while Hitler was 'very sincere'.)[412] Hitler should be given a chance; Germany should be given a chance. But too many chances were given, and too little attention was paid to the wickedness of the regime. Specifically, in the context of my own concerns, too little attention was paid to the persecution of the Jews.

The positions of the appeasers connected, for a time, with more widely held sentiments. That the Versailles Treaty should be revised in Germany's favour became the common sense of the political classes, and accommodating Germany in this respect became a principle of British foreign policy. This desire to accommodate, to 'do justice to Germany',[413] which in due course went beyond treaty revision, was derived from several distinct elements. There was a *realpolitik* readiness to trade Eastern Europe for guarantees in respect of the Empire. There was a fear of communism, believed to be far worse than anything of which Germany, even the Germany of the Third Reich, was capable. (Halifax assured Hitler in 1937 that 'there was a much greater degree of understanding of all his work on [combating Communism] than there had been some time ago'.)[414] For some it was a matter of racial solidarity, the Anglo-Saxons or Teutons against the Slavs, a proper indulgence towards the one, and implacable hostility to the other. There was a horror of war (Chamberlain said, 'Armed conflict between nations is a nightmare to me'),[415] and a sense that anti-appeasers were thus 'warmongers', guilty of 'war-lust', desiring the dangers they warned against.[416] There was also a sense of ideals and values shared by the British and the Germans, a wish to foster alliances, *rapprochements*, Anglo–German cooperation, which was not, even post-1933, wholly one-sided. (There was some talk by Hitler too, in the early years of his rule, of an Anglo–German alliance.)[417] But there was also a lack of imagination, an absence of any adequate conception of evil. It was assumed that the world was made up of reasonable men. Chamberlain had been Lord Mayor of Birmingham; he regarded Hitler and Mussolini as if they had been Lord Mayors of Liverpool and Manchester.[418]

It has been suggested that anti-Semitism was never far below the surface of appeasement.[419] Certainly, there was an indifference among many appeasers to the persecution of the Jews, a conviction that Germany's internal affairs were 'not our business',[420] and a readiness to dismiss it with excuses (they recognized that it was an obstacle to better relations with Germany).[421] It was exaggerated, a matter of 'mountains out of molehills',[422] or comprised the acts of undisciplined subordinates, 'a few isolated acts of violence',[423] or was an understandable response to an excessive and malign Jewish presence in German national life. The Jews, in some sense, 'had it coming'; the 'birds were coming home to roost'.[424] It would pass; it was not a permanent feature of Hitler's Germany. It was a reaction to external pressure and denunciation; Germany would come to terms with the Jews if left alone.[425] Nazi anti-Semitism had a certain radicalizing effect on some English appeasers, giving their social prejudices against Jews a racial edge.[426] But while appeasement did indeed come to appeal to the basest emotions, the character of that appeal largely shut out anti-Semitism itself. Appeasement meant servility in the face of real power, offering concessions from a position of weakness;[427] anti-Semitism, which is often false heroics in the face of illusory power, sat uneasily with it. And Neville Chamberlain himself was not an anti-Semite.[428]

There was immense institutional support for the policy of appeasement. It was not, however, a conspiracy, even though the members of the 'Cliveden Set'—a loose, pro-appeasement coterie of the influential and the powerful, grouped around Waldorf and Nancy Astor, and their country home, Cliveden—came to be regarded as conspirators. In 1937, the cartoonist David Low mocked them as the 'Shiver Sisters', their programme 'Any Sort of Peace at Any Sort of Price'. It is only at the margins of their activities that one comes across vocal anti-Semitism—in Nancy Astor's gift of mimicry, for example, which apparently extended to playing socially insecure Jewish businessmen (though she was hardly alone in that).[429] She was also, however, chronically suspicious of Jews; on occasions, the manner in which she voiced her suspicions encouraged people to think her slightly unhinged.[430] As late as in 1938, she was rebuking the Jews for their anti-Germanism, warning them 'not to allow themselves to be got at by the Communists as has too often been the case in the past'.[431] Her frequent outbursts against Jews often exceeded the quotidian anti-Semitism of her class. (Belloc may have been a bad influence on her in this respect.)[432] She was franker, for sure, at a dinner, commending Weizmann to the table, in his presence, as 'the only decent Jew I have ever met'. But she was also more gullible, swallowing whole the anti-Semitic fantasy of Jewish power, at the very time when all the evidence pointed in the other direction, to utter, hopeless, Jewish powerlessness. In New York, about to sail for England, she complained to reporters of 'the appalling anti-German propaganda here', and warning, 'If the Jews are behind [it], they've gone too far. And it will react on them.'[433] While these views were not incompatible with appeasement, they were not integral to it—or not, at least, in all its versions.

Appeasement became a degraded thing, from a tendency towards propitiation to utter defeatism.[434] The intensifying persecution of the Jews,[435] and the invasion of Czechoslovakia in breach of the Munich agreement, lost Germany most of its sympathy, leaving only the doughtiest pro-Germans to advocate the cause of 'peace'.[436] The day after Germany's invasion of Poland, the Tory anti-appeaser Duff Cooper ran into the Duke of Westminster, who 'began immediately to abuse the Jews' and 'rejoiced that we were not yet at war'. If war *did* come, it would be the Jews' fault—and Duff Cooper's.[437] This sat unhappily with newspaper coverage of the persecution of the Jews, especially given that the press was almost united in its condemnation.[438] Indeed, reports of pogroms, of street violence, of *Kristallnacht*, administered shocks to the public,

dislodging preconceptions, if not universally,[439] nor always for long enough
or with the best practical consequences. Reversions to pre-existing attitudes followed soon enough; the shocks did not seem to have any cumulative effect (*pace* Taylor), and accompanied a burgeoning sentiment of
anti-Semitism in England itself.[440]

The question of immigration

Broadly speaking, in the first half of the twentieth century, discussions in
England about immigration were discussions about *Jewish* immigration.
Legislation was framed with Jewish immigrants in mind. Prior to the 1905
Act, immigration control was within the executive power of the state—a
matter of the 'Royal Prerogative'.[441] The 1905 Act introduced port controls,
but was limited to groups travelling in steerage class. The poor, the sick, and
the criminal were to be denied admission. Immigrants were to be encouraged to regard England as a country of transit only. The 1914 Aliens
Restriction Act required foreign nationals to register with police, and
allowed for their deportation. The 1919 amending Act extended the 1914
Act's wartime emergency powers and added further restrictions, among
which was one that prohibited aliens from changing their names (s. 7(1)).
The Act was passed amid much discussion about 'Bolshevik sympathisers',
taken to be disproportionately Jewish in origin. In the twenty years that
followed, governments set immigration policy in part by reference to the
1919 Act and in part under their executive powers. The government
retained broad discretion on what immigrants, or what classes of immigrants
it would allow into the country.

Between 1933 and 1939, British policy changed several times. From the
Nazi accession to power until March 1938, and against an undertaking from
the Jewish community that refugees would not be a burden on the state,[442]
no specific restrictions on Jewish immigration were imposed. By the end of
this period, there were about 10,000 refugees in the country, and another
4,000 had re-emigrated. From March 1938 to November 1938 (*Kristallnacht*), a visa system was introduced, which significantly slowed down
the rate of arrival of immigrants. From November 1938 to the outbreak
of war, entry procedures were relaxed, on the ostensible understanding that
temporary refuge was being granted prior to re-emigration abroad.[443] In
September 1939, there were about 70,000 Jewish refugees, most of them
having arrived within the previous fifteen to eighteen months.[444] These
were not anti-Semitic policies, though the irrational fear that the refugees

would stimulate anti-Semitism and the indifference to Jewish suffering in Germany were sentiments that loitered, so to speak, in anti-Semitism's antechamber.

Certainly, among legislators and civil servants, there was some anti-Semitic sentiment, and much hard-heartedness.[445] The anti-Semitism, of course, substantially preceded 1933. Parliamentary debates on immigration even in the mid-1920s had an anti-Semitic colouring, with talk about 'hook-nosed patriots', 'alien revolutionary agitators', and so on.[446] A decade later, there were Conservative MPs ready to express their opposition to German-Jewish immigration in comparably anti-Semitic language: the Jews are 'clannish', they take the jobs of native Britons, their business practices are sharp, when not positively dishonest, every alien brought here displaces a British subject, and so on.[447] Among government ministers and civil servants, the concern was to ensure that the impact of Jewish refugees on English life was kept to a minimum. It was also assumed that there was a limit that it would not be safe to exceed, though this perceived national limit was usually not quantified as an actual figure. Civil servants in the Home Office, however, appeared to believe that the limit had been reached by the start of the war, and that offering even temporary refuge to Jews thereafter would have calamitous consequences.[448]

The press tended to combine condemnation of Nazi persecution with expressions of concern about the impact of refugees. Certainly, the persecution was not regarded as sufficient in itself to entitle the persecuted to a refuge in England (a sentiment shared by policymakers, however divided they may otherwise have been on the correct approach to the refugee problem).[449] 'Foreign Jews', complained the Daily Express, 'are overrunning the country.'[450] Public opinion was divided. Among those hostile to the Jewish immigrants, it became common in hostile circles to refer to 'refu-Jews'.[451] The more extravagantly hostile warned of the danger to the 'minds and morals' of 'Christian England', and pointed to an (imaginary) decline in newspaper standards.[452] The 'invasion' of these 'friendly aliens' was taken to be as dangerous an assault as the one threatened by Germany itself; they enjoy a 'regime of privilege'; in Golders Green, St John's Wood, and Hampstead (or 'St Johann's Wood, Finchley Strasse, and Britisch West Hampstead'), alien names had ousted British ones; the 'process of squeeze-out and muscle-in' was said to have begun.[453] It was this kind of sentiment, expressed at that time, that prompted Weitzmann to declare that for the six million Jews in East Central Europe the world was divided into places in which they were

not allowed to live and places to which they were not allowed entry.[454] At
11.00 a.m., all British visas granted to enemy nationals prior to the outbreak
of war automatically ceased to be valid. The Jews were trapped.[455]

World War II

Writing in 1942, I. Rennap observed that in the previous decade, anti-
Semitism in Britain had become a force 'seriously to be reckoned with', and
that since the outbreak of war, 'anti-Jewish feeling has spread further to an
alarming degree'.[456] Rennap was a Jewish member of the Communist Party,
and very ready to find the worst in a capitalist democracy. But his assessment
of the intensification of the problem can be trusted. 'Nearly everyone,'
concluded a wartime Mass Observation report, 'is latently somewhat anti-
Semitic.'[457]

Policy

This is not a history of the period, nor even a study of the formation of
particular policy decisions bearing on Jews (on which much has already
been written). My questions instead are the following: (a) what did Britain
do to aid the Jews, and (b) if not enough was done, to what extent was anti-
Semitism to blame? By 'aid' I mean facilitate the admission of Jewish
refugees either to Britain or British-administered Palestine, and intervene
in the killing process—often referred to as the 'bombing the railway lines to
Auschwitz' option. In summary, as to admission, there was successful
opposition to doing anything, or anything very much, from the Home
Office in respect of admission to Britain, and from the Foreign Office in
respect of Palestine. And there was cross-departmental opposition to admission at the Anglo-American Bermuda Conference convened in April
1943 to discuss Jewish refugees. As to interventions in the killing process,
there was successful opposition to intervention in the killing process from
the military planners. Given all this, then, the second question arises. To
what extent was anti-Semitism to blame?

There was one good, credible argument advanced in support of non-
admission and/or non-intervention, and that was that nothing should be
done to impede victory. Government policy was to win the war, and that
meant not diverting resources to any other end. Call this the 'supremacy
of prosecuting the war' argument. Weizmann wrote to Lord Halifax in
November 1939, protesting about the bar on entry to Palestine 'at a time

when almost two million Polish Jews are completely crushed under the Nazi occupation regime'. Halifax replied, 'we are putting our whole energy into a life-and-death struggle with Nazi Germany, the persecutor of Jews in Central Europe, and by ridding Europe of the present German regime we hope to render a supreme service to the Jewish people'.[458] Bombing of the camps would have killed the prisoners; bombing of the railway lines would have meant only minor disruption. Any such bombing represented a diversion of military equipment and personnel to non-military purposes. Some historians concur, at least in relation to the bombing of the railway lines. Martin Gilbert, for example, argues that the Nazi killing machine had the power and the will to continue behind German lines until Germany itself was overrun.[459] The supremacy of prosecuting the war argument was misused, however, when advanced as a blanket justification for inaction. For example, notwithstanding that it was evident within months of the outbreak of war that the anticipated support from Palestinian Arabs was not forthcoming, ships containing illegal Jewish immigrants were turned back, with disastrous consequences for the passengers. The *Salvador* sank on 12 December 1940, and over 200 refugees drowned. The *Struma* sank on 24 February 1942 with one survivor out of more than 750 passengers.

Of course, there were also positively bad arguments, principal among them that the Jews should not be treated as a special case and, relatedly, that nothing should be done to increase domestic anti-Semitism. The Jews were to be regarded as nationals of existing states. To treat them as members of a distinct Jewish nationality would merely play into the hands of 'the extreme Zionist campaign', a civil servant warned.[460] It might even encourage the view that war was being fought on behalf of Jewish interests.[461] It would be wrong to give them preferential treatment.[462] This was a failure of imagination, a failure to understand that because the Nazis were singling out the Jews, it was appropriate for the Allies to do so as well. A failure of a different order was involved in the assumption that aiding Jews would cause anti-Semitism. Even if there was a risk of this, why not take it?[463] It was taken for granted that an increase in Jewish immigration would cause anti-Semitism, that this anti-Semitism was already at a dangerous level and could get worse, that it could not be combated, and was a sufficient reason to keep Jews out of Britain. In September 1942, for example, Herbert Morrison, the Home Secretary, explained that if more Jews were allowed in, it might 'stir up an unpleasant degree of anti-Semitism (of which there is a fair amount just below the surface), and that would be bad for the country and for the Jewish community'.[464] Whenever the admission of refugees was considered, the argument was made that there were signs of an increase in anti-Semitism at home, the fear of fostering anti-Semitism thereby oddly leading to the adoption of policies injurious to Jews. Among the other bad ('demonstrably false')[465] arguments deployed to justify inaction, the argument that the risk of infiltration by Nazi spies counted against a more generous admissions policy was much heard,[466] as was the argument that the RAF did not have the purely technical ability to disrupt the killing process in the death camps.[467]

In addition to both good and bad arguments, there was also heartlessness, in full. When the *Salvador* sank, the head of the Refugee Section of the Foreign Office noted: 'There could have been no more opportune disaster from the point of view of stopping this traffic.'[468] Jewish children from Vichy France were denied admission to Britain in 1942, when deportation to Poland was the known, certain alternative. 'It seems to me wrong', asserted the most senior civil servant at the Home Office, 'to support bringing children into this country at present.'[469] Historians reading through the civil servants' memoranda have assembled the most incriminating notes. 'What is disturbing is the apparent readiness of the new Colonial Secretary to take Jewish agency sob-stuff at face value.' 'The Jews have spoilt their case by laying it on too thick for years past.' 'A disproportionate amount of the time of this [Foreign] Office is wasted on dealing with these wailing Jews.'[470] This was a heartlessness that played to stereotypical conceptions of Jews, inevitably. 'Jewish leaders would be well advised to face realities,' wrote a Conservative MP to *The Times*, 'and not to seek to over-exploit sympathies aroused by Nazi beastliness at a time when Jews are not alone in suffering wrongs...'[471] When assessing the situation in Occupied Europe, one had to 'allow for the customary Jewish exaggeration'.[472] During the 19 May debate, a government minister quoted Macaulay on the effect of distress on the human mind. It 'makes even wise men unstable, unreasonable, credulous, eager for immediate relief, heedless of remote consequences'.[473] William Cavendish-Bentinck, chairman of the Joint Intelligence Committee, on 27 August 1943, wrote: 'The Poles, and to a far greater extent the Jews, tend to exaggerate German atrocities in order to stoke us up.'[474] 'The Jews have no sense of humour, and no sense of proportion', a Colonial Office civil servant complained, in 1940.[475] Jewish protest could safely be disregarded. As a matter of *realpolitik*, certainly, the Jews' support could be taken for granted. They did not have to be accommodated. 'When it comes to the point,' noted a civil servant, 'the Jews will never hamper us to put the Germans on the throne.'[476]

We are approaching the question of anti-Semitism. But pause. The leaders of Anglo-Jewry were anxious to demonstrate their commitment to the greater good; they did not want to be seen as focusing on 'narrow' Jewish interests alone. And when they failed, as they mostly did, to convince the authorities to come to the aid of Europe's Jews, they were themselves not inclined to regard their failure as the product of anti-Semitism.[477] Lewis Namier, for example, having failed to persuade a Colonial Office official to allow Rumanian immigrants into Palestine, concluded that it was because of 'mere official reservations and not expressions of ill-will or indifference'.[478] Churchill was sometimes readier to name as anti-Semitic official obstructiveness. Writing to Lord Cranbourne in July 1942 on the subject of a specifically Jewish military force to fight as part of the Allied armies (which he supported, but which the War Office and the Colonial Office opposed):

> The strength of opinion in the United States is very great, and we shall suffer in many ways there by indulging the British military authorities' and Colonial Office officials' bias in favour of the Arabs and against the Jews. Now that these people are in direct danger, we should certainly give them a chance to defend themselves. . . . It may be necessary to make an example of these anti-Semitic officers, and others in high places. If three or four of them were recalled and dismissed, and the reasons given, it would have a salutary effect.[479]

On the very day that Namier was at the Colonial Office pleading for the Romanian refugees, the prime minister was writing to a friend warning him 'against drifting into the usual anti-Zionist and anti-Semitic channel which it is customary for British officers to follow'.[480]

Yet *was* there anti-Semitism? It seems reasonable to find anti-Semitism in expressions of hostility towards Jews; when Jewish suffering was denied, minimized or dismissed; when rescue action could have been taken within stated policy, but was not taken; when patently bad arguments were used to justify policies injurious to the Jews; when Jews were regarded as no less Britain's enemies than the Germans, because of Zionist sentiment in Palestine;[481] or where credible witnesses found anti-Semitism. Examples abound. Anthony Eden, the Foreign Secretary, was 'immovable on the subject of Palestine', his private secretary wrote, because 'he loves Arabs and hates Jews'.[482] The director of Internment Operations was apt to indulge 'in a tirade against refugees, Jews and voluntary agencies'.[483] A Foreign Office civil servant deprecated propaganda reports on Nazi crimes against Jews as the 'air for the Jew String'.[484] Yet it also seems fair to conclude with Michael Marrus that anti-Semitism was not decisive in blocking aid to the Jews.[485] It stemmed instead from what Bernard Wasserstein describes as the 'limited horizons of bureaucratic thinking',[486] which Martin Gilbert in turn casts as 'the principle of non-obligation'.[487]

Domestic sentiment

'It is a matter of common knowledge', wrote Harold Laski in the *New Statesman* in 1943, 'that anti-Semitism has grown significantly in Britain during the war.'[488] The claim that the Jews had promoted the war itself did not survive for long, and most of the evidence suggests that only dedicated fascists and fascist-sympathizers tended to believe it.[489] (They were responsible for the anti-Semitic scribbling over government propaganda posters, 'Your courage; Your cheerfulness; Your resolution; Will bring JEW Victory', and the anti-Semitic graffiti on walls and in railway carriages, 'Jews War', 'This is a Jewish war', 'Get rid of the Jews', 'Smash the Jewish press and the peace is yours', 'Smash Jews shops', 'P.J.' or 'Perish Judah', etc.)[490] But there were more minor, though offensive, allegations repeatedly made against Jews throughout the hostilities—principally, that a disproportionate number of Jews were cowards and/or black-market racketeers and profiteers. That is to say, Jews were accused of being army shirkers, overstayers in air-raid shelters, and voluntary refugees from London, and of trading in unregulated goods and overcharging for scarce goods.

Though the bombing of London in the second year of the war led many of the city's inhabitants to leave for safer destinations, rumours circulated among those who stayed that a disproportionate number leaving were Jews (they were the ones who 'fled first and fastest'). Those that stayed were said to sit all day in air-raid shelters. A correspondent of the *Hackney and Kingsland Gazette*, a local North London newspaper, wrote in: 'From personal observations, I should say that 90 per cent of those who recline nightly on Tube platforms are of the Jewish persuasion... Besides males with black patriarchical beards, the observer cannot fail to detect a considerable number of robust and obviously well-nourished men.'[491] There is a deliberately 'educated' tone adopted here; the reference to well-nourished men alludes both to shirkers and black marketeers. George Orwell went to investigate the rumour about aid raid shelters: '*Not* all Jews, but I think a higher proportion of Jews than one would normally see in a crowd of this size. What is bad about Jews is that they are not only conspicuous, but go out of their way to make themselves so.'[492] The Board of Deputies undertook an investigation into whether Jews were guilty of crowding into the air-raid shelters and underground tube stations. A non-Jew was appointed, and found (wrote the then president of the Board) that 'in those districts where Jews lived in large numbers they behaved just as well as the British people as a whole'.[493] There were also allegations that Jews were under-represented in the armed forces, reprising similar allegations made during World War I.[494] The journalist Douglas Reed, writing in 1942, claimed that he had seen in Sussex 'a community of Jews down from London', that 'the men seem exempt from war service' and 'the women wear expensive mink coats'.[495] In summary, it was said that the Jews were physical cowards; that they lacked the selflessness to volunteer their lives to a cause that offered them no chance of profit; and that they were incapable of military discipline. 'Windy Yids', dockers jeered early on in the war at a civil defence unit made up mainly of Jews.[496]

A disproportionate number of Jews were also said to be black-market racketeers. Many were identified as Jews simply on the basis that they had 'Jewish names'. The defamation was disseminated by literature, leaflets, whispering campaigns, and letters to the press; it was, it has been argued, the most important element in English wartime hostility to Jews.[497] Black marketeers and profiteers were seen as closely related. The *Daily Mirror* columnist, 'Cassandra', attacked alleged Jewish trading malpractices. A privately printed circular alleged that Jews were going round farms buying chickens and eggs for sale at inflated prices in London.[498] It was often also said that the reported convictions of Jews for economic crimes were only a fraction of total convictions, 'because some suppressive influence seems to intervene'.[499] The Board of Deputies undertook an investigation, and found that the numbers of Jews and non-Jews prosecuted for black-market offences were proportionate to the numbers of Jewish and non-Jewish traders as a whole.[500] People were, of course, ambivalent about the black market. On the one hand, it represented a source of supply of goods that otherwise would not have been available, and there was irritation at what was perceived as the fussy, bureaucratic regulation of rationing. On the other hand, the black marketeers themselves were disliked—they exploited scarcity; they favoured those who could afford their goods over those who most needed them; they were making money while others were dying. Lewis

Namier's mordant remark catches the complicity of anti-Semitism with just this ambivalence: 'It's not the black market that gives Jews a bad name, it's Jews who give the black market a bad name.' By 'Jews', of course, he meant 'anti-Semitism'.[501] The quickest way to make a thing unpopular, a wartime observer noted, was to call it Jewish.[502] In conformity with the Board's partial adoption of anti-Semitic accusations, at a public meeting, a Board spokesman condemned the 'many weak and wicked Jewish traders attracted to the black market'.[503]

In addition to these, Laski listed others: the Jews fill the air with protests against their misfortunes, they lack a sense of proportion, they lack dignity, they are over-insistent about their own tragedy at a time of general supreme tragedy; they irritate ministers because they complicate our relations with the Arabs; they irritate social workers because they do not fit into the formulae applicable to the general population; they irritate landladies and hoteliers, businessmen and administrators, with their demands and their expectations; they are noisy, pushy, attention-seeking, and so on, and so forth. But against these accumulating complaints (which, granted, often were no more than grumbles), there is also evidence of a certain restraint shown by some people at least, one that derived from a new understanding of the lethal nature of anti-Semitism. It was not so much the sense that the mildest remarks could 'lead to' murderous actions (though David Low's celebrated wartime cartoon made just this point), but rather that such remarks were no longer appropriate in the context of actions laying waste to whole communities. Elias Canetti, in Amersham during the war, was present on a private occasion when an anti-Semitic remark was made by a Romanian émigré. It took the form of a 'Jewish joke, but so dressed up that I could not be directly offended'. Such remarks had not been made in his presence before, and never were by any Englishmen or women of his acquaintance, 'because [it was understood that] there was a war on against people who behaved like that'.[504]

How to make sense of anti-Semitism in this wartime period? In the East End, it has been suggested, adversity created harmony. Although anti-Semitism did not disappear, it was never more than a local phenomenon, and directed at individuals rather than Jewry as a whole. Drawing a balance sheet of Jewish–Gentile relations is always difficult and also a dangerous pursuit. Generalizing even about an area or a town is hard enough, given the diversity of human responses. Applying this on a national scale becomes near impossible. Nevertheless, it would appear that there was a general fixation on matters Jewish. Several phases in English wartime anti-Semitism have been identified. In the first months, low morale led to hostility towards Jews; there was a certain amount of defeatist anti-Semitism, but it did not amount to a serious threat to the Jewish community. Between April and August 1940, a panic about the existence of a 'fifth column' ('refuspies') in England generated a xenophobia damaging to Jewish refugees, and dismaying to Jews in general. Anti-Semitism thus increased somewhat, though not to any dangerous level. Through 1941 and into 1942, food and other shortages provided the context for the emergence of rumours about Jewish black-market activities, and profiteering. Anti-Semitism was said to be at its highest level across this period, although it was contained by news of the genocidal turn taken by the Nazi persecutions. Thus it was in early 1943 that the Jewish community became most concerned about the danger of domestic anti-Semitism; but thereafter their concern receded, though it revived in November 1944, when Lord Moyne was assassinated in Palestine by the dissident Zionist group, *Lehi*. Government fears of domestic anti-Semitic discontent never materialized. 'There is', George Orwell wrote mid-way through the war, 'a certain amount of antisemitism. One is constantly coming on pockets of it, not violent, but pronounced enough to be disquieting. The Jews are supposed to dodge military service, to be the worst offenders on the Black Market etc. etc. I have heard this kind of talk even from country people who had probably never seen a Jew in their lives.' 'But,' Orwell added, 'no one wants actually to *do* anything to the Jews.'[505] It was part of the texture of everyday life,[506] not a mobilized sentiment, liable to be translated into action.

In a contribution in the last year of the war to a 'symposium' on the future of the Jews, Edward Hulton (1906–88), the founder of the pioneering illustrated newspaper, *Picture Post*, asked the question, is anti-Semitism growing in Britain today? 'It is growing somewhat at the moment', was his answer. He offered three reasons. Though Hitler is our enemy, a certain amount of what he has said about the Jews has 'stuck'; some 'not very desirable' Jewish refugees 'have upset the British people'; strong feelings of patriotism have led to questions being asked about foreign Jewish contributions to the war effort. 'Well-established Jews in Britain', Hulton recommended, should 'exert themselves to the full to keep their people up to the highest standards'. A 'powerful new Jewish organisation' is required for this purpose, 'a kind of self-disciplinary body, like the Law Society'. The Jews 'must decide upon the most meticulous observation of the social contract'.

Hulton went on to deprecate the Zionist solution. It is a counsel of despair; the land is too small and meagre in resources ever to become a genuine independent state; establishing a Jewish state would be an injustice to the Palestinian Arabs.[507] Hulton had been a member of the 1941 Committee, a group of progressive politicians, publishers, novelists, journalists, and other public figures, who met to discuss the efficient prosecution of the war and the principles of post-war reconstruction. During the war, Hulton provided the initial funding for the Home Guard training school, and briefly organized the private supply of weapons from the USA. He welcomed the 1945 Labour government.[508] Hulton was perhaps typical of nobody other than himself, but it is tempting to find in the views of this liberal-minded Englishman—a genuine concern about anti-Semitism, a conviction that there was (so to speak) something in it, and the recommendation that it be addressed, at least in part, by Jewish self-policing—a certain perspective representative of his time and class.

Post war

A crime novel published in 1945, *Death in Duplicate*, related the life and death of the Jewish master criminal and moneylender, Isaac Levant, the mystery of his violent end solved by the intrepid Detective Inspector McCarthy. Levant, or 'Sleek Ikey', is the 'controlling brain, the evil genius' behind a criminal conspiracy; he has a 'strange power over women'; he is like 'a vicious animal, scenting blood', a 'cold, deadly, slimy thing', 'more than enough to make an honest man cough blood'. His violent murder is 'just retribution'.[509] What inferences may be drawn from the fact that such a work could appear in the last year of the war—and, indeed, be reprinted by demand within months of first publication? Perhaps that its author, John G. Brandon, was a complaisant anti-Semite eager to meet the demands of a substantial, equally anti-Semitic readership; perhaps that the conventions of crime genre fiction are so strong that they will generate novels with Jewish villains even in the very year of the liberation of the death camps. This doubly overstates, but there is something in each inference. In any event, *Death in Duplicate* somewhat gives the lie to the common belief that the Nazi persecution, especially in its final, genocidal stage, made anti-Semitism in England impossible.[510] Indeed, one could compile a *sottisier* of anti-Semitic remarks made, and passages from books published, in the initial post-war years. I offer three examples.

First, five years after the end of the war and the liberation of the death camps, a highly praised work of literary criticism, *The Novel in France*, noted the Jews' 'pronounced characteristic' of 'rootlessness', and observed of one of the main characters in Proust's *À la Recherche du Temps Perdu*, '[Swann] shares with Marcel himself a tendency—it is another very unpleasant racial characteristic—to regard women as a "commodity" which has its price...'[511] The author, Martin Turnell, was born in 1908, read Modern Languages and English Literature at Cambridge, qualified as a solicitor, did his war service on the Continent in the Intelligence Corps, and for many years worked at the BBC. *The Novel in France* was published by a well-known house, Hamish Hamilton, and then published in paperback by Penguin in 1962. It remained in print for many years.

Second, and appearing in the same year as Turnell's work, the popular historian Sir Charles Petrie published his autobiography, *Chapters of My Life*. Petrie (1895–1977) recalled his early years in Liverpool where his father was the local leader of the Conservative Party. 'There were many Jews in the city, but there was no anti-Semitic feeling', he wrote. 'No one would have dreamed of objecting to men like Alderman Louis Cohen on the score of their race or religion.' Petrie had been an appeaser, and was also for a time a member of Oswald Mosley's January Club—described by one historian of the period as a 'Blackshirt front organisation'. Mosley failed, according to Petrie, because his 'continued flirtation with Hitler and Mussolini' caused his movement to be regarded as 'something not far removed from a conspiracy'. In addition, 'there was grave mistrust among the more sober-minded of the implications of his anti-Semitic policy'. And then, in the blandest manner imaginable, Petrie comments, 'It is true that the Jewish problem is a very real one, and it is not to be solved by ignoring it.' Mosley's problem was merely that his 'attitude' towards it 'did him much more harm than good'.[512]

Third, in 1951, the literary critic and scholar M. C. Bradbrook published *Shakespeare and Elizabethan Poetry*, in which she made certain observations on *The Merchant of Venice*, including the following on the likely influences on Shylock's disposition:

> The present generation has been taught by bitter examples that persecution breeds criminals, and sometimes criminals of so violent and perverted a nature that their only end, in a world that does not believe in the efficacy of forcible baptism, would seem to be despair. The concentration camps of Nazi Germany bred many heroes and martyrs, but also a few Shylocks.[513]

This is *so* incoherent that it seems to fail even the test of coherence required to qualify as anti-Semitic. But by collapsing an imputed vengefulness into murderous criminality, Bradbrook recycles an anti-Semitic commonplace; in the sheer tactlessness of her observation, she displays considerable insensitivity to very fresh Jewish suffering.[514]

Noel Annan was wrong, then, when he reported that after 1945 'it became bad form and was regarded as disgusting to talk in a derogatory way about Jews...The kind of anti-Semitic remarks common enough among Keynes's and Harold Nicolson's circles disappeared.'[515] For sure, in these first post-war years there was a somewhat greater sensitivity to the consequences of anti-Semitism than had been generally in evidence in the 1930s, but this sensitivity was not especially reflective, and, in certain respects, the sense that Britain had fought a good war against the Jews' genocidal enemies even encouraged a certain freedom to speak ill of Jews, either out of resentment at what was perceived as the absence of due Jewish gratitude or in the confident belief that the right to speak thus had been earned in consequence of the war effort itself. Hitler did not make anti-Semitism impossible.[516]

Within the general context of modern English anti-Semitism, there are three noteworthy post-war anti-Semitic passages worthy of recording, the final years of the Mandate, the trajectory of the fascist and Far Right parties in the 1950s and 1960s, and the controversy over the War Crimes Act 1991. Given the visibility of Israel in the contemporary period, it is noteworthy that the Suez Affair did not precipitate any fourth anti-Semitic episode. Indeed, Israel's role was barely remarked on by opponents of the military adventure. The historian Michael Howard, for example, writes of his 'anguish' at the time: 'It was not so much that the affair marked the end of Britain as a Great Power: it marked our end as a *good* power, one that could normally be expected to act honourably.' He contrasts Munich and Iraq—'understandable if deplorable acts of *realpolitik*', in contrast with the 'sheer irrationality' of the Suez adventure. But Israel's role does not figure in his assessment.[517]

The founding of the State of Israel

Relations between the British government and the Yishuv, seriously damaged by the 1939 White Paper, deteriorated still further during the war. Affronted by Jewish anger at British policy, and the steps taken by the Jewish Agency to frustrate it, the colonial administrators resorted to

increasingly abusive language when describing the Zionists, often comparing them to the Nazis. In his reports to London, the High Commissioner,
Sir Harold MacMichael, referred to the Jewish Agency as a 'Zionist juggernaut', a '*Todt* organisation', and pursuing the objective of a 'national
socialist state'.[518] In 1945, the then Director Of Education, Jerome Farrell,
complained of the Zionists' 'intellectual pride and political intolerance',
noting in a memorandum on Mandate education policy, 'the ideological
resemblance between Zionism and Nazism is becoming more marked'. And
later: 'Judaism is now a neotheism which leads to that racial self-worship
which Albert Rosenberg [*sic*] borrowed from the Jews for Nordic ends.'[519]
Of course, there were Zionists more than ready to return the compliment,
describing the British in Palestine as no better than, or successors to, the
Nazis.[520]

And then, during the three years between the end of the war and the
founding of the Jewish State, relations broke down completely. An unofficial state of war came into existence between the various Zionist paramilitary organizations and the Mandate administration, one that was marked by
acts of terror and of collective punishment. Violent incidents in Palestine
resonated in Britain. The blowing up of the King David Hotel, the location
of the secretariat of the Mandatory Administration and the British Army, on
22 July 1946, and the hanging and booby-trapping of two British NCOs in
July 1947, led to riots against Jews, and damage to Jewish property, in parts
of London, Liverpool, and Manchester, and elsewhere.[521] Synagogues were
damaged, Jewish shop windows were smashed, and cemeteries were desecrated. British Jews were everywhere suspected of 'dual loyalties'. The
British Foreign Secretary, Ernest Bevin, told the American Secretary of
State that the execution of the soldiers 'would never be forgotten', and that
'anti-Jewish feeling in England was now greater than it had been in a
hundred years'.[522] After the booby-trapping, recalled the then government
minister Hugh Dalton, 'I went absolutely cold towards the Jews in Palestine,
and didn't care what happened to them in their fight with the Arabs.'[523] In
the month following the hangings of the soldiers, editorials appeared in a
provincial newspaper condemning the Anglo-Jewish community. The first
of them rejoiced that 'only a handful of Jews bespoil the population of our
borough', and contentedly accepted the anticipated characterization of this
'outburst' as 'anti-Semitic' ('it is intended to be'). It continued by complaining that the Jews were 'the worst black market offenders', and urging
them to 'use their ill-gotten wealth' to 'dissuade' their American 'brothers'

from giving money to help 'European Jewish scum' immigrate to Palestine. It concluded:

> There is a growing feeling that Britain is in the grip of the Jews. There are more Jewish MPs than at any time in British history ... the Jews, indeed, are a plague on Britain ... Violence may be the only way to bring them to the sense of their responsibility to the country in which they live.

A subsequent editorial defended the first one. The newspaper proprietor, James Caunt was prosecuted for seditious libel, and accused by the prosecutor of seeking to stir race violence by promoting feelings of ill will and hostility between different classes of the King's subjects. He was speedily acquitted following a less than neutral summing-up by the judge.[524] In May 1948, the newspaper proprietor Esmond Rothermere was heard to observe that he 'had had the greatest difficulty in getting his *Daily Mail* people to write an article in support of the Jews or rather in criticism of our backing of the Arabs. They say that any such line would harm the paper, because of the strength of anti-semitism in the country.'[525] While old Nazi-sympathizers remained implacable in their opposition to Zionism,[526] the political journalist John Simpson writes more generally of the 'almost Nazi-like anti-Semitism in Britain' during this time.[527]

Relations between Britain and the United States were also put under strain by events in Palestine. The Labour administration was indignant at what it perceived as American interference, which it attributed to the power of the American Jewish vote. It flatly rejected the 1946 American proposal to admit 100,000 refugees into Palestine. (The notion, now current, that Israel was established in consequence of Western guilt about the Holocaust is fatuous.) The government minister most angered by the Americans was Ernest Bevin. He was in control of British policy on the Mandate; it was 'his' policy, and he interpreted challenges to it as challenges to his authority. Whoever disagreed with him was his enemy.[528] He liked to say of Palestine in his early days as Foreign Secretary, 'If I don't get a settlement, I'll eat my hat',[529] but in the end, he merely blamed the Jews, or 'international Jewry'.[530] According to Richard Crossman, 'it was the stubborn refusal of the Yishuv to be grateful for his protection and to conform to the plans he had made for them that finally tipped him into overt antisemitism'. What is more, 'nothing could shake his *idée fixe* that the British position in the Middle East was threatened by a Jewish–Communist conspiracy'.[531]

Bevin appeared to believe that the Zionists would ally with Stalin against British imperial interests once they had gained statehood. 'I am sure [the Russians] are convinced that by immigration they can pour in sufficient indoctrinated Jews', he wrote, 'to turn [Palestine] into a communist state in a very short time.' And he added, 'The New York Jews have been doing [the Russians'] work for them.'[532] He was worried, according to Wm. Roger Louis, that the Jews would damage his relations with both the Arabs and the Americans.[533] At a London embassy party in June 1948, Harold Nicolson reported Bevin remarking as follows: 'Nobody is going to tell him that in principle it does not pay better to remain friends with 200 million Moslems than with 200 thousand Jews, "to say nothing of the oil".'[534] But the anti-Semitism seems to have been there too—though his biographer, Alan Bullock, makes the best case for Bevin possible, observing that when the Foreign Secretary became the principal target for Zionist propaganda, identifying him with the Nazi image, he not unnaturally resented it.[535] Churchill, however, was ready to accuse Bevin of a 'very strong and direct streak of bias and prejudice': 'I do not feel any great confidence that he has not got a prejudice against the Jews in Palestine.'[536]

The question arises, is it indecent to deplore the anti-Semitic aspect to the response to the King David Hotel and Deir Yassin atrocities? On 22 July 1946, nearly one hundred people were killed, and about fifty were injured, when the Irgun, a dissident Jewish terrorist group, dynamited the hotel's south wing. The casualties comprised senior British and Jewish officials, and Arabs and other private individuals in the hotel at the time. It was the deadliest single act of terror so far in the Mandate's history. Everyone in the civil administration or army had a friend or acquaintance killed at the King David.[537] Just under two years later, between 9 and 11 April 1948, the Irgun perpetrated a massacre at the Arab village of Deir Yassin, killing between 100 and 120 villagers, mostly civilians (including many women and children), both in the course, and following the successful conclusion, of an assault upon the village. Deir Yassin had signed a non-belligerency pact with its Jewish neighbours and had barred entry to foreign irregulars. Benny Morris concludes that the 'dissident' Irgun members did not go in with the intention of committing a massacre, but 'lost their heads during the protracted combat'. It had from the outset, however, been their intention to expel the villagers. The massacre was immediately condemned by the mainstream Jewish authorities.[538]

Four days after the King David Hotel attack, General Sir Evelyn Barker, the
G.O.C. in Palestine, circulated a letter, marked 'Restricted', to his officers:

> The Jewish community cannot be absolved from the long series of outrages
> culminating in the blowing up of the Government offices in the King David
> Hotel, causing grievous loss of life . . . I am determined that they shall suffer
> punishment and be made aware of the contempt and loathing with which we
> regard their conduct. . . . I have decided . . . you will put out of bounds to all
> ranks all Jewish places of entertainment, cafés, restaurants, shops and private
> dwellings. No British soldier is to have any intercourse with any Jew . . .

Barker concluded, the army would thereby 'be punishing the Jews in a
way the race dislikes as much as any—by striking at their pockets'. The
letter did not remain private for very long. The Irgun printed it on posters.
In a Commons debate, a minister dissociated the government from Barker's
boycott instruction to his officers. Nonetheless, Barker affirmed his stance
several months later. It was not expressed in the emotion of the moment.
He wrote to an intimate correspondent, 'They do hate having their pockets
touched, as I said in my letter. I hope the Arabs will no longer think we are
afraid to hang Jews.' And in a still further letter, he wrote: 'these bloody
Jews. Yes I loathe the lot—whether they be Zionists or not. Why should we
be afraid of saying we hate them—it's time this damned race knew what we
think of them—loathsome people.' Before his departure, Barker urinated
on the soil of Palestine in a gesture of contemptuous disrespect.[539] As for
Deir Yassin, on 18 May 1948 the atrocity prompted Sir John Troutbeck, the
head of the British Middle East Office in Cairo, to describe it 'as a warning
of what the Jew will do to gain his purpose'. Later that year, he told Bevin
that the Americans were responsible for the creation of a gangster state
headed by 'an utterly unscrupulous set of leaders'.[540]

To return, now, to the question. Barker's and Troutbeck's responses
drew on familiar anti-Semitic prejudices. All Jews play their part in the
worst deeds of a few of them; Jews are greedy and materialistic, or self-
seeking and amoral. These are stock sentiments, and they therefore cannot
be respected as moral responses to immoral acts. It seems reasonable to
conclude that Barker was already an anti-Semite on 22 July 1946, and
Troutbeck, on 18 May 1948. If Barker's letter was 'written on the spur of
the moment', as Barker later claimed,[541] it was also written out of convictions long held. The atrocity gave him the opportunity to voice these
convictions in protected circumstances. Barker's instruction would have

punished many Jews innocent of even tacit support for the atrocity, let alone collusion with its perpetrators. He anticipated that it would also 'inflict some hardship on the troops'. It follows that his response was irrational and injurious. It can be deplored without qualifying censure of the atrocity itself. Likewise the remarks of Lieutenant-Colonel Richard Webb, following an attack on a roadblock that left two British soldiers dead, and ten wounded. 'These bloody Jews—we saved their skins in Alamein and other places and then they do this to us', he railed to journalists. They are a 'despicable race'. Remarks such as these did not emerge from a void. 'There was a lot of loose anti-Semitic talk among Army officers at parties', a British intelligence officer commented; another contemporary observer noted the 'rampant anti-Semitism among the British troops'.[542] There was also uncontrolled, retaliatory violence by deserters and other mavericks, including the bombing of the Jewish Agency complex on 1 March 1948. An offshoot of Mosley's British League of Ex-Servicemen claimed responsibility, quoting from the *Protocols*, and condemning the 'vile Jew', who intended to create 'a centre for international intrigue' under 'the cloak of Zionist ideals'.[543] Mosley himself tried hard during this time to exploit anti-Semitic tensions in London's East End, but with no real success.[544]

Fascism

After the war, fascism lingered on, a malign, minority pursuit, a kind of pernicious hobby for a few, utterly marginal types, mostly still in thrall to Nazism and the memory of the Führer—though some of the more realistic 'race nationalists' worried that overt Hitler-worship somewhat limited their electoral appeal.[545] The BUF's politics had become a political absurdity. Many BUF members hid their pre-war connection with Mosley, sometimes keeping their identity secret for the rest of their lives; others returned to worship at Mosley's feet; one or two engaged in random acts of terror against Jewish targets.[546] Far Right activists continued, at first, to be preoccupied with Jews, and spent much time deploring the Nuremberg Trials;[547] for a few decades, their attention shifted to New Commonwealth immigrants ('Keep Brixton White');[548] they now focus their incitements on Britain's Muslim populations. They have no political theory; they have few policies; they are mostly angry talk and violence, unredeemed by occasional invoking of Bellocian 'distributism', 'national revolution', 'folkish radicalism',[549] 'Racial-Nationalist Folk State',[550] and the doctrines of sociobiologists[551]—not to mention 'cultural revolution', 'racial and cultural heritage', 'the moral and spiritual sickness [of] Western civilisation', etc.[552]

In these post-war years, Mosley and his supporters laboured in denials of his anti-Semitism: 'Mosley's not anti-Jewish, the Jews are anti-Mosley', 'he doesn't hate Jews for what they are, only for what they do', etc.[553] He fought the 1959 election on one issue, London's West Indian community. He promised to close down the Black brothels, jail the black vice-kings, and protect the rights of white tenants. 'Deport them—in a humane, British way', Mosley would tell the small groups who gathered to hear him. And they would respond: 'Dirty niggers! Fucking spades! Baboons!' Hecklers would be met with cries, 'Jew-boy! Israel! Fucking Jew.'[554] In 1962, two Mosley supporters were convicted of public order offences for shouting 'Down with the fucking Jews' and 'Get out you Black bastards' at a rally in Bethnal Green. Ten years later, it was much more likely that they would be shouting only the latter slogan, and other slogans like it.[555] Anti-Semitism had become something of a minority taste among the members of Far Right groups,[556] while racist attacks on New Commonwealth immigrants acquired much greater salience. In the 1970s and 80s, the politics of the Far Right comprised the sum of two grievances, 'Black crime' and 'Jewish control';[557] now, the grievances relate to 'Islamic crime' and 'Jewish control'. In the 1950s and 60s, the talk was about 'Africans and Pakis', and 'Paki bashing', about the 'invasion' of 'our' country and 'immigration', and 'asylum seekers', about crime getting 'out of control', and about 'degeneracy', 'our people', and 'patriotism'. The smart talk now is of 'ZOG', of the 'New World Order', of 'World Government', of the 'survival of Western civilization', of 'free speech', of the 'Holohoax', of 'white Europeans', of the 'liberal establishment', of 'Zionists' rather than the 'ordinary Jew',[558] of 'international Zionism', the 'Zionist conspiracy', and the 'bandit state' of Israel. 'We are anti-Zionist and anti-Communist', declared a Far Right activist in 1974, 'We stand for race and nation.'[559] Much of this latter talk comes from the United States. 'White supremacism' is the stated goal.

The successors to the BUF periodically engaged and engage with parliamentary democracy, made and make opportunistic attempts to distance themselves from their fascist antecedents, had and have more or less intimate relations with paramilitary elements, and behind them, criminal elements.[560] They were and are monitored by the intelligence services and their activities were and are publicized by specialist journalists or *Searchlight* magazine. They were and are led by their ideological predisposition towards extra-parliamentary activities, and were and are limited by the Führer-complex of their leaders, and by the sectarianism that plagues all marginal groups. Theirs was and remains an anti-politics of violence and intimidation, of graffiti and anonymous leaflets, and provocative marches through 'minority' areas, all in the service of hopeless, ugly aspirations. In the first decades of the post-war period, the Far Right's preoccupations with 'repatriation' of British citizens of Afro-Caribbean descent, its 'Little England' hostility to the European Community, and its campaigns for the return of the death penalty, though calculated to broaden its appeal, failed to do so. The main political party of the Far Right, the BNP, has however recently enjoyed some modest electoral successes.

Anti-Semitic activity on the Far Right was and largely remains criminal in character, when not merely abusive ('the yids, the yids, we gotta get rid of the yids').[561] We know about it mainly because it figures in crime statistics and news stories. English anti-Semitism came to be considered during this period as a matter for the police. In 1962, for example, Colin Jordan, a leader of the National Socialist Movement, was charged with using insulting words likely to cause a breach of the peace. ('The 3 September [was] the blackest day in British history... Jews of the world rejoiced... our real enemies [are] world Jewry and its associates in this country';[562] 'We are National Socialists and we are anti-Jewish and we are proud of it.')[563] There was a spate of London synagogue burnings in the mid- to late 1960s for which neo-Nazi groups were held responsible. In March 1965, one synagogue was burned to the ground. In April, a synagogue was damaged by fire, and an arson attempt was made on another one. In June there were petrol bomb attacks on three further synagogues. In July, there were arson attempts on four synagogues, and serious fires at two others. In March 1966, there were petrol bomb attacks on a synagogue. Eighteen months later, there was a serious fire at a synagogue. In addition, there were arson attempts on several provincial synagogues and prayer houses, and a serious fire at a Jewish school in Manchester. All this activity was accompanied by swastikas on synagogue walls, broken synagogue windows, and gravestone desecrations.[564] Low-level anti-Semitic violence persisted. To take a representative, relatively recent year, in 2004, among other recorded serious assaults, a Southampton gang shattered a Jewish teenager's jaw and shouted anti-Semitic abuse at him, a North London synagogue was fire-bombed, swastikas and 'SS' insignia were daubed on gravestones at a Jewish cemetery, 'Happy Kristallnacht, Combat 18' and 'Jews Out' graffiti were painted on a doctor's surgery, and a Jewish organization in London received hate mail bearing swastikas and a booklet, 'The Holocaust. A Jewish Lie.'[565] From time to time, attempts are made by Far Right parties to 'tone down', or even disavow, their anti-Semitism. They complain that 'anti-Semitism' is 'simply a political smear word'; they embrace instead 'anti-Zionism'. They engage in what Michael Billig terms a game of 'peek-a-boo', deploying frankly anti-Semitic language at one moment, and then retreating into code words at the next moment.[566]

Consider the life of the career neo-Nazi, John Tyndall (1934–2005). He was a national serviceman, and then had various clerical jobs until becoming fully engaged in fascist politics. His admiration of Hitler ('Hitler was right') was the cause of some anxiety to fellow right-wingers, who regarded it as an electoral liability. He joined the League of Empire loyalists in 1956, founded the British National Party in 1960, then the British National Socialist Movement in 1962, and then the British National Movement. He was for a time in the 1960s deputy national organizer of Spearhead, and deputy commander of a private army modelled on the SA. He was leader of the National Front in the 1970s, and then the New National Front, which became the British National Party. He was expelled, reinstated, expelled. Spearhead disappeared as a party but continued as a monthly magazine, which Tyndall continued to edit until his death. He was jailed in 1966 for possession of offensive weapons, jailed in 1986 for incitement of racial hatred, and was awaiting trial on further incitement charges when he died. 'The Jews'—this 'cancerous microbe'—were a life-long obsession. '[Their] removal from Britain must be a cardinal aim of the new order.' In later years, he tended to substitute coded references to 'Zionism', to deflect charges of racism. Tyndall believed that he was the chosen leader of a master race; he also regarded himself as an intellectual, and assumed the burden of 'synthesizing' the British fascist tradition.[567] This is a melancholy chronicle of a wasted, hating, ridiculous life.[568]

Overall, the activities of these groups and individuals counted for very little; they occupied the most marginal of presences in the post-war public imagination. So marginal, indeed, that it seems most accurate to think of them as altogether sealed off from everything that was mainstream and conventional in political life. This impression remains correct, I think, even on closer investigation. Yet what is one to make of the following, taken from a *Daily Telegraph* 'leader' appearing in 1983, on the occasion of the release of Home Office files on Mosley and his Fascist movement in the mid-1930s?

> Mosley's Fascist philosophy contained much with a strong appeal to the heirs of a number of British political traditions. He invoked the national spirit at a time when patriotism was weak; he attacked irresponsible capitalism and egalitarian socialism; even his opposition to the Jews (until it became palpably vulgar and brutal) struck a certain chord, for the Jews, by the very nature of their history, were thought (before the holocaust) to represent the cosmopolitan principle and to be associated, on the one hand, with international banking and, on the other, with international revolution.[569]

It is the evasions that count the most in this passage. It's not that Mosley was actually right, we are meant to understand, only that his philosophy had a 'strong appeal', his opposition to the Jews 'struck a certain chord', the Jews were 'thought to represent', etc. But the implication remains that there was something valuable in Mosley's position, one with which the *Telegraph* wished to associate itself. Not altogether sealed off, then.

War Crimes Act 1991

The historian David Cesarani has written authoritatively on this topic. In the immediate post-war years, the British government recruited Eastern Europeans in Displaced Persons ('DP') camps to address a chronic domestic labour shortage. These were known as European Voluntary Worker ('EVW') schemes. Among these immigrants were many who had fought for the Nazis; within that number, there were many who had committed war crimes. That this was so was a matter of indifference to the civil servants in charge of the schemes. (For example: an entire Ukrainian *Waffen-SS* division was brought to England from Italy in 1947.) They lived undetected for many years, until a campaign to bring them to justice was launched. A group of Jewish and non-Jewish public figures, mainly Members of Parliament, led the campaign. It required legislation making some slight, technical adjustments to existing criminal law. (Opponents of the measure maintained that it criminalized actions that were not criminal when committed—the so-called 'retrospective legislation' objection.) By the time the campaign was won, and further obstacles were overcome, only two prosecutions were possible. One was abandoned in January 1997 because of the defendant's ill-health; in the other, the defendant was convicted on 1 April 1999 on two counts of murder.

There are two elements in this story relevant to the concerns of the present chapter.

First, the principle of selection back in 1946–8 was itself anti-Semitic. It was not just that Jewish DPs were unwelcome; they were consistently excluded from all the labour recruitment schemes. This was poorly concealed in self-contradictory formulations:

> there will be no discrimination on grounds of nationality ... *but* for the time being, the Ministry of Labour wants to concentrate on certain national- ities ... [italics added]

And:

> [we should] recruit from the whole body of DPs without regard to nationality, *except that* we should exclude Jews and Polish men because of the opposition from public opinion at home, and persons whom we acknowledge to be Soviet citizens, because of the certainty of trouble with the Soviets if we recruit such people. [italics added]

The reason given was fear of stimulating anti-Semitism ('a real risk of a wave of anti-semitic feeling in this country', noted a Cabinet Minute); an un- acknowledged further reason was anti-Semitism itself. The assumption that the very presence of Jews causes Jew-hatred is itself anti-Semitic—it amounts to nothing other than the proposition, 'to know the Jews is to hate them'. To warn of an increase in anti-Semitism can sometimes be a tactic of anti-Semites:[570] in effect, 'efforts to help Jews are exposing them to hostility, so stop helping them'. Of course, anti-Semites do not have a monopoly on such opinions, which can in any event be disguised in ostensibly neutral or even sympathetic formulations—say, regarding the need to maintain public order, or to serve the best interests of the existing Jewish population, etc. In fact, however, the policy of limiting Jewish immigration was but one aspect of post-war English anti-Semitism, and took its place alongside other aspects—the anti-Jewish riots of 1947, the local but intense public agitation for the repatriation of Jewish refugees, certain reservations expressed regarding the fairness of the Nuremberg trials, the vigorous campaign against the Jewish method of animal slaughter, and the renewal of wartime allegations against Jews of financial impropriety.

Secondly, and four decades later, the political opposition to the war crimes campaign was largely couched in anti-Semitic terms. The cam- paigners, their political and media opponents claimed, placed revenge above justice—certainly, above mercy. Their 'search for vengeance' was unseemly. Their values were 'Jewish' and 'alien', rather than 'Christian' and 'British'. Their demand for a 'specially-made law', one that would lead to the staging of 'show trials', was 'revolting to most British Christians'. Was there not something distasteful, it was asked, about the activities of 'Nazi hunters', still more 'international Nazi-hunters and their assorted sympathizers'? They were 'zealots', 'merciless', and 'motivated by hatred and revenge'. Their 'fanaticism' and 'thirst for vengeance' were 'unappeasable'. The 'culture of revenge seems to be at the heart of all Jewish or at least Israeli philosophy'. Their actions would 'revive anti-Semitism'. The campaigners were well-organized, it was further said, and succeeded notwithstanding the actual merits of their case. These 'self-appointed Jewish activists' constituted a 'lobby', one that had as its ultimate object the protecting of Israel from attack. An MP warned, 'there is a powerful Jewish lobby in the media'. The lobby was motivated not by any sense of justice but by the opportunities for pro-Israel propaganda the campaign presented. The critics of the legislation themselves went on the attack against Israel. It was also possible to detect intimations of the blood libel. 'Nazi-hunting', declared a newspaper editorial, is the 'new and frankly distasteful blood sport'. 'Would we prosecute the Israeli soldier', one MP asked, 'who savagely beat to death a fifteen-year-old Palestinian boy if that soldier came to stay in this country?'[571]

Shechita

Of course, this 300-odd-year history cannot quite be parcelled into self-contained episodes. Take *shechita*, for example. *Shechita*, or the slaughter of animals in accordance with Jewish law, that is to say by an incision to the throat while the animal is conscious, has long received the attention of both anti-Semitic agitators and animal welfare activists. The agitators have seized upon the issue as a means of both broadening their appeal and giving credibility to their most lurid allegation, the blood libel or 'ritual murder' (*shechita* is commonly referred to as 'ritual slaughter').[572] Anti-*shechita* sentiments were a staple of Nazi propaganda; they are now a staple of neo-Nazi propaganda. That the Jews treat animals barbarically is evidence that they treat Gentiles, whom they are said to regard as no better than animals, in a like manner whenever possible.[573]

In England, *shechita* has been the subject of public debate for about 150 years, and organized Anglo-Jewry has been stalwart in its defence,[574] leading to complaints by both animal welfare organizations and anti-Semitic groups about the Jews' financial and political 'behind-the-scenes' influence.[575] Anti-*shechita* controversies arise only intermittently,[576] usually prompted by a public inquiry or the publication of a report by an animal welfare organization. These controversies mix animal welfare and anti-Semitic positions in various combinations. When *shechita* was first publicly reviewed, in the mid-nineteenth century, it was in the context of respect for, and defence towards, the sensibilities of Jews. The phrase 'ritual slaughter' was avoided and the more neutral 'Jewish mode of slaughter' was used.[577] Fifty years later, the phrases in general use were 'the Jewish method' and 'Jewish rules about slaughtering', similarly unexceptionable.[578] The chairman of the 1904 Admiralty Committee Inquiry addressed the president of the Shechita Board: 'we thoroughly recognise the fact that the Jews have every desire to slaughter their animals in a humane manner'.[579] But in a pamphlet published by the Humanitarian League in the same year as the Admiralty report (which itself decided against *shechita*), Judaism stood indicted: 'any religion whose observances cannot be reconciled with the modern standard of humanity stands self-condemned as a barbarous survival of barbarous times'.[580] Thereafter, and for many decades, anti-Semitic language figured markedly in anti-*shechita* campaigns, and anti-*shechita* activists became careless about the support they solicited. In overstating their case—for example, by over-praising the alternative to *shechita*, stunning prior to incision—they encouraged the implication that Jews are wantonly cruel.

The anti-Semitic component of anti-*shechita* agitation was especially strong in the 1930s and during the wartime years.[581] Pro-Nazi activists infiltrated both the Anti-Vivisection League and the Animal Defence Society; many pro-Nazi groups campaigned against *shechita*, and implied that Jews also practised the ritual murder of Gentiles.[582] Consider this passage from *Jewish 'Kosher': Should it be permitted to survive in a new Britain?*, a short book published in 1944:

> The infiltration of Jews into this country in the interval between the pamphlet's completion [May 1943] and the present time has been terrific ... assuming the victory of the Allies and the prospective, seething, stabilized increase in the British-Jewish population... the practice of Kosher [i.e., *shechita*]...will swamp that of the Humane Killer all over Europe.... the ancient infamy of the Kosher... the strangle-hold of the Jewish Rabbis [must be] relaxed... the further flooding clamouring Jewish millions... Slash at the tentacles of the

embedded monstrosity . . . the hush-hush policy—the sort of spider's web of conspiratorial silence lulling the mentally indolent and gullible into a cradle-song . . . 'The Jewish business is not slaughter—it's murder!' . . . the Jews enjoy our all-too-lavish hospitality . . . England made an infamous bargain, and sold the Innocents . . . There are sympathetic Jews, but they are ruled out by the powers which direct Jewish action . . . the profits of Shechita are important items to Jewish revenue . . . unless we awake in time to stem it . . . there will be a determined post-war attempt by powerful Jewish elements to rush universality of the Kosher method, by legislation.[583]

The author, Mary Dudley Ward, had close links with the Animal Defence Society and the RSPCA.[584] When, four years later, the RSPCA published its own pamphlet, *Legalised Cruelty*, it piously explained that it had in previous years refrained from campaigning against *shechita* for fear of exacerbating anti-Semitic sentiment: 'when Jewish slaughter was attacked for political (pro-Fascist) purposes, the Society scrupulously stayed aloof'. In the immediate aftermath of the war, however, self-restraint was abandoned, and the pamphlet attacked 'Jewish slaughter' with images of sinister-looking knife-wielding Jews and in the most lurid language ('persistent barbarity', 'barbarities', 'barbarous practices', 'the coming of the slaughterer with his knife', etc.).[585] Connections between 'ritual slaughter' and 'ritual murder' continued to be made, of course. In 1962, a Lincolnshire vicar wrote to the publisher Victor Gollancz protesting about *shechita*, and commented: 'Can you wonder that the Little St. Hugh legend arose in this diocese?'[586]

Throughout the 150-year history of anti-*shechita* campaigning in England, the animal welfare arguments have remained the same. The state may not play favourites among religions. Jews and Muslims should have the same right as everyone else to debate forms of slaughter. But they are not entitled to a veto on legislation. To privilege the opinions of non-scientists over scientists on the matter of animal welfare is irrational. The general public has a legitimate interest in the protection of animals from excessive suffering. Many Jews are likely to feel hard done by, and they will doubtless complain. But they will not have been treated unfairly if their case for exemption from the rule is based solely on religious practice. Nobody is bound to eat meat.[587] These arguments are in turn met with counter-arguments. The effect on the animal is marginal, and there is no compelling government interest in banning a marginally inferior practice (if that is what it is—many *shechita* advocates insist upon its humaneness). By contrast, the religious interest in practising that form of slaughter *is* compelling.[588] Throughout the same period, the anti-Semitic account of *shechita* has similarly remained the same. *Shechita* is a barbaric practice of a barbaric religion. The Jews are primitive and inhumane. Ritual slaughter derives from a 'slavish interpretation of Mosaic law'; it is 'sheer bloody murder'; 'Jews demand their grisly sacrifices'; it is an 'alien practice'; it 'offends against moral sense';[589] Jews are 'blood-thirsty' and 'blood-drinking' people;[590] they practice 'ritual throat-cutting' and 'flout our laws';[591] *shechita* is 'an alien custom';[592] it is 'distasteful and inappropriate in this country';[593] 'Jewish ritual slaughter, or call it ritual murder if you like'.[594] The language is tribal, *our* virtues celebrated in the execration of *their* vices. Great offence is taken, therefore, at the fact that meat rejected by the Jews as unfit for their own consumption is routinely sold to butchers serving the general public.[595]

To what extent did specifically anti-Semitic anti-*shechita* positions reflect broader social hostility to Jews? In continental Europe, it would seem, the correlation was quite close.[596] Until the late nineteenth century, for example, German animal protection campaigners paid little attention to *shechita*. Slaughterhouse reforms routinely exempted Jews; kosher butchering was allowed notwithstanding stunning laws. But then things changed. *Shechita* became controversial. It assumed a central place in the Reichstag debates of 1899 and 1900. It engaged the interest of a broad cross-section of the German middle-class. There was, inevitably, a small group of Jews who promoted universal stunning laws. Why such a radical enlargement of focus, and such a swift change from the indifferent to the actively hostile? The campaign against kosher butchering vibrated sympathetically with more general themes of the time: a concern with Jewish particularity and brutality, a desire to eradicate deviance from society, a longing to return to a 'utopian' past, and an anxiety concerning political, economic and social changes. The scientific character of the campaign and its widespread audience, indeed, lent respectability to these themes.[597] In England, by contrast, the correlation was slightly less close (though still related), because programmatic, politically activist anti-Semitism, always a minority pursuit, rarely resonated with the broader English public. Anti-*shechita* controversies tend to engage the attentions of no more than the two relevant groups, animal welfare campaigners and opportunist anti-Semites. Statements by campaigners or anti-Semites to the effect that *shechita* is opposed by a majority of the population should be viewed with caution, and in any event are difficult to assess.[598]

Reflections on the character of these moments

What conclusions can be drawn about modern English anti-Semitism—that is to say, the anti-Semitism of that long, 300-year-period, from the Readmission to the Six Day War?

To begin with, that it could be verbally aggressive, without ever endangering the lives or physical well-being of Anglo-Jewry. England was not a violent place for Jews. There was slander and abuse, and on occasion, intimidation too. But there was no terror, and no murder—this was an anti-Semitism 'with the boots off'.[599] Moreover, anti-Semitism tended to originate in civil society. There was no state-sponsored persecution, and only very few hostile legislative assaults;[600] politicians who took antagonistic positions towards Jews were rarely able to translate their hostility into law, even when they wished to do so (and that includes Cabinet ministers—say, Joynson-Hicks in the 1920s, and Bevin in the late 1940s). The Aliens Act did not achieve the anti-Semites' purpose. Jewish immigration had already passed its peak, and the bulk of the new arrivals were thereafter in any event admitted without inspection.[601] Though the *Jewish Chronicle* was right to fear that the announced Aliens Act in 1904 would foster 'an anti-Semitic sentiment under Government patronage',[602] these fears did not materialize. The Marconi Affair did not 'take off' precisely because state institutions held back; indeed, the then prime minister, H. H. Asquith, put the whole weight of the Liberal Party machine behind the Jewish accused.[603] The few financial scandals in the 1980s that involved Jews likewise lacked any real anti-Semitic resonance.[604]

Within civil society, hostility to Jews was not the province of any particular group or class. It was both diffuse and weak. It was also complicated by other sentiments. It was sometimes difficult to distinguish hostility to Jews from a more generalized hostility to foreigners.[605] One consequence was that there was little space for the development of a more vigorous, more actively malign anti-Semitism, led by coteries of dedicated Jew-haters. The crises did not lead to the birth of any anti-Semitic movements or collective mobilization against Anglo-Jewry. There was no substantial political party at war with the Jews—the British Union of Fascists, thoroughly unpleasant and menacing, was easily seen off, and never commanded serious support. Anti-Semitism remained essentially *unorganized*.[606] There was no developed, politically mobilized racial politics directed at Jews—which is not to say, in particular, that at moments of panic about Jewish immigration there were not paranoid fears of race-corruption. But at different times, anti-Semitism informed the politics of both Left and Right parties and groupings—the Left, during the last decades of the nineteenth century (Bulgaria, 'sweating', the Boer War), the Right during the first decades of the twentieth century (the pre-Great War financial scandals, the Bolshevik Revolution, inter-war fascism), while Left and Right made common cause against the Jews from time to time (say, immigration).

English anti-Semitism of a more than unreflective, habitual kind was limited in two distinct respects. First, it was mostly an aspect of a larger political anxiety or concern. Rarely was a hostile position to be explained solely by reference to anti-Semitism. Arguments about admission to the legislature, and earlier and later arguments about admission to the country, were mere deformations of deeper arguments about the nature of England. Was it to be singular or plural, Christian or multi-cultural? Was it a settled, established society, or a work in progress?[607] The plight of the Christian nations subject to the Ottomans, say, or the plight of the native workers of London's East End, were of independent concern. And anti-Semitism was not, in spite of what many Zionists suspected, the exclusive cause of British official hostility to Zionism; indeed, it often did no more than add 'colour' to a political view based as much upon traditional attitudes towards Arabs.[608] Secondly, anti-Semitism was dependent upon larger events, and in particular moments of political crisis, to sustain itself; it did not quite have the strength of appeal to subsist in the public sphere as a distinct, continuous theme in its own right. It would be a stretch to claim that anti-Semitism was an *ideological* constant in English political life. The intensity of anti-Semitic articles in England's Catholic press, for example, is broadly to be related to particular external events, rather than reflecting a constant Catholic obsession.[609] The combined effect of these limitations—implicated in larger concerns, only flaring up in moments of political crisis—was to deny to the minority of activist anti-Semites the opening for building an anti-Semitic movement.

Anti-Semitic charges and tropes were dynamic, circulating in the culture, available as a resource in new contexts. Though anti-Jewish scandals and controversies might pass without leaving a mark (the Jew Bill affair has been described as a 'curious interlude . . . with no lasting effects whatsoever'),[610] the charges and tropes subsisted, though often in a condition of latency. Once launched, that is to say, they then acquired their own life, and recurred. For example, 'sweating', a charge made against Jews in the context of anti-alien agitation at the end of the nineteenth century, was then taken up half a century later in a quite different context, by Maule Ramsay: 'money that was once British . . . is now being used by international financiers in the City of London to sweat the Polish worker and keep the British worker out of a job'.[611] The charge that Jews start wars for profit, which originated in the Boer War, was then taken up both by Oswald Mosley and by leftist and pacifist groups.[612] The ILP journal, the *Forward*, for example, attacked 'the Jewish control of British foreign policy' and international Jewish finance.[613] In July and August 1939, *Peace News* carried comments about Jewish 'war plots' to disseminate false information about Nazi atrocities, with the object of securing popular support for an anti-Nazi war.[614] These remarks drew on even older motifs—Jews are timid, they contrive to have others fight for them, they are faint-hearted, cowardly.[615] The charge that Jews control the newspapers, either as owners or advertisers, with the power both to silence or smear their critics and illegitimately influence public opinion, has likewise been a staple of anti-Semitic discourse. To E. A. Freeman, writing in the aftermath of his polemical assaults on Disraeli, the Jews 'controlled the press of half the world';[616] in the Boer War, the complaint was that the 'German Jew Press' defamed the war's critics as 'unpatriotic';[617] in present times, it is the Zionist Press that is said to smear Israel's critics as anti-Semitic.

The master trope, that there are 'good Jews' and 'bad Jews', has been continuous in the political culture for at least the last hundred years. It does not evidence ambivalence about Jews, it is itself an anti-Semitic construction that permits some acknowledgement of reality (how can *all* Jews be bad?), and restates the Christian promise of redemption for a saving remnant (Romans 9:27). On the Right, the bad Jews were broadly 'international' (foreign or of foreign origin), 'disloyal', and 'pushy', while the good Jews were reliably loyal and modest subjects. On the Left, the bad Jews were foreign indigents and local sweaters (anti-alien agitation), plutocrats and international financiers (Boer War, World Wars I and II),[618] anti-Zionists (pre-World War II), and Zionists (post-World War II), while the good Jews were the 'unionizable' working-class, socialist Jews, Zionists,[619] then anti-Zionists. During World War II, distrust of 'Jewish atrocity stories' was to be found on the Left as well as the Right.[620]

Each moment in anti-Semitism's history may be understood both as an epitome of what has already passed and as a new development. Fear of one Jew with foreign antecedents (Disraeli) becomes fear of foreign Jews in general (Randlords, Russian immigrants), and then in due course becomes fear of all Jews, the international conspiracy.

6

The Mentality of Modern English Anti-Semitism

So much for the history. The rest of this book is less concerned with events, more with *mentalités*. Just as every country has its own tradition of political thinking,[1] so every country has its own traditions of *non*-thinking and *pseudo*-thinking. It is the anti-Semitic aspects of unthinking England that concern me first; the pseudo-thinking I address later in this chapter. *By mentalité* I understand a certain kind of spectrum: at one end background expectancies, shared understandings, habits of mind, unstated cultural assumptions, and the like, through to elaborated positions, systems of thought, and *their* like, at the other end. In the middle range, there are proverbs, maxims, legends, and other propositions of a rudimentary nature, through to explicit theories embraced by intellectuals and/or acted upon by institutions.[2] Something of the spread in this middle range may be captured in the distinction between *attitudes* and *opinions*.[3] My focus throughout the chapter tends towards the examination of anti-Semitic positions that are derived from assumptions partly subconscious and partly conscious, and moreover are collectively held, that is to say recurrent and pervasive in English society across the period under examination. I am concerned with the character of the regularities or uniformities of English anti-Semitism between the mid-1660s and the mid-1960s, for which purpose I assume the existence of a determinate and distinctive English *mentalité*.[4]

An 'unthinking' anti-Semitism

There have been no anti-Semitic atrocities in England since the Readmission. Jews have not been terrorized. They have not had to 'sit on packed suitcases', ready to flee at a moment's notice. Anglo-Jewish families were spared the Holocaust. It challenged them as spectators; they had reason to fear the consequences of an invasion; wartime domestic anti-Semitism kept them in a state of anxiety. But that is all. Indeed, English Jews' civil liberties have never been threatened, nor has their security even been put in jeopardy. Jews have not been legislated against; the closest they came to such a horror was the Aliens Act of 1905 (which was not close at all). Notwithstanding the efforts of anti-Semitic zealots, ever only few in number and marginal in influence, modern English anti-Semitism has been an elusive, low-key affair, perhaps best understood as an anti-Semitism of minor, uneven inhibition on Jewish ambition and self-esteem.[5]

Upon his appointment in 1937 as Secretary of State for War, Leslie Hore-Belisha (1893–1957) recorded in his diary a political colleague's warning, 'the military element might be very unyielding and they might try to make it difficult for me as a Jew'.[6] 'Making difficulties' for this or that Jew was the furthest that modern English anti-Semitism tended to go in its practical applications, though the desire to 'make difficulties' derives from a whole set of mostly unarticulated sentiments about Jews in general. It is often as covert as it is tacit. When it undertakes assaults, they tend to be oblique, and somewhat insidious. A striking example: in the late 1930s, the then prime minister, Neville Chamberlain, used the right-wing newspaper *Truth* to make anti-Semitic attacks on opponents of his appeasement policy. Though he had no disclosed connection with the newspaper, its editor operated under his direction. After Munich, *Truth* described Chamberlain's enemies as Jewish and/or communist traitors to Britain's true interests, which lay in friendship with Germany. 'No appreciable section of British opinion', it declared, 'desires to reconquer Berlin for the Jews.' And, it went on, newspapers that urged otherwise inhabited the 'Jew-infested sink of Fleet Street'.[7] Chamberlain would never himself have articulated such sentiments, expressed with such vulgar extremism. *Truth* was not itself representative of modern English anti-Semitism; its language was too violent, and its politics, too distant from received opinion. It was instead Chamberlain's use of the newspaper that disclosed something about the way in which Jews have often been harried in England—that is, by indirection, by means that permit a certain distance between bully and bullied.

This anti-Semitism demoralizes Jews, encouraging them to accept that they have certain talents, certain resources, the possession of which is not quite consistent with an ideal conception of what it is to be English. They may be admired for their superior acumen and industry, for their communal cohesiveness, and for being influential beyond their numbers. Most of all, they may be admired for a certain single-minded ambition. ('Within his not extensive limits the Jew succeeds, and nobody succeeds like him . . . In the popular Hebrew mind true Judaism has come to mean the art of getting on—of making the most of this world and completely ignoring any other. At what a cost!')[8] Modern English anti-Semitism is thus often ambiguous in its expression, and when named as anti-Semitic, it is often defended as being humorous or ironic in intention. Jews are then thought to expose themselves as a literal-minded, unhumorous people, incapable of taking a joke. (The joke is always, of course, at the expense of the Jew, and is made without expectation that he himself will find it amusing.)[9] Why do they treat everything so seriously? Jews will be insulted, and the insult misrepresented as a joke, or even as an irony at anti-Semitism's own expense. Jews will be excluded, and the exclusion denied. It is also a story of an anti-Semitism that shrinks from being named anti-Semitic.

'It is the common belief', declared an Anglo-Jewish writer in the early 1930s, 'that there is no anti-Semitism in the British Isles.' This belief is wrong, he went on to explain. Jews are 'not openly attacked'; they are instead 'by a thousand signs, and by ways not always conscious, edged on the one side, excluded'. It is a 'form of almost automatic anti-Semitism'. The 'taint of Jewry' in England means 'exclusion from garden-parties, refusal of certain cherished intimacies, and occasional light-hearted sneers'.[10] We may distinguish between an anti-Semitism of condescension or contempt, and one of apprehension or fear. There are anti-Semites who look down on 'the Jews'; there are anti-Semites who are frightened by 'the Jews'. There are also anti-Semites, of course, who manage to combine the two—they both scorn Jews and are obsessed by what they imagine to be Jewish power. Throughout most of English history, it is the anti-Semitism of condescension and not the anti-Semitism of apprehension, which has prevailed. (An eighteenth-century writer noted 'the slight contempt [the Jews'] religion lies under'.)[11] In England, for example, when the Talmud was attacked, it tended to be for its 'logical mistakes, scholastic torture and absurd thinking';[12] on the Continent, by contrast, it was attacked for teaching Gentile-hatred and even ritual murder. (I return to this topic in the next chapter.) However antagonistic English perspectives on the Jews may from time to time be, they are almost always unintimidated—think, say, of Beatrice Webb as she reports to her diary on a 'decidedly vulgar little Jew with much push', or reports in a letter to her husband Sidney on a 'conceited Philistine successful Jew of low mental and moral type'.[13] The 'most remarkable part' of the typical Jew's character may well be—to adapt some lines from Thomas Sheridan's play, *The Duenna* (1775)—'his passion for deceit and tricks of cunning'. But (and measure the qualifier, because in it lies the distinctiveness of English anti-Semitism), 'the fool predominates so much over the knave', he is 'generally the dupe of his own art'. He thus becomes a 'fair subject for contempt and ridicule'.[14] (The bamboozling of pretentious Jews was a theme in eighteenth-century English culture; see the second plate of William Hogarth's *A Harlot's Progress*, for example.)[15] The typical English anti-Semite believes that he has taken the measure of the Jew; he doesn't get stuck on the subject, and he is unafraid. Jews can be faced down; they are not an ungovernable threat; they are not, in Martin Luther's phrase, 'lords of the world'.[16] The Jews can be the subject of a certain kind of smart conversation—'In England, no one really is anti-Semitic.' Youghal shook his head. 'I know a great many Jews who are.'[17]— but the tone is typically one of command, not resentment. Only the exceptionally *a*typical English anti-Semite—the self-publishing Joseph Banister, say—will refer to Jews as 'our conquerors', and even in his case, the statement is made more for rhetorical effect than anything else.[18] 'The English', observed a late nineteenth-century English commentator on the European 'anti-Semitic movement', 'produce types perfectly well able to take care of themselves in the struggle for existence with the Semite'.[19] The Jews can be defeated—the lesson of 1290. (There is an obvious irony in the fact that the minor nature of modern English anti-Semitism is made possible, in part, by the radicalism of early medieval English anti-Semitism.) To fear the Jews is beneath an Englishman; the 'outspoken' anti-Semite has almost always been an exceptional figure in English society. This is a theme that runs through discussions of anti-Semitism by writers and journals not conspicuous for their friendly feelings towards Jews.

It is not Jew-hatred that we must write of, but Jew-*distrust*. Is it that the Jews will never be wholly accepted; they will never be considered 'wholly English' (whatever that might mean)?[20] But even that may go too far. Perhaps it is Jew-wariness, accompanied by a certain disdain. It is a story of snub and insult, sly whisper and innuendo, deceit and self-deception. Jews born in England quickly learn how to identify this Jew-wariness. It discomforts them, and it encourages among them a certain anxious conformism. They live with a continuous experience of constraint, one that makes them reluctant, for example, to test the limits of what they perceive as English tolerance. They may admonish each other, 'Keep your head down', 'Don't make trouble', 'Don't make waves.'[21] (From an Anglo-Jewish auto-biography of the late 1930s: 'He hugged the belief that nobody could suspect his origins. He was not ashamed of them, of course, but one need not rub them in, need one?')[22] The Jew living in England is always conscious of his Jewishness;[23] it can be an impediment to Jews who 'want to get on'. This anti-Semitism, so modest as to be invisible much of the time, is also powerful enough to influence the very formation of modern Anglo-Jewish identity. Its understanding of 'the Jew' has contributed to Jewish self-understanding. It is a horizon of aspiration for Jews. The English Jew is what he is in part because of English anti-Semitism. Each Jew strives to earn the reputation enjoyed by all Jews: clever, resourceful, and commercially and forensically astute. It is also a judgement on Jews, more unambiguously hostile, but easily internalized: they are uncultured, money-minded, 'clannish', aloof, incapable of altruism, unpatriotic, 'nervous', 'low'. All this is what 'everyone knows'. Newspaper items on the Jews mostly recycled given 'knowledge' about them; a *Times* series in 1924 on 'Alien'—that is, Jewish—'London', for example, is little more than a compendium of clichés. East End Jews are 'unassimilable', 'secretive', and 'excitable'; they 'lack the quality of comradeship', 'never tire of trying to get something for nothing', and have poor personal hygiene.[24] A journalist writing fifteen years later of Anglo-Jewry in general could assert, without fear of challenge, that the Jews were flamboyant, exclusive, and sycophantic.[25] And throughout all such maunderings, one finds this same, leading note of condescension.

Consider the following instances, across a period of seventy years. In 1863, Robert Cecil reviewed a book by a German anti-Semite for the *Saturday Review*. Cecil (later on, as Lord Salisbury, prime minister of three Conservative administrations) was condescending towards the author, mockingly referring to the work, *Judaism Among Strangers*, as an 'effusion':

> [It] is a curious book. Its reasoning is very similar to that which may be found in *Coningsby* or *Tancred*, only that it is written from exactly the opposite point of view. It is a full acknowledgment of the supremacy to which the children of Israel are gradually attaining, only in a tone not of national complaisance, but of Gentile terror. In the author's view, the Jews are becoming masters of the world ... he proves to his own satisfaction that, anatomically speaking, a Jew is a white

nigger ... [The Jew's] heaviest crime of all is that he never wears his hat—which according to our author, is the symbol of freedom—straight up in a dignified manner upon his brow, but always lets it drop upon the back of his head.[26]

All very silly, is the implication. (His own 'take' on the subject of Jewish mastery is best represented in this remark, made in 1868 to a parliamentary colleague: 'Matters seem very critical, a woman on the throne and a Jew adventurer who found out the secret of getting around her.')[27] Fourteen or so years later, the journal *Truth* pondered England's near-escape from an 'Anglo-Hebrew conspiracy' to 'drift us into a war in favour of the continuance of Semitic rule in Europe, not in the interests of England, but on account of affinity of race and feeling between the Jews and the Turks'. The conspiracy has failed, 'owing to the strong common sense of Englishmen'. 'The conspirators fancied that they had landed us, when we were only toying with the bait', the journal noted with satisfaction.[28] At the end of the century, the *Spectator* addressed the subject, 'The Dread of the Jew', noting the terror inspired by the Jews 'on the Continent'. This was 'absurd and unreasonable'; the complaints against the Jews do not stand up to scrutiny (though 'we confess to finding very disagreeable forms of Asiatic luxury'). If the Jews are really so terrible, the leader-writer observed, 'the only plan would be to slaughter [them], and thus make a real end of the so-called parasitic race. Half-measures will be of no avail.' He concluded:

> There is no need to be afraid of the Jews. They are clever and vigorous no doubt, but only a decadent race need be afraid of them. In a living polity like ours or that of the Americans, they form a useful element in the population, and may teach us some useful lessons. They constitute no danger to the State. ... The nation that cannot tolerate the Jews, and becomes deeply inspired by the anti-Semitic terror, is not the nation that will win. If we cannot resist the Jew without a resort to persecution, depend upon it we shall not long be fit to rank as an Imperial Power.[29]

Of course, these sentiments are quite compatible with expressions of concern about the 'admirable shrewdness' of Jews in business ('The Jew always triumphs!'),[30] or even the influence Jewish financiers wield over governments. Just this combination of confidence and apprehension, contempt and wariness, is evident in Frank Harris's short story, 'Mr Jacob's Philosophy', for example. Published in 1913, it relates an encounter between the narrator and 'a short, stout little man, with the heavy beaked nose and pendulous jowl of his tribe'. This Mr Jacob expounds his 'philosophy', an account of the power that Jews enjoy in the contemporary world because of their love of money and their great ability in getting it. 'Everyvere de Jew is master', he explains. 'And in anoder hundert years you vill see vonders: you vill all be serfants of de Jew, or his slaves.' The narrator 'lazily sips on [his] Mocha', as he listens to all this, but at the end of the story is taken aback by Jacob's 'abominable leer'.[31]

The next item is also from the *Spectator*. It appeared in 1922, on the election of a new Conservative government:

> We sincerely hope that the British government will not follow the advice which is sure to be given by the world-wise to beware of offending International Jewry. In the first place, a large part of International and British Jewry is immune from the Zionist bacillus, though it greatly dreads the disease. Next, we shall never get on satisfactory terms with Jewish financiers by showing ourselves afraid of them... *Besides, we are not financially dependent on International Jewish capital. We can paddle our own canoe in the hidden river of gold and paper.*[32] [Italics added]

One can trace a certain diminution in confidence, of course. But the sentiment broadly remains: the Jews may be strong, but we are also strong—perhaps even stronger than them. And we can see through their plots. Writing in 1925, for example, Stephen Graham, the *Times'* Russia correspondent, dismissed the Politburo member Grigory Zinoviev *'alias Apfelbaum'*, as a 'wretched little German Jew'. He is so keen to conceal his origins, Graham commented, yet 'everybody does know his real name' and his 'antics are the laughing-stock of the world'.[33] This kind of conviction, that Britain is powerful enough to see through Jewish plots, was even the position taken by the BUF in its early years. 'The English... are strong enough to ignore—or absorb—the Jews', a BUF publication explained, 'but in Germany they remain a constant intellectual provocation to a people always sensitive to the newness of their nationhood.'[34] And last, consider the autobiography of Admiral Sir Barry Domvile (1878–1971), a confirmed anti-Semite, and open admirer of the Nazis. In *By and Large* (1936), he condescends towards Jews, precisely as if aware that to admit to anything more aggressive would be to merit a *Spectator*-type rebuke. It would betray, that is, a certain feebleness of spirit, an unmanly hysteria, inappropriate in an Englishman. So—at an international conference he notices 'a clever little Jew'; in Palestine, he records the marriage of High Commissioner Samuel's son to 'a Jaffa Jewess'; visiting the concentration camp at Dachau, he finds no evidence to support the tale of 'a British

Jew-boy' about the ill-treatment of prisoners. He finds the German 'Jews not wanted' banners to be in 'bad taste' and to give 'great and unnecessary offence to foreign tourists'; he acknowledges that the Nazis have behaved towards the Jews 'with great harshness and tactlessness'. But they do not deserve the 'sloppy sentimental attitude' shown them here in England. Jewish influence in 'big business and the Press' directs our attention to Nazi behaviour; 'if we were not such a tolerant race there would have been trouble long ago'.[35]

It is perhaps not surprising, then, that in English political and cultural life the Jew has rarely figured as 'the enemy within'. Though there is a sense of, say, certain London suburbs having taken on a Jewish character, there is not the sense that Jews have captured them, no sense of a Jewish stronghold, a 'no go' area for non-Jews. Rarely have English non-Jews entertained the thought that they are not masters in their own home. There is nothing that is monomanic about this anti-Semitism. The typical English anti-Semite does not see Jews in every hiding place and under every disguise; he is not an obsessive; he is not at risk of being driven *mad* by his consciousness of Jews.[36] Anti-Semitism is rarely burdensome to him. Modern English anti-Semitism is best characterized as a prejudice rather than a preoccupation. It is consistent with a lazy reflex, a casual remark, and rarely reaches the intensity of a deliberate, persistent, active animus. 'To be an anti-Semite', wrote the Nazi anti-Semite Robert Ley in 1945, just before he killed himself in Allied captivity, 'is to occupy oneself with the Jewish question.'[37] More precisely: to be occupied *by* it, to live indefinitely in its intimacy.[38] Anti-Semites of this kind pressed for action; they worked to promote hostility; they committed themselves to campaigns; they put the Jews, and Jewish power, at the centre of their mental universe. For condescension, they substituted hatred; for contempt, they substituted fear; and they made themselves dizzy with fantasies of conspiracy. Their animus became a career; for some, it was also an obsession. They were anti-Semitism's vanguard; they became bores on the subject of the Jews.[39] There were few anti-Semites of this kind in England. This sense that England was not receptive to anything other than a causal, dismissive disregard for Jews (or a prejudiced curiosity, as if specimens of some exotic species)[40] was a cause for exasperation among the few anti-Semitic intellectuals that England possessed. In his book *The Jews* (1922, 1937), for example, Hilaire Belloc acknowledged that the 'English reader' might find what he had to say in his own work 'fantastic', but insisted that were his book 'put into the hands of a jury chosen from the various nationalities of Europe and the United States it would be found too moderate in its estimate of the peril it postulated'.[41] I return to Belloc below.

It is often difficult in England to identify precisely when anti-Semitism is at work. Consider the story of Leslie Hore-Belisha's resignation. At the beginning of 1940, Neville Chamberlain, then still prime minister, was considering putting Hore-Belisha in charge of the Ministry of Information. He was at the time Secretary of State for War, and was antagonizing the senior military with his criticisms of their conduct of the war.[42] He had also attracted the attention of anti-Semites: the right-wing journalist Collin Brooks described him in his diaries as '*le* Disraeli *de nos jours*', 'greatly disliked in the City, as a pushing Jew', 'a Bond Street bum boy', and a 'pushing Jew boy'.[43] The then Foreign Secretary, Lord Halifax, expressed mild doubts about the proposed new appointment. Chamberlain sounded out other Cabinet members and the editor of *The Sunday Times*. Reactions were on the whole favourable. So he invited Hore-Belisha to see him at 2.45 p.m. on 4 January, intending to offer him the job. But after the morning Cabinet meeting, Halifax stayed behind to insist that he and his advisers were strongly against the appointment. It would have a bad effect on the neutrals both because Hore-Belisha was a Jew and because his methods would let down British prestige. It had in fact previously been suggested that the appointment of a Jew would diminish the Ministry in American eyes, and so Chamberlain had checked with the former Ambassador to the United States. He 'had dismissed the suggestion at once as entirely baseless', Chamberlain later reported. Even so, given Halifax's vehemence, the prime minister did not feel that the offer could be made, and instead offered him the Board of Trade. Hore-Belisha turned him down, and his career was broken. A critic of the government told the Commons: 'The Prime Minister denies that the Secretary of State was dismissed because he was a Jew. He cannot deny that the prejudice against him was because he was a Jew.'[44] The generality of Anglo-Jewry agreed, it would seem.[45] Within days of his resignation, the anti-Semitic *Truth*, which was widely read in Conservative Party circles,[46] published an anti-Semitic attack on him, alleging shady business dealings, and the editor sent copies of the issue to all the members of both the Commons and the Lords.[47] General Ironside, the then Chief of the Imperial General Staff, referred to Hore-Belisha as 'Horeb Belisha';[48] during his 'peace' campaign, Mosley liked to attack Hore-Belisha as a 'Jewish warmonger'.[49] English anti-Semitism sometimes has to be teased out; it may also need to be weighed as one factor among several when seeking an explanation of particular events.

I take the novelist W. M. Thackeray (1811–63) to be typical of the quotidian modern English anti-Semite. Thackeray was a satirist, and a ready exploiter of received stereotypical representatives of social classes and types, Jews among them. He did not, in any event, care for Jews or 'members of the Hebrew persuasion'. He shrank with distaste from the money-power represented by the Rothschilds; he was similarly fastidious when contemplating 'greasy Jew writ-bearers'. He delighted in reproducing in prose pseudo-Jewish accents and movements. He doubted whether any Jew could be a gentleman. His regard for the *belle Juive*—'dark-eyed Hebrew maidens'—was not a true exception to his generally adverse view of Jews. He regularly caricatured and mocked them, and cared even less for the Old Testament, which he believed to be sanguinary and cruel, and alien to the spirit of Christianity. But he shrank from the persecution of Jews. He was ready to mock those displays of 'Christian zeal' that required 'burning a Jew or shooting a heretic'. He was ready to deplore the 'foul-mouthed illiberality of the bigots' who were quick to 'hunt down . . . a Jew'. He was not inclined to think that Jews, taken in the round, were in any serious respect worse than Gentiles. He was able to see the irrationality of Jew-hatred in others; he resented accusations that his lampoons, his ridicule, amounted to Jew-baiting. He was adamant that 'God's sun shines over us all Jews, Heathen Turks, Methodists, Catholics, Church-of-England men . . . ' Men must be allowed to 'worship God their own way'. Lady Louisa de Rothschild, who spent time with him on a Rhine steamer, recorded in her diary that they spent time talking about Jews 'of whom he has a bad opinion', but that he himself seemed to be 'a good and honest man'. He was not a 'programmatic anti-Semite', concludes S. S. Prawer, the authority on Thackeray in this respect. He takes Thackeray's perspectives on Jews to be typical of the writer's society.[50]

One hundred years later, nothing much had changed. Let me return to Kingsley Amis, in many respects comparable to Thackeray as a novelist. Like Thackeray, he too was unhappy at accusations of anti-Semitism. For example, writing to Anthony Thwaite, who had parodied Amis's autobiography, *Memoirs* (1991) ('Gave lunch to Thwaite again. Of course he's Yorkshire, which means he never attempts to pay his share of the bill. A bit of a Hebrew really'), Amis remarked, 'I roared with laughter at your evocation of a Thwaite para . . . but went a bit quiet at the Hebrew bit; not really my style, I hope.' Amis was also quick to condemn anti-Semitism publicly. In a 1962 letter to the *Spectator*, commenting on its columnist's declaration that it was 'everyone's job to correct the mistaken idea that it is somehow smart to be anti-Semitic', Amis wrote: 'It may be tedious and not with-it to say so, but anti-Semitism in any form, including the fashionable one of anti-anti-anti-Semitism, must be combated.' And thirty years later, he recalled with pride the intolerance towards anti-Semitism shown by his school. *But* also like Thackeray, though with much less frequency, he was drawn to speculations about Jews and Jewish characteristics. 'The great Jewish vice is glibness, fluency . . . also possibly just bullshit, as in Marx, Freud, Marcuse. Pity L. Ron Hubbard not.' And 'It's rather like being a Jew, no matter what you do or don't do, you can't help being one.' Or, 'He's a decent sort of shag, John Goldblatt by name—though he ate a couple of pork chops unhesitatingly enough.' In his private letters to Phillip Larkin, he made fantastically offensive references to Jews, in the broader idiom of a deliberately mad style of writing: 'Did you realise L Riding was a Yank Yid etc? . . . Well, of course, she was a joooo, and a yangck, and a womb'un, so we must make allowances BEFORE WE CUT HER ARMS AND LEGS OFF.' Or, 'Chaplin is a horse's arse. He's a Jeeeew, you see. Like the Marx Brothers. Like Danny Kaye.' Martin Amis recalls asking his father, 'What's it like, being mildly anti-Semitic? What's it feel like?' Amis replies: 'Very mild, as you say. If I'm watching the end of some new arts programme I might notice the Jewish names in the credits and think, Ah, there's another one. Or: Oh I see. There's another one.' Martin: 'And that's all?' Kingsley: 'More or less. You just notice them. You wouldn't want anyone to *do* anything about it. You'd be horrified by that.' Anti-Semitism also provided Amis with opportunities to be provocative. 'I've finally worked out why I don't like Americans', Amis told his son. 'Because everyone there is either a Jew or a hick.' Or he would ask: 'What's that you're reading? Some *Jew*?' Yet Kingsley Amis, like Thackeray, similarly could not be considered a 'programmatic anti-Semite'—he hated too indiscriminately, and too weakly.[51]

Of scoffs and scorns

Christians took the Jews to task for scoffing at Jesus. The Jewish priests and mob mocked his teachings, and then mocked his suffering. They were heartless and cruel. Their contempt, a trope of the Passion, was a staple of the religious literature of the late medieval, and early modern, periods:

When as in fair Jerusalem Our Saviour Christ did live,
And for the sins of all the world His own dear life did give;
The wicked Jews, with scoffs and scorns, did daily him molest,
That never till he left his life Our Saviour could not rest.
Repent, therefore, O England! Repent while you have space;
And do not (like the wicked Jews) despise God's proffered Grace.[52]

Though the 'scoffs and scorns' were 'daily', they were continuous with the more brutal, and ultimately lethal, treatment meted out to Jesus by the Jews. What began in disparagement ended in murder, though disparagement need not always end thus. It was not like that for England's Jews, for example. In modern England, by which I mean, for the purposes of my typology of English anti-Semitisms, the 1660s to the 1960s, the quotidian, hostile perspective on the Jews was almost entirely an affair of disparagement or 'scoffs and scorns'. It is a phrase that neatly encapsulates that combination of insult and condescension most characteristic of the English anti-Semitism under review in this, and the previous, chapter.

Scoffs and scorns, which are predicated on a sense of *difference*, may be evidence of nothing more than a certain amused contempt. I have several proof texts for this proposition: a World War I memoir, Adrian Bell's *Corduroy*, a passage from one of Macaulay's letters, a Balliol College rhyme, and then, by way of identifying the limit of this perspective, a short prose piece of Virginia Woolf's and a remark of a Cambridge don.

Major Vivian Gilbert, author of *The Romance of the Last Crusade* (1923), subtitled, 'With Allenby to Jerusalem', records an encounter with a battalion of the Royal Fusiliers ordered to guard the plains below Jerusalem, following the city's fall to the British in December 1917. 'This battalion was made up entirely of Jews, recruited in England, America and Palestine', he writes. 'It was nicknamed by our men the "Royal *Jewsiliers*".' And 'the Jordan High-landers'. Their battle cry was said to be, 'No advance without security.' Gilbert concludes his account with a commendation. 'As a matter of fact they did extremely fine work and possessed an extremely nice lot of officers.'[53] This mild joshing, if objected to, would be sure to draw a kind of puzzled dismay—surely you realize it's only a joke? It would be graceless to take offence.

Corduroy (1930) records the flight of a young man from London into the peace of the Suffolk countryside. It was immensely popular; it went through many editions; there were several sequels. It was particularly prized during World War II, and a Penguin edition was to be found in the kit of many British servicemen. Jewish poultry-buyers figure in one chapter. A queer exotic presence on market day, they present a striking contrast to the harmonies of country life. They are 'voluble', 'of unpleasing countenances', and wear 'East End suits and patent leather shoes ornamentally inlaid'. Their 'chattering', 'jabbering', and 'gesticulating' perplexes the 'simple rustics' who watch them 'for want of a better entertainment'. These locals are slow, pacific, genial, and they regard the Jews with an unthreatened and tolerant bemusement. Bell identifies himself with these perspectives, but gives them an anti-Semitic twist.[54] In choosing 'country' over 'town', and locating the Jews among the least attractive aspects of the latter, Bell is conforming to a preference very deep in English culture.[55]

The condescension is quite consistent with an active concern for Jewish civil rights. A different class, and a different period, for sure, but a passage from one of Macaulay's letters helps make this point. Shortly after his maiden speech in favour of removing Jewish disabilities, he received a party invitation, as he related to his sister. 'I am going to the fancy ball of—the Jew. He met me in the street, and implored me to come. "You need not dress ιore than for an evening party. You had better come. You will be delighted. It will be so very pretty." ' He then reported on the party a week later. He meets an 'angel of a Jewess' in a Highland plaid. He leaves at about 1 a.m., and walks quietly home. 'But it was some time before I could get to sleep. The sound of fiddles was in mine ears, and gaudy dresses, and black hair, and Jewish noses, were fluctuating up and down before mine eyes.'[56] There is an implication in this letter that these Jews are merely imitating social forms that they have not quite made their own. They have therefore made themselves slightly ridiculous.[57]

But the scoffing is not always so poised. Virginia Woolf also wrote up a social encounter with a Jew, one Mrs Loeb. It was a very disagreeable experience. This 'fat Jewess' 'fawned upon us, flattered us and wheedled us'. 'It seemed as though she wished to ingratiate herself with her guests and expected to be kicked by them.' Though rich, she is vulgar and ostentatious and, above all, ingratiating. And so on. There is a rhetoric of perceptiveness at play in the passage, which invites appreciation of the detailed realization of a singular presence. But it is no more than a compilation of clichés about Jews—their physical grossness, their dubiously acquired wealth, their oleaginous cuisine, their ignominious desire to please, their unutterable vulgarity. There is a shift here from the easier, lazier contempt of Bell's rural folk, or the handsome, public-spirited tolerance of Macaulay. Woolf does not merely find herself in the presence of a Jew, she is *unwillingly* in the Jew's presence. Noel

Annan's reference to Bloomsbury's 'faint contempt for Jews so characteristic of their class'[58] does not quite capture the experience of recoil and suffocation this passage intimates.

According to the *Daily Telegraph* obituary of Liam Hudson, the British experimental psychologist who died on 19 February 2005:

> His career at Cambridge started unpromisingly when, as a research student at Emmanuel College, he was placed next to the college Master, an historian, at dinner. On hearing that Hudson was interested in intelligence tests, the Master said: 'Huh! Devices invented by the Jews for the advancement of Jews.'
>
> 'Offered, I now realise, as a provocation,' Hudson wrote later, 'the remark blighted my relation with Emmanuel College . . .'[59]

Hudson was too generous to the Master, Edward Welbourne, whose remark was an *anti-Semitic* provocation. Why would Jews be in favour of intelligence tests? They overvalue intelligence, it is what they're good at, and so they would want to promote it as a value. They are incapable of judgement; they do not value character. Whatever is measurable, and therefore admits of competitive ranking, works to their advantage. But the truly valuable things in life cannot be measured—cannot be priced.[60] The German-Jewish historian, George L. Mosse, also had a story about Welbourne. Having completed his secondary education at a boarding school, he was interviewed by Welbourne. 'I told him what I thought of studying, he said to me: "You people become journalists, not historians." '[61] Welbourne was an academic of some standing. His 'High Table' disparagements of Jews, of which there are other examples,[62] is a version of what is often referred to as 'polite' anti-Semitism, typically expressed, wrote George Eliot, by the remark, 'I never did like the Jews.'[63] It is here that one encounters the authentic tones of modern English anti-Semitism. It always contains a note of contempt. It is given intermittent elaboration—as it was by Welbourne himself, apparently.[64] But it is not susceptible to systematic exposition; it was never elevated into a doctrine.

Beyond Welbourne—that is to say, beyond the boundary that his remark helps to demarcate—the scoffing and scorning is angry, even menacing. Consider, for example, this diary entry from 1920: 'A Jew may be a loyal Englishman and passionately patriotic, but he is intellectually apart from us and will never be purely and simply English.'[65] The author, Austen Chamberlain (1863–1937), was then Chancellor of the Exchequer, and the Jew to whom he referred was his Cabinet colleague, the Secretary of State for

India, Edwin Samuel Montagu (1879–1924). The diary entry was prompted by a debate on 8 July 1920 in the House of Commons. The debate concerned the conduct of General Dyer, the senior officer responsible for the 1919 Amritsar massacre, when many hundreds of unarmed men, women, and children were fired on by British Indian Army troops. Chamberlain noted: 'Our party has always disliked and distrusted [Montagu]. On this occasion all their English and racial feeling was stirred to passionate display... A Jew, a foreigner, rounding on an Englishman and throwing him to the wolves—that was the feeling.' And then he makes his point about patriotic and loyal Jews. The strain of dealing with the Dyer affair had by then already taken a heavy toll. Montagu had suffered a nervous breakdown earlier in the year, and the debate itself destroyed his career. He was a liberal and a political reformer, and was horrified by Dyer's actions. To one of Dyer's more scrupulous supporters, however, the questions for the House were somewhat different: '(a) Is it English to break a man who tried to do his duty? (b) Is a British General to be downed at the bidding of a crooked Jew?'[66]

What about the terrain beyond verbal violence? The English anti-Semitism I am exploring stops well short of it, and may be taken to survey it with distaste. Violence against Jews is what other nations do; in England, anti-Semitic violence is almost always confined to fiction—say, to certain jocosities in a short story by Saki (1870–1916),[67] or to a murder mystery by Dorothy L. Sayers (1893–1957). Sayers's *Whose Body?* (1923), her first novel, opens with the discovery of a dead body in a Battersea flat. At about the same time, a man disappears from his Central London home. The corpse in the flat resembles, but is not, the man who has disappeared. The murderer of the one makes use of the corpse of the other (available to him, because he is a doctor) in order to conceal his crime. The murderer's motive is in part revenge, in part a desire to commit the perfect crime. Many years before, the victim married the woman also loved by the murderer. The victim is the Jewish financier, Sir Reuben Levy; the murderer is a celebrated surgeon, Sir Julian Freke. He had 'his aristocratic nose put out of joint by a little Jewish nobody'.[68] Lord Peter Wimsey exposes the murderer, and has diverting conversations about the deceased with his mother, the Duchess, along the way. There are two perspectives on the Jews at work in the novel, the Duchess's (which is also the perspective of the novel itself), and the murderer's. To the Duchess, Levy is a faintly comic character. He had some difficulty persuading his prospective parents-in-law of his suitability. 'Of course, we're all Jews nowadays, and they wouldn't have minded so much if he'd pretended to be something else. I'm sure some Jews are very good people, and personally I'd much rather they believed something, though of course it must be very inconvenient, what with not working on Saturdays and circumcising the poor little babies...' She twitters on.[69] The murderer, by contrast, hated the deceased. He would have liked to have disregarded him, but he couldn't, because Levy bested him. The resentment almost overwhelmed him, and so he had to act. He had to kill Levy. And this, the novel plainly affirms, goes too far. It is in this respect both an instance of one kind of anti-Semitism and an interrogation of certain other kinds. Indeed, it is in this drawing back from a notion of anti-Semitic excess that Sayers most acutely captures the limits of a specifically *English* anti-Semitism. The present chapter is an exploration of everything that falls short of these limits.

Remarks and insults

There is a tendency in England towards the making of anti-Semitic remarks. A 'remark' is more than a thoughtless aside, less than a deliberate intervention. It doesn't just slip out; but there is nothing programmatic about it either. It is an appeal to what is understood, to what goes without saying. Harold Abrahams says in the film *Chariots of Fire* that you catch English anti-Semitism 'on the edge of a remark'.[70] The remark is often absurd, unpredictable—and quite unanswerable. Consider the following example. The Australian composer Arthur Benjamin (1893–1960) won an open scholarship to London's Royal College of Music at the age of eighteen. For composition, he had Charles Villiers Stanford (1852–1924), whom he considered a great teacher. Villiers, he reported, remarked to him once: 'You Jews can't write long tunes!'[71]

The most pointed kind of remark is the insult. There are many ways to insult a person. The simplest is to address a dismissive or disparaging remark direct to him; a more complex way is to address the remark to others in his presence. Anti-Semites insult Jews in both these ways. They are insulting to Jews; and they talk and write about Jews in insulting terms. The philosopher and Talmudist Emmanuel Levinas (1906–95) understood anti-Semitism to be in its essence an insult; he wrote of the 'insult of anti-Semitism'.[72] Every version of anti-Semitism insults Jews, that is to say comprises that active, radical withholding of respect on which an insult is predicated.

The BUF's newspaper, *Blackshirt*, was incontinent in its insults: 'oily, material, swaggering Jew', 'pot-bellied, sneering, money-mad Jew', and so on.[73] But insults do not need to be quite so crass, especially when the very word 'Jew' itself has insulting meanings. To characterize a person, for example, as 'a vain, blasphemous, tricky Jew' is to assert *both* that he is discreditably vain, etc. and discreditably Jewish, *and* that he is discreditably vain etc. precisely because he is a Jew.[74] 'Don't Jew me' says one Englishman to another when they bargain, complained a nineteenth-century Jewish pamphleteer. 'Jew', he wrote, had become synonymous with 'rogue'. And again: 'the very name of Jew conveys implicitly the ideas of fraud, deception and superstition'.[75] 'You use me like a Jew' was at one time an available complaint to anyone acting selfishly, exploitatively. 'You are a regular Jew.'[76] Discreditable classes or activities were referred to as if in the sole occupancy of Jews—to moneylenders, say, as 'the Jews'.[77] Then there are synonyms that tie the Jews to what is taken to be the most ignominiously criminal or sordid aspects of their history or character—'Christ-killer', chief among them.[78] And there are also the standard compounds, 'crafty Jew', 'rich Jew', and so on. The adjectives do not qualify—it is not a matter of 'these Jews rather than those Jews', but 'all Jews'.[79] New compounds emerge from time to time; T. S. Eliot, for example, gave 'free-thinking Jews' a certain currency. Often, the noun is used rather than the adjective to give a certain contemptuous emphasis—as in the common disparaging references during the years of Edward VII's reign to his 'Jew friends'.[80] It was also common for Far Right publicists to talk of 'the Jew Marx',[81] 'the Jew Disraeli', 'the Jew Einstein', etc.[82] Cockney rhyming slang is fertile with pejorative terms for 'Jew' and 'Yid': 'five to two', 'kangaroo', 'front wheel skid', 'tea pot lid', etc.[83] Inevitably, 'Shylock' and 'Fagin' were and continue to be much used—a Jew might be described as 'a Fagin', or 'a second Shylock'.[84] These insults take everything for granted; they barely invite assent, because they *assume* assent. They still inhabit the language, though they have a more restricted life than they once did.

Isaiah Berlin was ruled unsuitable to give the BBC Reith Lectures in 1952, notwithstanding the immense success of his radio talks earlier that year, 'Freedom and its betrayal'. His literary trustee Henry Hardy, in the introduction to the edited version of these talks, is compelled to comment: 'There is no evidence, at any rate, that anti-Semitism was at work.' By which he means *both* that there is no reason to suppose that the decision was motivated by anti-Semitism *and* that while the decision may indeed have been motivated by anti-Semitism, this must remain conjecture because of the absence of evidence. We are approaching a distinctly English practice here: that grey, indistinct region where insult may be intended without being understood or even received and insult may be claimed without being intended. Here are examples of some insults, each with a certain resonance, a certain representative quality:

- In general chatter, at a Bloomsbury circle gathering, a question was asked, addressed to all those assembled. A pause. And then, loudly, Virginia Woolf instructed, pointing to her husband, Leonard: 'Let the Jew answer.' To which Leonard replied: 'I won't answer until you ask me properly.'[85]

- In 1931, a Jewish mayor is elected for Stepney, in London's East End. She takes her seat in the council chamber amid cries from the Labour Party benches of 'Shylock'. When two new Jewish aldermen are introduced, a spectator cries out, 'I have had enough of this. You're all a bunch of yids.'[86]

- In the course of reminiscences of London in the 1930s: 'With a friend I used to go to listen to trials at the Old Bailey, London's criminal court, and whenever someone with a Jewish name testified, the judge invariably asked, "Is he English? Can he understand the English language?"'[87]

- In the first month or so of World War II, there was a small scandal involving Robert Boothby, a Tory politician who was a well-known supporter of the new prime minister, Winston Churchill. Boothby had been demanding the unfreezing of Czech assets, for which (as it turned out) he had received a commission. One of Churchill's political enemies wrote of Boothby's contact, one Richard Weineger: 'He is a trader in finance and is *as ready as Jews always have been* to pull up his stumps and flit to safer places with his wealth.'[88]

- In a confidential Foreign Office review of UK–Israel relations, written in 1950, the then ambassador, Sir Alexander Knox Helm, wrote: '[Israel's] greatest disability remains the more disagreeable features of the Jewish character, with an inability to realise that the obtaining of the farthing does not necessarily mean the best bargain, that in an imperfect world unrelieved seriousness is not a virtue, and perhaps above all, that strength is not always best displayed through force.'[89]

- The English playwright John Osborne wrote in his autobiography of a period in his life when he was separated from his then wife, and his belief that she would return to him, leaving the person for whom she had left him. This rival was a 'Jewish dentist in Derby'.[90]

There is a certain range, then. But all these insults trade on received understandings of Jews, they take for granted a complicity with their audience, some are comic in their effect (or intended to be comic), and all assume a certain moral and/or social superiority. Most of all, these insults are all offensive; they take for granted that Jews are fair game. They may be insulted with impunity.[91] Some of the insults are indistinct, if not subtle. You don't see them coming; and when they have passed, you're still not sure quite what they were. And this creates uneasiness, wariness. Reading the signs right can be difficult—you may never know.

Of course, it is not all indirection and ambiguity. There is chanting at football matches that leaves nothing to doubt: at a match against Manchester United, Arsenal fans chanted 'Send the Jews to Auschwitz'; West Ham fans at a Tottenham Hotspur match chanted 'I'd rather be a Paki than a Jew ... I've got a foreskin, haven't you, fucking Jew'; during a Barnet FC match against Arsenal, there were chants about 'gassing', 'Hitler' and 'Yids'. Groups of Chelsea fans have sung, 'Gas a Jew, Jew, Jew, put him in the oven, cook him through.' These chants, recorded in 2006–7, are instances of a different kind of anti-Semitic invective—raw, challenging, tribal.[92]

Jokes

Jokes about Jews are another form of collective abuse. Much English anti-Semitism is expressed in an ostensibly humorous register. Opposition to the Jew Bill mixed atrocity tales about Jews with vicious humour at the Jews' expense; an 'inexhaustible torrent of ribaldry against the Jew Bill', a contemporary commentator noted, 'daily overflows us fro the press'.[93] In the following century, *Punch* mocked Jews in somewhat less intemperate, because less threatened, language. The *Jewish Chronicle*'s complaint, that '*Punch* repeatedly fell foul of the whole Jewish people, with the virulence of true fanaticism',[94] misread the magazine's lazy, often sneering condescension for something more preoccupied, more *engaged*. There was nothing obsessive in *Punch*'s disparagement of Disraeli in 1848:

> A Curly-headed Jew-boy some years ago was I,
> And through the streets of London 'Old Clo' I used to dry,

But now I am a member, I speechifies and votes,
I've given up all my dealings in left-off hats and coats;
In a creditable manner I hope I fills my sheat,
Though I vonce vas but a Jew-boy vot whistled through the street.[95]

This was malice, for sure, but not of a 'fanatical' kind. (Gibes like this were perhaps in Disraeli's mind when he wrote in *Tancred* of Jews being 'born to hereditary insult'.)[96] *Punch* was ready, indeed, to mock Disraeli's own fantasies about Jewish power: 'The novel of Coningsby clearly discloses / The pride of the world are the children of Moses.' How absurd, is the implication, that Disraeli should write thus about 'the tribe of Old Clo'!'[97] George Eliot, with this kind of verse in mind, was suitably disparaging about 'the form of wit that identifies Moses with the advertising sheet'.[98] Humour of this sort remained current for many decades; it was still in circulation during World War II.[99] Of the specifically Edwardian vogue for comic postcards, the Jew was represented as grotesque, his manner ludicrous, and his character, avaricious, dishonest, and devious.[100] In an early issue of the satirical magazine *Private Eye*, the announcement of a spoof 'City of London Festival of Money' explains that the event commemorates the crime of a city trader now buried in 'the Church of St. Simeon Goldberg-by-Expenside, the Guild Church of the Worshipful Company of Money Spinners'.[101] If one adds stinginess, social pretension, a tendency to extravagant hand gestures,[102] an odd accent (the celebrated 'Jewish intonation', etc.)[103] and physical ugliness (the celebrated 'Jewish nose', etc.),[104] the humorous account of the Jew is complete. One from my own childhood can be taken to represent all such jokes: 'How do you get 20 Jews into a Mini? Throw a halfpenny in to it.' Jokes like this one were widespread in my primary school, and no doubt in many others too. They fell within the genre that makes a stock character the comic butt. They are mostly brief narratives, or take a question-and-answer form, but there are also jokes that turn on comic accents or comic gestures—jokes like this are everywhere in *Punch*, but for literary instances see Ezra Pound's Canto xxxv ('The tale of the perfect schnorrer: a peautiful chewisch poy . . . ')[105] and T. S. Eliot's 'saggy bending of the knees / And elbows, with the palms turned out'.[106] In its more developed form, it is comedy, especially the Roman New comedy. And then there are cartoons, of course. The humour tends to be contemptuous rather than deliberately cruel, dismissive rather than intimidated. Jews are disagreeable but risible, or if detestable, ludicrous too. The 'Auschwitz joke', for example, has not established itself in English culture.[107] Crueller English anti-Semites, however, derive pleasure from the torture-tales of medieval times. 'The same healthy instinct' that led Pharaoh to turn out the Jews, observed the Nazi-sympathizing Viscount Lymington, 'drove our ancestors to practise medieval dentistry on medieval moneylenders'.[108]

The outer limit of 'humorous' anti-Semitism is exemplified in a nasty book by the journalist T. W. H. Crosland, *The Fine Old Hebrew Gentleman* (1922). Crosland was an associate of Lord Alfred Douglas, contributing to his anti-Semitic scandal sheet, *Plain English*.[109] He explains in a Postscript to the book that it is 'written without malice and with more of an eye to the humour of life than the tragedy of it'. Some opening verses set the tone: 'They say to the minor: "Thix hundred per thent." / They say to the widow: "My dear, bring us cover," and they suck and suck till the blood be spent. / So they may guzzle and save and fatten and limp from Poland into Mayfair . . . ' The book thereafter consists of many jokey references to 'Aby and Ikey', comical appropriations of Hebrew and Yiddish words ('chacham', 'schemoz-zle'), renderings of Jewish speech, 'Jew stories' and cod-aphorisms of Jewish finance, and invitations to identify Jewish 'men of genius', poets, and the like. Though the tone is more one of disparagement than of fear, Crosland also maintains 'the community that was once considered a joke has come to be considered a menace'. And, he adds, the British Empire is largely a Jew-ruled Empire. The Jews are 'within a stride' of achieving 'mastership' in Britain. 'If we permit them to take that stride, the more fools we.' Notwithstanding this evidence of a certain preoccupation with Jews, Crosland is anxious to insist, 'I am not one of those who sees a Jew in every bush.'[110]

Last, and independently of jokes, there are witticisms. Witticisms at Jews' expense come very easily to the English imagination. Recorded in the diary of A. L. Rowse (1903–97), scholar and man of letters, is a witticism in praise of a late colleague: 'I remember his election in Common Room: Warden Pember saying that he was ultimately of Jewish extraction, but that the extraction was complete.'[111] It is a common enough phrase 'of Jewish extraction'. Its meaning lies in what it subtracts from the word 'Jewish'. He is not a Jew in any sense that sets him apart, he is not an identifying Jew, there is a Jew in the background—a parent, or a grandparent—but that is not to be held against him, does not define who he is. The witticism is to take this phrase and render it as literal, bringing out this latent sense. A person who is described, or describes himself, as being of 'Jewish extraction' is someone endeavouring to extract himself from his Jewishness. To make himself instead, perhaps, 'a very English type'. There is a tinge of malice, but not very much. But it is also just. It is interesting how Rowse places against the Jewishness the alternative of Englishness, quite unreflectively. If Dannreuther had described himself to the warden of being 'of Jewish extraction' and the warden had replied to him, 'well, in your case, the extraction is complete', I can imagine Dannreuther colouring. It is not insulting, but it is quite close to being insulting. It is not anti-Semitic, though it grates slightly on a Jewish ear (it grates on mine, at least). The warden would probably not have made the remark to Dannreuther himself.

A Jewish friend recalls his schooldays. There was only one other Jewish boy in his school. They became best friends ('You Jews always stick together!'). One day the new deputy headmaster took assembly. After the announcements, with no instruction, the two boys knew to get up and walk the length of the hall to leave. After the prayers, the hall doors were flung open, and the deputy head declared, 'Would the chosen people now come forth!' (The phrase 'chosen people' is rarely ever used in friendship.)[112] It was an essay in humour. It also intimated a certain resentment at the Jews' claim to a superior position in a different hierarchy—the deputy head might be immensely more powerful than two schoolboys, but as a mere Gentile . . . The comedy of this Jewish assertion of 'chosenness' had many registers. There was, for example, the comedy of Leonard's courtship of Virginia. The prospects of marriage were good, a friend of Virginia's thought, save that Woolf was a Jew, and his 'family are chosen beyond anything'.[113]

Jewish jokes are reflexive, returning on themselves, commenting on their own comedy. They are self-knowing. And thus there are Jewish jokes about the telling of Jewish jokes. They mock Jewish argumentativeness. They mock Jewish attempts, in the most hopeless of circumstances, to placate authority, to follow civilized forms of behaviour, or to avoid trouble. Such is the potential of Jewish jokes, their compressed power, their reach into the depths of Jewish suffering, that they may be related, without absurdity, to the greatest work of the Jewish humorists, to Sholom Aleichem and others—indeed even to that greatest of Jewish jokes, the Book of Job. Jewish jokes are authoritative. Jewish jokes are continuous with Jews' lives. Jewish jokes and anti-Semitic jokes touch at certain points—for example, in the malicious jokes told in the United States about 'JAPs' (Jewish American Princesses).[114]

What should we make of these remarks, insults, and jokes?
They speak for a stance that is unthreatened, relaxed. (Neo-Nazis apparently do not tell many anti-Semitic jokes, because Jews are too hateful to them to be fit subjects for humour.)[115] They assume a certain comfort about Jews, an

essential inequality. They imply a judgement; they are assertions of power. The maker of the remark, the insulter, the author of the witticism, may be taken to declare: I have nothing to fear from Jews. I can approach them unarmed. I can risk offending them, because they are of no account. I am released from the observance of my own code of good manners. See how unworthy they are, I do not have to behave decently towards them. My bad behaviour then becomes confirmation of nothing other than their disgrace. It reflects ill on them, not me. It is a gesture of exclusion: they may think that they have been accepted, but they are wrong. The remarks are comfortably within the limits, so to speak, of the 'sayable'. They draw on what everybody already knows about the Jews; they are not original observations. There is no holding the maker or author to personal account, because they merely recycle given slanders. Even when one Jew alone is addressed, all Jews are encompassed. It is not personal, because the insult reduces the insulted person to a mere instance of the despised collective entity, Jewry. This entity behaves in a certain way; he is taken to behave in that way too, by virtue of belonging to it. The insult is thus derived from group defamation. It deploys the words in which a whole people are customarily described.

The jokes, as much as the insults, are both aggressive and sour. There is no delight in absurdity; there is no happiness, no comical incongruity. They are contemptuous; the Jews are neither desired nor hated.[116] They are often tasteless. 'I stayed at the Metropole at Brighton; there wasn't enough foreskin there to cover a thrupenny-bit.'[117] According to Max Beerbohm, 'the [English public's] laughter at Jews' may be 'a survival of the old Jew-baiting' and second, they are 'foreigners, strangers, and the public has never got used to them': in combination, 'delight in suffering, contempt for the unfamiliar'.[118] It is self-congratulatory. The 'sudden glory' of laughter is prompted most often, observed Thomas Hobbes, among men by the 'apprehension of some deformed thing in another, by comparison whereof they suddenly applaud themselves'. Hobbes thinks little of people who are engaged thus. 'Of great minds', he writes, 'one of the proper works is to help and free others from scorn.' Anti-Semitic jokes are the work, by contrast, of small minds.[119] They contain the defence: 'only joking'. They are instances of hate speech uttered with a smile. They comprise the means by which anti-Semitism can be expressed, when 'serious' expressions might be deprecated. They evade censure.[120] Its current defensiveness is evoked in this meta-joke: 'How does a joke made by a Gentile about Jews begin? With a glance over the shoulder.'[121]

English culture thus made available many insults to direct at Jews. These insults were often merely offensive, almost contentless, perhaps given point by some allusion to a Jewish religious practice (frequently, circumcision) or religious prohibition (say, against the eating of pork). On occasion, they touched on an established theme of modern English anti-Semitism, the questioning of whether Jews could be loyal both to their own people and to their adopted nation. But they rarely were delivered to a general audience. It was as if a tacit distinction between public and private discourse on the matter of the Jews was honoured. The former was usually restrained, moderate, 'balanced'; the latter was looser, mocking, disparaging.

Jews are supposed to be unable to take a joke, and this puts them at a disadvantage, because being able to do so is prized in the culture. In December 1802, Jewish members of a theatre audience protested when in the course of the play they were watching insulting references to Jews were made. The press reaction to these protests was indignant and uncomprehending. 'What prescriptive right', asked the *Monthly Mirror*, have 'these men . . . to except to the universally admitted license of the stage to place in a humorous, and even ludicrous point of view the peculiarities, local and characteristic, which discover themselves in the common intercourse of men and manners?' Didn't they understand that it was all a harmless joke?[122] In June 2001, a Jewish City trader who was ordered to wear an Adolf Hitler uniform as a joke punishment for being late for work won substantial damages after claiming racial discrimination. Laurent Weinberger, whose grandmother died in Auschwitz, received an estimated £500,000 from the international money broker Tullett & Tokyo Liberty on the eve of an employment tribunal hearing. On refusing to wear the costume, Weinberger had been moved from his department and told to take a pay cut. Two weeks later he resigned. Mr Weinberger was called 'Jew Boy' and 'Yiddo' by one of his bosses. He also claimed that he was told he should make up for lost time when he took Jewish holidays. Brokers would also place a skullcap on top of the television when a Jew appeared on financial bulletins. In separate incidents, a Welsh trader was made to wear a Bo Peep costume because of his country's association with sheep, and a Northern Irish Protestant was given a pope costume. The firm said that Mr Weinberger, who worked there for six years, had joined in the 'banter', calling some colleagues a 'fat Scot' or 'yocks' if they were not Jewish. It claimed that such language was 'horseplay'.[123]

The effect on Jews is doubly damaging. There is the immediate, wounding impact, diminishing of self-esteem. And then there is the fact that they constitute a distraction. Jews are drawn to the work of seeking to controvert lies (insults are usually also false accusations), rather than to creative self-realization. Dictionaries become battlegrounds.[124] It became common, for a while, for Jews to refer to themselves as 'Israelite' or 'Hebrew' rather than 'Jews'.[125] Jews struggle against the prejudice expressed towards them in the very language that they themselves would otherwise wish to adopt in self-description.

Snubs, bullying, and exclusions

'I boldly confess', remarked Charles Lamb in his great essay, 'Imperfect sympathies' (1821), 'that I do not relish the approximation of Jew and Christian which has become so fashionable. The reciprocal endearments have, to me, something hypocritical and unnatural in them. I do not like to see the Church and Synagogue kissing...'[126] One hundred or so years later, a new friend of the then undergraduate Rosalind Franklin was warned off by another undergraduate, 'I don't know what you see in Ros—you know she is a Jew, don't you?'[127] Lamb and the anonymous undergraduate may both be said to have been discomforted by the abridging of the given social distance between Jews and Christians. By 'social distance' I mean the tacitly understood degrees of knowledge and intimacy that characterize relations between individuals, and between classes and groups.[128] The chief significance of social distance is in connection with the maintenance of status or with a person's standing; its counter-concept is of course 'social mobility'. Social scientists believe that the 'fellow-feeling and understanding'[129] between groups is measurable. In a typical scale, at one end there is, 'I would marry', or 'I would have as my regular friends'; towards the other end, 'I would decline to speak to', and then further towards that end, 'I would debar from the Presidency', and 'I would decline to work with in the same office' and at the end, 'I would have live outside my country.'[130] We live together, and yet we also live apart. If we are brought in closer physical proximity than social distance would allow, we often feel awkward, even tongue-tied. The following is an instance of precisely this experience. It records a visit at the turn of the twentieth century by the daughter of a leading Liberal politician to a wealthy Parisian Jewish household:

I wish I wasn't bored by what ought to amuse me...we have so little in common—it is hard to find anything to talk about...Tomorrow we can taste the joys of freedom & stringy meat & a vagabond life in the Quartier Latin free from Semitic patronage & hot rooms, constraints & orchids & champagne![131]

But there is also a moral—an *ostensibly* moral—aspect to this concept of social distance. Conforming to the rules of social distance is one way of showing respect to others. There is, then, a notion of 'proper distance', of how members of groups should relate to each other. 'Knowing one's place' is an aspect of treating others with the respect they claim, even if not due to them. This explains in part the active antipathy often provoked when social distance is breached. It is an antipathy expressed in a variety of ways. In a Frankfurt synagogue, a white-bearded man addresses Deronda, who 'had a strongly resistant feeling: he was inclined to shake off the touch of [the man's] arm'. The old man is presumptuous; Deronda is repelled by this unsought intimacy. He responds 'coldly': 'I am an Englishman.' Englishmen and women of an anti-Semitic inclination tended to respond more forcefully than Deronda to such overtures, resorting instead to snubs, to bullying, and to restrictions and exclusions, when making their own socially annihilating response, 'we are English'.

A snub is a response to a social solecism, an unjustified claim to attention—an attempt to violate the proper social distance between the parties. 'Will it not be infinitely disgusting to our County-Gentlemen', speculated an opponent of the Jew Bill, 'to have Jews mix'd amongst them?', while another observed of the Jews that they had grown 'very familiar' since the passing of the Bill.[132] Sir Richard Burton observed of 'the Hebrew', 'we should enjoy his society but for a certain coarseness of manner, and especially an offensive familiarity, which seems almost peculiar to him'.[133] The Jews, an anti-Semite complained in the 1930s, are 'blind to all lines of demarcation'. They make themselves 'conspicuous', 'drawing attention to themselves by loud clothes, loud cars and loud behaviour'.[134] This 'offensive familiarity' (often also described as 'pushiness') or 'blindness' is often met with a kind of inflamed condescension, somewhat akin to an insult, typically delivered with some hauteur. It is also akin to an act of expulsion, the driving away of a person who presumes on a circle of acquaintance.[135] (Called upon to justify the snub, circle members might say: 'We are without prejudice, but we are entitled to choose our company.' Alternatively, and more simply: 'He/she is not one of us.')[136] 'Antisemitism...was and is a just and legitimate reaction against the preposterous arrogance of the New

Jew', wrote an English observer in 1896. 'The main and most general cause of the dislike for Jews at present is their lack of tact.'[137] In 1901, Arnold White warned of the 'danger to the Empire' of the 'influence of foreign Jews on bad smart society'. (The only reason the Press ignores the problem, he added, is the 'remorseless control exercised by society and by Jews over the expression of public opinion hostile to them'.)[138] Lord Northcliffe told his editor to keep Jews out of the *Daily Mail's* 'Society' column: 'What with the Ecksteins, Sassoons and Mosenthals, we shall soon have to set the column in Yiddish.'[139] Jews often found themselves thus treated, because very few of them 'knew their place', and those who did were rarely prepared to 'keep' to it. They were not radicals; their ambition was no greater than to be accepted. They wished to 'pass'. ('Social position is the object of our modern Jew's real worship', mocked a Manchester newspaper, in 1876.)[140]

Jews had to be thick-skinned, to persevere in the face of frequent rebuff,[141] to be prepared for mockery of what was perceived as their obsequiousness; if they finally turned nasty, attacking their social superiors, it was attributed to frustrated ambition.[142] They offended equally when cowering or domineering. As the *Spectator* explained to its readership, 'the Jew has been obliged to make use of flattery and insolence to get his daily bread, and he discards neither when he gets rich'.[143] The world in which they lived was made up of notional, enclosed communities, the entrances to which were guarded by gatekeepers, and the Jews themselves were often no more than anxious, ingratiating supplicants. Some *were* accepted, in consequence of what Charles Booth described as 'the slow decay of the unwritten law of social prejudice'[144]—but only 'up to a point'; compromises were often reached (not a peerage for the useful Jewish financier, say, but a baronetcy for his baptized school-boy son).[145] The perception of Jews as somehow *petitioners*, dependent on the favour of society, caused them to be held in a kind of sardonic contempt, one that extended to society itself, if it so relaxed its standards as to let too many of them in. The exposure of social pretension then combined with the exposure of degraded social standards. This is the drama of Trollope's novels *The Way we Live Now* and *The Prime Minister*, for example. The latter's Mr Wharton QC muses, 'The world was changing around him every day. Royalty was marrying out of its degree. Peers' sons were looking only for money. And, more than that, peers' daughters were bestowing themselves on Jews and shopkeepers.'[146] A comparable contempt for Jews allied to self-contempt for reliance on Jewish money is also to be found in Thackeray: 'And we then leave the Jew (what we wish he'd leave us, / But we fear to no purpose) *a lone* in his glory.'[147] We need Rothschild's money, and so we must ignominiously suffer his presence.

These mostly diffuse sentiments achieved a certain concentration of expression in relation to the 'appropriateness' of Edward, the Prince of Wales, keeping company with 'rich, vulgar' Jews. Indeed, given that personal friendships in general were denied to the monarch, how could exceptions in favour of Jews be justified? The question was asked: 'What right have such people to force themselves in our society?' Queen Victoria warned her son: 'If you ever become King, you will find all these friends most inconvenient, and you will have to break with them all.' They were *parvenus*; their intolerable pretensions to equality with established members of society, and worse, their claim on the attention of the Prince of Wales, caused immense, perplexed offence. They might receive titles; they could not claim any honour. Their influence was degrading and coarsening. 'Why should [Edward] prefer to associate with Jews?' one courtier wondered, with some anguish. Edward was perceived to have taken on Jewish traits. A courtier claimed to notice a 'German-Jewish accent'. 'I wonder where [the king] got it', he pondered. 'Perhaps from his creditors.' They were not conventional court Jews, utterly beholden to their sovereign, mere instruments of his rule; *he* was beholden to *them*. Or so it seemed. To the sycophantic T. H. S. Escott, writing in 1908, 'the incorporation of the Hebrews into the august parts of the social fabric has been paid for at a certain moral price'. Though the 'great Jews' have 'appropriated the graces and the virtues of English lords', the 'highest sections of the polite world have voluntarily placed themselves under the Hebrew hegemony'. The Jews have become 'the favourites of fortune and the depositaries of power'. But when Edward VII died, and his son succeeded to the throne, another courtier confidently predicted, 'There will be a regular sweep of the people who used to be about the Court, the Jews and the second-rate women that the King preferred to his aristocracy because they amused him.' Within months, an observer was contentedly noting, 'harlots and Jews have been exchanged for tutors and governesses'. (A Max Beerbohm cartoon of the time has five Jewish figures anxiously wondering, 'Are we as welcome as ever?') And during the war, as we have seen, many well-to-do Jews of German origin were exposed to humiliating rebuffs. For example, Sir Edgar Speyer and his wife, it is related, 'were cut, pointedly and deliberately, by friends who in the summer had been staying with them and enjoying their hospitality'. Speyer responded to many such snubs by withdrawing from his public positions and immigrating to the United States.[148]

The concept of social distance, then, has considerable utility. It helps in the explication, say, of certain responses to the later career of Benjamin Disraeli. The abuse directed at him during his 1874–80 ministry derived at least in part from the belief, tacitly but widely held, that Anglo-Jewry was coming on 'too fast' in English society, conquering too many lofty positions too quickly—a Jew as prime minister, what next? One of Disraeli's critics complained, 'a single Jew' is 'mould[ing] the whole policy of Christendom to Jewish aims', and making 'it friendly to the friends and hostile to the foes of Judea'.[149] But it could not be denied, Disraeli declared his position; he could be argued with, voted against, snubbed, even. Hostility towards him was consistent, for example, with the expression of friendly, or at least neutral, sentiments towards the Rothschilds.[150] But 'social distance' has its limits as a concept. This sense of a troubling shortening of distance, of Jews advancing across social terrain once exclusively 'English', can give way to a sense of distance's utter collapse, of Jews taking control of society (and even of the 'BrYiddish Empire'),[151] not *visibly*, through command of its parliamentary institutions, but *invisibly*, through its financial and media institutions ('the Jew does not appear, for he does not care much to work openly').[152] This generates social emotions of much greater destructive power—not a manageable resentment towards identifiable, exceptional Jews, occupying lofty positions, but an *un*manageable fear of an *un*identifiable Jewish cabal (or lobby, or conspiracy), everywhere in control, but nowhere in evidence. When 'Jewish bankers' become the enemy then 'social distance' ceases to have explanatory value. One cannot snub the Elders of Zion.

It is across the final decades of the nineteenth century, then, that these two quite distinct positions come into distinct focus. Antagonism towards the Disraeli of the mid- to late 1870s is the furthest the first kind of position, the one explicable by reference to the concept of social distance, can go. Any further, and it passes over to the second position, which can only be explicated by concepts drawn from the vocabulary of social paranoia. It is indicative of the general character of English anti-Semitism that so much of it *can* be understood by reference to the policing of, and resentments at the infractions of, 'social distance'. Jews remained mostly *visible* to English anti-Semites.

The anti-Semitic snub is not, by contrast, always visible to its target. In 1935 the philosopher and lawyer H. L. A. Hart, of Jewish parentage, applied to become a member of the Oxford and Cambridge Club; in 1971, he applied for the position of Master of Hertford College, Oxford University. On both occasions, he was rejected, in each case, at least in part, because he was a Jew. In the first case, the rejection was thought to be as much about his lack of the right class and social connections as about his Jewishness. In the second case, the rejection was thought to be as much about Hart's unwillingness to attend chapel services (other than on special occasions) and his insistence upon living outside college. And yet. In the first case, the person who proposed Hart confirmed that the club committee did not 'dare' to go against 'a section of the club [that] was violently anti-Semitic'. In the second case, no less than the former prime minister, Harold Macmillan, confirmed to Hart that anti-Semitism was indeed a factor in the decision to reject him. When Hart was elected principal of Brasenose, another Oxford college, a Hertford don was heard to remark that the fellows had chosen 'Hirsch', a German-Jewish version of Hart's name.[153]

Bullying is an aggravated version of the snub. It is continuous, and coercive. With the snub, an actual claim is summarily rejected; with bullying, an imputed claim becomes the pretext for persistent harrying. The one is an act of exclusion; the other, a hunting down and a trapping. We have reached the point at which the English public school falls to be considered. 'In the life of an Englishman no period is more important than the years he spends at a public school', wrote the Old Etonian, Duff Cooper;[154] it has the 'largest share', asserted a nineteenth report, 'in moulding the character of an English Gentleman'.[155] In its worship of athletics, good form,[156] physical discomfort, and futile ritual,[157] bullying was of course taken for granted. The young Robert Cecil wrote despairingly from Eton to his father: 'I am bullied from morning to night without ceasing.' Repeated punching and kicking, and pulling of hair, of course, but also pelting with food, spitting, smashing possessions, tearing and burning personal books— all this, and more, Salisbury endured.[158] His experience was typical. Jewish boys often did at least as badly. Here is Froude on Disraeli: 'At an early age it was decided that he must go to school, but where it was not easy to decide. English boys were rough and prejudiced, and a Jewish lad would be likely to have a hard time among them.'[159] At Harrow school, in the early years of the twentieth century, the Jewish boys were known as 'the damned Jews'; there was always a 'background of anti-Semitic feeling'.[160] 'As a successful young sportsman', recalls one former pupil (1943–7), 'I clearly remember a master shouting, "knock the Jew boy off the ball".'[161] Testimonies of Jews bullied as children at school, and not only public schools,[162] throng memoirs of the period.[163] These experiences—the 'Jew hunts', the casual violence, the disparagements and insults, the laboured, wounding humour[164]—duly made their way into literature and film. In an early scene in Lindsay Anderson's film *If . . .* (1968) there is this exchange: 'Quiet!' 'Look at fatso's blubber! It's disgusting, it's a disease. Christ! I'm infected. I've got elephantitis!' 'Go on Keating, get out! Fatso hasn't got elephantitis, he's just a fat Jew!'[165]

The bullying of Jewish schoolchildren derived in part from the belief that Jews are not good at games, which in turn has several aspects. They are individualists, not 'team-players'; they do not play fair; they are physically weak; they are cowards. Jews are intellectual and self-seeking, brainy and commercial. They are not 'sporting'; they are 'too clever by half'. (That vice, 'cleverness'—the Jews 'are the cleverest people in the world', complained one anti-Semite. But, he added, much good it does them!)[166] Much school bullying was justified as punishment for these vices. It was an aggravated version of what Orwell referred to as 'the attitude of the rugger-playing prefect toward the school swot'.[167] The attitude reflected a culture of athleticism, and a disdain for mere intellectual acuteness.[168] In this culture, one plays to win, but not for oneself, for one's 'side'. Sport is taken to be the test of 'character'. 'All peoples have their play, but none of the great modern nations have built it up in quite the same way into a rule of life and a national code', wrote a German visitor to Britain in the 1920s.[169] It had, of course, an imperial aspect. In the words of an English public school headmaster, speaking at the end of the nineteenth century: 'In the history of the British Empire, it is written that England has owed her sovereignty to her sports.' This is because, he explained, of 'the pluck, the energy, the perseverance, the good temper, the self-control, the discipline, the co-operation, the *esprit de corps*', that are all necessary conditions for success at games.[170] Of course, when Jews defeated expectations, they were handsomely rewarded. They became invisible as Jews; they were *accepted*:

> As a public-school master I may remark that I have several times observed that Jewish boys at a public school who happen to be good athletes, and thus find open to them the readiest road to the esteem of their schoolfellows, display far

less of the 'Jewish ethos' than other less fortunate Jewish boys. The average Gentile boy simply does not reckon them as Jews at all, whatever their physiognomy and their surnames may be.[171]

It was this sense of an unparticularized but distasteful 'Jewish ethos' that doubtless lay beneath much of the anti-Semitic sentiment among the public schoolboys of the period. Ferdinand Mount, for example, writing about his post-war school days, noted: 'We are anti-Semitic in a vague, dismal way, perhaps because we are ignorant of the subject, although we know perfectly well what Hitler did.'[172]

If bullying is in some sense the opposite of the snub, social exclusions and restrictions are generalized versions of the snub. They are, of course, exercises of power.[173] These 'disabilities' were a central feature of Anglo-Jewish life in the eighteenth century and in the first half of the nineteenth century;[174] in the century that followed, they gradually lost their centrality. Partial or complete exclusions from golf, tennis, motor, and dining clubs, public school quotas ('all places for boys not of the Christian faith have been filled'),[175] restaurant and hostel advertisements that stated, 'Jews not catered for', advertisements for secretaries, clerks, and shop assistants that specified 'Jews need not apply', 'No Jewesses', 'No Jews entertained', and so on, did not have the same weight as exclusions from the Houses of Commons and Lords. But they were no doubt humiliating to Jews all the same.[176] One Jewish applicant was met with this exasperated response from the golf club committee: 'Can't you take a hint? Do we have to be more pointed? If you apply for membership, we will blackball you.'[177] The exclusion of Jews from Finchley Golf Club took on a political character when a local newspaper pointed out that the membership committee comprised 'prominent Conservatives', leading to a swing of Jewish voters towards the Liberal party in the local elections that followed shortly thereafter.[178] Even in the 1960s, these practices were quite widespread, though rarely openly avowed. A series of *Jewish Chronicle* investigations in 1960 and 1961 found that golf club secretaries tended to deny the existence of formal quotas or bans, often in the face of incontrovertible evidence of their existence ('We would not say we bar Jews, we just prefer not to take them'), while head teachers more robustly defended them as appropriate to their schools' Christian character, and meeting the requirements of both Christian and Jewish parents (the latter, because it was said they themselves did not want their children to be at predominantly Jewish schools).[179]

Such disabilities added to, and in some sense validated, Jews' poor reputation; they 'lowered them in the scale of society', it was said, 'and degraded them in the eyes of their fellow subjects'. Circumventing them offered no relief, what is more, because it made Jews look like 'tricksters'.[180] (There are many good Jewish jokes about Jews who deny their religion to get into 'restricted' clubs and schools.) Similarly, what conclusions could be drawn from adverts in London's East End press, such as 'Rooms to let, every convenience, quiet house, Jews and children objected to'?[181] Only that Jews were objectionable—personally disagreeable, perhaps, with habits that made them unsuitable, even unappealing, as tenants. These sentiments were not limited to any particular social class. Jews were excluded in the 1920s from many Oxford University clubs too.[182] And in the 1950s, officials of the Cambridge University Appointments' Board were required to defend themselves when extracts from their private notes concerning two Jewish undergraduates were made public:

> Not very appetizing looking—short and Jewy with wet palms but seems a versatile chap and quite a figure anyhow in the bridge and chess world.
>
> I fear an unattractive chap—if only because one is instinctively drawn to feel this about the chosen race from which he must surely stem. Small, sallow, raven hair and fleshy nose.[183]

The second official added the observation, 'I think more of the reaction of potential employers than my own, of course.' Of course.

Exclusions and restrictions of an informal nature, when acknowledged, were often contested. Proposals to exclude or restrict, lacking the authority of established practice, often failed. For example, Henrietta Barnett (1851–1936), the social reformer, early advocate of women's suffrage, and promoter of schemes to improve the lives of working-class girls and women, was not an admirer of Jews (she 'loved them not', she confided to her friend, for their selfishness), and wanted to limit Jewish access to Toynbee Hall, a university settlement in London's East End, where students could work in the holidays to relieve the lives of the poor. Her proposal was rejected. 'With regard to the Jews,' commented the Hall's warden, 'Mrs Barnett has suggested some frigid scheme of demarcation by which [they] should use the place within certain stated hours. This is absolutely impracticable.'[184] There was little scope in nineteenth-century England (still less, in the century that followed), for new 'frigid schemes'. Indeed, a sense developed that there was something ignominious about institutions maintaining restrictions, as if they feared those they sought to exclude. Certainly they came to be seen as risking isolation themselves from civil society. An advocate of the removal of the residual religious disabilities at Oxford and Cambridge Universities explained: 'I believe the removal of tests would tend to perpetuate our great institutions. . . . I am a Churchman because I believe the Church of England right; but I deprecate the University hiding itself in any little nook of prejudice out of the general spirit of the community.'[185]

In his biography of the philosopher A. J. Ayer, Ben Rogers tells of a provision in Eton's governing statute requiring fathers of Collegers (the school's scholars) to be British by birth. Hearing of this in 1960, Ayer, an Old Etonian, wrote to the headmaster asking when and why this particular provision had been added. The answer given was 1945, in order to ensure that the College did not admit 'too many boys who, though themselves British subjects, were alien in outlook and difficult to assimilate into the intimate life of college'. The fear was that the 'over-maturity' of 'sons of Southern Europeans and Middle Easterners' might 'exert a most undesirable influence' on British boys. Ayer replied that this had 'the flavour of anti-Semitism'. Following a private meeting, at which it was conceded that the provision had been aimed primarily at Jews (because they were 'too clever' or 'clever in the wrong way'), it was agreed that the provision would be repealed within a year, and that in return Ayer would not 'go public' on the matter. But the year passed and nothing happened. Then, by chance, Ayer ran into a senior Conservative Party politician, and raised it with him. He in turn raised it with the then prime minister, Harold Macmillan. An Old Collager himself, Macmillan wrote to the School complaining of the anti-Semitic tone of the statute. Within a month, it was repealed. Ayer was jubilant. His wife recalled, 'It was a once in a lifetime triumph; it meant *everything* to him.'[186] The Eton decision was an exclusion, which is a kind of snub, defended by an insult.

Of course, the most radical exclusion of all is expulsion. From time to time, and especially in the mid-twentieth century, the more radical English anti-Semites, pondering the 1290 precedent, entertained the thought that the Jews might be expelled once again—perhaps despatched to Madagascar.[187] This was silly, vicious stuff, the polar opposite to the resolved, sovereign act of Edward's, the fantasy of individuals who were marginal even among the coteries that comprised the extra-parliamentary Far Right. Jews have never—not even for a moment—been at risk of any second physical expulsion from England. But there has been, as a continuous aspect of English anti-Semitism, a kind of pushing-away of Jews ('Go back to Palestine!'),[188] a conceptual expulsion of them which amounts among other things to the proposition, a 'Jew' cannot be an 'Englishman'.[189] This gesture of exclusion from the national polity, one that operates by a kind of mental reservation, and regards Jews as in some sense apart from and alien to an idealized England and English values and characteristics,[190] has had a long life.

Here are some examples. An anti-Jew Bill pamphleteer asserted, as if driven to affirm the obvious only by the outrage upon it by the passing of the 1753 Bill, 'Jews cannot be incorporated with Englishmen, without violating whatever Englishmen hold sacred.'[191] Eighty years later, the position had not changed among anti-emancipationists. 'You cannot call them English, even though they are born among us', asserted a Tory MP in 1830. 'They are no more Englishmen (in the sense, at least, of civil identification) than they are Romans, Poles or Russians, among who we also find them.' And three years later, another Tory MP explained, 'A Jew could never be made an Englishman, even though he be born here.'[192] Frank Harrison Hill, in his series of articles, 'The Political Adventures of Lord Beaconsfield' (1878), insisted of Disraeli, 'he is in almost every essential point far more of a Venetian and a Jew than of an Englishman'. 'He has been true to the Jewish people who are really his country and church . . . his career has not been . . . that of an English statesman, but rather that of a foreign political adventurer.'[193] In 1905, Winston Churchill published a biography of his father, Lord Randolph Churchill. A hostile review appeared in the *Daily Telegraph*. The review enraged Churchill's uncle, the Duke of Marlborough, who wrote to the newspaper a letter of protest. He described the review as 'essentially un-English', a phrase, as he later explained to Churchill, intended to be 'a devastating reference' to the Jewish origins of the newspaper's proprietor, Levy Lawson, recently ennobled by Balfour as Lord Burnham. Marlborough hoped to 'administer a good and sound trouncing to that dirty little Hebrew'.[194] In April 1927, the Jewish Philip Sassoon, Under-Secretary of State for Air, expressed in the House of Commons some security concerns about a visit by MPs to an airplane construction site. A Labour MP shouted at him: 'You are insulting us; you are no Briton; you are a foreigner.'[195] Here is a letter from the *Cambridgeshire Times*, 18 October 1940: 'It is really scandalous when honest born British citizens are staying in London and facing it, that the Jewish element should come down here [to Cambridge] and throw themselves on the public expense.'[196] Asked about his liability for the legal costs of his victorious adversaries in the libel action he brought in 2000, the anti-Semitic David Irving responded, 'Undoubtedly they will come for their pound of flesh, but they will find I'm made of British beef.'[197] This sense of an Englishness embattled, and at risk of being overwhelmed, is strong in the late nineteenth and early twentieth century. When the actual, given England departs too desperately from the idealized, fantasy England, the search for those responsible for the gap ends with the Jews. Jewish influence or power is the cause of English decline; for the nation to be great again, the 'Jewish problem' must be addressed.

Gentlemen and Jews

The question of what constitutes a 'gentleman' is an element in the conversation that England has had with itself over the centuries; it is a cultural constant subject to endless refinement and comment. It is in English literature, perhaps, that the ideal has been most fully explored. In the nineteenth century, the concept served to unify the nation; the status of the gentleman was the horizon of aspiration for its citizens.[198] The ideal of the 'gentleman' has now faded, perhaps to invisibility. It might have reached this point of extinction in the 1960s, the end of the period under review in this chapter.[199] At pretty much any earlier time in England's history, however, the 'gentleman' would have been understood to be modest, diffident, well-mannered. He 'plays the game'; he is an amateur. He has character, if not unusual intellect. He does not make a display of himself; he conceals his abilities. He shrinks from originality. Art, music, and literature make him somewhat uncomfortable. The notion is somewhat class-bound; it was working-class shorthand for a male member of the upper-middle class.[200] But it was also very elevated, especially in eighteenth-century France. The *philosophes* constructed an ideal of seeking happiness upon this earth, tolerance of one's fellow man, and the pursuit of progress through scientific knowledge, and gave it the name, '*Gentleman anglais*'.[201]

Throughout much of this period, the question of whether a Jew could ever be a gentleman was an aspect of this conversation. The intolerable problem for Jews was that while to be a gentleman required a great deal of money, the getting of it was deprecated. Mostly, it was taken for granted that a Jew could not be a gentleman—a view shared by Jewish anti-Semites such as Otto Weininger.[202] Whatever else may be said of Jews, however estimable their qualities, however lamentable their sufferings, they are not, nor can they be, gentlemen. The phrase 'Jewish gentleman' begs for an ironic tone, or even a sneer.[203] In every century, the point is made (though sometimes also contested). In Maria Edgeworth's *Harrington*, for example, the objectionable Lady de Brantefield declares, 'A Jew, perhaps—gentleman, I deny; no Jew ever was or ever will be a gentleman.'[204] Jews get it wrong; they do not know the code. They insist on their position, or they are over-familiar. They are not unreflective virtuosos, that is, of social distance. Lady Halifax confided to her diary, upon her husband succeeding Lord Reading as Viceroy of India in 1926: 'It gets on my nerves to be called "Your Excellency", which I am sure is overdone by the ex-Reading staff. One hardly ever calls the K and Q "Your Majesty"; it seems to me rather vulgar.'[205]

It was in mid- to late-nineteenth-century fiction that the question of whether a Jew could be a gentleman was most thoroughly explored. In Anthony Trollope's novels, which represent the most sustained literary exploration of what he termed 'this difficult word',[206] the Jew is usually the antitype to the gentleman. The villain of *The Prime Minister*, Ferdinand Lopez, for example, 'knows how to look and talk like a gentleman' and claims to be one, but is soon revealed to be nothing but a Jew-adventurer— a stranger, apparently foreign, without discernible parentage, clever and adept at modern languages, who says awkward and impertinent things but is also a schemer, a cajoling bully, a speculator, a swindler, a liar, and a cheat. Though 'he had lived nearly all his life in England', Lopez 'had not quite acquired that knowledge of the ways in which things are done which is so general among men of a certain class'. He is 'selfish', 'void' of 'principle', 'utterly unmanly', 'a lie from head to foot'.[207] Nevertheless, according to Shirley Robin Letwin, Trollope concludes that the most perfect instance of an English gentleman is the foreign Jewish woman, Mme Max Goesler. Though this has an air of deliberate paradox, it was an established trope in the mid- to late Victorian era that one might find 'gentlemen' in the unlikeliest of places. When Sir David Salomons became Lord Mayor, *The Times* reported this exchange between a Church dignitary and the Prince Consort: 'Thank goodness, Your Royal Highness, we've got a gentleman in the civic chair at last.' 'Yes my lord, but you had to go beyond the pale of Christendom to find him.'[208] In George Eliot, we find that a Jew may be *better* than a gentleman. To be a 'gentleman' is a repudiated horizon of expectation in the novel. Deronda says, early on, 'I should like to be a gentleman.' 'I am a gentleman, Cath. We expect you to marry a gentleman', says Miss Arrowpoint's father, when told of his daughter's intention to marry the musician Klesmer.[209] Grandcourt is of course a gentleman, a man who is never rude except on purpose, and whose assumption of rank is automatic.[210] This setting off of the Jew against the English gentleman is the drama of *Daniel Deronda*. (Henry James contrives to be offensive about Jews *and* gentlemen in his fictional dialogue on the novel.) In George du Maurier's *Trilby*, the Jew is a kind of negative imprint of the English gentleman. Svengali speaks several languages, mixing them up charmlessly in individual sentences. His clothes are showy. He has lustreless hair, which falls down behind his ears on to his shoulders 'in that musician-like way that is so offensive to the normal Englishman'. His voice is thin and mean and harsh, and on occasion breaks into a disagreeable falsetto. He hisses. He is a 'great artist', a 'truly phenomenal artist', and his love of his art is his one virtue. Even here, however, he is incapable of doing justice to the 'highest and best music'—to Handel, Bach, Beethoven. He either fawns or bullies, and he is often 'grossly impertinent'. When he cringes, it is with a mock humility full of sardonic threats. He is always ready to vex, frighten, or torment anybody or anything smaller or weaker than himself. He has no heart, no conscience, no tenderness, no manliness. He has no honour; he is full of self-conceit. He is unchivalrous. He is a physical coward. He behaves ignominiously to a disadvantaged enemy ('being an Oriental Israelite Hebrew Jew, he [was] not able to resist the temptation of spitting in his face') but he is also 'cowed' by the 'stern, choleric, invincible blue eye of the hated northern Gentile'. He is a 'blackguard'. He is morally unclean.[211] It is perhaps only to Dickens, alone among the significant novelists of the nineteenth century, that the question of what constituted a gentleman was not of absorbing interest.[212]

It was not until 1932 that Anglo-Jewry volunteered a participant in this conversation; until then, Jewish men, whatever their position or wealth, were suppliants, not interlocutors. Then Harold Laski published 'The danger of being a gentleman: Reflections on the ruling class in England'.[213] Laski was a Jewish intellectual, and leading member of the Labour Party. He went too far; he was too clever; he spoke too much. British officials referred to him as a 'snivelling Hebrew'; the Labour politician Hugh Dalton called him 'an undersized Semite'; the Conservative *National Review* observed, 'anything less like the British working man than an international Jew could not well be imagined; he has no idea about the land he happened to be born in'; an obituary mentioned 'an alien mind imbued and impregnated with an alien philosophy'.[214]

Laski explains in his essay that the ideal of the gentleman is peculiarly English. The gentleman is, rather than does. His attitude towards life is one of indifferent receptivity. He is interested in nothing in a professional way. He must not concern himself with the sordid business of earning a living. He should have gone to Eton or Harrow, and then Oxford or Cambridge. He must know how to ride and shoot and cast a fly. He should have a club, and belong to the Conservative Party. He should play most games in some fashion, but none so well that he is thereby distinguished from his fellows. He should believe that the cultivation of sport is the secret of national greatness, but hold that professionalism ruins sport's true spirit. He should know nothing of political economy; he should not be enthusiastic about religion. He must find speech difficult, and eloquence impossible. He is sceptical of the thinker, and refuses to think in terms of principle. He is never so driven by a purpose as to be its slave. He never doubts his superiority over other people. If he travels abroad, he must return without the deformation of a broadened mind. He has the habit of graceful command, and enjoys the exercise of power. He keeps his word; he has a shrewd, worldly wisdom; he has a sense of obligation towards those whom he rules. His genius for compromise has given him control of England for at least 200 years. He regards himself as the final term of human evolution; until recently, the world was inclined to agree. In the period of his apogee he was indeed a better ruler than any of his rivals. *But*—his characteristics are a public danger whenever quantitative knowledge, unremitting effort, vivid imagination, or organized planning is required. He is unequal to the foreign challenge to English industrial supremacy; he is bewildered by modern democracy. He is a commercial and political failure, complacent and thickheaded. He is no more than a costly, if decorative, appendage to a civilization in which he is functionally useless. The prestige of his superiority has gone. Yet it is not certain that a more admirable type will replace him. The leader of the future is likely to take clemency for weakness and to have no time for the open mind. He has a horror of a various civilization and he means by 'freedom' only a stronger kind of chain.

Does Laski write all this, in the current cant phrase, 'as a Jew'? It is a considered, witty piece. There is also a slightly bruised sense of defining himself against the character of the gentleman. He is everything the gentleman is not; the gentleman is everything that he is not. Several decades later, the spokesmen for the 'gentleman' had their revenge. Discoursing on the concept of the English gentleman, the genealogist Sir Iain Moncreiffe observed of Laski, 'Foreigners at heart, like the late Harold Laski who wrote *The Danger of Being a Gentleman*, . . . could never begin to understand them [i.e. gentlemen].'[215] 'Foreigner' is of course code for 'Jew'—a 'foreigner at heart' is a person who though British-born, is incapable of a British perspective. This contempt, which sometimes intensifies and becomes a kind of angry scornfulness, is typical of English anti-Semitism.

Middle ground: ideological versions of contempt

It does not, then, lavish attention on Jews. Diderot remarked that the English believed in God '*un peu*';[216] one might also say, they hated Jews '*un peu*'. Theirs was not an anti-Semitism, then, likely to foster Jew-hatred of an elaborated or ideological character. In the eighteenth century, the furthest extent that English anti-Semitism moved in such a direction was when the Deists sought, in William Paley's phrase, to 'wound Christianity through the sides of Judaism'.[217] Though it was thus a somewhat compromised and opportunistic endeavour,[218] it was taken up and developed on the Continent to damaging effect. What the English Deists initiated, Continental philosophers continued. And then, about a hundred years later, certain English writers and publicists, operating at a much lower intellectual level to their eighteenth-century forebears, contributed to the formation of race thinking, which in turn, and once again, was taken up and developed on the Continent, by writers and publicists who themselves operated at a much lower intellectual level than *their* eighteenth-century forebears. In each case, in relation both to Deism and to racism, the effect of the move abroad (so to speak) was to convert what was an essentially condescending perspective on Jews to a perspective that was more threatened, and therefore much more belligerent.

English Deism was radical, innovative, the harbinger of great changes in the European mentality.[219] God's activity was taken to be limited to bringing the world into existence. All true revealed religion aspires to the condition of natural religion—that is, a doctrine of 'universal benevolence',[220] stripped of all local, temporal limitations. Natural religion, which is as old as the world, is to be distinguished from 'artificial theology' and 'superstitious devotion'.[221] Christianity is valid only to the extent that it is a 'republication of the Law of Nature'.[222] Granting the diversity of position among individual Deists, they shared certain fundamentals: a plea for free rational inquiry; an assertion of reason's pre-eminence; the rejection of religious privilege, revelation, and miracles; a conception of the purity of primitive religion and its corruption by priestcraft.[223] According to John Toland's *Christianity not Mysterious* (1696), Jesus Christ taught reasonable worship and pure morals. He stripped the truth of all external types and ceremonies, and made it obvious to people with even the meanest capacities. His disciples maintained this simplicity, but then Jews and Gentiles introduced abuses. The Jews, still attached to their Levitical rites and feasts, introduced comparable formalities and ceremonies into Christian practices. But this was as nothing compared to the injury done to true religion by Gentiles. Still attached to their mysteries, they likewise set up mysteries in Christianity. These pagan mystic rites were imported into Christianity to its great loss.[224] Other Deists took a harsher line on the Jewish contribution to Christianity's formation.[225] The Jews' claims made in respect of the composition of the Bible are false. It does not comprise God's revelation; it is instead the product of the Jews copying other peoples, especially the Egyptians.[226] Books do not assist, in any event save as instances of reasoning: if they refuse to reason, and instead insist upon their revelatory properties, they are useless. 'Nothing but reasoning can improve reason, and no book can improve my reason in any point, but as it gives me convincing proofs of its reasonableness...'[227] What is more, biblical morality is highly questionable. We should not, wrote Shaftesbury, 'view with satisfaction the punishments inflicted by human hands on...aliens and idolaters'.[228]

The Deists disparaged Judaism as the first instance of revealed religion; they disparaged Jewish influence in the early history of the Church; they disparaged the authority of the Bible; they disparaged biblical and modern Jews, the former for the vices exposed by their own Scriptures, the latter, for the implacability of their attachment to their absurd faith, and for their 'pretence' that the Talmud, 'the mere invention of modern Jews', had been 'secretly given to Moses at Mount Sinai'.[229] The Jews were vulgar and unoriginal, and they were mired in superstition and barbarity. To one Deist, they were 'the proudest and most lying nation in the world'; 'ignorance and superstition, pride, injustice, and barbarity were [their] peculiar characteristics'.[230] To another Deist, they were 'an illiterate, barbarous and ridiculous people' with whom God had to deal by using 'craft rather than reason'.[231] Their bigotry, their fanaticism and their violence, were utterly deplorable; they were altogether wretched. Christianity, which derived from this crude, cruel culture, was not to be taken seriously.[232] Ridicule was the Deists' principal rhetorical device,[233] and the Jews were their principal targets. God chose the Jews, Anthony Collins explained, for much the same reason that Socrates chose the 'ill-conditioned' Xantippe for his wife: that is, 'to exercise and declare his extreme patience to the world'.[234]

Consider Thomas Morgan's work, *The Moral Philosopher* (1738). It is a dialogue between a Christian Deist and a Christian Jew, and is thus a partly secularized instance of the medieval *Adversus Judaeos* genre. Morgan was condemned in his lifetime for his 'very deep prejudice against Old Testament history, and all the Characters of Persons therein contained'.[235] The work has a strongly Marcionite quality; it seeks to establish that one can be a Christian 'without being a Jew'. It asserts against the 'Judaizing Christians' that 'things merely positive, ritual and ceremonial', are not 'necessary Parts of Religion'. Christianity, the 'most complete and perfect Scheme of moral Truth and Righteousness', does not need Judaism, a 'dead weight', and a 'most gross and carnal Institution'. Morgan's account of the Jews is hostile in the extreme. They are 'reserv'd, sullen, morose and severe, [and cannot] bear any thing of Wit and Humour'; 'Blindness, Bigotry and Enthusiasm [is] the incurable Distemper of that wretched People'; Israel was a 'wretched and wicked Nation'. They were 'Egyptianized' in Egypt, coming 'out of their Bondage with all the Prejudices and Wrong Impressions that they had contracted in that most wretched, enslav'd and Priest-ridden Country'. By their wickedness, the Jews forfeited God's promises to them—promises that they foolishly believed to be unconditional. 'How much they were mistaken' in this respect, Morgan observes, 'Time has sufficiently demonstrated.' Their belief that they were 'the special Favourites of Heaven', that they would 'succeed in all their Enterprises' and 'make themselves the Masters of the whole World', and that God would give them 'uttermost Parts of the Earth for [their] Possession', was their 'national Delusion'. In fact, the Jews were 'set up by Providence as an Example to the World . . . of the natural Effects and Consequences of Ignorance, Superstition, Presumption and Immorality'. As they were when they left Egypt, so they were when God Himself finally left them, 'an everlasting Name of Reproach, and eternal Scandal to the Profession of Religion, without moral Goodness or any rational Dependence on God and Providence'. They were the crucifiers of Jesus, a 'victim to popular Superstition, Rage and Phrenzy'. The Jewish Christian does not put up much of a fight: 'We are agreed, that the People of Israel at first, and their Remains afterwards, called Jews, were a most untoward, grossly ignorant, amazingly superstitious, and desperately wicked Generation of Men . . . '[236]

The French then took up the Deists' views, and developed their anti-Semitic potential. Voltaire led the way, greedily receiving their endeavours and magnifying them,[237] but he was not alone in this respect.[238] D'Holbach's *L'esprit du Judaisme* (1770), for example, added venomous passages about the Jews not to be found in Anthony Collins's *Discourse* (1724).[239] The judgement that English Deists inaugurated modern anti-Semitism,[240] though commonly and on the whole justly made, needs to be qualified by reference both to the Deists' appropriation of critical Jewish perspectives on the Resurrection and on Jesus' divinity and miracles,[241] and to the innovative and immense influential critique of Judaism by Baruch Spinoza. The post-Christian Deists in turn adopted and derided Jewish positions, always mockingly, condescendingly; the post-Jewish Spinoza repudiated Judaism in its entirety and without reservation, forensically. In the history of modern anti-Semitism, Spinoza has the weightier presence by far.[242]

In any event, the English atheist positions that came out of Deism were rarely anti-Semitic themselves. English atheism, from Hume through Paine,[243] and then from Mill to Russell and on to Monty Python's *The Life of Brian*, has been even-handed in its rejection of Judaism and Christianity. The trajectory has been towards an ever more complete rejection of religion as such, 'that vast moth-eaten musical brocade / Created to pretend we never die . . . '[244] The most radical step was the first one. Hume exposed as a mere fiction the universal human nature on which the Deists founded their natural religion; his scepticism attacked the foundations of natural no less than revealed religion.[245] Paine, while conventionally scandalized by the behaviour of the ancient Israelites, dismissed both Old and New Testament as equivalent frauds.[246] 'Finding . . . no halting place in Deism,' wrote J. S. Mill of his father, James, 'he remained in a state of perplexity, until, doubtless after many struggles, he yielded to the conviction that concerning the origin of things nothing whatever can be known.' And then Mill adds the lethal note, 'the *ne plus ultra* of wickedness he considered to be embodied in what is commonly presented to mankind as the creed of Christianity'.[247] This wickedness was taken by most liberal-minded sceptics and atheists to include the persecution of non-Christians.[248] In his *History of Western Philosophy* (1946), Bertrand Russell identifies neutrally the Jewish elements in Christianity's formation, and makes neither especially deprecatory remarks about Judaism nor any supersessionist argument in favour of

Christianity. He is also clear about the character of Christian anti-Semitism.[249] In *Against All Gods* (2007), A. C. Grayling runs Judaism and Christianity together, and is pretty rude about both.[250]

What then of racism? Nineteenth- and early twentieth-century English anti-Semitism is not merely to be located within the broader racism of the period. Of course, what has been described as the 'virulence of race prejudice' in mid-nineteenth century Britain, its belief in racial determinism, provides something of a context. But the prejudiced conceptualizing of Jewish character and identity had a more specific and distinct provenance than the Victorian habit of generalizing about 'inferior' races.[251] In the pre-history of those discredited, bogus racial entities, the Aryan and the Semitic, may be found the Hebraic and Hellenic ideal types with some genuine if usually overstated cultural weight—especially when taken to stand for belief and intelligence, the sacred and the secular, as polarities in European thought.[252] English intellectuals contributed to the elaboration of both pairings, though not in the one-sided way typical of Continental writers. The principal English contribution to the discourse of the Hebraic and the Hellenic was made in a work that was not deprecatory of Jews (Matthew Arnold's *Culture and Anarchy*), written by a self-declared enemy of 'all one-sidedness and oppression',[253] while the principal English contributions to the pseudo-science of Semitic racial identity were made in one case by a man convinced that the Jews would shortly become extinct (Robert Knox), and in the other case, by a former Jew who celebrated in his fiction occult Jewish power (Benjamin Disraeli).

The deconstruction of the Christian civilization of the West into its Jewish and Greek components has mostly been a literary, when not a merely belletristic, exercise. It has had specific applications, of course. Jewish writers who wanted to break with traditional themes of *Galut* (exile) and *ge'ulah* (redemption),[254] for example, used the alternative binarism of the Hebraic and Hellenic the better to stage their agonistic encounters between Jerusalem and Athens. Matthew Arnold deployed these categories in *Culture and Anarchy* (1869) for the quite different purpose of addressing certain deformations in English politics and culture. He wanted his chapters on Hebraism and Hellenism to 'form a kind of centre for English thought and speculation on the matters treated in them'.[255] His master argument is that there are two sides to us, a 'thinking' side and a 'doing' side, which roughly correspond to the two aspects of our cultural inheritance, the Hellenic and the Hebraic. 'The uppermost idea with Hellenism is to see things as they really are; the uppermost idea with Hebraism is conduct and obedience.' Or in an alternative formulation, 'the governing idea of Hellenism is spontaneity of consciousness; that of Hebraism, strictness of conscience'. The tendency in England, says Arnold, has been to favour the latter; we are a nation 'nourished and reared in Hebraising'.[256] This has had many unhappy consequences, chief among which is 'Philistinism'. While we must Hellenize today, we may need to Hebraize tomorrow. Yet 'the aim and end of both Hebraism and Hellenism is ... one and the same'. Arnold makes no essential distinction between Judaism and the English forms of Christianity. He writes of 'the Hebrew, both of the Old and of the New Testament'. His concern throughout is with Christianity, barely with Judaism at all.

Arnold was not a systematic thinker; indeed, he tended to make a virtue of his dislike of 'system'.[257] He was therefore able, with clear conscience, to contribute to the confusions of his times regarding the supposed connections between racial, ethnological, and linguistic phenomena.[258] His race-talk tended to stimulate in him prejudicial remarks about the Jews, though of a constrained kind. In *Culture and Anarchy*, when he allowed race to intrude into his reasoning, he lapsed into both insult ('[the Hebrews were] an Oriental and polygamous nation ... whose wisest king had seven hundred wives and three hundred concubines') and a corresponding, immoderate praise ('the delicate and apprehensive genius of the Indo-European race, the race which invented the Muses, and chivalry and the Madonna').[259] The opening paragraph of *Literature and Dogma* (1873) frivolously disparages the prime minister, 'Mr Disraeli, treating Hellenic things with the scornful negligence natural to a Hebrew ...' A subsequent passage more hostilely disparages Jews in general as a 'petty, unsuccessful, unamiable people, without politics, without science, without art, without charm'. They are 'unattractive, nay repellent', and 'insignificant' in 'everything', save for one, 'extraordinary distinction', and that is their gift to humanity of the Bible, which is 'three-fourths of human life'.[260]

However, Arnold also tended to assert mankind's fundamental unity (and in particular to emphasize affinities between the English and the Hebrew people, the 'peculiar Semitico-Saxon mixture which makes the typical Englishman'),[261] and to mock or otherwise deprecate those race theories that tended towards opposing positions.[262] He repeatedly affirmed Christianity's origin in Judaism (notwithstanding that Jesus had a 'new and different way of putting things'), and he praised 'Israel's' 'signal witness'.[263] He even wrote, with somewhat clichéd pathos, of Israel's suffering, 'thy temple in ruins, thy reign over, thine office done, thy children dispersed, thy teeth drawn, thy shekels of silver and gold plundered'.[264] Much more consequentially, he did not confuse cultural categories, or ideal types, with actual, empirical communities of people, inevitably of mixed provenance. This conviction that European history and culture was to be understood in terms of a fluctuating but always constitutive combination of the Hebraic and the Hellenic was then taken up by Arnold's successors,[265] and became a cultural commonplace, subject only to the most inconsequential of occasional dissents.[266]

The 'scientific' discourse in England reflected and furthered the preoccupations of pan-European race 'science'. Robert Knox was the principal British contributor to this science, in his *Races of Man: A fragment* (London, 1850). Knox had little to say about Jews, and though what he said was mostly adverse, he attributed no particular power to them. There are, in ample measure, misconceptions about Jews in Knox's work. Some of these misconceptions recycle the oldest of anti-Semitic canards: 'To what extent the dreadful lepra afflicts the race [of gypsies] I know not; the Jew is, I think, also subject to it; races no doubt have their peculiar diseases'; 'the gipsy [sic] has made up his mind, like the Jews, to do no work, but to live by the industry of others'; etc. But, and this is what, matters: 'my opinion is that they [the Jews] are becoming extinct'.[267] Knox wrote dismissively: 'the theory of *Coningsby* is not merely a fable as applied to the real and undoubted Jew, but is absolutely refuted by history'.[268] This 'theory', advanced by a character in this novel, the impressive Sidonia, is that the Jews comprise a pure, flourishing race, exceptional in every respect, and dominant in the politics and culture of Europe. 'The world is governed by very different personages from what is imagined by those who are not behind the scenes.'[269]

Anti-Semites seized on this piece of bravado (or 'naughty joke')[270] as confirming the existence of an international Jewish conspiracy;[271] the fantastic Sidonia's boasts, treated as admissions on which complete reliance can be placed, continue to be cited by anti-Semites today.[272] Jewish publicists were from the outset careful to dissociate themselves from it.[273] It is indeed an empty fiction. In his own name, Disraeli offered a very diluted version of Sidonia's thesis a few years later. 'There is no race at this present', he wrote in his biography of the Tory politician, George Bentinck, 'that so much delights, and fascinates, and elevates, and ennobles Europe, as the Jewish.' They are an eternal people. 'The world has by this time discovered that it is impossible to destroy the Jews.' It is an 'inexorable law of nature which has decreed that a superior race shall never be destroyed or absorbed by an inferior one'.[274] And then, in 1870, he repudiated all talk of 'Semites' and 'Aryans', mocking it in his novel *Lothair* (1870). The absurd Mr Phoebus, an artist dedicated to 'Aryan principles', deplores 'Semitism' for destroying art and warns, 'Nothing can be done until the Aryan races are extricated from Semitism.'[275]

In the undergrowth of late Victorian and Edwardian culture there was much talk about race, and racial concepts steadily infiltrated the language of social science and policy administration[276]—as well as promoting on occasion somewhat ludicrous research (for example, into the 'fundamental character' of the 'Jewish facial expression').[277] Eugenicist positions gave a scientific basis to contempt for, and fear of pollution by, certain ethnic groups. But there was no ready consensus among eugenicists that the Jews were to be counted among these despised, dangerous groups. Among the measures to be taken to improve the quality of the nation's racial stock by influencing the breeding rates of different sections of the population, were the Jews to be encouraged, or discouraged?[278] Galton, for example, favoured selective immigration by Jews, among others.[279] Just as race language was not always used with exclusionary connotations,[280] so there were eugenicists who argued in favour of *mixing* the races.[281] They asked the old questions, in their own specialist language, with no striking advance in real originality: would the Jews 'maintain themselves as a group apart', 'a nation within a nation?' A bias against Jewish immigration, say, could be perceived in certain eugenicists' research, notwithstanding the ostensible rigour of their methodology.[282] But neither race-talk nor eugenics-talk became programmatic in English political discourse, though they each sanctioned a great deal of crassness.[283] The 'English governing class', Chesterton correctly observed, generally abstained from calling on 'the absurd deity of race'.[284] Elazar Barkan has described the scientific repudiation of racism in the inter-war period. It required more than an attack by scientists on popular misconceptions; science itself needed to be purged. The belief in the biological validity of race as a concept had to be eliminated from scientific discourse. By the end of this period, race typology as causally effective had been largely discredited, racial differentiation had retreated to physical characteristics, and racially discriminatory action came to be viewed as racist.[285]

The only substantial contribution of an English intellectual to the racist-conspiracist anti-Semitism that emerged in late nineteenth-century Continental Europe was made by Houston Stewart Chamberlain (1855–1927), but he did not make that contribution in England. ('The mere thought of England and the English makes me unhappy', he wrote.)[286] His *The Foundations of the Nineteenth Century* (1899), one of the principal texts of German racism,[287] was written in German and published in Munich. It preaches the 'antagonism of races', and the 'irreconcilability' of the religious ideals of Judaism and Christianity.[288] It sets the Teutons ('we Teutons'),[289] a free, self-governing people, against the Jews, heteronomous legalists. It detaches Jesus from the Jews and associates them with Marxism, liberalism, finance capitalism, materialism, and Catholicism. The inhabitants of Northern Europe have become the makers of the world's history, yet we are inclined to underestimate our own powers and exaggerate the importance of the Jewish influence. The usual treatment of the 'Jewish Question' is thus always superficial. Though the problem of Judaism in our midst is one of the most difficult and dangerous questions of the day, so threateningly perilous that indeed we live in a 'Jewish age', the solution is with us. The Teuton can, 'whenever we please', 'emancipate us from Judaism'.[290] In this 1,100 page work, Chamberlain recites many of the anti-Semitic commonplaces in circulation at the time, and in earlier periods; he was a plunderer, or ransacker, of other anti-Semitic writers, Drumont among them.[291] His separation of the Galilean Jesus from Judaism revives early Christian de-Judaized accounts of Jesus, which in due course encouraged the notion of a Semitic Judea and a more Aryan Galilee.[292] 'Practically all branches of our life', he lamented, 'have become more or less willing slaves to the Jews.' The Jews are an 'alien element', a 'state inside the state'. 'The Jew', and 'all that is derived from the Jewish mind, corrodes and disintegrates what is best in us.' The 'struggle' between Teuton and Jew is intensified by 'the annihilation of distances which furthers intercourse'. Their racial identity, which is indelible, can be detected by small children ('especially girls'), even though the 'learned' may often miss it, and confuse Jew with non-Jew.[293] He disparaged the Jews ('born dogmatists and fanatics', 'poor in religious instinct', 'materialists', crucifiers of Christ, 'historically narrow and deliberately intolerant', 'the Jewish religion of terror', 'Jewish-heathen', 'monolaters' rather than monotheists, 'Semitic half-castes', etc.),[294] and disparaged the nations who submitted to their influence. He hated

England, for example, because it had 'studied politics with a Jew for a quarter century' (i.e., Disraeli), and because Jewish financial interests prevailed there. He hated 'English sentimentalising' about 'the poor', and about 'persecuted Jews'.[295] The Kaiser praised him: 'You explain what was obscure . . . '[296]

Foundations is a puerile and bombastic work, bogus in scholarship and enslaved to an utterly incoherent notion of 'race', yet it appears to have found a somewhat receptive audience among the pre-World War I English intelligentsia, as well as being a huge success in Germany itself.[297] George Bernard Shaw, for example, praised the English edition of Chamberlain's work in the left-wing *Fabian News*, though he deprecated the extravagance of its anti-Semitism. There is no battle between the Teuton and Chaos, Shaw argued, and the enemy is not the Jew but the British greengrocer, with his 'short round skull', his militarism and his mediocrity.[298] Chamberlain himself, at one time at least, rejected the title of anti-Semite. 'I have remarkably many Jews or half-Jews for friends, with whom I am very close', he once remarked. He also once said that one did not have to be an anti-Semite 'in the odious sense of the word' to hold that 'all journalism is Jewish filth'. Very late in life, he embraced Nazism, and praised Hitler's position on the Jews.[299]

These considerations raise the question, how do we define the engagement of English intellectuals with anti-Semitism?

A 'thinking' anti-Semitism?

In the course of confiding to his private notebook his plans for the Jews ('by fire, fusion or explosion the Jews must disappear'), the French socialist P. J. Proudhon concluded, 'What the peoples of the middle ages hated by instinct, I hate upon reflection, and irrevocably.'[300] In every generation, there have been intellectuals ready, 'upon reflection', to renew anti-Semitism—from the twelfth-century cleric Thomas of Monmouth to the contemporary Nobel laureate José Saramago.[301] As I argued in Chapter 1, various anti-Semitisms have been promoted over time by both the learned and the pseudo-learned.[302] So even if it is merely a trespasser in intellectual history, anti-Semitism has earned its place in the history of intellectuals. The question for this part of the chapter is, what has been the specifically English contribution to this history?

The absence of any significant anti-Semitic aspect in the major intellectual engagements of the period

There is no significant anti-Semitic aspect to any of the major topics that engaged and divided the religious, cultural or political imagination of England between the mid-seventeenth and the mid-twentieth century—a large claim, but a true one. Consider, for example, the topics that set England to war against itself in the nineteenth century. Anti-Semites had no purchase on the debates that raged on the truth of Christianity, on the origins of the universe and of man, and on the authorship of the Bible; they did not participate in the debates between free traders and protectionists; they barely figured in the anguished reflections on the injuries inflicted by the 'industrial spirit', or in the idealizations of the Middle Ages and the *agon* of country *versus* city. They played no part in the agitation for an expanded franchise, or in the challenge of labour and the growth of trades' unionism. Even the topic of race, as we have seen, only glanced at Jews; the Victorian engagement with race had an imperial complexion, and when it divided intellectuals, it tended to do so in relation to colonial insurrections—say, India in 1857, or Jamaica in 1865.[303] Anti-Semitism in England tended instead to attach itself to more immediate, and less culturally fundamental issues—scandals, controversies, panic, fears, and the like—and then, mostly those with a foreign-policy character.

There was no version of anti-Semitism, then, that amounted to an animating concern, still less a preoccupation, of most of the coteries and groups that populated civil society in the nineteenth and twentieth centuries. Jews were at most the object of a kind of occasional, quizzical speculation. John Maynard Keynes, for example, displayed a certain intrigued interest in Jews. From time to time he applied received characterizations of Jews, but in novel or unusual contexts; he was also prone to amateur speculations about the distinctive nature of the Jewish mind. He was ready, that is, to mock the Jewish race's love for the principle of compound interest, or to doubt that communism makes Jews less avaricious;[304] he was inclined to describe Edwin Montagu as an Oriental, equipped, nevertheless, with the intellectual technique and atmosphere of the West.[305] He had Jewry pinned down, the object of his lazy, amused surveys, uninformed, dispassionate, and above all deriving from his own supreme self-confidence. But he did not offer a developed, hostile 'theory' of the Jews. He did not contribute to the elaboration of antagonistic responses to some (already prejudicially) posed 'Jewish Question'. The anti-Semites who *were* engaged in such sterile pursuits tended to live in groups somewhat isolated from the main intellectual currents in civil society; the absence of first-rate intellectual support for anti-Semitism was a great constraint on the development of any programmatic, campaigning, mainstream anti-Semitic movement in England.[306] English anti-Semites could not elicit from the given prejudices of the majority a programme that would appeal to more than a miniscule minority; they did not have the brainpower to make the latent manifest.

Types of English anti-Semitic intellectual

That is not to say that England was altogether without intellectuals who adopted anti-Semitic positions or sentiments. For purposes of exposition, we can identify the following relevant types:

- There are anti-Semitic thinkers, politically engaged anti-Semitic intellectuals, and campaigners against Jews, of major cultural status or authority. They contribute to the formation of an ideologically substantial, programmatic anti-Semitism, or they give express philosophical sanction to received anti-Semitic notions.[307] (*Type A*)

- There are anti-Semitic thinkers, politically engaged anti-Semitic intellectuals, and campaigners against Jews, of lesser cultural status or authority. These are still men and women of consequence, however. (For example, the anti-Semites Hilaire Belloc and G. K. Chesterton, typical of this class, were the most influential Catholic intellectuals of the 1930s.)[308] (*Type B*)

- Then, as a subset of type B, there are activist anti-Semitic pamphleteers, speechmakers, and polemicists, that is to say writers and public figures who address, in a hostile spirit, specific public issues concerning Jews, usually of an immediate, pressing political character. Most are hacks, and while some may be established, serious writers, none has the standing of the type A anti-Semitic intellectual. (*Type B1*)

- There are also, as a further subset of type B, anti-Semitic intellectuals and writers, whose antagonistic stance towards the Jews is thematic in their work, but who tend not to intervene in public scandal or controversy, or to be aligned with parties or movements. As with type B1, these intellectuals and writers are *not* of major cultural status. (*Type B2*)

- Then there are intellectuals and writers whose work is marked by occasional, disobliging anti-Semitic observations, characteristically expressed on private occasions—say, in conversation or in correspondence. When these observations are made in a public forum, they are typically opportunistic, surprising, undeveloped, and personal. (*Type C*)

- Last, there are intellectuals and writers who are genuinely engaged with the phenomenon of anti-Semitism, but are yet also compromised by it. Some among them attempt a theory of the Jews. (*Type D*)

Not since the eighteenth century have there been anti-Semitic English intellectuals of the cultural or political first rank. There have not been, that is, any *type A* English intellectuals. Nor have there been anti-Semitic English intellectuals who have played a decisive role *as anti-Semites* in the cultural or political life of their times. English intellectuals were no more resistant to the casual Jew-scorn of the ambient culture than any other group. But to take that scorn and, so to speak, *do* something with it, to treat it as the raw material for the creation of something ambitious and reflective, something with explanatory value (however fantastical it might be)—that was altogether a different matter.

Type A

Surveying French anti-Semitic intellectuals may best highlight English deficiencies.

France's anti-Semitic intellectuals gave Jew-hatred political and cultural dignity and influence; at the end of the nineteenth century, for that moment at least, the Dreyfus Affair came to define the most essential character of modern anti-Semitism. It preoccupied France—'nobody talks about anything else', commented a police report.[309] In defining their respective positions, French intellectuals drew on the deepest currents of thinking about their country as both nation and republic. France became a 'laboratory', in which the 'original political syntheses of our time were created'.[310] Among the anti-Dreyfusards, the interventions of the writer Maurice Barrès (1862–1923) most endure, because they constitute at an intellectually elevated level a negative imprint, so to speak, of the modern understanding of citizenship, of a liberal political order, of cosmopolitanism, of the type of the intellectual, and of the critical spirit (the *esprit d'analyse*).[311] 'The Jews have no native land in the sense that we understand it', he wrote. 'For us, a homeland implies the soil, our ancestors, the land of our dead. For them, it is only the place where they find the greatest profits.' To this self-described 'advocate of the dead',[312] contemporary France was not a democracy, it was a plutocracy, and the Jews were the master-plutocrats. 'If the state is not the powerful master, it is the slave of the bank; no middle ground is possible.' Having once been persecuted, the Jews now were tyrants; 'Semitic high finance' owned the public wealth.[313] Barrès admired the anti-Semite Drumont, because 'je suis né nationaliste'. 'Votre à bas les Juifs ne me choque pas.'[314]

'There is only a probability that Dreyfus is innocent,' Barrès wrote, 'but it is absolutely certain that France is innocent.'[315] He exulted in Dreyfus's ceremonial humiliation: it was the 'parade of Judas', a spectacle 'more exciting than the guillotine'.[316] The Jews should be deprived of their political rights; they did not belong to the nation. They were not 'united by the common legends, traditions, habits' that made Frenchmen French; they worked instead 'to transform the national consciousness according to their own sentiments'.[317] Barrès's prose communicated the sentiment: we are embattled, engaged in a life-and-death struggle; victory is far from certain; the fight for the collective self is by necessity uncompromising, not least because it is self-constituting.[318] One does not sacrifice the peace and unity of a nation for the sake of one individual, even if he is innocent.[319] Barrès insisted upon the assimilation of standards of truth to group loyalties. He set authority against truth, order against justice, exclusivism against universalism, social instinct against reason ('savouring deeply the instinctive pleasures of being part of a flock'),[320] and thereby defined for the Dreyfusard intellectuals the very values to which *they* could cleave. Everything that Barrès stood for, Zola stood against, everything that Barrès championed, Zola execrated, and vice versa. Each was the other's principal adversary.[321] There was in some sense an equality of arms in these engagements (which explains, among other things, why the Surrealists were moved to stage a public trial of Barrès in 1921),[322] one to be found nowhere else in the history of the contests between Jews and their enemies.[323]

To somewhat enlarge the range of comparators, add Germany and Russia. Consider anti-Semitism's ideological lineage in Germany; consider the friendship between one of Russia's leading novelists and man of letters, and one of its leading statesmen, anti-Semites both. Whom did England have to set against a Kant, a Hegel, and a Marx?[324] Or against a Dostoyevsky in the intimacy of his relations with Konstantin Pobedonostsev?[325] It had no one. An anti-Semitic philosophical tradition of the first order, a precedent-setting anti-Semitic event that divided the nation's intellectuals and had Europe-wide resonance, an alliance between a first-class anti-Semitic intellectual and an anti-Semitic statesman of immense influence—against these forms of anti-Semitic activity, each one engaging intellectuals of great prestige, England made an admirably poor showing.[326]

Type B

There are several anti-Semites among English writers and intellectuals of more minor cultural status. Principal among them were William Cobbett (1762(?)–1835) and Hilaire Belloc (1870–1953). Their work disclosed a preoccupation with Jews; they were also polemicists, and made anti-Semitic interventions in matters of public controversy. They are not, however, to be dismissed as cranks. Their contemporaries esteemed them; Cobbett in particular enjoyed an immense popularity and influence during his lifetime, and has a substantial posthumous reputation.[327] They had good minds— though only just about, perhaps.

In the work of William Cobbett, Jew-hatred is everywhere.[328] In *Rural Rides* (1830), he execrates Jews at every turn. The Jews have supplanted many of the old gentry. A town is estimable because it is without Jew-looking fellows with dandy coats, dirty shirts, and half-heels to their shoes. To be a financier is to act the part of a Jew. The Jew-system has swept all the little gentry, the small farmers, and the domestic manufacturers away. A group on horseback appear, by their hook-noses and round eyes, and by the long and sooty necks of the women, to be for the greater part Jews and Jewesses.[329] In the *Paper Against Gold* (1812), Cobbett elaborates a fantasy of Jewish economic vice, the 'tricks and connivances carried on by the means of paper money', out of a report of the suicide of the Jewish financier Abraham Goldsmid, 'the great Jew money-dealer'. His suicide was prompted by the loss of part of his wealth, 'a truly Jew-like motive for the commission of an act—at which human nature shudders'.[330] In *Good Friday; or the Murder of Jesus Christ by the Jews* (London, 1830), the killing of Jesus is said to have been a 'savage murder, committed after long premeditation, effected by hypocrisy and bribery and perjury' etc.[331] Thereafter, Cobbett proposed, the Jews damaged France and killed Poland with their deist and atheist 'reason'. They are a people 'living in all the filthiness of *usury and increase*', 'extortioners by habit and almost by instinct'.[332] In a parliamentary debate, Cobbett challenged a fellow Member to 'produce a Jew who ever dug, or who ever made his own coat or his own shoes, or who did anything at all, except get all the money he could from the pockets of the people'.[333] And Cobbett was ready to fantasize about Jewish crimes, for example alleging that in the 1771 Chelsea case (see Chapter 3), the Jewish criminals had mutilated the servant's body after murdering him.

Cobbett was regarded at the time as 'the sauciest' opponent of the removal of Jewish disabilities. The Jews did not merit 'any immunities, any privileges, any possessions in house, land or water, any civil or political rights', he argued. 'They should, everywhere, be deemed aliens and always at the absolute disposal of the sovereign power of the state, as completely as any inanimate substance.'[334] Certainly, his verbal assaults on the Jews were highly unusual among the writers and intellectuals of his time.[335] Yet his hatred of the Jews, so persistent, so unrelenting in its articulation, was but one hatred among many hatreds. 'His principle is repulsion, his nature contradiction, he is made up of mere antipathies', wrote the essayist William Hazlitt, 'an Ishmaelite indeed without a fellow'.[336] He took every public figure, Jew or Gentile, to be corrupt.[337] In consequence, anti-Semitism itself never acquired the status of a master-principle in his work. To write about Cobbett as a political thinker is misconceived, because he never thought at all; any study of his political 'ideas' must be an analysis of his likes and dislikes; his great failure was a failure of understanding; he was unable to render systematic, and therefore shareable with others, his prejudices.[338] This did not, of course, damage his standing to generations of admirers. Lewis Melville, for example, writes in *The Life and Letters of William Cobbett in England and America* (1913) that Cobbett's 'opinions on the Bill to give civil rights to Jews make amusing reading today', and then quotes from Cobbett's notes for his speech: 'Jew has always been synonymous with sharper, cheat, rogue. This has been the case with no other race of mankind. Rothschild married his own niece. They will flock in upon us from all countries.'[339] In general, readers of Cobbett who celebrated his qualities as a 'great Englishman' did not see his anti-Semitism,[340] nor did readers who sought to appropriate him for the political Left.[341] He was admired by anti-Semites, though, and acknowledged by them as one of their own.[342] More importantly, his anti-Semitism exercised a certain diffuse influence on radicals in the early to mid-nineteenth century, if only at the level of vocabulary.[343]

Hilaire Belloc was preoccupied with Jews, and would tell anyone ready to listen what he thought of them. They provoked him: 'the Jew cannot help feeling superior', he complained.[344] He had been an early anti-Dreyfusard;[345] the Jewish Question was a 'pressing problem'; the quarrel between the Jews and the West had 'cosmic' properties.[346] He regarded the Russian Revolution to be the work of a 'handful of aliens' and England to have been in 'alliance' with 'international Jewry' throughout modern times.[347] The modern communist movement, he wrote in 1937, 'was inspired and is directed by Jews'; the Revolution itself he described as 'the Jewish experiment in Russia'.[348] He protested the 'convention forbidding public allusion to the Jewish question'.[349] He was indeed in advance of his time as a conspiracist, observing in his novel *Emmanuel Burden* (1904), 'Whatever rules the world, it is not we.'[350] (He saw conspiracies wherever he looked, rewriting the history of the English Reformation as an Edwardian scandal—a puppet monarch, a plutocracy, a conspiracy of 'new millionaires', the 'real power in one hand, the nominal power in another', 'usury', a 'story of avarice', 'bribes', etc.)[351] He committed to poetry the anti-Semitic trope that British soldiers died to advance Jewish financial interests in South Africa.[352] He wrote the fictional history of a Jewish swindler, I. Z. Barnett, in a series of novels, archly celebrating his business triumphs, his control of the press, and his ultimate elevation to the peerage as Lord Lambeth. Belloc then strained, but failed, to elevate the inconsequential Marconi affair into a scandal of Dreyfus-like proportions. Somewhat like the Monica Lewinsky affair, the Marconi affair became an obsession for a certain kind of reactionary. There was no deliberate Jewish conspiracy, Belloc conceded; merely 'something fatally coincident with the presence of an alien race' (or a 'well-organised . . . organic, natural and even subconscious force . . . the force of national feeling'). Writing in 1911, he recommended a policy of 'privilege' (that is, 'segregation'), in preference to the alternative policies of 'absorption' or 'exclusion', to resolve the friction between 'the Jew and the European'. Under these arrangements, Jews would have their names entered on a register (false names to be punished by law), but would be exempt from military service.[353] He defended himself, when giving evidence to the Marconi Select Committee, against the charge of having 'an antipathy to Jews'. He had Jewish friends; he was not hostile to 'Jews as Jews'; the 'racial Jewish element in cosmopolitan finance' was 'large' but not 'indispensable', and if it became 'mainly Gentile', he would continue to attack it. What is more, he said, he often addressed 'audiences of Jews, always of poor Jews' on the 'grave problem in the near future—friction between Jew and Gentile'.[354]

Unsuccessful as a polemicist, Belloc also attempted a more discursive, more reflective, assault upon the Jews. He attempted, that is, a reasoned account of anti-Semitism, and a programme for the solution of the Jewish Problem, as he perceived it, in his book *The Jews* (1922, 1937). With an elaborate display of balance, a dedication to his Jewish secretary, 'the best and most intimate of our Jewish friends', dismissal of the 'mania' of anti-Semitism, and chapters on causes of friction on 'their' side and on 'ours', he rejected both assimilation (the 'pretence of common citizenship') and Zionism (how could 'a Jew govern Golgotha'?), and instead called for a 'full recognition of separate nationality', a kind of apartheid *avant la lettre*.[355] His fictional I. Z. Barnett routinely violated the 'subtle barrier that separates individuals and races from one another';[356] Belloc's segregation proposals for 'the Jewish stranger'[357] would ensure that these violations ceased. What was important was that the Jews be made visible again. Emancipation, and name changes, allowed the Jews (with their 'characteristic power of superficial mutation')[358] to disappear into Gentile society, while at the same time maintaining their own invisible connections. They had infiltrated everywhere, sometimes in close alliance with Freemasonry, which the Jews had inaugurated and whose ritual is Jewish in character.[359] They should come back out into the open, where they can be seen and recognized for what they are. There was little that was original in this (it was a line pursued by the *New Witness*,[360] a journal influential in Anglo-Catholic circles),[361] save for the intimation of the need for legislative intervention. In the 1970s, the National Front took a Bellocian position on the Jews: 'We will work for the peaceful separation of [the Jews] from the British Community.'[362]

In November 1938, Belloc wrote to the press asking sceptical questions about a report on an especially brutal incident of Nazi violence against Jews. The story was not 'impossible', he acknowledged, but how do we know for certain? If it is false, how can we believe anything the anti-Nazi side had to say? We must 'bolt out the truth'. He asked for further evidence, and then some weeks later announced that no corroborating evidence had been offered, and therefore that the bulk of readers should be 'chary of accepting such stories in the future'.[363] This established the methods of denial that later generations of Holocaust deniers would adopt. Yet, in a private letter, written in 1924, Belloc insisted: 'There is not in the whole mass of my written books and articles, there is not in any one of my lectures (many of which have been delivered to Jewish bodies by special request because of the interest I have taken) there is not, I say, in any one of the great mass of writings and statements extending now over twenty years, a single line in which a Jew has been attacked as a Jew or in which the vast majority of their race, suffering and poor, has received, I will not say an insult from my pen or tongue, but anything which could be construed as dislike.' And yet—the historian A. J. P. Taylor judged Belloc to be 'our only anti-Semitic writer', indicating thereby both the absurdity of Belloc's self-assessment and the invisibility even to one so intimate with English history and culture as Taylor of *other* English 'writers'' anti-Semitism.[364]

Type B1

William Prynne was first and chief among anti-Semitic polemicists; others emerged to challenge the Jews at moments of particular Anglo-Jewish visibility. I listed these moments, and identified some of the polemicists in Chapter 5—Arnold White, the 'anti-alienist', is a good example of the type. He wrote extensively about Jews, mostly warning against the 'waxing power of the Jewish race', 'a foreign antipathetic race', and the 'undesirable and hurtful' consequences for the 'English people' of the immigration of 'debased and impoverished Jews from the slums of the Russian Ghetto'.[365] He was as troubled by rich Jews as poor ones: 'It is impossible to watch without a shudder the union of alien Jew finance with English bad smart society.' The power of the German Jew, he warned, is both 'non-moral and immense'. (Of course, White made an exception for the 'good Jews', of which there are 'many'.)[366] White's interventions were rooted in what he understood to be the given, and most urgent, circumstances of his day. Perhaps the most substantial figure of this type, however, and the most surprising one, is the economist and public intellectual, J. A. Hobson (1858–1940).

Hobson stands quite apart from the generality of hacks and obsessives that populate the category. He made anti-Semitic interventions in two overlapping political episodes, addressing the cause of poverty and the cause of war in the contexts of Eastern European Jewish immigration to London, and Jewish participation in the economy and politics of South Africa. That is to say, he wrote pejoratively about poor Jews *and* rich Jews, about the Jewish immigrant as industrial competitor, and the Jewish financier as warmonger. In *Problems of Poverty* (1891–1913), he described 'the foreign Jew' as a terrible competitor, the ideal 'economic' man, the 'fittest' person to survive in trade competition. He is almost void of social morality. His superior calculating intellect, a national heritage, is used unsparingly to enable him to take advantage of every weakness, folly, and vice of society. He craves the position of a sweating-master, the lowest step in a ladder that may lead to a life of magnificence, supported out of usury.[367] The poor Jew is thus merely the rich Jew without funds. These latter Jews, Hobson explained elsewhere, were promoting the conflict with the Boers. In articles subsequently published as *The War in South Africa* (1900), Hobson wrote with special distaste of Johannesburg, the 'New Jerusalem', where the 'large presence of the chosen people' is inescapable. These Jews do not engage in direct political agitation; they let others do that sort of thing. For whom, then, Hobson asks, are we fighting? It is the Jews—or a 'small group of international financiers, chiefly German in origin and Jewish in race', a 'little ring of international financiers', 'financial foreigners', 'foreign Jews', a 'foreign host', 'a small international oligarchy', or 'syndicate'? The Jews have a 'monopoly of the economic power'; they control politics and legislation by bribery and other persuasive arts. They have added to their other businesses the business of politics.[368] Jews figured only infrequently in Hobson's work thereafter; in the book itself, he worried that telling the truth about war might be read as an appeal to 'the ignominious passion of *Judenhetze*'.[369] In *Democracy After the War* (1918), though, he restated his thesis on the Boer War but made no express reference to them.[370] In *God and Mammon* (1931), however, he described the Jewish businessman's distinctive qualities as skilful profiteering, hard bargaining, and usurious loans. Judaism aids moneymaking by promoting a sense of 'chosenness'.[371] By 1938, perhaps with the Nazi persecutions in his mind, he avoided any discussion of the role of Jews in his earlier account of the Boer War, though he described it as a turning-point in his own career.[372] The anti-Semitic aspect of Hobson's work had some influence among leftists, especially those in Independent Labour Party circles.[373]

Hobson was exceptional, however. The generality of anti-Semitic polemicists were of a substantially inferior character. Consider, for example, Goldwin Smith (1823–1910), a self-described 'liberal of the Old School'[374] and a committed, respectable Jew-hater.[375] His first academic appointment was as Regius Professor of modern history at Oxford University; in 1868, he became professor of English and constitutional history at Cornell University; in 1871, he moved to Toronto, where he died. The American journal, the *Independent*, described him in 1906 as 'the leading and almost the only exponent of anti-Semitism in the English-speaking world'.[376] He held elaborated, hostile views of Jews and Judaism. Jewish intelligence can be destructive; Jews monopolize 'the high places' of the nations; they represent the forces of materialism; their religion as well as their interest is 'essentially conservative', and 'with social progress they can have no sympathy'. In their 'tribal arrogance', the Jews think of themselves as 'chosen', and regard Gentiles as 'unclean', yet they are themselves parasites and natural exploiters of others. They are an 'anti-national money power'.[377] Edward I, 'the best of kings', did well to expel them.[378] Jewish writers have overstated the violence of Russia's pogroms, and misrepresented the motives of the Christian mob.[379] Jews merit the description given to them by Tacitus, Juvenal, and Gibbon as enemies of mankind.[380] Smith celebrated the 'great anti-Semitic revolt' of his times.[381] He accepted the designation 'anti-Semite', if the term meant 'fear of political, social and financial influence'. He had, he explained, no 'religious antipathy' towards Jews, but then added some objections to 'Jewish monotheism'.[382] Though he would 'ride his anti-Semitic hobby', his literary executor conceded, he was also aware of the risk of appearing an obsessive. 'These Jews hang together', Smith explained. 'There is a tacit understanding amongst them. A real danger lurks beneath their efforts. I don't like to say too much on this subject. I don't like to appear to be ventilating a craze; but that it is a fact, I am convinced...'[383] Goldwin Smith's work comprises one of the more dismal public performances of a mid- to late-nineteenth-century liberal intellectual.

Leo Maxse (1864–1932), editor of the *National Review*, was an ardent Dreyfusard and excoriator of anti-Semites in the late 1890s, and an ardent anti-Semite and excoriator of the 'International Jew' in the late 1910s. The Dreyfus case was 'the most atrocious conspiracy to be found in human history', one devised by the French Army and abetted by the 'savages of the anti-Semitic press'. Dreyfus was 'the martyr of a miscarriage of justice'.[384] Twenty years later, Maxse was fulminating against conspiracies of another kind. There was an 'irresistible, if invisible tie' between Independent Labour and the International Jew. The Bolshevik, who is the agent of the Boche, leads us back to the International Jew, who himself has lately embraced German or pro-German positions. He rules, regardless of who is ostensibly in power. At one time his name was Rothschild; then he was called Speyer; now he is Cassel or Mond or Montagu, 'for aught we know'. Here is the mystery of the 'Hidden Hand'. To identify the trend of British policy, one merely has to ask, 'What does the International Jew want?' Maxse was certain that he was not an anti-Semite: the 'imputation leaves us stone-cold'. He had no prejudice against Jews as such, and he positively admired the 'national Jews'. The International Jew, however, lies near the heart of every international problem, which remains unintelligible unless we realize his role.[385]

In Nesta H. Webster's plot-theory of history everything of consequence that happens is willed by secret collectives, operating against the interests of the majority. Webster (1876–1960) regarded it as the task of the historian to expose conspirators. Her works have been used to explain Napoleon's invasion of Egypt, the fall of the Ottoman Empire, and the creation of the State of Israel.[386] Her *Secret Societies and Subversive Movements* (1924) summarizes her main arguments. The East, she writes, is the cradle of secret societies; the causes of revolution lie not in popular discontent, but in deep-laid conspiracies. The 'Jewish' or 'perverted Cabala', is the inspiration of all 'subversive sects' hostile to Christianity. The Jews crucified Jesus, abusing him with 'abominable calumnies' in both Cabala and Talmud; they persist today in their assaults on Christianity. The Jews, or Cabalistic doctrines at least, are behind the other secret societies—the Gnostics, the Templars, the Rosicrucians, the Libertines, the Freemasons, and the Illuminati. Jewish influence on modern revolutions is both 'financial' and 'occult'; while Jews did not create every revolutionary movement, they knew how to make use of them for their own ends. The Jews are also behind 'the most dangerous form of psychoanalysis', the film industry, drug trafficking, and the other 'minor subversive movements' of today. The Jews' hope of world domination is 'very real'; they were the first pogromists; they have brought their suffering down on their own heads; they will always cry 'persecution' unless 'they are placed above the law, and allowed to occupy everywhere a privileged position'; the whole educational political and social world is permeated with Jewish influence. Webster was an undisciplined reader, relying partly on anti-Semitic works and partly upon 'Jewish authority'. She was touchy about her reputation, denied that she was an anti-Semite, and resented the charge that writers like her were 'victims of an obsession' (in her view, a charge made by people who do not accept what they cannot see). She enjoyed a substantial readership, and Winston Churchill cited her with approval in his 1920 article, 'Zionism versus Bolshevism'.[387] In a series of articles written for *The Patriot* in the late 1930s, she warned against war with Germany, writing with great ardour about Hitler, a man of brilliant intelligence, courage, and patriotism. (He 'writes in no spirit of Jew-baiting, but as a bacteriologist calmly examining through his microscope the action of certain noxious bacilli . . .'.) She made light of the Nazi persecution of the Jews, mostly misreported by newspapers and radio broadcasts controlled by

Jews, while acknowledging that perhaps Hitler's methods were not quite England's. Nazism merely replicates Jewish 'race-ism', in any event—and no people of any country wish for war except Bolsheviks and Jews.[388] She considered herself to be a member of the 'Christian intelligentsia', the 'main obstacle to [the Jews'] dream of world-power', and the 'sole bar to the enslavement of the proletariat'. She spoke for 'the powers of light', in 'eternal conflict' with 'the veritable powers of darkness'.[389] She was engaged, she explained in her autobiography, in a 'prolonged contest with...unseen powers'.[390] She continues to be read.[391]

Anthony M. Ludovici (1882–1971), anti-Feminist, exponent of Nietzsche[392] and the 'philosophy of the White Man',[393] was prominent in all the groups established by the right-wing activist Lord Lymington; he was the available intellectual.[394] He is unknown today, though he has his supporters, and they maintain a website which contains many of his works. He was the pseudonymous author (writing under the name 'Cobbett') of a work that appeared in 1938, *Jews, and the Jews in England*. Today's Jews, he writes there, are the near descendants of the Semites, a desert people. They belong to Asia. They are race-conscious and nomadic, and despise the foreigner and the stranger. They are averse to productive labour; they have a congenital dislike for hard work. They have a peculiar genius for finance; they also have a tendency towards socialism. The Jew today is at the forefront of every international movement. His feelings of inferiority produce a longing for ascendancy. Non-Semitic Europeans recognize the Jew as a type. All Jews share an irreducible physical and psychological kernel; they belong to a distinct order of mankind. The Jews of medieval England exploited the people often quite intolerably. They were a cloud of harpies, dropped on the country by the Normans, an invading and victorious dynasty. Upon being denied the opportunities of usury, they resorted to clipping and adulterating the coinage. They were expelled when England's kings themselves became English, and were no longer willing to abet the exploitation of their subjects. These Jews were responsible for an influx of Semitic blood into the population, which explains why certain Englishmen today have a conspicuous Semitic appearance. The debates on the removal of Jewish disabilities were lamentably superficial: they assumed a religious distinction only, rather than a racial one. The Jews are a disruptive or disintegrating force within the body of any nation among whom they settle. England is being Judaized. We must avoid intermarrying with Jews; we must also exclude Jews from all positions that afford opportunities to modify the character and customs of the nation. The author's tone is irenic, and he makes great play of his fair-mindedness, while dismissing 'excuses made by the Jews and by Liberal Gentiles'.[395] In an earlier work, *Man: An Indictment* (1927), published under his own name, Ludovici had made a case for segregation of the Jews in their own interest. 'Our kindness and familiarity are causing the Jews to relax their rules about cross-breeding with Gentiles', he wrote. This is 'perhaps the cruellest scourge that has ever been imposed upon the Jewish race'.[396]

Douglas Reed (1895–1976), the *Times'* Berlin correspondent until 1938, was a prolific writer, with a mainstream publisher for many years. His work was influential in the mid- to late-1930s;[397] during the war, he was foreign editor for a large newspaper group,[398] and was a noteworthy figure (George Orwell referred to the 'large public for which [Reed] caters');[399] he retained a substantial readership in the 1940s and 1950s; he is unread now, save by neo-Nazis and the like.[400] He was anti-Hitler but not anti-Nazi, and championed the dissident National Socialist Otto Strasser (1897–1974). His argument with Hitler was that he was bent on war against England, was neither a genuine National Socialist nor a genuine anti-Semite,[401] and was nothing but a 'puppet'.[402] Reed's argument with the Jews is similarly easy to summarize. Judaism was 'anti-Gentile'; the Jews would 'not allow themselves to assimilate';[403] Nazi discrimination was but a pale imitation of the Jewish original; the Russian Revolution was masterminded by non-Russian Jews in the pay of the German government;[404] the 'Zionist Empire' came into existence as a partner to the 'Communist Empire';[405] Zionism is a 'secret conspiracy for power and territory, pursued in all great countries of the world through power over public men';[406] opponents of Zionism risked their careers and even their lives when taking a stand against 'the Jewish cause'.[407] Reed was an early Holocaust denier.[408] In the early to mid-1950s, Reed wrote the posthumously published *The Controversy of Zion*. It describes Moses as a racial mass-murderer, Judaism as a fossil doctrine of self-segregation from mankind, the Old Testament as a political plan of world domination, the Zionists as controlling Gentile governments, and world Jewry as directed by a secret 'Talmudic government'. It holds the *Protocols* to be authentic by the conclusive test of subsequent events, Zionism to be a new form of messianism, and the Zionists to be seeking the extermination of the Arabs in accordance with biblical precedent. The book is almost unreadable; it would seem that it was almost unread—though not because of the 'virtual law of heresy which has prevented open discussion of the

"Jewish Question" '.[409] Unread, until, that is, it was picked up by one Ahmad Thomson, who used it to make his own case against the Jews and Zionism. I consider Thomson in Chapter 8.

Although these anti-Semites make something of a group, comprising in one aspect a single sequence (William Cobbett to Goldwin Smith to Douglas Reed) and in another aspect a series of cohorts (Goldwin Smith and E. A. Freeman, or Hilaire Belloc, Nesta Webster, and Anthony Ludovici), they wrote without much reference to each other, and almost never made common cause. They conformed, that is, to the rules governing anti-Semitic intellectual life in England: it will be *discontinuous*, it will be *marginal*, and it will be *mediocre*. There is no enlivening tradition; there is no appeal to individual talent. At most, some of these intellectuals, when hunting their Jewish quarry, possessed a certain sense that they were operating in the vicinity of other intellectuals of their kind—but no more. The liberal anti-Semite E. A. Freeman wrote to a correspondent:

> Mrs. Gurney has a small niece called Polly Hooper who says to her father, 'Good night, father; I hope you will sleep well, and that everybody will sleep well, *except the Jews*.' She dreamed also that she was chased by a lion, 'and it was a Jewish lion.' So I told her, if the Jewish lion came again, to call on Goldwin Smith, and he would help her.[410]

A few compliments, camaraderie expressed in private correspondence, perhaps a brief coming-together in the pursuit of some hapless Jewish public figure or in an endeavour to talk up some possible scandal; even so, the polemicizing activities of England's anti-Semitic intelligentsia remained a mostly solitary affair. There was no English polemicist after Prynne, then, who had the standing or influence of France's Edouard Drumont, the author of the immense bestseller, *La France Juive*, and editor of the mass circulation journal, *Libre Parole*. The absurd and vicious Joseph Banister, say, with his low print-run *England under the Jews*, might have wanted to make England 'extremely uncomfortable for the Chosen Ones',[411] but he failed utterly; the equally absurd and vicious Drumont, by contrast, for a time was able to make France's Jews very uncomfortable indeed. His anti-Semitism comprised a discourse of aggressive complaint, both defeated and defiant, utterly gloomy and yet insouciantly triumphalist. The Jews control everything; we can remove them by an act of will. 'A brave captain' will vanquish the Jewish capitalists and bankers.[412] They are the kings of the epoch, our masters, France itself has become Jewish—and yet, all will be well.

Type B2

The best example of an intellectual and writer whose antagonistic stance towards the Jews is thematic in his or her work, but who mostly held back from intervening in public scandal or controversy, is Arnold Toynbee. Toynbee published the first three volumes of his *A Study of History* in 1933, the next three in 1939, and the third batch in 1954. A two-volume abridgment by D. C. Somervell itself appeared in instalments, the first volume in 1946, and the second in 1957. There was also a one-volume abridgment, revised by the author and Jane Caplan, published in 1972. *A Study of History*, in all its versions, is both a typology of civilizations and a reflection on the 'senseless criminality of human affairs'.[413]

According to Toynbee, in both *A Study of History* and its two-volume abridgment, Hebrew nomads drifted into the Syrian dependencies of Egypt out of the no-man's-land of the North Arabian Steppe. The Jews are the products of this Syriac society. They became sedentary tillers. In the power of their spiritual understanding, they surpassed the military might of the Philistines and the maritime might of the Phoenicians. They have not sought after those things that the Gentile seeks, but sought instead the kingdom of God. The Philistines and the Phoenicians have disappeared; the Jews remain. They are impervious to the alchemy to which 'we Gentiles' succumb. They are fossilized relics of Syriac civilization, an extinct society. They became fossilized upon their rejection of the claims made on Jesus' behalf; in Paul, Judaism lost its life. They survive as a mere diaspora. The petrified religion that holds them together has lost its message for mankind. They are not 'living representatives of the species'; they are not 'going concerns'. Israel idolized itself as 'the Chosen People'. This was an error to which they had been led by their discovery of the one true God. This discovery gave them no more than a momentary spiritual eminence. Though the discovery of monotheism was a divine gift, it was not a privilege conferred upon them by God in an everlasting covenant.

The Jews are intensely conscious of their immeasurable superiority to other men. They have been preserved in the medium of their religious idiosyncrasies; they have been exposed to religious discrimination; they have learned to hold their own in hostile environments; they excel in trade and finance, to which their activities have been confined. Indeed, they are ubiquitous as men of business. The Jews have only recently achieved legal emancipation; they have yet to achieve moral emancipation. Judaism promotes fanaticism, intolerance, and arrogance among its adherents.

Jews are not as other men. They rise to superhuman heights in one dimension only to shrivel to a sub-human level in another dimension. The economic advances achieved by the West in modern times can be described with equal appropriateness as 'modernization' or 'Judaization'. The Jews' ill-repute is thus not mere libel. The Gentile who is disgusted and ashamed at the behaviour of his anti-Semitic fellow *Goyim* is also embarrassed at finding himself constrained to admit that there is some truth in the caricature they draw to justify their bestiality.

The Old Testament is the source of race-thinking; its own race-thinking is savage, fanatical, and ferocious. European imperialism derived its authority from the Israelites' biblically recorded conviction that God had instigated them to exterminate the Canaanites. The Jews themselves became racialists when they adopted Zionism. The Zionist attempt to revive Hebrew as a living vernacular is a perverse undertaking, the product of a nationalistic craze for distinctiveness and cultural self-sufficiency, an attempt to conjure intelligible speech out of the silence of the grave. Israel was established by force of arms, supported by a guilty West, and at great injustice to the Palestinian Arabs. Nazi depravity thus led to unprecedented sufferings of both innocent Jewish victims and an innocent Arab victim. The Jews' immediate reaction to their own experience was to become persecutors in their own turn. They seized a *Lebensraum* for themselves. The lesson they learned was not to eschew but to imitate some of the evil deeds committed by the Nazis against them. The gravest crime of the Nazis was not their extermination of a majority of the Jews, but that they had caused the remnant to stumble.

In the last volume, 'Reconsiderations', published in 1961, Toynbee addresses certain criticisms of his account of the Jews. He praises them for providing a model for preserving national identity without a state. He then observes that by holding themselves apart from the rest of mankind, they expose themselves to risk of injury. The host of meticulous observances to which they commit themselves are irrational and spiritually unprofitable. They must move towards the surrendering of all national particularities. The Zionists are thus travelling in entirely the wrong direction. Toynbee confirms that he has not changed his view of Zionism, and the Zionists are indeed 'disciples of the Nazis', though, 'on second thoughts', it may be true that the vehemence of his condemnation has been 'out of proportion to the magnitude of Zionism's guilt'. He draws towards an end his reflections on the Jews thus: 'I have never felt any inclination to be anti-Semitic. There have always been more Jews than Arabs in my circle of friends.' And anti-Semitism itself is but a 'left-handed' acknowledgement of the validity of the Jews' own claim to uniqueness, a claim that amounts to no more than an objectionable pretension.[414] In the one volume abridgment,[415] Judaism is described as totalitarian in its monotheism. Israel's policy of national and religious exclusivity must be 'renounced forthwith'.[416]

Toynbee's work was a principal focus of Jewish apologetics in the 1950s and 1960s.[417] It has left no trace on historical writing; it received the almost universal condemnation of historians;[418] it is now mentioned only to be dismissed.[419]

Type C

We have arrived at what might be termed the normative anti-Semitism of English writers and intellectuals. It is an anti-Semitism without pretension, and consistent with the character, and limits, of modern English anti-Semitism itself. The anti-Semitic expression is usually unremarkable in its formulation; it rarely derives from any special preoccupation of its author. It tends to be intemperate yet also passionless, flip and unpondered. It mostly completes itself in angry humour rather than any programme for action. It often derives from a kind of lazy contempt; it is often merely an instance of a more generalized malice. It can be expostulatory, but it is essentially private. The writer may indeed take particular care to keep it out of his published work, confining his anti-Semitic observations to a diary or to conversation.[420] Certainly, it is unable to take the measure of violence against Jews; it stands in perplexity before exterminatory anti-Semitism.

Consider, for example, Thomas Carlyle (1795–1881), the Victorian sage and man of letters. Infuriated by a bill to remove Jewish disabilities, he wrote to his friend Richard Monckton Milnes: 'How can a real Jew, by possibility, try to be a senator, or even Citizen of any country, except his own wretched Palestine, whither all his steps and efforts tend?' Carlyle later cursed Benjamin Disraeli as 'a cursed old Jew not worth his weight in bacon'.[421] His biographer, J. A. Froude, records him once remarking, as he stood outside Rothschild's Hyde Park Corner mansion:

> I do not mean that I want King John back again, but if you ask me which mode of treating these people to have been the nearest to the will of the Almighty about them—to build them palaces like that, or to take the pincers for them, I declare for the pincers.[422]

'Carlyle', wrote Froude, 'detested Jews.'[423] But his stance towards them was characterized by little more than a kind of malicious, grim frivolity. (The 'little more' was his Deist conviction that Christianity had to cast off its 'Hebrew old clothes' in order fully to reveal itself in the 'Heart of Nature and of Man forevermore'.)[424] The New England sage R. W. Emerson, who came to know Carlyle well, was inclined to dismiss his more reactionary rants. They were 'no more than could be expected' from someone who 'purposely made exaggerated statements merely to astonish his listeners'.[425] (None of this is to disregard the argument that Carlyle's celebration of the hero, his contempt for democracy, and his racism, give him a place in the genealogy of fascism.)[426]

Now here is the philosopher Bertrand Russell (1872–1970), writing from gaol to his lover Ottoline Morrell, on 18 August 1918:

> I hate being all tidy like a book in a library where no one reads—Prison is horribly like that—Imagine if you knew you were a delicious book, and some Jew millionaire bought you and bound you uniform with a lot of others and stuck you up in a shelf behind glass, where you merely illustrated the completeness of his System—and no anarchist was allowed to read you—That is what one feels like.[427]

The 'Jew millionaire' was like other millionaires, except more so. He was the millionaire type uncomplicated by culture or religious sentiment. He was vulgar, and philistine, and acquisitive, and quite the wrong owner of precious, valuable things like books. He was also the kind of person who was a good butt for jokes. Russell's remark, of course, is no more than a conceit. He does not suppose that either he or Ottoline will ever be the prisoner of a 'Jew millionaire'; the Jews do not have that kind of power. Russell's malicious remark was trivial, inconsequential, but it proved to be continuous with an inability to grasp the determinate character of a rather more lethal version of anti-Semitism.

Somewhat in the manner of Carlyle, the writer A. N. Wilson (b. 1950) has made a number of disobliging remarks about Jews, about Judaism, and about Israel. Wilson is a biographer, historian, novelist, and newspaper columnist. He may also be regarded as an artist of the 'remark'. From his *Belloc*: 'We all know that the Jews regard themselves as a separate group within society. And yet there remains something unacceptable about Gentiles sharing the view Jews take of themselves.'[428] (Wilson's defence of Belloc's anti-Semitism is itself indefensible.)[429] From his *Milton*: '[among other] unattractive things about Judaism [is its] cult of racial superiority'.[430] From a newspaper article: 'hate filled paranoias of Judaism'.[431] Wilson's hostility to Israel and the Zionist project on occasion[432] exceeds proper boundaries: '[Israel is guilty of] the poisoning of water supplies',[433] 'Israel never was a state, and it can only be defended by constant war.'[434] But what does this add up to, when taken with everything else that Wilson has said, and written about the Jews? First, and particularly in his journalism, a desire to 'stir things up', to run counter to a perceived consensus, and to meet the editorial pressure on every newspaper columnist to be provocative, memorable, and opinionated. But secondly, and notwithstanding this, there is a commonplace quality about these remarks. The hostile things he has to say are mostly nothing more than received opinion among anti-Semites. Indeed, not even fiction stimulates Wilson to think fresh thoughts about Jews—the heroine of his novel, *My Name is Legion* (2004), is an intense, dark-haired Jewish beauty named Rachel Pearl.[435]

Russell's anti-Semitism was not distinctively his own; it was not what made him Bertrand Russell. He had, one might say, no public relationship as an intellectual with anti-Semitism.[436] Carlyle's gibes were, on occasion, a good deal more splenetic than Russell's, but as expressions of hostility they came to the same thing—contempt for Jews, or certain kinds of Jews, or the Jewish project that is Israel. The remarks are ugly, sometimes worse than ugly. But they lead nowhere. They are also consistent with more original perspectives—less hostile, more curious and open—on Jews and the Jewish tradition. In Carlyle's *Sartor Resartus*, for example, the most fantastical of his works, with its cod-exposition of the 'clothes philosophy' of the imaginary Dr Teufelsdröckh, Carlyle has informed fun mocking the 'cabalistico-sartorial' fancies of Talmudists concerning 'Paradise and fig-leaves'. (He also gets in a dig at the 'Old-Clothes Jewry' of Monmouth Street.)[437] As for Wilson, he has written with generous sympathy about first-century Judaism. The Old Testament is the record of an evolving religious consciousness without equal in the literature of the world; the Pharisees were 'among the most virtuous men who had ever lived'; the problem of theodicy haunted the Jews until the twentieth century, 'when unimaginable suffering was to be their destiny'. Indeed: 'to be a Jew is to suffer'.[438] This sense of the absence of a distinctively intellectual version of modern English anti-Semitism is implicit in observations made by the historian Lewis Namier in a pamphlet published in the late 1930s, when an altogether more dangerous kind of anti-Semitism menaced Jews. In England, Namier wrote, Jews got the fairest deal. But that did not inhibit the making of remarks to Jews that were hurtful and untrue.[439]

Type D

The peer and leading politician, David Lindsay, attended a party hosted by Lord Rothschild in 1900:

> I have studied the anti-semite question with some attention, always hoping to stem an ignoble movement: but when confronted by the herd of Ickleheimers, Raphaels, Sassoons and the rest of the breed, my emotions gain the better of logic and injustice, while I feel some sympathy with Lueger and Drumont—John Burns, by the way, says the Jew is the tapeworm of civilisation.[440]

It is a contest between a certain fine feeling of distaste and more generous and rational impulses. The self-satisfaction runs quite deep, because Lindsay is plainly impressed both by his 'emotions' and by his 'logic'. But the sympathy expressed with Continental anti-Semitism was somewhat unusual. The more typical English anti-Semite tended to regard as vulgar and extravagant what he identified as 'anti-Semitism', which he distinguished from his own rational reservations about Jews. The former was taken to be characteristic of a certain kind of Continental European sensibility, one that is excitable, immoderate, ideological. It is one thing to maintain one's distance from Jews, deprecating the pushier or ostentatious among them, ensuring that they keep to their place (and being ready to remind them of it, should they appear to forget). It is quite another to polemicize against them, legislating away their civil rights, confining them in ghettoes and causing their women and children to suffer. This is to cause pain of a kind that every decent person must deplore. During periods when this latter, more dangerous, anti-Semitism is active, anti-Semites of the former kind will often do what they can to help Jews, if only to demonstrate to themselves the utter distinctness of their own animus (but that is perhaps to be uncharitable). Many English anti-Semites deplore 'anti-Semitism'. And so when they aim to exclude Jews from their institutions, or limit their number, they will draw the excluded and restricted categories so wide as to exclude or restrict others too, and they will do so half-persuaded, half-believing, that it is indeed their intention not to exclude or restrict Jews, but only some kinds of Jews, or not Jews at all, save for those who by mischance happen to qualify on grounds other than their religion. But Jews who see through this (and most do) are insulted, both by the policy, and by the amateur, easy self-deception that accompanies it.

Or take C. R. Ashbee (1863–1942), the architect and designer, and from 1918 to 1923, the civic adviser to what became the British Mandate administration in Palestine. There is absent from his memoir, *A Palestine Notebook 1918–1923* (1923), any fresh 'take' on the Zionist project, and instead one finds a recycling of the most tired and generally hostile clichés concerning Jewish capabilities and power. And this, despite being thrust into a milieu positively teeming with Jews—with Jews, what is more, who were (so to speak) vigorously, and emphatically Jewish. Yet all that Ashbee, himself the son of a Jewish mother, can report is that the Jew is unthinkable without the bargain; that he has a 'gift of apparent self-obliteration'; that he can swiftly disguise himself in the cloak of any nationality; and that his spiritual and intellectual arrogance is his curse, and has made him hated. Ashbee is against a Jewish National Home, because the world needs the cosmopolitanism of the Jew; he is a 'fermentator' and a 'wanderer'. Yet the Jews want the British in Palestine, and they will get their way—'it will not be the first time that English instinct has been like wax in their hands'. And so on, and so tediously forth.[441] It is as if there is something in the culture that inhibits all originality of perspective on Jews, Jewish projects, or Judaism—other, that is, for those unusual individuals utterly absorbed with such matters, either creatively or in a spirit of intense enmity.

The *type D* writers and intellectuals are within the broad category suggested by these two instances; in the structuring of their divided perspective on Jews they are closest to quotidian, unreflective modern English anti-Semitism. They might use pejorative language, make anti-Jewish jokes, or generally write deprecatingly about Jews, yet they will also maintain cordial relations with Jewish colleagues (sometimes, the very colleagues whom they have privately abused),[442] deplore 'anti-Semitism', and intervene to protest at anti-Semitic discrimination or persecution. This dislike of both Jews and of anti-Semitism is something of an English cultural reflex. 'Thank God, I have no prejudices,' ruminated an advocate of the removal of Jewish disabilities, 'but I do hate the Jews.'[443] W. M. Thackeray, ready with his own contempt for Jews, was also contemptuous of an excessive, unreasoning anti-Semitism:

> 'Odious people,' said Mrs. Bürcke, looking at the pair that Mrs. Löwe was driving; 'odious, vulgar horse!' . . . 'Roman-nosed beast! I shouldn't wonder but that the horse is a Jew too!'[444]

Mrs Bürcke, ludicrous to Thackeray both as female and German, exposes her stupidity in her comically overstated Jew-hatred. Wyndham Lewis made the point most succinctly, in his book *Hitler* (1931): 'a pinch of malice certainly, but no "antisemitism" for the love of Mike!' The Nazis 'take the Jews too seriously'.[445] The anti-Semite Collin Brooks thereafter made the point most unreflectively, when he dismissed Captain Ramsay MP in a 1940 diary entry as 'the conventional anti-Jew fanatic, tracing all our woes back to the *Protocols of Zion*, which most people, even anti-Semites, believe to be forged'.[446]

Harold Nicolson (1886–1968), the diplomat, Member of Parliament, and writer, is representative of this type. He supported Mosley until the latter took a definite turn towards fascism.[447] He then took an anti-appeasement position, and defined the war's purpose as saving humanity from the 'rubber truncheon and the concentration camp'.[448] He was sympathetic to Zionism, but felt keenly Britain's 'humiliation' in 1948 and deplored the 'ghetto thugs' who that year had assassinated the UN mediator, Count Berna-dotte.[449] In an early diary entry, Nicolson notes an evening spent with Virginia and Leonard Woolf. Nicolson wanted to argue that removing restrictions on Foreign Office entry might cause a 'flood' 'by clever Jews', but 'it was a little difficult to argue this point frankly with Leonard there'. In 1938, he notes information of the humiliations inflicted on Austria's Jews. Later that year, he notes Unity Mitford's adoration of Hitler, and her desire to have 'the Jews be made to eat grass'. When in December 1942 a young Jewish officer arrives to commandeer the family country home, Nicolson remarks, 'recalling how but three days before I had stood in tribute to the martyred Jews of Poland, I was most polite to Captain Rubinstein'. It is 'more disgraceful than ever', he records in March 1944, 'to see the Americans with East End Jewish girls, shouting among [the] unhappy and recumbent' people sheltering from air raids. In the following year, Nicolson notes 'a Jewess in a paper cup strolling down St James's turning a rattle'. During the General Election, Nicolson blames on the Jews the *Daily Mirror*'s contribution to anti-Tory Party sentiment in the Armed Forces. The *Mirror*'s board was composed mainly of Jews, he thought. This promotion of a 'general distrust of authority', which he deplores, Nicolson attributes to 'the Jewish capacity for destruction', which 'is really illimit-able'. And then, as if discovering in himself just this commonplace senti-ment, he remarks, 'Although I loathe antisemitism, I do dislike Jews.'[450]

George Orwell had a considerable interest in anti-Semitism, one that was much more developed than Nicolson's. In a 1944 review, he called for 'a full inquiry into the prevalence of anti-Semitism', observing, 'the fact that we should probably find that anti-Semitism of various kinds is alarmingly common, and that educated people are not in the least immune from it, ought not to deter us'.[451] He was vigilant for anti-Semitism in writers whose work he was reviewing.[452] He was also quick to spot moments of change and modification in anti-Semitic sentiment. In a short piece on *Trilby*, he contrasted the anti-Semitism of the 1890s with that of his own times, in which 'the English', being 'less sure of themselves, [are] less confident that stupidity always wins in the end'. This meant a change in the 'prevailing form of anti-Semitism', one not 'altogether for the better'.[453] He found the conspiracist, persecutory anti-Semitism of the 1930s a menace, and Mosley's domestic version of it ridiculous as well as unpleasant. In a March 1936 diary entry about a BUF rally he noted: 'The blame for everything was put upon mysterious international gangs of Jews who are said to be financing, among other things, the British Labour Party...'[454] News of the destruction of the Jews was a reminder of fascism's true nature, Orwell explained elsewhere, and of what the Allies were fighting against.[455] Conspiracy-talk was what the Nazis were about; it should have no place in England.[456] Zionism, however, encouraged Orwell into some of his own conspiracy talk. In conversation with strongly pro-Zionist journalist colleagues, Orwell described Zionists as 'a bunch of Wardour Street Jews who have a controlling influence over the British press'.[457] Malcolm Muggeridge regarded Orwell as 'at heart strongly anti-Semitic';[458] to Christopher Hitchens, Orwell's 'suspicion of Jews' was one of his 'inherited prejudices'.[459]

H. G. Wells occupies a distinctive place within this category of *type D* intellectuals. It would almost be sufficient to write of him that he was an anti-Semite. In *The Future in America* (1906), he argues that the Jews make a ghetto for themselves wherever they go.[460] In *A Short History of the World* (1922), he writes that 'the struggle of Aryan, Semitic and Egyptian ideas and methods' goes on 'through all the rest of history, and continues to this day', and that 'the rivalry of Aryan and Semite', which merged itself in 'the conflict of Gentile and Jew', exercises an influence on the conflicts of today.[461] In the fantasy *All Aboard For Ararat* (1940), God Himself repudiates the Jews: 'These Chosen People! The time they have given me!'[462] In *The Outlook for Homo Sapiens* (1942), he argues that the Jews' separatism, their implacable national egotism, has been the cause of all the persecutions that have been visited on them; Gentile intolerance is a response to the cult of the Chosen People. The Jews must assimilate, or their troubles will intensify. Judaism is an 'aggressive and vindictive conspiracy'; Isaiah is 'extraordinarily like the rantings of some Nazi propagandist'.[463] But it would also be possible to write of Wells that he was an anti-anti-Semite. He also argues in Outlook, for example, that belief in the occult powers of the Jews is delusional, and that conspiracy talk is insane. Jewish nationalism is just like every other nationalism, and it must end, just like all nationalisms must end, for the sake of the species.[464] In Liberalism and Its Party (1913) he writes about the Marconi Affair, and the impression it created of a 'pervading baseness',[465] without any anti-Semitic innuendo. In The Rights of Man (1940), the rejection of Nazi anti-Semitism is too complete to allow a case for its Jewish provenance.[466] In Tono-Bungay, it is taken to be an indication of George Ponderevo's moral fecklessness that on his voyage to West Africa he panders to the first mate's anti-Semitism.[467] In A Short History of the World (1922) he praises 'the last of the Hebrew prophets' for 'creating a free conscience for mankind', and writes of Isaiah that the 'prophetic voice rises to a pitch of splendid anticipation and foreshadows the whole earth united and at peace under God'.[468]

None of this is to be explained by 'ambivalence'. It is not enough to say that he is divided about the Jews, feeling both sympathy and hostility, nor that he divides up the Jews, distinguishing between the 'good' and the 'bad'. And nor is his work to be recuperated as merely representative of a liberal anti-Semitism. It is instead radically incoherent. In Anticipations (1902), for example, the objections to Jews are so radically qualified, either by describing them as 'alleged' ('the alleged termite in the woodwork, the Jew'), or by attributing them equally to non-Jews ('there are Gentile faces just as coarse and gross'), or by introducing them speculatively ('if the Jew has a certain incurable tendency to social parasitism . . . '), that a curiously self-cancelling meaning is communicated.[469] All the received ideas about Jews, etc., and not just the antagonistic ones, play across his prose, and Wells does little to discipline them. He writes one thing, and then another, and then a third thing. He will write, it sometimes seems, almost anything about the Jews. In his writing, almost everything that could be said about the Jews is said. The term 'the Jews' is for Wells a most capacious signifier, available to be filled by him as he chooses, as if on a whim. He wrote about Jews in contexts where doing so was unnecessary;[470] but what he then said tended to be banal, and somewhat enervated. He could not get his miscellaneous views about Jews to cohere.

Falling outside this kind of divided perspective were those non-*type D* writers and intellectuals whose posture amounted to deploring and justifying the persecution of the Jews, and to a claim to independence and objectivity of judgement ostensibly demonstrated by their readiness to write not just about Jews but about 'anti-Semitism' too. Goldwin Smith's chapter on 'The Jewish Question', in his *Questions of the Day* (London, 1897), for example, addresses 'Jewish ascendancy and the anti-Semitic movement provoked by it'.[471] Chesterton, writing in 1917 about 1290 (in his *Short History of England*) commended the 'just and conscientious' Edward I, never more truly 'representative' of his people than when he expelled the Jews, 'as powerful as they were unpopular'. They were 'the capitalists of their age' (in my second-hand copy of the book, the original owner has added in the margin, 'as now'). They were exploiters and exploited; they were oppressors and oppressed. This '*mutual* charge of tyranny', Chesterton writes, 'is the Semitic trouble in all times'. It is a nicely balanced formulation, one that appeals to a kind of fair-to-both-sides, 'six of one, half a dozen of the other', sentiment, but it does not quite survive the paragraph, because Chesterton adds that when Edward 'flung the alien financiers out of the land', he was both 'knight errant' and 'tender father of his people'.[472]

Some reasons for this absence of any significant anti-Semitic aspect in the major intellectual engagements of the period

The medieval historian R. I. Moore, in his important and original work, *The Formation of a Persecuting Society* (1987), argues that the development of persecution in all its forms, including the persecution of the Jews, in the European Middle Ages was an aspect of the tremendous extension of the power and influence of the literate, and therefore inseparable from their great and positive achievements.[473] Moore considers this to be as true of England as of anywhere else in Europe. But when this 'persecuting society' returned in Europe, as it did in the late nineteenth century, and once again was led by intellectuals, England, and in particular *its* 'literate', did not enrol. It is time to ask why this was so. Three reasons suggest themselves; there are no doubt others.

British supremacy

Ask the question 'what was new about anti-Semitism in the late nineteenth century?' and the answer will *not* be, characterizing Jews as superstitious, legalistic, unscrupulous, and misanthropic, or holding them responsible for hate crimes against Christians, or even blaming them for the death of Jesus. These defamations were in circulation then, for sure—and they continue to circulate today. But they were hardly new. What *was* new was the belief that Jews were somehow in charge of modern affairs. Secretly, sinisterly, beyond the reach of the law and even of governments, they were plotting, or already enjoying, global power. This anti-Semitism was thus no longer confined to descriptions of the Jews' unregenerate condition; it also offered an account of the allegedly determinative part that they played in the modern world. The modern anti-Semites told this story. While for centuries the coercive apparatuses of Church and State had contained the Jews, and thereby limited the evil they could do, when the ghetto walls fell, the Jews suddenly found themselves unfettered, unconstrained, and free to combine against the world and to dominate it. Christian Europe, newly secularized, was ill equipped to confront this immense, indeed immeasurable, escalation in the threat posed by the Jews ('the Jewish peril'). Indeed, it was walking, unaware, to enslavement. And this happened without anybody noticing— except, that is, the anti-Semites, who shouted warnings at the tops of their voices, and then suffered agonies of frustration as their message went unheeded. Anti-Semitism thus ceased to be a justification of Jewish subor- dination to Gentiles; it became instead an exposure of Gentile subordination to the Jews. And it ceased to address a problem *within* medieval life; it instead addressed the problem *of* modern life.

Though this transformed anti-Semitism had considerable reach, it failed to make headway in England, a fact noticed by English commentators in the 1890s.[474] In part, this was because so much of the world was under English rule, and in part it was because so much of modernity was of England's making. For most of the modern period (say, until the mid-twentieth century), not only were the English in control of their own lives, they were also in control of the lives of millions of other people. The question in England towards the end of the nineteenth century, and then continuing into the first half of the twentieth century, was not 'who is ruling us?', but rather, 'for how long can we continue to rule others?' Likewise, when English intellectuals deplored the rule of the 'cash-nexus' they could not— not even remotely—attribute it to the Jews. It was too intimately a creation of England itself. It was in some fundamental sense the author of most of modern life's perplexities and terrors. If as a general, minimum proposition it is true to say of conspiracy theories that they appeal to people who believe that they are not in control of their own lives *but that someone else is*, it is easy to see how slight an appeal such theories would have in a strong, self-confident imperial culture,[475] unreflectively persuaded of the truth of the proposition that, all things considered, it was better to have Englishmen rule the world than foreigners.[476]

British political culture was based on an unprecedented set of achievements. Britain was the most successful liberal capitalist state. The hundred-year or so period, from the loss of the American colonies to the first Great Depression and the Third Reform Act, saw the world triumph of British arms, commerce, industry, and ideas.[477] Among the Great Powers, it was the greatest power. At the zenith of their empire, the British ruled between a fifth and a quarter of humanity.[478] At its maximum extent between the world wars, the British Empire covered more than 13 million square miles, approximately 23 per cent of the world's land surface.[479] Never was the map redder;[480] Britain was top nation, ruler of the world.[481] Reporting on events celebrating Queen Victoria's Diamond Jubilee, a *Times* journalist enthused about 'the mightiest and most beneficial Empire ever known in the annals of mankind'.[482] It was a world-state, the central fact in the first global political economy.[483] 'The element of fear was singularly lacking in Victorian England', observed the intellectual historian, Crane Brinton.[484] This element is similarly lacking in Victorian anti-Semitism too—even Goldwin Smith was ready to acknowledge that 'England', being 'a great commercial country', could 'digest the Jewish element now'.[485] Across the nineteenth century, and until the calamities of World War I and the triumph of the Bolsheviks in 1917, Britain and the world order for which it stood, was just too successful, was doing just too well, to prompt the questions that the then dominant version of anti-Semitism was purporting to answer. The national reverses were too quickly remedied, the economic slumps were too limited in duration, and most of all, were too readily intelligible by reference to more proximate causes, to provide the conditions for the emergence of the modern, most pretentious version of anti-Semitism, the one summed up by the slogan 'The Jews are our misfortune.' Even the crises of the inter-war years failed to precipitate any substantial lurch to the anti-Semitic, extra-Parliamentary Right.[486] National self-assurance was essentially undentable, notwithstanding local, short-term reverses and defeats.[487] Prosperity, a commanding position in the world, the dignity and might of being the pre-eminent imperial power, unequalled in human history—why should the Jews be feared? The world had been made over in Britain's image.

It was only in the aftermath of World War II that the British, exhausted and in debt, were fully drawn to the contemplation of national decline (there had been thoughts of decline in earlier decades, of course, while even in the immediate post-war period Britain remained an imperial state and a world power). But it was at a moment that followed such disaster for the Jews that to entertain the thought that in some sense they might have had a hand in this loss of mastery was beyond even the absurdities tolerated by anti-Semitism. This was the moment in European history, more than any other moment, which illuminated the utter defencelessness, the impotence, of the Jews. For the more confirmed anti-Semites, of course, the moment quickly passed, and they recovered their faith in Jewish power. 'It is a tragedy', grieved Barry Domvile in 1947, 'that the British people have been so ill-informed on this crucial matter', the power of the 'sinister agency', the 'Judeo-Masonic combination'.[488] But anti-Semites like Domvile had by then become utterly marginal and discredited figures in England's political culture.

The English ideology

England was, and may still be, unreceptive to ideology and ideologists, if 'ideology' is understood as an elaborated world-view, both philosophical and programmatic, advanced by intellectuals, with its object the transformation of the state, or its mobilization against an economic class or religious group. This particular unreceptiveness is an aspect of a broader mistrust of general concepts,[489] and a pride in seeing through the pretentious, the snobbish, and the dishonest[490]—what George Eliot referred to as the 'solidity and directness of the English mind'.[491] One benefit has been to inhibit the development of any of the more fantastic and menacing anti-Semitisms; another, however, has been to encourage the disparaging of the 'Jewish intellectual', or indeed any preference for 'cleverness' over 'character'. Walter Bagehot, for example, praising what he described as 'a proper stupidity' as against mere 'cleverness', made his point by reference to 'Mr. Disraeli, the witty orator, the exceedingly clever *littérateur*, the versatile politician'. 'All England . . . has made up its mind that the stupidest country gentleman would be a better Home Secretary than the accomplished descendent of the "Caucasian race".'[492]

'Ideology' can be given a more capacious description, however. It can be used as a summary term for that bundle of values, ideals and enmities that comprise the self-understanding of an institution or entity—say, a church, or a political party, or even a nation. In this sense, 'ideology' is the answer that members of the institution or entity would give if asked to explain their beliefs. Even when offered by the most reflective and thoughtful of such members, the answer would not be fully worked-out; it would always have a quality of the tacit, the taken-for-granted. It is possible to speak of the 'English ideology', then, or the 'French ideology', in much the same way that it was once the style to speak of the 'English mind', or the 'French mind'. Of course, even the subtlest account of such phenomena risks deficiency: it may not admit all relevant exceptions, it may not include all relevant aspects. But that does not mean one should not try. Certainly, in any study of English anti-Semitisms, it would be a far greater deficiency were no account at all given of the 'English ideology'—and in particular those aspects that have a bearing on the formation of hostile perspectives on Jews and Judaism. I have attempted this, in both the present and certain of the previous, chapters. But the question arises, what of those aspects of the English ideology that may be said to have *inhibited* the formation of certain types of anti-Semitism? There is no doubt that Jews have been net beneficiaries of the English ideology.

We can identify, straight away, a certain privileging of 'common sense', 'fairness', and 'tolerance'. These are not bogus values, though they are complex in their formulations and often compromised in their application. 'Common sense', for example, is helpful because it shrinks from all political extravagance, including that of an anti-Semitic character. It is 'common sense' to be concerned only with the immediate and the foreseeable, and to disregard whatever does not bear directly and patently on material interests. At its most prejudiced, of course, it causes a kind of blindness to everything that falls outside that narrow compass. It can be exasperating, then. But it also constrains dangerous enthusiasms—the enthusiasms of conspiracy-minded anti-Semites, for example.[493] Their appeals to mysterious cabals, lethal plots, and the like, do not 'stand to reason'. They fail in their appeal to 'common sense'. But it is 'fairness' (or 'fair play') that is perhaps the master value of the English ideology.[494] 'Tolerance' is merely an important derivative of this value—as, say, is the ideal of the 'good sport', the person who does not take unfair advantage of others, and who is not quick to take offence.

It is to the principle of 'fairness' or 'fair play' that appeal is typically made in protest at acts of perceived injustice. In Trollope's *The Prime Minister*, for example, it is to Mr Wharton's credit that he 'tried to be fair on the subject [of Lopez]. It might be that it was a prejudice . . . '[495] That the notion of 'fair play' could have ludicrous applications—'the spirit of fair play and of just dealings with native races . . . has made our government always tolerated, and in most cases welcomed'[496]—is only evidence of its weight in English self-understanding. This colonialist self-understanding was put under particular strain in the Mandate context. 'It does not seem to have occurred to the Zionists', observed the committee of inquiry into the 1920 Arab riots, 'that it is possible for an English official to have a personal dislike for a type and yet do his duty conscientiously in spite of it.' A senior British official a few years later expressed the belief that 'the Palestine policy' could only be achieved if it was 'implemented by pure-bred Britishers whose justice and impartiality could not be questioned'.[497] Impartiality was often confused during the Mandate with even-handedness, which may with justice be satirized in this context as the principle that a conflict is best resolved by adjudicating in favour of none of the parties to it.

What then of tolerance? A principle of religious tolerance emerged across the most troubled decades of the seventeenth century, gathering up Jews among others in its embrace. There was a very strong English showing in the development of theories of toleration; it became a central aspect of the nation's political common sense, an aspect of how it differentiated itself from other, rival nations.[498] As early as in 1688, James II was able to declare that it had long been 'constant sense and opinion that conscience ought not to be constrained nor people forced in matters of mere religion'. Intolerance spoils trade, depopulates countries and discourages strangers, without ever attaining its object.[499] Further arguments supporting the principle and practice of toleration were also developed, then and in later centuries: that religious belief requires inward assent, which cannot be coerced; that 'revealed truths', conveyed to us by books, are 'liable to the common and natural obscurities and difficulties incidental to words';[500] that human beings should be respected as rational, autonomous agents; that a 'free market in ideas' has considerable utility; that the state should be neutral between the various conceptions of the good held by its citizens.[501] In addition, the eighteenth century contributed a certain contempt for the intolerant, an intolerance of intolerance. There was an Enlightenment scorn for medievalism, taken to include among its evil effects the persecution of Jews, and a broader mistrust of all fanaticism, 'that baleful love of truth'.[502] This eighteenth-century disparagement duly made its way into nineteenth-century historiography.[503] In addition to these positions, which benefited the Jewish community among other minority groups, a further set of positions were taken across the same extended period positively promoting the toleration of Jews. For example, it was said that it was wrong to 'add affliction to the afflicted'; though the Jews had been a rebellious people, they had long since expiated their offence.[504] The high value to be placed upon the principle of tolerance on occasion prompted a certain rueful pride. At the 1856 AGM of the RSPCA, for example, a critic of 'the Jewish system of slaughtering animals' observed with regret, 'till an Act of Parliament is passed, which I do not think likely, because *this is a country of perfect toleration*, we shall continue [to be] unable to interfere'.[505]

There was no substantial dissent from the English ideology by its intelligentsia, which never found itself in permanent conflict with the Church and the ruling classes. Indeed, their first challenge upon emergence as a distinct class in the eighteenth century was the *defence* of the reformed polity.[506] They provided a contingent of non-conformists, without whom orthodoxy would stifle all criticism of institutions and values. But their polemics have always been closer to actual experience and less inclined to the purely speculative than the intellectuals on the Continent; they were never isolated from the rich and the powerful, and demands for reform were met quickly enough for the political, economic system itself not to be called into question.[507] They were given a position in the elite and they did not dream of total upheaval; they did not burn for revolution.[508] Political thought in England has mostly been aligned with existing institutions; it is coincident with reality.[509] English intellectuals tended not to exceed the general consensus; if they made their times significant, they did not do so by forming public opinion.[510] England's merely social intolerance kills no one, roots out no opinions, but induces men to disguise them, or to abstain from any active effort for their diffusion. 'Heretical opinions', wrote J. S. Mill 'do not perceptibly gain, or even lose, ground in each decade or generation; they never blaze out far and wide, but continue to smoulder in the narrow circles of thinking and studious persons among whom they originate.'[511]

In the last decades of the nineteenth century, English writers came to view with some complacency the treatment of England's Jews, as against their persecutions elsewhere. 'London has always held out hands of toleration, if not of welcome, to the alien', wrote Walter Besant in 1903.[512] An anonymous contributor to the *London Quarterly Review*, distinguished between the Jew-hatred in Russia and Germany on the one hand, and the tolerance shown to Jews in England. In explaining the circumstances in which the new 'manifestations of race hatred' have arisen in Germany ('Jew-baiting is out of date'), the author displays some sympathy with the race-haters. The Jew was once 'hunted about the streets like a dog'. But 'now, he begins to hold his head high; he regards himself as our equal, if not our superior'. Yesterday, the Jew was the German's 'servant'; 'today, in an increasingly significant sense, he bids fair to become his master'. This 'ill-fated race has sought and found few friends'. Their 'ostentatious luxury, the unscrupulous use of every means of self-aggrandisement, the insults offered by the Jewish press to the Christian religion, the vulgar and almost unbear-able arrogance of the Jews themselves'—all this is intolerable. And yet . . . if the Jews were as bad as is said, 'their ruthless and total extermination would have become a necessity to the human race'. They are not; it is not. The persecutions and indignities visited upon the Jews cannot be justified. As for England, though it was not as prompt as it might have been to alleviate the disabilities of the Jews, 'we are [now] in advance of most other nations in the policy of justice and liberty'.[513]

Departures from this policy could thus be condemned as 'un-English'. When Colonel Wedgwood rose in the House of Commons debate on the Aliens Restriction Bill to oppose the clause that prevented an alien from changing his name, he was able to condemn the proposed measure as 'particularly un-English and unintelligent, because it pursues these unfor-tunate people with unbridled hate'. The point seemed obvious to him. 'The best way of turning a bad German into a good Englishman is to allow his name to be changed.' Indeed, 'the sooner you allow the alien element to assume English names and the higher English characteristics the better it will be for the whole country'.[514] English Jews likewise tended to appeal to 'English' values when persecutory or defamatory sentiments threatened their communal well-being[515]—though sometimes franker, or more des-pairing assessments of the English character prevailed.[516] The point should thus not be overstated. Common sense, fairness, and tolerance did not operate as a bar on all anti-Semitic sentiment. Sometimes, indeed, appeals to 'fair play' were made for a directly anti-Semitic purpose—the Jews do not believe in fair play, they engage in 'sharp practices', etc.[517] And often, the merest gesture was made in the direction of English values before the articulating of the most full-blooded expressions of Jew-hatred. 'The com-pilers [of *The Jews' Who's Who*] have no complaint to make of Jews as such,' H. H. Beamish piously explained, 'but Judaism is incompatible with English sincerity and single-mindedness.'[518] 'I do not say that there are no honourable and upright Jews,' Nesta Webster declared, with her own gesture towards fair-mindedness, 'but I do maintain that the spirit of fair play which is the essence of the British character is not the characteristic of the Jewish race in general.'[519] Always, then, this fair-minded acknowledgement of a saving remnant, coupled with commonplace anti-Semitic disparagements. 'He is modest, clean, free from the oiliness of most Jews', noted a World War II diarist. 'My opinion on his race rises to par.'[520]

A subtler offence is ostensible fair-mindedness in respect of an unquestionably bad cause. Representing, with a pronounced display of impartiality, anti-Semitic positions as merely one 'side' in what is cast as a 'debate', has long been a tactic among anti-Semitic controversialists. Sometimes, but then for more complicated reasons, this also becomes the tactic of individuals and entities not otherwise tainted by anti-Semitism. During the Damascus blood-libel affair, for example, *The Times* refused to take sides, over the course of its extended coverage setting out the cases for and against the Jews' guilt with a neutrality exasperating to its Jewish readers. It allowed space to correspondence debating the truth of the blood libel, printing many contributions disparaging of Judaism, as well as others in its defence. Tory sentiment seems to have been behind this unwarranted even-handedness—hostility to the then Whig government, and opposition to the cause of Jewish emancipation. Many of the reader's letters it published were frankly anti-Semitic. A 'leader' went so far as to assert that the affair put in question the future of Jewry as a whole. The 'very existence of the Jewish religion and of the Jews as a separate clan of the community' depends upon the outcome of the case: 'Admitting for the moment [the accusations to be true], then the Jewish religion must at once disappear from the face of the earth. No honourable or honest man could remain a member of such a community.' 'We shall await the issue,' *The Times* concluded, 'as the whole of Europe and the civilised world will do, with intense interest.'[521]

Lastly, a case has been made that the specific character of English toleration exercised a limiting, and in certain respects, repressive influence on Anglo-Jewish freedom. It was a tolerance of condescension, and inhospitable to diversity. English society itself was monolithic and exclusive: Jews could either join it on given terms, or live outside it, free of undue hardship. Jews who wished to embrace received English values were permitted to do so, and to reap the rewards; other Jews, who wished to stand apart, were permitted to do so, but paid a small price in social exclusion. What Jews were *not* able to do was to play a full, participating part in English society on their *own* terms, it is argued. They were themselves intolerant of outsiders (that is to say, of non-Jews); why then should they be tolerated? To participate meant to some degree withdrawing from Jewish society. Jews had to make a choice. The merit of the tolerance was in permitting the choice; the vice of the tolerance was in requiring it. Toleration was thus 'qualified, hedged around with reservations, and ultimately ambiguous'.[522] This was an 'anti-Semitism of tolerance'.[523]

English philo-Semitism

It was in keeping with Ford Madox Ford's conviction in the 'broad, tolerant, humanitarian, practical optimistic thing which is [English] public opinion', that he should welcome the poor immigrant Jews of Odessa, among whom might be 'another Disraeli, the man who will help England muddle through'.[524] But independently of this capacious generosity of spirit, there was also an English philo-Semitism, one derived from strong religious and intellectual traditions, directly or indirectly sympathetic to Jews, Judaism, and Jewish history, and which had the effect of hampering the expression of overt, ideological anti-Semitism, making it appear discreditable, and causing many of those who might otherwise have been most drawn to its embrace to disavow it. By contrast, in neither France, Germany nor Russia was there a discursive philo-Semitism sufficiently robust and unqualified to check the appeal of anti-Semitism to the intelligentsia. This is not to say that Germany, for example, was without its philo-Semites, with their appeals to 'the legacy of Lessing',[525] and so on, only that they were isolated as a counter-force, rather than speaking for the common sense of the culture.

There was in England, of course, the whole dissenting, Protestant ferment of the seventeenth century, with its 'Judaizing' tendencies and its millenarian expectations,[526] if not always pro-Jewish, certainly tending to the temporal advantage of Jews.[527] There was the academic study of Judaism, a staple of Tudor humanism as much as of nineteenth- and early twentieth-century university scholarship. In the 1770s, an anti-Deist defence was made of the Jews, 'neither more ignorant, nor more barbarous, nor more superstitious than other people';[528] the defence of the Pharisees in the work of Travers Herford was particularly important;[529] there were serious, sympathetic accounts of post-biblical Jewish history—see, for example, H. H. Milman's *History of the Jews*, 4th edn, 1866. In the works of Joseph Priestley (1733–1804), one finds friendly, open engagements with Jews, conversionist in tendency, but rational and fair-minded; his *Letters to the Jews* (1786–7) and *Address to the Jews* (1799) are exemplary instances of inter-faith dialogue.[530] There were ready, generous acknowledgements of the role played by Jews in the development of international commerce and the circulation and exchange of ideas.[531] There was early, committed, practical support for the Zionist project in Palestine. In Part II of the *Letters*, Priestly urges his Jewish readers, 'According to Moses, your return to your country is always in your own power. Do your part, and your merciful God and father will not delay to do his.'[532] Priestley's tough-mindedness was one aspect of Christian encouragement to Jewish settlement; there were also across the centuries somewhat more visionary dreams composed of the temporal restoration of the Jews to Palestine, exercises in speculative Zionism before the term itself was invented.[533] David Hartley combined the practical with the visionary in his *Observations on Man* (1791), holding it 'probable that the Jews will be restored to Palestine' partly because Scripture prophesied it, and partly because they 'are treated with contempt and harshness and sometimes with great cruelty by the nations amongst whom they sojourn', and thus are no doubt ready to 'return to their own land'.[534] There was the study of Christian anti-Semitism, transformed, if not altogether initiated by, the Rev. James Parkes (1896–1981). Parkes was a champion of Jewish causes, and a person who 'spoke as a Jew',[535] somewhat in the manner of Keti'ah. There was also a pervasive, popular admiration for certain values regarded as specifically Jewish, including sobriety, enterprise, family loyalty, and philanthropy, and a notion that the Jews had suffered deeply and unfairly for their faith.[536] Champions of Jewish emancipation offered these praises, among others; the Jews 'are entitled to our best consideration'.[537] And there were public demonstrations of concern for Jewish suffering—the 1840 Mansion House meeting to protest the Damascus blood libel, the 1882 Mansion House and 1890 Guildhall meetings to protest the persecutions in Russia, the Queen's Hall, London, rally in June 1933 to 'express in unequivocal terms the nation's abhorrence at the anti-Jewish persecutions in Germany',[538] and the 17 December 1942 House of Commons protest at the Nazi genocide. English philo-Semitism, the authors of a recent study have concluded, has been a 'significant force' in English society.[539]

Relatedly, there was also a sense, somewhat supersessionist in character, of the Jewish nation as the precursor and model for the English nation. England was taken to have a special place in the providential scheme of history, analogous to the position held by the ancient Israelites. It was an elect nation; it had its own distinct covenant with God.[540] The Puritans regarded their struggle as akin to the Maccabean uprising; the Levellers called their opponents 'Amalekites'.[541] 'Israel' was conceived in allegorical relation to England—see, for example, the poetry of William Blake, or John Dryden's 'Absalom and Achitophel' (1681), or the lines from Daniel Defoe's 'The True-Born Englishman' (1700): 'In this to ancient Israel well compared, / Eternal murmurs are among them heard'. England's struggles parallel the struggles of ancient Israel. 'England too, equally with any Judah whatsoever,' writes Thomas Carlyle, 'has a History that is Divine, an Eternal Providence presiding over every step of it...'[542] The English themselves are as the chosen race—'the chosen race and sons of England', declaims Edmund Burke in his speech urging conciliation with the American colonies.[543] George Eliot made the same points, but without the supersessionism, commending the 'affinities of disposition between our own race and the Jewish'.[544] These forms of identification could lead in several directions, towards position hostile or sympathetic to Jews, or unstable combinations of both.[545]

Jewish publicists tended to play on England's reputation for tolerance when drawing the attention of the English public to anti-Semitic persecutions abroad. In the pamphlet put out by the Russo-Jewish Committee of London, *The Persecution of the Jews in Russia* (1891), for example, much was made of the contrast between the condition of England's Jews and Russia's; that the former should be treated in like manner as the latter 'is so utterly impossible in free England, that [even the thought] may easily raise a smile'; the burden on Russian Jewry of discriminatory and oppressive laws all 'Englishmen would consider utterly intolerable'; it 'is unnecessary here in England to argue elaborately that the ordinary Russian Jews are not fiends in human shape...'; and so on.[546] The freedom that Jews enjoyed in England was a matter of national pride. Hall Caine's *Scapegoat* (1890), for example, contrasts a benighted Morocco, where Jews are the objects of Muslim contempt and oppression, with England, a land of 'white-hearted men', where a 'Jewish man may find rest for the soles of his feet'.[547]

A conjuncture that is shifting?

How is one to characterize the contemporary engagement of English intellectuals with anti-Semitism? Many are willing to take up positions without regard to their anti-Semitic resonance; many have only the patchiest knowledge of Jews, of Jewish history, of Judaism; many are hostile to Israel and to the Zionist project. These positions may be preparatory of the emergence of a new, ideologically charged anti-Semitism. Its absence in the modern period has been merely conjunctural; it is not an immutable aspect of English culture and history. The conjuncture may now have shifted. The possibility that this may be so is evident in the course taken by the blood libel since the Readmission. It subsisted, but mostly in minority milieus; it rarely figured in mainstream political discourse, save to be contested; however, it is now being deployed in a new 'anti-Zionist' assault on the Jewish State (as we saw in Chapter 4).

A normative rejection

In the eighteenth century, the objection to the blood libel was first framed as a public order issue. In 1732, a pamphlet appeared accusing London's Jews of murdering a Jewish mother and child on the ground that the father was Christian. Attacks on Jews followed, and so, in due course, the author was prosecuted for criminal libel. The court convicted him. Pamphlets of this kind, the court decided, 'raise tumults and disorders among the people and inflame them with an universal spirit of barbarity against a whole body of men, as if guilty of crimes scarce practicable and totally incredible'.[548] In the 1760s, the objection was then framed as an antiquarian and historical issue. Percy's *Reliques of Ancient English Poetry* (1765) pours scorn on the Jews' 'supposed practice' of 'crucifying or otherwise murdering Christian children'. 'The whole charge' is 'groundless and malicious'.[549] In the 1770s the objection was then framed as a theological issue, in the context of a broader defence of Christianity against Voltaire's attack on it. Contrary to the French Deist's claim, the Jews were not 'the devourers of human flesh' or the makers of 'human sacrifices'.[550] About seventy years later, it was framed as a foreign-policy issue. The allegation against the Jews of Damascus excited immense opprobrium, with diplomatic interventions, speeches in the House of Commons, widespread censure in the press, and well-attended public meetings. Alexander McCaul, an Anglican cleric and the spiritual leader of the London Society For Promoting Christianity Amongst the Jews, published *Reasons for Believing that the Charge Lately Revived against the Jewish People is a Baseless Falsehood* (1840), and dedicated it with royal permission to Queen Victoria. One newspaper acknowledged the English precedent: 'the monkish legend [of Hugh of Lincoln] is certainly the origin of the miserable farce got up in Syria'.[551]

In the following decades, a scholarly and journalistic consensus emerged. The blood libel was the product of primitive, superstitious times; it was entirely false. In 1863, Bernard Cracroft, writing in the *Westminster Review*, described the 'strange stories' that were 'invented', and soon 'pervaded Europe' that 'the Jews crucified the innocent children of Christian parents'.[552] In 1879, George Eliot noted, among the consequences of holding that the Jews were cursed, the 'taking it as certain that they killed and ate babies'.[553] In 1883, Charles H. H. Wright published 'The Jews and the Malicious Charge of Human Sacrifice', in the journal *The Nineteenth Century*. The blood libel, he wrote, was a product of 'anti-Semitic agitation', designed to inflame 'common prejudices against the Jewish race'. It was employed as a pretext to seize Jewish property and frustrate Jewish creditors. It has been periodically 'renewed', noted Wright, by 'men with the reputation of scholarship'.[554] In the same year, the *Graphic* reported on the Tisza-Esler trial, dismissing the court proceedings as unjust, and the charges themselves as groundless. The case was nothing more than 'an excuse for an outbreak of fierce hatred'.[555] In 1890, H. C. Lea published *Chapters from the Religious History of Spain connected with the Inquisition*. He listed the blood libels from Norwich onwards, describing them as wild stories and the product of human credulity and intolerance. As for the affair of 'Santo Niño de la Guardia', it is impossible to construct a connected and coherent story, and difficult to avoid the conclusion that there was no murdered child.[556] In 1896, Emil Reich, writing in the journal, the *Nineteenth Century*, condemned the 'revival of the old calumny that Jews need the blood of Christians for the preparation of their Passover bread'.[557] In 1893, W. E. H. Lecky noted that 'even the old calumny that the Jews are accustomed at Easter to murder Christian children in order to mix their blood with the Passover bread is still living in many parts of Europe'.[558] In 1899, the anti-Semitic Arnold White described the blood libel as an 'insane fancy'.[559] And then, in 1909, an English translation of a work by the German theologian Hermann Strack, *The Jew and Human Sacrifice*, appeared. Strack was a committed campaigner against the blood libel. 'I hope my book will make its way in English-speaking lands,' he wrote, 'and help to discredit the propagation of the abominable blood accusation.'[560]

In 1939, Wyndham Lewis described with some complacency the 'anti-Semite of the European Continent': he regards the Jew as the 'villain of the piece', he 'betrayed once—the supreme betrayal' and 'will betray again', and, of course, 'he eats Christian children'. 'We' are different, 'thank heaven'. We are 'more tolerant', and 'less fanatic'.[561]

Intermittent restatements

Wyndham Lewis somewhat overstated his case. If we put to one side stray mentions and anecdotal evidence,[562] a privately printed pamphlet, 'Jewish Cruelty in London' (which took up the case of a little girl accidentally run over by a Jewish cabman in 1882),[563] and a somewhat odd reference in a 1942 debate in the House of Lords on libel law reform,[564] several nineteenth- and twentieth-century restatements in England of the blood libel may be identified.

First, across the last decades of the nineteenth century, it was proposed that exceptional, primitive Jews, or even a specific Jewish sect, may have been guilty of murder. Some anti-Jewish controversialists promoted this 'theory of the fanatical sect' during the Damascus Affair.[565] In his *History of the Jews*, Milman commented: 'Great parts of this story refutes itself, but I have already admitted the possibility that among the ignorant and fanatic Jews there might be some who, exasperated by the constant repetition of this charge, might brood over it so long as at length to be tempted to its perpetration.'[566] The editor of *The Misrule of Henry III* (1887), an anthology of extracts from Henrician chronicles, commented on a passage from Matthew Paris, 'This extract is given as an example of many statements of the kind to be found in the chronicles. If the tale seems incredible we may imagine how incredible the dynamite plots will seem six hundred years hence.'[567] Rogue Jews then, rogue anarchists now, is the implication. Then in 1896, in their edition of Thomas of Monmouth's work, Jessop and James, while dismissing Jewish ritual murder as no more than 'an appalling and destructive myth', and condemning Thomas for 'first stirr[ing] up that mighty wave of superstitious credulity, unreasoning hate, and insatiable ferocity, which has not yet spent itself', yet conclude by speculating that a Jew might well have committed the crime, motivated by 'a mad hatred of a dominant system, or a reversion to half-forgotten practices of a darker age'.[568] The theory of the fanatical sect persisted, and was rehearsed in a journal article written at the outbreak of World War I. The author remarked of the 'great ritual murder trail at Kief' that while Beilis was innocent, he was 'involved in the murder', that the wounds on the dead Christian child's body had 'some sort of mystic significance', and that another Jew had probably done the deed, though it was 'another matter' whether for 'ritual purposes or not'. The Russian government made a mistake in 'fight[ing] the Jews on the count of the murder of a Christian child'. The real quarrel is not over the death of a few children, but with the 'Jewish business spirit'. It is no more than a 'curiosity' if 'among the illiterate and savage Jews that dwell in the remoter parts of the Pale there should exist dark sects in whose rites child-sacrifice, Moloch worship, and the like, are practised'. It is noteworthy that the Jewish people had the power to procure a 'not guilty' verdict. Since the Jews have never been found sacrificing Christian children in England or America, the 'Anglo-Saxon race' believes that ritual murder is a myth.[569]

Secondly, in or about late 1871 or early 1872, Richard Burton (1821–90), the explorer, diplomat, translator, and man of letters, wrote a posthumously published book, *The Jew, the Gypsy and El Islam*, in which he argued that ritual murder was part of Jewish doctrine. He writes, he explains, from the Aryan point of view. The Jews have a distinct existence, and are a power in every European capital. Their faith and practice convinced them of their immeasurable superiority. They were ready to dare and to do everything against all who were not of their own blood. Of all Europeans, the Englishman knows least about the Jews—though even he may be dimly aware that they alone spurn honest toil, and engage in usury. The Englishman therefore attributes to bigotry and fanaticism the persecutions they have suffered; he does not consider that it might be the direct result of some intolerable wrong committed by them; he does not consider, that is, that they are persecuted because they make away with children. Yet they do, and what began no doubt as random acts of vengeance, through human perversity and over time became a semi-religious rite. (Indeed, Gentile blood is mixed into cakes prepared for Passover.) What is more, how could the Talmud's cruel and vindictive teaching do anything other than bear fruit in crime and atrocities? Burton concludes by listing events of ritual murder: in 1135 [*sic*], the Jews crucified a boy at Norwich; in 1166, they crucified a boy at Ponthosa; in 1250, the Jews of Saragossa nailed a child to the wall in the form of a cross; and so on. The Jews of Damascus were of course guilty of the murder of Friar Thomas and his servant.[570] Twice Burton made some attempt to publish his manuscript, but never did. His widow then indicated that she would publish it, but died before doing so. It finally appeared, in truncated form, in 1898; the excluded parts were considered to be too objectionable to be made available to the public.[571] Several years later, the complete manuscript came into the possession of the Board of Deputies, where it remains.[572]

Thirdly, there was the horror of Jack the Ripper. Between August and November 1888 the killer known as Jack the Ripper murdered five prostitutes in the East End of London. He was never apprehended; his identity remains a mystery. For a time, suspicions were directed towards the Jews. It couldn't be a local man; the murders were alien to the English style of crime. The second weekend in September, Jews were threatened, abused, and assaulted.[573] A message had been scrawled near the site of the fourth murder: THE JUWES ARE NOT THE MEN THAT WILL BE BLAMED FOR NOTHING.[574] A few days later, a letter was published in *The Times*. The correspondent wrote from Vienna and told of the trial in 1884 of a 'Galician Jew named Ritter' for the murder and mutilation of a 'Christian woman in a village near Cracow':

> The mutilation was like that perpetrated on the body of the woman Chapman [one of the Ripper's victims], and at the trial numbers of witnesses deposed that among certain fanatical Jews there existed a superstition to the effect that if a Jew become intimate with a Christian woman he would atone for his offence by slaying and mutilating the object of his passion. Sundry passages of the Talmud were quoted which, according to the witnesses, expressly sanctioned this form of atonement.

The letter-writer added that the man was convicted, only for a retrial to be ordered by the appeal court. A further conviction followed, with a further order for retrial, and a still further conviction, at which point the appeal court quashed the sentence. The Chief Rabbi protested to the newspaper: 'The tragedies enacted in the East End are sufficiently distressing, without the revival of moribund fables and the importation of prejudices abhorrent to the English nation.' The *Jewish Chronicle* added its voice in condemnation of the letter.[575] None of this, however, stymied speculation. Rumours circulated concerning harsh punishments prescribed in the Talmud for prostitutes. *Schochets* were viewed with particular suspicion. A mender of leather shoes and bookbindings, John Pizer, was arrested early on, but released without charge. He was described in a police notice as 'a man of Jewish forebears'; a newspaper report described him as 'half man, half beast...a ghoulish creature, stalking with deadly Jewish cunning'.[576] This anti-Jewish whisper-propaganda was at least in part the product of the broader anti-Jewish immigrant or 'anti-alien' sentiment then current in London's East End.[577]

Fourthly, in the 1920s and 1930s the blood libel gained some ground. This was partly the work of the widely read conspiracy theorist, Nesta Webster: 'If ignorant superstition is found on the side of the persecutors, still more amazing superstition is found on the side of the persecuted.... Demonology in Europe was in fact an essentially Jewish science.... The cult of evil is a reality.'[578] Another factor was the relaunching of the La Guardia blood libel in two works of popular history, Rafael Sabatini's *Torquemada and the Spanish Inquisition* (1913) and William Walsh's *Isabella of Spain* (1931). To Sabatini, 'the affair of the Holy Infant of la Guardia must to a certain extent remain in the category of historic mysteries'. He rejected the ritual murder allegation, but left open the possibility that a crime had indeed been committed, even an act of sorcery.[579] Walsh was rather stronger than Sabatini, writing about 'Jewish plutocracy', 'Jewish millionaires', and offering a qualified defence of the charge of ritual murder and host dese-cration, and a defence of the Expulsion. He praises Isabella for preventing the Jews destroying the Christian civilization of Europe.[580] Yet another factor was Montague Summers's *The History of Witchcraft and Demonology* (1926), which listed martyred children, starting with 'S. William of Norwich'. Until the nineteenth century, it relates, there were prosecutions for the 'practice of the dark and hideous traditions of Hebrew magic'. 'Of the cases of ritual murder commonly listed, the evidence is quite conclusive that the body, and especially the blood, of the victim was used for magical purposes.' In all such cases, 'the underlying precept', Summers explains, is the 'Mosaic law', 'for the life of all flesh is the blood thereof'.[581] Summers's book was republished in paperback as recently as in 1973, by Routledge and Kegan Paul. Further still, the propagation of the blood libel was assisted by the efforts of Arnold Leese (1878–1956), to the distress of British Jewry.[582] Each year's ritual murder, Leese explained, was part of a plan designed to recover Palestine (an early reconciliation of the medieval libel with a modern anti-Zionism).[583] Leese's pamphlet is cribbed by many post-war blood libellers—an Egyptian publication, *The Danger of World Jewry to Islam and Christianity* (1960), draws heavily on him, for example. The author writes, 'The God of the Jews is not content with animal sacrifices; he must be appeased with human sacrifices.'[584] The pamphlet itself is available on several Islamist sites.[585]

Lastly, in John Harvey's *The Plantagenets* (1948). 'Added to economic difficulties caused by the presence of this alien body [i.e., the Jews]', Harvey explains, 'was a series of most sinister crimes committed against Christian children, including murder (allegedly ritual) and forcible circumcision'. Those Jews convicted of such offences were fairly tried. 'There was no question of mob-violence or lynch-law; no mass-condemnations, and a scrupulous adherence to form. In law, the evidence of the public records on this case in unassailable.' But 'a stronger argument is perhaps to be found' for the truth of the allegations 'in the poignancy and pathos of the considerable literature of the subject'. Harvey instances *The Prioress's Tale* and a 'series of exquisite folk-songs'.[586] Harvey was deeply involved in pro-Nazi activities in the 1930s.[587] His book was available as a mass-market paperback in the Fontana/Collins series, 'British Monarchy'.[588] Following protests in 1984, the publishers confirmed that the book would be allowed to go out of print.[589] Barely two decades later, Paulin's poem 'Crossfire' was published in a mainstream national newspaper, and Churchill's play *Seven Jewish Children* was both performed on the London stage and published by the *Guardian* online in a performed version. There were protests in each case, of course, but here, to no avail.

It is time to turn to contemporary anti-Zionism.

7

Contemporary Secular Anti-Zionisms

And so we come to the fourth of the English anti-Semitisms. The received term for it is 'the new antisemitism',[1] though it has also been named 'neo-antisemitism',[2] 'Euro-anti-Semitism'[3] and 'a postmodern version of Jew-hatred'.[4] It first emerged in the late 1960s and early 1970s in consequence of the Six Day War,[5] but became hegemonic in the 1990s and 2000s in consequence of certain developments mostly unrelated to the Middle East. It is to be distinguished from the 'old antisemitism' because it takes Israel and the Zionist project as its collective term for the Jews, because its geographic hub is Western Europe, because it is adopted by people who profess deep hostility to anti-Semitism, because self-identified Jews are among its advocates, and because it comes from the Left—indeed, has become part of the common sense among people of a broadly progressive temper. It is taken to be continuous with the 'old antisemitism' in its principal stratagems and tropes, while novel in its specific focus upon the Jewish State—uniquely evil and without the right to exist.[6] It demonizes Jewish nationalists in place of Jewish usurers, Jewish capitalists, and Jewish communists. This 'new' or 'renewed' or resurgent or 'realigned'[7] anti-Semitism is a malicious aggravation of somewhat more rational, though contestable, positions. That is to say, it is hostile to Zionism or to a new version of Zionism. In its milder form, it seeks to fix the world's attention on the injustices of the Occupation (always, with a capital 'O') and upon a new, land-hungry, triumphalist, religious-fundamentalist Zionism.[8] It is distinguishable from the Zionist critique of this new Zionism[9] in its indifference to the complexity of the historical record, and its one-eyed refusal to find fault with any party other than Israel. In its stronger form, it recasts the 1948 War as an originary act of persecution perpetrated by the fledgling

Jewish State upon the Palestinians (the 'Naqba'). In both forms it tends to seize upon misjudgements and acts of injustice as proof of fundamental iniquity. It is best understood as adversarial to a Jewish project, in the sense defined in Chapter 1, though polluted by irrationality. The term 'new antisemitism' misses this, and so I will instead refer to the present ideological challenge to Israel, the Jewish State, as 'contemporary anti-Zionism'. Within this contemporary anti-Zionism there may be found (a) a secular, leftist, or post-leftist anti-Zionism ('the new anti-Zionism'), and (b) Muslim, Jewish, and Christian anti-Zionisms (collectively, 'confessional anti-Zionisms').

Contemporary anti-Zionism in England has certain specifically English characteristics.

To begin with, it is embedded in a distinct history. British interest in the Middle East stemmed in substantial part from both 'balance of power' and imperial preoccupations. Intervention in the region was required to see off threats by the French, the Russians, and then the Germans; a substantial presence in the region was required to secure the route to India and meet the Indian government's own interests as a regional power.[10] Further, it was in Britain that the first non-Jewish efforts to restore the Jews to political sovereignty in Palestine were undertaken; it was in Britain that the 'dispensational' Christian Zionism that now dominates American Fundamentalist Protestantism originated.[11] 'Palestine remains in our minds a special land, lying above and beyond purely political thoughts', wrote J. Ramsay MacDonald in 1922.[12] It was Britain that promised the Jews a home in Palestine; it was Britain's General Allenby who entered Jerusalem as conqueror in 1918; it was Britain that occupied Palestine under the terms of a League of Nations Mandate; it was Britain that undertook, in partnership with France and Israel, the invasion of Egypt and brief occupation of the Suez Canal in 1956. As early as in 1902, it was possible for an observer to comment that in no other country were there 'so many interesting phases associated with the progress and development of Zionism as in England'.[13] In the decades that followed, these 'phases' only became more intimately associated with England. Its connection with Zionism is unique in intensity, longevity, and fruitfulness.[14] As a result, anti-Zionist positions tainted by anti-Semitism were already circulating in England in the aftermath of World War I.[15] In the matter of anti-Semitic anti-Zionism, then, England arrived first—even though the more proximate origin of contemporary global anti-Semitic anti-Zionism may be found in the Soviet polemics of the post-World War II period.

Contemporary English anti-Zionism is distinct in combining a hegemonic, or near-hegemonic 'new anti-Zionism' with three vigorous confessional anti-Zionisms: the Muslim, the Jewish, and the Christian. They are all compromised, though not to the same extent, by their adoption of anti-Semitic language and by their readiness to make common cause with unembarrassed anti-Semites. (For example, the defeated Labour candidate's Jewishness was given an ugly prominence in a 2005 General Election campaign.)[16] These distinct anti-Zionisms are all strongly represented in the English public sphere. England is an alternative Anglophone site for American anti-Zionists; it has become home to Israeli anti-Zionists; it is home to several Palestinian writers, intellectuals, and academics; it was home, and to a diminished extent remains home, to radical Islamists from abroad, many of whom are committed to an ideology of global conflict between Muslims and non-Muslims.[17] One should be careful, however, not to overstate its presence. It has not become—or not yet become—a staple of what might be termed current public doctrine; it is not a part of some broad national consciousness.

Nevertheless, anti-Zionist activism is especially strong in England, where something amounting to an 'anti-Israel lobby' operates.[18] This lobby has been especially active in promoting boycotts of Israel.[19] After some preliminary exclusionary activity in 2002,[20] there followed calls for academic boycotts (AUT in 2005, NATFHE in 2006, UCU, 2007 and recurring), a cultural boycott (John Berger and others),[21] and a boycott of the Israel Medical Association (letter to the *Guardian*).[22] Boycott resolutions were also passed in 2007 at the conferences of the National Union of Journalists,[23] the TGWU section of UNITE, and the public servants' union UNISON. In 2007, the charity War on Want funded a pamphlet, 'Towards a Global Movement for Palestine', calling for a boycott of Israel.[24] There was a boycott threat against Israeli architects and construction companies ('Architects and Planners for Justice in Palestine' in 2006).[25] The Palestinian boycott movement itself emerged in response to the initiatives of English boycotters.[26] The depth of support for these initiatives tends, however, to be overstated by both supporters[27] and opponents.[28] In 2007, the boycott movement suffered a major reverse when the UCU abandoned its boycott resolutions on legal advice that a boycott would be racially discriminatory and therefore illegal.[29] This advice did not, however, cause the boycott movement itself to reflect upon the ethics of a strategy thus condemned, nor deter the UCU's own executive committee from proposing a boycott resolution the following year, which was then passed by the union at its conference, only to be abandoned once again later on in the year.[30] The conflict between boycotters and anti-boycotters continues.

To identify these specificities is not, of course, to divorce English anti-Zionism from the inter-continental anti-Zionist phenomenon. Nor is it to make of it an utterly novel phenomenon, though I am here concerned only with the contemporary period—by which I mean the period from the aftermath of the Six Day War through to the shifting, evolving present.

A regional conflict, a global preoccupation

Why has one conflict, of the approximately forty armed conflicts being fought in approximately thirty countries at present,[31] received so much attention? And why has that attention now predominantly taken the form of radical partisanship with one side?

Disproportionalities

This is a regional conflict, one of several in the Middle East (among others, the Arab–Persian conflict, the Sunni–Shi'ite conflict, the Kurdish conflicts, the conflicts in the Sudan, the nationalist–Islamist conflict within many Arab states, and so on).[32] It has been going on for about 120 years. It is a conflict between two rival communities, fought out on a land over which both sides have religious, historical, and property claims. The relative strength of the primary parties has changed; the relative strength of the sponsoring parties has also changed. That is to say, while the USA and Israel have each prospered, the Arab States have stagnated and the USSR has disappeared. The conflict may resolve itself over time, though there are many reasons to be pessimistic. In its latest phase, the Jewish State is in possession of the land west of the Jordan River and in control of a hostile, recalcitrant Palestinian population numbering several millions. This recent asymmetry in power has been misread as the outcome of a plan on the part of the now dominant party, rather than the product of complex, contingent historical circumstances. In the received account, Israel has force but not justice on its side, and the Palestinians, justice but not force. Heartless might is taken to confront pitiable right.

It has been cogently argued that this conflict has been almost irrelevant since the end of the Cold War, that global dependence on Middle Eastern oil is declining (today the region produces under 30 per cent of the world's crude oil), that resolution of the conflict would do little or nothing to calm the other conflicts in the Middle East from Algeria to Iraq, and that it is a mistake to attribute real military strength to Middle Eastern societies whose populations can sustain excellent insurgencies but not modern military forces. Arab–Israeli catastrophism is therefore wrong twice over—first, because the conflict is merely one of several in the region, and secondly, because the Levant itself is just not that important any more.[33]

Yet the conviction that the Israel–Palestinian conflict is fundamental to the future of the world, and has properties that makes it utterly different from every other conflict in the Middle East (indeed, in the world), runs too deep to be touched by such realities. The broad attention it receives from the media, the degree of interest in it shown by the political classes, and the significance attached to it in the world at large, is immense—'enduring and obsessive,' according to one informed observer.[34] By comparison, other causes of international concern—say, China's role in the twenty-first century, the 30 million Africans with AIDS, or the emergence of Russia as a gangster state[35]—barely register in European political consciousness. In 2003, an EU poll of 7,500 Europeans found that Israel was considered the greatest threat to world peace.[36] This belief in the threat *posed* by Israel is usually accompanied by indifference to threats *facing* Israel. In its sovereign invulnerability, Israel is held to constitute a global menace.

This preoccupation has not always led to the taking of positions adverse to the Jewish State—and certainly not, across a longer period, positions adverse to the Zionist project. For several reasons, the region has long engaged the West's imagination.

First, it is the 'Holy Land'. For the Jews the land itself is holy; for Christians it contains places in which sacred history was enacted; for Muslims it contains the third holiest city. The Jews were constituted as a nation in the land; the Christians were constituted as a faith; the Arabs added it to their roster of conquests, settling it and converting its indigenous inhabitants. Jerusalem is the focus of Jewish worship, and the site of its former Temples; it was the place of Christ's death and resurrection; it was the first focus (or *qibla*) of Muslim worship and, by tradition, the place from which Muhammad ascended.[37] The history of the Holy Land may be characterized as consisting of extended periods of stagnation punctuated by moments of extreme violence. It has long attracted pilgrims and travellers, writers and intellectuals, and more recently, the world's media.

Secondly, for several centuries it has had strategic value to the great powers; it is the point of maximum collision between 'West' and 'East'; it is the junction of three continents.[38] There has always thus been an international aspect to Middle Eastern affairs. Rarely have the nations or peoples of the region exercised autonomy; the question for them instead has been: is it to be one, or more than one, great power interfering in our affairs? The early twentieth-century conflict in Palestine was a local affair between the Mandate Power, the Zionists, and the Palestinians until the early 1930s. Thereafter, the conflict was internationalized in stages:[39] the advent of Hitler, which increased the demand for immigration and encouraged challenges to British rule; the 1938 London conference, to which representatives of Arab states were invited, thereby sanctioning the intervention of a number of sovereign states in the affairs of a territory under British control; the involvement of the USA in 1946; the involvement of the UN in 1947–8; the American–Soviet collusion in 1956 to wreck British and French power and influence in the region; the superpower confrontation in the Six Day War; and now, with the collapse of the Soviet Union, American hegemony, and a site of conflict between Europe and the USA. It has become a commonplace that this conflict is the creation of Europe and that Europe is suffering in consequence of the absence of any resolution to it. It was fashioned by us; it is hurting us. It is therefore, doubly, 'our' problem.

Thirdly, the Jews comprise one of the interested parties. Martin Buber once remarked, 'everything we Jews do takes place on a stage'.[40] It was a complaint—even, an exasperated one. The complaint is a common one now, most usually made by Jews in respect of the Jewish State. Some among them tend to attribute to anti-Semitism this rendering of every Jewish action as a spectacle for the world's consumption. They are often right, but never completely so; many times, they are just wrong. The 'audience' is not always hostile; and even when it is, the hostility may have more complex causes. The survival into the twenty-first century of this minor people of the ancient world is generally regarded as noteworthy, even miraculous. The contribution of the Jews to the cultural formation of the West is out of all proportion to their numbers, and this too is a topic of wide-ranging interest. But it is the *manner* of the Jews' survival, and the *character* of their contribution, that in combination now constitute the greatest challenge to understanding, a challenge posed most directly by Israel's very existence, let alone its constitutional nature, and let alone its politics. *Everyone*, so to speak, has a theory. A common one runs something like the following. The Jews introduced two sets of values: a universalist morality and the obligation to work for human progress. The world expects the Jews to exemplify these values; Israel has inherited that expectation. Jews were victims for 2,000 years; they preached justice, and thus made everyone else feel deficient; what the West expected from the Jews of the past, it expects from Israel today.[41] This super-attentiveness to their words and deeds tends, in any event, to be a source of wonder to Jews. 'Each Jew knows how thoroughly ordinary he is', wrote Milton Himmelfarb. 'Yet taken together, we seem caught up in things great and inexplicable. Big things seem to happen around us and to us.'[42]

Fourthly, the Israel–Palestinian conflict draws very many spectators, who then report back what they see and hear to news-hungry media outlets. There are several reasons why journalists and their employers find the conflict appealing: the region is both accessible and fairly safe; there is very little censorship; both sides are very willing to speak.[43] The current interest in the region, mediated by normative media values, sustains an account of Israel, the Palestinians, and the 120-year conflict between Arab and Jewish nationalisms, which is ahistorical, moralizing, and unnuanced. In earlier times, the Yishuv, and after 1948, the State of Israel, were the net beneficiaries of these tendencies; nowadays, they work to Israel's disadvantage.

Though these considerations explain the particular intensity of interest in the Israel–Palestinian conflict they do not quite explain its current political complexion. They do not, that is, account for that combination of progressive and confessional anti-Zionisms that characterizes contemporary hostility to the Jewish State.

Progressive anti-Zionism, or 'the new anti-Zionism'

An outline of progressive anti-Semitism

Reactionaries have always been frank about their anti-Semitism. In late nineteenth-century France, for example, they banded together in groups bearing names such as *Ligue Antisémitique, Comité Ouvrier Antijuif, Ligue Antijuive, Union des Voyageurs Français Antisémites pour la Défense du Commerce et de l'Industrie*, and *Jeunnesse Antisémitique et Nationaliste*. 'We are anti-Semitic and nationalist', an anti-Dreyfusard announced, addressing a large meeting at the height of the Affair.[44] Liberal and leftist anti-Semites were different. They did not acknowledge—still less, advertise—their anti-Semitism. This remains the case today.

It is somewhat counter-intuitive to posit a *liberal* anti-Semitism. It is in conflict with: the liberal version of the State, in which all citizens are equal; the liberal version of civil society, in which diversity of affiliation is encouraged; the historical role played by liberalism in promoting political and religious freedoms; the investment of generations of Jews in (what broadly may be defined as) the liberal project;[45] the hostility of many anti-Semites to liberalism, which they regard as somehow infected by the 'Jewish spirit'; the fact that the defence of Jews and the defence of liberalism have often been allied activities.

Still, there *is* a liberal anti-Semitism—though there is a risk that it can be overstated.[46] It was found in certain formulations of the emancipation project, when accompanied by a desire to 'improve' the Jews—to promote their 'civic betterment'. Emancipation was there expected to inculcate sentiments of civic morality; it would regenerate the Jews, and make them useful. They were to be denationalized and secularized. Jewish communal structures would not be permitted to duplicate (and certainly not usurp) the functions of the state. 'Jews as individuals deserve everything, Jews as a nation, nothing', argued de Clermont-Tonnere, one of the Jews' principal advocates in the emancipation debate in Revolutionary France. He added, 'Within the state there can be neither a separate political body nor an order. There can only be the individual citizen.'[47] The emancipation process would not just free the Jews from legal constraints; it would also free them from Judaism. Intermarriage was to be promoted, Yiddish abolished, the Talmud repudiated, and rabbinic authority curtailed. The Jews should convert and disperse, their friends recommended. And they should change the nature of their economic activity. If they refused, then they would thereby exclude themselves from the new polity. Following emancipation, this almost universal condescension towards the Jews was liable to turn into hatred, when the Jews were held to have failed to meet expectations.[48] There continue to be liberals provoked into anti-Semitism by the failure of Jews to conform to liberalism's requirements. Judaism can itself make some liberals uncomfortable. Liberals also now tend to favour supra-state structures—international courts, federated structures, and so on. They wish mankind to 'cast away the yoke of national prejudices' (Rousseau).[49] These sentiments now tend to encourage a mild anti-Zionism. Formerly, the liberal wished the Jew to dissolve in the solvent of the state; he now wishes to dissolve the Jewish State in the solvent of the Middle East. In a secularized version of the Christian critique of Judaism, Zionism is taken to be a repudiation of a kind of 'universal humaneness'.[50]

It is similarly counter-intuitive to posit a leftist anti-Semitism—certainly, leftists themselves think so. 'All progressive mankind are the allies of the Jews', declared the communist MP, Willie Gallacher, 'anti-Semitic propaganda is anti-working-class propaganda'.[51] Yet there were, to begin with, extended periods of disengagement between the Left and the Jews. In France, for example, the disengagement lasted from the decree of 28 September 1791, the emancipation of the Jews by the Constituent Assembly, until some time into the Dreyfus Affair.[52] More importantly, there have also always been leftists ready to find reasons to tolerate the Jew-hatred of others—say, as the primitive, spontaneous anti-capitalism of the masses,[53] as a transitional stage to a more fully developed class-consciousness (anti-Semitism as 'the road to socialism'),[54] or merely the better to ingratiate themselves with their audience.[55] There are also anti-Semitic tropes *specifically* leftist in character, the product of a *'socialisme nuancé d'antisemitisme'*.[56] Just as there were anti-Semites on the Right ready to identify Jews with communist subversion, so there were anti-Semites on the Left who habitually identified Jews with a sinister and predatory capitalism. The recasting of Zionism as a cause of anti-Semitism, rather than a Jewish response to it, is a specifically leftist contribution to anti-Semitic doctrine.[57] Many leftists set their own values (secular, collectivist, internationalist, universalist) against perceived 'Jewish' values (religious, individualist, nationalist, particularist), to the disadvantage of the Jews. They looked askance at what they understood to be Judaism's merely national religion, its merely national deity.[58] They were affronted by that 'collective subjectivity',[59] the Jewish people. That to be an anti-Semite was not the very *worst* thing one might be was something many on the Left were quite ready to concede, even in the late 1930s. *The Jewish Question*, a *Left Book Club* volume published in 1937, appealed to its readers: 'Hate the Jew if you must, but do not allow your hatred to make you the victim of the Fascist who, on the plea that he also hates the Jew, makes you his accomplice in worse crimes.'[60] In its most degenerate, that is to say Soviet, condition, leftist anti-Semitism travestied every leftist value. 'Internationalism', remarked the Soviet satirist Alexander Zinoviev, 'is when the

Russian, the Georgian, the Ukrainian, the Chuvash, the Uzbek and others get together to strike at the Jews.'[61]

There has been little self-examination by the Left into this constitutive anti-Semitism—none, at any rate, comparable in quality and depth, say, to Christian self-examination in respect of Christianity's constitutive anti-Semitism. Rowan Williams, the archbishop of Canterbury, has written of the right of the Jew to call the Christian to account.[62] The Left recognizes no comparable right, and in consequence leaves unexamined troubling aspects of its history, among which is the fact that in the last decades of the twentieth century so many disappointed or demoralized leftists drifted into anti-Semitic politics.[63] This failure of inquiry is in part attributable to the survival of a certain *anti*-anti-Semitic rhetoric on the Left (how could any person on the Left be anything other than hostile to anti-Semitism?), the belief that its professed good intentions excuse it from self-scrutiny, and the further, equally self-serving belief that anti-Semitism is characteristic only of the Right.[64] Yet one need look no further or later than Stalin, who set the precedent for authorizing attacks on the anti-Semitism of others while at the same time promoting his own anti-Semitic policies,[65] to see that such a rhetoric is quite consistent with the adoption of anti-Semitic positions—indeed, even assists to promote them.

The emergence of progressive anti-Zionism

In 1969 and 1972 the exiled Palestinian activist and writer Khalid Kishtainy published two books about English perspectives on the Israel–Palestinian conflict, *Verdict in Absentia* (Beirut, 1969) and *The New Statesman and the Middle East* (Beirut, 1972). Kishtainy complained: Zionism has massive resources of talent, funds, and public relations; the World Zionist Organization is unmatched in its propaganda activities; the American pro-Israel lobby is one of the most influential pressure groups in the world; the Zionists suppress critical or dissenting publications. A preponderant Zionist representation, the slavery of the advertising agent, the general anti-Arab milieu, the fear of Zionist intimidation and the 'anti-Semitism blackmail' or 'smear' together ensure that the press is firmly pro-Israel. Its double standards are everywhere in evidence. In consequence, the Arab intelligentsia despairs at reaching the political mind of the West.[66] The *New Statesman* has supported justice everywhere in the world except in Palestine. Its support for the Zionist project goes back to 1914. The Arab case went by default.

Zionist contributors who wrote lengthy essays for the magazine balanced pre-Nazi period support for a binational state.[67] The magazine favoured cooperation between the two communities over support for the majority community. In the 1930s, the magazine took a marked Zionist turn. A Jewish Palestine or a Jewish part of Palestine became the Middle Eastern 'New Statesmanship'. The *New Statesman* backed the *Hagana* during the 1948 War, which was likened to the Spanish Civil War; part of the magazine's case against the Arabs was that they had defied the UN partition resolution. It has always been 'Zionophile'; it suppressed the Arab voice almost completely, allowing it only the occasional off-stage whimper. The British press is preoccupied with Israel's achievements.[68]

Now go forward forty years. A journalist in *Al-Ahram*[69] rejoices that 'a greater understanding of the plight of the Palestinians at the hands of the Israelis seems to be emerging in news coverage and some op-ed articles', and 'mainstream news coverage of the events in the occupied territories is no longer parroting Israeli propaganda'. He cites among others Robert Fisk of the *Independent* (who begged readers to 'understand the injustice of the Middle East'), Jonathan Cook of the *Guardian* ('the shift in tone has been led by the writers who could not avert their eyes from such disturbing images as Mohamed Al-Dura being killed cold-bloodedly by the Israelis'), Alexei Sayle ('The violent creation of the state of Israel and the subsequent oppression of the Palestinian people [is] one of the great injustices of our age'),[70] and David Goldberg ('You cannot subjugate, demonise and dispossess another people, and treat them as second-class citizens without one day reaping the whirlwind'). The journalist relates this shift to the impact of the Second Intifada, though in truth it took place a little more gradually, and in consequence of events within the preceding decades. Palestinian terrorism in the 1970s, the UN 'Zionism is racism' resolution in 1975, Israel's invasion of Lebanon in 1982, the collapse of the socialist project in the late 1980s, and European demographic changes in the 1990s, all contributed. The fact of a shift, in any event, is widely acknowledged; the British press is now preoccupied with Israel's crimes. It continues to be a source of dismay, even anguish, to liberal-minded Zionist Jews. 'Why', asks the Anglo-Jewish scholar and activist Colin Shindler, 'has progressive humankind turned its back on Zionism?'[71]

Kishtainy somewhat overstated the extent of progressive indifference to the Palestinian Arab cause,[72] while Shindler slightly overstates the extent of progressive support for it. But neither Kishtainy's judgement nor Shindler's can be substantially faulted, and it is therefore worth examining the reasons for the radical change of perspective registered in the remarks of these two engaged commentators. Let me isolate for examination one of these reasons: the failure of the progressive cause itself. (There are other reasons, of course, and not least among them, Israel's own conduct. For many observers, this is a sufficient reason.[73] But in itself, it explains little of the content of the new anti-Zionism, nor the intensity of conviction it commands among anti-Zionists, for many of whom anti-Zionism is a comprehensive political stance, complete in itself.)

The causes of the defeat and disintegration of socialism are complex. In addition to the failure of the Soviet Union, there was the failure of the leftist opposition to the Soviet Union, the failure of Third World liberation movements, and the continuing (though crisis-ridden) success of the capitalist economies of the West. There were also more proximate causes, chief among which were the appearance of Solzhenitsyn's *Gulag Archipelago*,[74] the emergence of the Polish Solidarity movement, and the murderous reign of Pol Pot in Cambodia. The collapse of the socialist project was ideological as well as geopolitical—perhaps, ideological *because* geopolitical. Acknowledging the 'bankruptcy of Marxism',[75] the 'collapse of Marxism',[76] or less enthusiastically, the 'theoretical defeat of the Left',[77] has now become a commonplace of contemporary political theory.[78] But it was an acknowledgement that was slow in coming. As late as 1978, the French Marxist philosopher Louis Althusser was writing, 'the crisis [of Marxism] has at last come to a head! It has at last become obvious to one and all! It is at last possible to begin the work of rectification and revision!'[79] But there was to be no further 'beginning'. The 'New Left' of the 1960s turned out to be the last Left. By 1989, the cause of the Left had expired, and in its place was to be found certain *boutique movements* and post-leftist accommodations with conventionally *liberal* and *reactionary* positions. One consequence of these developments was that 'New Left' anti-Zionism mutated into the 'new' anti-Zionism of present times.

The *boutique movements* are the products of a certain scaling back of political ambitions, a championing of more limited or 'local' causes. Scattered sets of issues and demands that do not add up to a unified vision or coherent ideology have instead cohered into what might be termed 'semi-ideologies'.[80] There are many of these semi-ideologies, among which can be numbered certain versions of feminism, ecologism,[81] Third Worldism, animal rights activism,[82] and organized support for various 'socialist' states or 'national liberation' movements. Each semi-ideology, which takes a variety of institutional forms, falls short of that programme of a general transformation of society that was socialism's goal. Each may be supported without reference to any other. This drift away from general revolutionary projects began in the late 1960s; in the decade that followed, the illusion of a shared purpose between these heterogeneous groupings and movements began to wane (for a time, for example, the PLO took its place alongside many other groups similarly engaged elsewhere in the world);[83] by the early 1990s, they had diverged to such an extent that they could no longer be contained within a single frame of reference.

As for the *appropriations of, and accommodations with, liberal positions*, the general abandonment of Marxist positions in favour of liberal or post-liberal ones is evident wherever one looks, but particularly evident, perhaps, among France's political theorists.[84] The 'class struggle' between 1848 and 1936 encouraged people on the Left to regard rights as mere abstractions, aspects of bourgeois ideology that concealed and legitimized the subordination of one class to another. But this supersession of rights by communism did not take place;[85] on the contrary, it was by exposing the absence of 'rights' in the Soviet Union and its satellites that communism was discredited.[86] A human rights discourse now dominates politics; there is a powerful human rights 'movement';[87] it is the new secular religion of our time;[88] politics itself has been juridified. Liberalism provides the terms and defines the tone in which both Europeans and Americans now address their political affairs.[89] The post-leftist appropriation of this discourse has been in the development of a 'transnational progressivism'[90] or anti-national cosmopolitanism. It deprecates unrestrained state sovereignty; it endorses international and transnational legal institutions; it champions human rights against national security considerations;[91] it accepts the liberal critique of imperialism. It sets pacific, post-capitalist, and collectivist (or communitarian) values against militarist, capitalist, and individualist ones. It esteems post-national, multiple, and pluralized forms of citizenship identities. It accords great value to the United Nations—notwithstanding its inability to enforce its decisions, and its refusal to make practical demands of its members to be democratic or respect the human rights of their citizens.[92] The effect is to maintain a certain challenge to normative liberalism, but on rather different terms than before. The new militant is not the party sectarian but the NGO activist—seen in least attractive aspect at the 2001 UN Conference Against Racism in Durban. This is, in any event, a

post-Left, one reconciled to the impossibility of revolutionary transform-
ations—the abolition of class, self-government in place of representative
government, and the common ownership of the means of production.[93]

Lastly, there are what I have termed the *appropriations of, and accommodations with, reactionary positions*. Over two centuries, progressive doctrines
wreaked many humiliations on national and religious sentiment.[94] No
more. In their support for radical Islam (the 'Red–Green alliance') former
leftists elide the secular/religious divide between Left and Right; in their
hatred of the United States they restate the anti-Americanism shared by Left
and Right for at least 150 years;[95] in their opposition to globalization or
'neoliberalism' or 'market fundamentalism', they make common cause with
extreme nationalists; many former leftists have abandoned the internationalism of the proletariat for the transnationalism of the Islamic *umma*.[96] The
impossibility of imagining a leftist alternative to the existing state of affairs,
namely the complete absence of a leftist programme, has encouraged the
embracing of *any* politics hostile to the world as it is. If we cannot make a
new world, we can at least tear down the present one. This is the nihilism of
the 'unreconstructed Left', 'pseudo-Left',[97] or 'Third Worldist' Left,[98]
though some of their positions have also begun to infect more mainstream
progressive politics.[99] This pure (in the sense of unqualified) oppositionism
emerged in the 1990s, and it is now pervasive among members of ostensibly
Leninist parties—victims of a deadening incapacity to think realistically
about the world as it is, and a cramped and dishonest unwillingness to
rethink, let alone abandon, their 'progressive' ideas about Third World
movements.[100] They are happy to treat with Far Right groupings, with
obscurantists and theocrats of all kinds, and of course with those anti-
Semites prepared to characterize their Jew-hatred as *anti*-globalist, or *anti*-
colonialist, or *anti*-American, or *anti*-racist. The origins of their positions in
Counter-Enlightenment polemic and nineteenth century and early twentieth-century racist execrations, is a matter of indifference to them—a
willed genealogical ignorance[101] that permits, for example, the ardent advocacy of boycotts of the Jewish State, notwithstanding the prominence of
boycotts in the millennial history of anti-Semitism. On the specific point of
the Far Left embracing the Far Right, there are of course precedents. In the
immediate post-war period, communist parties all over Eastern Europe
began to court former members of pre-war fascist movements. It was in
accordance with the policy of the *Machtergreifung*, the 'power grab'. The
communists willingly put on national costume in order to succeed. In their

desire to portray themselves as an indigenous political movement they passed over the problems confronting the Jewish population. During the very earliest phase of communism's reach for power in Eastern Europe, the Party had made a clear choice between Jews and their local enemies. Patriotic, indeed nationalist, popular sentiment was tapped to safeguard the rule of the Party. If such sentiments—among the Russians, the Ukrainians, the Romanians, or the Poles—came with a mixture of xenophobia or anti-Semitism, so be it. Poland's communist authorities, for example, acquiesced in Polish society's violently expressed desire to render the country *Judenrein*.[102]

As heterogeneous as these developments have been, they share certain antagonisms—specifically, an antagonism towards America, and a broader antagonism towards 'imperialism'. These antagonisms comprise the points of contact between old-style leftists and their new allies among the specialist or boutique campaigners, the reactionaries and the liberals. They also reflect even broader currents of political opinion and sentiment. I will return to anti-Americanism and anti-imperialism towards the end of the next chapter; they are the political antagonisms common to practically all contemporary anti-Zionisms.

Anti-Zionism is widespread in this post-Left world. It is itself a *boutique movement*, one among many 'causes' available to be taken up. The 'fight for Palestine' appears to some to be the successor to the 'fight for socialism'. It is in this respect a self-standing cause, unrelated to any larger project of human liberation, unrelated indeed to any particular politics, and this has made it especially vulnerable to anti-Semitism. In its allegations against Israel of human rights abuses, war crimes, breaches of humanitarian law, and the like, it appropriates and develops *liberal positions*. In its appropriation of the language of nationalism and of Islamic radicalism, it accommodates itself to *reactionary positions*, among which is Jew-hatred. The Palestinian cause has become a preoccupation for many, connecting the governing classes with their traditional enemies on Left and Right.[103] Bernard-Henry Lévy has rhapsodized on the theme of Marxism's collapse: 'All the orphaned theories, all these little dark stars fallen from doctrinaire galaxies, all this scattered debris, these directionless iron filings in search of a new magnet.'[104] Anti-Zionism is one such magnet—perhaps now even the principal one. This 'anti-Zionism' is ideological in the sense that it is an unstable combination of ideas and representations in which the reality of its subject, Israel and the Zionist project, is conceived in a partial and distorted form.[105] Every act hostile to Israel is an affirmation of progressive political values. Israel has become, in Phyllis Chesler's phrase, a 'crime against the Left'.[106] The tacit slogan of the anti-Zionist is 'the less Israel, the more peace'.[107]

There are two distinct positions taken in the politics of the new anti-Zionism. Each is predicated on the illegitimacy of the Zionist enterprise. Each holds that Israel was established by the dispossession of the Palestinian people, that it was enlarged by aggressive wars waged against militarily inferior forces, and that it is maintained by oppression and brutality. Each maintains that the militarily powerful Jewish State is not to be confused with the powerlessness of pre-1948 Jewry, and that it is precisely this confusion that Israel fosters as a cover for its oppression of the Palestinians. None concedes that the Palestinians are the authors, to any extent, of their current plight. Among much relevant history that is ignored or overlooked, most contemporary anti-Zionists ignore or overlook, say, pre-1948 Palestinian Arab violence against Jews, the Palestinians' repeated rejection of partition, the UN partition resolution, the Arab states' decision to confine Palestinians in camps and deny them civil rights, the expulsion of Jews from Arab lands, Egypt's responsibility for the start of the Six Day War, and Jordan's decision to participate in it. Pure victim confronts egregious oppressor, and the effect is to criminalize Zionism.

At this point, the new anti-Zionism divides.

'Re-partition' anti-Zionism (also known as the 'two state solution'), acknowledges that there is now a state, recognized in international law, and the established polity of an Israeli people. This is an anti-Zionism that accepts that there is 'no going back', so to speak. 'The fantasy of somehow removing Israel and its people is equally unthinkable', explained Edward Said:

> Yes, they can be made to withdraw from occupied territories, but it is a dream to expect that 'they' will disappear or go back to Poland, Russia, America. There is now an Israeli nationalism and a society independent of what we think and independent of the diaspora.[108]

Even if the first Zionists were colonialists, their descendants would have rights; they could not be expelled from the places where their lives have become rooted.[109] But while this anti-Zionism submits to the regime of practical politics, it is ready to deal with Israel in a harsh manner, and as if it were still in some sense a provisional state. It is an anti-Zionism *very* ready indeed to redraw Israel's borders.[110] This anti-Zionism is consistent with a slightly older and still more radical version, which denied everything to

Israel and practically everything to its Jewish citizens. 'It is impossible to justify the continuance of the State of Israel', wrote Christopher Mayhew and Michael Adams in 1975, 'on legal, historical or moral grounds.' The 'Palestinian formula', which would allow only those Jews now living in Israel to remain in the new Palestinian state if they were 'prepared to renounce Zionism', though 'attractive in principle', was alas 'not practicable for the time being', they explained. 'There is no immediate alternative to the continued existence, in one form or another, of the State of Israel.'[111]

'Liquidation' anti-Zionism (also known as the 'one state solution'), regards the specifically Jewish character of Israel as objectionably illiberal *or* unIslamist, and argues for a state of all its citizens (that is, Jewish and non-Jewish), *or* an Islamic state. It rejects what one British Islamist describes as 'the suicidal illusion of [Palestinian] statehood'.[112] This is an anti-Zionism that in its secular version converges with certain *'post*-Zionist' positions taken both in Israel itself[113] and elsewhere.[114] In both its secular and Islamist version, however, it amounts to the cancellation of the last surviving Jewish political project of the twentieth century, the State of Israel. It denies statehood to the Jewish people; it does not address the wishes of Jewish— or indeed, Arab—Israelis; it is indifferent to the fate of those Israeli Jews who might choose to live as citizens in this new state;[115] it is indifferent to the sincerity of Palestinian statements regarding what Jews might expect under such arrangements; it does not even consider whether a state with a substantial Islamist Muslim population is capable of sustaining secular institutions protective of minorities (the example of Lebanon does not encourage optimism).[116] It is obvious to all but those ideologically committed to a 'one-state solution' that the animosities and fears that now exist between the two sides rule it out of contention.[117] 'Do you think', Edward Said was once asked, 'a Jewish minority would be treated fairly in a binational state?' And Said replied:

> I worry about that. The history of minorities in the Middle East has not been as bad as in Europe, but I wonder what would happen. It worries me a great deal. The question of what is going to be the fate of the Jews is very difficult for me. I really don't know. It worries me.[118]

There is a position between the 'repartitionist' and 'liquidationist', namely the 'bi-nationalist' one, which envisages the Jewish state surrendering its sovereignty in favour of membership alongside the Palestinians of a confessionally divided state. It was for a time promoted by reference to the (now somewhat forlorn) example of Lebanon.[119] Before the foundation of the State it was the position of a group of Zionists who made their home at the Hebrew University of Jerusalem, but it failed to attract any significant Arab support.[120] There is, in practical terms, little to distinguish 'repartition anti-Zionism' from the proposals championed at first by the Israeli peace camp and now commanding broad Israeli support. What is distinctive about repartition anti-Zionists lies rather in the readiness of some of them to use anti-Semitic tropes, and in their antipathy towards the Zionist enterprise.

Liquidation anti-Zionism, which was promoted by the PLO for many years, gave way in the 1990s to re-partition anti-Zionism, but then staged a comeback at the beginning of the twenty-first century. This was in consequence of the emergence of an uncompromising Islamist opposition to Israel, of the collapse of the Palestinian national movement, and of the belief that the many Israeli settlements in the West Bank and Gaza (and the measures taken to secure them) made a separate Palestinian state unfeasible. The Islamist opposition—say, the frankly anti-Semitic parties, Hamas and Hezbollah—remained unreconciled to Israel's existence, wished it harm, and were committed to an account of its power and standing that was utterly dependent on classical anti-Semitic tropes and texts. The Palestinians themselves seemed further than ever before from possessing the collective self-discipline, and the constructive engagement in building state institutions, necessary to achieving statehood. This collapse of Palestinian morale appeared irreversible.

The reach of these new anti-Zionist positions is of course by no means complete. If only in consequence of the disintegration of the Left, many different positions are taken on Israel and the Zionist project, not all of them hostile. The more sympathetic positions, in turn, are not taken merely by older leftists,[121] unable or unwilling to shrug off their earlier support for Israel; they are also taken by leftists who came to political maturity during the post-Six Day War period. Statements to the effect that the 'chattering classes' are uniformly hostile to Israel[122] overstate the position by some margin. Indeed, even within the historic Far Left, there are parties—the Socialist Party,[123] say, and the AWL[124]—that favour a two-state solution and have taken a stand against boycott initiatives. The Euston Manifesto Group,[125] a coalition of Left-liberals (self-described as 'democrats and progressives'), is well known for its nuanced position on Israel and the Zionist project, one that recognizes the right of both the Israeli and the Palestinian peoples to self-determination within the framework of a two-state solution, and rejects any resolution of the Israel–Palestinian conflict that subordinates or eliminates the legitimate rights and interests of either one of its parties to the other.[126] The scholar-activist Fred Halliday eschews sectarian perspectives in his extensive writings on the Middle East.[127] There are leftists who have begun to acknowledge anti-Semitism as an emerging problem within their own groupings.[128] And there are coalitions of groups and individuals who have come together for the specific purpose of opposing this received, progressive anti-Zionism (for example, 'Engage', which is an activist Web-based network that came into existence to fight university boycotting, and campaigns against leftist anti-Semitism,[129] and the Parliamentary Committee Against Antisemitism, which in 2006 published a report on its inquiry into antisemitism in the UK, chaired by the Labour MP and former government minister Denis MacShane).[130]

This heterogeneity of positions taken within the Left, or what was once the Left, has in turn to be understood in the context of a still broader range of opinion and position on the Israel–Palestinian conflict. One of the more significant positions in this range might be described as 'realist'—that is, a position on the conflict that is neither especially drawn, nor antagonistic, towards Israel and the Zionist project. It analyses the conflict in terms essentially no different to those it applies to foreign affairs generally. The shift in overall perspective that Kishtainy and Shindler noted, and that I endorse, is not a simple affair. But in summary it is as follows. Positions sympathetic to Israel have substantially diminished in their salience; by contrast, positions hostile to Israel have substantially grown; and the 'realist' perspective on the conflict now casts a rather more sceptical eye towards Israel than at any time since the last, bitter months of the Mandate. This is not to say, however, that were Kishtainy once again to survey the scene he would be content. He would not. And there are many partisans of the Arab or Palestinian cause who continue to perceive great bias in Israel's favour, both in government policy and media perspective. Still, that there *has* been a shift—a substantial one, at that—away from broadly pro-Israel positions only very few would deny. The question for this chapter is whether, and if so to what extent, this shift has led to the emergence of any new versions of anti-Semitism.

Institutional forms of the 'new anti-Zionism'

The institutional forms taken by the 'new Zionism' broadly correspond to the boutique/liberal-Left/pseudo-Left divisions outlined above. Most, if not all of the specifically 'pro-Palestinian' organizations, websites, and blogs, are anti-Zionist. The distinction between the liberal-leftist and the pseudo-leftist approximates to the one between certain parliamentary parties and a Leninist extra-parliamentary party—that is, the Labour Party and the Liberal Democrats on the one hand, and the Socialist Workers Party on the other. (The 'Respect' party is an anomaly—an ostensibly parliamentary party largely controlled, or once controlled, by a non-parliamentary party—I return to it below.) These distinctions are not perfect, but for the purposes of exposition, they just about work.

Boutique movements

The 'boutique movements' comprise certain charities, formally constituted pressure groups, and campaigning networks—often loose associations of individuals. Among these, the 'Palestine Solidarity Campaign' (PSC) is especially prominent.

The PSC, which was founded in 1982, describes itself as 'an independent, non-governmental and non-party political organisation with members from many communities across Britain'. It claims to be the largest and most active campaigning organization in the UK on the 'issue of Palestine'. It aims to build an 'effective mass campaign, organising protests, political lobbying and raising public awareness'. It exists to display 'solidarity with the Palestinian people' (a phrase which appears repeatedly in its literature). It has an activist, engaged membership, and is structured like a political party—it holds conferences at which motions are proposed for adoption, and so on. It has affiliations with other groups, though it does not appear to be affiliated to any particular Palestinian party. It stands for a passionate, if diffuse, commitment to the 'cause' of Palestine. There is implicit in its politics a desire to see the end of Israel, if not Israelis.

It describes its three 'core values' as (1) 'supporting the Palestinian right of return as stipulated in UN Resolution 194' (2) organizing 'campaigns, demonstrations and public meetings in the UK'; and (3) working to 'highlight the human rights abuses committed by the Israelis' and to 'raise awareness on the issue of Palestine to the general public'. Neither (2) nor (3) are in fact core values; indeed, they are not 'values' at all. If one seeks the political objective towards which the activities at (2) and (3) are directed, one can look only to (1), the endorsement of 194. This resolution was passed on 11 December 1948. It was passed in the middle of the war between the newly founded state of Israel and the armies of Syria, Jordan, Egypt, Lebanon, and Iraq, and small expeditionary forces from other Arab countries, including Yemen and Saudi Arabia.[131] The relevant article is art. 11, which resolves that:

> the refugees wishing to return to their homes *and live at peace with their neighbours* should be permitted to do so *at the earliest practicable date*, and that compensation should be paid for the property of those choosing not to return and for loss of or damage to property which, under principles of international law or in equity, should be made good by the Governments or authorities responsible. [Italics added]

Israel accepted the resolution; most of the Arab states voted against it. Other articles resolved to set up a 'Conciliation Commission' (art. 2), requested the Commission to establish 'contact between the parties [to the conflict] themselves' (art. 4), and resolved both that the Holy Places should be under 'UN supervision' (art. 7), and that 'the Jerusalem area' should be under 'UN control' (art. 8). The representatives of France, Turkey, and the United States of America who made up the Conciliation Commission laboured in vain. Most of the provisions of the resolution remain unacceptable to the generality of Arab states, with the exception now perhaps of Egypt and Jordan with whom Israel has peace treaties.

Article 11 does *not* comprise a 'right of return'. The resolution was passed by the General Assembly, and it is therefore non-binding or 'recommendatory' in character. It is confined to those refugees prepared to live at peace with their neighbours, and even this limited class may only return at the earliest practicable date. Who is to determine which refugees are willing to live in peace, and how is it to be done? Who is to determine the earliest practicable date, and how is *that* to be done? In mid-June 1948, for example, the new Israeli government refused to readmit Palestinian refugees because it believed that elements among them would resume hostilities and seek to reverse the outcome of the war.[132] The PSC's overstatement of 194 is common enough;[133] a more rational statement of its meaning, in the context of a final settlement, is contained in art. 7 of the Geneva Peace Accord.[134] (Leading Palestinians have acknowledged that there can be no 'blanket' right of return into Israel for the refugees;[135] a case has also been made for the Palestinian 'right of return' to be reinterpreted as a right to settle in a *Palestinian* state, rather than within Israel.)[136] But there is a broader point. The PSC is remarkable for being a campaigning organization that has no declared final position. It is not working towards a defined solution to the Israel–Palestinian conflict. It appears to have no position on the one-state versus two-state solution, though the implication of its 'right of return' position is that there would be two Palestinian states and no state at all for the Jewish people.[137]

The liberal-Left

Anti-Zionism in the parties of the Left and Centre-Left has had a mixed fortune in recent decades. It was much stronger in the Labour Party, for example, during its years of opposition, especially in the 1980s. It remains at most an aspect of broader party policy, and characteristic of more radical positions that are often held by activists, not the party as a whole—at a certain point, the activist breaks with party consensus, and then disciplinary action beckons. These activists often display a vehemence about Israel (the sinful nature of its origins, its continuing crimes, the power of the Jewish lobby in sustaining it, etc.) that sits uncomfortably with the relative moderation of their typical position on the resolution of the conflict (a two-state solution, Israel secure within its pre-1967 borders, a 'right of return' limited to symbolic numbers and otherwise satisfied by the payment of compensation, etc.). The Occupation looms large in their considerations; they are motivated by dismay at the spectacle of Palestinian suffering and Israeli oppression rather than by any more specifically ideological loyalties, although in the last few years, electoral calculations have come into play too.[138]

Among several available examples of these themes, remarks made by two senior Liberal Democrat politicians may be taken to be representative of the liberal-Left perspective.

Jenny Tonge (b. 1941) was a Liberal Democrat MP from 1997 until 2005, and she is now a member of the House of Lords. In January 2004, she was sacked from her front bench position for remarks about Palestinian suicide bombers. She had told a pro-Palestinian lobby: 'If I had to live in that situation—and I say that advisedly—I might just consider becoming one myself.'[139] A little later on, Tonge wrote in a Web diary for the BBC: 'Suicide bombers are born out of despair and the desire to resist occupation, laced with religious belief. Civilian targets are chosen because there is simply no way of getting at military targets.'[140] This excuse-making, or 'apologetic discourse'—say, the claim that it is 'injustices' that 'drive men and women to commit' 'moral obscenities'[141]—is often misrepresented as a search for 'root causes'. Perfunctory acknowledgement is followed by an extensive plea in mitigation.[142] Just before the 2005 general election, in response to a question from the *Guardian*. 'My proudest achievement since the 2001 general election: Highlighting the plight of the Palestinians under occupation by Israel, by making a speech expressing empathy for suicide bombers—looking for the cause of terrorism.'[143] On Wednesday 20 September 2006, at the Liberal Democrat Party conference, Jenny Tonge said: 'I said, and I would repeat it now: if I had had to live through that as a Palestinian over decades and I was being given no hope for the future whatsoever I might have considered being a suicide bomber.' And then: 'I condemn terrorism, whether it comes from bomber pilots dropping bombs on Iraq or Afghanistan or Lebanon or whether it's a suicide bomber.' 'The suicide bomber is prepared to give his life, the bomber pilot goes home for a beer in the bar afterwards. That is the only difference.' She added, 'The pro-Israel lobby has got its grips on the Western world, its financial grips. I think they have probably got a certain grip on our party.'[144] In a speech in the House of Lords in December 2006, explaining her comments, she insisted that she both defended Israel's right to exist and its right to defend itself.[145] Liberal Democrat Matthew Harris pointed out that the party had received no large donations from Jewish or other pro-Israeli donors within the last five years.[146]

Chris Davies, the Liberal Democrat MEP, was e-mailed by a Jewish correspondent who told him that she disagreed with comments he had made claiming that the people who had suffered in Auschwitz seemed 'not to care that they have themselves become oppressors'.[147] She complained that he appeared to 'equate the situation of the Palestinian people' with 'the Jewish victims of the Holocaust'. She criticized him for supporting 'Muslim extremists and haters of Israel', and she contrasted Israel's treatment of homosexuals with their treatment elsewhere in the Middle East. Davies responded: 'Sounds like racism to me. I hope you are enjoying wallowing in your own filth.' In a subsequent e-mail to her, he wrote that if he stood for re-election he would highlight 'the racist policies of apartheid being put into practice by an Israeli Government'. He added: 'I shall denounce the influence of the Jewish lobby that seems to have far too great a say over the political decision-making process in many countries.'[148] When these exchanges were made public, he first explained that he had received many other emails, variously calling him 'anti semitic', 'scumbag', 'Jew hater', and comparing him with excrement, and he invited the woman to dissociate herself from 'the filthy apartheid policies being practiced' by Israel. But then party officials appear to have intervened, and he thereupon offered a

'fulsome apology'. He explained that he didn't know the difference between referring to the 'pro-Israel lobby' and the 'Jewish lobby'. 'I'm quite
prepared to accept that I don't understand the semantics of some of these
things.'[149] Some months later, Davies offered the following reflections on
the affair:

> Some of my remarks led to me being denounced as 'anti-Semitic' in the UK's
> Jewish newspapers. But as the *Economist* pointed out on 13 January 2007,
> defenders of Israel routinely accuse critics of being 'anti-Semitic' for saying
> things that are commonplace in Israel's own internal debate. My party leader,
> Sir Menzies Campbell, has voiced his personal conviction that the views
> I have expressed are not 'anti-Semitic'—and we need not even discuss
> whether Palestinians are Semites too! I am not an anti Semite, nor am
> I anti-Israel, or anti-Jew. I think anyone who denies the holocaust is a fool
> and I do not support any act of violence. I understand why the Palestinians try
> to strike back. But I cannot agree with such actions. I am one of the few
> Western politicians to have met with Hamas elected representatives and told
> them to their face that they should recognise the State of Israel and the 1967
> borders, that violence offers no solution, and that attempts to shell Israeli
> towns is both indefensible and self-defeating.[150]

It would seem that for both Tonge and Davies, talk about the 'Jewish lobby',
the invoking of Auschwitz, the assumption that all 'Jews' think alike,
the generally intemperate language, even the misleading reference to 'Jewish
newspapers',[151] support nothing more controversial than a mainstream
position on the resolution of the Israel–Palestinian conflict.

Though there was disquiet in her party over her 'pro-Israel lobby'
remarks, Tonge was not expelled. The party leader described her remarks
as 'unacceptable' and 'contrary to the principles of the party', and said that
they cast 'an unjustified slur on its leadership'. He wrote to the baroness,
saying the remarks had 'clear anti-Semitic connotations'.[152] The internal
debate drew on all the usual tropes and counter-tropes, though with
occasional reference to the other side being 'illiberal'.[153] On 5 May, Davies
resigned as leader of the British Liberal Democrat MEPs. 'I apologise for the
language and tone of my email, which was unacceptable and without
justification.'[154] In December 2006, the leader of the party, Sir Menzies
Campbell, announced that no further action would be taken against Davies,
as 'he did not intend any antisemitic inference to be drawn, nor do his
remarks when fairly read and in context support such an inference'.[155]

No ready inference from these affairs should be drawn concerning the Liberal Democrat Party's general position on Israel, save perhaps that it can no longer be said of the party now what was said of the Liberal Party in the 1970s: that it is 'perhaps the most deeply committed to Israel of all the parties'.[156] At its 2007 conference, the Party passed by a large majority a motion condemning the academic boycott of Israel. Tonge, who said that she was 'not anti-Semitic' but 'anti-injustice', opposed the motion.[157]

The Far Left

The non-regime Communist Party, and certainly the semi-clandestine Leninist Party, is practically extinct as a political force in Europe and the Americas.[158] If the remnants of these parties are to subsist at all, it is by attaching themselves to larger groups or movements. In recent times, the principal such candidates have been drawn from Islamic politics. They matter, because their influence extends beyond their own membership. This vulnerability—amounting at times to a capitulation—to Islamist positions takes its place at the end of a sequence of 'leftist' engagements with Islam that begins with the rather positive Soviet encounter in the aftermath of the 1917 Revolution, then deteriorates with the many conflicts between Islamist and Communist groups, but revives again in the early years of the New Left, with its extravagant praise for Arab socialism and corresponding denigration of Israel.[159]

Trotskyism has always been particularly strong as a component of the British Far Left;[160] and within the British Trotskyist groups, there has been a significant engagement with Zionism, Israel, and Islam. This is in part because the British administration of the Mandate made Zionism a local concern for all British political parties, in part because one of the principal ideologues of British Trotskyist politics was the Jewish Yigal Gluckstein, who was born in Palestine in 1917 and emigrated to Britain in 1946 (whereupon he changed his name to 'Tony Cliff'); and in part because the largest British Trotskyist party, the Socialist Workers Party, found opportunities for influence in an alliance with radical Islamism. The Trotskyist parties inherited from their founders and forebears a disparagement of Islam,[161] a hostile conception of Zionism as an alternative to socialist revolution, and a view of anti-Semitism as unconnected with Islam. What these parties made of this legacy can be analysed in four historical phases.

In the first phase, which runs from the 1920s through to the inauguration of the Cold War and the founding of the State of Israel, the partially anti-Jewish character of Arab resistance to Jewish immigration and settlement is acknowledged; the operating distinction is between the masses and the leaders; the Jewish masses are taken to be dominated by Zionist leaders, the Arab masses dominated by anti-Jewish feudal elements and clerical fascist elements; British imperialism is the enemy. The Jews must renounce exclusivism—and the Arabs, anti-Jewish terror. The Arab national movement has bred chauvinist, fascist, and particularly anti-Jewish ideas.[162] Over the decade before his death in 1940, Trotsky himself made several contributions to the formulation of these positions, acknowledging (for example) the role of 'reactionary Mohammedans and anti-Semitic pogromists' in the 1929 Arab riots.[163] There is no such thing, he argued, as the notion that any one group has more claim to land than any other group.[164] Such a notion is inconsistent with any thoroughgoing internationalism. In the *second* phase (essentially, post-war to 1967), Israel comes to be viewed as in alliance with the West; in consequence of Suez, Israel is seen as in the service of British and French imperialism; but Suez matters more to liberal England than it does to the Trotskyists, for whom Khrushchev's Secret Speech and the Hungarian Uprising in the same year was rather more significant.[165] (Hungary for a time preoccupied and divided the Far Left, with 7,000 members deserting the British Communist Party alone.)[166] The solution is minority autonomy within a Republic of Workers and Peasants of the Arab East.[167] In the *third* phase, the 'New Left' emerges, promoting a doctrine of 'national liberation' in which Israel plays the part of oppressor (though the Israel–Palestinian conflict is regarded as just one among several Third World conflicts); the hostility to 'Zionism' deepens as the prospects fade of detaching the Jewish Israeli masses from the national project; the goal comes to be defined as 'the Palestinian revolution';[168] a distinction is maintained between secular Palestinians and the Islamist radicals; one secular democratic state for the whole of Palestine is the goal of leftist endeavour;[169] the Soviet Union continues to exercise considerable influence, building alliances within the Arab world and propagandizing against Zionism to communist parties in the West.[170] These positions were taken within a considerably broader internationalist perspective. Israel did not *dominate* Far Left politics; indeed, for much of the time, it barely figured at all[171] (save, perhaps, for the Workers Revolutionary Party, a tiny group).[172] The anti-Zionism of this third phase somewhat petered out in the mid- to late 1980s. It generated its own, distinctive slogans, such as the German anti-Zionist 'Schlaegt die Zionisten tot, macht den Nahen Osten rot' ('Kill the Zionists dead, make the Near East red').[173]

We are now in the *fourth* phase. America and Israel emerge from a generalized West as the principal enemies of peace; the distinction between the secular and the Islamist gradually collapses; a class analysis of the Arab–Israeli conflict disappears; Israel is denied any legitimacy; Zionism is viewed with a hostile perplexity. This phase is inaugurated by the SWP pamphlet 'The prophet and the proletariat' (1994).[174] It argues that Islamism can challenge 'imperialism' and that while Islamists are not allies, socialists may be able to influence them. It says nothing about the anti-Semitic element in much Islamist ideology, while professing readiness to defend 'gays, Berbers or Copts'. Political opportunism, and the habit of operating through broad-based front organizations, led the SWP to abandon this somewhat detached position in favour of an open and uncritical alliance with radical Islamist elements.[175] By 2005, therefore, the SWP's declared ambition became 'to strengthen the basis for continuing political cooperation between the left and British Muslims'.[176] And in February 2007, *Socialist Worker* reported with enthusiasm that Hamas and Hezbollah would be sending delegates to the following month's 'anti-war conference' in Cairo.[177] The desire to find common ground with the Islamists was unquenchable.[178] And there are indeed, certain parallels between revolutionary socialism and Islamism,[179] not least in a common execration of the United States of America. This sense that the Qur'an is engaged in a battle with Capital and therefore deserves some support, now appears to be quite strong on the Left.[180]

The new anti-Zionism as campaign

On 30 May 2007 the union of university teachers, the UCU, passed two boycott resolutions. Resolution 30 endorsed the call for an academic boycott of Israel by a Palestinian boycott group, PACBI.[181] It also committed union funds to promoting it on campuses. But it did not commit the union itself to a boycott. Resolution 31 condemned the USA and EU boycott of the Palestininian National Authority (PA) (that is, the 'suspension of aid'). There was symmetry here. Resolution 30 called for a boycott; 31 called for the ending of a boycott. Israel's universities, which are liberal institutions, were to be shunned; the government of the PA, which was then controlled by Hamas, a party committed to the destruction of Israel, was to be embraced.

These resolutions were successors to boycott resolutions passed by the predecessor academic unions, the AUT in 2005, and NATFHE in 2006. The AUT resolutions purported to justify a boycott of named Israeli universities by making specific allegations against them. The NATFHE resolution, which was much like UCU resolution 30, 'invited members to consider their own responsibility for ensuring equity and non-discrimination in contacts with Israeli educational institutions or individuals and to consider the appropriateness of a boycott of those that do not publicly dissociate themselves from such policies'. The AUT resolutions were reversed following a special conference; the NATFHE resolution lapsed upon the union's dissolution only a few days later. The UCU resolutions also took their place in a greater series of anti-Israel boycott resolutions.

The supporters of the UCU resolutions argued that a boycott was justified on two grounds. First, Israel's universities are complicit in its misdeeds. Some boycotters alleged active complicity. Others alleged a complicity that arises either through failure to condemn the State's misdeeds or because the universities are themselves organs of the State. Secondly, Israel's misdeeds justify the boycott regardless of the universities' own complicity in them. The universities, it was said, are an important aspect of the prestige that Israel enjoys in the world, and this prestige is not deserved because of its treatment of the Palestinians.

Israel's misdeeds for these purposes (according to PACBI) comprise the 'ethnic cleansing' during the 1948 War, the 'military occupation and colonisation' following the 1967 War, and the 'entrenched system of racial discrimination and segregation against the Palestinian citizens of Israel'. That is to say, the 'misdeeds' are constitutive of the State itself, and can only be remedied by Israel embracing its own extinction. PACBI desires academics worldwide to boycott Israel's universities until Israel itself disappears. Of course, the boycotters were challenged: why Israel, when there are so many more oppressive states in the world? They gave three answers.

First, because Israel is a democracy, the entire people are to be associated with the actions of the government. Secondly, because Israel purports to respect law and human rights, it should be sanctioned when it acts unlawfully and in breach of the human rights in its power to uphold. Thirdly, because Jewish culture holds education and scholarship in high regard, an academic boycott of Israel would be more likely to have the desired political effect than in other countries.[182] The first two answers disclosed a misunderstanding of the nature of democratic accountability. Democracies make rulers accountable to the people; they do not make the people accountable to third parties. To think otherwise is to embrace a pseudo-democratic version of the notion of collective national guilt, to permit to tyrannies what is forbidden to democracies, and to overlook the fact that *every* state purports to respect 'human rights'. The third answer was fatuous. The reasoning appeared to be, Jews are clever and esteem learning, and so a boycott would hurt them in a special and distinctive way.[183]

The boycotters then argued, in defence of the UCU resolution, that it was institutional, rather than personal. It was limited, one of them argued, to 'joint research, conferences or other collaborative activity'[184]—as if these were enterprises transacted with corporate entities and not individual scholars. The boycotters neglected to consider the implications of their stance—including its implications for the very many Arab Israelis and Palestinians studying at Israeli universities. Were they to abandon their studies, and withdraw from their universities?[185] And what of the fruits of Israeli university research? Consider the new surgical techniques developed in Israeli medical faculties for treating the survivors among the victims of suicide bombers, their limbs lacerated or amputated by explosive mixed with steel nuts and nails and sometimes poison too, to ensure that haemorrhaging occurs even more swiftly?[186] Were these techniques, with potentially wide application, to be disregarded by doctors among the boycotters?

It may be enough to say, 'The boycotters were wrong.' They failed to make out their case. Their reasoning was not 'philosophically respect-able',[187] and they themselves, in their obsessive and fascinated enmity, merited mockery.[188] But this does not quite meet the case. The boycotters were not just adopting bad politics, which in turn was derived from faulty thinking. There was an edge of malice to their campaign. Their desire to hurt, to punish, outstripped their ability to identify precisely and consen-sually either their targets or their objectives. All Israeli universities without exception? All academics within those universities? Israeli academics in non-Israeli universities? Israeli universities but not Israeli academics?[189] There were similar difficulties in identifying objectives, though there were some irreconcilables ready to acknowledge that their aim was the isolation and ultimate disappearance of the Jewish State.[190] It was not certain, however, that they spoke for the boycott movement. And so the question arises—does this malice have a name? I will suggest an answer later on in the chapter.

The ADL 2007 Survey found that of those surveyed in the UK, 42 per cent strongly supported/somewhat supported, and 37 per cent strongly opposed/somewhat opposed, efforts by UK-based organizations to boycott Israel. Respondents over the age of forty-five were much more likely than other segments of the population to 'strongly oppose' the efforts to boycott Israel.[191] On 28 September 2007, the UCU issued a press release declaring that, upon legal advice, an academic boycott would be unlawful and could not be implemented. 'Making a call to boycott Israeli institutions would run a serious risk of infringing discrimination legislation', the union explained, and was also 'outside the aims and objects of the UCU'.[192] Given this advice, the resolute pursuit nonetheless of a boycott strategy by elements in the union, resulting in the passing of further boycott motions, led one critic of the UCU to conclude that it had become institutionally racist.[193]

The new anti-Zionism in the public sphere

By the 'public sphere' I mean that fraction of the 'sayable' in the culture that is more than merely privately in circulation. It defines the public conversation; it determines what range of comment can get a hearing, what is given authority by being published—and what, by contrast, is ruled out of public contention. In 1913, for example, it was possible to 'say' this:

> The Jews are not Christians nor Europeans, and can never be, without absolutely ceasing to be what they are. . . . Here we have a vast tribal organisation of Asiatic heathens, devoted to gain and domination according to ideas which you can read in the Pentateuch, alien to our beliefs, alien to our codes, alien to our very humanity.[194]

The editor of the *New Witness* was content to publish this letter—perhaps, more than content, given his own anti-Semitism. But the magazine was widely read, and more than a coterie. In 1930 it was possible in a national newspaper to 'say' this:

> All thinking people are aware that the present world depression is a direct result of the Jewish intrigue, as they are also aware that the wave of moral laxity, the debasement of the decencies of life, and the general undermining of the body politic originate from . . . the same source.[195]

The editor of the *Daily Express* was content to publish this letter in his newspaper. There is no reason to suppose that it commanded general assent;

it is enough that it was considered to represent a point of view entitled to be heard. Within the broad category of what is 'sayable' is the subcategory of what is taken to be 'obvious' at any given time. A contemporary journalist, writing in another national newspaper, wrote the following:

> [Walt and Mearsheimer] have caused one of the most extraordinary political storms over the Middle East in recent American history by stating what to many non-Americans is obvious: that the US has been willing to set aside its own security and that of many of its allies in order to advance the interests of Israel, that Israel is a liability in the 'war on terror', that the biggest Israeli lobby group, Aipac (the American Israel Public Affairs Committee), is in fact the agent of a foreign government and has a stranglehold on Congress—so much so that US policy towards Israel is not debated there—and that the lobby monitors and condemns academics who are critical of Israel.[196]

This is from an article by the journalist Robert Fisk, published in the *Independent* newspaper, bearing the title, 'United States of Israel?'

The new anti-Zionism has acquired some ascendancy in the public sphere. It conditions reporting on the Israel–Palestinian conflict in the general news media;[197] it is represented in websites (e.g., *Electronic Jihad*); there are Internet journals (*Counterpunch*); there are bloggers; and there are 'comment' posters[198] and email respondents[199] to opinion pieces written by columnists and commentators. Indicative of this ascendancy is the character of the reporting in the UK media of Israel's sixtieth anniversary. According to research undertaken by 'Just Journalism', the strongest theme in the coverage was that Israel was created at the expense of the Palestinians; another theme was that Israel does not seek peace. There were divergences in 'message' across media outlets, with the *Guardian*, the *Independent*, and the BBC News website containing the highest volume of negative coverage.[200]

This new anti-Zionism both feeds and is fed by a considerable quantity of misreporting—for example, of the Jenin incursion by the IDF in April 2002. To the *Guardian*, Israel's actions in Jenin were 'every bit as repellent' as Osama bin Laden's attack on New York on September 11. 'Rarely in more than a decade of war reporting from Bosnia, Chechnya, Sierra Leone, Kosovo, have I seen such deliberate destruction, such disrespect for human life', reported the *Times*' correspondent in Jenin. It was 'a monstrous war crime', reported the *Independent*, '[the IDF] has killed and injured hundreds of Palestinians'. A. N. Wilson declared, 'we are talking here of massacre, and a cover-up, of genocide'. An 'enormous slaughter . . . has overwhelmed the

Palestinians', said Robert Fisk.[201] Yet Fatah officials themselves referred to Jenin as the 'capital of suicide';[202] it was a centre of murderous terrorist activity; there was no massacre.[203] There were no acknowledgements of error when the truth could no longer be denied. On the contrary, reports of a massacre continued—in the *Guardian*[204] and elsewhere. John Pilger claimed, '[In April 2002] Israeli troops demolished most of the Jenin refugee camp; an unconfirmed number of people were bulldozed to death in their homes' (the weasel word is 'unconfirmed').[205] Though Jenin was typical of the reporting of the Israel–Palestinian conflict, rarely had the misrepresentation of reality been quite so egregious, the consequences for a true understanding of that conflict quite so destructive.[206] The 'massacre' story, so resilient, survived its refutation.

The *Guardian* has played a distinctive part in the dissemination of the new anti-Zionism.[207] No single item, or series of items, can be taken as representative beyond rational dispute, but the following indicates a certain tone and perspective. On 20 October 2004, two items appeared in the newspaper. One concerned a report on racism and anti-Semitism that had just been submitted to France's interior ministry; the other was a comment piece by Simon Tisdall, 'Bush and Kerry dance to the tune of Ariel Sharon'. According to the report, there had been a greater number of anti-Semitic threats and attacks in France in the first nine months of 2004 than in the whole of 2003. Cemeteries had been desecrated, synagogues had been firebombed, Jewish-owned property had been sprayed with swastika graffiti, and Jewish children had been verbally abused at their schools. All this was not just the work of the Far Right and disaffected youths of North African origin, the report concluded. The comment piece, two pages earlier, accompanied items about the then imminent US presidential elections. Sharon has led Bush 'by the nose', wrote Tisdall. He has 'mesmerised' him. He 'eggs on' the US in its confrontation with Israel's enemies, Iran and Syria. Sharon policy is Bush policy; 'Mr Sharon calls the shots.' Kerry is unlikely to be any better, as his existing record indicates. 'The guileful Mr Sharon . . . must be laughing all the way to the West Bank.'[208] Sharon is the Jew as puppet master or Svengali, dictating the decisions of the political leaders of great nations. Were Bush free of Sharon's influence, Tisdall supposes, his stance on Israel would be different. But he then acknowledges that the presidential candidate John Kerry, whose will he does not allege to have been similarly overborne, has a very similar position to Bush's. If this is so, why is it so? Tisdall cannot explain, because he suggests no cause for

American support of Israel other than Sharon's guile in respect of its president. Tisdall relies on an anti-Semitic trope to indicate what lies at the root of USA–Israel relations—and of course, it lets him down. The *Guardian* both reports on and fosters anti-Semitic sentiment. And when it published online both a videoed version of Caryll Churchill's *Seven Jewish Children* and a condemnation of the play's anti-Semitic tropes, it achieved the singular result of both promoting and challenging anti-Semitism at one and the same time.[209]

The BBC has likewise played its own part in the establishment of this anti-Zionist ascendancy. In March 2006, for example, the corporation's governors censured the BBC's online news service for a report about the Israel–Palestinian conflict because it misrepresented UN resolution 242 as requiring Israel's unconditional withdrawal from the Occupied Territories.[210] The BBC commissioned an investigation into its reporting of Middle East affairs, but then refused to make it public. This was typical of a certain mulishness on the Corporation's part, an intransigence extreme enough, in fact, to cause the BBC to refuse to remove a patently anti-Semitic posting from one of its websites. The 'message board moderators' explained that the posting did not 'contravene the House Rules'.[211] The House Rules give the moderators the discretion to reject postings that are 'racist, abusive or otherwise objectionable'.[212] This is the posting, signed by 'Iron Naz':

> Zionism is a racist ideology where jews are given supremacy over all other races and faiths. This is found in the Talmud. There is a law called Baba Mezia which allows jews to lie as long as its to non-jews. Many pro jewish supporters will cringe at this being exposed because they know it exists, yet they keep quiet about it . . . The Law of Baba Mezia!! Tsk tsk tsk! It's in the Talmud.[213]

In a second posting in the same thread, in response to objections, Iron Naz, wrote:

> I only follow what the respected scholars of Islam say. The Baba Mezia law specifically states you can lie to non-jews, and non-jews, or gentiles, are inferior in all ways to jews . . . chosen people to these guys means anyone who isn't chosen can be killed and/or treated worse then animals.[214]

This 'law' is a fabrication. There is nothing in this tractate of the Talmud that permits Jews to lie to non-Jews. There is, however, a relevant passage in another tractate, *Baba Kama*. In an account of a rabbinic dispute, the first rabbi cited expresses the opinion that if a person is questioned by a corrupt tax collector who is also a publican (and in the context, necessarily a non-Jew), it is permitted to answer untruthfully. The second rabbi then overrules him, stating that even in these circumstances a person cannot lie. This rabbi is the great Rabbi Akiva, whose ruling is authoritative.[215] Further, there is nothing in the Talmud that allows Jews to kill non-Jews or 'treat them worse than animals'.

The new anti-Zionism as anti-Semitism

In his *Art of Always Being Right*, the German philosopher Arthur Schopenhauer (1788–1860) identified the stratagems most likely to deliver victory to a controversialist, however weak his thesis. One of these stratagems is to put the adversary's argument 'into some odious category'. It is often said by Israel's critics that just this stratagem is used against them when they are accused of anti-Semitism. Is this true?

There are two approaches to this question. The first examines the extent to which holders of anti-Israel views *also* hold anti-Semitic views. The second examines the extent to which anti-Israel views are themselves coloured by anti-Semitism. The best instance of the first approach is Edward H. Kaplan and Charles A. Small's 2006 paper, 'Anti-Israel sentiment predicts anti-Semitism in Europe'.[216]

Drawing on research undertaken by the Anti-Defamation League, Kaplan and Small analyse polling responses to a set of 'anti-Semitic statements' and a set of 'anti-Israel' statements. These are the anti-Semitic statements, eleven in all:

> The Jews don't care what happens to anyone but their own kind; Jews are more willing than others to use shady practices to get what they want; Jews are more loyal to Israel than to this country; Jews have too much power in the business world; Jews have lots of irritating faults; Jews stick together more than other (citizens of respondent's country of residence); Jews always like to be at the head of things; Jews have too much power in international financial markets; Jews have too much power in our country today; Jewish business people are so shrewd that others do not have a fair chance to compete; Jews are not as honest as other business people.

And these are the 'anti-Israel' statements, four in all:

> The Israeli treatment of the Palestinians is similar to South Africa's treatment of blacks during apartheid; the Israelis are more responsible than the Palestinians

for the past three years of violence in Israel, the West Bank and the Gaza Strip; during military activities inside the West Bank and Gaza Strip, the Israeli Defence Forces intentionally target Palestinian civilians; there is some justification for Palestinian suicide bombers who target Israeli civilians.

The statements are not, of course, of equal gravity—that the IDF sets out to kill Palestinian civilians is a far more serious charge than that the Israelis bear the greater responsibility for violent incidents. In any event, the authors conclude 'the prevalence of those harboring (self-reported) anti-Semitic views consistently increases with respondents' degree of anti-Israel sentiment, even after controlling for other factors'.[217] Among those with the most extreme anti-Israel sentiments in the survey ('anti-Israel' index scores of 4), 56 per cent report anti-Semitic leanings. The greater the anti-Israel sentiment, the greater the anti-Semitism—save that *some* anti-Israel sentiment, they say, can be sustained without *any* anti-Semitism.

It is an attractive approach. The anti-Semitic statements are indeed unquestionably anti-Semitic; the difficult question of whether the anti-*Israel* statements are anti-Semitic is left open; the correlation exercise is neutral; the conclusion is not counter-intuitive—one would expect Jew-hatred and immoderate hostility to Israel to make a pair. But its appeal is also its limitation. It is not enough to say of someone that his perspective on Israel is so hostile that it is likely that he is also an anti-Semite. This does not serve as a response to his arguments; it does not serve as a characterization of his position. If there is a 56 per cent chance that he is an anti-Semite, there is a 44 per cent chance that he is not. Certainly, this is not in itself a reason to hold back from examining whether certain anti-Israel sentiments are in themselves anti-Semitic, or are coloured by anti-Semitism. There are good grounds for such an examination. The 'anti-Israel' statement that relates the treatment of Palestinians to the treatment of Apartheid South Africa's Black population, for example, may well be derived, if only in part, from the broader 'anti-Semitic' statements that 'Jews don't care what happens to anyone but their own kind' and 'Jews always like to be at the head of things.' This kind of examination, the second of the two approaches outlined above, is the one—with due acknowledgement to the value of the first approach—adopted in this chapter.

In the received wisdom, anti-Zionists merely take the side of the Palestinians in their dispute with Israel. It is a cause of some perplexity to many that this can amount to anti-Semitism. Their response, when not limited to a flat denial that their position is anti-Semitic, typically consists of some combination of the following: we are good people; we are politically progressive; there are Jews who agree with us; we have Jewish friends; the Jews/Israelis who accuse us of anti-Semitism are not sincere, and are merely using the charge as a means of deflecting criticism of Israel/Zionism; we are the real victims, and there is a McCarthyite-style witch-hunt against so-called anti-Semites.

In consequence of the general belief that charges of anti-Semitism are thrown about promiscuously, there is a tendency for thoughtful people to be circumspect when reflecting on contemporary anti-Zionism. It is right that this should be so. The charge of anti-Semitism is a very serious one; it should be made only as a last resort. It is important not to confuse a bad argument with a bad *and* anti-Semitic one. While every anti-Semitic argument is also a bad argument, not every bad argument is anti-Semitic. While there is therefore no doubt that immense abuse has been heaped on Jews in the name of anti-Zionism, much of what gives offence is no more than ordinary politics—even Herzlian politics. If one puts to one side the vocational anti-Semites, who have discovered the expediency of casting their Jew-hatred in the language of Israel-hatred, and asks the question, in relation to discourse about Israel, 'when does anti-Semitism arise?', it is possible to examine certain indices. There will be simple cases: 'new anti-Zionists' in thrall to conspiracy fantasies, blood libels, and Holocaust denial, and ready to find in Israel's abuse of its power over Palestinians a fresh application of Jewish abuse of power, anti-Semitism's master trope. Certainly, 'anti-Zionism' has become a cover for much anti-Semitic abuse and Jew-baiting. 'Zionist' is now principal among the circumlocutions[218] that substitute for 'Jewish' in anti-Semitic rhetoric. In this sense, it has given anti-Semitism a future. Certainly too, much anti-Zionist comment one hears today has absorbed the language of Nazi and Soviet anti-Semitism.[219] If one listens carefully enough, one can hear it. But this does not exhaust the sum of all cases of anti-Semitic anti-Zionism. If anti-Semitism represents a boundary, then it is a fuzzy one, marking a band of uncertainty.

Resonances with anti-Semitism's history

On 11 January 2009, about 15,000 English Jews assembled in Trafalgar Square to demonstrate in support of Israel. There was a small counter-demonstration on the day, made up of pro-Hamas protesters, who chanted in the direction of the massed Jews, 'How many children have you killed today?' The war in Gaza was at its height, and there had been many

Palestinian civilian casualties, among them children. Hamas for its part had been firing missiles into Israel for several years, several of which had hit schools and nurseries. It was not the first time that London's Jews had been accused of child-murder. Take another example. Statements to the effect that criticisms of Jews or Jewish projects require courage, and are difficult to make public because of Jewish control of the media, are long-standing tropes of anti-Semitic discourse. ('It would not be an exaggeration', wrote Nesta H. Webster, 'to say that there is hardly a periodical in this country . . . that dares to speak out freely on questions in which the interests of the Jews are involved.')[220] Such recapitulations, as we have seen, are now routinely made by or on behalf of certain kinds of critics of Israel. The question arises: how is one to gauge the resonances with anti-Semitism's history in contemporary anti-Israel and anti-Zionist discourse? Are they mere coincidences to be dismissed, or do they disclose elements of continuity between history and discourse, or even a certain indebtedness of the one to the other? Take a simple example. Is it right to assimilate to the anti-Semitic theological paradigm of an Old Testament 'vengeful God' and a New Testament 'loving God', the characterization of Israel's 'collective punishment' of the Palestinians as 'vengeance'?[221] Certainly, the author of this characterization benefits from the buried force of the word, one that helps him make his case for a boycott of the Jewish State. The semantic affinities always add their own weight to the argument; sometimes, they even make the argument.

Calls to boycott Israel, for sure, both resonate with historical anti-Semitic campaigns against Jews and draw on the language of anti-Semitic polemic. Indeed, to generations earlier than the present one, it could be taken for granted that anti-Semites would especially favour the boycott, because it most completely expressed anti-Semitism's project of repudiation and exclusion of Jews. Protesting at the very end of the nineteenth century against the anti-Semitic character of the SDF newspaper *Justice*, a correspondent made just this point:

> I should like to ask our anti-Semitic writers, 'What are the lessons they wish to propagate?' They tell us that our social and political evils are due to Jew-capitalists and the existence of Jews generally. What is the remedy? They have left it to be answered by inference, not daring to openly avow it. The boycott, in a word, anti-Semitism . . . [222]

One hundred years on, the anti-Semitic character of boycotts directed at Jews or groups of Jews can no longer be taken for granted.

Historically, the Jews were boycotted for one or more of the following reasons: to protect the Gentile community from Jewish conversionary influence; to protect the Gentile community from being corrupted by Jews or otherwise injured by them; to protect Gentile traders or labourers from Jewish competition; to maintain Gentile ascendancy by prohibiting Gentiles from taking employment with Jews; as a public act of disapproval of alleged Jewish wrongdoing; to coerce Jews into acting contrary to their interest; as a means of ostracizing from the nation a people considered to be ethnically alien or ambiguous;[223] as a preliminary step towards expulsion. Anti-Semitic polemicists invariably seek, among other things, to promote the boycotting or shunning of Jews—something recognized by the police in the Leese case (see Chapter 6; he was tried for 'rendering His Majesty's Jewish subjects of the Jewish faith liable to suspicion, affront and boycott').[224] Consider, in this context, the following significant moments.

In medieval times, Christians were not allowed to enter a Jewish synagogue; they were not allowed to celebrate a holiday with Jews; they were not allowed to go as guests to Jewish banquets. Anyone who violated these provisions, and was thus 'defiled by [the Jews'] impieties', was in turn to be shunned by Christians. Popes from time to time instructed the faithful to boycott Jews to achieve specific purposes—for example, to apply pressure on them to surrender property mortgaged by the Church.[225] Both patristic and medieval Church texts also affirm a more general rejection or boycott. 'How dare Christians have the slightest intercourse with Jews, those most miserable of all men', asked St John Chrysostom (c.347–407). 'Flee then, from their assemblies, fly from their houses...'[226] 'The Godly Fathers do not wish us to have any association with the Jews', pronounced a twelfth-century Byzantine text. 'There is no communion between light and darkness.'[227] Christians risked contamination by contact with Jews; they should not 'Judaize', because it was wrong to have fellowship with God's enemies.[228] The English Church was especially active in excluding or 'boycotting' Jews—recall the directions of the 1222 Canterbury Council, and Bishop Grosseteste's pastoral circular (see Chapter 3). Boycotts were often preparatory to physical attacks and/or to expulsions.

The boycotting of Jewish shops and businesses was an aspect of anti-Semitic activity in France in the 1890s, and figured prominently during the 1898 anti-Semitic riots. The *Ligue Antisémitique Française*, which had been agitating for a boycott for some time, presented itself as a radical Left-wing organization. One of its leaders asserted, 'anti-Semitism is essentially socialist', and its economic programme consisted of opposition to (Jewish-owned) department stores in favour of small traders and artisans. It called for Jews to be deprived of French citizenship, to be banned from public positions, and to be expelled from France. A Social Catholic Congress passed resolutions in 1889 enjoining members not to marry Jews, not to read Jewish newspapers, and not to have any commercial relations with Jews. Other Catholic groups passed boycott resolutions at congresses in 1895 and 1898. It was during that latter year that the boycott campaign ignited. It ceased to be merely the programme of ideologically driven anti-Semites; it became the common sense of a substantial fraction of the general population. Customers were urged, 'For the honour and salvation of France, buy nothing from the Jews'; stickers appeared on shop walls, 'Never buy from a Jew. Keep France for the French. Drive out the Jews from France', 'Blacklist them!' and 'European and Arab Frenchmen, don't buy anything from the Jews!' Vigilante brigades were organized to photograph and denounce non-Jews who patronized Jewish shops. The local anti-Semitic press published lists of shops and businesses owned by Jews. Of all the campaigns mounted by anti-Semites, the boycott campaign was the most serious and sustained one.[229] It had a specifically leftist provenance. The French socialist, P.-J. Proudhon (1809–65), was an early advocate of boycotting Jews, and called for their exclusion from all kinds of employment and the closure of their synagogues. 'In the end, it will be necessary', he said, to 'send this race back to Asia or exterminate it'.[230]

In Limerick, in 1904, a local priest, Father Creagh, incited a boycott of the local Jewish population. 'It is madness', he declared, 'for a people to allow an evil to grow in their midst that will eventually cause them ruin.' He had received complaints from shopkeepers about the unwelcome competition from Jewish peddlers. The Jews 'force themselves and their goods upon the people, and the people are blind as to their tricks'. Economic sanctions were imposed; orders were given to the Jews' customers and creditors not to buy their goods and to repay their loans. The boycott was accompanied by violent demonstrations against the Jews, and considerable intimidation. They confronted chanting crowds: 'Down with the Jews: they kill our innocent children!' 'Death to the Jews!' and 'We must hunt them out.' Stones were thrown at the community's rabbi. Jewish children were ostracized in the schools. The local newspaper, which supported the boycott, counselled restraint. 'If the people do not want the Jews, then leave them severely alone.' The affair received widespread notice in the international press. Creagh himself was quick to deprecate the violence he had incited, and instead advised his congregation, 'keep away from them [i.e., the Jews], and let them go to whatever country they came from . . .'. The Jews, he added, 'have proved themselves to be the enemies of every country in Europe, and every nation had to defend itself against them'. The boycott lasted for many months, causing great hardship to local Jewish families, several of whom left for abroad. The Jewish community of Limerick never recovered; the Board of Deputies' response to the boycott was especially feeble.[231]

In the very first weeks of the Third Reich, on 1 April 1933, Hitler ordered a boycott of Jewish shops, banks, offices, and department stores, and Jewish doctors and lawyers. The Nazi Party had by then been pursuing a boycott campaign against the Jews for several years; boycott propaganda had hit Jewish businesses hard. On the day, signs were posted 'Don't Buy from Jews' and 'The Jews Are Our Misfortune'. The boycott was announced as a 'defensive measure'. Uniformed Nazis, some armed with rifles, stationed themselves in front of Jewish business premises, and barred customers from entry. Cars circulated in the street broadcasting slogans condemning buying from Jews. The Nazi boycott was intended to isolate German Jews from their non-Jewish fellow citizens. Some Jews, anxious to demonstrate to their erstwhile customers their patriotic credentials wore military decorations, but to no avail. A new wave of violent boycotts broke against Jewish businesses in the summer of 1935. The anti-Jewish boycott was a process, not a series of individual events. In mid-March 1938, upon the *Anschluss* with Germany, Austria's Jewish merchants faced a boycott, enforced by thugs in brown shirts or by marauding youths wearing the swastika armband, ready to take savage reprisals against those who ignored or defied them. These Nazi-devised boycotts followed earlier anti-Semitic boycott initiatives in Germany,[232] and occurred in a broader Central and East European context of boycotting and excluding Jews—'cold pogroms', as they were termed.[233] Fascist hooliganism in London's East End repeatedly attempted to replicate the Nazi boycott. Jewish shops were picketed and customers intimidated. Gangs chanted, 'Buy from people who celebrate Christmas', 'Why buy goods from stinking Jews?' and 'Boycott the Jews'. Bills were posted on the shops, 'Keep away. These Jews are here to rob you', 'Boycott Jewish shops', and 'Come in and be robbed. These Jews want your money.' In October 1938, a local newspaper reported that in consequence of the 'Fascist terror' 'large numbers of Jews, owning shops and houses, have been forced to leave the district'.[234] Fascists doggedly persisted in the post-war period with their boycott campaigns. In the early 1960s, for example, Colin Jordan's newspaper, *National Socialist*, contained appeals to its readers to boycott Jewish goods, amid articles attacking ritual slaughter and threatening Jews with Nazi justice, and pictures of children said to have been butchered by the Stern Gang.[235]

The boycott of Palestine's Jews and then of the Jewish State itself has a long history. In September 1929, shortly after the massacres of Jews in Hebron, Safed, and elsewhere, Jerusalem Arab students, with the authority of the Moslem Supreme Council, called for a boycott of Jewish businesses: 'O Arab! Remember that the Jew is your strongest enemy and the enemy of your ancestors since olden times.'[236] Indeed, boycotting became a reflex of the Palestinian Arab leadership throughout the Mandate period.[237] On 2 November 1945, the anniversary of the Balfour Declaration, the worst anti-Jewish pogrom in Cairo's history took place. Demonstrators broke into the Jewish Quarter, plundered houses and shops, and set fire to the Ashkenazi synagogue. Four hundred people were injured, and a policeman was killed. In Alexandria, at least five people were killed in the course of even more violent riots that a British Embassy official described as 'clearly anti-Jewish'. A few weeks later, Islamist newspapers launched an attack on Egypt's Jews, describing them as capitalists, bloodsuckers, white-slave traders, arms' traffickers, capitalists, and (of course) Zionists. They called for a boycott of Jewish goods.[238] In the same year, the Arab League initiated a boycott of Jewish Palestinian businesses. It prohibited Arab states from doing business both with 'Zionists'/'Jews'[239] and with any third parties who themselves might be doing business with Zionists. The object was to isolate and weaken the Palestinian Jewish community. One year later, the ban was extended to prohibit contact with 'anything Jewish' (as the *Palestine Post* reported, quoting a League announcement). Arab Boycott Offices were established in many of the Arab countries. Saudi Arabia, for example, issued boycott regulations in 1952 prohibiting importers from dealing with any businesses owned or controlled by Jews and which employed Jews.[240] The boycott made no distinction of principle between Israeli enterprises and non-Israeli enterprises that employed Jews.[241] In the 1970s, the USA made compliance with the boycott illegal; most European states, on the other hand, colluded with it. Britain's record was especially ignominious in this respect: Jews were dismissed from companies and required to resign directorships, and to withdraw from investments or participate in banking deals, at the behest of boycotting Arab countries, and a bill intended to outlaw such discriminatory pressure was killed in 1978 by the then government for fear that it would adversely affect the nation's commercial interests.[242] This economic warfare continues to the present day.[243] It is destructive and self-destructive.

Given this history, it might be thought that critics and adversaries of the Jewish State would be deterred from wielding the weapon of the boycott. Certainly, the boycott initiatives of the early twenty-first century reminded Jews, and historically literate people of goodwill, of those earlier occasions when entire Jewish communities were isolated and shunned. Ghada Karmi, for example, in the very course of denying that the boycott call was anti-Semitic, evoked precisely these memories, when she urged that 'all efforts should be directed toward boycotting all Israeli institutions. Only when Israel is made a pariah state, as happened with South Africa, will its people understand that they cannot trample on another people's rights without penalty.'[244] By 'its people' Karmi refers to the Jewish population of Israel, and possibly Jewish supporters of Israel elsewhere too. Her use of the word 'pariah' requires no gloss.

What happens when people are boycotted? The ordinary courtesies of life are no longer extended to them. They are not acknowledged in the street; their goods are not bought, their services are not employed; invitations they hitherto could rely upon dry up; they find themselves isolated in company. The boycott is an act of violence, though of a paradoxical kind—one of recoil and exclusion rather than assault. The boycotted person is pushed away by the 'general horror and common hate'.[245] It is a denial, amongst other things, of the boycotted person's freedom of expression. Expression is one of the principal means by which we realize ourselves. It is by speaking or writing that we discover who we are; in conversing with others we are constructing ourselves.[246] To limit or deny self-expression is thus an attack at the root of what it is to be human. Of course, freedom of expression must incorporate freedom of address. It is not sufficient for the exercise of my freedom of expression for me simply to be free to speak. What matters to me is that people should also be free to hear me. There should at least be the possibility of dialogue. Boycotts put a barrier in front of the speaker. He can speak but he is prevented from communicating. When he addresses another, that other turns away. The boycott thus announces a certain moral distaste; it is always self-congratulatory. 'I am too fine a person to have anything to do with those people', the boycotter says to himself. 'They will have to reform themselves before I am ready to admit them back into my circle. Contact with them is intolerable to me.' Boycotting is thus an activity especially susceptible to hypocrisy. It implies moral judgements on both boycotter and boycotted.

The academic boycott was a denial of Israeli academics' freedom of expression; it was an attempt at censorship; it did not derive from any criteria capable of being applied universally; it was but the latest in a millennial series of campaigns to isolate Jewish communities—in this case, the Jewish community living in Israel; it was inconsistent with the general academic and political principles the boycotters professed to espouse; it punished indiscriminately—Israeli nationality was the only criterion; Jews would suffer disproportionately; it was not directed towards the achieving of any specific, achievable goals. The campaign was, in a word, *irrational*. It should not have been a matter of controversy (though it *was* a matter of controversy) to define this irrational campaign against Jews and the Jewish State as anti-Semitic—it was unfair, it was intellectually and morally frivolous, and it was continuous with historical anti-Semitic discourse and practice.[247]

The conspiracy trope

It is in reliance on the conspiracy trope that the contemporary anti-Zionist comes closest to the position of the anti-Semite using anti-Zionism merely as a cover. It is the simplest kind of anti-Semitic anti-Zionism that both denies that the Jews have any national rights and yet also insists that Jews work internationally to further their collective interests. For such anti-Zionists, the Jews are a conspiracy, not a nation. Israel is merely an external aspect of that conspiracy. It is 'the capital of an elusive and omnipresent empire'.[248]

Conspiracy theories are, however, notoriously the province of cranks. To admit to a conspiracy perspective on the world is to own up to political moronism. Most accounts of Jewish power therefore draw back from any full embrace of the notion of a Jewish conspiracy, while hinting at it, or disavowing and invoking it at the same time. There are many variations to this dance.

One variation, for example, is to argue that try as they might, the Jews are too disorganized to be conspirators. This was the argument of Dennis Sewell's 'A kosher conspiracy?' in the 14 January 2002 issue of the *New Statesman*. 'When one looks at the array of pro-Israel organisations

in Britain, one is struck not by their cohesion so much as their fragmenta-
tion.... The truth is that the "Zionist lobby" does exist, but is a clueless
bunch.' Yet on the cover of the magazine there was a picture of a gold Star
of David above a supine Union Jack, the Star's lower triangle piercing the
flag like a dagger. This resonated with very traditional anti-Semitic iconography and language.[249]

Another variation is to exchange the major term 'conspiracy' for the
minor one, 'cabal'. The post-war anti-Semitic newspaper *Candour* was fond
of referring to 'the dominant Money Power', a 'supranational body operating from New York and working closely with Moscow', as a 'cabal'.[250]
But this was within the mostly closed *milieu* of the anti-Semitic underworld.
In the days prior to the launch of the second Iraq war, however, the term
surfaced in a mainstream journal. During the course of an interview with
the magazine *Vanity Fair*, the 'senior member of the House of Commons,
Tam Dalyell', said that 'Blair is unduly influenced by a cabal of Jewish
advisers. He mentions Mandelson, Lord Levy and Jack Straw.'[251] Dalyell
was a Labour MP and an opponent of the Iraq war. When challenged,
Dalyell explained 'the cabal I referred to was American', and then named
seven Bush advisers, six of whom were Jewish. 'It's the Jewish Institute for
National Security Affairs combined with Christian fundamentalists.' He also
dropped Straw and Mandelson from his Anglo-Jewish cabal. There is 'one
person about whom I am extremely concerned and I have to be blunt about
it. That is Lord Levy, Mr Blair's official representative in the Middle East.'
(It was not the first time in English history that the patriotism of a Jewish
political figure was called into question.)[252] Elsewhere, Dalyell explained
that he was 'worried about my country being led up the garden path on a
Likudnik, Sharon agenda'.[253] 'Cabal' was correctly taken to have anti-
Semitic connotations;[254] it cannot now be used in relation to Jews *without*
anti-Semitic connotations;[255] the OED cites, and endorses, Dr Johnson's
gloss on the word, 'something less than a conspiracy'; Dalyell himself
conceded that 'cabal' was 'at least linguistically, a misjudgment'.[256] He
rejected, however, the charge of anti-Semitism. 'The idea of me being
anti-Semitic is total rubbish. I have Jewish friends. I have been on holiday
in Israel, and I have written endless affectionate obituaries for Jewish
people.'[257] And elsewhere, 'I am not going to be labelled anti-Semitic.
My children worked on a kibbutz.'[258]

'Jewish conspiracy' beliefs sometimes prove too hard altogether to repudiate. At the 2007 AGM of the PSC, for example, a resolution was tabled

that contained—after much throat-clearing on the differences between anti-Zionism and anti-Semitism, and the wickedness of those who say otherwise—a paragraph rejecting talk of the 'Jewish lobby' and 'Jewish power'.[259] That objections to imperialism have often been deformed by anti-Semitic sentiment is a commonplace among historians and political scientists;[260] the deformations are also acknowledged from time to time by activists too. But not on this occasion, and specifically not in relation to objections to Zionism. The resolution was rejected.[261] In the debate on this resolution lies the irresolution of the new anti-Zionists before the Jewish conspiracy trope.

If conspiracy, in its baldest and most unqualified form, is usually a step too far, attributing improper influence to Jewish lobbies through their use of money is a very common accusation. There is little difference in this respect between the fulminating of the Social Democratic Federation newspaper in the 1880s against the 'Jew moneylenders who now control every Foreign Office in Europe', and the fulminating of the Workers Revolutionary Party newspaper in the 1970s against 'Britain, who sold the Palestinian people out to Zionist money power'.[262] In April 2008, George Galloway 'warned that the Jewish lobby was also working against the election of Ken Livingstone because of his support for the Muslim community of the capital'.[263] In a House of Lords debate a few weeks after her speech about the 'pro-Israel lobby', Tonge asked, 'Why can Israel continue its actions when other countries have sanctions imposed, or are invaded, for less?' And she continued:

> My recent contention that a factor in all this is the activity of the pro-Israel lobby operating in the West has got me into big trouble, and led to accusations of anti-Semitism. I would like to sincerely apologise to colleagues in my party and elsewhere, and to Jewish people all over the country, who may have misunderstood my remarks. I beg leave to try to explain them.
>
> 'The Israel Lobby' is the title of a paper written by Professors Mearsheimer and Walt of Chicago and Harvard universities. It is not the only paper on the subject. It is well researched and authoritative. The authors conclude that the lobby exerts a huge influence on US politicians and foreign policy. That is their conclusion and anyone can draw their own.
>
> Let us remember that the lobby to which they refer is not composed simply of Zionists. There are many neo-conservatives and right-wing Christian evangelists in that lobby's huge, wide coalition of people. Criticism of the lobby therefore cannot be called anti-Semitic.
>
> It is not anti-Semitic to criticise either the lobby or the actions of the Israeli Government. It may be said that to do so is simply used as an excuse to

be anti-Semitic, which I accept; I have heard that said many times. Yet the reverse is also true.

Accusations of anti-Semitism can be used as a smokescreen to shield the actions of Israel from censure and to silence her opponents. I am not anti-Semitic—I will challenge anyone who accuses me of that disgusting sentiment—but I am horrified by decades of inaction by the international community in dealing with the occupation of Palestine, and the damage that that is doing to the Jewish diaspora, who contribute so much to all our lives.

Tonge concluded: 'The Holocaust was the worst event in human history; we must never forget it. But, in making amends for that terrible event, we cannot condemn millions of innocent Palestinians to humiliation and poverty in what seems like perpetuity.'[264]

Shadowy, powerful forces are suppressing the truth about Israel; the 'Israel lobby' will stifle criticism of Israel whenever it can.[265] Ordinary people are brave if they face down threats or dangers that have the capacity to cow or intimidate them; critics of the 'Lobby', by contrast, are taken to be 'brave' merely by virtue of the object of their criticism. During the Danish cartoon crisis of February 2006, for example, when British editors were nervously declining to publish the cartoons in their own newspapers, the *Guardian* ran a two-part series on the Israel/apartheid trope. Reviewing the pieces, and the reactions to them, the 'Readers' Editor' complacently noted 'many [readers] applauded [the author of the pieces, Chris] McGreal for his "courage", a word that cropped up quite often, and congratulated the *Guardian* for publishing the articles'.[266] Criticized for baiting a Jewish journalist in February 2005 by comparing him to a German war criminal, Ken Livingstone defended himself by referring to the pre-war pro-fascist sympathies record of the journalist's employers and by hinting that he was being punished for his stance on Israel. '[Israel's policies] are . . . fuelling anger and violence across the world. For a mayor of London not to speak out against such injustice would not only be wrong—but would also ignore the threat it poses to the security of all Londoners.'[267] But 'speaking out', Livingstone implied, carried a cost. It might attract criticism.

One of the principal tools of the 'lobby' is taken to be the 'smear'. 'The trouble is that anyone who dares criticise the Zionist operation', Dalyell told one newspaper, 'is immediately labelled anti-Semitic.'[268] (This is a common enough complaint—'we *soi-disant* anti-Semites for daring to protest about soldiers shooting at kids'; it is 'the usual trick'.)[269] Elsewhere it was observed, 'Mr Dalyell said that he now expects to be victimised because he raised a "whisper of criticism" about the influence which Jewish advisers hold on Tony Blair, the Prime minister, and George Bush, the President of the US.'[270] The MP Clare Short complained at the premiere of a piece of music written in memory of Rachel Corrie that 'there has been the usual campaign to silence even a cantata to commemorate a young woman who gave her life in order to stand for justice'.[271] According to the press announcement of Alan Hart's book *Zionism: The real enemy of the Jews*, 'Alan believes that nothing is more important for justice and peace than ending the silence of troubled mainstream Diaspora Jews on the matter of Israel's behaviour.' The 'lobby' is an affront to national pride: 'our cowardly subservience to the all-powerful pro-Israel lobby in America'.[272] It does not just silence, it also punishes. According to Robert Fisk, 'Noam Chomsky, America's foremost moral philosopher and linguistics academic' is 'so critical of Israel that he does not even have a regular newspaper column'.[273] The musician Gilad Atzmon's 'fearless tirades against Zionism—the ideology behind the Israeli state—have cost him in terms of lost gigs and constant vigilance about personal security', reports the SWP journal, *Socialist Worker*.[274] This is an old trope. Things are bad, much worse than they were, it is now almost impossible to be heard, Jewish/Zionist power is almost overwhelming... Douglas Reed made similar points in 1942:

> None thought to intimidate Dickens, by attacks in the Press, by the yelping and yapping of 'anti-Semite,' from setting in a book a Jewish character, Fagin, of a type as familiar today as in his time and long before. Truth could be spoken then. We were neither mealy-mouthed nor chicken-hearted.[275]

That Reed made this claim in a book published by the well-known, mainstream house of Jonathan Cape, no more fazed him than does the ready and extensive media access enjoyed by Israel's critics. 'Courage' has become a posture. Indeed, the specific property, 'courage', is taken to attach itself to *any* adversarial stance towards the 'lobby', regardless of the absence of actual risk.

There is in reality something of a gap between the actual operation of representative Jewish bodies and the rhetoric of 'Jewish lobby'. In the summer of 2005, Foreign and Home Office officials debated whether Sheikh Qaradawi should be allowed into the UK. Mayor Livingstone had invited him the previous year, and this had prompted the submission of a dossier by a coalition of minorities (Hindus, Jews, Gays) detailing his views on non-Muslims, homosexuals, and so on. On 14 July 2005, a Foreign

Office civil servant, Mockbul Ali, circulated a memorandum, recommending that Qaradawi not be excluded:

> A significant number of the accusations against Qaradawi seemed to have been as a result of a dossier compiled by the Board of Deputies, based on information from Middle East Media Research Institute (MEMRI). The founding President of MEMRI is retired Colonel Yigal Carmon, who served for 22 years in Israel's military intelligence service. MEMRI is regularly criticised for selective translation of Arabic reports.... [Excluding Qaradawi] could also fuel media reports of conspiracy theories—especially in the UK Muslim media—about the involvement of Jewish lobby groups and their influence on British government policy.[276]

In fact, the objections to Qaradawi had *not* just come from Jews or 'Jewish lobby groups'. Furthermore, much of the material had been drawn from Qaradawi's own website. So what was at work here? There was an acknowledgement of the importance of a Muslim lobby ('the UK Muslim media'), one that must not be antagonized. There was a representation that objections to the cleric came solely from the Jewish lobby. There was a further representation that this lobby relies upon tainted sources. And there was a recommendation that the lobby's objections should be disregarded. But the critical point is that it was taken for granted that while allowing Qaradawi in to the UK could be done *without any adverse political consequences*, excluding him carried various risks. Ali raised the spectre of Jewish 'influence' precisely in order to *support* the case for the cleric's admission. Objections from the Jews could be ignored. 'Jewish lobby' talk had never seemed quite so threadbare as here.

Control of the media

In 1975, Christopher Mayhew and Michael Adams published *Publish It Not: The Middle East cover-up*. Mayhew (1915–97) was a former Labour government minister, and Adams (1920–2005) was a journalist and film-maker. They were prime movers in CAABU, the Council for the Advancement of Arab–British Understanding, which they had set up in 1967. Their book was republished in 1989, and then again in 2006 with an introduction by Tim Llewellyn, a former BBC journalist and CAABU board member. In a favourable review of the republished book in the *Tablet*, Adams and Mayhew were praised for their efforts to counter 'the power of the Zionist lobby at every level of British society'.[277]

The authors argue that supporters of Israel created and then propagated myths concerning the 'Palestine problem' in order to conceal the truth about the cruelties and injustices that the Israelis inflicted, and continue to inflict, on the Palestinians. Since the 1973 War, however, Israel's critics have been listened to more readily. Arguments that once were dismissed as 'Arab propaganda' are now regarded as 'self-evident'. In their 1989 Preface, they note a trend towards even more balanced news coverage, which they attribute in part to books written in the previous decade exposing the Zionist myths and in part to the impact of television. The Zionist lobby no longer enjoys the easy domination it once had over Labour Party policy. However, 'everyone who criticises Israel publicly, whether Jew or Gentile, must expect to pay some penalty, even in the more relaxed climate of today'.[278]

According to Llewellyn, though there has indeed been a shift in public opinion, it is not enough to influence Britain's political leaders or the heads of its most influential institutions. The same forces are at work ensuring that the British public are kept in ignorance of the true facts. 'No alien polity', he writes, 'has so successfully penetrated the British government and British institutions during the past 90 years as the Zionist movement and its manifestation as the state of Israel.' 'The Zionists have manipulated British systems as expertly as maestros', and the audience has been 'spellbound'. They have 'suborned Britain's civil structures, including government, parliament and press'. (To 'suborn' means to induce a person by bribery to commit perjury or some other crime.) The BBC operates in a climate of fear. 'The Zionist lobby in all its devious forms' propagates misinformation about the history of the Israel–Palestinian conflict. The Union of Jewish Students 'elbows and induces Zionistically inclined undergraduates towards influential positions in British public life'. The Board of Deputies of British Jews is an 'influential lobby of the Zionist Great and Good'. The Israelis and their friends 'fight fiercely, expertly and without quarter. Nowhere is this more true than with the press and broadcasters'. They lean hard on reporters and bureau chiefs, making complaints and suggestions for stories. They hold 'schmoozing lunches, the cocktails flavoured with menace'. The accusation of anti-Semitism is the ready-to-hand smear of the Zionists and their friends if they think Israel is receiving a tough press. The mainstream media refuses to report the truth of the so-called 'Arab–Israeli dispute', which is nothing more than 'settler-colonialists stealing the lands and stamping on the rights of the indigenous people'. What is the explanation for this state of affairs?

Llewellyn cannot say. 'Nowhere in *Publish It Not* is this Zionist force and its captive hold on the British establishment *quite* satisfactorily explained. I cannot explain it myself.'[279]

That it might in part be attributable to the merits of the Zionist cause lies beyond Llewellyn's understanding, as it lies beyond Mayhew's and Adams's. Such influence as the Arab nations are able to exercise by the use of the 'oil weapon'[280] tends to be celebrated by Mayhew and Adams, or noted without comment; the influence that Israel, and Jewish supporters of Israel, are able to exercise to the Jewish State's advantage is regarded, by contrast, with suspicion and usually treated as in some sense illegitimate. Mayhew, Adams, and Llewellyn all decline, however, to make the leap into the full-blown anti-Semitic fantasy of Jewish control of the media. In an appendix to the 2006 edition, one Shelby Tucker contributes a short account of the 'pervasive Zionist control of our media' and 'the extent and effectiveness of its indoctrinating power'. His piece is entitled 'Hidden hands?'

Good Jews, bad Jews, and Jewish self-incrimination

The wish to have bad Jews confess, to catch them owning up to their mysterious, murderous crimes, lies behind the relentless torturing of them in medieval legal proceedings to 'confess correctly',[281] and the fictions of voluntary and involuntary admission and self-condemnation that litter the history of anti-Semitism. The *Protocols* are merely the most completely realized product of just such a wish; there are many other such products. Jewish admissions of wickedness comprise a trope of anti-Semitic discourse; each one is the equivalent of a soliloquy addressed to the audience by the Jewish villain in a melodrama. 'A certain honest Jew named Henriquez once remarked,' wrote Joseph Banister, ' "We are a walking lie, because we cheat all nations whose franchise we have accepted." '[282] 'Dr. Oscar Levy says,' reports the anti-Semitic T. W. H. Crosland (see Chapter 6): ' "We Jews are today nothing else than the world's seducers, its destroyers, its incendiaries, its executioners." '[283] 'I will begin', writes William Joyce, 'with the intelligent criticism of the Jewish race by one of its own illustrious members ... '[284] A Jew asserts it, contrary to the Jewish interest, so it must be true. The Jews are best slain with their own sword.[285] In the evolution of this trope, several distinct stages may be identified (I am returning here, as I said I would, to a topic I first raised in the Preface). In each stage, the anti-Semites may be imagined responding to sceptics and people of goodwill: 'Look the Jews *admit* it! They hate Gentiles and want to kill them or rule over them.'

Voltaire, taking the Hebrew Scriptures' prohibition of human blood sacrifice as evidence that the practice was widespread, gleefully insisted, 'No historical detail is better attested; a nation can only be judged by its own archives.'[286] A 1924 leaflet published by the Britons Publishing Society invited electors, 'Before casting your vote for Mond read what the Jews say of themselves...' It quoted statements by Jews to the effect that a Jew cannot be an Englishman.[287] And here, for example, is a passage from a contemporary Islamist work, available in London: 'The Jews admit that fashion is one of the three things they used to westernise our girls...'[288] And it is an American neo-Nazi group, of course, that now publishes Samuel Roth's mad book of hatred, *Jews Must Live*. Study the Jews' own scriptures, read what they themselves write, listen to what they themselves say—*they admit it*! These statements attributed to Jews comprise simple acknowledgements of guilt as well as more complex self-incriminating statements. In many instances, the acknowledgements are just false and the statements are fabricated; in other cases, the acknowledgements are given too much weight and the meanings of the statements are misrepresented.

The Gospels, and in particular Matthew, comprise the *first stage*. A combination of direct speech and ostensibly authoritative citation or quotation from Jewish teachings serves to incriminate both Judaism and the Jews themselves. The chief priests, the elders, and the Jewish multitude all respond to Pilate's 'I am innocent of the blood of this just person', with a ready, glad assumption of responsibility for Jesus' death, 'His blood be on us and on our children.' It is a confession of guilt, binding on all the generations. Somewhat earlier, in the Sermon on the Mount, Jesus says, 'Ye have heard that it hath been said, "Thou shalt love thy neighbour, and hate thine enemy." But I say...' (5:43–4). The impression given is that Jesus is quoting from the Hebrew Scriptures. But while the instruction 'love thy neighbour' is indeed a quotation from Leviticus (19:18), the instruction 'hate thine enemy' is a complete invention.[289]

The *second stage* coincides with the first appearance of the blood libel. Its promoters relied in part on reported or mendacious admissions by Jewish converts,[290] and in part on admissions extracted from Jews under extreme torture. The thirteenth-century French monk Thomas Cantipratanus wrote that the Jews use Christian blood as a means of cure, and that it must be true because 'I heard that a very learned Jew, who was converted to the faith of our times, [had said words to that effect].'[291] In his extended polemic against the Jews, *Fortalitium Fidei* (1464), the Spanish Inquisitor, Alonso Espina, claims that the truth of the blood libel was confirmed to him by a 'Jew by the name of Emanuel'.[292] In addition to relying upon Theobald of Cambridge, Thomas of Monmouth gives a self-incriminating speech to one of William's murderers:

> the detection of the truth [of William's death] will bring a very extreme peril upon us all. Indeed, *through the fault of our imprudence, and not undeservedly*, our race will be utterly driven out from all parts of England, and—what is even more to be dreaded—we, our wives and our little ones will be given as prey to the barbarians, we shall be delivered up to death, we shall be exterminated, and our name will become a reproach to all people for ever.[293]

He does not merely admit the crime, he implicates the whole of Anglo-Jewry in its commission, and he prescribes their punishment—extermination. The Jews write their own death sentence, thereby exculpating their victims of blame when they execute it.

Anti-Semites were left unsatisfied with admissions of misanthropy from individual Jews. Where, they wondered, could this hatred of Christians be found in authoritative Jewish texts? This question prompted the *third stage*, an assault on the Talmud. In Christian Europe,[294] the earliest such assaults, mostly conducted by converted Jews,[295] occurred during the same period that the blood libel took hold in the medieval imagination. By the beginning of the sixteenth century, the association of the Jews with their books was absolute.[296] Proof of the Jews' iniquity could thus be found in the iniquity of these books. A leading figure in this distinct assault on Jews and Judaism was one Johann Andreas Eisenmenger.[297] His *Judaism Exposed* (1711) was an immense work of misrepresentation, mistranslation, and (on occasion) fabrication. It went through many editions. Its essential argument was that the Jews are permitted by their religion to commit any excess against non-Jews, whom they are taught to hate. They regard all non-Jews as Amalekites.[298] He wrote, in support of a particular libel on Jews, 'I heard it myself from a convert.'[299] One hundred and fifty years later, Eisenmenger's work was plagiarized by August Röhling, a professor of theology at the German University in Prague, in his *Talmud Jew* (1871). It went through six printings between 1871 and 1877.[300] (One Catholic group alone distributed no less than 38,000 copies of the sixth reprint *gratis* in Westphalia.)[301] He gave evidence in 1883 at the Tisza-Eszlar blood-libel trial that Jews practise ritual murder.[302] Röhling enjoyed the protection and patronage of the local archbishop.[303] But in 1885, Rabbi Joseph S. Bloch (1850–1923) accused him of incompetence and of fabricating texts. Röhling sued the rabbi for libel, but fled the city just a few days before the trial was due to begin.[304] The defaming of the Talmud has been a practice of anti-Semites, aided by renegade Jews, from the Middle Ages right up to the Nazi period and beyond.[305] Defamatory publications with titles such as *The Fruits of the Torah-Inspired Ideology of Israel* and *Judaism from a Theoretical and Practical Perspective: An anthology from the Torah and the Talmud*, now circulate widely in the Arab and Muslim world and are now being exported back to the West.[306]

Then, towards the end of the nineteenth century, the *fourth stage* was reached: the allegation of a world Jewish conspiracy. It wasn't enough that Jews were said to plot the murder of Christian children; it wasn't even enough that their religion was said to have instructed them to hate non-Jews; their plotting and their hatred had also to be directed towards some immense goal—nothing less than global domination. In his *Diary of a Writer*, for example, Dostoyevsky puts quotation marks around this ostensibly scriptural injunction to the Jews: 'Step out of the family of nations... exterminate the rest, or make slaves of them, or exploit them. Have faith in the conquest of the whole world; adhere to the belief that everything will submit to thee. Loathe strictly everything', etc. And Dostoyevsky then triumphantly comments: 'Such is the essence of that [state within a state]...' Yet the passage was a complete fabrication—indeed, one of Dostoyevsky's own making. It is to be found neither in the Hebrew Scriptures nor in the Talmud.[307] One may identify a rule here. The more extravagant the allegation against the Jews, the greater the dependence on forms of confession—here, fiction and fabrication.[308] The fiction was supplied by Benjamin Disraeli, and the most notorious fabrication, by agents of Tsarist Russia. Sidonia, a character in Disraeli's *Coningsby* (1844), advances the thesis that the Jews comprise a pure, flourishing race, exceptional in every respect, and dominant in the politics and culture of Europe. He tells the young hero of the novel, 'The world is governed by very different personages from what is imagined by those who are not behind the scenes.'[309] Anti-Semites seized on this piece of bravado as confirmation of the existence of an international Jewish conspiracy.[310] The Tsarist fabrication consisted of a memorandum attributed to the Jews, the *Protocols*—a 'how to conquer the world book' in twenty-four short chapters. This too went through many editions and, notwithstanding several books and even legal actions exposing its utter falsity, it remains in circulation today. Henry Ford alleged that during World War I a 'prominent Jew' had once confided in him that the Jews controlled the world through their control of gold, and that only the Jews could stop the war. Ford was foolish enough, upon being challenged, to offer the name of this Jew, who then successfully sued him for libel.[311] (Statements made by the anti-Semitic Henry Ford are attributed to 'the Jewish Harry Ford' in a book found at the London offices of the Muslim World League.)[312] In addition, a fresh kind of fabrication emerged: the apparent endorsement by prominent figures of positions taken by anti-Semites. Benjamin Franklin, for example, was said to have denounced the Jews as 'vampires' and called for their expulsion from the United States. A Nazi 'research' institute fabricated this document: among many others, Captain Ramsay dutifully parroted it in his *The Nameless War* (1952).[313]

We are now in the *fifth stage*. Incriminatory quotations are a staple of anti-Zionism. These quotations are partly the old ones, mostly updated by substituting 'Zionist' for 'Jew',[314] and partly new ones. They are a mix of fabricated quotations (including fictitious endorsements from prominent figures such as Nelson Mandela), and genuine quotations that are given undue weight. These quotations serve as substitutes for reasoned argument. Edward Said, for example, wrote of 'the Zionist slogan formulated by Israel Zangwill for Palestine...a land without people, for a people without land'.[315] Yet this was *not* a slogan of the Zionist movement, it was *not* formulated by Zangwill, and when it *was* used, it mostly was with the indefinite article, 'a land without *a* people'—i.e., a distinct national grouping.[316] Misquotations are central to anti-Zionist polemic, and so it is not surprising to find them in Said's work.[317] On one website (miftah.org), in an item entitled 'In Their Own Words', one may read: 'Following is a compilation of selected quotations from prominent Israeli and Zionist figures that embodies the discourse of hatred, racism, and rejection that nurtured Israeli society throughout the short existence of Israel.'[318] On the website, 'San Francisco Independent Media', there is an article entitled '23 Reasons to Condemn Zionism', all of which comprise incriminatory quotations.

'Why then, apart from the general Moslem unrest,' asked J. Ramsay MacDonald, writing in 1922, 'is there friction between Jew and Arab?' 'Much of it is propaganda. Every foolish statement made by Jews is passed from lip to lip and is amplified in the passing.'[319] The misuse by one side of statements made by the other, though doubtless a staple of all political conflicts, was an early feature of the conflict between Jews and Arabs in Mandate Palestine. Nothing has changed. Among the most frequently cited of the genuine quotations is this one from Herzl, taken here from Tariq Ali's book *The Clash of Fundamentalisms* (London, 2003), but to be read in many other places too:[320]

> [Ethnic cleansing] had always been part of the Zionist project. In 1895, Herzl wrote in his diary: 'We shall try to spirit the penniless population across the border by procuring employment for it in the transit countries, while denying it any employment in our country ... Both the process of expropriation and the removal of the poor must be carried out discreetly and circumspectly.'[321]

This and related incriminatory quotations are deployed to make a case that this is what all Zionists thought; this was integral to Zionism; this was the master plan; it would have been implemented in 1948 regardless of context; present-day Israelis are guilty; the state has no legitimacy therefore.

The historian Derek J. Penslar has given this diary entry of Herzl's[322] particularly close attention.[323] His argument, in summary, is as follows. Herzl addressed the question of the Palestinian Arabs on three principal occasions: in the diary entry of 12 June 1895 quoted above; in a draft charter he prepared in 1901, under which owners of land bought for occupation by Jews may be resettled elsewhere; and in his novel *Altneuland* ('Old New Land') (1902). Each reflects a distinct perspective on transfer/Arab rights in the Jewish State. None was acted upon; none defined Zionist policy. The diary entry, according to Penslar, was a 'narcissistic fantasy', composed during his 'celebrated manic fit';[324] the draft charter was never even debated, let alone executed, and in any event assumed that the Jews would be subject to Ottoman rule; the novel was a fantasy of a different, more public kind, anticipating a substantial, though subordinate Arab presence in the imagined Jewish State. Notwithstanding what Penslar describes as the 'voyeuristic zeal'[325] with which the diary entry typically is now seized upon, it is no more than one moment in a much greater and more complex story. But the interpretation of the diary entry does not end here. The historian Efraim Karsh, noting that the entry makes no express mention of either Arabs or Palestine, concludes that Herzl in fact had South America in mind, and not Palestine. A careful reading of his diaries for that month reveals, says Karsh, that Herzl did not consider Palestine to be the future site of Jewish resettlement at all.[326] The question of Zionism and 'transfer' may not, then, be resolved by incriminatory quotations—or, for that matter, exculpatory ones (of which, incidentally, there would appear to be far more).[327]

More typically, outright fabrications are combined with genuine but misleading quotations:

> Unlike [Tony Blair], the Israelis at least are honest. 'We must use terror, assassination, intimidation, land confiscation and the cutting of all social services to rid the Galilee of its Arab population,' said Israel's founding prime minister, David Ben-Gurion. Half a century later, Ariel Sharon said, 'It is the duty of Israeli leaders to explain to public opinion . . . that there can be no Zionism, colonisation or Jewish state without the eviction of the Arabs and the expropriation of their lands.' The current prime minister, Ehud Olmert, told the US Congress: 'I believe in our people's eternal and historic right to this *entire* land [his emphasis].'[328]

In this column by John Pilger, quotations from Ben Gurion, Israel's first and most revered prime minister, Ariel Sharon, its most reviled one, and Ehud Olmert, its then current one, are meant to be indicative of what 'Israelis' intend. When these prime ministers speak, Israel speaks, and Zionism speaks. The quotations amount to a confession of iniquity. The foundation of the State, and its continued existence, is predicated on criminality—frankly acknowledged, or 'honest', criminality. Pilger's piece is both an instance of a certain kind of 'new anti-Zionist' discourse and an instance of a contemporary journalism that is typically polemical, bitter, and dismissive.[329] Pilger is well known for the extravagance of his rhetoric, and to take him with more than a certain degree of seriousness is to lack seriousness oneself (to borrow a formulation of Henry James's).[330]

Of his three quotations, the first is a fabrication. Neither Ben Gurion nor anybody else said those words. They have been circulating on anti-Zionist websites for a while, attributed to one Israel Koenig.[331] Koenig was author of the 'Koenig Report'[332] a paper prepared by an Israeli civil servant in the mid-1970s regarding the Arabs of Galilee. The then government repudiated Koenig's paper. It is in many respects an ugly document,[333] but nowhere in it does he write the words attributed to him (or anything like these words). It is most likely that the fabrication came into existence over time, probably in the following way. There were rumours of the existence of the report before it was leaked to the newspapers, where it was published as a scoop. Hostile, inaccurate précis of the report were doubtless already in circulation. Over time, these précis became more and more inaccurate, more and more hostile to its author. At some point, someone decided to put inverted commas around the précis, at which point it ceased to be a false summary *of* the report and became instead a false quotation *from* it.

The second quotation is a misattribution, and a misrepresentation of its true, contextual meaning. It is taken from an op-ed column in the Israeli daily newspaper *Yediot Ahronot* of 4 July 1972. At the time, Ariel Sharon was head of the IDF's southern command. Even given Israel's relatively open political culture, it would have been surprising to find him publicly calling for the eviction of Arabs from their homes and for the expropriation of their land. He did not do so, though it is common enough in anti-Zionist discourse to attribute blood-curdling statements to him.[334] Yeshayahu Ben-Porat, a journalist and commentator, in fact wrote the words. In the column from which the quotation has been taken, Ben-Porat called on the government to recognize honestly the implications of occupation. Though some anti-Zionist websites make the same mistake in attribution as Pilger does,[335] most of them mistakenly attribute it to one 'Yoram Bar-Porath',[336] relying on the authority of an article by the French Holocaust denier Roger Garaudy, in the *Journal of Historical Review*.[337] Others misattribute it to Yoram Ben-Porath, a Hebrew University professor of economics and a leading figure in the Israeli peace movement who died in the early 1990s.[338]

The third quotation is a correct attribution, but a misrepresentation so egregious that it reverses Olmert's meaning. Ehud Olmert is—in the language of Israeli politics—a 'prince' of the right-wing Revisionist Zionist movement. He is the son of a leader of the Irgun pre-independence militia and was a Likud Party Member of Israel's parliament, the Knesset. The young Olmert was undoubtedly raised to believe in the Jewish people's historic right to the Land of Israel. The Irgun's symbol showed the map of the 'greater' land of Israel—Mandatory Palestine and Transjordan—with a rifle in a clenched fist superimposed. Its motto 'Rak Kach'—'Only Thus'— makes the point even clearer. Pilger's choice of Olmert's words is entirely consistent with this heritage. But what Olmert went on to say, in this speech given to a joint meeting of the US Congress on 24 May, gave the lie to Pilger's account of his views. He expressly surrendered the ambition that Pilger attributed to him.[339] 'We have to relinquish part of our dream to leave room for the dream of others, so that all of us can enjoy a better future.' This sentence does not figure in Pilger's exposition.

Pilger's sequence of quotations was almost certainly lifted from an article written by Edward S. Herman, and posted on the Internet some twelve or so days before his own column appeared in the *New Statesman*. Herman is a long-time writing-partner of Noam Chomsky's.[340] And so the incriminatory quotations are recycled. In due course, the editor of the *New Statesman* acknowledged the errors in Pilger's column. Pilger added his own note to the acknowledgement:

> The academic source for a quotation of David Ben-Gurion I used in my piece now believes it is incorrect. This referred to the expulsion of the Arab population from the Galilee in 1948. It is worth adding that the sentiments expressed were not extraordinary. Ben-Gurion, in his war diaries and elsewhere, showed an obsession with the expulsion or compulsory transfer of the Palestinians from their homeland. The Israeli historian Benny Morris wrote: 'arriving at the scene, David Ben-Gurion, Israel's first prime minister, was asked by General Allon, "What shall we do with the Arabs?" ' Ben-Gurion, wrote Morris, 'made a dismissive, energetic gesture with his hand and said, "Expel them." '[341]

Saying nothing about the quotations attributed to Sharon and Olmert, Pilger withdraws the one attributed to Ben-Gurion, and substitutes another one. Almost certainly, this statement is correct. *But* it does not relate to the 'Arabs' in general. It relates instead to the Arab population of Lydda and Ramle, two Arab towns on the road from Tel Aviv to Jerusalem, and it was made during the 1948 War. The sentences in Morris's essay that immediately precede the passage quoted by Pilger make this clear:

> There was shooting in Lydda. According to the best account of that meeting, someone, possibly Allon, proposed expelling the inhabitants of the two towns. Ben-Gurion said nothing, and no decision was taken.

Then, Morris continues, after the meeting was over, Ben-Gurion made the gesture attributed to him, and orders were given to transport the inhabitants of the towns towards the Arab Legion lines. But that is not the end of the story. As the expulsions were taking place, the Israeli minister for Minority Affairs arrived and was shocked by what he saw. The following day he reported to Foreign Minister Shertok. Shertok and Ben-Gurion then agreed guidelines for Israeli military behaviour towards the civilian population. Inhabitants who wished to leave would be free to do so; the Israeli authorities would not be obliged to procure food for those who remained; women, children, the sick and the aged must not be forced to leave; monasteries and churches are not to be damaged. These guidelines were converted into an order to the Israeli military operational HQ. A week before, the deputy chief of staff had issued an order to the entire army, 'outside of actual hostilities it is forbidden . . . to expel Arab inhabitants...without special permission or an express order from the Defence Minister in every specific case. Anyone violating this order will be put on trial.' Neither this order, nor the later guidelines, was effective to halt the exodus from Lydda and Ramle, partly because the local Israeli military forces remained bent on expulsion, and partly because the inhabitants hoped to find safety behind Arab lines. It was the biggest expulsion operation of the 1948 War. It was also a consequence of the war. So far from it representing State policy, it was implemented behind the Cabinet's back. Israel never adopted a general policy of expulsion, which explains why 160,000 Arabs remained, and became citizens in 1949 (accounting for more than 15 per cent of the population).[342]

A criminal justice system that relies on confessions can make the police corrupt and prosecutors lazy.[343] It is also the mark of state terror: during the Soviet Great Terror of the 1930s, confessions were highly prized, and obtained by various coercive means, including torture.[344] The practice of incriminatory quotation in political debate is also dangerous, if not as lethal. It is not, of course, confined to anti-Semitic discourse,[345] nor is it limited to one side in the Israel–Palestinian conflict.[346] Quotations can never be substitutes for the hard work of analysis and exposition. Even when the quotation is genuine, it is almost always made to do more work than can properly be expected of it. Certainly, no single statement, nor even some dozen or so statements, can be adequate to encompass the entire history and ideology of Zionism. The history is too complex, and the ideology too fractured, for this to be possible.

There is a related tendency in anti-Zionist polemicizing to detach complicating statements from Zionism's discursive history, in order to preserve an adverse judgement, unrelieved, unmitigated. Tariq Ali, for example, refers only to Ahad Ha'am as 'the Jewish thinker' when he cites him as 'demoli[shing]' the 'Zionist fundamentalist myth' that Palestine was a land without a people for a people without a land.[347] But Ahad Ha'am was himself a Zionist, and the criticism was part of the self-interrogation of the movement. This is the opposite of the self-incrimination move; it misrepresents self-interrogation as external critique, the better to maintain Zionism's own essential wickedness. To preserve the character of anti-Zionism's indictment of a Zionism of its own construction, the plurality of Zionist perspectives must be reduced to a discreditable singularity.

Counter-accounts, counter-histories

There is a tendency among friends of Israel engaged in its defence to assert, at a particular point in an argument, 'Of course, we are not asserting that every criticism of Israel is anti-Semitic', and to leave it at that. They do not invite any such criticism; they rarely themselves offer any criticism. The statement functions as a device, a general acknowledgement of imperfection, one that forestalls rather that initiates specific objections to a policy or practice. But though it may serve in the context of public debate, and constitutes a fair enough riposte at the low level at which anti-Israel polemicizing is mostly conducted, it is inadequate for present purposes. So let me pose the following question. What kind of *non*-anti-Semitic criticisms *can* be made? Consider, for example, Israel's occupation of the lands conquered in the Six Day War. It is relevant to the formation of the new anti-Zionism; it has given immense impetus to anti-Zionism in general.

The criticism of the administration of the Occupied (or 'Disputed') Territories must begin with the humiliations inflicted on the occupied population. These are humiliations transacted within a general denial of self-government, that especially intolerable circumscription of autonomy imposed by any enemy entity on a subject population. Every occupation in this sense may be conceived as a prison;[348] it interferes, writes Mourid Barghouti with little overstatement, in every aspect of life and of death.[349] The rights enjoyed by those citizens of the occupying power who live, or move about, in the occupied land will always appear in painful contrast with the lack of rights of those whose land is being occupied. If only for this reason, there is no such thing as an enlightened or benign occupation.[350] Israel may indeed have built the first universities in Gaza and the West Bank, it may have brought electricity to small villages there,[351] it may at first instance even have been welcomed by many as a relief following the years of occupation by Egypt of Gaza and Jordan of the West Bank,[352] but none of these reforms and improvements to the lives of the Palestinians can transform a condition of oppression into one of freedom. Occupations institutionalize inequality between rulers and ruled; they encourage abuses, even acts of baseness.[353] They announce to a subject-people, 'We are the masters here.'[354] And to this general characteristic of all occupations must be added the specific burdens of checkpoints, curfews, closures, permits, and all those other limitations on movement that are imposed without accountability. Israel's occupation is no different in these respects to any other occupation. The Six Day War is now entering its fifth decade.

The burden of Israel's occupation has been exacerbated by the general deterioration in relations between Israelis and Palestinians in the last twenty-five or so years. Targeted assassinations have killed bystanders.[355] The shootings (live rounds and rubber bullets), beatings, and tear gas, have injured many thousands of Palestinians; the punitive destruction of private property has made many hundreds of Palestinians homeless; the uprooting of orchards and fields, the destruction of factories, workshops, and hot-houses, has robbed many thousands of Palestinians of their means of liveli-hood; the confiscation of vehicles, the house searches, the demands for the production of papers and the examinations of personal effects, the shaming of parents in the presence of their children, are no doubt both demoralizing and enraging. The 'Security fence' (or 'Wall'), however much intended as a non-violent response to Palestinian violence, has generated its own oppres-sions—'land-grabs,' the separating of neighbours, the looming ugliness of the structure itself. It is, at the very least, a most disruptive act of self-defence.

These criticisms can be developed further by a consideration of why Israel is still in any part of the Occupied Territories. Having conquered them in 1967, it retains a substantial part of them, and has until very recently appeared to want to hold on to them regardless of the wishes of the Palestinians. It has recklessly ignored the fact that it is not alone.[356] Israel is still there partly because instead of actively pursuing peace in the aftermath of the Six Day War it has waited for overtures from its enemies,[357] and partly in consequence of the settlements built there in the last forty years. Instead of administering the territories as conquered land in accordance with the relevant international conventions, it has financed the settlement activity of mainly national-religious Zionists (who have promoted a version of Zion-ism that in certain respects breaks with the pre-existing Zionist consensus). It built homes for its Jewish citizens, who thereupon shared the land with non-citizens in conditions of the grossest inequality. And this settlement project produced, and continues to produce, its own, further oppressions. The construction of settlements requires the confiscation of land; connect-ing settlements to each other and to Israel itself requires the building of roads that cut through Palestinian land;[358] defending the settlements means, among other things, the imposition of circuitous travel routes on Palestin-ians. These settlements, moreover, unless capable of justification on security grounds, are probably in themselves unlawful (unlike the occupation itself),[359] both in international law and in municipal law.[360]

The occupation has harmed both Israeli and Palestinian societies. From the Palestinian side, it has fostered a culture of dependency *and* terrorist violence. That is to say, there has been a double absence: an absence of any sustained independent economic development and an absence of any sustained acts of non-violent civil disobedience. The two are related, as the collapse of the first Intifada, and the character of the second Intifada, demonstrated—the one, an uprising of mostly unarmed Palestinian civilians against Israeli soldiers, the other, a campaign by armed Palestinian militias against unarmed Israeli civilians.[361] From Israel's side, the occupation has damaged the ideal of a democratic state governed by the rule of law. The Occupied Territories are not 'abroad'; there cannot be a state in which the rule of law applies only in part. Unless it is universal, the rule of law is nowhere, and that inferior thing, a set of privileges, exists in its place.[362]

None of these criticisms, in my view, is anti-Semitic. Many of them seem to me simply to be true, and what is true cannot be anti-Semitic. Nor are these criticisms anti-Zionist. They would not have surprised Ben Gurion, who predicted in the immediate aftermath of the Six Day War disaster for the Jewish State if it did not immediately give back all the territory it had just won, with the exception of East Jerusalem.[363] The criticisms can thus be derived from a classical Zionist position, even a Herzlian[364] one—Herzl spoke of Zionism as a 'moral, lawful, humanitarian movement'.[365] In his address at the 2006 Rabin memorial rally, David Grossman spoke of Palestinians as an 'oppressed, occupied people bereft of hope'. But he also said: 'I am totally secular, and yet in my eyes the establishment and the very existence of the State of Israel is a miracle of sorts that happened to us as a nation—a political, national, human miracle.' The miracle was:

> the opportunity to establish . . . a state that is efficient, democratic, which abides by Jewish and universal values; a state that would be a national home and haven, but not only a haven, also a place that would offer a new meaning to Jewish existence; a state that holds as an integral and essential part of its Jewish identity and its Jewish ethos, the observance of full equality and respect for its non-Jewish citizens.[366]

For sure, the criticisms are also in certain respects one-sided, a mere accumulation of everything that is wrong that may plausibly be regarded as Israel's fault. The Israel–Palestinian conflict is treated as melodrama rather than tragedy; total innocence confronts total guilt.

The criticisms say nothing, for example, about the inadequacies of the Palestinians' own political leadership: most catastrophically of all, its failure at any time in the last eighty years to foster the creation of a body politic— to commit, that is, to state-building. It was always the struggle against Zionism that was pressing, while the establishing of a state could be postponed to some later date.[367] The institutionalized thievery and violence of the Palestinian Authority under Arafat's reign subverted the very possibility of a Palestinian state. Billions of dollars were stolen; 'monopolies' were established for the benefit of Arafat's cronies;[368] immense funds were disbursed on armaments and for the maintenance of private militias. In its first three years, there were just about the same number of Palestinian deaths in PA gaols as there were in Israeli gaols in twenty years.[369] Torture by Palestinian security forces of prisoners was rife.[370] The cause of this endemic corruption,[371] which only became worse when Hamas assumed power,[372] cannot be laid wholly at Israel's door.[373] An 'all-or-nothing-at-all-ism', no more than self-defeating maximalist posturing, has driven the Palestinians into more and more desperate conditions, and these conditions in turn have become the justification for grosser and grosser acts of pseudo-redemptive violence—like the gambler who places bets at longer and longer odds in order to recover the ever-increasing volume of his losses. Is there any doubt that had Israel offered *in July 1967* to vacate the whole of Gaza and the West Bank in return for peace with the Palestinians and the Arab states, the offer would have been rejected? The criticisms also say nothing about the anti-Semitism that saturates accounts of Israel and the Israelis in the Palestinian media—the harshest *and* the most knowledgeable critic of Israel's Occupation, Amira Hass, has noticed that among Palestinians the negative associations of the word 'Jew' are 'not limited to the occupation and the expulsion'.[374] Such things stifle hopes for coexistence, and further encourage an Israeli Right already ready to indulge its own fantasies of the ineradicable, radical Jew-hatred of 'the Arabs'.

Lastly, these criticisms say nothing about the deforming burden carried by the State and its citizens of the refusal by its neighbours to accept its existence, or (in the case of Egypt and Jordan) accept it on terms that permit genuine friendship and cooperation. The burden was already heavy in 1948, at the moment of the State's founding. It must not be forgotten that the first generation of Israeli citizens came to their State with experience in full of riot, murder, and destruction. The inaugural moments of the State left 1 per cent of its Jewish population dead; the secretary general of the Arab League had promised the Jews 'a war of extermination and a momentous massacre'.[375] It is precisely this burden that has generated the national imperative to build and maintain an army of overwhelming capability; it is precisely this burden that has generated the conviction that Israel cannot afford to lose any battle (let alone, war) and that its security must be pursued above all other considerations. It is hard to gauge what measure of fear and anxiety, what profundity of intuition of 'disastrous defeat or failure',[376] contributed to the formation of the Israeli national identity—but to deny it altogether, to equivocate over its reality, or to disparage it as an irrational 'obsession with security',[377] is surely to omit an essential element in the explanation of this 120-year conflict. The overwhelmingly superior force of the Israelis has not meant that the injuries have been confined to one side alone; a sense of persecution, victimization, even vulnerability, is experienced by both sides.[378] Palestinian misery is not the fault of Israel alone; Israeli misery is not entirely self-authored.

What happens when the one-sidedness of these criticisms is left uncorrected, and is instead pressed further?

First, as the following examples indicate, the character of the criticisms becomes irrational. 'US backing for Israeli policies of expansion of the Israeli State and oppression of the Palestinian people is *the major cause* of bitter division and violence in the world' (Clare Short, former Labour government minister);[379] Israel/Palestine is 'the most inflammatory conflict on the planet' (Seamus Milne, *Guardian* journalist);[380] 'the Middle East . . . is key to peace in the world' (Jenny Tonge, Liberal Democrat politician);[381] '[until Israel withdraws from the Palestinian territories] most of the world will be in terrible, terrible trouble' (Vanessa Redgrave);[382] 'Unless Israel withdraws to its 1967 borders, I fear for peace, not only in Israel and Palestine but in the whole world' (Bishop Riah Abu El-Assal, the former Anglican bishop of Jerusalem);[383] 'Israel has gone beyond just war crimes. It is horrific what is going on there. Many of us would like to talk about it as some kind of Holocaust which the world will eventually wake up to, much too late, of course, as they did with the last one' (Professor Mona Baker, who in June 2002 sacked two academics from the board of her journal for the offence of being Israeli);[384] 'the Zionist state remains the cause of more regional grievance and sheer terror than all the Muslim states combined' (John Pilger, in the *New Statesman*).[385] None of these judgements withstand the most cursory scrutiny; they all trade on ignorance. Several assume, wrongly, that 'Palestine' motivates the perpetrators of the major terrorist atrocities of recent times.[386] In their preoccupation with Israel's offences, imagined and real, they disregard calamities elsewhere in the Muslim world of many greater orders of magnitude.[387]

Secondly, and in consequence, the criticisms drift towards an objection to the very existence of the State of Israel, however constituted, and within whatever borders. Israel as such becomes the problem—its inescapable history, its intolerable presence.[388] It is a 'mistake';[389] it is not a 'viable presence'.[390] It is a 'racist state that has come into existence through ethnic cleansing and theft and sustained itself through war and expansion. . . . [The two-state solution] negates the legitimate rights and interests of Palestinians, while upholding an entirely illegitimate and spurious claim by Zionists based on biblical exegesis and racial domination.'[391] 'The Zionists . . . stole Palestine from its people and have been persecuting them for more than sixty years in a regime that is many times worse than the defunct Apartheid regime of South Africa.'[392] A newspaper columnist, Richard Stott, wrote: 'The Jewish people have suffered many horrors. They have also given a great deal to the world in every area of human endeavour, the arts, sciences and everything in between. Yet somehow when they are transformed into Israeli politicians and military men, they become something terrible. Blinkered, barbaric killers with little regard for the suffering of innocents who happen to be on the other side of the border.'[393] Israelis are unacceptable Jews; Israel is an unacceptable state.

The criticisms, that is, take on an 'anti-Zionist' complexion. They support a larger narrative that amounts to a hostile rewriting of the history of Israel and the Zionist movement. The rewriting of the Jews' history has been the practice of their adversaries since ancient times. In present times, it is the obsession of Holocaust deniers and the weakness of many anti-Zionists. These rewritings are termed 'counter-histories'. Their function is polemical. They cast the Jews as criminals; they distort the Jews' self-image through the deconstruction of their memory.[394] There is a quality of counter-history in much writing about Israel and the Zionist project now. Especially salient in this counter-history—which has become the received narrative—is the proposition that there was no Arab, and in particular no Palestinian, participation in the Nazi genocide of the Jews. This has indeed become a staple of anti-Zionist polemic: the Palestinians are paying the price of exclusively Western guilt.

And yet...the Arab rejection of the Peel Commission partition proposal, a rejection that in turn led to the punitive restrictions on Jewish immigration into Palestine, was a calamity for European Jewry. Haj Amin al-Husseini (1895–1974), the most prominent Palestinian political and religious leader of his time, the chairman of the Supreme Muslim Council and the Grand Mufti of Jerusalem, worked for the Nazis in Berlin from 1941 to 1945, broadcasting Nazi propaganda to the Arab world, obstructing wartime Jewish emigration from Europe, and helping to raise a collaborationist Muslim brigade in Bosnia. There was substantial Palestinian Arab sympathy for the Nazi cause, a boycotting by Palestinians of the local force raised by the British to aid the war effort, and significant Arab Nazi activism. Further, there was Arab participation in Holocaust-era violence against Jews, mainly in consequence of Nazi, fascist, and Vichy persecutions of Jews in the Arab lands of the southern shore of the Mediterranean; and there were terrible pogroms in Iraq and elsewhere in the Arab world. The Holocaust was *not* solely a European story, then.[395] These contributions to the Nazi war-effort produced some dividends for later Arab efforts against Jewish settlements and population centres in Palestine. The chief bomb-maker for the Husseini-affiliated irregular Palestinian troops, Fawzi al-Kutab, learned his craft in an SS course in Nazi Germany. His work included a truck-bombing on 22 February 1948 in the centre of the Jewish part of Jerusalem, killing fifty-eight people and seriously wounding thirty-two others.[396]

The Zionist/Nazi trope

There was a certain vogue, at one time, to account for the Nazi genocide as a kind of Crucifixion. The Jews were crucified by Nazi Germany it was said. The Jews were millennially accused of crucifying Jesus; but it is they who have been crucified, by Jesus' own followers. The rebuke was to Christianity, and the Christian legacy of Jew-hatred Nazism inherited and then radicalized. This trope of the 'crucified Jews', to be found in both writing and painting that addressed the Holocaust, effects an inversion, the persecuted becoming persecutor. An event that defines Christian identity is appropriated to an account of a radically different event, one that brings shame on Christianity and calls into question its moral purpose. If Christian worship and belief can lead to genocide, should one not shrink from the religion in horror? A similar mechanism is at work in the current vogue to account for the Israel–Palestinian conflict as a kind of Holocaust. It is a companion to the 'Israel is doing to the Palestinians what the Jews did to Jesus' trope, which also has a certain currency now.

The 'Jews as Nazis' trope, or 'Holocaust inversion'[397] is very common in the iconography of the new anti-Zionism—the Star of David morphing into the Swastika, Israeli leaders morphing into Hitler, IDF soldiers morphing into jackbooted stormtroopers, Palestinians as victims of a new Holocaust, etc. In 1968, the drawing of analogies between Israel and the Nazis was a deliberate provocation; in the mid-to late 1970s, it was one of the tactics used by anti-Zionist groups to demoralize Jewish students on English campuses;[398] by 2003, it had become a reflex. In 1968, the journalist Michael Adams, active in the Council for the Advancement of Arab–British Understanding ('CAABU'), contributed a piece to the *Guardian* about the occupied territories: 'I had my ups and downs during four years as a prisoner of war in Germany, but the Germans never treated me as harshly as the Israelis are treating the Arabs of the Gaza Strip . . .' The outcry in response to the piece was so great that the then editor told Adams that he regretted publishing it.[399] By 2003, however, when Ray Davies, a Labour councillor in Wales, was reported as remarking, 'Hitler's Nazi regime occupied Europe for four years only. Palestine and the West Bank have been occupied for 40 years',[400] he was merely making a connection that was commonplace.

The playing of the 'Hitler card' has become a common move in political debate;[401] whatever is disliked is described as 'Fascist'. Nazi iniquities now comprise a fund for the polemically incontinent to draw upon in the abuse of enemies and adversaries.[402] In Israel, it tends to be the Zionist Right that draws on this language; in Europe, it is the anti-Zionist Left.[403] This is almost always a discreditable move. It is made by Hamas, for example, in its Charter (see arts. 20 and 31).[404] The move is particularly common in online discussions. According to *Godwin's Law*, as the discussion continues, the probability of a comparison involving Nazis or Hitler approaches 1. The law has encouraged the practice among Usenet newsgroups of ending the thread once such a comparison is made.

The Zionist/Nazi trope compounds several distinct defamations:

- *The 'Zionists' and the Nazis are said to share the Fascist ideology.* State worship, and concepts of 'chosenness' and blood kinship, are said equally to dominate Nazi and Zionist thinking. Nazis and 'Zionists' are said to share other values too—a preoccupation with 'discipline', for example.[405] (These particular defamations have the most remote derivation, dating back to smart, pre–war commonplaces about the Nazis' indebtedness to the Jewish conception of 'chosenness'.)[406]

- *The 'Zionists' are said to have been complicit with the Nazis in the Holocaust.* 'Zionists' are said to have collaborated with the Nazis; they are said to have bargained with the Nazis; they are said to have been indifferent to the fate of the Jews trapped on the Continent; the Nazis and the 'Zionists' are said to have agreed that the Jews had to leave Europe; the Nazis and the 'Zionists' are said to have been similarly scornful of the Diaspora Jew. The 'Zionists' financed the genocide;[407] they misled the Jewish masses; they had a role in organizing the mass destruction of Jews.[408] In consequence, 'Zionism' was responsible, or partly responsible, for the Holocaust.

- *The 'Zionists' are said to be to the Palestinians what the Nazis were to the Jews.* It was common for the PLO to declare, 'The Zionist rulers today appear before the world as the inheritors of Nazism and Fascism.'[409] Hamas now competes with, and indeed exceeds, this rhetoric: 'We have no alternative but to pool all our forces and energies to face this despicable Nazi-Tartar invasion.'[410] Political commentators and columnists in the West likewise pitch in: 'In 1935, Goebbels said: "Many intellectuals are trying to help the Jews with the ancient phrase, 'The Jew is also a man'. Yes, he is a man, but what sort of man? The flea is also an animal!" Today, Semites treat the Arab brother as the flea, or the "other".'[411]

The implications? There can be no compromise with Zionism, because it is the expression in collective political form of the principle of evil. 'Zionists', understood to comprise all who favour Israel's continued existence, are complicit in Israel's Nazi-like crimes, and thus merit extreme opprobrium. Israel deserves the same fate as Nazi Germany; 'Zionists' are not entitled to complain if they are treated harshly, or even injured or killed. The nation is evil; its (Jewish) citizens are evil, or abet evil; Diaspora Jewry is made up of complicit bystanders or worse.[412] So anti-Semitism has returned in the guise of anti-Nazism.[413] There are a number of aspects to this trope.

First, it is historical nonsense. The Nazis were not Zionist; the Zionists were not Nazi. To the Jews, Zionist and non-Zionist alike, a Nazi victory would have been the ultimate catastrophe. The Zionists, of course, wanted to leave Germany for Palestine. The Nazis were anti-Semites; the Zionists wanted a life for Jews free of anti-Semitism. Some Nazis were keen to see Jews go—though others wanted to kill them all where they stood, and still others wanted to confine them in 'reservations'.[414] The 12,000 German Jews who left for Palestine between 1933 and 1937 under the Transfer Agreement were 12,000 Jews saved. The Nazis did not want a state for the Jews. It would give legal protection to Jews throughout the world. 'Germany has an interest in strengthening the Arab world as a counterweight against such a possible increase in power for world Jewry', declared Germany's foreign minister, von Neurath.[415] These policy positions flowed from Hitler's own doctrinal opposition to Zionism:

> while Zionism tries to make the other part of the world believe that the national self-consciousness of the Jew finds satisfaction in the creation of a Palestinian State, the Jews again most slyly dupe the stupid *goyim*. They have no thought of building up a Jewish State in Palestine, so that they might perhaps inhabit it, but they only want a central organisation of their international world cheating, endowed with prerogatives, withdrawn from the seizure of others: a refuge for convicted rascals and a high school for future rogues.[416]

In his interview with the Mufti on 30 November 1941, Hitler explained, 'Germany stood for uncompromising war against Jews. That naturally included active opposition to the Jewish national home in Palestine, which was nothing other than a centre, in the form of a state, for the exercise of destructive influence by Jewish interests.'[417] By contrast, on the day Britain declared war, the Jewish Agency declared its total support; even the Revisionists, who had been conducting an anti-British campaign following the White Paper, declared a truce, and then offered military assistance.[418] During the war, the Nazi Press Office instructed the German press to replace 'anti-Semitism' with such expressions as 'opposition to Jews', 'hostility to Jews', and 'anti-Judaism', for fear of 'destroying our relationships with non-Jewish Semites—namely, the pan-Arab world which is so important to us'.[419]

Secondly, it has a distinct provenance, originating in Soviet polemic. Zionism as the new Nazism became the major trope in 1960s and 1970s Soviet anti-Semitism, spawning many articles, pamphlets, and books. For example, at the UN on 14 October 1965, the Soviet Union and Poland opposed a proposal that the Charter of Human Rights should contain a clause banning anti-Semitism. Instead, they pressed for an amendment classifying Zionism, Nazism, and Neo-Nazism (in that order) as racial crimes.[420] This was taken up in Arab political discourse. For example, on 16 October 1973, Anwar Sadat declared 'our war is a continuation of humanity's war against Fascism and Nazism; for, by its racist claims and its reasoning of expansion through brute force, Zionism is nothing but a feeble replica of Fascism and Nazism which is contemptible rather than frightening and calls for disdain rather than hatred'. As in the Soviet precedent, the trope is on occasion rather frivolously deployed. Later on, in the same speech, Sadat announced, 'we are prepared . . . to attend an international peace conference'. And four years later, in a speech to the Knesset, he declared: 'In all sincerity I tell you we welcome you among us with full security and safety.'[421] Again, as in Soviet precedent, the trope is subjected to an uncontrolled inflation of language. 'Zionism is only another face of Nazism, but rather a double Nazism', wrote a correspondent for *Al-Ahram*. 'Israel is racist, Sharon is racist, the Israelis are racist. They are more racist than the Nazis', declared President Assad of Syria.[422]

Thirdly, it is the latest version of that much older trope, 'persecuted Jews become persecutors'. Consider the sermon preached by Herbert of Losinga, the bishop of Norwich (d. 1119), 'On the birthday of our Lord'.[423] He says that he intends to relate a story, one that he learned from a faithful report. There was a certain city of the Greeks in which Jews and Christians dwelt together. The Jews, and in particular their children, were thus exposed to Christian teaching. In consequence, on the holy day of Easter a Jewish boy went to Church and received Communion. He then went home and told his mother what he had done. She was very angry with him, and told his father. He was even angrier, and threw his son into a furnace and then sealed up its mouth. This was too much for the mother, and she ran to her Christian neighbours for help. They raced to the furnace, broke it open, and pulled the child out. He was alive, safe, and unharmed. It was a miracle of the Virgin. Herbert concludes the story:

> Forthwith there followed a most just vengeance on the heads of the Jews; and they who would not believe in the Incarnate Word were all alike burned in the aforesaid furnace.

Though his are the only extant sermons of an English bishop of this period, Herbert's sermons have been taken to reflect the general tendencies of the times. He and his contemporaries were using the same sources. He was no intellectual innovator; his sermons are derived from the writings of others; he was quite unoriginal. This story was itself one of the most popular of all medieval sermon-stories, in the most popular of genres, the miracles of the Virgin.[424] It is likely that Herbert took the anecdote from Gregory of Tours.

Gregory expressly relates it to the story in the Book of Daniel of the three children in the Nebuchadnezzar's furnace. The Jews are now the perpetrators of what once was done to them.[425] This has become a familiar trope of anti-Semitic anti-Zionism, where for 'Babylonians', read 'Nazis' and for 'Christians' read 'Palestinians'.

Fourthly, it now coexists with, and draws (perhaps remote) strength from, a certain contemporary tendency to strive for provocative formulations in the writing of the Holocaust's history, one that entails injudicious analogies, and a readiness to blur the line between victim and perpetrator. Representative of this tendency, in ways relevant to the topic of this part of the present chapter, is Norman Davies' considerable work, *Europe* (1996). It is marked by an occasional glibness of tone, and a somewhat wayward ambition to write with originality and political point. Davies is a historian of strong opinions, and offers a personal view of Europe's history. In a passage on the French Revolution, he compares the murderous ingenuity of French Republican officers in Nantes with the murderous ingenuity of Nazi officers in occupied Poland.[426] Somewhat later in the book, he records that on 13 July 1942, members of German Reserve Police Battalion 101, following the orders of their SS officers, murdered about 1,500 Jewish men, women, and children in the Polish town, Otwock. He ponders, what would Jews do if given such a command? Jewish policemen in the Nazis' ghettoes, and Jewish *Sonderkommandos* in the death camps, cooperated in heinous acts. Worse, in post-war Eastern Europe, 'the notorious communist Security Office (UB) [which] contained a disproportionate number of Jews (or rather ex-Jews)' committed many terrible crimes.[427]

Lastly, it comprises an insult—let me associate you with what you hold to be most obnoxious, most polluted. Within your own world, today, what is it that you most loathe? The Nazis who murdered your parents, your siblings, and your children?—Well, *you* are Nazis. And in earlier times, in medieval times? The pig you are prohibited from consuming? Well, *you* are pigs. The antecedent to the 'Jewish Nazi' insult is the '*Judensau*' or 'Jewish pig' insult. The former is as common now as was the latter in the late Middle Ages.[428] While the medieval mind holds the Jews to be no better than pigs,[429] in the contemporary imagination they are no better than Nazis. The medieval mind presents the pig as progenitor or nurturer of the Jew;[430] in the contemporary imagination, Hitler is the progenitor or nurturer of the Jew.[431] The medieval mind holds Jew-pigs to be child-murderers;[432] in the contemporary imagination, Jew-Nazis are child-murderers.

It follows from the above that it is an understatement to dismiss the Jew/ Nazi tropes as *mere* abuse. Yet one British commentator complains that too much is made of them—and for certain, that they are not anti-Semitic:

> analogies with Nazi Germany . . . should be deplored on grounds of both historical truth and taste. But are they anti-Semitic as opposed to just plain obnoxious? Those who resort to them know they are bogus, but they understand their shock value and hope to shame and anger Israel and its supporters into modifying their behaviour.[433]

Compare Salmawy's defence of the blood libel (see Chapter 2). The notion that what are acknowledged to be misconceived insults are nonetheless likely to be persuasive, or otherwise likely to modify the behaviour of the insulted party, is somewhat odd.

So unreflective is the use of the Nazi/Zionist trope that it is even used by activists quick to deplore analogies with Nazism in every other context. Take Tariq Ali, for example:

> From the moment of its foundation, the Zionist leaders of Israel were determined to depopulate the country. They wanted a home that matched the myth they had fostered in Europe of a 'land without a people.' The Palestinians were now a non-people. Those who could not be driven out were treated like *Untermenschen*.[434]

Now compare that very specific invocation of Nazism ('*Untermenschen*') with this passage from the same book, *The Clash of Fundamentalisms* (2003):

> Ever since the Second World War the name of Hitler and his philosophy has been recklessly invoked to drum up public support for Western wars. . . . During the First Oil War (Suez) in 1956, Britain characterised the Egyptian leader, Gamel Abdel Nasser, as the 'Hitler on the Nile;' for the duration of the Third Oil War (*a.k.a.* the Gulf War) the Hitler badge was pinned on the lapel of the Iraqi leader, Saddam Hussein. . . . When Madeleine Albright decided that a war was needed in Kosovo . . . the Serbian leader was provided with the familiar sobriquet: Milosevic became Hitler. It was inevitable that, sooner or later, an apologist for the latest war would describe the latest enemy as 'fascist.' The metamorphosis is triggered only when the 'fascists' are opposed to US interests. . . . To dress all new enemies in the black shirts and leather jackets of European fascism is grotesque.[435]

In this second passage, Ali is deploring the use of the term 'Islamo-fascism'.

On 25 January 2007, the Edinburgh branch of the Palestine Solidarity Campaign staged a performance of Jim Allen's play, *Perdition*. The performance took place two days before Holocaust Memorial Day, and during the week when events commemorating the Holocaust were taking place. The PSC advertised the performance on the HMD Trust website. There were protests, and the advert was removed. This in turn provoked protests from the PSC and others. One protester characterized it as a 'ban on discussion of Palestine'; another protester wrote, 'I am deeply shocked...that the Holocaust Memorial Trust is seeking to narrow the focus of Holocaust Memorial Day in order to exclude any discussion of the past role of Zionists in collaborating with Nazism and the present role of Zionism in ethnically cleansing the Palestinian people.'[436]

Perdition was written twenty years earlier, in 1987, for performance at a London theatre, the Royal Court. The author described it as 'the most lethal attack on Zionism ever written'.[437] It is a fictional version of a libel case tried in Israel in 1954–5. It had been alleged against the claimant, Rudolf Kasztner, that when on the wartime Rescue Committee in Budapest he had collaborated with the Nazis to save himself, his family, and certain Zionist leaders, while deserting the Jews in his charge. Kasztner sued his accuser, winning only token damages at trial. He appealed, but was assassinated before being more generously vindicated in Israel's Supreme Court. This was a quarrel *within* the Zionist movement. Kasztner's adversary came from the Zionist Right; Kasztner himself was part of Labour Zionist.[438] In Allen's play, Ruth Kaplan, an Israeli pacifist and civil rights activist living in London, is the defendant in libel proceedings brought by Dr Yaron. The action concerns a pamphlet written by Kaplan accusing Yaron, a Hungarian Jew and Holocaust survivor, of Nazi collaboration. At the end of the trial, which Kaplan wins, Yaron remarks, 'When I sat in that witness box, *I* was on trial.' The play also puts Zionism and Israel on trial. In a final twist, Yaron reveals that he sued Kaplan in order to expose himself. As if in imitation of a show trial,[439] the play treats this ploy of Yaron's as a kind of expiation through confession. Jewish Zionist self-accuser and Jewish anti-Zionist accuser thereby make common cause in condemnation of Zionism's history and ideology.

Yaron is the fictional representative of a Zionist conspiracy. The conspirators at first colluded in the Nazi persecution of the Jews, and then attempted to conceal news of the massacres (for fear that the news might have persuaded 'other countries to open doors to Jewish refugees').[440] Such private protests as were made by the Zionists were made only 'so that after the war they would be able to say that everything possible had been done'.[441] Zionists were ready to sacrifice the generality of European Jewry in order to foster the environment for a Jewish state. 'Our Zionist tradition compelled us to save the few out of the many', says Yaron.[442] The Zionists wanted to salvage 'the best biological material'.[443] Jews would have resisted the Nazis, had their Zionist leaders not manipulated them into acquiescence. 'The Nazis controlled the Councils, the Councils controlled the Jews.'[444] It was the Zionists' 'policy' to 'mak[e] deals with the Nazis both before and during World War II'.[445] They sought 'a special relationship' with Hitler.[446] The Zionists trapped in Europe were also cowards, willing to trade Jewish lives for their own. They 'bought their own lives with the price of silence'.[447] Other Zionist leaders simply 'sat out [the war] in Palestine'.[448] Zionism is racist, and therefore ideologically predisposed to favour Nazism.

This is the play's account of the Holocaust:

> The sheer physical task of uprooting six million people, of removing them from their homes in towns and cities, herding them into ghettoes and marching them to the collecting points, and finally shipping them on special trains to the death camps would have been impossible. What made it possible was the presence of Jewish leaders who carried out the instructions of the Nazis.[449]

How *could* it have happened? Was it because the Nazis were able to outwit the Jews, at every turn,[450] taking them by surprise (and who could fail to be surprised by the Nazis' plans?), a victory over the Jews secured by cunning and ruthlessness? Did the awesome power of the Nazis' totalitarian structures have a crippling effect on the human personality?[451] Was it because the Holocaust was an incremental process, each stage misunderstood as the final one? In the camps themselves, was the 'Jewish will to resist' sapped by the transience of the population, the absence of outside resistance committees, and so on?[452] Had passivity become an aspect of the Jewish response to a hostile environment, learned over hundreds of years, a strategy of placatory acquiescence, a 'vocation for surrender'?[453] Or was it the 'Jewish tradition of trusting God, princes, laws and contracts'?[454] The question of resistance is complex, incapable of a single answer, immensely difficult, and painful, too—almost intolerably so.[455] There *was* resistance: uprisings in ghettoes, revolts in death camps, and Jewish participation in partisan movements.[456] There were also instances of escape, though the Nazis could rely on the refusal of individuals to take flight, if flight meant abandoning parents or children.[457] And last of all—and only as a specific and limited question, asked solely in respect of those Jews confined in ghettoes prior to transportation and murder—was it because the Jewish Councils assisted the Nazis in their work?

The last question is the only one that interests Allen. The answer to it is that there was a diversity of official or organized Jewish responses, and among those who *did* do the Nazis' work, *none did so as collaborators*.[458] They did not assist the Nazis in combating the underground. The Councils and the underground agreed that the existence of the ghettoes was to be prolonged for as long as possible and that an uprising was only to take place at the moment of final liquidation. The clashes between the Councils and the underground only took place when there was a disagreement between them on whether underground activities jeopardized the policy of maintaining the ghettoes. Neither the Councils nor the underground could affect the ultimate survival of the Jewish masses in the ghettoes.[459] Further, it is simply a lie to assert that there were Zionists who preferred that Jewish refugees perish rather than permit them to be diverted to destinations other than Palestine.[460] Certainly, as a recent study of the Holocaust in Hungary concludes, the members of the Budapest Rescue Committee were themselves captives and victims of the SS and the Reich's merciless extermination machine.[461] Primo Levi once judged the confusing of murderers with their victims to be 'a moral disease *or* an aesthetic affectation *or* a sinister sign of complicity'.[462] In Allen's case—that is to say, in the case of *Perdition*—the confusing of Nazis with Jewish Zionists evidences both a 'moral disease' and a certain aesthetic affectation, as well as also deriving from a broader political confusion or bewilderment.

The Bolshevik anti-Zionist stands in momentary perplexity before the Holocaust and is forced to wonder whether the Zionists were right in their assessment of the lethal character of European anti-Semitism and the consequent need for a Jewish homeland.[463] He enters a moment of crisis, contemplating history's defeat of his programme for the Jews.[464] And then the consoling answer dawns—the Holocaust happened only because the Zionist leaders of the Jews *allowed* it to happen, and because the Jewish people submitted to it. A self-serving 'Holocaust falsification' comes to his aid, comparable to the value of Holocaust denial to the *Protocols* affirmer. 'The Jews lived in close-knit communities and did what their Elders, their leaders, told them',[465] Jim Allen's prosecutorial defence lawyer explains. These 'Elders', the powerful Jews, 'strangled all mass activity',[466] and thus sacrificed the powerless Jews. Were it not for that, catastrophe would have been avoided. But the Zionists made a strategic mistake. They are not safer in their Jewish State: 'The Arab countries can absorb defeat', the defence lawyer adds. 'Israel cannot. In which case the temptation to use nuclear weapons will be great. Then what? Another holocaust? Computerized, clean, more efficient? You [i.e., the Jews] should have stayed in Europe...'[467] The Bolsheviks were right after all. Zionism is a dead-end for the Jews. Literally, a dead end—it ultimately will cause their death.

In the event, the play was not performed at the Royal Court. The author and director alleged that it had been banned, in consequence of pressure from a 'clique' able to 'buy their own way'.[468] The theatre's artistic director responded, however, that he had merely 'lost confidence in the play's credibility'.[469]

Anti-Zionism as anti-racism/anti-Judaism

The twentieth century witnessed both the greatest assault *of* racism, and the greatest assault *on* racism. The racism of the Nazis destroyed almost an entire people; anti-colonial movements struggled to liberate entire continents. The Nazis demonstrated racism's genocidal capacities; the anti-colonial movements exposed racism's modern institutional forms, imperialism and colonialism. In consequence, racism became the worst offence; it was shorthand for all that was wrong in the world; whatever could be described as racist had to be rejected. 'Anti-racism' became the founding position of all liberal-Left politics. In recent times, its meaning has expanded somewhat, and it is now commonly understood to comprise any stance of disrespect by a dominant or majority group towards a subordinate or minority group.

This expansion of meaning has been accompanied by certain further developments of particular relevance to Jews. Anti-Semitism has faded from general political consciousness; Zionism has come to be characterized as racist; 'Islamophobia' has come to be regarded by many as the worst, or most threatening, of contemporary racisms; Judaism has begun to attract censure as racist. The effect of these developments has been to put Jews, and in particular those Jews with an attachment to Israel, on the wrong side of what is taken to be the critical political divide, that is, between racists and anti-racists. Each development requires examination. Though this chapter is concerned with England, much of the history has more general application to Europe.

Anti-Semitism faded from political consciousness in the 1970s   There were several reasons for this development. It was, in part, because the Six Day War presented the world with a compelling demonstration of the martial powers of the Jewish State. It was no longer necessary to worry about the Jews. In some fundamental, unspoken sense, the conclusion was drawn, 'they can look after themselves'. This is perhaps the explanation for anti-Semitism often being omitted from the anti-racism and diversity training[470] that is now common in the public and voluntary sectors. It was also, in part, because the political Right grew preoccupied with an undifferentiated Afro-Caribbean and Asian immigration to Britain, conceived as a densely populated, overcrowded, small island, at risk of being 'swamped' by 'people with a different culture'.[471] As the authors of a study of the 'new racism' wrote, 'although anti-Semitism, anti-Irish racism and other forms of chauvinism sometimes feature, the main thrust is against black people'.[472] It was in part, because the kind of people most likely to be troubled by racism stopped thinking about anti-Semitism. It was treated as a component of an outdated ideology, a 'relic',[473] merely an aspect of the pre-history of contemporary racist groupings, a prejudice that thus had lost its capacity to injure. And it was also because, in consequence of a certain post-war obsession with Nazism,[474] the Holocaust came to condition the understanding of anti-Semitism. Anti-Semitism, that is, was understood to comprise state-sponsored violence, one that starts at street level and ends in death camps, speaks German, and has its ideological home on the Right. A new illiteracy thus developed in the decades that followed concerning anti-Semitic language and iconography, which precisely was *not* state-sponsored, did *not* speak German, and did *not* have its ideological home on the Right. While it is, for example, an overstatement to characterize as 'anti-Semitic attacks'[475] the Labour Party election posters in 2005 associating the Conservative Party politicians, Michael Howard and Oliver Letwin, with pigs and (in the case of Howard) Shylock,[476] the posters evidenced a culpable ignorance of anti-Semitism's long pre-Holocaust history.

Zionism came to be characterized as racist   In the same decade, and as no coincidence, just as anti-Semitism faded away, so anti-Zionism emerged, and Zionism came to be characterized as 'racist.' This characterization has persisted, its two symbolic moments being the 1975 'Zionism is racism' resolution at the United Nations, which denied to the Jews in Palestine the right to their own state,[477] and the 2001 UN Conference Against Racism in Durban, a festival of anti-Israel, anti-Zionist, anti-Semitic hatred.[478] While the conference drew together the tropes of the new anti-Zionism, and boosted the morale of its champions, it also exposed them to hostile scrutiny.[479] A constant theme was the indictment of Zionist 'racism' and the dismissal of Jew-hatred. A delegate from Iran, for example, called Zionism 'the greatest manifestation of racism' while demanding that anti-Semitism be struck from the conference's official register of bigotries because it is not a 'contemporary form of racism'.[480] Recent developments at the UN have been no less discouraging. Only *Jewish* nationalism is condemned—just as in earlier times, it was only Jewish *capitalism* that was condemned. The anti-Semitic pedigree of the 'Zionism is racism' resolution should not have been hard to spot.[481] Resentment towards what is considered to be Jewish exclusiveness is very ancient indeed. It is a note sounded very early on in the history of Christianity. 'And [Peter] said unto them, Ye know how that it is an unlawful thing for a man that is a Jew to keep company, or come unto one of another nation; but God hath shewed me that I should not call any man common or unclean' (Acts 10:28).

'Islamophobia' came to be regarded as the worst, or most threatening, of contemporary racisms   'Islamophobia', by which was meant irrational hostility to Muslims and to Islam, was added in the 1990s to the class of racisms. It was taken to be rife: on a representative occasion, Ken Livingstone referred to a media 'orgy of Islamophobia'.[482] Islamophobia would turn ordinary Muslims into terrorists, it was suggested.[483] It was also taken to be threatening in the same degree as the threat posed by anti-Semitism to Europe's Jews in the 1930s. 'Muslims are the new Jews', announced a *Times* columnist.[484] These claims were, and remain, somewhat overstated.[485] Further, allegations of Islamophobia have had several unhappy consequences: the violent intimidation of people perceived to be 'Islamophobes', and a consequent chilling effect on free speech;[486] the suppression of any consideration of Islamic anti-Semitism on the basis that the topic is itself in some sense 'racist';[487] and a victim mentality among British Muslims.[488] A more critical perspective is in consequence now emerging on 'Islamophobia', though it remains a minority one.[489]

Judaism itself began to attract censure as racist   It is now commonly suggested that Judaism, or in another formulation, the Old Testament, is at the root of

Zionist criminality. John Pilger writes of 'the Biblo-ethnic cleansers in Israel'.[490] George Monbiot writes, 'the Mosaic doctrine of *terra nullius* (the inhabitants possess no legal rights to their land), which permitted the Lord's appointed to "smite the corners of Moab, and destroy all the children of Sheth", has become the founding creed of the usurper all over the world. It continues to inform the land seizures in modern Israel, seeking now to turn itself into a walled garden . . . '[491] These positions, published respectively in the *New Statesman* and the *Guardian*, are also being taken elsewhere in Europe. The Nobel laureate José Saramago has written, 'Israel is a racist state by virtue of Judaism's monstrous doctrines—racist not just against the Palestinians, but against the entire world, which it seeks to manipulate and abuse.'[492] The Norwegian novelist, Jostein Gaarder, author of *Sophie's World*, contributed this observation, 'To act as God's chosen people is not only foolish and arrogant, it is a crime against humanity. We call it racism.'[493] 'Election', or 'chosenness', is inherently racist, and justifies the brutal treatment of the non-elect.[494] This is a developing theme among certain Jewish anti-Zionists;[495] it is common in the Arab world, where the casual defamation of Jews extends to a similarly casual defamation of their religion.[496] It is no different in character to the anti-Semitic execrations of the 'Law of Moses' and the 'Jewish character', in the aftermath of the Russian Revolution.[497] It dehistoricizes the Hebrew Scriptures, as Daniel and Jonathan Boyarin argue, holding historically and materially defined local practices of a culture far away and long ago as responsible for the colonial practices of cultures entirely other to it, simply because those later cultures used those practices as their authorization. It also exonerates European Christian society, the religious hegemonic system for virtually all of the imperialist, racist, and even genocidal societies of the West, and it disregards the rabbinic ruling that the scriptural injunction against the Canaanites was limited to those particular people in that particular place and time, and is thus no longer applicable.[498]

Anti-racism is especially, though somewhat counter-intuitively, susceptible to anti-Semitic pollution. Jews now fall foul of anti-racists, and on occasion need to invoke the protection of anti-race discrimination legislation *against* trades unions and other elements on the self-identifying political Left.[499] Anti-Judaism is the most problematic aspect of this most problematic of currents. It is made up of bad arguments; it resonates in anti-Semitism's history; it draws on anti-Semitic tropes. There is no such thing as a 'Mosaic' doctrine of *terra nullius*. Characterizing Judaism as a religion of conquest requires disregarding all the passages in the Hebrew Scriptures that teach respect for the stranger (for example, Exodus 23:9, and Leviticus 19:33–4). It also requires disregarding the refusal of the *Tanach* to treat the injunctions to extirpate Amalek and the Canaanites as precedent-establishing. These injunctions no more enjoin murder and conquest than does the *Akedah* mandate child sacrifice. On the contrary, they teach precisely that no other people may be treated thus, just as the *Akedah* teaches that no other child may be treated thus. In any event, characterizing Zionism as a derivative of Judaism disregards the *dis*connection between the secular Zionists and the *Tanach*. The later, religious Zionist critique of the Labour Zionists is precisely that they built a country with a Judaic void in its heart; they built a nationalism without reclaiming Judaism.[500] But they did not come to Palestine armed. Their ambition, as Ruth Wisse has correctly observed, was to subdue with the plough the land that both Christians and Muslims had conquered with a sword.[501] Violence took them by surprise—and then, falteringly at first, they responded.

Within the history of anti-Semitism, this attack on Judaism has three distinct sources. First, there is an Enlightenment source, though the 'new' anti-Zionist' version is a departure from Voltaire in two respects: there is no hostility to Mohammed here, and anti-Zionism is grafted onto anti-Judaism. Secondly, there is a more proximate Soviet source. In officially sponsored books such as *Judaism without Embellishment* (1963), *Judaism and Zionism* (1968), Judaism was travestied as a doctrine that teaches thievery, betrayal, and perfidy, and a poisonous hatred for all other peoples. Zionism, wrote the author of these works, teaches 'the chauvinistic idea of the God-chosenness of the Jewish people'. Another text, *The School of Obscurantism* (1972), published in the official bulletin of the Soviet Information Office in Paris, explained that Judaism's sacred books are the source of the 'racism' and 'atrocities' committed by Israel and 'international Zionism'.[502] Third, there is a contemporary Islamist source, most succinctly expressed by a senior Muslim cleric on Al-Manar: 'There is no such thing as Zionism, there is only Judaism.'[503]

As I have argued, contemporary anti-Semitism escapes notice in part because it is somewhat different to the Nazi model. It is *not* state-sponsored and it is *not* violent (not in the main, that is). Indeed, this contemporary anti-Semitism is consistent with expressions of piety towards the dead of the

Holocaust. The *pre*-Nazi history of anti-Semitism has been lost. This is a cultural amnesia that resists cure. There is an unwillingness to learn about, or to acknowledge, the diverse versions of anti-Semitism that preceded the Nazi one. This unwillingness has a strategic value. To limit anti-Semitism to its Nazi variant permits the argument: 'I cannot be an anti-Semite, I am a person of the Left, the history of the Leftist struggle against anti-Semitism speaks through me.' This argument, or versions of it, is much used now. Karl Lueger once declared, 'I decide who is a Jew.'[504] The new anti-Zionists may be taken to declare, 'We decide who is an anti-Semite.' Anti-Semitism is a bulky presence in the history and consciousness of the West. The notion that it was somehow dispelled, or overcome, in the few years following the Holocaust is false, as is the related notion that anti-Semitism has no influence on anti-Zionist positions nowadays. *Of course* some of the rhetoric of anti-Israel movements contains anti-Semitic themes.[505] Anti-Semitism continues to confront Jews both as a menace and as a puzzle.

New anti-Zionists and the phenomenon of 'fellow travelling'

In 2005, three Jewish members of the National Union of Students resigned from their positions in the union. One of them, Luciana Berger, the then 'anti-racism convenor', explained her position to the union's conference:

> This year, a comment was made in a Student Union saying that burning down a synagogue is a rational act. When asked to comment, NEC members could not even bring themselves to condemn that statement. Over five months ago serious complaints were lodged about antisemitic comments made by an NEC member in a public meeting. There is yet to be any form of official response to these complaints. . . . While I accuse no one of antisemitism, this year NUS has been a bystander to Jew-hatred.[506]

The question arises, is it right to characterize as anti-Semitic those adverse stances towards Israel and the Zionist project that are derived from false facts, and/or are malicious, and/or are taken without regard to Jewish objections, and/or resonate with anti-Semitism's history and/or deploy anti-Semitic tropes? Mostly, the answer is 'yes'—particularly when several of these features are combined. But in certain instances, the answer might be, 'no'—or 'not quite'.

First, the affirmative answer might be a tactical mistake. It might be received as merely abusive—no more than a piece of name-calling. It often serves as a mere provocation, inviting the tedious riposte, 'I am not an anti-Semite, indeed I deplore anti-Semitism, I am instead a partisan of the Palestinians, you are making a false accusation of anti-Semitism to squash my unanswerable case, etc.' Why, then, take this step, one which almost always signals the end of any useful exchange of views, and instead inaugurates the trading of insults, the argument no longer being about the coherence of the stance, but instead about the respective moral character of its advocates and critics?[507]

Secondly, the affirmative answer might be premature. Anti-Semitic anti-Zionism is so much part of the *zeitgeist*, it is reasonable to assume that many of the people who draw upon its tropes do so without reflection. If they are open to correction when the provenance of their language is pointed out to them, they are not anti-Semites. Anti-Semites are obdurate in their Jew-hatred. They display their anti-Semitism as much in their defences and counter-charges to accusations of anti-Semitism as in their discoursing about Israel, the Jewish Lobby, and Jews. They defend by accusation, relying on well-understood tropes of Jewish infamy—the Jews' use of their political or financial power to silence truth-tellers, the exploitation of their historic suffering to gain present-day advantages, a ready resort to character-assassination or smear, and so on.

Finally, a 'yes' risks lumping together two kinds of people. For the first kind, anti-Semitism determines their positions; they embrace Jew hatred; they acknowledge and welcome the anti-Semitism of others. For the second kind, anti-Semitism is not relevant to the positions that they take; they do not recoil from anti-Semitism when they encounter it; they are insensitive to the presence of anti-Semitism in their own positions or in the positions that they support. They may not be anti-Semites themselves, but they collude with anti-Semitism. They are often found defending anti-Semites—not guilty of the offence themselves, but quick to champion others who *are* guilty of it. The distinction I am drawing is between the culpable adoption of anti-Semitism and a culpable indifference towards it. Many 'new anti-Zionists' bear this latter, lesser responsibility. They share space with anti-Semites, untroubled by the company that they keep; they comprise a species of 'fellow traveller' ('bystander' does not quite do the vice justice), the kind of person ready to overlook or excuse everything that is vicious in the cause he supports, the protagonists he admires.

The Soviet analogy

The first fellow travellers were the early supporters of the Bolshevik revolution.[508] They were non-Party progressives who had, in Trotsky's phrase, 'turned their eyes eastwards'[509] (though over time that came to include China—and then they turned westward, to Cuba). Mostly, they were intellectuals, in the broadest sense of the term. 'Fellow traveller' did not at first have pejorative overtones; many progressives were happy to describe themselves thus.[510] The fellow travellers of the Soviet Union (FTSUs) share many traits with those new anti-Zionists who are also anti-Semitism's fellow travellers (FTASs).[511]

They tend to be similarly reality-denying in their perspectives on Russia/Palestine. The FTSUs romanticized; they propagandized; they misled. They sent despatches from Russia intended to dispel hostile impressions; they colluded in 'conducted tours', when shown only what Party-minders presented. Famines, mass deportations, show trials, slave labour camps, killings—all were suppressed or excused. ('All [will] be right when the new civilisation [is] stabilised...')[512] Russia only wants peace, whereas the Western democracies are warmongers and imperialists. The FTASs perform similar services for Ahmadinejad,[513] for Hezbollah, and for Hamas. They deny the reality of anti-Semitism in the West; they regard it as either invented to suppress criticism of Israel, or else a misnamed European Muslim indignation. They deny the reality of anti-Semitism in the Middle East; when they acknowledge it at all, they regard it as no more than a polemical extravagance. Anti-Semitic violence that cannot be denied they deplore 'here', while excusing it 'there'. Similarly, FTSUs tended to find the one-party state acceptable 'there', i.e., in Russia, but not 'here', i.e., in the West. In the received sentiment, it was a solution for them, not for us; we do not need, or even want, it for ourselves; we are different here.

The effect in each case is to encourage a terror-apologism. To the FTSUs, the indiscriminate murder of the kulaks was a necessary harshness. Violence inflicted either in defence or in pursuit of the revolution, and repression in the name of worthy ends, was worthy of endorsement. Similarly, to the FTASs, the indiscriminate killings of Jews by Palestinian suicide bombers are taken to be necessary protests, appropriate retaliations. Indeed, for some these acts of murder are not crimes, but sanctified acts of resistance.[514] They demand respect, not condemnation. We are invited to find a language free of condescension that will allow us to understand why in a world of rampant inequality and injustice people are driven to do things we hate.[515] Suicide bombing is not an *act* of injustice, it is a *response* to injustice. Indeed, it is an involuntary response ('driven')—'when life is a living hell what's wrong with going to heaven in a ball of fire?... The wonder is that there are not more such acts of self-immolation, not that they occur at all.'[516] These FTASs reject the proposition that setting out to destroy random members of a culture one finds unacceptable is an indefensible project.[517]

Tolerance can lead to a certain sycophancy. Consider, for example, the dean of Canterbury, writing in 1942: 'Stalin was calm, composed, simple. Not lacking in humour. Direct in speech, untouched by the slightest suspicion of pomposity. There was nothing cruel or dramatic... about Stalin's face. Just steady purpose and a kindly geniality.'[518] Similarly, provided that the leader's anti-Israel credentials are solid, anything else will be excused. There is even a certain sycophancy shown towards anti-Semitic tyrants and party leaders. It follows that, conversely, opposition to the favoured entity, the Soviet Union or Palestine, cannot be tolerated on any terms. As David Caute has explained, FTSUs caused the 'non-official' Soviet intelligentsia to despair. 'In their darkest hours', he writes, 'they heard themselves condemned by their own kind, by foreigners who shared their own idealistic traditions and whose immunity from imprisonment or death was due solely to the accident of nationality.'[519] There is an equivalent indifference to reformists in the Arab/Muslim world. In addition, the characterization of every criticism of the Soviet Union as 'Red-baiting', and of supporters of the Soviet Union as 'McCarthyism', resonates in the characterization of every criticism of any Islamist position as 'Islamophobia'.

It should not be thought, however, that the connection between FTSUs and FTASs exists merely at the level of analogy. FTSUs were indifferent to Soviet anti-Semitism; FTASs are indifferent to contemporary anti-Semitic tropes mostly derived from the Soviet precedent. Anti-Semitism, that is, is what makes a unity of the two at the level of content.

In the very year of the Soviet system's collapse, Soviet anti-Zionism was credibly considered the greatest threat to Israel and Jews generally.[520] The Soviet Union was the first non-Arab country after World War II to initiate a hate campaign against Jews. It was disguised as a campaign against 'Zionists'.[521] Some 230 books 'exposing' the Zionist–Masonic conspiracy against Russia and the world were published in the Soviet Union between 1969 and 1985, with a combined print-run of 9.4 million copies.[522] The current anti-Zionism consists of variations on themes introduced by the Soviet Union.[523]

Though its Ministry of Information only began to use the term 'anti-Zionist' systematically after the Six Day War,[524] it was used intermittently from as early as 1949. This 'anti-Zionism' survived the collapse of the Soviet system: in 1994, 18 per cent of polled Moscow residents agreed or were inclined to agree that a global 'Zionist' plot against Russia existed.[525] Soviet anti-Zionism comprised a combination of Russian anti-Semitism, Bolshevik anti-Zionism, and Soviet opposition to the Zionist project.

Tolerating anti-Semitism

Many anti-Zionist polemicists tend to deny the anti-Semitic aspects of much contemporary hostility to Israel and the Zionist cause. The denial is typically accompanied by a formulaic condemnation of anti-Semitism, and a counter-charge that the allegation of anti-Semitism is nothing more than a diversionary tactic.[526] The denial is also often frivolously advanced, without any real thought being given to the possibility that anti-Semitism might taint the defended anti-Zionist position. Even when it is pondered, the denial is often derived from a misunderstanding of anti-Semitism, which is typically considered to come only from the Right, to be State-sponsored, and to speak German. The massive presence of the Holocaust, that is, has occluded the pre-Nazi history of anti-Semitism—that is to say, what might be termed a *hypermnesia* in respect of the former has promoted an *amnesia* in respect of the latter.[527]

There are two kinds of denier.[528] The denier in good faith *cannot* see the anti-Semitism, while the bad faith denier *will not* acknowledge it. In either case, the complaint of anti-Semitism is taken to be just a ruse by Jews and other defenders of Israel. Tariq Ali's indignation is representative: 'The campaign against the supposed new "anti-semitism" in Europe today is basically a cynical ploy on the part of the Israeli Government to seal off the Zionist state from any criticism of its regular and consistent brutality against the Palestinians.'[529] Anti-Semitism is not a problem, not to be taken seriously, no longer a real threat. The anti-Semitism of the Hamas Charter 'has been repeatedly disavowed in recent years by Hamas leaders, specifically in relation to the anti-Jewish tropes'.[530] And Israel is practically invulnerable. 'To say that the Zionist state is threatened by any Arab country is pure demagogy.'[531] Once evacuated of historical meaning, 'anti-Semitism' is then available to be turned against the Jews. 'Israeli racism [is] a virulent form of anti-semitism';[532] Israel's 2006 War in Lebanon was pursued by 'politicians, generals and soldiers' who were 'consumed with burning revulsion for all their non-Jewish Semite neighbours'.[533] And then, this commonplace of anti-Zionist discourse: that to hold that Jews are one people apart, regardless of the countries in which they live and of which they are citizens, is itself anti-Semitic. Lastly, the Arab Muslim world cannot be anti-Semitic because Arabs themselves are Semitic—a piece of semantic nonsense that is much deployed now.

A more elaborated denial of anti-Semitism was evident in a recent controversy over a political cartoon. On 27 January 2003, the *Independent* published a cartoon on its op-ed page showing Ariel Sharon, Israel's prime minister, eating a Palestinian child. Helicopter gunships, circling above newly wrecked Palestinian homes, broadcast the message 'Sharon... Vote Sharon... Vote.' Sharon himself, as if responding to an objection, snarls: 'What's wrong... You never seen a politician kissing babies before?'

A complaint was made about the cartoon to the Press Complaints Commission (PCC) on behalf of the Israel Embassy and Mr Sharon himself. The PCC administers the voluntary system of self-regulation in the newspaper industry. It was argued that the cartoon was anti-Semitic and therefore breached clause 13 of the PCC Code. This is the clause that prohibits prejudicial or pejorative reference to a person's religion. Anti-Semitism tainted the cartoon because it introduced the blood libel into an attack on Sharon. The intention of the cartoonist was irrelevant. One can no more suppress allusion to the blood libel in an image of a Jew consuming a Gentile child, than one can suppress the echo of a voice sounding in a canyon. The cartoon was thus a prejudicial reference to Sharon's religion. It encouraged readers to think the worse of the prime minister by identifying him not just (say) as the architect of the invasion of Lebanon and the sponsor of the settlement movement, but as a Jew, and thus capable of murdering children for no better reason than that to do so would appeal to his fellow Jews. And what could be *more* 'prejudicial' than to associate the Jewish leader of the Jewish State with the blood libel? The letter of complaint made the point that the blood libel was once again in wide circulation in the world, and that it was therefore imperative that it should not be given any foothold in Britain—and certainly not in a mainstream, national newspaper. If it did, other cartoons would follow.[534]

The editor, Simon Kelner, responded by insisting that the cartoon was only about Sharon and not about Jews in general. He said that it was 'hard-hitting comment', which justified the use of an appalling and gruesome image. He also said that it was not the cartoonist's intention to allude to the blood libel. The cartoon alluded solely to Goya's 'Saturn Devouring his Children'.[535] Were the PCC to uphold the complaint, it would compromise the newspaper's freedom of speech. In a later exchange of letters, just before the PCC met to adjudicate on the complaint, the editor added a further defence of the cartoon. The child being eaten was not Palestinian, but Israeli, and represented the Israeli electorate. To this opportunistic misreading of the cartoon, one that was quite inconsistent with the other arguments advanced in its defence, the editor added the observation that he himself was a Jew and was therefore well-qualified to determine whether it was anti-Semitic and, in his judgement, it was not. 'I am unashamed about publishing' the cartoon, he wrote. In the range of available responses, this was the most defiant, and the least rational. Peter Wilby's response in respect of a similarly provocative image (the *New Statesman*'s 'Kosher conspiracy'), though inadequate, had more to commend it: 'The cover was not intended to be anti-Semitic; the *New Statesman* is vigorously opposed to racism in all its forms. But it used images and words in such a way as to create unwittingly the impression that the New Statesman was following an anti-Semitic tradition . . . '[536]

The PCC rejected the complaint. In its initial, draft adjudication, it reasoned that there was a disagreement about whether the cartoon was anti-Semitic, and given this, that it should not itself seek to resolve the question. In any event, it added, both editor and cartoonist denied any anti-Semitic intent. The adjudication was then redrafted to correct the impression given by the draft that the mere existence of a disagreement as to the meaning of the cartoon had led the PCC to reject the complaint.[537] It did not, however, make any finding on the meaning of the cartoon. If the cartoon was acceptable to the editor and his colleagues on the newspaper, then it was acceptable to the PCC. This was an unseemly abdication of responsibility, inconsistent with the very reason for the PCC's existence. The adjudication went on to note that 'the Code does not cover complaints about alleged discrimination against groups of people'—a statement inconsistent with adjudications of comparable complaints.[538] A short while after the complaint was rejected, the cartoonist was awarded a prize.[539] He defended himself:

> Do I believe, or was I trying to suggest, that Sharon actually eats babies? Of course not—one of the other benefits of the borrowed image was that it was sited squarely in the field of allegory. My cartoon was intended as a caricature

of a specific person, Sharon, in the guise of a figure from classical myth who, I hoped, couldn't be farther from any Jewish stereotype.[540]

Let me turn now to the *downplaying* of, or *indifference* towards, anti-Semitism. Often, when the anti-Semitic aspect of a particular remark or political programme is pointed out, the response is dismissive, as if anti-Semitism itself is of no consequence. The implication is that the characterizing of the remark or programme as anti-Semitic is to miss their 'point'. Parties who make these remarks, adopt these programmes, do not mean what they say when they use anti-Semitic language.[541] Hamas's Jew-hating desire to eradicate Israel, for example, is taken to be nothing more than a misconceived 'maximalism', a regrettable 'weakness' of Palestinian nationalism, one that indeed is to the disadvantage of the Palestinians rather than their enemies.[542] The appropriate tone in which to consider President Ahmadinejad's genocidal threats and his Holocaust Denial is one of wry understatement.[543] And so on. As long as it does not have Hitler's name attached to it, murderous acts and even genocidal threats against Jews tend to be ignored or allowed to pass.[544] The ritualized murder of the journalist Daniel Pearl, for example tended to be represented in the Western media as anything other than the killing of a Jew for the crime of being Jewish.[545] Jewish participants at the 2001 Durban Conference noted with alarm the indifference of human rights activists to the anti-Semitism on display there. 'Their almost uniform response', writes Ken Stern, 'was either to encourage it or to let it pass without speaking out.'[546]

In an article written for the *London Review of Books* during the Summer 2006 war between Israel and Hezbollah, Charles Glass compared Israel's occupation of Lebanon with the Nazi occupation of France, and observed that while Hezbollah relied on 'the weapons of the weak', among which were 'suicide bombers', it 'used them intelligently'. Glass also noted Hezbollah's 'uncompromising political programme'.[547] A reader wrote in to observe that Nasrallah, the leader of the 'Party of God' was 'not simply a resistance fighter'; he was also 'an anti-Semite with fantasies of genocide'. Citing anti-Semitic statements attributed to Nasrallah, he suggested that Glass did not seem to care about any of that, which made his 'defence of Hizbullah' 'beyond the pale'. Glass responded that the statements attributed to Nasrallah were 'in all likelihood fabrications'. He did not, however, respond squarely to the characterization of Nasrallah as an anti-Semite. I wrote in to draw his attention, and the attention of the *LRB*'s readers, to Amal Saad-Ghorayeb's *Hizbullah: Politics and religion* (2002), which I suggested might be a reliable source for Nasrallah's, and Hezbollah's, anti-Semitism. Saad-Ghorayeb deals at length with the party's 'anti-Judaism' (as she terms it), and quotes extensively from the writings and speeches of its leaders. I observed that the implication of Glass's letter was that Goodheart was wrong to describe Nasrallah, and by extension Hezbollah, as anti-Semitic. I invited Glass to confirm that that was indeed his position, and, if it was, to comment on the material assembled by Saad-Ghorayeb. Glass took some time to respond. He had taken the trouble, he explained, to check with Saad-Ghorayeb an anti-Semitic remark she attributed to Nasrallah in her book. She had confirmed to him, he reported, that the footnoted reference for the remark was a 'mistake', and 'therefore, until someone discovers where and when Nasrallah uttered the words above, the case is unproved'. He added that he was 'agnostic on Nasrallah's alleged anti-Semitism' and as far as Hezbollah itself was concerned, 'anti-semitism was irrelevant to my original article, which concerned Hezbollah's role in Lebanese political life'. In each instance, Glass ducked the question of anti-Semitism. Now, there can be no sensible denying that Hezbollah is an anti-Semitic party. Nasrallah's own anti-Semitism seems similarly beyond dispute. And Hezbollah's anti-Semitism is far from 'irrelevant' to Lebanese political life, not least because it influences the party's posture towards Israel. Glass's 'agnosticism' is better described as indifference.[548]

Finally, and most problematically, there is the position of *justification* of anti-Semitism in particular contexts. If it cannot be denied, or dismissed, then it will be justified. It is the fault of the Jews. The Jews bring suffering upon themselves. This suffering is perhaps a little arbitrary, and on occasion even excessive, but—essentially—it is merited. This was an old argument,[549] revived in the late 1960s in defence of African-American or 'Black' anti-Semitism, which was said not to be rooted in the irrational Jew-hatred of the Christian Middle Ages but in the 'concrete fact of oppression by Jews of Blacks in the ghetto'. It was, it was claimed, 'an *earned* anti-Semitism',[550] at least in part. The British journalist, Jonathan Cook, writing in 2003, distinguished the 'modern phenomenon' of 'Muslims retaliating against fellow Jewish citizens for Israel's military strategies against the Palestinians' from 'traditional European anti-Semitism'.[551] Further, the weak cannot be racist—this is an established trope of anti-racist discourse.[552] Elsewhere, Cook offered an explanation of anti-Semitism that relates Jewish services to medieval aristocrats to Israel's services to today's United States. In each case, the justified anger of the general population against their rulers has been displaced onto the Jews.[553] Cook argues that Israel has three reasons for promoting fears of anti-Semitism: to stifle all criticism of Israel; to deter Israeli Jews from leaving Israel; to incriminate Muslims and put Israel on the 'right' side in the war against terror. The implication is that there is no anti-Semitism; the whole matter is a scare. Hence the all-party British parliamentary report into anti-Semitism in the UK was merely 'preposterous'.[554] Cook's piece is subtitled 'How Israel is engineering the "Clash of Civilizations"'. There is some tension between the two positions—anti-Semitism exists, but it is the fault of the Jews; anti-Semitism doesn't exist, it is an illusion created by the Jews. In another piece, Cook attempts to reconcile these positions:

> Israel [has] a product it desperately needs to sell (*aliyah*) that few Jews want to buy. The 'new anti-Semitism' is Israel's marketing strategy at its most aggressive. But more worrying is evidence that, in the absence of 'Jew hatred', Israel may be encouraging a climate of anti-Semitism to make its case to the diaspora more convincing. . . . The 'new anti-Semitism', *whether real or imagined*, is the only sales pitch Israel has that still works.[555] [italics added]

The reconciliation fails.

It is at best a mind-clouding compassion for Palestinian suffering; it is more often a deliberate stupidity, a refusal to learn, to understand—a reconnecting with anti-Semitic discourse in ignorance, willed if not feigned. The risk of anti-Semitism is not important to these fellow travellers. They write and say things that they should not. They do not care, or they care in the wrong way, about complaints of anti-Semitism.

'As regards a "fellow-traveller",' observed Trotsky, 'the question always comes up—how far will he go?'[556] The question should be posed of FTASs. Some FTASs are willing to sit alongside anti-Semites in the interests of a wider cause. Some FTASs are willing to use anti-Semitic tropes and when challenged, to bluff it out—Tam Dalyell, for example,[557] or Ted Honderich.[558] Some give a 'free pass' to interviewees with a record of making anti-Semitic statements—Madeleine Bunting, for example, in her interview with Sheikh Qaradawi.[559] Some will pander to the anti-Semitic prejudices of their audience—George Galloway, for example, in interviews with Arabic media speaks of 'the right wing Zionist press' and 'the newspapers and news media which are controlled by Zionism', while to English broadcasters, the talk is merely of 'the right wing media'.[560]

David Caute thinks that the history of fellow travelling reached a 'dead end'[561] with the disillusionment of the Left about Cuba. He is wrong about this, I think. Indeed, even old-style fellow travelling persists—there is still irrational support for regimes perceived to be anti-American, still the denial or minimizing of any non-American crimes (Cambodia, Serbia), still the mocking of the West's claims to superiority, still the promotion of an undifferentiated Western 'guilt'. Some FTSUs, indeed, have merely adopted these positions in support of political Islam. But there is also something new, a fellow travelling with specifically anti-Semitic positions taken by Israel's most aggressive enemies. These fellow travellers find their political vocation in 'judgement-passing' on Israel and its friends, and 'excuse-making'[562] for Israel's enemies. This often leads to misjudgements and follies.

I now turn to the three confessional anti-Zionisms.

8

Contemporary Confessional Anti-Zionisms, and a Conclusion

The anti-Zionism in Britain's diverse Muslim communities, in its more homogeneous Jewish communities, and in the various Christian denominations, substantially draws upon what I have termed the new anti-Zionism. But these confessional anti-Zionisms have their own distinct properties too, deriving both from the particularity of their connection with the Israel–Palestinian conflict, and in the religious self-understanding that accompanies their perspective on it. In summary:

- Anglo-Muslim anti-Zionism is characterized by fellow-feeling with the Palestinian Muslim population and by diffusely Islamist perspectives on Jews, Israel, and the Israel–Palestinian conflict. These perspectives are often informed by conspiracist beliefs.[1]

- Anglo-Jewish anti-Zionism is characterized by assumed guilt and anger at what is perceived as oppressive Israeli behaviour, and by non-nationalist, mostly universalist perspectives on Judaism and the Jewish people.

- Anglo-Christian anti-Zionism is characterized by an intense consciousness of the role of the Holy Places in the Christian Scriptures, by the historical Anglican presence in Jerusalem, and by a distaste for Christian Zionism that expresses itself in part in the restating of supersessionist perspectives on Judaism and the Jews.

Of the three, Jewish anti-Zionism is the least religiously inflected and therefore the closest in content to the new anti-Zionism; Muslim anti-Zionism is the most polluted by anti-Semitic tropes and language; Christian anti-Zionism has the most complex, and most specifically English, history.

Muslim anti-Zionism

Until the mid-1950s, opposition to the Zionist project was mainly an affair of Arab solidarity in the Middle East itself, and of solidarity with Arabs among elements in the West. The non-Arab, specifically Muslim, engagement with the Israel–Palestinian conflict by comparison was limited to Britain, and was rather slight and ineffectual. (A July 1917 meeting held in London by the Central Islamic Society, protesting what was perceived as the Zionist movement's growing influence within the British government, was given short shrift by the Foreign Office, dismissing the petition that followed the meeting as the product of a 'crew of seditionists'.)[2] Then, from the mid-1950s through to the 1970s, opposition to Israel took on a certain Third World, pro-Soviet colouring. There was much talk, for a time, of 'Arab socialism'. This dwindled, just as Soviet support dwindled, and the Soviet Union itself then disappeared. Between the 1970s and the 2000s, the 'secular' and 'revolutionary socialist' gave way to the 'Islamic', and non-Arab Muslim investment in the Israel–Palestinian conflict expanded. At the same time, an Islamically informed anti-Semitic anti-Zionism gained salience.

In the nineteenth century, Indian soldiers in the British armed forces and Yemeni and Somali seamen settled in London and Liverpool. A more extensive migration of Muslims to Britain and elsewhere in Europe began in the 1950s, in consequence partly of decolonization and partly of greater European prosperity and the demand for labour. Among the Western European states, citizenship has been most easily obtained in Britain.[3] Over the last few decades, the British Muslim population has grown substantially, and now stands at about 2 million. British Muslim communities first came to political consciousness (though not to political power)[4] in consequence of the Rushdie Affair; many among an entire generation of young Muslims[5] were radicalized by events in Bosnia and Chechnya;[6] the same Muslim communities were then put on the defensive by the London bombing on 7 July 2006, while a few young Muslims comprised the perpetrators of the atrocity.[7] Notwithstanding this emergence of British Muslims as a political constituency (one no longer taken for granted by the Labour Party, to which for some time they gave strong, mostly unreciprocated loyalty), it has been hard for some commentators to draw their political profile without descending into alarmism. It would seem that a certain appreciation of values and institutions identified as typically British[8] can coexist with an angry rejection of values and institutions identified as typically Western. Likewise, certain tentative forays into the parliamentary political process can coexist with the rejection of any normative political engagement in favour of other forms of political action. In consequence of this new Muslim activism, which is often articulated in the language of grievance, new words have been added to the political lexicon—principal among them, 'Islamophobia'. It is an activism, broadly Islamist in orientation, which has been adept at converting the frustrations of young men into political energy.[9]

There is an account—troubling or encouraging, according to perspective—of Muslim demographic growth in Europe leading to a 'deWesternizing' of the continent. The spectre of the Arab as military invader *of* Europe has given way to the spectre of the Muslim as a separatist presence *in* Europe. This is simplified politics, not least because it overlooks, among many other things, the diversity and complexity of actual Muslim communities; the existence of a much longer-term Muslim presence and influence in the West, and the appeal to Muslims of those characteristics recently acquired by the West, such as the separation of Church and State, a 'human rights' culture, democracy, freedom of expression, and so on. 'Eurabia' is not inevitable, or perhaps even likely;[10] rather more likely is the emergence of a theory of the legitimacy and practice of a minority Islam.[11] It is also objectionable politics, because it assumes that every person of Muslim origin is the (in effect) genetic 'carrier' of a certain anti-Western cultural and religious perspective—an assumption that is racist in its implications.[12] The Islam supposed by both certain fundamentalists and by their enemies, namely a body of closed norms followed by members of a single, transnational community who have no other affiliations, is fantasy only.[13]

There would appear, however to be something of an 'English exception' to the general truth that most Muslims in Europe aspire to integration,[14] and this in turn has fostered the development of distinctively English versions of contemporary European Muslim anti-Zionism. The distinction between Israelis and Jews, or between 'Zionists' and Jews, rarely figures in this anti-Zionism[15]—indeed, the term 'anti-Zionism' thus does not quite capture the sentiment. In the *Guardian*, for example, the Muslim journalist Faisal Bodi argued that Israel had no right to exist. God did not intend his promise to Abraham to be used as an excuse to take by force and chicanery a land lawfully inhabited and owned by others. Bodi went on:

The idea that Israel is some kind of religious birthright has only imprisoned Jews in a never-ending cycle of conflict. The 'promise' breeds an arrogance which institutionalises the inferiority of other peoples and generates atrocities against them with alarming regularity. It allows soldiers to defy their consciences and blast unarmed schoolchildren.

The alternative to Jewish 'self-reproach', Bodi concluded, is 'perpetual war'.[16] Similar expressions of hostility towards Israel are sometimes accompanied by somewhat rosy accounts of Jewish life under Muslim rule. More commonly, however, they affirm misconceptions about Jews and Jewish power.

There is a reflex to blame 'Zionists' or a 'Zionist' or 'pro-Israeli' agenda, or 'Islamophobia', for anything disliked. The Islamic Human Rights Commission, a London-based NGO, explains that the Western conception of human rights (which it deprecates) was 'politically motivated, and led by advocates with narrow political agendas of their own'. 'The idea of a universal definition of human rights', it adds, 'can be dated back to the proposal of an International Bill of Rights of Man in 1945 by Hersch Lauterpecht [sic], a leading Zionist.'[17] A BBC documentary critical of bodies claiming to represent British Muslims fund-raising activities for Palestinians was, the Muslim Council of Britain spokesman said, 'more interested in furthering a pro-Israeli agenda than assessing the work of Muslim organisations in the UK'. He added, 'the BBC should not allow itself to be used by highly placed supporters of Israel in the British media'.[18] Jewish control of the media has become a pervasive theme in this discourse.[19] Another body that makes (a highly challengeable) claim to represent British Muslims, the Muslim Public Affairs Committee, warned visitors to its website that 'the power of the Zionists is unlimited, they will manoeuvre and plot from every angle to stifle any open debate about the racist political ideology of Zionism and the threat upon us all'.[20] 'Unlimited power' is precisely the theme purveyed by versions of the *Protocols*,[21] and other inflammatory, anti-Semitic material,[22] available in mosques and Islamic educational institutions and bookshops in London and the provinces.[23] 'Jewish conspiracy' theories are common in Islamist circles, in the UK and elsewhere.

Holocaust denial must also figure in any account of British Muslim anti-Zionism. A recent survey found that only 22 per cent agreed that the Holocaust happened 'as history teaches'. The rest were as follows: it has been exaggerated (17 per cent), never heard of it (23 per cent), no opinion (24 per cent), didn't happen (2 per cent), don't know (6 per cent).[24]

According to a government-funded report, some teachers are reluctant to teach it for fear of offending Muslim students whose 'beliefs' include Holocaust denial.[25] It is in this context that the MCB's boycott of Holocaust Memorial Day, maintained for several years, has to be interpreted.[26] (In 2009, the MCB resumed its boycott of Holocaust Memorial Day, explaining that the day will be used to 'silence criticism of Israel'.)[27] Holocaust denial appears to be a relatively recent arrival in British Muslim politics—at the time of the Bosnian crisis, the tendency was to invoke the Holocaust as a precedent for persecution of European Muslims.[28]

And this, in turn, provides the context not just for political campaigning of the conventional, parliamentary kind,[29] but also for acts of terror, random acts of violence, intimidatory leafleting, and abuse and sloganeering, directed at Jews from time to time. A rabbinical student was stabbed on a London bus in 2002 by a Muslim man who said, upon being arrested, 'Israel are the murderers. They kill women and children, so I stabbed him.'[30] Leaflets, for example, were left on cars outside a London school in 2002, attacking the 'Zionist Crusader conspiracy to control the world and propagate evil'. The General Union of Palestinian Students circulated a pamphlet describing Jews as 'vampires'. An Arabic language poster was put up at Manchester University that read 'Slaughter the Jews'.[31] A note was left in a phone box in London, which read 'Not only should bloody Jew boy Israel to [sic] be wiped off the map but America too! Fucking dirty Jew boys and yanks—get out of our lands (& Britain is one of our lands) or British Islam will kick you out.' The home and vehicle of a Jewish man in London were daubed with a swastika and the words 'Kill all Jews' and 'Allah'. A Lubavitch 'Happy Passover' stand at a Manchester supermarket was plastered with posters showing a suicide bomber with the words 'Happy Passover from al-Qaeda'. A Jewish man was walking to synagogue in London when a group of Asian men shouted 'Jewish scumbag, go back to the camps' and directed Nazi salutes at him.[32] In London's Stamford Hill, densely populated with Orthodox Jews, graffiti appeared in May 2008 calling for *jihad*, described as the only solution for Israel.[33] The full list, if not quite endless, would run on for several pages.

It is not all emotional solidarity, unreflective animus, anger, and violence. This Muslim anti-Zionism also finds more discursive expression in texts such as Ahmad Thomson's *The Next World Order*, published by the Al-Aqsa Press in Beirut, in 1994. Thomson is a London barrister, a former Rhodesian, and a convert to Islam. He is the deputy chairman of the

Association of Muslim Lawyers and the editor of the journal *Muslim Lawyer*. He submitted memoranda on behalf of the Association to Parliament in which he wrote about 'Khazar Zionists'.[34] In 2005, it was reported that the government had consulted him on issues concerning Muslims.[35] He is a prolific author, and London and provincial libraries stock several of his books.[36] *The Next World Order* sets out to establish that the Jews' claim to the Holy Land, derived from allegedly historical rights, is false. The Holy Land has been the land of the 'Muslims' from time immemorial; the establishing of 'the final Islam of the Prophet Muhammad' was therefore not an invasion of previously held 'Jewish' or 'Christian' land. The whole of Israel is therefore 'occupied territory'. Israel is a cancer. The Jews invented the term 'anti-Semitism' as a means of obscuring the fact that they are not Semites but Khazars, and thus have no racial connection to the Holy Land. Since the fifteenth century, virtually all the money circulating in society has passed through the Jewish banking system; and since then, too, there has always been a centre of Talmudic or Jewish government. Communism and Zionism share a secret purpose. During the first half of the twentieth century, the one dominated Russian politics, and the other dominated American politics. The figure of '6 million' must be a monstrous exaggeration of the number of Jews dead in World War II. Further, for the last three years of the war, East European communists were in charge of the concentration camps, and as everyone knows, there were many Jews among their ranks. Still, the Zionists benefited from the sympathy generated by the circulation of information about what had allegedly been going on in Europe's concentration camps. Like any spider's web, the Jewish economic web is a masterpiece, but in the end it will be blown away, and Israel along with it.[37]

Now compare a Palestinian anti-Zionism—English, by virtue of exile. Ghada Karmi was born in the Jerusalem suburb of Katamon. She arrived with her family in London in 1949, where they settled in Golders Green. Her father had made the decision, for the sake of their safety, and through a sense of 'impending disaster', to take them away from their Palestinian home.[38] She had a conventional middle-class English education, counted Jews among her friends, qualified as a doctor, married and then divorced an Englishman. She became involved in pro-Palestinian politics after the Six Day War. She remains an activist, and campaigns for a boycott of Israel. Her 'tortured love affair' with Palestine, she says, has lasted 'a lifetime'.[39] She has written two books, *In Search of Fatima* (2002) and *Married to Another Man:*

Israel's dilemma in Palestine (2007). The first is autobiographical; the second makes the case for a 'one-state' solution. Her perspective, which is broadly secular, casts Israel as the 'perpetrator', and the Palestinians as the 'victim'.[40] She has found her vocation in working to 'put right a huge injustice of which [she] was also a victim'.[41]

Karmi considers herself free of any anti-Semitism animus. She writes that as a schoolgirl she 'unthinkingly adopted my parents' lack of hostility towards Jews'.[42] She is, however, deeply hostile to Israel and the Zionist project. In the matter of a 'solution' to the Israel–Palestinian conflict, she is indifferent to the wishes of Israeli Jews. 'Only by bringing the Zionist project to an end would the conflict also be ended', she explains.[43] The 'best solution to this intractable problem is to turn the clock back before there was any Jewish state and rerun history as if from there'.[44] By conceding the right of return to Palestinians, Israel would repent the crimes committed by Zionism and thereby undo the state that it had created.[45] The Palestinians were 'forced' into terrorism;[46] the frontline states were 'dragged into wars';[47] Israel was 'instrumental in creating Islamic fundamentalism'.[48] For Karmi, the precondition of 'peace' is that Israel accepts exclusive responsibility for everything bad that has happened to the Palestinians in the last sixty years.

She writes of the spectacle of the 'scenes of wild rejoicing as Israeli crowds swarmed all over the Wailing Wall', following the fall of East Jerusalem in the Six Day War. 'Israel's leaders announced that Jerusalem would be theirs forever. What a curious, disturbing sight, I thought, to see the gleaming Dome of the Rock, one of Islam's most famous shrines, become the backdrop to this alien horde of black-robed rabbis and soldiers.' Karmi erases the relevant Jewish history in this dismissive, contemptuous account of the 'alien horde'. The 'Western Wall' was one of the retaining walls that defined the platform (or 'Mount') on which the Temple was constructed. It is the only wall now standing; the Roman general Titus destroyed the Temple and ploughed over the site in 70 CE.[49] When the Arabs conquered Jerusalem in 638 CE, the Dome was built on the site of the razed Temple. It is the supreme architectural statement of Islamic supersessionism.[50] Among the Grand Mufti's many intransigencies in the 1920s was his refusal to acknowledge the Jewish right of prayer at the Wall; the 1931 Report of the Commission on the Western Wall, which recognized 'Moslem owner-ship of the Wall without any limitation' but permitted limited facilities to Jews for worship, was condemned as 'the infidel decision'.[51] In 1948, the majority of the population was Jewish, and probably had been so for about a hundred years.[52] But the war led to the expulsion of many of the city's Jewish residents, and their synagogues were converted into homes for Arab families.[53] Palestinian leaders have claimed that neither Solomon's Temple nor Herod's Temple ever existed on the site. In a 2007 interview, the then Palestinian Justice Minister Taysir Tamimi stated: 'About these so-called two temples, they never existed, certainly not on the Haram al-Sharif.'[54] These positions are creeping into the discourse of the new anti-Zionism. Tim Llewellyn writes of Haram al-Sharif that it is 'one of Islam's holiest sites, known incorrectly as the Temple Mount'.[55]

There are certain parallels in Karmi's writings with Thomson's. Karmi entertains the Khazar fantasy (but it has been a staple of anti-Zionism since at least the 1940s);[56] she entertains the trope of Jewish control of the media; she asks 'Who controls America?' answering it in paragraphs headed 'Israel in Control';[57] she flirts with the 'dual loyalty' canard;[58] and she does more than flirt with the Zionism/Nazism trope.[59] Unlike Thomson, Karmi is alive to a certain kind of snobbish, money-minded anti-Semitism typical at one time among the English middle- and upper-middle classes.[60] She also acknowledges Arab 'paranoia' about the Jews,[61] but she is not ready, however, to name it anti-Semitism. 'Anti-Semitism', she writes, 'hardly seems an appropriate term . . . since the Arabs are semites.'[62]

On 1 February 2007, a Muslim man, Abdul Saleem, was found guilty of stirring up racial hatred during a protest against the publication of cartoons depicting the prophet Muhammad. Saleem was filmed chanting '7/7 on its way' and 'Europe you will pay with your blood' as demonstrators marched from the Regents Park mosque to the Danish embassy. Saleem told the trial that, while his words could be seen as 'threatening', he had not intended to be. He said he was repeating slogans 'because everyone else was saying [them]' (my italics).[63] The impression is sometimes given that within the various Muslim communities that comprise the British Muslim population, 'everyone is saying' anti-Israel, anti-Zionist slogans. Claims are often made to this effect.[64] Is this true?

Opinion polls help, though there is a somewhat illusory appearance of precision about these statistics, characteristic of all surveys:[65]

- *The February 2006 Populus report on attitudes of British Muslims.*[66] Only a bare majority (52 per cent) supported the right of the state of Israel to exist, 30 per cent did not. Thirty-one per cent thought that the Muslim Community should participate in Holocaust Memorial day, while 56 per cent said they should not (21 per cent said they shouldn't because of Israeli treatment of Palestine, 12 per cent because it ignored Muslim suffering, 20 per cent for unspecified other reasons, 4 per cent said they didn't believe the Holocaust happened). Fifty-eight per cent of British Muslims thought that English Jews supported Israel right or wrong, 20 per cent disagreed. Fifty-seven per cent thought they had no interest in the plight of the Palestinians, 21 per cent disagreed. Fifty-three per cent thought that the Jewish community had too much influence on foreign policy, 46 per cent thought that the Jewish community were in league with Freemasons to control the media and politics, and 37 per cent thought they were legitimate targets as part of the struggle for justice in the Middle East.[67]

- *The April 2006 Channel 4 Despatches survey of British Muslim attitudes, based on 1,000 telephone interviews conducted in March and April 2006.* Forty-five per cent of Muslims asked, agreed that 9/11 was perpetrated by an America–Israel conspiracy. Of Muslims aged between twenty-five and forty-one, the figure is 51 per cent; second-generation Muslims (50 per cent) are more likely than first-generation Muslims (42 per cent) to believe it was a conspiracy.[68] (This particular fantasy—as distinct from most other fantasies about Jewish power—has caused much distress to al-Qaeda's leadership).[69]

- The 2007 Policy Exchange report, *Living Apart Together: British Muslims and the paradox of multiculturalism.* Only 18 per cent of Muslims questioned knew the name of the Chairman of the Palestinian Authority, and only 14 per cent knew the name of Israel's prime minister. When asked to name an organization that represented British Muslims, only 6 per cent identified the Muslim Council of Britain; 51 per cent believed that no organization represented their views as Muslims. However, the report identifies a marked increase in religiosity among the younger generation, indicated, inter alia, by 'an increase in anti-Western and anti-Semitic attitudes in Muslim literature and websites'. This religiosity is politicized. Most Muslims do not subscribe to Holocaust denial or other anti-Semitic positions, 'but this kind of sentiment seems to be on the rise'.[70]

On 7 September 2007, the London *Times* reported that almost half of Britain's mosques are under the control of the Deobandi 'sect', one of whose leading imams, Riyadh ul Haq, 'supports armed jihad and preaches contempt for Jews, Christians and Hindus'.[71] During the course of one sermon, he explained to his audience that the Jews are 'all the same'. And he explained, 'they've monopolised everything: the Holocaust, God, money, interest, usury, the world economy, the media, political institutions . . . they monopolised tyranny and oppression as well. And injustice.' In a sermon on 'Jewish fundamentalism', this British-educated imam argued that no one should be surprised that 'the terrorist Israeli Government' continues to murder Muslims with impunity, because of the peoples of the earth, the ones that hate the Muslims the most are the Jews and the idolaters. And lest someone claims that this is anti-Semitic, it is Allah, the creator of the Semites, who says this in the Qur'an. What is more, the Jewish professor Israel Shahak has written a book exposing the true teachings of extremist Judaism. He shows that a Jew is generally allowed to kill a non-Jew without fear of punishment either in this world or the next. This, and many other examples drawn from their texts, ul Haq adds, explains the 'Jewish mentality' and the Jews' relationship with the Muslims of Palestine. There were no Jews in Hebron before 1967; but when the Jews occupied the land illegally, just over 400 Israeli settlers moved in. The massacre there on 25 February 1994 of twenty-nine Palestinians, and the injury of very many more, was carried out by a typical religious Jew, and was endorsed by 50 per cent of the Israeli public. Many religious Jews do not want peace; they are not even satisfied with what they have got. They want the whole of Lebanon, the whole of Syria, they want Jordan, and they want Kuwait as well. Muslims are said to be fundamentalists and extremists, but it is the *Jews* who are, at their most representative, fundamentalists and extremists.[72]

Contrary to the imam, however, it is rarely appropriate to take individual acts as representative of *any* community, including his own—certainly, not individual acts of terrorism, or the incitement of terrorism, or acts of generalized violence, or even individual sermons, however extravagantly phrased. On the other hand, such activities are not wholly maverick; they require some collective effort, however modest, and they are nurtured within communities in which a sense of injustice and grievance may be pervasive.[73] Incidents of violence almost always take place within a larger context of hostility. This hostility is in turn inculcated both by the general circulation of wildly inaccurate accounts of the Israel–Palestinian conflict and by a distinctively Muslim teaching of contempt in respect of Jews— abusive and uncomplimentary, and in certain instances, ostensibly sanctioned by the Qur'an. Also not to be ignored, of course, is incitement from abroad. According to a senior European Commission official, a full 50 per cent of anti-Semitic incidents on the European continent are connected to radical Islamic elements.[74] Monica Ali, a close, engaged observer, finds anti-Semitism everywhere in London's Muslim East End;[75] Jews appear to be more intensely hated, however, in specifically Islamist circles;[76] the most absurd rumours find purchase (for example, in relation to 9/11).[77] The combined effect is to create an atmosphere in which anything is possible, everything is justified. It is an atmosphere to which radical preachers in mosques have made a signal contribution.[78]

Consider the career of Abu Hamza (b. 1958). In 1997, he was appointed preacher at Finsbury Park mosque. He sent men from the mosque to Yemen for training; others were despatched elsewhere for similar purposes. The tapes of his addresses circulated widely; he extended the hospitality of the Finsbury Park Mosque to suicide murderers and other terrorists. According to him, the 9/11 killers were martyrs acting in self-defence. Kamel Bourgass, who lived in the Finsbury Park mosque, was convicted of plotting to make ricin poison for an attack in London. Asif Mohammed Hanif and Omar Khan Sharif, regular worshippers at the mosque, were the suicide-murderers in the 30 April 2003 attack on Mike's bar, Tel Aviv.[79] Hamza himself was convicted in February 2006 of inciting murder and race-hate against Jews and in addition, of one terrorism offence. Hamza was the leading figure in the small Salafi group, 'Supporters of Shari'ah' ('SOS'). SOS blamed 9/11 on the Jews: 'Zionists are the only beneficiaries from this plot! ... The towers are owned by a Jew. It is reported that 4000 Jews did not go to work at the World Trade Centre on that day', etc.[80]

According to Hamza, Jews in the UK and the US 'control [the] money supply'. Friends of Israel have hijacked UK foreign policy.[81] Jews are 'blasphemous, traitors and dirty'.[82] They are 'sons of monkeys'.[83] Western politicians 'all know their roles as they are slaves of the Jews ... they hate the Jews more than we do, but the Jews own them'.[84] The Jews control the news media. They are responsible for the anti-terrorism laws. They have started all the world's wars. The Jews 'wanted to deceive [Hitler]', and 'some were dealing with the Allies against him'. Hitler punished them. The day is fast approaching when Muslims will have to kill all the Jews. This will be in accordance of a prophecy of Mohammed's. All the Jews will be killed; the Jewish State will be destroyed. The earth will curse them; none will survive. Palestine will be the biggest Jewish graveyard. That is where they should be buried. At his trial, Hamza described the existence of the State of Israel as an 'abomination', and said that his statements about the Jews could be justified 'scientifically'.[85] His defence lawyer told the jury that speeches in which

Hamza appeared to be calling on Muslims to kill Jews were direct quotations from the Hadith.[86] For some time, Hamza had been in regular contact with British intelligence agencies, playing a double game of ostensible cooperation and continuing terror-related activities. He took their advice on the content of his speeches, substituting 'Zionists' for 'Jews' as his verbal targets.[87]

If Hamza was a conman,[88] he was one who exercised considerable authority and enjoyed considerable appeal.[89] Nor can he be dismissed as wholly aberrant. For example, another Muslim cleric, Abdullah al-Faisal, was given a seven-year jail sentence in February 2003 for soliciting murder and inciting racial hatred. 'The people who are ruling the world unfortunately happen to be the Jews, who are the henchman of the dajal [anti-Christ].'[90] 'Jews', Faisal preached, 'should be killed...as by Hitler.' Video and audiotapes of his sermons circulated widely; hundreds of Muslims, it was said, attended his lectures in mosques across Britain.[91] In one of his tapes, 'No Peace with the Jews', recorded at a July 2001 event in Luton, he lists nineteen reasons why Muslims cannot have peace with the 'filthy Jews', such as 'they are evil to the core' and 'deceitful by nature'. He jokes, to appreciative laughter, 'How did the Jews get back at Hitler? They sent him back the gas bill.' The tape ends with a question-and-answer session. 'Should we hate Jews and when we see them on the street, should we beat them up?' Al-Faisal replies, 'You have no choice but to hate them. How do you fight the Jews? You kill the Jews.'[92]

Perhaps rather more significant, before his arrest in London in October 2002, was the Jordanian preacher, Abu Qatada al-Filistani. In the late 1990s and early 2000s, Abu Qatada was in direct contact with numerous members and supporters of al-Qaeda. The reach and the depth of his influence among terrorist groups was said to have been 'formidable, even incalculable'. In one of his sermons, he preached:

> In Jewish law, when a Jew enters a village in war or peace it is his duty to rape the land, take kill [sic] the men and turn the women into slaves. He will take the land and the money and that is what that religion says. This war is for existence, to exist or not exist. You see the West supports that state [Israel], they are on their side. The west says it is an economic relationship but it is not.

He continued, 'There will be a great battle', and 'the saviour will come back to this earth, the king with an army in the sky, killing the Jews, to wipe them out and rid of the planet of the Jews'.[93]

Some time in 2008, Hizb-ut-Tahrir removed from its website a pamphlet that asserted of 'the Jews' that they were 'cowards', 'a people of money and not a people of fighting'.[94] The removal of this pamphlet, *The Muslim Umma will never submit to the Jews*, should perhaps be viewed as a sign of hope.

Jewish anti-Zionism

Modern Jewish politics was a response to, and an attempt to address, the 'Jewish Question'; it emerged out of ideological divisions within Jewish communities in the mid- to late nineteenth century. The combined effects of the Holocaust and the foundation of the State of Israel brought this politics to an end. For two decades thereafter there was no Jewish politics. Ideological differences within Jewish communities following the Six Day War then caused a *re*-emergence of Jewish politics. This is best described as *contemporary* Jewish politics. It is a response to, and an attempt to address, the 'Israel Question'. Contemporary Jewish anti-Zionism is best interpreted as occupying a set of positions within this new Jewish politics.

The shift from the 'modern' to the 'contemporary' has a complex history.

Towards the end of the nineteenth century, there was an upsurge in collective enthusiasms within the Jewish world,[95] and a break with traditional religious and communal life.[96] The precipitating events were the 1881 pogroms in Russia, taken by many Jews to confirm the failure of the emancipation project. The divisions within Jewish communities caused by this new and perhaps clearer-eyed understanding of their predicament grew over succeeding decades. Intra-communal conflict reached maximum intensity in the inter-war period of the twentieth century. It was, for example, the Jewish sections of the Communist Party in revolutionary Russia that led the fight against Zionism; if it were not for these sections, the liquidation of the Zionist movement would have been a slower process.[97]

The 'Jewish Question' was several questions, not just one. Are Jews to be defined as a nation or a religion—and then, what version of Judaism, what kind of Jewish nation? How should Jewish history be understood, and what aspects of it speak to contemporary concerns? Where, how, and with whom should Jews live, 'here' in the Diaspora, 'there' in Palestine—and with what minority/majority rights and status? In what language or languages should they express themselves as Jews? With what broader political movements, if any, should they ally? From what broader ideologies should they take direction? How should anti-Semitism be combated—by Jewish solidarity or proletarian solidarity?[98] A divided, inventive, and almost always struggling Jewish Left took every possible position between the polarities of class and nation, revolution and exodus, Lenin and Weizmann, Moscow and Jerusalem. The most refined reasoning—say, Gershom Scholem's insistence that he was a Zionist, not a Jewish nationalist, or Buber's insistence that he was a Hebrew Humanist, and not a nationalist[99]—often emerged in the most desperate of circumstances. There was often, of course, an anti-Semitic aspect to formulations of the Jewish Question, the very term itself being used to make the point that the Jews were an anomalous, troubling presence in Europe. And in response to such uses Jewish publicists would then insist: 'There should be no Jewish Question.'[100] But there *was*, and it persisted.

Though modern Jewish politics was not confined to the Left, it was easy to believe otherwise. It took multiple institutional forms. There were Jewish political parties and groups, Jewish 'sections' in non-Jewish political parties, philanthropic organizations, labour unions with a predominantly Jewish membership, trade associations, clubs and reading circles, newspapers and journals.[101] The variety was immense; the level of engagement was intense. In 1920s Poland, for example, there were no less than six socialist Zionist parties;[102] there were also substantial anti-Zionist groupings, and a broader anti-, or non-Zionist sentiment, particularly in Western Europe and the United States. The contending institutions of *contemporary* Jewish politics are radically different. On the one hand, there is the massive fact of the Jewish State. On the other, the political life of Diaspora Jewry is much attenuated—especially in Europe. There are communal bodies, one or two research institutions, some ad hoc pressure groups, and there are charities. But that is all. The principal oppositionist bodies that identify themselves as Jewish—in England, 'Jews for Justice for Palestinians', 'Independent Jewish Voices', and one or two others—are marginal to their community and tend to speak in sectarian tones.

The Nazis destroyed the Yiddish-speaking Jewish nation that inhabited parts of Central and Eastern Europe,[103] and many of the ideological positions taken by those Jews perished with them. The very possibility of Jewish politics suffered an immense blow; Zionism was the only Jewish political ideology to arise in Eastern Europe that survived.[104] Many leftists of Jewish origin surrendered their Jewish identity in favour of their leftist politics; other Jews merely abandoned their Jewish politics and either chose or had forced upon them the consolations of private life, the *a*politics of quietism.

In the decades immediately following the war, the Jews in the Soviet bloc were prisoners; the Jews of Muslim lands were expelled; the Jews of Israel built their state; the Jews of Western Europe and America reconciled themselves to their good fortune. And then came the Six Day War, and with it, the emergence of a new Jewish politics—a contemporary Jewish politics.

The 'Israel Question' is similarly plural. The Six Day War that reintroduced the possibility of a Jewish politics by posing the question, what should be done with this newly conquered land? If returned, on what terms; and if retained, by what right? These questions led to still further ones, of a more historical nature. Most concerned the differences and similarities between the 1967 War and the 1948 War. Were they both wars of Jewish survival? Were Israel's adversaries on both occasions the authors of their own calamity? What were Israel's peacemaking responsibilities in the aftermath of these wars, and did it meet them? And what, indeed, were Israel's responsibilities towards those unwillingly under its control, and did it meet those responsibilities, too? And still further questions arose. Can Israel be both Jewish and democratic? What are Diaspora Jewry's obligations to Israel? And by reference to what (Jewish?) principles were these obligations to be defined?[105] These questions together came to constitute a new Jewish politics in the making.[106]

The character of the contemporary Jewish anti-Zionist

There have always been distinct strands in the Jewish objection to Zionism. It has been regarded as inconsistent with Jewish teaching (the *'religious objection'*), with Jews' obligations to their countries of citizenship (the *'patriotic objection'*), and with projects of universal emancipation both/either from capitalism (the *'leftist objection'*) and/or ethnic or religious particularism (the *'liberal objection'*).

In the pre-1948 period, every one of these objections counted for a great deal. The religious objection existed in both Orthodox and Reform or Liberal versions. The patriotic objection, which was often advanced in tandem with the religious one, was made by substantial fractions of the Jewish communities of most Western European nations, and of the United States.[107] Indeed, antipathy to Zionism was one of the few positions (according to Michael B. Oren) around which, in the early 1900s, most of American Jewry could rally.[108] In Germany, meanwhile, in addition to the patriotic objection commanding the unreflective, commonsense allegiance of the generality of the nation's Jewry it was also given considerable theological depth by the German thinker Herman Cohen (1842–1919).[109] The liberal objection was to the effect that Zionism represented an attempt—no more, actually, than the latest in a series of such attempts in Jewish history—to distance the Western Jew from Western culture.[110] The leftist objection was advanced by both the Third and the Fourth Internationals, that is, the Stalinist and the Trotskyist wings of the revolutionary communist movement. All these objections faded upon the establishing of the Jewish State; not all at once, but over time. The religious objection was chastened by the ready accommodation reached with the State by the non-Zionist religious parties; the patriotic objection disappeared almost completely, as Jews found it possible to be citizens of their own country while also taking a fond pride in the achievements of another, Israel; the leftist objection faded before the spectacle of the Jewish remnants of the Holocaust rebuilding their lives as they built a state. Non-Zionists became no less ardent for the safety and success of the young State as the Zionists themselves;[111] the obdurately anti-Zionist tended to keep their own counsel. The argument was over; a new reality had emerged. 'In the 1920s,' wrote Leonard Woolf 'I was against Zionism . . . ' 'But,' he went on, 'in politics and history once something has been done radically to change the past into a new present, you must not act upon a situation which no longer exists, but upon the facts that face one.' And he concluded, post-1948, 'Zionism and anti-Zionism had become irrelevant.'[112]

And there matters stood until 1967; it took a short war to rescue anti-Zionism from 'irrelevance' (for Jews, at least). In the late 1960s, for a variety of reasons, the leftist objection re-emerged among young Jews who belonged to the New Left.[113] It was thought necessary to 'shatter' Zionism to release the revolutionary potential of the Israeli working class; a 'dialectical relationship' was perceived between the struggle against Zionism in Israel and the struggle for social revolution within the Arab world.[114] Religious and patriotic objections to Zionism, however, continued to count for nothing. Then, in 1989 or thereabouts, the socialist project was all but abandoned and the radical transformation of society was ruled out of question. And it is at this moment that contemporary Jewish anti-Zionism emerges (though there were early intimations of its emergence in certain positions taken by Diaspora Jews on the 1982 Lebanon War). The leftist objections wither, while the religious objection is revived—though in radically reformulated terms. This new Jewish anti-Zionism inaugurates a return for many Jews to some kind of Jewish identity. They no longer seek, as with previous generations, to relieve themselves of the burden of their Jewish origins;[115] rather, they reassume the burden, in order further to burden their fellow Jews. It is a return conditioned by many factors, of course. It is in part an involuntary response to what is taken to be Israel's importunacy of people of Jewish descent; it is in part also deliberately assumed for its value in the context of pro-Palestinian activism;[116] and lastly, it is in part the result of a certain post-leftist searching for new allegiances or affiliations. 'I find in anti-Zionism', writes Mike Marqusee, 'emancipation both as a Jew and as a human being.'[117]

The reformulation of the religious objection has two aspects. First, it is framed in terms of 'justice', understood to be a distinctly Jewish concept. The Palestinian cause is 'just'; Israel's cause is 'unjust'. Secondly, it is framed in terms of universalist allegiances, similarly understood to be Jewish in character. Let me take these in turn.

First, there is the objection in the name of justice. The 'Independent Jewish Voices' (*IJV*) opening statement in 2007, for example, endeavoured to 'reclaim' the 'tradition of Jewish support for universal freedoms, human rights and social justice'. 'Judaism', it continued, 'means nothing if it does not mean social justice.' And Moses' instruction to Israel was cited, 'Justice, justice shall you pursue' (Deuteronomy 16:20). This instruction 'is a compass bearing for all humanity'.[118] 'As a Jew, I feel a particular duty to oppose the injustice that is done to Palestinians', said one *IJV* signatory.[119] 'Israel's actions betray Jewish ethical traditions', assert a Jewish pro-boycott group.[120] The anti-Zionist is not just a Jew like other Jews; his dissent from normative Zionist loyalties makes him a *better* Jew. He restores Judaism's good name; to be a good Jew one has to be an anti-Zionist. Eric Hobsbawm, for example, explained when *IJV* was launched: 'It is important for non-Jews to know that there are Jews ... who do not agree with the apparent consensus within the Jewish community that the only good Jew is one who supports Israel.'[121] This refusal to 'support' Israel leads to the formulation: 'Israel is one thing, Jewry another.'[122] So far from Zionism being inextricably implicated in Jewish identity, fidelity to Judaism demands that Israel be criticized and one's distance from Zionism be affirmed. The public repudiation of the 'right of return', guaranteed to Jews by Israel in one of its earliest pieces of legislation, was considered to be one important such affirmation.[123]

Secondly, there is the objection in the name of universalism. The national project has debased the Jewish character by making it ordinary. The true Jew is the universalist—indeed, the one who paradoxically has disavowed all 'the trappings of linguistic, religious, and national identity'.[124] This contentless 'Jewishness' then becomes pure subjectivity.[125] Statehood, nationality, race, and ethnicity—each one is a false icon. 'Jewish particularism' of every kind must be rejected; Jews should not cut themselves off from their fellow students, workmates, and neighbours;[126] Jews should seek a 'Jewishness not sealed behind walls of conviction, but open to the infinite possibilities of tomorrow'.[127] Jews should be exemplary intellectuals. They must reject every particularism, and especially the particularity of the national, in favour of the universal.[128] The ambition is captured in Karl Krauss's slogan, 'Through dissolution to redemption!'[129] It must be the Jewish quality to have no qualities at all; assimilation is a 'renunciation of characteristics'; Jews are to be distinctive as exemplars of pure humanity.[130] This was a commonplace of a certain kind of nineteenth-century Jewish intellectual.[131] The Jewish anti-Zionists say with Lord Byron, Mankind our country—Israel but the grave.[132] And they say with Stephen Dedalus, 'You talk to [us] of nationality, language, religion. [We] shall try to fly by those nets.'[133] Israel is a test of their commitment to a cosmopolitan identity. Once, it was a test of their patriotism; now, it is a test of their freedom from all patriotisms—all loyalties smaller than to an indivisible human race. The only Jewish nationalism that is acceptable is an *extra*nationalism; the only Zionism, a renunciation of Jewish statehood. *IJV*'s principles, one of its founders explained, include 'putting human rights first; repudiating all forms of racism; and giving equal priority to Palestinians and Israelis in their quest for a better future'. These are 'principles that unite people of goodwill'; 'group or ethnic loyalty', by contrast, is *not* a principle—or not a worthy one, at least.[134] Contrary to Freud, whose own stance towards Zionism was somewhat reserved,[135] but who affirmed 'I have never lost the feeling of solidarity with my people', these Jews play no favourites.[136] Many anti-Zionist Jews do not consider themselves bound by an obligation of loyalty to *any* Jewish project. Indeed, they are not drawn to any such enterprises. Their ties to Israel are at most ones of affection;[137] more usually, they are strong in their denial of a tie.[138]

These Jewish anti-Zionists claim to speak as the moral conscience of the Jewish people. They no longer assert, as their revolutionary forebears once did, 'We regard ourselves as men, not Jews.'[139] Instead, they play the part of scourges of the Jewish State. While the position of scourge can be an honourable one, it is rarely free of difficulty. Many Jewish anti-Zionist scourges find themselves mired in difficulty. The 'scourge' is a kind of moralizer, namely a public person who prides himself on the ability to discern the good and the evil. He makes judgements on others, and profits by so doing; he puts himself on the right side of the fence. Moralizing provides the moralizer with recognition of his own existence and confirmation of his own value. A moralizer has a good conscience and is satisfied by his own self-righteousness.[140] The Jewish anti-Zionist scourge is not a self-hater; he is enfolded in self-admiration. He is in step with the best opinion.[141] He holds that the truth is to be arrived at by inverting the 'us = good' and 'other = bad' binarism.[142] He finds virtue in opposing his own community; he takes the other point of view. He writes counter-histories of his own people. It is not enough for him to disagree, or even refute; he must expose the worst bad faith, the most ignoble motives, the grossest crimes. He must *discredit*.

There is thus a quality of rage in much Jewish anti-Zionist writing. Consider, for example, Oren Ben-Dor, an Israeli academic who teaches Legal and Political Philosophy at Southampton University. In his view, the State of Israel should be 'reconfigured'. Israel is a 'terrorist state like no other' because it 'hides [its] primordial immorality [by] foster[ing] an image of victimhood'. 'Israel', he writes, 'was created through terror and it needs terror to cover-up its core immorality.' 'In 1948, most of the non-Jewish indigenous people were ethnically cleansed from the part of Palestine which became Israel. This action was carefully planned.' Israel has pursued a 'successful campaign to silence criticism of its initial and continuing dispossession of the indigenous Palestinians'. The Palestinians have 'no option but to resort to violent resistance'. 'Silence about the immoral core of Israeli statehood makes us all complicit in breeding the terrorism that threatens a catastrophe which could tear the world apart.' 'The main problem in Palestine [is] Zionism':

> Hamas' voice as a blunt denial of the 'right of Israel to exist' has indeed a belligerent tone to it, signalling destruction and annihilation. However, understanding this voice as an ethical cry to the world to not allow Israel the right to persist in its racist self-definition is a much better way of articulating the moral message.

Given these positions, it is perhaps inevitable that Ben-Dor should also maintain 'the U.S. is a captive of Zionism'.[143]

The rage is given less histrionic expression in the work of Ilan Pappe, another Israeli who has now made his home at an English university. He has written a book characterizing the two-way, mostly forced transfer of populations during the 1947–8 fighting between Jews and Arabs as a one-way, comprehensive 'master plan', devised by the Zionist movement in advance of hostilities and executed under cover of war.[144] Every Zionist reference to 'transfer' is treated as evidence of the plan; every Zionist disavowal of transfer is treated as an act of dissembling. Every Arab declaration of war against the Jews is treated indulgently, as mere rhetoric; every Arab claim of persecution is accepted without challenge. Every Zionist atrocity is treated as part of a transfer plan; every Arab atrocity is treated as a defensive response to Zionist aggression or is erased from the historical record.[145] The Palestinian refugees from Israel are represented as the victims of an historic injustice, and the pathos of their unsought and undeserved condition moves Pappe to indignant eloquence; the many hundreds of thousands of Jewish refugees from Arab countries, on the other hand, displaced by a combination of coordinated action by the League of Arab States, of state-sanctioned discriminatory and repressive measures, and of popular violence,[146] barely figure in his narratives.

Jewish anti-Zionist moralizers attract the praise of Israel's adversaries and enemies;[147] they are perceived by them to be an admirable, embattled remnant. They are credited with knowing the truth about Israel, the truth about Jews. The ex-Israeli Akiva Orr, wrote Tariq Ali admiringly, 'had long abandoned Israeli patriotism, but he had been an insider and knew a great deal'.[148] Ilan Pappe has received the kind of praise usually reserved for dissident truth-tellers in totalitarian societies. This esteem tempts some Jewish anti-Zionists into a certain kind of posturing. It takes 'guts' to speak out, says one, Alexei Sayle.[149] This 'speaking out'—always that, never merely 'speaking'—encourages overstatement. A group describing itself as 'Jews for Boycotting Israeli Goods' writes 'the continuing occupation and exploitation of Palestinian land is a major obstacle to peace for Israelis and Arabs alike *which has global implications for world peace*' (my italics).[150] Even though *IJV* comprises a group of people with very good access to the public sphere, they lent support to the trope that Jews endeavour to suppress the truth about Israel. They had been 'silenced', they claimed, reduced to muteness by allegations of 'disloyalty' or 'self-hatred'. Several months after its launch, however, a member of the steering committee resigned, remarking 'I've become aware how little in touch with the Anglo-Jewish community so many of its people are, when they make the good old Board of Deputies the axis of evil.'[151]

So much for contemporary Jewish anti-Zionism, most broadly conceived. Within it, however, a distinction may be made between the Israeli or ex-Israeli perspective, on the one hand, and the Diaspora Jewish perspective, on the other. The writings of Akiva Orr and Uri Davis may be read as representative of the former perspective, and the writings of Jacqueline Rose as representative of the latter perspective. There are of course others who could have been chosen, both Israeli and Diaspora Jews.

Akiva Orr argues that to be Jewish is to be religious; there is no such thing as a secular Jewish identity. Only those who keep the *mitzvoth* remain 'indisputably Jews'; the tenets of Judaism cannot be secularized. Zionism, which is predicated on such a project of secularization, has failed. The secular Jewish State has been unable to provide its Jewish citizens with a new, secular Jewish identity. The failure was inevitable. 'Zionism' is no more than a heresy of Judaism and the ethnocentrism of Jewish Israelis. The 'dominant criterion of personal and political behaviour' should instead be the 'well being' of 'humanity as a whole and not one's self, nation, or God'. The anthropocentric should take the place of the theocentric, the ethnocentric, *and* the egocentric.[152] Orr's fellow Israeli, Uri Davis, has adopted a somewhat more legalistic stance in his writings. He has three objections to Israel. First, political Zionists founded it, and political Zionism is an objectionable political ideology. Secondly, the circumstances of its founding caused great hardship to Palestinians. Thirdly, its character as a 'Jewish State' puts its non-Jewish citizens at a substantial juridical disadvantage. Each of Davis's objections is to what he regards as an aspect of racism. Zionist ideology is racist; Israeli conduct towards the Palestinians in 1948 was racist; Israel's laws are racist. It is this last aspect that for Davis justifies the term 'Apartheid'. Apartheid is racism regulated in law, he says. In consequence, Israel does not deserve to exist; it should be 'dismantled'. It should be replaced by a 'confederal, federal or unitary state for all of its citizens and Palestinian refugees', namely a 'democratic Palestine'. Davis describes political Zionism as an 'abomination' and a 'crime'.[153] He works hard to keep at bay those acknowledgements of complexity and nuance that from time to time surface in his work; he may intuit that his harsh, un-nuanced condemnations lack sophistication, balance, and even justice.

Jacqueline Rose has written three books with an anti-Zionist perspective: *States of Fantasy* (1996), *The Question of Zion* (2005), and *The Last Resistance*

(2007). She seeks, she says, to 'revive the story of internal Jewish dissent'.[154] In the 1996 book, in which she describes herself as 'a Jewish woman', and as a 'Jewish critic who wishes to address Israel as an outsider', she writes that Israel 'desires its potential citizens—exiled, diaspora Jewry—to come home, with as much fervour as it banishes the former occupants of its land from their own dream of statehood'.[155] In the 2005 book, she describes herself as a 'Jewish writer'.[156] Israel, she writes, is one of the most powerful military nations in the world, yet it presents itself as vulnerable and on the defensive. It suppresses dissent.[157] Though Zionism emerged out of the legitimate desire of a persecuted people for a homeland, the creation of Israel in 1948 led to a historic injustice against the Palestinians still awaiting redress. A straight line may be drawn from the seventeenth-century heretic, Shabtai Zvi, mystic and false messiah, to the Zionism of the late nineteenth and the twentieth century. Jewish messianism is material and carnal as well as spiritual, fully embodied in political time. It is a notion of redemption as bound up with ruin, dread, and catastrophe. With the birth of Israel, nationalism became the new messianism. Messianism colours Zionism, including secular Zionism, at every turn. This is 'chilling'.[158] We cannot relegate messianism, she continues, to the religious Zionists and the Ortho- dox anti-Zionists. The compulsion to fight the Arab people is entirely self- authored.[159] Arab aggression is either a response to Jewish settlement of the land or dispossession. The Palestinians are the inadvertent objects of a struggle that, while in one sense is all to do with land, in another sense, has nothing to do with the Palestinians themselves at all.[160] The remedy? Rose is committed, she writes, to Palestinian self-determination *or* to full political and civic equality.[161] But though she does not quite know her own mind on these alternatives, she is certain that absent one or other of them, there will be catastrophe—Israel cannot secure its own future.

The question of anti-Semitism

Jewish anti-Zionists tend to misrepresent the nature of the prophetic trad- ition, which celebrates Jewish self-government and preaches the link be- tween righteousness *and the holding of the land*;[162] they wrongly assume that group loyalty is inconsistent with the ethical life, and that universalist moral foundations cannot sustain a version of nationalism;[163] they fall into contra- diction when they hold that while dispersion is good for the Jews, it is bad for the Palestinians, and when they demand of the Jews that they disavow 'nationalism', while valuing the Palestinians' 'continuing struggle for just-ice';[164] and though there is indeed a messianic aspect to one version of religious Zionism, they mistakenly hold it to be a necessary feature of all religious Zionisms,[165] and indeed of Zionism in its secular versions too.[166] (They are also mistaken in thinking that Jewish messianism in any event implies a claim to Jewish political hegemony[167]—indeed, to some Jewish thinkers it meant the positive disavowal of sovereignty.)[168] None of these objections, of course, imply a judgement on Jewish anti-Zionists that they are anti-Semitic. Is such a judgement tenable, ever?

Struggling with the nakedly anti-Semitic character of Stalin's defamatory attacks on him, and the threat of the physical extermination of the Jews, Trotsky was driven to acknowledge, 'I have lived my whole life outside Jewish circles', and he then circled the Jewish Question, rejecting all solutions other than 'revolutionary struggle'—in 1937–8, a hopeless, even contentless option.[169] Many Jewish anti-Zionists hold back from making such an acknowledgement, though they could (and perhaps should) do so, before they too circle today's 'Jewish Question'. Trotsky maintained that his disconnectedness from Jews 'did not mean that he had the right to be blind to the Jewish problem'.[170] He did not, however, assert that he had any special insight into it, merely because he was a Jew by birth. He most certainly did not assert that he spoke on behalf of the Jews or of Judaism when he offered his views. Indeed, he rarely spoke or wrote on any issue as a Jew. 'I am a Social Democrat,' he once declared, 'and that's all.'[171] He would have acknowledged that he was not only without that quality known among Jews as *ahavat Zion* (yearning for, love of, Zion),[172] but also the fundamental quality of *ahavat Israel* (love of the Jewish people). He was not, however, an anti-Semite. What is more, he could smell anti-Semitism in others. Contemporary Jewish anti-Zionists, however, have lost the sense for it. They struggle, mostly incompetently, to understand it; they struggle, mostly incompetently, against it; many are themselves susceptible to its tropes and turns of phrase. Their perspectives *on* anti-Semitism are defect-ive; their contributions *to* anti-Semitism are significant.

Jewish anti-Zionist *perspectives* on anti-Semitism tend to be derived from one or more of the following propositions: anti-Semitism is caused by Israel; anti-Semitism should not preoccupy Jews; contemporary anti-Sem-itism is trivial, and need not be taken seriously; many ostensibly anti-Semitic acts and/or language are not in reality Jew-hating; the anti-Semites happen to be right about the 'Israel Lobby'. Jewish anti-Semites sometimes find themselves viewing Jewish events through the eyes of the anti-Semite.[173]

Anti-Semitism is caused by Israel   For most anti-Zionists, such anti-Semitism as now afflicts Jews is largely engendered by Israel. To Tony Judt, 'today, non-Israeli Jews feel themselves once again exposed to criticism and vulnerable to attack for things they didn't do, but this time it is a Jewish state, not a Christian one, which is holding them hostage for its own actions'. If Israel behaved better, Jews would fare better; Israel is bad for the Jews.[174] (German Jews once similarly complained about East European Jews.)[175] To Sabby Sagall, insofar as the Israeli leadership claims to speak for all Jews, and the majority unfortunately accept the claim, anti-Zionism tends to appear as anti-Semitism. Only when a majority of Jews speak out against Israel will that 'anti-Semitism' be defeated.[176] He is certain, however, that anti-Zionism is not anti-Semitism.[177] And to Anne Karpf, a *Guardian* journalist and contributor to an *IJV* volume of essays, Arab Holocaust denial is merely the natural consequence of a kind of Holocaust overemphasis:

> Since the Jewish genocide is used so shamelessly in legitimation of Israeli policy towards the Palestinians, it's hardly surprising if many Arabs and Muslims respond either with Holocaust denial or by trying to appropriate the Holocaust themselves. In a mirror-image of Arabs-are-Nazis, Zionism-is-Nazism: they accuse Israel of acting like Nazis even while they represent Jews in the crude and offensive stereotypes used by Nazi propaganda.[178]

Karpf does not grasp the autonomy of anti-Semitic discourse; she does not acknowledge the moral responsibility of anti-Semites for their anti-Semitism; she does not put 'Arab and Muslim' post-war Holocaust denial in the context of Arab and Muslim pre-war anti-Semitism. To Jacqueline Rose, while anti-Semitism is not *caused* by Israel's policies, without a clear critique of Israel today, there is no chance of defeating it. Anti-Semitism is thereafter not examined in her 2005 book, other than by reference to Zionism's complicity with it. When opportunities for such an examination arise, she avoids them.

Anti-Semitism should not preoccupy Jews   There has always been within Judaism, and therefore within Jewish politics, a certain tension between the 'universal' and the 'particular'. In response to any public call made by a Jew on behalf of other Jews, another Jew is likely to comment that the call should not be restricted to Jews and should extend more widely. This is the small change of intra-Jewish controversy.[179] Jewish critics of Zionism have always argued that Jewish nationalism neglects the universal in favour of the particular.

Contemporary anti-Semitism is trivial, and need not be taken seriously   'There's a great deal of criticism of Israel which spills over into odious anti-Semitism', says Dan Judelson, chair of Jews for Justice for Palestinians. 'It's not a type of deep-seated, visceral hatred of the Jews; it's just intellectual laziness.'[180] And of course, Jews do not need protection from the intellectually lazy; the intellectually lazy, in their indolence, pose no threat. It is asylum seekers, Muslims, and black people who bear the brunt of today's racism.[181] Many of the attacks on Jews in Europe and elsewhere, Tony Judt says, are 'misdirected efforts' by young Muslims to get back at Israel. Uri Davis writes approvingly of the UN 1975 resolution and the WCAR 2001 conference.[182] Anti-Semitism is no longer a serious problem for Jews; it is now a marginal, insignificant phenomenon. It is not to be confused with anything that is truly 'evil'. 'Every time someone smears anti-Semitic graffiti on a synagogue wall in France,' writes Judt, 'we are warned that "the unique evil" is with us once more, that it is 1938 all over again. We are losing the capacity to distinguish between the normal sins and follies of mankind—stupidity, prejudice, opportunism, demagogy, and fanaticism— and genuine evil.'[183]

Many ostensibly anti-Semitic acts and/or language are not in reality Jew-hating   Attacks on Israel, or even upon Jews, by Palestinians or those sympathetic to the Palestinian cause, are rarely to be construed as anti-Semitic. When Israel claims that it acts in the name of all Jews, there are some among its enemies ready to take the claim at face value, and strike at Jewish targets outside Israel. They cannot be criticized for doing so. These attacks are motivated by political outrage, not bigotry.[184] Anti-Semitism in the Arab countries must be distinguished from its Western European counterpart. Suicide bombing is the reaction to Israeli action; 'the roots of the problem [are] the human rights abuses, daily humiliations and overwhelming frustrations...in the occupied territories'.[185] The bombing of a synagogue in Paris, for example, is reprisal for an incursion into the West Bank. 'Racism' legitimizes the powerful's oppression of the weak; the 'weak' Palestinians by definition cannot be racist towards the powerful Israelis.[186] False accusations of anti-Semitism have led a few of the falsely accused to embrace some anti-Semitic tropes. The occasional anti-Semitic remark can be dealt with swiftly. For example, Tam Dalyell's 'anti-Semitic outburst', said one Jewish anti-Zionist, would be 'decisively reject[ed]' by 'the anti-war movement and the left'.[187]

The anti-Semites happen to be right about the 'Israel Lobby'   In a speech at Chicago University, given in October 2007, Tony Judt said:

> If you stand up here and say, as I am saying and someone else will probably say as well, that there is an Israel lobby, that there is . . . there are a set of Jewish organizations, who do work, both in front of the scenes and behind the scenes, to prevent certain kinds of conversations, certain kinds of criticism and so on, you are coming very close to saying that there is a *de facto* conspiracy or if you like plot or collaboration to prevent public policy moving in a certain way or to push it in a certain way—and that sounds an awful lot like, you know, the Protocols of the Elders of Zion and the conspiratorial theory of the Zionist Occupational Government and so on—well if it sounds like it it's unfortunate, but that's just how it is. We cannot calibrate the truths that we're willing to speak, if we think they're true, according to the idiocies of people who happen to agree with us for their reasons.[188]

Judt's odd, misconceived remarks bring me to the Jewish anti-Zionist *contributions* to anti-Semitism—in summary, both to affirm the truth of certain anti-Semitic positions (or positions with anti-Semitic implications) and to protect the holders of those positions from charges of anti-Semitism.

To Lynne Segal, Palestinians are the new Jews, and their suffering evokes Jewish suffering in the worst periods of anti-Semitism in Europe.[189] But Jacqueline Rose goes further, and affirms the Israel/Nazi analogy. 'The suffering of a woman on the edge of the pit with her child during the Nazi era', she writes, 'and a Palestinian woman refused access to a hospital through a checkpoint and whose unborn baby dies as a result, *is the same*' (italics added).[190] How, she asks, did one of the most persecuted peoples of the world come to embody some of the worst cruelties of the modern nation-state?[191] Israel inscribes at its heart the very version of nationhood from which the Jewish people had had to flee.[192] What should one make of the use by self-identifying Jews of the Jew/Nazi trope? It has a distant relation to that tendency in foundational Jewish texts to collapse the ostensibly inconsequential into the grievously consequential, condemning both with a similar ferocity. One finds in the Talmud, for example, the following formulation: anyone who does *x* (something ostensibly minor), it is as if he has done y (something indisputably major), and thus has merited z (the punishment for the most major of offences). In some usages, the trope also derives from a specifically Jewish conviction that Jews should have nothing to do with power, which is in its nature unjust. Nazism is thus merely the most realized expression of power; *every* exercise of power has a certain Nazi quality. In some other usages, it is an aspect of that overheated, intemperate intra- and inter-communal polemicizing that characterizes Israeli public life. And why not characterize one's opponents as utterly iniquitous, without saving quality or merit? It has been the Jewish way in polemic for centuries.

What then of the protection, or cover, given by Jews to anti-Semitic positions? 'Nothing infuriates Zionists more than the arguments of anti-Zionist Jews', wrote the SWP activist and journalist Paul Foot:

> who have such a courageous and principled history. The essence of the intellectual case for Zionism is that its opponents are anti-Semitic. But when Jews...speak out against Zionism, and especially if they denounce Israeli imperialism and defend the victims of it, how can they be accused of anti-semitism?[193]

It was noted in the context of the boycott agitations, not least because the boycotters themselves loudly insisted upon it, that the boycott cause had Jewish supporters. Though not advancing fresh arguments in favour of a boycott, these Jews made two distinctive contributions to the boycott campaign. First, they maintained that as Jews they were under a moral duty to campaign for a boycott. Their Jewish conscience required them, they claimed, to side with Israel's enemies. Secondly, they gave cover to non-Jewish boycotters accused of anti-Semitism.[194] How could these non-Jews be anti-Semitic, when Jews took their line too? Anti-Semitism, they intimated, ceases to be anti-Semitic when adopted by a Jew. These absurd, ignominious positions attracted only a few Jews, though they were much exploited by the boycott movement.

Most Jewish anti-Zionists reach anti-Semitism by the thoughtless deployment of the new anti-Zionism's vulgarities. A few reach anti-Semitism, however, by reviving rather older libels on Judaism. In *The unJewish State* (1983), Akiva Orr characterizes Judaism as subordinating morality, society and justice to God, and characterizes God as demanding of Jews that they carry out immoral, antisocial, and unjust acts, like sacrificing their own children to him, merely to test the strength of their conviction.[195] Israel

Shahak's *Jewish History, Jewish Religion* (1997) sought to trace the most discreditable aspects of Zionism in Jewish religious laws concerning the treatment of non-Jews. The book is published by Pluto Press, which was founded in London in 1969 as a publishing arm of International Socialism, the forerunner of the Socialist Workers Party in the UK. In 1979, however, it broke with the party, 'and became truly independent'.[196] It publishes, according to its website, 'the very best in progressive, critical thinking', and it describes Shahak as a 'voice of conscience'. Shahak composed tracts worthy of Eisenmenger and Röhling—only to be praised for his scholarship by people who knew nothing either of his sources or his way with them.[197]

The distinction between a perspective and a contribution is not absolute. A perspective can of course also be a contribution.

Beyond the everyday Jewish anti-Zionists lurk a few maverick figures, Gilad Atzmon chief among them. Atzmon is a jazz musician, much lionized by the SWP.[198] 'Zionists have imposed a blindness on the world', he says. 'It's time to hit back with literature, prose, music, cinema. Everything goes.' 'It's time to establish a clear association between colonialism and the Zionist lobby. It's my duty to make that association widely known.'[199] His incontinent, malicious verbalizing, which has no connection to real thought, is of significance only because he nonetheless continues to be admired in anti-Zionist circles.[200] Oren Ben-Dor is a particular champion of Atzmon's 'endeavours'.[201]

Representativeness

Jewish anti-Zionists find nothing appealing about the principle of Jewish self-government; they find little of value in the project of maintaining the existence and integrity of the Jewish state. While most Jewish anti-Zionists are realists about Israel, they tend to be idealists about the Palestinians. Many acknowledge that Israel is still too substantial a presence, too *fixed*, to be dislodged; all are engaged by the Palestinian 'struggle', which excites their imagination and engages their sympathies. In the Israeli, they see nothing of the state-building pioneer, they see only the predatory land-grabber and people-expeller; in the Palestinian, they see nothing of the defeated aggressor, they see only the victim. Indeed, the Palestinians are mostly represented as somewhat spectral vessels of pure suffering.

In these respects, they are with the *zeitgeist*. Jacqueline Rose, for example, happily acknowledges, 'I am with the *zeitgeist*.'[202] She has the sense that Zionism—understood to be ethnicist, separatist, particularist, 'messianist', a reactionary nationalism—is out of step with the times. Tony Judt has most recently made just this case. Israel, Judt argues, denominates and ranks its citizens according to ethno-religious criteria, which makes it an oddity among 'modern nations', *or alternatively* among 'democratic states'. It has imported a typically late-nineteenth-century separatist project into a world that has moved on, a world of individual rights, open frontiers, and international law. The very idea of a 'Jewish state' is from another time and place, the twilight of the continental empires, when Europe's subject peoples dreamed of forming 'nation-states'. In the contemporary world, where nations and peoples increasingly intermingle and intermarry at will; where cultural and national impediments to communication have all but collapsed; where more and more of us have multiple elective identities and would feel falsely constrained if we had to answer to just one of them, Israel is an anachronism. *Alternatively*, if this does not characterize the world as a whole, but only the world of open, pluralist democracies, engaged in a 'clash of cultures' with belligerently intolerant, faith-driven ethno-states, Israel risks falling into the wrong camp. A binational state is the solution.[203] Zionism is a dead end; the Jewish State must cease to define itself as Jewish.[204] She must, that is, dissolve herself. Judt does not entertain the question of whether this proposal would be welcomed by the majority of Israel's citizens.[205] Nor does he seem to be aware that he is rehearsing an argument within Jewish politics that is at least 140 years old—since the very emergence of modern Jewish politics, there has always been a position that finds in the modern the very negation of the national.[206] Needless to say, he is also rehearsing an argument within an *anti*-Jewish politics that is several millennia old. The Jews hold themselves apart, they will not assimilate, etc.[207]

But if this is now the *zeitgeist*, it is not—or not yet, at least—the Jewish *zeitgeist*. Anti-Zionism remains a minority position within the Jewish community. In a survey of Anglo-Jewish opinion conducted in 2004, 47 per cent of those questioned agreed with the statement 'I am a Zionist', and 78 per cent agreed with the statement 'I care deeply about Israel'. The gap between the final two figures is attributable to the commonly held conviction that one can only describe oneself as a Zionist if one intends to emigrate to Israel.[208]

Christian anti-Zionism

England itself is no longer a Christian country: by the 1990s, only about a tenth of the population in England was in regular contact with any Church.[209] But it remains institutionally Christian. There are several kinds of English Christians—Roman Catholics, Anglicans, and members of the Nonconformist Churches. Several of these denominations, though originating in England, are now international in character. All are intensely engaged with the Israel–Palestinian conflict. The Anglican Bishopric of Jerusalem incorporates the Sabeel Ecumenical Liberation Theology Center ('*sabeel*' means 'the way' in Arabic). It has the support of leading Anglican clerics.[210]

In a specifically English context, Christian anti-Zionism is to be distinguished from other confessional anti-Zionisms on several grounds.

First, the Christian understanding of the region as 'the Holy Land' is distinct from Judaism's and Islam's understandings. Part of Christianity's struggle against Judaism is in the contest over the sacred quality of the land. The connection between Judaism and the land is intimate; many of the commandments a Jew can only perform when actually there. By contrast, while Galilee, Bethlehem, and Jerusalem are all places with immense resonance to Christians, they do not have theological meaning. Christ has taken the place of the Temple. He preaches the kingdom of God, not the kingdom of Israel. His message transcends the land. Jerusalem and the 'Holy Land' itself have been made irrelevant in God's redemptive purposes.[211] Jewish anti-Zionists, by contrast, tend to be divided on the continuing significance of *Eretz Israel* to their sense of what it is to be Jewish today.

Secondly, a negative theological weight is attached by some Christian anti-Zionists to the Jewish return to sovereign power in the Holy Land. The establishment of the Jewish State represents a challenge to the received Christian understanding of the Jews' loss of Jerusalem as a punishment for their rejection of Jesus, and the new religion of Christianity as superseding Judaism itself. There are Christian anti-Zionists who find this challenge intolerable. They are especially angry about the Zionist or pro-Israel positions taken by certain Christian denominations in the United States, which they consider in many instances to be theologically perverse, elevating 'Israel' above the 'Church'. According to the divine plan, the Jews were supposed to have no future. The Anglican George Herbert's poem 'The

Jews', for example, though it pushes empathy for its subjects to the Christian limit, is typical in its acknowledgement of the Jews' sterility: 'Poor nation, whose sweet sap and juice / Our scions have purloined, and left you dry . . . '[212] What to make, then, of the State of Israel, in which Jewish 'sap and juice' runs so freely? Jewish and Muslim anti-Zionists are, of course, indifferent to such considerations.

Thirdly, there is a substantial and lengthy history of Anglican involvement in Palestine, the 'bible' to the British Empire's 'sword' in Barbara Tuchman's pairing.[213] There is a continuous line, from the seventeenth to the twentieth centuries, of English advocates of Jewish restoration in the Holy Land—ardent Christians who looked forward to a revivified and gloriously rebuilt New Jerusalem,[214] and who took God's covenant with Abraham to be absolute, unlimited, and for the benefit of an 'Israel properly descended out of Jacob's loins'.[215] It became their mission to restore the land to its lawful owners, and thereby assist in fulfilling Biblical prophecy.[216] An Anglican bishopric in Jerusalem was established in 1841, with a converted Jew consecrated as its first bishop. Many early Christian Zionists worked through the London Society for Promoting Christianity, an Anglican organization and, later on in the nineteeth century, the Palestine Expedition Fund. The history bears heavily on the minds of contemporary anti-Zionists. 'Lord Shaftesbury', writes one, 'inspired a generation of Joshuas.'[217] The Anglo-Christian Zionism of the nineteenth and early twentieth centuries, which by then had mostly abandoned its conversionist ambitions, is held by its critics to have played a large part in defining the terms of the subsequent Israel–Palestinian conflict.[218] The history does not go all one way, however. The English missionaries in Mandate Palestine, for example, were taken by at least one observer to be 'almost to a man, if not actually anti-Semitic, at any rate anti-Zionist'.[219] Anglican sympathies in Mandate times were with the Arabs; in 1937, a group of leading Anglican theologians, constituted as the 'Archbishops' Commission', very firmly restated received doctrine by declaring, 'the Church is not only "the Israel of God", it is also the "elect race"'.[220]

Fourthly, the Queen is the Head of the Church of England. Its bishops are legislators, and sit in the House of Lords. The Church of England can act *corporately*: it has a 'General Synod'. Most Christian denominations have their own religious institutions, their own hierarchy. By contrast, there are no Jewish or Muslim clerics with the right to sit in the House of Lords. Though one branch of the Anglo-Jewish Orthodox community, in imitation of the Anglican model, has a 'Chief Rabbi', he does not have the authority of the archbishop of Canterbury. The Muslim community is altogether without a religious hierarchy.

Fifthly, this anti-Zionism is expressed in specifically Christian language and imagery. Christian anti-Zionists typically call for 'compassion', and an 'unhardening of the heart'.[221] They cite Jesus' 'Blessed are the peacemakers' (Matthew 5:9). Some are also ready to describe Palestinian suffering in language borrowed from accounts of the Passion of Christ, thereby rendering Israel as successor to Jesus' Jewish tormentors: 'Palestine has become one huge Golgotha. The Israeli government crucifixion system is operating daily. Palestine has become the place of the skull.'[222] Jewish anti-Zionists, by contrast, draw on the *Tanach* to recall Jews to their most elevated spiritual qualities, while Muslim anti-Zionists cite the Qur'an and the Hadiths as evidence of Jewish treachery.

Anglo-Christian perspectives on Israel and the Zionist project are no longer influenced by the history of Anglican involvement in the Middle East. They are instead influenced, in an unqualifiedly negative way, by the current involvement of American Christian Zionists. In their open letter to the prime minister, the archbishops of Canterbury and York wrote:

> Within the wider Christian community we also have theological work to do to counter those interpretations of the Scriptures from outside the mainstream of the tradition which appear to have become increasingly influential in fostering an uncritical and one-sided approach to the future of the Holy Land.[223]

By which is meant: 'The Americans have got it wrong, and this is damaging the prospects for peace in the Middle East.' There is a flavour here of the greater political and cultural confrontation between Europe and the United States, and this is evident in other texts by English Christians too.[224]

A restated supersessionism

It is in Christianity that for the first time in the world's history Jew-hatred becomes *sanctified*. As against the pagan confrontation with the Jews, which was mostly voluntary and occasional, the Christian Church was *compelled* to confront the Jews. Though Jews were a significant presence in the pagan world, they were objectionable but not important to the pagan anti-Semite; to the Christian Church, by contrast, Jews were immensely objectionable and immensely important, even though numerically insignificant. When anti-Semitism began again in Christian culture, then, it was thus more attention-seeking than in pagan times. Its claims regarding the Jews were more importunate, more extreme. It constituted the Jews and Judaism, collectively, as *the* enemy of the good, the true, and the beautiful. This new, Christian anti-Semitism was always endemic, and sometimes epidemic.[225] The Church Father John Chrysostom (347–407), a principal contributor to the patristic enterprise of vilification of the Jews,[226] wrote, 'If the Jewish rites are holy and venerable, our way of life must be false. But if our way is true, as indeed it is, theirs is fraudulent.'[227] Here, and in the perplexity and anger at Jewish rejection of the apostolic mission, is the germinating seed of Christian anti-Semitism.

A systematized, hostile conception of Judaism, the Jews, and Jewish history, thus became part of Christianity. Anti-Semitism is consistent with normative Christian perspectives—indeed, it was assumed for a *very* long time to be a necessary consequence of them. (Christian slave-owners had to work somewhat harder to find scriptural justifications for holding Africans in servitude.)[228] Anti-Semitism is not a repudiation of Christianity; it is not un-Christian.[229] But Christianity is not constitutively anti-Semitic. It is not *credal*—neither the Apostles' Creed nor the Nicene Creed, which appear in Anglican Books of Common Prayer, refer to Jews.[230] Anti-Semitism is a contingent and not a necessary truth about Christianity; there are possible worlds in which Christianity is *not* anti-Semitic. Indeed, Christianity is predicated on a refusal to distinguish between Jew and Gentile, a refusal that has on many occasions moved Christians to take a stand against the persecution of Jews.[231] It should be possible to say 'Jesus is Messiah' without saying at the same time, 'and the Jews be damned'.[232] If Christianity provides a pretext for hating Jews, then, it may also provide the means of overcoming this hatred.[233] There is much to overcome, however.

In the first centuries following its establishment, the Christian Church developed a doctrine regarding the Jews that became known as the *Adversus Judaeos* discourse or the teaching of contempt.[234] Among its elements were the following:

• *Reinterpretation of the Tanach.* The Church is the fulfilment of Israel's prophecies and aspirations, as expressed in Israel's own Scriptures.[235] They are thus proleptic texts, their persons and events to be read as types or prefigurations of the persons and events of the 'New Testament'.

The 'Old Testament' is but 'a book of shadows, given on loan, until the coming of Christ'.[236] The Jews' own texts concede the truth of Christianity's claims, but the Jews perversely, or blindly, deny them. They read literally or 'carnally'; Hebrew, properly understood, is a Christian language;[237] the 'Old Testament' is likewise a Christian book.[238] The Jews' rejection of Jesus is of a piece with their misreading of their Scriptures. This rejection is itself prefigured—while the Christians are Abel, Isaac, and Jacob, the Jews are Cain, Ishmael, and Esau.[239] Indeed, in one formulation, the Christians are the 'true Israelites' and the Jews, the 'Amalekites'.[240] Just as philosophy was a schoolmaster to bring the Greek mind to Christ, so the Law should have brought the Jews to him. It was a preparation only, intended to pave the way towards perfection in Christ.[241]

- *The providential punishment of the Jews.* Rejecters of Christ, their land has rejected them. Their dispersion is proof of their wickedness. Their exile sets the seal on all prophecies that they would be punished for their deicide.[242] They subsist in a state of spiritual ignominy; they are a divinely disgraced people. The destruction of the Temple, the burning of Jerusalem, and the 'unexampled state in which the Jews have ever since continued',[243] prove their wrongdoing. Jerusalem was the Deicide city, and its fall was commemorated in medieval Church liturgy.[244] By the Jews' wickedness they have earned their misfortune;[245] their guilt has consigned them to 'perpetual serfdom'.[246] They wander, a race accursed, an object of contempt to all other peoples. They are the people of Cain, smitten by the divine malediction. It is God's revenge upon them for the killing of His son. Any effort to ameliorate their condition is contrary to divine justice; the Jews *should* be miserable, because they crucified Jesus. The modern political doctrine of Zionism is to be deprecated, both because it endeavours to improve the divinely ordained condition of the Jews and because it affirms the continued vibrancy of Jewish collective existence.[247] The Jews are God's enemies; they have been cursed for crucifying His Son; they cannot lift that curse by any mere act of national will.

- *A 'supersessionist' or 'replacement' theology.* With the new covenant, the old one is obsolete (see ch. 8, Hebrews).[248] The Church has displaced Israel. It is the new and true Israel. Christianity is the true Judaism. It is eternally young. God has abandoned the Jews; they have been dismissed from the service of the Revelation.[249] God has 'transferred his favour' to 'worshippers far more faithful' than the Jews.[250] They are the forsaken nation, no longer God's own people.[251] They are to be regarded as sons of Hagar, the slave woman, and not sons of Sarah, the free woman (Galatians 4:21–8). They are not inheritors of the promise made to their father, Abraham. Not all who are descended from Israel belong to Israel (Romans 9:6). Jewish history ends with the appearance on the world stage of Christianity, and that Jews continue to exist thereafter is nothing more than a curiosity. Though different positions are taken on the merit of what has been superseded,[252] all agree that salvation can only come through Christ. This Christian triumphalism would not allow Judaism's self-understandings. That the Jews continue to resist the truth is evidence only of their wilful stubbornness. They are an irrational, superstitious, and obstinate people.[253] (This supersessionism exists in secular versions too.)[254]

The Church assumed the role of inspired interpreter of Jewish action and Jewish destiny.[255] The teaching of the doctrine of contempt was not a constant throughout Christianity's history. It remained underdeveloped for the first 1,000 years;[256] it became an aspect of the Church's governing perspective only in the twelfth century. In the centuries that followed, different emphases emerged, reflecting the many distinct and conflicting beliefs held by Christians. The charge of deicide (another aspect of the teaching of contempt) tended to be prominent in the Catholic Church, while the charge of legalism (a still further aspect) was more persuasive to Protestant Christians.[257] By the late nineteenth century,[258] the teaching had been all but abandoned in the Anglophone world—at least, at the level of Bible scholarship.[259] However, the more general notions of the Jew as Christianity's great antagonist, and of Judaism itself as that 'Other' that Christianity overturns,[260] have not altogether disappeared from the stock of received wisdom that is the common heritage of those nations that comprise 'the West'.

While Christian anti-Semitism is not now what it once was, it would be wrong to say, as one Israeli historian has asserted, that 'the Christian debate that started nineteen hundred years ago, in our day came to a conciliatory close'.[261] To the contrary—this 'debate' has somewhat revived in certain versions of Christian anti-Zionism for which the existence of a sovereign Jewish State is a challenge, specifically, to the doctrines of supersessionism and the providential punishment of the Jews.[262] More broadly, the State has compelled all Christians to re-address 'the meaning of Israel'.[263]

While Christian anti-Zionism is the pursuit of activists, inevitably a minority within their various denominations, it also has a normative theological aspect that speaks to *all* Christians. This aspect is what might be termed a revived, even somewhat politicized, supersessionism. It tends to understand Zionism only as a response to anti-Semitism (and then to criticize it for its inadequacy as a response, and even its replication of anti-Semitism's own themes).[264] It argues for the incompatibility of Zionism with Christianity; it even presumes to argue for the incompatibility of Zionism with Judaism.[265] It is stimulated both by dismay at Jewish political resurgence[266] and by antagonism towards American premillenialist dispensationalism. Dispensationalism holds that God has separate purposes for the Jews and the Church; the millennium will mark the culmination of God's purposes for Israel; the Jews remain God's chosen people; there will be a final restoration of the Jews to Zion; God will judge the world on the basis of how it has treated the Jews.[267] 'Theology really matters, and if the theology is wrong, the consequences are disastrous', one Christian critic of Zionism has written.[268] The Anglican Church in general endeavours to steer a middle course between dispensationalism and supersessionism.

This 'middle course' is exemplarily evident in the archbishop of Canterbury's 2004 lecture at Sabeel. For sure, he granted, 'Christian Zionism' is a 'deeply eccentric form of Christian theology'. However, the existence of Israel is of positive theological significance, and this because the existence of the Jews as a people is itself a theologically positive matter. Israel's being as a people is still, and in spite of all, a gift to the community of nations. Israel is called to be the 'paradigm nation', the example held up to all nations of how a people live in obedience to God and justice with one another. While the modern political reality of Israel is not biblical Israel, it is ideally one of the conditions for biblical Israel's message and witness to be alive in the world today. It is wrong, furthermore, to challenge Israel in the name of a Christian universalism that tries to dispense with the specifics of the history of revelation. What then of the Israel–Palestinian conflict? The State of Israel has had to sustain its existence against enemies who would not grant its right to exist. Yet if the land has to be defended by a ceaseless struggle that has the effect of distorting the very fabric of the common life, it ceases to be a 'sacramental' mark of God's calling. There is now this risk. Moreover, the causes of the conflict lie less with aggressive neighbours than with broader failures to tackle regional stability. Bad and unscriptural Christian theologies become part of the problem, theologies that collude with the violence of either side.[269]

In the following year, the Church of England published *Countering Terrorism: Power, violence and democracy post 9/11*. On the one hand, it argued that American Christian Zionists derive their position from a reading of the books of Daniel, Ezekiel, and Revelation that 'European Christian scholars would regard as unwarranted'.[270] The place that premillennialists give to the founding of the state of Israel in God's purpose has no real foundation in the biblical narrative. What is more, 'it creates amongst Arabs, particularly Christian Arabs, a deep sense of resentment and unfairness that the faith they share with American Christians has been used against them'.[271] The State of Israel should be understood in terms of international law—that is, its creation was a purely secular event, and without spiritual significance.[272] On the other hand, in affirming a continuing role for the people of Israel, dispensationalism is 'more biblical' than traditional Christian supersessionism. It is truer to Romans 9–11, in which Paul confirms that God has not broken his promise, and has not abandoned his people.

Christian anti-Zionists, and many Christian critics of Zionism, by contrast, take a straightforwardly supersessionist line. Kenneth Cragg, for example, argues that 'By Christian reckonings, we are bound to disallow any extension from biblical Israel to Zionist Israel of promises, claims or meanings that flout the New Testament principle of divinely consistent love and universal grace.'[273] The Bible needs to be interpreted by reference to what he terms the 'Christ-criterion'.[274] It must, writes a Palestinian Christian, 'be de-Zionized'.[275] The Rev. Stephen Sizer is among the champions of Christian anti-Zionism in England. He is an Evangelical Christian, a Surrey parish vicar, and the chairman of the International Bible Society (UK). His book *Anti-Zionism: Road-map to Armageddon?* (2004) builds upon his repudiation of his own earlier Christian Zionism.[276] Contrary to received opinion, he insists, not all evangelicals are Zionist. He is a 'Covenantalist', postulating two covenants, one with the Jews, and a later one with the Church. The second covenant has superseded the first one. 'Under the first, Adam failed, under the second, Jesus triumphed in our place.'[277] He dismisses dispensationalism as 'heretical and cultic'.[278] Christian Zionists misapply injunctions and promises concerning the ancient Jews to the State of Israel rather than to the Church. They are at fault in rejecting the normative typological reading of the Old Testament. They show an 'uncritical tolerance of rabbinic Judaism'.[279] They are further at fault in disavowing 'missionizing' to the Jews. They invert supersessionist doctrine, by holding that Israel will succeed the church, and that the 'church age' itself is almost over. They do not understand that Jews who reject Jesus Christ are outside the covenant of grace and are now to be regarded as children of Hagar (Galatians 4:21–8). Sizer writes that 'unbelieving Jewish people' are 'loved by God but cut off from God's people'.[280] He has recently explained, however, that he 'categorically reject[s] any position that threatens the integrity of Israel as a sovereign nation'.[281]

Palestinian Christian theologians go further, skirting Marcionite themes. (The second-century theologian Marcion heretically identified two Gods, an Old Testament one, and a New Testament one, and rejected the first in favour of the second.) Christians must 'assert their faith in a universal God of justice and mercy', one theologian explains, 'and not in a tribal deity of vengeance and favouritism'.[282] 'Many of our Palestinian Christians wanted to abandon the Bible, particularly the Old Testament, which was being used against them', writes Father Ateek. They have a 'problem with the Bible'. 'The establishment of the State of Israel was a seismic tremor of enormous magnitude that has shaken the very foundation of their beliefs.'[283] But, he continues, as Christians, we cannot do our theology outside of the Bible. We need to find in the Bible the God of justice, the God who is concerned with the oppressed, who is concerned with the Palestinians as the oppressed. We do this by interrogating the Incarnation. It is to be understood as an answer to the 'claims of messianic fulfilment used by Jews and Western Christians to oppress and destroy us'.[284] This is a 'Palestinian liberation theology'.[285] The conflict over Palestine should thus very specifically *not* be interpreted in religious terms. It is instead a struggle undertaken by Palestinians for their homeland. They believe that they can achieve a full expression of their religious life by sharing the land; Jews likewise should adopt this belief.

Political activity

Countering Terrorism immensely overstates the part played by Israel in the Middle East:

> There can be little doubt that one of the major obstacles to the establishment of democracy in most Arab countries is the recent history of the Middle East

and, in particular, the role played in the popular imagination by the state of Israel. The creation of the state of Israel, at a time when other Arab states were achieving their independence, and the subsequent wars and Arab defeats have been a significant inhibiting factor in the region's political development. These events have enabled many Arab states to live in a perpetual state of emergency that justifies, on the one hand the development of military re-gimes, and on the other hand security-focused states, neither of which is conducive to democracy.[286]

This widely held view gives impetus to specifically Christian political activity, which, in addition to condemning various actions and initiatives by Israel ('the Apartheid wall'), has a dual institutional focus, consisting, first, of fundraising for the relief of Palestinian poverty and hardship and, sec-ondly, of campaigns to divest from companies doing certain kinds of business with Israel. The fundraising is conducted by charities that have an intense, but not exclusive, focus on the Israel–Palestinian conflict. One of the principal such charities is 'Christian Aid'. The divestment campaign began in September 2004, with a 'statement' by the Anglican Peace and Justice Network. It condemned the unwillingness of 'the Israeli government to recognize the rights of the Palestinians to a sovereign state to be created in the West Bank—which includes East Jerusalem—and Gaza', and called for an unqualified, unconditional 'right of return for Palestinian refugees'.[287] The statement was adopted in June 2005 by the Anglican Consultative Council, which recommended to Anglicans worldwide a policy of divestment from companies that 'contribute to Israel's occupation of the Palestinian territories'.[288] The Anglican General Synod, in turn, endorsed the request from the Episcopal Church in Jerusalem to disinvest from 'companies profiting from the illegal occu-pation'.[289] The archbishop of Canterbury supported the decision.[290] The debate focused on one company, Caterpillar, which manufactures bull-dozers. On 7 March 2006, however, the Ethical Investment Advisory Group of the Church of England unanimously voted against divesting the Caterpillar stock.[291]

An Anglican priest who supported the divestment campaign explained:

I have sat with a mother and her children and heard her speak of what it is like to have 50 tons of bulldozer coming through her front room unannounced in the middle of the night. The Synod acted in solidarity with the vulnerable. To call this anti-Semitism is facile nonsense.[292]

The question of anti-Semitism

Within the various denominations, it is the Church of England that is most divided—publicly, at least—over the Israel–Palestinian conflict. Partisans of each side to the conflict can point both to achievements and reverses. For example, in the September following the General Synod's divestment vote, and the EIAG's recommendation on Caterpillar, the archbishop of Canterbury and Israel's two Chief Rabbis signed an agreement that, among other things, acknowledged Israel's right to live within secure and internationally recognized borders and to defend itself by all legal means.[293] This was taken as a reverse for Christian anti-Zionists, and deprecated by the Anglican bishop of Jerusalem (as reported in the *Jerusalem Post*): 'Senior people of the Church of England informed me that the whole event came to appease Rabbi Jonathan Sacks, Israel and the Jewish lobby because of what happened at the Synod of the Church of England regarding the issue of divestment', Bishop Riah said.[294]

As with other contemporary anti-Zionisms, Christian anti-Zionism is concerned with injustice to Palestinians and with Palestinian suffering. Kenneth Cragg's work is the product of decades of reflection on the Israel–Palestinian conflict, and of many years living in the region. Stephen Sizer's work has the merit of clearly setting out the issues that divide the two sides, and furthermore doing so without the rancour or sheer nastiness of tone typical of the polemics in the conflict. Ateek's 'liberation theology' merits a careful, respectful reading; his endeavour to address Jewish readers by a reading of their own Scriptures can only be welcomed. He writes, 'the preservation of Israel as a Jewish state is important not only to Israeli Jews but to Jews all over the world. I believe that we must honour their wish and accept it.'[295]

There are difficulties, of course, with their respective positions. There is a certain tendency to accord Palestinian suffering theological significance, which then allows false scriptural parallels. There is also an implication that, independently of the wrongdoing of particular Zionists, Zionism itself is morally debasing—'happily, *many* in Judaism and *some* within Zionism live . . . in alertness to universal norms' (italics added).[296] And there is too ready an embrace of supersessionist positions, with the consequence that Israel's very existence can appear theologically perverse. There are also the deficiencies common to other anti-Zionisms, principal among which is the refusal to confront anti-Semitism and atrocity in the Palestinian Arab opposition to Zionism. (Ateek, for example, glosses the 1929 massacre in Hebron as 'armed resistance'.)[297] The readiness, too, to defame Zionism as 'racist', while relying on 'courageous'[298] Jewish critics of Israel as a counter to any charge of anti-Semitism.[299] And one cannot rule out the basest of Christian charges against the Jews—the 2007 ADL Survey found that 22 per cent of those surveyed in the UK either 'strongly agreed' or 'somewhat agreed' that the Jews are responsible for the death of Jesus.[300]

Representativeness

It is hard to say how common these positions are. They probably reflect a consensus among Palestinian Christians, though not among English Christians, where the broadest current might better be defined as *non*-Zionist— concerned, sensitive to the claims of all the interested parties, eager for peace and reconciliation, but broadly unsympathetic to Israel's stated positions.[301] A poll conducted of its Roman Catholic readers by *The Tablet* in December 2006, for example, produced these results, among others: 79.4 per cent disagreed with the proposition that the security wall is needed to protect the population of the Holy Land from suicide bombers. Substantial majorities agreed that the Churches should support international efforts to arrive at a two-state solution between the Israelis and the Palestinians (80.4 per cent), campaign for the dismantling of the security wall (77.6 per cent), call for the removal of Jewish West Bank settlements (75 per cent), and disinvest from companies whose products are used by the Israeli government in the occupied territories (68.5 per cent). By contrast, only a bare majority believed that the Churches should call on the Palestinians to recognize Israel and renounce violence (57.3 per cent). Only 21.2 per cent of readers agreed that Israel is engaged in a struggle for its survival and support its efforts to root out its enemies.[302]

New and confessional anti-Zionisms in combination

There is plainly an overlap between these anti-Zionisms—even, a certain reciprocal indebtedness. Much of the language used to describe the Israel– Palestinian conflict is common to all. They are similarly ready to find explanations for Arab terrorism, while holding the essential character of the Zionist project to be expressed by the Deir Yasin massacre—comparable in its significance and ultimate effect to the Holocaust itself.[303] They embrace the Nazi/Zionist trope in their judgements on Israel[304]—though some Christian anti-Zionists make of the State of Israel the successor to Herod too.[305] There is also a common reaching back, and reaching across, to earlier and other anti-Zionist positions. There are affiliations between the adherents of these anti-Zionisms, who come together for the sake of a march, a movement, or even a new party. And there are replications, too—among Jewish anti-Zionists, there are precisely the same 'boutique', 'liberal-Left', and 'pseudo-Left' elements as in the new anti-Zionism. Such is the overlap, such are the affiliations, such is the extent of the replication, these anti-Zionisms on occasion have the appearance of a single project.

Consider, for example, the character of the connection between Muslim anti-Zionism and that version of the new anti-Zionism associated with the Far Left. Institutionally, it could not be closer. It bears several names, principal among which are the Stop the War Coalition (STWC) and the Respect Party. This is a development of the last decade. The 1994 SWP pamphlet argued that the Left has 'at all costs' to preserve its own political independence and that it must subject Islamist leaders to public criticism both for their domestic policies and their shortcomings in 'the struggle against imperialism'. However, the SWP did not hold to this position, opting instead for an opportunistic merging with Islamist groups, the stifling of criticism of their leaders, and the exploitation of communalist politics[306] (all of which eventually produced tensions within the party). These initiatives acquired an international dimension, with SWP and Respect leaders meeting with Hamas and Hezbollah leaders at 'anti-war' conferences in Cairo in 2003 and 2007. The 2nd Cairo Declaration of 2003, for example, identified 'the Zionist plan' as the 'establishment of the greater State of Israel from to Nile to Euphrates'; it condemned pressure on Arab nations to 'acknowledge the legitimacy of the racist Zionist entity'; it also condemned 'Israel's direct role in the occupation of Iraq'; it opposed all 'normalisation with the Zionist entity'.[307] (The Declaration was posted on the STWC website; John Rees, the national secretary of Respect was the vice-president, Europe, of the Conference.) The SWP has taken to celebrating Hamas victories.[308] The intimacy of connection between the SWP and specifically Iranian interests has excited alarm elsewhere on the Far Left.[309] It is a 'long war' strategy that is being pursued.[310] The SWP has always been most successful when operating through front organizations, pursuing 'single issue' campaigns.[311] In the late 1970s, it was the Right to Work Campaign and the Anti-Nazi League;[312] in the 2000s, it has been the STWC and the Respect Party.

Respect does not have an adequate perspective on the Israel–Palestinian conflict.[313] Yvonne Ridley, a national council member and party candidate in the 2005 General Election, told Imperial College students in February 2006: '[Respect] is a Zionist-free party . . . if there was any Zionism in the Respect Party they [sic] would be hunted down and kicked out. We have no time for Zionists.' By contrast, all the mainstream parties are 'riddled with Zionists'. The Labour government, she added, supports 'that disgusting little watchdog of America that is festering in the Middle East'. 'Israel is a vile little state. It's propped up by America. It cannot survive without American money.'[314] During the 2006 war between Israel and Hezbollah, an excited George Galloway declared, 'Hezbollah is not and has never been a terrorist organisation; it is the legitimate national resistance movement of Lebanon.' And then, with even greater emotion, 'I glorify the Hezbollah national resistance movement, and I glorify the leader of Hezbollah, Sheikh Sayyed Hassan Nasrallah.'[315]

Insofar as the STWC has a position on the Israel–Palestinian conflict, it can be found in *Stop the War* (London, 2005), a book celebrating the Coalition and written by its leaders, Andrew Murray and Lindsey German. (Murray is a member of the Communist Party of Great Britain, while Lindsey German is a member of the SWP; the USSR's demise made the Stalinist/Trotskyist conflict redundant.) The authors are proud, they write, of the STWC's association with the Muslim Association of Britain (MAB). The MAB is taking the lead in introducing a more assertive Muslim intervention in British politics. It has been branded as a reactionary fundamentalist organization, as a front for Egyptian terrorists, and as anti-Semitic. None of these charges is true, the authors insist. MAB's objectives are clear and reasonable; the MAB and its leaders should also be acquitted of the charge of anti-Semitism. MAB leaders, like almost everyone in the Middle East, regard Palestine as existing not merely in the West Bank and Gaza but throughout its historic territory. It is not in itself anti-Semitic to regard Israel as an historic aberration that has brought vast suffering on the Arab peoples of the Middle East and proved a dead end for Jewish people worldwide. A single secular democratic state is not an anti-Semitic objective. (Murray and German skate over the fact that the MAB does not want to see a *secular* state take the place of Israel, the West Bank and Gaza.) STWC stands for justice for the Palestinians, and would support anything the Palestinians themselves recognize as such. (By contrast, the STWC 'was careful', the authors write, 'to avoid taking a position on the Kashmir question, another issue dear to many Muslims worldwide.... Likewise, we did not become engaged with the Chechen question...') The authors ponder, what would be anti-Semitic? Policies that call for the expulsion of Israelis or the killing of Jews are anti-Semitic, as are conspiracy theories. No British Jew bears any responsibility for the policy of the Israeli government. Such conspiracy theories as are mouthed occasionally by young Muslims are rooted in 'European Christian reaction'. STWC, the authors insist, has addressed all legitimate concerns. It is entirely hostile to anti-Semitism. Notwithstanding the attacks on the MAB by the *Observer* and by 'Zionist MPs like Louise Ellman', it was clear, German and Murray argue, that MAB's real offence was to have helped mobilize millions of Muslims against imperialism. On one of the pages devoted to their discussion of anti-Semitism, German and Murray incorporate a photograph of a child holding a cardboard sign, 'ISRAEL STOP KILLING CHILDREN!'[316]

The combinations are rarely frictionless, and sometimes they cause considerable discomfort. Some Jews participating in STW rallies, for example, complained of anti-Semitic chants from fellow-protesters: 'to be surrounded by hate-filled chanting and images in which anti-Israel and anti-Jewish imagery were blurred left us feeling deeply alienated'.[317] Another Jewish activist at a 2002 Trafalgar Square rally for Palestine reported:

> the overwhelming feeling that I got from the mainstream British Left that day was not so much solidarity with the Palestinians as virulent hostility towards Israel, and by extension towards anyone who didn't express shame to be Jewish or utterly reject a Jewish state.[318]

Though Jewish anti-Zionists may use language, promote activities, and endorse positions, that are highly problematical, and though, further, they are ready to ally with other anti-Zionist groups that nurse more violent ambitions against Israel and Jews, they mostly draw the line of acceptable politics somewhere further away from the plainly anti-Semitic than most other anti-Zionists.

The universities comprise prime sites for collaboration between anti-Zionist groupings.[319] There are the distinct Islamist groups, of course. 'In my own college [King's, London]', one academic reported, 'there were posters quoting a famous verse from the Hadith urging the murder of Jews, to the last of them, wherever they are.'[320] And according to one formerly Islamist student:

> on campuses we used the platform of the Islamic Society to call for the destruction of Israel and the rejection of the West, and to promote an Islamist alternative. At Queen Mary and Westfield College, for example, we held debates with the Jewish Society during which [fellow Islamists] often referred to the 'bastard state of Israel'.[321]

But these anti-Zionist positions are also shared with leftist groups. England's universities have been described by a former union of Jewish Students activist as laboratories for the changing vocabulary of contemporary anti-Semitism.[322] Israel would appear to lack legitimacy in parts of the academic world.[323]

There is similarly mixed company in what might be termed the anti-Zionist underworld. Consider this report of protesters outside the main Marks and Spencer department store in central London:

> One woman in religious Muslim attire standing next to us . . . screamed at the top of her voice to the Israel supporters, 'You Jews destroyed my country, Iraq.' Someone asked her what Israel had to do with Iraq and she screeched, 'You killed sixty of my family in Iraq.' She was asked how sixty Iraqis were killed by Israelis and she said 'Israel—USA! Same thing! And now you will take over Iran!' . . . Then came the chorus of really quite terrifyingly angry English people with their shouted mantras of 'You people invented terrorism in Palestine', 'Israel is expanding every day and will soon own the whole Middle East!' . . . 'Israel is slaughtering thousands of Palestinians every day.' . . . [Another protester] said, 'I love and revere the suicide bombers. Every time I hear of a suicide bomb going off I wish it had been eighty or ninety Jews instead of a pitiful handful.' He then went on to shout at everyone around him every time someone tried to speak . . . 'You people have been trying to acquire land across the entire globe and will soon own every nation if you are not stopped!'[324]

It is not impossible to imagine some crossover between the universities and this underworld. In a letter to the *Jewish Chronicle*, published in August 1994, a Union of Jewish Students organizer explained what was going on in English universities:

> In January at a meeting of the School of Oriental and African studies a Hizb al-Tahrir activist stated: 'Let's be open about this—the Koran does not mention Zionists, it mentions Jews. They are our enemy and, *insha allah*, we shall kill them.' And at the City University, one of Hizb al-Tahrir's

leaders... announced to his audience: 'The Holocaust is a fabrication.' In a leaflet distributed on one university campus this year, Jews are referred to as 'the lowliest people on earth', and in another leaflet Judaism (not Zionism) is called 'a purely racist doctrine'.[325]

The situation has not improved.

Beyond 'new' and 'confessional' anti-Zionisms

Beyond these combinations of 'new' and 'confessional' anti-Zionisms, we may identify a more diffuse antagonism towards Israel and the Zionist project, especially as an aspect of that broadest contemporary current of political emotion, 'anti-Americanism' (though the leftist version of this hostility tends to name it as 'anti-imperialism'). These sentiments, in their commonest expressions, often tend to take a problematic turn in the direction of anti-Semitism. The very turn itself makes many Jews uncomfortable—not all Jews, for sure, but typically those who possess a sense of anti-Semitism's history and have an attachment to Israel.

The specifically leftist hostility to the United States derives from a set of inherited, mostly Cold War reflexes. It celebrates adversarial stances towards America as commendable 'resistance' to the world's only imperial power. To be anti-imperialist is to be anti-American. United States' imperialism combines an aggressive political pursuit of its national interest with a similarly aggressive pursuit of economic globalization. It is self-regarding; it subordinates the world to its own interests. It is the world's only hegemonic power. In this perspective, the world now consists of one empire, its allies, and its victims; this empire or 'dominant power'[326] is always in the wrong; any nation or entity with which it is in an antagonistic relation must be supported;[327] those who cooperate with the empire are best characterized as being in active or tacit collusion with it, and are often no more than 'bribed hangers-on'.[328] It is an anti-imperialism that is reluctant to identify ideological enemies in the Third World, a place conceived as pure suffering, just as the West is conceived as pure exploitation. Imperialism is the cause of this suffering; in its absence, Third World nations would grow and prosper. Western intervention will thus always be wrong; 'real' change can only come from 'below', not through imperial interventions.[329] Western interventionism, which nowadays comes packaged as 'humanitarian', is only the latest form of imperialism, the 'new' imperialism. It is intolerable to this perspective that Europe and America are the only parts of the world that are simultaneously peaceful, powerful, and prosperous.[330]

Within such a perspective, the Jewish State is doubly at fault. It is itself aggressively imperialist, and it aids USA imperialist aggression ('militaristic Israel, kept in place by the requirements of a militaristic America... [Israel] depends for its existence on the American establishment responsible for the bombing of Vietnam, Fallujah, and a variety of similar adventures').[331] It is regarded as a colonizing movement, by implication acting on behalf of another power or powers. Israel itself, it is said, is bound to expand as a condition of its existence. While in the immediate post-war period, when imperial Britain was in conflict with militant Zionism, the Yishuv benefited from a leftist anti-imperialism,[332] from the 1956 Suez Campaign, Israel was regarded as allied with the West, and from the Six Day War, as allied with the USA. Israel has come to symbolize global US-centred imperialism just as, for some, Jews once symbolized the evils of capitalism.[333]

(These positions, of course, do not take into account much of the relevant history. Zionism does not seek an empire; it wishes to build a nation. In its origins, it was without substantial connection to the major states of the day; it was instead a spontaneous, non-governmental movement, merely seeking to win over governments to its side.[334] It was neither funded nor even consistently supported by any major state until the 1970s. There have been instances of *expansion*—from the UN partition plan borders to the 1949 armistice borders, from those armistice borders to the conquests of 1967, and the invasion and occupation of Lebanon. But there have also been instances of *contraction*—the evacuation from the Sinai following the peace treaty with Egypt, the departure from Lebanon, and the 'disengagement' from Gaza.)

Anti-imperialism is susceptible to anti-Semitic pollution; contemporary anti-Semitism has been termed the 'anti-imperialism of fools'.[335] The decline of leftism across the nineteenth and twentieth centuries is marked by the following passage: from commitment to an ideal (world revolution) to commitment to an empire (the USSR and its satellites), and then from commitment to that empire to hatred of another empire (the USA and its allies). It now finds ideological peace in the execration of the United States and one particular ally, Israel.[336] Its politics amount to no more than the pseudo-religious principle, 'America is the source of all that is wicked in the world.' 'Imperialism' is simply understood as 'America abroad'. The effect is to wink at the most immense crimes committed by entities other than, or unsupported by, the USA.[337] This critique of America contrives to uphold *both* international principles *and* principles of state sovereignty, defending tyrannies against American-led intervention on either or both grounds, opportunistically. But it would be a mistake to conceive of these anti-imperialist positions as being limited to the Left, or what once was the Left. The animus towards America is not now, nor has it ever been, an aspect of 'progressive' politics alone.

North America has loomed large in the European imagination since the sixteenth century. Though it has not been conceived in ways that have been entirely friendly, it is only in the last century that the United States as a political entity has experienced European enmity. Mere opposition to the USA's 'concrete interventions [and] specific depredations'[338] could not in itself foster, or sustain, this generalized 'anti-Americanism'. The discourse of first-class European intellectuals on the United States has, throughout its history, typically been *sub*-intellectual in character, that is to say a matter of received ideas, stale tropes, and the like. It mixes condescension and alarm, and defines America as Europe's dystopian 'other'. It is taken to be Europe's 'counterworld', its 'alter ego'.[339] It is a discourse of disparagement, and it derives from a certain kind of ignorance, a 'thick' ignorance,[340] a perfect instance of which is Tom Paulin's observation that 'the United States contains millions of blockishly reactionary people'.[341] What Paulin offers is an old libel masquerading as a fresh insight. The *political* enmity of specific European nations towards the United States reflected divisions within the continent—the World Wars I and II, in which West and East confronted the Prussian or Nazi Centre, and the Cold War, in which the Capitalist West confronted the Communist East. A *pan*-European political enmity, by contrast, only emerged in the aftermath of the collapse of the Soviet Union—that is to say, after the moment that promised both continental unification and the rule of a single 'hyper-power'. This enmity developed in consequence of different perspectives on the nature of the confrontation with Islam. European anti-Americanism finds itself in uncomfortable proximity to a non-European anti-'Westernism'. Its enemies see the West as a single political and cultural entity; the United States is taken to speak for the West as a whole.[342]

Where precisely, then, do Israel and the Jews fit in with this anti-Americanism? America's relationship with Israel has been given several distinct formulations, each one more at risk of anti-Semitic pollution than the one before.

The alliance between the USA and Israel reflects the common values of the two nations   America and Israel comprise a pair,[343] hence the 'wild popularity' of the latter among the population of the former.[344] The two nations are taken to share certain characteristics. In some versions of this formulation, these common characteristics overlap with anti-Semitic accounts of the Jews. They are two strong states, each hostile to internationalist and transnationalist currents. They stand against Europe's 'shared political mentality', which is taken to embrace the pacification of class conflicts through the welfare state, the pacification of religious conflicts through the privatization of faith, and the pacification of national conflicts through the self-restriction of individual state-sovereignty.[345] (To one UCU member, writing in the *Guardian*, they are also beneficiaries of similar 'unbreachable taboos', that is 'anti-Americanism and criticism of the Israeli state and its occupation of Palestine'.)[346] This formulation (of shared values) has been rejected both by traditional US isolationists and foreign-policy commentators who adopt a 'realist' perspective regarding America's national interest. Mearsheimer and Walt, for example, straightforwardly assert, 'in the event that Israel was conquered... America's... core political values would [not] be jeopardized'.[347] By this, I take them to mean that America's core values are not Israel's—since were the two nations to have common values, a defeat of one would indeed represent a setback for the other.

The alliance serves USA interests   As Polly Toynbee puts it, 'Ugly Israel is the Middle Eastern representative of ugly America.'[348] George Galloway describes Israel as 'the West's settler-state sentinel'.[349] Tariq Ali writes, 'The Arab east is today the venue of a dual occupation: the US–Israeli occupation of Palestine and Iraq.'[350] These positions broadly reflect the thesis of Noam Chomsky's book *Fateful Triangle* (London, 1999). The US is Israel's patron. Israel is a 'strategic asset' for the USA, fulfilling US goals in the region and performing dirty work that the US itself is unable to undertake. It is a US military base; it is so integrated into the US military economy, it is indistinguishable from it. The USA is the master and Israel is the servant.[351] This is a Cold War perspective that has survived the passing of the Cold War itself (during which period the Americans would not countenance any defeat of Israel by Soviet-backed military forces).[352] Israel's defenders also sometimes adopt modified versions of just this position, identifying Israeli actions that served America's interests,[353] in order to challenge the thesis that the alliance serves Israel's interests instead.

The alliance serves Israel's interests It is now argued both by demagogues (Buchanan)[354] and academics (Walt and Mearsheimer, in various iterations),[355] with varying degrees of nuance, that the 'Jewish lobby' or the 'Israel lobby' controls American foreign policy, contrary to America's national interest. The reasoning, which commands considerable support,[356] is as follows. America supports Israel; supporting Israel supports neither America's national interest nor morality; America would not pursue policies contrary to its national interest or to morality if it was in charge of its own decision-making processes; some other entity must therefore be in control of American foreign policy; that entity is the one that promotes support for Israel, the 'Israel Lobby' or 'the Lobby'; this is now the most powerful lobby in Washington; it is the most powerful lobby that has ever existed. While Walt and Mearsheimer flirt with conspiracy motifs, they also insist that their position is unlike any position influenced by the *Protocols* and, of course, they deny any anti-Semitic intent.[357] Yet they overstate Israel's offences, its power, and its contribution to global insecurity; they wrongly agglomerate the USA entities campaigning in Israel's interests ('the Israel Lobby') and then overstate this agglomerated entity's influence; they dismiss the influence on policy of pro-Israel American public opinion;[358] they disregard the contribution of 'non-Lobby' entities and constituencies to foreign policy decisions that they hold to be in Israel's, but not the USA's, interest (e.g., the decision to go to war against Iraq); they disregard the failures of the 'Lobby' to achieve identified objectives; they disregard the offences and misjudgements of the Palestinian 'movement', most broadly conceived, while overstating the offences of the Zionist movement and of Israel (on occasion, by simple misrepresentation);[359] they attach little or no weight to anti-Semitism as a contemporary phenomenon;[360] and, finally, without troubling to do any research of their own,[361] they substitute for the complex, multi-causal explanation of America's current foreign policy crisis an essentially mono-causal, Judeo-centric, and therefore misleading explanation—it is the fault of 'the Lobby'.[362] Their response to criticism has tended to consist of more strident affirmations of their position, just as their assessments of recent events have become even less nuanced ('the lobby...would have preferred to kill Freeman's appointment without leaving any fingerprints').[363] At times, they talk just like anti-Semites talk.

The 14 January 2002 *New Statesman* piece (see Chapter 7) was followed by a relatively understated piece a few months later in the political journal *Prospect* in which the 'lobby'—not all-powerful, but too powerful—was said to 'distort' USA foreign policy.[364] There has been a gradual coarsening of views. In April 2006 Abdurrahman Jafar, the Respect mayoral candidate for London, asserted that 'Israel has been formulating and directing UK and US foreign policy.'[365] His fellow Respect politician, Yvonne Ridley, proposed that while Israel held the Palestinian people under military occupation, it held the Americans under political occupation.[366] Perry Anderson, writing in the British periodical *New Left Review*, maintained that 'the Middle East is the one part of the world where the US political system, as presently constituted, *cannot* act according to a rational calculus of national interest', which he attributed to 'the grip of the Israeli lobby, drawing strength from the powerful Jewish community in the US, on the American political and media system'. Anderson then footnotes 'the outstanding work of John Mearsheimer and Stephen Walt [that] has finally broken this silence'.[367] These views both strengthen, and reflect, sentiments more widely held. And so, in the 2007 ADL Survey, 34 per cent of those surveyed in the UK agreed with the statement that American Jews control US Middle Eastern policy.[368] At the end of 2007, in the aftermath of the defeats of the boycott initiatives, anti-Zionist campaigners adopted a new tack, complaining about the influence of the 'Israel lobby' on British politics—or the 'israeli infiltration of British Parliament', which followed upon 'the zionist plague that has engulfed Congress', as one group phrased it.[369] Allegations against members of Labour Friends of Israel and Conservative Friends of Israel of 'dual loyalties'[370] were made. It was also said that these parliamentary interest groups were responsible for 'scandals' in British political life.[371]

The alliance serves the Jews' interests   The Jews, their first loyalty to Israel, are taken to control the Congress, the Pentagon, the banks, the universities, and the media. Having captured the hyperpower, they now rule the world. This is an old view—at least a hundred years old, but most developed by the Nazis ('the Jew holds sway in America').[372] The Mufti was an early promoter of this perspective among Arab audiences. In 1942, on the occasion of American troops landing in North Africa, he declared, 'the Americans are the willing slaves of the Jews, and as such the enemies of

Islam and the Arabs'.[373] 'No one ever thought', he declared in March 1944, 'that 140 million Americans would become tools in Jewish hands ... '[374] This sinister perspective, so productive of the most lethal anti-Semitism, becomes banal, though not altogether harmless, in the observations of Richard Dawkins, interviewed by the *Guardian* about his campaign on behalf of atheists in the United States: 'When you think about how fantastically successful the Jewish lobby has been, though, in fact, they are less numerous I am told—religious Jews anyway—than atheists *and [yet they] more or less monopolise American foreign policy* as far as many people can see. So if atheists could achieve a small fraction of that influence, the world would be a better place' (italics added).[375]

In each of these formulations, the 'turn' towards anti-Semitism is easy enough to spot. There is a pejorative characterization of Jews in the first formulation, a pejorative characterization of Israel in the second formulation, and fantasies of conspiracy, manipulation, and control by Israel or by the Jews, in the third and fourth formulations. To the extent that these formulations resonate with anti-Semitism's history, they give comfort to anti-Semites; to the extent that they draw on anti-Semitic tropes they are themselves polluted by anti-Semitism. But while it is true that hostility to America and hostility to Jews possess certain structural similarities,[376] and indeed that there is something deeply dispiriting about contemporary leftist anti-Americanism in general, Max Horkheimer went too far when he asserted that everywhere one finds anti-Americanism, anti-Semitism is also prevalent.[377]

Conclusion

Israel is the only state in the world whose legitimacy is widely denied and whose destruction is publicly advocated and threatened;[378] Israelis are the only citizens of a state whose indiscriminate murder is widely considered justifiable. Now, these sentiments are both sufficiently irrational and sufficiently serious in their practical implications, to merit urgent, considered reflection. And during the course of that process of reflection, the pondering of the relation between the history of anti-Semitism and the datum of Israel as the Jewish State is bound to arise. When reflecting upon the character of contemporary Israel-hatred, then, the question of anti-Semitism cannot be avoided.

Anti-Semitism is implicated in contemporary anti-Zionism in much the same way as it was implicated in the anti-Bolshevism of the 1920s. It is as difficult for today's anti-Zionist to evade anti-Semitism as it was for the anti-Bolshevist of ninety years ago. Bolshevik Jews in alliance with New York were fomenting world unrest; the world would not be safe unless they were defeated, or at least contained. Zionist Jews in alliance with Washington are the cause of global instability; the world will not be safe unless they are defeated, or at least contained. And there are even broader continuities, contemporary anti-Zionist discourse with earlier discourses, their anti-Semitism instantly recognizable, unarguably present. Consider this speech by Karl Lueger (1844–1910), the anti-Semitic Mayor of Vienna:

> The chief generator of anti-Semitism is the *Jewish liberal press*. Its corruption and monstrous terrorism was bound to give rise to a counter-movement ... We do not shout 'Hep, Hep', but we object to *Christians* being oppressed and we object to *the old Austrian Empire* being replaced by a *new Jewish Empire*. It is not hatred for the individual, not hatred for *the poor, the small Jew*. No, gentlemen, we do not hate anything except the *oppressive big capital that is in the hands of the Jews*.[379]

Now modify it thus (and what follows could come from any one of a thousand speeches or columns written within the discourse of the new anti-Zionism):

> The chief generator of anti-Semitism is *Israel*. Its corruption and monstrous terrorism was bound to give rise to a counter-movement ... We do not shout 'Hep, Hep', but we object to *Palestinians* being oppressed and we object to *Palestine* being replaced by *Israel*. It is not hatred for the individual, not hatred for *the anti-Zionist Jew*. No, gentlemen, we do not hate anything except *the oppressive Jewish State, the State of Israel*.

The structure is identical—this identifying of a powerful Jewish entity as the single cause of Gentile disempowerment, the shifting of responsibility for anti-Semitism onto that Jewish entity, and the saving acknowledgement of another, virtuous class of Jew.[380]

Leftist and reactionary anti-Semites can agree on the Jews' deplorable commercialism; leftist and liberal anti-Semites can agree on the Jews' deplorable solidarity; liberal and reactionary anti-Semites can agree on the Jews' deplorable radicalism. There is one cause, that all—leftist, liberal *and* reactionary—anti-Semites can agree upon, however, and that is 'anti-Zionism'. Contemporary anti-Semitism mostly speaks the language of anti-Zionism; most anti-Semites are now 'anti-Zionists'.[381] I have not concerned myself with these 'anti-Zionists' in this chapter—even though the anti-Zionists that I *have* examined have on occasion made common cause with them. There are of course anti-Semites who have merely adopted anti-Zionism as a disguise for their Jew-hatred, and in order to claim respectability for their views[382] or to evade laws against anti-Semitic activity.[383] These are Jew-haters whose 'anti-Zionism' is nothing more than a posture—convenient camouflage:

> [Belloc] was not a Nationalist in our sense of the word, although he was clearly a patriot... Nevertheless, he did recognise the enemies of the Nation—Capitalists, Marxists, Zionists...[384]

By the mid-1950s, the English Far Right had woken up to the advantages of attacking 'Zionists' rather than 'Jews': 'if we attack Zionists, no one can say we're anti-Jewish, can they? Even some Jews are anti-Israel.'[385] 'Zionism' was just a new word for an old project. The Jews are evil, their efforts to acquire power must be stymied... this is the drift of the argument. The 'Zionist' is the 'Jew' by another name—a mere code word, serving the same purpose to the present generation of anti-Semites as 'international' and 'cosmopolitan' did for earlier generations.[386] Zionism is regarded merely as the most recent Jewish crime of choice. Contemporary Jewry now bears the accusations hitherto directed by acknowledged anti-Semites at earlier generations of Jews: they are said to be bloodthirsty child-killers, global conspirators and the enemies of humanity.[387] There is a certain strategy being pursued by the Far Right, attacking Israel and Zionism rather than the usual, discredited rant about Jews. In their 'struggle for the mind', neo-Nazis considered this to be quite clever, this appropriating of hostility to Israel.[388] The exploitation of the Palestine question has been a consistent theme in Far Right politics for several decades.[389]

We have seen that contemporary anti-Zionism is a heterogeneous phenomenon. It requires some elaborating; it cannot be reduced to a formula. It is to be found within received, progressive opinion (the 'new anti-Zionism'); it is generated by the conflict in the Middle East between Israelis and Palestinians, a conflict that resonates in the wider Arab and Muslim world; it is the means by which some Jews have come to position themselves in relation both to their Judaism and their 'Jewishness'; it is also part of a broader Christian deprecation of collective Jewish endeavour, especially in the 'Holy Land'.

These are not reducible to types of vigorous partisanship with or sponsorship of the Palestinian cause; they are distinct *ideological* positions.

As a result, anti-Zionism, and in particular the 'new anti-Zionism', has become part of the common sense of present times, an aspect of the *zeitgeist*. It inhabits those grooves along which received thought—and *non*-thought— moves. It is, so to speak, the spontaneous philosophy of a substantial fraction of those who do not philosophize,[390] and the spontaneous history of many of those who know no history. It is expressed by reference to 'what everyone knows about Israel', and 'what everybody knows about Zionism'—the 'non-negotiables for any right-thinking decent person', as one journalist put it, dissenting.[391] The content of its expressions no longer has to be verified. Anti-Zionist positions are thus rarely articulated at the level of explicit, elaborated analysis; they are more typically articulated at the level of the trope. These tropes are often 'partial truths' as defined in Chapter 3, that is, charges with some foundation in fact, but characterized by overstatement, suppression, 'singling-out', and malice. They purvey ideologically structured lies employing empirical truths.[392]

Anti-Zionists should want to avoid anti-Semitism; they should be prepared when appropriate to modify both their language and their substantive positions. Anti-Semitism is objectionable because it is stupid and wicked. It is never an analysis. It always goes wrong. It is an unjustifiable attack on Jews. Specifically, in the context of the Israel–Palestinian conflict, it impedes a peace settlement. Indeed, there is no 'peace settlement' that will satisfy anti-Semites, other than the destruction of Israel, the Jew among the nations. Israelis often do not hear the Palestinian case precisely because anti-Semitism distorts it.

Anti-Zionists should also be ready to listen to Jews who find anti-Semitism in contemporary anti-Zionist positions. Yet listening to Jews on the subject of anti-Semitism is not popular. Many people, indeed, now regard being Jewish as an obstacle to the understanding of anti-Semitism. Jews are too quick, it is often suggested, to cry anti-Semitism. Their over-readiness is perceived to derive from many sources: they cannot be 'objective';[393] they overestimate the threat to Israel;[394] they are by their nature complainers; they are over-sensitive; they are too quick to make judgements; and so on. Jews are not allowed to bear witness to anti-Semitism's existence, nor of the nature of their suffering. They are not accepted as arbiters of what constitutes new instances of anti-Semitism. Complaints of anti-Semitism have instead become legitimate occasions for gestures of exasperation. 'I'm fed up', complained one newspaper columnist, 'with being called an anti-Semite.'[395]

This resistance to giving Jews a voice on the matter of anti-Semitism is somewhat against the contemporary practice of defining racism in subjective terms. The 1999 *Stephen Lawrence Inquiry* (known as the 'MacPherson Report'), which introduced into public discourse the concept of 'institutional racism', recommended that a 'racist incident' be defined as 'any incident which is perceived to be racist by the victim or any other person'. 'Racist incidents' comprised both crimes and non-crimes, in policing terms; the definition was to be 'universally adopted by the police, local government and other relevant agencies'.[396] In the following year, the Crown Prosecution Service announced that it had adopted the new definition of racist incident. It is as if race has become knowledge, or at least the precondition for knowledge—as Mary Lefkowitz expresses it, the Cartesian 'I think, therefore I am', being replaced by 'I am, therefore I know.'[397]

Yet one does not need to follow the MacPherson line to accept that anti-Semitism has features of particular interest to anyone born a Jew.[398] Since anti-Semitism disproportionately afflicts Jews, it is also reasonable to suppose that they are likely to know more about it than non-Jews.[399] If it is true that Jews sometimes find anti-Semitism where there is none, it is only because they tend to be among the first to identify it when it *is* present. They have a strong claim to be arbiters on questions of anti-Semitism. But it is not the best claim. *That* claim can only be made by those Jews *and* non-Jews whose conclusions are informed by fair-mindedness, an ability to give proper weight to the relevant evidence, and a thorough understanding of the character and history of anti-Semitism. Of course, such Jews and non-Jews will take very seriously indeed Jewish testimony.

★★★

The *Pirke Aboth* enjoins Jews to read the Torah so as to be ready with arguments to controvert the heretic.[400] The implication is that heretics are susceptible to reason; there is thus at least the possibility that they may be returned to truth. Anti-Semites, however, are not heretics. They are antagonists of a different, less reputable kind. While circumstances may cause them to abandon their hatred, they cannot be *debated* into giving it up.[401] They will not acknowledge 'Jews as they are'—to quote the title of a late-nineteenth-century work of apologetics.[402] They are not susceptible to the presentation of contrary evidence.[403] They will not accede to unchallenge-able facts—say, the real number of alien immigrants in turn-of-the-century England,[404] or the disproportionately high number of Jewish soldiers enlisted in the Tsarist Russian army,[405] or killed on active service in World War I,[406] or serving in the British Army in both World Wars,[407] or the disproportionately low number of Jewish criminals in turn-of-the-century New York, over which a veritable war of statistics was waged.[408] Nor will they accede to incontrovertible arguments—say, that it is irrational to regard Jews as both capitalist *and* communist, mainstays *and* subverters of the established order, the most powerful *and* the most contemptible, worse than Nazis *and* fabricators of Nazi atrocities. They will not acknowledge their error, even when what they have emphatically denied possible in due course occurs—say, the passing of the Aliens Act, notwithstanding Arnold White's insistence a few years' earlier that 'the irresistible weight of Jewish influence' would make 'restrictive legislation' 'hopeless'.[409] Generations of Jews have railed impotently against the anti-Semitic fantasy of corporate, malign 'Jewish influence';[410] generations of rabbis have affirmed the scrip-tural prohibition against blood consumption.[411] When Herbert Samuel stood up in the House of Commons on 14 February 1917 to declare, 'There never has been any hidden hand', he could have saved himself the trouble.[412] 'We have sought to educate the public as to the facts about Jews', the president of the Board of Deputies wrote plaintively in 1939, 'and to show that they have been worthy of their citizenship.'[413] And so on, and so forth. And all this, because what characterizes anti-Semites is not so much their falsehoods and their misbeliefs as the malice with which they promote them. They hate Jews. The errors in logic, in history and theology, in politics and sociology, come later. I have therefore not written this book to controvert them; it is not an exercise in advocacy; I do not expect any anti-Semites who persevere with *Trials of the Diaspora* to change their views.

Across these eight chapters, I have mostly been engaged in the explication of nonsense—pernicious nonsense, at that. Has there been any merit in the exercise? I hope so; I have committed a great deal of time to it. There is some value in studying anti-Semitism, if only as an instance of how ideas become effective forces in history.[414] And while nonsense is just nonsense, the academic study of nonsense can be scholarship.[415] But in such a case, to study is to immerse oneself in muck. Anti-Semitism is a sewer.[416] This is my second book on the subject and I intend it to be my last.

Notes

INTRODUCTION

1. 'We are rather sensitive: others have made us so...': Israel Mattuck, 'Why are Jews so touchy?', *Sunday Express*, 24 June 1928.
2. A point made to me by Bernard Harrison.
3. See 'Terror and abuse in a London street', *Guardian*, 3 May 2002.
4. Alain Finkielkraut's *The Imaginary Jew* (Lincoln, NA, 1994) begins with an account of 'the typical scene of humiliation'. See pp. 3 and 6.
5. See William Miller, *Faking It* (Cambridge, 2003), p. 140.
6. Her contact with non-Jews was itself probably quite limited. I do not think, for example, that she had ever visited the home of a non-Jewish family. She never mentioned to me the existence of any non-Jewish friends or acquaintances. In this, her experience appears to have been typical of East End Jews of her generation. See Tony Kushner, 'Jew and non-Jew in the East End of London' in Geoffrey Alderman and Colin Holmes (eds.), *Outsiders and Outcasts* (London, 1993), pp. 38–9.
7. See Jerry White, *Rothschild Buildings* (London, 2003), p. 134; Eugene C. Black, *The Social Politics of Anglo-Jewry 1880–1920* (Oxford, 1988), pp. 220–1; Alan Lee, 'Aspects of the working-class response to the Jews in Britain, 1880–1914' in Kenneth Lunn (ed.), *Hosts, Immigrants and Minorities* (London, 1980), p. 121. It was an old rhyme, popular in the eighteenth century: Frank Felsenstein, *Anti-Semitic Stereotypes* (Baltimore, MD, 1995), p. 150. One of James H. Robb's interviewees related how he and his friends, when schoolboys, had stoned Jewish boys as they came out of school: *Working-Class Anti-Semite* (London, 1954), p. 111. On the separate lives lived by Jews and non-Jews in the East End at that time, see Tony Kushner, *The Persistence of Prejudice* (Manchester, 1989), p. 48, and Todd M. Endelman, *Radical Assimilation in English Jewish History 1656–1945* (Bloomington, IN, 1990), p. 176.
8. 'Who killed Christ?' was the question addressed at school to Louis Golding by his schoolmates: *Hitler Through the Ages* (London, n.d.), p. 17. Golding records the response: 'We did, with a butcher's knife... Our manoeuvres were thrust and counter-thrust in a game hallowed by tradition, but by no sacerdotal fury.' See also Bryan Magee, *Clouds of Glory* (London, 2003),

pp. 24–5, and Emanuel Litvinoff, *Journey Through a Small Planet* (London, 2008), p. 22. William Rubinstein records this exchange: 'Who killed Christ?' 'I did, and I'll bloody well kill you too if I catch you.' See *A History of Jews in the English-Speaking World: Great Britain* (London, 1996), p. 243.

9. On the experiences of Jewish civilian evacuees, see Tony Kushner, *The Persistence of Prejudice* (Manchester, 1989), pp. 65–77; Todd M. Endelman, *The Jews of Britain 1656–2000* (Berkeley, CA, 2002), pp. 222–4; Geoffrey Alderman, *Modern British Jewry* (Oxford, 1992), pp. 299–300; Richard Weight, *Patriots* (London, 2002), pp. 82–3.

10. 'Stories about Jews being asked about their horns abound.' Tony Kushner, *The Persistence of Prejudice* (Manchester, 1989), p. 69.

11. On armed forces wartime anti-Semitism, see ibid., pp. 123–5.

12. Richard Ingrams, *Observer*, 13 July 2003.

13. See David Sylvester, *Memoirs of a Pet Lamb* (London, 2002), p. 26; John Gross, *A Double Thread* (London, 2001), pp. 182–6.

14. Chris Baldick, *The Social Mission of English Criticism 1848–1932* (Oxford, 1987), pp. 26, 124; but see Robert Conquest, *The Dragons of Expectation* (London, 2005), p. 40 (mere 'English Department philosophy').

15. *Contribution to the Critique of Political Economy* (London, 1971), pp. 20–1.

16. Matthew Arnold, 'A French critic on Goethe', quoted in Chris Baldick, *The Social Mission of English Criticism 1848–1932* (Oxford, 1987), p. 38.

17. Ian MacKillop, *F. R. Leavis: A life in criticism* (London, 1997), p. 93.

18. See Q. D. Leavis, 'Leslie Stephen: Cambridge critic' in F. R. Leavis, *A Selection from 'Scrutiny'* (Cambridge, 1968), vol. 1, pp. 22–31.

19. *English Literature in Our Time and the University* (London, 1969), p. 8.

20. Ibid., p. 14.

21. See Chris Baldick, *The Social Mission of English Criticism 1848–1932* (Oxford, 1987), p. 96.

22. Q. D. Leavis, 'A critical theory of Jane Austen's writings' in F. R. Leavis, *A Selection from 'Scrutiny'* (Cambridge, 1968), vol. 2, p. 1.

23. Ibid., p. 47.

24. See F. R. Leavis, 'The responsible critic, or the function of criticism at any time' in ibid., pp. 292–3. The poem is a determinate thing; it is *there*. Social context is indeterminate; it is an illusion.

25. See, for example, Raymond Williams, *Politics and Letters* (London, 1979), p. 45.

26. 'Eliot . . . was the man really responsible for introducing into Cambridge a set of ideas that both shocked and satisfied.' E. M. W. Tillyard, *The Muse Unchained* (London, 1958), p. 98.

27. See my *T. S. Eliot, Anti-Semitism, and Literary Form* (London, 2003), pp. 205–8.

28. This is not to say, of course, that there were not instances of anti-Semitism among Faculty members. 'In 1970 I was in my first year as an undergraduate at Cambridge. I remember sitting in a somewhat sparsely attended public lecture being given by a senior member of the faculty of English, during which he

remarked, quite without irony—as if irony would have helped!—that "the trouble with Hitler was that he made intelligent anti-Semitism impossible for ever after".' David Simpson, 'New broom at Fawlty Towers' in Bruce Robbins (ed.), *Intellectuals: Aesthetics, politics, academics* (Minneapolis, MN, 1990), p. 270.

29. *Lessons of the Masters* (Cambridge, MA, 2005), pp. 142–3.

30. 'A kind of survivor', *Language and Silence* (London, 1969), p. 131.

31. Though Israel is an 'indispensable miracle', in the sense that its emergence and achievements defy rational expectation, Steiner also considers it to be 'normal', commonplace, vulgar—'armed to the teeth, a land for the bourse and the Mafiosi, as are all other lands'. 'Where Jeremiah thundered, there are topless bars.' The existence of nations breeds mutual loathing; there is nothing to say in favour of the 'barbed-wire idiocy of frontiers'. All wars are territorial: what are ideologies but territories of the mind? Judaism would survive the ruin of the state of Israel, because its 'election' is one of wandering. The Jewish condition is a 'singularity' etc. See *Errata* (London, 1997), pp. 48–60. Steiner is wobbly on quite basic aspects of Jewish belief and practice. It is not true, for example, that for the 'Orthodox . . . A Jew, a veritable Jew, is one who observes the several hundred ritual, liturgical ordinances . . .' He also confuses 'reformed' and 'liberal' Jews with 'occasional' Jews. See *My Unwritten Books* (London, 2008), pp. 89, 91. In this most recent work, many of the contradictory, received notions about Jews, Judaism, and Zionism that are currently in circulation jostle, unexamined. The Orthodox are literalists, yet the interpretation of the Talmud is endless; New York is both the financial metropolis and the capital of Judaism; Israel is a nationalist, sometimes aggressive and repressive society, but it has to be; anti-Zionism is a defensible option but it is also now used to mask anti-Semitism; and so on. Steiner concludes, 'I had hoped to hammer out these arguments in a full-scale work. I lacked the clarity of vision to do so' (ibid., p. 116). One cannot but respect the straightforwardness of this admission.

32. See the Preface and the Postscript to the 2nd edn of my *T. S. Eliot, Anti-Semitism, and Literary Form* (London, 2003), pp. xi–xv and 302–35.

33. 'I do not consider that Irving's claim to have been the victim of a conspiracy in which both the Defendants were implicated is established by the evidence placed before me': *The Irving Judgment* (London, 2000), p. 20.

34. Ibid., p. 343.

35. Christopher Browning, 'Historians and Holocaust denial in the courtroom' in John K. Roth and Elisabeth Maxwell, *Remembering for the Future: The Holocaust in an age of genocide* (New York, 2001), vol. 1, p. 775.

36. *The Irving Judgment* (London, 2000), pp. 62–3.

37. For example, as to the fact, scale, and systematic nature of the killing of the Jews in the East by shooting and, secondly, the gassing of Jews from Poland and from Europe in the Reinhard death camps. See *The Irving Judgment* (London, 2000), p. 167, and see also pp. 210 and 344–6. He also modified his 'position'

on Auschwitz, from unqualified denial of any gas chambers to a concession that gassing of human beings took place on a limited scale (ibid., pp. 167–8).

38. *The Irving Judgment* (London, 2000), p. 347.

39. See Richard Evans, *Lying about Hitler* (New York, 2001), p. 234. Six years later, the Austrians jailed Irving for Holocaust denial. He equivocated on his views prior to trial, but then reaffirmed them following sentence. See, for example, Katy Duke, 'Irving barred from speaking to media', *Guardian*, 7 March 2006. In a subsequent interview, he changed his position again, reverting to views held several decades ago. 'Irving now concedes that the Holocaust happened— and there were "some" gassings at Auschwitz—but he insists Hitler had no idea it was going on.' Johann Hari, 'The last believer', *Independent*, 15 January 2009.

40. See Kate Taylor, *Holocaust Denial: The David Irving trial and international revisionism* (London, 2000), p. 40.

41. Pierre Vidal-Naquet, *Assassins of Memory* (New York, 1992), p. 24.

42. Arthur Hertzberg, 'Foreword' in Michael Shermer and Alex Grobman, *Denying the Holocaust* (Berkeley, CA, 2002), p. xiii.

43. See D. D. Guttenplan, *The Holocaust on Trial* (London, 2001), p. 81.

44. Marc Augé, *Oblivion* (Minneapolis, MN, 2004), p. 87.

45. *The Imaginary Jew* (Lincoln, NA, 1994), p. 7.

46. Ibid., p. 34.

47. In France, by contrast, the battle against Holocaust denial was one of the strategic nodes of French cultural life in the 1980s. See Jeffrey Mehlman, 'Foreword' in Pierre Vidal-Naquet, *Assassins of Memory* (New York, 1992), p. xxi; Alain Finkielkraut, *The Future of a Negation* (Lincoln, NA, 1998), pp. 77–8.

48. See, for example, Anthony Julius and Simon Schama, 'John Berger is wrong', posted on the *Guardian* website 'Comment is Free', on 22 December 2006.

49. *T. S. Eliot, Anti-Semitism, and Literary Form* (London, 2003), pp. 144–5.

50. T. S. Eliot, *A Choice of Kipling's Verse* (London, 1987), pp. 258–9.

51. See Nigel Copsey, *Contemporary British Fascism* (London, 2008), pp. 71–2; Nick Ryan, *Homeland* (London, 2004), pp. 64–5, 134.

52. Nesta Webster, *Secret Societies and Subversive Movements* (London, 1924), pp. 395–6; Nigel Copsey, 'John Amery', *Patterns of Prejudice*, 36/2 (2002), 20; Saul Friedländer, 'Europe's inner demons' in Robert Wistrich (ed.), *Demonizing the Other* (Amsterdam, 1999), p. 219; 'Not a single announcement will reach the public without our control.' *Protocol* XII, para 4, p. 32.

53. Peter Hitchens, *The Abolition of Britain* (London, 2000), p. xxvii.

54. Harry G. Frankfurt, *On Bullshit* (Princeton, NJ, 2005), pp. 33–4.

55. John Clive, *Not By Fact Alone* (London, 1989), pp. 4–5.

56. Heribert Adam and Kogila Moodley, *Seeking Mandela* (London, 2005), p. 159.

57. But not in *all* respects. For an analysis of certain French precedents, see Nicholas C. Vincent, 'Jews, Poitevins, and the bishop of Winchester, 1231–1234' in

Diana Wood (ed.), *Studies in Church History: Christianity and Judaism* (Oxford, 1992), vol. 29, pp. 130–1.

58. Anthony Bale, *The Jew in the Medieval Book* (Cambridge, 2006), p. 17.
59. Patricia Skinner, 'Jews in medieval Britain and Europe' in Patricia Skinner (ed.), *The Jews in Medieval Britain* (Woodbridge, 2003), p. 9.
60. Colin Richmond, 'Englishness and medieval Anglo-Jewry' in Tony Kushner (ed.), *The Jewish Heritage in British History: Englishness and Jewishness* (London, 1992), pp. 49–50.
61. W. B. Yeats, 'Church and State', *The Poems*, Daniel Albright (ed.) (London, 1990), p. 333.
62. Robin R. Mundill, *England's Jewish Solution: Experiment and Expulsion: 1262–1290* (Cambridge, 1998), p. 51.
63. Zefira Entin Rokéah, 'The State, the Church, and the Jews in medieval England' in Shmuel Almog (ed.), *Antisemitism through the Ages* (Oxford, 1988), p. 116.
64. Francis James Child (ed.), *The English and Scottish Popular Ballads* (New York, 1888), vol. 3, pp. 233–54. Oddly, Nick Groom regards the ballad as among those possessing 'all the rude vigour of the anecdote—they are without discursive history'. See *The Making of Percy's 'Reliques'* (Oxford, 1999), p. 45.
65. H. Michelson, *The Jew in Early English Literature* (New York, 1972), p. 41.
66. Selig Brodetsky, *Memoirs from Ghetto to Israel* (London, 1960), p. 19.
67. See Richard Holt, *Sport and the British* (Oxford, 1989), p. 133.
68. Todd M. Endelman, *The Jews of Britain 1656–2000* (Berkeley, CA, 2002), p. 9. Endelman is writing of modern Anglo-Jewish history; his remarks apply *a fortiori* to the history of modern English anti-Semitism.
69. See Simon Schama, 'Virtual annihilation' in Ron Rosenbaum (ed.), *Those Who Forget the Past* (New York, 2004), p. 356.
70. Gilles Kepel, *The Roots of Radical Islam* (London, 2005), p. 13.
71. See, for example, Fawwaz Trabulsi, 'The Palestine problem: Zionism and imperialism in the Middle East', *New Left Review*, 57 (September–October 1969), 86–7.
72. On 13 May 1948, following heavy fighting, approximately 120 residents and defenders of the kibbutz Kfar Etzion were massacred by elements of the Arab Legion and Arab irregulars to whom they had surrendered. See Benny Morris, *Righteous Victims* (New York, 2001), p. 214; Benny Morris, *The Road to Jerusalem* (London, 2002), pp. 138–9; Idith Zertal and Akiva Eldar, *Lords of the Land* (New York, 2007), p. 5; Amnon Rubinstein, *From Herzl to Rabin* (New York, 2000), p. 113.
73. See, for example, 'Stop the War Coalition' Newsletter 1040: 'The previous Newsletter no. 1039 gave the impression that the Stop the War Coalition has taken a position on the Tibet issue. This is not the case . . . '
74. Kenneth S. Stern, *Why Campus Anti-Israel Activity Flunks 'Bigotry 101'* (AJC, 2002), p. 4.

75. On the UNCHR, see Irwin Cotler, 'Why single out Israel?', *globeandmail.com*, 21 June 2007; J. P. Staff, 'Ban Ki-Moon slams UNHCR decision on Israel', *Jerusalem Post*, 21 June 2007; Jackson Diehl, 'a shadow on the human rights movement', *Washington Post*, 25 June 2007; David Aaronovitch, 'UN expert? No, a conspiracy crank', *The Times*, 15 April 2008.

76. Fred Halliday, *Nation and Religion in the Middle East* (London, 2000), p. 45.

77. John Pilger, 'An important marker has been passed', *New Statesman*, 23 August 2007.

78. For example: 'Millions of activists have come to see an organic link between the occupation and colonization of Palestine and diverse and pressing global issues ranging from the war on Iraq to global poverty.' Mazin Qumsiyeh, 'Boycott Israel', *Global Agenda: The Magazine of World Economic Forum Meeting*, 2006, formerly at <http://www.globalagendamagazine.com/2006/Qumsiyeh.asp>.

79. See David Mamet, *The Wicked Son* (New York, 2006), p. 15; Petronella Wyatt, 'Poisonous prejudice', *Spectator*, 8 December 2001.

80. See Isabel Oakeshott and Chris Gourlay, 'Anti-Semitism rules come in at universities', *The Times*, 25 March 2007.

81. Nigel Copsey, *Contemporary British Fascism* (London, 2008), p. 92.

82. Denis MacShane, *Globalising Hatred* (London, 2008), p. 22.

83. House of Lords, 5 December 2006, <http://www.publications.parliament. uk/pa/ld200607/ldhansrd/text/61205-0008.htm#06120574000047>.

84. Jonathan Scott, 'What the Dutch taught us', *Times Literary Supplement*, 16 March 2001, p. 6.

85. Joseph Jacobs, *The Jewish Question 1875–1884. Bibliographical Hand-List* (London, 1885), p. v.

86. 'Progress or return?' and 'Why we remain Jews', *Jewish Philosophy and the Crisis of Modernity* (New York, 1997), pp. 92, 320–1. Cf. 'Formerly there were persecutions *pur et simple*. No one cared to find another name for it. Now there is *Antisemitism*.' Emil Reich, 'The Jew-baiting on the Continent', *Nineteenth Century*, 40 (July–December 1896), 422.

87. 'Even in the post-1933 period, it is best to speak in the plural of German anti-Semitisms.' Christopher Browning, *Ordinary Men* (London, 2001), p. 198.

88. *Pace* Nicholas De Lange, 'The origins of modern Anti-Semitism: Ancient evidence and modern interpretations' in Sander L. Gilman and Steven T. Katz (eds.), *Anti-Semitism in Times of Crisis* (New York, 1991), p. 23. Note: 'the addition of the suffix "ism" does not automatically transform a term into an ideology'. Michael Freeden, *Ideologies and Political Theory* (Oxford, 1996), p. 7. Max Horkheimer and Theodor W. Adorno, *Dialectic of Enlightenment* (London, 1972), p. 171, go too far in the other direction, however: 'There is no genuine anti-Semitism.'

89. Does 'shyster', for example, have anti-Semitic connotations? See *King v Lewis and ors* [2004] EWHC 168 (QB) 6 February 2004, and Matt Scott, 'Chelsea accuse former owner Bates of racism', *Guardian*, 18 August 2006. Does

accusing Jews of pursuing a 'global plot' to rule the world amount to 'propagating... racial enmity'? See Kenneth S. Stern, *Antisemitism Today* (New York, 2006), p. 105. Is it defamatory to describe an anti-Zionist activist as anti-Semitic? See Benjamin Weinthal, 'Anti-Zionism a trope of anti-Semitism', *Jerusalem Post*, 4 September 2008. On the subject generally, see Jonathan Marwil, 'Accusations of Antisemitism' in Richard S. Levy (ed.), *Antisemitism: A historical encyclopedia of prejudice and persecution* (Santa Barbara, CA, 2005), vol. 1, pp. 23–4.

90. See Peter Beaumont, 'The new anti-Semitism?', *Observer*, 17 February 2002; Seamus Milne, 'This slur of anti-Semitism is used to defend repression', *Guardian*, 9 May 2002; Patrick J. Buchanan, 'Whose war?', *American Conservative*, 24 March 2003; Ken Livingstone, 'An attack on voters' rights', *Guardian*, 1 March 2006.

91. See Louise Brown, 'Professor suing York U.', *Toronto Star*, 22 November 2006.

92. 'It is quite possible I may be called an antisemite for writing [this book]. I must put up with that. But I have never had any truck with antisemitism, and find the persecution of the Jews in Central Europe as crying a disgrace to humanity as their imposition upon the Arabs has been.' J. M. N. Jeffries, *Palestine: The reality* (London, 1939), p. xvii.

93. See Jonathan Hess, *Germans, Jews and the Claims of Modernity* (New Haven, NJ, 2002), pp. 173–4, 193–6.

94. See Norman Davies, *God's Playground: A history of Poland* (Oxford, 2005), vol. 2, p. 51. Staaszic was given the sobriquet, 'the old Jew baiter'.

95. *New Witness*, 2 January/13 February 1913.

96. Martin Gilbert, *Sir Horace Rumbold* (London, 1973), p. 49.

97. Michael B. Oren, *Power, Faith and Fantasy: America in the Middle East, 1776 to the present* (New York, 2007), pp. 374, 386.

98. See John A. Garrard, *The English and Immigration 1880–1910* (Oxford, 1971), pp. 67, 75; Eugene C. Black, *The Social Politics of Anglo-Jewry 1880–1920* (Oxford, 1988), pp. 271–5.

99. Alan Lee, 'Aspects of the working-class response to the Jews in Britain, 1880–1914' in Kenneth Lunn (ed.), *Hosts, Immigrants and Minorities* (London, 1980), p. 119.

100. See I. Rennap, *Anti-Semitism and the Jewish Question* (London, 1942), pp. 101–2.

101. See Berel Lang, 'Self-description and the anti-Semite: Denying privileged access' in Ron Rosenbaum (ed.), *Those Who Forget the Past* (New York, 2004), pp. 91–5.

102. But see G. R. Searle, 'Critics of Edwardian society: The case of the radical Right' in Alan O'Day (ed.), *The Edwardian Age* (London, 1979), p. 92.

103. *The Alien Menace* (London, 1932), pp. vii, 3, 124.

104. Ernst L. Freud (ed.), *The Letters of Sigmund Freud and Arnold Zweig* (London, 1970), p. 3. For a short account of Zweig's life, see David Caute, *The Fellow-Travellers* (London, 1988), pp. 304–6.

105. See *The Interpretation of Dreams* (London, 1954), pp. 196–7. Freud writes of 'the increasing importance of the effects of the anti-Semitic movement upon our emotional life helped to fix the thoughts and feelings of those early days'. It is in the same part of the book that Freud tells the story of his father's unheroic encounter with an anti-Semite.

106. 'Analysis of a phobia in a five-year-old boy ("Little Hans")', *Case Studies I* (London, 1977), pp. 198–9.

107. *Civilisation and its Discontents* (London, 1973), p. 51.

108. Ernst L. Freud (ed.), *The Letters of Sigmund Freud and Arnold Zweig* (London, 1970), p. 91.

109. 'Have we fulfilled our mission?' in Joseph Leftwich (ed.), *Great Yiddish Writers of the Twentieth Century* (Northvale, NJ, 1987), p. 67.

110. See Ramin Jahanbegloo, *Conversations with Isaiah Berlin* (London, 1992), p. 118.

111. See Pierre Vidal-Naquet, *Assassins of Memory* (New York, 1992), p. 140.

112. See John Felstiner, 'The voice of the "Other" in Paul Celan' in Robert Wistrich (ed.), *Demonizing the Other* (Amsterdam, 1999), p. 250.

113. Freud was 'over concerned' with anti-Semitism, Leo Strauss suggested. See 'Freud on Moses and monotheism', *Jewish Philosophy and the Crisis of Modernity* (New York, 1997), pp. 286–7.

114. See Peter Gay, *A Godless Jew* (New Haven, 1987), p. 150; Marthe Robert, *From Oedipus to Moses* (London, 1977), pp. 133–67; Morris Raphael Cohen, *Reflections of a Wondering Jew* (New York, 1950), p. 146.

115. See *The Thirteenth Tribe* (London, 1976).

116. Quotations seem so much *safer*. 'That is why I have made extensive use of quotations. Attitudes are elusive. Try to define them and you lose their essence, their special colour and tone.' Walter E. Houghton, *The Victorian Frame of Mind* (New Haven, CT, 1974), p. xv.

117. *The Fateful Triangle* (London, 1999), pp. 123–4.

118. Chomsky cites no source for this statement. There is, in any event, no such entity as 'the rabbinate', if by that is meant some single council, capable of giving Vatican-style rulings. There is an implication in Ehud Sprinzak, *The Ascendance of Israel's Radical Right* (Oxford, 1991), p. 271, that one rabbi, Israel Ariel, in a Gush Emunim pamphlet, endorsed the Lebanon War as divinely supported ('God was behind the Israeli army when it entered Lebanon . . .'), but this falls short of *milhemet mitzvah*, and Rabbi Ariel does not speak for any 'rabbinate'. Not even the far Right demagogue Rabbi Meir Kahane called for a *milhemet mitzvah* to regain the Promised Land: ibid., p. 223.

119. The articles appeared in the 28 September 1981, 9 July, and 3 September 1982 issues of *Nekuda*.

120. See Ehud Sprinzak, *The Ascendance of Israel's Radical Right* (Oxford, 1991), pp. 88, 122; Idith Zertal and Akiva Eldar, *Lords of the Land* (New York, 2007), pp. 219–21.

121. See Amnon Rubinstein, *From Herzl to Rabin* (New York, 2000), pp. 124–6, 139–43.

122. '[On the alleged anti-Semitism of the Black Panthers:] There is no doubt that an assiduous search would reveal anti-Semitic statements by black militants, just as there is no doubt that the black movements have always welcomed support by Jews and other whites. There is also no doubt that by applying the same technique, one could "prove" that Israel is a racist state bent on genocide... Some might interpret this as rather cynical and even deceitful. What is true in one case is no less true in the other.' Noam Chomsky, 'Israel and the new Left' in Mordecai Chertoff (ed.), *The New Left and the Jews* (New York, 1971), pp. 216–17.

123. On the misleading tendency of the Israeli revisionist historians to privilege words over actions, see Anita Shapira, 'The strategies of historical revisionism' in Anita Shapira and Derek J. Penslar (eds.), *Israeli Historical Revisionism From Left to Right* (London, 2003), p. 70.

124. It has been taken to be one of the defects of Israeli historical revisionism that it treats the Israeli establishment, and in certain instances, the Zionist movement itself, as a monolith, which it then indicts, by reference to selected quotations, as speaking a 'uniform discourse of blood'. See Daniel Gutwein, 'Left and Right post-Zionism and the privatisation of Israeli collective memory' and Anita Shapira, 'The strategies of historical revisionism' both in Anita Shapira and Derek J. Penslar (eds.), *Israeli Historical Revisionism From Left to Right* (London, 2003), pp. 20–1, 69–71.

125. *Being and Time* (Oxford, 1962), pp. 191–2.

126. See, for example, Hugh Kearney, *The British Isles* (Cambridge, 1995), pp. 1–12. But note Todd M. Endelman, *The Jews of Britain 1656–2000* (Berkeley, CA, 2002), p. 12: 'The history of the Jews in Britain is overwhelmingly the history of Jews who lived in *English* cities, London in particular.'

127. William Chester Jordan, *Europe in the High Middle Ages* (London, 2002), p. 48.

128. John A. Garrard, *The English and Immigration 1880–1910* (Oxford, 1971), p. 69; Richard Thurlow, *Fascism in Modern Britain* (London, 2000), pp. viii, xi, 82; Eugene C. Black, *The Social Politics of Anglo-Jewry 1880–1920* (Oxford, 1988), pp. 372–3; Stephen Dorril, *Blackshirt* (London, 2006), pp. 380, 410–11; Geoff Dench, Kate Gavron, and Michael Young, *The New East End* (London, 2006), pp. 16–17.

129. On a Mancunian-inflected anti-Semitism, for example, see Bill Williams, *The Making of Manchester Jewry 1740–1875* (Manchester, 1985), pp. 9–10, 27–8, 39. An anti-Semitic twist was given to local manufacturers' fears of 'travelling plagiarists'—industrial spies—who would sell manufacturing secrets to foreign rivals. Jews, taken to be foreigners themselves and with an international network, were prime suspects.

130. See Yonah Alexander, 'Terrorism in the twenty-first century: Threats and responses', *DePaul Business Law Journal* (Fall 1999/Spring 2000), 65.

131. Cecil Roth, 'England in Jewish history', The Lucien Wolf Memorial Lecture, The Jewish Historical Society of England, London, 1949, p. 15 ('the antiquarian can with difficulty assemble a few minor instances to qualify the rule').

132. See David Cesarani, 'The study of antisemitism in Britain: Trends and perspectives' in Michael Brown (ed.), *Approaches to Antisemitism* (New York, 1994), p. 250. Historians outside this Anglo-Jewish coterie were readier to name English society as anti-Semitic. See for example L. S. Sutherland, 'Samson Gideon and the reduction of interest, 1749–50', *Economic History Review*, 16/1 (1946), 15, on 'the anti-Semitism of English society and George II'.

133. David Cesarani, 'Dual heritage or duel of heritages? Englishness and Jewishness in the heritage industry' and David Katz, 'The marginalization of early modern Anglo-Jewish history' both in Tony Kushner (ed.), *The Jewish Heritage in British History* (London, 1992), pp. 33–4, 61.

134. Geoffrey Alderman, *Modern British Jewry* (Oxford, 1992), pp. 265, 318.

135. David Cesarani, 'The study of antisemitism in Britain: Trends and perspectives' in Michael Brown (ed.), *Approaches to Antisemitism* (New York, 1994), p. 260.

136. Abraham Gilam, *The Emancipation of the Jews in England 1830–1860* (New York, 1982), p. 65; Aubrey Newman, *The Board of Deputies of British Jews 1760–1985* (London, 1987), p. 9. The Board's ignominious abstention from the campaign had already been noted by the Anglo-Jewish historian James Picciotto, writing in 1875. The Board members 'in their corporate capacity displayed much timidity and acted as if they were fettered by a dread of responsibility and by a lack of funds'. *Sketches of Anglo-Jewish History* (London, 1956), p. 120.

137. David Feldman, *Englishmen and Jews* (London, 1994), pp. 129–32; Geoffrey Alderman, *Modern British Jewry* (Oxford, 1992), p. 137; John A. Garrard, *The English and Immigration 1880–1910* (Oxford, 1971), p. 112; Tony Kushner, *The Persistence of Prejudice* (Manchester, 1989), pp. 164–5.

138. Todd M. Endelman, *The Jews of Britain 1656–2000* (Berkeley, CA, 2002), p. 171.

139. Geoffrey Alderman, *Modern British Jewry* (Oxford, 1992), p. 238.

140. Elaine R. Smith, 'Jewish responses to political antisemitism and fascism in the East End of London, 1920–1939' in Tony Kushner and Kenneth Lunn (eds.), *Traditions of Intolerance* (Manchester, 1989), pp. 63–5; Aubrey Newman, *The Board of Deputies of British Jews 1760–1985* (London, 1987), p. 25; Gisela C. Lebzelter, *Political Anti-Semitism in England 1918–1939* (London, 1978), p. 169; David Cesarani, 'Great Britain' in David S. Wyman (ed.), *The World Reacts to the Holocaust* (Baltimore, MA, 1996), pp. 604–5; Todd M. Endelman, *The Jews of Britain 1656–2000* (Berkeley, CA, 2002), pp. 209–10.

141. Todd M. Endelman, *The Jews of Britain 1656–2000* (Berkeley, CA, 2002), pp. 212–13.

142. Richard Bolchover, *British Jewry and the Holocaust* (Cambridge, 1993), pp. 59–60.

143. David Cesarani, *The Jewish Chronicle and Anglo-Jewry 1841–1991* (Cambridge, 1994), pp. 19, 27, 39, 54, 56, 216.

144. Todd M. Endelman, *The Jews of Britain 1656–2000* (Berkeley, CA, 2002), p. 225.

145. Bernard Wasserstein, *Britain and the Jews of Europe 1939–1945* (Oxford, 1988), p. 128. 'Although Anglo-Jewry appeared to be a self-confident minority . . . it proved reluctant to take public action when confronted with open hatred.' Gisela C. Lebzelter, *Political Anti-Semitism in England 1918–1939* (London, 1978), p. 138.

146. See Geoffrey Alderman, *London Jewry and London Politics 1889–1986* (London, 1989), p. 100.

147. Meier Sompolinsky, *The British Government and the Holocaust* (Brighton, 1999), p. 212. See also Tony Kushner, *The Persistence of Prejudice* (Manchester, 1989), pp. 177–8. On the pre-war Board displaying a 'remarkable submissiveness to the anti-Semitic campaign', see Gisela C. Lebzelter, *Political Anti-Semitism in England 1918–1939* (London, 1978), p. 149. For a defence of pre-war Board policy, see Neville Laski, *Jewish Rights and Jewish Wrongs* (London, 1939), pp. 130–5.

148. See Richard Bolchover, *British Jewry and the Holocaust* (Cambridge, 1993), pp. 42–4, 47, 50, 52.

149. 'The defence activities of Anglo-Jewry in their entirety expose most convincingly the myth constantly advanced by anti-Semites, that Jewry constitutes a closely-knit corporate entity.' Gisela C. Lebzelter, *Political Anti-Semitism in England 1918–1939* (London, 1978), p. 154.

150. Geoffrey Alderman, *Modern British Jewry* (Oxford, 1992), pp. 241, 254.

151. Ibid., p. 290.

152. See Geoff Dench, *Minorities in the Open Society* (London, 1987), pp. 45, 48.

153. See, for example, the Introduction to Bryan Cheyette and Nadia Valman (eds.), *The Image of the Jew in European Liberal Culture* (London, 2004), pp. 1–26. The editors write, at p. 22, of 'the racism of liberal English discourse'. In 'Jewish stereotyping and English literature 1875–1920: Towards a political analysis', Bryan Cheyette writes, 'British liberal culture created an anti-semitism in its own image.' Cheyette appears to believe that it is the 'good Jew'/'bad Jew' binarism that gives 'liberal anti-Semitism' its particular character, which he contrasts with 'illiberal Judeophobia'. See Tony Kushner and Kenneth Lunn (eds.), *Traditions of Intolerance* (Manchester, 1989), pp. 26–7.

154. 'We can see in Fagin . . . many aspects of the complex negative stereotype of the Jew that, *despite the persuasive liberalism of the age*, persisted as a feature of English popular culture . . .' (italics added). Frank Felsenstein, *Anti-Semitic Stereotypes* (Baltimore, MD, 1995), p. 238.

155. Tony Kushner, *The Persistence of Prejudice* (Manchester, 1989), pp. 161, 164; Richard Bolchover, *British Jewry and the Holocaust* (Cambridge, 1993), pp. 42, 79, 106, 145. See also Nadia Valman, 'Semitism and criticism: Victorian Anglo-Jewish literary history', *Victorian Literature and Culture*, 27 (1999), 241.

156. Bryan Cheyette, 'Introduction' in *Between 'Race' and Culture* (Stanford, CA, 1996), p. 12 ('apparently benevolent liberalism'); Tony Kushner, *The Persistence of Prejudice* (Manchester, 1989), p. vi; Tony Kushner and Kenneth Lunn, 'Introduction' in Tony Kushner and Kenneth Lunn (eds.), *Traditions of Intolerance* (Manchester, 1989), pp. 7, 8. On the other hand: 'This does not mean . . . that the supposed decency, humanitarianism or liberalism of the British with regard to the Jews should be rejected as insignificant. The actual belief that Britain was all of these things did affect reality.' Tony Kushner, *The Persistence of Prejudice* (Manchester, 1989), pp. 201–2.

157. There was, however, little evidence in works such as Tony Kushner, *The Holocaust and the Liberal Imagination* (Oxford, 1994) or Bryan Cheyette and Nadia Valman (eds.), *The Image of the Jew in European Liberal Culture* (London, 2004) of any understanding of liberalism's complex history, either as doctrine or state form. It is hard to know, for example, what to make of this judgement: 'we need to reinterpret the attitudes and policies of Ernest Bevin. Long seen as a pathological, gutter antisemite, Bevin in his crude way was merely advocating a liberal attitude.' Tony Kushner, 'Remembering to forget: Racism and anti-racism in postwar Britain' in Bryan Cheyette and Laura Marcus (eds.), *Modernity, Culture and 'the Jew'* (Oxford, 1998), p. 234. Pamela Shatzkes notes 'a certain parochialism' in Kushner's work, and the work of other 'revisionist historians'. She criticizes 'their simplistic characterisation of a deeply complex society as "liberal", an epithet which is then used loosely as a term of abuse'. See *Holocaust and Rescue* (London, 2002), pp. 18–19. Liberalism has been better understood outside the Anglo-Jewish academic *milieu*. Irene Tucker's *A Probable State* (Chicago, 2000), for example, is a valuable exploration of the relations between liberalism and the form and history of the realist novel.

158. Deborah Cohen, 'Who was who? Race and Jews in turn-of-the-century Britain', *Journal of British Studies*, 41 (October 2002), 483.

159. Cecil Roth, 'England in Jewish history', Lucien Wolf Memorial Lecture, Jewish Historical Society of England, London, 1949, p. 5.

160. Tony Kushner, 'The impact of British anti-semitism, 1918–1940' in David Cesarani (ed.), *The Making of Anglo-Jewry* (Oxford, 1990), pp. 191–7.

161. Todd M. Endelman, *The Jews of Britain 1656–2000* (Berkeley, CA, 2002), pp. 201–2, 269. See also Frank Felsenstein, *Anti-Semitic Stereotypes* (Baltimore, MD, 1995), p. 1, expressly dissenting from Roth, whom he claims, 'smoothed over (and at times consciously chose to ignore) the extensive undergrowth of anti-Semitic allusion that permeates the rhetoric of 18th century English popular culture'.

162. *Anglo-Jewish Letters 1158–1917* (London, 1938), p. 105.

163. See David Feldman, *Englishmen and Jews* (London, 1994), pp. 13–14, 136.

164. See David Cesarani, 'Great Britain' in David S. Wyman (ed.), *The World Reacts to the Holocaust* (Baltimore, MD, 1996), pp. 257, 260–1, 265. James Shapiro argues that 'anti-Semitism' and 'philo-Semitism' are 'anachronistic terms, inventions of nineteenth-century racial theory', 'fundamentally ill-suited for gauging what transpired three hundred years earlier': *Shakespeare and the Jews* (New York, 1996), p. 11. Frank Felsenstein, while acknowledging that 'anti-Semitism' is an 'inappropriate term' in the context of the eighteenth century and 'other historical periods', concludes, 'no alternative word has really taken its place': *Anti-Semitic Stereotypes* (Baltimore, MD, 1995), p. 8.

165. Bryan Cheyette, 'Introduction' in *Between 'Race' and Culture* (Stanford, CA, 1996), p. 4; Tony Kushner, *The Persistence of Prejudice* (Manchester, 1989), p. vi. Kushner later suggests that 'the ambivalence in attitudes towards Jews' shows the 'danger of relying *too heavily* on concepts such as philo- and anti-semitism' (italics added). However, 'antisemitism' is a 'useful tool in analysing the various forms of reactions to Jews in the 1939–1945 era in Britain' (pp. 4, 8).

166. See James Shapiro, *Shakespeare and the Jews* (New York, 1996), p. 38. While Shapiro is no more a native English academic than is Endelman, their work is continuous with many of the themes explored in the best new work undertaken by Anglo-Jewish scholars.

167. Bryan Cheyette, *Constructions of 'the Jew' in English Literature and Society* (Cambridge, 1993), p. xi; Nadia Valman, *The Jewess in Nineteenth Century British Culture* (Cambridge, 2007), p. 4; Nadia Valman, 'Semitism and criticism: Victorian Anglo-Jewish literary history', *Victorian Literature and Culture* (1999), p. 242. But note: 'All Jewish racial representations can, of course, be said to be ultimately "antisemitic".' Bryan Cheyette, 'Introduction' in *Between 'Race' and Culture* (Stanford, CA, 1996), p. 14.

168. Bryan Cheyette, *Constructions of 'the Jew' in English Literature and Society* (Cambridge, 1993), p. xi.

169. Tony Kushner, 'Offending the memory? The Holocaust and pressure group politics' in Tony Kushner and Nadia Valman (eds.), *Philosemitism, Antisemitism, and 'the Jews'* (Aldershot, 2004), p. 262; Tony Kushner, 'Remembering to forget: Racism and anti-racism in postwar Britain' in Bryan Cheyette and Laura Marcus (eds.), *Modernity, Culture and 'the Jew'* (Oxford, 1998), pp. 226–41.

170. Bryan Cheyette, 'Introduction' in *Between 'Race' and Culture* (Stanford, CA, 1996), p. 14.

171. See *The Jews in the History of England* (Oxford, 1996), pp. vii–xi.

172. See, for example, Michael Galchinsky, 'Jewish and other questions in the age of empire' in Bryan Cheyette and Nadia Valman (eds.), *The Image of the Jew in European Liberal Culture* (London, 2004), p. 57.

173. *A History of Jews in the English-Speaking World: Great Britain* (London, 1996), pp. 2, 5, 6, 8–9, 11, 12, 13, 28, 30, 35, 36, 56, 59–60, 66, 85, 90, 201, 215, 294–5, 367–8. Rubinstein developed some of his arguments on contemporary anti-Zionism in *Israel, the Jews, and the West* (London, 2008). His broad position on the subordinate character of English anti-Semitism is everywhere implicit in a later work, co-authored with Hilary L. Rubinstein, *Philosemitism: Admiration and support in the English-speaking world for Jews, 1840–1939* (London, 1999). But see Michael Ragussis, 'The "secret" of English anti-Semitism: Anglo-Jewish studies and Victorian studies', *Victorian Studies*, Winter (1997), 296–7, controverting Rubinstein ('the subtle but nonetheless widespread, powerful and deeply ingrained forms of anti-Semitism that are an important part of English history and culture. The writing of European history should not be staged as a contest . . . ').

174. Richard Cumberland, 'Prologue' in *The Jew* (London, 1794).

175. Jan Herben, 'Thomas G. Masaryk, Jews and anti-Semitism' in *Thomas G. Masaryk and the Jews*, trans. Benjamin Epstein (New York, 1949), pp. 15.

176. Jeffrey Herf, *The Jewish Enemy* (Cambridge, MA, 2006), p. 6; Louis H. Feldman, 'Anti-Semitism in the Ancient World' in David Berger (ed.), *History and Hate* (Philadelphia, PA, 1986), p. 30; Erich Gruen, *Heritage and Hellenism* (Berkeley, CA, 1998), p. 43 ('numbers game').

177. Geoffrey G. Field, 'Anti-Semitism with the boots off' in Herbert A. Strauss (ed.), *Hostages of Modernization* (Berlin, 1993), p. 323.

178. See Andrew Sharf, *The British Press and Jews under Nazi Rule* (London, 1964), p. 4; Ulrike Ehet, 'Catholics and antisemitism in Germany and England 1918–1939', University of London, 2005 (unpublished PhD thesis), pp. 44–5.

179. In a House of Lords debate on Jewish emancipation, for example, the bishop of Oxford insisted that 'the silence pervading the country' on the question was 'the crushed silence of great indignation and great apprehension'. See Hansard, Parl. Debs. (series 3) vol. 98, col. 1380 (1848). In the event, he was wrong—the silence was merely indifference. But the meaning of silence is not always so readily divined. On the problem of 'silence' in the classical world, see Nicholas de Lange 'The origins of modern anti-Semitism' in Sander L. Gilman and Steven T. Katz (eds.), *Anti-Semitism in Times of Crisis* (New York, 1991), p. 24.

180. *Anti-Semitism in British Society 1876–1939* (New York, 1979), p. 220.

181. See, for example, the 'Report of the All-Party Parliamentary Inquiry into Antisemitism', September 2006, pp. 7–23, <http://thepcaa.org/Report.pdf>; Joanna Bale and Anthony Browne, 'Attacks on Jews soar since Lebanon', *The Times*, 2 September 2006; Hillel Fendel, 'Anti-Semitic hate wave rolls across Britain and Australia', *Arutz Sheva*, 6 September 2006; 'City "has high anti-Semitic rate" ', *BBC News* 7, September 2006, <http://news.bbc.co.uk/1/hi/england/manchester/5322878.stm>; Vanessa Bulkacz, 'Record anti-Semitism weighs heavily on British Jews', 14 September 2007,

<jewishjournal.com>; Denis MacShane, 'The writing is on the synagogue wall', *The Times*, 16 February 2009.

182. Walter Laqueur, *The Changing Face of Antisemitism* (New York, 2006), p. ix; Richard Littlejohn, 'The new anti-Semitism', *Daily Mail*, 7 July 2007; Bernard Lewis, 'The new anti-Semitism', *The American Scholar*, 75/1 (2006); Yigal Hai, ' "Alarming" rise reported in attacks on Jews in 2006', *Ha'aretz*, 15 April 2007.

I. ENMITIES

1. See St Augustine, *City of God* (London, 1972), p. 828.
2. See Sylvia Haim (ed.), *Arab Nationalism: An anthology* (London, 1976), p. 101.
3. Bernard Lewis, *Semites and Anti-Semites* (London, 1986), p. 166.
4. See, for example, Norman Rose, *A Senseless, Squalid War* (London, 2009), p. 177.
5. See Helmut Walser Smith, *The Butcher's Tale* (New York, 2002), p. 29.
6. See Antony Beevor and Artemis Cooper, *Paris after the Liberation: 1940–1949* (London, 2004), pp. 79–80.
7. Lloyd P. Gartner, *The Jewish Immigrant in England 1870–1914* (London, 2001), p. 36.
8. See Hermann L. Strack, *The Jew and Human Sacrifice* (London, 1909), p. 222; Léon Poliakov, *The History of Anti-Semitism* (London, 1974) vol. 1, p. 62; S. W. Baron, *A Social and Religious History of the Jews*, 2nd edn (New York, 1967), vol. 11, p. 147.
9. See Jonathan Hess, *Germans, Jews and the Claims of Modernity* (New Haven, NJ, 2002), p. 198.
10. See, for example, Daniel J. Goldhagen, *Hitler's Willing Executioners* (London, 1997), p. 299.
11. Helmut Walser Smith, *The Butcher's Tale* (New York, 2002), p. 132.
12. Max Horkheimer and Theodor W. Adorno, *Dialectic of Enlightenment* (London, 1972), p. 170.
13. Jewish opportunists in medieval England assisted the Crown in its spoliation of the Jews. See Cecil Roth, *A History of the Jews in England*, 3rd edn (Oxford, 1978), p. 46, and Richard Vaughan (ed.), *Chronicles of Matthew Paris* (New York, 1984), p. 215.
14. See Oscar I. Janowsky, *People at Bay* (London, 1938), pp. 123–4.
15. 'Les Juifs ne sont grands, que parce que nous sommes à genoux! Levons-nous!' See Nelly Wilson, *Bernard-Lazare* (Cambridge, 1978), p. 67. Goebbels declared: 'Every Jew is our enemy.' Mark Mazower, *Hitler's Empire* (London, 2008), p. 374.
16. See Stephen Frosh, *Hate and the 'Jewish Science'* (London, 2005), p. 59.

17. Jeffrey Herf, *The Jewish Enemy* (Cambridge, MA, 2006), pp. 7, 37, 265; David Bagchi, 'Catholic anti-Judaism in Reformation Germany: The case of Johann Eck' in Diana Wood (ed.), *Studies in Church History* (Oxford, 1992), vol. 29, p. 255.
18. See Jeffrey Herf, *The Jewish Enemy* (Cambridge, MA, 2006), pp. vii, 5.
19. 'The myth of the Jewish world-conspiracy', *Commentary*, 41/6 (1966), 41.
20. See Stephen Dorril, *Blackshirt* (London, 2006), pp. 324, 402.
21. Hilaire Belloc, *The Jews* (London, 1922), p. 3; see Bernard Glassman, *Protean Prejudice: Anti-Semitism in England's Age of Reason* (Atlanta, GA, 1998), p. 6.
22. Jeffrey Herf, *The Jewish Enemy* (Cambridge, MA, 2006), p. 209.
23. Jan T. Gross, *Fear* (New York, 2006), p. 247. There were precedents: Simon M. Dubnow, *History of the Jews in Poland and Russia* (Bergenfield, NJ, 2000), pp. 22–3.
24. Carl Schmitt, *The Concept of the Political* (Chicago, 1996), p. 28. I acknowledge the eccentricity of deploying Schmitt in an argument about rational enmity towards Jews. See Omer Bartov, *Mirrors of Destruction* (Oxford, 2000), pp. 143–8.
25. *The Jewish State* (London, 1972), p. 76.
26. *Reflections on Exile and Other Literary and Cultural Essays* (London, 2001), pp. xxxiv, 547.
27. See T. R. Fyvel, *George Orwell* (London, 1982), p. 71.
28. See David Drake, *French Intellectuals and Politics from the Dreyfus Affair to the Occupation* (London, 2005), p. 4.
29. See Alain Finkielkraut, 'The religion of humanity and the sin of the Jews', *Azure*, 21 (Summer 5765/2005), 23.
30. See Edward W. Said, 'U.S. intellectuals and Middle East politics' in Bruce Robbins (ed.), *Intellectuals: Aesthetics, politics, academics* (Minneapolis, 1990), p. 149.
31. Alain Finkielkraut, 'The religion of humanity and the sin of the Jews', *Azure*, 21 (Summer 5765/2005).
32. See *Freedom's Battle* (New York, 2008), pp. 48, 56–7, 64–5, 76–7. Lord Byron was exceptional among the philhellenes for his refusal to whitewash Greek affairs.
33. See T. R. Fyvel, *George Orwell* (London, 1982), p. 71.
34. Paul Frosh, 'The glamour of the Boycott', *Engage*, 3 November 2006.
35. Angus Howarth, 'MP sparks fury with her view on bombers', *Scotsman*, 23 January 2004.
36. Carl Schmitt, *The Concept of the Political* (Chicago, 1996), p. 27.
37. R. W. Southern, *The Making of the Middle Ages* (London, 1993), p. 49; Thomas Asbridge, *The First Crusade* (London, 2004), p. 18.
38. Cf. Edmund Burke, 'Speech on conciliation with the colonies', *Selected Works* (Indianapolis, IN, 1999), vol. 1, p. 251.
39. See Pinchas Hacohen Peli, 'Responses to anti-Semitism in Midrashic literature' in Sander L. Gilman and Steven T. Katz (eds.), *Anti-Semitism in Times of Crisis* (New York, 1991), pp. 103–14, and Susan Neiman, *Evil in Modern Thought*

(Princeton, NJ, 2002), p. 253. See also the note to Exodus 17:8–16, in Adele Berlin and Marc Zvi Brettler, *The Jewish Study Bible* (Oxford, 2004), p. 142. But cf. the note to Deuteronomy 25:17–19, p. 423: 'Amalek came to symbolise *any enemy* of the Jews' (italics added). The commentary to Exodus is by Jeffrey H. Tigay; the commentary to Deuteronomy is by Bernard M. Levinson. Two commentators, two views.

40. See Richard Bolchover, *British Jewry and the Holocaust* (Cambridge, 1993), pp. 84, 96. Cf. Leon Wieseltier, 'Against ethnic panic: Hitler's is dead' in Ron Rosenbaum (ed.), *Those Who Forget the Past* (New York, 2004), pp. 181–3.

41. See Tom Segev, *Elvis in Jerusalem* (New York, 2002), p. 6. For examples see Elliot Horowitz, *Reckless Rites* (Princeton, NJ, 2006), pp. 1, 3, and 5–6, and Fred Halliday, *Islam and the Myth of Confrontation* (London, 2003), pp. 187–92.

42. See Ehud Sprinzak, *The Ascendance of Israel's Radical Right* (Oxford, 1991), pp. 123–4, 269–70; Laura Blumenfeld, *Revenge* (London, 2002), pp. 54–5.

43. See Dina Porat, ' "Amalek's Accomplices": Blaming Zionism for the Holocaust: Anti-Zionist ultra-orthodoxy in Israel during the 1980s', *Journal of Contemporary History*, 27 (1992) 695–729; Aviezer Ravitsky, 'Munkács and Jerusalem', and Shlomo Avineri, 'Zionism and the Jewish religious tradition' both in Shmuel Almog, Jehuda Reinharz, and Anita Shapira (eds.), *Zionism and Religion* (Hanover, NH, 1998), p. 80.

44. Nachmanides, *Commentary on the Torah: Exodus* (New York, 1973), p. 177.

45. Rashi glosses the verse 'And when King of Arad the Canaanite, which dwelt in the south, heard that Israel...' (Numbers 21:1) as a reference to Amalek. There is no reference to Amalek in the verse itself. He says of the Amalekites that they 'changed their language, and spoke in the Canaanite tongue...*but they were not Canaanites*' (italics added). See R. Avrohom Davis (trans.), *The Metsudah Chumash/Rashi* (Lakewood, NJ, 2002), vol. 4, pp. 275–6.

46. Nachmanides, *Commentary on the Torah: Exodus* (New York, 1973), p. 243.

47. See Daniel Boyarin, *Intertextuality and the Reading of Midrash* (Bloomington, IN, 1994), pp. 92, 108, 128. The direction of Midrashic interpretation is from the concrete to the concrete; it fills in Scriptural 'gaps'; it is a continuation of the literary activity that engendered the Scriptures themselves.

48. See, for example, Nahum M. Sarna, *Exploring Exodus* (New York, 1996), p. 121. But this was not all. 'When all the nations heard [of God's visitation upon the Egyptians], they trembled. Philistia, Edom, and Moab, and the inhabitants of Canaan melted away from before the terror of the Eternal, and from the Glory of His Majesty, whereas Amalek came from afar as if to make himself master over God.' Nachmanides, *Commentary on the Torah: Exodus* (New York, 1973), p. 248. Amalek, says the Midrash, was also an adviser to Pharaoh: *Midrash Rabbah: Exodus* (London, 1983), p. 325.

49. *Midrash Rabbah: Numbers (II)* (London, 1983), p. 507.

50. He is 'Israel's evil strap'. *Midrash Rabbah: Numbers (II)* (London, 1983), p. 685 (and see also p. 769); *Midrash Rabbah: Exodus* (London, 1983), pp. 317, 319.

51. However, the *nature* of the war waged against him is unique to him, and is not comparable to any war waged against any Canaanite nation. See, on this point, *Midrash Rabbah: Numbers (II)* (London, 1983), pp. 685 and 769. The Midrash cites Deuteronomy 2:4–5: 'Ye are to pass through the coast of your brethren the children of Esau, which dwell in Seir... Meddle not with them; for I will not give you of their land, no, not so much as a foot breadth; because I have given mount Seir unto Esau for a possession.' And later, it is supposed that God addressed the Israelites: 'They are *like* Canaanites to you...'

52. Louis Jacobs, *The Jewish Religion: A companion* (Oxford, 1995), p. 23. See also, for this 'allegorized notion', Elliot Horowitz, *Reckless Rites* (Princeton, NJ, 2006), pp. 134–5. Alternatively, he is the type of all Israel's enemies, and is singled out for punishment only as a deterrent to others. See Moses Maimonides, *The Guide of the Perplexed* (Chicago, 1963), vol. 2, p. 566.

53. Rashi's gloss on Amalek, citing Amos 1:11: 'For three transgressions of Edom, and for four, I will not turn away the punishment thereof; because he did pursue his brother with the sword, and did cast off all pit, and his anger did tear perpetually, and he kept his wrath for ever.' See R. Avrohom Davis (trans.), *The Metsudah Chumash/Rashi* (Lakewood, NJ, 2002), Shemos-Beshalach 17:16, p. 225.

54. Midian and Amalekite raiders attack the Israelites in the period of the judges (Judges 3:13, 6:3 and 33, 7:12); the Amalekite King Agag causes King Saul's downfall (1 Samuel 15); an Amalekite thereafter kills Saul (2 Samuel 1:8–10); David engages with the Amalekites, and after an initial reverse, defeats them (1 Samuel 30); the tribe of Simeon finishes them off (1 Chronicles 42–3).

55. Brian M. Britt, 'Erasing Amalek: Remembering to forget with Derrida and biblical tradition' in Yvonne Sherwood (ed.), *Derrida's Bible* (New York, 2004), pp. 65–6.

56. See Richard Breitman, *The Architect of Genocide: Himmler and the Final Solution* (London, 2004), p. 189.

57. See Debórah Dwork and Robert Jan Van Pelt, *Holocaust: A history* (London, 2003), pp. 303–4.

58. See Danielle Knafo, 'Anti-Semitism in the clinical setting: Transference and countertransference dimensions', *Journal of the American Psychoanalytical Association* 47 (1999), 57–60.

59. See Ulrike Ehet, 'Catholics and Antisemitism in Germany and England 1918–1939', unpublished PhD thesis, University of London, 2005, p. 170.

60. See Robert Wistrich, *Anti-Semitism* (London, 1991), p. 57.

61. See Nathan Rotenstreich, 'For and against emancipation', *Leo Baeck Institute Year Book*, London, 1959, pp. 17–18.

62. See J. S. Mill, 'On Liberty', *Three Essays* (Oxford, 1975), p. 12.

63. See Leon Volovici, *Nationalist Ideology & Antisemitism* (Oxford, 1991), pp. 19-20.

64. See Nelly Wilson, *Bernard-Lazare* (Cambridge, 1978), p. 72.

65. See J. S. McClelland (ed.), *The French Right* (London, 1971), p. 181.

66. See Philippa Foot, 'Virtues and vices' in Roger Crisp and Michael Slote (eds.), *Virtue Ethics* (Oxford, 1997), pp. 174–5.

67. See Paul Frosh, 'The glamour of the boycott', *Engage*, 3 November 2006.

68. Jan T. Gross, *Fear* (New York, 2006), p. 69.

69. Leon Trotsky, *1905* (London, 1973), p. 151.

70. See Mark Roseman, *The Villa, the Lake, the Meeting* (London, 2002), p. 23.

71. See *Obedience to Authority* (London, 2004) pp. 166–8.

72. Uli Linke, *Blood and Nation: The European aesthetics of race* (Philadelphia, PA, 1999), p. 150.

73. See Richard Evans, *The Coming of the Third Reich* (London, 2003), pp. 183, 223, 431–2.

74. Simon Sebag Montefiore, *Stalin: The court of the Red Tsar* (London, 2004), p. 576.

75. See Leslie Mitchell, *The Whig World* (London, 2005), p. 74.

76. Martin Amis, *Koba the Dread* (London, 2002), p. 218.

77. Jonathan Judaken, *Jean-Paul Sartre and the Jewish Question* (Nebraska, 2006), p. 67.

78. Bernard Lewis, *Semites and Anti-Semites* (London, 1986), pp. 204–5.

79. Annual Report 2000–2001, The Stephen Roth Institute for the Study of Contemporary Antisemitism and Racism.

80. *Infidel* (London, 2007), p. 47.

81. See Fritz Stern, *Gold and Iron* (London, 1977), p. 392.

82. Richard Sennett, *The Fall of Public Man* (London, 1986), p. 244.

83. Franz Neumann, 'Anxiety and politics', *The Democratic and the Authoritarian State* (New York, 1964), p. 287.

84. See R. Patai (ed.), *The Complete Diaries of Theodor Herzl* (London, 1960), vol. 4, p. 1603.

85. Hansard, Parl. Debs. (series 3) vol. 98, cols. 1379–80 (1848).

86. R. Travers Herford, *Christianity in Talmud and Midrash* (London, 1903), pp. 359, 393.

87. See Jonathan Hess, *Germans, Jews and the Claims of Modernity* (New Haven, NJ, 2002), pp. 101–2.

88. *Daniel Deronda* (Oxford, 1998), p. 544.

89. *The Diary of a Writer* (Salt Lake City, UT, 1985), p. 645.

90. Otto Fenichel, 'Elements of a psychoanalytic theory of anti-Semitism' in Ernst Simmel (ed.), *Anti-Semitism: A social disease* (New York, 1946), p. 35.

91. *Anti-Semite and Jew* (New York, 1995), p. 26.

92. Franz Neumann, 'Anxiety and politics', *The Democratic and the Authoritarian State* (New York, 1964), p. 287. Cf., 'For all those who have been unsuccessful in the battle of life, National Socialism is the great worker of magic.' Hermann Rauschning, *The Voice of Destruction* (New York, 1940), pp. 221–2.

93. Edgar Morin, *Rumour in Orléans* (London, 1971), p. 157.

94. See Earl Hopper, 'The problem of context in group: Analytic psychotherapy', *The Social Unconscious* (London, 2003), p. 120.

95. See Joseph Jacobs (ed.), *The Jews of Angevin England* (London, 1893), p. 113.

96. See Earl Hopper, 'The problem of context in group: Analytic psychotherapy', *The Social Unconscious* (London, 2003), p. 113.

97. Max Horkheimer, 'Sociological background of the psychoanalytic approach' in Ernst Simmel (ed.), *Anti-Semitism: A social disease* (New York, 1946), p. 4.

98. See Kate Barrows, *Envy* (London, 2002), p. 54.

99. 'Scientific experiences of a European scholar in America' in Donald Fleming and Bernard Bailyn (eds.), *The Intellectual Migration* (Cambridge, MA, 1969), pp. 367–8; Joseph Epstein, *Envy* (Oxford, 2003), pp. 60–1.

100. See Kate Barrows, *Envy* (London, 2002), p. 11.

101. Christopher Browning, *The Origins of the Final Solution* (Nebraska, 2004), p. 175.

102. See Nelly Wilson, *Bernard-Lazare* (Cambridge, 1978), p. 209.

103. R. I. Moore, 'Anti-Semitism and the birth of Europe' in Diana Wood (ed.), *Studies in Church History* (Oxford, 1992), vol. 29, pp. 50–2.

104. See Ulrike Ehet, 'Catholics and antisemitism in Germany and England 1918–1939', unpublished PhD thesis, University of London, 2005, p. 137.

105. T. W. Adorno, 'Anti-Semitism and fascist propaganda' in Ernst Simmel (ed.), *Anti-Semitism* (New York, 1946), p. 127; Slavoj Žižek, *Did Somebody Say Totalitarianism?* (London, 2001), p. 149.

106. See Slavoj Žižek, *Did Somebody Say Totalitarianism?* (London, 2001), p. 138.

107. *The Modern Jew* (London, 1899), pp. ix–x, xvi.

108. See Richard Griffiths, *Patriotism Perverted: Captain Ramsay* (London, 1998), p. 61.

109. Ibid., p. 28; Colin Holmes, 'Alexander Ratcliffe, militant protestant and antisemite' in Tony Kushner and Kenneth Lunn (eds.), *Traditions of Intolerance* (Manchester, 1989), p. 204.

110. See Tony Kushner, *We Europeans?* (London, 2004), p. 174.

111. Jean-Paul Sartre, *Anti-Semite and Jew* (New York, 1995), p. 40.

112. See Claire Hirshfield, 'The Anglo-Boer War and the issue of Jewish culpability', *Journal of Contemporary History*, 15 (1980), 623.

113. See 'The testament of an Anti-Semite' in Moshe Zimmermann, *Wilhelm Marr* (Oxford, 1986), p. 151.

114. *An Essay Concerning Human Understanding* (New York, 1959), vol. 2, p. 431.

115. Jean-Denis Bredin, *The Affair: The case of Alfred Dreyfus* (London, 1987), p. 28. 'Houston Stewart Chamberlain praised Hitler in 1923, "the great simplifier of all problems".' John Lukacs, *The Hitler of History* (London, 2002), p. 252.

116. See Mark Strauss, 'Who hates the Jews now?', *Spectator*, 29 November 2003.

117. Cf. 2 Corinthians 3:14.

118. See Neil Baldwin, *Henry Ford and the Jews* (New York, 2001), p. 144.

119. Richard Hofstadter, 'The paranoid style in American politics' in *The Paranoid Style in American Politics and Other Essays* (New York, 1967), p. 3.

120. Canto LXXIV, 'The Pisan Cantos', *The Cantos* (London, 1975), p. 430.

121. Franz Neumann, 'Anxiety and politics', *The Democratic and the Authoritarian State* (New York, 1964), p. 287.

122. That is, Hitler. See Ian Kershaw, *Hitler: Nemesis 1936–1945* (London, 2001), p. 841.

123. Theodore Abel, *Why Hitler Came Into Power* (Cambridge, MA, 1968), pp. 160–1.

124. Wolfgang Hochheimer, 'Lessening of prejudice through education and prevention of antisemitism' in Werner Bergmann (ed.), *Error Without Trial* (Berlin, 1988), p. 529.

125. See Gustave Le Bon, *The Crowd: A study of the popular mind* (Atlanta, GA, 1982), p. 113.

126. Theodore Abel, *Why Hitler Came into Power* (Cambridge, MA, 1986), p. 117.

127. Christopher Browning, *The Origins of the Final Solution* (Nebraska, 2004), pp. 226, 232, 251–2. Cf. Gerald Reitlinger, *The Final Solution*, 2nd edn (London, 1968), pp. 198 and 204, on the 'queer intellectual riff-raff' and 'lost legion of unemployed intellectuals' that comprised the commanders of the *Einsatzgruppen*.

128. For some examples, see Richard Thurlow, *Fascism in Modern Britain* (London, 2000), pp. 58, 84, 135.

129. Paul Lawrence Rose, *German Question/Jewish Question* (Princeton, NJ, 1990), p. 281.

130. *Out of Step* (Hollywood, CA, n.d.), pp. 50–1.

131. See Nigel Copsey, *Contemporary British Fascism* (London, 2008), p. 8.

132. Michael Billig, *Fascists* (London, 1978), pp. 119, 133.

133. Seamus Perry (ed.), *Coleridge's Notebooks* (London, 2002), p. 110.

134. See Susan Jacoby, *The Age of American Unreason* (New York, 2008), pp. 210–41.

135. See Haig Bosmajian, *The Language of Oppression* (Washington, DC, 1974), pp. 12–13.

136. Isaiah Berlin, 'L. B. Namier', *Personal Impressions* (London, 1980), p. 65.

137. See, for example, Roger Eatwell, 'The Holocaust denial' in Luciano Cheles et al. (eds.), *Neo-Fascism in Europe* (London, 1991), p. 137.

138. See Ron Rosenbaum, *Explaining Hitler* (London, 1999), p. 222.

139. James H. Robb, *Working-Class Anti-Semite* (London, 1954), pp. 52, 98.

140. See Plato, *Phaedo* (Oxford, 1996), pp. 43–4.

141. Max Horkheimer, 'Sociological background of the psychoanalytic approach' in Ernst Simmel (ed.), *Anti-Semitism* (New York, 1946), p. 4.

142. William D. Rubinstein, *Elites and the Wealthy in Modern British History* (New York, 1987), p. 342.

143. See Robert Musil, 'On stupidity', *Precision and Soul* (Chicago, 1994), p. 275.

144. David Baker, *Ideology of Obsession* (London, 1996), p. 178.

145. *Economy and Class Structure of German Fascism* (London, 1978), p. 152.

146. See Robert Jan Van Pelt, *The Case for Auschwitz* (Bloomington, IN, 2002), p. 432.

147. See Ron Rosenbaum, *Explaining Hitler* (London, 1999), pp. 68–77.

148. T. W. Adorno, 'Anti-Semitism and fascist propaganda' in Ernst Simmel (ed.), *Anti-Semitism* (New York, 1946), p. 130.

149. See Norman Davies, *Europe* (London, 1997), pp. 500–1.

150. Gustave Le Bon, *The Crowd* (Atlanta, GA, 1982), p. 121.

151. Hannah Arendt, *The Origins of Totalitarianism* (New York, 1976), p. 87.

152. Richard I. Cohen, 'Recurrent images in French antisemitism' in Robert Wistrich (ed.), *Demonizing the Other* (Amsterdam, 1999), p. 188.

153. *Twilight Over England* (London, 1992), p. 9.

154. Richard Dawkins, *The Selfish Gene* (Oxford, 1989), pp. 192–4; John Gray, *Heresies* (London, 2004), p. 69.

155. See my *T. S. Eliot, Anti-Semitism, and Literary Form*, 2nd edn (London, 2003).

156. See Todd M. Endelman, *The Jews of Georgian England 1714–1830* (Philadelphia, 1979), p. 90.

157. See Alain Besançon, *A Century of Horrors* (Wilmington, DE, 2007), p. 92.

158. See, for example, Peter A. French, 'Unchosen moral evil and moral responsibility' in Aleksander Jokić (ed.), *War Crimes and Collective Wrongdoing* (Oxford, 2001), pp. 36, 40. 'The average Balkan war criminal is not a moron, nor a brute . . .'

159. See Richard Overy, *The Dictators* (London, 2005), p. 19. Auschwitz had nothing to do with capitalism or any other economic system, wrote Jean Améry. It was the monstrous product of sick minds and perverted souls. *At the Mind's Limits* (New York, 1986), p. 15.

160. *Politics and Passion* (New Haven, 2004), p. 2.

161. For anti-Semitism as a virus, see Robert S. Wistrich, *Anti-Semitism* (London, 1991), p. xxii.

162. *Zettel* (Oxford, 1967), p. 69/69e. 'In philosophizing, we may not terminate a disease of thought (*Denkkrankheit*). It must run its natural course, and slow cure is all important.'

163. See Alain Besançon, *A Century of Horrors* (Wilmington, DE, 2007), p. 16.

164. See, for example, Paul Johnson, 'The anti-Semitic disease', *Commentary*, June (2005), 33–8. Anti-Semitism 'makes no more sense than malaria or meningitis'. But note: 'There is need for a great deal more careful research on the problems of continuity and transmission.' Nicholas de Lange, 'The origins of modern anti-Semitism' in Sander L. Gilman and Steven T. Katz (eds.), *Anti-Semitism in Times of Crisis* (New York, 1991), p. 34.

165. Leon Trotsky, *1905* (London, 1973), p. 149.

166. *The Crowd* (Atlanta, GA, 1982), p. 23.

167. See Edgar Morin, *Rumour in Orléans* (London, 1971).

168. See Peter Goldie, *On Personality* (London, 2004), p. 46.

169. See Edgar Morin, *Rumour in Orléans* (London, 1971), p. 142.

170. See Charles Taylor, *Modern Social Imaginaries* (London, 2004), p. 23; Michel Foucault, *The Archaeology of Knowledge* (London, 1974), p. 129 ('the law of what can be said').

171. See Susan Neiman, *Evil in Modern Thought* (Princeton, NJ, 2002), pp. 292–9.

172. Nigel Copsey, 'John Amery', *Patterns of Prejudice*, 36/2 (2002), 26.

173. Geoffrey Alderman, *Modern British Jewry* (Oxford, 1992), p. 134.

174. (London, 1950), p. 12.

175. 'Address to the Society of B'nai Brith', *Psychological Writings and Letters* (New York, 1995), p. 267; Sander L. Gilman, *Jewish Self-Hatred* (Baltimore, MD, 1986), p. 251.

176. See *Totem and Taboo* (London, 1960), p. xi. But see also 'Death and us' in David Meghnani (ed.), *Freud and Judaism* (London, 1993), pp. 3–53.

177. See Yosef Hayim Yerushalmi, *Freud's Moses* (New Haven, CT, 1991), p. 13.

178. The literature on this topic is extensive. See, for example, Janine Chasseguet-Smirgel, 'Some thoughts on Freud's attitude during the Nazi period' in David Meghnani (ed.), *Freud and Judaism* (London, 1993), p. 76 (on Freud's 'fidelity to his Jewish heritage').

179. Ernst L. Freud (ed.), *The Letters of Sigmund Freud and Arnold Zweig* (London, 1970), p. 102.

180. Mark Edmundson, *The Death of Sigmund Freud* (London, 2007), pp. 149–50, 198.

181. See Peter Gay, *A Godless Jew* (New Haven, 1987), p. 149; Robert S. Wistrich, *The Jews of Vienna in the Age of Franz Joseph* (Oxford, 1990), p. 582. Freud was defensive about its impact on his fellow Jews. It would not affect the generality of Jews; the book is for a minority with no faith to lose; to fail to publish would be cowardly, a reproach now directed at Jews (which he would therefore disprove by publication of the book); the truth should not be slighted in defence of national interests. See Peter Gay, *Freud* (London, 1988), pp. 633–7.

182. Freud described himself in a letter to Oskar Pfister as a 'completely godless Jew'. See Yosef Hayim Yerushalmi, *Freud's Moses* (New Haven, CT, 1991), p. 8.

183. 'Freud on Moses and monotheism', *Jewish Philosophy and the Crisis of Modernity* (New York, 1997), pp. 286–8. In this sense, Spinoza was *not* a 'good Jew'. See 'Why we remain Jews', *Jewish Philosophy and the Crisis of Modernity* (New York, 1997), p. 318. Cf. 'The fact that, within a Jewish historical context, I have arrived at a positive evaluation of Freud's intentions in *Moses and Monotheism* does not mean that I necessarily share any of his views on Jews or Judaism.' Yosef Hayim Yerushalmi, *Freud's Moses* (New Haven, CT, 1991), p. xviii.

184. 'As a Jew myself, who supported the state of Israel from its earliest days, I am grieved to ask the question, but I must: will they [i.e., the Israelis] never learn?' Gerald Kaufman, *Daily Mail*, 23 July 2006.

185. 'Freedom from ghetto thinking', *Freud's Vienna and Other Essays* (New York, 1989), pp. 243–71.

186. See Marcel Liebman, *Born Jewish* (London, 2005), p. 169.

187. Hyam Isaacs, *Ceremonies, Customs, Rites and Traditions of the Jews* (London, 1836), pp. iii–vi. See also Todd M. Endelman, *Radical Assimilation in English Jewish History 1656–1945* (Bloomington, IN, 1990), p. 166.

188. See Jane Irwin (ed.), *George Eliot's 'Daniel Deronda' Notebooks* (Cambridge, 1996), p. 88.

189. See Eli Lederhendler, *The Road to Modern Jewish Politics* (Oxford, 1989), pp. 105–6.

190. Paul Lawrence Rose, *German Question/Jewish Question* (Princeton, NJ, 1990), p. 159.

191. Ruth Wisse, *Jews and Power* (New York, 2007), p. 74.

192. See Heiko A. Oberman, *The Roots of Anti-Semitism* (Philadelphia, 1984), pp. 11, 32–7, 55, and 66–70. Following Pfefferkorn's conversion, he 'confessed' to conspiring with Jewish associates to poison an archbishop, an Elector, and thirteen other Christians. S. W. Baron, *A Social and Religious History of the Jews*, 2nd edn (New York, 1967), vol. 11, p. 159.

193. H. Graetz, *Popular History of the Jews* (New York, 1923), vol. 5, p. 515; Jonathan Frankel, *The Damascus Affair* (Cambridge, 1997), p. 268; James Picciotto, *Sketches of Anglo-Jewish History* (London, 1956), p. 345; S. W. Baron, *A Social and Religious History of the Jews*, 2nd edn (New York, 1967), vol. 11, p. 157.

194. H. C. Lea, *Chapters from the Religious History of Spain Connected with the Inquisition* (London, 1890), pp. 448–9.

195. David Meghnagi, 'Editor's note' and Freud, Sigmund, 'Death and us' in David Meghnagi (ed.), *Freud and Judaism* (London, 1993), p. 52; Kurt Lewin, 'Self-hatred among Jews', *Contemporary Jewish Record*, 4 (1941), 224–5; David Forgacs, 'Building the body of the nation' in Bryan Cheyette and Nadia Valman (eds.), *The Image of the Jew in European Liberal Culture* (London, 2004), p. 103.

196. Yehezkel Kaufman, 'Anti-Semitic stereotypes in Zionism', *Commentary*, 7 (1949), 240.

197. Sander L. Gilman, *Jewish Self-Hatred* (Baltimore, MD, 1986), p. 2.

198. See Robert S. Wistrich, *The Jews of Vienna in the Age of Franz Joseph* (Oxford, 1990), p. 193.

199. See Aharon Appelfeld, *Beyond Despair* (New York, 1994), pp. 6, 47, 76–7; Emanuel Litvinoff, *Journey Through a Small Planet* (London, 2008), p. 174.

200. See Geoffrey G. Field, *Evangelist of Race* (New York, 1981), p. 52.

201. See *Sex and Character* (London, 1906), pp. 304–5.

202. Bernhard Berliner, 'On some religious motifs of anti-Semitism' in Ernst Simmel (ed.), *Anti-Semitism* (New York, 1946), p. 80.

203. Heinrich Graetz, *Popular History of the Jews* (New York, 1923), vol. 5, p. 543.

204. See Robert S. Wistrich, 'Anti-Zionism and antisemitism' in Michael Fineberg, Shimon Samuels, and Mark Weitzman (eds.), *Antisemitism* (London, 2007), p. 9.

205. Bernard Lewis, *Semites and Anti-Semites* (London, 1986), p. 124; *The Jews of Islam* (London, 1984), p. 86.

206. R. Po-Chia Hsia, *Trent 1475* (New Haven, 1992), p. 100; Elisheva Carlebach, *Divided Souls* (New Haven, 2001), p. 35.

207. Lauren Fogle, 'Between Christianity and Judaism: The identity of converted Jews in medieval London', *Essays in Medieval Studies*, 22 (2005), 108, 110–12.

208. Elisheva Carlebach, *Divided Souls* (New Haven, 2001), p. 38.

209. David Frankfurter, *Evil Incarnate* (Princeton, NJ, 2006), p. 186. 'An apostate! A renegade! Someone who comes up with the stuff, the secrets, the list of the enemy camp's dirty tricks, in his beggar's bag.' Bernard-Henri Lévy, *American Vertigo* (New York, 2006), p. 208.

210. Sander L. Gilman, *Jewish Self-Hatred* (Baltimore, MD, 1986), p. 32.

211. *Barry Lyndon* (Oxford, 1999), p. 160.

212. 'The anti-Semitic movement', *Punch*, 29 January 1881.

213. See Jacob Katz, *From Prejudice to Destruction: Anti-Semitism 1700–1933* (Cambridge, MA, 1980), p. 118.

214. *Jews Must Live* (Arlington, VA, 1964), p. 17.

215. Sidney Whitman, 'The anti-Semitic movement', *Contemporary Review*, 63 (May 1983), 712.

216. Hermann L. Strack, *The Jew and Human Sacrifice* (London, 1909), p. 148; but contrast pp. 239–50. For an example, see S. W. Baron, *A Social and Religious History of the Jews,* 2nd edn (New York, 1967), vol. 11, p. 153. See also Joseph Bloch, *My Reminiscences* (New York, 1973), pp. 402–7, 450, 456, 462–6, 562.

217. Petrus Alfonsi, *Dialogue Against the Jews* (Washington, DC, 2006), p. 10; Judah M. Rosenthal, 'The Talmud on trial', *Jewish Quarterly Review*, 47 (1956), 63.

218. Petrus Alfonsi, *Dialogue Against the Jews* (Washington, DC, 2006), p. 40.

219. Steven F. Kruger, *The Spectral Jew* (Minneapolis, MN, 2006), p. 166.

220. Elisheva Carlebach, *Divided Souls* (New Haven, 2001), p. 45; James Parkes, *Voyage of Discoveries* (London, 1969), p. 141 ('all the false accusations which had led to the deaths of tens of thousands of Jews had come from Jewish converts to Christianity').

221. Solomon Grayzel, *The Church and the Jews in the XIIIth Century: 1254–1314* (New York, 1989), p. 98. But see Cecil Roth, *The Ritual Murder Libel and the Jew: The report by Cardinal Lorenzo Ganganelli* (London, n.d.), p. 81.

222. Simon M. Dubnow, *History of the Jews in Poland and Russia* (Bergenfield, NJ, 2000), p. 83.

223. Norman Cohn, *Warrant for Genocide* (London, 1967), pp. 53–5.

224. David I. Goldstein, *Dostoyevsky and the Jews* (Austin, Texas, 1981), pp. 96–7, 122–4. Dostoyevsky was the dedicatee of the second edition of the work.

225. Hans Rogger, *Jewish Policies and Right-Wing Politics in Imperial Russia* (London, 1986), p. 22.

226. Walter Laqueur, *The Changing Face of Antisemitism* (New York, 2006), p. 82.

227. Steven G. Marks, *How Russia Shaped the Modern World* (Princeton, NJ, 2003), pp. 157–8; Norman Cohn, *Warrant for Genocide* (London, 1967), pp. 105–6.

228. Dubnow gives further examples in *History of the Jews in Poland and Russia* (Bergenfield, NJ, 2000), pp. 232, 236–7, 436. See too Charles H. H. Wright, 'The Jews and the malicious charge of Human Sacrifice', *The Nineteenth Century*, 81 (November 1883), 769, 774. But there were also converts who gave evidence for defendants at blood libel trials, and confirmed as experts (that is, former Jews) that there was nothing in the ritual murder allegation.

229. See Elisheva Carlebach, *Divided Souls* (New Haven, 2001), p. 21.

230. See ibid., pp. 12–13.

231. R. I. Moore, 'Anti-Semitism and the birth of Europe' in Diana Wood (ed.), *Studies in Church History* (Oxford, 1992), vol. 29, p. 52; Robert Chazan, *The Jews of Medieval Western Christendom* (Cambridge, 2006), p. 63.

232. S. W. Baron, *A Social and Religious History of the Jews* (New York, 1965), vol. 9, p. 270, fn. 12.

233. Ibid., p. 64; Jeremy Cohen, 'Christian theology and anti-Jewish violence in the Middle Ages: Connections and disjunctions' in Anna Sapir Abulafia (ed.), *Religious Violence between Christians and Jews* (New York, 2002), p. 53.

234. Heinrich Graetz, *Popular History of the Jews* (New York, 1923), vol. 3, pp. 342–3; but see Yvonne Friedman, 'Anti-Talmudic invective from Peter the Venerable to Nicholas Donin (1144–1244)' in G. Dahan (ed.), *Le Brûlement du Talmud à Paris, 1242–1244* (Paris, 1999), p. 187.

235. Israel J. Yuval, *Two Nations in Your Womb* (Berkeley, 2006), pp. 280–3; Judah M. Rosenthal, 'The Talmud on trial', *Jewish Quarterly Review* 47 (1956), 70.

236. Gilbert Dahan, *The Christian Polemic against the Jews in the Middle Ages* (Notre Dame, IN, 1998), pp. 31, 32, 84.

237. See Jeremy Cohen, 'Christian theology and anti-Jewish violence in the Middle Ages' in Anna Sapir Abulafia (ed.), *Religious Violence between Christians and Jews* (New York, 2002), p. 54.

238. Judah M. Rosenthal, 'The Talmud on trial', *Jewish Quarterly Review* 47 (1956), 69.

239. Yvonne Friedman, 'Anti-Talmudic invective from Peter the Venerable to Nicholas Donin (1144–1244)' in G. Dahan (ed.), *Le Brûlement du Talmud à Paris, 1242–1244* (Paris, 1999), p. 181.

240. S. W. Baron, *A Social and Religious History of the Jews* (New York, 1965), vol. 9, pp. 80–1.

241. See Jeremy Cohen, *The Friars and the Jews* (Ithaca, 1982), pp. 60–1, and fn. 19, and pp. 71–2.

242. Judah M. Rosenthal, 'The Talmud on trial', *Jewish Quarterly Review*, 47 (1956), 70.

243. Lesley Smith, 'William of Auvergne and the Jews' in Diana Wood (ed.), *Studies in Church History*, (Oxford, 1992), vol. 29, pp. 113–14.

244. See Léon Poliakov, *The History of Anti-Semitism* (London, 1974), vol. 2, p. 69, fn. 22.

245. Nathan Lopes Cardozo, *Thoughts to Ponder* (Jerusalem, 2006), p. 46.

246. II:17. See R. Travers Herford (ed.), *Sayings of the Fathers* (New York, 1975), p. 58.

247. See Donald Davie (ed.), *The Psalms in English* (London, 1996), p. 130.

248. See ibid., p. 1; Laurance Wieder (ed.), *The Poets' Book of Psalms* (New York, 1995), p. 7; Robert Alter, *The Book of Psalms* (New York, 2007), p. 3.

249. See *Avodah Zarah* 19b.

250. *Daniel Deronda* (Oxford, 1998), p. 620; Irene Tucker, *A Probable State* (Chicago, 2000), p. 35.

251. *Secret Societies and Subversive Movements* (London, 1924), pp. 393–4, 401.

252. *Germany and England* (Arabi, LA, n.d.), pp. 19–20.

253. Ibid., pp. 32–3. Webster was very taken with Walter Rathenau's remark, 'Three hundred men, all acquainted with each other, control the economic destiny of the Continent.' *The Surrender of an Empire* (London, 1931), p. 122.

254. *Desert Highway* (London, 1944), pp. viii, 43–4.

255. See Richard Bolchover, *British Jewry and the Holocaust* (Cambridge, 1993), pp. 115–16, on Anglo-Jewry's 'policy of cultic gratitude', 'gratitude strategy', and 'ritualistic expressions of gratitude' for favourable statements by non-Jewish national figures.

256. Martin Gilbert, *Churchill and the Jews* (London, 2007), p. 1.

257. 'I would like to create a politics of anti-anti-Semitism . . .' Denis MacShane, *Globalising Hatred* (London, 2008), pp. ix, 17, 157. The Russian intellectual Peter Struve (1870–1944) described himself as an '*a*-Semite', neither *anti*- nor *philo*-Semitic. See Paul Berline, 'Russian religious philosophers and the Jews', *Jewish Social Studies*, 9/4 (1947), 301, 303.

258. Wyndham Lewis, *The Jews: Are they human?* (London, 1939), pp. 8, 15–16, 28, 30.

259. Mr. B. Osborne. Hansard, Parl. Debs. (series 3) vol. 125, col. 91 (1853).

260. See Paul Berline, 'Russian religious philosophers and the Jews', *Jewish Social Studies*, 9/4 (1947), 273.

261. *After the Victorians* (London, 2005), pp. 359–60.

262. Frank Stern, 'The revival of antisemitism in united Germany' in Michael Brown (ed.), *Approaches to Antisemitism* (New York, 1994), p. 88.

263. T. H. S. Escott, *King Edward and his Court* (London, 1908), p. 212. See also Moshe Rosman, *How Jewish Is Jewish History?* (Oxford, 2007), p. 79.

264. 'Israel Among the Nations', *The Forum*, 16 (December 1893), 447–8. See also Paul Lawrence Rose, *German Question/Jewish Question* (Princeton, NJ, 1990), pp. 76–7.

265. Paul Lawrence Rose, *German Question/Jewish Question* (Princeton, NJ, 1990), p. 91.

266. Mortimer Ostow, 'A contribution to the study of antisemitism' in Werner Bergmann (ed.), *Error Without Trial* (Berlin, 1988), pp. 57–66; Michael Burleigh, *Earthly Powers* (London, 2005), pp. 434–6.

267. Edmund Wilson, *A Piece of My Mind* (London, 1957), p. 74; David Cesarani, 'Reporting anti-semitism' in Sîan Jones *et al.*, *Cultures of Ambivalence and Contempt* (London, 1998), p. 248 ('so called philosemitism').

268. 'The group round Lenin', *The Times*, 22 November 1919. Four days later, 'Judaeus' wrote in: 'No one can doubt the friendly feelings of Philojudaeus' towards the Jews. His letter, however... does them some injustice...'

269. Duke of Devonshire, 1923. See Michael J. Cohen, *Churchill and the Jews* (London, 2003), p. 50.

270. John Corry, *A Satirical View of London at the Commencement of the Nineteenth Century* (London, 1801), p. 47; see David S. Katz, *The Jews in the History of England* (1996), p. 293.

271. Pierre Birnbaum, *Anti-Semitism in France* (Oxford, 1992), pp. 182–7.

272. For an example of an ambiguous philo-Semitism, see Hillel J. Kieval, *Languages of Community* (Berkeley, CA, 2000), ch. 9.

273. See Geoffrey Wheatcroft, *The Controversy of Zion* (Reading, MA, 1996), p. xi.

274. Paul Lawrence Rose, *German Question/Jewish Question* (Princeton, NJ, 1990), p. 6.

275. 'The soul of man under socialism', *Complete Works* (London, 1966), p. 1079; David Theo Goldberg, 'The power of tolerance' in Tony Kushner and Nadia Valman (eds.), *Philosemitism, Antisemitism, and 'the Jews'* (Aldershot, 2004), pp. 34–7 ('a form of bad faith').

276. *The Social Problem* (London, 1902), p. 197.

277. *The Jew as Pariah* (New York, 1978), p. 60. See also J.-P. Sartre, *Anti-Semite and Jew* (New York, 1995), pp. 76–7.

278. See H. R. S. van der Veen, *Jewish Characters in Eighteenth Century English Fiction and Drama* (Groningen, 1935), pp. 230–1.

279. *Collected Poems* (London, 1979), pp. 180–1.

280. See also *The Strings are False* (London, 2007), pp. 18–19, 107, 199.

281. Peter Longerich, *The Unwritten Order* (Stroud, Gloucestershire, 2001), pp. 15–16; John Lukacs, *The Hitler of History* (London, 2002), pp. 48, 192–4.

282. David Bankier, 'The use of antisemitism in Nazi wartime propaganda' in Michael Berenbaum and Abraham J. Peck (eds.), *The Holocaust and History* (Bloomington, IN, 2002), pp. 43–4.

283. See Mark Roseman, *The Villa, the Lake, the Meeting* (London, 2002), p. 56.

284. Phillipe Burrin, *Nazi Anti-Semitism* (New York, 2005), p. 82.

285. See Franklin H. Littel, 'The other crimes of Adolf Hitler' in Michael Berenbaum and Abraham J. Peck (eds.), *The Holocaust and History* (Bloomington, IN, 2002), p. 228. And see, for an example of the citing of Zechariah for just this purpose: Menasseh ben Israel, *Vindiciae Judaeorum* (1656), in Lucien Wolf (ed.), *Menasseh ben Israel's Mission to Oliver Cromwell* (London, 1901), p. 115.

286. Steven F. Kruger, *The Spectral Jew* (Minneapolis, MN, 2006), p. 81; Leonard B. Glick, *Marked In Your Flesh* (Oxford, 2005), p. 42.

287. See Peter Schäfer, *Judeophobia* (Cambridge, MA, 1997), ch. 5.

288. Ibid., p. 118.

289. See Juvenal, *Saturae* XIV in Menachem Stern (ed.), *Greek and Latin Authors on Jews and Judaism* (Jerusalem, 1980), vol. 2, pp. 102–3.

290. See Benno Müller-Hill, 'Human genetics and the mass murder of Jew, Gypsies, and others' in Michael Berenbaum and Abraham J. Peck (eds.), *The Holocaust and History* (Bloomington, IN, 2002), p. 108.

291. Debórah Dwork and Robert Jan Van Pelt, *Holocaust* (London, 2003), p. 348.

292. See, for example, Martin Gilbert, *The Righteous* (London, 2002), pp. 154, 184–5, 201–2, 341. There were also involuntary rescuers, who were drawn into acts of rescue by ties of family or physical proximity, to other rescuers; child rescuers, a sub-set of involuntary rescuers, but with their own additional motives—a sense of adventure, a desire to please their parents, and so on. See Eva Fogelman, 'The rescuer self' in Michael Berenbaum and Abraham J. Peck (eds.), *The Holocaust and History* (Bloomington, IN, 2002), pp. 667–72.

293. See Sander L. Gilman, *Jewish Self-Hatred* (Baltimore, MD, 1986), pp. 33–56.

294. Steven G. Marks, *How Russia Shaped the Modern World* (Princeton, NJ, 2003), p. 147.

295. See Norman Cohn, *Warrant for Genocide* (London, 1967), p. 111.

296. See Theodore Abel, *Why Hitler Came into Power* (Cambridge, MA, 1986), pp. 160–1.

297. I have drawn these contradictory propositions from a table in Daniel J. Levinson and R. Nevitt Sanford, 'A scale for the measurement of anti-Semitism' in Werner Bergmann (ed.), *Error Without Trial* (Berlin, 1988), pp. 475–7.

298. See Raphael Israeli, 'Anti-Jewish attitudes in the Arabic media, 1975–1981' in Robert S. Wistrich (ed.), *Anti-Zionism and Antisemitism in the Contemporary World* (New York, 1990), p. 104.

299. *In the Time of Nations* (London, 1994), pp. 74–5.

300. See Werner Bergmann, 'Group theory and ethnic relations' in Werner Bergmann (ed.), *Error Without Trial* (Berlin, 1988), p. 140.

301. See William Graham Sumner, *Folkways* (New York, 1906), ch. 1. Sumner regarded the Jews as 'ethnocentric' (p. 14). That Sumner was wrong, however, detracts nothing from the truth of Kant's observation, 'nowhere does human nature appear less admirable than in the relationships which exist between peoples'. 'On the common saying: "This may be true in theory,

but it does not apply in practice"' in Hans Reiss (ed.), *Kant's Political Writings* (Cambridge, 1970), p. 91.

302. George M. Fredrickson, *Racism* (Princeton, NJ, 2002), p. 5.
303. See Bernard-Henri Lévy, *Sartre: The philosopher of the twentieth century* (Cambridge, 2003), p. 299.
304. Antony Beevor and Artemis Cooper, *Paris after the Liberation: 1940–1949* (London, 2004), p. 13.
305. Otto Fenichel, 'Elements of a psychoanalytic theory of anti-Semitism' in Ernst Simmel (ed.), *Anti-Semitism* (New York, 1946), p. 39.
306. Cf. '[Leon Poliakov's] thesis . . . that the root of the process was hatred, seemed in my eyes to be an antiquated supposition. The bureaucrats, I already knew, were not "haters".' Raoul Hilberg, *The Politics of Memory* (Chicago, 1996), p. 70.
307. Lucy S. Dawidowicz, *The Holocaust and the Historians* (Cambridge, MA, 1981), p. 9. In the Nazi period, 'the concept of the Jew as an enemy lost all realistic meaning. President Roosevelt became a Jew and the English leaders of the war likewise became Jews; in other words, the Jew was omnipresent, secreted in everyone inimical to Germany. The Jew became *the* enemy absolute.' Otto Fenichel, 'Elements of a psychoanalytic theory of anti-Semitism' in Ernst Simmel (ed.), *Anti-Semitism* (New York, 1946), p. 38.
308. See Michael Burns, *France and the Dreyfus Affair* (New York, 1999), pp. 122–3, 130–1.
309. See Andrew Roberts, *Hitler and Churchill* (London, 2003), pp. 136, 140.
310. Michael Marrus, *The Holocaust in History* (London, 1989), pp. 186, 188.
311. See, for example, Joe Hillaby, 'The ritual-child-murder accusation: Its dissemination and Harold of Gloucester', *Transactions of the J.H.S.E.*, 34 (1994–6), 77–8. The monks of St Peter's, Gloucester falsified the year, though not the day or month, of Harold of Gloucester's death so as to make it coincide with Passion Sunday.
312. See Sander L. Gilman, *Jewish Self-Hatred* (Baltimore, MD, 1986), p. 277.
313. George L. Mosse, *Towards the Final Solution* (Madison, Wisconsin, 1985), pp. 233–5.
314. See George M. Fredrickson, *Racism* (Princeton, NJ, 2002), pp. 140, 154.
315. Léon Poliakov, *The Aryan Myth* (New York, 1974), p. 193.
316. See Steven T. Katz, 'The Holocaust' in Michael Berenbaum and Abraham J. Peck (eds.), *The Holocaust and History* (Bloomington, IN, 2002), pp. 57–8.
317. Debórah Dwork and Robert Jan Van Pelt, *Holocaust: A history* (London, 2003), pp. 260–1.
318. George M. Fredrickson, *Racism* (Princeton, NJ, 2002), p. 128.
319. See Tzvetan Todorov, 'Letter from Paris', *Salmagundi*, 88–9 (Fall 1990–Winter 1991), 48.
320. George M. Fredrickson, *Racism* (Princeton, NJ, 2002), p. 135.

321. Joseph Jacobs, 'On the racial characteristics of modern Jews', *Journal of the Anthropological Institute of Great Britain and Ireland*, 15 (1886), 54.

322. Richard Griffiths, *The Use of Abuse* (Providence, RI, 1991), pp. 50-1.

323. See Franz Neumann, 'Anxiety and politics', *The Democratic and the Authoritarian State* (New York, 1964), p. 279.

324. See William D. Rubinstein, *Elites and the Wealthy in Modern British History* (New York, 1987), pp. 340-1.

325. For example, of the Jewish communities in late 1930s Central and Eastern Europe: 'A united, organized and ably led group of Jewish merchants and artisans might prove a force to be reckoned with. But that is rarely in evidence. Instead we find *a harried and terror-stricken mass of unorganised and undisciplined individuals* . . . No traces of the pooled wisdom and magical power of the Elders of Zion were in evidence along the route traversed by this writer' (my italics). Oscar I. Janowsky, *People at Bay* (London, 1938), pp. 134, 182.

326. The editors of Henry Ford's *Dearborn Independent*, for example, when broaching 'The Jewish question: Fact or fancy?' on 12 June 1920, declared that they were at a disadvantage, because of the 'supersensitiveness of Jews and non-Jews concerning the whole matter . . . [who] would prefer to keep it in the hazy borderlands of their thought, shrouded in silence'. See Neil Baldwin, *Henry Ford and the Jews* (New York, 2001), p. 129.

327. Richard Landes, 'The massacres of 1010: On the origins of popular anti-Jewish violence in Western Europe' in Jeremy Cohen (ed.), *From Witness to Witchcraft* (Wiesbaden, 1996), pp. 79-80, 93.

328. Elisheva Carlebach, *Divided Souls* (New Haven, 2001), p. 182.

329. See Jacob Katz, *From Prejudice to Destruction* (Cambridge, MA, 1980), p. 88.

330. See Samuel M. Osgood, *French Royalism under the Third and Fourth Republics* (The Hague, 1960), p. 61.

331. *The Nameless War* (London, 1952), p. 22.

332. Daniel Pipes, *Conspiracy* (New York, 1997), p. 40.

333. Norman Cohn, *Warrant for Genocide* (London, 1967), pp. 33-6.

334. Ibid., p. 109.

335. Ibid., pp. 138-9.

336. Cesare G. De Michelis, *The Non-Existent Manuscript* (Lincoln, NA, 2004), pp. 49-50. The two texts were taken to be reciprocally validating of each other: p. 111.

337. Ibid., pp. 6-7.

338. Ibid., pp. 11-12.

339. Norman Cohn, *Warrant for Genocide* (London, 1967), p. 119.

340. In the 1903 version, published in a St. Petersburg daily newspaper, the title was given as 'The Protocols of the sessions of the "World Alliance of Freemasons and of the Sages of Zion"'. See Cesare G. De Michelis, *The Non-Existent Manuscript* (Lincoln, NA, 2004), p. 7. For an overview, see Jacob Katz, *From Prejudice to Destruction* (Cambridge, MA, 1980), ch. 11. Islamist anti-Semites

have taken up this antagonism towards Freemasons, in part because the Freemasons are taken to exalt Solomon above all other prophets. See V. S. Naipaul, *Among the Believers* (London, 2001), p. 238.

341. Protocol III, para. 10—the Protocols are widely available on the Internet.

342. Protocol I, para. 15.

343. Protocol III, para. 1, and Protocol VII, para. 5.

344. Protocol XI, para. 4.

345. See Cesare G. De Michelis, *The Non-Existent Manuscript* (Lincoln, NA, 2004), pp. 14, 15, 47–8, 64, 113–14, 124.

346. Norman Cohn, *Warrant for Genocide* (London, 1967), pp. 118–19.

347. Ibid., pp. 71, 152–3.

348. See *Palestine: The land of three faiths* (London, 1923), p. 188.

349. T. W. H. Crosland, *The Fine Old Hebrew Gentleman* (London, 1922), p. 31. See also Hilary Blume, 'A study of anti-Semitic groups in Britain, 1918–1940', unpublished D. Phil thesis, University of Sussex, 1971, pp. 62–4.

350. Norman Cohn, *Warrant for Genocide* (London, 1967), pp. 136–8.

351. See Neil Baldwin, *Henry Ford and the Jews* (New York, 2001).

352. Nathan Weinstock, *Histoire des chiens: La dhimmitude dans le conflit israélo-palestinien* (Paris, 2004), p. 127; Tom Segev, *One Palestine, Complete* (London, 2000), p. 217.

353. Daniel Pipes, *Conspiracy* (New York, 1997), pp. 5–6.

354. Robert Rockaway, '*The Jews Cannot Defeat Me*': *The anti-Jewish campaign of Louis Farrakhan and the Nation of Islam* (Tel Aviv, 1995), p. 18. 'At almost every Farrakhan appearance, speech or rally, his followers display and sell copies of the *Protocols*... and Henry Ford's *The International Jew*...' (p. 25).

355. David Goodman, *The 'Protocols of the Elders of Zion', Aum, and Antisemitism in Japan*, Posen Papers in Contemporary Antisemitism no. 2, The Vidal Sassoon International Center for the Study of Antisemitism, The Hebrew University of Jerusalem (2005).

356. See Emanuel Litvinoff (ed.), *Soviet Anti-Semitism: The Paris trial* (London, 1974), pp. 9–11.

357. Lord Sydenham, letter to the *Spectator*, 27 August 1921, as set out in the *Protocols*, p. 60.

358. See Norman Cohn, *Warrant for Genocide* (London, 1967), p. 182.

359. Elżbieta Ettinger, *Hannah Arendt: Martin Heidegger* (New Haven, 1995), p. 48.

360. *Black England* (London, 1977), pp. 65–8.

361. Mark Roseman, *The Villa, the Lake, the Meeting* (London, 2002), pp. 108–18.

362. Steven G. Marks, *How Russia Shaped the Modern World* (Princeton, NJ, 2003), p. 164.

363. *Warrant for Genocide* (London, 1967), p. 17.

364. See Emanuele Ottolenghi, ' "The lie that will not die": Confronting the *Protocols of the Elders of Zion* in the 21st Century', *Transatlantic Institute*, 2007.

365. '[T]he Lobby's activities are not a conspiracy of the sort depicted in tracts like the *Protocols of the Elders of Zion*. For the most part, the individuals and groups that comprise it are only doing what other special interest groups do, but doing it very much better.' John Mearsheimer and Stephen Walt, 'The Israel lobby', *LRB*, 23 March 2006.

366. Maurice Oleander, *The Languages of Paradise* (Cambridge, MA, 2008), pp. 13, 18; Léon Poliakov, *The Aryan Myth* (New York, 1974), p. 1.

367. See David Fromkin, *A Peace to End All Peace* (London, 2003), pp. 41–3.

368. See Kenneth Lunn, 'Political anti-Semitism before 1914: Fascism's heritage?' in Kenneth Lunn and Richard C. Thurlow (eds.), *British Fascism* (London, 1980), p. 26.

369. Richard Griffiths, *Patriotism Perverted* (London, 1998), pp. 83, 91.

370. See Kenneth Lunn, 'Political anti-Semitism before 1914: Fascism's heritage?' in Kenneth Lunn and Richard C. Thurlow (eds.), *British Fascism* (London, 1980), p. 29.

371. *The Thirty-Nine Steps* (London, 1994), p. 14.

372. *Selected Poems* (New York, 1964), p. 35.

373. Alain Finkielkraut, *In the Name of Humanity* (London, 2001), p. 46.

374. F. Borkenau, *The Totalitarian Enemy* (London, 1939), p. 138.

375. *The Language of the Third Reich* (London, 2000), p. 135. '[The Nazi regime was] the only regime that . . . had no other clear principle except murderous hatred of the Jews, for "Aryan" had no clear meaning other than "non-Jewish".' Leo Strauss, 'Preface to Spinoza's *Critique of Religion*', *Jewish Philosophy and the Crisis of Modernity* (New York, 1997), p. 139.

376. *The House That Hitler Built* (London, 1937), pp. v, 261.

377. See Peter Longerich, *The Unwritten Order* (Stroud, Gloucestershire, 2001), p. 22.

378. John Lukacs, *The Hitler of History* (London, 2002), pp. 182–3. 'Hitler's entire political career was guided by his obsession with "the Jew".' Omer Bartov, 'The new antisemitism' in David Kertzer (ed.), *Old Demons, New Debates* (New York, 2005), p. 13.

379. Richard Overy, *Interrogations* (London, 2002), p. 185.

380. Ibid., p. 494.

381. Sebastian Haffner, *The Meaning of Hitler* (London, 1997), p. 83.

382. Leon Trotsky: Isaac Deutscher, *The Prophet Outcast: Trotsky 1929–1940* (Oxford, 1970), p. 154; F. Borkenau, *The Totalitarian Enemy* (London, 1939), pp. 171–2.

383. Leonard Woolf, *Quack, Quack!* (London, 1935), p. 70.

384. Leon Trotsky, 'Imperialism and anti-Semitism' (1940), *On the Jewish Question* (London, 1970), p. 30.

385. Louis W. Bondy, *Racketeers of Hatred* (London, 1946), pp. 7–8.

386. Sebastian Haffner, *The Meaning of Hitler* (London, 1997), p. 125.

387. Ibid., p. 60.

388. F. Borkenau, *The Totalitarian Enemy* (London, 1939), p. 166; Richard Bessel, *Nazism and War* (London, 2004), p. 3.

389. Fritz Stern, 'Subtle silence and its consequences' in Henning Tewes and Jonathan Wright (eds.), *Liberalism, Anti-Semitism and Democracy* (Oxford, 2001), p. 6.

390. Thomas Mann, 'The fall of the European Jews' in J. J. Lynx (ed.), *The Future of the Jews* (London, 1945), p. 13.

391. See Richard Evans, *The Coming of the Third Reich* (London, 2003), pp. 457, 459.

392. *The War Commentaries* (London, 1987), p. 162.

393. See Nicholas Fraser, *The Voice of Modern Hatred* (London, 2000), p. 35.

394. See Joachim Fest, *Inside Hitler's Bunker* (London, 2004), pp. 24, 41, 125, 129, 133, 165–7; Karl Jaspers, *The Question of German Guilt* (New York, 2000), p. 63.

395. Joachim Fest, *Inside Hitler's Bunker* (London, 2004), p. 125.

396. Ibid., p. 167.

397. Ibid., p. 82.

398. See Richard Bessel, *Nazism and War* (London, 2004), p. 1.

399. Yehuda Bauer, *Rethinking the Holocaust* (New Haven, 2001), p. 267; Lucy S. Dawidowicz, *The Holocaust and the Historians* (Cambridge, MA, 1981), pp. 19–20; Mark Mazower, *Hitler's Empire* (London, 2008), p. 12.

400. See Mr Justice Gray, *The Irving Judgment* (London, 2000), p. 239.

401. See Ronald L. Nettler, *Past Trials and Present Tribulations* (Oxford, 1987), pp. 86–7.

402. See Alain Finkielkraut, *The Future of a Negation* (Lincoln, NA, 1998), pp. 24–8.

403. See Robert Satloff, 'The Holocaust's Arab heroes', *Washington Post*, 8 October 2006.

404. Ronald Eissens, 'Common ground for hatemongers: Incitement on the Internet' in Michael Fineberg, Shimon Samuels, and Mark Weitzman (eds.), *Antisemitism* (London, 2007), p. 111.

405. Pierre Vidal-Naquet, *Assassins of Memory* (New York, 1992), p. 20.

406. Ibid., p. 87.

407. See Nicholas Fraser, *The Voice of Modern Hatred* (London, 2000), p. 131.

408. See Kate Taylor, *Holocaust Denial* (London, 2000), p. 63; David Irving, *Hitler's War* (London, 1991), p. 148, footnote; Richard Evans, *Lying about Hitler* (New York, 2001), pp. 67–8.

409. See Richard Evans, *Lying about Hitler* (New York, 2001), p. 135.

410. Gregg Rickman, 'Taking stock: Combating anti-Semitism in the OSCE region', 7 February 2008, <http://csce.gov/index.cfm?FuseAction=ContentRecords. ViewWitness&ContentRecord_id=931&ContentType=D&ContentRecord Type=D&ParentType=H&CFID=18849146&CFTOKEN=53>; 'Action heroes', *Daily Telegraph*, 2 June 2007.

411. Alain Finkielkraut, *The Imaginary Jew* (Lincoln, NA, 1994), p. 164.

412. Graffiti sprayed on Hove Progressive Synagogue and on a bus shelter near where Jews live in Brighton, in August 2006. See Jon Pike, 'The left needs consistent, anti-racist action', *Engage*, 19 August 2006. See also Yaniv Salama-Scheer, 'Synagogue in Chicago vandalized', *Jerusalem Post*, 5 April 2007.

413. Luciana Berger, 'Why I had to resign', *Guardian*, 15 April 2005.

414. Isaac Landman, 'Canards', *The Universal Jewish Encyclopedia* (New York, 1941), vol. 3, pp. 1–10.

415. See Susan Neiman, *Evil in Modern Thought* (Princeton, NJ, 2002), p. 9.

416. Cf. '[Weininger's] remarkable book, *Sex and Character* (1903) . . . treated Jews and women with equal hostility and overwhelmed them with the same insults.' Sigmund Freud, 'Analysis of a phobia in a five-year-old boy ("Little Hans")', *Case Studies I* (London, 1977), p. 198, fn. 2.

417. Dan Pattir, 'Graphic anti-Semitism', *Jerusalem Post*, 12 February 2006.

418. 'More light! More light!' in Hilda Schiff (ed.), *Holocaust Poetry* (London, 1995), p. 99.

419. Ernst Simmel, 'Anti-Semitism and mass psychopathology' in Ernst Simmel (ed.), *Anti-Semitism* (New York, 1946), pp. 33–4; Paul Berline, 'Russian religious philosophers and the Jews', *Jewish Social Studies*, 9/4 (1947) 282.

420. Louis Golding, *Hitler Through the Ages* (London, n.d.), p. 10.

421. See J. S. Mill, 'Representative government', *Three Essays* (Oxford, 1975), p. 167.

422. For the purposes of constructing an anti-type, I have drawn on Quentin Skinner's account of the rational agent, in 'Interpretation, rationality and truth', *Visions of Politics (1)* (Cambridge, 2002), pp. 31–2.

2. DEFAMATIONS

1. I. R. Polak, 'Mendel Bejlis' in Benjamin Epstein (trans.), *Thomas G. Masaryk and the Jews* (New York, 1949), p. 262; Léon Poliakov, *The History of Anti-Semitism* (London, 1975), vol. 3, p. 416.

2. See Kenneth Stow, *Jewish Dogs* (Stanford, CA, 2006), p. 28; Heiko A. Ober-man, *The Roots of Anti-Semitism* (Philadelphia, 1984), pp. 41–2; Dermot Keogh, *Jews in Twentieth Century Ireland* (Cork, 1998), p. 28; Geoffrey G. Field, *Evangelist of Race: The Germanic vision of Houston Stewart Chamberlain* (New York, 1981), p. 90; Daniel Pipes, *Conspiracy* (New York, 1997), p. 6; Emanuel Litvinoff (ed.), *Soviet Anti-Semitism: The Paris trial* (London, 1974), p. 15; Pierre Birnbaum, *Anti-Semitism in France* (Oxford, 1992), p. 205.

3. L. E. Goodman, *God of Abraham* (Oxford, 1996), p. 228; Maimonides, *The Guide of the Perplexed* (Chicago, 1963), vol. 2, pp. 529–30. See also William K. Gilders, *Blood Ritual in the Hebrew Bible* (Baltimore, 2004) and David Biale, *Blood and Belief* (Berkeley, CA, 2007), pp. 19–22.

4. Hermann L. Strack, *The Jew and Human Sacrifice* (London, 1909), p. 129; Peggy McCracken, *The Curse of Eve, the Wound of the Hero* (Philadelphia, 2003), p. ix.

5. Maimonides, *The Guide of the Perplexed* (Chicago, 1963), vol. 2, pp. 517–18, 585–6, 612; R. H. Charles (trans.), *The Book of Jubilees* (London, 1917), VI:13–14, p. 62.

6. S. W. Baron, *A Social and Religious History of the Jews*, 2nd edn (New York, 1967), vol. 11, p. 153; Sander L. Gilman, *Jewish Self-Hatred* (Baltimore, MD, 1986), p. 75.

7. See Robert Bartlett, *England under the Norman and Angevin Kings: 1075–1225* (Oxford, 2000), p. 356.

8. Steven F. Kruger, *The Spectral Jew* (Minneapolis, MN, 2006), p. 82.

9. See B. Netanyahu, *The Origins of the Inquisition in Fifteenth Century Spain*, 2nd edn (New York, 2001), pp. 821–30.

10. Ezekiel Leikin, *The Beilis Transcripts* (Northvale, NJ, 1993), p. 212.

11. Leonard B. Glick, *Marked In Your Flesh* (Oxford, 2005), pp. 98–9.

12. Kenneth Stow, *Jewish Dogs* (Stanford, CA, 2006), p. 122.

13. Helmut Walser Smith, *The Butcher's Tale* (New York, 2002), p. 110.

14. Leonard B. Glick, *Marked In Your Flesh* (Oxford, 2005), p. 100.

15. Jan T. Gross, *Fear* (New York, 2006), p. 74.

16. See B. Netanyahu, *The Origins of the Inquisition in Fifteenth Century Spain*, 2nd edn (New York, 2001), p. 823.

17. Hermann L. Strack, *The Jew and Human Sacrifice* (London, 1909), p. xiv.

18. Jonathan Frankel, *The Damascus Affair* (Cambridge, 1997), p. 264.

19. Uli Linke, *Blood and Nation: The European aesthetics of race* (Philadelphia, PA, 1999), p. 165. See also Simon M. Dubnow, *History of the Jews in Poland and Russia* (Bergenfield, NJ, 2000), p. 83.

20. See Cecil Roth, 'The feast of Purim and the origins of the blood accusation' in Alan Dundes (ed.), *The Blood Libel Legend* (Madison, WI, 1991), p. 268. See also Hermann L. Strack, *The Jew and Human Sacrifice* (London, 1909), pp. 63–5.

21. R. Po-Chia Hsia, *Trent 1475* (New Haven, 1992), p. 89.

22. See Helmut Walser Smith, *The Butcher's Tale* (New York, 2002), p. 17.

23. Simon M. Dubnow, *History of the Jews in Poland and Russia* (Bergenfield, NJ, 2000), p. 36; S. W. Baron, *A Social and Religious History of the Jews*, 2nd edn (New York, 1967), vol 11, p. 151.

24. Robert Bartlett, *England under the Norman and Angevin Kings: 1075–1225* (Oxford, 2000), p. 357.

25. See Zenon Guldon and Jacek Wijacka, 'The accusation of ritual murder in Poland 1500–1800' in Gershon David Hundert (ed.), *Polin: Jews in early modern Poland* (London, 1997), p. 123.

26. 'Blood libel', *Encyclopedia Judaica* (Jerusalem, 1972), vol. 4, p. 1123.

27. See Otto Fenichel, 'Elements of a psychoanalytic theory of anti-Semitism' in Ernst Simmel (ed.), *Anti-Semitism* (New York, 1946), pp. 57–8.

28. See Elliot Horowitz, *Reckless Rites* (Princeton, NJ, 2006), p. 12.

29. But not, according to Elliot Horowitz, *always* misunderstood. See *Reckless Rites* (Princeton, NJ, 2006), p. 18.

30. *Ecclesiastical History* (Eugene, OR, 2003), pp. xviii, 296–7; Elliot Horowitz, *Reckless Rites* (Princeton, NJ, 2006), pp. 213–17.

31. Kenneth Stow, *Jewish Dogs* (Stanford, CA, 2006), p. 60.

32. See Jeremy Cohen, *Sanctifying the Name* (Philadelphia, PA, 2004).

33. Ibid., p. 74.

34. Kenneth Stow, *Jewish Dogs* (Stanford, CA, 2006), p. 26. It was more likely that, in many cases, what motivated these desperate Jews was the wish not to be killed by their enemies. See Abraham Gross, 'Historical and Halakhic aspects of the mass martyrdom in Mainz: An integrative approach' in Yom Tov Assis *et al.* (eds.), *Facing the Cross* (Jerusalem, 2000), p. xv.

35. Robin R. Mundill, *England's Jewish Solution* (Cambridge, 1998), p. 53.

36. Israel J. Yuval, 'Vengeance and damnation, blood and defamation', *Zion*, 58/1 (1993), viii.

37. See Jeremy Cohen, 'Christian theology and anti-Jewish violence in the Middle Ages: Connections and disjunctions' in Anna Sapir Abulafia, *Religious Violence between Christians and Jews* (New York, 2002), p. 51.

38. See Ernst Rychnovsky, 'The struggle against the ritual murder superstition' in Benjamin Epstein (trans.), *Thomas G. Masaryk and the Jews* (New York, 1949), p. 192.

39. See Augustus Jessopp and M. R. James (eds.), *The Life and Miracles of St William of Norwich by Thomas of Monmouth* (Cambridge, 1896), p. 240 ('iudeos in se quasi mortem Christi reiterantes').

40. See also my *T. S. Eliot, Anti-Semitism, and Literary Form*, 2nd edn (London, 2003), pp. 70–1.

41. See Evelyn M. Simpson and George R. Potter (eds.), *The Sermons of John Donne* (Berkeley, CA, 1953), vol. 6, p. 199.

42. Ian Bradley, 'Sacrifice' in Adrian Hastings (ed.), *The Oxford Companion to Christian Thought* (Oxford, 2000), p. 637.

43. Adrian Hastings, 'Blood' in Adrian Hastings (ed.), *The Oxford Companion to Christian Thought* (Oxford, 2000), p. 76.

44. Henry Bettenson (ed.), *Documents of the Christian Church* (Oxford, 1967), p. 308.

45. Jaroslav Pelikan, *The Christian Tradition* (Chicago, 1978), vol. 3, pp. 203–4.

46. David Biale, *Blood and Belief* (Berkeley, CA, 2007), pp. 57–61.

47. Miri Rubin, *Corpus Christi* (Cambridge, 1991), p. 347.

48. Jacques Le Goff, *My Quest for the Middle Ages* (Edinburgh, 2003), p. 69.

49. Leah Sinanoglou, 'The Christ Child as sacrifice', *Speculum*, 48 (1973), 499.

50. Jaroslav Pelikan, *The Christian Tradition* (Chicago, 1978), vol. 3, pp. 184–5.

51. *The Complete English Poems*, John Tobin (ed.) (London, 1991), pp. 97–8.

52. Evelyn M. Simpson and George R. Potter (eds.), *The Sermons of John Donne* (Berkeley, CA, 1953), vol. 6, p. 237.

53. *My Quest for the Middle Ages* (Edinburgh, 2003), p. 92.

54. Bettina Bildhauer, *Medieval Blood* (Cardiff, 2006), p. 155.

55. Leah Sinanoglou, 'The Christ Child as sacrifice', *Speculum*, 48 (1973), 491.

56. Miri Rubin, *Gentile Tales* (New Haven, 1999), p. 32.

57. Jaroslav Pelikan, *The Christian Tradition* (Chicago, 1978), vol. 3, p. 201.

58. Bettina Bildhauer, *Medieval Blood* (Cardiff, 2006), p. 17.

59. Uli Linke, *Blood and Nation* (Philadelphia, PA, 1999), p. 125.

60. See Rowan Williams, *Tokens of Trust* (Norwich, 2007), pp. 113–14.

61. 'The displaying of the Popish Mass' in Rev. John Ayre (ed.), *Prayers and Other Pieces of Thomas Brecon* (Cambridge, 1844), pp. 280–1.

62. Jeremy Cohen, *The Friars and the Jews* (Ithaca, 1982), p. 239.

63. W. E. H. Lecky, *History of European Morals from Augustus to Charlemagne* (London, 1869), vol. 1, p. 415.

64. See Simon M. Dubnow, *History of the Jews in Poland and Russia* (Bergenfield, NJ, 2000), p. 38.

65. Catherine Gallagher and Stephen Greenblatt, *Practising New Historicism* (Chicago, 2000), p. 94.

66. See R. Po-Chia Hsia, *Trent 1475* (New Haven, 1992), p. xix.

67. See Heinz Schrekenberg, *The Jews in Christian Art* (New York, 1996), pp. 259–60, figs. 4 and 6–8.

68. Catherine Gallagher and Stephen Greenblatt, *Practising New Historicism* (Chicago, 2000), p. 93.

69. Mordechai Breuer, 'The Black Death and antisemitism' in Shmuel Almog (ed.), *Antisemitism Through the Ages* (Oxford, 1988), pp. 140, 150. It was frequently said, however, that the poison was made from the hearts of Christians and fragments of the Host: Norman Cantor, *In the Wake of the Plague* (London, 2001), p. 155. See also J. F. K. Hecker, *The Black Death* (London, 1888), a work first translated into English in 1833. The book was powerful in its condemnation of anti-Semitic excesses, and was reviewed favourably in the *National Standard*, a sheet that also carried Thackeray's anti-Semitic lampoons of the Rothschilds. See S. S. Prawer, *Israel at Vanity Fair* (Leiden, 1992), pp. 17–29.

70. Norman Cantor, *In the Wake of the Plague* (London, 2001), pp. 156–7.

71. S. W. Baron, *A Social and Religious History of the Jews*, 2nd edn (New York, 1967), vol. 11, p. 167.

72. See Michel Winock, *Nationalism, Anti-Semitism, and Fascism in France* (Stanford, CA, 1998), p. 91. See also David Carroll, *French Literary Fascism* (Princeton, NJ, 1995), p. 175.

73. Hans Rogger, 'Conclusion and overview' in John D. Klier and Shlomo Lambroza (eds.), *Pogroms* (Cambridge, 1992), p. 339.

74. Leon Trotsky, 'Thermidor and anti-Semitism' (1937), *On the Jewish Question* (London, 1970), p. 25.

75. Richard Bessel, *Nazism and War* (London, 2004), p. 172.

76. Protocol X, para. 19. See also Daniel Pipes, *Conspiracy* (New York, 1997), p. 54.

77. Richard S. Levy, 'Introduction' in Richard S. Levy (ed.), *Antisemitism in the Modern World* (Lexington, MA, 1991), p. 1; Daniel Pipes, *Conspiracy* (New York, 1997), p. 3.

78. See Menachem Klein, 'Arafat as a Palestinian icon', *Palestine-Israel Journal*, 11/3–4 (2004/5), and John Lichfield, 'French try to quash rumours that Israeli agents killed Arafat', *Independent*, 18 November 2004, or just type 'Arafat poisoned' in the Google search box.

79. *England under the Jews* (London, 1907), p. 23. See also A. H. Lane, *The Alien Menace* (London, 1932), p. 53; William Joyce, *Twilight Over England* (London, 1992), p. 104.

80. Edward J. Bristow, *Prostitution and Prejudice* (New York, 1983), pp. 4–5, 45–6, 82, 250–1; Joseph Banister, *England under the Jews* (London, 1907), pp. 6–7.

81. Menasseh ben Israel, *Vindiciae Judaeorum* (1656), in Lucien Wolf (ed.), *Menasseh ben Israel's Mission to Oliver Cromwell* (London, 1901), p. 115.

82. Joseph Jacobs, 'The Damascus Affair of 1840 and the Jews of America', *Publications of the American Jewish Historical Society*, 10 (1902), 124.

83. See 'Blood libel', *Encyclopedia Judaica* (Jerusalem, 1972), vol. 4, p. 1120–31; Emily Rose, 'Ritual murder (medieval)' and Hillel J. Kieval, 'Ritual murder (modern)' in Richard S. Levy (ed.), *Antisemitism* (Santa Barbara, CA, 2005), pp. 602–8.

84. Shelby Brown, *Late Carthaginian Child Sacrifice* (Sheffield, 1991), pp. 25, 155. These charges against Christianity were revived in the nineteenth century by the German radical anti-Christian, Georg Friedrich Daumer (1800–75). See Léon Poliakov, *The History of Anti-Semitism* (London, 1975), vol. 3, p. 411. Daumer's work was taken seriously in its day, and earned even Marx's endorsement:<http://www.marxists.org/archive/marx/works/1847/11/30. htm>. Daumer regarded the Damascus trial as evidence that the Jews had not been able to purge Judaism of this primitive cult. See Jonathan Frankel, *The Damascus Affair* (Cambridge, 1997), p. 412.

85. See R. Po-Chia Hsia, *The Myth of Ritual Murder* (New Haven, 1988), pp. 57–65.

86. Bettina Bildhauer, *Medieval Blood* (Cardiff, 2006), p. 164; Jeremy Cohen, *Christ Killers* (Oxford, 2007), p. 110.

87. Robert Chazan, *The Jews of Medieval Western Christendom* (Cambridge, 2006), p. 137.

88. Ibid., p. 191.

89. Robin R. Mundill, *England's Jewish Solution: Experiment and expulsion: 1262–1290* (Cambridge, 1998), p. 52.

90. B. Netanyahu, *The Origins of the Inquisition in Fifteenth Century Spain*, 2nd edn (New York, 2001), pp. 833, 1089–92.

91. See Léon Poliakov, *The History of Anti-Semitism* (London, 1974), vol. 2, p. 145.

92. Innocent III's condemnation was concerned specifically with ritual cannibalism, and not ritual murder (that is, crucifixion). Langmuir suggests that the

pope's 'silence could easily be interpreted as tacit permission to continue crucifixion allegations'. See Gavin I. Langmuir, *Towards a Definition of Antisemitism* (Berkeley, CA, 1990), p. 260.

93. See Robert Chazan, 'The Bray incident of 1192', *Proceedings of the American Academy for Jewish Research*, 28 (1969), 10–11, 13, 14.

94. See Heiko A. Oberman, *The Roots of Anti-Semitism* (Philadelphia, 1984), p. 37.

95. See Paul Lawrence Rose, *German Question/Jewish Question* (Princeton, NJ, 1990), p. 7.

96. Livia Bitton-Jackson, 'Myth and negative Jewish stereotypes' in Michael Brown (ed.), *Approaches to Antisemitism* (New York, 1994), p. 238.

97. John Edwards, 'Ritual murder in the Siglo de Oro: Lope de Vega's *El Niño Inocente de La Guardia*', The Proceedings of the Tenth British Conference on Judeo-Spanish Studies, 29 June–1 July 1997, Annette Benaim (ed.), Dept. of Hispanic Studies, Queen Mary and Westfield College, University of London, p. 86.

98. S. W. Baron, *A Social and Religious History of the Jews*, 2nd edn (New York, 1967), vol. 11, p. 156.

99. Alexander Samson, 'Anti-Semitism, class and Lope de Vega's *El Niño Inocente de la Guardia*', *Hispanic Research Journal*, 3/2 (2002), 111.

100. John Edwards, 'Why the Spanish Inquisition?' in Diana Wood (ed.), *Studies in Church History* (Oxford, 1992), vol. 29, p. 234.

101. B. Netanyahu, *The Origins of the Inquisition in Fifteenth Century Spain*, 2nd edn (New York, 2001), pp. 1035, 1091.

102. James Given, 'The Inquisitors of Languedoc and the medieval technology of power', *American Historical Review*, 94/II (1989), 351.

103. H. C. Lea, *Chapters from the Religious History of Spain connected with the Inquisition* (London, 1890), p. 464.

104. Alexander Samson, 'Anti-Semitism, class and Lope de Vega's *El Niño Inocente de la Guardia*', *Hispanic Research Journal*, 3/2 (2002), 111.

105. Anthony J. Farrell, Preface to Lope de Vega, *El Niño Inocente de la Guardia* (London, 1985), p. xvi. In 1954, a Spanish theologian published a book affirming the libel: Léon Poliakov, *The History of Anti-Semitism* (London, 1974), vol. 2, p. 377.

106. See Arthur Hertzberg, *The French Enlightenment and the Jews* (New York, 1968), pp. 20, 34.

107. Zenon Guldon and Jacek Wijacka, 'The accusation of ritual murder in Poland 1500–1800' in Gershon David Hundert (ed.), *Polin* (London, 1997), p. 98. Norman Davies somewhat understates the significance of the record. See *God's Playground* (Oxford, 2005), vol. 1, p. 148. This is all he has to say on the blood libel.

108. 'Most of these accusations took place at a time when ritual murder trials in Western Europe had been consigned to history.' Zenon Guldon and Jacek Wijacka, 'The accusation of ritual murder in Poland 1500–1800' in Gershon

David Hundert (ed.), *Polin* (London, 1997), pp. 139–40. See also Simon M. Dubnow, *History of the Jews in Poland and Russia* (Bergenfield, NJ, 2000), pp. 45, 77–9, 83–7, 119.

109. Simon M. Dubnow, *History of the Jews in Poland and Russia* (Bergenfield, NJ, 2000), p. 86.

110. In 1399, the Jews of Poznań (then part of Poland) were accused of host desecration. Thirteen elders of the community, and one woman, were roasted alive on a slow fire. The community was further punished by the imposition of an 'eternal fine', paid annually to the local Domnicans. The fine was still being exacted in the eighteenth century. See Simon M. Dubnow, *History of the Jews in Poland and Russia* (Bergenfield, NJ, 2000), p. 22.

111. Simon M. Dubnow, *History of the Jews in Poland and Russia* (Bergenfield, NJ, 2000), pp. 43, 83; Louis W. Bondy, *Racketeers of Hatred* (London, 1946), p. 67.

112. Louis Jacobs, 'Blood Libel' in *The Jewish Religion: A companion* (Oxford, 1995).

113. Zenon Guldon and Jacek Wijacka, 'The accusation of ritual murder in Poland 1500–1800' in Gershon David Hundert (ed.), *Polin* (London, 1997), pp. 125–8.

114. Cecil Roth, *The Ritual Murder Libel and the Jew: the report by Cardinal Lorenzo Ganganelli* (London, n.d), p. 25.

115. Zenon Guldon and Jacek Wijacka, 'The accusation of ritual murder in Poland 1500–1800' in Gershon David Hundert (ed.), *Polin* (London, 1997), p. 140.

116. Keely Strauter-Halstead, 'Jews as middleman minorities in rural Poland' in Robert Blobaum (ed.), *Antisemitism and Its Opponents in Modern Poland* (Ithaca, NY, 2005), p. 46.

117. See Heinz Schrekenberg, *The Jews in Christian Art* (New York, 1996), pp. 273–91, figs. 1–16.

118. Uli Linke, *Blood and Nation* (Philadelphia, PA, 1999), p. 151.

119. The mural was next to Frankfurt's busiest gate. It was painted at the end of the fifteenth century, and restored in 1678. See David Frankfurter, *Evil Incarnate* (Princeton, NJ, 2006), pp. 205–6.

120. Kenneth Stow, *Jewish Dogs* (Stanford, CA, 2006), p. 59.

121. See Kenneth Stow, *Jewish Dogs* (Stanford, CA, 2006), *passim*.

122. For an example, see Heiko A. Oberman, *The Roots of Anti-Semitism* (Philadelphia, 1984), p. 99.

123. See Richard S. Levy (ed.), *Antisemitism in the Modern World* (Lexington, MA, 1991), pp. 33–6.

124. See Kenneth Stow, *Jewish Dogs* (Stanford, CA, 2006), p. 38. For a somewhat critical account of the role of the Catholic Church in combating the blood libel, see Massimo Introvigne, 'The Catholic Church and the blood libel myth: A complicated story', *Covenant*, 2/1 (2007).

125. Gavin I. Langmuir, *Towards a Definition of Antisemitism* (Berkeley, CA, 1990), p. 287.

126. See Richard S. Levy (ed.), *Antisemitism in the Modern World* (Lexington, MA, 1991), p. 36.

127. Y. Harkabi, *Arab Attitudes to Israel* (Jerusalem, 1972), p. 271.

128. Ibid., p. 274.

129. Gustav Le Bon, *The Crowd* (Atlanta, GA, 1982), pp. 23, 25.

130. Robert Chazan, *Church, State, and Jew in the Middle Ages* (West Orange, NJ, 1980), pp. 93 and 125–6.

131. 'Blood libel', *Encyclopedia Judaica* (Jerusalem, 1972), vol. 4, p. 1129.

132. Heiko A. Oberman, *The Roots of Anti-Semitism* (Philadelphia, 1984), p. 35.

133. This compromises Ganganelli's report, because he must acknowledge that Simon of Trent and Andreas of Rinn were indeed martyred—though he does all he can, notwithstanding this acknowledgement both to cast doubt on these stories and to deny their representative status. See Cecil Roth, *The Ritual Murder Libel and the Jew: The report by Cardinal Lorenzo Ganganelli* (London, n.d.), pp. 85–6. It was only in 1965 that the Church repudiated the Trent blood libel (see 'Blood libel', *Encyclopedia Judaica* (Jerusalem, 1972), vol. 4, p. 1124). It was only in 1984 that the cult of Andreas was suppressed.

134. See Ernst Rychnovsky, 'The struggle against the ritual murder superstition' in Benjamin Epstein (trans.), *Thomas G. Masaryk and the Jews* (New York, 1949), p. 211; Jonathan Frankel, *The Damascus Affair* (Cambridge, 1997), pp. 261–4.

135. *Philosophical Dictionary* (London, 2004), pp. 40, 256–7. Voltaire was 'obsessed with ritual murder'. Léon Poliakov, *The History of Anti-Semitism* (London, 1975), vol. 3, p. 89.

136. Paul Lawrence Rose, *German Question/Jewish Question* (Princeton, NJ, 1990), pp. 45–50, 256–9, 314–15.

137. Léon Poliakov, *The History of Anti-Semitism* (London, 1975), vol. 3, p. 79.

138. See my *Transgressions* (London, 2002), pp. 154–5.

139. Jan Herben, 'Thomas G. Masaryk, Jews and anti-Semitism' in Benjamin Epstein (trans.), *Thomas G. Masaryk and the Jews* (New York, 1949), p. 3.

140. Jacob Barnai, ' "Blood libels" in the Ottoman Empire of the fifteenth to nineteenth centuries' in Shmuel Almog (ed.), *Antisemitism Through the Ages* (Oxford, 1988), pp. 191–2.

141. Tudor Parfitt, 'The year of the "Pride of Israel" ' in Sonia and V. D. Lipman (eds.), *The Century of Moses Montefiore* (London, 1985), p. 144.

142. Harriet Martineau, *Eastern Life* (Philadelphia, 1848), p. 497.

143. Tudor Parfitt, 'The year of the "Pride of Israel" ' in Sonia and V. D. Lipman (eds.), *The Century of Moses Montefiore* (London, 1985), p. 133.

144. Bernard Lewis, *The Jews of Islam* (London, 1984), p. 159.

145. Albert H. Hyamson, 'The Damascus Affair—1840', *Transactions of the J.H.S.E.*, 16 (1940), 47.

146. Tudor Parfitt, 'The year of the "Pride of Israel" ' in Sonia and V. D. Lipman (eds.), *The Century of Moses Montefiore* (London, 1985), p. 131.

147. See Albert H. Hyamson, 'The Damascus Affair—1840', *Transactions of the J.H.S.E.*, 16 (1940), 47. Ratti-Menton was 'a heartless and conscienceless fortune-hunter' and a 'downright rascal and arch-enemy of the Jews'. H. Graetz, *Popular History of the Jews* (New York, 1923), vol. 5, p. 505.

148. But see 'The year of the "Pride of Israel" ' in Sonia and V. D. Lipman (eds.), *The Century of Moses Montefiore* (London, 1985), p. 138.

149. Jonathan Frankel, *The Damascus Affair* (Cambridge, 1997), p. 56.

150. Ibid., p. 24.

151. Tudor Parfitt, 'The year of the "Pride of Israel" ' in Sonia and V. D. Lipman (eds.), *The Century of Moses Montefiore* (London, 1985), p. 142.

152. Albert H. Hyamson, 'The Damascus Affair—1840', *Transactions of the J.H.S.E.*, 16 (1940), 67.

153. Jonathan Frankel, *The Damascus Affair* (Cambridge, 1997), p. 390.

154. Tudor Parfitt, 'The year of the "Pride of Israel" ' in Sonia and V. D. Lipman (eds.), *The Century of Moses Montefiore* (London, 1985), p. 131.

155. Palmerston stamped on Werry very hard. The consul, he wrote, 'must either be wholly uninformed of what passes in the city in which you are stationed, or else evinces . . . an entire want of those principles and sentiments which ought to distinguish a British agent'. Albert H. Hyamson, 'The Damascus Affair—1840', *Transactions of the J.H.S.E.*, 16 (1940), 50–4, 58. See also Jonathan Frankel, *The Damascus Affair* (Cambridge, 1997), pp. 53–4.

156. *Rome and Jerusalem* (New York, 1958), p. 31; Ken Koltun-Fromm, *Moses Hess and Modern Jewish Identity* (Bloomington, IN, 2001), pp. 46–7, 52.

157. Léon Poliakov, *The History of Anti-Semitism* (London, 1975), vol. 3, p. 349.

158. Luke Owen Pike, *A History of Crime in England* (London, 1873), vol. I, pp. 194–5.

159. 'The year of the "Pride of Israel" ' in Sonia and V. D. Lipman (eds.), *The Century of Moses Montefiore* (London, 1985), pp. 144–5.

160. Helmut Walser Smith, *The Butcher's Tale* (New York, 2002), p. 123.

161. Eugen Weber, *My France* (Cambridge, MA, 1991), pp. 288 and 387, fn. 12.

162. Cecil Roth, *The Ritual Murder Libel and the Jew: The report by Cardinal Lorenzo Ganganelli* (London, n.d), p. 16.

163. See Hillel J. Kieval, 'Ritual murder (modern)' in Richard S. Levy (ed.), *Antisemitism* (Santa Barbara, CA, 2005), p. 607.

164. Daniel J. Goldhagen, *Hitler's Willing Executioners* (London, 1997), p. 64.

165. See Jan Herben, 'Thomas G. Masaryk, Jews and anti-Semitism' in Benjamin Epstein (trans.), *Thomas G. Masaryk and the Jews* (New York, 1949), pp. 9–10.

166. Arnold J. Band, 'Refractions of the blood libel in modern literature' in *Studies in Modern Jewish Literature* (Philadelphia, PA, 2003), p. 317.

167. See David Biale, *Blood and Belief* (Berkeley, CA, 2007), pp. 129–30.

168. Hans Rogger, *Jewish Policies and Right-Wing Politics in Imperial Russia* (London, 1986), p. 1.

169. Stephen Wilson, *Ideology and Experience* (London, 1982), p. 479.

170. Charles H. H. Wright, 'The Jews and the malicious charge of human sacrifice', *The Nineteenth Century*, 81 (November 1883), 753, 758, 765, 778.

171. See the translator's footnote, Solomon Maimon, *An Autobiography* (London, 1888), pp. 17–18.

172. Shlomo Lambroza, 'The pogroms of 1903–1906' in John D. Klier and Shlomo Lambroza (eds.), *Pogroms* (Cambridge, 1992), pp. 196–7; Robert S. Wistrich, *The Jews of Vienna in the Age of Franz Joseph* (Oxford, 1990), p. 296.

173. See David Biale, *Blood and Belief* (Berkeley, CA, 2007), pp. 129–38, 169–75.

174. Shlomo Lambroza, 'The pogroms of 1903–1906' in John D. Klier and Shlomo Lambroza (eds.), *Pogroms* (Cambridge, 1992), p. 204; Helmut Walser Smith, *The Butcher's Tale* (New York, 2002), pp. 29–30, 56.

175. Helmut Walser Smith, *The Butcher's Tale* (New York, 2002), p. 117.

176. See Uli Linke, *Blood and Nation* (Philadelphia, PA, 1999), pp. 201–6.

177. Hillel J. Kieval, *Languages of Community* (Berkeley, CA, 2000), p. 112.

178. Steven Beller, 'The world of yesterday revisited: Nostalgia, memory, and the Jews of fin-de-siècle Vienna', *Jewish Social Studies*, 2 (1996), 47.

179. Hillel J. Kieval, *Languages of Community* (Berkeley, CA, 2000), p. 168.

180. See Ernst Rychnovsky, 'The struggle against the ritual murder superstition' in Benjamin Epstein (trans.), *Thomas G. Masaryk and the Jews* (New York, 1949), pp. 189–94.

181. Karel Čapek, *President Masaryk Tells His Story* (London, 1934), p. 187; R. W. Seton-Watson, *Masaryk in England* (London, 1943), p. 15.

182. Joël et Dan Kotek, *Au nom de l'antisionisme* (Bruxelles, 2005), p. 32.

183. Ezekiel Leikin, *The Beilis Transcripts* (Northvale, NJ, 1993), pp. 9, 12, 14–16, 39.

184. Shari Schwartz (ed.), *Scapegoat on Trial* (New York, 1992), pp. 38, 205.

185. Hans Rogger, *Jewish Policies and Right-Wing Politics in Imperial Russia* (London, 1986), pp. 48, 55.

186. Ezekiel Leikin, *The Beilis Transcripts* (Northvale, NJ, 1993), p. 164.

187. <http://en.wikipedia.org/wiki/Menahem_Mendel_Beilis> contains a link to the periodical http://www.personal-plus.net/article.php?ida=453.

188. Anshel Pfeffer, 'Grave near Kiev is reminder of 20th century's only blood libel', *Ha'aretz*, 9 February 2008.

189. Stephen Wilson, *Ideology and Experience* (London, 1982), p. 411, but see also pp. 551–3.

190. Shlomo Lambroza, 'The pogroms of 1903–1906' in John D. Klier and Shlomo Lambroza (eds.), *Pogroms* (Cambridge, 1992), p. 214. See also Simon M. Dubnow, *History of the Jews in Poland and Russia* (Bergenfield, NJ, 2000), pp. 451–7.

191. John D. Klier and Shlomo Lambroza, 'The pogroms of 1881–1884' in John D. Klier and Shlomo Lambroza (eds.), *Pogroms* (Cambridge, 1992), pp. 40–2.

192. Peter Pulzer, *Jews and the German State* (Detroit, MI, 2003), p. 141.

193. N. Kornev, 'Julius Streicher—Nazi King of Smut', *New Masses*, 27 August 1935, p. 11.

194. Shlomo Glickstein, *The Forgeries and Falsifications in the Anti-Semitic Literature and My Lawsuit against Julius Streicher and Company* (New York, 1939), pp. 51–2; Dennis E. Showalter, *Little Man, What Now?* (Hamden, CT, 1982), p. 103.

195. Randall L. Bytwerk, *Julius Streicher* (New York, 1983), pp. 12–13, 129.

196. See Dennis E. Showalter, *Little Man, What Now?* (Hamden, CT, 1982), pp. 104–8.

197. See Louis W. Bondy, *Racketeers of Hatred* (London, 1946), pp. 58–9; David Biale, *Blood and Belief* (Berkeley, CA, 2007), pp. 123–6.

198. Saul Friedländer, *Nazi Germany and the Jews: The years of persecution 1933–1939* (London, 1997), pp. 123–4.

199. See Haig Bosmajian, *The Language of Oppression* (Washington, DC, 1974), pp. 23–4.

200. David Biale, *Blood and Belief* (Berkeley, CA, 2007), p. 125; Uli Linke, *Blood and Nation* (Philadelphia, PA, 1999), p. 200.

201. Jonathan Frankel, *The Damascus Affair* (Cambridge, 1997), p. 431.

202. Stephen Dorril, *Blackshirt* (London, 2006), p. 283.

203. Martin Gilbert, *The Holocaust* (London, 1987), p. 518; Cecil Roth, 'England in Jewish history', The Lucien Wolf Memorial Lecture, The Jewish Historical Society of England, London, 1949, p. 15; Raul Hillberg, *The Destruction of the European Jews* (New York, 1985), vol. 3, p. 1022.

204. Raul Hillberg, *The Destruction of the European Jews* (New York, 1985), vol. 3, pp. 1021–2.

205. David Faber, *Speaking for England* (London, 2005), p. 471.

206. Robert Satloff, *Among the Righteous* (New York, 2006), p. 84.

207. Jan T. Gross, *Fear* (New York, 2006), p. 93.

208. Martin Gilbert, *The Holocaust* (London, 1987), p. 819.

209. See Jan T. Gross, *Fear* (New York, 2006), pp. 73–80.

210. Michael C. Steinlauf, 'Poland' in David S. Wyman (ed.), *The World Reacts to the Holocaust* (Baltimore, 1996), pp. 111–12.

211. Jan T. Gross, *Fear* (New York, 2006), p. 119.

212. See Jeffrey Herf, 'Foreword' in Matthias Küntzel, *Jihad and Jew-Hatred* (New York, 2007), p. vii.

213. Robert S. Wistrich, *Anti-Semitism* (London, 1991), pp. 206–7, 234–6; Gabriel Schoenfeld, *The Return of Anti-Semitism* (San Francisco, 2004), pp. 14–15, 17–20, 35–6; Rivka Yadlin, *An Arrogant Oppressive Spirit* (Oxford, 1989), pp. 97–8; David I. Kertzer, 'The modern use of ancient lies', *NY Times*, 9 May 2002; Menachem Milsom, 'What is Arab antisemitism?', MEMRI Special Report—no. 26, 27 February 2004.

214. See Benny Morris, *Righteous Victims* (New York, 2001), p. 91.

215. See F. H. Kisch, *Palestine Diary* (London, 1938), pp. 112, 390.

216. See Joël and Dan Kotek, *Au nom de l'antisionisme* (Bruxelles, 2005), p. 82.

217. Ibid., p. 83.
218. See Livnat Holtzman and Eliezer Schlossberg, 'Fundamentals of the modern Muslim–Jewish polemic', *Israel Affairs*, 12/1 (2006), 14–15; Y. Harkabi, *Arab Attitudes to Israel* (Jerusalem, 1972), p. 271.
219. Gabriel Schoenfeld, *The Return of Anti-Semitism* (San Francisco, 2004), pp. 19–20; Kenneth R. Timmerman, *Preachers of Hate* (New York, 2004), pp. 70–3; Reuven Erlich, 'Anti-Semitism in the contemporary Middle East', Intelligence and Terrorism Information Center at the Center for Special Studies, Jerusalem, April 2004, pp. 64–5; Raphael Israeli, 'Anti-Jewish attitudes in the Arabic media, 1975–1981' in Robert S. Wistrich (ed.), *Anti-Zionism and Antisemitism in the Contemporary World* (New York, 1990), p. 118.
220. See Arieh Stav, *Peace: The Arabian caricature* (Jerusalem, 1999), p. 232.
221. Kenneth R. Timmerman, *Preachers of Hate* (New York, 2004), pp. 71–2. See also Itamar Radai, 'On the road to Damascus: Bashar al-Asad, Israel, and the Jews', Posen Papers in Contemporary Antisemitism, no. 9, The Vidal Sassoon International Center for the Study of Antisemitism, The Hebrew University of Jerusalem, 2007, p. 4.
222. Itamar Radai, 'On the road to Damascus: Bashar al-Asad, Israel, and the Jews', Posen Papers in Contemporary Antisemitism, no. 9, The Vidal Sassoon International Center for the Study of Antisemitism, The Hebrew University of Jerusalem, 2007, p. 4.
223. Jonathan Frankel, *The Damascus Affair* (Cambridge, 1997), p. 418, and fns. 57–9.
224. Y. Harkabi, *Arab Attitudes to Israel* (Jerusalem, 1972), pp. 270–1.
225. In a Ruprecht cartoon, 'The day of vengeance is coming', a German man, cradling a bloodied infant, shakes his fist at a disappearing car of Jews. See Dennis E. Showalter, *Little Man, What Now?* (Hamden, CT, 1982), pp. 59–68, 146. In another cartoon, three Jews drink the blood of a woman they have tied to the ground. Ruprecht also exploited blood imagery to represent more general, and financially motivated, homicidal Jewish tendencies. In a wartime cartoon he pictures a sack of 'Jewish war profits' floating on a sea of blood. See Randall L. Bytwerk, *Julius Streicher* (New York, 1983), pp. 55–6, 105, 126–9, 140.
226. See Pierre-André Taguieff, *Prêcheurs de haine* (Paris, 2004), p. 119. The pamphlet was circulated at a conference held in April 2002 in Strasbourg, entitled 'Antisemitism, racism, xenophobia, intolerance—everyone's concern'.
227. The Soviets pointed the way. See Emanuel Litvinoff (ed.), *Soviet Anti-Semitism: The Paris trial* (London, 1974), p. 12. But cf. Yeshayahu Nir, *The Arab–Israeli Conflict in Soviet Caricatures 1967–1973* (Tel Aviv, 1976), p. 80.
228. See <www.seconddraft.org>. Israeli responsibility for the death continues to be asserted: Emma Williams, *It's Easier to Reach Heaven than the End of the Street* (London, 2006), pp. 46–7.
229. See <http://memri.org/bin/articles.cgi?Page=archives&Area=sd&ID=SP76304 #_edn3>.

230. See MEMRI *Special Dispatch Series—no. 1011,* <http://memri.org/bin/articles. cgi?Page=archives&Area=sd&ID=SP101105>.

231. Raphael Israeli, *Poison* (Lanham, MD, 2002).

232. See <http://www.freearabvoice.org/aidsInfection.htm>; Kenneth S. Stern, *Antisemitism Today* (New York, 2006), p. 58.

233. 'Hillary Clinton criticises Mrs Arafat', *BBC News,* 12 November 1999.

234. 'Barefaced lies': Benny Morris, *Righteous Victims* (New York, 2001), p. 665.

235. See Joël and Dan Kotek, *Au nom de l'antisionisme* (Bruxelles, 2005), pp. 44–6.

236. Arieh Stav, *Peace: The Arabian caricature* (Jerusalem, 1999), pp. 232–7; Reuven Erlich, 'Anti-Semitism in the contemporary Middle East', Intelligence and Terrorism Information Center at the Center for Special Studies, Jerusalem, April 2004, pp. 38, 139–40.

237. For text and video, see <http://www.mideasttruth.com/adtvtxt.html>.

238. Anton La Guardia, 'Saudi newspaper editor retracts "Jewish vampire" article', *Daily Telegraph,* March 2002.

239. Livnat Holtzman and Eliezer Schlossberg, 'Fundamentals of the modern Muslim–Jewish Polemic', *Israel Affairs,* 12/1 (2006), 14.

240. See Yossef Bodansky, *Islamic Anti-Semitism as a Political Instrument* (Houston, TX, 1999), p. 163.

241. David Aaronovitch, 'The new anti-Semitism', *Observer,* 22 June 2003.

242. Joël and Dan Kotek, *Au nom de l'antisionisme* (Bruxelles, 2005), p. 108.

243. Ibid., p. 71.

244. See 'Major anti-Semitic motifs in Arab cartoons: An interview with Joël Kotek', Jerusalem Centre for Public Affairs, no. 21, 1 June 2004/12 Sivan 5764. See also Jeremy Cohen, *Christ Killers* (Oxford, 2007), pp. 115–16.

245. Khalid Kishtainy, *Arab Political Humour* (London, 1985) *passim,* but especially p. 8.

246. See <http://en.wikipedia.org/wiki/Naji_Salim_al-Ali>. Thomas Friedman suspects that the assassination was the work of Arafat: *From Beirut to Jerusalem* (London, 1998), p. 369. Two years before the assassination, Kishtainy wrote of the 'revenge squads despatched from the Middle East to the four corners of the world'. *Arab Political Humour* (London, 1985), p. ix.

247. '[Of the cartoonist:] il est . . . contraire à son éthique et sa déontologie propres de faire mentir son crayon.' Joël and Dan Kotek, *Au nom de l'antisionisme* (Bruxelles, 2005), p. 47.

248. Hansard, 4 July 2001. See also *Parliamentary Debates,* Vol. 475, no. 95, 15 May 2008, col. 1587. At Stop the War rallies, children were given inked, cardboard posters with the legend, 'ISRAEL STOP KILLING CHILDREN'. See Andrew Murray and Lindsey German, *Stop the War* (London, 2005), p. 83.

249. 'Palestinian children send messages to passive Arab leaders', formerly at <http://www.palestine-info.co.uk/am/publish/article_19562.shtml>.

250. '[Quoting a leaflet circulated in the constituency:] "Note there are 300,000 Jews in Britain but over 2 million Muslims in Britain. The Jewish community

has over 20 declared MPs while the Muslims have only one MP." The implication was that people should be elected on the basis of religion rather than any other criterion. I believe that these people thought that I was Jewish because I am in the Parliamentary Labour Friends of Israel. I am not, but whether I am or am not Jewish is irrelevant...' See Hansard, 4 July 2001, <http://www.publications.parliament.uk/pa/cm200102/cmhansrd/vo010704/halltext/10704h02.htm#10704h02_spnew0>. See also Melanie Phillips, *Londonistan* (London, 2006), p. 246.

251. See, for example, 'In order to present Israeli state and society as evil incarnate, [Hezbollah] clearly feels that it must specify the atrocities committed by Israel in its public discourse. It frequently avails itself of the depiction of the Israeli as one who commits such heinous crimes as "slaughtering children" and, even more morally repugnant, as one who "rips open pregnant women's stomachs" and bets on the sex of the embryos.' Amal Saad-Ghorayeb, *Hizbu'llah: Politics and religion* (London, 2002), p. 136.

252. Itamar Radai, 'From father to son: Attitudes to Jews and Israel, in Asad's Syria', Analysis of Current Trends in Antisemitism, no. 29, The Vidal Sassoon International Center for the Study of Antisemitism, The Hebrew University of Jerusalem, 2007, p. 29.

253. Rory McCarthy, ' "They were targeting the children": Gaza factions hit new level of horror', *Guardian*, 12 December 2006.

254. 'Since the establishment of the PLO, the Palestinian national movement has sanctified the principle of armed struggle, sometimes to the point where it becomes the end rather than the means. From there, it's a short leap to sanctifying anyone with a weapon, even if that "weapon" is a human being.' Amira Hass, *Reporting from Ramallah* (New York, 2003), p. 183.

255. A small example. On the BBC Radio 4 programme *Today*, the claim was made that a young Arab-Israeli conscripted into the IDF had been imprisoned for refusing to shoot Palestinian children. See Kirsty Scott, 'Thought for the Day ends in apology', *Guardian*, 18 February 2005. 'The BBC said it had been "unable to find any evidence to support the story" told by the Rev Dr John Bell.' *Independent*, 18 February 2005.

256. See, for example, <http://www.heretical.com/British/jews1290.html>. See also Philip de Vier, *Blood Ritual* (Hillsboro, WV, 2001), as quoted in David Frankfurter, *Evil Incarnate* (Princeton, NJ, 2006), p. 163: 'The brutal murder of little Simon kept coming back to my mind... then a stark reality dawned... Most of these were children, entirely helpless to defend themselves against a gang of savage child-abusing killers...' etc.

257. William Korey, *The Soviet Cage* (New York, 1973), p. 82.

258. Semyon Reznik, *The Nazification of Russia* (Washington, DC, 1996), pp. 126, 163–74.

259. Robert S. Wistrich, *Anti-Semitism* (London, 1991), pp. 166, 292 (fn. 23).

260. Semyon Reznik, *The Nazification of Russia* (Washington, DC, 1996), pp. 126, 163.

261. Formerly at <http://www.bbc.co.uk/radio4/today/listenagain/zthursday_2005 0217.shtml>. This BBC Radio 4 news item reported on 17 February 2005 that Jewish leaders in Moscow were about to sue the MPs for signing the letter.

262. Yael Branovsky, 'Russian blood libel: Jews use children's blood for matzot', *Ynet News*, 19 March 2008.

263. Some Arab intellectuals have openly deprecated the use of the blood libel. 'It is also important, in this regard, that we refrain from succumbing to such myths as the *Protocols of the Elders of Zion* and the use of Christian blood in Jewish rituals.' Osama El-Baz, 'Contaminated goods', *Al-Ahram Weekly on-line*, 2–8 January 2003, <http://weekly.ahram.org.eg/2003/619/focus. htm>. The article describes Mr El-Baz as chief political advisor to President Hosni Mubarak. See also Bernard Lewis, *Semites and Anti-Semites* (London, 1986), p. 208, and Menachem Milsom, 'What is Arab antisemitism?', MEMRI Special Report—no. 26, 27 February 2004.

264. Kate Clark, 'Interpreting Egypt's anti-Semitic cartoons', *BBC News*, 10 August 2003, <http://news.bbc.co.uk/1/hi/world/middle_east/3136059. stm>.

265. Thomas Asbridge, *The First Crusade* (London, 2004), 87, quoting from the Mainz Chronicle, written by an anonymous Mainz Jew soon after 1096.

266. See Joshua Trachtenberg, *The Devil and the Jews* (Philadelphia, 1983), pp. 101–6, and Léon Poliakov, *The History of Anti-Semitism* (London, 1974), vol. 1, pp. 104–5. But cf.: 'The charge of ritual murder, the blood libel, as well as the accusations that Jews desecrated the host and poisoned wells, first appeared in medieval Europe only in the twelfth and thirteenth centuries.' Jeremy Cohen, 'Traditional prejudice and religious reform: The theological and historical foundations of Luther's anti-Judaism' in Sander L. Gilman and Steven T. Katz (eds.), *Anti-Semitism in Times of Crisis* (New York, 1991), p. 96.

267. Cecil Roth, *The Ritual Murder Libel and the Jew: The report by Cardinal Lorenzo Ganganelli* (London, n.d.), p. 90.

268. Baruch Knei-Paz, *The Social and Political Thought of Leon Trotsky* (Oxford, 1979), p. 546.

3. MEDIEVAL ENGLISH ANTI-SEMITISM

1. There is no evidence of Jewish settlement in Anglo-Saxon England. This absence, notwithstanding the closeness of connections between England and the Rhineland, and the considerable international trading activity of Rhineland Jews, is attributable, perhaps, to their exclusion from England by royal decree: James Campbell, 'Was it infancy in England? Some Questions of comparison' in Michael Jones and Malcolm Vale (eds.), *England and her Neighbours 1066–1453* (London, 1989), p. 14. The Conquest itself was an

event for which some English anti-Semites held the Jews responsible. See Louis W. Bondy, *Racketeers of Hatred* (London, 1946), pp. 168–9.

2. Cecil Roth, *The Intellectual Activities of Medieval English Jewry* (London, n.d.), pp. 12–18, 65–9, 71; Zefira Entin Rokéah, 'The State, the Church, and the Jews in medieval England' in Shmuel Almog (ed.), *Antisemitism Through the Ages* (Oxford, 1988), p. 100.

3. H. G. Richardson, *The English Jewry under Angevin Kings* (London, 1960), p. 26.

4. B. Netanyahu, *The Origins of the Inquisition in Fifteenth Century Spain*, 2nd edn (New York, 2001), pp. 836–9; Simon M. Dubnow, *History of the Jews in Poland and Russia* (Bergenfield, NJ, 2000), p. 43.

5. Cecil Roth, *A History of the Jews in England*, 3rd edn (Oxford, 1978), pp. 47–8.

6. Paul Brand, 'Jews and the law in England 1275–1290', *English Historical Review*, 115 (2000), 1139. Brand unhelpfully distinguishes between charters (good—'privileges') and legislation (bad—'restrictions').

7. F. Pollock and F. W. Maitland, *The History of English Law before the Time of Edward I*, 2nd edn (Cambridge, 1968), vol. 1, p. 474.

8. Norman Cantor, *The Sacred Chain* (New York, 1994), p. 168.

9. Joseph Jacobs (ed.), *The Jews of Angevin England* (London, 1893), pp. 136, 213.

10. Paul Brand, 'Jews and the law in England 1275–1290', *English Historical Review* 115 (2000), 1142. Brand considers this to be a development in English jurisprudential thinking about the Jews.

11. F. Pollock and F. W. Maitland, *The History of English Law before the Time of Edward I*, 2nd edn (Cambridge, 1968), vol. 1, p. 468.

12. Quoted ibid. See also Gavin Langmuir, 'The Jews and the archives of Angevin England', *Traditio*, 19 (1963), 201, on the 'extreme rightlessness' of the Jews 'vis-à-vis the king'.

13. Robin R. Mundill, *England's Jewish Solution* (Cambridge, 1998), p. 54.

14. Cecil Roth, *A History of the Jews in England*, 3rd edn (Oxford, 1978), p. 33.

15. F. Pollock and F. W. Maitland, *The History of English Law before the Time of Edward I*, 2nd edn (Cambridge, 1968), vol. 1, p. 472.

16. Gilbert Dahan, *The Christian Polemic against the Jews in the Middle Ages* (Notre Dame, IN, 1998), p. 13. However: 'Even [John and Henry III] realised that their controls [over the Jews] were circumscribed by custom.' S. W. Baron, *A Social and Religious History of the Jews* (New York, 1965), vol. 10, p. 55.

17. Robert C. Stacey, 'The conversion of Jews to Christianity in thirteenth-century England', *Speculum*, 67 (1992), 271.

18. Robert Bartlett, *England Under the Norman and Angevin Kings: 1075–1225* (Oxford, 2000), p. 352.

19. Robin R. Mundill, *England's Jewish Solution* (Cambridge, 1998), pp. 53–7. Thomas à Becket's successor complained, 'if a Jew or a layman of the lowest grade be killed, justice is done, but this is not the case with a priest'. Michael Adler, *Jews of Medieval England* (London, 1939), p. 50.

20. Joe Hillaby, 'Jewish colonisation in the twelfth century' in Patricia Skinner (ed.), *Jews in Medieval Britain* (Woodbridge, 2003), pp. 15, 23.

21. H. G. Richardson, *The English Jewry under Angevin Kings* (London, 1960), p. 3.

22. Joe Hillaby, 'Jewish colonisation in the twelfth century' in Patricia Skinner (ed.), *Jews in Medieval Britain* (Woodbridge, 2003), pp. 28–9.

23. Robin R. Mundill, *England's Jewish Solution* (Cambridge, 1998), pp. 204–8. See also S. W. Baron, *A Social and Religious History of the Jews*, 2nd edn (New York, 1967), vol. 11, p. 186, on the wealthy Jew of Hereford who, at his daughter's wedding in 1286, allegedly entertained his Christian friends in high style.

24. H. G. Richardson, *The English Jewry under Angevin Kings* (London, 1960), pp. 46–7.

25. See Zefira Entin Rokéah, 'Crime and Jews in late thirteenth-century England', *Hebrew Union College Annual* (Cincinnati, 1985), vol. 55.

26. Augustus Jessopp and M. R. James (eds.), *The Life and Miracles of St William of Norwich by Thomas of Monmouth* (Cambridge, 1896), p. 70.

27. Rabbi Meir ben Baruch of Rothenburg (1215–93). Zefira Entin Rokéah, 'Money and the hangman in late-thirteenth-century England (Part I)', *Transactions of the J.H.S.E.*, 31 (1988–90), 83.

28. Richard Vaughan (ed.), *Chronicles of Matthew Paris* (New York, 1984), p. 214; Richard Vaughan, *Matthew Paris* (1958), p. 143.

29. Augustus Jessopp and M. R. James (eds.), *The Life and Miracles of St William of Norwich by Thomas of Monmouth* (Cambridge, 1896), p. 28. The discrepancy between the two accounts is explored in John McCulloh, 'Jewish ritual murder', *Speculum* 72 (1997), 713.

30. Joseph Jacobs, 'St William of Norwich', *The Jewish Quarterly Review*, 9 (1897), 750. Jacobs proposes that the boy fell into a cataleptic fit while his family were themselves crucifying him, a 'process ... which, to their minds, had brought salvation and sanctity to the whole world. William was a martyr to Christian, not Jewish, bigotry.'

31. V. D. Lipman proposes a sex-crime, the perpetrator probably being a Christian: *The Jews of Medieval Norwich* (London, 1967), pp. 55–6.

32. There is no official account of the trial. See Zefira Entin Rokéah, 'The Jewish church-robbers and Host desecrators of Norwich (ca. 1285)', *Revue des Études juives*, 141 (juill.–déc. 1982), 338.

33. Augustus Jessopp and M. R. James (eds.), *The Life and Miracles of St William of Norwich by Thomas of Monmouth* (Cambridge, 1896), pp. xi and xxi.

34. Joe Hillaby, 'The ritual-child-murder accusation: Its dissemination and Harold of Gloucester', *Transactions of the J.H.S.E.*, 34 (1994–6), 71–2.

35. It had, writes H. G. Richardson, 'a long anti-Semitic tradition'. See *The English Jewry under Angevin Kings* (London, 1960), p. 186. 'Norwich [was] a city long noted for its anti-Semitism': Zefira Entin Rokéah, 'The Jewish church-robbers and Host desecrators of Norwich (ca. 1285)', *Revue des Études juives*, 141 (juill.–déc. 1982), 335.

36. Zefira Entin Rokéah, 'Crime and Jews in late thirteenth-century England: Some cases and comments', *Hebrew Union College Annual* (Cincinnati, 1985), vol. 55, pp. 119–20. '[S]uch accusations about church-robbing having been made, the anti-Semitic residents of Norwich were only too glad to report them and emphasize the role of the Jews': Zefira Entin Rokéah, 'The Jewish church-robbers and Host desecrators of Norwich (ca. 1285)', *Revue des Études juives*, 141 (juill.–déc. 1982), p. 351.

37. There are fifteenth-century rood screens that depict William as a martyr in churches at Litcham and Lodden. Miri Rubin, 'William of Norwich' in Edward Kessler and Neil Wenborn, *A Dictionary of Jewish–Christian Relations* (Cambridge, 2005), p. 445.

38. See Joseph Jacobs (ed.), *The Jews of Angevin England* (London, 1893), pp. 45–7.

39. Ibid., p. 46.

40. See Joe Hillaby, 'The ritual-child-murder accusation: Its dissemination and Harold of Gloucester', *Transactions of the J.H.S.E.*, 34 (1994–6), 74–5.

41. *Chronicle of the Abbey of Bury St Edmunds* (Oxford, 1998), p. 15.

42. Kenneth Stow, *Jewish Dogs* (Stanford, CA, 2006), pp. 61–2.

43. Zefira Entin Rokéah, 'The State, the Church, and the Jews in medieval England' in Shmuel Almog (ed.), *Antisemitism Through the Ages* (Oxford, 1988), p. 107. See also Michael Adler, *Jews of Medieval England* (London, 1939), pp. 185–6.

44. R. Po-Chia Hsia, *Trent 1475* (New Haven, 1992), p. 87; Slisheva Carlebach, *Divided Souls* (New Haven, 2001), pp. 145–6.

45. Richard of Devizes, *Chronicle* (Cambridge, Ontario, 2000), pp. 48–52.

46. Cecil Roth, *A History of the Jews in England*, 3rd edn (Oxford, 1978), pp. 21–2, fn. 1.

47. J. W. F. Hill, *Medieval Lincoln* (Cambridge, 1948), p. 223.

48. Zefira Entin Rokéah, 'The State, the Church, and the Jews in medieval England' in Shmuel Almog (ed.), *Antisemitism Through the Ages* (Oxford, 1988), p. 108.

49. Ibid.

50. Nicholas C. Vincent, 'Jews, Poitevins, and the Bishop of Winchester, 1231–1234' in Diana Wood (ed.), *Studies in Church History* (Oxford, 1992), vol. 29, pp. 128–9.

51. Zefira Entin Rokéah, 'The Jewish church-robbers and Host desecrators of Norwich (ca. 1285)', *Revue des Études juives*, 141 (juill.–déc. 1982), pp. 340–1, 345.

52. V. D. Lipman, *The Jews of Medieval Norwich* (London, 1967), pp. 59–63; Zefira Entin Rokéah, 'The Jewish church-robbers and Host desecrators of Norwich (ca. 1285)', *Revue des Études juives*, 141 (juill.–déc. 1982), 340–6.

53. J. A. Giles (trans.), *Matthew Paris's English History* (London, 1853), vol. 2, pp. 21–2.

54. S. W. Baron, *A Social and Religious History of the Jews* (New York, 1965), vol. 10, p. 107.

55. Gavin I. Langmuir, *Towards a Definition of Antisemitism* (Berkeley, CA, 1990), p. 259.

56. Thos. R. Howitt, *Jew's Court and the Legend of Little St Hugh of Lincoln* (Leeds, 1911).

57. Ibid., p. 12.

58. J. W. F. Hill, *Medieval Lincoln* (Cambridge, 1948), pp. 228–32.

59. 'End of "Little St Hugh" legend', *The Times*, 15 October 1959.

60. See Zefira Entin Rokéah, 'The State, the Church, and the Jews in medieval England' in Shmuel Almog (ed.), *Antisemitism Through the Ages* (Oxford, 1988), p. 110.

61. Ibid.

62. 'The Deacon and the Jewess; or Apostasy at common law' in H. A. L. Fisher (ed.), *The Collected Papers of Frederic William Maitland* (Cambridge, 1911), vol. 1, p. 400.

63. S. W. Baron, *A Social and Religious History of the Jews* (New York, 1965), vol. 10, p. 111.

64. Zefira Entin Rokéah, 'Crime and Jews in late thirteenth-century England', *Hebrew Union College Annual* (Cincinnati, 1985), vol. 55, pp. 109–10, 119; H. G. Richardson, *The English Jewry under Angevin Kings* (London, 1960), pp. 217, 221.

65. H. G. Richardson, *The English Jewry under Angevin Kings* (London, 1960), pp. 221–2.

66. Ibid., p. 219.

67. 'There is no evidence whatsoever from the records [of criminal cases in general] of a deliberate or a concerted effort to incriminate Jews, with the sole and very obvious exception of the charges raised against Jews in 1278–1279 in connection with coinage offences.' Zefira Entin Rokéah, 'Crime and Jews in late thirteenth-century England', *Hebrew Union College Annual* (Cincinnati, 1985), vol. 55, p. 123.

68. Michael Adler, *Jews of Medieval England* (London, 1939), p. 19; Zefira Entin Rokéah, 'Money and the hangman in late-thirteenth-century England (Part I)', *Transactions of the J.H.S.E.*, 31 (1988–90), 98–9.

69. Zefira Entin Rokéah, 'Money and the hangman in late-thirteenth-century England (Part II)', *Transactions of the J.H.S.E.*, 32 (1990–2), 160.

70. Cf.: 'Institutional racism is in our view primarily apparent in what we have seen and heard in the following areas: . . . (b) countrywide in the disparity in stop and search figures.' Sir William MacPherson, *The Stephen Lawrence Inquiry* (London, 1999), para. 6.45.

71. Zefira Entin Rokéah, 'Money and the hangman in late-thirteenth-century England (Part I)', *Transactions of the J.H.S.E.*, 31 (1988–90), 96.

72. H. G. Richardson, *The English Jewry under Angevin Kings* (London, 1960), p. 218.

73. Ibid., pp. 218–19.

74. Leon Simon (ed.), *Selected Essays of Ahad Ha'am* (New York, 1962), p. 203; Leon Simon, *Ahad Ha'am: A biography* (London, 1960), p. 111.

75. To Gavin Langmuir, by contrast, anti-Semitism's defining quality is that it deals in fabrications and not partial-truths. See *Towards a Definition of Antisemitism* (Berkeley, CA, 1990), p. 11. For Colin Holmes, the anti-Semites' use of partial-truths means that what he terms the 'scapegoat theory' of anti-Semitism is wrong. Jews were not merely 'innocent recipients of hostility, whose activities and interests were essentially irrelevant to an understanding of [anti-Semitic] situations'. There is a 'core' of truth, which is then 'simplified and distorted'. *Anti-Semitism in British Society 1876–1939* (New York, 1979), pp. 30–5.

76. See François Furet and Ernst Nolte, *Fascism and Communism* (Lincoln, NA, 2001), pp. 22, 28, 36–7, 41–2.

77. The charge was made in the context of defending the Incarnation—how could the Jews mock the enfleshment of God when they themselves, etc. See Anna Sapir Abulafia, 'Bodies in the Jewish–Christian debate' in Sarah Kay and Miri Rubin (eds.), *Framing Medieval Bodies* (Manchester, 1994), pp. 126–9. See also Judah M. Rosenthal, 'The Talmud on trial', *Jewish Quarterly Review* 47 (1956), 63, and George Foot Moore, 'Christian writers on Judaism', *Harvard Theological Review*, 14/3 (1921), 202. For a nineteenth-century instance of Talmud-mockery, see Goldwin Smith, 'The Jewish question', *Questions of the Day* (London, 1897), pp. 266–7. It would appear that it was dissenting Jews who first made these charges against the Talmud: see Petrus Alfonsi, *Dialogue Against the Jews* (Washington, DC, 2006), pp. 29–32.

78. On the concept of 'transformative interpretation' in the reading of Jewish texts, see Josef Stern, 'Maimonides on Amalek, self-corrective mechanisms, and the war against idolatry' in Jonathan W. Malino (ed.), *Judaism and Modernity* (Burlington, VT, 2004), p. 381. On anthropomorphisms in the *Tanach* and the Talmud generally, see 'Anthropomorphism', *Encyclopedia Judaica* (Jerusalem, 1972), vol. 3, pp. 50–8.

79. Amos Funkenstein, *Perceptions of Jewish History* (Berkeley, CA, 1993), pp. 88–90. 'The purpose of everyone endowed with intellect should be wholly directed to rejecting corporeality with respect to God. . . . He who affirms that God . . . has positive attributes . . . has abolished his belief in the existence of the deity without being aware of it.' Moses Maimonides, *The Guide of the Perplexed* (Chicago, 1963), vol. 1, pp. 61, 144. 'The Holy Scriptures use the language of

the common people.' Solomon Maimon, *An Autobiography* (London, 1888), pp. 123–4.

80. Robert S. Wistrich, *The Jews of Vienna in the Age of Franz Joseph* (Oxford, 1990), p. 67; Jan T. Gross, *Fear* (New York, 2006), pp. 226–39, 245.

81. Michael Adler, *Jews of Medieval England* (London, 1939), pp. 226, 228.

82. According to the chronicler, seven teeth were pulled before the Jew relented. See J. A. Giles (trans.), *Roger of Wendover's Flowers of History* (London, 1854), vol. 2, pp. 252–3, and Michael Adler, *Jews of Medieval England* (London, 1939), p. 201–2.

83. Robert Southey, *Letters from England* (Gloucester, 1984), p. 392.

84. Robert Bartlett, *England Under the Norman and Angevin Kings: 1075–1225* (Oxford, 2000), p. 352.

85. Cecil Roth, *A History of the Jews in England*, 3rd edn (Oxford, 1978), p. 35.

86. Michael Adler, *Jews of Medieval England* (London, 1939), p. 159.

87. S. W. Baron, *A Social and Religious History of the Jews*, 2nd edn (New York, 1967), vol. 11, p. 202.

88. Miri Rubin, 'The person in the form: Medieval challenges to bodily "order"' in Sarah Kay and Miri Rubin (eds.), *Framing Medieval Bodies* (Manchester, 1994), p. 108.

89. The exception appears to be in Lynn, where the chronicler William of Newbury reports that 'young foreigners' committed the murders. They had escaped back abroad, apparently, before the king's officers could detain them. William comments (and we may be right to hear irony), 'the inhabitants of the place, when they were interrogated about the matter by the officials, attributed the deed to the foreigners who had already gone away'. See Joseph Jacobs (ed.), *The Jews of Angevin England* (London, 1893) p. 115.

90. Thomas Asbridge, *The First Crusade* (London, 2004), p. 86.

91. Henry Hart Milman, *History of the Jews* (London, 1866), vol. 3, p. 179.

92. See Joe Hillaby, 'Jewish colonisation in the twelfth century' in Patricia Skinner (ed.), *Jews in Medieval Britain* (Woodbridge, 2003), p. 29.

93. Joseph Jacobs (ed.), *The Jews of Angevin England* (London, 1893), p. 101.

94. Ibid.

95. See 'Ballad of the Wolf' in Eisig Silberschlag, *Saul Tschernichowsky* (New York, 1968), p. 185.

96. Cf. Jan T. Gross, *Fear* (New York, 2006), pp. 108, 111, 159–60, 163.

97. Hugh M. Thomas, 'Portrait of a medieval anti-Semite', *The Haskins Society Journal*, 5 (1993), 10.

98. See S. W. Baron, *A Social and Religious History of the Jews* (New York, 1965), vol. 10, p. 152.

99. William of Newbury writes that Benedict 'met with a most wretched end [in London]' while Josce 'escaping with difficulty, returned to York'. Another source has Benedict dying in Northampton. See Joseph Jacobs (ed.), *The Jews of Angevin England* (London, 1893), pp. 106, 118.

100. In William of Newbury's account. See Joseph Jacobs (ed.), *The Jews of Angevin England* (London, 1893), p. 127.

101. R. B. Dobson, 'The Jews of medieval York and the massacre of march 1190', Borthwick Papers no. 45 (York, 1974).

102. Joseph Jacobs (ed.), *The Jews of Angevin England* (London, 1893), p. 131.

103. Ibid., pp. 217–18.

104. J. R. Maddicott, *Simon de Montfort* (Cambridge, 1994), p. 15.

105. Robert C. Stacey, 'The conversion of Jews to Christianity in thirteenth-century England', *Speculum* 67 (1992), 272.

106. *A History of the Jews in England*, 3rd edn (Oxford, 1978), pp. 58, 61.

107. J. R. Maddicott, *Simon de Montfort* (Cambridge, 1994), p. 15.

108. Cecil Roth, *A History of the Jews in England*, 3rd edn (Oxford, 1978), pp. 57–8.

109. Michael Adler, *Jews of Medieval England* (London, 1939), p. 79.

110. Ibid., p. 220.

111. Robin R. Mundill, *England's Jewish Solution* (Cambridge, 1998), pp. 42–3.

112. William Chester Jordan, *Europe in the High Middle Ages* (London, 2002), p. 238.

113. Max Weber, *The Protestant Ethic and the Rise of Capitalism* (London, 1974), pp. 165–6.

114. R. H. Tawney, *Religion and the Rise of Capitalism* (London, 1972), p. 55.

115. See Joseph Jacobs (ed.), *The Jews of Angevin England* (London, 1893), p. xix.

116. H. G. Richardson, *The English Jewry under Angevin Kings* (London, 1960), pp. 60–3, 65–6, 121.

117. See David Carpenter, *The Struggle for Mastery* (London, 2004), pp. 41–2.

118. Ibid., p. 41.

119. See S. W. Baron, *A Social and Religious History of the Jews* (New York, 1965), vol. 10, pp. 94–5.

120. Joseph Jacobs (ed.), *The Jews of Angevin England* (London, 1893), pp. 156–9.

121. Cecil Roth, *A History of the Jews in England*, 3rd edn (Oxford, 1978), p. 17.

122. See Robert C. Stacey, '1240–60: A watershed in Anglo-Jewish relations?', *Historical Research*, 61/145 (1988), 136–7.

123. Robin R. Mundill, *England's Jewish Solution* (Cambridge, 1998), p. 92.

124. Ibid., p. 100.

125. See Michael Adler, *Jews of Medieval England* (London, 1939), p. 64.

126. See Joseph Jacobs (ed.), *The Jews of Angevin England* (London, 1893), p. 47.

127. *A History of the Jews in England*, 3rd edn (Oxford, 1978), p. 50.

128. See Paul Brand, 'Jews and the law in England 1275–1290', *English Historical Review* 115 (2000), 1153, and cf. Robin R. Mundill, *England's Jewish Solution* (Cambridge, 1998), pp. 124–45.

129. Bernard Lewis, *Semites and Anti-Semites* (London, 1986), p. 91; Bernard Lewis, *The Jews of Islam* (London, 1984), p. 25; S. W. Baron, *A Social and Religious History of the Jews*, 2nd edn (New York, 1957), vol. 3, pp. 139–40;

S. W. Baron, *A Social and Religious History of the Jews*, 2nd edn (New York, 1967), vol. 11, p. 97.

130. Robin R. Mundill, *England's Jewish Solution* (Cambridge, 1998), pp. 120–1.

131. Ibid., pp. 10, 95.

132. J. A. Cannon, 'Jews' in John Cannon (ed.), *The Oxford Companion to British History* (Oxford, 1997), p. 533.

133. Paul Brand, 'Jews and the law in England 1275–1290', *English Historical Review*, 115 (2000), 1153; Marc Morris, *A Great and Terrible King* (London, 2008), pp. 126–7.

134. Cecil Roth, *A History of the Jews in England*, 3rd edn (Oxford, 1978), p. 73.

135. Robin R. Mundill, *England's Jewish Solution* (Cambridge, 1998), p. 119.

136. S. W. Baron, *A Social and Religious History of the Jews* (New York, 1965), vol. 10, p. 109.

137. Oscar I. Janowsky, *People at Bay* (London, 1938), pp. 64–7.

138. See Edgar Samuel, 'Diamonds and pieces of eight', *At the End of the Earth* (London, 2004), pp. 256–7.

139. See Michael Prestwich, 'The Ordinances of 1311 and the politics of the early fourteenth century' in John Taylor and Wendy Childs (eds.), *Politics and Crisis in Fourteenth-Century England* (Gloucester, 1990), pp. 3–4.

140. Robert C. Stacey, 'The conversion of Jews to Christianity in thirteenth-century England', *Speculum*, 67 (1992), 264.

141. Miri Rubin, 'Religious culture in town and country' in David Abulafia, Michael Franklin, and Miri Rubin (eds.), *Church and City 1000–1500* (Cambridge, 2002), p. 12.

142. Richard Vaughan (ed.), *Chronicles of Matthew Paris* (New York, 1984), pp. 214–15.

143. The deacon had converted in order to marry a Jewish woman. See F. W. Maitland, 'The Deacon and the Jewess; or Apostasy at common law' in H. A. L. Fisher (ed.), *The Collected Papers of Frederic William Maitland* (Cambridge, 1911), vol. 1, pp. 385–406. A later convert, a former Dominican, died in prison: Robin R. Mundill, *England's Jewish Solution* (Cambridge, 1998), p. 48.

144. Colin Richmond, 'Englishness and medieval Anglo-Jewry' in Tony Kushner (ed.), *The Jewish Heritage in British History* (London, 1992), p. 51. The archbishop was the king's half-brother.

145. See Paul Brand, 'Jews and the law in England 1275–1290', *English Historical Review* 115 (2000), 1142.

146. See J. H. Strawley, *Robert Grosseteste* (Lincoln, 1966), p. 7.

147. See R. W. Southern, *Robert Grosseteste*, 2nd edn (Oxford, 1992), pp. 246–7.

148. Robert Chazan, *The Jews of Medieval Western Christendom* (Cambridge, 2006), pp. 44–51.

149. Jocelin of Brakelond, *Chronicle of the Abbey of Bury St Edmunds* (Oxford, 1998), p. 10.

150. *Chronicle of the Abbey of Bury St Edmunds* (Oxford, 1998), pp. 41–2.

151. Jocelin of Brakelond, *Chronicle of the Abbey of Bury St Edmunds* (Oxford, 1998), p. 42.

152. But see Robin Mundill, *England's Jewish Solution* (Cambridge, 1998), pp. 61–2.

153. At the time of the Expulsion, the Archbishop of York wrote to his diocese threatening with excommunication anyone who molested the Jews: Robin R. Mundill, *England's Jewish Solution* (Cambridge, 1998), pp. 254–5.

154. Cecil Roth, *A History of the Jews in England*, 3rd edn (Oxford, 1978), p. 11.

155. Robin R. Mundill, *England's Jewish Solution* (Cambridge, 1998), pp. 37–8, 41, 44, 45–6, and 110; F. Pollock and F. W. Maitland, *The History of English Law before the Time of Edward I*, 2nd edn (Cambridge, 1968), vol. 2, pp. 123–4.

156. On occasion, even Popes were ready to intervene. In 1199, Innocent III ordered the abbot of the Leicester convent to provide for a converted Jew 'who had lost his noble patron by death'. See C. R. Cheney and Mary G. Cheney, *The Letters of Pope Innocent III Concerning England and Wales* (Oxford, 1967), p. 29.

157. See Joseph Jacobs (ed.), *The Jews of Angevin England* (London, 1893), p. 106.

158. See F. D. Logan, 'Thirteen London Jews and conversion to Christianity', *Bulletin of the Institute of Historical Research*, 45 (1972).

159. See Robert C. Stacey, 'The conversion of Jews to Christianity in thirteenth-century England', *Speculum*, 67 (1992).

160. Miri Rubin, *Charity & Community in Medieval Cambridge* (Cambridge, 2002), p. 108.

161. H. R. Trevor-Roper, *The European Witch-Craze of the 16th and 17th Centuries* (London, 1969), pp. 33–4; Jeremy Cohen, *The Friars and the Jews* (Ithaca, 1982), p. 13.

162. Or possibly members of both orders: Jeremy Cohen, *The Friars and the Jews* (Ithaca, 1982), pp. 42–3.

163. F. D. Logan, 'Thirteen London Jews and conversion to Christianity', *Bulletin of the Institute of Historical Research*, 45 (1972), 220.

164. Michael Adler, *Jews of Medieval England* (London, 1939), p. 97. Solomon Grayzel thought it likely that the letter from Pope Honorius IV reproving backsliding English clergy originated with a request to him by Peckham for a policy statement on the Jews. See *The Church and the Jews in the XIIIth Century: 1254–1314* (New York, 1989), p. 160, fn. 2.

165. Robin R. Mundill, *England's Jewish Solution* (Cambridge, 1998), p. 47.

166. Jonathan Riley-Smith, 'Christian violence and the Crusades' in Anna Sapir Abulafia (ed.), *Religious Violence between Christians and Jews* (New York, 2002), p. 11.

167. S. W. Baron, *A Social and Religious History of the Jews*, 2nd edn (New York, 1967), vol. 11, pp. 204–5.

168. See Michael Adler, 'The medieval Jews of Exeter', *Transactions of the Devon-shire Association for the Advancement of Science, Literature, and Art*, 63 (1931), 221–40.

169. Cecil Roth, *A History of the Jews in England*, 3rd edn (Oxford, 1978), p. 39.

170. Ibid., p. 42. On Langton, see also H. G. Richardson, *The English Jewry under Angevin Kings* (London, 1960), pp. 182–7.

171. Zefira Entin Rokéah, 'The State, the Church, and the Jews in medieval England' in Shmuel Almog (ed.), *Antisemitism Through the Ages* (Oxford, 1988), p. 113.

172. Cecil Roth, *A History of the Jews in England*, 3rd edn (Oxford, 1978), p. 40; S. W. Baron, *A Social and Religious History of the Jews* (New York, 1965), vol. 9, p. 29. 'England was the first country to follow the lead of the Lateran Council and to order, in 1218, all Jews to wear on their outer garments two white tables made of linen or parchment.' S. W. Baron, *A Social and Religious History of the Jews*, 2nd edn (New York, 1967), vol. 11, p. 98.

173. Zefira Entin Rokéah, 'The State, the Church, and the Jews in medieval England' in Shmuel Almog (ed.), *Antisemitism Through the Ages* (Oxford, 1988), p. 113.

174. Ibid.

175. S. W. Baron, *A Social and Religious History of the Jews* (New York, 1965), vol. 9, p. 26.

176. Ibid., p. 16.

177. See, for example, Robin R. Mundill, *England's Jewish Solution* (Cambridge, 1998), p. 50.

178. Nicholas C. Vincent, 'Jews, Poitevins, and the Bishop of Winchester, 1231–1234' in Diana Wood (ed.), *Studies in Church History* (Oxford, 1992), vol. 29, p. 120.

179. James Picciotto, *Sketches of Anglo-Jewish History* (London, 1956), p. 11.

180. Cecil Roth, *A History of the Jews in England*, 3rd edn (Oxford, 1978), p. 42.

181. The circular is extracted in W. H. Hutton (ed.), *The Misrule of Henry III* (London, 1887), p. 12.

182. Zefira Entin Rokéah, 'The State, the Church, and the Jews in medieval England' in Shmuel Almog (ed.), *Antisemitism Through the Ages* (Oxford, 1988), p. 112.

183. Gavin Langmuir, 'The Jews and the archives of Angevin England', *Traditio*, 19 (1963), 228.

184. John Edwards, 'The Church and the Jews in medieval England' in Patricia Skinner (ed.), *Jews in Medieval Britain* (Woodbridge, 2003), pp. 86, 90–2, 94.

185. See Robert C. Stacey, '1240–60: A watershed in Anglo-Jewish relations?', *Historical Research*, 61/145 (1988), 147. In 1245, for example, the bishop of London forbade all Christians from selling food to the Jews of London. In 1286, the Bishop of Hereford threatened with excommunication any

Christians who attended a local Jewish wedding: Michael Adler, *Jews of Medieval England* (London, 1939), p. 27. Such boycotts, if carried out, would have made Jewish life in England unbearable: S. W. Baron, *A Social and Religious History of the Jews* (New York, 1965), vol. 10, p. 102.

186. See H. G. Richardson, *The English Jewry under Angevin Kings* (London, 1960), pp. 182–97.

187. Michael Adler, *Jews of Medieval England* (London, 1939), p. 226.

188. Pope Gregory IX sent letters in June 1239 to the Kings of France, England, Portugal, Navarre, Aragon, Leon, and Castile, ordering them to investigate 'the books of the Jews' (i.e., the Talmud). Only the French King acted on this instruction, and following a public inquisition, copies of the Talmud were duly burned in Paris in 1242. Henry III either ignored the letter or never received it. See Lesley Smith, 'William of Auvergne and the Jews' in Diana Wood (ed.), *Studies in Church History* (Oxford, 1992), vol. 29, pp. 114–16.

189. See Robin R. Mundill, *England's Jewish Solution* (Cambridge, 1998), p. 32. See also Michael Adler, *Jews of Medieval England* (London, 1939), pp. 39–40. Henry III may have seized books simply in order to sell them back to their original Jewish owners: S. W. Baron, *A Social and Religious History of the Jews* (New York, 1965), vol. 9, p. 67.

190. Joseph Jacobs (ed.), *The Jews of Angevin England* (London, 1893), p. 6. H. G. Richardson suggests that this is 'no more than an idle tale': *The English Jewry under Angevin Kings* (London, 1960), p. 24. Gilbert Dahan, on the other hand, takes it seriously: *The Christian Polemic against the Jews in the Middle Ages* (Notre Dame, IN, 1998), pp. 21–2.

191. For Gilbert's intellectual debt to Anselm, see Anna Sapir Abulafia, 'Theology and the commercial revolution: Guibert of Nogent, St Anselm and the Jews of Northern France' in David Abulafia, Michael Franklin, and Miri Rubin (eds.), *Church and City 1000–1500* (Cambridge, 2002), pp. 23–4.

192. Joseph Jacobs (ed.), *The Jews of Angevin England* (London, 1893), pp. 7–12.

193. Cecil Roth, *A History of the Jews in England*, 3rd edn (Oxford, 1978), p. 5; Beryl Smalley, *The Study of the Bible in the Middle Ages* (Notre Dame, IN, 1982), pp. 77–8. Was there really a debate? See Jeremy Cohen, *The Friars and the Jews* (Ithaca, 1982), p. 26. In the twelfth century, further, a Rabbi Benjamin of Cambridge might have debated an apostate. See Cecil Roth, *The Intellectual Activities of Medieval English Jewry* (London, n.d.), pp. 31–2.

194. Gilbert Dahan, *The Christian Polemic against the Jews in the Middle Ages* (Notre Dame, IN, 1998), p. 56.

195. Joseph Jacobs (ed.), *The Jews of Angevin England* (London, 1893), pp. 179–82.

196. See Gilbert Dahan, *The Christian Polemic against the Jews in the Middle Ages* (Notre Dame, IN, 1998), pp. 81–4. The shift is not clear-cut. In his *Dialogue Against the Jews*, Bartholomew, Bishop of Exeter (d. 1184), attacking rabbinic interpretation of the 'Old Testament', condemns the Jews' 'serpentine wile[s]': Beryl Smalley, *The Study of the Bible in the Middle Ages* (Notre Dame, IN,

1982), pp. 170–1. But Peter of Cornwall's (d. 1221) *Dialogue* (1208) is more pacific. Dahan *Christian Polemic*, p. 62; R. W. Hunt, 'The Disputation of Peter of Cornwall against Symon the Jew' in R. W. Hunt *et al.* (eds.), *Studies in Medieval History Presented to Frederick Maurice Powicke* (Oxford, 1948), p. 151.

197. Jacques Le Goff, *Intellectuals in the Middle Ages* (Oxford, 1993), pp. 6, 10.

198. S. W. Baron, *A Social and Religious History of the Jews* (New York, 1965), vol. 10, p. 102.

199. See Gilbert Dahan, *The Christian Polemic against the Jews in the Middle Ages* (Notre Dame, IN, 1998), p. 47.

200. See ibid., p. 65.

201. Robert Chazan, *The Jews of Medieval Western Christendom* (Cambridge, 2006), p. 6.

202. Amos Funkenstein, 'Anti-Jewish propaganda: Pagan, medieval, and modern', *The Jerusalem Quarterly*, 19 (Spring 1981), 64. In the twelfth century, 'anti-Jewish propaganda changed... in quantity and quality'.

203. But see R. W. Hunt, 'The Disputation of Peter of Cornwall against Symon the Jew' in R. W. Hunt *et al.* (eds.), *Studies in Medieval History Presented to Frederick Maurice Powicke* (Oxford, 1948), pp. 146–7. Peter of Cornwall, writing in about 1208, claims to have converted his adversary.

204. Beryl Smalley, *The Study of the Bible in the Middle Ages* (Notre Dame, IN, 1982), p. 181.

205. See Gilbert Dahan, *The Christian Polemic against the Jews in the Middle Ages* (Notre Dame, IN, 1998), pp. 107–8.

206. James McEvoy, *Robert Grosseteste* (Oxford, 2000), pp. 10–11; see also Beryl Smalley, *The Study of the Bible in the Middle Ages* (Notre Dame, IN, 1982), p. 235.

207. See Anna Sapir Abulafia, 'Theology and the commercial revolution: Guibert of Nogent, St. Anselm and the Jews of Northern France' in David Abulafia, Michael Franklin, and Miri Rubin (eds.), *Church and City 1000–1500* (Cambridge, 2002), pp. 30, 33, 39.

208. Norman Cantor, *Medieval Lives* (New York, 1995), pp. 120, 125.

209. J. H. Strawley, *Robert Grosseteste* (Lincoln, 1966), p. 9.

210. James McEvoy, *Robert Grosseteste* (Oxford, 2000), pp. 101–2. *De cessatione legalium* had a wide circulation and many manuscript copies were made. In the three centuries that followed, it continued to influence English opinion. Lee M. Friedman, *Robert Grosseteste and the Jews* (Cambridge, MA, 1934), pp. 21–2. Compare Herbert de Losinga's treatment of the episode of Jesus and the moneychangers, read as representing the Expulsion of the Jews from the cognition of Christ's incarnation, and the subversion by the Jewish priests of the laws of Moses. See James W. Alexander, 'Herbert of Norwich 1091–1119' in William M. Bowsky (ed.), *Studies in Medieval and Renaissance History* (Lincoln, NA, 1969), vol. 6, p. 190.

211. James McEvoy, *Robert Grosseteste* (Oxford, 2000), p. 106; Beryl Smalley, 'The Biblical Scholar' in D. A. Callus (ed.), *Robert Grosseteste* (Oxford, 1955), p. 81.

212. Robert C. Stacey, 'The conversion of Jews to Christianity in thirteenth-century England', *Speculum*, 67 (1992), 269.

213. Colin Richmond, 'Englishness and medieval Anglo-Jewry' in Tony Kushner (ed.), *The Jewish Heritage in British History: Englishness and Jewishness* (London, 1992), pp. 42–3.

214. Joan Greatrex, 'Monastic charity for Jewish converts' in Diana Wood (ed.), *Studies in Church History* (Oxford, 1992), vol. 29, p. 135.

215. Robert C. Stacey, 'The conversion of Jews to Christianity in thirteenth-century England', *Speculum*, 67 (1992), 265.

216. S. W. Baron, *A Social and Religious History of the Jews*, 2nd edn (New York, 1967), vol. 11, p. 98; Robert Bartlett, *England Under the Norman and Angevin Kings: 1075–1225* (Oxford, 2000), p. 354.

217. S. W. Baron, *A Social and Religious History of the Jews* (New York, 1965), vol. 10, p. 110.

218. Henry took the Cross on 6 March 1250, but did not sail for the Holy Land. See Simon Lloyd, 'King Henry III, the Crusade and the Mediterranean' in Michael Jones and Malcolm Vale (eds.), *England and her Neighbours 1066–1453* (London, 1989), p. 99. 'Henry's interest in the Jews was almost morbid. He could not do without them, and at times tried to be just to them. He was keenly interested in attempts to convert them. But in times of stress, when he was apt to take refuge from his anxieties or his conscience in religious exercises, the ruthless exploitation of the Jews would seem to him a duty as well as a means of profit.' F. M. Powicke, *King Henry III and the Lord Edward* (Oxford, 1947), p. 313.

219. Zefira Entin Rokéah, 'The State, the Church, and the Jews in medieval England' in Shmuel Almog (ed.), *Antisemitism Through the Ages* (Oxford, 1988), pp. 114–15.

220. Robin R. Mundill, *England's Jewish Solution* (Cambridge, 1998), p. 58.

221. T. F. Tout, *Edward I* (London, 1893), p. 69.

222. H. G. Richardson, 'Glanville Continued', *The Law Quarterly Review*, 215 (1938), 392–4; F. M. Powicke, *King Henry III and the Lord Edward* (Oxford, 1947), p. 125.

223. Michael Adler, *Jews of Medieval England* (London, 1939), p. 127.

224. Joan Greatrex, 'Monastic charity for Jewish converts' in Diana Wood (ed.), *Studies in Church History* (Oxford, 1992), vol. 29, p. 142. Robert C. Stacey, '1240–60: A watershed in Anglo–Jewish relations?', *Historical Research*, 61/145 (1988), 140, gives the date as 1255.

225. Robert C. Stacey, '1240–60: A watershed in Anglo–Jewish relations?', *Historical Research*, 61/145 (1988), 141.

226. Robin R. Mundill, *England's Jewish Solution* (Cambridge, 1998), p. 265.

227. Ibid., p. 80.

228. Ibid., p. 9.

229. Ibid., p. 254.

230. For an analysis of the parameters, see ibid., pp. 26–7.

231. Zefira Entin Rokéah, 'Crime and Jews in late thirteenth-century England', *Hebrew Union College Annual* (Cincinnati, 1985), vol. 55, p. 131.

232. S. W. Baron, *A Social and Religious History of the Jews* (New York, 1965), vol. 10, p. 65.

233. Robin R. Mundill, *England's Jewish Solution* (Cambridge, 1998), p. 14.

234. See Jacques Le Goff, *Your Money or Your Life* (New York, 1990), p. 49.

235. Joseph Jacobs (ed.), *The Jews of Angevin England* (London, 1893), p. xiii.

236. T. F. Tout, *Edward I* (London, 1893), p. 161; Michael Adler, *Jews of Medieval England* (London, 1939), p. 95.

237. Robin R. Mundill, *England's Jewish Solution* (Cambridge, 1998), pp. 63–4.

238. Colin Richmond, 'Englishness and medieval Anglo-Jewry' in Tony Kushner (ed.), *The Jewish Heritage in British History* (London, 1992), p. 44.

239. Solomon Grayzel, *The Church and the Jews in the XIIIth Century: 1254–1314* (New York, 1989), p. 295. The exchange is dated May–July 1285.

240. Kenneth R. Stow, 'The popes and Jewish money' in Diana Wood (ed.), *Studies in Church History*, (Oxford, 1992), vol. 29, p. 239.

241. Cf. H. R. Trevor-Roper, *The European Witch-Craze of the 16th and 17th Centuries* (London, 1969), p. 38.

242. See, for example, Sophia Menache, 'The king, the Church and the Jews', *Journal of Medieval History*, 13 (1987).

243. Colin Richmond, review of Robin R. Mundill, *England's Jewish Solution* (Cambridge, 1998), <www.history.ac.uk/reviews/paper/mundhill.html>.

244. Sophie Menache, 'The king, the Church and the Jews: Some considerations on the expulsions from England and France', *Journal of Medieval History*, 13 (1987), 223–6.

245. William Chester Jordan, *Europe in the High Middle Ages* (London, 2002), p. 317.

246. Robin R. Mundill, *England's Jewish Solution* (Cambridge, 1998), pp. 247–8.

247. Ibid., pp. 257–9.

248. Zefira Entin Rokéah, 'Crime and Jews in late thirteenth-century England', *Hebrew Union College Annual* (Cincinnati, 1985), vol. 55, p. 131.

249. Kenneth R. Stow, 'The popes and Jewish money' in Diana Wood (ed.), *Studies in Church History* (Oxford, 1992), vol. 29, p. 240.

250. Robin R. Mundill, *England's Jewish Solution* (Cambridge, 1998), p. 255.

251. H. G. Richardson, *The English Jewry under Angevin Kings* (London, 1960), p. 167.

252. Jeremy Cohen, *The Friars and the Jews* (Ithaca, 1982), p. 14. 'The Franciscan Henry of Wadstone played an instrumental role in securing a decree forbidding Jewish ownership of freeholds in England, and the register of the Grey Friars of London notes owing to his efforts all Jews were finally expelled from England' (ibid., p. 43).

253. Jacques Le Goff, *Your Money or Your Life* (New York, 1990), pp. 14–15.

254. Ibid., pp. 10, 21.
255. See Robert C. Stacey, '1240–60: A watershed in Anglo–Jewish relations?', *Historical Research*, 61/145 (1988), pp. 146–7 for a discussion of the impact on the Jews of this aspect of thirteenth century sentiment.
256. Marc Saperstein, *Moments of Crisis in Jewish–Christian Relations* (London, 1989), pp. 22–4.
257. Marc Morris, *A Great and Terrible King* (London, 2008), p. 371.
258. Patricia Skinner, 'Jews in medieval Britain and Europe' in Patricia Skinner (ed.), *Jews in Medieval Britain* (Woodbridge, 2003), p. 3.
259. R. I. Moore, 'Anti-Semitism and the birth of Europe' in Diana Wood (ed.), *Studies in Church History* (Oxford, 1992), vol. 29, p. 36.
260. See Robin R. Mundill, *England's Jewish Solution* (Cambridge, 1998), pp. 2–4. According to James Howell, writing in 1633, the Jews were 'expelled for villainies and cheatings, for clipping coins, poisoning of waters, and counterfeiting of seals'. See Edgar Rosenberg, *From Shylock to Svengali* (Stanford, CA, 1960), p. 26. Note the reading back into thirteenth-century English history of the much later, Continental allegation of well-poisoning.
261. Nathan Osterman, 'The controversy over the proposed readmission of the Jews to England (1655)', *Jewish Social Studies*, 3 (July 1941), 305.
262. *A History of Crime in England* (London, 1873), vol. 1, p. 184.
263. See Geoffrey Hartman, *Scars of the Spirit* (New York, 2002), pp. 173–4, on Germany's post-Holocaust 'culture-guilt'.
264. 'I don't want to wallop anybody, even Jews. The best thing is to kick them out, like King Edward Longshanks of famous memory.' W. R. W. Stephens, *The Life and Letters of Edward A. Freeman* (London, 1895), vol. 2, p. 428. See also Joseph Banister, *England under the Jews* (London, 1907), p. 33; William Joyce, *Twilight Over England* (London, 1992), p. 15; Stephen Dorril, *Blackshirt* (London, 2006), p. 425; Martin Pugh, *'Hurrah for the Blackshirts'* (London, 2005), p. 239.
265. See 'Thomas of Monmouth: Detector of ritual murder', *Towards a Definition of Antisemitism* (Berkeley, CA, 1990), pp. 232–5.
266. Joe Hillaby, 'The ritual-child-murder accusation: Its dissemination and Harold of Gloucester', *Transactions of the J.H.S.E.*, 34 (1994–6), 70–3.
267. Benedicta Ward, *Miracles and the Medieval Mind* (Aldershot, Hants, 1987), p. 69.
268. See Michael Adler, *Jews of Medieval England* (London, 1939), p. 60.
269. F. Pollock and F. W. Maitland, *The History of English Law before the Time of Edward I*, 2nd edn (Cambridge, 1968), vol. 1, pp. 470–1; J. C. Holt, *The Northerners* (Oxford, 1992), p. 195. The 'anti-Semitism was caused by money-lending' trope is challenged in Michael Toch, 'The economic activities of German Jews in the 10th to 12th centuries' in Yom Tov Assis et al. (eds.), *Facing the Cross* (Jerusalem, 2000), pp. viii–ix.
270. Robin R. Mundill, *England's Jewish Solution* (Cambridge, 1998), p. 117.

271. For example, while perpetual fee-rents owed by Christians to Jews were abolished in 1269, fee-rents owed to Christians remained valid and enforceable. Robert C. Stacey, '1240–60: A watershed in Anglo–Jewish relations?', *Historical Research*, 61/145(1988), 145.

272. Ibid., 140, 142.

273. See Hugh M. Thomas, 'Portrait of a medieval anti-Semite' in Robert B. Patterson (ed.), *The Haskins Society Journal*, 5 (1993).

274. Cecil Roth, *A History of the Jews in England*, 3rd edn (Oxford, 1978), p. 32.

275. 'Thus, in after generations, when no Jew was left in England, it was from the poetical descriptions of this half-legendary event [the Lincoln blood-libel] that a large part of the population received its impression of the despised race.' Ibid., p. 57.

4. ENGLISH LITERARY ANTI-SEMITISM

1. See 'England the Ninth of Ab', *Opportunities that Pass* (London, 2005), pp. 114–18.

2. See Robert C. Stacey, '1240–60: A watershed in Anglo–Jewish relations?', *Historical Research*, 61/145 (1988), 149–50.

3. See James Simpson, *The Oxford English Literary History*, Vol. 2: *1350–1547 Reform and Cultural Revolution* (Oxford, 2002), p. 4. This, says Simpson, is the 'formal' definition of literature. There are, he adds, at least four plausible other definitions: 'functional' (i.e., designed to entertain), 'positivist' (i.e., regarded as literature by readers and writers), 'discursive' (i.e., subversive of discursive norms), and last, at some distance from an historically 'true' account (i.e., either verisimilar or fabulous).

4. See Northrop Frye, *The Myth of Deliverance* (Toronto, 1983), p. 11.

5. Derek Attridge, *The Singularity of Literature* (London, 2004), p. 11.

6. René Wellek and Austin Warren, *Theory of Literature* (London, 1976), p. 156; Geoffrey Hartman, *Scars of the Spirit* (New York, 2002), p. 227.

7. Michel Butor, *Inventory* (London, 1970), p. 27.

8. Alastair Fowler, 'The two histories' in David Perkins (ed.), *Theoretical Issues in Literary History* (Cambridge, MA, 1991), pp. 121, 123.

9. *Daniel Deronda* (Oxford, 1998), p. 309.

10. Raymond Williams, *Keywords* (London, 1976), pp. 150–4; J. Hillis Miller, *On Literature* (London, 2002), *passim*.

11. E. R. Curtius, *European Literature and the Latin Middle Ages* (Princeton, NJ, 1973), pp. 70–1, 79, 105, 197; Roland Barthes, 'The old rhetoric: An aide-mémoire', *The Semiotic Challenge* (Berkeley, CA, 1994), pp. 67–72; Omer Bartov, *The 'Jew' in Cinema* (Bloomington, IN, 2005), p. x.

12. Bernard Lewis, *Semites and Anti-Semites* (London, 1986), p. 97.

13. Edgar Rosenberg, 'The Jew in Western drama', *Bulletin of the New York Public Library*, 72/7 (1968), 455; H. Michelson, *The Jew in Early English Literature* (New York, 1972), pp. 149–50.

14. William Austin, *Letters from London* (Boston, 1804); David S. Katz, *The Jews in the History of England* (1996), p. 293.

15. See Leo Lowenthal, *Literature, Popular Culture, and Society* (Palo Alto, CA, 1961), p. xi.

16. Cf. Leslie Stephen, *English Literature and Society in the Eighteenth Century* (London, 1963), p. 35.

17. See Simon M. Dubnow, *History of the Jews in Poland and Russia* (Bergenfield, NJ, 2000), pp. 436–7.

18. *Complete Poems* (London, 1928), p. 131.

19. See Lope de Vega, *Plays: One* (London, 2001), pp. 105–75.

20. Jeffrey Herf, *The Jewish Enemy* (Cambridge, MA, 2006), pp. 14–15.

21. See Czeslaw Milosz, 'Dedication', *New and Collected Poems 1931–2001* (New York, 2003), p. 77.

22. *The Arcades Project* (Cambridge, MA, 2002), p. 331.

23. See Umberto Eco, *On Literature* (London, 2006), pp. 8–9, 11.

24. But see James Shapiro, *Shakespeare and the Jews* (New York, 1996), pp. 2, 9, 43, 100–11.

25. See J. Hillis Miller, *On Literature* (London, 2002), pp. 55–7.

26. Todd M. Endelman, *The Jews of Britain 1656–2000* (Berkeley, CA, 2002), p. 206.

27. On Jewish stereotypes, see Edgar Rosenberg, *From Shylock to Svengali* (Stanford, CA, 1960). On literary stereotypes in general, see Nicholas McDowell, 'Early modern stereotypes and the rise of English: Jonson, Dryden, Arnold, Eliot', *Critical Quarterly*, 48/3 (2006), 25–34.

28. See Mario Praz, *The Romantic Agony* (London, 1966), pp. 90–2.

29. But see also my 'Dickens the lawbreaker', *Critical Quarterly*, 40/3 (1998), 57–63.

30. Catherine Gallagher and Stephen Greenblatt, *Practising New Historicism* (Chicago, 2000), p. 17. For an exploration of the relationship between medieval 'urban legends' about Jews and medieval plays on related topics, see Jody Enders, *Death by Drama and Other Medieval Urban Legends* (Chicago, 2002), pp. 118–30.

31. Catherine Gallagher and Stephen Greenblatt, *Practising New Historicism* (Chicago, 2000), p. 7.

32. See Neil R. Davison, ' "The Jew" as Homme/Femme-Fatale: Jewish (Art)-ifice, *Trilby*, and Dreyfus', *Jewish Social Studies*, 8:2/3 (2002), 73, 80. Frank Felsenstein's *Anti-Semitic Stereotypes* (Baltimore, MD, 1995), analyses, without distinguishing the literary from the non-literary, an 'intertextual discourse' (p. 245) hostile to Jews.

33. *Ulysses* (London, 1971), p. 205. 'Chime', in the sense of 'expressing *subordinate* accord' (see *OED*, 2nd edn (Oxford, 1989), vol. III, p. 121, col. 1, 8c), is not quite right.

34. Neil R. Davison, ' "The Jew" as Homme/Femme-Fatale: Jewish (Art)ifice, *Trilby*, and Dreyfus', *Jewish Social Studies*, 8:2/3 (2002), 77, 101–6; Daniel Pick, *Svengali's Web* (New Haven, 2000), pp. 188–93.

35. See Daniel Pick, *Svengali's Web* (New Haven, 2000), p. 129.

36. See Jules Zanger, 'A sympathetic vibration: Dracula and the Jews', *ELT*, 34:1 (1991); Judith Halberstam, 'Technologies of monstrosity: Bram Stoker's *Dracula*' in Glennis Byron (ed.), *Dracula: Contemporary critical essays* (London, 1999); Sarah Gracombe, 'Converting Trilby', *Nineteenth Century Literature*, 58/1 (2003), 95; Daniel Pick, *Svengali's Web* (New Haven, 2000), p. 4. Pick goes further, reading *Trilby* epiphenomenally, 'a reflection of intensely conflicting Victorian attitudes to Jewish–Gentile relations in an age of growing "toleration" ': ibid., p. 15.

37. See Ludwig Lewisohn (ed.), *Among the Nations* (Philadelphia, 1948), pp. 137–222.

38. See Adam Kirsch, *Benjamin Disraeli* (New York, 2008), *passim*.

39. *The Jews' Who's Who* (London, 1920), p. 137.

40. Victor Erlich, *Russian Formalism* (The Hague, 1965), p. 171.

41. David Perkins, 'Literary history and the themes of literature' in Werner Sollors (ed.), *The Return of Thematic Criticism* (Cambridge, MA, 1993), p. 115; Alastair Fowler, 'The two histories' in David Perkins (ed.), *Theoretical Issues in Literary History* (Cambridge, MA, 1991), p. 121.

42. Augustus Jessopp and M. R. James (eds.), *The Life and Miracles of St William of Norwich by Thomas of Monmouth* (Cambridge, 1896), p. x and fn. 2, and p. xiii.

43. And therefore a work of history too. See Paul Meyvaert, 'Bede the scholar' in Gerald Bonner (ed.), *Famulus Christi* (London, 1976), p. 53.

44. W. H. Auden, 'The Guilty Vicarage', *The Dyer's Hand* (London, 1975), p. 154.

45. Augustus Jessopp and M. R. James (eds.), *The Life and Miracles of St William of Norwich by Thomas of Monmouth* (Cambridge, 1896), p. 58.

46. *Ghosts and Other Plays* (London, 1973), p. 21.

47. Gavin Langmuir, *Towards a Definition of Antisemitism* (Berkeley, CA, 1990), p. 209. Joyce 'regarded the English interest in crime in the shape of the detective story as exceptionally ludicrous'. See Frank Budgen, *James Joyce and the Making of 'Ulysses'* (Oxford, 1972), p. 191.

48. See Julian Symons, *Mortal Consequences* (New York, 1977), pp. 8, 178–80.

49. The anti-Semite Douglas Reed appealed to the 'English passion for thrillers' when he asked, 'Whodunit?' 'Who told us, this is the road to peace, and led us straight to war? Who took our savings, destroyed our businesses, and sent our sons and daughters away?' It is 'international bankers', and 'international power-seeking groups'—that is, the Jews. *Lest We Regret* (London, 1943), pp. 86–7, 109.

50. 'The Guilty Vicarage', *The Dyer's Hand* (London, 1975), p. 151.

51. The Welsh Thomas of Monmouth may have come to Norwich in the company of Geoffrey of Monmouth. See Augustus Jessopp and M. R. James (eds.), *The Life and Miracles of St William of Norwich by Thomas of Monmouth*

(Cambridge, 1896), p. ix. Geoffrey finished the final draft of his *History* in 1147 (or somewhat earlier, by 1139, according to David Carpenter, *The Struggle for Mastery* (London, 2004), p. 20); he addressed his *Vita Merlina* to the bishop of Lincoln in 1149. Thomas began writing his account of William of Norwich in 1149/50 and completed it in 1172/3. See Gavin Langmuir, 'Thomas of Monmouth: Detector of ritual murder', *Towards a Definition of Antisemitism* (Berkeley, CA, 1990), p. 209.

52. Roger Sherman Loomis, *The Development of Arthurian Romance* (London, 1963), pp. 29, 35–40.

53. Norman Cantor, *The Sacred Chain* (New York, 1994), pp. 172–3.

54. Roger Sherman Loomis (ed.), *Arthurian Literature in the Middle Ages* (Oxford, 1959), p. xv.

55. See ibid.

56. Robert W. Ackerman, 'English rimed and prose romances' in Roger Sherman Loomis (ed.), *Arthurian Literature in the Middle Ages* (Oxford, 1959), p. 480.

57. Roger Sherman Loomis, *The Development of Arthurian Romance* (London, 1963), p. 13; Theodore Ziolkowski, 'Wagner's *Parsifal* between mystery and mummery; or Race, class, and gender in Bayreuth' in Werner Sollors (ed.), *The Return of Thematic Criticism* (Cambridge, MA, 1993), p. 269; James Simpson, *The Oxford English Literary History*, vol. 2: *1350–1547 Reform and Cultural Revolution* (Oxford, 2002), p. 106.

58. *The Castle of Otranto*, in *Four Gothic Novels* (Oxford, 1994), pp. 11–14.

59. Ibid., 8.

60. G. K. Anderson, 'Popular survivals of the Wandering Jew in England' in Galit Hasan-Rokem and Alan Dundes (eds.), *The Wandering Jew* (Bloomington, IN, 1986), p. 77.

61. See J. A. Giles (trans.), *Roger of Wendover's Flowers of History* (London, 1854), vol. II, pp. 512–14.

62. See G. K. Anderson, *The Legend of the Wandering Jew* (London, 1991), p. 124.

63. Ibid., p. 62.

64. See G. K. Anderson, 'Popular survivals of the Wandering Jew in England' in Galit Hasan-Rokem and Alan Dundes (eds.), *The Wandering Jew* (Bloomington, IN, 1986), p. 85.

65. Ibid., p. 79.

66. See ibid., p. 87.

67. See G. K. Anderson, *The Legend of the Wandering Jew* (London, 1991), pp. 106–27.

68. See Rudyard Kipling, 'The Wandering Jew' and 'Jews in Shushan', *Life's Handicap* (1891).

69. G. K. Anderson, *The Legend of the Wandering Jew* (London, 1991), p. 178.

70. *The Monk*, in *Four Gothic Novels* (Oxford, 1994), pp. 253–70.

71. G. K. Anderson, *The Legend of the Wandering Jew* (London, 1991), p. 179.

72. See Adam Kirsch, *Benjamin Disraeli* (New York, 2008), pp. 124–9.

73. G. K. Anderson, 'Popular survivals of the Wandering Jew in England' in Galit Hasan-Rokem and Alan Dundes (eds.), *The Wandering Jew* (Bloomington, IN, 1986), pp. 77–8, 91–6; Richard I. Cohen, 'The "Wandering Jew" from medieval legend to modern metaphor' in Barbara Kirshenblatt-Gimblett (ed.), *The Art of Being Jewish in Modern Times* (Philadelphia, 2008) p. 165.

74. See G. K. Anderson, *The Legend of the Wandering Jew* (London, 1991), p. 94. According to Anthony S. Wohl, however, 'the Wandering Jew was very much alive as a popular folk legend in the 1870s'. 'Ben Juju' in Todd M. Endelman and Tony Kushner (eds.), *Disraeli's Jewishness* (London, 2002), p. 153.

75. 'A man by pain and thought compelled to live, / Yet loathing life till anger is appeased...' etc. See *Poetical Works*, Thomas Hutchinson and Ernest de Selincourt (eds.) (Oxford, 1971), p. 62.

76. In other hands, the theme of perpetual wandering became the means by which world history could be surveyed. See G. K. Anderson, *The Legend of the Wandering Jew* (London, 1991), pp. 148–50. It was also useful to conclude an account of great wickedness. See Fred Botting, *Gothic* (London, 1996), pp. 107–8. Jewish writers also adopted it for their own, essentially apologetic, purposes. See G. K. Anderson, *The Legend of the Wandering Jew* (London, 1991), p. 299.

77. *Helena* (London, 1963), pp. 148–50.

78. See Miri Rubin, *Corpus Christi* (Cambridge, 1991), pp. 345–6; Anthony Bale, *The Jew in the Medieval Book* (Cambridge, 2006), pp. 27–9.

79. John T. Appleby (ed.), *Chronicon Richardi Divisensis de Tempore Regis Richardi Primi* (London, 1963), pp. 67–8.

80. *Serious Entertainments* (Chicago, 1977), pp. 6, 145–6, 160, 176, 177–8, 204.

81. See Philip Brett, 'Toeing the line', *Musical Times*, 137/1843 (1996), 9–10.

82. Neil C. Hultin, 'The Cruel Jew's Wife', *Folklore*, 99/2 (1988), 197.

83. Robert Darnton, *George Washington's False Teeth* (New York, 2003), pp. 53–4.

84. Thomas Percy, *Reliques of Ancient English Poetry* (New York, n.d.), p. 2.

85. See Miri Rubin, 'The person in the form' in Sarah Kay and Miri Rubin (eds.), *Framing Medieval Bodies* (Manchester, 1994), p. 114.

86. *Reliques of Ancient English Poetry* (New York, n.d.), pp. 54–60.

87. Victor Erlich, *Russian Formalism* (The Hague, 1965), pp. 260–1.

88. Geoffrey Hartman, *Scars of the Spirit* (New York, 2002), p. 4.

89. See, for example, Douglas Reed, *All Our Tomorrows* (London, 1942), p. 318.

90. See Harold Fisch, *The Dual Image* (New York, 1971), p. 23.

91. See Geoffrey Hartman, *A Scholar's Tale* (New York, 2007), p. 60.

92. Miri Rubin, *Gentile Tales* (New Haven, 1999), p. 1.

93. See David Bevington (ed.), *Medieval Drama* (London, 1975), pp. 754–88.

94. *The Croxton Play of the Sacrament*, l. 963, David Bevington (ed.), *Medieval Drama* (London, 1975), pp. 763, 787, 779, 780.

95. See Miri Rubin, *Corpus Christi* (Cambridge, 1991), pp. 122, 126.

96. *The Croxton Play of the Sacrament*, David Bevington (ed.), *Medieval Drama* (London, 1975), p. 757.
97. Jacques Le Goff, *Medieval Civilization* (Oxford, 1990), pp. 157–9.
98. *The Book of Margery Kempe* (London, 1994), pp. 230–3; Douglas Gray, 'Popular religion and late medieval English literature' in Piero Boitani and Anna Torti (eds.), *Religion in the Poetry and Drama of the Late Middle Ages in England* (Cambridge, 1990), p. 25.
99. For other instances, see Jeremy Cohen, *Christ Killers* (Oxford, 2007), pp. 125–35. It is said that Margery was so moved by the thought of Christ's Passion that in church she would often burst into tears and roar with anguish, to the confusion of the preaching friars. On one such occasion, and in response to a priest ('Damsel, Jesus is dead long since'), she retorted, 'His death is as fresh to me as if he had died this same day.' Douglas Gray, *Themes and Images in the Medieval English Religious Lyric* (London, 1972), p. 27.
100. See Douglas Gray, *Themes and Images in the Medieval English Religious Lyric* (London, 1972), p. 81.
101. See ibid., pp. 136–8.
102. See ibid., p. 140.
103. *Piers the Ploughman* (London, 1966), pp. 203–4, 218–20.
104. David Bevington (ed.), *Medieval Drama* (London, 1975), pp. 891, 897.
105. Ibid., pp. 536–52.
106. *Margery Kempe's Dissenting Fictions* (University Park, PA, 1994), p. 70.
107. *Revelations of Divine Love* (London, 1998), pp. 3, 51, 54, 55, 61, 71, 79–80, 105, 112, 147.
108. Ibid., p. 87.
109. Douglas Gray, *Themes and Images in the Medieval English Religious Lyric* (London, 1972), p. 221; Louis L. Martz, *The Poetry of Meditation* (New Haven, CT, 1976), pp. 82–3.
110. *The Complete English Poems*, John Tobin (ed.) (London, 1991), p. 160.
111. 'Divine Meditations', 11, ll. 1–8, *The Complete English Poems*, A. J. Smith (ed.) (London, 1986), p. 313.
112. John Donne, 'The Progress of the Soul', l. 77, ibid., p. 179.
113. For example: Bk. 1, Canto 1.2, Edmund Spenser, *The Faerie Queen*, Thomas P. Roche, Jr (ed.) (London, 1987), p. 41; John Donne, 'Crucifying' and 'The Cross', *The Complete English Poems*, A. J. Smith (ed.) (London, 1986), pp. 307–8, 326–7; John Milton, 'The Passion' and 'Upon the Circumcision', *The Complete Poems*, John Leonard (ed.) (London, 1998), pp. 12–16; Richard Crashaw, 'The Office of the Holy Cross' and 'On the Wounds of Our Crucified Lord', Edward Hutton (ed.), *The English Poems of Richard Crashaw* (London, 1901), pp. 19–31, 35. And note: 'After the Reformation, there is little innovation in the tradition of the Passion and Crucifixion. References occur throughout English literature, but most are conventional reflections...' Esther Quinn and John R. Donahue, 'Passion, Cross' in David Lyle Jeffrey

(ed.), *A Dictionary of Biblical Tradition in English Literature* (Grand Rapids, MI, 1992), p. 585.

114. As in Henry Vaughan's devotional handbook, *The Mount of Olives* (1652), for example: 'Call to mind his wearisome journeys, continual afflictions, the malice and scorn he underwent, the persecutions and reproaches laid upon him, his strong cries and tears in the days of his flesh, his spiritual agony and sweating of blood, with the implacable fury of his enemies, and his own unspeakable humility...' See Louis L. Martz, *The Poetry of Meditation* (New Haven, CT, 1976), pp. 85, 92–4.

115. 'In Excelsis', *Complete Poems* (London, 1928), p. 122.

116. There were seven editions in as many months, and the one-volume edition, which appeared in February 1894, sold 10,000 copies in one week. Brian Masters, *Now Barabbas Was A Rotter* (London, 1978), p. 130.

117. *Barabbas* (London, 1894), pp. 55, 57, 77, 83, 91, 108, 230, 238, 248, 267, 410, 411.

118. *The Man Born To Be King* (London, 1946), pp. 22, 112, 113, 267, 281, 286, 302.

119. David Bevington (ed.), *Medieval Drama* (London, 1975), p. 557.

120. See David S. Katz, *The Jews in the History of England 1485–1850* (Oxford, 1996), p. 81.

121. In John Webster's *The Devil's Law Case* (1623), the Neapolitan merchant Romelio disguises himself as a Jewish doctor in order to kill his enemy. He tells the audience that he is thereby 'play[ing] with his own shadow'. He will be 'a rare Italianated Jew', capable of poisoning a friend, coining money, betraying a town to the Turk, and eating a politician, digesting him 'to nothing but pure blood'. See Edgar Rosenberg, 'The Jew in Western drama', *Bulletin of the New York Public Library*, 72/7 (1968), 450–1.

122. Sigmund Freud, 'The theme of the three caskets', *On Creativity and the Unconscious* (New York, 1958), p. 63.

123. See R. Mohrlang, 'Love' in Gerald F. Hawthorne, Ralph P. Martin, and Daniel G. Reid (eds.), *Dictionary of Paul and His Letters* (Leicester, 1993), pp. 575–8.

124. See Jonathan Bate (ed.), *The Romantics on Shakespeare* (London, 1992), p. 457.

125. Jonathan Bate, *The Genius of Shakespeare* (London, 1997), p. 159. But contrast Northrop Frye, *The Myth of Deliverance* (Toronto, 1983), p. 26.

126. 'Our sympathies are repulsed and defeated in all directions', wrote Hazlitt. The play, wrote Coleridge, 'baffles the strong indignant claims of justice'. See Jonathan Bate (ed.), *The Romantics on Shakespeare* (London, 1992), p. 453.

127. See ibid., p. 456.

128. Ibid., p. 457.

129. See David Seymour, 'Letter from Shylock: Reflections on my case (authorship attributed to Shylock "the Jew")', *Law and Critique*, 8/2 (1997), 215–22.

130. *Samson Agonistes* (ll. 102–5), in Stephen Orgel and Jonathan Goldberg (eds.), *John Milton* (Oxford, 1991), p. 675.

131. See Jonathan Bate (ed.), *The Romantics on Shakespeare* (London, 1992), pp. 166, 181–2, 188, 266, 282, 460.

132. Jonathan Bate, *The Genius of Shakespeare* (London, 1997), pp. 159, 202–3, 241, 297, 302, 315, 327–40.

133. See Jonathan Bate (ed.), *The Romantics on Shakespeare* (London, 1992), pp. 282, 287.

134. See ibid., p. 454.

135. See Brian Vickers (ed.), *Shakespeare* (London, 1981), vol. 6, pp. 30–1, 325.

136. *Anna Karenina* (London, 2006), p. 768.

137. See Milan Kundera, *The Curtain* (New York, 2007), pp. 152–3.

138. See 'Hysterical phantasies and their relation to bisexuality', *On Psychopathology* (London, 1979), p. 92; J. Laplanche and J.-B. Pontalis, *The Language of Psychoanalysis* (London, 1973), p. 76.

139. See Jonathan Bate (ed.), *The Romantics on Shakespeare* (London, 1992), pp. 282–3.

140. See Nadia Valman, *The Jewess in Nineteenth Century British Culture* (Cambridge, 2007), p. 2 ('From the medieval ballad of the Jew's daughter ... to Shakespeare's uncertain apostate Jessica, the Jewess held a marginal place in English literary history. In the nineteenth century, however, she became a literary preoccupation').

141. See Daniel Pick, *Faces of Degeneration* (Cambridge, 1989), p. 94.

142. Miri Rubin, *Gentile Tales* (New Haven, 1999), p. 71; John Gross, *Shylock* (London, 1992), pp. 58–9.

143. Ibid., pp. 8–20; Jeremy Cohen, *Christ Killers* (Oxford, 2007), pp. 103–6.

144. See Jonathan Bate (ed.), *The Romantics on Shakespeare* (London, 1992), p. 458.

145. Stephen Graham, *Russia in Division* (London, 1925), p. 97.

146. H. R. Woudhuysen (ed.), *Samuel Johnson on Shakespeare* (London, 1989), p. 125.

147. *The Ring and the Book* (London, 1981), Book VI, ll. 1908–14, p. 317.

148. Northrop Frye, *The Myth of Deliverance* (Toronto, 1983), p. 26.

149. 'Comedy' in Wylie Sypher (ed.), *Comedy* (New York, 1956), p. 4; Erich Segal, *The Death of Comedy* (Cambridge, MA, 2001), p. 25.

150. Northrop Frye, *Anatomy of Criticism* (Princeton, NJ, 1971), pp. 172, 175–6.

151. *Totem and Taboo* (London, 1960), p. 140.

152. *Shylock is Shakespeare* (Chicago, 2006), p. 1.

153. See G. A. Cranfield, 'The "London Evening-Post" and the Jew Bill of 1753', *Historical Journal*, 8/1 (1965), 22; James Shapiro, *Shakespeare and the Jews* (New York, 1996), pp. 213–24.

154. 'I believe I am quoting Shakespeare, who would be banned from the BBC if he lived today; was he not bawdy in his talk, and an anti-Semite?' Douglas Reed, *All Our Tomorrows* (London, 1942), p. 130.

155. See Frank Felsenstein, *Anti-Semitic Stereotypes* (Baltimore, MD, 1995), pp. 78–85.

156. Paul Salzman (ed.), *An Anthology of Elizabethan Prose Fiction* (Oxford, 1998), pp. 288–99; Edgar Rosenberg, 'The Jew in Western drama', *Bulletin of the New York Public Library*, 72/7 (1968), 450–5.

157. *Roxana* (London, 1987), pp. 150–60.

158. Ibid., p. 361.

159. Ibid., p. 379.

160. See Pat Rogers, 'Nameless names: Pope, Curll and the uses of anonymity', *New Literary History*, 33/2 (2002).

161. *Works* (London, 1824), vol. 7, pp. 270–6.

162. David Biale, *Blood and Belief* (Berkeley, CA, 2007), p. 99.

163. See Michael Mack, *German Idealism and the Jew* (Chicago, 2003), p. 12.

164. *The Ring and the Book* (London, 1981), Book XII, ll. 838–40, pp. 627–8.

165. 'Prologue', *The Jew* (London, 1794).

166. *The Jew* (London, 1794), pp. 6–7, 13, 73.

167. H. R. S. van der Veen, *Jewish Characters in Eighteenth Century English Fiction and Drama* (Groningen, 1935), pp. 229–30.

168. John Sutherland, *Stephen Spender* (London, 2005), p. 17.

169. *Harrington* (Toronto, ON, 2004), pp. 70, 290.

170. Ibid., p. 291; Catherine Gallagher, *Nobody's Story* (Berkeley, CA, 1995), p. 311.

171. *The Absentee* (London, 1999), pp. 48–52.

172. *Harrington* (Toronto, ON, 2004), p. 17; Catherine Gallagher, *Nobody's Story* (Berkeley, CA, 1995), p. 311.

173. *Ivanhoe* (London, 1986), pp. 8, 165.

174. Ibid., p. 512.

175. Jacques Le Goff, *My Quest for the Middle Ages* (Edinburgh, 2003), p. 2.

176. *Ivanhoe* (London, 1986), pp. 49–51, 69–70, 80, 225, 226.

177. Ibid., pp. 79, 82.

178. Anthony Trollope, *Nina Balatka* (Oxford, 1991), pp. 82–3.

179. *The Rock* (London, 1934), p. 44; Anthony Julius, *T. S. Eliot, Anti-Semitism, and Literary Form*, 2nd edn (London, 2003), pp. 196–7.

180. *Trial of a Judge* (London, 1938), pp. 16–17, 18; John Sutherland, *Stephen Spender* (London, 2005), pp. 234–6.

181. *Trial of a Judge* (London, 1938), pp. 19, 28, 93.

182. *Geneva* (London, 1946), p. 72.

183. See my *T. S. Eliot, Anti-Semitism, and Literary Form*, 2nd edn (London, 2003), pp. 81–5.

184. *The Berlin Novels* (London, 1999), pp. 74, 226, 254–5, 279, 304, 344, 381–2, 409, 431–2, 435, 455, 460, 470, 485.

185. *The Life of Charles Dickens* (London, 1969), vol. 1, p. 90.

186. F. R. and Q. D. Leavis, *Dickens the Novelist* (London, 1994), p. 153.

187. *Practising New Historicism* (Chicago, 2000), pp. 176–8.

188. *Oliver Twist* (New York, 1993), p. 139.

189. Ibid., p. 131.

190. Jeannie Duckworth, *Fagin's Children* (London, 2002), p. 27.

191. Norman Cohn, 'The myth of the Jewish world-conspiracy', *Commentary*, 41/6 (1966), 39.

192. Daniel Pick, *Svengali's Web* (New Haven, 2000), pp. 136–7.

193. *Oliver Twist* (New York, 1993), p. 91.

194. Ibid., p. 132.

195. Ibid., p. 311.

196. Ibid., pp. 73, 125, 231.

197. Ibid., p. 351.

198. See John Forster, *The Life of Charles Dickens* (London, 1969), vol. 1, pp. 79, 87.

199. William Empson, 'The symbolism of Dickens', and John Bayley, 'Oliver Twist: "Things as they really are"' both in John Gross and Gabriel Pearson (eds.), *Dickens and the Twentieth Century* (London, 1962), pp. 13, 55; John R. Reed, *Dickens and Thackeray* (Athens, OH, 1995), pp. 85–6; Peter Ackroyd, *Introduction to Dickens* (London, 1991), p. 10.

200. *The Melodramatic Imagination* (New Haven, CT, 1995), pp. viii–ix, 5, 11–12, 25, 28, 32, 38, 39, 43, 56, 119, 121–2, 124, 168, 206.

201. See Adena Rosmarin, *The Power of Genre* (Minneapolis, MN, 1985), p. 106.

202. *Chesterton on Dickens* (London, 1992), pp. 3, 10–11, 38; Deborah Heller, 'The outcast as villain and victim' in Derek Cohen and Deborah Heller (eds.), *Jewish Presences in English Literature* (Montreal, 1990), p. 49.

203. See Miri Rubin, *Gentile Tales* (New Haven, 1999), pp. 24–6.

204. *Our Mutual Friend* (London, 1997), p. 428.

205. John Forster, *The Life of Charles Dickens* (London, 1969), vol. 2, p. 291.

206. *Our Mutual Friend* (London, 1997), pp. 429, 712.

207. See Fred Kaplan, *Dickens* (London, 1989), pp. 472–3.

208. John O'Connor, *Shakespearean Afterlives* (Cambridge, 2005), pp. 95–147; John Gross, *Shylock* (London, 1992), pp. 164, 197.

209. A 2005 Labour Party election poster represented the then leader of the Conservative Party, the Jewish Michael Howard, as a Fagin-type character, swinging a gold watch, and boasting, 'I can spend the same money twice.' See Toby Helm, 'Labour drops flying pigs and "Fagin" posters', *Daily Telegraph*, 1 February 2005.

210. See S. S. Prawer, *Israel at Vanity Fair* (Leiden, 1992), pp. 409, 424.

211. *The Way We Live Now* (Oxford, 1991), p. 68.

212. *The Prime Minister* (London, 2004), pp. 35, 39, 126, 136, 259, 261, 386, 404, 424, 477. On Jews looking like Portuguese, see Robert Southey *Letters from England* (Gloucester, 1984), p. 396.

213. J. W. Cross, *George Eliot's Life* (London, n.d.), p. 555; Rosemary Ashton, *George Eliot* (London, 1997), p. 350.

214. On the colonialist aspect of Deronda's project, see Kenneth M. Newton, 'Second sight: Is Edward Said right about Daniel Deronda?', *TLS*, 9 May 2008, pp. 14–15.

215. Alexander Welsh, 'The later novels' in George Levine (ed.), *The Cambridge Companion to George Eliot* (Cambridge, 2001), p. 69; Kathryn Hughes, *George Eliot* (London, 1999), p. 448.

216. David Carroll (ed.), *George Eliot* (London, 1971), p. 383; Laurence Lerner, 'Daniel Deronda: George Eliot's struggle with realism' in Alice Shalvi (ed.), *Daniel Deronda* (Jerusalem, 1976), pp. 89–109.

217. Irene Tucker, *A Probable State* (Chicago, 2000), p. 31.

218. *Daniel Deronda* (Oxford, 1998), p. 4.

219. See H. M. Daleski, 'Owning and disowning' in Alice Shalvi (ed.), *Daniel Deronda* (Jerusalem, 1976).

220. *Daniel Deronda* (Oxford, 1998), p. 462.

221. See Barry Qualls, 'George Eliot and religion' in George Levine (ed.), *The Cambridge Companion to George Eliot* (Cambridge, 2001), p. 133.

222. Irene Tucker, *A Probable State* (Chicago, 2000), p. 115.

223. See *Selected Critical Writings* (Oxford, 2000), pp. 317–18.

224. Ibid., p. 113; Bernard Semmel, *George Eliot and the Politics of National Inheritance* (Oxford, 1994), pp. 4, 17–19, 28. 'Scott's Rebecca' is mentioned in *Daniel Deronda* (Oxford, 1998), p. 305.

225. *Daniel Deronda* (Oxford, 1998), p. 310. See also the list of anti-Semitic misconceptions at p. 452.

226. Ibid., p. 14. Cf. her reference to Mirah as a 'little Jewess': ibid., p. 502.

227. Ibid., p. 309.

228. Shmuel Werses, 'The Jewish reception of *Daniel Deronda*' in Alice Shalvi (ed.), *Daniel Deronda* (Jerusalem, 1976), p. 16.

229. David Kaufmann, *George Eliot and Judaism* (London, 1877), p. 61.

230. *Daniel Deronda* (Oxford, 1998), pp. 176, 306.

231. Sonja A. Sackman, 'Culture and subcultures', *Administrative Science Quarterly*, 37 (1992).

232. *Felix Holt* (London, 1995), pp. 29–31, 401.

233. See Alfred Schutz, 'The Stranger', *Collected Papers II* (The Hague, 1976), p. 95.

234. *Ivanhoe* (London, 1986), pp. 226, 295, 300, 324. On the cliché of the 'gloomy, obscurantist Middle Ages', see Jacques Le Goff, *My Quest for the Middle Ages* (Edinburgh, 2003), p. 4.

235. *Ivanhoe* (London, 1986), p. 69.

236. See *S/Z* (New York, 1974), pp. 19–20, 97, 100, 160, 185.

237. See Frank Kermode, *Essays on Fiction 1971–1982* (London, 1983), p. 121.

238. Lewes responded to Blackwood: 'You are surprised at her knowledge of the Jews? But only learned Rabbis are so profoundly versed in Jewish history and literature as she is.' Rosemary Ashton, *George Eliot* (London, 1997), p. 355. Cf. '*Daniel Deronda* amazed [Freud] by its knowledge of Jewish intimate ways that "we speak of only among ourselves".' Ernest Jones, *The Life and Work of Sigmund Freud* (London, 1974), p. 166.

239. On Eliot's friendship with Emanuel Deutsch (1829–1873), see Rosemary Ashton, *George Eliot* (London, 1997), pp. 304, 335. On Eliot's friendship with David Mocatta, see Jane Irwin (ed.), *George Eliot's 'Daniel Deronda' Notebooks* (Cambridge, 1996), p. xxxi.

240. See Jane Irwin (ed.), *George Eliot's 'Daniel Deronda' Notebooks* (Cambridge, 1996).

241. *Daniel Deronda* (Oxford, 1998), p. 177.

242. *George Eliot and Judaism* (London, 1877), pp. 76, 81–2, 90.

243. *Daniel Deronda* (Oxford, 1998), p. 306.

244. Ibid., p. 688.

245. See William Baker, *George Eliot and Judaism* (Salzburg, 1975), p. 3.

246. See David Carroll (ed.), *George Eliot* (London, 1971), pp. 368, 371, 374, 377, 438.

247. See ibid., pp. 364–5.

248. J. W. Cross, *George Eliot's Life* (London, n.d.), p. 563.

249. Matthijs van Boxsel, *The Encyclopedia of Stupidity* (London, 2003), p. 109.

250. *Daniel Deronda* (Oxford, 1998), p. 194.

251. *Middlemarch* (Oxford, 1998), p. 182.

252. See David Carroll (ed.), *George Eliot* (London, 1971), pp. 404–5.

253. *Daniel Deronda* (Oxford, 1998), pp. 37, 39, 40.

254. Ibid., p. 35.

255. Ibid., p. 155.

256. *Bouvard et Pécuchet* (Paris, 1979), p. 485.

257. See Julian Barnes, *Flaubert's Parrot* (London, 1992), pp. 96, 127.

258. Milan Kundera, *The Curtain* (New York, 2007), p. 127.

259. *Impressions of Theophrastus Such* (London, 1995), p. 135.

260. Ibid., pp. 144, 148, 152.

261. See Jonathan Culler, *Flaubert* (London, 1974), pp. 157–85.

262. *Selected Literary Criticism* (London, 1968), p. 187.

263. Paul Lawrence Rose, *German Question/Jewish Question* (Princeton, NJ, 1990), p. 3.

264. Michael N. Dobkowski, *The Tarnished Dream* (Westport, CT, 1979), pp. 22–3.

265. Jean Radford, 'The woman and the Jew' in Bryan Cheyette and Laura Marcus (eds.), *Modernity, Culture and 'the Jew'* (Oxford, 1998), p. 95. Richardson somewhat modified her position in her later novels. See Maren Linett, 'The wrong material', *Journal of Modern Literature* 23/2 (1999).

266. 'But there were no hooked noses; no one in the least like Shylock. What *were* Jews? How did [Shatov] know the room was full of them?' *Deadlock*, *Pilgrimage 3* (London, 1979), p. 127.

267. Ibid., p. 93, 151.

268. Ibid., p. 193.

269. Jean Radford, 'The woman and the Jew' in Bryan Cheyette and Laura Marcus (eds.), *Modernity, Culture and 'the Jew'* (Oxford, 1998), pp. 99, 101.

270. *The Scapegoat* (London, n.d.), pp. 123, 147, 167, 212. Nevertheless, wrote the *Illustrated London News* in the year following publication, the novel was 'hailed by the most intelligent and influential members of the respectable Jewish community in London as a real service to the cause of justice and mercy'. See Anne and Roger Cowen, *Victorian Jews through British Eyes* (Oxford, 1986), p. 132.

271. Rudyard Kipling, *Life's Handicap* (London, 1987), pp. 260-3.

272. *Trilby* (Oxford, 1998), p. 298.

273. Ibid., pp. 27, 254.

274. See Sarah Gracombe, 'Converting Trilby', *Nineteenth Century Literature*, 58/1 (2003), 80.

275. Nina Auerbach, *Woman and the Demon* (Cambridge, MA, 1982), p. 18.

276. S. S. Prawer, *Israel at Vanity Fair* (Leiden, 1992), pp. 112-14; R. C. McCail, 'The genesis of Du Maurier's *Trilby*', *Forum of Modern Languages Studies*, 13 (1977), 12-15; David Lodge, *Author, Author* (London, 2005), pp. 222-3.

277. *The Collected Essays, Journalism and Letters* (London, 1968), vol. 4, p. 292.

278. *Trilby* (Oxford, 1998), p. 11.

279. Ibid., p. 87.

280. Ibid., p. 91.

281. Ibid., pp. 92-3.

282. Ibid., p. 299, and see Daniel Pick, *Svengali's Web* (New Haven, 2000), p. 23.

283. George Taylor, 'Svengali: Mesmerist and aesthete' in Richard Foulkes (ed.), *British Theatre in the 1890s* (Cambridge, 1992), p. 101.

284. *Trilby* (Oxford, 1998), pp. 298-9.

285. Ibid., pp. 16, 211, 255-6, 258, 265, 299; Daniel Pick, *Svengali's Web* (New Haven, 2000), pp. 148-51; Edmund Wilson, *A Piece of My Mind* (London, 1957), pp. 78-9;

286. See Ken Gelder, *Reading the Vampire* (London, 1994), pp. 25-7, 30; Mario Praz, *The Romantic Agony* (London, 1966), pp. 95-7; Clive Leatherdale, *Dracula* (London, 1985), pp. 47-54.

287. *Nicholas Nickleby* (London, 2003), p. 172.

288. *Dracula* (Oxford, 1996), p. 80.

289. Ibid., pp. 39, 45, 177-8, 190, 214, 239, 306. Stoker dismissed the Wandering Jew as a mere legend. See *Famous Impostors* (1910), pp. 107-20.

290. David Biale, *Blood and Belief* (Berkeley, CA, 2007), pp. 129, 172. Strack noted the widespread superstition concerning vampires, especially in Prussia. *The Jew and Human Sacrifice* (London, 1909), p. 96.

291. See David Biale, *Blood and Belief* (Berkeley, CA, 2007), p. 144. The vampire motif recurs in late twentieth-century anti-Semitism: Michael Billig, *Fascists* (London, 1978), p. 181.

292. George du Maurier, *Trilby* (Oxford, 1998), p. vii-viii; L. Edward Purcell, 'Trilby and Trilby-Mania', *Journal of Popular Culture*, 11/1 (1977), 62-76; Daniel Pick, *Svengali's Web* (New Haven, 2000), p. 2; Clive Leatherdale, *Dracula* (London, 1985), p. 11.

293. Ken Gelder, *Reading the Vampire* (London, 1994), pp. 13–14; Nina Auerbach, *Woman and the Demon* (Cambridge, MA, 1982), p. 16.

294. *Trilby* (Oxford, 1998), p. 282.

295. Ibid., pp. 73, 92.

296. Ibid., p. 7.

297. Jonathan H. Grossman, 'The mythic Svengali: Anti-aestheticism in *Trilby*', *Studies in the Novel*, 28/ 4 (1996), 533; See Sarah Gracombe, 'Converting Trilby: Du Maurier on Englishness, Jewishness, and culture', *Nineteenth Century Literature*, 58/1 (2003), 92–4.

298. *Dracula* (Oxford, 1996), pp. 20, 32, 50, 51, 349; Clive Leatherdale, *Dracula* (London, 1985), p. 32; William Thomas McBride, 'Dracula and Mephistopheles: Shyster Vampires', *Literature Film Quarterly*, 18/2 (1990), 116–17.

299. See Stephen D. Arata, 'The Occidental tourist: *Dracula* and the anxiety of reverse colonisation' in Glennis Byron (ed.), *Dracula: Contemporary critical essays* (London, 1999), p. 123; *Dracula* (Oxford, 1996), p. 28.

300. *Dracula* (Oxford, 1996), p. 349; Daniel Pick, *Faces of Degeneration* (Cambridge, 1989), p. 73.

301. Judith Halberstam, 'Technologies of monstrosity' in Glennis Byron (ed.), *Dracula* (London, 1999), pp. 178, 183.

302. Ibid., p. 178.

303. *Tono-Bungay* (London, 2005), p. 147.

304. *Experiment in Autobiography* (London, 1934), vol. 1, p. 53.

305. *Tono-Bungay* (London, 2005), pp. 332, 335, 336.

306. Ibid., pp. 16, 66.

307. Ibid., p. 10.

308. London is the 'capital of a kingdom of Bladesovers . . . parasitically occupied, insidiously replaced by alien, unsympathetic and irresponsible elements . . .' See ibid., pp. 100–3.

309. 'In those days I had ideas about Aryans extraordinarily like Mr. Hitler's. The more I hear of him the more I am convinced that his mind is almost the twin of my thirteen year old mind in 1879; but heard through a megaphone and— implemented. . . . [The Aryans'] ultimate triumphs everywhere squared accounts with the Jews, against which people I had a subconscious dissatisfaction because of their disproportionate share of holy writ. . . . But unlike Hitler I had no feelings about the contemporary Jew.' This neutrality was abandoned by the time Wells reached his mid-20s. He writes of a Jewish friend, 'We argued endlessly about the Jewish question, upon which he sought continually to enlighten me. But I have always refused to be enlightened and sympathetic about the Jewish question. From my cosmopolitan standpoint it is a question that ought not to exist.' *Experiment in Autobiography* (London, 1934), vol. 1, pp. 100, 353.

310. *Raffles* (London, 2003), pp. xxi, xxxv–xxxvi, xli–xlii.

311. Julian Symons, *Mortal Consequences* (New York, 1977), p. 89.

312. *Raffles: The amateur cracksman* (London, 2003), pp. 7–8.
313. ' "We are adventurers," said Raffles gravely.' 'Nine Points of the Law', *Raffles: The amateur cracksman* (London, 2003), p. 89.
314. Ibid., pp. 23–4.
315. Ibid., pp. 26, 37.
316. Derek Attridge, 'Introduction' in Derek Attridge (ed.), *James Joyce's Ulysses* (Oxford, 2004), p. 3; Hugh Kenner, *Joyce's Voices* (Rochester, NY, 2007), p. xii.
317. See Declan Kiberd, *Inventing Ireland* (London, 1996), p. 327.
318. Wyndham Lewis, *Time and Western Man* (Santa Rose, CA, 1993), p. 74.
319. *Ulysses* (London, 1971), pp. 602–3.
320. Ibid., p. 637.
321. Hugh Kenner, *Joyce's Voices* (Rochester, NY, 2007), p. 61.
322. Frank Budgen, *James Joyce and the Making of 'Ulysses'* (Oxford, 1972), p. 15.
323. Forrest Read (ed.), *Pound/Joyce* (New York, 1970), p. 197.
324. Declan Kiberd, *Inventing Ireland* (London, 1996), p. 342.
325. Derek Attridge, 'Introduction' in Derek Attridge (ed.), *James Joyce's Ulysses* (Oxford, 2004), p. 3.
326. *Ivanhoe* (London, 1986), p. 34.
327. 'Royal Hibernian Academy "Ecce Homo" ' (1899), in James Joyce, *The Critical Writings*, Ellsworthy Mason and Richard Ellmann (eds.) (New York, 1964), p. 34.
328. Edward George Bulwer-Lytton, *Leila* (Holicong, PA, n.d.), pp. 9, 33, 39–44, 153, 165, 171, 176, 236.
329. Anthony Trollope, *The Way We Live Now* (Oxford, 1991), p. 31.
330. John Sutherland, 'Is Melmotte Jewish?', *Is Heathcliff a Murderer?* (Oxford, 1996), p. 162; Nadia Valman, *The Jewess in Nineteenth Century British Culture* (Cambridge, 2007), pp. 137–8.
331. Michael Ragussis, *Figures of Conversion* (London, 1995), p. 242.
332. David Carroll (ed.), *George Eliot* (London, 1971), p. 420. '[Theodora:] I have never disliked the Jews, as some people do; I am not like Pulcheria, who sees a Jew in every bush. I wish there were one; I would cultivate shrubbery! I have known too many clever and charming Jews; I have known none that were not clever' (ibid., p. 423).
333. See Declan Kiberd's note on 'Penelope', *Ulysses* (London, 1992), p. 1183.
334. *Daniel Deronda* (Oxford, 1998), p. 91.
335. Forrest Read (ed.), *Pound/Joyce* (New York, 1970), pp. 139, 145.
336. See Gillian Beer, *The Romance* (London, 1970), p. 77.
337. Maurice Samuel, 'Bloom of Bloomusalem', *The Reflex*, February 1929, p. 12.
338. *Ulysses* (London, 1971), p. 40.
339. Ibid., p. 336.
340. Forrest Read (ed.), *Pound/Joyce* (New York, 1970), p. 194.
341. See Declan Kiberd's note on 'Penelope', *Ulysses* (London, 1992), p. 1184.

342. See Wyndham Lewis, *Time and Western Man* (Santa Rose, CA, 1993), pp. 94, 98–9 ('[Joyce] has certainly contributed nothing to the literature of the Jew').

343. See S. L. Goldberg, *The Classical Temper* (London, 1961), p. 145.

344. Cheryl Herr, 'Art and life, nature and culture', in Derek Attridge (ed.), *James Joyce's Ulysses* (Oxford, 2004), p. 67.

345. Steven Connor, *Theory and Cultural Value* (Oxford, 1971), p. 203.

346. See Marilyn Reizbaum, 'Weininger and the Bloom of Jewish self-hatred in Joyce's *Ulysses*' in Nancy A. Harrowitz and Barbara Hyams (eds.), *Jews and Gender* (Philadelphia, 1995).

347. 'Joyce: The (r)use of writing' in Derek Attridge and Daniel Ferrer (eds.), *Post-Structuralist Joyce* (Cambridge, 1984), pp. 15–17. Cf.: 'Shaw was right to talk of the negativity of Ulysses in relation to its treatment of the human subject.' Stephen Heath, 'Ambiviolences' in Derek Attridge and Daniel Ferrer (eds.), *Post-Structuralist Joyce* (Cambridge, 1984), p. 38.

348. *Ulysses* (London, 1971), p. 213.

349. André Topia, 'The matrix and the echo: Intertextuality in *Ulysses*' in Derek Attridge and Daniel Ferrer (eds.), *Post-Structuralist Joyce* (Cambridge, 1984), p. 104.

350. 'The nothingness of personality', *The Total Library* (London, 1999), pp. 3, 5.

351. Stephen Heath, 'Ambiviolences' in Derek Attridge and Daniel Ferrer (eds.), *Post-Structuralist Joyce* (Cambridge, 1984), p. 33.

352. Milan Kundera, *The Curtain* (New York, 2007), p. 167.

353. See Jeremy Adler, *Franz Kafka* (London, 2001), p. 18.

354. Wyndham Lewis, *Time and Western Man* (Santa Rose, CA, 1993), pp. 73–110.

355. *Ulysses*, proposed Ezra Pound, is a '*sottisier gigantesque*', and the product of Joyce's research into '*l'homme type, la généralisation la plus général*'. Forrest Read (ed.), *Pound/Joyce* (New York, 1970), p. 205.

356. *Ulysses* (London, 1971), p. 336.

357. *Daniel Deronda* (Oxford, 1998), p. 323.

358. Ibid., p. 326.

359. Ibid., p. 337.

360. Marvin Magalaner, 'The anti-Semitic Limerick incidents and Joyce's "Bloomsday"', *PMLA*, 68/5 (1953), 1220.

361. *Ulysses* (London, 1971), p. 82.

362. Edmund Wilson, *Axel's Castle* (London, 1974), p. 178.

363. *Ulysses* (London, 1971), p. 302.

364. Maurice Samuel, 'Bloom of Bloomusalem', *The Reflex*, February 1929, p. 14.

365. *The Classical Temper* (London, 1961), pp. 124, 173, 258, 277.

366. See Nikos Stangos, 'How could speech exhaust the meaning of speech?', *Pure Reason* (London, 2007), p. 30.

367. *Ulysses* (London, 1971), p. 304. Cf.: 'Of course, Mr. Bloom proceeded to stipulate, you must look at both sides of the question. It is hard to lay down any hard and fast rules as to right and wrong...' Ibid., p. 563.

368. Leo Bersani, 'Against *Ulysses*' in Derek Attridge (ed.), *James Joyce's Ulysses: A casebook* (Oxford, 2004), p. 210.

369. See Ira B. Nadel, *Joyce and the Jews* (London, 1989), pp. 135–6.

370. Richard Ellmann (ed.), *Selected Letters of James Joyce* (London, 1975), p. 138, and fn. 1.

371. *Ulysses* (London, 1971), p. 27.

372. Ibid., pp. 39–40.

373. See Thomas Goodwin, 'Of Christ the mediator', *Works* (London, 1863), vol. 5, p. 427.

374. Natania Rosenfeld, 'James Joyce's womanly wandering Jew' in Nancy A. Harrowitz and Barbara Hyams (eds.), *Jews and Gender* (Philadelphia, 1995), p. 221.

375. *Ulysses* (London, 1971), p. 302.

376. Ibid., p. 464.

377. Ibid., pp. 329–41. The list of names is a little eccentric. See Robert Martin Adams, *Surface and Symbol* (New York, 1967), pp. 197–8.

378. *Ulysses* (London, 1971), pp. 563–4.

379. Ibid., p. 613.

380. See Steven Connor, *Theory and Cultural Value* (Oxford, 1971), p. 219.

381. Milan Kundera, *The Curtain* (New York, 2007), p. 161.

382. Daphne du Maurier, *The Progress of Julius* (London, 1975), p. 263.

383. *Experience* (London, 2001), pp. 93, 229, 309. Kingsley, responding to a critical review in the *New York Times*, wrote to Philip Larkin, 'Boy, they really believe lit. makes statements.' Zachary Leader (ed.), *The Letters of Kingsley Amis* (London, 2000), p. 1004.

384. Zachary Leader (ed.), *The Letters of Kingsley Amis* (London, 2000), p. 28.

385. Martin Amis, *Experience* (London, 2001), p. 178.

386. 'Political Verse', *Writing to the Moment* (London, 1996), p. 105.

387. The 'al Dura affair' has become a scandal. See Anne-Elisabeth Moutet, 'L'Affaire Enderlin', *Weekly Standard*, 7 July 2008.

388. *Independent*, 2 October 2000.

389. See Martin Gilbert, *The Holocaust* (London, 1987), pp. 187–8.

390. Roderick Stackelberg and Sally A. Winkle, *The Nazi Germany Sourcebook* (London, 2002), p. 370.

391. J. S. McClelland (ed.), *The French Right* (London, 1970), p. 111; Sander L. Gilman, *Jewish Self-Hatred* (Baltimore, MD, 1986), p. 60.

392. Compare: 'The Zionist objective was (and is)...To persuade "dumb goy" Parliamentary politicians that there is a need for even more repressive race relations legislation which would have the effect... of rendering public criticism of Zionist Jewry a criminal offence.' Martin Webster, 'Media Zionists show their hand', *Spearhead*, May 1976: Henri Stellman, 'The ideologies of Anti-Zionism: 1881 to the present day', University of London PhD, 1982. And cf.: 'our alien invaders regard the native English as belonging

to a vastly inferior breed'. Joseph Banister, *England under the Jews* (London, 1907), p. 40.

393. Cf. Sander L. Gilman, *Jewish Self-Hatred* (Baltimore, MD, 1986), p. 242.

394. Augustus Jessopp and M. R. James (eds.), *The Life and Miracles of St William of Norwich by Thomas of Monmouth* (Cambridge, 1896), pp. 32–3.

395. See Joseph Jacobs (ed.), *The Jews of Angevin England* (London, 1893), p. 19.

396. Pierre Birnbaum, *Anti-Semitism in France* (Oxford, 1992), p. 112.

397. 'Shooting Niagara: And after?', *Critical and Miscellaneous Essays* (London, n.d.), vol. 7, p. 209.

398. Sean O'Hagan, 'The sound and the fury', *Observer*, 20 January 2002.

399. *A Global Report from the Coalition to Stop the Use of Child Soldiers* (London, 2001), pp. 287–90; David Horovitz, *Still Life with Bombers: Israel in the age of terrorism* (New York, 2004), pp. 10–11; Barbara Victor, *Army of Roses* (London, 2004), p. 267.

400. Shragai Nadav, 'The roots of Palestinian hatred', *Ha'aretz*, 13 May 2001, and 'Shin Bet nabs killer of baby Shalhevet Pas', *Ha'aretz*, 10 December 2002; *Daily Telegraph*, 3 May 2004.

401. *Ireland and the English Crisis* (Newcastle Upon Tyne, 1984), p. 27.

402. *LRB*, 2 January 2003; *Guardian*, 8 January 2003.

403. <http://www.guardian.co.uk/stage/video/2009/apr/25/seven-jewish-children-caryl-churchill>. See also Dave Rich and Mark Gardner, 'The blood libel brought up to date', *Guardian*, *CiF*, 1 May 2008.

5. MODERN ENGLISH ANTI-SEMITISM

1. Michael Marrus, *The Holocaust in History* (London, 1989), p. 28.

2. But see Kenneth Rose, *Elusive Rothschild* (London, 2003), p. 62 ('all Jews almost everywhere learn to live with the mild sort of anti-Semitism which afflicts so many people, even the liberal-minded').

3. Meir Michaelis, 'The Holocaust in Italy: Areas of inquiry' in Michael Berenbaum and Abraham J. Peck (eds.), *The Holocaust and History* (Bloomington, IN, 2002), p. 439; Antonio Alberti Semi, 'Psychopathology of everyday antisemitism' in David Meghnani (ed.), *Freud and Judaism* (London, 1993), pp. 142–3.

4. David S. Katz, *The Jews in the History of England 1485–1850* (Oxford, 1996), pp. 1–106.

5. See Steven F. Kruger, *The Spectral Jew* (Minneapolis, MN, 2006), pp. xvii–xx.

6. David S. Katz, *The Jews in the History of England 1485–1850* (Oxford, 1996), p. 108, fn. 3.

7. In John Marston's *The Malcontent* (1603), the duke is a master poisoner, 'no Jew, pothecary politician better' (V, iii, ll. 31–2); Edgar Rosenberg, *From Shylock to Svengali* (Stanford, CA, 1960), p. 26.

8. Evelyn M. Simpson and George R. Potter (eds.), *The Sermons of John Donne* (Berkeley, CA, 1953), vol. 6, p. 334; Jeanne Shami, 'Donne, anti-Jewish rhetoric, and the English Church in 1621' in Chanita Goodblatt and Howard Kreisel (eds.), *Tradition, Heterodoxy and Religious Culture* (Beer-Sheva, 2006), pp. 46–7. Donne mistakenly ascribes to Jews a version of his own Christian belief in the redemptive power of blood. So elsewhere, he makes a typological connection between Ezekiel's God, who addresses Jerusalem, relating how He saw it polluted in its own blood, and washed it (Ezekiel 16:6 and 9), and Jesus, who washes the Church in his own blood. But in Ezekiel the washing is with water. *There*, the blood is washed off; *here*, the Church is immersed in God's own blood, though it 'washes white'. See Evelyn M. Simpson and George R. Potter (eds.), *The Sermons of John Donne* (Berkeley, CA, 1953), vol. 6, p. 65.

9. Nathan Osterman, 'The controversy over the proposed readmission of the Jews to England (1655)', *Jewish Social Studies*, 3/3 (1941), 325–6.

10. See Avrom Saltman, *The Jewish Question in 1655* (Ramat-Gan, 1995), p. 58.

11. Steven F. Kruger, *The Spectral Jew* (Minneapolis, MN, 2006), p. 140.

12. Thomas Dekker, *The Witch of Edmonton*, II.i. ll. 6–8, Frederick Bowers (ed.), *The Dramatic Works of Thomas Dekker* (Cambridge, 1966), vol. 3, p. 506.

13. The clergyman John Traske (*c.*1585–1636) was imprisoned, whipped, mutilated, and branded with the letter 'J', for his advocacy of 'Jewish opinions'. See Nicholas McDowell, 'The stigmatizing of Puritans as Jews in Jacobean England', *Renaissance Studies*, 19/3 (2005), 348–52.

14. See Douglas J. Culver, *Albion and Ariel* (New York, 1995), p. 77.

15. Achsah Guibbory, 'The Church of England, Judaism, and the Jewish Temple in early modern England' in Chanita Goodblatt and Howard Kreisel (eds.), *Tradition, Heterodoxy and Religious Culture* (Beer-Sheva, 2006), pp. 15–17.

16. See Reid Barbour, *John Selden* (Toronto, 2003), pp. 8, 13–14, 112–13, 240, 272, 300, 353, 355, 358.

17. Ibid., pp. 218–19, 222, 356.

18. Achsah Guibbory, 'The Church of England, Judaism, and the Jewish Temple in early modern England' in Chanita Goodblatt and Howard Kreisel (eds.), *Tradition, Heterodoxy and Religious Culture* (Beer-Sheva, 2006), pp. 12–14.

19. See Hugh Kearneym, *The British Isles* (Cambridge, 1995), pp. 168–73.

20. See Bernard Glassman, *Protean Prejudice* (Atlanta, GA, 1998), *passim*.

21. David S. Katz, *The Jews in the History of England 1485–1850* (Oxford, 1996), pp. 106, 92, 96, 105–6.

22. *The conversion and persecution of Eve Cohen, now called Elizabeth Verboon, a person of quality of the Jewish religion, who was baptized the 10th of October 1680, at St. Martin's in the Fields, by the Right Reverend Father in God, William, Lord Bishop of St. Asaph* (London, 1680).

23. *The Jews of Georgian England 1714–1830* (Philadelphia, 1979), p. 87; Frank Felsenstein, *Anti-Semitic Stereotypes* (Baltimore, MD, 1995), *passim*; Bernard Glassman, *Protean Prejudice* (Atlanta, GA, 1998), *passim*; James Picciotto,

Sketches of Anglo-Jewish History (London, 1956), pp. 90, 170 ('the great bulk of the ancient people were eyed by the British *vulgus* as outcasts with whom it was discreditable to consort').

24. Todd M. Endelman, *The Jews of Georgian England 1714–1830* (Philadelphia, 1979), p. 93.

25. 'Is it possible that Donne could have given credit to this absurd legend!' George Whalley (ed.), *The Collected Works of Samuel Taylor Coleridge: Marginalia II* (London, 1984), p. 274.

26. See David S. Katz, *The Jews in the History of England* (1996), pp. 292–3.

27. *Letters from England* (Gloucester, 1984), pp. 394–5, 398.

28. James H. Robb, *Working-Class Anti-Semite* (London, 1954), pp. 98–100, 106–7, 109, 111, 120, 137. An interviewee assigned by James H. Robb to the 'tolerant group' regarded himself as exceptional in the neighbourhood in not being anti-Semitic. The charge that Jews burned down their commercial property for the insurance was then sixty or seventy years old. In 1898, insurance companies announced that they would no longer insure against fire in London's East End. Samuel Montagu regarded the decision as motivated by anti-Semitism. See Daniel Gutwein, *The Divided Elite* (Leiden, 1992), p. 274.

29. See *Chance Witness* (London, 2003), p. 222.

30. David S. Katz, *The Jews in the History of England 1485–1850* (Oxford, 1996), p. 125.

31. Nathan Osterman, 'The Controversy over the proposed readmission of the Jews to England (1655)', *Jewish Social Studies*, 3/3 (1941), 302.

32. David S. Katz, *The Jews in the History of England 1485–1850* (Oxford, 1996), pp. 140–1.

33. Ibid., pp. 146–54, 170–2.

34. Ibid., p. 109.

35. Nathan Osterman, 'The controversy over the proposed readmission of the Jews to England (1655)', *Jewish Social Studies*, 3/3 (1941), 308.

36. M. Wilensky, 'The literary controversy in 1656 concerning the return of the Jews to England', *Proceedings of the American Academy for Jewish Research*, 20 (1951), 363, 365, 372, 376.

37. Avrom Saltman, *The Jewish Question in 1655* (Ramat-Gan, 1995), p. 31.

38. William Lamont, *Puritanism and Historical Controversy* (London, 1996), pp. 16–25, 60–1, 87.

39. Avrom Saltman, *The Jewish Question in 1655* (Ramat-Gan, 1995), p. 121.

40. Julian Barnes, 'Holy hysteria', *NYRB*, 10 April 2003.

41. Cecil Roth, 'England the Ninth of Ab', *Opportunities that Pass* (London, 2005), p. 114.

42. Nathan Osterman, 'The controversy over the proposed readmission of the Jews to England (1655)', *Jewish Social Studies*, 3/3 (1941), 315–16.

43. David S. Katz, *The Jews in the History of England 1485–1850* (Oxford, 1996), p. 129. According to Avrom Saltman, Prynne also intended converts to be excluded. See *The Jewish Question in 1655* (Ramat-Gan, 1995), p. 112.

44. See Avrom Saltman, *The Jewish Question in 1655* (Ramat-Gan, 1995), pp. 19–20, 109. 'Froward', which means 'perverse, ill-shaped', is also the name of the Jewish torturers' servant in the Wakefield 'Buffeting'. See David Bevington (ed.), *Medieval Drama* (London, 1975), p. 548.

45. Avrom Saltman, *The Jewish Question in 1655* (Ramat-Gan, 1995), pp. 19, 27–9, 89–91, 129, 133, 135, 136–7, 149, 159, 167, 170–1.

46. Nathan Osterman, 'The controversy over the proposed readmission of the Jews to England (1655)', *Jewish Social Studies*, 3/3 (1941), 318.

47. M. Wilensky, 'The literary controversy in 1656 concerning the return of the Jews to England', *Proceedings of the American Academy for Jewish Research*, 20 (1951), 383.

48. Lucien Wolf (ed.), *Menasseh ben Israel's Mission to Oliver Cromwell* (London, 1901), p. 114.

49. Thomas W. Perry, *Public Opinion, Propaganda, and Politics in Eighteenth-Century England* (Cambridge, MA, 1962), p. 5.

50. David S. Katz, *The Jews in the History of England* (1996), p. 244.

51. *The Parliamentary History of England*, vol. 14, 1747–53, cols. 1365–431; Bernard Glassman, *Protean Prejudice* (Atlanta, GA, 1998), pp. 185–7.

52. M. C. N. Salbstein, *The Emancipation of the Jews in Britain* (London, 1982), p. 45.

53. Thomas W. Perry, *Public Opinion, Propaganda, and Politics in Eighteenth-Century England* (Cambridge, MA, 1962), pp. 3, 8, 39–40, 50, 55, 65, 75, 83, 93, 97–8, 107, 112, 118, 120–1, 194–6; David S. Katz, *The Jews in the History of England* (1996), p. 246; Isaiah Schachar, *The Judensau* (London, 1974), p. 63 and plates 58a and 60b; Bernard Glassman, *Protean Prejudice* (Atlanta, GA, 1998), pp. 195–201; Todd M. Endelman, *The Jews of Georgian England 1714–1830* (Philadelphia, 1979), pp. 89, 194; G. A. Cranfield, 'The "London Evening-Post" and the Jew Bill of 1753', *Historical Journal*, 8/1 (1965), 18, 20, 21.

54. Thomas W. Perry, *Public Opinion, Propaganda, and Politics in Eighteenth-Century England* (Cambridge, MA, 1962), pp. 79–80, 126, 131, 142, 194; James Picciotto, *Sketches of Anglo-Jewish History* (London, 1956), pp. 84–5.

55. David S. Katz, *The Jews in the History of England* (1996), pp. 246, 248. 'It would be a mistake to regard the agitation of 1753 as an outbreak of anti-Semitism.' Allan Peskin, 'England's Jewish Naturalisation Bill of 1753', *Historia Judaica*, 19 (April 1957), 28.

56. G. A. Cranfield, 'The "London Evening-Post" and the Jew Bill of 1753', *Historical Journal*, 8/1 (1965), 16.

57. See David S. Katz, *The Jews in the History of England* (1996), p. 240.

58. See Allan Peskin, 'England's Jewish Naturalisation Bill of 1753', *Historia Judaica*, 19 (April 1957), 16.

59. Charles Egan, *The Status of the Jews in England* (London, 1848), p. 34.

60. Henry Hart Milman, *The History of the Jews*, 4th edn (London, 1866), vol. 3, p. 398.

61. *Public Opinion, Propaganda, and Politics in Eighteenth-Century England* (Cambridge, MA, 1962), pp. 14, 31–3, 85, 179–80.
62. *Letters from England* (Gloucester, 1984), p. 393.
63. M. C. N. Salbstein *The Emancipation of the Jews in Britain* (London, 1982), p. 165.
64. Geoffrey Alderman, *Modern British Jewry* (Oxford, 1992), p. 3.
65. M. C. N. Salbstein, *The Emancipation of the Jews in Britain* (London, 1982), p. 217.
66. Israel Finestein, 'Some modern themes in the emancipation debate in early Victorian England' in Jonathan Sacks (ed.), *Tradition and Transition* (London, 1986), pp. 134–6; David Vital, *A People Apart* (Oxford, 1999), pp. 178–9.
67. See Elie Kedourie, *The Crossman Confessions and Other Essays* (London, 1984), p. 49.
68. See ibid.
69. Charles Egan, *The Status of the Jews in England* (London, 1848), pp. 40–1.
70. See ibid., p. 70.
71. Hansard, Parl. Debs. (series 3) vol. 98, cols. 1342–3, 1344, 1374, 1375, 1377 (1848); Hansard, Parl. Debs. (series 3) vol. 125, cols. 79, 84 (1853); M. C. N. Salbstein, *The Emancipation of the Jews in Britain* (London, 1982), pp. 73–5; Abraham Gilam, *The Emancipation of the Jews in England 1830–1860* (New York, 1982), p. 24.
72. M. C. N. Salbstein, *The Emancipation of the Jews in Britain* (London, 1982), p. 230.
73. Mr Drummond, Hansard, Parl. Debs. (series 3) vol. 125, col. 95 (1853).
74. The bishop of Oxford. See Israel Finestein, 'Some modern themes in the emancipation debate in early Victorian England' in Jonathan Sacks (ed.), *Tradition and Transition* (London, 1986), p. 139.
75. M. C. N. Salbstein, *The Emancipation of the Jews in Britain* (London, 1982), pp. 130, 143, 147, 158; Abraham Gilam, *The Emancipation of the Jews in England 1830–1860* (New York, 1982), p. 90.
76. G. Otto Trevelyan, *The Life and Letters of Lord Macaulay* (New York, 1877), vol. 1, p. 146; Charles Egan, *The Status of the Jews in England* (London, 1848), p. 60; Abraham Gilam, *The Emancipation of the Jews in England 1830–1860* (New York, 1982), pp. 87, 136–7; David Feldman, *Englishmen and Jews* (London, 1994), p. 32.
77. See G. Otto Trevelyan, *The Life and Letters of Lord Macaulay* (New York, 1877), vol. 1, pp. 152–3.
78. See Charles Egan, *The Status of the Jews in England* (London, 1848), pp. 84–5.
79. Lord John Russell. See M. C. N. Salbstein, *The Emancipation of the Jews in Britain* (London, 1982), p. 130.
80. Abraham Gilam, *The Emancipation of the Jews in England 1830–1860* (New York, 1982), p. 72.
81. *Lectures on the Relation between Law and Opinion in England during the Nineteenth Century* (London, 1905), p. 343.

82. See M. C. N. Salbstein, *The Emancipation of the Jews in Britain* (London, 1982), pp. 151, 165, 170–1.

83. See Edgar Feuchtwanger, ' "Jew Feelings" and Realpolitik' in Todd M. Endelman and Tony Kushner (eds.), *Disraeli's Jewishness* (London, 2002), pp. 184–5.

84. David S. Katz, *The Jews in the History of England 1485–1850* (Oxford, 1996), p. 162; M. C. N. Salbstein, *The Emancipation of the Jews in Britain* (London, 1982), pp. 50–1.

85. See Abraham Gilam, *The Emancipation of the Jews in England 1830–1860* (New York, 1982), pp. 10, 83.

86. M. C. N. Salbstein, *The Emancipation of the Jews in Britain* (London, 1982), p. 57.

87. See Todd M. Endelman, *The Jews of Britain 1656–2000* (Berkeley, CA, 2002), pp. 2, 9.

88. See Nathan Osterman, 'The controversy over the proposed readmission of the Jews to England (1655)', *Jewish Social Studies*, 3/3 (1941), 305, 309.

89. See R. W. Davis, 'Disraeli, the Rothschilds and antisemitism' in Todd M. Endelman and Tony Kushner (eds.), *Disraeli's Jewishness* (London, 2002), pp. 176–8.

90. See M. C. N. Salbstein, *The Emancipation of the Jews in Britain* (London, 1982), pp. 65–6.

91. See Anthony S. Wohl, 'Ben Juju' in Todd M. Endelman and Tony Kushner (eds.), *Disraeli's Jewishness* (London, 2002), p. 107.

92. Michael Walzer, *Politics and Passion* (New Haven, 2004), pp. 28–9.

93. See Abraham Gilam, *The Emancipation of the Jews in England 1830–1860* (New York, 1982), pp. 97–8. See also David Feldman, *Englishmen and Jews* (London, 1994), pp. 75–7.

94. Abraham Gilam *The Emancipation of the Jews in England 1830–1860* (New York, 1982), p. 65.

95. J. H. Stallard, *London Pauperism Amongst Jews and Christians* (London, 1867), p. 4.

96. See Alan Sykes, *The Radical Right in Britain* (London, 2005), p. 32.

97. Goldwin Smith, 'England's abandonment of the Protectorate of Turkey', *Contemporary Review*, 31 (February 1878), 617.

98. David Fromkin, *A Peace to End All Peace* (London, 2003), pp. 27, 75.

99. Gary J. Bass, *Freedom's Battle* (New York, 2008), p. 240; John Vincent, *Disraeli* (Oxford, 1990), p. 13.

100. Edgar Feuchtwanger, ' "Jew Feelings" and Realpolitik' in Todd M. Endelman and Tony Kushner (eds.), *Disraeli's Jewishness* (London, 2002), pp. 187, 195.

101. See Daniel Gutwein, *The Divided Elite* (Leiden, 1992), p. 325.

102. See J. A. Froude, *Lord Beaconsfield* (London, 1890), pp. 63–4, and Robert Blake, *Disraeli* (London, 1967), pp. 123–6. O'Connell was a committed supporter of Jewish emancipation. See M. C. N. Salbstein, *The Emancipation of the Jews in Britain* (London, 1982), pp. 123–4.

103. See R. W. Davis, 'Disraeli, the Rothschilds and antisemitism' in Todd M. Endelman and Tony Kushner (eds.), *Disraeli's Jewishness* (London, 2002), p. 172.

104. 'Ben Juju' in Todd M. Endelman and Tony Kushner (eds.), *Disraeli's Jewishness* (London, 2002), p. 106.

105. J. A. Froude, *Lord Beaconsfield* (London, 1890), p. 37.

106. See Daniel Pick, *Svengali's Web* (New Haven, 2000), p. 130.

107. See Anthony S. Wohl, 'Ben Juju' in Todd M. Endelman and Tony Kushner (eds.), *Disraeli's Jewishness* (London, 2002), p. 116.

108. Ibid., pp. 105–61; Anne and Roger Cowen, *Victorian Jews through British Eyes* (Oxford, 1986), p. 30.

109. See William Morris, *News from Nowhere and Other Writings* (London, 1998), pp. 396–8.

110. See E. A. Freeman, 'The English People in relation to the Eastern Question', *Contemporary Review*, 29 (February 1877), 489, 510. '[Freeman] was a philanthropist and a sincere patriot', and subscribed to 'the principles of civil and religious freedom, humanity and justice'. He was a 'man of sturdy independence of character, irrepressible zeal for simple truth, and unvarnished plainness of speech'. W. R. W. Stephens, *The Life and Letters of Edward A. Freeman* (London, 1895), vol. 1, pp. 208, 357.

111. See David Feldman, *Englishmen and Jews* (London, 1994), p. 102.

112. Leopold Glückstein, *The Eastern Question and the Jews* (London, 1876), pp. 5–6. Gladstone responded to the pamphlet in a letter to the *Jewish Chronicle*, 13 October 1876. He 'deplored' the manner in which 'Judaic sympathies', which were not restricted to 'the circle of professed Judaism', were acting on the Eastern Question.

113. W. R. W. Stephens, *The Life and Letters of Edward A. Freeman* (London, 1895), vol. 2, p. 389.

114. David Feldman, *Englishmen and Jews* (London, 1994), p. 103.

115. Edgar Feuchtwanger, ' "Jew Feelings" and Realpolitik' in Todd M. Endelman and Tony Kushner (eds.), *Disraeli's Jewishness* (London, 2002), p. 184.

116. W. R. W. Stephens, *The Life and Letters of Edward A. Freeman* (London, 1895), vol. 2, p. 138.

117. Ann Pottinger Saab, 'Disraeli, Judaism, and the Eastern Question', *The International History Review*, 10/4 (November 1988), 570–1.

118. Stanley Weintraub, *Disraeli* (London, 1993), pp. xi, 567 ('Gladstone's tame historian', '[his] favourite historian'); Edgar Feuchtwanger, ' "Jew Feelings" and Realpolitik' in Todd M. Endelman and Tony Kushner (eds.), *Disraeli's Jewishness* (London, 2002), p. 184.

119. 'The progress of personal rule', *Nineteenth Century*, 21 (November 1881), p. 792.

120. *Lord Beaconsfield* (London, 1890), pp. 4, 41, 84, 108, 170, 261.

121. *A Short History of England* (London, 1917), pp. 226, 234.

122. See Richard Ollard, *A Man of Contradictions: A life of A. L. Rowse* (London, 1999), p. 94.
123. Pierre Birnbaum, *Anti-Semitism in France* (Oxford, 1992), p. 14.
124. 'The political adventures of Lord Beaconsfield', *Fortnightly Review*, 23 (April 1878) (I), 477–8, 480, 482, 484, 486; (May 1878) (II), pp. 691, 704, 706; (June 1878) (III), pp. 868–9; (August 1878) (IV), pp. 268, 269.
125. Jamie Camplin, *The Rise of the Plutocrats* (London, 1978), pp. 49–50.
126. Nicholas Owen, 'Critics of empire in Britain' in Judith M. Brown and Wm. Roger Louis (eds.), *The Oxford History of the British Empire: The twentieth century* (Oxford, 1999), p. 190.
127. *Justice*, 3 November 1899.
128. See Thomas Pakenham, *The Boer War* (London, 1992), pp. xvi–xvii, 88–9, 116, 384.
129. Ibid., pp. 250, 388.
130. Claire Hirshfield, 'The Anglo-Boer War and the issue of Jewish culpability', *Journal of Contemporary History*, 15 (1980), 622.
131. L. T. Hobhouse, *Democracy and Reaction* (Brighton, Sussex, 1972), pp. 70, 179.
132. *The Jews* (London, 1922), p. 50.
133. See R. W. Davis, 'Disraeli, the Rothschilds and antisemitism' in Todd M. Endelman and Tony Kushner (eds.), *Disraeli's Jewishness* (London, 2002), pp. 163–4; Claire Hirshfield, 'The Anglo-Boer War and the issue of Jewish culpability,' *Journal of Contemporary History*, 15 (1980), 628–9.
134. *Reynolds's Newspaper*, 12 November 1899.
135. Ibid., 25 February 1900.
136. *Justice*, 17 May 1890.
137. Claire Hirshfield, 'The Anglo-Boer War and the issue of Jewish culpability', *Journal of Contemporary History*, 15 (1980), 621.
138. See John A. Garrard, *The English and Immigration 1880–1910* (Oxford, 1971), p. 191.
139. See Geoffrey Wheatcroft, *The Randlords* (London, 1985), p. 206.
140. *Justice*, 21 January 1893.
141. Ibid., 5 July 1890. Ironically, at about the same time, the diplomat Sir Horace Rumbold (1864–1941), was complaining about the pro-*Boer* sentiments of the 'Jewish controlled' Viennese newspapers. They had 'peculiar reason to speak well of England where there is an almost total absence of anti-Semitism'. Martin Gilbert, *Sir Horace Rumbold* (London, 1973), p. 34.
142. *Justice*, 21 January 1893.
143. Ibid., 7 and 14 October 1899.
144. Claire Hirshfield, 'The Anglo-Boer War and the issue of Jewish culpability', *Journal of Contemporary History*, 15 (1980), 622.
145. *Justice*, 14 October 1899.
146. Ibid., 28 October 1899.

147. See Claire Hirshfield, 'The Anglo-Boer War and the issue of Jewish culpability', *Journal of Contemporary History*, 15 (1980), 621.

148. *Justice*, 4 November 1899.

149. Ibid., 7 October 1899.

150. Ibid., 4 November 1899.

151. See ibid., 28 October 1899.

152. Ibid., 21 October 1899.

153. Ibid., 11 November 1899. On 'Rich-Jew anti-Semitism', see Geoffrey Alderman, *Modern British Jewry* (Oxford, 1992), pp. 192–3.

154. *Justice*, 7 October 1899.

155. Ibid., 11 November 1899.

156. John Burns, *War against the Two Republics* ('Stop the War' Committee, London, 1900), pp. 4, 6. See also G. R. Searle, *Corruption in British Politics 1895–1930* (Oxford, 1994), p. 69.

157. 'The Trail of the Financial Serpent', London, 1900, p. 7.

158. *ILP News*, October 1899.

159. Report of Proceedings of the Thirty-Third Annual Trades Union Congress, held in the Town Hall, Princess Street, Huddersfield, 3–8 September 1900, pp. 54–5.

160. Hansard, Parl. Debs. (Commons) (series 4) vol. 77, pp. 125–6, 186 (17–18 October 1899).

161. Claire Hirshfield, 'The Anglo-Boer War and the issue of Jewish culpability', *Journal of Contemporary History*, 15 (1980), 624.

162. Lloyd P. Gartner, *The Jewish Immigrant in England 1870–1914* (London, 2001), p. ix.

163. John A. Garrard, *The English and Immigration 1880–1910* (Oxford, 1971), pp. 27–8.

164. Ibid., pp. 105–8.

165. See Bernard Harris, 'Anti-alienism, health and social reform in late-Victorian and Edwardian Britain', *Patterns of Prejudice*, 31/4 (1977), 6.

166. See John A. Garrard, *The English and Immigration 1880–1910* (Oxford, 1971), p. 18.

167. See Bernard Harris, 'Anti-alienism, health and social reform in late-Victorian and Edwardian Britain', *Patterns of Prejudice*, 31/4 (1977), 9.

168. G. S. Reaney, 'The moral aspect' in Arnold White (ed.), *The Destitute Alien in Great Britain* (London, 1892), pp. 87–8.

169. See Bill Williams, 'The anti-Semitism of tolerance' in Alan J. Kidd and K.W. Roberts (eds.), *City, Class and Culture* (Manchester, 1985), p. 86.

170. Montague Crackanthorpe, 'Should government interfere?' in Arnold White (ed.), *The Destitute Alien in Great Britain* (London, 1892), p. 59.

171. See John A. Garrard, *The English and Immigration 1880–1910* (Oxford, 1971), p. 162.

172. R. H. Sherard, *The White Slaves of England* (London, 1897), pp. 112, 114.

173. See Colin Holmes, *John Bull's Island* (London, 1988), p. 69.

174. See Norman Bentwich and Helen Bentwich, *Mandate Memories 1918–1948* (London, 1965), p. 142.

175. John A. Garrard, *The English and Immigration 1880–1910* (Oxford, 1971), pp. 24–5.

176. Ibid., p. 53.

177. See Geoffrey Alderman, *Modern British Jewry* (Oxford, 1992), p. 167.

178. John A. Garrard, *The English and Immigration 1880–1910* (Oxford, 1971), pp. 53, 61.

179. Ibid., p. 56; Bill Williams, 'The anti-Semitism of tolerance' in Alan J. Kidd and K. W. Roberts (eds.), *City, Class and Culture* (Manchester, 1985), p. 87.

180. 'Introductory' in Arnold White (ed.), *The Destitute Alien in Great Britain* (London, 1892), p. 1.

181. 'A Typical Alien Immigrant', *Contemporary Review*, 73 (February 1898), 241.

182. John A. Garrard, *The English and Immigration 1880–1910* (Oxford, 1971), p. 50; David Feldman, *Englishmen and Jews* (London, 1994), p. 166.

183. See Stephen D. Arata, 'The Occidental tourist' in Glennis Byron (ed.), *Dracula* (London, 1999), p. 123; *Dracula* (Oxford, 1996).

184. Lloyd P. Gartner, *The Jewish Immigrant in England 1870–1914* (London, 2001), p. 278.

185. *England under the Jews* (London, 1907), p. 68. See also Bernard Harris, 'Anti-alienism, health and social reform in late-Victorian and Edwardian Britain', *Patterns of Prejudice*, 31/4 (1977), 7.

186. *England under the Jews* (London, 1907), pp. ii, iii, 10, 22, 25, 40, 77, 86, 162, 170, 191; Colin Holmes, *Anti-Semitism in British Society 1876–1939* (New York, 1979), pp. 39–42.

187. Karl Pearson and Margaret Moul, 'The problem of alien immigration into Great Britain, illustrated by an examination of Russian and Polish Jewish children', *Annals of Eugenics*, vol. 1, 1925–6, p. 7.

188. John A. Garrard, *The English and Immigration 1880–1910* (Oxford, 1971), pp. 109–11.

189. Ibid., pp. 39, 51, 56, 62.

190. Colin Holmes, *John Bull's Island* (London, 1988), p. 70.

191. See Lloyd P. Gartner, *The Jewish Immigrant in England 1870–1914* (London, 2001), p. 62.

192. John A. Garrard, *The English and Immigration 1880–1910* (Oxford, 1971), pp. 33, 41.

193. Steve Cohen, 'Anti-Semitism, immigration controls and the welfare state', *Critical Social Policy*, 5/13 (1985), 75–6.

194. See ibid., p. 76.

195. See John A. Garrard, *The English and Immigration 1880–1910* (Oxford, 1971), p. 189.

196. See Steve Cohen, 'Anti-semitism, immigration controls and the welfare state', *Critical Social Policy*, 5/13 (1985), 76.

197. John A. Garrard, *The English and Immigration 1880–1910* (Oxford, 1971), p. 164.

198. Ibid., p. 176.

199. Ibid., p. 183.

200. See Steve Cohen, 'Anti-Semitism, immigration controls and the welfare state', *Critical Social Policy*, 5/134 (1985), 77.

201. Hansard, Parl. Debs. (series 4) vol. 133, cols. 1149–50, 1158, 1159 (1904). See also Kenneth D. Brown, *John Burns* (London, 1977), p. 92 ('an almost pathological dislike of Jews').

202. William Kent, *John Burns* (London, 1950), p. 106.

203. See, for example, G. D. H. Cole's Fabian pamphlet, *John Burns* (London, 1943), pp. 5, 26, 35, which notes Burns's 'ardent "pro-Boer"' position, and while acknowledging 'all his faults', does not find among them hatred of Jews.

204. 'This policy of the Tory Government is dictated by the Jewish financiers who ordered them to make the South African war...Premier Balfour does not spend his week-ends in the houses of great Jewish money-lenders for nothing.' 'The Tory anti-Jew Bill', *Reynold's Newspaper*, 23 April 1905.

205. John A. Garrard, *The English and Immigration 1880–1910* (Oxford, 1971), pp. 135–6.

206. Lloyd P. Gartner, *The Jewish Immigrant in England 1870–1914* (London, 2001), pp. 18, 24–5, 49–50.

207. John A. Garrard, *The English and Immigration 1880–1910* (Oxford, 1971), pp. 24–5.

208. See ibid., p. 67.

209. Lloyd P. Gartner, *The Jewish Immigrant in England 1870–1914* (London, 2001), p. 55; Todd M. Endelman, *The Jews of Britain 1656–2000* (Berkeley, CA, 2002), p. 173; David Cesarani, *The Jewish Chronicle and Anglo-Jewry 1841–1991* (Cambridge, 1994), p. 75 (on the restrictionist Jewish MP for Limehouse, Harry Samuels).

210. See John A. Garrard, *The English and Immigration 1880–1910* (Oxford, 1971), p. 66.

211. Ibid., pp. 59, 64.

212. See ibid., pp. 64–5.

213. Bernard Harris, 'Anti-alienism, health and social reform in late-Victorian and Edwardian Britain', *Patterns of Prejudice*, 31/4 (1977), 16.

214. C. Russell and H. S. Lewis, *The Jew in London* (London, 1900), p. 138.

215. *My Apprenticeship* (Cambridge, 1979), p. 331.

216. See John A. Garrard, *The English and Immigration 1880–1910* (Oxford, 1971), pp. 29, 158–60, 167; Lloyd P. Gartner, *The Jewish Immigrant in England 1870–1914* (London, 2001), pp. 65, 93, 276 ('a misleading nexus').

217. John A. Garrard, *The English and Immigration 1880–1910* (Oxford, 1971), p. 66.

218. Lloyd P. Gartner, *The Jewish Immigrant in England 1870–1914* (London, 2001), p. 277.

219. John A. Garrard, *The English and Immigration 1880–1910* (Oxford, 1971), pp. 87, 94–6, 102.

220. See Chaim Bermant, *The Cousinhood* (London, 1971), p. 287.

221. See Leonard Stein, *The Balfour Declaration* (London, 1961), p. 42.

222. G. R. Searle, *Corruption in British Politics 1895–1930* (Oxford, 1994), p. 339. See, for example, T. W. H. Crosland, *The Fine Old Hebrew Gentleman* (London, 1922), pp. 120–4.

223. G. R. Searle, *Corruption in British Politics 1895–1930* (Oxford, 1994), pp. 207, 209.

224. Ibid., p. 211.

225. Geoffrey Alderman, *London Jewry and London Politics 1889–1986* (London, 1989), pp. 62–3.

226. Eugene C. Black, *The Social Politics of Anglo-Jewry 1880–1920* (Oxford, 1988), p. 374.

227. Selig Brodetsky, *Memoirs from Ghetto to Israel* (London, 1960), p. 88.

228. Colin Holmes, *John Bull's Island* (London, 1988), pp. 104–5.

229. Tony Kushner, 'Jew and non-Jew in the East End of London' in Geoffrey Alderman and Colin Holmes (eds.), *Outsiders and Outcasts* (London, 1993), pp. 41–2.

230. See C. C. Aronsfeld, 'German Jews in Victorian England', *Leo Baeck Institute Year Book* (1962), p. 327.

231. See C. C. Aronsfeld, 'Jewish enemy aliens in England during the First World War', *Jewish Social Studies*, 18/4 (1956), 276.

232. See ibid., p. 280.

233. Ibid., p. 277.

234. 23 November 1917; see Sharman Kadish, *Bolsheviks and British Jews* (London, 1992), p. 10.

235. Ibid., pp. 21, 26.

236. 'The horrors of Bolshevism', *The Times*, 14 November 1919.

237. See Sharman Kadish, *Bolsheviks and British Jews* (London, 1992), p. 18.

238. See F. H. Kisch, *Palestine Diary* (London, 1938), p. 154.

239. William D. Rubinstein, 'Henry Page Croft and the National Liberal Party 1917–1922', *Journal of Contemporary History*, 9/1 (1974), 143–4.

240. 'Sanity and Semitism', *New Witness*, 13 April 1923, p. 225.

241. See Markku Ruotsila, *British and American Anticommunism before the Cold War* (London, 2001), p. 171.

242. Ulrike Ehet, 'Catholics and antisemitism in Germany and England 1918–1939', unpublished PhD thesis, University of London, 2005, p. 83.

243. Todd M. Endelman, *Radical Assimilation in English Jewish History 1656–1945* (Bloomington, IN, 1990), p. 142.

244. G. R. Searle, *Corruption in British Politics 1895–1930* (Oxford, 1994), pp. 248–52, 268–70.

245. Gisela C. Lebzelter, *Political Anti-Semitism in England 1918–1939* (London, 1978), pp. 14–16.

246. Sharman Kadish, *Bolsheviks and British Jews* (London, 1992), p. 34; Gisela C. Lebzelter, *Political Anti-Semitism in England 1918–1939* (London, 1978), p. 22.

247. See Maurice Cowling, *The Impact of Labour 1920–1924* (Cambridge, 2005), p. 84.

248. Philip Graves, *Palestine: The land of three faiths* (London, 1923), p. 239.

249. Gisela C. Lebzelter, *Political Anti-Semitism in England 1918–1939* (London, 1978), p. 21.

250. 7 August 1917. See Gisela C. Lebzelter, *Political Anti-Semitism in England 1918–1939* (London, 1978), pp. 14–15.

251. See ibid., p. 55.

252. See Viscount Samuel, *Memoirs* (London, 1945), p. 147: genuine sympathy with the Jews; commitment to the regeneration of the land; precaution against threats to national self-interest.

253. Blanche E. C. Dugdale, *Arthur James Balfour: Years 1906–1930* (London, 1939), p. 268.

254. George Galloway, *I'm Not the Only One* (London, 2004), p. 31.

255. *Cross Roads to Israel* (London, 1965), p. 18.

256. Leonard Stein, *The Balfour Declaration* (London, 1961), p. 165.

257. *Arthur James Balfour: Years 1906–1930* (London, 1939), p. 159.

258. Speech in the House of Lords, 21 June 1922, quoted ibid., p. 160.

259. *Arthur James Balfour: Years 1848–1905* (London, 1939), p. 327.

260. Ruddock F. Mackay, *Balfour* (Oxford, 1985), p. 317.

261. *Arthur James Balfour: Years 1906–1930* (London, 1939), pp. 173, 325–7.

262. Leonard Stein, *The Balfour Declaration* (London, 1961), pp. 69–80, 172–6, 220, 316–17, 445–8, 497–8, 516, 566, 578; Virginia H. Hein, *The British Followers of Theodor Herzl* (New York, 1987), p. 26. Lord Curzon, a senior member of the Lloyd George government which in 1917 approved the Balfour Declaration, was 'implacably' opposed to Zionism, but was not an anti-Semite: Kenneth Rose, *Superior Person* (New York, 1969), pp. 89–90.

263. *The Case of the Anti-Zionists: A reply* (London 1917), p. 1.

264. Louis Golding, *Those Ancient Lands* (London, 1928), p. 254. See also Todd M. Endelman, *The Jews of Britain 1656–2000* (Berkeley, CA, 2002), pp. 188–95.

265. On the confrontation between the two men, see, for example, Tom Segev, *Elvis in Jerusalem* (New York, 2002), pp. 20–1.

266. R. Travers Herford, *Talmud and Apocrypha* (New York, 1971), p. 94.

267. Geoffrey Alderman, *London Jewry and London Politics 1889–1986* (London, 1989), p. 65.

268. 'Chaim Weizmann', *Personal Impressions* (London, 1980), pp. 36–7.

269. Daniel Gutwein, *The Divided Elite* (Leiden, 1992), p. 359.

270. See David Fromkin, *A Peace to End All Peace* (London, 2003), p. 294. He knew, however, that he was the object of anti-Semitic sentiment. Eugene Black, 'Edwin Montagu', *Transactions of the J.H.S.E.*, 30 (1987–8), 213.

271. Eugene Black, 'Edwin Montagu', *Transactions of the J.H.S.E.*, 30 (1987–8), 214.

272. Daniel Gutwein, *The Divided Elite* (Leiden, 1992), p. 366.

273. Lucy Cohen, *Some Recollections of Claude Goldsmid Montefiore 1858–1938* (London, 1940), pp. 14–15, 138, 212, 227, 253; Claude Montefiore, 'Is Judaism a tribal religion?' *Contemporary Review*, 42 (September 1882), 379.

274. Charles Egan, *The Status of the Jews in England* (London, 1848), p. 57.

275. See Horace B. Samuel, *Unholy Memories of the Holy Land* (London, 1930), pp. 10–11.

276. *The Jews* (London, 1922), p. 235.

277. See Peter Hyman, *1 out of 10* (London, 2005), pp. 70–1.

278. See <http://www.adl.org/anti_semitism/European_Attitudes_Survey_July-2007.pdf>. Switzerland had the lowest percentage (44%), and Austria and Belgium, the highest (54%).

279. Leonard Stein, *The Balfour Declaration* (London, 1961), pp. 76, 80.

280. *Arthur James Balfour: Years 1906–1930* (London, 1939), p. 157.

281. Eugene C. Black, *The Social Politics of Anglo-Jewry 1880–1920* (Oxford, 1988), p. 303.

282. Geoffrey Alderman, 'The political impact of Zionism in the East End before 1940' in Aubrey Newman (ed.), *The Jewish East End 1840–1939* (London, 1981), pp. 229–30; Todd M. Endelman, *The Jews of Britain 1656–2000* (Berkeley, CA, 2002), p. 195.

283. Meyer W. Weisgal (ed.), *The Letters and Papers of Chaim Weizmann* (Oxford, 1977), vol. 10, p. 98. See also the reference to 'our enemies, Jewish and non-Jewish', in vol. 11, p. 66. The letters date from the early 1920s.

284. David Cesarani, 'Joynson-Hicks and the radical right in England after the First World War' in Tony Kushner and Kenneth Lunn (eds.), *Traditions of Intolerance* (Manchester, 1989), pp. 123–6; Maurice Cowling, *The Impact of Labour 1920–1924* (Cambridge, 2005), pp. 49, 75–87.

285. David Cesarani, 'Anti-Zionist politics and political antisemitism in Britain, 1920–1924', *Patterns of Prejudice*, 23/1 (1989).

286. Ibid., p. 38.

287. Ibid.

288. Ibid., p. 30.

289. Ibid.

290. See ibid., p. 32.

291. *Catholic Herald*, 31 March 1923.

292. Meyer W. Weisgal (ed.), *The Letters and Papers of Chaim Weizmann* (Oxford, 1977), vol. 11, pp. 24, 133.

293. 'Occupied Enemy Territory Administration'. It came to an end on
     1 July 1920, when Sir Herbert Samuel assumed office as the first High
     Commissioner of Palestine.
294. Norman Rose, *A Senseless, Squalid War* (London, 2009), pp. 20, 30–1. There
     were OETA officials who 'looked down on the people in their care as a
     tiresome gaggle of yids and wogs'. Christopher Sykes, *Cross Roads to Israel*
     (London, 1965), pp. 37–8. '[In 1921] General Congreve issued an army order
     which referred at one point to "the grasping policy of the Zionist extrem-
     ists".' Martin Gilbert, *Winston S. Churchill: The stricken world 1916–1922*
     (London, 1975), p. 641. Twenty years later, the situation had not altered—
     at least, according to Churchill. He told Roosevelt in 1942 that he was
     'strongly wedded to the Zionist policy', which would be assisted by the
     dismissal of 'anti-Semite officers and others in high places'. Bernard Wasser-
     stein, *Britain and the Jews of Europe 1939–1945* (Oxford, 1988), p. 32.
295. *New Statesman*, 13 December 1919, pp. 320–1.
296. Bernard Wasserstein, *The British in Palestine* (Oxford, 1991), pp. 22, 45–6,
     48–9.
297. See Richard Crossman, *A Nation Reborn* (London, 1960), p. 38.
298. *Flourishing: Letters 1928–1946* (London, 2004), p. 685.
299. Norman Bentwich and Helen Bentwich, *Mandate Memories 1918–1948*
     (London, 1965), pp. 57–8. On talk of 'Bolshevik Jews', see also Jenifer Glyn
     (ed.), *Tidings from Zion* (London, 2000), p. 99.
300. Jenifer Glyn (ed.), *Tidings from Zion* (London, 2000), pp. 41–2, 67, 70. 'The
     Jewish population in Palestine . . . thought that, after the Balfour Declaration,
     it was the duty of Lord Allenby and his staff to promote the immigration and
     settlement of Jews on the land, to give Jews autonomy, and to make Hebrew
     an official language. If an officer resisted the pressure, he was regarded as an
     anti-Semite, or at least an enemy of Zionism.' Norman Bentwich, *Mandate
     Memories 1918–1948* (London, 1965), p. 46. But cf. F. H. Kisch, the chairman
     of the Palestine Zionist Executive, 1923–31, on E. T. Richmond: *Palestine
     Diary* (London, 1938), pp. 34–5 ('sincere'), 47, 62, 64, 87, 113, 455 ('fanatical
     although sincere partisan').
301. See Bernard Wasserstein, *The British in Palestine* (Oxford, 1991), p. 67.
302. Barbara Board, *Reporting from Palestine 1943–1944* (Nottingham, 2008), p. 125.
303. Tom Segev, *One Palestine, Complete* (London, 2000), pp. 9, 331, 480; Bernard
     Wasserstein, *The British in Palestine* (Oxford, 1991), pp. 23, 61.
304. Horace B. Samuel, *Unholy Memories of the Holy Land* (London, 1930), pp. 50,
     62–3.
305. Meyer W. Weisgal (ed.), *The Letters and Papers of Chaim Weizmann* (Oxford,
     1977), vol. 11, p. 220.
306. Bernard Wasserstein, *The British in Palestine* (Oxford, 1991), pp. 11–12, 96,
     98–100, 143–7, 157; David Fromkin, *A Peace to End All Peace* (London, 2003),
     p. 518; Horace B. Samuel, *Unholy Memories of the Holy Land* (London, 1930),

p. 68; E. T. Richmond, ' "England" in Palestine', *Nineteenth Century* (July 1925), 46–51, and 'Dictatorship in the Holy Land', *Nineteenth Century* (February 1938), 186–92.

307. Philip Graves, *Palestine: The land of three faiths* (London, 1923), pp. 3, 47, 237, 186, 153, 243, 239, 246.

308. Richard Crossman, *A Nation Reborn* (London, 1960), pp. 66–7.

309. Christopher Sykes, *Cross Roads to Israel* (London, 1965), p. 140.

310. Chaim Weizmann, *Trial and Error* (London, 1949), pp. 410–11. According to Joseph Gorny, she also feared that handing Palestine to the Jews would cause 'the rapid decay of Christianity'. *The British Labour Movement and Zionism 1917–1948* (London, 1983), p. 77.

311. See Joseph Gorny, *The British Labour Movement and Zionism 1917–1948* (London, 1983), p. 99.

312. Tom Segev, *One Palestine, Complete* (London, 2000), p. 414.

313. See Bernard Lewis, *Semites and Anti-Semites* (London, 1986), p. 143.

314. Sir George Rendel, *The Sword and the Olive* (London, 1957), pp. 70, 76; Elie Kedourie, *Islam in the Modern World* (London, 1980), pp. 67–9, 105, 109, 113–19, 124, 125, 133–4, 136, 145–8, 161, 167, 240.

315. Elie Kedourie, *Islam in the Modern World* (London, 1980), p. 71.

316. See Andrew Sharf, *The British Press and Jews under Nazi Rule* (London, 1964), p. 37.

317. Tom Segev, *One Palestine, Complete* (London, 2000), p. 436.

318. The White Paper can be accessed at <http://avalon.law.yale.edu/subject_menus/mideast.asp>.

319. Ghada Karmi, *In Search of Fatima* (London, 2004), p. 372, and *Married to Another Man* (London, 2007), p. 119.

320. John Marlowe, *Rebellion in Palestine* (London, 1946), p. 215.

321. Christopher Sykes, *Cross Roads to Israel* (London, 1965), p. 239.

322. See Martin Gilbert, *Auschwitz and the Allies* (London, 2001), p. 171.

323. *Palestine: The reality* (London, 1939), p. 183.

324. See ibid., p. 710.

325. Malcolm Muggeridge, *The Thirties* (London, 1989), p. 243.

326. A. J. P. Taylor, *English History 1914–1945* (Oxford, 1965), pp. 419–20.

327. Kenneth Lunn, 'Political anti-Semitism before 1914: Fascism's heritage?' in Kenneth Lunn and Richard C. Thurlow (eds.), *British Fascism* (London, 1980), pp. 20–40; Tony Kushner, 'Beyond the Pale? British reactions to Nazi anti-Semitism, 1933–1939', *Immigrants and Minorities*, 8 (1989), 143.

328. Richard Griffiths, *Patriotism Perverted* (London, 1998), p. 29.

329. Franklin Reid Gannon, *The British Press and Germany 1936–1939* (Oxford, 1971), pp. 226–8.

330. *Warrant for Genocide* (London, 1967), p. 18; Michael Billig, *Fascists* (London, 1978), pp. 98–9; Richard Thurlow, *Fascism in Modern Britain* (London, 2000), pp. 33, 57; Stephen Dorril, *Blackshirt* (London, 2006), pp. 72–80.

331. William D. Rubinstein, *Elites and the Wealthy in Modern British History* (New York, 1987), p. 344; Michael Barkun, *A Culture of Conspiracy* (Berkeley, CA, 2003), pp. 141–57.

332. Richard C. Thurlow, 'The return of Jeremiah: The rejected knowledge of Sir Oswald Mosley in the 1930s' in Kenneth Lunn and Richard C. Thurlow (eds.), *British Fascism* (London, 1980), p. 101.

333. 'Sanity and Semitism', *New Witness*, 13 April 1923, p. 221.

334. See Michael J. Cohen, *Churchill and the Jews* (London, 2003), p. 111.

335. G. C. Webber, *The Ideology of the British Right* (London, 1986), pp. 17–18.

336. According to Hilary Blume, 'A study of anti-Semitic groups in Britain, 1918–1940', unpublished D. Phil thesis, University of Sussex, 1971, p. 53, it was the publication of the *Protocols* that first provided anti-Semites 'with the impetus to organise themselves'.

337. See G. C. Webber, 'Intolerance and discretion: Conservatives and British fascism, 1918–1926' in Tony Kushner and Kenneth Lunn (eds.), *Traditions of Intolerance* (Manchester, 1989), pp. 155–72.

338. On the Anglo-Catholic community in this respect, see Ulrike Ehet. 'Catholics and antisemitism in Germany and England 1918–1939', unpublished PhD thesis, University of London, 2005, p. 157. Tony Kushner writes of the 'generally harmonious 1920s'. *The Persistence of Prejudice* (Manchester, 1989), p. 165.

339. Martin Pugh, *'Hurrah for the Blackshirts'* (London, 2005), p. 28. It kept the *Protocols* in print, and it confined its membership to Aryans who could demonstrate that 'their ancestry is free from Jewish taint'. See Gisela C. Lebzelter, *Political Anti-Semitism in England 1918–1939* (London, 1978), pp. 49, 58.

340. Gisela C. Lebzelter, *Political Anti-Semitism in England 1918–1939* (London, 1978), pp. 50–1.

341. See David Cesarani, 'Joynson-Hicks and the radical Right in England after the First World War' in Tony Kushner and Kenneth Lunn (eds.), *Traditions of Intolerance* (Manchester, 1989), pp. 118–39; H. A. Taylor, *Jix—Viscount Brentford* (London, 1933), pp. 101–2; Geoffrey Alderman, *Modern British Jewry* (Oxford, 1992), p. 263; Martin Gilbert, *Churchill and the Jews* (London, 2007), p. 78; Martin Pugh, *'Hurrah for the Blackshirts'* (London, 2005), pp. 59, 215. Joynson-Hicks disappointed admirers. See Nesta H. Webster, *The Surrender of an Empire* (London, 1931), pp. 255–6. For a dissenting view on Joynson-Hicks, see W. D. Rubinstein, *A History of Jews in the English-Speaking World: Great Britain* (London, 1996), pp. 272–7.

342. See Maurice Cowling, *The Impact of Labour 1920–1924* (Cambridge, 2005), p. 75.

343. Andrew Roberts, *Eminent Churchillians* (London, 1994), p. 190.

344. Stephen Dorril, *Blackshirt* (London, 2006), pp. 5, 95.

345. A. W. B. Simpson, *In the Highest Degree Odious* (Oxford, 1994), p. 124. In the 1950s, Mosley thought it would be a 'good thing' if his Union Movement had

'some Jewish members'. See Trevor Grundy, *Memoir of a Fascist Childhood* (London, 1999), p. 123.

346. Alan Sykes, *The Radical Right in Britain* (London, 2005), p. 65.

347. A. W. B. Simpson, *In the Highest Degree Odious* (Oxford, 1994), p. 125; Stephen Dorril, *Blackshirt* (London, 2006), p. 320; N. Nugent, 'The ideas of the British Union of Fascists' in Neill Nugent and Roger King (eds.), *The British Right* (Westmead, Hants, 1977), pp. 149, 150.

348. David Pryce-Jones, *Unity Mitford: A quest* (London, 1976), pp. 142–3.

349. Alan Sykes, *The Radical Right in Britain* (London, 2005), pp. 65–6.

350. Robert Skidelsky, *Interests and Obsessions* (London, 1993), pp. xi–xii, 181–3, 187, 197. 'I was loath to admit', Skidelsky concedes, 'that he had a dark side' (p. xii). See also Stephen Dorril, *Blackshirt* (London, 2006), p. 493.

351. *Tomorrow We Live* (London, 1939), pp. 64–5.

352. See Maurice Cowling, *Religion and Public Doctrine in Modern England* (Cambridge, 1980), vol. 1, p. 339.

353. Graham Macklin, *Very Deeply Dyed in Black* (London, 2008), pp. 116–19.

354. *Mosley: Right or wrong?* (London, 1961), pp. 131–3.

355. See *My Answer* (London, 1946), pp. 22–3, 107–10; Richard Thurlow, *Fascism in Modern Britain* (London, 2000), pp. 162–3.

356. Louis W. Bondy, *Racketeers of Hatred* (London, 1946), pp. 148–9; Richard Griffiths, *Patriotism Perverted* (London, 1998), pp. 88, 100–1, 111, 121.

357. *The Nameless War* (London, 1952), pp. 11, 17, 21–2, 24, 31, 33, 54, 85, 89–90. On the 'Jew-Wise' in general, see Richard Thurlow, *Fascism in Modern Britain* (London, 2000), pp. 54–60.

358. *Out of Step* (Hollywood, CA, n.d.)

359. See Gisela C. Lebzelter, *Political Anti-Semitism in England 1918–1939* (London, 1978), pp. 68–85; Louis W. Bondy, *Racketeers of Hatred: Julius Streicher and the Jew-Baiters' International* (London, 1946), p. 251. Douglas Reed took up this theme after the war: see *Somewhere South of Suez* (London, 1950), p. 341. 'Mosley's advent was a disaster to Fascist development in Britain.' Arnold Spencer Leese, *Out of Step* (Hollywood, CA, n.d.), p. 52.

360. See Louis W. Bondy, *Racketeers of Hatred* (London, 1946), pp. 60, 157.

361. Richard Griffiths, *Patriotism Perverted* (London, 1998), p. 48.

362. See Colin Holmes, *Anti-Semitism in British Society 1876–1939* (New York, 1979), pp. 170–2.

363. Richard Griffiths, *Patriotism Perverted* (London, 1998), pp. 39–41.

364. *From Admiral to Cabin Boy* (London, 1947), pp. 80, 86.

365. Richard Griffiths, *Patriotism Perverted* (London, 1998), pp. 47, 87. 'The Anglo-German Brotherhood', ostensibly concerned with promoting understanding between the clergy and laity of the German and English Churches, merged with the Link in 1939. See ibid., p. 51. On A. K. Chesterton generally, see Martin Walker, *The National Front* (London, 1977), pp. 28–30.

366. Richard Thurlow, *Fascism in Modern Britain* (London, 2000), p. vii.

367. Alice Kaplan, *The Collaborator* (Chicago, 2000), p. 11.

368. Markku Ruotsila, 'The antisemitism of the Eighth Duke of Northumberland's the *Patriot*, 1922–1930', *Journal of Contemporary History*, 39/1 (2004), 72, 77, 90.

369. Ibid., pp. 79–81, 86. See also Martin Pugh, *'Hurrah for the Blackshirts'* (London, 2005), pp. 78–9.

370. See Oswald Mosley, *My Answer* (London, 1946), p. 109. Mosley was a strong anti-Zionist from the early 1920s. See Stephen Dorril, *Blackshirt* (London, 2006), pp. 65, 376.

371. Hilary Blume, 'A study of anti-Semitic groups in Britain, 1918–1940', unpublished D. Phil thesis, University of Sussex, 1971, p. 73.

372. *Germany and England* (Arabi, LA, n.d.), p. 34.

373. *The Surrender of an Empire* (London, 1931), pp. 360, 365.

374. Richard Griffiths, *Patriotism Perverted* (London, 1998), p. 111.

375. See ibid., pp. 24–6, 131.

376. *Twilight Over England* (London, 1992), pp. 49, 125–6.

377. See N. Nugent, 'Post-war fascism?' in Kenneth Lunn and Richard C. Thurlow (eds.), *British Fascism* (London, 1980), p. 212.

378. Martin Walker, *The National Front* (London, 1977), p. 41.

379. N. Nugent, 'Post-war fascism?' in Kenneth Lunn and Richard C. Thurlow (eds.), *British Fascism* (London, 1980), p. 218.

380. Martin Walker, *The National Front* (London, 1977), p. 192 (and see also p. 90).

381. 'Trotsky on England', *Essays in Biography* (London, 1961), p. 74.

382. Thomas P. Linehan, 'The British Union of Fascists in Hackney and Stoke Newington 1939–1940', in Geoffrey Alderman and Colin Holmes (eds.), *Outsiders and Outcasts* (London, 1993), p. 162; Gisela C. Lebzelter, *Political Anti-Semitism in England 1918–1939* (London, 1978), p. 37.

383. Bryan Magee, *Clouds of Glory* (London, 2003), p. 314.

384. Stephen Dorril, *Blackshirt* (London, 2006), p. 479. Other fascist groups also used labels: 'Scratch a Bolshie and find a Jew', 'Britons! Do not allow Jews to tamper with white girls'. Martin Pugh, *'Hurrah for the Blackshirts'* (London, 2005), p. 70.

385. Gisela C. Lebzelter, *Political Anti-Semitism in England 1918–1939* (London, 1978), pp. 95, 96.

386. Ibid., p. 41.

387. Todd M. Endelman, *The Jews of Britain 1656–2000* (Berkeley, CA, 2002), p. 203.

388. Thomas P. Linehan, 'The British Union of Fascists in Hackney and Stoke Newington 1939–1940', in Geoffrey Alderman and Colin Holmes (eds.), *Outsiders and Outcasts* (London, 1993), p. 155.

389. Ibid., pp. 144–5, 153.

390. See Gisela C. Lebzelter, *Political Anti-Semitism in England 1918–1939* (London, 1978), p. 39.

391. Thomas P. Linehan, 'The British Union of Fascists in Hackney and Stoke Newington 1939–1940', in Geoffrey Alderman and Colin Holmes (eds.), *Outsiders and Outcasts* (London, 1993), p. 150.

392. Ibid., p. 163.

393. Ibid., pp. 148–9.

394. See Martin Pugh, *'Hurrah for the Blackshirts'* (London, 2005), pp. 11–12.

395. Richard Griffiths, *Patriotism Perverted* (London, 1998), p. 170.

396. See ibid., p. 69; Tony Kushner, *The Persistence of Prejudice* (Manchester, 1989), p. 15.

397. See Robert Skidelsky, *Interests and Obsessions* (London, 1993), p. 203; Richard Griffiths, *Patriotism Perverted* (London, 1998), pp. 183–7.

398. See Richard Griffiths, *Patriotism Perverted* (London, 1998), p. 1.

399. G. C. Webber, *The Ideology of the British Right* (London, 1986), p. 136.

400. See Robert Skidelsky, *Interests and Obsessions* (London, 1993), pp. 205–6.

401. See Louis W. Bondy, *Racketeers of Hatred* (London, 1946), p. 159. 'I want everyone to know, I am a Jew hater', she told the readers of *Der Stürmer*. See Noel Annan, *Our Age* (London, 1990), p. 204.

402. Robert Skidelsky, *Interests and Obsessions* (London, 1993), p. 206.

403. G. C. Webber, *The Ideology of the British Right* (London, 1986), p. 57.

404. See Louis W Bondy, *Racketeers of Hatred* (London, 1946), p. 149; G. C. Webber, *The Ideology of the British Right* (London, 1986), p. 125.

405. Tony Kushner, 'The paradox of prejudice: the impact of organised antisemitism in Britain during an anti-Nazi war', in Tony Kushner and Kenneth Lunn (eds.), *Traditions of Intolerance* (Manchester, 1989), p. 75.

406. See ibid., pp. 72–84.

407. See Sidney Aster (ed.), *Appeasement and All Souls* (Cambridge, 2004), p. 24.

408. See Martin Gilbert, *The Roots of Appeasement* (New York, 1966), p. xi. Gilbert distinguishes between 'old' appeasement, which he broadly endorses, and 'new' appeasement, which he condemns. See his final chapter, 'Epilogue: Munich and the new appeasement'.

409. Martin Gilbert and Richard Gott, *The Appeasers* (London, 2000), pp. vii, 183.

410. Norman Rose, *The Cliveden Set* (London, 2001), pp. 196–7.

411. Ibid., p. 194.

412. See Elie Kedourie, 'Lord Halifax, Conservative', *The Crossman Confessions and Other Essays* (London, 1984), p. 34.

413. Ian Kershaw, *Making Friends with Hitler* (London, 2004), p. 63.

414. See Elie Kedourie, 'Lord Halifax, Conservative', *The Crossman Confessions and Other Essays* (London, 1984), p. 34.

415. See Frank McDonagh, *Hitler, Chamberlain and Appeasement* (Cambridge, 2002), p. 58.

416. Duff Cooper, *Old Men Forget* (London, 1953), pp. 183, 200; Sidney Aster (ed.), *Appeasement and All Souls* (Cambridge, 2004), p. 205.
417. Frank McDonagh, *Hitler, Chamberlain and Appeasement* (Cambridge, 2002), p. 19.
418. Duff Cooper, *Old Men Forget* (London, 1953), p. 200.
419. Martin Gilbert and Richard Gott, *The Appeasers* (London, 2000), p. 26.
420. See Andrew Sharf, *The British Press and Jews under Nazi Rule* (London, 1964), p. 41.
421. Ian Kershaw, *Making Friends with Hitler* (London, 2004), pp. 147, 230–1.
422. See Richard Griffiths, *Patriotism Perverted* (London, 1998), p. 15.
423. Ian Kershaw, *Making Friends with Hitler* (London, 2004), p. 59.
424. Richard Griffiths, *Patriotism Perverted* (London, 1998), p. 27.
425. Martin Gilbert, *The Roots of Appeasement* (New York, 1966), pp. 146, 162–3.
426. See Ian Kershaw, *Making Friends with Hitler* (London, 2004), pp. 55, 146–7, 228–9.
427. Ibid., p. 50.
428. On his dismay at the Nazi persecutions, and his support for the policy of expanding temporary refuge for Jews following the events of November 1938, see Louise London, *Whitehall and the Jews 1933–1948* (Cambridge, 2000), pp. 14, 105–8, 110–13.
429. See Victoria Glendinning, *Leonard Woolf* (London, 2006), p. 154.
430. Harold Nicolson, *Diaries and Letters: 1930–39* (London, 1966), p. 327; Norman Rose, *The Cliveden Set* (London, 2001), p. 183.
431. See Gisela C. Lebzelter, *Political Anti-Semitism in England 1918–1939* (London, 1978), p. 158.
432. See John Grigg, *Nancy Astor* (London, 1980), p. 114.
433. Norman Rose, *The Cliveden Set* (London, 2001), pp. 37, 122.
434. Duff Cooper, *Old Men Forget* (London, 1953), p. 171.
435. See Andrew Sharf, *The British Press and Jews under Nazi Rule* (London, 1964), pp. 65, 67.
436. Martin Gilbert and Richard Gott, *The Appeasers* (London, 2000), pp. 218, 233.
437. Duff Cooper, *Old Men Forget* (London, 1953), pp. 258–9.
438. Andrew Sharf, *The British Press and Jews under Nazi Rule* (London, 1964), pp. 23, 58, 77, 87, 155, 193.
439. N. J. Crowson, *Fleet Street, Press Barons and Politics: The journals of Collins Brooks, 1932–1940* (Cambridge, 1998), p. 229.
440. Richard Griffiths, *Patriotism Perverted* (London, 1998), p. 27.
441. Jack Beatson, 'Aliens, enemy aliens, and friendly enemy aliens' in Jack Beatson and Reinhard Zimmerman (eds.), *Jurists Uprooted* (Oxford, 2004), pp. 79–84; *Mark v Mark* (2005) UKHL 42, (2006) 1 AC 98.
442. Louise London, *Whitehall and the Jews, 1933–1948* (Cambridge, 2000), p. 28.
443. See David Cesarani, 'Great Britain' in David S. Wyman (ed.), *The World Reacts to the Holocaust* (Baltimore, MA, 1996), p. 603.

444. Louise London, *Whitehall and the Jews 1933–1948* (Cambridge, 2000), pp. 12, 59 ('in early 1938, an estimated 10,000 Jewish refugees were present').

445. Or lack of 'generosity': ibid., pp. 14–15, 256.

446. See Colin Holmes, *John Bull's Island* (London, 1988), pp. 112–14, 140.

447. See Richard Griffiths, *Patriotism Perverted* (London, 1998), pp. 19–20, 146.

448. Louise London, 'British responses to the plight of Jews in Europe 1933–1945' in Michael Berenbaum and Abraham J. Peck (eds.), *The Holocaust and History* (Bloomington, IN, 2002), pp. 515–16.

449. See Louise London, *Whitehall and the Jews 1933–1948* (Cambridge, 2000), pp. 8, 14, 126.

450. See Andrew Sharf, *The British Press and Jews under Nazi Rule* (London, 1964), p. 168.

451. Richard Griffiths, *Patriotism Perverted* (London, 1998), p. 21.

452. Nesta H. Webster, *Germany and England* (Arabi, LA, n.d.), p. 21.

453. Douglas Reed, *All Our Tomorrows* (London, 1942), pp. 283–4, 296; *A Prophet at Home* (London, 1941), p. 23.

454. Fritz Stern, *Five Germanys I Have Known* (New York, 2006), p. 143.

455. 'It was the British Government which took the lead in barring the escape-routes from Europe against Jewish refugees.' Bernard Wasserstein, *Britain and the Jews of Europe 1939–1945* (Oxford, 1988), p. 345.

456. *Anti-Semitism and the Jewish Question* (London, 1942), pp. 100–1; Henry Srebrnik, 'The British Communist Party's National Jewish Committee' in Tony Kushner and Kenneth Lunn (eds.), *The Politics of Marginality* (London, 1990), pp. 82–96.

457. Bernard Wasserstein, *Britain and the Jews of Europe 1939–1945* (Oxford, 1988), pp. 90, 116–17.

458. See Andrew Roberts, *'The Holy Fox': The life of Lord Halifax* (London, 1997), pp. 155–6.

459. *Auschwitz and the Allies* (London, 2001), p. viii. 'However much it may be disparaged now, the argument that real rescue could only come from an Allied victory was compelling and persuasive.' Michael Marrus, *The Holocaust in History* (London, 1989), p. 172.

460. See Martin Gilbert, *Auschwitz and the Allies* (London, 2001), p. 74.

461. Bernard Wasserstein, *Britain and the Jews of Europe 1939–1945* (Oxford, 1988), p. 163.

462. See Meier Sompolinsky, *The British Government and the Holocaust* (Brighton, 1999), p. 203.

463. Martin Gilbert, *Auschwitz and the Allies* (London, 2001), p. 140.

464. See ibid., p. 77.

465. Michael Marrus, *The Holocaust in History* (London, 1989), p. 193.

466. Bernard Wasserstein, *Britain and the Jews of Europe 1939–1945* (Oxford, 1988), pp. 49, 88, 147.

467. See ibid., pp. 308–19.

468. See Martin Gilbert, *Auschwitz and the Allies* (London, 2001), p. 21.

469. See ibid., p. 77.

470. See ibid., pp. 99, 312.

471. See ibid., p. 129.

472. See ibid., p. 290.

473. See ibid., p. 138.

474. See ibid., p. 150. Cavendish-Bentinck was ambassador to Poland after the War. For his response to post-War anti-Semitism see Jan T. Gross, *Fear* (New York, 2006), pp. 138–9.

475. Bernard Wasserstein, *Britain and the Jews of Europe 1939–1945* (Oxford, 1988), p. 69.

476. Ibid., p. 37.

477. Pamela Shatzkes, See *Holocaust and Rescue* (London, 2002), p. 239.

478. See Martin Gilbert, *Auschwitz and the Allies* (London, 2001), p. 76.

479. See ibid., pp. 48–9.

480. See ibid., p. 76; Martin Gilbert, *Churchill and the Jews* (London, 2007), p. 190.

481. See Bernard Wasserstein, *Britain and the Jews of Europe 1939–1945* (Oxford, 1988), pp. 50–1.

482. Ibid., p. 34. Eden himself acknowledged in a private note, 'I prefer Arabs to Jews.'

483. Ibid., p. 97.

484. Ibid., p. 297. See also Norman Rose, *A Senseless, Squalid War* (London, 2009), p. 63.

485. *The Holocaust in History* (London, 1989), p. 166.

486. *Britain and the Jews of Europe 1939–1945* (Oxford, 1988), pp. 132, 350.

487. *Auschwitz and the Allies* (London, 2001), p. 24.

488. 'A Note on anti-Semitism', *New Statesman*, 13 February 1943, p. 107.

489. A Mass-Observation poll in November 1939 found that 17% of the population were cynical about Britain's war aims, 'including many statements that it was "for the Jews"'. Tony Kushner, *The Persistence of Prejudice* (Manchester, 1989), p. 19.

490. Ibid., p. 17; Angus Calder, *The People's War* (London, 1992), p. 167; Aaron Goldman, 'The resurgence of antisemitism in Britain during World War II', *Jewish Social Studies*, 46/1 (1984), 39.

491. 21 October 1940. See I. Rennap, *Anti-Semitism and the Jewish Question* (London, 1942), p. 109.

492. Richard Overy, *The Battle* (London, 2000), pp. 101–2.

493. Selig Brodetsky, *Memoirs from Ghetto to Israel* (London, 1960), pp. 202–3.

494. Steven J. Zipperstein, *Elusive Prophet* (London, 1993), p. 296.

495. *All Our Tomorrows* (London, 1942), p. 39.

496. Tony Kushner, *The Persistence of Prejudice* (Manchester, 1989), p. 52.

497. Ibid., pp. 120, 122; M. Corbett Ashley, 'Great Britain and the Jews' in J. J. Lynx (ed.), *The Future of the Jews* (London, 1945), pp. 111–12.

498. Bernard Wasserstein, *Britain and the Jews of Europe 1939–1945* (Oxford, 1988), pp. 117–20.

499. See, for example, Douglas Reed, *All Our Tomorrows* (London, 1942), p. 148.

500. Selig Brodetsky, *Memoirs from Ghetto to Israel* (London, 1960), p. 203.

501. See John Gross, *A Double Thread* (London, 2001), p. 70.

502. See Aaron Goldman, 'The resurgence of antisemitism in Britain during World War II', *Jewish Social Studies*, 46/1 (1984), 41.

503. Richard Bolchover, *British Jewry and the Holocaust* (Cambridge, 1993), p. 48.

504. Elias Canetti, *Party in the Blitz* (London, 2005), p. 73.

505. Tony Kushner, *The Persistence of Prejudice* (Manchester, 1989), pp. 55, 57, 76, 78, 101, 101–5, 117; Tony Kushner, 'The paradox of prejudice' in Tony Kushner and Kenneth Lunn (eds.), *Traditions of Intolerance* (Manchester, 1989), 79; George Orwell, 'London Letter to *Partisan Review*', *The Collected Essays, Journalism and Letters* (London, 1968), vol. 2, p. 209.

506. Mary Kenny, *Germany Calling* (Dublin, 2003), p. 197.

507. 'The Jew in the World of the Future' in J. J. Lynx (ed.), *The Future of the Jews* (London, 1945), pp. 51–3, 56.

508. Colin Seymour-Ure, 'Sir Edward George Warris Hulton', *Oxford Dictionary of National Biography* (Oxford University Press, 2004; online edn, Jan 2008).

509. *Death in Duplicate* (London, 1945), pp. 33, 34, 79, 161, 162.

510. 'When the war ended and the secrets of Belsen and Auschwitz were exposed, the Jews enjoyed a brief popularity.' John Rae, *The Custard Boys* (London, 1960), p. 55; 'Among educated people, anti-Semitism is held to be an unforgivable sin...It is not at present possible, indeed, that anti-Semitism should become respectable.' George Orwell, 'Anti-Semitism in Britain', April 1945, in *I Belong to the Left* (London, 1998), p. 66.

511. *The Novel in France* (London, 1962), p. 368.

512. *Chapters of Life* (London, 1950), pp. 21, 168; Philip Rees, 'Changing interpretations of British FASCISM: A bibliographical survey' in Kenneth Lunn and Richard C. Thurlow (eds.), *British Fascism* (London, 1980), p. 195.

513. M. C. Bradbrook, *Shakespeare and Elizabethan Poetry* (London, 1951), p. 175.

514. See John Gross, *Shylock* (London, 1992), pp. 316–17.

515. Noel Annan, *Our Age* (London, 1990), p. 208.

516. See David A. Hollinger, *Science, Jews, and Secular Culture* (Princeton, NJ, 1996), pp. 9, 26–7.

517. Michael Howard, *Captain Professor* (London, 2006), p. 155.

518. See Ronald W. Zweig, *Britain and Palestine during the Second World War* (London, 1986), p. 167.

519. Naomi Shepherd, *Ploughing Sand* (London, 1999), pp. 158, 171, 177–8; Angus Calder, *The People's War* (London, 1992), p. 499. Benny Morris, *The Road to Jerusalem* (London, 2002), pp. 24, 82, 221, 226–7 (on General Sir John Glubb's

fondness for relating 'Jewish'—by which he meant 'Israeli'—behaviour to Nazism). Glubb was commander of the Arab Legion, 1939–56. Reporting the Moyne assassination, *The Times* worried that 'the Jews' risked 'contamination' by Nazism.

520. David Cesarani, *Justice Delayed* (London, 2000), p. 166.

521. Norman Rose, *A Senseless, Squalid War* (London, 2009), pp. 166–8; David Leitch, 'Explosion at the King David Hotel' in Michael Sissons and Philip French (eds.), *Age of Austerity 1945–1951* (London, 1964), pp. 74–5.

522. Wm. Roger Louis, 'British imperialism and the end of the Palestine Mandate' in Wm. Roger Louis and Robert W. Stookey (eds.), *The End of the Palestine Mandate* (London, 1986), p. 19.

523. *High Tide and After* (London, 1962), p. 190.

524. David Leitch, 'Explosion at the King David Hotel' in Michael Sissons and Philip French (eds.), *Age of Austerity 1945–1951* (London, 1964), pp. 75–7; Anthony Lester and Geoffrey Bindman, *Race and Law* (London, 1972), pp. 347–9.

525. Harold Nicolson, *Diaries and Letters: 1945–62* (London, 1968), p. 140.

526. See, for example, Admiral Sir Barry Domvile, *From Admiral to Cabin Boy* (London, 1947), pp. 21, 54, 147–8.

527. *Days from a Different World* (London, 2005), p. 300. See also Simon Garfield, *Our Hidden Lives* (London, 2004), pp. 321, 430, 432.

528. See Wm. Roger Louis, 'British imperialism and the end of the Palestine Mandate' in Wm. Roger Louis and Robert W. Stookey (eds.), *The End of the Palestine Mandate* (London, 1986), pp. 1–2.

529. Hugh Dalton, *High Tide and After* (London, 1962), p. 147.

530. See Wm. Roger Louis, *Ends of British Imperialism* (London, 2006), p. 443.

531. Richard Crossman, *A Nation Reborn* (London, 1960), pp. 69–70. 'For Bevin the step from anti-Zionist to anti-Jew was instinctive.' Norman Bentwich and Helen Bentwich, *Mandate Memories 1918–1948* (London, 1965), p. 176. See also Christopher Mayhew, *Time to Explain* (London, 1987), pp. 119–20. In *Publish It Not: The Middle East cover-up* (1975), pp. 19, 40–1, however, Mayhew argued that Bevin was *not* an anti-Semite, though the Foreign Secretary's 'plain speaking enabled the Zionists to misrepresent him' as one. On Bevin's grievance at perceived Jewish ingratitude, see James McDonald, *My Mission in Israel* (New York, 1951), p. 25.

532. See Wm. Roger Louis, 'British imperialism and the end of the Palestine Mandate' in Wm. Roger Louis and Robert W. Stookey (eds.), *The End of the Palestine Mandate* (London, 1986), p. 23.

533. *Ends of British Imperialism* (London, 2006), p. 427.

534. Harold Nicolson, *Diaries and Letters: 1945–62* (London, 1968), p. 145.

535. Alan Bullock, *Ernest Bevin Foreign Secretary* (Oxford, 1985), pp. 182–3. Wm. Roger Louis concurs. 'As Alan Bullock has pointed out, Bevin reached the age of sixty four before anyone suspected him of harbouring an anti-Jewish

prejudice.' *Ends of British Imperialism* (London, 2006), p. 419. See also Norman Rose, *A Senseless, Squalid War* (London, 2009), p. 83.

536. Martin Gilbert, *Churchill and the Jews* (London, 2007), p. 275.

537. A warning had been given, but in one version, it was disregarded. 'We aren't here to take orders from Jews', a very senior British official is said to have responded. 'We give *them* orders.' The official communiqué insisted that the warning came too late. See David Leitch, 'Explosion at the King David Hotel' in Michael Sissons and Philip French (eds.), *Age of Austerity 1945– 1951* (London, 1964), p. 60. Nicholas Bethell argues, however, that this version—which he attributes to Menachem Begin—is false. The official himself 'flatly denied it', and sued a London newspaper for repeating it, winning an apology. See *The Palestine Triangle* (London, 1979), pp. 264–6, 279. See also Norman Rose, *A Senseless, Squalid War* (London, 2009), p. 116.

538. Benny Morris, *The Birth of the Palestinian Refugee Problem Revisited* (Cambridge, 2004), pp. 237–9.

539. Wm. Roger Louis, 'British imperialism and the end of the Palestine Mandate' in Wm. Roger Louis and Robert W. Stookey (eds.), *The End of the Palestine Mandate* (London, 1986), pp. 10, 12; Norman Rose, *A Senseless, Squalid War* (London, 2009), pp. 108–9, 117–18; John Simpson, *Days from a Different World* (London, 2005), p. 300; Tom Segev, *One Palestine, Complete* (London, 2000), pp. 479–80; David Leitch, 'Explosion at the King David Hotel' in Michael Sissons and Philip French (eds.), *Age of Austerity 1945–1951* (London, 1964), pp. 60, 71–2.

540. Wm. Roger Louis, *Ends of British Imperialism* (London, 2006), pp. 445–6.

541. Nicholas Bethell, *The Palestine Triangle* (London, 1979), p. 267.

542. Ibid., pp. 280–1; Norman Rose, *A Senseless, Squalid War* (London, 2009), pp. 147–8.

543. Norman Rose, *A Senseless, Squalid War* (London, 2009), pp. 186–7; see also Graham Macklin, *Very Deeply Dyed in Black* (London, 2008), pp. 45–7 ('the Palestine factor').

544. Graham Macklin, *Very Deeply Dyed in Black* (London, 2008), p. 48.

545. Gerry Gable, 'The Far Right in contemporary Britain' in Luciano Cheles *et al.* (eds.), *Neo-Fascism in Europe* (London, 1991), p. 247; Nigel Copsey, *Contemporary British Fascism* (London, 2008), p. 11.

546. Richard Thurlow, *Fascism in Modern Britain* (London, 2000), p. xii; Graham Macklin, *Very Deeply Dyed in Black* (London, 2008), pp. 9–14, 39–40.

547. Graham Macklin, *Very Deeply Dyed in Black* (London, 2008), pp. 127–9, 132.

548. Ibid., p. 67.

549. Nigel Copsey, *Contemporary British Fascism* (London, 2008), p. 157; Alan Sykes, *The Radical Right in Britain* (London, 2005) pp. 117–18.

550. N. Nugent, 'The political parties of the extreme Right', in Neill Nugent and Roger King (eds.), *The British Right* (Westmead, Hants, 1977), p. 167.

551. Richard Thurlow, 'The developing British fascist interpretation of race, culture and evolution' in Julie V. Gottleib and Thomas P. Lineham (eds.), *The Culture of Fascism* (London, 2004), p. 71.

552. See Steven Woodridge, 'Purifying the nation: Critiques of cultural decadence and decline in British neo-fascist ideology' in Julie V. Gottleib and Thomas P. Lineham (eds.), *The Culture of Fascism* (London, 2004), pp. 137–42.

553. See Trevor Grundy, *Memoir of a Fascist Childhood* (London, 1999), pp. 49, 65.

554. Dan Jacobson, 'Plague spot', *Time of Arrival and Other Essays* (New York, 1962), pp. 64–7.

555. Martin Walker, *The National Front* (London, 1977), p. 43.

556. It remained, however, central to the deep structure of Far Right and Fascist thinking. See Michael Billig, *Fascists* (London, 1978), pp. 41, 127–36.

557. See Gerry Gable, 'The Far Right in contemporary Britain' in Luciano Cheles *et al.* (eds.), *Neo-Fascism in Europe* (London, 1991), pp. 256–8, 246.

558. Nigel Copsey, *Contemporary British Fascism* (London, 2008), p. 89.

559. N. Nugent, 'The political parties of the extreme Right' in Neill Nugent and Roger King (eds.), *The British Right* (Westmead, Hants, 1977), pp. 173, 188.

560. Nick Ryan, *Homeland* (London, 2004), chs. 1–2.

561. Stephen Dorril, *Blackshirt* (London, 2006), p. 579. Expulsion was a policy of John Tyndall's Greater Britain movement: 'The removal of the Jews from Britain must be a cardinal aim of the new order...' N. Nugent, 'The political parties of the extreme Right' in Neill Nugent and Roger King (eds.), *The British Right* (Westmead, Hants, 1977), p. 168.

562. Anthony Lester and Geoffrey Bindman, *Race and Law* (London, 1972), p. 352.

563. 'Anti-Jewish and proud', *Guardian*, 13 October 1962.

564. Chaim Bermant, *Troubled Eden* (London, 1969), pp. 259–60.

565. See Community Security Trust, *Antisemitic Incidents Report 2004* (London, 2005).

566. See Michael Billig, *Fascists* (London, 1978), pp. 165–9, 175, 177–9, 186, 196, 207, 298–9, 305.

567. See Richard Thurlow, 'The developing British fascist interpretation of race, culture and evolution' in Julie V. Gottleib and Thomas P. Lineham (eds.), *The Culture of Fascism* (London, 2004), p. 72.

568. Nigel Copsey, *Contemporary British Fascism* (London, 2008), pp. 14, 16, 88–93; Martin Walker, *The National Front* (London, 1977), pp. 35, 39, 69–70, 72; and see the obituaries in *The Times*, the *Guardian*, and the *Daily Telegraph*, 20 July 2005.

569. 'The Mosley Moral', *Daily Telegraph*, 10 November 1983.

570. See, for example, N. J. Crowson, *Fleet Street, Press Barons and Politics* (Cambridge, 1998), p. 240.

571. David Cesarani, *Justice Delayed* (London, 2000), pp. 4–5, 74–81, 166–9, 201, 204–5, 210–14, 218–19, 221–4, 228, 230, 254, 257, 260–3.

572. Robin Judd, 'The politics of beef', *Jewish Social Studies*, New Series, 10/1 (2003), 124–5.

573. See David Biale, *Blood and Belief* (Berkeley, CA, 2007), pp. 127–8.

574. See Geoffrey Alderman, 'Power, authority and status in British Jewry' in Geoffrey Alderman and Colin Holmes (eds.), *Outsiders and Outcasts* (London, 1993); Tony Kushner, 'Stunning intolerance', *Jewish Quarterly* (Spring 1989).

575. Tony Kushner, 'Stunning intolerance', *Jewish Quarterly* (Spring 1989), 20; Roger Charlton and Ronald Kaye, 'The politics of slaughter', *New Community*, 12/3 (1985), 494.

576. Tony Kushner, 'Stunning intolerance', *Jewish Quarterly* (Spring 1989), 16.

577. See *The Annual Report of the Royal Society for the Prevention of Cruelty to Animals etc.* (London, 1856), p. 9. The report goes on, 'the practise of unnecessary cruelty is not confined to Jewish butchers. Your committee believes that cruelty prevails very largely in slaughtering animals generally . . .' (ibid., p. 10).

578. *Committee on Humane Slaughter* (London, 1904), pp. 9, 12, 15, 20, 21, 25, 27 ('the Jewish method of slaughter is a cruel method'), 34, 42 ('Jewish mode'), 52 ('what I might call the religious portion of the killing'), 53, 55 ('the Jewish fashion'), 57. In the Report itself, there is a reference to 'animals slaughtered according to Jewish rites'. *Report of the Committee appointed by the Admiralty, etc.* (London, 1904), p. 13.

579. *Committee on Humane Slaughter* (London, 1904), p. 51. The Committee concluded, 'all animals without exception should be stunned'. *Report of the Committee appointed by the Admiralty, etc.* (London, 1904), p. 6, para. 6 (a), and pp. 10–11, para. 12.

580. Ernest Bell, 'The humane slaughtering of animals', *Humanitarian League* (London, 1904), p. 13.

581. See Tony Kushner, *The Persistence of Prejudice* (Manchester, 1989), pp. 94–5.

582. See Richard Griffiths, *Patriotism Perverted* (London, 1998), pp. 64, 110; Martin Pugh, *'Hurrah for the Blackshirts'* (London, 2005), p. 231.

583. M. Dudley Ward, *Jewish 'Kosher': Should it be permitted to survive in a new Britain?* (Ilfracombe, 1944), pp. 4–5, 9, 10, 24, 28, 30, 41, 43.

584. Tony Kushner, 'Stunning intolerance', *Jewish Quarterly* (Spring 1989), 18.

585. *Legalised Cruelty* (London, October 1948). However, acording to Tony Kushner, 'The impact of British anti-semitism, 1918–1940' in David Cesarani (ed.), *The Making of Anglo-Jewry* (Oxford, 1990), p. 203, the RSPCA 'exploited anti-semitism to try to reach [its] goal of banning *shechita*'.

586. See Tony Kushner, 'Heritage and ethnicity' in Tony Kushner (ed.), *The Jewish Heritage in British History* (London, 1992), pp. 16–17.

587. Brian Barry, *Culture and Equality* (Cambridge MA, 2001), pp. 32–6, 45–6, 295–6, 303–4; David Miller, 'Liberalism, equal opportunities and cultural commitments', and Simon Caney, 'Equal treatment, exceptions and cultural diversity' both in Paul Kelly (ed.), *Multiculturalism Reconsidered* (Cambridge,

2002), pp. 56, 82–3; Linda Barclay, 'Liberalism and diversity' in Frank Johnson and Michael Smith (eds.), *The Oxford Handbook of Contemporary Philosophy* (Oxford, 2005), p. 159; *Report on the Welfare of Livestock when Slaughtered by Religious Methods*, FAWC, 1995.

588. Linda Barclay, 'Liberalism and diversity' in Frank Johnson and Michael Smith (eds.), *The Oxford Handbook of Contemporary Philosophy* (Oxford, 2005), p. 160; Neville Kesselman, 'Challenges to Shechita and its protection by government and legislation in late twentieth century Britain', unpublished MA thesis, University of London, September 2001, pp. 2–49.

589. See Brian Klug, 'Ritual murmur', *Patterns of Prejudice*, 23/2 (1989), 23.

590. Robin Judd, 'The politics of beef', *Jewish Social Studies*, New Series, 10/1 (2003), 126.

591. Letter, *The Times*, 9 May 1978.

592. David McCalden, 'Alien cruelty to British animals', *Spearhead*, May 1974.

593. Letter, *Independent*, 2 September 1987.

594. Quoted in Tony Kushner, 'Stunning intolerance', *Jewish Quarterly* (Spring 1989), 17.

595. This grievance was voiced as early as the 9th century. See Avrom Saltman, *The Jewish Question in 1655* (Ramat-Gan, 1995), p. 247.

596. See Michael F. Metcalf, 'Regulating slaughter', *Patterns of Prejudice*, 23/3 (1989), 32–47.

597. Robin Judd, 'The politics of beef', *Jewish Social Studies*, New Series, 10/1 (2003), 122–4.

598. 'The vast majority of people in Europe agree that pre-stunning is more humane . . .' 'Humane slaughter', RSPCA, 16 April 1981. 'The fact remains that the vast majority of people in this country today are utterly opposed to this inhumane and cruel method of slaughter.' Letter, *Daily Telegraph*, 21 January 1969. Opinion polls that seek to establish high levels of opposition to 'ritual slaughter' are often criticized for the skewed framing of the questions and their prejudicial language. See Roger Charlton and Ronald Kaye, 'The politics of slaughter', *New Community*, 12/3 (1985), 498.

599. Geoffrey G. Field, 'Anti-Semitism with the boots off' in Herbert A. Strauss (ed.), *Hostages of Modernization* (Berlin, 1993), pp. 294–325.

600. Tony Kushner intimates a dissent from this proposition, but instances only the Aliens Act, and then, with qualifications. He also quotes a Board of Deputies member, who warned in 1938 of the possibility of 'anti-Jewish legislation in this country'. See *The Persistence of Prejudice* (Manchester, 1989), pp. 10–11, 13.

601. Geoffrey Alderman, *London Jewry and London Politics 1889–1986* (London, 1989), pp. 42–3.

602. David Cesarani, *The Jewish Chronicle and Anglo-Jewry 1841–1991* (Cambridge, 1994), p. 98.

603. Richard Shannon, *The Crisis of Imperialism 1865–1915* (London, 1974), pp. 446–7.

604. See Todd M. Endelman, *The Jews of Britain 1656–2000* (Berkeley, CA, 2002), p. 244.

605. Jack Beatson, 'Aliens, enemy aliens, and friendly enemy aliens' in Jack Beatson and Reinhard Zimmerman (eds.), *Jurists Uprooted* (Oxford, 2004), p. 77.

606. See Tony Kushner, 'The impact of British anti-semitism, 1918–1940' in David Cesarani (ed.), *The Making of Anglo-Jewry* (Oxford, 1990), p. 192.

607. Jose Harris, *Private Lives, Public Spirit: Britain 1870–1914* (London, 1994), pp. 16–17.

608. Bernard Wasserstein, *The British in Palestine* (Oxford, 1991), p. 12.

609. Ulrike Ehet, 'Catholics and antisemitism in Germany and England 1918–1939', unpublished PhD thesis, University of London, 2005, p. 59.

610. See G. A. Cranfield, 'The "London Evening-Post" and the Jew Bill of 1753', *Historical Journal*, 8/1 (1965), 30.

611. See Richard Griffiths, *Patriotism Perverted* (London, 1998), p. 56.

612. See Robert Skidelsky, 'Reflections on Mosley and British fascism' in Kenneth Lunn and Richard C. Thurlow (eds.), *British Fascism* (London, 1980), p. 90, for Mosley's debt to the 'radical tradition of anti-semitism, dating from the late nineteenth-century, which stressed the role of "cosmopolitan" Jewish finance in the generation of both depressions and wars'.

613. See Tony Kushner, *The Persistence of Prejudice* (Manchester, 1989), pp. 85, 91.

614. Richard Griffiths, *Patriotism Perverted* (London, 1998), p. 29.

615. See Elliot Horowitz, *Reckless Rites* (Princeton, NJ, 2006), pp. 198–201.

616. W. R. W. Stephens, *The Life and Letters of Edward A. Freeman* (London, 1895), vol. 2, p. 254.

617. See Stephen Koss (ed.), *The Pro-Boers* (London, 1973), p. 149.

618. Tony Kushner, *The Persistence of Prejudice* (Manchester, 1989), pp. 85–8.

619. '[The Labour leader George Lansbury] distinguished between the egotistical rich Jews who were against "the re-establishment of a Jewish kingdom", and the poor masses, who yearned for deliverance . . .' Joseph Gorny, *The British Labour Movement and Zionism 1917–1948* (London, 1983), p. 22.

620. Tony Kushner, *The Persistence of Prejudice* (Manchester, 1989), p. 88.

6. THE MENTALITY OF MODERN ENGLISH ANTI-SEMITISM

1. Raymond Aron, *The Opium of the Intellectuals* (New Brunswick, NJ, 2001), p. 216; Mark Lilla, 'The legitimacy of the Liberal Age' in Mark Lilla (ed.), *New French Thought* (Princeton, NJ, 1994), p. 3.

2. See Peter Berger and Thomas Luckmann, *The Social Construction of Reality* (London, 1991), pp. 112–13.

3. Daniel J. Levinson and R. Nevitt Sanford, 'A scale for the measurement of anti-Semitism' in Werner Bergmann (ed.), *Error Without Trial: Psychological research on antisemitism* (Berlin, 1988), pp. 472–3.

4. See G. E. R. Lloyd, *Demystifying Mentalities* (Cambridge, 1990), pp. 4–5, 135, 138.

5. 'I live in a constant and ever-present dread that I may not be able to give my children this essential equipment [i.e., cultural knowledge] that is a Jew's greatest weapon to fight the perpetual battle against the inherent inferiority complex of their race and against the disability of being a Jew.' 'Because I am a Jew I am afraid', *Daily Express*, 17 March 1931.

6. R. J. Minney, *The Private Papers of Hore-Belisha* (London, 1960), pp. 17, 164; Ian R. Grimwood, *A Little Chit of a Fellow* (Lewes, 2006), pp. 63, 144.

7. Richard Cockett, *Twilight of Truth* (London, 1989), pp. 9–11, 162–4; Martin Pugh, *'Hurrah for the Blackshirts'* (London, 2005), p. 233.

8. Fred J. Dowset, 'Both sides of Jewish character', *Westminster Review*, 130 (July–December 1888), 152, 154.

9. John Diamond, 'Dressing up as Hitler isn't funny', *Telegraph*, 11 February 2001.

10. Humbert Wolfe, *Now a Stranger* (London, 1933), pp. 116, 125–6.

11. See Todd M. Endelman, *The Jews of Georgian England 1714–1830* (Philadelphia, 1979), p. 117.

12. A. Neubauer, 'Notes on the race-types of the Jews', *Journal of the Anthropological Institute of Great Britain and Ireland*, 15 (1886), 20; Matthew Arnold, *Literature and Dogma* (London, 1876), pp. 143, 145, 156, 161; James Ogden, *Isaac D'Israeli* (1969), p. 194. Alexander McCaul was careful to explain in the 'advertisement' to *The Old Paths* (London, 1854), that when criticizing the Talmud for, inter alia, 'intolerance to other nations', he had 'carefully avoided the tone in which Eisenmenger and others have treated this subject': see p. vii. Contrast T. W. H. Crosland, *The Fine Old Hebrew Gentleman* (London, 1922), pp. 41–4, however; and see also Frank Felsenstein, *Anti-Semitic Stereotypes* (Baltimore, MD, 1995), p. 180. For an English defence of the Talmud, see John Mills, *The British Jews* (London, 1853), pp. 356–413.

13. Norman and Jeanne MacKenzie, *The Diary of Beatrice Webb* (Cambridge, MA, 1982–1985), vol. 2, p. 323; Norman MacKenzie (ed.), *The Letters of Sidney and Beatrice Webb* (Cambridge, 1978), vol. 1, p. 324.

14. Thomas Sheridan, *Dramatic Works* (London, 1902), pp. 40, 95.

15. Frank Felsenstein, *Anti-Semitic Stereotypes* (Baltimore, MD, 1995), pp. 53–5.

16. Paul Lawrence Rose, *German Question/Jewish Question* (Princeton, NJ, 1990), p. 6.

17. 'Saki', *The Unbearable Bassington*, *The Complete Saki* (London, 1982), p. 605.

18. *England under the Jews* (London, 1907), p. 169.

19. Sidney Whitman, 'The anti-Semitic movement', *Contemporary Review*, 63 (May 1983), 709.

20. 'Jonathan Wilson, 'How I became a Jewish writer in America', in Derek Rubin (ed.), *Who We Are: On being (and not being) a Jewish American writer* (New York, 2005), pp. 156–7.

21. See Frederic Raphael, *A Spoilt Boy* (London, 2003), pp. 56, 187.

22. Humbert Wolfe, *The Upward Anguish* (London, 1938), p. 47.

23. Ramin Jahanbegloo, *Conversations with Isaiah Berlin* (London, 1992), p. 87.

24. 'Alien London', *The Times*, 27 November–8 December 1924.

25. Ronald Lewin, 'John Bull and the Jews', *London Mercury*, April 1939.

26. *Saturday Review*, 21 November 1863, p. 684. On Salisbury's attitude towards the Jews, see Andrew Roberts, *Salisbury* (London, 2000), pp. 70–1, 478–9.

27. Andrew Roberts, *Salisbury* (London, 2000), p. 116.

28. 'Jews and Mahometans', *Truth*, 22 November 1877.

29. *Spectator*, 9 September 1899, pp. 338–9.

30. Marie Corelli, *The Sorrows of Satan* (London, 1998), p. 98.

31. *Unpath'd Waters* (London, 1913), pp. 180, 184, 192.

32. See David Cesarani, 'Anti-Zionism in Britain 1922–2002' in Jeffrey Herf (ed.), *Anti-Semitism and Anti-Zionism in Historical Perspective* (London, 2007), p. 121.

33. *Russia in Division* (London, 1925), p. 284. Graham got the name wrong, in the event.

34. See A. W. B. Simpson, *In the Highest Degree Odious* (Oxford, 1994), pp. 121–2. The BUF's main publicist, Raven Thompson mocked the 'incompetence and greed of our financial masters', combining contempt and paranoia in a single sentence. See N. Nugent, 'The ideas of the British Union of Fascists' in Neill Nugent and Roger King (eds.), *The British Right* (Westmead, Hants, 1977), p. 151.

35. Sir Barry Domvile, *By and Large* (London, 1936), pp. 107, 141, 242–3, 245–7. Domvile was not nearly so poised in his 1947 volume, *From Admiral to Cabin Boy*, which recounts his experiences as a detainee in Brixton gaol through the war under regulation 18B. 'Judmas', the 'Judaeo-Masonic combination', was to blame for all his woes, and the world's. See pp. 15, 22, 26–7, etc.

36. See Edmund Wilson, *A Piece of My Mind* (London, 1957), pp. 72–3.

37. Richard Overy, *Interrogations* (London, 2002), p. 483.

38. See David Carroll, *French Literary Fascism* (Princeton, NJ, 1995), p. 200.

39. Wyndham Lewis, *The Jews: Are They Human?* (London, 1939), p. 28.

40. See, for example, Daphne du Maurier, *The Progress of Julius* (London, 1975), p. 146.

41. *The Jews* (London, 1922), p. viii. Unity Mitford, no intellectual, complained, 'The English have no notion of the Jewish danger.' The 'struggle' to educate 'the British public' about the Jews' 'true dreadfulness' was 'extremely hard'. See Stephen Dorril, *Blackshirt* (London, 2006), pp. 346–7.

42. See J. P. Harris, 'Two war ministers', *War and Society*, 6/1 (1988).

43. N. J. Crowson, *Fleet Street, Press Barons and Politics* (Cambridge, 1998), pp. 39, 259, 262–3. See also Richard Griffiths, *Patriotism Perverted* (London, 1998), pp. 105, 108, 195–7; Colin Richmond, *Campaigner Against Antisemitism* (London, 2005), pp. 145–6.

44. See Martin Gilbert and Richard Gott, *The Appeasers* (London, 2000), pp. 348–9; Bernard Wasserstein, *Britain and the Jews of Europe 1939–1945* (Oxford, 1988),

p. 93; Tony Kushner, *The Persistence of Prejudice* (Manchester, 1989), pp. 3–5; Iain Macleod, *Neville Chamberlain* (London, 1961), pp. 286–7 ('To Chamberlain as to Halifax anti-Semitism was alien and repugnant').

45. Richard Bolchover, *British Jewry and the Holocaust* (Cambridge, 1993), p. 97.

46. See Tony Kushner, *The Persistence of Prejudice* (Manchester, 1989), pp. 81–3.

47. R. J. Minney, *The Private Papers of Hore-Belisha* (London, 1960), pp. 287–8; Ian R. Grimwood, *A Little Chit of a Fellow* (Lewes, 2006), pp. 169–74.

48. Stephen Dorril, *Blackshirt* (London, 2006), p. 482.

49. Ibid., p. 475.

50. S. S. Prawer, *Israel at Vanity Fair* (Leiden, 1992), pp. 1, 11, 18–19, 29, 36, 41, 55–6, 59, 66, 76, 87, 103–4, 119, 127 ('the Jews murdered [Jesus] for questioning their exclusive claims to divine favour . . . I dislike the Old Testament . . .'), 183, 218–19, 241, 242, 244, 324–5 ('swarms of Hebrew gentlemen'), 338–41 ('I don't believe that God ordered the Israelites to butcher Canaan'), 349 ('What is it to be a gentleman?'), 385–6.

51. Zachary Leader (ed.), *The Letters of Kingsley Amis* (London, 2000), pp. 320 ('The editor of the Jewish Quarterly hasn't said yet whether he wants a full-length article from me . . . Yes I am mad, I know. No, I'm not a Yidd'), 523, 611–12, 726, 728 ('The pork-chop chap has no pork-chop chip, is easy to deal with'), 943, 961, 1070–1, 1104, 1118; *Memoirs* (London, 1991), p. 30; J. G. Ballard, *Miracles of Life* (London, 2008), p. 196.

52. See G. K. Anderson, *The Legend of the Wandering Jew* (London, 1991), p. 61.

53. *The Romance of the Last Crusade* (New York, 1929), pp. 181–2, 180.

54. *Corduroy* (London, 2000), pp. 104–5.

55. See, for an example of the preference, Edward Horne, *A Job Well Done* (Lewes, Sussex, 2003), p. 109. See also Louise London, *Whitehall and the Jews 1933–1948* (Cambridge, 2000), p. 276 ('one of the stereotypes most entrenched in British official thinking was of Jews as incorrigibly urban and incapable of settling to agricultural work'), and Simon Garfield, *We Are At War* (London, 2006), p. 121 ('the idea that Jews cannot settle happily on the land').

56. G. Otto Trevelyan, *The Life and Letters of Lord Macaulay* (New York, 1877), vol. 1, pp. 194, 201–3.

57. An Oxford University undergraduate song: 'The things that a fellow don't do / They haven't been told to the Board School boy / They haven't been revealed to the Jew.' Thomas Weber, 'Anti-Semitism and philo-Semitism among the British and German elites', *English Historical Review*, 118/475 (2003), 107.

58. *Our Age* (London, 1990), p. 77.

59. 21 March 2005.

60. Hudson was tougher on Welbourne when he repeated the story in 'The Life of the Mind', The Tanner Lectures on Human Values, delivered at Yale University, 14 and 15 April 1997, <http://www.tannerlectures.utah.edu>.

61. George L. Mosse, *Confronting History* (Madison, Wisconsin, 2000), p. 94.

62. '[In Oxford, c.1955] I encountered an anti-Semitism couched in humour, but nonetheless brazen... The romantic ideal I had formed of Britain... was sobered by this encounter.' Heiko A. Oberman, *The Roots of Anti-Semitism* (Philadelphia, 1984), p. ix.

63. *Impressions of Theophrastus Such* (London, 1995), p. 146.

64. See Maurice Cowling, *Religion and Public Doctrine in Modern England* (Cambridge, 1980), vol. 1, pp. 61–72.

65. Sir Charles Petrie, *The Life and Letters of the Right Honourable Sir Austen Chamberlain KG, PC, MP* (London, 1940), vol. 2, pp. 152–3.

66. Nigel Collett, *The Butcher of Amritsar* (London, 2007), pp. 342, 375, 379–80. Nesta Webster was an ardent Dyer supporter. See *The Surrender of an Empire* (London, 1931), pp. 161–2.

67. 'We are going to massacre every Jew in the neighbourhood.' 'The Unrest-Cure', *The Complete Saki* (London, 1982), p. 131.

68. *Whose Body?* (London, 1995), p. 170.

69. Ibid., pp. 20, 23, 41–3, 49–50, 56, 59–60, 64, 110, 162, 170.

70. See Christopher Hitchens, *Love, Poverty and War* (New York, 2005), p. 329.

71. The story is taken from a sleeve note, written by Calum MacDonald, to the *Lyrita* label recording of Benjamin's Symphony and other works.

72. *Beyond the Verse* (London, 1994), p. 9.

73. See Stephen Dorril, *Blackshirt* (London, 2006), p. 263.

74. See Richard Davenbrook-Hines, *Letters from Oxford* (London, 2006), p. xxvii.

75. Todd M. Endelman, *Radical Assimilation in English Jewish History 1656–1945* (Bloomington, IN, 1990), pp. 44, 98; Louis Golding, *Hitler Through the Ages* (London, n.d.), pp. 21–2; Bryan Magee, *Growing Up in a War* (London, 2007), p. 88.

76. See Geoffrey Hughes, *Swearing* (London, 1998), pp. 130–1.

77. See S. S. Prawer, *Israel at Vanity Fair* (Leiden, 1992), p. 116; Selig Brodetsky, *Memoirs from Ghetto to Israel* (London, 1960), p. 51.

78. Jonothon Green, 'Anti-Semitic insults,' *Engage Journal*, no. 5, September 2007.

79. Bernard Glassman, *Protean Prejudice* (Atlanta, GA, 1998), pp. 73, 159–60, 163, 178–80, 183.

80. See Norman Rose, *The Cliveden Set* (London, 2001), p. 19; '[Mandate officials] always call everything "Jew" instead of "Jewish"—it doesn't matter really, but it jars. Jew-boys, Jew Government, Jew villages etc.' Jenifer Glyn (ed.), *Tidings from Zion* (London, 2000), p. 110.

81. 'The Progress of World Revolution', *The Patriot*, 1 October 1925.

82. William Joyce, *Twilight Over England* (London, 1992), pp. 22, 123.

83. Geoffrey Hughes, *Swearing* (London, 1998), pp. 135–7.

84. Bernard Glassman, *Protean Prejudice* (Atlanta, GA, 1998), pp. 73, 159–60, 163, 178–80, 183.

85. That Leonard's friends—Harold Nicolson, Vita Sackville-West, T. S. Eliot—'moderated' their anti-Semitism in his presence, makes Virginia's insult more

complicated. See F. M. Leventhal, 'Leonard Woolf' in Susan Pedersen and Peter Mandler (eds.), *After the Victorians* (London, 1994), p. 152. 'Virginia, one gathers, was fond of making Bloomsbury-style bad-taste jokes at the expense of Leonard's Jewishness, and the fact that she allowed herself to do so, knowing he would not be seriously offended, seems to be proof of her great trust in him.' P. N. Furbank, 'The love of a pessimist', *NYRB*, 21 December 2006, p. 46.

86. Elaine R. Smith, 'Jewish responses to political antisemitism and fascism in the East End of London, 1920–1939' in Tony Kushner and Kenneth Lunn (eds.), *Traditions of Intolerance* (Manchester, 1989), p. 55.

87. George L. Mosse, *Confronting History* (Madison, Wisconsin, 2000), p. 125.

88. Andrew Roberts, *Eminent Churchillians* (London, 1994), p. 190; Barry Domvile, *From Admiral to Cabin Boy* (London, 1947), p. 73.

89. See Neil Lochery, *Loaded Dice* (London, 2007), pp. 30–1, 165. A British ambassador described the Jews' 'skill in money management' as their 'chief weapon of defence against persecution over many hundreds of years'.

90. *Looking Back* (London, 1999), pp. 278, 325.

91. See James Parkes, *Voyage of Discoveries* (London, 1969), p. 100.

92. See John Mann MP and Johnny Cohen, *Anti-Semitism in European Football*, The Parliamentary Committee Against Antisemitism (London, 2008).

93. See G. A. Cranfield, 'The "London Evening-Post" and the Jew Bill of 1753', *Historical Journal*, 8/1 (1965), 22; R. J. Robson, *The Oxfordshire Election of 1754* (Oxford, 1949), p. 87.

94. 'Refuted slanders revived', *Jewish Chronicle*, 25 October 1861.

95. See Adam Kirsch, *Benjamin Disraeli* (New York, 2008), p. 31; Anne and Roger Cowen, *Victorian Jews through British Eyes* (Oxford, 1986), p. 4.

96. *Novels and Tales* (London, 1881), vol. 9, p. 389.

97. Anne and Roger Cowen, *Victorian Jews through British Eyes* (Oxford, 1986), pp. 7, 12, 17.

98. *Daniel Deronda* (Oxford, 1998), pp. 177, 396.

99. Tony Kushner, *The Persistence of Prejudice* (Manchester, 1989), pp. 131–2.

100. Esther Pearlman, 'The representation of Jews on Edwardian postcards' in Bryan Cheyette and Nadia Valman (eds.), *The Image of the Jew in European Liberal Culture* (London, 2004), pp. 217–42.

101. *Private Eye*, 8 February 1963, p. 12.

102. See H. Michelson, *The Jew in Early English Literature* (New York, 1972), p. 58.

103. '[John Gielgud's] jewish intonation [as Shylock] was perfect without exaggeration'. N. J. Crowson, *Fleet Street, Press Barons and Politics* (Cambridge, 1998), p. 207.

104. On meeting her future husband Sidney, Beatrice Webb noted his 'Jewish nose, prominent eyes and mouth, black hair, somewhat unkempt...' On later, more loving, reflection, the hair was 'thick' and 'wavy', the eyes 'large, kindly [and] grey',' and the nose—'Roman'. See *My Apprenticeship* (Cambridge, 1979), p. 408, and *Our Partnership* (London, 1948), p. 5.

105. *The Cantos* (London, 1981), p. 174.

106. 'Burbank with a Baedeker: Bleistein with a Cigar', *Selected Poems* (New York, 1964), p. 34. Whitechapel was referred to as 'the land of waving palms'. James H. Robb, *Working-Class Anti-Semite* (London, 1954), p. 99.

107. See Alan Dundes and Thomas Hauschild, 'Auschwitz jokes', *Western Folklore*, 42/4 (1983), 249–60; Alan Dundes and Uli Linke, 'More on Auschwitz jokes', *Folklore*, 99/1 (1988), 3–10.

108. Viscount Lymington, *Ich Dien* (London, 1931), pp. 52–3.

109. Colin Holmes, *Anti-Semitism in British Society 1876–1939* (New York, 1979), p. 308, fn. 123.

110. *The Fine Old Hebrew Gentleman* (London, 1922), pp. 9, 18, 25–6, 33, 67, 72–7, 99, 159, 160.

111. Richard Ollard (ed.), *The Diaries of A. L. Rowse* (London, 2004), p. 112.

112. See George Orwell, 'Anti-Semitism in Britain', April 1945, in *I Belong to the Left* (London, 1998), p. 64. '[Noting Edward VII's friendship with Jews:] I wonder whether any of the chosen people will get any honours...' Martin Gilbert, *Sir Horace Rumbold* (London, 1973), p. 44.

113. See Victoria Glendinning, *Leonard Woolf* (London, 2006), p. 146.

114. See Jim Holt, *Stop Me If You've Heard This* (New York, 2008), p. 76.

115. John J. Ray, 'Is Antisemitism a cognitive simplification?' in Werner Bergmann (ed.), *Error Without Trial* (Berlin, 1988), p. 131.

116. See Thomas Hobbes, *Leviathan* (London, 1968), Pt I, ch. 6, p. 120.

117. See Richard Griffiths, *Patriotism Perverted* (London, 1998), p. 12.

118. Max Beerbohm, *Selected Prose* (Boston, 1970), p. 217.

119. *Leviathan* (London, 1968), Pt I, ch. 6, p. 125.

120. See Anthony S. Wohl, 'Ben Juju' in Todd M. Endelman and Tony Kushner (eds.), *Disraeli's Jewishness* (London, 2002), pp. 107–8.

121. See Jim Holt, *Stop Me If You've Heard This* (New York, 2008), p. 99.

122. Todd M. Endelman, *The Jews of Georgian England 1714–1830* (Philadelphia, 1979), p. 217.

123. *The Times*, 26 June 2001; *Jewish Telegraphic Agency*, 31 January 2001.

124. See 'Action over definitions of "Jew" fails', *The Times*, 6 July 1973; Jonothon Green, 'Anti-Semitic insults', *Engage Journal*, no. 5, September 2007.

125. See Bernard Susser, 'The nineteenth century constitution of the Sunderland congregation', *Transactions of the J.H.S.E.*, 40 (2005), 8–9.

126. See Todd M. Endelman, *The Jews of Georgian England 1714–1830* (Philadelphia, 1979), p. 109.

127. Brenda Maddox, *Rosalind Franklin* (London, 2002), p. 49.

128. See Robert E. Park, 'The concept of social distance as applied to the study of racial attitudes and racial relations', *Journal of Applied Sociology*, 8 (1924), 339–44; Robert E. Park, 'The concept of position in sociology', *Papers and Proceedings of the American Sociological Society*, 20 (1926), 1–14; Emory S. Bogardus, 'Social distance and its origins', *Journal of Applied Sociology*, 9

(1925), 216–26; Emory S. Bogardus, 'Social distance in the city', *Proceedings and Publications of the American Sociological Society*, 20 (1926), 40–6; Emory S. Bogardus, 'A social distance scale', *Sociology and Social Research*, 17 (1933), 265–71; Harry C. Triandis and Leigh Minturn Triandis, 'Race, social class, religion, and nationality as determinants of social distance' in Werner Bergmann (ed.), *Error Without Trial* (Berlin, 1988), pp. 501–16.

129. Emory S. Bogardus, 'Social distance in the city', *Proceedings and Publications of the American Sociological Society*, 20 (1926), 40.

130. Emory S. Bogardus, 'A social distance scale,' *Sociology and Social Research*, 17 (1933), 266–9.

131. Peter Stansky, *Sassoon: The worlds of Philip and Sybil* (New Haven, NJ, 2003), p. 15.

132. See G. A. Cranfield, 'The "London Evening-Post" and the Jew Bill of 1753', *Historical Journal*, 8/1 (1965), 18, 21.

133. *The Jew, the Gypsy, and El Islam* (Palmdale, CA, 2000), p. 17. 'The westernized Jew [has a] pathetic desire to be friendly.' Wyndham Lewis, *The Jews: Are They Human?* (London, 1939), p. 12.

134. A. K. Chesterton, 'The apotheosis of the Jew', *British Union Quarterly*, 1 (January–July 1937), 51, 52.

135. See Leslie Mitchell, *The Whig World* (London, 2005), pp. 16–17, 24–6.

136. See Robert E. Park, 'The concept of social distance as applied to the study of racial attitudes and racial relations', *Journal of Applied Sociology*, 8 (1924), 343.

137. Emil Reich, 'The Jew-baiting on the Continent', *Nineteenth Century*, 40 (July–December 1896), 432, 434.

138. *Efficiency and Empire* (London, 1901), p. 80.

139. See G. R. Searle, *Corruption in British Politics 1895–1930* (Oxford, 1994), p. 26. For Northcliffe's 'dislike of Jews', and his 'belief in racial stereotypes', see A. J. A. Morris, *The Scaremongers* (London, 1984), p. 347, and Stephen Koss, *The Rise and Fall of the Political Press in Britain* (London, 1984), vol. 2, pp. 208–9.

140. See Bill Williams, 'The anti-Semitism of tolerance' in Alan J. Kidd and K.W. Roberts (eds.), *City, Class and Culture* (Manchester, 1985), p. 80.

141. Anthony Allfrey, *Edward VII and his Jewish Court* (London, 1991), p. 11.

142. Frank Harrison Hill, 'The political adventures of Lord Beaconsfield', *Fortnightly Review*, May 1878 (II), pp. 702, 703.

143. 'The just pride of the Jew', *Spectator*, 14 June 1902, p. 910.

144. *Charles Booth's London* (London, 1971), p. 201; David Englander, 'Booth's Jews: The presentation of Jews and Judaism in *Life and Labour of the People in London*', *Victorian Studies*, 32/4 (1989), 556.

145. See L. S. Sutherland, 'Samson Gideon and the reduction of interest, 1749–50', *Economic History Review*, 16/1 (1946), 15.

146. *The Prime Minister* (London, 2004), p. 75.

147. See S. S. Prawer, *Israel at Vanity Fair* (Leiden, 1992), p. 18.

148. See Anthony Allfrey, *Edward VII and his Jewish Court* (London, 1991), pp. 22–3, 101, 184, 248; C. C. Aronsfeld, 'German Jews in Victorian England', *Leo Baeck Institute Year Book*, 1962, p. 315; Beatrice Webb, *My Apprenticeship* (Cambridge, 1979), pp. 50–5; Jamie Camplin, *The Rise of the Plutocrats* (London, 1978), pp. 142, 158; Lewis Coser, *Greedy Institutions* (New York, 74), pp. 34–40; T. H. S. Escott, *King Edward and his Court* (London, 1908), pp. 26, 209, 212–13, 217; G. R. Searle, *Corruption in British Politics 1895–1930* (Oxford, 1994), pp. 28, 98; C. C. Aronsfeld, 'Jewish enemy aliens in England during the First World War', *Jewish Social Studies*, 18/4 (1956), 281–2; Chaim Bermant, *The Cousinhood* (London, 1971), p. 217; Simon Heffer, *Power and Place: The political consequences of King Edward VII* (London, 1998), pp. 27, 124.

149. See Anthony S. Wohl, 'Ben Juju' in Todd M. Endelman and Tony Kushner (eds.), *Disraeli's Jewishness* (London, 2002), pp. 110, 115.

150. See R. W. Davis, 'Disraeli, the Rothschilds and antisemitism', ibid., pp. 162–79. The Rothschilds also provoked rather more modern fears much earlier in the century. The MP Thomas Duncombe remarked in a speech to the House of Commons on 18 February 1828 that he 'trusted that the duke of Wellington . . . would not allow the finances of this great country to be controlled any longer by a Jew'. His sally was met with laughter. See *The Parliamentary Debates*, vol. XVIII, pp. 542–3.

151. See Ulrike Ehet, 'Catholics and antisemitism in Germany and England 1918–1939', unpublished PhD thesis, University of London, 2005 p. 172.

152. See ibid., p. 185.

153. See Nicola Lacey, *A Life of H. L. A. Hart* (Oxford, 2004), pp. 54–5, 312–14.

154. Duff Cooper, *Old Men Forget* (London, 1953), p. 18.

155. See Martin J. Wiener, *English Culture and the Decline of the Industrial Spirit 1850–1980* (Cambridge, 1981), p. 17; Goldwin Smith, *A Trip to England* (Toronto, 1891), p. 53.

156. Lytton Strachey, *Eminent Victorians* (London, 1986), p. 187.

157. Louis MacNeice, *The Strings are False* (London, 2007), p. 80.

158. Andrew Roberts, *Salisbury* (London, 2000), pp. 10–11.

159. *Lord Beaconsfield* (London, 1890), p. 13; Benjamin Disraeli, *Vivian Grey* and *Contarini Fleming, Novels and Tales* (London, 1881), vol. 1, pp. 9–10, and vol. 3, pp. 36–7; Adam Kirsch, *Benjamin Disraeli* (New York, 2008), pp. 28–30.

160. R. W. Johnson, 'Young brutes', *London Review of Books*, 23 February 2006; Todd M. Endelman, *Radical Assimilation in English Jewish History 1656–1945* (Bloomington, IN, 1990), pp. 98–9, 139, 141, 195.

161. Cyril Wick, letter to *Jewish Chronicle*, 16 May 2008.

162. Barry Rubin and Judith Roumani, 'An interview with Robert Wistrich', *Covenant*, 1/3 (October 2007/Cheshvan 5768).

163. According to a *Jewish Chronicle* story, 'considerable evidence' of the bullying of Jewish schoolchildren was submitted to 'a certain organisation' which

prepared a report on the subject in or about 1961. See 'The Public Schools (3)', *Jewish Chronicle*, 3 February 1961. But see W. D. Rubinstein, *A History of Jews in the English-Speaking World: Great Britain* (London, 1996), pp. 127–30. Frederic Raphael makes a nice distinction between 'bullying' and 'persecution' in *A Spoilt Boy* (London, 2003), pp. 244–5 ('The bullied child is never reminded of his solidarity with anyone else'). See also Chaim Bermant, *The Cousinhood* (London, 1971), pp. 389–91, Kenneth Rose, *Elusive Rothschild* (London, 2003), pp. 27, 29, 62, and Al Alvarez, *Where Did It All Go Right?* (London, 1999), pp. 73–4. And see George Orwell, 'Anti-Semitism in Britain', April 1945, in *I Belong to the Left* (London, 1998), p. 67 ('a Jewish boy at a public school almost invariably had a bad time').

164. See Todd M. Endelman, *Radical Assimilation in English Jewish History 1656–1945* (Bloomington, IN, 1990), p. 99; Emanuel Litvinoff, *Journey Through a Small Planet* (London, 2008), p. 172.

165. Screenplay, p. 15, accompanying the DVD, released by Paramount Pictures in 2007. But compare George L. Mosse, *Confronting History* (Madison, Wisconsin, 2000), pp. 82–3.

166. See Benny Morris, *The Road to Jerusalem* (London, 2002), p. 225.

167. 'As I please', *The Collected Essays, Journalism and Letters* (London, 1968), vol. 4, p. 293.

168. Richard Holt, *Sport and the British* (Oxford, 1989), p. 82.

169. See ibid., pp. 1, 93.

170. See ibid., p. 205.

171. Arnold Toynbee, *A Study of History*, abridged by D. C. Somervell, 2 vols. (Oxford, 1960), vol. 2, p. 136.

172. Ferdinand Mount, *Cold Cream* (London, 2008), 31.

173. Ian Hacking, 'The archaeology of Michel Foucault', *Historical Ontology* (Cambridge, MA, 2002), p. 76.

174. Todd M. Endelman, *The Jews of Georgian England 1714–1830* (Philadelphia, 1979), pp. 270–1.

175. Highgate School. See *Private Eye*, 6 June 1969, issue 195, p. 4.

176. See Todd M. Endelman, *The Jews of Britain 1656–2000* (Berkeley, CA, 2002), pp. 199, 243; Gisela C. Lebzelter, *Political Anti-Semitism in England 1918–1939* (London, 1978), pp. 32–4; Tony Kushner, *The Persistence of Prejudice* (Manchester, 1989), p. 96; Tony Kushner, 'The impact of British anti-semitism, 1918–1940' in David Cesarani (ed.), *The Making of Anglo-Jewry* (Oxford, 1990), pp. 201–2 ('anti-Semitism of exclusion').

177. 'Golf Clubs and Jews (1)', *Jewish Chronicle*, 3 February 1961.

178. Geoffrey Alderman, *London Jewry and London Politics 1889–1986* (London, 1989), pp. 108–9.

179. 'Golf Clubs and Jews (1)–(4)', 'The Public Schools, (1)–(3)', *Jewish Chronicle*, 20 and 27 January, and 3 February 1961.

180. See Abraham Gilam, *The Emancipation of the Jews in England 1830–1860* (New York, 1982), p. 15.

181. Jerry White, *Rothschild Buildings* (London, 2003), p. 62; Lloyd P. Gartner, *The Jewish Immigrant in England 1870–1914* (London, 2001), p. 107; Colin Holmes, *John Bull's Island* (London, 1988), pp. 69–70.

182. Nicola Lacey, *A Life of H. L. A. Hart* (Oxford, 2004), p. 35.

183. Stephen Aris, *The Jews in Business* (London, 1970), pp. 209–10.

184. Seth Koven, 'Henrietta Barnett' in Susan Pedersen and Peter Mandler (eds.), *After the Victorians* (London, 1994), pp. 43, 52.

185. See Israel Finestein, 'Religious disabilities at Oxford and Cambridge' in *Anglo-Jewry in Changing Times* (London, 1999), p. 115.

186. Ben Rogers, *A. J. Ayer* (London, 2000), pp. 270–1.

187. Alan Sykes, *The Radical Right in Britain* (London, 2005), p. 50.

188. See Emanuel Litvinoff, *Journey Through a Small Planet* (London, 2008), pp. 94, 172–3.

189. Douglas Reed, *A Prophet at Home* (London, 1941), p. 121.

190. See David Baker, *Ideology of Obsession* (London, 1996), p. 37.

191. Thomas W. Perry, *Public Opinion, Propaganda, and Politics in Eighteenth-Century England* (Cambridge, MA., 1962), p. 108.

192. See Todd M. Endelman, *The Jews of Georgian England 1714–1830* (Philadelphia, 1979), pp. 93–4.

193. 'The political adventures of Lord Beaconsfield', *Fortnightly Review*, April 1878 (I), pp. 483, 492.

194. Martin Gilbert, *Churchill and the Jews* (London, 2007), p. 13. 'I employed the word "un-English" in my letter with the intention of conveying the idea that no one but a Foreign Jew [*sic*] wd have permitted himself to commit such an error, and any one of English birth wd have shrunk fro such a course.' Randolph Churchill, *Winston S. Churchill: Companion Volume II* (London, 1969), p. 490.

195. Peter Stansky, *Sassoon: The worlds of Philip and Sybil* (New Haven, NJ, 2003), p. 122.

196. See I. Rennap, *Anti-Semitism and the Jewish Question* (London, 1942), p. 110.

197. See Richard Evans, *Lying about Hitler* (New York, 2001), p. 230.

198. Philip Mason, *The English Gentleman* (London, 1993), pp. 10–12; Noel Annan, *Our Age* (London, 1990), pp. 19–36; Maurice Samuel, *The Gentleman and the Jew* (New York, 1950), pp. 38–9. There were dissents, of course. See Walter E. Houghton, *The Victorian Frame of Mind* (New Haven, CT, 1974), p. 185.

199. Christopher Meyer, *DC Confidential* (London, 2006), p. 2; Charles Moore, 'The Spectator's notes', *The Spectator*, 9 October 2004.

200. See Stefan Collini, 'R. H. Tawney', *English Pasts* (Oxford, 1999), p. 192.

201. Ira O. Wade, *The Intellectual Origins of the French Enlightenment* (Princeton, NJ, 1971), p. 47.

202. *Sex and Character* (London, 1906), p. 308.

203. See Victoria Glendinning, *Leonard Woolf* (London, 2006), p. 14.

204. Yet the exemplary Mr Montenero has 'the indescribable air' of a 'gentle-man—dignified, courteous and free from affectation'. *Harrington* (Toronto, ON, 2004), pp. 142, 186. Cf.: 'It [is] declared by the spirit and history of our laws, that the possession of a property, not connected with especial duties, a property not fiduciary or official, but arbitrary and unconditional, was in the light of our forefathers the brand of a Jew and an alien; not the distinction, not the right, or honour, of an English baron or gentleman.' S. T. Coleridge, *On the Constitution of the Church and State* (London, 1972), pp. 31–2.

205. See Elie Kedourie, 'Lord Halifax, Conservative', *The Crossman Confessions and Other Essays* (London, 1984), pp. 31–2. 'By encouraging these habits the Readings clearly showed that they were not patrician.'

206. *The Prime Minister* (London, 2004), p. 10.

207. Ibid., pp. 10, 30–3, 37, 43, 88, 210–11, 371, 464, 477, 497, 514, 606.

208. See Anthony Allfrey, *Edward VII and his Jewish Court* (London, 1991), p. 19.

209. *Daniel Deronda* (Oxford, 1998), pp. 146, 210.

210. Christopher Hitchens, *Letters to a Young Contrarian* (Oxford, 2001), p. 69; G. K. Chesterton, *Chesterton on Dickens* (London, 1992), p. 126.

211. *Trilby* (Oxford, 1998), pp. 11–12, 23, 41–2, 49, 73, 77, 97, 170, 245.

212. See G. K. Chesterton, *Heretics* (New York, 2006), p. 115.

213. *The Danger of Being a Gentleman and Other Essays* (London, 1940), pp. 13–31.

214. Eric Hobsbawm, 'The Left's megaphone', *Uncommon People* (London, 1999), p. 189; Tony Kushner, *The Persistence of Prejudice* (Manchester, 1989), p. 84; Maurice Cowling, *Religion and Public Doctrine in Modern England* (Cambridge, 1980), vol. 3, p. 527.

215. See Douglas Sutherland, *The English Gentleman* (London, 1980), pp. vii, xi.

216. See Susan Neiman, *Evil in Modern Thought* (Princeton, NJ, 2002), p. 150.

217. Henry Hart Milman, *The History of the Jews*, 4th edn (London, 1866), vol. 3, p. 396.

218. Norman L. Torrey, *Voltaire and the English Deists* (New Haven, NJ, 1930), p. 108.

219. Roy Porter, 'The Enlightenment in England' in Roy Porter and Mikuláš Teich (eds.), *The Enlightenment in National Context* (Cambridge, 1981), pp. 1–18; Shmuel Almog, 'The borrowed identity' in Robert Wistrich (ed.), *Demonizing the Other* (Amsterdam, 1999), p. 135.

220. Henry St John Bolingbroke, 'Essays on human knowledge', *Works* (Philadelphia, PA, 1841), vol. 3, p. 396.

221. Henry St John Bolingbroke, 'Fragments or minutes of essay', ibid., vol. 4, p. 273.

222. See Ernst Cassirer, *The Philosophy of the Enlightenment* (Princeton, NJ, 1968), p. 173.

223. James A. Herrick, *The Radical Rhetoric of the English Deists* (Columbia, SC, 1997), pp. 23, 26–39.

224. Philip McGuinness, Alan Harrison, and Richard Kearney, *John Toland's 'Christianity not Mysterious'* (Dublin, 1997), p. 92.

225. Bernard Glassman, *Protean Prejudice* (Atlanta, GA, 1998), pp. 19–21.

226. Arthur Hertzberg, *The French Enlightenment and the Jews* (New York, 1968), p. 38; Bernard Glassman, *Protean Prejudice* (Atlanta, GA, 1998), pp. 4–5; Jacob Katz, *From Prejudice to Destruction* (Cambridge, MA, 1980), p. 28.

227. Matthew Tindall (1657–1733). Henry Bettenson (ed.), *Documents of the Christian Church* (Oxford, 1967), pp. 311–12.

228. See Jacob Katz, *From Prejudice to Destruction* (Cambridge, MA, 1980), p. 29.

229. James A. Herrick, *The Radical Rhetoric of the English Deists* (Columbia, SC, 1997), pp. 138–41, 188–90; Anthony Collins, *Discourse of the Ground and Reasons of the Christian Religion* (London, 1737), p. 105.

230. Henry St John Bolingbroke, 'Fragments or minutes of essay', *Works* (Philadelphia, PA, 1841), vol. 4, p. 241; 'A letter on one of Archbishop Tillotson's sermons', ibid., vol. 3, p. 22.

231. Anthony Collins, *A Discourse of Free Thinking* (London, 1713), pp. 157–8. See also Arthur Hertzberg, *The French Enlightenment and the Jews* (New York, 1968), p. 38, and Bernard Glassman, *Protean Prejudice* (Atlanta, GA, 1998), pp. 22–3.

232. Robert Darnton, *George Washington's False Teeth* (New York, 2003), p. 81.

233. See James A. Herrick, *The Radical Rhetoric of the English Deists* (Columbia, SC, 1997), pp. 52–63.

234. Anthony Collins, *A Discourse of Free Thinking* (London, 1713), p. 157.

235. See Introduction, *The Moral Philosopher* (London, 1995), p. viii.

236. *The Moral Philosopher* (London, 1995), pp. v, 21, 96–7, 142, 248, 254, 255, 257, 258, 265, 290, 325, 353, 359.

237. Norman L. Torrey, *Voltaire and the English Deists* (New Haven, NJ, 1930), pp. 200–1.

238. Jacob Katz, *From Prejudice to Destruction* (Cambridge, MA, 1980), p. 33; Arthur Hertzberg, *The French Enlightenment and the Jews* (New York, 1968), p. 39. One English cleric blamed the deists for Voltaire's own 'many cruel and ill-grounded aspersions on the Jewish nation and religion'. See Norman L. Torrey, *Voltaire and the English Deists* (New Haven, NJ, 1930), p. 113.

239. See Arthur Hertzberg, *The French Enlightenment and the Jews* (New York, 1968), p. 310, fn. 120.

240. See Otto D Kulka, 'The Critique of Judaism in modern European thought' in Robert Wistrich (ed.), *Demonizing the Other* (Amsterdam, 1999), pp. 199–200.

241. See Thomas Woolston, *Six Discourses on the Miracles of Our Saviour* (1727–1729), extracted in John Martin Creed and John Sandwith Boys Smith (eds.), *Religious Thought in the Eighteenth Century* (Cambridge, 1934), pp. 66–7;

Bernard Glassman, *Protean Prejudice* (Atlanta, GA, 1998), pp. 12, 22–3; James A. Herrick, *The Radical Rhetoric of the English Deists* (Columbia, SC, 1997), pp. 85–6.

242. One acknowledged by historically minded anti-Semitic intellectuals. 'Jews who celebrate the birth of Spinoza might as well celebrate the rending of the veil of the Temple or the conversion of St. Paul.' Goldwin Smith, 'Can Jews be patriots?', *Nineteenth Century*, 3 (May 1878), 884.

243. See *The Age of Reason* (New York, 2004), p. 22,

244. Philip Larkin, 'Aubade', *Collected Poems* (London, 1988), p. 208.

245. Ernst Cassirer, *The Philosophy of the Enlightenment* (Princeton, NJ, 1968), pp. 178, 181.

246. *The Age of Reason* (New York, 2004), pp. 34, 38, 90, 93, 102–3, 114–15, 181–2, 183.

247. J. S. Mill, *Autobiography* (Oxford, 1971), pp. 26–7.

248. See Richard H. Popkin, 'Hume and Isaac de Pinto', *Texas Studies in Literature and Language*, 12/3 (1970), 417, quoting a letter of Hume's which deprecates the 'misguided zeal of the Christians'. See also Bernard Cracroft, 'The Jews of Western Europe', *Westminster Review*, New series, 23 (April 1863), 434–6, 470.

249. *History of Western Philosophy* (London, 1961), pp. 311–24, 423.

250. See *Against All Gods* (London, 2007), pp. 29–30. But compare Bryan Magee, *Confessions of a Philosopher* (London, 1997), p. 444: 'Of the religions I studied, the one I found least worthy of intellectual respect was Judaism.' And John Weightman, *Reading the Bible* (London, 2003), pp. 10, 32, 34. He has always 'harboured a grievance' against the 'Old Testament'. It gives him a 'terrible sense of claustrophobia'. It sanctions 'massacre' and 'racialism'. God demands his 'pound of flesh' and 'shows no respect for human life'. Ezra's policy anticipates the measures of the Nazis, etc.

251. Christine Bolt, *Victorian Attitudes to Race* (London, 1971), pp. 56, 75, 188; Léon Poliakov, *The Aryan Myth* (New York, 1974), p. 223.

252. David J. DeLaura, *Hebrew and Hellene in Victorian England* (Austin, TX, 1969), p. xvii.

253. *On the Study of Celtic Literature* (London, 1910), p. 17.

254. Moses Hess, *Rome and Jerusalem* (New York, 1958), p. 46; Eisig Silberschlag, *Saul Tschernichowsky* (New York, 1968), pp. 41–3.

255. See David J. DeLaura, *Hebrew and Hellene in Victorian England* (Austin, TX, 1969), p. 173.

256. Matthew Arnold, *Culture and Anarchy* (New Haven, 1994), p. 26.

257. See Lionel Trilling, *Matthew Arnold* (London, 1974), p. 9.

258. See, for example, *On the Study of Celtic Literature* (London, 1910), pp. 25–7, 101, 115. Wyndham Lewis, *The Lion and the Fox* (London, 1966), pp. 306, 320 (Arnold's 'nonsense-book'). And see Maurice Oleander, *The Languages of Paradise* (Cambridge, MA, 2008), pp. 11–13.

259. See Stefan Collini (ed.), *Culture and Anarchy and other writings* (Cambridge, 1993), p. 168.

260. *Literature and Dogma* (London, 1876), pp. 1, 58–9.

261. *On the Study of Celtic Literature* (London, 1910), pp. 25, 70; *Culture and Anarchy* (New Haven, 1994), p. 122.

262. *Literature and Dogma* (London, 1876), pp. 122–5, 290; *On the Study of Celtic Literature* (London, 1910), pp. 67–8.

263. See, for example, *Literature and Dogma* (London, 1876), pp. 41, 57, 83–7, 90–1, 366.

264. Ibid., p. 376.

265. See, for example, Oscar Wilde, 'The rise of historical criticism', *Complete Works* (London, 1966), p. 1147 ('the function of ancient Italy was . . . to blend into one elemental creed the spiritual aspirations of Aryan and Semite').

266. 'Its dreadful that we should accept [the Jews] as the impresarios of our religious dreamland instead of the Greeks.' 'Saki', *The Unbearable Bassington*, *The Complete Saki* (London, 1982), p. 605.

267. *Races of Man: A fragment* (London, 1850), pp. 106, 108, 140.

268. Ibid., pp. 131–2.

269. Benjamin Disraeli, *Coningsby* (London, 1983), pp. 232, 273.

270. Norman Cohn, *Warrant for Genocide* (London, 1967), p. 32.

271. Houston Stewart Chamberlain, *The Foundations of the Nineteenth Century* (London, 1911), p. 271; Douglas Reed, *The Controversy of Zion* (Durban, Natal, 1978), pp. 165–75.

272. <http://holywar.org>.

273. Israel Finestein, 'Jewish emancipationists in Victorian England' in *Anglo-Jewry in Changing Times* (London, 1999), p. 87.

274. *Lord George Bentinck* (London, 1852), pp. 482–507.

275. *Novels and Tales* (London, 1881), vol. 10, pp. 136–7, 139; Adam Kirsch, *Benjamin Disraeli* (New York, 2008), p. 194.

276. Deborah Cohen, 'Who was who? Race and Jews in turn-of-the-century Britain', *Journal of British Studies*, 41 (October 2002), 461.

277. See R. N. Salaman, 'Heredity and the Jew', *Journal of Genetics*, 1/3 (August 1911), 289–90.

278. See Marek Kohn, *The Race Gallery* (London, 1995), p. 33.

279. George L. Mosse, *Towards the Final Solution* (Madison, Wisconsin, 1985), p. 74.

280. See, for example, James Bryce, *Race Sentiment as a Factor in History* (London, 1915).

281. See Frank H. Hankins, *The Racial Basis of Civilization* (New York, 1926), *passim*.

282. Karl Pearson and Margaret Moul, 'The problem of alien immigration into Great Britain, illustrated by an examination of Russian and Polish Jewish

children', *Annals of Eugenics*, 1 (1925–6), 6, 127. And see Elazar Barkan, *The Retreat of Scientific Racism* (Cambridge, 1992), pp. 156–7.

283. See, as a striking postwar example, Eliot Slater, 'A note on Jewish–Christian intermarriage', *Eugenics Review* (April 1947), 17–21 (when the 'differences between Jews and non-Jews . . . disappear', 'the potentiality for anti-Semitism [will also] disappear').

284. G. K. Chesterton, *Heretics* (New York, 2006), p. 92.

285. *The Retreat of Scientific Racism* (Cambridge, 1992), p. 3.

286. See Geoffrey G. Field, *Evangelist of Race* (New York, 1981), p. 32.

287. Ibid., p. 224.

288. *The Foundations of the Nineteenth Century* (London, 1911), vol. 2, pp. 69, 279.

289. Ibid., p. 482.

290. Ibid., vol. 1, pp. lxv, lxxviii–lxxix, 116, 250, 330; vol. 2, p. 495; Martin Woodroffe, 'Racial theories of history and politics' in Paul Kennedy and Anthony Nicholls (eds.), *Nationalist and Racialist Movements in Britain and Germany before 1914* (London, 1981), p. 152.

291. Geoffrey G. Field, *Evangelist of Race* (New York, 1981), pp. 173, 199.

292. Maurice Oleander, *The Languages of Paradise* (Cambridge, MA, 2008), p. 14; Léon Poliakov, *The Aryan Myth* (New York, 1974), p. 101.

293. Geza Vermes, *The Passion* (London, 2005), pp. 72, 118–19; *The Foundations of the Nineteenth Century* (London, 1911), vol. 1, pp. 11, 201–47, 330, 336, 345, 537, 578; vol. 2, p. 483.

294. Ibid., vol. 1, pp. 120, 214, 225, 255, 425; vol. 2, pp. 46, 93, 111, 246.

295. Geoffrey G. Field, *Evangelist of Race* (New York, 1981), pp. 116, 359.

296. See Léon Poliakov, *The Aryan Myth* (New York, 1974), p. 319.

297. Colin Holmes, 'Houston Stewart Chamberlain in Great Britain', *Wiener Library Bulletin*, New Series no. 19, 24/2 (1970), 31, 34; Geoffrey G. Field, *Evangelist of Race* (New York, 1981), p. 226. Weininger made admiring references to him in *Sex and Character* (London, 1906), pp. 303, 312.

298. Geoffrey G. Field, *Evangelist of Race* (New York, 1981), pp. 464–5.

299. Ibid., pp. 99, 155, 439–42.

300. George Lichtheim, 'Socialism and the Jews', *Collected Essays* (New York, 1973), p. 425.

301. Robert Alter, 'From myth to murder', *New Republic*, 20 May 1991; Paul Berman, 'Bigotry in print: Crowds chant murder. Something's changed' in Ron Rosenbaum (ed.), *Those Who Forget the Past* (New York, 2004), p. 19.

302. R. I. Moore, 'Anti-Semitism and the birth of Europe' in Diana Wood (ed.), *Studies in Church History* (Oxford, 1992), vol. 29, pp. 44–5.

303. Christine Bolt, *Victorian Attitudes to Race* (London, 1971), pp. 75–108, 157–205, 208–9, 215; Daniel Pick, *Faces of Degeneration* (Cambridge, 1989), pp. 21, 37.

304. See Robert Skidelsky, *John Maynard Keynes 1883–1946* (London, 2004), pp. 373–4.

305. 'Edwin Montagu', *Essays in Biography* (London, 1961), p. 50.
306. See Gisela C. Lebzelter, *Political Anti-Semitism in England 1918–1939* (London, 1978), pp. 173–4.
307. See Nathan Rotenstreich, *The Recurring Pattern* (London, 1963), pp. 16–22.
308. Ulrike Ehet, 'Catholics and antisemitism in Germany and England 1918–1939', unpublished PhD thesis, University of London, 2005, p. 176.
309. Pierre Birnbaum, *Anti-Semitism in France* (Oxford, 1992), p. 1.
310. Zeev Sternhell, *Neither Right nor Left* (Princeton, NJ, 1986), p. 14.
311. Eugen Weber, *My France* (Cambridge, MA, 1991), p. 239.
312. See Daniel Pick, *Faces of Degeneration* (Cambridge, 1989), p. 99.
313. See Michael Burns, *France and the Dreyfus Affair* (New York, 1999), p. 7; Pierre Birnbaum, *Anti-Semitism in France* (Oxford, 1992), p. 93.
314. See Nelly Wilson, *Bernard-Lazare* (Cambridge, 1978), pp. 67–8. Barrès later changed his mind, responsive to the sacrifices of the Great War and the ideology of the *union sacrée*: 'the Jewish desire to be absorbed and become as one with the soul of France' has been attained. See *The Soul of France* (London, 1915), p. 6; *The Faith of France* (London, 1918), pp. 1–2, 9, 14, 63–89, 254–5; David Drake, *French Intellectuals and Politics from the Dreyfus Affair to the Occupation* (London, 2005), pp. 52–5.
315. See Michael Curtis, *Three Against the Republic* (Princeton, NJ, 1959), pp. 149, 187, 194, 203.
316. See Michael Burns, *France and the Dreyfus Affair* (New York, 1999), p. 51.
317. See Michael Curtis, *Three Against the Republic* (Princeton, NJ, 1959), pp. 203–5.
318. See David Carroll, *French Literary Fascism* (Princeton, NJ, 1995), p. 26.
319. Nelly Wilson, *Bernard-Lazare* (Cambridge, 1978), p. 278.
320. See Zeev Sternhell, *Neither Right nor Left* (Princeton, NJ, 1986), p. 37.
321. David Drake, *French Intellectuals and Politics from the Dreyfus Affair to the Occupation* (London, 2005), pp. 23, 26–7; Richard Griffiths, *The Use of Abuse* (Providence, RI, 1991), pp. 47, 115.
322. Maurice Nadeau, *The History of Surrealism* (London, 1973), pp. 69–71; Pierre Birnbaum, *Anti-Semitism in France* (Oxford, 1992), p. 262.
323. See Zeev Sternhell, *Neither Right nor Left* (Princeton, NJ, 1986), p. 6, on the 'remarkably high intellectual standard of French fascist literature and thought'.
324. Immanuel Kant, *Anthropology from a Pragmatic Point of View* (Carbondale, IL, 1978), pp. 33, 60, 101–2; *The Conflict of the Faculties* (Lincoln, Nebraska, 1992), pp. 113–21; *Religion Within the Limits of Reason Alone* (New York, 1960), pp. 74, 116–17; Nathan Rotenstreich, *The Recurring Pattern* (London, 1963), pp. 24, 30, 37; Paul Lawrence Rose, *German Question/Jewish Question* (Princeton, NJ, 1990), pp. 96–7, 110–12, 122, 132, 254–5; Karl Marx, *Early Writings* (London, 1975), pp. 211–42; Otto Weininger, *Sex and Character* (London, 1906), p. 328; Jonathan Hess, *Germans, Jews and the Claims of Modernity* (New Haven, NJ, 2002), pp. 140–4; William J. Brazill, *The Young Hegelians*

(New Haven, NJ, 1970), pp. 201–2; Nathan Rotenstreich, 'For and against emancipation', *Leo Baeck Institute Year Book*, London, 1959; David Vital, *A People Apart* (Oxford, 1999), pp. 190–4; Michael Mack, *German Idealism and the Jew* (Chicago, 2003), pp. 6–12; Ernst Cassirer, *Kant's Life and Thought* (New Haven, NJ, 1981), pp. 388–9.

325. Andrzej Walicki, *A History of Russian Thought* (Oxford, 1988), pp. 297–300, and 320; Nicholas V. Riasanovsky, *Russia and the West in the Teaching of the Slavophiles* (Gloucester, MA, 1965), pp. 114–17; David I. Goldstein, *Dostoyevsky and the Jews* (Austin, Texas, 1981), pp. 91–2, 93–5, 144, 155–8; Paul Berline, 'Russian religious philosophers and the Jews', *Jewish Social Studies*, 9/4 (1947), 271–2; F. M. Dostoyevsky, *The Diary of a Writer* (Salt Lake City, UT, 1985), pp. 3, 105, 246, 355, 419, 423, 430–2, 458, 637–60, 779–83; Joseph Frank, *Dostoyevsky: The mantle of the prophet 1871–1881* (Princeton, NJ, 2002), pp. 301–3, 423, 433, 669–70; F. M. Dostoyevsky, *The Brothers Karamazov* (London, 2003), p. 746; Robert F. Byrnes, *Pobedonostov* (Bloomington, IN, 1968), pp. 93–104, 206–7, 209, 290; Konstantin P. Pobedonostov, *Reflections of a Russian Statesman* (Ann Arbor, MI, 1965), p. 65. Joseph Frank and David I. Goldstein (eds.), *Selected Letters of Fyodor Dostoyevsky* (London, 1987), p. 480; W. E. H. Lecky, 'Israel among the nations,' *The Forum*, 16 (December 1893), 442–3; John A. Dyche, 'The Jewish workman', *Contemporary Review*, 73 (January 1898), 38; Arnold White, 'A typical alien immigrant', *Contemporary Review*, 73 (February 1898), 244; Russo-Jewish Committee of London, *The Persecution of the Jews in Russia* (London, 1891), pp. 35–6; Arnold White, *The Modern Jew* (London, 1899), p. 15.

326. See Geoffrey G. Field, 'Anti-Semitism with the boots off' in Herbert A. Strauss (ed.), *Hostages of Modernization* (Berlin, 1993), pp. 296–7 ('neither a long nor a distinguished list').

327. William D. Rubinstein, *Elites and the Wealthy in Modern British History* (New York, 1987), p. 353.

328. Frank Felsenstein, *Anti-Semitic Stereotypes* (Baltimore, MD, 1995), pp. 231–7; William D. Rubinstein, *Elites and the Wealthy in Modern British History* (New York, 1987), pp. 351–2.

329. *Rural Rides* (London, 1967), pp. 119, 342, 345, 395, 402.

330. *Paper Against Gold* (1844, New York), p. 121; Mark L. Shoenfeld, 'Abraham Goldsmid: Money magician' in Sheila A. Spector (ed.), *British Romanticism and the Jews* (London, 2002), pp. 46–53; David S. Katz, *The Jews in the History of England* (1996), pp. 287–8.

331. See David Vital, *A People Apart: The Jews in Europe 1789–1939* (Oxford, 1999), pp. 186–7.

332. M. C. N. Salbstein, *The Emancipation of the Jews in Britain* (London, 1982), pp. 67, 68–9.

333. Ibid., p. 67. See also Abraham Gilam, *The Emancipation of the Jews in England 1830–1860* (New York, 1982), p. 53.

334. See Michael Ragussis, *Figures of Conversion* (London, 1995), pp. 22–3.

335. See M. C. N. Salbstein, *The Emancipation of the Jews in Britain* (London, 1982), p. 67; Frank Felsenstein, *Anti-Semitic Stereotypes* (Baltimore, MD, 1995), p. 237.

336. *Cobbett: Prose and poetry*, A. M. D. Hughes (ed.) (Oxford, 1923), p. 7.

337. Lewis Melville, *The Life and Letters of William Cobbett in England and America* (London, 1913), vol. 1, p. 267.

338. See Crane Brinton, *English Political Thought in the Nineteenth Century* (New York, 1962), pp. 61–74.

339. *The Life and Letters of William Cobbett in England and America* (London, 1913), vol. 1, pp. 20–1.

340. See Martin J. Wiener, *English Culture and the Decline of the Industrial Spirit 1850–1980* (Cambridge, 1981), pp. 106, 118; Richard Ingrams, *The Life and Adventures of William Cobbett* (London, 2006), pp. 112, 170, 210, 222.

341. G. D. H. Cole, *The Life of William Cobbett* (London, 1924), writes about Cobbett's hatred of the 'stock-jobber' (p. 11), but not about his hatred of the Jews; Alun Howkins and C. Ian Dyck, '"The Time's alteration": Popular ballads, rural radicalism and William Cobbett', *History Workshop*, 23/1 (1987), 20–38, consider Cobbett's 'attacks on tea drinking and eating potatoes', which have caused 'difficulty' for 'even the most sympathetic writers on Cobbett' (see p. 30). They too are silent on the anti-Semitism.

342. Sir Richard F. Burton, *The Jew, the Gypsy, and El Islam* (Palmdale, CA, 2000), p. 23.

343. See for example the passage quoted in Gareth Stedman Jones, *Languages of Class* (Cambridge, 1983), p. 104, from the *Northern Star*, 4 August 1838: 'All these and one hundred minor grievances, subservient to the same grand end (of making the working classes beasts of burden... to the aristocracy, Jewocracy, Millocracy, Shopocracy and every other Ocracy which feeds on human vitals...' See also W. D. Rubinstein, *A History of Jews in the English-Speaking World: Great Britain* (London, 1996), pp. 51–4, 58.

344. *The Jews* (London, 1922), p. 301.

345. Jay P. Corrin, *G. K. Chesterton and Hilaire Belloc* (London, 1981), p. 14.

346. *The Battleground Syria and Palestine* (London, 1936), p. 245.

347. Ibid., pp. 286, 325.

348. *The Jews* (Palmdale, CA, 1998), p. 21; *The Jews* (London, 1922), p. 181.

349. Ibid., p. 53.

350. *Emmanuel Burden* (London, 1927), p. 189.

351. *Characters of the Reformation* (Rockford, IL, 1992), pp. 58, 80, 102, 107, 175, ('the successive conspiracies of the wealthier classes') 204; *How the Reformation Happened* (Rockford, IL, 1992), pp. 35, 92, 111–12, 155–9, 173–6.

352. See John A. Garrard, *The English and Immigration 1880–1910* (Oxford, 1971), p. 17.

353. 'The Jewish Question: IV, The peril', *The Eye-Witness*, 28 September 1911, p. 459; 'The Jewish Question: VIII, The end—privilege', *The Eye-Witness*, 26 October 1911, p. 588; 'The Jewish nation and the war', *New Witness*, 31 January 1918, p. 317.

354. *Evidence from the Select Committee on Marconi's Wireless Telegraph Company Limited, Agreement (1913)*, 12 June 1913, p. 427.

355. *The Jews* (London, 1922), pp. 3–4, 10, 39, 149, 244; *The Jews* (Palmdale, CA, 1998), pp. 38–9. Cf.: 'Imagine the awful shock to the medieval Crusaders if they had foreseen the Christian kingdoms of England, France and Italy withdrawing Jerusalem from Islam in order to hand it over to the representatives of those who crucified Jesus of Nazareth...' Norman and Jeanne MacKenzie, *The Diary of Beatrice Webb* (Cambridge, MA, 1982–1985), vol. 4, p. 229.

356. *Emmanuel Burden* (London, 1927), p. 117.

357. *The Jews* (London, 1922), p. 249.

358. Ibid., p. 33.

359. Ibid., pp. 47, 223.

360. See 'Samuel *versus* Semitism', *New Witness*, 1 May 1913, pp. 801–2.

361. Ulrike Ehet, 'Catholics and antisemitism in Germany and England 1918–1939', unpublished PhD thesis, University of London, 2005, p. 47.

362. See Michael Billig, *Fascists* (London, 1978), p. 132.

363. See Andrew Sharf, *The British Press and Jews under Nazi Rule* (London, 1964), pp. 81–4.

364. 'Palmerston and Disraeli' in Norman F. Cantor and Michael S. Werthman (eds.), *The English Tradition* (New York, 1967), vol. 2, p. 256.

365. *The Modern Jew* (London, 1899), 'Preface', and pp. xi, 88.

366. *Efficiency and Empire* (London, 1901), pp. 78–81.

367. *Problems of Poverty* (London, 1913), pp. 60, 98. Roberto Romani regards these observations as evidencing Hobson's 'scant respect for traditional economic virtues'. *National Character and Public Spirit in Britain and France 1750–1914* (Cambridge, 2002), p. 264. He was no doubt indebted to Charles Booth's account of East End Jews' 'Always enlightened selfishness'. *Charles Booth's London* (London, 1971), p. 226.

368. *The War in South Africa* (London, 1900), pp. 11, 12, 189–97, 217, 228.

369. Ibid., p. 189.

370. *Democracy after the War* (London, 1918), pp. 85–7.

371. *God and Mammon* (London, 1931), pp. 10, 40–1.

372. *Confessions of an Economic Heretic* (London, 1938), pp. 59, 61.

373. Stephen Dorril, *Blackshirt* (London, 2006), pp. 78–80. H. N. Brailsford, *The Life-Work of J. A. Hobson* (London, 1948), pp. 3, 7–8, characterizes *The War in South Africa* as a 'powerful topical book' about 'Big business'. Hobson did not suppose 'a conscious conspiracy of this kind among capitalists to be a frequent occurrence'. According to Peter Clarke, Hobson was not anti-Semitic,

because his claim that 'Rhodes and the German Jews of the Rand manipulated British policy to their own advantage' was empirical, not axiomatic. *Liberals and Social Democrats* (Cambridge, 1981), p. 92.

374. *Loyalty, Aristocracy and Jingoism* (Toronto, 1896), pp. 10, 81; see also *Questions of the Day* (London, 1897), pp. v–xiii.

375. Colin Holmes, 'A "liberal" antisemite', *Patterns of Prejudice*, 6/5 (1972), 30.

376. See Naomi Cohen, *Encounter with Emancipation* (Philadelphia, PA, 1984), p. 278; Gerald Tulchinsky, 'Goldwin Smith' in Alan Davies (ed.), *Antisemitism in Canada: History and interpretation* (Waterloo, Canada, 1992), p. 68.

377. 'The Jewish Question', *Questions of the Day* (London, 1897), pp. 258, 262, 265, 270–1, 275, 279, 280; 'England's abandonment of the Protectorate of Turkey', *Contemporary Review*, 31 (February 1878), 618.

378. *The United Kingdom* (Toronto, 1899), vol. 1, pp. 46, 108–11; 'New light on the Jewish Question', *North American Review*, 417 (August 1891), 137.

379. 'The Jewish Question', *Questions of the Day* (London, 1897), pp. 241–51.

380. Ibid., pp. 241–51.

381. 'New light on the Jewish Question', *North American Review*, 417 (August 1891), 129.

382. Arnold Haultain (ed.), *Goldwin Smith's Correspondence* (London, n.d.), p. 441. The Jews must be 'derabbinised', and give up circumcision. 'New light on the Jewish Question', *North American Review*, 417 (August 1891), 141.

383. Arnold Haultain (ed.), *Goldwin Smith: His life and opinions* (London, n.d.), pp. 125–6.

384. 'The key to the mystery', *National Review*, 32/188 (1898), 274, 277, 283; 'Russia and Captain Dreyfus', *National Review*, 32/189 (1898), 358, 360, 366, 367; 'Some international aspects of the Dreyfus scandal', *National Review*, 32/192 (1899), 740–1. See also Robert Tombs, ' "Lesser breeds without the law": The Brtitish establishment and the Dreyfus affair, 1894–1899', *Historical Journal*, 41/2 (1998), 495–510.

385. 'The chameleon of the Rue Nitot', *National Review*, 73/435 (1919), 365, 366; 'The Second Treaty of Versailles', *National Review*, 73/438 (1919), 819–20, 844. See also A. J. A. Morris, *The Scaremongers* (London, 1984), pp. 226–7, 269.

386. Martha F. Lee, 'Nesta Webster', *Journal of Women's History*, 17/3 (2005), 96.

387. 'The schemes of the International Jews . . . this world-wide conspiracy . . . played, as a modern writer, Mrs Webster, has so ably shown, a definitely recognisable part in the tragedy of the French Revolution . . .' 'Zionism versus Bolshevism: A struggle for the soul of the Jewish people', *Illustrated Sunday Herald*, 8 February 1920.

388. *Germany and England* (Arabi, LA, n.d.), pp. 20, 22–3, 24, 25, 27, 31.

389. *Secret Societies and Subversive Movements* (London, 1924), pp. 391, 405.

390. *Spacious Days* (London, 1949), p. 191.

391. See, for example, on the American politician, Pat Robertson: Jacob Heilbrunn, 'His anti-Semitic sources', *NYRB*, 20 April 1995.

392. *Who is to be Master of the World?* (London, 1909).

393. *Enemies of Women* (London, 1948), p. 1.

394. Dan Stone, *Breeding Superman* (Liverpool, 2002), pp. 33–61; Richard Griffiths, *Patriotism Perverted* (London, 1998), pp. 53, 139 (Ludovici was a 'fervent anti-Semite'); Martin Pugh, *'Hurrah for the Blackshirts'* (London, 2005), pp. 13–14, 16–17; Alan Sykes, *The Radical Right in Britain* (London, 2005) p. 91; Dan Stone, 'The Far Right and the back-to-the-land-movement' in Julie V. Gottleib and Thomas P. Lineham (eds.), *The Culture of Fascism* (London, 2004), p. 190.

395. *Jews, and the Jews in England* (London, 1938), pp. 3–4, 26–7, 45, 53–4, 67, 72, 77, 81, 85, 89, 94, 99, 115–16. Mosley also alluded to Cobbett when he denounced the transformation of 'Merrie England' into a 'sweatshop and a slum'. See Martin J. Wiener, *English Culture and the Decline of the Industrial Spirit 1850–1980* (Cambridge, 1981), p. 107.

396. *Man: An indictment* (London, 1927), p. 309.

397. See Tony Kushner, 'Beyond the pale? British reactions to Nazi Anti-Semitism, 1933–1939', *Immigrants and Minorities*, 8 (1989), 151–2. According to W. D. Rubinstein, certain of Reed's works were 'enormously popular'. *A History of Jews in the English-Speaking World: Great Britain* (London, 1996), p. 308.

398. Tony Kushner, 'The paradox of prejudice' in Tony Kushner and Kenneth Lunn (eds.), *Traditions of Intolerance* (Manchester, 1989), p. 81.

399. *The Observer Years* (London, 2003), p. 94. The *Jewish Chronicle* noted with dismay that Reed's war books had 'gained praise from unexpected quarters'. Tony Kushner, *The Persistence of Prejudice* (Manchester, 1989), p. 100.

400. Michael Billig, 'Methodology and scholarship in understanding ideological explanation' in Clive Seale (ed.), *Social Research Methods* (London, 2003), p. 16; *Fascists* (London, 1978), p. 187.

401. *Nemesis?* (London, 1940), p. 67; *Somewhere South of Suez* (London, 1950), p. 190.

402. *Lest We Regret* (London, 1943), p. 109.

403. Ibid., p. 246.

404. *Nemesis?* (London, 1940), pp. 214–15, 249; *All Our Tomorrows* (London, 1942), p. 87; *Lest We Regret* (London, 1943), p 259.

405. *The Prisoner of Ottawa* (London, 1953), pp. 40–1, 148, 150.

406. *Somewhere South of Suez* (London, 1950), pp. 37, 327, 357, 427.

407. *All Our Tomorrows* (London, 1942), p. 201.

408. *A Prophet at Home* (London, 1941), p. 94; *All Our Tomorrows* (London, 1942), p. 299; *Lest We Regret* (London, 1943), pp 250–4; *The Prisoner of Ottawa* (London, 1953), p. 141.

409. *The Controversy of Zion* (Durban, Natal, 1978), p. 492.

410. W. R. W. Stephens, *The Life and Letters of Edward A. Freeman* (London, 1895), vol. 2, p. 235. Italics in the original text.

411. *England under the Jews* (London, 1907), p. iii.

412. Richard I. Cohen, 'Recurrent images in French antisemitism' in Robert Wistrich (ed.), *Demonizing the Other* (Amsterdam, 1999), p. 188; Richard Griffiths, *The Use of Abuse* (Providence, RI, 1991), p. 48.

413. Arnold Toynbee, *A Study of History*, 1 vol. edn, revised and abridged by Arnold Toynbee and Jane Caplan (Oxford, 1972), p. 11.

414. Arnold Toynbee, *A Study of History* (Oxford, 1933; 1939; 1954, 1961), vol. 1, pp. 51, 82–3, 91, 209–12, 211, 214, 246–7; vol. 2, pp. 53–5, 93, 211–27, 235–6, 240–8, 252–4; vol. 3, p. 49; vol. 4, pp. 1, 225, 228, 236, 246, 262–3, 510; vol. 5, pp. 71–4, 126, 389–90, 543–4, 658; vol. 6, pp. 8, 70–1, 95, 124; vol. 7, pp. 75, 393; vol. 8, pp. 108, 185, 258–9, 272–313 ('The Modern West and the Jews'), 576, 601, 626; vol. 9, pp. 86–8, 437; vol. 12, pp. 209–17, 292–300, 477–517, 597 (a fn.: 'I am particularly grateful to Rabbi J. B. Agus for testifying that "I am most certainly not" an anti-Semite'), 622–4, 627–8. In Annexes VII–XIII to vol. 12, Agus comments on three aspects of Toynbee's treatment of the Jews, including his use of the word 'fossil'. *A Study of History*, 2 vol. edn, abridged by D. C. Somervell (Oxford, 1960), vol. 1, pp. 26–7, 94, 135–7, 304, 310, 386, 388–9, 433–5, 485, 502–3, 508, 522.

415. See Elie Kedourie, 'Arnold J. Toynbee', *The Crossman Confessions and Other Essays* (London, 1984), p. 199.

416. Arnold Toynbee, *A Study of History*, 1 vol. edn, revised and abridged by Arnold Toynbee and Jane Caplan (Oxford, 1972), pp. 65–9, 232–3, 336, 339–41, 420

417. Nathan Rotenstreich, *The Recurring Pattern* (London, 1963), pp. 76–121; Harry Sacher, 'Dr. Toynbee and the Jews', *Zionist Portraits and Other Essays* (London, 1959), pp. 252–9.

418. J. H. Plumb, *The Death of the Past* (London, 2004), p. 136, and 'The historian's dilemma' in J. H. Plumb (ed.), *Crisis in the Humanities* (London, 1964), p. 32; H. R. Trevor-Roper, 'Arnold Toynbee's Millenium', *Encounter*, 8 (January–June 1957) ('untrue, illogical and dogmatic').

419. Alan Ryan, 'Arnold J. Toynbee', *New Republic*, 8 July 1989; Richard Davenbrook-Hines, *Letters from Oxford* (London, 2006), p. 152.

420. As did, for example, the travel writer H. V. Morton (1892–1979). 'He was anti-democratic, anti-Semitic, racist. . . . he was careful not to let any of these prejudices leak into his books.' Michael Bartholomew, *In Search of H. V. Morton* (London, 2004), p. 227. For respectful references to Jews in his travel books, see *In the Steps of the Master* (London, 2001), pp. 37–41, 66–8.

421. See Simon Heffer, *Moral Desperado* (London, 1995), pp. 263, 379.

422. See Montagu Frank Modder, *The Jew in the Literature of England* (New York, 1960), pp. 171–2.

423. *Lord Beaconsfield* (London, 1890), p. 84.

424. 'Shooting Niagara: And after?', *Critical and Miscellaneous Essays* (London, n.d.), vol. 7, p. 225.

425. See Rupert Christiansen, *The Visitors* (London, 2000), p. 127.

426. Leonard Woolf, *Quack, Quack!* (London, 1935), p. 123; Bertrand Russell, 'The ancestry of fascism', *Let the People Think* (London, 1941), p. 71; G. K. Chesterton, *The End of the Armistice* (London, 1940); J. L. Borges, *The Total Library* (London, 1999), pp. 414–15; Frederic E. Faverty, *Matthew Arnold: The ethnologist* (Evanston, IL, 1951), pp. 15, 195; but see John Clive, *Not By Fact Alone* (London, 1989), pp. 86–7.

427. Bertrand Russell, *Autobiography* (London, 1971), vol. 2, p. 92. 'Bolshevism is a close, tyrannical bureaucracy, with a spy system more elaborate and terrible than the Tsar's, and an aristocracy as insolent and unfeeling, composed of Americanised Jews.' See Ronald W. Clark, *The Life of Bertrand Russell* (London, 1978), p. 473. In 1924, on a tour through the United States, Russell stayed with the philosopher H. M. Kallen, described in a letter to Ottoline Morrell as 'a Jew whose friends are all Jews. All were kind, but I began to long for the uncircumcised.' Ray Monk, *Bertrand Russell: The ghost of madness, 1921–1970* (New York, 2001), p. 36.

428. *Belloc* (London, 1986), p. 269.

429. Ibid., pp. 262, 383; but see *After the Victorians* (London, 2005), p. 120.

430. *Milton* (Oxford, 1983), p. 252.

431. *Daily Telegraph*, 10 April 2004.

432. But see *After the Victorians* (London, 2005), pp. 495–7.

433. *Evening Standard*, 15 April 2002.

434. 'The tragic reality of Israel', *Evening Standard*, 22 October 2001.

435. She is 'the young, dark-haired, intense woman' (p. 6), '[t]he dark-haired, intense young woman, Rachel' (p. 6—again), 'Rachel, the intense young woman' (p. 7), 'Rachel Pearl, the one whom the Superior thought an intense young woman' (p. 8), etc.

436. See Norman Geras, *Solidarity in the Conversation of Humankind* (London, 1995), p. 2.

437. *Sartor Resartus* (London, 1901), pp. 29, 60, and 192.

438. *Jesus* (London, 1992), pp. 29, 11, 13.

439. *The Jews* (London, n.d.), p. 6.

440. See Thomas Weber, 'Anti-Semitism and philo-Semitism among the British and German elites', *English Historical Review*, 18/475 (2003), 107–8.

441. *A Palestine Notebook 1918–1923* (New York, 1923), pp. ix, xi, 36, 68, 164–5.

442. The Conservative MP, 'Chips' Channon, wrote of Leslie Hore-Belisha, 'he is an oily man, half a Jew, an opportunist, with the Semitic flair for publicity'. On another occasion, writing of Hore-Belisha's performance at a lunch, Channon records, 'suddenly Leslie became "the Jew boy", bungling and self-important . . .' Chips found Hore-Belisha's home 'snug and luxurious, like the boite of a well-kept tart. And it is a touch Jewish.' But then he adds,

'He is a brilliant minister.' Channon was Hore-Belisha's friend, after a fashion, and mostly admired his political skills and judgement. See Robert Rhodes James (ed.), *Chips: The diaries of Sir Henry Channon* (London, 1967), pp. 23–4, 120, 155, 181, 228–31 ('I admire his jaunty courage'), 334, 341, 344, 471.

443. See Abraham Gilam, *The Emancipation of the Jews in England 1830–1860* (New York, 1982), p. 53.

444. 'Little Spitz' (1841). See S. S. Prawer, *Israel at Vanity Fair* (Leiden, 1992), p. 93.

445. See Charles Ferrall, *Modernist Writing and Reactionary Politics* (Cambridge, 2001), p. 151.

446. N. J. Crowson, *Fleet Street, Press Barons and Politics* (Cambridge, 1998), p. 269.

447. *Diaries and Letters: 1930–39* (London, 1966), p. 97.

448. See Sidney Aster (ed.), *Appeasement and All Souls* (Cambridge, 2004), pp. 230–1.

449. *Diaries and Letters: 1945–62* (London, 1968), pp. 139, 149.

450. *Diaries and Letters: 1930–39* (London, 1966), pp. 53, 347–8; *1939–45* (London, 1967), pp. 268, 353, 456, 469.

451. See George Orwell, *The Observer Years* (London, 2003), pp. 104–6.

452. See, for example, ibid., p. 154.

453. 'As I please', *The Collected Essays, Journalism and Letters* (London, 1968), vol. 4, p. 293.

454. 'The Road to Wigan Pier Diary', *Orwell's England* (London, 2001), p. 35.

455. *The War Commentaries* (London, 1987), p. 188.

456. Ibid., p. 158.

457. T. R. Fyvel, *George Orwell* (London, 1982), p. 140. Wardour Street was the home of the British film industry.

458. Ibid., p. 178, disagrees.

459. *Orwell's Victory* (London, 2002), p. 7. See also Bernard Crick, *George Orwell* (London, 1980), p. 307.

460. *The Future in America* (London, 1987), p. 149.

461. *A Short History of the World* (London, 2006), pp. 86, 140.

462. *All Aboard For Ararat* (London, 1940), p. 18.

463. *The Outlook for Homo Sapiens* (London, 1942), p. 77.

464. Ibid., pp. 76–88, 282–4.

465. *Liberalism and Its Party* (London, 1913), p. 2.

466. *The Rights of Man* (London, 1940), pp. 32, 62.

467. ' "Romanian Jew, isn't he?" I said. He nodded darkly and almost forbiddingly. More would have been too much. The thing was said. But from that time forth I knew that he and I were friends.' *Tono-Bungay* (London, 2005), p. 323.

468. *A Short History of the World* (London, 2006), pp. 101, 107.

469. *Anticipations* (Mineola, NY, 1999), pp. 177–8.

470. C. F. G. Masterman, *The Condition of England* (London, 1909), pp. 46–8, 203–4, 208, 236–7, and 240–1, traverses much of the same ground as *Tono-Bungay*, but without referring to Jews.

471. *Questions of the Day* (London, 1897), p. 241.

472. *A Short History of England* (London, 1917), pp. 108–9.

473. R. I. Moore, *The Formation of a Persecuting Society* (Oxford, 1987), p. 153.

474. Emil Reich, 'The Jew-baiting on the Continent', *Nineteenth Century*, 40 (July–December 1896), 425.

475. See Gisela C. Lebzelter, 'Anti-Semitism: A focal point for the British Radical Right' in Paul Kennedy and Anthony Nicholls (eds.), *Nationalist and Racialist Movements in Britain and Germany before 1914* (London, 1981), p. 103.

476. A view attributed to Keynes by his biographer, Robert Skidelsky in *John Maynard Keynes 1883–1946* (London, 2004), p. 57.

477. See Robert Skidelsky, *Interests and Obsessions* (London, 1993), pp. 108–9.

478. Niall Ferguson, *Colossus* (London, 2005), p. 15.

479. Ibid.

480. Jason Tomes, *Balfour and Foreign Policy* (Cambridge, 2002), p. 2.

481. Christopher Hill, *Some Intellectual Consequences of the English Revolution* (London, 1997), p. 3.

482. Gregory Fremont-Barnes, *The Boer War 1899–1902* (Oxford, 2003), p. 75.

483. David Marquand, *Britain since 1918* (London, 2008), p. 38.

484. *English Political Thought in the Nineteenth Century* (New York, 1962), p. 178.

485. 'Can Jews be patriots?', *Nineteenth Century*, 3 (May 1878), 885. Thirteenth-century England, by contrast, could *not* 'digest' the Jews, and found 'the oppression of the Jewish usurers intolerable'.

486. Alastair Hamilton, *The Appeal of Fascism* (London, 1971), p. 257.

487. John Keegan, *The Battle for History* (London, 1997), p. 13.

488. *From Admiral to Cabin Boy* (London, 1947), p. 80.

489. John Morley, *On Compromise* (London, 1888), pp. 5–6; Robert Skidelsky, *Interests and Obsessions* (London, 1993), 145.

490. See Stefan Collini, 'With friends like these: John Carey and Noel Annan', *English Pasts* (Oxford, 1999), p. 289.

491. *Selected Critical Writings* (Oxford, 2000), p. 20.

492. 'Letters on the French coup d'état of 1851' in Norman St John Stevas (ed.), *Bagehot's Historical Essays* (London, 1971), pp. 409–10.

493. Geoffrey G. Field, 'Anti-Semitism with the boots off' in Herbert A. Strauss (ed.), *Hostages of Modernization* (Berlin, 1993), pp. 324–5.

494. See Peter Mandler, *The English National Stereotype* (London, 2006), pp. 166, 174, 182, 191, 235.

495. *The Prime Minister* (London, 2004), p. 110.

496. W. A. McArthur, 'The imperial aspect' in Arnold White (ed.), *The Destitute Alien in Great Britain* (London, 1892), p. 132.

497. See Bernard Wasserstein, *The British in Palestine* (Oxford, 1991), pp. 66, 149.

498. Michael Ragussis, *Figures of Conversion* (London, 1995), p. 3.

499. Henry Bettenson (ed.), *Documents of the Christian Church* (Oxford, 1967), p. 298. To deny non-Christian witnesses the right to swear oaths in court

according to their own faith would obstruct the adjudication of business disputes, the Lord Chief Justice decided in 1744. Further, to hold that the law should treat such persons as if they were 'perpetual enemies' would 'at once destroy all that trade and commerce from which this nation reaps such great benefits'. See M. C. N. Salbstein, *The Emancipation of the Jews in Britain* (London, 1982), p. 31.

500. John Locke, *An Essay Concerning Human Understanding* (New York, 1959), vol. 2, p. 121.

501. John Horton, 'Toleration' in David Miller (ed.), *The Blackwell Encyclopedia of Political Thought* (Oxford, 1991), p. 522.

502. A phrase of the French philosopher Alain's. See André Comte-Sponville, *A Short Treatise on the Great Virtues* (London, 2003), p. 164.

503. For example: (1) 'The Jews were always crucifying boys, as everyone knew, and were now and again slaughtered for it.' F. W. Maitland 'The Deacon and the Jewess' in H. A. L. Fisher (ed.), *The Collected Papers of Frederic William Maitland* (Cambridge, 1911), vol. 1, p. 400; (2) 'They were accused of foul crimes, such as murdering and crucifying Christian children, and occasional outbursts of Christian fanaticism had involved them in outrage and massacre.' T. F. Tout, *Edward I* (1893), p. 160.

504. W. K. Jordan, *The Development of Religious Toleration in England* (London, 1938), vol. 3, pp. 211, 530.

505. *The Annual Report of the Royal Society for the Prevention of Cruelty to Animals etc.* (London, 1856), pp. 34–5.

506. Roy Porter, *The Enlightenment* (London, 2001), pp. 50–1; Gertrude Himmelfarb, *The Roads to Modernity* (New York, 2004), pp. 50–1.

507. See *The Opium of the Intellectuals* (New Brunswick, NJ, 2001), p. 215.

508. Noel Annan, *Our Age* (London, 1990), p. 7.

509. Raymond Aron, *The Opium of the Intellectuals* (New Brunswick, NJ, 2001), p. 28.

510. Cf. Noel Annan, *Our Age* (London, 1990), p. 3.

511. 'On Liberty', *Three Essays* (Oxford, 1975), pp. 13, 41–2.

512. *East London* (London, 1903), p. 187.

513. 'The Jewish Question', *London Quarterly Review*, 59 (October 1882–January 1883), 94–119.

514. But then, as if to demonstrate that English 'fair play' could be bent in the direction of intolerance and oppression too, a champion of the bill smoothly insisted, 'I do not treat the Park Lane alien any different from the alien in the East End.' These aliens have 'aroused the antipathy of the British public', they have 'kept themselves aloof', and 'while underselling the British workman' they are 'ever ready to take advantage of the asylum we have given them'. And he concluded, 'Treat them all alike, rich and poor. I would like to see England rid of aliens from top to bottom.' *The Parliamentary Debates (Official Report)*, 5th Series, vol. 37, 1919, Commons, cols. 1230–2, 1240.

515. See Lucien Wolf, 'Prefatory Note', *The Myth of the Jewish Menace in World Affairs* (New York, 1921). In John Galsworthy's *Loyalties*, the Jewish de Levis demands 'Give me fair play.' See Ludwig Lewisohn (ed.), *Among the Nations* (Philadelphia, 1948), p. 174.

516. 'The motive-power of this anti-alien agitation is race hatred and that instinct so peculiar to Englishmen which impels them to glorify the powerful and the strong and to deride and persecute the poorer and weaker peoples who might need their sympathy.' John Dyche, 'The Jewish workman', *Contemporary Review*, 73 (January 1898), 35, 50.

517. See Simon Garfield, *Our Hidden Lives* (London, 2004), pp. 166, 169, 257, for examples of such complaints.

518. *The Jews' Who's Who* (London 1920), p. 3.

519. *Secret Societies and Subversive Movements* (London, 1924), p. 398.

520. See Simon Garfield, *We Are at War* (London, 2006), p. 51.

521. Jonathan Frankel, *The Damascus Affair* (Cambridge, 1997), pp. 146, 207–11, 253, 259, 264–6.

522. Todd M. Endelman, *Radical Assimilation in English Jewish History 1656–1945* (Bloomington, IN, 1990), pp. 3, 21, 208–9.

523. See Bill Williams, 'The anti-Semitism of Tolerance' in Alan J. Kidd and K.W. Roberts (eds.), *City, Class and Culture* (Manchester, 1985); Tony Kushner, *The Persistence of Prejudice* (Manchester, 1989), p. 92.

524. *England and the English* (Manchester, 2003), pp. 278, 308.

525. See Peter Pulzer, *The Rise of Political Anti-Semitism in Germany and Austria* (New York, 1964), p. 337.

526. David S. Katz, *Philo-Semitism and the Readmission of the Jews to England 1603–1655* (Oxford, 1982), ch. 1.

527. Todd M. Endelman, *The Jews of Georgian England 1714–1830* (Philadelphia, 1979), p. 52.

528. 'Critical remarks on some passages of Voltaire', *Gentleman's Magazine*, 40 (October 1770), 459. See also 40 (October 1770), 554; 41 (February 1771), 108, 203–4, 299–300; 42 (January 1772), 9–11; (May 1772), 214–15; (August 1772), 356–7; 43 (February 1773), 81.

529. See R. Travers Herford, 'What the world owed to the Pharisees' (London, 1919), an address to the Jewish Historical Society.

530. The 'Address' describes the Jews as 'worshippers of the one true God', an 'appellation unhappily not as yet applicable to the great body of Christians; *Letters to the Jews, Part II* addresses the Jews as "brethren in the belief of the unity of God"'.

531. See David Vital, *A People Apart* (Oxford, 1999), p. 39.

532. *Letters to the Jews, Part II* (London, 1787), p. 42.

533. See Jeanne Shami, 'Donne, anti-Jewish rhetoric, and the English Church in 1621' in Chanita Goodblatt and Howard Kreisel (eds.), *Tradition, Heterodoxy and Religious Culture* (Beer-Sheva, 2006), pp. 34–43.

534. *Observations on Man* (Washington, DC, 1998), vol. 2, pp. 373–4. Hartley offers seven reasons in all.

535. Haim Chertok, *He also Spoke as a Jew* (London, 2006), p. 368 ('a thoroughly "bejewed" Christian'). Colin Richmond, *Campaigner Against Antisemitism* (London, 2005), p. 69.

536. See Solomon Rappaport, *Jew and Gentile: The philo-Semitic aspect* (New York, 1980), p. 94.

537. The Marquess of Lansdowne. Hansard, Parl. Debs. (series 3) vol. 98, col. 1336 (1848).

538. See W. D. Rubinstein, *A History of Jews in the English-Speaking World: Great Britain* (London, 1996), p. 330.

539. William D. Rubinstein and Hilary L. Rubinstein, *Philosemitism: Admiration and support in the English-speaking world for Jews, 1840–1939* (London, 1999), p. ix.

540. See Douglas J. Culver, *Albion and Ariel* (New York, 1995), pp. 30–1, 52; Léon Poliakov, *The Aryan Myth* (New York, 1974), pp. 42–5.

541. See Douglas J. Culver, *Albion and Ariel* (New York, 1995), p. 156.

542. 'Shooting Niagara: And after?' *Critical and Miscellaneous Essays* (London, n.d.), vol. 7, p. 222.

543. 'Speech on conciliation with the colonies', *Selected Works* (Indianapolis, IN, 1999), vol. 1, p. 287.

544. 'The Modern Hep! Hep! Hep!', *Impressions of Theophrastus Such* (London, 1995), p. 142.

545. Eric Michael Reisenauer, 'Anti-Jewish philosemitism', *British Scholar*, 1 (2008), 103.

546. Russo-Jewish Committee of London, *The Persecution of the Jews in Russia* (London, 1891), pp. 3–4, 34.

547. *The Scapegoat* (London, n.d.), p. 155.

548. *Rex v Osborne*, H. S. Q. Henriques, *The Jews and the English Law* (London, 1908), pp. 9–10.

549. *Reliques of Ancient English Poetry* (New York, n.d.), vol. 1, p. 54.

550. 'Critical remarks on some passages of Voltaire', *Gentleman's Magazine*, 42 (January 1772), 9–11; (May 1772), 214–15; (August 1772), 356–7.

551. Jonathan Frankel, *The Damascus Affair* (Cambridge, 1997), pp. 126, 143–4, 194–6, 207.

552. 'The Jews of Western Europe', *Westminster Review*, New series, 23 (April 1863), 450.

553. 'The Modern Hep! Hep! Hep!', *Impressions of Theophrastus Such* (London, 1995), p. 143.

554. 'The Jews and the malicious charge of human sacrifice', *The Nineteenth Century*, 81 (November 1883), 757, 765, 768–9. Cf.: 'the cruel fancy that the Jews sacrifice Christian children and spread pestilence'. Goldwin Smith, 'The Jewish Question', *Questions of the Day* (London, 1897), p. 262.

555. See Anne and Roger Cowen, *Victorian Jews through British Eyes* (Oxford, 1986), pp. 158–60.

556. *Chapters from the Religious History of Spain connected with the Inquisition* (London, 1890).

557. 'The Jew-baiting on the Continent', *Nineteenth Century*, 40 (July–December 1896), 423.

558. W. E. H. Lecky, 'Israel among the nations', *The Forum*, 16 (December 1893), 443.

559. *The Modern Jew* (London, 1899), p. 121.

560. Hermann L. Strack, *The Jew and Human Sacrifice* (London, 1909), p. xv.

561. Wyndham Lewis, *The Jews: Are They Human?* (London, 1939), p. 54.

562. 'Refuted slanders revived', and 'The Mystery of Metz', *Jewish Chronicle*, 25 October 1861 and 14 February 1862; W. D. Rubinstein, *A History of Jews in the English-Speaking World: Great Britain* (London, 1996), p. 289; Frank Flesenstein, *Anti-Semitic Stereotypes* (Baltimore, MD, 1995), p. xiii.

563. See Joseph Jacobs, *The Jewish Question 1875–1884: Bibliographical hand-list* (London, 1885), p. 44.

564. 'If you wish to utter a collective libel or slander, those libelled or slandered have no remedy. For example, if a newspaper were to talk about the odious practice of ritual murder among Jews I doubt if anybody could bring any action at all, and if he did, people would say, "Why are you so sensitive on this point; what have you got to conceal?" ' See Hansard, HL (series 5) vol. 122, col. 575 (1942). The implication appears to be that the 'ritual murder' libel is true.

565. Jonathan Frankel, *The Damascus Affair* (Cambridge, 1997), p. 266.

566. Henry Hart Milman, *History of the Jews* (London, 1866), vol. 3, p. 249.

567. W. H. Hutton (ed.), *The Misrule of Henry III* (London, 1887), p. 91.

568. Augustus Jessopp and M. R. James (eds.), *The Life and Miracles of St William of Norwich by Thomas of Monmouth* (Cambridge, 1896), pp. lxxviii–lxxix.

569. Stephen Graham, 'Russia and the Jews', *English Review*, 19 (December 1914–March 1915), 325–8.

570. Sir Richard F. Burton, *The Jew, the Gypsy, and El Islam* (Palmdale, CA, 2000), pp. 3, 5, 9, 17, 21, 26–8, 62, 88, 92–8. See also Dane Kennedy, *A Highly Civilised Man* (Cambridge, MA, 2005), pp. 185–91.

571. See 'Sir Richard Burton's manuscripts', *The Times*, 28 March 1911.

572. See Geoffrey Alderman and Colin Holmes, 'The Burton Book', *Journal of the Royal Asiatic Society*, series 3, 18/1 (2008), 8–13; *Anti-Semitism in British Society 1876–1939* (New York, 1979), pp. 49–62.

573. Jerry White, *Rothschild Buildings* (London, 2003), p. 25.

574. Terence Sharkey, *Jack the Ripper* (London, 1987), p. 45.

575. David Cesarani, *The Jewish Chronicle and Anglo-Jewry 1841–1991* (Cambridge, 1994), p. 81.

576. Terence Sharkey, *Jack the Ripper* (London, 1987), pp. 114–16, 124–6.

577. Gisela C. Lebzelter, *Political Anti-Semitism in England 1918–1939* (London, 1978), p. 8.

578. *Secret Societies and Subversive Movements* (London, 1924), pp. 79–80, 83–4.

579. *Torquemada and the Spanish Inquisition*, 8th edn (London, 1937), pp. 248, 270, 275.

580. *Isabella of Spain* (1935), pp. 258, 265, 356, 357, 437, 439, 440, 470, 542.

581. *The History of Witchcraft and Demonology* (London, 1973), pp. 161–2, 172, 195–7. This is a typical anti-Semitic inversion. The full passage affirms the Jewish prohibition of the consumption of blood: 'Ye shall eat the blood of no manner of flesh: for the life of all flesh is the blood thereof: whosoever eateth it shall be cut off' (Leviticus 17:14). James Parkes took the witchcraft explanation seriously: Colin Richmond, *Campaigner Against Antisemitism* (London, 2005), pp. 262–3.

582. See Louis Golding, *Hitler Through the Ages* (London, n.d.), p. 61; but see also his *Those Ancient Lands* (London, 1928), p. 27. The Britons Publishing Society published a pamphlet promoting the blood libel, 'The Jews' Ritual Slaughter' in 1923. See Hilary Blume, 'A study of anti-Semitic groups in Britain, 1918–1940', unpublished D. Phil thesis, University of Sussex, 1971, p. 66.

583. *My Irrelevant Defence, Being Meditations Inside Gaol And Out On Jewish Ritual Murder* (London, 1938), p. 3. John Morell, 'Arnold Leese and the Imperial Fascist League' in Kenneth Lunn and Richard C. Thurlow (eds.), *British Fascism* (London, 1980), p. 62.

584. Y. Harkabi, *Arab Attitudes to Israel* (Jerusalem, 1972), pp. 273–4.

585. Joël et Dan Kotek, *Au nom de l'antisionisme* (Bruxelles, 2005), p. 44.

586. *The Plantagenets* (London, 1972), pp. 119–20.

587. Tony Kushner, *The Persistence of Prejudice* (Manchester, 1989), p. 45.

588. Colin Holmes and Tony Kushner, 'The charge is ritual murder', *Jewish Chronicle*, 29 March 1985.

589. Ibid.

7. CONTEMPORARY SECULAR ANTI-ZIONISMS

1. Kenneth S. Stern, *Antisemitism Today* (New York, 2006); Bernard Harrison, *The Resurgence of Anti-Semitism* (New York, 2006); Fiamma Nirenstein, *Terror* (Hanover, NH, 2005); Irwin Cotler, 'The new Antisemitism' in Michael Fineberg, Shimon Samuels, and Mark Weitzman (eds.), *Antisemitism* (London, 2007), pp. 15–32; Matti Bunzl, *Anti-Semitism and Islamophobia* (Chicago, 2007); Phyllis Chesler, *The New Anti-Semitism* (San Francisco, CA, 2003); Gabriel Schoenfeld, *The Return of Anti-Semitism* (San Francisco, 2004); Abraham H. Foxman, *Never Again?* (New York, 2003); Mark Gardner, 'The Zionists are our misfortune', *Democratiya* (Autumn 2007); Yehonatan Tommer and Tzvi Fleischer, 'Hate's revival: What's new about the "new antisemitism"?', *AIR* (May 2007); Alvin H. Rosenfeld, '"Progressive" Jewish thought and the new anti-Semitism',

American Jewish Committee (August 2006); Denis MacShane, 'The new antisemitism', *Washington Post*, 4 September 2007 and *Globalising Hatred* (London, 2008); Mitchell Cohen, 'Anti-Semitism and the Left that doesn't learn', *Dissent* (Fall 2007); *Report of the All-Party Parliamentary Inquiry into Antisemitism* (London, September 2006); Omer Bartov, 'The New Antisemitism' in David Kertzer (ed.), *Old Demons, New Debates* (New York, 2005).

2. Denis MacShane, *Globalising Hatred* (London, 2008), p. viii.

3. Imre Kertesz, 'The freedom of Bedlam', *signandsight*, 22 August 2006.

4. See Moshe Rosman, *How Jewish Is Jewish History?* (Oxford, 2007), p. 75.

5. See Seymour Martin Lipset, 'The return of anti-Semitism as a political force' in Irving Howe and Carl Gershman (eds.), *Israel, the Arabs & the Middle East* (New York, 1972), pp. 390–427. Israel's success caused discomfort. See Michael Frayn, 'My dear Israel', *Observer*, 25 June 1967: 'What makes your behaviour all the more perplexing is that when the war commenced you enjoyed the approval and sympathy of polite society as a whole.'

6. See Natan Sharansky with Ron Dermer, *The Case for Democracy* (New York, 2006), pp. 224–5.

7. William D. Rubinstein, *The Left, the Right, and the Jews* (London, 1982), pp. 77–114.

8. See Ehud Sprinzak, *The Ascendance of Israel's Radical Right* (Oxford, 1991).

9. See Arthur Hertzberg, *The Fate of Zionism* (New York, 2003), pp. xi, 1–9.

10. Elie Kedourie, *Islam in the Modern World* (London, 1980), p. 233.

11. See Stephen Sizer, *Christian Zionism* (Downers Grove, IL, 2004), pp. 42–60.

12. 'Zionism and Palestine', *Contemporary Review* (April 1922), 434.

13. See Virginia H. Hein, *The British Followers of Theodor Herzl* (New York, 1987), p. 28.

14. Douglas J. Culver, *Albion and Ariel* (New York, 1995), p. 23; Virginia H. Hein, *The British Followers of Theodor Herzl* (New York, 1987), p. 168.

15. See David Cesarani, 'Anti-Zionist politics and political antisemitism in Britain, 1920–1924', *Patterns of Prejudice*, 23/1 (1989).

16. Oona King, *House Music* (London, 2007), p. 261; *Report of the All-Party Parliamentary Inquiry into Antisemitism* (London, September 2006), p. 22.

17. Hence the popularity of the designation for London, 'Londonistan', coined by French security officials. They intended a criticism of British laxity regarding Islamic groups. It has been over-used, and now has a pejorative edge, collapsing many, properly distinct, aspects of British-Muslim life into a single terrorist or proto-terrorist paradigm. See Rageh Omar, *Only Half of Me* (London, 2007), pp. 29–32.

18. David Hirsh, 'Anti-Zionism and antisemitism', YIISA Working Paper #1, 2008; Jonathan Spyer, 'The anti-Israel lobby', *Guardian*, 8 February 2007.

19. David Newman, 'Britain and the academic boycott of Israel', *Israel Journal of Foreign Affairs*, 2/2 (2008), 45–55.

20. See Andy Beckett, 'It's water on stone—in the end the stone wears out', *Guardian*, 12 December 2002.

21. Charlotte Higgins, 'John Berger rallies artists for cultural boycott of Israel', *Guardian*, 15 December 2006.

22. 21 April 2007. The *British Medical Journal* conducted a poll on the boycott question, following publication of papers both in favour of, and against, a boycott. The vote was 77% against, 23% in favour. See <http://www.bmj. com/cgi/content/extract/335/7611/124>.

23. Stephen Brook, 'NUJ abandons Israel boycott', *Guardian*, 10 July 2007.

24. See <http://stopthewall.org/news/boycot.shtml>.

25. Oliver Duff, Rob Sharp, and Eric Silver, 'Architects threaten to boycott Israel over "apartheid" barrier', *Independent*, 10 February 2006; Hugh Muir, 'Top architects accuse Israelis of oppression', *Guardian*, 26 May 2007.

26. Peter Beaumont, 'To boycott or not: The new Israeli question', *Observer*, 10 June 2007.

27. John Pilger, 'An important marker has been passed', *New Statesman*, 23 August 2007.

28. Emanuele Ottolenghi, 'British Journalism vs. Israel', *Commentary*, 4 May 2007; Gerald Steinberg, 'Anti-Israel boycotts: A British disease', *The Jewish Week*, 18 May 2007; 'Battle for Britain', *Ha'aretz*, 27 May 2007; Gerald M. Steinberg, 'Britain's obsessive boycotters', *Jerusalem Post*, 30 May 2007. But see Ron Prosor, 'Britain is a hot-bed of anti-Israeli sentiment', *Daily Telegraph*, 10 June 2008.

29. James Meikle, 'Lecturers drop Israeli universities boycott call after legal advice', *Guardian*, 29 September 2007. But see Jonny Paul, 'UCL Professor: "Terror Palestinians' Moral Right"', *Jerusalem Post*, 27 January 2008.

30. Anthea Lipsett, 'Union committee to reconsider Israeli academics boycott', *Guardian*, 27 March 2008; Anthea Lipsett, 'Lecturer union urges moral review of Israeli college links', *Guardian*, 29 May 2008; Eve Garrard 'Passing Motion 25', *Normblog*, 29 May 2008. The conference rejected an amendment requiring a ballot of the UCU membership before any call to boycott Israelis. At the first executive meeting of the UCU following the conference, the motion was remitted to a committee for further consideration. See Jonny Paul, 'Academic trade union wavers on implementing decision to boycott Israeli academia', *Jerusalem Post*, 15 June 2008.

31. See Olivia Ball and Paul Gready, *The No-Nonsense Guide to Human Rights* (Oxford, 2006), pp. 56-7.

32. Martin Kramer, 'The myth of linkage', *MESH*, 12 June 2008.

33. Edward Luttwak, 'The middle of nowhere', *Prospect*, May 2007; Shahar Smooha, 'All the dreams we had are now gone', *Ha'retz*, July 2007. But see Niall Ferguson, 'Yes, the Mideast matters', *LA Times*, 18 June 2007.

34. Anton La Guardia, *Holy Land, Unholy War* (London, 2002), p. 370.

35. See Thérèse Delpech, *Savage Century* (Washington, DC, 2007), pp. 84, 96, 121, 129, 133-44.

36. Peter Beaumont, 'Israel outraged as EU poll names it a threat to peace', *Observer*, 2 November 2003.

37. Unmentioned in the Qu'ran by name, it is understood to be the 'Furthest Mosque', mentioned at 17:1. See Waleed El-Ansary, 'The economics of terrorism' in Joseph E. B. Lumbard (ed.), *Islam, Fundamentalism, and the Betrayal of Tradition* (Bloomington, IN, 2004), pp. 215-16.

38. See Barbara Tuchman, *Bible and Sword* (London, 1982), p. viii.

39. See Elie Kedourie, 'The Arab-Israeli Conflict', *Arabic Political Memoirs and Other Studies* (London, 1974), pp. 218-30.

40. Nahum N. Glatzer and Paul Mendes-Flohr (eds.), *The Letters of Martin Buber* (New York, 1991), p. 146.

41. See Thomas Friedman, *From Beirut to Jerusalem* (London, 1998), pp. 431-5.

42. *The Jews of Modernity* (New York, 1973), p. 359.

43. See Anton La Guardia, *Holy Land, Unholy War* (London, 2002), pp. 376-8.

44. Pierre Birnbaum, *The Anti-Semitic Moment* (New York, 2003), pp. 135, 142, 144, 243-4.

45. See, for example, Steven Beller, *Vienna and the Jews 1867-1938* (Cambridge, 1989), pp. 122-7.

46. See David Feldman, 'Was modernity good for the Jews?' in Bryan Cheyette and Laura Marcus (eds.), *Modernity, Culture and 'the jew'* (Oxford, 1998), pp. 176-7.

47. See Jacob Katz, *From Prejudice to Destruction* (Cambridge, MA, 1980), p. 109.

48. Meir Michaelis, 'The Holocaust in Italy' in Michael Berenbaum and Abraham J. Peck (eds.), *The Holocaust and History* (Bloomington, IN, 2002), p. 449.

49. See Steven Lukes, *Liberals and Cannibals* (London, 2003), p. 6.

50. Michael Burleigh, *Sacred Causes* (London, 2006), p. 105.

51. I. Rennap, *Anti-Semitism and the Jewish Question* (London, 1942), pp. 9-10. Cf.: 'Antisemitism comes more naturally to people of Conservative tendency.' George Orwell, 'Notes on nationalism', October 1945, in *I Belong to the Left* (London, 1998), p. 152.

52. The Left was probably the most vociferous source of attacks on Jews until the 1890s. Eugen Weber, *My France* (Cambridge, MA, 1991), p. 290.

53. Jonathan Frankel, *Prophecy and Politics* (Cambridge, 1984), pp. 100-1, 113-14; Theodore H. Friedgut, 'Soviet anti-Zionism: Origins, forms, and development' in Robert S. Wistrich (ed.), *Anti-Zionism and Antisemitism in the Contemporary World* (New York, 1990), p. 29.

54. Eugen Weber, *My France* (Cambridge, MA, 1991), p. 289; Dan Diner, *America in the Eyes of the Germans* (Princeton, NJ, 1996), p. 67; David Carroll, *French Literary Fascism* (Princeton, NJ, 1995), p. 241.

55. Pierre Birnbaum, *The Anti-Semitic Moment* (New York, 2003), p. 99.

56. Nelly Wilson, *Bernard-Lazare* (Cambridge, 1978), p. 219.

57. Ben Cohen, 'The persistence of anti-Semitism on the British Left', *Jewish Political Studies Review*, 16/3–4 (2004).

58. Friedrich Engels, 'Anti-Dühring', *Marx and Engels on Religion* (Amsterdam, The Netherlands, 2002), p. 148.

59. Leon Wieseltier, 'What is not to be done', *New Republic*, 27 October 2003.

60. George Sacks, *The Jewish Question* (London, 1937), p. 87.

61. See Emmanuel Levinas, *Beyond the Verse* (London, 1994), p. 191.

62. 'Holy Land and Holy People', a Lecture at the 5th International Sabeel Conference, 14 April 2004. See <http://www.archbishopofcanterbury.org/sermons_speeches/2004/040414.html>.

63. Roger Garaudy in France, Horst Mahler in Germany, and Ohta Ryu in Japan. Garaudy, formerly a member of the French Communist Party, was convicted of Holocaust denial and racial defamation by a French court in 1998. Mahler was a former Red Army Faction member, and now belongs to the Far Right National Democratic Party. He is a Holocaust denier: <http://www.spiegel.de/international/germany/0,1518,550430,00.html>. On Ryu, see David Goodman, *The 'Protocols of the Elders of Zion', Aum, and Antisemitism in Japan*, Posen Papers in Contemporary Antisemitism, no. 2, The Vidal Sassoon International Center for the Study of Antisemitism, The Hebrew University of Jerusalem (2005), pp. 9–11.

64. See, for example, Seamus Milne, 'This slur of anti-Semitism is used to defend repression', *Guardian*, 9 May 2002.

65. Simon Sebag Montefiore, *Stalin: The court of the Red Tsar* (London, 2004), pp. 561, 624.

66. *Verdict in Absentia* (Beirut, 1969), pp. 21, 27, 33, 57, 63–4, 68, 86, 87–99.

67. 'The possibility of mixing two communities of entirely different background and orientation and the creation of a test-tube new nation was something which could not fail in its appeal to people who viewed national questions with dislike.' *The New Statesman and the Middle East* (Beirut, 1972), p. 27.

68. Ibid., pp. 103–4, 113.

69. Omayma Abdel-Latif, 'Covering the Intifada', *Al-Ahram Weekly On-line*, 23–9 November 2000, Issue no. 509.

70. 'I've got what it takes to lead the PLO: Jewish good looks', *Independent*, 3 October 2000.

71. *What do Zionists Believe?* (London, 2007), pp. 1–2, 64–72.

72. The 'valiant defenders of the Arabs' rights' (J. M. N. Jeffries' phrase) were not quite as consistently unsuccessful as they made out. The 1939 White Paper, for example, was an immense success for the Arab interest, in the then received understanding of the term. See *Palestine: The reality* (London, 1939), p. 578. See also Joseph Gorny, *The British Labour Movement and Zionism 1917–1948* (London, 1983), p. 150. Nevertheless, Labour Party support for Israel in the 1950s and 1960s was quite solid. See Hugh Dalton, *High Tide and After* (London, 1962), p. 387. In 1966, the then former foreign minister of Israel, Golda Meir,

opened the Labour Party Conference. See Neil Lochery, *Loaded Dice* (London, 2007), p. 118.

73. Daphna Baram, *Disenchantment* (London, 2004), p. 14.

74. Sunil Khilnani, 'The end of ideology and the critique of Marxism' in Lawrence D. Kritzman (ed.), *The Columbia History of Twentieth-Century French Thought* (New York, 2006), p. 193.

75. Julia Kristeva, *Nations without Nationalism* (New York, 1993), p. 2.

76. Brian Barry, *Culture and Equality* (Cambridge, MA, 2001), p. 4.

77. Slavoj Žižek, *Did Somebody Say Totalitarianism?* (London, 2001), p. 3.

78. Perry Anderson, 'Renewals', *New Left Review*, January–February 2000.

79. 'Marx in his limits', *Philosophy of the Encounter* (London, 2006), p. 10. In the same year, Althusser dismissed the 'theoretical vapidities of human rights ideologies'. 'Philosophy and Marxism', ibid, p. 288. The Left now acknowledges 'the idea of rights might have something to teach us'. Phillipe Raynaud, 'Bourdieu' in Mark Lilla (ed.), *New French Thought* (Princeton, NJ, 1994), p. 69.

80. See Fred Halliday, *Islam and the Myth of Confrontation* (London, 2003), p. 160. A 'semi-ideology' is a 'body of ideas that, like gender and racial prejudice, is often articulated in conjunction with others that have a greater potential to function independently'. See also Michael Freeden, *Ideologies and Political Theory* (Oxford, 1996), p. 485.

81. Paul Berman, *Power and the Idealists* (New York, 2005), p. 73.

82. Mark Lilla, 'The legitimacy of the Liberal Age' in Mark Lilla (ed.), *New French Thought* (Princeton, NJ, 1994), p. 14.

83. Paul Berman, *Power and the Idealists* (New York, 2005), p. 6.

84. See Mark Lilla (ed.), *New French Thought* (Princeton, NJ, 1994).

85. Luc Ferry and Alain Renaut, 'How to think about rights' in Mark Lilla (ed.), *New French Thought* (Princeton, NJ, 1994), pp. 149, 150.

86. See Tony Judt, *Postwar* (London, 2005), p. 577.

87. Desmond M. Tutu, 'Foreword' to Olivia Ball and Paul Gready, *The No-Nonsense Guide to Human Rights* (Oxford, 2006), p. 5.

88. Irwin Cotler, 'The new antisemitism' in Michael Fineberg, Shimon Samuels, and Mark Weitzman (eds.), *Antisemitism* (London, 2007), p. 22.

89. Pierre Manet, 'The contest for command' in Mark Lilla (ed.), *New French Thought* (Princeton, NJ, 1994), p. 178. Cf.: 'Rights talk . . . is our natural language.' Michael Walzer, *Politics and Passion* (New Haven, 2004), p. 45. Cf.: 'There is simply no other legitimating set of ideas besides liberal democracy that is broadly accepted in the world today.' Francis Fukayama, *After the Neocons* (London, 2006), p. 130. 'There is no grand alternative to liberal democratic society.' Fred Halliday, *Two Hours that Shook the World* (London, 2002), p. 182.

90. John Fonte, 'Liberal Democracy vs. Transnational Progressivism', *Orbis* (Summer 2002).

91. Michael Ignatieff, 'Is the human rights era ending?', *New York Times*, 5 February 2002.
92. See Francis Fukayama, *After the Neocons* (London, 2006), pp. 157–8.
93. 'I think one of the things the left ought to give up is the idea that there's some other system waiting in the wings instead of capitalism.' Gareth Stedman Jones, <http://www.pbs.org/heavenonearth/interviews_jones.html>.
94. Julia Kristeva, *Nations without Nationalism* (New York, 1993), p. 2.
95. Richard Wolin, *The Seduction of Unreason* (Princeton, 2004), pp. 278–314; Dan Diner, *America in the Eyes of the Germans* (Princeton, NJ, 1996), pp. 38, 64; Martin J. Wiener, *English Culture and the Decline of the Industrial Spirit 1850–1980* (Cambridge, 1981), pp. 88–90, 142.
96. Tony Judt, *Postwar* (London, 2005), p. 784; Malise Ruthven, A *Fury for God* (London, 2002), pp. 130–1.
97. Nick Cohen, 'Ken has a lot to be sorry for', *Observer*, 20 February 2005; Micha Odenheimer, 'Vicious circles closing in: An interview with Thomas von der Osten-Sacken', *Ha'aretz*, 4 October 2002.
98. Olivier Roy, *The Politics of Chaos in the Middle East* (New York, 2008), pp. 5, 32.
99. Micha Odenheimer, 'Vicious circles closing in: An interview with Thomas von der Osten-Sacken', *Ha'aretz*, 4 October 2002.
100. See John Lukacs, *George Kennan* (New Haven, 2007), p. 77.
101. See Richard Wolin, *The Seduction of Unreason* (Princeton, 2004), p. 301.
102. See Jan T. Gross, *Fear* (New York, 2006), pp. 223–4, 259.
103. Chris Patten, *Not Quite the Diplomat* (London, 2006), p. 196.
104. Bernard-Henri Lévy, *American Vertigo* (New York, 2006), p. 9.
105. See Louis Althusser, 'Marx in his limits', *Philosophy of the Encounter* (London, 2006), p. 135.
106. *The New Anti-Semitism* (San Francisco, CA, 2003), p. 187.
107. See Manfred Gerstenfeld, 'Language as a tool against Jews and Israel: An interview with Georges-Elia Sarfati', *Post-Holocaust and Anti-Semitism*, Jerusalem Center for Public Affairs, no. 17 1 February 2004.
108. *The End of the Peace Process* (New York, 2000), p. 230.
109. Chaim Gans, 'The Palestinian right of return and the justice of Zionism', *Theoretical Inquiries in Law*, 5/2 (2004), 281.
110. Perry Anderson, 'Scurrying towards Bethlehem', *New Left Review*, (July–August 2001); Tariq Ali, 'Mid-point in the Middle East?', *New Left Review* (March–April 2006).
111. *Publish it Not: The Middle East cover-up* (Oxford, 2006), pp. 195–7.
112. Soumaya Ghannoushi, 'Chasing a ghost', *CiF Guardian*, 27 November 2007.
113. See, for example, Itamar Rabinovich, *Waging Peace* (Princeton, 2004), p. 256 and Shlomo Avineri, 'Post-Zionism doesn't exist', *Ha'aretz*, 7 July 2007. For a reconciliation of the liberal and Jewish imperatives in Israel's political

character, see Ruth Gavison, 'On the Jewish right to sovereignty', *Azure*, (Summer 5763/2003), 70–108.

114. See, for example, Judith Butler, 'The charge of anti-Semitism: Jews, Israel and the risks of public critique' in Ron Rosenbaum (ed.), *Those Who Forget the Past* (New York, 2004), pp. 438–50.

115. Chaim Gans, 'The Palestinian right of return and the justice of Zionism', *Theoretical Inquiries in Law*, 5/2 (2004), 275.

116. Michael Hirst, 'Rise in radical Islam last straw for Lebanon's Christians', *Sunday Telegraph*, 31 March 2007.

117. See Fred Halliday, *Two Hours that Shook the World* (London, 2002), p. 137.

118. Ari Shavit, 'My right of return', *Ha'aretz*, 18 August 2000; cf. the complacency of Fawwaz Trabulsi, 'The Palestine problem: Zionism and imperialism in the Middle East', *New Left Review*, 1/57 (1969), 86–7. In 'a united republic of the Middle East . . . the rights of the Jewish minority should be dealt with along the same lines as those of other minorities (the Kurds of Iraq and Syria and the Africans of Southern Sudan)'.

119. Charles Douglas-Home, *The Arabs and Israel* (London, 1968), p. 117.

120. See Ghada Karmi, *In Search of Fatima* (London, 2004), p. 43.

121. Steven Schwarzschild, 'Jean-Paul Sartre as Jew' in Menachem Kellner (ed.), *The Pursuit of the Ideal* (New York, 1990), p. 169; Jonathan Judaken, *Jean-Paul Sartre and the Jewish Question* (Nebraska, 2006), ch. 6.

122. John Torode, 'Diary', *Spectator*, 25 August 2007.

123. 'Boycotts of Israel: Will they help the Palestinians?', *The Socialist*, 14 June 2007.

124. See 'Why "hate Israel" agitation is no service to the Palestinians' <http://www.workersliberty.org/node/view/340#comment-586>.

125. See <http://www.eustonmanifesto.org/>.

126. See para. 7 of the Manifesto at <http://eustonmanifesto.org/?page_id=132>.

127. For example, 'Tibet, Palestine and the politics of failure', *openDemocracy*,·9 May 2008, <http://www.opendemocracy.net/article/tibet-palestine-and-the-politics-of-failure>.

128. E.g., see Andy Newman, 'Anti-Semitism is a real problem', <http://www.socialistunity.com/?p=1687#comment-40995>; David T., 'International Jewry', <http://hurryupharry.bloghouse.net/archives/2008/02/07/international_jewry.php>.

129. See 'Arm yourself with the arguments—Engage', <http://www.engageonline.org.uk/blog/article.php?id=648>.

130. <http://www.thepcaa.org/report.html>.

131. Benny Morris, *Righteous Victims* (New York, 2001), p. 191.

132. See Colin Shindler, *What do Zionists Believe?* (London, 2007), p. 2; Benny Morris, 'The ignorance at the heart of an innuendo: And now for some facts', *The New Republic* (May 2006).

133. See the website of the ENOUGH! Coalition: 'The United Nations asserted the refugees' right to return home in 1948, but Israel has refused to allow this. Meanwhile the refugee population has grown to over four million, one of the largest in the world, many of whom live in camps waiting for international law to be upheld.' <http://www.waronwant.org/?lid=13692>. See also: 'UN resolution 194 demands their [i.e., Palestinian refugees'] immediate return to their homes.' Soumaya Ghannoushi, 'Chasing a ghost', *CiF Guardian*, 27 November 2007.

134. Formerly at <http://www.geneva-accord.org/Accord.aspx?FolderID=33 &lang=en>. It calls for full compensation of Palestinians who lost property in 1948, but it leaves the entry of refugees into Israeli territory to the discretion of the Israeli government.

135. See Sari Nusseibeh with Anthony David, *Once Upon a Country* (New York, 2007), p. 446.

136. See Jonathan Rynhold, 'The second half of the refugee equation', *Ha'aretz*, November 2007.

137. See Amos Oz, 'No right of return, but Israel must offer a solution', *Theglobeandmail.com*, 12 May 2007.

138. See 'Labour and British Muslims: Can we dream the same dream?', *Muslim Weekly*, no. 58.

139. 'Tonge sacked over suicide comment', *BBC News*, 23 January 2004, <http:// news.bbc.co.uk/1/hi/uk_politics/3421669.stm>. She later observed: 'I totally supported Charles Kennedy in what he had to do in reaction to the tabloids' interpretation of what I said. He had to distance the party as a whole from support for terrorists.' BBC Radio 4, 'Today', Webchat: Wednesday 18 February 2004, <http://www.bbc.co.uk/radio4/today/webchat/webchat_ tonge.shtml>.

140. <http://www.bbc.co.uk/radio4/today/reports/international/tonge_ 20040217. shtml>.

141. See Terry Eagleton, *Ideology* (London, 2007), p. xiii.

142. See Simon R. Cottee, 'Excusing Terror', *Journal of Human Rights*, 5 (2006), 149–62.

143. 'Dr Jennifer Tonge', *Guardian*, 4 April 2005, <http://politics.guardian.co.uk/ mpsuncovered/story/0,9396,1448403,00.html>.

144. 'Ms Tonge's outburst comes despite the conference overwhelmingly passing a motion on Wednesday condemning the Israeli military action in Lebanon as "disproportionate".' 'Tonge condemned for Israel remark', *BBC News*, 21 September 2006, <http://news.bbc.co.uk/1/hi/uk_politics/5366870.stm>. See also Letter to the Editor, *The Times*, 23 September 2006. 'Tonge "in trouble" over comments', *BBC News*, 27 November 2006, <http://news. bbc.co.uk/1/hi/uk_politics/6186966.stm>.

145. House of Lords, 5 December 2006, <http://www.publications.parliament. uk/pa/ld200607/ldhansrd/text/61205-0009.htm>.

146. Matthew Harris, 'Baroness Tonge and the "pro-Israeli lobby" ', *Engage*, 25 September 2006, http://www.engageonline.org.uk/blog/article.php?id=666. Tonge's claim was similar to the anti-Semitic Leopold Maxse's in 1898. He alleged that the Liberals were 'at the mercy' of 'semi-educated plutocrats', i.e., Jews. See G. R. Searle, *Corruption in British Politics 1895–1930* (Oxford, 1994), p. 90.

147. 'I visited Auschwitz last year, and it is very difficult to understand why those whose history is one of such terrible oppression appear not to care that they have themselves become oppressors.' 'NEWS RELEASE: Date: 18 April 2006 STOP ISRAELI APARTHEID POLICIES SAYS LIB DEM EURO-MP', <http://www.chrisdaviesmep.org.uk/other/Palestine.htm>.

148. The emails are reproduced in Alex Sholem, 'MEP disciplined over slur', *TotallyJewish.com*, 4 May 2006, <http://www.totallyjewish.com/news/national/?content_id=3403>.

149. 'I wish to extend a fulsome apology for my remarks to [this correspondent]. It was wholly unacceptable for me to use the language and tone that I did. I deeply regret the obvious offence that my remarks will have caused. However much I may disagree with someone else's political views, I accept that there is absolutely no justification for making the comments I did.' See ibid.

150. From the section of the website 'Palestine', 17 January 2007, <http://www.chrisdaviesmep.org.uk/other/Palestine.htm>. 'On Monday, [Davies] told [radio] listeners: "[The correspondent] justified her own policies towards Israel by describing the Palestinians as effectively sub-human. I just exploded . . . " ' David Aaronovitch, 'Lib-Dem Tonge's Illiberal fans', *Jewish Chronicle*, 1 December 2006.

151. See David Hirsh, 'Jews do not all think the same', and 'Revenge of the Jewish lobby?' *Guardian*, *CiF*, 26 April and 5 May 2006.

152. 'Tonge "in trouble" over comments', *BBC News*, 27 November 2006, <http://news.bbc.co.uk/1/hi/uk_politics/6186966.stm>.

153. Matthew Harris, 'Baroness Tonge and the "pro-Israeli lobby" ', *Engage*, 25 September 2006.

154. <http://www.libdems.org.uk/news/resignation-statement-by-chris-davies-mep.10111.html>. See also 'Lib Dem resigns in row over remarks', *BBC News*, 4 May 2006, <http://news.bbc.co.uk/1/hi/uk_politics/4974808.stm>.

155. Rachel Fletcher, 'Tonge resigns as charity trustee', *Jewish Chronicle*, 1 December 2006.

156. *Publish it Not: The Middle East cover-up* (Oxford, 2006), p. 38.

157. Bernard Josephs, 'Union leaders condemn calls for Israel boycott and so do leading Liberal Democrats', *Jewish Chronicle*, 21 September 2007.

158. Eric Hobsbawm, 'Cadres', *London Review of Books*, 26 April 2007, p. 25.

159. See Mordecai Chertoff, 'The new left and the newer leftists' in Mordecai Chertoff (ed.), *The New Left and the Jews* (New York, 1971), p. 195.

160. Paul Berman, *Power and the Idealists* (New York, 2005), p. 174; Ben Cohen, 'The persistence of anti-Semitism on the British Left', *Jewish Political Studies Review*, 16/3–4 (2004).

161. Karl Marx and Friedrich Engels, *Marx and Engels on Religion* (Amsterdam, The Netherlands, 2002), pp. 120, 125, 317.

162. Tony Cliff, 'British policy in Palestine', *New International*, October 1938, <http://www.marxists.org/archive/cliff/works/1938/10/britpol.htm> and 'The Jewish–Arab Conflict,' *New International*, November 1938, <http://www.marxists.org/archive/cliff/works/1938/11/jew-arab.htm>.

163. Leon Trotsky, 'On the Jewish Problem' (1932), *On the Jewish Question* (London, 1970), p. 18. Trotsky distinguishes his position from that of the official Communist Party line, which interpreted the 1929 events as the revolutionary uprising of the oppressed Arab masses.

164. 'National topography will become a part of the planned economy. There will be great migrations, which will occur not through compulsion, but by the demand of certain nationalities or parts of nationalities. The dispersed Jews who will want to reassemble in the same community will find their place under the sun, as will the Arabs and all other scattered nations.' Ibid., pp. 18, 20–1; Isaac Deutscher, *The Prophet Outcast* (Oxford, 1970), p. 369, fn. 1; Irving Howe, *Trotsky* (London, 1978), p. 155.

165. See John Callaghan, *The Far Left in British Politics* (Oxford 1987), pp. 68–72.

166. Bryan D. Palmer, *E.P. Thompson* (London, 1994), p. 73. Suez kept some otherwise terminally disaffected CP members in the Party. See John Callaghan, *The Far Left in British Politics* (Oxford 1987), p. 169.

167. Tony Cliff, 'A new British provocation in Palestine', *Fourth International*, September 1946, <http://www.marxists.org/archive/cliff/works/1946/07/provocation.htm>. It would seem that Cliff did not alter his position substantially in the 20 years that followed. See 'The struggle in the Middle East' in Tariq Ali (ed.), *The New Revolutionaries* (New York, 1969), pp. 219–37.

168. See Edward W. Said, *Peace and Its Discontents* (New York, 1995), p. 77.

169. 'Mid-East War: What we think', *Socialist Worker*, 20 October 1973; Chris Harman, *In The Heat Of The Struggle* (London, 1993), p. 102.

170. 'Belsen comes to Beirut', *Socialist Worker*, 25 September 1982; Chris Harman, *In The Heat Of The Struggle* (London, 1993), p. 202.

171. Such was their insignificance, neither Israel, Zionism, nor the Palestinian cause, figured in the two standard surveys of Far Left politics in Britain. See John Callaghan, *British Trotskyism* (Oxford, 1984), and *The Far Left in British Politics* (Oxford 1987).

172. See John Callaghan, *The Far Left in British Politics* (Oxford 1987), p. 80.

173. Russell A. Berman, 'From "Left-fascism" to campus antisemitism: Radicalism as reaction', *Democratiya*, 13 (Summer 2008), <http://www.democratiya.com/review.asp?reviews_id=158>.

174. See <http://www.marxists.de/religion/harman/index.htm>.

175. This was so, notwithstanding occasional throat-clearing. E.g.: 'As revolutionary socialists we have many ideological differences with Hizbollah, which is an Islamist party . . . ' 'Against the US-Israeli War on Lebanon', 31 July 2006; <http://www.swp.org.uk/lebanon.php>.

176. Andrew Murray and Lindsey German, *Stop the War* (London, 2005), p. 82.

177. John Rees, 'Plans in place for biggest Cairo Conference against war yet', *Socialist Worker*, 7 February 2007.

178. Dave Crouch, 'Bolsheviks and Islam: Religious rights', *Socialist Review* (December 2003).

179. Walter Laqueur, *Voices of Terror* (New York), pp. 388–9, 398; V. S. Naipaul, *Among the Believers* (London, 2001), p. 90.

180. See Terry Eagleton, *Ideology* (London, 2007), pp. xvii–xviii.

181. See <http://www.pacbi.org/campaign_statement.htm>.

182. Tom Hickey, writing in favour of a boycott in the *British Medical Journal*, 335 (2007), 124, 125.

183. See Shalom Lappin, 'Of boycotts and exceptionalism', <http://normblog.typepad.com/normblog/2007/08/of-boycotts-and.html>.

184. Ghada Karmi, 'Weapon of the weak', *Ha'aretz*, 14 July 2007.

185. 'New pariah on the block', *Economist*, 13 September 2007.

186. See Fiamma Nirenstein, *Terror* (Hanover, NH, 2005), p. 139.

187. Martha Nussbaum, 'Against academic boycotts', *Dissent* (Spring 2007); Eve Garrard, 'Excluding Israelis: An intellectual anatomy of the academic boycott', *Z Word*, February 2008, <http://www.z-word.com/z-word-essays/excluding-israelis%253A-an-intellectual-anatomy-of-the-academic-boycott.html>; Ben Cohen, 'The ideological foundations of the boycott movement', *American Jewish Committee*, September 2007.

188. See Eve Garrard, 'Portrait of the Union as an old stalker', 30 March 2008, and 'The boycotter's decalogue', 23 April 2008, <http://normblog.typepad.com/normblog/2008/04/the-boycotters.html>.

189. Baruch Kimmerling, 'The meaning of academic boycott', *Borderlands e-journal*, 2/3 (2003).

190. Ghada Karmi, 'Weapon of the weak', *Ha'aretz*, 14 July 2007. Emma Clancy, 'Israel boycott campaign momentum grows', *Green Left online*, 27 July 2007, <http://www.greenleft.org.au/2007/719/37305>.

191. See <http://www.adl.org/anti_semitism/European_Attitudes_Survey_July-2007.pdf >.

192. See 'Israel boycott illegal and cannot be implemented UCU tells members', <http://www.ucu.org.uk/index.cfm?articleid=2829>.

193. See Michael Rubenstein, 'Antisemitism and the UCU', *Equal Opportunities Review*, no. 178 (July 2008).

194. *New Witness*, 16 January 1913, p. 341.

195. See Gisela C. Lebzelter, *Political Anti-Semitism in England 1918–1939* (London, 1978), p. 30.

196. 'United States of Israel?', *Independent*, 27 April 2006.

197. So, the intense focus in anti-Zionist discourse on the Deir Yasin atrocity, and the disregarding of the Kfar Etzion atrocity, is replicated in Jeremy Bowen's account of the 1967 War. See *Six Days* (London, 2003), pp. 7 and 340. Bowen was BBC Middle East correspondent.

198. See the comments following Anthony Julius and Simon Schama, 'John Berger is wrong', 22 December 2006, <http://commentisfree.guardian.co. uk/anthony_julius_and_simon_schama/2006/12/bergerboycott.html>. See also David Aaronovitch, 'Another day of Internet abuse', *The Times*, 22 January 2008.

199. Nick Cohen, *What's Left? How liberals lost their way* (London, 2007), pp. 333–5.

200. <http://www.justjournalism.com>.

201. Tom Gross, 'Jeningrad: What the British media said' in Ron Rosenbaum (ed.), *Those Who Forget the Past* (New York, 2004), pp. 135–44; Daphna Baram, *Disenchantment* (London, 2004), pp. 237–51.

202. Jeffrey Goldberg, *Prisoners* (New York, 2006), p. 281.

203. 'Human Rights Watch found no evidence to sustain claims of massacres or large-scale extrajudicial executions by the IDF in Jenin refugee camp.' 'Jenin: IDF military operations', *Human Rights Watch*, May 2002, see <http://www. hrw/legacy/reports/2002/israel3/>

204. Taji Mustafa, 'Cameron got it wrong', *CiF*, *Guardian*, 9 July 2007 ('the massacre in Jenin').

205. *The New Rulers of the World* (London, 2003), p. 147.

206. Fiamma Nirenstein, *Terror: The new anti-Semitism and the war against the West* (Hanover, NH, 2005), p. 166.

207. Colin Shindler, 'Reading the *Guardian*' in Tudor Parfitt with Yulia Egorova (eds.), *Jews, Muslims and Mass Media* (London, 2004).

208. Jon Henley, 'Spread of racism could kill French democracy', and Simon Tisdall, 'Bush and Kerry dance to the tune of Ariel Sharon', *Guardian*, 20 October 2004, pp. 15, 17.

209. Dave Rich and Mark Gardner, 'The blood libel brought up to date', *Guardian*, *CiF*, 1 May 2008.

210. Ben Dowell, 'BBC online censured for biased Israel story', *Guardian*, 8 March 2006.

211. See <http://hurryupharry.bloghouse.net/archives/2007/07/13/racist_lies_on_bbc_noticeboard.php>.

212. The House Rules can be found by following the links from the '5 Live' homepage. See <http://www.bbc.co.uk/dna/mbfivelive/>.

213. <http://hurryupharry.bloghouse.net/archives/2007/07/13/racist_lies_on_bbc_noticeboard.php>; 'Anti-Semitic slur doesn't bother BBC', *Jewish Tribune*, 19 July 2007; Leon Symons, 'Anger as BBC refuses to ban racist posting', *Jewish Chronicle*, 24 August 2007.

214. See Melanie Phillips, 'The BBC's own war on the Jews', *Jewish Chronicle*, 20 July 2007.

215. E. W. Kirzner (trans.), *Baba Kama* (London, 1990), p. 113a.

216. Edward H. Kaplan and Charles A. Small, 'Anti-Israel sentiment predicts anti-Semitism in Europe', *Journal Of Conflict Resolution*, 50/4 (2006), 548–61.

217. Ibid., p. 560.

218. 'East Coast' and 'New York', are common American substitutes for 'Jews'. See Walter Laqueur, *The Changing Face of Antisemitism* (New York, 2006), p. 131.

219. Ruth R. Wisse, 'On ignoring anti-Semitism' in Ron Rosenbaum (ed.), *Those Who Forget the Past* (New York, 2004), p. 192.

220. *Secret Societies and Subversive Movements* (London, 1924), p. 395; 'The very term "international financier" can now only be used with extreme caution.' Nesta H. Webster, *The Surrender of an Empire* (London, 1931), pp. 19–20.

221. See Paul Stewart, 'Work, employment and society today', *Work, Employment and Society* 18/4 (2004), 661.

222. *Justice*, 11 November 1899.

223. See Hillel J. Kieval, *Languages of Community* (Berkeley, CA, 2000), p. 189, on the *Nekupu°jte od židu°* ('Do not buy from Jews') campaign in 1892 in Bohemia.

224. Anthony Lester and Geoffrey Bindman, *Race and Law* (London, 1972), p. 349.

225. Solomon Grayzel, *The Church and the Jews in the XIIIth Century: 1254–1314* (New York, 1989), pp. 223–4.

226. See Victor J. Seidler, *Jewish Philosophy and Western Culture* (London, 2007), p. 12.

227. Amonon Linder (ed.), *The Jews in the Legal Sources of the Early Middle Ages* (Detroit, MI, 1997), pp. 185, 193.

228. Solomon Grayzel, *The Church and the Jews in the XIIIth Century: 1254–1314* (New York, 1989), p. 17.

229. See Stephen Wilson, *Ideology and Experience* (London, 1982), pp. 116, 120, 141, 180–3, 283–5, 420, 526, 700, 735; Pierre Birnbaum, *The Anti-Semitic Moment* (New York, 2003), pp. 82, 135, 188, 287–8; Emil Reich, 'The Jew-baiting on the Continent', *Nineteenth Century*, 40 (July–December 1896), 427.

230. Jonathan Judaken, *Jean-Paul Sartre and the Jewish Question* (Nebraska, 2006), p. 12; George Lichtheim, 'Socialism and the Jews', *Collected Essays* (New York, 1973), p. 425.

231. Dermot Keogh and Andrew McCarthy, *Limerick Boycott 1904* (Cork, 2005), pp. 39, 69; Dermot Keogh, *Jews in Twentieth Century Ireland* (Cork, 1998), pp. 26–53; Ira B. Nadel, *Joyce and the Jews* (London, 1989), pp. 59–60, 190; Paul Bew, *Ireland: The politics of enmity 1789–2006* (Oxford, 2007), p. 364; Cormac Ó Gráda, *Jewish Ireland in the Age of Joyce* (Princeton, NJ, 2006), pp. 192–4; Todd M. Endelman, *The Jews of Britain 1656–2000* (Berkeley, CA, 2002), p. 171.

232. Edwin Black, *The Transfer Agreement* (New York, 2001), pp. 25–6; Thomas Weber, 'Anti-Semitism and philo-Semitism among the British and German Elites: Oxford and Heidelberg before the First World War', *English Historical Review*, 118/475 (2003), 93.

233. Avraham Barkai, *From Boycott to Annihilation* (London, 1989), pp. 17–25, 56, 64; Oscar I. Janowsky, *People at Bay* (London, 1938), pp. 6, 50–2, 56–7, 62, 69, 72, 84, 86.

234. Gisela C. Lebzelter, *Political Anti-Semitism in England 1918–1939* (London, 1978), pp. 39–40.

235. George Thayer, *The British Political Fringe* (London, 1965), pp. 24–5.

236. Aaron J. Sarna, *Boycott and Blacklist* (Totowa, NJ, 1986), pp. 5–6; Gil Feiler, *From Boycott to Economic Cooperation* (London, 1998), pp. 21–7.

237. See Christopher Sykes, *Cross Roads to Israel* (London, 1965), pp. 68, 72–3, 83, 93, 124, 149, 192–3 ('their favourite political manoeuvre'), 200, 230–1. In 1971, General Sir John Glubb, the former commander of the Arab Legion, wrote of the Arabs' 'disastrous habit of boycotting political inquiries'. See Benny Morris, *The Road to Jerusalem* (London, 2002), p. 31.

238. Matthias Küntzel, *Jihad and Jew-Hatred* (New York, 2007), p. 7.

239. 'The terms "Jews" and "Zionists" were used in the declaration interchangeably.' Gil Feiler, *From Boycott to Economic Cooperation* (London, 1998), p. 25.

240. Aaron J. Sarna, *Boycott and Blacklist* (Totowa, NJ, 1986), pp. 14–15.

241. Ibid., p. 49; Gil Feiler, *From Boycott to Economic Cooperation* (London, 1998), pp. 96–9.

242. Aaron J. Sarna, *Boycott and Blacklist* (Totowa, NJ, 1986), pp. 22–3, 143–54; Gil Feiler, *From Boycott to Economic Cooperation* (London, 1998), pp. 4–5, 136, 209–19.

243. Sharon Wrobel, 'Dubai bans Israel from international forum', *Jerusalem Post*, 15 October 2007; 'Arab delegates meet in Syria-based office to discuss boycott of Israel', *IHT*, 6 November 2007.

244. 'Weapon of the weak', *Ha'aretz*, 14 July 2007.

245. Robert Browning, *The Ring and the Book* (London, 1981), Book VI, l. 1912, p. 317.

246. See E. Doyle McCarthy, *Knowledge as Culture* (London, 1996), p. 77.

247. See Bernard Harrison, 'Israel, anti-semitism, and free speech', *American Jewish Committee*, October 2007, pp. 13, 16, 32.

248. See Alain Finkielkraut, *The Imaginary Jew* (Lincoln, NA, 1994), p. 160.

249. The editor apologised: *New Statesman*, 11 February 2002; Bernard Harrison, *The Resurgence of Anti-Semitism* (New York, 2006), ch. 2, *passim*.

250. See George Thayer, *The British Political Fringe* (London, 1965), p. 62.

251. *Vanity Fair*, June 2003, p. 227. There had been a certain amount of 'cabal' talk in the air: Patrick J. Buchanan, 'Whose War?', *American Conservative*, 24 March 2003.

252. Dalyell's remarks, in their scepticism concerning the patriotism of Blair's Jewish advisers, were comparable to remarks made during an earlier anti-Zionist moment in English politics, 1922 to 1924. It is Lord Levy who drew Dalyell's fire; then, it was the Jewish Sir Alfred Mond. 'Despite the many virtues and great abilities of Sir Alfred Mond', observed the *Morning Post*, 'we would like to see purely British representatives in a purely British parliament.' See David Cesarani, 'Continuities and discontinuities in anti-Zionism in Britain, 1922–2002', *Journal of Israeli History*, 25/1 (2006).

253. Nicholas Watt, 'Dalyell may face race hatred inquiry', *Guardian*, 5 May 2003.

254. Jonathan Freedland, *Jacob's Gift* (London, 2005), p. 351.

255. See 'A question of language', <http://www.newint.org/issue372/facts. htm>.

256. *Jewish Chronicle*, 20 June 2003.

257. *Herald*, 5 May 2003.

258. *Daily Telegraph*, 4 May 2003.

259. *Engage*, 12 March 2007.

260. Bernard Semmel, *The Liberal Idea and the Demons of Empire* (Baltimore, MD, 1993), pp. 12–13, 85–7, 111–12, 177.

261. See 'The PSC AGM 2007 commits members to uniting with broad forces to campaign to end Israeli occupation', *PSC*, 15 March 2007.

262. See Ben Cohen, 'The persistence of anti-Semitism on the British Left', *Jewish Political Studies Review*, 16/3–4 (2004).

263. 'Democracy indispensable for Pakistan: British MP', *Associated Press of Pakistan*, 22 April 2008, <http://www.app.com.pk/en_/index.php?option=com_content &task=view&id=36242&Itemid=2>.

264. House of Lords, 5 December 2006, <http://www.publications.parliament. uk/pa/ld200607/ldhansrd/text/61205-0009.htm>. 'I am beginning to understand the power of the Israel lobby, active here as well as in the USA, with AIPAC, the Friends of Israel and the Board of Deputies. They take vindictive actions against people who oppose and criticise the lobby, getting them removed from positions that they hold and preventing them from speaking—even on unrelated subjects in my case. . . . They make constant accusations of anti-Semitism when no such sentiment exists to silence Israel's critics.' Speech in the House of Lords, 2 July 2008, <http://www.publications. parliament.uk/pa/ld200708/ldhansrd/text/80702-0012.htm>.

265. Protest at being 'silenced' is one of the tropes of contemporary politics: '[After 9/11] the central issue again is silence.' John Pilger, *The New Rulers of the World* (London, 2003), pp. 163–4. 'Authorised versions' of contemporary history 'censor by omission'. There is a 'great silence, unbroken by the incessant din of the media age' regarding the West's—and in particular, the USA's great crimes. John Pilger, *Freedom Next Time* (London, 2006), p. 6.

266. Ian Mayes 'Open door', *Guardian*, 13 February 2006. But cf.: 'It is a long time since criticism could be regarded as a proof of courage, at least in our free Western societies.' Raymond Aron, *The Opium of the Intellectuals* (New Brunswick, NJ, 2001), p. 212.

267. Ken Livingstone, 'This is about Israel, not anti-semitism', *Guardian*, 4 March 2005. See also Charles Moore, 'How Livingstone turned a racist remark into a cause célèbre', *Daily Telegraph*, 4 March 2006 ('I know of no evidence that Mr Livingstone is personally anti-Semitic, but this whole saga shows that he is not politically averse to being seen to be rude to Jews. Why would that be?'). In the matter of anti-Zionism, Livingstone has a certain form. See Geoffrey Alderman, *London Jewry and London Politics 1889–1986* (London, 1989), pp. 132–7.

268. *The Herald*, 5 May 2003.

269. Taki, 'Rich rewards', *Spectator*, 24 February 2001; Martin Rowson, 'Dark Magic', *Index on Censorship*, 38/1 (2009), 163.

270. *The Scotsman*, 5 May 2003.

271. <http://weepingskies.blogspot.com/2005/10/our-patrons-say.html>.

272. Brian Reade, 'Douglas Alexander's Gaza aid pledge typifies Britain's cowardly subservience to US pro-Israel lobby', *Daily Mirror*, 5 March 2009.

273. *Independent*, 27 April 2006.

274. 'Gilad Atzmon: "Zionism is my enemy" ', *Socialist Worker*, 5 June 2004.

275. *All Our Tomorrows* (London, 1942), p. 290. 'By the time the World War in which [Rupert Brooke] died was resumed, no Englishman of his class and kind would have thought of writing anything which would set the critics yelping the dread name "anti-Semite".' *A Prophet at Home* (London, 1941), p. 100.

276. See Martin Bright, *When Progressives Treat with Reactionaries* (London, 2006), pp. 55–6. On Ali himself, see Nick Cohen, *Waiting for the Etonians* (London, 2009), pp. 150–1.

277. Trevor Mostyn, review in *The Tablet*, 27 May 2006.

278. *Publish it Not: The Middle East cover-up* (Oxford, 2006), p. 75.

279. Ibid., pp. ix–xxxv. In an article protesting the BBC's refusal to broadcast a charity appeal for Gazan Palestinians, he asked: 'The big question that remains is this: what are the suits scared of? Why do BBC managers try to second-guess our government and even outreach it in grovelling to the United States and Israel?' 'This cowardly decision betrays the values the corporation stands for', *Observer*, 25 January 2009.

280. See *Publish it Not: The Middle East cover-up* (Oxford, 2006), pp. 157–63.

281. See R. Po-Chia Hsia, *Trent 1475* (New Haven, 1992), pp. 45, and 84–5 (italics added).

282. *England under the Jews* (London, 1907), p. 38.

283. *The Fine Old Hebrew Gentleman* (London, 1922), p. 16. Levy was a prominent publicist for Nietzsche in the 1920s and 30s, and adopted what he took to be

the German philosopher's perspective on the Jews. See *The Idiocy of Idealism* (London, 1940), p. 134, and Dan Stone, *Breeding Superman* (Liverpool, 2002), pp. 12–32.

284. 'It is characteristic of the Jewish superiority complex to make such a brazen admission of Jewish faults.' *Twilight Over England* (London, 1992), p. 86.

285. Petrus Alfonsi, *Dialogue Against the Jews* (Washington, DC, 2006), p. 44.

286. *Philosophical Dictionary* (London, 2004), pp. 40, 256–7; Paul Lawrence Rose, *German Question/Jewish Question* (Princeton, NJ, 1990), pp. 46–7.

287. Hilary Blume, 'A study of anti-Semitic Groups in Britain, 1918–1940', unpublished D. Phil thesis, University of Sussex, 1971, p. 77.

288. See Denis MacEoin, *The Hijacking of British Islam* (London, 2007), p. 73.

289. See Milton Himmelfarb, *The Jews of Modernity* (New York, 1973), p. 199. The editors of the Authorised Version do their best with 'hate thine enemy', citing a verse in Deuteronomy about the Ammonites and Moabites, 'Thou shalt not seek their peace nor their prosperity all thy days'. This falls somewhat short of a duty to hate them (23:6). More importantly, it precedes the celebrated verse: 'Thou shalt not abhor an Egyptian, because thou wast a stranger in his land' (23:7).

290. A late nineteenth-century Austrian champion of the blood libel, the parish priest, Joseph Deckert, boasted that he had in his possession the letters of a converted Jew who had been a witness to several ritual murders. See Joseph Bloch, *My Reminiscences* (New York, 1973), pp. 387, 395.

291. Hermann L. Strack, *The Jew and Human Sacrifice* (London, 1909), pp. 174–5.

292. B. Netanyahu, *The Origins of the Inquisition in Fifteenth Century Spain*, 2nd edn (New York, 2001), pp. 826–7; Jacob Barnai, ' "Blood libels" in the Ottoman Empire of the fifteenth to nineteenth centuries' in Shmuel Almog (ed.), *Antisemitism Through the Ages* (Oxford, 1988), p. 192.

293. Augustus Jessopp and M. R. James (eds.), *The Life and Miracles of St William of Norwich by Thomas of Monmouth* (Cambridge, 1896), p. 25 (my italics).

294. Attacks on the Talmud by Karaite and Muslim theologians preceded the Christian attacks by several centuries. See Judah M. Rosenthal, 'The Talmud on Trial', *Jewish Quarterly Review*, 47 (1956), 63–4.

295. Steven F. Kruger, *The Spectral Jew* (Minneapolis, MN, 2006), p. 181; Judah M. Rosenthal, 'The Talmud on Trial', *Jewish Quarterly Review*, 47 (1956), 62.

296. Sander L. Gilman, *Jewish Self-Hatred* (Baltimore, MD, 1986), p. 33.

297. George Foot Moore, 'Christian writers on Judaism', *Harvard Theological Review*, 14/3 (1921), 213–14 ('Eisenmenger is the notorious source of almost everything that has been written since his time in defamation of the Talmud or in derision of Jewish superstitions').

298. Walter Laqueur, *The Changing Face of Antisemitism* (New York, 2006), p. 59.

299. Elisheva Carlebach, *Divided Souls* (New Haven, 2001), p. 214.

300. Peter Pulzer, *Jews and the German State* (Detroit, MI, 2003), p. 140.

301. Ibid.

302. See Robert S. Wistrich, *The Jews of Vienna in the Age of Franz Joseph* (Oxford, 1990), p. 281.

303. Jan Herben, 'Thomas G. Masaryk, Jews and Anti-Semitism' in Benjamin Epstein (trans.), *Thomas G. Masaryk and the Jews* (New York, 1949), p. 9.

304. Joseph Bloch, *My Reminiscences* (New York, 1973), pp. 84–135; Ernst Rychnovsky, 'The struggle against the ritual murder superstition' in Benjamin Epstein (trans.), *Thomas G. Masaryk and the Jews* (New York, 1949), p. 199.

305. Walter Laqueur, *The Changing Face of Antisemitism* (New York, 2006), p. 153; Abraham H. Foxman, *Never Again?* (New York, 2003), pp. 9–10; Ira B. Nadel, *Joyce and the Jews* (London, 1989), pp. 118–19; Charles H. H. Wright, 'The Jews and the malicious charge of human sacrifice', *The Nineteenth Century*, 81 (November 1883), 772–8. Nesta Webster added the Cabala to the Talmud as barriers separating the Jews from the 'rest of the human race'. 'It is in the Cabala, still more than in the Talmud, that the Judaic dream of world-domination recurs with the greatest persistence.' *Secret Societies and Subversive Movements* (London, 1924), p. 370.

306. Itamar Radai, 'From father to son: Attitudes to Jews and Israel in Asad's Syria', Analysis of Current Trends in Antisemitism, no. 29, The Vidal Sassoon International Center for the Study of Antisemitism, The Hebrew University of Jerusalem, 2007, pp. 15–20; Rivka Yadlin, *An Arrogant Oppressive Spirit: Anti-Zionism as anti-Judaism in Egypt* (Oxford, 1989), pp. 87–8; Abraham H. Foxman, *Never Again?* (New York, 2003), pp. 9–10.

307. *The Diary of a Writer* (Salt Lake City, UT, 1985), p. 646; David I. Goldstein, *Dostoyevsky and the Jews* (Austin, TX, 1981), pp. 123–5.

308. Not only fiction and fabrication, though. Otto Weininger's work, *Sex and Character* (1903), was also much cited in this period. Barbara Hyams and Nancy A. Harrowitz, 'A critical introduction to the history of Weininger reception' in Nancy A. Harrowitz and Barbara Hyams (eds.), *Jews and Gender* (Philadelphia, PN, 1995), p. 10.

309. Benjamin Disraeli, *Coningsby* (London, 1983), pp. 232, 273. Disraeli modified his language in *Lord George Bentinck* (London, 1852). The Jews are 'the human family that has contributed most to human happiness'. See ch. XXIV, p. 482.

310. <http://holywar.org>.

311. Neil Baldwin, *Henry Ford and the Jews* (New York, 2001), pp. 164, 236–7. Nesta Webster relies on Ford's claim in *Secret Societies and Subversive Movements* (London, 1924), p. 366.

312. See Denis MacEoin, *The Hijacking of British Islam* (London, 2007), p. 73.

313. See Gabriel Schoenfeld, *The Return of Anti-Semitism* (San Francisco, 2004), pp. 15–16; *The Nameless War* (London, 1952), p. 117.

314. Y. Harkabi, *Arab Attitudes to Israel* (Jerusalem, 1972), pp. 272–5; Semyon Reznik, *The Nazification of Russia* (Washington, DC, 1996), p. 39.

315. *The Question of Palestine* (London, 1980), p. 9.

316. See Diana Muir, 'A land without a people for a people without a land', *Middle East Quarterly* (Spring 2008), 55–62 ('it is not evident that this was ever the slogan of any Zionist organization or that it was employed by any of the movement's leading figures. A mere handful of the outpouring of pre-state Zionist articles and books use it. For a phrase that is so widely ascribed to Zionist leaders, it is remarkably hard to find in the historical record').

317. See Cameron S. Brown, 'Answering Edward Said's *The Question of Palestine*', *Israel Affairs*, 13/1 (2007), 71–6.

318. 'In their own words', 11 March 2003, <http://www.miftah.org/Display.cfm?DocId=1837&CategoryId=21>.

319. 'Zionism and Palestine', *Contemporary Review* (April 1922), 437.

320. 'One can learn a great deal from pronouncements made by strategically important Zionist leaders.' Edward W. Said, 'Zionism from the standpoint of its victims' in Anne McClintock, Aamir Mufti, and Ella Shohat (eds.), *Dangerous Liaisons* (Minneapolis, 1997), pp. 25, 32.

321. *The Clash of Fundamentalisms* (London, 2003), p. 94. The diary entry had been circulating for some time. See Fawwaz Trabulsi, 'The Palestine problem: Zionism and imperialism in the Middle East', *New Left Review*, 57 (September–October 1969), 55.

322. See Raphael Patai (ed.), *The Complete Diaries of Theodor Herzl* (New York, 1960), vol. 1, p. 88.

323. Derek J. Penslar, 'Historians, Herzl and the Palestinian Arabs', *Israel in History* (London, 2007), pp. 51–61; Cameron S. Brown, 'Answering Edward Said's *The Question of Palestine*', *Israel Affairs*, 13/1 (2007), 71–6.

324. Derek J. Penslar, 'Historians, Herzl and the Palestinian Arabs', *Israel in History* (London, 2007), pp. 52, 57–9.

325. Ibid., p. 60.

326. 'Benny Morris and the myths of post-Zionist history' in Edward Alexander and Paul Bogdanor (eds.), *The Jewish Divide Over Israel* (London, 2006), pp. 251–2.

327. Benny Morris, 'The ignorance at the heart of an innuendo: And now for some facts', *New Republic* (May 2006).

328. John Pilger, 'The real threat we face is Blair', *New Statesman*, 21 August 2006.

329. See John Lloyd, *What the Media Are Doing To Our Politics* (London, 2004), p. 102.

330. See 'Charles Baudelaire', *Selected Literary Criticism* (London, 1968), p. 55.

331. See, for example, 'The true face of Israel: Let's learn from history and see how new generations are raised', <http://truefaceofisrael.blogspot.com/>; 'In their own words', 11 March 2003, <http://www.miftah.org/Display.cfm?DocId=1837&CategoryId=21>; 'Have you seen these Jewish quotes?', Stormfront.org, 13 May 2002, <http://www.stormfront.org/forum/showthread.php?t=21968>.

332. Israel Koenig, 'The Koenig Report', *Journal of Palestine Studies*, 6/1 (1976). Though the report was secret, it was leaked, and appeared in an Israeli newspaper on 7 September 1976. The version in the *Journal* is an English translation. It is taken to be an 'inadvertent' and 'unguarded' confirmation of 'the assumptions of Zionism' in Edward Said, *The Question of Palestine* (London, 1980), pp. 107–11.

333. See Ahmad H. Sa'di, 'The Koenig Report and Israeli policy towards the Palestinian minority, 1965–1976: Old wine in new bottles', *Arab Studies Quarterly* (Summer 2003).

334. Itamar Radai, 'On the road to Damascus: Bashar al-Asad, Israel, and the Jews', Posen Papers in Contemporary Antisemitism, no. 9, The Vidal Sassoon International Center for the Study of Antisemitism, The Hebrew University of Jerusalem, 2007, p. 13.

335. See 'The Jewish State's final solution: The assault on Gaza (James Petras)', July 2006, <http://canadiandimension.com/articles/2006/07/17/568/>.

336. See 'In their own words', 11 March 2003, <http://www.miftah.org/Display.cfm?DocId=1837&CategoryId=21>. Zachary Wales, 'Looking for Shalit', 1 July 2006, The Electronic Intifada, <http://electronicintifada.net/v2/article4882.shtml>.

337. Roger Garaudy, 'The myth of a land without a people for a people without a land', Institute for Historical Review, <http://www.ihr.org/jhr/v18/v18n5p38_Garaudy.html>.

338. Obituary, 'Yoram Ben-Porath, 55; A Top Israeli Academic', *New York Times*, 19 October 1992.

339. <http://www.pmo.gov.il/PMOEng/Communication/PMSpeaks/speechcong240506.htm>.

340. 'Ethnic cleansing: Constructive, benign, and nefarious' (Kafka Era Studies, no. 1), <http://www.zmag.org/content/showarticle.cfm?ItemID=10731>.

341. *New Statesman*, 3 October 2006. Pilger's comment follows upon an 'Editor's note' which accepts that the first two quotations were 'misattributed'. The first quotation, as a fabrication, is a very special kind of misattribution.

342. Benny Morris, 'Operation Dani and the Palestinian Exodus from Lydda and Ramle in 1948', *Middle East Journal*, 40/1 (1986), 82, 91, 102, 109; 'And now for some facts', *New Republic*, 8 May 2006.

343. Soviet Russian jurisprudence of the 1930s regarded 'the defendants' statements in state crimes . . . as the main evidence, the most important, crucial evidence'. See Arkady Vaksberg, *The Prosecutor and the Prey* (London, 1990), p. 161.

344. Alain Besançon, *A Century of Horrors* (Wilmington, DE, 2007), p. 8.

345. David Caute, *The Fellow-Travellers* (London, 1988), p. 298.

346. Thomas Friedman, *From Beirut to Jerusalem* (London, 1998), p. 524.

347. Tariq Ali, *The Clash of Fundamentalisms* (London, 2003), p. 90. Adam Shatz refers to 'the other Zionism' of Ahad Ha'am in *Prophets Outcast* (New York,

2004), p. 29. 'Can you be a non-Zionist Zionist? Grossman, I think, comes close.' 'I have ... wanted to revive the early Jewish voices—Martin Buber, Hans Kohn, Hannah Arendt and Ahad Ha'am, some of whom called themselves Zionists—who sounded the critique, uttered the warnings that have become all the more prescient today.' Jacqueline Rose, *The Last Resistance* (London, 2007), pp. 121, 198.

348. See David Grossman, *The Yellow Wind* (London, 1988), pp. 63–4, 96.

349. *I Saw Ramallah* (New York, 2000), p. 48.

350. See Thomas Friedman, *From Beirut to Jerusalem* (London, 1998), pp. 257, 360.

351. Jeffrey Goldberg, *Prisoners* (New York, 2006), pp. 99, 218–19, 233.

352. See Amos Elon, 'War without end', *NYRB*, 15 July 2004.

353. See Jeffrey Goldberg, *Prisoners* (New York, 2006), pp. 118, 212. See also Michael Sfard, 'Why Israel's "seruvniks" say enough is enough', *Observer* 19 May 2002.

354. Mourid Barghouti, *I Saw Ramallah* (New York, 2000), p. 141.

355. Richard Ben Cramer, *How Israel Lost* (New York, 2004), pp. 35–8.

356. Amos Elon, 'War without end', *NYRB*, 15 July 2004.

357. Walter Laqueur, *No End to War* (New York, 2006), pp. 99–100.

358. These road construction projects have often meant the demolition of private homes that stand across the designated route. See Amira Hass, *Reporting from Ramallah* (New York, 2003), p. 52.

359. 'There is nothing in either the [UN] Charter or general international law which leads one to suppose that military occupation, pending a peace treaty, is illegal.' Rosalyn Higgins, 'The June War: The United Nations and legal background' in John Norton Moore (ed.), *The Arab–Israeli Conflict* (Princeton NJ, 1977), p. 553.

360. Steven Erlanger, 'Israeli map says West Bank posts sit on Arab land', *New York Times*, 21 November 2006; Nadav Shragai, 'Blow to settlement movement', *Ha'aretz*, 23 November 2006; Steven Erlanger, 'West Bank sites on private land, data shows', *New York Times*, 14 March 2007.

361. Yossi Klein Halevi, 'Israel's moral war', 'Perspectives from Israel', *American Jewish Committee*, 8 September 2004. The Second Intifada 'was a catastrophic slapdash brawl without leadership, strategy or ideas; it was a ruinous and sanguinary fit of madness'. Sari Nusseibeh with Anthony David, *Once Upon a Country* (New York, 2007), p. 429.

362. Amira Hass, *Drinking the Sea at Gaza* (London, 1999), p. 4; Amira Hass, *Reporting from Ramallah* (New York, 2003), pp. 22–3, 26; Jeffrey Goldberg, *Prisoners* (New York, 2006), p. 126. Administrative detentions, for example, are incompatible with the rule of law.

363. See Arthur Hertzberg, *The Fate of Zionism* (New York, 2003), pp. x–xi.

364. Steven Beller, *Herzl* (London, 2004), p. x.

365. See Amnon Rubinstein, *From Herzl to Rabin* (New York, 2000), p. 4.

366. 'David Grossman's speech at the Rabin memorial', *Haaretz*, 6 November 2006.

367. See Shlomo Avineri, 'For Palestinians, a coherent body politic is wanting', *Daily Star*, 18 July 2007.

368. Amira Hass, *Drinking the Sea at Gaza* (London, 1999), pp. 301, 305.

369. Fred Halliday, *Nation and Religion in the Middle East* (London, 2000), p. 23; Richard Ben Cramer, *How Israel Lost* (New York, 2004), pp. 116–28.

370. Ulrike Putz, 'A visit to Fatah's torture chamber', *Der Spiegel* (international edition), 21 June 2007.

371. David Samuels, 'In a ruined country: How Yasir Arafat destroyed Palestine', *Atlantic Monthly*, 296/2 (2005), 60–91.

372. Josh Mitnick, 'Palestinian minister admits aid millions lost', *Daily Telegraph*, 11 March 2007.

373. Sari Nusseibeh with Anthony David, *Once Upon a Country* (New York, 2007), p. 487.

374. Amira Hass, *Drinking the Sea at Gaza* (London, 1999), pp. 205–6.

375. Benny Morris, *Righteous Victims* (New York, 2001), p. 219.

376. See Leo Strauss, *Jewish Philosophy and the Crisis of Modernity* (New York, 1997), p. 413.

377. Samia Khoury, 'Foreword' and Jonathan Kuttab, 'Biblical justice, law, and the Occupation' in Naim Ateek et al. (eds.), *Faith and the Intifada* (New York, 1992), pp. vii, 95.

378. Amira Hass, *Drinking the Sea at Gaza* (London, 1999), pp. 23, 120.

379. <http://weepingskies.blogspot.com/2005/10/our-patrons-say.html>. At a UN conference in August 2007, Short proposed that Israel 'undermines the international community's reaction to global warming'. See Daniel Schwammenthal, *Wall Street Journal*, 3 September 2007.

380. 'Britain's standing is now at a nadir in the Middle East', *Guardian*, 16 March 2006.

381. BBC Radio 4, 'Today', Webchat: Wednesday 18 February 2004, <http://www.bbc.co.uk/radio4/today/webchat/webchat_tonge.shtml>.

382. Joel Clark, 'Redgrave given an easy ride', *Jewish Chronicle*, 8 December 2006.

383. 'For world peace, Israel must pull out', *Church Times*, 24 March 2006.

384. Charlotte Edwardes, 'Fury as academics are sacked for being Israeli', *Daily Telegraph*, 7 July 2002.

385. 'John Pilger on Terror in Palestine', *New Statesman*, 22 March 2004.

386. It is an error to regard the architects of the 9/11 massacres as motivated by concern for Palestine. See *The 9/11 Commission Report* (New York, 2004), pp. 47–8, 51, 70.

387. See Ben Dror Yemini, 'And the world is silent', *Maariv*, 27 September 2006. The article is translated in three texts at <http://imshin.net/?p=448>, <http://imshin.net/?p=451>, and <http://imshin.net/?p=452>; Gadi Taub, 'Genocide against

Muslims', 27 September 2006, <http://www.gaditaub.com/eblog/genocide-against-muslims/>.

388. Melanie Phillips, *Londonistan* (London, 2006), p. 205.

389. Richard Cohen, 'Hunker down with history', *Washington Post*, 18 July 2006.

390. 'Rees lays it on the line', *Weekly Worker*, 488, Thursday July 10 2003.

391. Richard Seymour, 'In the name of decency: The contortions of the pro-war Left', *International Socialism*, Issue no. 113.

392. Azzam al-Tamimi, 'A compliment from the devil', *Muslim Weekly*, 5–11 January 2007.

393. 'Blind to the obvious', *Sunday Mirror*, 30 July 2006.

394. Amos Funkenstein, *Perceptions of Jewish History* (Berkeley, CA, 1993), p. 36.

395. Ghada Karmi, *In Search of Fatima* (London, 2004), p. 372, *Married to Another Man* (London, 2007), p. 119, and 'Where is the global outcry at this continuing cruelty?', *Guardian*, 15 May 2006; Norman Rose, *A Senseless, Squalid War* (London, 2009), pp. 44, 53–5, 185, 209; Robert Satloff, *Among the Righteous* (New York, 2006), pp. 18, 79, 81–3, 86–90, 96, 160; Lucy S. Dawidowicz, 'Could America have rescued Europe's Jews?', *What Is the Use of Jewish History?* (New York, 1992), p. 178; Bernard Lewis, *Semites and Anti-Semites* (London, 1986), pp. 143, 147, 149, 156–8, and 'The new anti-Semitism', *The American Scholar*, 75/1 (2006); Arthur Hertzberg (ed.), *The Zionist Idea: A historical analysis and reader* (New York, 1977), pp. 585, 587; Zvi Elpeleg, *The Grand Mufti: Haj Amin Al-Hussaini* (London, 1993), pp. xv, 59, 70–3, 179; Bernard Wasserstein, *The British in Palestine* (Oxford, 1991), pp. 237–8; Robert Irwin, *For Lust of Knowing* (London, 2006), p. 228; Matthias Küntzel, *Jihad and Jew-Hatred* (New York, 2007), pp. 31, 35, 36, 41, 45, 47, 69, 'National socialism and the Arab world', <www.matthiaskuentzel.de>, and 'Interview', *Democratiya*, 13 (Summer 2008); Baruch Kimmerling, 'Israel's culture of martyrdom', *The Nation*, 10 January 2005; Jeffrey Herf, *The Jewish Enemy* (Cambridge, MA, 2006), pp. 173, 179–80; Benny Morris, *Righteous Victims* (New York, 2001), p. 201; Daniel Carpi, 'The diplomatic negotiations over the transfer of Jewish children from Croatia to Turkey and Palestine in 1943', *Yad Vashem Studies*, 12 (1977), 112–15, 123–4; Fred Halliday, *Islam and the Myth of Confrontation* (London, 2003), p. 166; David Yisraeli, 'The Third Reich and Palestine' in Elie Kedourie and Sylvia Haim (eds.), *Palestine and Israel in the 19th and 20th Centuries* (London, 1982), p. 110; Joseph B. Schechtman, *The Mufti and the Fuehrer* (New York, 1965), pp. 152, 157; 'Bishop Riah Abu El-Assal: "We are the true heirs"', *The Dallas Morning News*, 13 November 2005; Elie Kedourie, *Arabic Political Memoirs and Other Studies* (London, 1974), p. 189, 'The sack of Basra and the Baghdad Farhud', ibid., pp. 298, 307–8, and *Islam in the Modern World* (London, 1980), p. 241; David Pryce-Jones, *The Closed Circle* (Chicago, 2002), pp. 206–7; Irwin Cotler, David Matas, and Stanley A. Urman, *Jewish Refugees from Arab Countries* (New York, 2007), section V (D); Hanna Batatu, *The Old Social Classes*

and the Revolutionary Movements in Iraq (London, 2004), p. 258; Arieh Stav, Peace: The Arabian caricature (Jerusalem, 1999), p. 119; Meir Litvak, 'The development of Arab anti-Semitism', Jerusalem Center for Public Affairs, no. 5, 30 Shevat 5763/2 February 2003.

396. Benny Morris, Righteous Victims (New York, 2001), p. 201.

397. See Manfred Gerstenfeld, 'Holocaust inversion: The portraying of Israel and Jews as Nazis', Jerusalem Center for Public Affairs, no. 55, 1 April 2007.

398. 'Anti-Zionism at British Campuses', IJA Research Report, July 1977; Alan Elsner, 'Race, tolerance and the NUS', New Statesman, 15 May 1977; Ann Hulbert and Peter Galison, 'Zionism, racism and free speech', Commentary (October 1978); A Correspondent, 'Anti-Zionism at British Universities', Patterns of Prejudice, 11/4 (1977); Jacob Gewirtz, 'The lie of Zionist–Nazi collaboration', Jewish Chronicle, 25 January 1980.

399. Daphna Baram, Disenchantment (London, 2004), p. 114. Adams also compared anti-Zionist Jews to the resistance movement against the Nazis in Germany. See Publish it Not: The Middle East cover-up (Oxford, 2006), p. 185.

400. Jamie Lyons, ' "Israel like Nazi Germany"—row spreads', icWales.icnetwork. co.uk, 3 January 2003.

401. See <http://www.fallacyfiles.org/adnazium.html>; Frank Furedi, 'What's behind the "new anti-Semitism"?', Spiked, 6 March 2007; Nick Cohen, Pretty Straight Guys (London, 2004), p. 81.

402. Anton La Guardia, Holy Land, Unholy War (London, 2002), p. 172; Idith Zertal and Akiva Eldar, Lords of the Land (New York, 2007), pp. 74–5, 135, 152, 215, 298.

403. Ehud Sprinzak, The Ascendance of Israel's Radical Right (Oxford, 1991), p. 75.

404. 'In their Nazi treatment, the Jews made no exception for women or children.... They deal with people as if they were the worst war criminals. Deportation from the homeland is a kind of murder' (art. 20). 'The Zionist Nazi activities against our people will not last for long' (art. 31).

405. Martin Gilbert, Auschwitz and the Allies (London, 2001), p. 164.

406. See, for example, W. R. Inge, 'Hitler's creed and others', Evening Standard, 8 December 1938.

407. Henri Stellman, 'The ideology of Anti-Zionism 1881 to the present day', unpublished PhD thesis, University of London, 1982.

408. See Lucy S. Dawidowicz, The Holocaust and the Historians (Cambridge, MA, 1981), pp. 86–7.

409. See Walter Laqueur and Barry Rubin (eds.), The Israel–Arab Reader (London, 2001), p. 315.

410. Article 32, Hamas Charter: see <www.mideastweb.org>.

411. Yasmin Alibhai-Brown, 'Nothing but anti-Arab racism can fully explain the behaviour of the Israelis', Independent, 17 July 2006.

412. See Bernard Harrison, The Resurgence of Anti-Semitism (New York, 2006), pp. 68–78.

413. See Omer Bartov, 'The new antisemitism' in David Kertzer (ed.), *Old Demons, New Debates* (New York, 2005), pp. 19, 25.

414. David Yisraeli, 'The Third Reich and Palestine' in Elie Kedourie and Sylvia Haim (eds.), *Palestine and Israel in the 19th and 20th Centuries* (London, 1982), pp. 104–5; Debórah Dwork and Robert Jan Van Pelt, *Holocaust: A history* (London, 2003), pp. 125, 208.

415. See Matthias Küntzel, 'National socialism and the Arab world', <www.matthiaskuentzel.de>.

416. R. Melka, 'Nazi Germany and the Palestine question' in Elie Kedourie and Sylvia Haim (eds.), *Palestine and Israel in the 19th and 20th Centuries* (London, 1982), p. 89; Jeffrey Herf, *The Jewish Enemy* (Cambridge, MA, 2006), pp. 73–6, 180–1, 244.

417. See R. Melka, 'Nazi Germany and the Palestine question' in Elie Kedourie and Sylvia Haim (eds.), *Palestine and Israel in the 19th and 20th Centuries* (London, 1982), p. 97; David Yisraeli, 'The Third Reich and Palestine', ibid, p. 104.

418. Benny Morris, *Righteous Victims* (New York, 2001), pp. 161, 166–7.

419. Jeffrey Herf, *The Jewish Enemy* (Cambridge, MA, 2006), pp. 76, 159–60.

420. Emanuel Litvinoff (ed.), *Soviet Anti-Semitism: The Paris trial* (London, 1974), p. 4.

421. See Walter Laqueur and Barry Rubin, *The Israel–Arab Reader* (London, 2001), pp. 150, 210.

422. Fiamma Nirenstein, *Terror* (Hanover, NH, 2005), p. 246.

423. Edward Goulburn and Henry Symons, *The Life, Letters, and Sermons of Bishop Herbert de Losinga* (Oxford, 1878), vol. 2, pp. 31–2.

424. James W. Alexander, 'Herbert of Norwich 1091–1119' in William M. Bowsky (ed.), *Studies in Medieval and Renaissance History* (Lincoln, NA, 1969), vol. 6, pp. 180–2, and 193–4.

425. Edward Goulburn and Henry Symons, *The Life, Letters, and Sermons of Bishop Herbert de Losinga* (Oxford, 1878), vol. 2, pp. 434–9.

426. *Europe: A history* (London, 1997), pp. 706–7.

427. Davies concludes by citing a study undertaken 'by a Jewish investigator . . . in the spirit of Jewish redemption', which found that in a town in Upper Silesia, every single commander and three-quarters of the local agents of the UB were of 'Jewish origin'. *Europe* (London, 1997), pp. 1022–3.

428. Isaiah Schachar, *The Judensau* (London, 1974); Heinz Schrekenberg, *The Jews in Christian Art* (New York, 1996), pp. 331–7, figs. 1–6; Jeremy Cohen, *Christ Killers* (Oxford, 2007), pp. 207–9.

429. Heinz Schrekenberg, *The Jews in Christian Art* (New York, 1996), p. 20.

430. Ibid., p. 333, fig. 1. Sometimes, the pig is the Jew's progeny. S. W. Baron, *A Social and Religious History of the Jews* (New York, 1967, 2nd. ed), vol. 11, p. 137.

431. Emanuel Litvinoff (ed.), *Jews in Eastern Europe: Israel in Soviet cartoons*, 4/4 (1970), 10, 11, 13, 34, 42, 48; Moshe Decter, *Israel and the Jews in the Soviet Mirror* (New York, 1967), pp. 4, 42, 43.

432. Isaiah Schachar, *The Judensau* (London, 1974), pp. 1, 24–5; Heinz Schreken-berg, *The Jews in Christian Art* (New York, 1996), pp. 332 and 335–7; Israel J. Yuval, *Two Nations in Your Womb* (Berkeley, 2006), pp. 127, 175; David Frankfurter, *Evil Incarnate* (Princeton, NJ, 2006), p. 206.

433. David Clark, 'Accusations of anti-semitic chic are poisonous intellectual thuggery', *Guardian*, 6 March 2006. Cf. Christopher Hitchens: 'One sign of modern anti-Semitism is the obsessive, nasty need of some people to compare Israel to Nazi Germany.' *Love, Poverty and War* (New York, 2005), p. 331.

434. *The Clash of Fundamentalisms* (London, 2003), p. 93.

435. Ibid., pp. 310–11.

436. Private e-mail communications to HMD Trust, 10.46 and 00.16, 22 January 2007.

437. David Cesarani, 'The perdition affair' in Robert S. Wistrich (ed.), *Anti-Zionism and Antisemitism in the Contemporary World* (New York, 1990), p. 54.

438. 'These men courageously ran both the intended and unintended risks of dealing with the persecutors of their people. They wanted to save Jewish lives *at any cost...*' Szabolcs Szita, *Trading in Lives?* (Budapest, 2005), p. 220.

439. See Otto Kirchheimer, *Political Justice* (Princeton, NJ, 1961), p. 108.

440. *Perdition* (London, 1987), p. 34.

441. Ibid., pp. 43–4.

442. Ibid., p. 63.

443. Ibid., p. 21. The phrase is put in the mouth of Kaplan's counsel, but as a quotation. The source of the quotation is not given.

444. Ibid., p. 48.

445. Ibid., p. 35.

446. Ibid., p. 36.

447. Ibid., p. 14.

448. Ibid., p. 45.

449. Ibid., p. 46.

450. See Yehuda Bauer, *The Holocaust in Historical Perspective* (London, 1978), p. 7.

451. See Michael Marrus, *The Holocaust in History* (London, 1989), pp. 130–1.

452. Gerald Reitlinger, *The Final Solution*, 2nd edn (London, 1968), p. 128; Primo Levi, *The Drowned and the Saved* (London, 1989), p. 24.

453. Michael Marrus, *The Holocaust in History* (London, 1989), p. 130.

454. Raoul Hilberg, *The Politics of Memory* (Chicago, 1996), pp. 126, 150–1.

455. See Michael Marrus, 'Good scholarship and good teaching' in Michael Brown (ed.), *Approaches to Antisemitism* (New York, 1994), pp. 123–5.

456. Leni Yahil, *The Holocaust* (Oxford, 1990), p. 458.

457. Gerald Reitlinger, *The Final Solution*, 2nd edn (London, 1968), pp. 220–1.

458. Michael Marrus, *The Holocaust in History* (London, 1989), p. 116.
459. See Yitzhak Arad, 'The armed Jewish resistance in Eastern Europe' in Berenbaum and Abraham J. Peck (eds.), *The Holocaust and History* (Bloomington, IN, 2002), p. 599.
460. See Bernard Wasserstein, *Britain and the Jews of Europe 1939–1945* (Oxford, 1988), p. 347.
461. Szabolcs Szita, *Trading in Lives?* (Budapest, 2005), p. 207.
462. See Norman Geras, *The Contract of Mutual Indifference* (London, 1998), p. 100.
463. See Michael Marrus, *The Holocaust in History* (London, 1989), pp. 139, 231.
464. Baruch Knei-Paz, *The Social and Political Thought of Leon Trotsky* (Oxford, 1979), pp. 554–5.
465. *Perdition* (London, 1987), p. 13.
466. Ibid., p. 45.
467. Ibid., p. 67; on her return to Prague, having escaped from the Auschwitz death march, Heda Margoulis was asked by her neighbour, 'Why have you come back?' Tony Judt, *Postwar* (London, 2005), p. 182.
468. See David Cesarani, 'The perdition affair' in Robert S. Wistrich (ed.), *Anti-Zionism and Antisemitism in the Contemporary World* (London, 1990), pp. 58–9.
469. *Guardian*, 13 March 1987; *Guardian*, 23 December 2004.
470. *Report of the All-Party Parliamentary Inquiry into Antisemitism* (London, September 2006), p. 4; Golda Zafer-Smith, 'Anti-Semitism and anti-discrimination training and practice', *International Journal of Human Rights*, 7/1 (2003), 118–20.
471. <http://www.margaretthatcher.org/speeches/displaydocument.asp?docid=103485>.
472. Paul Gordon and Francesca Klug, *New Right, New Racism* (London, 1986), p. viii.
473. Martin Barker, *The New Racism* (London, 1982), p. 25.
474. See François Furet and Ernst Nolte, *Fascism and Communism* (Lincoln, NA, 2001), pp. 16–17.
475. See Walter Laqueur, *The Changing Face of Antisemitism* (New York, 2006), p. 149.
476. See Matthew Tempest, 'Blair combats anti-Semitism claims', *Guardian*, 18 February 2005.
477. See Fred Halliday, *Two Hours that Shook the World* (London, 2002), p. 135. The resolution, and the campaign of which it was the product, 'was pernicious and in the end backfired'.
478. Anton La Guardia, *Holy Land, Unholy War* (London, 2002), p. 372; Shimon Samuels, 'The Durban Protocols: Globalisation of the new antisemitism' in Michael Fineberg, Shimon Samuels, and Mark Weitzman (eds.), *Antisemitism: The generic hatred* (London, 2007), p. 45.
479. See Michael C. Kotzin, 'The new anti-Semitism,' *JUF/JFMC*, 2004, p. 5.

480. Arch Puddington, 'The wages of Durban', *Commentary* (November 2001), 30.

481. Fred Halliday, *100 Myths About the Middle East* (London, 2005), p. 199.

482. Munira Mirza, Abi Senthilkumaran, and Zein Ja'far, *Living Apart Together* (London, 2007), p. 64.

483. David Harrison, 'Media "contributing to rise of Islamophobia"', *Daily Telegraph*, 10 September 2006.

484. India Knight, 'Muslims are the new Jews', *The Times*, 15 October 2006.

485. See Munira Mirza, Abi Senthilkumaran, and Zein Ja'far, *Living Apart Together: British Muslims and the paradox of multiculturalism* (London, 2007), pp. 64–6; Kenan Malik, 'Are Muslims hated?', *Channel 4*, 8 January 2005, <www. kenanmalik.com>.

486. Christopher Hitchens, 'The war within Islam', *Slate*, 19 February 2007.

487. Sean O'Neill, 'University is accused of censoring anti-Semitic Islam lecture', *The Times*, 15 March 2007.

488. Munira Mirza, Abi Senthilkumaran, and Zein Ja'far, *Living Apart Together* (London, 2007), p. 71.

489. 'Full text: Writers' statement on cartoons', *BBC News*, 1 March 2006, <http://news.bbc.co.uk/1/hi/world/europe/4764730.stm>.

490. 'Despatches: The real threat we face is Blair', *New Statesman*, 21 August 2006.

491. 'Driven out of Eden', *Guardian*, 5 August 2003.

492. Todd Gitlin, 'The rough beast returns', *Motherjones.com*, 17 June 2002.

493. See the *Wikipedia* entry 'Norwegian Jostein Gaarder controversy'; Assaf Uni, 'Norway up in arms after author asserts Israel has lost right to exist', *Ha'aretz*, 12 August 2006.

494. 'The history of election is, for the most part, a very sorry one. When the Israelites invaded the land of Canaan, etc.' Jeremy Cott, 'The Biblical problem of election', *Journal of Ecumenical Studies*, 21/2 (1984), 201. Cott does not limit the doctrine to Judaism, however. For a critique of Cott, specifically in relation to Judaism, see Joel S. Kaminsky, 'Did election imply the mistreatment of non-Israelites?', *Harvard Theological Review*, 96/4 (2003).

495. Gabriel Piterberg, 'Erasures', *New Left Review*, July–August 2001, in Adam Shatz (ed.), *Prophets Outcast* (New York, 2004), p. 147.

496. Itamar Radai, 'From father to son: Attitudes to Jews and Israel in Asad's Syria', Analysis of Current Trends in Antisemitism, no. 29, The Vidal Sassoon International Center for the Study of Antisemitism, The Hebrew University of Jerusalem, 2007, p. 2.

497. 'Verax', 'The Mosaic law in politics', *The Times*, 27 November 1919.

498. 'Diaspora: Generation and the ground of Jewish identity', *Critical Inquiry* 19 (Summer 1993), 709–10; Joel S. Kaminsky, 'Did election imply the mistreatment of non-Israelites?' *Harvard Theological Review*, 96/4 (2003), 403–5. But for a more radical reading of Scriptural texts, from within a Jewish perspective, see Norman Solomon, 'Reading intolerant texts in a tolerant society' in

Tony Kushner and Nadia Valman (eds.), *Philosemitism, Antisemitism, and 'the Jews'* (Aldershot, 2004), pp. 49–68 ('somehow, one must find the courage to say No!').

499. James Meikle, 'Lecturers drop Israeli universities boycott call after legal advice', *Guardian*, 29 September 2007.

500. Thomas Friedman, *From Beirut to Jerusalem* (London, 1998), p. 315.

501. *Jews and Power* (New York, 2007), p. 115.

502. See William Korey, *The Soviet Cage* (New York, 1973), pp. 80–1, 146, 161, 304–5; Tony Judt, *Postwar* (London, 2005), p. 186; Walter Laqueur, *The Changing Face of Antisemitism* (New York, 2006), p. 178.

503. Avi Jorisch, *Beacon of Hatred* (Washington, DC, 2004), p. 64.

504. See Steven Beller, *Vienna and the Jews 1867–1938* (Cambridge, 1989), pp. 195, 198.

505. Fred Halliday, *100 Myths About the Middle East* (London, 2005), pp. 198–9.

506. See Geoffrey Short, 'Antisemitism on campus' in Michael Fineberg, Shimon Samuels, and Mark Weitzman (eds.), *Antisemitism* (London, 2007), p. 122.

507. Jon Pike, 'Honderich on terrorism', *Democratiya* (November–December 2005).

508. David Caute, *The Fellow-Travellers* (London, 1988), p. 1.

509. See Isaac Deutscher, *The Prophet Outcast* (Oxford, 1970), p. 433.

510. See David Caute, *The Fellow-Travellers* (London, 1988), p. 21.

511. See Simon R. Cottee, 'The culture of denial', *Journal of Human Rights*, 4 (2005), 1291–31.

512. David Caute, *The Fellow-Travellers* (London, 1988), pp. 77, 109–10, 191, ch. 4; Norman and Jeanne MacKenzie, *The Diary of Beatrice Webb* (Cambridge, MA, 1982–1985), vol. 4, p. 420. Webb is summarizing Harold Laski's views.

513. Ben White, 'History, myths, and all the news that's fit to print', *Palestine Chronicle*, 10 January 2006 ('It could be argued . . . that the comments made by Ahmadinejad in recent months are not anti-Semitic . . .'); John Pilger, 'The lies of Hiroshima live on, props in the war crimes of the 20th century', *Guardian*, 8 August 2008 ('Iran's president Mahmoud Ahmadinejad never threatened to "wipe Israel off the map" '); Jonathan Steele, 'If Iran is ready to talk, the US must do so unconditionally', *Guardian*, 2 June 2006 ('He was not making a military threat'). Walt and Mearsheimer adopt Steele's reading: *The Israel Lobby* (London, 2007), pp. 98, 387. Cf.: David Aaronovich, 'You don't have to be paranoid to want to take these lunatics at their word', *The Times*, 12 June 2006; Christopher Hitchens, 'The Cole Report', <http://www.slate.com/id/2140947/>; Matthias Küntzel, 'Unholy hatreds: Holocaust denial and antisemitism in Iran', Posen Papers in Contemporary Antisemitism no. 8, The Vidal Sassoon International Center for the Study of Antisemitism, The Hebrew University of Jerusalem (2007).

514. Ted Honderich, *After the Terror*, 2nd edn (Edinburgh, 2003), pp. 151, 156, 167.

515. Jacqueline Rose, *The Last Resistance* (London, 2007), p. 135.

516. George Galloway, *I'm Not the Only One* (London, 2004), p. 37.

517. Susan Neiman, *Evil in Modern Thought* (Princeton, NJ, 2002), p. 284.

518. Quoted in David Caute, *The Fellow-Travellers* (London, 1988), p. 95.

519. *The Fellow-Travellers* (London, 1988), pp. 13–14.

520. See, for example, Yehuda Bauer, 'Antisemitism and Anti-Zionism: New and old' in Robert S. Wistrich (ed.), *Anti-Zionism and Antisemitism in the Contemporary World* (New York, 1990), pp. 200–1.

521. Bernard Lewis, *Semites and Anti-Semites* (London, 1986), p. 35; Tony Judt, *Postwar* (London, 2005), pp. 183–7; Semyon Reznik, *The Nazification of Russia* (Washington, DC, 1996), pp. 35–47.

522. Semyon Reznik, *The Nazification of Russia* (Washington, DC, 1996), p. 49.

523. See Alain Finkielkraut, *The Imaginary Jew* (Lincoln, NA, 1994), pp. 154–6.

524. Emanuel Litvinoff (ed.), *Jews in Eastern Europe: Israel in Soviet cartoons*, 4/4 (1970).

525. Robert J. Brym, *The Jews of Moscow, Kiev and Minsk* (New York, 1994), pp. 41, 48.

526. Emanuel Litvinoff (ed.), *Soviet Anti-Semitism: The Paris trial* (London, 1974), p. 13.

527. See Alain Besançon, *A Century of Horrors* (Wilmington, DE, 2007), p. xiv.

528. See Oliver Kamm, 'Chomsky and holocaust denial', 1 November 2004, <http://timesonline.typepad.com/oliver_kamm>.

529. 'Notes on anti-Semitism, Zionism, and Palestine', *Counterpunch*, 4 March 2004.

530. Seamus Milne, <http://commentisfree.guardian.co.uk/david_hirsh/2008/03/half-truths_cannot_aid_peace.html#comment-1182965>, comment 1182965. The Charter remains unamended at the time of writing. Milne does not cite any instances of disavowal, nor does he address the broader question of anti-Semitism in, say, Hamas-controlled TV broadcasts. See also <http://hurryupharry.bloghouse.net/archives/2008/03/07/hirsh_v_milne_on_cif.php>.

531. Tariq Ali, 'Notes on anti-Semitism, Zionism, and Palestine', *Counterpunch*, 4 March 2004: 'the truth is that Israel today is not in existential danger'. Tony Judt, 'The "Problem of Evil" in Postwar Europe', *NYRB*, 14 February 2008, p. 35.

532. John Pilger, letter, *Guardian*, 10 October 2003.

533. Yasmin Alibhai-Brown, 'Nothing but anti-Arab racism can fully explain the behaviour of the Israelis', *Independent*, 17 July 2006.

534. In the *Guardian*, 19 July 2006, a cartoon pictured a black-gloved fist, with knuckle-duster Stars of David, punching the bloody head of a young boy, while a Hizbullah wasp hovered overhead; <http://hurryupharry.bloghouse.net/archives/2006/07/20/guardian_or_der_sturmer.php>.

535. An ironic defence, as well as an inept one, not least because Jews were commonly portrayed in the Middle Ages as the children of Saturn (and Saturn in turn was often portrayed bearing 'Jewish' characteristics). Saturn was the god of disaster, and associated with meanness, and the harshness of business life. See Heinz Schrekenberg, *The Jews in Christian Art* (New York, 1996), pp. 330–1, figs. 1–2.

536. *New Statesman*, 11 February 2002.

537. The adjudication can be read at <http://www.pcc.org.uk/news/index.html?article=MjA5OA==>.

538. 'The Association of Greater London Older Women complained that an article in the August 6–13 1997 issue of *Time Out*... contained language which was prejudicial and pejorative in breach of Clause 15 (Discrimination) of the Code of Practice.' The PCC upheld the complaint. The 'columnist's humorous remarks... were clearly distressing to the elderly and to those with mental health problems', <http://www.pcc.org.uk/news/index.html?article=MTk1Mw>.

539. 'Independent cartoonist wins award', *Independent*, 27 November 2003.

540. See Tim Benson, 'The Twice-Promised Land: A cartoonists perspective (1917–2004)', *The Political Cartoon Society*, <http://www.politicalcartoon.co.uk/html/history/twice_promised_land.html>.

541. Cf.: 'It's not smart to pretend that they don't mean what they say.' Michael Walzer, 'Response to Jerome Slater: The Lebanon War', *Dissent* (Winter 2007). See also Omer Bartov, 'The new antisemitism' in David Kertzer (ed.), *Old Demons, New Debates* (New York, 2005), pp. 10–11.

542. Tariq Ali, 'Mid-point in the Middle East?', *New Left Review* (March–April 2006).

543. 'Mr Ahmadinejad may not know much about the Holocaust. But he certainly knows how to work a crowd.' Simon Tisdall, 'Ahmadinejad roadshow seduces an adoring public', *Guardian*, 19 August 2006; Ewen MacAskill, Simon Tisdall, and Robert Tait, 'Lone Jewish MP confronts Ahmadinejad on Holocaust but stresses loyalty to Iran', *Guardian*, 28 June 2006 ('controversial Holocaust statements').

544. See Omer Bartov, 'The new antisemitism' in David Kertzer (ed.), *Old Demons, New Debates* (New York, 2005), pp. 11, 15.

545. See ibid., pp. 22–3.

546. Kenneth S. Stern, *Antisemitism Today* (New York, 2006), p. 30.

547. See Eugene Goodheart, 'The London Review of Hezbollah', *Dissent* (Winter 2007). Glass's article appeared in the 17 August 2006 issue of the *London Review of Books*. The cited (and other relevant) correspondence then appeared in the 5 October, 19 October 2006, 4 January, and 25 January 2007 *LRB*.

548. Fred Halliday, 'A Lebanese fragment: Two days with Hizbollah', *openDemocracy*, 20 July 2006; Jeffrey Goldberg, 'In The Party Of God', *New Yorker*, 14–21 October 2002; Avi Jorisch, *Beacon of Hatred* (Washington, DC, 2004),

pp. 57, 63; 'France pulls plug on Arab network', *BBC News*, 14 December 2004, <http://news.bbc.co.uk/1/hi/world/europe/4093579.stm>; 'Argentine prosecutors seek Iran arrests', *Guardian*, 25 October 2006; Stephen Schwartz (ed.), *Hassan Nasrallah* (New York, 2006), pp. 21, 54–5. It is not *just* an anti-Semitic party, of course: Judith Palmer Harik, *Hezbollah: The changing face of terrorism* (London, 2005).

549. In fifteenth-century Italy, for example, certain violent disorders in which Jews were killed and injured were blamed on the Jews themselves. As the bishop of Cremona explained, the Jews had provoked their tormentors 'by their crimes, perfidy, iniquity, abomination and dishonest mode of living'. S. W. Baron, *A Social and Religious History of the Jews*, 2nd edn (New York, 1967), vol. 11, p. 33.

550. See Mordecai Chertoff, 'The new left and the newer leftists' in Mordecai Chertoff (ed.), *The New Left and the Jews* (New York, 1971), p. 177.

551. 'The new anti-Semitism?', *The Electronic Intifada*, 3 June 2003, <http://www.jkcook.net/Articles1/0002.htm>; Mark Mazower, 'Anti-Semitism is not the real danger to Jews today', *The Times*, 27 November 2003.

552. Joseph Harker, 'Of course all white people are racist', *Guardian*, 3 July 2002.

553. 'Lessons of history', *Al-Ahram Weekly,* 27 November–3 December 2003.

554. 'From the new "anti-Semitism" to nuclear Holocaust', *Counterpunch*, 23–4 September 2006.

555. 'Selling anti-Semitism', *Al-Ahram Weekly*, 10–16 October 2002.

556. *Literature and Revolution* (Ann Arbor, 1960), p. 58.

557. Nicholas Watt, 'Dalyell may face race hatred inquiry', *Guardian*, 5 May 2003.

558. In the second edition of *After the Terror* (Edinburgh, 2003), he complains that he has been accused of anti-Semitism, and that this accusation was sufficient to cause the German edition of his book to be withdrawn by its publishers. He cites Jürgen Habermas, 'Banning a Book': 'I can find nothing in the text to justify [this] charge.' But Habermas adds: 'there are generalizing statements that made me groan slightly when I read them: "Having been the principal victims of racism in history, Jews now seem to have learned from their abusers." Sentences like this can always be used for anti-Semitic purposes, even against the author's intention, if they are taken out context without any attempt to explain them.'

559. 'Friendly fire', *Guardian*, 29 October 2005.

560. 'The leadership of the Stop-The-War Coalition has been under attack in the right wing Zionist press...': 'British Labour MP George Galloway tells *Al Bawaba* Arab movement mobilizing for his defense', *Al Bawaba*, 29 April 2003, <http://www.albawaba.com/en/main/163382/&searchWords=galloway>. In an interview broadcast on 17 November 2005 on Al-Jazeera satellite TV: 'I was re-elected despite all the efforts made by the British government, the

Zionist movement and the newspapers and news media which are controlled by Zionism.' Galloway spoke in English, with simultaneous Arabic translation. See: <http://normblog.typepad.com/normblog/2005/11/galloways_poiso.html>. But in an interview with Sky, it was just 'the right wing media'. 'Galloway talks to Sky', *Sky News*, 23 April 2003, <http://news.sky.com/skynews/article/0,,30800-12295068,00.html>. And here is Galloway on Syrian TV, 31 July 2005: 'Two of your beautiful daughters are in the hands of foreigners—Jerusalem and Baghdad. The foreigners are doing to your daughters as they will. The daughters are crying for help, and the Arab world is silent. And some of them are collaborating with the rape of these two beautiful Arab daughters. Why? Because they are too weak and too corrupt to do anything about it.' MEMRI Special Dispatch Series, no. 948, 3 August 2005.

561. *The Fellow-Travellers* (London, 1988), p. 420.
562. See Nick Cohen, *What's Left? How liberals lost their way* (London, 2007), p. 107.

8. CONTEMPORARY CONFESSIONAL ANTI-ZIONISMS, AND A CONCLUSION

1. 'Conspiracy theories abound in the Muslim community, many of them piggy-backing on an underlying notion of an American-Israeli bogeyman.' Zia Haider Rahman, 'Time to confront the Muslim conspiracists', *Daily Telegraph*, 6 June 2007.
2. Jonathan Schneer, 'Origins of the Balfour Declaration: An unexplored dimension', *Report of the Oxford Centre for Hebrew and Jewish Studies, Academic Year 2006–2007*, pp. 7–8.
3. Ira M. Lapidus, *A History of Islamic Societies*, 2nd edn (Cambridge, 2006), pp. 789–91, 799.
4. Ziauddin Sardar, *Desperately Seeking Paradise* (London, 2004), pp. 282–3.
5. Ed Husain, *The Islamist* (London, 2007), p. 91.
6. See, for example, Moazzam Begg, *Enemy Combatant* (London, 2007), pp. 61, 83.
7. See Anthony McRoy, *From Rushdie to 7/7* (London, 2006), pp. 7–67.
8. Moazzam Begg, *Enemy Combatant* (London, 2007), p. 381.
9. Thérèse Delpech, *Savage Century* (Washington, DC, 2007), p. 86.
10. See Niall Ferguson, *Colossus* (London, 2005) pp. xxiv–xxv.
11. Olivier Roy, *Secularism Confronts Islam* (New York, 2007), p. 51.
12. Ibid., p. 65.
13. See ibid., p. 42: 'The vision of a Muslim world united under the banner of Islam and storming the West makes no sense.' See also Olivier Roy, *The Politics of Chaos in the Middle East* (New York, 2008), p. 158.

14 'Muslims in Europe: Economic worries top concerns about religious and cultural identity: Few signs of backlash from Western Europeans', *Pew Global Attitudes Project*, 6 July 2006.

15. Ed Husain, *The Islamist* (London, 2007), p. 251.

16. 'Israel simply has no right to exist', *Guardian*, 3 January 2001.

17. 'Human rights, justice, and Muslims in the modern world', 7 May 2000, <http://www.ihrc.org.uk/show.php?id=10>.

18. Martin Bright, 'Muslim leaders in feud with the BBC', *Observer*, 14 August 2005.

19. See, e.g., Anthony McRoy, *From Rushdie to 7/7* (London, 2006), pp. 19, 178.

20. <http://www.mpacuk.org/content/view/4/1235/103/>.

21. Damian Thompson, 'Ancient fantasies that infect the Internet and inspire suicide bombers', *Daily Telegraph*, 6 August 2005.

22. Antony Barnett, 'Bookshop's messages of racist hate', *Observer*, 4 February 2007.

23. See Denis MacEoin, *The Hijacking of British Islam* (London, 2007), *passim*.

24. *Attitudes to Living in Britain: A survey of Muslim opinion*, GfK NOP Social Research, April 2006.

25. Laura Clark, 'Teachers drop the Holocaust to avoid offending Muslims', *Daily Mail*, 2 April 2007. Shortly after 9/11, a survey disclosed that not a single module, text, or programme for the teaching of the Holocaust, even within the context of twentieth-century history, existed in the Arab world. Robert Satloff, *Among the Righteous* (New York, 2006), p. 4.

26. Notwithstanding the efforts of a sizeable minority of MCB members who wanted it lifted to repair relations between British Muslims and Jews. See John Ware, 'MCB in the dock', *Prospect* (December 2006). The MCB voted in December 2007 to end its boycott. See Vikram Dodd, 'Muslim Council ends boycott of Holocaust memorial day', *Guardian*, 3 December 2007.

27. 'Muslim Council of Britain boycotts Holocaust day', *Guardian*, 26 January 2009.

28. See Anthony McRoy, *From Rushdie to 7/7* (London, 2006), pp. 23, 26.

29. See ibid., pp. 183–4.

30. 'Muslim who stabbed Jew to be detained in hospital', *Guardian*, 19 September 2002.

31. See The Community Security Trust, *Antisemitic Incidents Report 2002* (London, 2002), pp. 5–8.

32. The Community Security Trust, *Antisemitic Incidents Report 2006* (London, 2007), pp. 9–11.

33. John Mann MP, Hansard, HC (series 6) vol. 475, no. 95, col. 1574 (15 May 2008).

34. See 'The Present Situation in the United Kingdom within the Global Context', Memorandum from the Association of Muslim Lawyers, Minutes of Evidence, Select Committee on Religious Offences in England and Wales, 14 July 2002.

35. See Toby Helm, 'Jews and Freemasons controlled war on Iraq, says No 10 adviser', *Daily Telegraph*, 12 September 2005.

36. James Brandon and Douglas Murray, *Hate on the State* (London, 2007), pp. 24, 31.

37. *The New World Order* (Beirut, 1994), pp. ix, xiii, 6, 10, 50, 109, 118, 141, 167, 169, 171, 189–95, 218, 226, 240, 263, 271, 311, 325, 335–6, 340, 353–4, 356, 360, 403, 411, 424–6, 461, 469, 470, 478, 512, 514, 517, 528, 535, 538, 545, 552, 556, 560, 575–6, 602, 618, 630, 631.

38. See *In Search of Fatima* (London, 2004), pp. 124–7.

39. Ibid., p. 380.

40. *Married to Another Man* (London, 2007), p. 257.

41. *In Search of Fatima* (London, 2004), p. 399.

42. Ibid., p. 244.

43. *Married to Another Man* (London, 2007), p. 230.

44. Ibid., p. 265.

45. Ibid., p. 257.

46. *In Search of Fatima* (London, 2004), p. 388.

47. *Married to Another Man* (London, 2007), p. 21.

48. Ibid., p. 41.

49. Simon Goldhill, *The Temple of Jerusalem* (London, 2006), pp. 6–7.

50. Ira M. Lapidus, *A History of Islamic Societies*, 2nd edn (Cambridge, 2006), p. 51.

51. See F. H. Kisch, *Palestine Diary* (London, 1938), pp. 342, 424, 433. The Commission recommended that no facilities be granted 'for any kind of seats for aged or infirm' Jews, that the use of the *sefer torah* be prohibited on the Sabbath, and the sounding of the *shofar* be prohibited at all times.

52. Dan Cohn-Sherbok, *The Politics of Apocalypse* (Oxford, 2006), p. 58. In 1896, for example, an estimated 28,110 Jews, 8,750 Christians, and 8,560 Muslims lived there. Amy Dockser Marcus, *Jerusalem 1913* (New York, 2008), p. 41.

53. Tom Segev, *1967* (London, 2007), p. 488.

54. Hershel Shanks, 'Biblical destruction', *Wall Street Journal*, 18 July 2007. See also Fiamma Nirenstein, *Terror* (Hanover, NH, 2005), p. 63.

55. *Publish it Not: The Middle East cover-up* (Oxford, 2006), p. xxix.

56. *Married to Another Man* (London, 2007), pp. 66–7; Rory Miller, *Divided Against Zion* (London, 2000), pp. 128–9.

57. *Married to Another Man* (London, 2007), pp. 92–103.

58. Ibid., pp. 81–3.

59. Ibid., p. 15.

60. See *In Search of Fatima* (London, 2004), pp. 14, 188–9, 234.

61. *Married to Another Man* (London, 2007), p. 94.

62. Ibid., pp. 48–9. Cf.: 'In Palestine there is no anti-Semitism for the simple fact that we are all Semites.' Munir Fasheh, 'Reclaiming identity and redefining ourselves' in Naim Ateek, Marc H. Ellis *et al.* (eds.), *Faith and the Intifada* (New York, 1992), p. 63.

63. 'Man convicted over cartoon protest', *Guardian*, 1 February 2007.

64. Fuad Nahdi, 'Tel Aviv first, then Manchester?', *Guardian*, 2 May 2003.

65. *Report of the All-Party Parliamentary Inquiry into Antisemitism* (London, September 2006), pp. 26–32 ('a minority of Islamist extremists in this country do incite hatred towards Jews').

66. *The Times*, 7 February 2006.

67. Ibid.

68. *Attitudes to Living in Britain: A survey of Muslim opinion*, GfK NOP Social Research, April 2006.

69. 'Al-Qaeda accuses Iran of 9/11 lie', *BBC News*, 22 April 2008, <http://news. bbc.co.uk/1/hi/world/middle_east/7361414.stm>.

70. Munira Mirza, Abi Senthilkumaran, and Zein Ja'far, *Living Apart Together* (London, 2007), pp. 6, 15, 31.

71. Andrew Norfolk, 'Hardline takeover of British mosques', *The Times*, 7 September 2007.

72. See <http://www.timesonline.co.uk/tol/comment/faith/article2402173.ece? token=null&offset=12>.

73. Speech by the director general of the Security Service, Dame Eliza Manningham-Buller, at Queen Mary's College, London, 9 November 2006.

74. Haviv Rettig, 'EU official: Half of European anti-Semitism related to radical Islam', *Jerusalem Post*, 2 February 2008.

75. Christopher Hitchens, 'Londonistan calling', *Vanity Fair*, June 2007 ('hatred of the Jews has become absolutely standard, all across the community').

76. Ed Husain, *The Islamist* (London, 2007), p. 54. See also pp. 80–1, 113, 171, 202.

77. Ibid., p. 206.

78. 'Undercover mosque', broadcast on Channel 4 on 15 January 2007, in the *Dispatches* series.

79. See Peter Clarke, 'Learning from experience: Counter terrorism in the UK since 9/11', *Policy Exchange*, London, 2007, p. 21.

80. See Anthony McRoy, *From Rushdie to 7/7* (London, 2006), pp. 38, 194.

81. 'Media controlled by Jews—Hamza', *BBC News*, 24 January 2006.

82. Duncan Gardham, 'Hamza "had Big Ben as terror target"', *Daily Telegraph*, 12 January 2006.

83. 'The preachings of Abu Hamza', *Guardian Unlimited*, <http://www.guardian. co.uk/terrorism/story/0,,1704312,00.html>.

84. Duncan Campbell, 'Cleric of hate', *Guardian*, 7 February 2006.

85. Sean O'Neill and Daniel McGrory, *The Suicide Factory* (London, 2006), pp. 63–4, 306; James Brandon, *Virtual Caliphates* (London, 2008), p. 2.

86. 'It was "bloodthirsty language", but far from being an incitement to do anything, the words were a prediction drawn from Scripture.' Sean O'Neill and Daniel McGrory, *The Suicide Factory* (London, 2006), p. 305.

87. Ibid., pp. 145, 192, 196.

88. See Rageh Omar, *Only Half of Me* (London, 2007), p. 124.

89. Simon Freeman, 'Abu Hamza jailed for seven years for inciting murder', *The Times*, 7 February 2006.

90. James Brandon, *Virtual Caliphates* (London, 2008), pp. 7–8.

91. Fred Attewill, 'Race hate preacher Faisal deported', *Guardian*, 25 May 2007.

92. Dominic Kennedy, 'Britain's sheikh of race hate', *The Times*, 4 February 2002.

93. James Brandon, *Virtual Caliphates* (London, 2008), pp. 14–15.

94. See Sarah Glazer, 'Anti-Semitism in Europe', *CQ Global Researcher*, 2/6 (2008), 160.

95. Jonathan Frankel, *Prophecy and Politics* (Cambridge, 1984), p. 79.

96. Eli Lederhendler, *The Road to Modern Jewish Politics* (Oxford, 1989), pp. 3, 5; Hillel J. Kieval, *Languages of Community* (Berkeley, CA, 2000), p. 26.

97. Zvi Gitelman, 'The evolution of Soviet anti-Zionism' in Robert S. Wistrich (ed.), *Anti-Zionism and Antisemitism in the Contemporary World* (New York, 1990), p. 15.

98. See Walter Laqueur, 'Zionism, the Marxist critique, and the Left' in Irving Howe and Carl Gershman (eds.), *Israel, the Arabs and the Middle East* (New York, 1972), p. 19.

99. Lionel Abel, *The Intellectual Follies* (New York, 1984), p. 256; Amnon Rubinstein, *From Herzl to Rabin* (New York, 2000), pp. 45–6. Buber said this 'in the midst of World War II'.

100. See Russo-Jewish Committee of London, *The Persecution of the Jews in Russia* (London, 1891), p. 39.

101. See Ezra Mendelsohn, *On Modern Jewish Politics* (Oxford, 1993), *passim*.

102. Ibid., p. 65.

103. Ibid., p. 141.

104. Steven J. Zipperstein, *Imagining Russian Jewry* (Seattle, WA, 1999), p. 4.

105. See Brian Klug, 'A time to speak out: Rethinking Jewish identity and solidarity with Israel' in Adam Shatz (ed.), *Prophets Outcast* (New York, 2004), pp. 378–92.

106. Philip Weiss, 'AIPAC alternative?' *Nation*, 23 April 2007.

107. Michael B. Oren, *Power, Faith and Fantasy* (New York, 2007), p. 351.

108. Ibid., p. 352.

109. See Mark Lilla, *The Stillborn God* (New York, 2007), pp. 241–2.

110. See Sander L. Gilman, *Jewish Self-Hatred* (Baltimore, MD, 1986), p. 237.

111. Eugene Goodheart, 'A non-Zionist reflects on the Israeli–Palestinian conflict', *Dissent* (Summer 2007).

112. Leonard Woolf, *An Autobiography 2: 1911–1969* (London, 1980), pp. 499–500.

113. However, 'during the pivotal sit-in at the Berkeley Administration building, a Chanukah service was conducted, and the *Hatikva* [Israel's national anthem] was sung'. Stanley Rothman and Robert S. Lichter, *Roots of Radicalism* (New York, 1982), p. 81.

114. Haim Hanegbi, Moshe Machover, and Akiva Orr, 'The class nature of Israeli society', *New Left Review*, no. 65 (January 1971), 12, 26.
115. See Stanley Rothman and Robert S. Lichter, *Roots of Radicalism* (New York, 1982), pp. 85, 110–11.
116. Or it may be both, and then more than either. See Lynne Segal, *Making Trouble* (London, 2007), pp. 214–15.
117. *If I Am Not For Myself: Journeys of an anti-Zionist Jew* (London, 2008), p. 289.
118. Brian Klug, 'Who speaks for Jews in England?', *Guardian*, 5 February 2007.
119. Martin Hodgson, 'British Jews break away from "pro-Israeli" Board of Deputies', *Independent*, 5 February 2007.
120. Letter, *Guardian*, 25 April 2007; letter, *Jewish Chronicle*, 27 April 2007.
121. Martin Hodgson, 'British Jews break away from "pro-Israeli" Board of Deputies', *Independent*, 5 February 2007.
122. Brian Klug, 'The myth of the new anti-Semitism', *Nation*, 2 February 2004.
123. 'We renounce Israeli rights', *Guardian*, 8 August 2002.
124. See Jacqueline Rose, 'Response to Edward Said' in Edward W. Said, *Freud and the Non-European* (London, 2003), p. 71. Rose describes this as a 'striking self-definition of a modern secular Jew'. The 'trappings' 'stripped away' are the 'untenable, most politically dangerous elements'. Cf.: 'My belated identification with Judaism was determined only by those aspects of the national Jewish character that are supra-national in character.' Letter from Margarete von Bendeman-Susman to Martin Buber, 29 March 1921, Nahum N. Glatzer and Paul Mendes-Flohr (eds.), *The Letters of Martin Buber* (New York, 1991), p. 257.
125. See Yosef Hayim Yerushalmi, *Freud's Moses* (New Haven, CT, 1991), p. 10.
126. *Born Jewish* (London, 2005), p. 176.
127. Jacqueline Rose, Introduction to Marcel Liebman, *Born Jewish* (London, 2005), p. xix.
128. See Alain Finkielkraut, *In the Name of Humanity* (London, 2001), p. 98.
129. Robert S. Wistrich, *The Jews of Vienna in the Age of Franz Joseph* (Oxford, 1990), p. 514.
130. See Steven Beller, *Vienna and the Jews 1867–1938* (Cambridge, 1989), p. 211.
131. See Paul Lawrence Rose, *German Question/Jewish Question* (Princeton, NJ, 1990), p. 142.
132. 'Oh! Weep for those' in Thomas L. Ashton (ed.), *Byron's Hebrew Melodies* (Austin, TX, 1972), p. 138. I have slightly modified the line.
133. See James Joyce, *A Portrait of the Artist as a Young Man* (New York, 2007), p. 179.
134. Brian Klug, 'Climate of the debate over Israel', <http://www.engageonline. org.uk/blog/article.php?id=1003>.
135. See Yosef Hayim Yerushalmi, *Freud's Moses* (New Haven, CT, 1991), pp. 12–14.
136. Alain Finkielkraut, *The Imaginary Jew* (Lincoln, NA, 1994), p. 136.

137. See Brian Klug, 'A time to speak out: Rethinking Jewish identity and solidarity with Israel' in Adam Shatz (ed.), *Prophets Outcast* (New York, 2004), p. 383.

138. Eric Hobsbawm, *Interesting Times* (London, 2002), p. 24.

139. See Jonathan Frankel, *Prophecy and Politics* (Cambridge, 1984), p. 52.

140. See Tzvetan Todorov, *Hope and Memory* (London, 2003), pp. 189, 196.

141. John Docker, ' "Sheer perversity": Anti-Zionism in the 1940s', *London Papers in Australian Studies*, no. 4, Menzies Centre for Australian studies, King's College London, 2001, p. 22.

142. See Tzvetan Todorov, *Hope and Memory* (London, 2003), p. 140.

143. 'Hamas' victory, a new hope?', *The Palestine Chronicle*, 1 February 2006; 'Who are the real terrorists in the Middle East?', *Independent*, 26 July 2006.

144. *The Ethnic Cleansing of Palestine* (Oxford, 2006), *passim*; *A History of Modern Palestine* (Cambridge, 2006), pp. 128–30.

145. See Seth Frantzman, 'Ethnic cleansing in Palestine?', *Jerusalem Post*, 16 August 2007. For example, Pappe mentions neither the 1929 massacre in Hebron nor the 1948 massacre in Kfar Etzion. Hebron is instead merely referred to as a 'biblical Jewish site', as if it had no *post*-biblical Jewish existence. See *The Ethnic Cleansing of Palestine* (Oxford, 2006), p. 43. See also his *A History of Modern Palestine* (Cambridge, 2006), pp. 90–2. For a further example of the elimination from history of the Hebron massacre, see Fawwaz Trabulsi, 'The Palestine problem: Zionism and imperialism in the Middle East', *New Left Review*, no. 57 (September–October 1969), 62.

146. See Irwin Cotler *et al.*, *Jewish Refugees from Arab Countries* (New York, 2007).

147. Even though Zionism—a 'settle-state ideology'—has now become hegemonic among the Jews, there are still some among them engaged 'in the vanguard, in the struggle for humanity'. See George Galloway, *I'm Not the Only One* (London, 2004), pp. 31–3.

148. *The Clash of Fundamentalisms* (London, 2003), p. 88. '[Akiva] became something of a guru for many of us aspiring Palestinian and Israeli activists.' Ghada Karmi, *In Search of Fatima* (London, 2004), p. 397.

149. 'I've got what it takes to lead the PLO: Jewish good looks', *Independent*, 3 October 2000.

150. Letter, *Guardian*, 25 April 2007.

151. Simon Rocker, 'Voices founder quits "out of touch" group', *Jewish Chronicle*, 16 November 2007.

152. *The unJewish State* (London, 1983), pp. 5–6, 237–8.

153. This language comes from *Apartheid Israel* (London, 2003), but note also the following, from his contribution to a July 2006 conference organized by the IHRC: '[I hope] that within the next decade or fifteen years the UN General Assembly will endorse a long overdue covenant, the covenant for the suppression of political Zionism as a crime against humanity.' See <http://www.ihrc.org.uk/060702/>.

154. 'Nation as trauma, Zionism as question: Jacqueline Rose interviewed', *open-Democracy*, 18 August 2005.
155. *States of Fantasy* (Oxford, 1996), pp. 2, 13.
156. *The Question of Zion* (Princeton, 2005), p. xviii. Two pages earlier, Rose describes herself as a 'Jewish woman'.
157. Not always consistently, though. Jacqueline Rose, for example, has maintained *both* that 'Israel silences dissent' and 'inside Israel [the Zionist dissenters'] voices have been mostly silenced' *and* that 'the voices of dissent and opposition are very strong inside Israel'. See *The Question of Zion* (Princeton, 2005), pp. 53, 69, and contrast John Sutherland, 'The ideas interview: Jacqueline Rose', *Guardian*, 28 November 2005. Rose also argues that the voices of the dissenting Zionist intellectuals (Buber, Scholem, Kohn, Arendt) 'inside Israel have been mostly silenced', though their vision has also 'returned to the centre of debate inside Israel'. *The Question of Zion* (Princeton, 2005), pp. 69, 86–7.
158. *The Question of Zion* (Princeton, 2005), p. 43.
159. 'Arab rights can be dismissed; the Arab people—only too visible—can or rather must be defeated, because any concession is repetition. Weakness always excites hate.' *The Question of Zion* (Princeton, 2005), p. 131.
160. *The Question of Zion* (Princeton, 2005), p. 133. Later, as if as an afterthought, Rose concedes, 'That the Arabs played their part in rendering... coexistence impossible is not in dispute' (ibid., p. 147). That Palestinian enmity also played a part in pushing Zionism towards the kind of nation she deplores is barely considered, however. Responding to Judah Magnes's proposals for limited Jewish autonomy, and no independent state, one of the leaders of the Arab *Istiqlal* (independence) Party wrote: 'In your opinions and proposals I can see nothing but a blatant provocation against the Arabs, who will allow nobody to share with them their natural rights... as to the Jews, they have no rights whatsoever except spiritual memories replete with catastrophes and woeful tales... It is, therefore, impossible to have a meeting between the leaders of the two peoples—the Arab and the Jewish' (see Amnon Rubinstein *From Herzl to Rabin* (New York, 2000), p. 68, and Norman Rose, *A Senseless, Squalid War* (London, 2009), p. 95). Rose expresses great sympathy for the stance taken by Magnes and his circle, but no understanding of the strength of the Arab opposition to it. 'Magnes proceeded to offer his hand, but found no one willing to take it.' Michael B. Oren, *Power, Faith and Fantasy* (New York, 2007), p. 437.
161. *The Question of Zion* (Princeton, 2005), p. 11.
162. Brian Klug tellingly omits the final clauses of the verse he quotes from Deuteronomy, which is as follows: 'That which is altogether just shalt thou follow, that thou mayest live, *and inherit the land which the LORD thy God giveth thee*' (italics added).
163. See Richard W. Miller, 'Nationalist morality and crimes against humanity' in Aleksander Jokić (ed.), *War Crimes and Collective Wrongdoing* (Oxford, 2001), p. 144 et seq.

164. Jacqueline Rose, *Guardian*, 2 January 2006.

165. See David Hartman, *Israelis and the Jewish Tradition* (New Haven, 2000), which argues for a religious Zionism 'grounded in a normative covenantal framework that is independent of messianism' (p. xi).

166. See Shlomo Avineri, 'Zionism and the Jewish religious tradition', and Yosef Salmon, 'Zionism and anti-Zionism in traditional Judaism in Eastern Europe' both in Shmuel Almog *et al.* (eds.), *Zionism and Religion* (Hanover, NH, 1998), pp. 3, 25.

167. See David Hartman, *Israelis and the Jewish Tradition* (New Haven, 2000), p. 82.

168. Mark Lilla, *The Stillborn God* (New York, 2007), pp. 241–2.

169. See 'Thermidor and Anti-Semitism' (1937), and 'Appeal to American Jews menaced by Fascism and anti-Semitism' (1938), *On the Jewish Question* (London, 1970), pp. 28–30.

170. 'Thermidor and Anti-Semitism' (1937), ibid., p. 28.

171. See Baruch Knei-Paz, *The Social and Political Thought of Leon Trotsky* (Oxford, 1979), pp. 533–9.

172. Colin Shindler, *What do Zionists Believe?* (London, 2007), p. 15.

173. See Kurt Lewin, 'Self-hatred among Jews', *Contemporary Jewish Record*, 4 (1941), 228.

174. 'Israel: The alternative', *NYRB*, 23 October 2003.

175. Kurt Lewin, 'Self-hatred among Jews', *Contemporary Jewish Record*, 4 (1941), 219.

176. Sabby Sagall, 'The Jewish Question', *Socialist Review* (July/August 2002).

177. *The Question of Zion* (Princeton, 2005), pp. 134–5.

178. 'Islamofascist slanders', *Guardian*, 4 November 2008.

179. Natan Sharansky, with Ron Dermer, *The Case for Democracy* (New York, 2006), p. xxix.

180. Sarah Glazer, 'Anti-Semitism in Europe', *CQ Global Researcher*, 2/6 (2008), 157.

181. Tony Greenstein, 'The seamy side of solidarity', *Guardian CiF*, 17 February 2007.

182. *Apartheid Israel* (London, 2003), pp. 3–4, 150, 176–7.

183. 'The "problem of evil" in postwar Europe', *NYRB*, 14 February 2008.

184. See Brian Klug, 'The myth of the new anti-Semitism', *Nation*, 2 February 2004.

185. Irene Bruegel, JFJP, letter to the *Guardian*, in support of Jenny Tonge, 24 January 2004.

186. Arthur Neslen, 'When an anti-Semite is not an anti-Semite', *Guardian, CiF*, 5 April 2007.

187. *Guardian*, 5 May 2003.

188. The speech is available by following the link on this web page: <http://mrzine.monthlyreview.org/freedom161007.html>; see also <http://www.engageonline.org.uk/blog/article.php?id=1488>. Compare this New Left

perspective: 'we have to use expressions which, taken by themselves, appear to resemble certain lines from *Mein Kampf*. As a result we shall feel the burden of being labelled anti-Semites and will be obliged to live "with" this insult, in the same way that the incurably ill live "with" their "ailment".' See Seymour Martin Lipset, 'The return of anti-Semitism as a political force' in Irving Howe and Carl Gershman (eds.), *Israel, the Arabs and the Middle East* (New York, 1972), p. 393.

189. Lynne Segal, *Making Trouble* (London, 2007), p. 244.

190. 'Nation as trauma, Zionism as question: Jacqueline Rose interviewed', *openDemocracy*, 18 August 2005.

191. *The Question of Zion* (Princeton, 2005), p. 116. See also pp. 145–6.

192. Ibid., p. 83.

193. 'Palestine's partisans', *Guardian*, 21 August 2002.

194. Ghada Karmi, 'Weapon of the weak', *Ha'aretz*, 14 July 2007; John Berger letter calling for cultural boycott, *Guardian*, 15 December 2006. This is a common enough tactic. For other campaigns, see Mary Lefkowitz, *History Lesson* (New Haven, NJ, 2008), pp. 61–2, 71, 85 (Black slave trade); Michael F. Metcalf, 'Regulating slaughter', *Patterns of Prejudice*, 23/3 (1989), 34 (*shechita*); Benjamin Weinthal, 'The hallmark of anti-Semitism', *Ha'aretz*, 19 September 2008 (German media discussion of Israel).

195. *The unJewish State* (London, 1983), p. 184.

196. See <http://www.plutobooks.com/shtml/aboutpluto.shtml>.

197. On Shahak, see Seth Farber, *Radicals, Rabbis and Peacemakers* (Monroe, ME, 2005), p. 183, and Gabriel Schoenfeld, *The Return of Anti-Semitism* (San Francisco, 2004), p. 134.

198. See, for example, <http://www.swappeal.org.uk/events/gilad.html>. It would appear that at one such event some SWP members criticized his anti-Semitism, and gave him a 'rough ride'. See <http://leninology.blogspot.com/2004/07/anti-fascist-and-anti-anti-semitic.html>. But he continues to be invited back.

199. 'Gilad Atzmon: "Zionism is my enemy"', *Socialist Worker*, 5 June 2004.

200. Chris Searles, 'Interview', *Morning Star*, 12 November 2007.

201. Oren Ben-Dor, 'The silencing of Oren Ben-Dor', *Counterpunch*, 15–16 March 2008.

202. 'Nation as trauma, Zionism as question: Jacqueline Rose interviewed', *openDemocracy*, 18 August 2005.

203. 'Israel: An alternative future', *NYRB*, 23 October 2003, anthologized in Adam Shatz (ed.), *Prophets Outcast* (New York, 2004), pp. 396–404. See also the correspondence in the *NYRB* 4 December 2003. Judt writes: 'After all that has happened, a binational state with an Arab majority could, as Amos Elon ruefully reminds us, very well look more like Zimbabwe than South Africa. But it doesn't have to be so.' 'After all that has happened' suggests that at some earlier moment, a binational state stood a somewhat better chance of

success. 'A bi-national state is not the alternative for Israel', writes Leon
Wieseltier. 'It is the alternative to Israel.' 'What is not to be done', *New
Republic*, 27 October 2003.

204. Gaby Wood, 'The new Jewish Question', *Observer*, 11 February 2007.

205. Michael Walzer, contribution to 'An alternative future: An exchange', *NYRB*
4 December 2003.

206. Jonathan Frankel, *Prophecy and Politics* (Cambridge, 1984), pp. 30–1. See also
Steven Beller, 'In Zion's hall of mirrors', *Patterns of Prejudice*, 41/2 (2007),
236–8 ('the American/Israeli strategy makes little sense in today's globalizing,
hi-tech world . . . the long-term hope for humanity cannot be the compromised model of the nation-state, but rather the inclusive, multiethnic and
multilateral, alternative, inspired in part by the *diasporic* Jewish experience').

207. For a late nineteenth-century example, see Anonymous, 'The Jewish
Question', *London Quarterly Review*, 59 (October 1882–January 1883), 106.
'Rightly or wrongly, the Gentile world, in its cosmopolitanism, is disposed to
resent this unyielding tribal exclusiveness, or, if not actually resent it, at any
rate to withhold its sympathy; and so in a thousand mouths the sentiments of
Voltaire and Gibbon find repeated utterance.'

208. See *The UJIA Study of Jewish Identity in the UK: A survey of Jewish parents*
(London, 2004). 'This would appear to represent a modest strengthening of
Zionist sentiment over the previous decade. In 1995, of Jews surveyed, 43 per
cent felt a strong attachment, and 38 per cent felt a moderate attachment, to
Israel. Thus while over 80 per cent of respondents expressed special feelings of
attachment to Israel, only 3 per cent expressed negative feelings.' Barry
Kosmin, Anthony Lerman, and Jacqueline Goldberg, *The Attachment of British
Jews to Israel*, JPR Report, no. 5, 1997.

209. David L. Edwards, *English Christianity* (London, 1998), pp. 3, 139.

210. Margaret Brearley, 'The Anglican Church, Jews and British multiculturalism', Posen Papers in Contemporary Antisemitism no. 6, The Vidal Sassoon
International Center for the Study of Antisemitism, The Hebrew University
of Jerusalem (2007), p. 5. Ateek has also offered an explanation of suicide
bombing. See Gershon Nerel, 'Anti-Zionism in the "Electronic Church" of
Palestinian Christianity', The Vidal Sassoon International Center for the
Study of Antisemitism, The Hebrew University of Jerusalem (2006),
pp. 14–15, 17–18.

211. Stephen Sizer, *Christian Zionism* (Downers Grove, IL, 2004), p. 170.

212. *The Complete English Poems*, John Tobin (ed.) (London, 1991), p. 143. Cf.: 'th'
Hebrew's royal stem / (That old dry stock) . . .' Richard Crashaw, 'sospetto
d'Herode', Edward Hutton (ed.), *The English Poems of Richard Crashaw*
(London, 1901), p. 93.

213. See Barbara W. Tuchman, *Bible and Sword* (London, 1982).

214. See Douglas J. Culver, *Albion and Ariel* (New York, 1995), p. 107.

215. See ibid., p. 109.

216. Dan Cohn-Sherbok, *The Politics of Apocalypse* (Oxford, 2006), pp. 3–11, 54, 141.

217. Stephen Sizer, *Christian Zionism* (Downers Grove, IL, 2004), p. 60.

218. Ibid., p. 17.

219. Horace B. Samuel, *Unholy Memories of the Holy Land* (London, 1930), p. 31.

220. Naomi Shepherd, *Ploughing Sand* (London, 1999), pp. 46–7.

221. Kenneth Cragg, *This Year in Jerusalem* (London, 1982), p. ii.

222. <http://www.sabeel.org/pdfs/2001%20Easter%20Message.htm>; Sarah Mandel, 'The radicals behind the Anglican Church', *Jerusalem Post*, 26 February 2006.

223. Letter to the prime minister from the archbishops of Canterbury and York, published in *The Times*, 30 June 2004.

224. 'Many would argue that present American policy in the Middle East has been distorted by pressure from Christian "fundamentalists". These Churches believe, alongside some Jewish fundamentalists, that the land-grabbing and ethnic cleansing described so vividly in the book of Joshua can be re-enacted today, with God's blessing, by the secular Israeli state.' Malcolm Guite, *What Do Christians Believe?* (London, 2006), pp. 104–5.

225. Bernard Lewis, *Semites and Anti-Semites* (London, 1986), p. 81.

226. Moshe Lazar, 'The lamb and the scapegoat: The dehumanisation of the Jews in medieval propaganda literature' in Sander L. Gilman and Steven T. Katz (eds.), *Anti-Semitism in Times of Crisis* (New York, 1991), p. 47.

227. See Jeremy Cohen, 'Traditional prejudice and religious reform: The theological and historical foundations of Luther's anti-Judaism' in Sander L. Gilman and Steven T. Katz (eds.), *Anti-Semitism in Times of Crisis* (New York, 1991), p. 86.

228. George M. Fredrickson, *Racism* (Princeton, NJ, 2002), pp. 42–3, 51–2.

229. Jules Isaac goes slightly too far, I think: 'A true Christian cannot be an anti-Semite; he simply has no right to be one.' And perhaps he then goes too far in the other direction: 'the vast majority of Christians are anti-Semites'. *The Teaching of Contempt* (New York, 1964), pp. 21, 24. Heiko A. Oberman, *The Roots of Anti-Semitism* (Philadelphia, 1984), p. 124, writes of the 'anti-Judaism inherent . . . in the Christian faith' (my italics), while the preacher of the papal household maintains that 'anti-Semitism . . . was not born out of fidelity to the Christian Scriptures, but out of infidelity to them'. Raniero Cantalamessa, 'In support of Jewish–Christian dialogue', *The Tablet*, 12 May 2007.

230. See Rowan Williams, *Tokens of Trust* (Norwich, 2007), pp. xi–xiii.

231. Said the students of the Cévenol school to the Vichy Minister of Education: 'We feel obliged to tell you that there are among us a certain number of Jews. But we make no distinction between Jews and non-Jews. It is contrary to the Gospel teaching.' The students added that, if the Jewish students were threatened with deportation, their non-Jewish fellows would hide them 'as best we can'. See Martin Gilbert, *The Righteous* (London, 2002), p. 336.

232. See Thomas A. Idinopulos and Roy Bowen Ward, 'Is Christology inherently anti-Semitic? A critical review of Rosemary Ruether's *Faith and Fratricide*', *Journal of American Academy of Religion*, 45/2 (1977), 203.

233. Rudolph M. Loewenstein, 'Anti-Semites in psychoanalysis' in Werner Bergmann (ed.), *Error Without Trial: Psychological research on antisemitism* (Berlin, 1988), p. 45.

234. Jules Isaac, *The Teaching of Contempt* (New York, 1964).

235. Krister Stendahl, 'Anti-Semitism' in Bruce Metzger and Michael D. Coogan (eds.), *The Oxford Companion to the Bible* (Oxford, 1993), p. 32.

236. Erasmus: Heiko A. Oberman, *The Roots of Anti-Semitism* (Philadelphia, 1984), p. 39.

237. See Anna Sapir Abulafia, 'Jewish carnality in twelfth century renaissance thought' in Diana Wood (ed.), *Studies in Church History* (Oxford, 1992), vol. 29, pp. 59, 75.

238. Heinz Schrekenberg, *The Jews in Christian Art* (New York, 1996), p. 16. This trope reaches its terminus in the teachings of the American Christian Identity movement, which regards Cain as the child of Eve and Satan, and the progenitor of the Jews (the 'two-seed' theory of creation). See Kenneth S. Stern, 'Understanding the summer of hate', 'Issues in National Affairs', *American Jewish Committee*, 8/1 (1999).

239. This list is not intended to be exhaustive. Esther, for example, was read typologically too, with the rejected Vashti standing for the Jews, and Queen Esther herself representing the vanquishing Christians. See James Shapiro, *Oberammergau* (London, 2000), p. 97.

240. See Elliot Horowitz, *Reckless Rites* (Princeton, NJ, 2006), p. 88.

241. Clement of Alexandria (*c*.200): Henry Bettenson (ed.), *Documents of the Christian Church* (Oxford, 1967), p. 6.

242. An eighteenth-century French abbé: 'Despite all their attempts, [the Jews] have not been able to succeed to this day in creating a nation, a state, and an established government of their own. The Jews are the objects of hatred and general indignation...' See Arthur Hertzberg, *The French Enlightenment and the Jews* (New York, 1968), p. 250.

243. Soame Jenyns, *View of the Internal Evidence of the Christian Religion* (1770), in John Martin Creed and John Sandwith Boys Smith (eds.), *Religious Thought in the Eighteenth Century* (Cambridge, 1934), p. 83.

244. Amnon Linder, 'Jews and Judaism in the eyes of Christian thinkers of the Middle Ages' in Jeremy Cohen (ed.), *From Witness to Witchcraft* (Wiesbaden, 1996), p. 117.

245. 'Carefully read over their Scriptures... and you shall know... that nothing happened that had not been predicted, if they should persevere in their obstinacy.' Minucius Felix, *Octavius* (*c*.160–250 CE?), <http://www.earlychristianwritings.com/text/octavius.html>.

246. Epistle of Innocent III, 15 July 1205, quoted in S. W. Baron, *A Social and Religious History of the Jews* (New York, 1965), vol. 9, p. 137. The formulation became canonical (ibid., p. 188).

247. On the anti-Zionism of the teaching of contempt, see Charlotte Klein, 'The theological dimensions of the State of Israel', *Journal of Ecumenical Studies*, 10/4 (1973), and her *Anti-Judaism in Christian Theology* (London, 1978), pp. 13, 18–19, 22. See also Norman Solomon, 'The Christian Churches on Israel and the Jews' in Robert S. Wistrich (ed.), *Anti-Zionism and Antisemitism in the Contemporary World* (New York, 1990). See also Edward Kessler, 'Jewish–Christian Relations: Past, present, future', Grosseteste Lecture 2005, Lincoln Cathedral, <www. lincolncathedral.com>.

248. There was an intricate debate, however, on the precise moment of supersession, and the implications for the practices of the early Christians in the first centuries following Jesus' death. See, for example, Beryl Smalley, 'The biblical scholar' in D. A. Callus (ed.), *Robert Grosseteste* (Oxford, 1955), pp. 90–4.

249. Cardinal Faulhaber, *Judaism, Christianity and Germany* (London, 1934), p. 5, quoted in Charlotte Klein, 'The theological dimensions of the State of Israel', *Journal of Ecumenical Studies*, 10/4 (1973), 704.

250. Tertullian, *Apology*: Morton Irving Seiden, *The Paradox of Hate* (New York, 1967), p. 136.

251. Martin Luther: Benjamin Nelson, *The Idea of Usury* (Chicago, 1969), p. 55.

252. See 'The Epistle of Barnabas' in Maxwell Staniforth and Andrew Louth (eds.), *Early Christian Writings* (London, 1987), pp. 155–8, 164–71.

253. See R. Po-Chia Hsia, *Trent 1475* (New Haven, 1992), p. 12.

254. See Nathan Rotenstreich, 'For and against emancipation', *Leo Baeck Institute Year Book* (London, 1959), pp. 6–7.

255. See Charlotte Klein, 'The theological dimensions of the State of Israel', *Journal of Ecumenical Studies*, 10/4 (1973), 702.

256. Gavin I. Langmuir, 'The faith of Christians and hostility to Jews' in Diana Wood (ed.), *Studies in Church History* (Oxford, 1992), vol. 29, p. 82.

257. Krister Stendahl, 'Anti-Semitism' in Bruce Metzger and Michael D. Coogan (eds.), *The Oxford Companion to the Bible* (Oxford, 1993), p. 33. Critics of the papacy adopted the anti-Jewish language of John: the Roman Church was 'the synagogue of Satan'. See John Wycliffe (1324–84): Henry Bettenson (ed.), *Documents of the Christian Church* (Oxford, 1967), p. 174. There were those on both sides of the religious divide in sixteenth- and seventeenth-century Europe who regarded the Jews and Judaism as proofs of the spiritual chaos of the time: Heiko A. Oberman, *The Roots of Anti-Semitism* (Philadelphia, 1984), p. 22.

258. 'The attitude on the Continent has always been different from that of the English speaking world.' Charlotte Klein, *Anti-Judaism in Christian Theology* (London, 1978), p.4.

259. 'There is a huge gap between the insights of biblical scholars and what usually gets purveyed from Christian pulpits.' Richard Harries, 'Judaism and Christianity' in Alister McGrath (ed.), *The Blackwell Encyclopedia of Modern Christian Thought* (Oxford, 1993), p. 285. The teaching of contempt persisted in France and Germany. See Charlotte Klein, *Anti-Judaism in Christian Theology* (London, 1978), p. 3.

260. See Rowan Williams, *Wrestling with Angels* (Bury St Edmunds, 2007), p. 71, summarizing 'the Christian, and more particularly Lutheran, account of Judaism'.

261. Israel J. Yuval, *Two Nations in Your Womb* (Berkeley, 2006), p. 20.

262. Gershon Nerel, 'Anti-Zionism in the "Electronic Church" of Palestinian Christianity', The Vidal Sassoon International Center for the Study of Antisemitism, The Hebrew University of Jerusalem (2006), p. 38; Charlotte Klein, 'The theological dimensions of the State of Israel', Journal of Ecumenical Studies, 10/4 (1973), 713–15.

263. Kenneth Cragg, *This Year in Jerusalem* (London, 1982), p. ii.

264. Ibid., p. 96.

265. Ibid., pp. 96–7; John Watson, *Listening to Islam* (Brighton, 2005), pp. 49–68; Naim Ateek, *Justice and only Justice* (New York, 1989), p. 101.

266. Lothar Kahn, *Mirrors of the Jewish Mind* (New York, 1968), p. 169.

267. Stephen Sizer, *Christian Zionism* (Downers Grove, IL, 2004), pp. 199, 203, 266.

268. David Peterson, 'Foreword' in Stephen Sizer, *Christian Zionism* (Downers Grove, IL, 2004), p. 7.

269. 'Holy Land and Holy People', a Lecture at the 5th International Sabeel Conference, 14 April 2004. See <http://www.archbishopofcanterbury.org/1175>. Williams hints in various places in his writings at his dissatisfaction with the simpler and less nuanced versions of supersessionism. See *Wrestling with Angels* (Bury St Edmunds, 2007), pp. 71, 91, 290, and *Tokens of Trust* (Norwich, 2007), pp. 59–60, 101–2, 121.

270. *Countering Terrorism* (2005), p. 44.

271. Ibid., p. 46.

272. 'For world peace, Israel must pull out', *Church Times*, 24 March 2006.

273. *This Year in Jerusalem* (London, 1982), p. 103.

274. Ibid., p. 104; Stephen Sizer, *Christian Zionism* (Downers Grove, IL, 2004), p. 204.

275. Nadia Abboushi, 'The Intifada and the Palestinian Churches' in Naim Ateek, Marc H. Ellis, and Rosemary Radford Ruether (eds.), *Faith and the Intifada* (New York, 1992), p. 59.

276. See Stephen Sizer, *Christian Zionism* (Downers Grove, IL, 2004), pp. 8–9.

277. Ibid., p. 266.

278. Ibid., p. 19.

279. Ibid., p. 260.

NOTES TO PAGES 569–572

280. Ibid., p. 262.

281. Letter, *Spectator*, 14 March 2009, p. 24.

282. Nadia Abboushi, 'The Intifada and the Palestinian Churches' in Naim Ateek *et al.* (eds.), *Faith and the Intifada* (New York, 1992), p. 59.

283. Naim Ateek, *Justice and only Justice* (New York, 1989), p. 77.

284. 'Introduction: The emergence of a Palestinian Christian theology' in Naim Ateek *et al.* (eds.), *Faith and the Intifada* (New York, 1992), pp. 3–5.

285. See his *Justice and only Justice* (New York, 1989), and 'Biblical perspectives on the land' in Naim Ateek *et al.* (eds.), *Faith and the Intifada* (New York, 1992), pp. 108–16.

286. *Countering Terrorism* (2005), pp. 61–2.

287. It offered, in somewhat formulaic terms, an assurance to 'the Israeli Jewish community of our concern for their security and safety, to be able to live without fear'. 'Give sight to the blind and freedom to the captives', <http://www.anglicancommunion.org/un/israeli_palestinian_conflict.htm>.

288. Formerly at <http://www.episcopalchurch.org/3577_63362_ENG_HTM.htm>.

289. Ruth Gledhill, 'synod in disinvestment snub to Israel', *The Times*, 7 February 2006.

290. See Nick Cohen, 'Arson, rape, massacres . . . and the strange silence of the archbishop', *Observer*, 5 March 2006. The archbishop of Canterbury, in a public letter addressed to the Chief Rabbi, insisted, 'no-one in the Synod would endorse anything that could even appear to endorse terrorist activities or anti-Semitic words or actions. But there is a real concern which we hope our Jewish and Israeli colleagues will help us address honestly and constructively.' <http://www.archbishopofcanterbury.org/1665>.

291. George Conger, 'Anglican advisors reject divestment', *Jerusalem Post*, 7 March 2007.

292. The Rev. Dr Giles Fraser, 'I'm not anti-Semitic and neither is the Synod', *Church Times*, 24 February 2006.

293. See Margaret Brearley, 'The Anglican Church, Jews and British multiculturalism', Posen Papers in Contemporary Antisemitism no. 6, The Vidal Sassoon International Center for the Study of Antisemitism, The Hebrew University of Jerusalem (2007), p. 8.

294. George Conger, 'Jewish–Anglican pact upsets Arab clerics', *Jerusalem Post*, 5 September 2006.

295. Naim Ateek, *Justice and Only Justice* (New York, 1989), p. 166.

296. Kenneth Cragg, *This Year in Jerusalem* (London, 1982), p. 104. Ateek proposes that 'the Palestinians seek peace with justice, while the Israeli Jews want peace with security'. *Justice and only Justice* (New York, 1989), p. 144.

297. See Naim Ateek, *Justice and only Justice* (New York, 1989), p. 29.

298. Ibid., p. 69.

299. Zionism is 'intrinsically racist'. The 'Jewish academic Uri Davis' has written probably the most detailed book on racism in Israel. 'Numerous other well known Jewish figures have been critical of Israel's apartheid policies.' Indeed, it is 'especially' Jewish critics who argue that the State 'continues to practice apartheid'. Stephen Sizer, *Christian Zionism* (Downers Grove, IL, 2004), pp. 205, 210, 211.

300. See <http://www.adl.org/anti_semitism/European_Attitudes_Survey_July-2007.pdf>. Only in Hungary was the percentage higher (26 per cent).

301. This would appear to be the position of Bishop Michael Nazir-Ali. See *Conviction and Conflict* (London, 2006), pp. 51–4.

302. See *The Tablet*, 16 December 2006. There were 2,815 responses.

303. 'Of course, there is a *quantitative* distinction... But there is no *qualitative* distinction: killing is killing.' See John Watson, *Listening to Islam* (Brighton, 2005), p. 66.

304. '... in Ramallah, in reality, was the suffering and deprivation that I could only imagine in Auschwitz.... No longer could I speak of the "matchless catastrophe of the Holocaust" without reference to the havoc wreaked by Israeli soldiers on the indigenous Palestinians. No longer could I hold Auschwitz up as the ultimate reference point which must inform our ways of being, etc.' *Church Times*, 24 January 2003.

305. Gershon Nerel, 'Anti-Zionism in the "Electronic Church" of Palestinian Christianity', The Vidal Sassoon International Center for the Study of Antisemitism, The Hebrew University of Jerusalem (2006), p. 22.

306. See Ed Husain, *The Islamist* (London, 2007), pp. 281–2.

307. <http://www.mdsweb.jp/international/cairo_sec/cairo2_dec.html>.

308. Simon Assaf, 'Hamas's victory in Gaza is a blow to Bush's plans', *Socialist Worker*, 20 June 2007.

309. See James Turley, 'Sickening apologetics', and Jim Moody, 'Giving excuses leads to active collaboration', *Weekly Worker*, 12 July 2007.

310. See Jonathan Spyer, 'The long war strategy', *Guardian*, 11 June 2007.

311. See John Callaghan, *The Far Left in British Politics* (Oxford 1987), p. viii.

312. Ibid., p. 102.

313. For a survey of the party, written before it foundered, see Eran Benedek, 'Britain's Respect Party', *Jewish Political Studies Review*, 19/3–4 (2007).

314. 'felixonline', issue 1344, 16 February 2006, <http://www.felixonline.co.uk/articles/2923/Taleban_kidnap_victim_Yvonne_Ridley_talks_to_Alon_Orbach>. The item is a report on a speech given by Ridley at Imperial College, London University.

315. 'Hizbollah is right to fight Zionist terror', *Socialist Worker*, 29 July 2006.

316. Andrew Murray and Lindsey German, *Stop the War* (London, 2005), pp. 82–9.

317. Reva Klein, Edie Friedman, Francesca Klug, letter to the *Guardian*, 1 October 2002.

318. Lucy Michaels, 'Fear and loathing', *New Internationalist*, October 2004.

319. See *Report of the All-Party Parliamentary Inquiry into Antisemitism* (London, September 2006), pp. 38-42. On campus anti-Semitism as a distinct ideological formation, see Russell A. Berman, 'From "Left-Fascism" to Campus Antisemitism', *Democratiya*, 13 (Summer 2008).

320. 'The state of the Jewish State: An interview with Professor Efraim Karsh', *Harvard Israel Review* (Spring 2004); James Brandon and Douglas Murray, *Hate on the State* (London, 2007), p. 11.

321. Ed Husain, *The Islamist* (London, 2007), p. 104.

322. Mitch Simons, 'Anti-Semitism on campus', Engage, <http://www.engageonline.org.uk/blog/article.php?id=632>. See also Melanie Phillips, *Londonistan* (London, 2006), pp. 149-52.

323. 'Of course, the only terrorist state in the Middle East is Israel...' Daniel Johnson, 'Allah's England?', *Commentary* (November 2006), 42.

324. 'I wish eighty or ninety Jews would die with each bomb', *JewishComment.com*, 11 October 2003.

325. See Geoffrey Short, 'Antisemitism on campus' in Michael Fineberg, Shimon Samuels, and Mark Weitzman (eds.), *Antisemitism* (London, 2007), p. 118.

326. John Pilger, *The New Rulers of the World* (London, 2003), p. 161.

327. Hugo Chavez, president of Venezuela, for example. As for Saddam, the Left was hostile to him when he was supported by the US, but defending him when attacked by the US. 'When America switched sides, the left switched sides.' Nick Cohen, *Pretty Straight Guys* (London, 2004), p. 125.

328. John Pilger, *The New Rulers of the World* (London, 2003), p. 11.

329. See Robin Blackburn, letter to the *TLS*, 18 and 25 August 2006.

330. See Thérèse Delpech, *Savage Century* (Washington, DC, 2007), p. 42.

331. Mark Steel, 'Book of the week', *Independent*, 6 June 2008.

332. Khalid Kishtainy, *The New Statesman and the Middle East* (Beirut, 1972), p. 65.

333. David Hirsh and Jon Pike, 'Know the boundaries', *Ha'aretz*, 24 January 2006.

334. Fred Halliday, *100 Myths About the Middle East* (London, 2005), pp. 133-4.

335. Mick Hume, 'The anti-imperialism of fools', *New Statesman*, 17 June 2002.

336. See Czeslaw Milosz, 'The Poor Poet', and 'Child of Europe', *New and Collected Poems 1931-2001* (New York, 2003), pp. 59, 84.

337. See Nick Cohen, *What's Left? How liberals lost their way* (London, 2007), pp. 117-19, 124.

338. Edward Said, 'Islam and the West are inadequate banners', *Guardian*, 16 September 2001.

339. Dan Diner, *America in the Eyes of the Germans* (Princeton, NJ, 1996), p. 5.

340. Bernard Henri-Lévy, *American Vertigo* (New York, 2006), p. 290.

341. *Writing to the Moment* (London, 1996), p. 134.

342. Thérèse Delpech, *Savage Century* (Washington, DC, 2007), p. 163.

343. David Brooks, 'Among the bourgeoisophobes', *Weekly Standard*, 15 April 2002.

344. Walter Russell Mead, 'The new Israel and the old', *Foreign Affairs* (July/August 2008).

345. Jürgen Habermas, *The Divided West* (Cambridge, 2006), pp. 45–6.

346. Priyamvada Gopal, 'A shameful silence', *Guardian*, 5 October 2007.

347. John J. Mearsheimer and Stephen M. Walt, *The Israel Lobby* (London, 2007), p. 338.

348. 'Say it loud: No more support until Israel agrees to pull out', *Guardian*, 24 October 2001.

349. *I'm Not the Only One* (London, 2004), p. 41.

350. 'Resistance is the first step towards Iraqi independence', *Guardian*, 3 November 2003.

351. Noam Chomsky, *Power and Terror* (London 2003), pp. 103, 115–16.

352. Henry Kissinger, *Crisis: The anatomy of two major foreign policy crises* (New York, 2003), p. 147.

353. Dore Gold, 'Understanding the US–Israel alliance', *Jerusalem Center for Public Affairs* (September 2007).

354. Lawrence F. Kaplan, 'Toxic talk on war', *Washington Post*, 18 February 2003.

355. 'The Israel lobby and US foreign policy' by Stephen Walt and John Mearsheimer was published as the lead item in the 23 March 2006 issue of the *London Review of Books*. In a break with its standard practice, the issue's front cover carried a long quotation from the piece. The work was then revised and published as a book, *The Israel Lobby and US Foreign Policy*, in 2007.

356. Nick Cohen, *Waiting for the Etonians* (London, 2009), p. 199.

357. See Ira Stoll, 'Two professors fail to clean up their act', *New York Sun*, 29 August 2007.

358. Walter Russell Mead, 'The new Israel and the old', *Foreign Affairs* (July/August 2008).

359. See for example *The Israel Lobby* (London, 2007), pp. 99 and 387, fn. 95. Mearsheimer and Walt misattribute to Ben Gurion a misattribution by Pappe to Allon. See Anthony Julius, 'Jewish anti-Zionism unravelled: The morality of vanity', *Z Word*, March 2008, fn. 45.

360. *The Israel Lobby and US Foreign Policy* (London, 2007), p. 146.

361. Jeffrey Goldberg, 'The usual suspect', *New Republic*, 8 October 2007.

362. David Remnick, 'The lobby', *The New Yorker*, 3 September 2007; Ben Fishman, 'Inside track: Missing the point', *National Interest*, 27 August 2007; Editorial, *The Jewish Daily Forward*, 22 August 2007; Jeffrey Goldberg, 'The usual suspect', *New Republic*, 8 October 2007—particularly good on Walt and Mearsheimer's 'Judeocentrism'; Bernard Harrison, *The Resurgence of Anti-Semitism* (New York, 2006), pp. 194–204.

363. John Mearsheimer, 'The lobby falters', *LRB*, 26 March 2009.

364. Michael Lind, 'The Israel lobby', *Prospect* (April 2002). But see also Michael Lind, 'Israel lobby part 3', *Prospect* (October 2002).

365. Abdurrahman Jafar, 'Time to be heard, time to be respected!' *Muslim Weekly*, 21–27 April 2006.

366. 'Egypt's judicial system', 20 July 2007, <http://yvonneridley.org/yvonne-ridley/articles/egypts-judicial-system-4.html>.

367. 'On the conjuncture', *New Left Review*, 48 (November/Decemeber 2007); Alan Johnson, 'Is Perry Anderson lost in the lobby?', *Guardian*, CiF, 30 January 2008.

368. See <http://www.adl.org/anti_semitism/European_Attitudes_Survey_July-2007.pdf>.

369. <http://www.itszone.co.uk/zone0/viewtopic.php?t=83004&postdays=0&postorder=asc&start=0>.

370. Stuart Littlewood, 'Gagged while Gaza is crushed', 12 January 2008, <http://redress.cc/stooges/slittlewood20080112>.

371. <http://fanonite.org/2008/01/18/uk-israel-lobby-in-the-spotlight/>.

372. See Dan Diner, *America in the Eyes of the Germans* (Princeton, NJ, 1996), pp. 62–3, 97.

373. Matthias Küntzel, *Jihad and Jew-Hatred* (New York, 2007), p. 35.

374. Joseph B. Schechtman, *The Mufti and the Fuehrer* (New York, 1965), p. 150.

375. Ewan MacAskill, 'Atheists arise', *Guardian*, 1 October 2007.

376. Alvin H. Rosenfeld, 'Anti-Americanism and anti-Semitism', *American Jewish Committee* (August 2003), 1.

377. Dan Diner, *America in the Eyes of the Germans* (Princeton, NJ, 1996), p. 20. See also Richard Wolin, *The Seduction of Unreason* (Princeton, 2004), pp. 300–1.

378. Michael Walzer, 'Response to Jerome Slater: The Lebanon War', *Dissent* (Winter 2007).

379. See Robert S. Wistrich, *The Jews of Vienna in the Age of Franz Joseph* (Oxford, 1990), p. 222.

380. See Mitchell Cohen, 'Anti-Semitism and the Left that doesn't learn', *Dissent* (Fall 2007).

381. 'On antisemitism within the Palestine Solidarity Movement', *Engage*, <http://www.engageonline.org.uk/blog/article.php?id=8>.

382. Bernard Lewis, 'The new anti-Semitism', *The American Scholar*, 75/1 (2006).

383. Emanuela Trevisan Semi, 'From Judeophobia to Islamophobia in the Italian media, with a special focus on the Northern League Party media' in Tudor Parfitt with Yulia Egorova (eds.), *Jews, Muslims and Mass Media* (London, 2004), p. 51.

384. Andrew Brons, 'Hilaire Belloc', *New Nation*, no. 6 (Winter 1984).

385. Trevor Grundy, *Memoir of a Fascist Childhood* (London, 1999), p. 92.

386. See Sander L. Gilman, *Jewish Self-Hatred* (Baltimore, MD, 1986), p. 178.

387. See Mitch Simons, 'Anti-Semitism on campus', Engage, <http://www.engageonline.org.uk/blog/article.php?id=632>.

388. Nick Ryan, *Homeland* (London, 2004), p. 302.

389. Gerry Gable, 'The Far Right in contemporary Britain' in Luciano Cheles, Ronnie Ferguson, and Michalina Vaughan (eds.), *Neo-Fascism in Europe* (London, 1991), pp. 252, 260.

390. Michel Foucault, *The Archaeology of Knowledge* (London, 1974), p. 136.

391. Andrew Anthony, *The Fallout* (London, 2007), p. 19.

392. Dan Diner, *America in the Eyes of the Germans* (Princeton, NJ, 1996), pp. 13, 91.

393. Greg Dyke, 'The BBC should never give in to pressure—or even be seen to', *Independent*, 12 December 2005.

394. Jon Snow, *Shooting History* (London, 2005), p. 73.

395. Deborah Orr, 'I'm fed up with being called an anti-Semite', *Independent*, 21 December 2001.

396. Sir William MacPherson, *The Stephen Lawrence Inquiry* (London, 1999), ch. 47, para. 12.

397. Mary Lefkowitz, *History Lesson* (New Haven, NJ, 2008), p. 122.

398. See Leonard Woolf, *Quack, Quack!* (London, 1935), p. 195.

399. See Per Ahlmark, 'Combatting old/new antisemitism', Speech at Yad Vashem, April 11, 2002. Ahlmark is the former Leader of the Swedish Liberal Party and deputy prime minister of Sweden.

400. II:19. See R. Travers Herford (ed.), *Sayings of the Fathers* (New York, 1975), p. 61.

401. Cf.: 'The presence in Germany of a vast amount of careful, scholarly work exposing the absurdities of Teuton worship had little effect on public thought.' Frank H. Hankins, *The Racial Basis of Civilization* (New York, 1926), p. 77. Josephus explained that he wrote *Against Apion* to 'demonstrate that those calumnies and reproaches which some have thrown upon our nation, are lies'. 'Against Apion', *Works* (London, 1818), vol. 4, p. 309.

402. Charles Kensington Salaman, *Jews As They Are* (London, 1882).

403. See Gisela C. Lebzelter, *Political Anti-Semitism in England 1918–1939* (London, 1978), pp. 144–6.

404. See John A. Dyche, 'The Jewish workman', *Contemporary Review*, 73 (January 1898), 36–7. Arnold White gave an unsatisfactory, but intransigent reply, in 'A typical alien immigrant', *Contemporary Review*, 73 (February 1898).

405. See Russo-Jewish Committee of London, *The Persecution of the Jews in Russia* (London, 1891), p. 33.

406. During World War I, many German Jews 'regarded their military service as the ultimate test Germany would demand of them, the one that would wipe out every last remnant of anti-Semitism'. They were wrong, of course. See Nahum N. Glatzer and Paul Mendes-Flohr (eds.), *The Letters of Martin Buber* (New York, 1991), p. 25, Omer Bartov, *Mirrors of Destruction* (Oxford, 2000), pp. 96–7, and Geoffrey G. Field, *Evangelist of Race* (New York, 1981), pp. 386–7. See also Neville Laski, *Jewish Rights and Jewish Wrongs* (London,

1939), p. 29, and David Cesarani, 'An embattled minority' in Tony Kushner and Kenneth Lunn (eds.), *The Politics of Marginality* (London, 1990), p. 65.

407. Tony Kushner, *The Persistence of Prejudice* (Manchester, 1989), p. 123.

408. Edward J. Bristow, *Prostitution and Prejudice* (New York, 1983), pp. 162–3.

409. Of course, White gave himself an escape route. The subject of legislation might be 'revived' if 'public opinion brings it to the front in a new and ominous form'. Jewish influence was 'irresistible'—and yet, it could be resisted, if only...See 'A typical alien immigrant', *Contemporary Review*, 73 (February 1898), 242.

410. 'There is no such thing as "Jewish influence" in politics, in the press, or in commerce, for the Jews have no combined action in these matters.' Hermann Adler, 'Jews and Judaism: A rejoinder', *Nineteenth Century*, 4 (July 1878), 135.

411. Jonathan Frankel, *The Damascus Affair* (Cambridge, 1997), pp. 221, 266.

412. See Gisela C. Lebzelter, *Political Anti-Semitism in England 1918–1939* (London, 1978), p. 14.

413. Neville Laski, *Jewish Rights and Jewish Wrongs* (London, 1939), p. 139.

414. See Max Weber, *The Protestant Ethic and the Rise of Capitalism* (London, 1974), p. 90.

415. The remark is attributed to the Talmudist Saul Lieberman, and the occasion, on introducing a lecture by Gershom Scholem. See Simon Schama, *Landscape and Memory* (London, 1996), p. 134, and <http://www.indopedia.org/Talk: Kabbalah.html#.22Nonsense.22_quote_of_Lieberman>.

416. See Robert Jan van Pelt, 'Dirty work: A personal reflection on the Irving trial' in Debra Kaufman, Gerald Herman, James Ross, and David Phillips (eds.), *From the Protocols of the Elders of Zion to Holocaust Denial Trials* (London, 2007), pp. 111–13.

Extract acknowledgements

We are grateful for permission to include the following extracts of verse by Tom Paulin in this book: from 'Killed in Crossfire', first published in the *Observer*, 18 February 2001, and from 'On Being Dealt the Anti-Semite Card', first published in the *London Review of Books*, 2 January 2003, reprinted by permission of Faith Evans Associates for the author.

We have made every effort to trace and contact all copyright holders before publication. If notified, the publisher will be pleased to rectify any errors or omissions at the earliest opportunity.

Index